JAPAN

PROFILE OF A NATION

revised edition

英文 日本小事典

改訂新版

JAPAN

PROFILE
OF
A
NATION
**revised
edition**

Published by Kodansha International Ltd.,
17-14 Otowa 1-chome,
Bunkyo-ku, Tokyo 112-8652
and Kodansha America Inc.

Distributed in the United States by Kodansha America Inc.,
575 Lexington Avenue, New York, NY 10022 and
in the United Kingdom and continental Europe
by Kodansha Europe Ltd.,
95, Aldwych, London WC2B 4JF.

99 00 01 02 10 9 8 7 6 5 4 3 2 1

ISBN4-4-7700-2384-7

Printed in Japan

Library of Congress Cataloging-in-Publication Data
A catalog record for this book is available
from the Library of Congress

Preface 刊行のことば

During the closing years of the twentieth century, we have seen worldwide interest in Japan grow as the nation takes on a more prominent and active role on the international stage. Many have felt the need for an accurate and reliable reference source that is both comprehensive and accessible to the general reader. With this in mind, JAPAN: PROFILE OF A NATION was compiled from the valuable and detailed resource *Japan: An Illustrated Encyclopedia* published by our parent company Kodansha Ltd. A generous selection of entries from this treasure trove of information has been reorganized into thematic sections such as Geography and Nature, History, Government and Diplomacy, Economy, Society, Culture, and Life. Cross-references are provided within the entry to lead the reader to related material, and an index of entry titles and key words is included as part of the supplementary materials. Those readers requiring more specialized information about Japan are advised to consult *Japan: An Illustrated Encyclopedia.*

We sincerely hope that the publication of this book will promote better international understanding through an authentic and fascinating portrayal of all that is Japan. The present edition has been updated to reflect the many political and economic changes that have taken place since this book was first published in 1995.

Kodansha International
March 1999

Organization | 構成

This book is divided into seven thematic sections which are further divided into a number of sub-sections. For example, the Society section consists of four parts: Social Environment, Education, Transportation, Mass Communications. Each of these sub-sections in turn comprises a number of in-depth entries on specific subjects.

Entry Titles and Sub-Headings | 見出し語と小見出し

Entry titles are, wherever possible, given in English followed by the same title in Japanese characters. In most cases the romanized equivalent of the Japanese title is included in parenthesis at the head of the entry. Where a romanized Japanese title is used for the main entry title, a parenthetical English translation is given when appropriate. Within many of the longer entries, sub-headings are used to indicate major divisions. A Japanese translation of each sub-heading is given to the right.

Romanization and Italicization | ローマ字表記とイタリック

Japanese words are spelled in this book according to the Hepburn system of romanization used in most English-language publications on Japan. Chinese words and names are given in the official pinyin system of romanization. Sanskrit is transliterated in the system most widely used in English-language scholarly publications.
Japanese words and other non-English words are italicized.

Cross-References | 参照項目

Cross-references are included within the entries themselves in the form of words set in SMALL CAPITALS to inform the reader that the book contains an entry on the subject named.

Money	通貨

Post-1945 yen values are followed by their US dollar equivalents, with the dollar figure based on the average exchange rate pertaining during the year or years in question.

Personal Names	人名

Japanese, Chinese, and Korean personal names are given surname first, the normal order used in those languages (e.g., Kawabata Yasunari rather than Yasunari Kawabata or Kawabata, Yasunari).

Aids for the Japanese Reader	英文読解の補助機能

To aid the Japanese reader in understanding the English text, the corresponding Japanese word has been inserted after some of the key English words.

Supplementary Materials	巻末資料

The following reference materials are presented in both English and Japanese at the back of the book.

- Constitution of Japan
- Selected treaties and international agreements

  Cairo Declaration

  Potsdam Declaration

  San Francisco Peace Treaty

  United States-Japan Security Treaty (1951)

  United States-Japan Security Treaty (1960)
- The Guidelines for U.S.-Japan Defense Cooperation
- Chronology of Japanese History
- Red List (a list of species and animals in danger of extinction)

Index	索引

The bilingual index includes entry titles and key words from the text.

CONTENTS 目次

CONTRIBUTORS

James C. ABEGGLEN	David HALE	Terry Edward MacDOUGALL
AKIYAMA Terukazu	Ivan P. HALL	Theodore McNELLY
Walter AMES	William B. HAUSER	MAKABE Tetsuo
J. L. ANDERSON	Benjamin H. HAZARD	John M. MAKI
AOKI Haruo	HIRANO Ken'ichirō	William P. MALM
ARAI Naoyuki	HIRASAWA Yutaka	MASUI Ken'ichi
James T. ARAKI	Leon HOLLERMAN	MATSUDA Osamu
ARAMAKI Shigeo	HOSOYA Chihiro	MERA Kōichi
Janet ASHBY	IKEDA Hiroko	MURATA Yoshio
Hans H. BAERWALD	IMAIZUMI Yoshinori	NAKAGAWA Toshihiko
BEFU Harumi	INOKUCHI Shōji	NAKAMURA Hajime
BEKKI Atsuhiko	ISHIYAMA Akira	NIIRA Satoshi
Andrea BOLTHO	ITŌ Nobuo	NIWATA Noriaki
Robert H. BROWER	Donald JENKINS	Agnes M. NIYEKAWA
Thomas W. CLEAVER	KANEKO Yoshimasa	NOGUCHI Yukio
Martin C. COLLCUTT	KARASAWA Tomitarō	Edward NORBECK
Walter Ames COMPTON	KARIYA Takehiko	ODA Takeo
Michael COOPER	KATA Kōji	OGAWA Yoshio
Ronald P. DORE	KATŌ Kōji	OGURA Michio
Heinrich DUMOULIN	KATŌ Tsuneo	Frank Masao OKAMURA
H. Byron EARHART	KAWAMOTO Takashi	OKAMURA Tadao
Earle ERNST	KIDA Hiroshi	ŌKI Yasue
Lee W. FARNSWORTH	KIMURA Kiyotaka	P. G. O'NEILL
Scott C. FLANAGAN	KŌNO Tomomi	ORITA Kōji
FUJII Toshiko	KOTANI Kōzō	ŌTSUKA Shigeru
FUKUDA Hideichi	KUDŌ Masanobu	ŌTSUKA Shigeru
FUKUI Haruhiro	KUMAKURA Isao	ŌTSUKA Sueko
FUKUSHIMA Yasuto	KURITA Ken	Allan PALMER
Robert GARFIAS	Edward J. LINCOLN	T. J. PEMPEL
Van C. GESSEL	Victor D. LIPPIT	David W. PLATH
Allan G. GRAPARD	Leonard LYNN	William V. RAPP
Willem A. GROOTAERS	Kathleen McCARTHY	

GEOGRAPHY and NATURE

地理・自然

国土	Land
地域・都市	Areas and Cities
動物・植物	Plants and Animals

Japan (Nippon or Nihon) 日本

Territory and Administrative Divisions
領土と行政区分

Area 面積

Japan consists of an archipelago 列島 extending approximately from northeast to southwest. It lies off the east coast of the Asian continent アジア大陸. The total land area is 377,829 square kilometers (145,880 sq mi), only slightly larger than that of Finland or Italy and about the same size as the US state of Montana. The four major islands of Japan are Hokkaidō, Honshū, Shikoku, and Kyūshū. Claimed by the Japanese, the northernmost islands of Kunashiri (Kunashir) 国後島, Etorofu (Iturup) 択捉島, the Habomai Islands 歯舞諸島, and Shikotan 色丹島 were occupied by the Soviet Union at the end of World War II and are still occupied by the Russian Federation. The Ogasawara Islands and Okinawa Islands, under American rule after World War II, were returned to Japan in 1968 and 1972, respectively. The areas of the main geographical divisions of Japan (including offshore islands under their administrative control) are as follows: Hokkaidō 北海道 83,451 sq km (32,220 sq mi), Honshū 本州 231,084 sq km (89,222 sq mi), Shikoku 四国 18,798 sq km (7,258 sq mi), Kyūshū 九州 42,155 sq km (16,276 sq mi), and Okinawa Prefecture 沖縄県 2,265 sq km (875 sq mi). Japan set its territorial limit at 12 nautical miles from the coast in 1977.

Population 人口

At the time of the Meiji Restoration 明治維新 (1868) Japan's population was about 33 million. In 1996 it was 124,914,373, seventh largest in the world. The

NORTH AMERICA

ASIA

JAPAN

Equator

AUSTRALIA

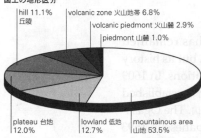

hill 11.1%
丘陵

volcanic zone 火山地帯 6.8%

volcanic piedmont 火山麓 2.9%

piedmont 山麓 1.0%

plateau 台地
12.0%

lowland 低地
12.7%

mountainous area
山地 53.5%

Source: Geographical Survey Institute.

population density 人口密度 per square kilometer (0.386 sq mi) was 331 persons in 1996. Although this figure is comparable to 372 persons (1992) in the Netherlands and 328 (1992) in Belgium, the density of the Japanese population per unit area under cultivation is the highest in the world, because over two-thirds of Japan is occupied by mountainous terrain, and alluvial plains 沖積平野 occupy only 13 percent.

The population was distributed comparatively equally all over the country about a century ago, when Japan was still predominantly agricultural. With industrialization, however, there was a strong tendency toward regional concentration. As a result, more than 40 percent of Japanese live in the three major urban areas of TŌKYŌ, ŌSAKA, and Nagoya. The Tōkyō Metropolitan Area 首都圏 in particular, although less than 2.0 percent in terms of area, has a concentration of 23.4 percent of the national population.

Formation of the Country 国家の成立

By the 4th century a sovereign court had emerged, which by conquest and alliance eventually unified the country. The Yamato court 大和朝廷 (ca 4th century–ca mid-7th century) repeatedly dispatched expeditionary forces to northeastern Honshū and succeeded in subduing it in the 7th century, thus establishing the prototype of a unified Japan consisting of Honshū, Shikoku, and Kyūshū. Under the Taika Reform 大化の改新 of 645, the *kokugun* system 国郡制 of administration was instituted, and the country was divided into 58 (later 66) provinces (*kuni* or *koku*) with subunits called *gun* (district). This division remained in effect nominally until the Meiji Restoration 明治維新 (1868). However, during the Edo period (1600–1868), the *bakuhan* (shogunate and

Population of Japan's Ten Largest Cities (1996)
日本の10大都市の人口

(in thousands)

Tōkyō 23 wards	7,817
Yokohama	3,281
Ōsaka	2,482
Nagoya	2,084
Sapporo	1,751
Kōbe	1,439
Kyōto	1,390
Fukuoka	1,234
Kawasaki	1,179
Hiroshima	1,088

domain) system 幕藩制 was superimposed on the *koku-gun* system.

Changes in Territory 領土の変遷

The territory of Japan 日本の領土 has remained essentially the same from the 7th century, but its history is nonetheless one of numerous modifications. In 1609 the *daimyō* 大名 of the Satsuma domain 薩摩藩 established control over the Ryūkyū Kingdom 琉球王国. The Ogasawara Islands were discovered by the Japanese in 1593 and were officially incorporated into Japan in 1876. Hokkaidō, once called Ezochi 蝦夷地, was settled by the Japanese in the Edo period. As trade developed with the Ainu people in the interior, the Japanese gradually made their way into the southern part of Sakhalin (J: Karafuto) 樺太 and the Kuril Islands 千島列島, where they came into conflict with the Russians. In 1875 Japan concluded the Treaty of St. Petersburg 樺太千島交換条約 with Russia and gave up the southern part of Sakhalin in exchange for the Kuril Islands. After the Sino-Japanese War of 1894–1895 日清戦争 Japan acquired Taiwan, and after the Russo-Japanese War 日露戦争 of 1905 it acquired the southern half of Sakhalin. It annexed Korea in 1910

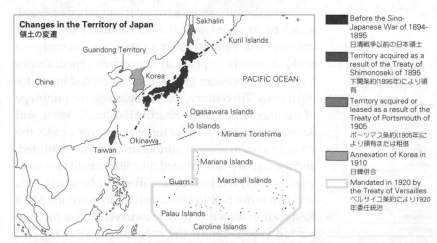

Changes in the Territory of Japan
領土の変遷

Sakhalin

Kuril Islands

Guandong Territory

China

Korea

PACIFIC OCEAN

Ogasawara Islands

Iō Islands

Minami Torishima

Okinawa

Taiwan

Mariana Islands

Guam

Marshall Islands

Palau Islands

Caroline Islands

■ Before the Sino-Japanese War of 1894-1895
日清戦争以前の日本領土

■ Territory acquired as a result of the Treaty of Shimonoseki of 1895
下関条約(1895年)により領有

■ Territory acquired or leased as a result of the Treaty of Portsmouth of 1905
ポーツマス条約(1905年)により領有または租借

■ Annexation of Korea in 1910
日韓併合

□ Mandated in 1920 by the Treaty of Versailles
ベルサイユ条約により1920年委任統治

and secured a mandate over former German territories in the South Sea Islands 南洋諸島 after World War I. Thus at the time of the outbreak of World War II, the total land area was 680,729 square kilometers (262,830 sq mi). However, after its defeat Japan was stripped of all territories acquired during its period of colonialism and, until the restoration of Okinawa 沖縄返還 in 1972, was left with essentially the four main islands.

▌Modern Prefectural System 府県制度

After the Meiji Restoration 明治維新 the country was administratively reorganized into the prefectural system 府県制度. Tōkyō, Ōsaka, and Kyōto were made *fu* (urban prefectures) 府 in 1871, and the rest of the country was divided into 302 *ken* (prefectures) 県. By 1888 this system had been integrated into a system of 3 *fu* and 43 *ken*. Hokkaidō was initially administered directly by the central government but later came to be treated equally with other prefectures, although it was called a *dō* (circuit) 道 rather than a *ken*. In 1943 Tōkyō Fu was designated as a special administrative area and named Tōkyō To 東京都 (officially translated as Tōkyō Metropolis). At present Japan is administratively divided into 1 *to* (Tōkyō To), 1 *dō* (Hokkaidō 北海道), 2 *fu* (Ōsaka Fu 大阪府 and Kyōto Fu 京都府), and 43 *ken*.

▌Natural Features of Japan 日本の自然
▌Topography 地形

The chief feature of the Japanese archipelago is its geological instability, including frequent volcanic activity 火山活動 and many earthquakes. Another distinctive characteristic of the topography is the fact that the Japanese archipelago is made up almost entirely of steep mountain districts with very few plains.

Mountains 山脈 High, precipitous mountains of about 1,500–3,000 meters (5,000–10,000 ft) run along the Pacific Ocean side of southwestern Japan. Deep, V-shaped valleys V字形の谷 are cut into these mountain

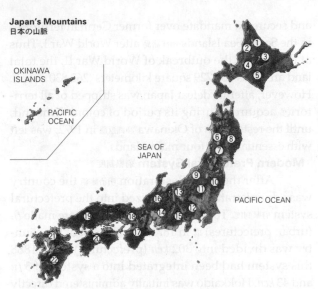

Japan's Mountains
日本の山脈

OKINAWA
ISLANDS

PACIFIC
OCEAN

SEA OF
JAPAN

PACIFIC OCEAN

① Kitami Mountains
② Teshio Mountains
③ Ishikari Mountains
④ Yūbari Mountains
⑤ Hidaka Mountains
⑥ Dewa Mountains
⑦ Ōu Mountains
⑧ Kitakami Mountains
⑨ Echigo Mountains
⑩ Abukuma Mountains
⑪ Mikuni Mountains
⑫ Kantō Mountains
⑬ Hida Mountains
⑭ Kiso Mountains
⑮ Akaishi Mountains
⑯ Ryōhaku Mountains
⑰ Kii Mountains
⑱ Tamba Mountains
⑲ Chūgoku Mountains
⑳ Shikoku Mountains
㉑ Tsukushi Mountains
㉒ Kyūshū Mountains

districts. The mountain ranges and mountainous districts of Akaishi 赤石山脈, Kii 紀伊, Shikoku, and Kyūshū are representative of this zone. In contrast, on the Sea of Japan side of southwestern Japan are groupings of plateaus and low mountain districts with a height of about 500–1,500 meters (1,600–5,000 ft), such as the Tamba, and Chūgoku mountain districts 丹波山地：中国山地; the Kibi Highland 吉備高原; and the Tsukushi Mountains 筑紫山地.

Volcanoes 火山 The large number and variety of volcanoes found throughout the Japanese archipelago constitute another remarkable feature. There have been 188 volcanoes active at some time or another since the Quaternary geological period 新生代第4期, and more than 40 of these remain active today. Among these are volcanoes that have had numerous violent eruptions, such as Asamayama 浅間山 and Bandaisan 磐梯山. Further, a special characteristic of Japan's volcano zone is the development of large craters or calderas such as those at Akan 阿寒, Daisetsu 大雪, Hakone 箱根, Aso 阿蘇, and Aira

Five Highest Mountains
主な山

Fujisan	3,776 m
Kitadake	3,192 m
Oku Hotakadake	3,190 m
Ainotake	3,189 m
Yarigatake	3,180 m

Atmospheric Pressure Configuration
気圧配置

Rainy season
梅雨

Okhotsk high

baiu front

North Pacific high

Midsummer
盛夏

North Pacific high

Typhoon season
台風

typhoon

Winter
冬

Siberian high

Aleutian low

始良. The caldera at Aso is on a scale unrivaled anywhere in the world.

Rivers 河川 A small number of large rivers, such as the Ishikarigawa 石狩川, Shinanogawa 信濃川, Tonegawa 利根川, Kisogawa 木曽川, Yodogawa 淀川, and Chikugogawa 筑後川, have fair-sized delta plains 沖積平野 at their mouths. Diluvial uplands 洪積台地 and river and marine terraces 河岸段丘：海岸段丘 have developed in many coastal areas of Japan, and these are utilized along with the plains for both agriculture and habitation.

Climate 気候

Located in the monsoon zone モンスーン地帯 of the eastern coast of the Asian continent, the most notable features of the climate of the Japanese archipelago are the wide range of yearly temperatures and the large amount of rainfall. However, because of the complexity of the land configuration, there are numerous regional differences throughout the seasons.

Spring 春 When low-pressure 低気圧 areas pass over the Pacific coast of Japan in March, the temperature rises with each rainfall. When low-pressure areas start to develop over the Sea of Japan 日本海, the strong wind from the south called *haru ichiban* (the first tidings of spring) 春一番 blows over Japan.

Summer 夏 The onset of the rainy season 梅雨 (*baiu* or *tsuyu*) takes place around 7 June. It starts in the southern part of Japan and moves northward. With the end of the rain around 20 July, the Ogasawara air masses 小笠原気団 blanket Japan, and the weather takes on a summer pattern. The peak of summer is late July, and the summer heat lingers on into mid-August.

Fall 秋 September is the typhoon season. Weather resembling that of the rainy season also occurs because of the autumnal rain fronts 秋雨前線. The weather clears in mid-October, and the winter winds start to blow.

Winter 冬 In December, when the atmospheric

pressure configuration 気圧配置 has completely changed to the winter pattern, northwest winds bring snow to the mountains and to the plains on the Sea of Japan side, and a dry wind blows on the Pacific Ocean side. The peak of winter comes around 25 January.

Life and Nature 生活と自然

The climate and the flora and fauna vary regionally, extending from the subarctic zone 亜寒帯 in the north to the subtropical zone 亜熱帯 in the south; there is also much seasonal change. An abundance of hot springs, which are popular as health resorts, accompany the many volcanoes.

Japan's seasonal changes and geological structure bring many natural disasters. Heavy rains due to the *baiu* front 梅雨前線 and the autumn typhoons bring about landslides, floods, and wind damage. Heavy winter precipitation causes snow damage as well as flooding and cold damage. In addition, major earthquakes strike somewhere in Japan every several decades. Typhoons and the *tsunami* (tidal waves) 津波 accompanying earthquakes also inflict damage on heavily populated, low-lying coastal areas.

Geological Structure 地質構造

The Japanese archipelago is a part of the island arc systems that border the eastern edge of the Asian continent アジア大陸. It occupies a position at the junction of four plates: the Pacific, North American, Eurasian, and Philippine Sea plates, which have reacted with each other over a long period to form complex arc-trench systems 島弧・海溝系.

Overall Topography 全体的な地勢

The Japanese archipelago itself is composed of five island arcs 島弧: from north to south, the Kuril Arc 千島弧, the Northeastern Honshū Arc 東北本州弧, the Izu-

Major Typhoons in Japan and Resultant Damage
主な台風とその被害

Rank	Name	Year	Dead or missing	Buildings damaged
1	Ise Bay Typhoon	1959	5,098	1,352,717
2	Makurazaki Typhoon	1945	3,746	446,897
3	Muroto Typhoon	1934	3,066	488,897
4	Typhoon Kathleen	1947	1,910	394,041
5	Tōya maru Typhoon	1954	1,761	371,043
6	Kanogawa Typhoon	1958	1,216	542,828

Source: Meteorological Agency.

Bonin Arc 伊豆・小笠原弧, the Southwestern Japan Arc 西南日本弧, and the Ryūkyū Arc 琉球弧, the last-named being connected to the Southwestern Japan Arc. Each of these arcs is convex oceanward, and they are accompanied on the ocean side by oceanic trenches or troughs, The arcs rarely exceed an altitude of 3,000 meters (10,000 ft), but the trenches are often as deep as 9,000 meters (30,000 ft). The Kuril, Northeastern Honshū, and Izu-Bonin arcs form a greater arc system, which is convex toward the west in general shape and which is often called the East Japan Arc 東日本島弧系. The Southwestern Japan and Ryūkyū arcs, which are collectively called the West Japan Arc 西日本島弧系, are a separate arc system. This system is truncated obliquely at its eastern margin by the great fault 断層 called the Itoigawa-Shizuoka Tectonic

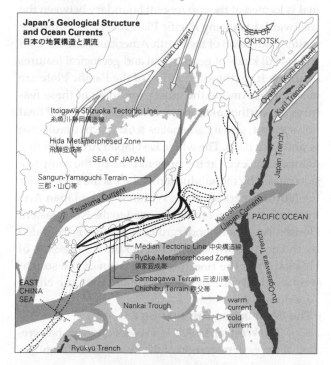

Japan's Geological Structure and Ocean Currents
日本の地質構造と潮流

Itoigawa-Shizuoka Tectonic Line
糸魚川・静岡構造線

Hida Metamorphosed Zone
飛騨変成帯

SEA OF JAPAN

Sangun-Yamaguchi Terrain
三郡・山口帯

Tsushima Current

SEA OF OKHOTSK

Liman Current

Oyashio (Kuril Current)

Kuril Trench

Japan Trench

Kuroshio (Japan Current)

PACIFIC OCEAN

Izu-Ogasawara Trench

Median Tectonic Line 中央構造線
Ryōke Metamorphosed Zone 領家変成帯
Sambagawa Terrain 三波川帯
Chichibu Terrain 秩父帯

EAST CHINA SEA

Nankai Trough

warm current
cold current

Ryūkyū Trench

Line 糸魚川・静岡構造線, which limits the western margin of the transversal depression called the Fossa Magna フォッサマグナ. The marginal seas—the Sea of Okhotsk オホーツク海, the Sea of Japan 日本海, and the Philippine Sea フィリピン海—that separate the arcs from the continent are one of the most characteristic topographic features. They are generally shallow seas, 3,000–4,000 meters (9,800–13,000 ft) in depth, but they are devoid of continental crust. In fact, oceanic crust exposes on the sea floor 海底 as a result of the fracturing and opening of the continental crust in Tertiary times 第3紀. The Okinawa Trough 沖縄トラフ behind the Ryūkyū Arc is now in the course of opening, representing the early stage of creation of a marginal sea 縁海.

The East Japan Arc 東日本島弧系

The East Japan Arc is an active island arc system that is located at the convergent boundary between the westward-advancing Pacific Plate 太平洋プレート and the western extension of the North American Plate 北アメリカプレート. All kinds of geophysical and geological features resulting from the subduction of the Pacific Plate are observable. Among the most prominent of these features are earthquakes 地震, volcanoes 火山, crustal heat flows 地殻熱流, gravity anomalies 重力異常, active faults 活動層, and folds 活褶曲. The whole East Japan Arc is suffering deformation even at the present time by the compression caused by the subduction of the Pacific Plate under the North American Plate. Within the East Japan Arc, the Kuril Arc is smoothly connected to the Northeastern Honshū Arc, but its underground structure is truncated by the north-south-running backbone range 脊梁 of Hokkaidō as the result of a collision of the southwestward-advancing Okhotsk Plate with the North American Plate.

The West Japan Arc 西日本島弧系

The West Japan Arc is an older orogenic belt created at the eastern margin of the Eurasian continent ユー

ラジア大陸 by successive subduction of accretionary complexes since Paleozoic times 古生代. The arc preserves the older geologic structures of pre-Tertiary rocks 先第3系岩石, on which several structural belts 構造帯 can be identified. The oldest belt, composed mostly of granitic 花崗岩 and gneissose rocks 片麻岩 in the Hida 飛驒 and Oki 隠岐 areas, which are probably of Precambrian age 先カンブリア時代, is considered to be a fragment of the Eurasian continent that separated and drifted oceanward with the opening of the Japan Sea about 15 million years ago. To this continental fragment, late Paleozoic 古生代後期 and Mesozoic 中生代 sediments and rocks were successively added, first, at about 400 million years ago, by the subduction of the Farallon Plate ファラロンプレート (which disappeared under the Asian continent at the end of the Paleozoic), then, during Mesozoic and Cenozoic times (about 250 to 30 million years ago), by the subduction of the Izanagi イザナギ, Kula クラ, and Pacific plates (all of which either disappeared or were displaced). These subductions are well witnessed by the existence of high pressure metamorphic rocks 高圧型変成岩, for example, in the Sangun 三郡変成帯 and Sambagawa terrains 三波川変成帯, which indicate the deep burial of the subducting plate. Presently the Philippine Sea Plate, advancing toward the north, is giving rise to a new arc-trench system, off the West Japan Arc, along the Nankai Trough-Ryūkyū Trench.

Theories of the Genesis of the Japanese Islands
日本列島成因の理論

The above interpretation is not the only theory for the genesis of the Japanese arcs. Another, entirely different, theory of continental accretion called collage tectonics コラージュ・テクトニクス has also been introduced. According to this theory, every structural belt 構造帯 of all the Japanese arcs represents an isolated fragment of continental rocks, called a terrane テレーン, which was displaced, together with the spreading ocean floor, and collided successively with preexisting continental masses or terranes to form a belt of fold mountains 褶曲山地. At present, both of these two theories are considered as alternatives for the genesis of the Japanese islands.

Sea of Japan (Nihonkai) 日本海

One of the three marginal seas (the others are the East China Sea 東シナ海 and the Sea of Okhotsk オホーツク海) around Japan. It is situated between the Asian continent and the Japanese archipelago and is connected to adjacent seas by the straits of Mamiya 間宮海峡, Sōya 宗谷, Tsugaru 津軽, Kammon 関門, and Tsushima 対馬. It is the smallest of the three seas (1,008,000 sq km; 389,000 sq mi) and the deepest (maximum depth: 3,712 m; 12,178 ft; average depth: 1,350 m; 4,430 ft). The Sea of Japan provides good fishing grounds and is an important factor in the heavy winter snowfalls on parts of Honshū.

Volcanoes (kazan) 火山

The many active volcanoes 活火山 in Japan form a part of the so-called circum-Pacific volcanic zone 環太平洋火山帯, which surrounds the Pacific Ocean. While volcanic eruptions 噴火 have significantly influenced the life of the Japanese people since earliest times, causing heavy loss of life, they have also produced beautiful natural views and features and provided fertile soil.

Distribution of Volcanoes 火山の分布

The volcanoes are located in a line that generally runs parallel to the Japanese archipelago. The eastern edge of volcano distribution in Hokkaidō and northern Honshū forms a line running almost parallel to the central mountain range that forms the backbone of the archipelago; to the west of this edge line, called the volcanic front 火山前線, volcanoes are distributed as far as the SEA OF JAPAN. The volcanic front turns abruptly south-

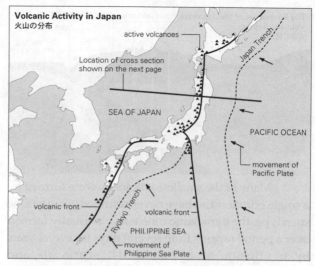

active volcanoes

Location of cross section
shown on the next page

SEA OF JAPAN

Japan Trench

PACIFIC OCEAN

movement of
Pacific Plate

volcanic front

Ryūkyū Trench

volcanic front

PHILIPPINE SEA

movement of
Philippine Sea Plate

ward in the northwest corner of the Kantō region of Honshū near Mt. Asama 浅間山 and, by way of the Yatsugatake volcano group, Fuji-Hakone-Izu National Park 富士箱根伊豆国立公園, and the eastern side of the Izu Peninsula 伊豆半島, goes through the Izu Islands to the volcanic islands of the Marianas マリアナ諸島. In southwestern Japan the distribution is not so dense, but a volcanic front runs across western Honshū, extends southward to central Kyūshū, and is connected to the volcanoes of Taiwan 台湾 by way of the Ryūkyū Islands. As of 1996 there were 86 active volcanoes in Japan.

Structure and Activity of Japanese Volcanoes
火山の構造と活動

Many Japanese volcanoes have a conical shape similar to that of Mt. Fuji 富士山, which has become a symbol of Japan. These volcanoes, called stratovolcanoes 成層火山, were formed by the alternate accumulation of lava flows 溶岩流 and of volcanic blocks and bombs 火山岩：火山弾 emitted from the summit crater 火口. One characteristic of this type of volcano is its profile, which consists of a beautiful exponential curve with wide, gentle skirts.

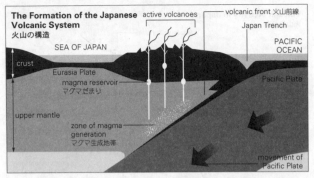

The Formation of the Japanese Volcanic System 火山の構造

SEA OF JAPAN

crust

Eurasia Plate

magma reservoir マグマだまり

upper mantle

zone of magma generation マグマ生成地帯

active volcanoes

volcanic front 火山前線

Japan Trench

PACIFIC OCEAN

Pacific Plate

movement of Pacific Plate

Many of the smallest volcanoes were formed by a single eruption and have never resumed activity. One such type, the pyroclastic cone 砕屑丘, is usually formed over a period ranging from several days to several years by an effusion 流出 of pumice 軽石, scoria 岩滓, and volcanic ash. Another type is the lava dome 溶岩ドーム, in which highly viscous lava is gradually pushed up as a huge mass. Most pyroclastic cones and lava domes are no more than 200 meters (650 ft) in height, and they often occur in groups.

Two rarer kinds of eruption activity are known for their destructive power. One is a large steam explosion 蒸気爆発, which is a characteristic feature of the stratovolcano toward the end of its life. In the 1888 eruption of Mt. Bandai 磐梯山, a series of violent explosions lasting several minutes each was followed by a huge landslide. The other type of destructive eruption is caused by the effusion of an enormous amount of magma onto the ground within a brief period. The foamy magma splits into pieces and is violently ejected as a mixture of rocks, pumice, volcanic ash, and gas known as a pyroclastic flow 火砕流.

In November 1990 there was an eruption at Fugendake 普賢岳, the highest peak of Unzendake 雲仙岳, which last erupted in 1792. During subsequent eruptions in 1991 pyroclastic flows claimed 44 lives.

▌Volcano Monitoring 火山観測

Microearthquakes and any change in the earth's crust are observed regularly and continuously at 19 active volcanoes throughout Japan, including Asama-yama 浅間山, Miharayama 三原山, Asosan 阿蘇山, and the Unzendake 雲仙岳 group. At these volcanoes instruments such as seismometers 地震計, tiltmeters 傾斜計, extensometers 伸縮計, and laser beams レーザー光線 are used to make precise measurements of any changes. The Global Positioning System (GPS) 汎地球測位システム, which uses artificial satellites 人工衛星, is also utilized to monitor conditions. Thus, it is unlikely that a major eruption could occur without some forewarning. However, means of preventing disasters stemming from volcanic eruptions remain inadequate, as volcanic eruptions are natural phenomena involving the release of huge amounts of energy.

Earthquakes (*jishin*) 地震

Earthquakes are a frequent phenomenon in Japan; nearly 10 percent of the energy released worldwide by earthquakes each year is concentrated in and around the Japanese islands. In the last century Japan has experienced 24 destructive earthquakes with magnitudes of 6 or higher on the scale used by the Meteorological Agency of Japan 気象庁. This scale roughly approximates the better-known Richter scale リヒタースケール used in the West. Both scales measure the magnitude of an earthquake by the energy released from its epicenter 震央.

Two major Japanese cities, Tōkyō and Kōbe, have been devastated by earthquakes in this century. The Tōkyō Earthquake of 1923 関東大震災, which was centered near metropolitan Tōkyō and Yokohama and estimated to be magnitude 7.9 on the Japanese scale, resulted in more than 140,000 deaths and billions of dollars in property loss. In Tōkyō alone it took the lives of more than 60,000 people, of whom more than 50,000 died in quake-related fires.

In January 1995, the Kōbe Earthquake 阪神・淡路大震災, with a magnitude of 7.2 and epicenter in the northern tip of the Awajishima, destroyed much of the Hanshin area, leaving a total of 6,430 dead.

Causes of Earthquakes in Japan
日本における地震の原因

The Tōkyō Earthquake was caused by movement along a fault, that is, a fracture in the earth's crust. The upper layer of the fault 断層 zone shifted about 6 meters (20 ft) east and about 3 meters (10 ft) south with respect to the lower layer. The surface of the earth moved upward and toward the Pacific Ocean. This same type of movement is seen in virtually every earthquake that occurs along the Pacific coast of Japan.

There are also "swarms," 群発地震 sustained periods of numerous small quakes. The longest recorded swarm took place in the mid-1960s at Matsushiro in Nagano Prefecture.

Earthquake activity in Japan is accompanied by various forms of crustal distortion and fault displacement depending on the geographic and geologic area involved. For example, the tips of such peninsulas as the Bōsō 房総半島, Miura 三浦半島, and Kii 紀伊半島, all of which jut out into the Pacific Ocean 太平洋, slowly sink into the ocean at the rate of 1 centimeter (0.4 in) a year, but a major earthquake would lift the tip to compensate instantly for the accumulated depression. On the other hand, earthquakes occurring in southwestern Japan,

Major Earthquakes in Japan since 1923
日本の主な地震

Earthquake	Date	Magnitude	Dead or missing
Tōkyō (Kantō) Earthquake	1923, 9	7.9	142,807
North Tango Earthquake	1927, 3	7.3	2,925
Sanriku Offshore Earthquake	1933, 3	8.1	3,008
Tottori Earthquake	1943, 9	7.2	1,083
Tōnankai Earthquake	1944, 12	7.9	998
Mikawa Earthquake	1945, 1	6.8	2,306
Nankai Earthquake	1946, 12	8.0	1,432
Fukui Earthquake	1948, 6	7.1	3,892
Niigata Earthquake	1964, 6	7.5	26
Tokachi Offshore Earthquake	1968, 5	7.9	52
Miyagi Offshore Earthquake	1978, 6	7.4	28
Central Sea of Japan Earthquake	1983, 5	7.7	104
Southwest Hokkaidō Offshore Earthquake	1993, 7	7.8	230
Kōbe (Hanshin-Awaji) Earthquake	1995, 1	7.2	6,430

Source: Fire Defense Agency; *Rika nempyō*.

west of the Fossa Magna フォッサマグナ, are created by sudden movements of the earth along an existing fault zone, and unlike earthquakes on the Pacific coast 太平洋岸, these quakes are not preceded by crustal movement 地殻変動.

The crustal distortion accompanying Pacific coast quakes is caused by mantle convection マントル対流 within the earth. In the southeastern Pacific Ocean there is a ridge 海嶺, toward which mantle convection surges from the earth's core and then moves horizontally toward Japan before creeping downward again to the core. When mantle flow gets into the core, the movement causes one plate プレート on the mantle to subduct, or dive under the other, and become absorbed in the underlying mantle. The involvement of peninsula tips in this movement causes their slow depression between earthquakes, the rate of depression being equal to the speed of mantle convection. The sudden upheaval of a peninsula's tip in an earthquake is due to "elastic rebound." 弾性反発

Pacific coastal areas are gradually compressed by mantle convection in the intervals between earthquakes, and in a large earthquake they rebound toward the Pacific. Accordingly, the greater the accumulation of pressure from the Pacific Ocean, the greater the probability that an earthquake will occur in the region.

Earthquake Prediction 地震予知

Since 1965, funds have been allocated for research on earthquake prediction 地震予知, most of it centering on characteristic crustal distortions. In 1969 the Meteoro-logical Agency, the Geographic Survey Institute 国土地理院, and several national universities

1) Areas for intensified observation 観測強化地域
   (A) Southern Kantō
   (B) Tōkai
2) Areas for specified observation 特定観測地域
   (C) Eastern Hokkaidō
   (D) Western Akita and north-western Yamagata
   (E) Eastern Miyagi and eastern Fukushima
   (F) South-western Niigata and northern Nagano
   (G) Western Nagano and eastern Gifu
   (H) Nagoya, Kyōto, Ōsaka, and Kōbe area
   (I) Eastern Shimane
   (J) Iyo Nada and Hyūga Nada area

Earthquake Observation Areas
地震観測地域

Okinawa Islands

Source: Coordinating Committee for Earthquake Prediction.

formed the Coordinating Committee for Earthquake Prediction 地震予知連絡会 to pool the results of their research. It was decided to conduct surveys over the entire area of Japan and to repeat measurements of geologic changes at short intervals by means of leveling 水準測量 and triangulation 三角測量 in comparatively small areas of the country deemed important, such as the southern Kantō area and the Tōkai region 東海地方 (Shizuoka 静岡 and Aichi 愛知 prefectures). Distortion and faulting also have been monitored continuously, using sensitive instruments such as the tiltmeter 傾斜計 and extensometer 伸縮計. It is known that microelastic impact waves 弾性衝撃波 are generated in considerable numbers before rock fractures under the accumulation of strain, which is thought to resemble foreshock activity preceding large earthquakes. The flow of heat that is transmitted from the core of the earth to the surface is closely related to crustal phenomena; further, terrestrial magnetism 地磁気 and earth current 地電流 are said to change in relation to a large earthquake. Therefore, these phenomena are being measured to determine if there is some connection that will contribute to earthquake prediction.

Three factors: when, where, and how severe are essential to earthquake prediction. Although quakes do occur periodically and are accompanied by characteristic crustal movements, the difficulties of predicting precisely when a quake will strike are not likely to be solved soon.

Most of the enormous damage accompanying large earthquakes comes from fire following building collapse, and also from the effects of *tsunami* 津波, a large sea wave. Earthquakes are particularly destructive in Japan because closely packed structures, usually of wood, make for inadequate firebreaks, while the popularity of small space heaters fueled by gas or kerosene 灯油 increases the chance of fire.

Hokkaidō 北海道

Hokkaidō
北海道

The northernmost and second largest of Japan's four main islands. It is separated from Honshū to the south by the Tsugaru Strait 津軽海峡 and bounded by the SEA OF JAPAN on the west, the Sea of Okhotsk on the northeast, and the Pacific Ocean on the south and east. Several mountain ranges cross Hokkaidō, and those belonging to the Ezo Mountains 蝦夷山地 run from north to south across the center of the island, separated into two strands by a series of basin areas. To the west of these mountains lies the broad Ishikari Plain 石狩平野. To the southwest of the plain is a long peninsula, which is the area closest to Honshū. The climate is unlike that of the rest of Japan, being notably colder and drier.

The prehistoric culture of Hokkaidō seems to have shared many of the characteristics of the early culture of Honshū, except that it lacked the culture of the Yayoi period 弥生時代 (ca 300 bc–ca ad 300). Hokkaidō, or Ezo, as it was known, was inhabited by the Ainu and not included in Japan proper. In the Edo period (1600–1868) the Matsumae domain 松前藩 was established in the extreme southwestern corner of the island. After the Meiji Restoration 明治維新 of 1868, the new government placed great emphasis on Hokkaidō's economic development, setting up the Hokkaidō Colonization Office (kaitakushi) 開拓使 and encouraging settlers to come from other parts of Japan. The name of the island was changed to Hokkaidō (literally, "Northern Sea Circuit") in 1869. The present prefectural form of administration was established in 1886.

The main agricultural crop is rice; grain and vegetable farming as well as dairy farming are active. Fishing and forestry have long been an important part of Hokkaidō's economy. They also form the basis for

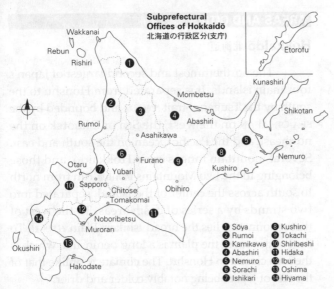

Subprefectural
Offices of Hokkaidō
北海道の行政区分(支庁)

Wakkanai
Rebun
Rishiri
❶
Mombetsu
Etorofu
Kunashiri
❷
❸
Abashiri
Shikotan
❹
Rumoi
Asahikawa
❺
Nemuro
Otaru
❻ Furano
❾
❽
Kushiro
❼ Yūbari
Sapporo
❿
Chitose
Obihiro
Tomakomai
⓬
⓫
Noboribetsu
⓮
Muroran
Okushiri
⓭
Hakodate

❶ Sōya   ❽ Kushiro
❷ Rumoi   ❾ Tokachi
❸ Kamikawa   ❿ Shiribeshi
❹ Abashiri   ⓫ Hidaka
❺ Nemuro   ⓬ Iburi
❻ Sorachi   ⓭ Oshima
❼ Ishikari   ⓮ Hiyama

much of Hokkaidō's industrial activity, including food-processing, woodworking, pulp, and paper industries.

Hokkaidō is noted for its dramatic and unspoiled scenery, which includes active volcanoes, large lakes, and vast virgin forests. Major tourist attractions are Shikotsu-Tōya 支笏洞爺, Akan 阿寒, Daisetsuzan 大雪山, Shiretoko 知床, Rishiri-Rebun-Sarobetsu 利尻礼文サロベツ, and Kushiro Shitsugen 釧路湿原 national parks. Area: 83,451 sq km (32,220 sq mi); pop: 5,684,842 in 1996; capital: Sapporo 札幌(市). Other major cities include Hakodate 函館(市), Asahikawa 旭川(市), Otaru 小樽(市), Muroran 室蘭(市), Tomakomai 苫小牧(市), Obihiro 帯広(市), and Kushiro 釧路(市).

Tōhoku region (Tōhoku *chihō*) 東北地方

Region encompassing the entire northeastern part of Honshū and consisting of Aomori 青森(県), Iwate 岩手(県), Akita 秋田(県), Yamagata 山形(県), Miyagi 宮城(県), and Fukushima 福島(県) prefectures. The region is largely mountainous, and most towns and cities are concentrated along the Pacific and SEA OF JAPAN coasts and in

Tōhoku region
東北地方

the centers of several basins. The climate is highly seasonal, with short summers and long winters.

The area is primarily an agricultural area and forestry and fishing are also important. There is some petroleum and natural-gas production, and the electrical appliance 電気機器, cement セメント, chemical 化学, pulp パルプ, and petroleum-refining 石油精製 industries have been developing. The principal city is Sendai 仙台. Area: 66,884 sq km (25,824 sq mi); pop: 9,865,006 in 1996.

Kantō region (Kantō *chihō*) 関東地方

Kantō region
関東地方

Located in east central Honshū, consisting of TŌKYŌ 東京(都), Chiba 千葉(県), Saitama 埼玉(県), Kanagawa 神奈川(県), Gumma 群馬(県), Ibaraki 茨城(県), and Tochigi 栃木(県) prefectures. This is Japan's most heavily populated region and is the political, economic, and cultural center of the nation. The regional center is the metropolitan area 首都圏 that includes Tōkyō, Yokohama 横浜(市), Kawasaki 川崎(市), and Chiba 千葉(市). The region is dominated by the Kantō Plain 関東平野.

The term Kantō (literally, "east of the barrier") originally referred to the area east of the barrier station 関所 at Ōsakayama 逢坂山 in what is now Ōtsu 大津, Shiga 滋賀 Prefecture; the term was used in contradistinction to the KANSAI REGION west of the station. The border was later moved twice, finally being set much farther east at the barrier station at Hakone 箱根 (in what is now Kanagawa Prefecture).

The Tōkyō-Yokohama district in the center of the region is Japan's leading commercial and industrial area. Agriculture plays a declining but still important role in the region's economy. Coastal fishing in the Pacific Ocean and Tōkyō Bay 東京湾 has declined because of increased pollution and land reclamation in Tōkyō Bay. Area: 32,418 sq km (12,517 sq mi); pop: 39,159,557 in 1996.

Tōkyō 東京[都]

Capital 首都 of Japan. Located on the Kantō Plain 関東平野, on the Pacific side of central Honshū. Bordered by the prefectures of Chiba 千葉(県) on the east, Saitama 埼玉(県) on the north, Yamanashi 山梨(県) on the west, and Kanagawa 神奈川(県) on the southwest, and by Tōkyō Bay 東京湾 on the southeast. Under its administration are islands scattered in the western Pacific, among them the Izu Islands 伊豆諸島 and the Ogasawara Islands 小笠原諸島.

Tōkyō Prefecture comprises the 23 wards (*ku* 区) of urban Tōkyō, 27 cities (*shi* 市), 1 county (*gun* 郡), and 4 island administrative units (*shichō* 支庁). The county and the island units contain 13 towns and villages (*chō* 町, *son* 村). Area: 2,183 sq km (843 sq mi); pop: 11,542,468 in 1996.

The residents of Tōkyō live in a total of 5,003,985 dwellings, with an average floor space of 63 square meters (678 sq ft). The average household has 2.3 members.

Geography and Climate 地形と気候

Tōkyō was known by the name Edo 江戸 (literally, "Rivergate") before the Meiji Restoration 明治維新 (1868), and the principal rivers of the Kantō region—the Edogawa 江戸川, Arakawa 荒川, and Sumidagawa 隅田川— still flow to the sea through eastern Tōkyō. Along the alluvial plains of the old river Tamagawa 多摩川, volcanic ash emitted from the Fuji-Hakone Volcanic Range 富士箱根火山帯 accumulated to form the Musashino Plateau 武蔵野台地, where the western wards (commonly known as the Yamanote 山手 district) and outlying districts are located. Some areas in the eastern wards (the *shitamachi* 下町 district) lie 2–3 meters (6.5–10 ft) below sea level.

The four seasons are sharply delineated, and the climate is generally mild, with the highest average monthly temperature in August (27.1°C; 80.8°F) and the lowest in January (5.2°C; 41.4°F). The annual precipitation 降水量 is 1,460 millimeters (57.5 in).

Fauna and Flora 動物と植物

   Pollution and unchecked land development ravaged the animal and plant population in Tōkyō Prefecture during the 1960s, but, with stricter pollution controls, 370 out of the approximately 500 bird species found throughout Japan have been sighted within Tōkyō. Other wildlife found in the mountainous areas include the Japanese serow ニホンカモシカ, raccoon dog タヌキ, fox キツネ, flying squirrel ムササビ and rabbit ウサギ.

   The official tree of Tōkyō is the ginkgo イチョウ, which is utilized as a shade tree throughout the city. Other common trees in Tōkyō include the cherry サクラ, zelkova ケヤキ, and Japanese oak カシ.

History 歴史

   During the 7th century Japan was divided into some 58 provinces, and Musashi Province 武蔵国 was established in what is today Tōkyō, Saitama, and eastern Kanagawa prefectures. Its administrative center was located in what is now the city of Fuchū, which served as the political center of the province for nearly 900 years. During the civil wars of the 15th century, the warrior Ōta Dōkan 太田道灌 (1432–1486) constructed the predecessor of Edo Castle at the present site of the Imperial Palace 皇居.

   After nearly a century of warfare, Toyotomi Hideyoshi 豊臣秀吉 (1537–1598) partially united the country and dispatched Tokugawa Ieyasu 徳川家康 (1543–1616) to Kantō in 1590 as lord of Edo Castle 江戸城. After Hideyoshi's death Ieyasu completed the unification of Japan and established the Tokugawa shogunate 徳川幕府 in Edo in 1603. He constructed a castle town 城下町 there with a *samurai* 侍 residential district on the castle's western side. To the east marshland

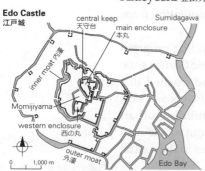

Edo Castle
江戸城

central keep
天守台

main enclosure
本丸

Sumidagawa

inner moat 内濠

Momijiyama

western enclosure
西の丸

outer moat
外濠

Edo Bay

0   1,000 m

was reclaimed, and a commercial and industrial area came into being. As the city flourished merchants and artisans flocked to Edo; the population reached one million by 1720, making Edo the largest city in the world at that time.

In 1867 the Tokugawa shogunate came to an end, and, with the Meiji Restoration 明治維新 the following year, Edo, renamed Tōkyō ("eastern capital"), became the national capital. The imperial family took up residence at Edo Castle in 1869. In the following years Tōkyō grew steadily in importance as the political, commercial, and financial center of Japan. Almost completely destroyed in the Tōkyō Earthquake of 1923 関東大震災, the city was largely rebuilt by 1930 and administratively enlarged in 1943, merging surrounding districts and suburbs into Tōkyō To 東京都 (Tōkyō Prefecture; officially, Tōkyō Metropolis).

Much of Tōkyō was destroyed during World War II by American bombing. After Japan's defeat Tōkyō remained the seat of government, with the General Headquarters (GHQ) 連合国最高司令官総司令部 of the Supreme Commander for the Allied Powers (SCAP) 連合国最高司令官 located there until the end of the Occupation 占領 in 1952. During the period of economic recovery starting in the 1950s, large enterprises increasingly concentrated their managerial operations in Tōkyō. This resulted in an increase in population from 6.3 million in 1950 to 9.7 million in 1960.

The city undertook a feverish building program in preparation for the 1964 Tōkyō Olympic Games 東京オリンピック, and by 1965 the population had reached 10.9 million, resulting in serious housing problems and skyrocketing land prices. A program of building urban subcenters 副都心 has since been carried out to alleviate the concentration of company head offices in the central Tōkyō area.

The reclaimed land in the Tōkyō Bay area has developed into seaside parks and sports facilities, and a major project for a waterfront subcenter 臨海副都心 is underway in this area.

Local and Traditional Industry 地場産業と伝統産業

Local industries were long centered in the three *shitamachi* 下町 wards of Taitō 台東(区), Sumida 墨田(区), and Arakawa 荒川(区), but in recent years are expanding to the surrounding wards, particularly Adachi 足立(区) and Katsushika 葛飾(区). Products include clothing, knitted goods, precious metals, toys, and leather goods. Among traditional industries, fabric making has been prominent. Cities within Tōkyō Prefecture such as Hachiōji 八王子(市), Ōme 青梅(市), and Musashi Murayama 武蔵村山(市) have been noted for the production of fabrics since the Edo period (1600–1868), and the island of Hachijōjima 八丈島 is noted for its *kihachijō* dyed fabric 黄八丈.

Modern Industry and Finance 現代の産業と金融

Tōkyō developed into a center of manufacturing and heavy industry from the Meiji period (1868–1912) until the end of World War II. After 1965, however, tertiary industries 第3次産業—commerce, finance, transportation, communication, wholesale and retail stores, and service industries—began to surpass secondary industries 第2次産業. As of 1995 tertiary industries constituted more than 70 percent of the total industries in Tōkyō. Tōkyō boasts a total of approximately 765,600 private enterprises employing nearly 8.2 million workers. Most of these enterprises are small and medium-sized enterprises 中小企業. The total output of Tōkyō Prefecture in fiscal 1995 was ¥19.7 trillion (US $209 billion).

As new office buildings take over the central part of the city, small shops and permanent residents have been forced out to suburban areas, creating the so-called doughnut phenomenon ドーナツ化現象. The pollution of

Employment Distribution by Industrial Sector (1995)
就業人口の産業別構成 (%)

	Japan	Tokyo
primary industries	6.0	0.5
secondary industries	31.6	25.6
tertiary industries	61.3	72.1
other	0.6	1.8

Source: National Census.

the 1970s also forced large manufacturing plants and related factories from the *shitamachi* lowlands to the outlying districts or to reclaimed land in Tōkyō Bay and adjacent prefectures. Most large Japanese corporations, foreign companies, and the national press and mass media have their head offices in Tōkyō; these are particularly concentrated in Chiyoda 千代田(区), Chūō 中央(区), and Minato 港(区) wards.

Another recent development has been the growth of the Shinjuku, Shibuya, and Ikebukuro districts. Now known as satellite city centers 副都心 or urban subcenters, they have become flourishing business and recreation districts. The doughnut phenomenon, originally confined to the old city center, has spread to these satellite centers, and between 1985 and 1990 the population of the 23 urban wards of Tōkyō Prefecture fell by 190,000.

Tōkyō is also a major financial center. The Tōkyō Stock Exchange 東京証券取引所 is one of the largest in the world in terms of aggregate market value and total sales, and deposits in Tōkyō banks constituted 24 percent of the nation's total deposits in 1993.

▌Transportation 交通

Airports 空港 Tōkyō is served by two international AIRPORTS: Tōkyō International Airport 東京国際空港 (commonly called Haneda Airport), the main terminal for domestic flights in the southern end of the city, and New Tōkyō International Airport 新東京国際空港 (commonly called Narita Airport), located 66 kilometers (41 mi) east of Tōkyō.

Railways and roads 鉄道・道路 The nation's main railway lines are concentrated in Tōkyō, with terminals at Tōkyō 東京(駅), Ueno 上野(駅), and Shinjuku 新宿(駅) stations. Trains for the west (Nagoya 名古屋, Kyōto 京都 Ōsaka 大阪,) leave from Tōkyō Station (Tōkaidō 東海道 and Tōkaidō SHINKANSEN 新幹線 lines); trains for Tōhoku 東北,

Railway Track Length in Tōkyō (1996)
東京都の鉄道営業延長

Type of railway	(km)
JR lines	299
Subways	225
Private lines	333
Monorails, streetcars	47
Total	904

Source: Tōkyō Metropolitan Government.

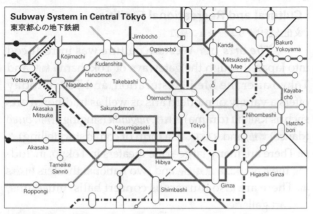

Hokkaidō 北海道, and Niigata 新潟 originate from Ueno Station (Tōhoku 東北, Jōban 常磐, Takasaki 高崎, and Jōetsu 上越 lines; the Tōhoku, Jōetsu and Hokuriku 北陸 (Nagano) Shinkansen lines originate from Tōkyō Station). From Shinjuku Station trains connect the city with the mountainous regions of central Japan (Chūō trunk line 中央本線).

The principal commuter railway lines 通勤列車路線 in Tōkyō are the Yamanote line 山手線, the Keihin Tōhoku line 京浜東北線, the Chūō line 中央線, and the Sōbu line 総武線. A network of private railway lines radiates outward from the principal stations on the Yamanote line, and 12 private and metro-politan SUBWAY lines have replaced the old network of streetcars. Tōkyō is also well served by bus lines, and expressways connect the city to various regions.

Education 教育

In recent years a number of colleges and universities have moved away from the crowded city, but Tōkyō is still a major educational center, with 78 junior colleges and 107 universities as of 1995. The city is also the location of numerous academic societies, including the Japan Academy 日本学士院 and the Japan Art Academy 日本芸術院.

Cultural and Recreational Facilities
文化及びリクリエーション施設

The arts 芸術 Western culture was introduced into Japan through the gateways of Yokohama 横浜 and Tōkyō after the Meiji Restoration, and Tōkyō today offers a variety of modern arts as well as traditional arts such as KABUKI (drama) 歌舞伎, *nagauta* (singing) 長唄, *buyō* (dance) 舞踊, and RAKUGO (a form of comic storytelling) 落語. There are many large-scale theaters in Tōkyō, including the Kabukiza 歌舞伎座 and two national theaters 国立劇場. There are also numerous concert halls, museums, and art galleries.

The media マスメディア Tōkyō is also a major information center. Eight general newspapers are published in Tōkyō (including four in English), as well as three economic and industrial newspapers and seven sports newspapers; an average of more than 6,676,000 newspaper copies were circulated each day in October 1996. In addition, it is estimated that roughly 2,400 monthly and weekly magazines were being published in Tōkyō in the early 1990s.

A large proportion of television programming also originates in Tōkyō from NHK and the five commercial channels.

Parks 公園 Although most parks are small by Western standards, a considerable number are scattered throughout Tōkyō. Major parks in central Tōkyō include the Imperial Palace grounds, Hibiya Park 日比谷公園, Ueno Park 上野公園, and the Meiji Shrine Outer Garden 明治神宮外苑. There are also some 10 zoological and botanical gardens in the metropolitan area. Major national parks in Tōkyō Prefecture include Chichibu-Tama National Park 秩父多摩国立公園, Ogasawara National Park 小笠原国立公園, and part of Fuji-Hakone-Izu National Park 富士箱根伊豆国立公園.

Points of Interest 観光名所

Situated in the center of Tōkyō and surrounded

Per-capita Park Area in Major Cities in the World and Six Major Cities in Japan
世界主要都市及びわが国6大都市の1人あたり公園面積　(m²)

London	30.4
New York	19.2
Montreal	13.1
Paris	12.2
Kita Kyūshū	8.9
Nagoya	6.0
Tōkyō	4.5
Yokohama	3.3
Ōsaka	3.0
Kyōto	2.7

Note: (1) Data on Japanese cities is based on a 1992 survey.
(2) Data on non-Japanese cities is based on a 1984 survey.
Source: Tōkyō Metropolitan Government.

by a moat 濠 and high stone walls is the Imperial Palace 皇居, still retaining vestiges of its former glory as the residence of the Tokugawa family 徳川氏. To the east lies the Ginza 銀座, an area known for its fine shops, department stores, and numerous restaurants, bars, and cabarets.

North of the Ginza is Nihombashi 日本橋, the commercial hub of the city, from which all distances from Tōkyō to places throughout Japan are measured. Nearby are the districts of Kanda 神田, renowned for its bookshops and universities, and Akihabara 秋葉原, famous for its discount stores selling all kinds of electrical appliances. Further to the north lie Ueno 上野 and Ueno Park 上野公園 that houses the Tōkyō National Museum 東京国立博物館, the National Science Museum 国立科学博物館, the National Museum of Western Art 国立西洋美術館, the Ueno Zoological Gardens 上野動物園, and the temple Kan'eiji 寛永寺. To the east of Ueno is the oldest temple in Tōkyō, Asakusa Kannon 浅草観音(浅草寺), in the heart of the *shitamachi* district, with its many shops still selling traditional handicrafts 伝統的手工芸品.

Another point of interest in the capital is the Diet Building 国会議事堂 in Nagatachō 永田町. Nearby Roppongi 六本木 and Azabu 麻布, situated close to Tōkyō Tower 東京タワー, house many foreign embassies. Neighboring Akasaka 赤坂 is known for its luxurious nightlife. Near Shibuya Station 渋谷駅 lie Meiji Shrine 明治神宮, Yoyogi Park 代々木公園, the National Stadium 国立競技場, and Harajuku 原宿, a fashionable district popular with young people.

The area around Shinjuku Station—which has the highest rate of passenger turnover in the country—is rapidly being developed, with restaurants and theaters in the Kabukichō 歌舞伎町 area on the eastern side of the station and numerous skyscrapers on the western side, including the new Tōkyō Metropolitan Government Offices 東京都庁舎 in the striking 48-story twin-tower building (243 m; 797 ft).

Chūbu region (Chūbu *chihō*) 中部地方

Chūbu region
中部地方

Encompassing Niigata 新潟(県), Toyama 富山(県), Ishikawa 石川(県), Fukui 福井(県), Yamanashi 山梨(県), Nagano 長野(県), Gifu 岐阜(県), Shizuoka 静岡(県), and Aichi 愛知(県) prefectures in central Honshū. Geographically divided into three districts: the Hokuriku region 北陸地方 on the SEA OF JAPAN side, the Central Highlands 中央高地 (or Tōsan 東山), and the Tōkai region 東海地方 on the Pacific seaboard. The region, largely mountainous, is dominated by the Japanese Alps 日本アルプス and contains numerous volcanoes including Mt. Fuji 富士山 (FUJISAN). Some of Japan's longest rivers, the Shinanogawa 信濃川, Kisogawa 木曽川, and Tenryūgawa 天竜川, flow through the region. The Niigata Plain 新潟平野 along the Sea of Japan is one of the largest rice-producing areas in Japan, and the Nōbi Plain 濃尾平野 on the Pacific coast is the most densely populated and highly industrialized area in this region. Numerous inland basins have very cold winters. The Pacific side is generally mild, and the Sea of Japan side has long snowy winters.

The Chūbu region includes three industrial areas (the Chūkyō Industrial Zone 中京工業地帯 and the Tōkai and Hokuriku industrial regions 東海工業地帯：北陸工業地帯). Among traditional products of the district are lacquer ware and ceramics. Agricultural products include rice 米, tea 茶, mandarin oranges ミカン, strawberries イチゴ, grapes ブドウ, peaches モモ, and apples リンゴ. Fishing is important all along its coast. The principal city of the region is Nagoya 名古屋市. Area: 66,778 sq km (25,783 sq mi) in 1992; pop: 21,286,176 in 1996.

Kinki region (Kinki *chihō*) 近畿地方

Located in west central Honshū and consisting of Ōsaka 大阪(府), Hyōgo 兵庫(県), Kyōto 京都(府), Shiga 滋賀(県), Mie 三重(県), Wakayama 和歌山(県), and Nara 奈良(県) prefectures. It is the nation's second most important industrial

Kinki region
近畿地方

region. The region's northern part is dominated by the Chūgoku Mountains 中国山地 and the Tamba Mountains 丹波山地, and the steep Kii Mountains 紀伊山地 lie to the south. The land is generally low between these ranges, with many small basins and numerous coastal plains on the Inland Sea 瀬戸内海, Ōsaka Bay 大阪湾, and the Kii Channel 紀伊水道. The Kii Peninsula 紀伊半島 is warm even in winter. The northern part of the region faces the SEA OF JAPAN and is noted for its heavy snowfall.

The Kyōto-Nara area was the cultural and political center of Japan in ancient days, but it lost its political significance after the capital was moved to Tōkyō in 1868. The Ōsaka-Kōbe district is the center of commerce and industry for western Japan. This area is called the Hanshin Industrial Zone 阪神工業地帯. Rice and citrus fruit 柑橘類 production, lumbering 製林業, and fishing 漁業 are important activities. Principal cities include ŌSAKA 大阪 (市), KYŌTO 京都(市), and Kōbe 神戸(市), one of the country's most important ports. Area: 33,095 sq km (12,778 sq mi) in 1992; pop: 22,226,969 in 1996.

Kansai region (Kansai *chihō*) 関西地方

A term loosely applied to the area centering on the cities of Ōsaka 大阪(市), Kyōto 京都(市), and Kōbe 神戸 (市). It is sometimes defined as equivalent to the KINKI REGION, but the latter is an official geographical designation with clearly defined boundaries. The term Kansai is rather a cultural and historical one, the definition of which has changed over the years. Kansai (literally, "west of the barrier") was first used sometime before the 10th century in contradistinction to the word Kantō. Kantō 関東 ("east of the barrier") referred to the area east of the barrier station 関所 at Ōsaka (in what is now Shiga Prefecture), and Kansai referred to the area west of the station. It was later fixed farther east at the barrier station at Hakone 箱根 (in what is now Kanagawa Prefecture).

The term is also used to describe local speech patterns (as in Kansai *ben* 関西弁 or Kansai *namari*) and manners and customs. See also KANTŌ REGION.

Kyōto 京都[市]

Capital of Kyōto Prefecture 京都府. The city is situated in southern Kyōto Prefecture, in the Kyōto fault basin 京都(地溝)盆地. The ancient capital of Japan from 794 to 1868, Kyōto, rich in historical sites, is today one of Japan's largest cities. Kyōto is renowned for its fine textiles and traditional products and is also a thriving center for industry.

Natural Features 地形

The low Tamba Mountains 丹波山地 surround the city to the north, east, and west. Two peaks, Hieizan 比叡山 and Atagoyama 愛宕山, dominate the northeast and northwest of the city. The rivers Kamogawa 鴨川 and Katsuragawa 桂川 flow through the central and western districts of the city. Kyōto's landlocked location accounts for its cold winters and hot summers. The annual average temperature is 15.2°C (59.4°F) and annual precipitation is 1,600 mm (63 in).

History 歴史

The Kyōto fault basin was first settled in the 7th century by the Hata family 秦氏, immigrants from Korea 渡来人. In 603 Kōryūji 広隆寺, the family temple of the Hata, was constructed at Uzumasa 太秦 in the western part of the basin. In 794 Kyōto, then called Heiankyō 平安京, became the capital of Japan. The plan of the new city was patterned after China's Tang dynasty 唐 (618–907) capital of Chang'an 長安 (modern Xi'an). Its rectangular shape measured 4.5 kilometers (2.8 mi) east to west and 5.2 kilometers (3.2 mi) north to south.

Kyōto was temporarily eclipsed as the center of national power by Kamakura 鎌倉 during the Kamakura period (1185–1333), but during the Muromachi period

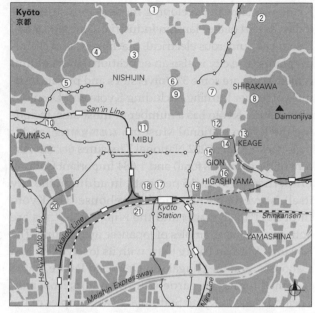

(1333–1568) a shogunate was established in Kyōto, and the city regained its status as the nation's political center. During the Ōnin War 応仁の乱 (1467–1477), which signaled the end of the Muromachi shogunate 室町幕府, a large part of the city was destroyed.

During the Edo period (1600–1868) the Tokugawa shogunate 徳川幕府 was firmly established in Edo (now Tōkyō) and the political focus of the country again shifted away from Kyōto. However, the city still prospered as an artistic, economic, and religious center. Particularly notable were fabrics such as *nishijin-ori* (brocade) 西陣織 and *yūzen-zome* (printed-silk) 友禅染, pottery 陶磁器, lacquer ware 漆器, doll making, and fan making. The city received a great blow when the capital was transferred to Tōkyō after the Meiji Restoration 明治維新 (1868), but responded with a rapid program of modernization.

▌Kyōto Today 今日の京都

Lacking a harbor and surrounding open land,

Kyōto was slow in developing modern industries, but today, as part of the Hanshin Industrial Zone 阪神工業地帯, Kyōto has numerous electrical, machinery, and chemical plants. The city is also an educational and cultural center. There are some 37 universities and private institutes of higher learning, including Kyōto and Dōshisha universities. Kyōto has a number of museums, including the Kyōto National Museum 京都国立博物館, and it possesses a total of 202 National Treasures 国宝 (20 percent of the country's total) and 1,684 Important Cultural Properties 重要文化財 (15 percent). In addition the city itself is a veritable historical storehouse. The Kyōto Imperial Palace 京都御所 and the Nijō Castle 二条城 are both remarkable examples of Japanese architecture. The Katsura Detached Palace 桂離宮 with its lovely pond and teahouses, and the Shugakuin Detached Palace 修学院離宮, famed for its fine garden, draw visitors from afar. Located close to Kyōto Station are two temples of the Jōdo Shin sect 浄土真宗, Nishi Honganji 西本願寺 and Higashi Honganji 東本願寺, both imposing examples of Buddhist architecture 寺院建築, as well as Tōji 東寺, noted for its five-tiered pagoda 五重塔.

East of the Kamogawa are the temple Kiyomizu-dera 清水寺, with its wooden platform built out over a deep gorge; the Yasaka Shrine 八坂神社, where the annual Gion Festival 祇園祭 is held in July; and the Heian Shrine, where the annual Jidai Festival 時代祭 is held in October. Other noted temples include Chion'in 知恩院; Ginkakuji 銀閣寺, built in 1482 and famed for its garden; and Nanzenji 南禅寺, situated in a pine grove east of the Heian Shrine 平安神宮. In the northern part of the city are the Kamo Shrines 賀茂神社, where the Aoi Festival 葵祭 is held in May each year. To the northwest are the Zen temple 禅寺 Daitokuji 大徳寺, with its priceless art objects; Kinkakuji 金閣寺, with its three-story golden pavilion 金閣; Ninnaji 仁和寺, renowned for its cherry blossoms; and

Kōryūji 広隆寺. The natural beauty of the Hozukyō gorge 保津峡, the Sagano 嵯峨野 district, and the hills of Takao 高雄 also attracts visitors. Kyōto is the national center for the tea ceremony 茶の湯 and flower arrangement 生け花 and is the birthplace of NŌ 能, *kyōgen* 狂言, KABUKI 歌舞伎, and other traditional performing arts 伝統芸能. Area: 610.2 sq km (235.6 sq mi); pop: 1,390,305 in 1996.

Ōsaka 大阪[市]

Capital of Ōsaka Prefecture 大阪府. The third largest city in Japan after TŌKYŌ and Yokohama, it is the financial center of western Japan. In the 7th and 8th centuries Ōsaka was a port for trade with China and the site of several imperial residences. The national unifier Toyotomi Hideyoshi 豊臣秀吉 (1537–1598) built Ōsaka Castle 大坂城 as his headquarters in 1583. In the Edo period (1600–1868) Ōsaka served as the entrepôt 集散地 for goods, especially tax rice 年貢米, for the entire nation and was called Japan's "kitchen." 天下の台所

Ōsaka is the center of the Hanshin Industrial Zone 阪神工業地帯. Its principal industries are textiles, chemicals, steel, machinery, and metal. Besides Ōsaka Castle, attractions include the Ōsaka Municipal Museum of Fine Arts 大阪市立美術館, the remains of the ancient capital of Naniwakyō 難波京, the temple Shitennōji 四天王寺, and the Sumiyoshi Shrine 住吉大社. Cultural attractions include the BUNRAKU 文楽 puppet theater as well as KABUKI 歌舞伎. Area: 220.5 sq km (85 sq mi); pop: 2,481,923 in 1996.

Chūgoku region (Chūgoku *chihō*) 中国地方

Encompasses the entire western tip of Honshū, comprising Hiroshima 広島(県), Okayama 岡山(県), Shimane 島根(県), Tottori 鳥取(県), and Yamaguchi 山口(県) prefectures. With the Chūgoku Mountains 中国山地 as the dividing line, the Inland Sea 瀬戸内海 side is called the San'yō region 山陽地方 and the SEA OF JAPAN side, the San'in region 山陰地

方. It is a mountainous region with many small basins and coastal plains. The most heavily populated areas are along the Inland Sea coast. The Inland Sea coast is a major area of industry and commerce. The Okayama Plain 岡山平野 and the coastal plains along the Sea of Japan are important rice-producing areas. The warm, dry climate of the Inland Sea coast is also ideal for citrus fruit 柑橘類 and grapes. The waters off the coast were once among Japan's richest fishing grounds, but catches have declined because of industrial pollution. The major cities are Hiroshima 広島(市) and Okayama 岡山(市). Area: 31,909 sq km (12,320 sq mi); pop: 7,763,515 in 1996.

Chūgoku region
中国地方

Shikoku region (Shikoku *chihō*) 四国地方

Region consisting of Shikoku, the smallest of Japan's four main islands, and numerous surrounding islands. Shikoku lies across the Inland Sea from western Honshū and across the Bungo Channel 豊後水道 from northeastern Kyūshū 九州. It consists of Kagawa 香川(県), Tokushima 徳島(県), Ehime 愛媛(県), and Kōchi 高知(県) prefectures. Shikoku's high mountains and steep slopes severely limit agriculture, habitation, and communication. The climate on the Pacific Ocean side of the island is subtropical and has heavy rainfall in summer.

Shikoku region
四国地方

Much of the island is a thinly populated agricultural region, with little large-scale industry. Two recently completed chains of bridges linking Shikoku with Honshū 本州-四国連絡橋 are expected to bring in many new industries. Extensive land reclamation in Kagawa and Tokushima prefectures should provide more room for this industrial expansion. The major cities are Takamatsu 高松(市) and Matsuyama 松山(市). Area: 18,798 sq km (7,258 sq mi); pop: 4,220,707 in 1996.

Kyūshū region (Kyūshū *chihō*) 九州地方

Region consisting of Kyūshū, the third largest

and southernmost of the four major islands of Japan, and surrounding islands. Kyūshū comprises Fukuoka 福岡(県), Nagasaki 長崎(県), Ōita 大分(県), Kumamoto 熊本(県), Miyazaki 宮崎(県), Saga 佐賀(県), and Kagoshima 鹿児島(県) prefectures. OKINAWA 沖縄県 PREFECTURE is sometimes included in the term Kyūshū. Geographically divided into north, central, and south Kyūshū, the region has a mountainous interior with numerous coastal plains, volcanoes, and hot springs. The climate is mild to subtropical with heavy precipitation.

Rice, tea, tobacco, sweet potatoes, and citrus fruit are the major crops, and stock farming, hog raising, and fishery also flourish. Heavy and chemical industries are concentrated in the Kita Kyūshū Industrial Zone 北九州工業地帯. The major cities are Kita Kyūshū 北九州(市) and Fukuoka 福岡(市). Area : 42,155 sq km (16,276 sq mi) ; pop: 13,420,578 in 1996.

Okinawa 沖縄[県]

Composed of a chain of some 60 islands generally referred to as the Ryūkyū Islands 琉球諸島 ; located south of Kyūshū and surrounded by the East China Sea 東シナ海 and the Pacific Ocean. The islands are generally subdivided into the Okinawa 沖縄, Miyako 宮古, Yaeyama 八重山, and Senkaku 尖閣 groups 諸島. Okinawa, the main island of the Okinawa group, is by far the largest in terms of both size and population and is the prefecture's economic, administrative, and cultural center. With the exception of the northern portion of the main island, most of the terrain is fairly level. The climate is subtropical 亜熱帯, with abundant rainfall; typhoons are frequent.

Okinawa has developed outside the framework of the Japanese state for much of its history. In the 15th century the Ryūkyūs developed into a unified kingdom, whose ruler paid tribute to the Chinese emperor. In

1609 the kingdom was conquered by the Shimazu family 島津氏 of the Satsuma domain 薩摩藩 (now Kagoshima Prefecture). However, tribute missions continued to be sent to China. After the Meiji Restoration 明治維新 (1868) the Japanese government claimed formal sovereignty over the Ryūkyūs and incorporated them as Okinawa Prefecture. This was not recognized by the Chinese until the conclusion of the Sino-Japanese War 日清戦争 in 1895. The invasion of Okinawa by American troops in 1945 resulted in some of the bloodiest fighting in World War II 第2次世界大戦, with great loss of life among the civilian population. The islands were administered by the American military from 1945 until 1972, at which time they were returned to Japan.

Economic development has been made difficult by the fact that much of Okinawa, including prime agricultural land, has been occupied by American military bases 米軍基地. Remoteness from mainland Japan and lack of fresh water have also hindered progress. Tourism is the primary source of revenue. Okinawa's warm climate, subtropical vegetation, and beaches, as well as its unique arts and handicrafts, attract visitors. The Okinawa International Ocean Exposition 沖縄国際海洋博覧会 was held here in 1975. Area: 2,265 sq km (875 sq mi) ; pop: 1,287,023 in 1996; capital: Naha 那覇(市). Other major cities include Okinawa 沖縄(市), Ginowan 宜野湾(市), and Urasoe 浦添(市).

Fujisan (Mt. Fuji) 富士山

The highest mountain (3,776 m; 12,388 ft) in Japan and the most loved by the Japanese. Located on the border of Shizuoka and Yamanashi prefectures in central Honshū, Fujisan boasts a superb conical form 円錐形 that has become famous throughout the world as a symbol of Japan and has inspired generations of Japanese artists and poets. Although dormant 活動休止状

態 since 1707, it is classified by geologists as an active volcano 活火山.

At the summit of Fujisan is a crater 火口 with a diameter of about 800 m (2,600 ft) and a depth of about 200 m (660 ft). The diameter at the base of the mountain, including the broad lava fields 溶岩原 of the piedmont zone 山麓地帯, is roughly 40–50 km (25–30 mi). Lava from Fujisan has been discovered in the seabed near Tagonoura, indicating that there is a vertical range in the lava distribution of nearly 4,000 m (13,100 ft).

In broad perspective Fujisan is part of the Fuji Volcanic Zone 富士火山帯. The timberline 樹木限界線 is found in the altitude range of 2,400–2,800 m (7,900–9,200 ft); between this line and the peak are naked slopes of lava and lapilli. Fujisan has few alpine plants compared with other mountains exceeding 2,500 meters (8,200 ft) in central Japan.

Climbing of Fujisan started as a religious practice. Adherents of Fujikō, a syncretic sect 習合宗派 with both Buddhist and Shintō elements, regard the mountain as sacred. The Shintō shrine Fujisan Hongū Sengen Jinja 富士山本宮浅間神社, whose main shrine is in the city of Fujinomiya 富士宮市, south of the mountain, also treats Fujisan as sacred. Nowadays many people climb Fujisan for pleasure. It is crowded with tens of thousands of climbers daily during the climbing season, which runs from 1 July to 31 August.

World Heritage Convention (Sekai Isan Jōyaku) 世界遺産条約

Formally named the Convention Concerning the Protection of the World Cultural and Natural Heritage 世界の文化遺産および自然遺産の保護に関する条約. An agreement adopted on 16 November 1972 by the 17th General Conference of UNESCO ユネスコ総会, for the purpose of protecting and preserving places and properties that are an irreplaceable part of the cultural heritage of all humanity. Included are: notable historical sites, memorials, groups of buildings, and so forth as well as natural areas that are specially worthy of preservation—the habitats of endangered species of plants and animals, to cite one example.

Japan ratified the convention on 30 June 1992 and was the 126th nation to do so. As of December 1998, 152 countries had ratified the convention, and a total of 582 World Heritage sites had been registered, including 9 in Japan. The Japanese sites (which include areas and groups of buildings) were Himeji Castle 姫路城 (resistered in 1993); Hōryūji and other temples in the same area 法隆寺地域の仏教建造物 (registered in 1993); part of Yakushima 屋久島, including and ancient cedar forest (1993); the Shirakami Mountains 白神山地 (1993); historic temples and shrines in and around Kyōto 古都京都の文化財 (1994); Villages containing *gasshō-zukuri*-style farmhouses around Shirakawa in northwestern Gifu Prefecture and Gokayama in Toyama Prefecture 合掌造り集落の白川郷と五箇山 (1995); the Atomic Bomb Dome 原爆ドーム in Hiroshima (1996); the Itsukushima Shrine 厳島神社 (1996); and the ancient temples and other historic monuments of Nara 古都奈良の文化財 (1998). The 22nd session of the World Heritage Committee 世界遺産委員会 was held in Kyōto in 1998.

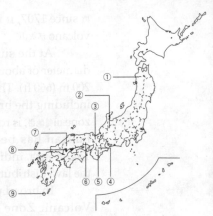

① Shirakami Mountains (1993)
② Villages of Shirakawa and Gokayama (1995)
③ Historic temples and shrines in and around Kyōto (1994)
④ Historic temples and shrines in and around Nara (1998)
⑤ Hōryūji, Hokkiji and other temples around Hōryūji Area (1993)
⑥ Himeji Castle (1993)
⑦ Atomic Bomb Dome (1996)
⑧ Itsukushima Shrine (1996)
⑨ Yakushima (1993)

PLANTS AND ANIMALS 動物・植物

Plants (*shokubutsu*) 植物

Extending north to south for some 3,500 kilometers (2,175 mi), the Japanese archipelago has a great diversity of climate and vegetation. Botanists estimate

- alpine vegetation
高山帯
- subalpine deciduous broad-leaved thicket
亜高山広葉落葉樹林
- subalpine coniferous forest
亜高山針葉樹林
- subarctic mixed broad-leaved deciduous and coniferous forest
亜北極広葉落葉林・針葉混合林
- cool-temperate broad-leaved deciduous forest
亜寒帯広葉落葉樹林
- warm-temperate coniferous forest
温帯針葉樹林
- warm-temperate broad-leaved evergreen forest
温帯広葉常緑樹林
- subtropical rain forest
亜熱帯雨林

that there are 5,000 to 6,000 native species 固有種 of plants.

Types of Plants in Japan
日本の植物の種類

In terms of plant distribution, Japan is included in the East Asian temperate zone 東アジア温帯 and may be roughly subdivided into the following five zones:

1. The subtropical zone 亜熱帯, which includes the Ryūkyū and Ogasawara island groups. Characteristic plants are the *gajumaru* (*Ficus microcarpa*) ガジュマル of the Ryūkyūs and the *himetsubaki* (*Schima wallichii*) ヒメツバキ of the Ogasawaras.

2. The warm-temperate zone 温帯 of broad-leaved evergreen forests 広葉常緑樹林帯, which covers the greater part of southern Honshū, Shikoku, and Kyūshū. The *yabutsubaki* (*Camellia japonica*) ヤブツバキ, the *shiinoki* (*Castanopsis sieboldii*) シイノキ, and the *kusu* (*Cinnamomum camphora*) クス are among its characteristic plants.

3. The cool-temperate zone 亜寒帯 of broad-leaved deciduous forests 広葉落葉樹林帯, which covers central and northern Honshū and the southwestern part of Hokkaidō. Characteristic plants include the *konara* (*Quercus serrata*) コナラ and the *buna* (*Fagus crenata*) ブナ.

4. The subalpine zone 亜高山帯, which includes central and northern Hokkaidō. Characteristic plants include the *kokemomo* (*Vaccinium vitis-idaea*) コケモモ and the *tōhi* (*Picea jezoensis*) トウヒ.

5. The alpine zone 高山帯, which covers the high-

lands of central Honshū and the central part of Hokkaidō, with the *haimatsu* (*Pinus pumila*) ハイマツ and *komakusa* (*Dicentra peregrina*) コマクサ among the characteristic plants.

Although some plants, like the *higambana* (*lycoris radiata*) ヒガンバナ, came to Japan very early in the nation's history, most of the naturalized plants 帰化植物 were introduced in rapid succession after the beginning of the Meiji period (1868–1912). The number of naturalized plants is said to be between 200 and 500. Although most came from Europe, the United States has in recent years become a major source.

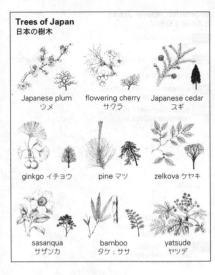

Trees of Japan
日本の樹木

Japanese plum
ウメ

flowering cherry
サクラ

Japanese cedar
スギ

ginkgo イチョウ

pine マツ

zelkova ケヤキ

sasanqua
サザンカ

bamboo
タケ：ササ

yatsude
ヤツデ

Floriculture plants developed in China and introduced to Japan by the Edo period include the *suisen* (narcissus) スイセン, the *asagao* (morning glory) アサガオ, the *kiku* (chrysanthemum) キク, the *ume* (Japanese plum) ウメ, the *momo* (peach) モモ, the *botan* (tree peony) ボタン.

Plants in Literature 文学と植物

The beauty of nature, embodied in the term *kachō fūgetsu* ("flowers, birds, wind, and moon") 花鳥風月, has been a principal theme in Japanese literature, especially WAKA (31-syllable poetry) 和歌 and HAIKU 俳句. The fact that flowers have been given first place in this phrase does not seem to be coincidental. *The Tale of Genji* 源氏物語, written about the year 1000 and noted for its superb descriptions of nature, makes reference to 101 kinds of plants. Frequent use of trees and plants in similes is often considered one of the characteristics of Japanese literature.

For the Japanese, nature has not only been an object of aesthetic appreciation but also an agent evoking intense poetic sentiments 詩心. They have loved flowers not so much for their fragrance and color as for their form and emotional import. An understanding of this attitude is essential to the appreciation of traditional Japanese literature.

Plants in the Visual Arts 芸術と植物

Pictorial and other arts in Japan have also traditionally relied heavily on the artist's sensitivity to nature and have generally tended toward the simple, compact, and sparely graceful. Traditional Japanese renditions of landscapes do not display the wide range of color seen in Western-style oil paintings. In sculpture, too, works are in general delicately carved and small in scale. Plants, flowers, and birds or their patterns are frequently reproduced in lifelike colors on fabric, lacquer ware, and ceramic ware. A love of natural form and an eagerness to express it ideally have been primary motives in the development of traditional Japanese arts, such as FLOWER ARRANGEMENT 華道, the TEA CEREMONY 茶の湯, tray landscapes 盆景, BONSAI 盆栽, and landscape gardening 造園.

Plants and Folklore 植物と民俗学

In the hope of avoiding natural disasters 自然災害, early people formulated sacred rites of exorcism, ablution, and divination. These mystico-religious activities and an awe of nature in general led people to see symbols of the divine in trees and flowers. An excellent example is the once widely practiced worship of primeval evergreen trees 常緑樹—pines マツ, cedars スギ, cypresses ヒノキ, and camphor trees クスノキ—which the early Japanese believed offered habitation (*yorishiro* 依代) to deities who descended from heaven. The practice of decorating the gates of houses with pine branches (*kadomatsu*) on New Year's Day 正月 (see NEW YEAR) derives from the belief that this was a means of welcoming deities.

Another folk custom involving flowers, the flower-viewing party 花見, also dates back to antiquity. An annual cherry-viewing party sponsored by the

Garden Flowers
園芸植物

chrysanthemums キク

irises ハナショウブ：カキツバタ

peonies ボタン：シャクヤク

imperial court became an established custom in the Heian period (794–1185). During the Edo period (1600–1868) the practice of holding annual flower-viewing parties spread among the common people. Besides the sakura, the *ume* (Japanese plum), *fuji* (wisteria) フジ, *kiku* (chrysanthemum), and *hasu* (lotus) ハス are common objects of viewing.

Plants and Religion 植物と宗教

The early Japanese worshiped nature as divine. They believed that natural features such as mountains, rivers, stones, and plants all had spirits and offered prayers to and sought salvation from them. For religious festivals, evergreen trees such as pines and *sakaki* (*Cleyera japonica*) サカキ were used because they were thought to be dwellings of gods, and marine products (seaweed, fish, and shellfish) and fresh farm vegetables were offered to the deities instead of animal flesh. These traditions survive in present-day Shintō 神道. Buddhism, which was introduced to Japan in about the 6th century, banned the destruction of living creatures, so flowers and plants were used for its rituals, a practice that is still followed.

Animals (*dōbutsu*) 動物

The Japanese islands are inhabited by Southeast Asiatic tropical animals 熱帯動物, Korean and Chinese temperate-zone animals 温帯動物, and Siberian subarctic animals シベリア亜寒帯動物. Japan's fauna 動物相 includes many species 種 and relicts 遺存種 not found in neighboring areas. Some of these relicts are found on Honshū, but a larger number inhabit the Ogasawara Islands and the islands south of Kyūshū.

Overall Characteristics 特徴

In zoogeographic terms, the sea south of central Honshū belongs to the Indo-Western Pacific region イ ンド-西太平洋地域, which is part of the tropical kingdom; it

Examples of Some Species Native to Japan (1)
日本産の動物

Amami rabbit アマミノクロウサギ
Body length 45 cm

Japanese mole アズマモグラ
Body length 12 cm, tail 2 cm

Amami spiny mouse トゲネズミ
Body length 13cm, tail 10 cm

Japanese shrew mole ヒミズ
Body length 10 cm, tail 4 cm

Iriomote cat イリオモテヤマネコ
Body length 60 cm

Japanese giant salamander
オオサンショウウオ
Maximum length with tail 1.2 m

Okinawa habu ハブ
Length 2 m

abounds in bright coral fish, sea snakes, and turtles and is inhabited by the dugong and the black finless porpoise スナメリ. The sea north of central Honshū belongs to the Northern Pacific region 北太平洋地域, part of the northern kingdom, which extends along the southern coast of the Aleutian Islands and the west coast of the United States down to California and is inhabited by the fur seal オットセイ, Steller's sea lion トド, and Baird's beaked whale ツチクジラ. Finally, Hokkaidō, which largely faces the Sea of Okhotsk, is visited occasionally by animals indigenous to the Arctic region 北極区, such as the walrus セイウチ.

In the zoogeographical division of the Japanese islands by land animals 陸生動物, the Ryūkyū Islands south of Amami Ōshima are sometimes regarded as part of the Oriental region 東洋区 extending from the Malayan Peninsula to India and sometimes as a transition zone from this region to the Palaearctic region 旧北区; the area north of Yakushima off southern Kyūshū is considered part of the Palaearctic region. The Ryūkyū Islands are inhabited mostly by tropical animals, such as the flying fox オオコウモリ, crested serpent eagle カンムリワシ, variable lizard トカゲ, and butterflies of the family Danaidae マダラチョウ. In mainland Japan (Honshū, Shikoku, and Kyūshū) and Hokkaidō, which belong to the Palaearctic region, two groups of animals are predominant: those of deciduous forests of Korea and central and northern China, such as the raccoon dog タヌキ, *shika* deer シカ, mandarin duck オシドリ, and hairstreak シジミチョウ; and those of coniferous forests of Siberia, such as the brown bear ヒグマ, pika ナキウサギ, hazel grouse エゾライチョウ, common lizard コモチカナヘビ, and nine-spined stickleback トミヨ.

Of these animals, those of the Korean and Chinese group are confined mostly to the Japanese mainland and those of the Siberian group to Hokkaidō.

The geological history of the Japanese islands, marked by repeated separation from and reunion with the Asian continent, is exceedingly complex, giving rise to a corresponding complexity of animal migration 動物分布.

For the protection of endangered species 絶滅危惧種, countermeasures such as the conservation of habitats 生息地保全, artificial breeding 人工増殖, and feeding have been reviewed by the Environment Agency 環境庁, and some proposals already have been implemented. In order to protect animals and insects, in 1979 the agency started a quinquennial survey of the status of animal populations.

Animals in Japanese Culture 日本文化と動物

Many of the beliefs and views held in Japan about various animals stem from native traditions, Buddhist sources, and the classic works of Chinese literature. Such traditional animal symbols as cranes and turtles (for felicity and long life) and swallows (for faithful return) were adopted from the Chinese by the Japanese ruling class in the protohistoric and ancient periods.

Until the late 19th century, the vast majority of Japanese people refrained from slaughtering animals and relied chiefly on fish and shellfish for animal protein. This practice derived mainly from Buddhist teachings. The Japanese view of animals includes the role played by *jikkan jūnishi,* or the sexagenary cycle 十干十二支. Even today, it is common practice to associate a person's character and fortune—based on his or her birth date—with those of the corresponding animal in the subcycles of 12 years of the sexagenary cycle. In addition, animals and flowers are often used in artistic and poetic descriptions to elicit a sense of time and season.

The Twelve Branches (*Jūnishi*)
十二支

Chinese character	*On* reading	Animal name	English
子	shi	ne	rat
丑	chū	ushi	ox
寅	in	tora	tiger
卯	bō	u	hare or rabbit
辰	shin	tatsu	dragon
巳	shi	mi	snake
午	go	uma	horse
未	bi	hitsuji	ram or sheep
申	shin	saru	monkey
酉	yū	tori	rooster
戌	jutsu	inu	dog
亥	gai	i	boar

pheasant キジ
Total length 60–80 cm

bush warbler ウグイス
Total length 15 cm

Japanese crested ibis トキ
Total length 70–80 cm

Japanese crane タンチョウ
Total length 140 cm

Birds (*chōrui*) 鳥類

About 490 species of birds inhabit Japan. However, there are relatively few endemic bird species as compared to mammals.

Endemic Species 日本特産種

The endemic mainland species are the long-tailed *yamadori* (copper pheasant) ヤマドリ, the red-cheeked *aogera* (Japanese green woodpecker) アオゲラ, the black-backed *seguro sekirei* (Japanese wagtail) セグロセキレイ, and the *kayakuguri* (Japanese accentor) カヤクグリ. Endemic species 特産種 of the outer islands of Japan include the following: the *meguro* (Bonin honeyeater; *Apalopteron familiare*) メグロ in the Ogasawara Islands; the *akakokko* (Izu Island thrush) アカコッコ in the Izu Islands and Yakushima; the *akahige* (Liukiu robin; *Erithacus komadori*) アカヒゲ; the *noguchigera* (Pryer's woodpecker) ノグチゲラ; the flightless rail, Yambaru *kuina* (*Rallus okinawae*), in the Ryūkyū Islands; and the *rurikakesu* (Lidth's jay; *Garrulus lidthi*) ルリカケス, which has bright chestnut and blue markings, in Amami Ōshima.

Seabirds 海鳥類

Among seabirds seldom seen outside Japan are the *ahōdori* (short-tailed albatross; *Diomedea albatrus*) アホウドリ found in Torishima and the Senkaku Islands; the *umineko* (black-tailed gull) ウミネコ, which breeds in Hokkaidō and Honshū; and the *kammuri umisuzume* (Japanese auk; *Synthliboramphus wumizusume*) カンムリウミスズメ, which breeds in the mainland and the Izu Islands.

Nonendemic Species 特産種以外の鳥類

Japan's nonendemic birds include the *tanchō* (Japanese crane) and the giant *shimafukurō* (fish owl; *Ketupa blakistoni*) シマフクロウ, which breed in Hokkaidō; the beautiful *oshidori* (mandarin duck); the *karugamo* (spotbill duck) カルガモ, found year round throughout Japan; the *sashiba* (gray-faced buzzard eagle) サシバ,

which breeds in the mainland; the mountain-dwelling *kumataka* (Hodgson's hawk eagle) クマタカ, a mainland inhabitant used for falconry; the *kijibato* (eastern turtle-dove; *Streptopelia orientalis*) キジバト and the *hiyodori* (brown-eared bulbul; *Hypsipetes amaurotis*) ヒヨドリ, found all over Japan; the sweet-voiced *uguisu* (bush warbler) ウグイス; the lemon-breasted *kibitaki* (narcissus flycatcher; *Ficedula narcissina*) キビタキ; the long-tailed *sankōchō* (black paradise flycatcher; *Terpsiphone atrocaudata*) サンコウチョウ; the trainable *ya-magara* (varied tit; *Parus varius*) ヤマガラ; and the nectar-sucking *mejiro* (Japanese white-eye; *Zosterops japonica*) メジロ.

Other birds worthy of mention are the *onaga* (azure-winged magpie; *Cyanopica cyana*) オナガ, the giant *ōwashi* (Steller's sea eagle; *Haliaeetus pelagicus*) オオワシ, the *umiu* (Temminck's cormorant; *Phalacrocorax filamentosus*) ウミウ, several species of *hototogisu*, the *akashōbin* (ruddy kingfisher; *Halcyon coromanda*) アカショウビン, the *raichō* (ptarmigan; *Lagopus mutus*) ライチョウ, the high-mountain-dwelling *iwahibari* (alpine accentor; *Prunella collaris*) イワヒバリ, and the *kiji* (common pheasant; *Phasianus colchicus*) キジ.

Natural monuments and protected species (*tennen kinembutsu*) 天然記念物

The term refers to natural objects and phenomena (including species of animals and plants) characteristic of or peculiar to Japan that have been designated for preservation under the Cultural Properties Law 文化財保護法 of 1950 or similar local laws. These include certain geologic or mineral formations 地質鉱物 and areas (other than national parks) of special historic, scenic, or scientific interest, as well as certain species of animals and plants found only in specific areas of Japan. Natural monuments and protected species are classified into two categories: those designated for preservation by the national government under the Cultural Properties Law and those set aside for protection by the laws of local public bodies such as prefectures, cities, towns, and villages. As of 1996, there were 955 legally designated natural monuments, 75 of which were further distinguished as "special natural monuments." 特別天然記念物

Protected Areas 保護区域

Areas of specific interest that have been set aside as *tennen kinembutsu* are classified under a number of official designations such as Nature Protection District 天然保護区域, Primeval Forest 原始林, and Shrine Forest 社叢. Nature Protection Districts include Lake Towada; the river Oirasegawa; the Kurobe gorge; the Oze, Torishima, and Kushiro bogs; and the island of Minami Iōjima. Primeval Forests include the Daisetsuzan area, the Sarugawa 沙流川 Headwaters Primeval Forest, and the Maruyama 円山 Primeval Forest (all in Hokkaidō); the Kasugayama Primeval Forest in Nara; and the Aso Kitamukidani 北向谷 Primeval Forest. One Shrine Forest is the Miyazaki Kashima Forest in Toyama Prefecture.

Plants and geologic formations 植物と地質

Certain rock-zone flora found in specific locations 特殊岩石地植物群落 and the boundary zones of distribution 生育限界 of certain plants found only in limited areas, such as the southern boundary zone of the Ehime iris in Yamaguchi Prefecture, are also classified as *tennen kinembutsu*. A great number of very old or very large individual trees have also been designated as natural monuments.

Geologic formations that have been designated as natural monuments include the group of cirques (deep, steep-walled basins) at Yakushidake, the limestone cave known as Akiyoshidō 秋芳洞 in Yamaguchi Prefecture, and the upthrust coasts of Kisakata 象潟 in Akita Prefecture. A number of unique mineral formations and fossil 化石 sites have also been designated.

Animals 動物

  Indigenous species 固有種 of Japanese wildlife designated as *tennen kinembu-tsu* include the Amami *no kurousagi* アマミノクロウサギ, the *meguro* (Bonin honeyeater) メグロ, and the giant salamander オオサンショウウオ. Other *tennen kinembutsu* include cranes and their migration grounds 渡来地 in Kagoshima Prefecture, the natural habitat 生息地 of sea bream in the waters of Tainoura in Chiba Prefecture, and the breeding grounds 繁殖地 of the horseshoe crab カブトガニ in the waters near Kasaoka, Okayama Prefecture. Naturalized species 帰化種 include the magpie カササギ, the turtledove, and domestic birds and animals, such as the *misaki* horse 岬馬 bred in Miyazaki Prefecture, Mishima cattle 見島牛 bred in Yamaguchi Prefecture, and the long-tailed cock (*onagadori* オナガドリ) bred in Kōchi Prefecture.

HISTORY

歴史

日本史

History of Japan

History of Japan: Overview (*nihonshi*: *gaisetsu*)
日本史：概説

Observers in Europe and the United States are naturally tempted to view Japanese history in terms of its encounters with the West. From this perspective, the "Christian Century" 「キリスト教の世紀」 from ca 1540 to ca 1640, and the century and a half from the arrival of Commodore Matthew Perry's ペリー司令長官 fleet and the "Opening of Japan" 開国 in the mid-19th century to the present, tend to be viewed as the major phases of Japanese history. The Japanese themselves, of course, see these periods of contact with the West, especially in modern times, as vital phases of their historical development, but they also look to their relations with the Asian continent アジア大陸. They prize the formative contacts with China and Korea in the premodern era and recall with regret Japan's imperialist aggression in Korea, China, and Manchuria in the period leading to World War II.

Despite the importance of these contacts with other societies, however, it is the unfolding history of the Japanese people within the islands of the Japanese archipelago 日本列島 itself that must take center stage in any discussion of the Japanese past. That past can be divided into seven major phases: prehistoric 先史, proto-historic 原史, ancient 古代, medieval 中世, early modern 近世, modern 近代, and contemporary 現代.

The Prehistoric Period 先史時代

Archaeologists usually divide the prehistoric phase into four major periods: a long paleolithic prece-ramic period 旧石器(先土器)時代 prior to ca 10,000 BC; the Jōmon period 縄文時代 (ca 10,000 BC–ca 300 BC), which saw the introduction of ceramics; the Yayoi period 弥生時代(ca 300 BC–ca AD 300), when metals and sedentary agriculture became widespread; and the Kofun period

古墳時代 (ca 300–710), age of the great tomb mounds and the beginnings of political centralization. However, this latter period, which was one of transition to the era of written records, is also known as the protohistoric period.

The first inhabitants of the Japanese islands were paleolithic hunter-gatherers from the continent who used sophisticated stone blades but had no ceramics or settled agriculture. This paleolithic culture persisted until the close of the Pleistocene epoch 更新世, about 13,000 years ago, when the Japanese climate ameliorated and sea levels began to rise. In these changing climatic circumstances a new culture began to overlay the older paleolithic culture. This new culture is known as Jōmon (literally, "cord marked") 縄文 from the magnificent pottery that characterized it. Although it has been commonly thought that the Jōmon people were hunter-gatherers who did not practice cultivation, recent research suggests that by about 1000 BC they had begun to cultivate rice.

From about 300 BC Jōmon culture was overlaid by a distinctly different culture, the Yayoi, characterized by less flamboyant ceramics, a knowledge of bronze and iron technologies, including fine weaponry, and the systematic development of wet-field rice agriculture 水稲農耕. These developments laid the basis for the strong martial current found in Japan's early history and for the agricultural way of life that profoundly shaped Japanese society into the modern era. They also contributed to greater social stratification and the emergence of a hierarchy of local clans 氏, ruling service groups 部, and slaves 奴婢.

The Protohistoric Period 原史時代

Before the close of the Yayoi period, from about the mid-3rd century, clans in the Yamato region 大和地方 and other areas of central and western Japan were building tomb mounds 古墳, for the burial of their chieftains.

The largest of these *kofun*, built in the Yamato region, are said to be the mausoleums of the first powerful political dynasty in Japan, the Yamato, which eventually asserted political control over the entire country.

By the end of the 7th century, the old clan society was being restructured and Japan was already well on the way to the articulation of a Chinese-inspired centralized imperial administration. The Asuka period 飛鳥時代 (593–710) marks the final phase of this transition between protohistory and history proper. The Asuka period dates from the establishment of the court of Empress Suiko 推古天皇 (r 593–628) in the Asuka region of Yamato. That same year (593) Prince Shōtoku 聖徳太子 (574–622) began to serve as her regent 摂政. For more than a century the area was the site for the palaces of the rulers of the Yamato lineage and the powerful *uji* 氏 supporting it. Buddhism 仏教 had been introduced to this region in the mid-6th century and it was here that Prince Shōtoku set the country on the course of centralized reform heralded in his Seventeen-Article Constitution 十七条憲法. The Japanese court sponsored Buddhism; built temples, palaces, and capitals after Korean and later Chinese models; began to write histories using Chinese characters 漢字; and laid out a blueprint for the *ritsuryō* (legal codes) system 律令制度.

The Ancient Period 古代

In 710 a magnificent new capital, called Heijōkyō 平城京 and modeled on the Chinese Tang dynasty 唐王朝 (618–907) capital at Chang'an 長安, was established at Nara. During the course of the Nara period 奈良時代 (710–794) Japan received even more direct cultural and technological influences from China. Japan's first chronicles, the *Kojiki* (712, Records of Ancient Matters) 「古事記」 and *Nihon shoki* (720, Chronicle of Japan) 「日本書紀」, were compiled at this time. Buddhism and Confucianism 儒教 were harnessed to support political authority, and temples were constructed in the capital and in each of the provinces (provincial temple 国分寺). Centralized systems for the administration of taxation, census, and landholding were instituted. By the closing years of the 8th century, however, the centralized imperial administration and public land allotment system 班田収授法 were showing signs of strain. Politics in Nara were upset by rivalries among nobles and clerics. In 784 Emperor Kammu 桓武天皇 (r 781–806) decided to make a new start and tried to revive the *ritsuryō* system by moving the capital to a new site. In 794 a new capital, called Heiankyō 平安京 (literally, "Capital of Peace and Tranquillity"), was established where the modern city of Kyōto 京都 now stands. This was to serve as the home of the imperial court 朝廷 and the capital of Japan until the 19th century, when the capital was moved to Edo 江戸, which was renamed Tōkyō 東京.

The period from 794 to 1185, is known as the Heian period 平安時代. It saw the full assimilation of Chinese culture and the flowering of an elegant courtly culture 宮廷文化. Politically, however, the imperial court came to be dominated by nobles of the Fujiwara family 藤原氏. In the absence of an effective centralized military system, warrior bands 武士団 began to assume more power, first in the provinces 地方 and then over the court itself when the Taira family 平氏 seized power in the capital in the mid-12th century.

The Medieval Period 中世

The Taira were overthrown in the Taira-Minamoto War 源平の争乱 in 1185 by warriors led by Minamoto no Yoritomo 源頼朝 (1147–1199), who was granted in 1192 the title of *seii tai shōgun* 征夷大将軍 and established a military government 武家政権, called the Kamakura shogunate 鎌倉幕府, in the small town of Kamakura in eastern Japan. The first four centuries of warrior domination, covering the Kamakura period 鎌倉時代 (1185–1333) and the Muromachi period 室町時代 (1333–1568), are usually described as Japan's feudal era 封建時代. The court was not displaced by the creation of a military government 武家政権 in Kamakura but its influence steadily weakened. The shogunate assumed control of the administration of justice, the imperial succession, and the defense of the country against the attempted Mongol invasions of Japan 蒙古襲来 in the late 13th century. Headed first by Yoritomo, the Kamakura shogunate was over-thrown in 1333 by a coalition led by Emperor Go-Daigo 後醍醐天皇 (r 1318–1339), who was seeking to restore direct imperial rule (Kemmu Restoration 建武の新政).

Go-Daigo himself was ousted in 1336 by Ashikaga Takauji 足利尊氏 (1305–1358), who had helped bring him to power. Takauji, using a rival emperor as a puppet sovereign, established a new shogunate in the Muromachi 室町 district of Kyōto. After several decades of civil war between the rival Northern and Southern courts 南北朝 the shogunate was put on a firm footing by Ashikaga Yoshimitsu 足利義満 (1358–1408), the third Ashikaga shōgun 足利将軍. Later Ashikaga shōguns were less successful in controlling the feudal coalition. Beginning with the Ōnin War 応仁の乱 (1467–1477), the country slipped into the century of sporadic civil war 内乱 known as the Warring States period 戦国時代 (Sengoku period; 1467–1568).

The Early Modern Period 近世

From the mid-16th century, a movement toward national reunification gradually emerged out of the violence of the warring feudal domains 戦国大名 and was carried through by three powerful hegemons, Oda Nobunaga 織田信長 (1534–1582), Toyotomi Hideyoshi 豊臣秀吉 (1537–1598), and Tokugawa Ieyasu 徳川家康 (1543–1616). The short but spectacular epoch during which Nobunaga and Hideyoshi established their military control over the country and began to reshape its feudal institutions is known as the Azuchi-Momoyama period 安土桃山時代 (1568–1600). This was an age of gold, grandeur, and openness to the outside world. Hideyoshi had visions of conquering Korea and establishing an enduring dynasty, though he lived to see his Korean invasions in 1592 and 1597 文禄・慶長の役 end in brutal failure. His death in 1598 left his heir vulnerable to rival *daimyō* 大名. One of these, Tokugawa Ieyasu, after a striking victory over pro-Toyotomi warriors at the Battle of Sekigahara 関ヶ原の戦い in 1600, assumed the title of *seii tai shōgun* 征夷大将軍 and established a powerful and enduring shogunate in the city of Edo 江戸 (now Tōkyō), ushering in the Edo period 江戸時代 (1600–1868) in Japanese history.

Ieyasu's victory gave him preponderant power and allowed him to rearrange the political map of Japan. He established a carefully balanced political structure known as the *bakuhan* (shogunate and domain) system 幕藩体制 in which the Tokugawa shogunate 徳川幕府 directly controlled Edo and the heartland of the country while the *daimyō* governed the 250 or so domains 藩. Ieyasu and his shogunal successors were able to maintain a strong centralized feudal structure by balancing the *daimyō* domains; enforcing status distinctions between *samurai*, merchants, artisans, and peasants 士農工商; instituting a hostage system of alternate-year attendance by *daimyō* in Edo 参勤交代; eradicating Christianity キリスト教; controlling contacts with the outside world, especially the West; and enforcing regulations for *samurai*, nobles, and temples. This structure was dominated by *samurai* and relied heavily on the tax yield of the peasants 年貢, but it also gave scope to the merchants 商人 of Edo, Ōsaka, Kyōto, and the castle towns 城下町 to develop commerce and a lively urban culture.

The Modern Period 近代

The Tokugawa system, oppressive as it was in

many respects, gave the country more than two centuries of peace and relative seclusion from the outside world (National Seclusion 鎖国). This was threatened in the 19th century as Russian, British, and American vessels began to probe Asian waters and press for trade with China and Japan. The shogunate's failure to "expel the barbarians 攘夷," the concession of unequal treaties 不平等条約, and the opening of ports 開港 after Perry's ペリー visit in 1853 set in motion a chain of events that led the powerful domains of Satsuma 薩摩, Chōshū 長州, and Tosa 土佐 to use the imperial court 朝廷 to challenge the shogunate, which was overthrown in the Meiji Restoration 明治維新 of 1868. The young *samurai* who carried through the restoration wanted to preserve, revitalize, and strengthen the country. This process moved ahead rapidly during the course of the Meiji period 明治時代 (1868–1912). The slogan of the new leadership of Japan was *fukoku kyōhei* 富国強兵 (Enrich the Country, Strengthen the Military). Japan adopted a constitution in 1889, opening the way to parliamentary government 議会政治. It achieved industrial progress and built up sufficient military power to defeat China in 1895 and Russia in 1905, and to annex Korea in 1910 日韓併合, emerging as the major imperialist power in East Asia.

The Taishō period 大正時代 (1912–1926) was marked by Japan's acceptance as a major power and a period of party government 政党内閣 sometimes known as Taishō Democracy 大正デモクラシー. The Shōwa period 昭和時代 (1926–1989) began on a note of optimism but quickly descended into military aggression in Manchuria 満州 and China and Japan's departure from the League of Nations 国際連盟. Ultranationalism 国粋主義 and political oppression at home eventually led to war with the United States and the Allied powers in Asia and the Pacific.

The Contemporary Era 現代

The defeat of Japan in 1945 under atomic clouds brought the Allied Occupation 連合国占領, demilitarization, dismantling of the old industrial combines 財閥, renunciation of divinity by the emperor 天皇人間宣言, a new constitution, democratization, and a new educational system. After a painful period of postwar rehabilitation, the Japanese economy began to surge ahead in the 1960s and 1970s. The Tōkyō Olympic Games 東京オリンピック in 1964 brought Japan renewed international recognition. The nation's continued prosperity has been based on the United States-Japan security treaties 日米安全保障条約, a consistent stress on economic growth 経済成長 and business-oriented policy making, an emphasis on education, and the frugality, energy, and sustained efforts of the Japanese people. In recent years the Japanese, under international pressure to liberalize trade 貿易自由化, have been moving from an export-oriented economy to one that is more accessible to foreign imports. This is part of a larger effort by the Japanese to overcome a strong historical tendency to view themselves as somehow unique and aloof from other nations. They are now attempting to truly internationalize 国際化 their society and bring it into fuller cooperation with an increasingly interdependent world.

History of Japan: By Historical Period
(*nihonshi*: *jidaishi*) 日本史：時代史

Jōmon period 縄文時代

(ca 10,000 BC–ca 300 BC; Jōmon *jidai*). Prehistoric period 先史時代 during which the peoples of Japan followed a hunting and gathering way of life. It was preceded by the Paleolithic period 旧石器時代 (pre–10,000 BC), from which it is distinguished by the presence of pottery, and was followed by the Yayoi period 弥生時代 (ca 300 BC–ca AD 300), the distinguishing characteristics of which are the use of metals and wet-rice cultivation 稲作.

The Jōmon period is studied in terms of six subperiods, although archaeologists are not in complete agreement over the dates of the various Jōmon phases. The Incipient Jōmon period 縄文草創期 (ca 10,000 BC–ca 7500 BC) is a transitional period, marked by the combining of pottery making with late paleolithic stone-working techniques. It is not clear how pottery making originated in Japan, but it is clear that the world's oldest known pottery dates from between 10,750 and 10,000 BC and was excavated from Fukui Cave 福井洞穴 in Nagasaki Prefecture 長崎県 and other sites in southern Japan. Whether introduced from the Asian mainland or locally developed, the appearance of pottery does not appear to have been caused by or to have resulted in immediate changes in paleolithic subsistence or settlement patterns.

Initial and Early Jōmon Periods 早期・前期縄文時代

The major innovation of the Initial Jōmon period (ca 7500 BC–ca 5000 BC) was the utilization of marine and coastal resources leading to the accumulation of the first shell mounds 貝塚. At this time the Jōmon cultural assemblage—including basic stone tool types, pit houses 竪穴住居, clay Jōmon figurines 土偶, and cord-marked (*jōmon*) pottery vessels 縄文土器—was also established. The evidence of shell middens indicates that the economy was well rounded: not only were fish and shellfish collected, but deer and wild pigs were hunted and wild seeds and plant foods were gathered. From this time Jōmon culture 縄文文化 was divided into two spheres, roughly corre-

Jōmon Period
縄文時代

Phase	Japanese Name	Dates
Incipient (Subearliest) Jōmon	Jōmon Sōsōki 縄文草創期	ca 10,000 BC–ca 7500 BC
Initial (Earliest) Jōmon	Jōmon Sōki 縄文早期	ca 7500 BC–ca 5000 BC
Early Jōmon	Jōmon Zenki 縄文前期	ca 5000 BC–ca 3500 BC
Middle Jōmon	Jōmon Chūki 縄文中期	ca 3500 BC–ca 2000 BC (ca 3500 BC–ca 2500 BC)
Late Jōmon	Jōmon Kōki 縄文後期	ca 2000 BC–ca 1000 BC (ca 2500 BC–ca 1000 BC)
Final (Latest) Jōmon	Jōmon Banki 縄文晩期	ca 1000 BC–ca 300 BC

Jōmon Pottery
縄文土器

A deep pot featuring the raised-line decorations and extravagant rim ornamentation characteristic of Middle-Jōmon period *kaen* pottery. Height 29 cm. Umataka site, Niigata Prefecture.

sponding to the deciduous forests 落葉樹林 of eastern Japan and the broadleaf evergreen forests 広葉常緑樹林 of the southwestern end of the archipelago, which preserved their differences until the end of the Jōmon period.

High sea levels caused by warm climates during the Early Jōmon period (ca 5000 BC–ca 3500 BC) turned coastal lowlands into tidal marshes, and huge accumulations of seashells and fish bones attest to the utilization of this resource through coastal gathering. In western Japan deep-sea fishing may also have been undertaken; similarities between the Sobata 曽畑 pottery of Kyūshū and comb-pattern pottery of Korea indicate that there was waterborne contact.

▌Middle, Late, and Final Jōmon 中期・後期・晩期縄文

The cultural center shifted from the coasts to the interior of the Kantō district 関東地方, where large semi-sedentary villages 準定住村 developed during the Middle Jōmon period (ca 3500 BC–ca 2500 BC; also dated as ca 3500 BC–ca 2000 BC). This may have been a result of improved methods of exploiting available plant resources. Most archaeologists feel, however, that although the economy of this period drew on a wide range of wild resources, it cannot be considered a true agricultural one. A strikingly elaborate pottery appeared during the period. In the Late Jōmon period (ca 2500 BC–ca 1000 BC; also dated as ca 2000 BC–ca 1000 BC) a more vigorous marine economy developed along the Pacific coast of eastern Japan. The fishermen of this period invented a vast array of tools and techniques that allowed them to undertake true deep-sea fishing. The Final Jōmon period (ca 1000 BC–ca 300 BC) saw the spread of a series of elaborate pottery styles—called Kamegaoka-type pottery 亀ヶ岡式土器—along the Pacific coast from northern Tōhoku to the Inland Sea 瀬戸内海 region. Throughout the Late and Final Jōmon periods, southwestern Japan was a largely separate cultural sphere. Ceramic similarities strongly suggest that there was regular contact between Kyūshū and western Japan and the Korean peninsula 朝鮮半島 during the Final Jōmon period.

The introduction of rice farming to Kyūshū and the rapid spread of Yayoi culture 弥生文化 brought an end to the Jōmon lifestyle. Remnants of the Jōmon tradition—called the Zoku Jōmon 続縄文—persisted in Hokkaidō until it developed into the Satsumon culture 擦文文化 in the 8th century.

Yayoi period 弥生時代

(ca 300 BC–ca AD 300; Yayoi *jidai*). Prehistoric period. The first period of intensive agriculture and bronze and iron use in Japanese prehistory, so called because of certain characteristic pottery discovered in the Yayoi section of Bunkyō Ward, Tōkyō, in 1884. Wet-rice technology, metallurgy, and other innovations were introduced piecemeal from the late-bronze-age cultures of the Korean peninsula into Kyūshū. From there, wet-rice cultivation 水稲耕作 spread rapidly throughout western Japan and some northern coastal regions during the Early Yayoi period 前期弥生時代 (ca 300 BC–ca 100 BC) and then gradually into northeastern Japan in the Middle Yayoi 中期弥生時代 (ca 100 BC–ca AD 100) and Late Yayoi 後期弥生時代 (ca 100–ca 300) periods. Bronzes 青銅, however, were confined to the west, and the ceramics of northeastern Yayoi exhibit strong persistence of the traditions of the Jōmon period (ca 10,000 BC–ca 300 BC). Northeastern agriculture probably also relied much more on such nonrice crops as millet, barley, and beans. In contrast to the earlier view of Yayoi as consisting of peaceful agricultural villages (such as the well-known Toro site 登呂遺跡), the period is increasingly seen as one of competition and warfare, as trends toward social stratification and polity formation took hold.

Settlement 集落

Villages in the Early Yayoi period were located near the low coastal marshlands, where rice was easily grown in diked fields with drainage canals. The grain harvest, carried out with a distinctive stone reaping knife, was supplemented with hunting, gathering, and shellfish collecting in the Jōmon pattern until the agricultural intensification of the Middle Yayoi period. The development of irrigation systems 灌漑 and iron-edged tools 鉄器 at that time allowed the expansion of cultivation onto drier land, and increased harvests stimulated a massive population explosion. The numerous Middle Yayoi villages of thatched pit houses 茅葺き竪穴住居 and raised granaries were often surrounded by substantial village ditches. These may have provided protection, and, from the Middle to the Late Yayoi period, settlements in upland defensive hilltop positions were common. Also, caches of bronze bells 銅鐸 are often found on hilltops in the eastern Seto region 瀬戸地方 (in what is now Aichi Prefecture 愛知県) overlooking fertile agricultural land. These may have been used in fertility rites 豊作祈願 within the agricultural cycle and buried for safekeeping between ceremonies.

Culture 文化

Many types of craft production of continental origin were established in Yayoi Japan: casting bronze in sandstone molds, pouring round and curved glass beads 勾玉 in molds, weaving paper mulberry and flax fibers, turning wooden bowls on lathes, and forging small iron tools. Native crafts included jasper and jade bead production, stone tool manufacture, and ceramic production. Many of the polished stone tools were used for working wood into architectural elements or other tools, such as pestles for pounding grain, hafts for the stone tools themselves, or hoes and spades. The Yayoi pottery 弥生土器 tradition is a transformation of the

Jōmon earthenware tradition with new techniques and shapes (long-necked jars, pedestaled bowls 高坏 <ruby>高坏<rt>たかつき</rt></ruby>) from the continent. Western Yayoi pottery is decorated with combed motifs, appliqués, raised bands, and some burnished surfaces. High pedestals and stepped rims characterize the more elaborate shapes. Northeastern Yayoi pottery continued the Jōmon cord-marking tradition on Yayoi shapes, but incised-line geometrics and appliqués were also popular. All these ceramics were unglazed and fired at low temperatures in open stacks.

Burials 埋葬

Each of three large regions exhibited particular burial patterns. In northeastern Japan secondary burials of exhumed bones were conducted, the remains being painted with ocher, placed in highly decorated jars, and buried, often collectively, in large pits. In the eastern Seto region collective primary burials in moated, mounded precincts probably represent prestigious family precincts. Adults were interred directly in pits or in wooden coffins; children were buried in small jars. These precincts are often clustered into cemeteries adjacent to the village. Western Seto had several different types of burial facilities. The practice of depositing goods with the deceased was carried out only in this region during the Yayoi period. Jar burials 甕棺葬 of adults are notable in north Kyūshū in addition to cist burials 石棺葬, both of which might have been covered by a low dolmen structure. All these might have been accompanied by grave goods consisting of bronze weapons 青銅武器, beads, and many Chinese tribute goods, such as bronze mirrors 青銅鏡. These were very much ceremonial and status goods, but the different shell bracelets worn on the arms of men and women are thought to distinguish gender.

Previously, the Yayoi period was differentiated from the Kofun period 古墳時代 (ca 300–710) by the presence of mounded tombs 古墳 in the latter. Several types of Yayoi mound burials, however, are now recognized, and the Kofun tradition is thought to have developed indigenously from these. The Yoshinogari mound burial 吉野ヶ里墳丘墓, recently excavated in Saga Prefecture 佐賀県, is one of the earliest, containing a jar burial with a continental sword and blue glass beads.

International Relations 国際関係

Kyūshū 九州 was drawn into the tribute and trade network of the Chinese Lelang (Lolang) commandery on the northern Korean peninsula 朝鮮半島. Via this network, foreign goods flowed into western Japan, and information about Yayoi culture and politics was inscribed in the Chinese dynastic histories. Relatively complex political units called *kuni* 国 are recorded, a number under the hegemony of Yamatai 邪馬台国, ruled by Queen Himiko 卑弥呼. The Yoshinogari site 吉野ヶ里遺跡 is thought to embody the level of development reflected in these descriptions, having a double-moated structure complete with palisade and watchtowers.

Kofun period 古墳時代

(ca 300–710; Kofun *jidai*). Protohistoric period during which large tumuli 古墳 were built for deceased members of the ruling elite. The period is variously dated as ca 250–552, ca 300–552, ca 300–645, ca 300–710, and so forth, and it may be divided into either two or three phases: Early 前期 (4th and 5th centuries) and Late 後期 (6th and 7th centuries), or Early (4th century), Middle 中期 (5th century), and Late (6th and 7th centuries). This book has adopted the three-phase division and the dates ca 300–710 for the period; thus, it encompasses the Asuka period 飛鳥時代 (593–710). The first state in Japan, Yamato 大和, emerged during the Kofun period, and diplomatic relations were established with the Korean states and the Chinese courts. Based on rice agriculture continuing from the Yayoi period (ca 300 BC–ca AD 300), the economy was reorganized in the late 5th century in the form of the *be* 部 system to provide the supplies necessary to support palace life. Buddhism was introduced from the kingdom of Paekche 百済 on the Korean peninsula in the mid-6th century, and the state administrative structure was reorganized on the Tang (T'ang) dynasty 唐朝 (618–907) model through the Taika Reform 大化の改新 in the mid-7th century.

Mounded Tombs 墳丘墓

The large tombs of the Kofun period resulted from the formation, in the late 3rd century, of a class society consisting of aristocrats and commoners. Social stratification is reflected in the size, labor required for construction, and isolation of the aristocratic burials in contrast to the humble graves of the masses—most of which are unknown. The tombs range in size from 15 meters (50 ft) in diameter to 32.3 hectares (79.8 acres) in area. A unique tomb shaped like an old-fashioned keyhole when viewed from above (front square and rear-round tomb mound 前方後円墳) was used for the burials of the highest-ranking members of the ruling elite. Many of these keyhole-shaped tombs are assigned as imperial mausolea of specific emperors listed in the early historical chronicles, the *Kojiki* and *Nihon shoki*, both compiled in the 8th century. Round tombs, present from the beginning of the period, served as burials for the lower-ranking aristocrats; from the early 6th century, they became family repositories clustered together in clan cemeteries on hillsides. Square tombs 方墳, also present from early on, became the preferred shape for the highest-ranking aristocratic burials at the end of the Kofun period.

The earliest tombs were built in the Kinai 畿内 (Kyōto-Ōsaka-Nara) region, spreading from there through the Inland Sea 瀬戸内海 to northern Kyūshū in

Main Types of Tomb Mounds
主な古墳の種類

empun 円墳
(round tomb mound)

hōfun 方墳
(square tomb mound)

zempō kōen fun 前方後円墳
(front-square and rear-round tomb mound)

zempō kōhō fun 前方後方墳
(front-square and rear-square tomb mound)

the 4th century and into other regions of western and eastern Japan thereafter. The predecessor of the mounded tomb was probably the Yayoi-period mound burial; but Yayoi mound burials did not often contain lavish grave goods, whereas sumptuous funerary deposits always occur in Kofun-period tombs. Burial facilities changed through time, at first consisting of a wooden coffin buried directly in the tomb summit or in a pit lined with stone slabs and covered ceiling rocks. Earthenware cylinders were often embedded in the tomb surface surrounding the burial, and some supported earthenware sculptures of shields, sunshades, and houses—symbolic representations to protect and/or house the spirit of the deceased. These cylinders and sculptures are called *haniwa* 埴輪. Later, stone coffins were used, and, finally, in the Late Kofun period, stone chambers 石室 with horizontal entrance passages were constructed. These allowed reentry into the chamber, leading to their development as family repositories and also contributing to the development of ideas about *yomi* 黄泉, the Japanese underworld.

The grave goods deposited in Kofunperiod tombs chronicle the changing nature of leadership and status during the period of state emergence. In the Early Kofun period, funerary goods were mainly ceremonial, with some iron weapons and armor, an indication that the deceased had considerable magico-religious powers as well as military might. The ceremonial goods consisted of bronze mirrors 青銅鏡, necklaces of curved and cylindrical beads made from precious jade and jasper, and other jasper and green-tuff ornaments including unusually shaped bracelets. Tomb contents from the Middle Kofun period—vast numbers of iron weapons and agricultural implements and imported gold ear ornaments, stoneware, and horse trappings in the continental style—attest to the rulers' limitless access to the resources of society and to new contacts with the Korean peninsula. The character of ritual objects changed dramatically from the carefully made jasper, jade, and green-tuff beads and bracelets to hoards of quickly roughed-out talc imitations of sheathed knives and daily objects. The significance of the knife imitations is still unknown. From the Late Kofun period on, in addition to personal ornaments and weapons worn by the deceased, *sue* ware 須恵器 and food were deposited to provide for the afterlife.

By the 6th century, tomb burial was not confined to the rulers per se but was afforded to all aristocrats; thus the sizes of the tombs were much smaller and the contents more religious than political in that they provided for the individual's existence in the next life. As Buddhism took hold, many elites invested their resources in temple building rather than tomb building for aggrandizement of their status. In combination with cremation, these trends led to the demise of tomb building by the end of the 7th century.

Formation of the State 国家の形成

It is known from Chinese chronicles that Japan housed many small polities called *kuni* at the end of the Yayoi period. Although one of these was named Yamatai 邪馬台国, it is still not known whether Yamatai and the early state of Yamato can be equated. Equally unclear is exactly when the Yamato polity became a state. Japanese historians speak of the Yamato court 大和朝廷 existing in the 4th century and tend toward recognizing a unified state in the mid- to late 5th century. Archaeologists tend to equate the mounded tomb culture (stratified society) with state organization. The appearance of horse trappings 馬具 in the 5th-century tombs led one school of Japanese scholars to postulate an invasion of "mounted warriors" from the Asian mainland, who subsequently formed the imperial

Yamato line. This horse-rider theory 騎馬民族説 of state formation has been adopted by many historians and woven into their accounts of Yamato development because it dovetails nicely with a break in the imperial genealogies as reconstructed from the chronicles. Archaeologists vehemently reject this hypothesis, saying that the material evidence on which the original thesis was based had been skewed to fit the theory.

In any case, it is clear both archaeologically and historically that the Japanese were in close contact with the continent from the late 4th century. Virtually all the grave goods in the early tombs, except for the stone ornaments, have Korean or Chinese prototypes, and many appear to have been imported. Contemporary Chinese records of the southern Chinese courts make mention of the Five Kings of Wa 倭の五王, who may be identifiable with some of the emperors known from the *Nihon shoki*. From 369, Yamato was in touch with Paekche 百済 on the Korean peninsula, and the court provided refuge for many skilled craftspeople and court functionaries during Paekche's retreat in the 5th century from invasions by Koguryŏ 高句麗—another northern peninsular state. It is the influx of knowledge and skills, which demanded the reorganization of court administration into the *be* 部 system, that contributed most significantly to the emergence of a strong centralized Yamato state in the 6th century.

Be is a word adopted from the Paekche language; however, in Paekche *be* were territorial administrative units, whereas in Yamato they were groups of people. The appointment of nobles to administer the *be* signaled the emergence of a service nobility, which gathered strength from its positions and formed the nuclei of emergent aristocratic clans, the *uji* 氏. It was once thought that *uji* were the primeval units of social organization, but now scholars see them as a late development and outgrowth of the *be* system. This system of administration was short-lived, being replaced in the mid-6th century by the Chinese administrative model.

▌Establishment of Palace 宮城の造営

The center of the Yamato state was the Kinai 畿内 area, especially the Nara Basin 奈良盆地 in the old province of Yamato. Imperial tombs and palaces, as identified in the chronicles, cluster mainly in the Nara Basin and the Ōsaka Plain. The location of the imperial residence changed with each new emperor, giving rise to what is known as the "shifting palace system." Actual palace buildings are unknown archaeologically before the 6th century, but the locations mentioned for earlier palaces coincide with areas of concentrated craft production and ritual remains. These provide the earliest evidence of urban conglomerates in the Nara Basin.

In the 6th century, elite domestic architecture was heavily influenced by Buddhist temple construction—especially in the use of roof tiles 瓦 and stone foundations. In the Asuka region of southern Nara, where most of the earliest temples were built, early imperial palaces such as the Asuka Itabuki Palace 飛鳥板蓋宮 of Empress Kōgyoku 皇極天皇 have been excavated. These have stone-lined drainage ditches and foundation stones upon which a wooden building was erected. This new style of architecture differed from the traditional thatched pit house in having load-bearing pillars integrated into a wooden-board wall structure.

In the mid-7th century, with the Taika Reform 大化の改新 initiating the sinicization of the administrative system, the Chinese gridded city plan was adopted. The first capital built on this model was Fujiwarakyō 藤原京, north of Asuka in the southern Nara Basin. In 710 the capital was moved to Heijōkyō 平城京 in the northern Nara Basin, marking the end of the Kofun period as here defined and leading into the fully historic Nara period 奈良時代 (710–794). Soon after the removal the court chronicles still extant today were compiled: the *Kojiki* in 712 and the *Nihon shoki* in 720. These documents were politically aimed at legitimizing the imperial and aristocratic families by recounting their genealogies and their forebears' roles in the development of the Yamato state. However, because they describe events for much of the Kofun period in mythological and semilegendary terms, and because the chronology is not reliable before 500, they must be used with great care in analysis of this period.

Asuka period 飛鳥時代

(593–710; Asuka *jidai*). Period in the history of Japan dated from 593, the year in which Empress Suiko 推古天皇 (r 593–628) was crowned and took up residence in the Toyura Palace 豊浦宮 in Asuka, Yamato Province 大和国 (now Nara Prefecture). Because written materials become more numerous from this time, the Asuka period is usually considered to coincide with the beginning of the historic age in Japan. The period also includes the decade after 645 when Emperor Kōtoku 孝徳天皇 (r 645–654) removed the capital to Naniwa 難波 (now the city of Ōsaka) and issued the edicts of the Taika Reform 大化の改新, and the interval commencing in 694 when Empress Jitō 持統天皇 (r 686–697) entered Fujiwarakyō 藤原京 and ending in 710 when the capital was shifted to Heijōkyō 平城京, marking the beginning of the Nara period 奈良時代 (710–794).

Buddhism and the Ascendancy of the Soga Family
仏教と蘇我氏の台頭

Asuka, a narrow area in the southeastern corner of the Nara Basin behind which rise the Yoshino Mountains, was the territory of the Soga family 蘇我氏, whose leaders possessed the title *omi* 臣 and served the Yamato court 大和朝廷 in the ministerial capacity of financial administrators and diplomats, and who were instrumental in introducing continental culture, in particular Buddhism, to Japan. As the leading *omi*, the Soga also held the right to provide consorts and wives to the imperial line. This right was later granted to the Mononobe family 物部氏 and the Nakatomi family 中臣氏, both of which held the title *muraji* 連 and which were, respectively, professional soldiers and proprietors of Shintō religious affairs 神事・祭祀. Fraternal succession to the throne was common, and was initially determined by consensus of heads of the leading families (*uji*).

The issue of the acceptance of Buddhism, reported in the historical chronicle *Nihon shoki* 「日本書紀」 to have been introduced in 552, became closely linked to rivalry between the Soga family on one side and the Mononobe and the Nakatomi on the other, over control of the process of kingmaking and the administration of court affairs. Buddhist ritual paraphernalia was brought from the continent by an embassy from the Korean kingdom of Paekche 百済 that had come to seek military aid in its struggle against Silla 新羅, another Korean kingdom. In addition to being a highly developed religion whose deities might be invoked to protect the nation, Buddhism held the potential of offering a broad range of cultural contributions, such as literacy, craftsmanship, and advanced forms of architecture. At the request of the emperor, but against the strong opposition of the Mononobe and Nakatomi, Soga no Iname 蘇我稲目 (d 570) agreed to worship the Buddhist ritual objects. Following the death of Emperor Yōmei 用明天皇 (r 585–587) rumor spread of a conspiracy by Mononobe no Moriya 物部守屋 to install a successor, and in 587 the Soga, led by Soga no Umako 蘇我馬子 and joined by many other major *uji*, attacked Moriya in his home, destroying him and his family and with them the chief opposition to Soga dominance at court and the acceptance of Buddhism.

Temples and the Cultural Role of Prince Shōtoku
寺院と聖徳太子の文化的役割

In 588, according to the *Nihon shoki*, Soga no Umako initiated construction of Asukadera 飛鳥寺, the first full-fledged *garan* 伽藍, or temple compound, in Japan. In 593, upon acceding to the throne, Empress Suiko 推古天皇 declared her acceptance of Buddhism and encouraged the building of temples. In the same year, again according to the *Nihon shoki*, Prince Shōtoku 聖徳太子 ordered the construction of Shitennōji 四天王寺. In 605 Shōtoku, who in 593 had been appointed regent 摂政 and crown prince 皇太子 to Suiko, took up residence in Ikaruga, an alluvial terrace in the northwest of the Nara Basin, and at about this time built the temple Ikarugadera 斑鳩寺 in fulfillment of the professed desire of his father, Emperor Yōmei. It is recorded that with the aid of Korean tutors Shōtoku studied Buddhist scriptures, on some of which he gave lectures and wrote detailed exegeses (*Sangyō gisho* 三経義疏). He is also credited with writing the now lost national histories *Tennōki* 「天皇記」 and *Kokki* 「国記」. In 604, he issued the Seventeen-Article Constitution 十七条憲法 and established the court ranks, *kan'i jūnikai* 冠位十二階, which was the first step in the process of replacing the *uji-kabane* 氏姓制度 system of hereditary titles assumed by leaders of *uji* with one based upon the merit of personal service to the sovereign.

The temples built at the direction of Shōtoku, including Shitennōji 四天王寺 and Ikarugadera 斑鳩寺, were laid out according to a plan then current in Paekche. A rectangular *garan*, or inner precinct—enclosed by a roofed corridor and entered from the south through the *chūmon* 中門, or middle gate—contains in a line on the long north–south axis a pagoda (*tō* 塔), a main hall (*kondō* 金堂, literally, "golden hall"), and, in some cases, a lecture hall (*kōdō* 講堂), the front of which was flush with the corridor marking the north perimeter of the precinct.

Destroyed by fire in 670, Ikarugadera was rebuilt toward the end of the century and renamed Hōryū Gakumonji 法隆学問寺 (Hōryū Temple of Learning; now called Hōryūji 法隆寺), following the practice of using sinicized names established by Emperor Temmu 天武天皇 (r 672–686) in 679. The new ground plan displays native innovation in the positioning of the pagoda and main hall. The long sides of the rectangular inner precinct run east to west, and a north–south line from the middle gate passes between the pagoda on the west side of the compound and the main hall on the east side.

The *Nihon shoki* reports that in 594, in the wake of Suiko's public promotion of Buddhism, the *omi* and *muraji*, who were the leading nobles at court, were vying with one another in the erection of temples. A census in 624 lists 46 temples attended by 816 monks and 569 nuns. There is mention in 680 of "the 24 temples of the capital" and in 690 of "the Seven Temples," at which resided 3,363 monks, or an average of 480 at large temples. The construction of Yakushiji 薬師寺 was ordered in 680 by Emperor Temmu when his consort, who later reigned as Empress Jitō 持統天皇, fell ill. Its monumental gilt bronze triad of the Buddha of healing, Yakushi 薬師如来 (Skt: Bhaiṣajyaguru), and the bodhisattvas of the sun, Nikkō 日光菩薩 (Skt: Sūryaprabha), and the moon, Gakkō 月光菩薩 (Skt: Candraprabha), were installed in 696. The inner precinct is rectangular with the main hall at its center and two pagodas, one disposed to the east and one to the west.

Imperial Palaces 宮城

It is thought that it was not until the Taika Reform of 645 and the introduction of Chinese-style palace design that emperors lived in residences substantially different from those of the leaders of powerful *uji*. Excavations at the site of the palace of Emperor Kōtoku 孝徳天皇, built between 645 and 653 in the capital city Naniwakyō 難波京, clearly show that it followed the Chinese model. There was a large compound (*chōdōin* 朝堂院) containing the Eight Ministries 八省 and behind it a smaller one, entered through a massive gate, that contained the quarters of the emperor. Similarly, reference in the annals to the great gates, gardens, hall of state (Daigokuden), ministry buildings, and imperial residence, and to the ceremonial events conducted at the emperor's court, indicate that Asuka Kiyomihara no Miya 飛鳥浄御原宮, constructed in 672 by Emperor Temmu 天武天皇, also introduced many features of Chinese palace design. However, it has not been determined where in the Asuka area the palace was situated, precluding verification by archaeological study. It was the custom during much of the Asuka period for each ruler to build one or more palaces, a practice that inhibited the development of a stable political order. Fujiwara no Miya 藤原宮, occupied by Empress Jitō 持統天皇 from 694 and until 710 by her successors, Mommu 文武天皇 (r 697–707) and Gemmei 元明天皇 (r 707–715), was the first multigenerational palace. It was situated in the northern part of the planned city Fujiwarakyō and was closely modeled, as was the grid layout of the city itself, on the Chinese pattern.

The Taika Reform 大化の改新

Following the deaths of Prince Shōtoku 聖徳太子 in 622 and Soga no Umako 蘇我馬子 in 626, manipulation by Soga family leaders in succession struggles became increasingly high-handed. Umako's son, Soga no Emishi 蘇我蝦夷 (d 645), intervened to force the accession of Emperor Jomei 舒明天皇 (r 629–641) over more logical candidates. In 643, the second year of the reign of Empress Kōgyoku 皇極天皇 (r 642–645; as Saimei 斉明天皇 she reigned again from 655 to 661), Soga no Iruka 蘇我入鹿, Emishi's son, schemed to have Jomei's prince, Furuhito no Ōe 古人大兄皇子, ascend the throne, and toward this end he forced the suicide of Prince Yamashiro no Ōe 山背大兄王, Shōtoku's eldest son and the leading candidate to succeed. In 645 Nakatomi no Kamatari 中臣鎌足 (later Fujiwara no Kamatari 藤原鎌足) and Prince Naka no Ōe 中大兄皇子, brother of Furuhito no Ōe and emperor as Tenji 天智天皇 from 661 to 672, played leading roles in a coup in which Soga no Iruka was assassinated, followed by the suicide of Emishi. The court was removed from Soga territory to Naniwa 難波, where its structure and functions were fully reorganized. Four edicts 四か条の詔 issued in 646 laid the basis for an ongoing process of reform and are termed, in the narrow sense, the Taika Reform. They dealt with land control and government structure and included limitations on the size of burial mounds (*kofun*). The implementation of these edicts required the definition of land boundaries (*jōri* system 条里制), a major system of roads, formation of local offices, a census and the levying of taxes (*so, yō,* and *chō* 租、庸・調), allotment of land to families and individuals responsible for cultivation (*handen shūju* system 班田収授の法), and the standardization of village size. By 649, eight state ministries, after the Chinese model, presided over by ministers, and a new system of 19 ranks for the nobility 冠位十九階 had been established.

The Reigns of Emperors Tenji and Temmu
天智天皇・天武天皇の治世

Domestic security in the wake of the Taika reforms was threatened by Silla 新羅, which was poised to conquer the entire Korean peninsula, so that the pace of reform slowed considerably after 650. An army was dispatched to the peninsula to defend Paekche 百済 against Silla and its powerful ally Tang (T'ang) dynasty 唐朝 (618–907) China. Empress Saimei 斉明天皇 went to Kyūshū to direct military operations but died there in 661, and during the reign of the succeeding emperor Tenji Japan was defeated in a decisive naval engagement with the

Tang in 663 and Paekche was vanquished (Battle of Hakusonkō 白村江の戦い). Hasty measures were taken to fortify north Kyūshū, but the Tang fleet was withdrawn.

Emperor Tenji expired in 672 and his son ascended the throne as Emperor Kōbun 弘文天皇. In the same year, however, Kōbun was defeated in battle (Jinshin Disturbance 壬申の乱) by Tenji's brother, who, as Emperor Temmu 天武天皇, made further reforms in the system of hiring provincial and central government bureaucrats, established in 684 a new system of eight court ranks (*yakusa no kabane* 八色の姓) under which the former high titles *omi* and *muraji* were displaced toward the bottom, and initiated the compilation of legal statutes that were distributed in 689 as the Asuka Kiyomihara Code 飛鳥浄御原令. The Asuka Kiyomihara Code was the first Japanese legal code that was divided into criminal laws 律 and administrative regulations 令, and it was the basis for the more comprehensive Taihō Code of 701 大宝律令.

Culture 文化

Although the Chinese system of writing was in use in Japan in the 6th century, the oldest extant inscriptions are on halos of Buddhist images of the early 7th century and on *mokkan* 木簡 (wooden tallies used for recording the receipt of goods) excavated from Asuka no Itabuki Palace 飛鳥板蓋宮, which was occupied around the mid-7th century by the empress who reigned as Kōgyoku 皇極天皇 and Saimei 斉明天皇. Paekche sent specialists in a number of fields, such as priests and diviners, temple builders, bronze casters, and roof tile makers; it also introduced to Japan the Confucian classics 儒教書, continental music and dance, and Chinese court ceremonies. Calendar makers arrived in 602 and by the 8th century the Chinese practice of using era names 年号 was fully established.

Reading and writing in Chinese spread among

the aristocracy and it is recorded in the introduction to the *Kaifūsō*「懐風藻」 (751), an anthology of Chinese poetry by Japanese, that Chinese verse was being written at the court of Emperor Tenji 天智天皇 in the mid-7th century. The use of Chinese characters 漢字 to denote Japanese words or syllables, the method employed to write the mid-8th-century anthology of Japanese poetry *Man'yōshū*「万葉集」, seems to have developed by the 7th century; it was by this means that the great early poets of the native tradition, such as Kakinomoto no Hitomaro 柿本人麻呂 and Nukata no Ōkimi 額田王, recorded their verses.

Almost all of the works of art that remain from the Asuka period are related to Buddhist worship. The Shaka (Śākyamuni) Triad 釈迦三尊像 (623) at Hōryūji by Kuratsukuri no Tori 鞍作止利, a work that is strongly influenced by Northern Wei 北魏 (386–535) sculptural style, is the earliest piece of Buddhist statuary that can be positively dated. Another important piece from about the same period is the seated bodhisattva at Chūgūji 中宮寺. An important example of painting of the 7th century is the Tamamushi Shrine 玉虫厨子, on whose panels are depicted scenes from the previous lives of the Buddha and other Buddhist scenes.

The culture developed late in the Asuka period is called the Hakuhō culture 白鳳文化. Outstanding examples of the culture are the east pagoda of Yakushiji 薬師寺東塔 and the Miroku Buddha 弥勒菩薩像 at Taimadera 当麻寺.

Nara period 奈良時代

(710–794; Nara *jidai*). The period during which the seat of government was at Heijōkyō 平城京 (now the city of Nara) in Yamato 大和 (now Nara Prefecture 奈良県). Strictly speaking, the Nara period began in 710, when the imperial capital was moved from Fujiwarakyō 藤原京, and ended in 784 with the transfer of the capital to Nagaokakyō 長岡京, excluding temporary removals to

Kuni no Miya 恭仁宮, Naniwakyō 難波京, and Shigaraki no Miya 紫香楽宮. Dates for the period are usually given as 710–794, however, to include the 10 years during which the capital was in Nagaoka. The period was characterized by the full implementation of the *ritsuryō* system 律令制度 of government; the establishment of Buddhism as the religion of the court and, by extension, of the state; and new heights in intellectual and cultural achievement, as exemplified in the building of the Great Hall 大仏殿 of the temple Tōdaiji 東大寺. Early in the period the central administration was able to exercise close control over the country, but during the middle of the period a power struggle broke out among the court nobility. Modifications in the land tenure system 土地保有制度, and the absconding from state lands of peasants overburdened by taxes, contributed to the breakdown of central authority.

Political Developments 政治的発展

The political history of the Nara period may be seen as a series of struggles for power that pitted the Fujiwara family 藤原氏 against factions composed of, among others, members of the Tachibana 橘氏 and Ōtomo families 大伴氏 in association with disaffected members of the imperial family. The leader of the government at the beginning of the Nara period was Fujiwara no Fuhito 藤原不比等. His daughter Kyūshi 宮子 was a consort of Emperor Mommu 文武天皇 (r 697–707), and Fuhito succeeded in establishing her son Obito 首 as crown prince. He further arranged for another daughter, Asukabehime 安宿媛 (Empress Kōmyō 光明天皇), to become Prince Obito's consort, thus assuring the continuing influence of the Fujiwara family.

However, when Fuhito died in 720 the political situation underwent drastic change, and the princess Toneri Shinnō 舎人親王 and Nagaya no Ō 長屋王 formed a faction to oppose the Fujiwara ascendancy. After Prince

Obito began his reign as Emperor Shōmu 聖武天皇 (r 724–749), a crisis developed over recognition of Asukabehime as Shōmu's empress. Nagaya no Ō was forced to commit suicide (Rebellion of Nagaya no Ō 長屋王の変), and Asukabehime became Empress Kōmyō. Fuhito's sons, Muchimaro 武智麻呂, Fusasaki 房前, Umakai 宇合, and Maro 麻呂, took control of the government, and it appeared that the era of a Fujiwara dispensation had begun. In 737, however, Fuhito's four sons died in a smallpox epidemic 天然痘.

The center of power now shifted to Tachibana no Moroe 橘諸兄 and Prince Suzuka no Ō 鈴鹿王 (brother of Nagaya no Ō), who were advised by the priest Gembō 玄昉 and Kibi no Makibi 吉備真備, former members of an embassy to China 遣唐使. They attempted to reform the administration by disbanding the provincial militia (the *kondei* system 健児) and reducing the number of district officials (*gunji* 郡司), but turmoil in the provinces weakened their position.

Emperor Shōmu 聖武天皇 was deeply disturbed by this course of events, and, in the hope that the powers of Buddha would bring an end to epidemic disease and social ills, in 741 he ordered the construction of temples and nunneries (*kokubunji* 国分寺) in every province. This undertaking was completed only after many years. In 743 he also ordered the construction of a gigantic statue of the Buddha Vairocana 毘盧遮那仏 so that the blessings of the Buddha would extend over the entire country. Completed in 752 at enormous expense, it was known as the Great Buddha 大仏 of Tōdaiji 東大寺.

Emperor Shōmu abdicated in 749 and was replaced by his daughter Empress Kōken 孝謙天皇 (r 749–758). An office (Shibichūdai 紫微中台) was established for the empress dowager Kōmyō 光明皇太后, and Fujiwara no Nakamaro 藤原仲麻呂 appeared in the political arena as administrator of her palace affairs.

Nakamaro disposed of his principal rival, Tachibana no Moroe 橘諸兄, in 756 on a charge of sedition. Emperor Shōmu's zeal in spreading Buddhism had imposed an intolerable burden on the peasantry, and, under the pretext of ameliorating their lot, Moroe's son Tachibana no Naramaro 橘奈良麻呂 attempted a coup in 757. Nakamaro foiled the coup, but, realizing that the plot had profited from peasant distress, he immediately reduced by half the most burdensome of the taxes, the *zōyō* 雑徭, which called for 60 days of labor each year. He also commuted the interest on all debts accumulated through the previous year. In 758 Nakamaro dispatched officials (*momikushi* 問民苦使) throughout the country to listen to the peasants' grievances and to give relief to the indigent. Within officialdom he encouraged the observance of filial piety and renamed official ranks and ministries in the Chinese manner. He publicly commended his grandfather Fuhito for his work in drawing up the Taihō Code 大宝律令 (701) and the Yōrō Code 養老律令 (718), and he belatedly enforced the latter in 757. The government, which had been dominated by Buddhism, now took on a more Confucian aspect.

However, the former reigning empress Kōken, who by 762 had gained ascendancy over her successor, Emperor Junnin 淳仁天皇 (r 757–764), was displeased with the new measures; she dismissed Nakamaro and instead relied heavily on the priest Dōkyō 道鏡, who she believed had cured her of an illness. In 764 Nakamaro instigated a rebellion but was captured and killed. Dōkyō was elevated to the rank of *dajō daijin zenji* 太政大臣禅師 (priestly grand minister of state) and given the title of *hōō* 法王 (priestly retired sovereign). With the appointment of his fellow monks as religious councillors (*hōsangi* 法参議), court politics was monopolized by the Buddhist clergy. Previous policies were reversed and Buddhism once again became supreme. Finally, on the basis of an oracle he claimed to have received at the Usa Hachiman Shrine 宇佐八幡宮, Dōkyō tried to have himself enthroned. He was thwarted by Fujiwara no Momokawa 藤原百川, Wake no Kiyomaro 和気清麻呂, and others. The empress Shōtoku 称徳天皇 (the name taken by Empress Kōken when she reascended the throne in 764) died without issue in 770, and Dōkyō was banished.

After the death of Shōtoku, Fujiwara no Momokawa and his followers successfully countered the attempts of Kibi no Makibi to enthrone the grandson of Emperor Temmu 天武天皇 (r 672–686) and installed instead the grandson of Emperor Tenji 天智天皇 (r 661–672), 62-year-old Prince Shirakabe 白壁王. As Emperor Kōnin 光仁天皇 (r 770–781), he was the last sovereign whose reign fell completely within the Nara period. His rule was distinguished by efforts to reduce national expenditures, to discipline officials and monks, and to rebuild farming villages. Government offices founded for the construction of religious edifices were reduced in size or abolished altogether. Sinecures established outside the *ritsuryō* administrative framework to provide income for officials were eliminated. In 780 the staffs of all government offices were reduced, and men conscripted from the provinces to work in the bureaucracy were allowed to return home. In order to encourage the return of dispossessed peasants who had left their homes to escape debts, a limit was set on the interest on borrowed seed rice (*suiko* 出挙). Tax payments to the national coffers continued to decrease, however, and the decay of the central government's authority was felt as far away as northeastern Japan, where the Ezo 蝦夷 tribes rose in rebellion. The rebellion spread to other areas and posed a grave problem for years afterward. In 781 Emperor Kōnin's crown prince acceded to the throne as Emperor Kammu 桓武天皇 (r 781–806), and it was he who was instrumental in moving the capital to Heiankyō in 794.

Society and Economy 社会と経済

The social structure in the Nara period conformed to the *ritsuryō* system, as set forth in the Taihō Code 大宝律令. The central government was headed by the Dajōkan 太政官 (Grand Council of State), which presided over eight ministries, and the country was divided into provinces (*kuni* or *koku* 国), which in turn were divided into districts (*gun* 郡), villages (*gō* 郷), and hamlets (*ri* 里). An early-Nara-period document lists 67 provinces, comprising 555 districts, 4,012 villages, and 12,036 hamlets. The provinces were administered by governors (*kokushi* 国司), who were sent out from the capital. All the people were considered the emperor's subjects and were expected to obey officials who acted in his name.

All rice land was declared public domain. Under the *handen shūju* system 班田収授制度 the land was redistributed every six years to all males and females over six years of age (five in Western reckoning). Men received 2 *tan* 反 (1 *tan* = 0.12 hectare or 0.3 acre), women two-thirds that amount. In order to ensure proper allocation of rice land, the census register was updated every six years. The authority of the imperial court at the time extended as far south as the islands off the coast of Kyūshū and as far north as Akitajō 秋田城 in what is now Akita Prefecture. The population within this area is estimated to have been about 5 to 6 million and the acreage of rice land about 601,000 *chō* 町 (721,200 hectares or 1.8 million acres; 1 *chō* = 10 *tan*); it is clear that even after taking into consideration the ratio of men to women, there was not enough arable land. Judging from historical materials, however, the *handen* system and the census registration seem to have been implemented throughout the country with little resistance. Holders of allotted rice land (*kubunden* 口分田) were liable to corvée (*zōyō* 雑徭), a rice tax (*so* 租), and a handicraft or local products tax (*chō* 調). There was also a handicraft or local products tax (*yō* 庸) in lieu of labor. To strengthen administrative and military communications with the provinces and to facilitate the payment of taxes, the government established a network of post stations (*eki-sei* 駅制) on the public roads connecting the capital and provincial seats of government. The rice and produce taxes that had hitherto been paid to local chieftains were now sent directly to the central government.

A faithful imitation of the Chinese system of government was bound to have negative side effects, for it was unsuited to Japan's agricultural reality. According to a document of 730, in the province of Awa 安房国 (now part of Chiba Prefecture) 412 out of 414 households were listed as being at the bare subsistence level. The figures for Echizen Province 越前国 (now part of Fukui Prefecture) in that year tell the same story: of 1,019 households, 996 were found to be poverty stricken. The tax burden fell most heavily on the peasants, and the number of those who absconded increased at an alarming rate.

At the same time, as a means of increasing revenue, there was a demand for an expansion of acreage under cultivation through the reclamation of land. This plan was to be implemented chiefly by provincial governors and district officials and would require a large-scale mobilization of peasant labor. Since the early 8th century, however, members of the royal family, the aristocracy, the great temples, local magnates, and, to a lesser extent, the peasants themselves had set about gaining control of uncultivated lands. It is believed that a large number of vagrant peasants supplied the labor for these private endeavors. The reclaimed lands were not subject to taxation under the *handen* system, but, as there was no clear title attaching to them, there were cases of reclaimed land being summarily placed by governors in the handen pool of rice lands.

In 723 the government issued the Sanze Isshin no Hō 三世一身法, a law declaring that reclaimed lands could be held in private hands for up to three generations, but that thenceforth they must be given over to the *handen* system. This law proved to be ineffective, however, and in 743, through the Konden Einen Shizai Hō 墾田永年私財法, the government permitted the privatization of reclaimed lands in perpetuity. As a consequence the aristocracy, the great temples, and local magnates naturally redoubled their efforts to reclaim land. Although the reclaimed lands 開墾地 were, in fact, subject to taxation, their loss to the public domain had grievous effects upon the *handen* system 班田制. Furthermore, the influence of members of the central power structure acting as private citizens was brought to bear upon the provincial populace through the medium of lands subject to reclamation. The fact that a large number of peasants were thus organized outside of the *ritsuryō* system 律令制度 into a labor force to develop land was a decisive factor in the evolution of society during and after the Nara period, for it created the basis for the formation of privately owned estates (*shōen* 荘園).

Diplomacy 外交

Embassies to Tang (T'ang; 618–907) China 遣唐使, which had been interrupted for some 30 years after the defeat of Japan by the combined armies of China and the Korean state Silla 新羅 in the Battle of Hakusonkō 白村江の戦い, were revived in 702, the year in which the Taihō Code 大宝律令 came into effect. During the Nara period eight embassies, six of which actually reached the continent, were commissioned. The purpose of sending embassies to China was, first, to profit from trade and absorb the culture, knowledge, and methods of an advanced society. Second, through the establishment of diplomatic relations the Japanese court hoped to gain a closer relationship with China than that enjoyed by other nations. Among students who accompanied these embassies, each of which numbered as many as 500 to 600 men, were Kibi no Makibi 吉備真備 and the priest Gembō 玄昉. Gembō returned with over 5,000 sutras, while Kibi no Makibi, who had studied Confucianism 儒教, military science, and ceremonial rites in China, set up an educational program for future government officials.

On their homeward journeys from China the missions were joined by numerous non-Japanese, and these men too had great influence upon the politics and culture of the time. Notable among them was the Chinese monk Ganjin 鑑真, transmitter of the teachings of the Ritsu sect 律宗, who established the Ordination Hall (Kaidan'in 戒壇院) at the temple Tōdaiji and founded the temple Tōshōdaiji 唐招提寺. There were also members of embassies who, because of their talents and facility with the Chinese language, were retained by the Tang court 唐朝 to serve as administrators. Among these was Abe no Nakamaro 阿倍仲麻呂.

Relations with Silla were not so felicitous. The Japanese insisted that Silla was a subject nation and referred to its embassies as tribute missions. However Silla, which had unified the Korean peninsula in the late 7th century, demanded that its dealings with Japan be conducted on a basis of equality. In 753, at a banquet held by the Tang imperial court, the embassies of Japan and Silla argued over which should sit closest to the representatives of the host nation. Relations deteriorated, and Fujiwara no Nakamaro 藤原仲麻呂 urged that a punitive force be dispatched to the peninsula. Before the plan was carried out, Nakamaro was removed from his position of power, but relations with Silla remained troubled throughout the Nara period.

In 727 an embassy from Bohai (Po-hai) 渤海, a nation situated north of the Korean peninsula, arrived in Japan. Bohai's diplomatic relations with both Silla and China were unstable, and it was anxious to form an alliance with Japan. Japan reciprocated Bohai's visit the following year and, treating it as a tributary nation, permitted it a lucrative trade. For the Japanese, Bohai was a convenient window through which to follow events on the continent. It was in this way that Japan learned of the An Lushan (An Lu-shan) Rebellion 安禄山の乱 (755) in China. More than 30 missions were exchanged by the two nations before Bohai lost its sovereignty in the 10th century.

Culture 文化

The ripening of Tempyō culture 天平文化, so termed after the era name 年号 for the years 729–749, owed much to the resumption of relations with Tang China. Visitors came to Japan from as far away as Central and West Asia, Indonesia, Vietnam, Malaysia, and India, contributing to the culture's vigor and diversity.

As receptive as Japan was to foreign influence, however, the culture of the period remained uniquely Japanese. The process of domestication of foreign influences is readily apparent in the development of a native writing system, for until Chinese characters 漢字 were imported Japan had no letters of its own. The *Nihon shoki* 「日本書紀」 (720, Chronicles of Japan) was actually written in Chinese (*kambun* 漢文), whereas the *Kojiki* 「古事記」 (712, Record of Ancient Matters) and the poetic anthology *Man'yōshū* 「万葉集」 (mid-8th century) employed various devices, among them the use of Chinese characters to represent similar-sounding Japanese syllables, to enable a concatenation of Chinese characters to be read in Japanese. This development was the result of a phenomenal increase in the production of manuscripts and books in Chinese during the 8th century. Contributing to this growth were the flourishing of Buddhism, which was accompanied by the copying of sutras and the writing of exegetic works, and the activities of the *ritsuryō* state itself, which relied chiefly on the use of Chinese characters to transmit information.

Influenced by the import of foreign cultural artifacts and the growth of Buddhism, an aristocratic culture flourished, characterized by impressive developments in the fine arts. Emperor Shōmu 聖武天皇 was the great patron of Tempyō culture, and objects made for his personal use, such as goblets, musical instruments, and other items, compose the heart of the collection of treasures at Shōsōin 正倉院. Employing materials gathered throughout Asia and applying technology that often required specialization of labor, a large number of these treasures were fabricated in Japan by immigrant artisans and by craftsmen assembled under the administration of the *ritsuryō* system. For the construction of each temple a special government bureau, such as the Zō-Tōdaiji-Shi 造東大寺司 (Bureau for the Erection of Tōdaiji), was formed in order to direct the huge labor required.

The Nara period marked the culmination, largely through state sponsorships, of the first great flowering of Japanese literature 日本文学 and the fine arts 美術, supplying the foundation upon which the pervasive domestication of continental culture was achieved in the Heian period (794–1185).

Heian period 平安時代

(794–1185; Heian *jidai*). As defined in this book, the Heian period is a span of nearly 400 years extending from 794, when Emperor Kammu 桓武天皇 established Heiankyō 平安京 (now Kyōto) as the imperial capital of Japan, to 1185, when Minamoto no Yoritomo's 源頼朝 forces defeated those of the Taira family 平氏, thus setting the stage for the establishment of the Kamakura shogunate 鎌倉幕府. The name of the period is taken from that of the capital and means "peace and tranquility." Some classifications begin the period in 781, the year of Kammu's accession to the throne, or in 784, when the capital was removed from Heijōkyō 平城京 (now Nara) to Nagaokakyō 長岡京; some end it in 1180, when Yoritomo took up arms and established his headquarters at Kamakura, or in 1183, when the Taira family fled Heiankyō before the advancing army of Minamoto no Yoshinaka 源義仲.

Heian has long been an established division of history, regarded as the apogee of the nation's aristocratic age, which produced one of the world's most exquisitely refined cultures. During Heian times, Japan fully assimilated the elements of Chinese society that the architects of the Japanese state had long emulated. While the Chinese ideals never died out completely, in economics, government, and cultural style, the Japanese created indigenous institutions that bore only a slight resemblance to Chinese prototypes.

From Nara to Nagaoka to Kyōto
奈良から長岡、そして京都へ

In 784 Emperor Kammu moved the capital from Heijōkyō (now Nara) northwest to Nagaokakyō, and only a decade later he moved it to Heiankyō. Political rivalries at court lay behind these removals. One major consideration was to escape the baneful influence of a Buddhist clergy that had come to exercise considerable influence in secular affairs, especially under the leadership of the priest Dōkyō 道鏡 during the reign of Empress Shōtoku 称徳天皇 (r 764–770).

There were other political problems. The Fujiwara family 藤原氏, then headed by Fujiwara no Momokawa 藤原百川 (732–779), was responsible for the exile of Dōkyō after Shōtoku's death and for the enthronement of Emperor Kōnin 光仁天皇 (r 770–781) and then arranged for Kammu to succeed by eliminating

Crown Prince Osabe 他戸親王. For the imperial house this represented a shift from the line of Emperor Temmu 天武天皇, which remained powerful around Nara, to that of Tenji 天智天皇, which was dominant in Yamashiro 山城, location of both Nagaokakyō and Heiankyō. Thus several factors—desire to escape Buddhist influence, desire to move into the area of Tenji-line strength, and fear of the spirits of the deceased Prince Osabe and his mother—motivated Kammu to move from Nara.

Momokawa's nephew Fujiwara no Tanetsugu 藤原種継 (737–785) was placed in charge of construction at Nagaokakyō, to which Kammu moved long before the city itself was completed. Tanetsugu supported Kammu's eldest son, Prince Ate 安殿親王, to succeed his father but was opposed by Crown Prince Sawara 早良親王. One night Tanetsugu was set upon and assassinated, and Sawara, among others, was implicated; exiled to Awaji 淡路, he died within a few weeks but always has been considered innocent. Sawara's figure seemed to haunt the court, and Kammu, fearful that several untoward events (including the deaths of his mother and empress) were the result of Sawara's vengeful spirit, ordered the construction of, and removal to, Heiankyō.

Ritsuryō System 律令制度

Heian political, social, and economic institutions were shaped by the *ritsuryō* system, based on the penal 律 and administrative 令 codes of Tang (T'ang) China 唐 (618–907). Ever since the time of Prince Shōtoku 聖徳太子 in the early 7th century, imperial house members and their close associates had sought to invoke august Chinese symbols of authority and power to assert their hegemony over society. By the early Nara period (710–794) they had succeeded in creating a reasonable approximation of the Chinese model, complete with a detailed administrative and penal code and an impressive capital that demonstrated the transcendent magnificence of the emperor.

Although it functioned imperfectly from the outset, the *ritsuryō* system remained the fountainhead of Japanese political and economic ideas, even during the Heian period, when considerable movement away from the system occurred. Especially entrenched was the concept of a "public" system of peasantry and land in the sense that they belonged to the emperor, as opposed to a system in which land and people were controlled by "private" interests. The latter had been the case under the earlier *uji* 氏 (powerful kin groups) society, and private interests reasserted control under the feudal system 封建制度 that developed over the course of the Heian period to replace the *ritsuryō* system.

Politics and Government 政治と政治体制

The political history of Heian Japan can be divided in several ways, most simply by postulating early and late Heian periods, divided near the mid-10th century. The early period represents various attempts to reinvigorate the *ritsuryō* system 律令制度, with its emperor-dominated polity and nationally controlled rice fields. In the late Heian period, systemic contradictions allowed Fujiwara regents 藤原摂政・関白 (and then retired sovereigns) to dominate the political system and *shōen* 荘園 (private landed estates) to become the principal form of landholding.

A more precise division of the period requires a four-phase scheme. In the first phase, which ended in the early 9th century, Kammu attempted to reinvigorate the *ritsuryō* system through various governmental reforms and military campaigns. His work was carried on by Emperor Saga 嵯峨天皇, who created certain extrastatutory offices outside the *ritsuryō* system to enhance government efficiency. These offices, however, created new avenues to power for nonimperial royal families, most important among them the Fujiwara, who had been a leading family in Nara times. Through skillful political maneuvering in several plots at court, the Fujiwara eliminated a number of rival families and drew close to the imperial house as regents (*sesshō* 摂政 or *kampaku* 関白).

In the second phase, from the late 9th century until 967, the imperial house managed to preserve power and authority in the face of the rise of the Fujiwara under Emperors Uda 宇多天皇, Daigo 醍醐天皇, and Murakami 村上天皇, all of whom ruled without Fujiwara "assistance." But the court faced both political and fiscal problems at this juncture. Daigo tried to solve the matter by regulating *shōen* and reforming provincial government and tax collection. But his efforts were in vain as court control of land and people continued to weaken due to the collaboration of local landholders with central nobles and religious institutions to create *shōen*.

The third phase is dated from 967, when Fujiwara no Saneyori 藤原実頼 became regent after a hiatus of 20 years. With the exile of his rival Minamoto no Takaakira 源高明 in 969, Saneyori was supreme. The next century was the period of Fujiwara regency politics (*sekkan seiji* 摂関政治), when the northern branch of the Fujiwara family established a permanent regency. Emperors were born of Fujiwara mothers and dominated by uncles, fathers-in-law, or grandfathers, in whose households they usually were raised. The two greatest Fujiwara regents were Fujiwara no Michinaga 藤原道長, father of four daughters married to emperors and grandfather of three emperors, and his son Fijiwara no Yorimichi 藤原頼通, who held the post of regent for 52 years.

The fourth phase of the Heian period is recognized as commencing when Go-Sanjō 後三条天皇, the first emperor in a century who had not been born of a Fujiwara mother, came to the throne in 1068. It is called the phase of *insei* 院政, or rule by "cloistered emperor," so named because three successive retired emperors—Shirakawa 白河天皇, Toba 鳥羽天皇, and Go-Shirakawa 後白河天皇—replaced emperors and also regents as the supreme political figures at Heiankyō, fully utilizing and expanding upon a private base of power for the imperial house created by Go-Sanjō.

This was a period of imperial revival, as the imperial house, no longer simply the repository of sovereignty as it had been under Fujiwara domination, regained control over the imperial position, reorganized itself into a strong private house with aristocratic and military clients, and competed with the Fujiwara and others for *shōen* acquisition.

The *ritsuryō* system virtually disappeared during this phase, however, as cliques of local powerful individuals threatened state control over lands, Buddhist institutions quarreled with each other and with the court, and public law and order broke down. The rising military class became increasingly necessary to maintain civil government even in Heiankyō, as demonstrated by the Hōgen Disturbance 保元の乱 (1156) and the Heiji Disturbance 平治の乱 (1160). One warrior-courtier, Taira no Kiyomori 平清盛, rose so high in court rank that some scholars postulate the existence of yet a fifth phase of the Heian period, one of Taira warrior domination, from 1160 to 1185.

Landholding System 土地保有制度

Facing a shaky hegemony over other *uji* 氏 at the Yamato court 大和朝廷 in the mid-7th century, the Yamato *uji*, or imperial family, centralized the government, establishing the *ritsuryō* system. At the core of the system was the idea of imperial control over both land and people, replacing earlier control by individual *uji*. The imperial house lacked the power to force others to accept the new arrangements and achieved acquiescence only by appointing other *uji* members to bureaucratic posts that allowed them to maintain their economic interests under the new system.

Under the *ritsuryō* system the government asserted the right to control and tax the land, which was allotted to free and slave cultivators, both male and female. Lands, which could be held throughout the recipient's lifetime, were pooled by household units for cultivation purposes. A complex system of land allotment required a census every six years to reallocate lands according to population increase or decrease in households. The state levied three kinds of taxes on cultivators: a rice tax (*so* 租), a tax in kind (*chō* 調), and corvée (*yōeki* 徭役), the heaviest burden of all, which was levied on males aged 17 to 65. Military duty also was required.

From the outset the system worked only imperfectly, largely due to compromises needed to maintain the support of great *uji*. The nobility and large temples had the capital to open new lands, and they were able to entice cultivators of allotment fields unable to sustain themselves on their own lands. The government, faced with the problem of increasing population demands without a concomitant increase in productive lands, could do little to stop this process. Although it announced a project in 722 to open new lands, little cooperation was forthcoming until a law the next year offered proprietary control for periods of one or three generations to those opening new fields (Sanze Isshin no Hō 三世一身の法). By 743 the government had to grant permanent ownership to anyone reclaiming new rice fields (Konden Einen Shizai Hō 墾田永年私財法).

These actions paved the way for extensive private land ownership by temples and nobles, a movement counter to the spirit of the *ritsuryō* system but supported by government officials who found it profitable. Several attempts to halt this development in the late Nara and early Heian periods failed, and reallotment was accomplished only twice in the 9th century, during which time noble lands, acquired through reclamation, purchase, occupation of abandoned fields, or placing them into vassalage, expanded. Many of these were in the form of *shōen*, and in 902 an edict was promulgated to stop their growth, but it succeeded only in curtailing lands of the imperial house.

Onerous *ritsuryō* levies forced peasants to abscond, to falsify census records, or to collude with temples or nobles to form *shōen*, seriously eroding the resources of the government. To alleviate the crisis, two major changes in the provincial government and taxation systems were introduced in the early 10th century. First, *ritsuryō* levies were now made on lands rather than individuals since the former were easier to calculate. A new administrative unit, called the *myō* 名, was established, a taxation unit on which both rent and corvée could be levied. The second change was that local administration was entrusted to governors or their deputies in return for a stipulated amount of tax revenue, calculated for each province.

Allotment no longer being practiced, all government lands—that is, taxable lands—were now listed as *kōden* 公田 ("public lands"). The amount for each province was set and divided for exploitative purposes into *myō*. Nonpublic lands were mostly *shōen*, and their growth over the 11th and 12th centuries was so great that by the end of the Heian period more than half the paddy fields were within *shōen* 荘園, forcing the nobility to look for ever more private land to replace declining public revenues. Although *kōden* survived well into the Kamakura period (1185–1333), the *ritsuryō* ideal of national control over people and land was long dead by the end of the 12th century.

Religion 宗教

Although escaping the undue influence of Buddhism was one of the reasons for removing the capital to Heiankyō, Emperor Kammu 桓武天皇 and his successors were not hostile to Buddhism. Buddhism flourished in Heian times, and in combination with native Shintō 神道 beliefs it dominated the religious and philosophical lives of the nobility. But Heian-period Buddhism differed from earlier Buddhism.

New forms of Buddhism were brought to the Heian court by two monks who had gone to China in search of Buddhist truth. Saichō 最澄, who had founded the temple Enryakuji 延暦寺 on Mt. Hiei (Hieizan 比叡山), established the Tendai sect 天台宗, dedicating himself to creating a monastic order that would truly serve the nation. Indeed, a large number of Japan's subsequent religious leaders came from the Tendai headquarters at Enryakuji. Situated in the critically dangerous northeast, from which it was believed evil spirits invaded, Enryakuji came to be regarded as the protector of the capital.

Kūkai 空海, better known by his posthumous name Kōbō Daishi 弘法大師, returned to found his temple on Mt. Kōya (Kōyasan) 高野山, far from the court in Kii Province 紀伊国 (now Wakayama Prefecture). Kūkai introduced tantric Buddhism into Japan in the form of the Shingon sect 真言宗. Because it emphasized rituals, incantations, and powerful visual representations of the Buddhist cosmology—in cosmic diagrams called *mandala* 曼陀羅—Shingon Buddhism proved immensely popular with the Japanese court, as a means of personal comfort and as a spur to artistic developments. Furthermore, Kūkai's own talents and strength of character helped to make esoteric Shingon more influential than Tendai among the nobility.

The headquarters of the new sects of Buddhism

were located outside the capital, reflecting Kammu's desire to avoid the negative influence of priests. Only two temples, both located far south of the palace near Heiankyō's main gate, were included in the original city plan, and other temples were constructed in the suburbs. But from mid-Heian times the aristocracy had built numerous private temples within the city, and monks from suburban temples were as common a sight in Heiankyō as they had been in Nara. In fact, they proved more threatening, for they often were armed.

Major temples recruited warrior-monks (sōhei 僧兵) for protection in bitter doctrinal disputes within and among temples and in conflicts over shōen 荘園 holdings. These monks were also effective in pressing demands at court, when they would march into the capital bearing the sacred palanquin of the protective Shintō deity associated with their temple. Ironically, it was the warrior-monks of Mt. Hiei 比叡山 at the capital's protective temple of Enryakuji 延暦寺 who most terrified the court and the citizens of Heiankyō 平安京. Yet despite occasional intimidation, the separation of religion and politics was largely maintained. The court nobles remained devout, however, and frequent pilgrimages to major Buddhist and Shintō institutions were common, even for emperors.

In Heian times Buddhism did not spread widely among commoners, but the faith began to be popularized through the belief in the saving grace of Amida 阿弥陀, the Buddha of Boundless Light, into whose Western Paradise 極楽 souls could be reborn. Amida supposedly made an original vow that all who called on his name— a practice known as nembutsu 念仏—would be welcome in the Western Paradise, or Pure Land (Pure Land Buddhism 浄土宗). This Pure Land doctrine was introduced from China in the 9th century by Ennin 円仁 and was popularized to some degree by Kūya 空也, who preached it in the streets. The most important Heian figure in Pure Land development was Genshin 源信, who wrote graphically of the horrors of hell and the delights of the Pure Land in his *Ōjōyōshū*「往生要集」.

Pure Land Buddhism achieved great popularity from mid-Heian times. The key to its popularity was the Mahāyāna Buddhist idea of *mappō* 末法, the concept that Buddhist law would develop through three stages after the death of the Buddha: prosperity of 500 years, decline of 1,000 years, and finally disappearance in the latter days (*mappō*). Once *mappō* began, widely believed in Japan to have been in 1052, it would not be sufficient to achieve enlightenment through one's own efforts, as most Buddhist sects preached; the only hope was faith in the saving grace of Amida. Thus, court nobles and ladies chanted the *nembutsu* with great fervor or built Amida halls 阿弥陀堂 within their residences to show their faith. The most famous example of such private Amida temples is the Phoenix Hall 鳳凰堂 of the Byōdōin 平等院 in Uji , which was built by Fujiwara no Yorimichi 藤原頼通.

Although Buddhism flourished in the Heian period, there was no strict sectarian division among devotees. Apart from members of the religious community itself, religious belief for most Japanese was highly eclectic. Courtiers seemingly made little distinction among different sects of Buddhism, Shintō beliefs, and imported Confucian lore centering on the pseudoscientific concepts of *yin* 陰 and *yang* 陽 and the "five elements 5行."

▌Literature 文学

The field of literature represented the height of the Heian creative spirit. As in other spheres, a convenient psychological dividing point in Heian literary history is the year 838, when the last official mission was sent to China. After that the Japanese, while continuing to value Chinese books, pictures, and other artifacts and while retaining Chinese philosophical tendencies, turned increasingly to a more native means of expression.

The outburst of literary creativity was made possible by the development of the *kana* 仮名 syllabary with its some 50 phonetic symbols 50音, which made writing much simpler. While it was now theoretically possible to write in Japanese without reliance on any Chinese characters 漢字, the Japanese had by this time borrowed such an enormous corpus of Chinese terms that in practice both *kana* and Chinese characters were used. Moreover, Heian courtiers remained intellectually committed to the written Chinese language, which they employed in private diaries, court records, and official documents, using *kana* only when composing Japanese poetry. Thus, the use of *kana* was left largely to court ladies, and by and large it was these women who produced the greatest works of Heian literature.

As direct interest in China waned, courtiers turned increasingly to the cultivation of the 31-syllable *waka* 和歌 poem. In fact, poetry composition became a crucial aspect of the world of the Heian courtier. Poetry competitions were held (some at imperial command), lovers commonly exchanged poems, and the inability to compose a credible poem or recognize a poetic allusion could condemn one to social disgrace. Although none matched the earlier *Man'yōshū*「万葉集」, anthologies of Japanese poetry were compiled, the *Kokin wakashū*「古今和歌集」being perhaps the greatest.

The *kana* syllabary was a stimulus to the creation of a native prose literature, of which there were essentially two types in Heian times, the *monogatari* (tale) 物語 and the *nikki* (diary) 日記. The former was a narrative tale, which reached unparalleled heights in Murasaki Shikibu's 紫式部 *Genji monogatari* (*Tale of Genji*)「源氏物語」, while the latter was more a record of intimate, private impressions of daily events at court. The two genres did share the common feature of interspersing poems throughout the narrative. In fact, one type of tale, the *uta monogatari* 歌物語, or poem tale, was little more than a large number of poems linked by brief introductory remarks. *Ise monogatari* (Tales of Ise) 「伊勢物語」, thought to be the best of this genre, is regarded as a classic of Japanese literature.

The *nikki* is regarded as having its beginning with *Tosa nikki* (Tosa Diary) 「土佐日記」, an account by Ki no Tsurayuki 紀貫之 of his trip to Tosa Province 土佐国 (now Kōchi Prefecture) in the early 10th century. The genre was later taken over by women, the two most representative works being the *Kagerō nikki* (The Gossamer Years) 「蜻蛉日記」 by the "mother of Michitsuna 道綱母" and *Murasaki Shikibu nikki* 「紫式部日記」 by the author of *Genji*.

In a slightly different vein from the diary is Sei Shōnagon's 清少納言 *Makura no sōshi* (Pillow Book) 「枕草子」, a collection of reminiscences, anecdotes, and very candid opinions about the world of the court. The tone is light and witty, expressing the ideal of amusement or delight that Heian courtiers referred to as *okashi* をかし, and it pioneered the popular genre of essays known as *zuihitsu* 随筆.

The *Tale of Genji* 「源氏物語」 remains the classic work of Japanese literature, a massive work in 54 chapters dealing with the life of the court and focusing on the hero, Hikaru Genji 光源氏, the "shining prince." In contrast to the *Pillow Book*—which stressed the aesthetic of *okashi*—*Genji* is the epitome of another Heian ideal, a sense of *mono no aware* もののあはれ, or the sadness inherent in the things of this world.

Art 美術

Heian art is usually divided into two periods hinging on the break in official relations with China in 838. The first 100-year period is known by one of two era names, Kōnin 弘仁 (810–824) or Jōgan 貞観 (859–877), and the last three centuries are called the Fujiwara age 藤原時代. In the Jōgan era Chinese influence remained strong, and the development of arts related to esoteric Buddhism 密教美術 was especially striking. The two major art forms were Buddhist sculpture 仏像 and mandalas 曼陀羅.

In the Jōgan era the Japanese began to rely on wood for their sculpture, moving away from early bronze, lacquer, and clay figures. It was common to carve an entire statue from one large block of wood, left unpainted except for the lips to preserve the natural aroma (sandalwood ビャクダン was especially favored). Decline of court patronage of the Buddhist establishment from the level evident in the Nara period reduced the necessity for massive Buddhist sculptures, which were as much nationalistic as religious, and consequently also reduced the need for large numbers of government artisans, so that from the Jōgan era the tendency toward individual craftsmen became strong. The two greatest examples of Jōgan sculpture are the Yakushi Nyorai (healing Buddha) 薬師如来 at Kyōto's Jingoji 神護寺 and the Shaka Nyorai (historical Buddha) 釈迦如来 at Murōji 室生寺, south of Nara.

Among the few surviving examples of early Heian painting are mandalas, used as aids in meditation, and fierce representations of Fudō Myōō 不動明王, a manifestation of the cosmic Buddha, always depicted as grotesque, muscular guardians who subdued enemies of the faith with the ropes and swords they usually carried.

Just as in literature, the art of the long period of Fujiwara domination shows great changes. One of the most important determinants of the new art was the growing popularity of Amida. Images of Amida 阿弥陀 became popular, the most remarkable being that sculpted by Jōchō 定朝 in the Phoenix Hall 鳳凰堂 of the Byōdōin 平等院. Amida's gentle and serene countenance contrasts with the more severe Buddhist figures of the Jōgan era. There were also sculptural representations of Amida coming to lead the believer to the Pure Land.

The most marked departure from earlier art forms was the development of secular painting, known as *yamato-e* 大和絵 or "Japanese (style) pictures" to distinguish them from "Chinese pictures" (*kara-e* 唐絵). Compared to the few earlier examples of religious portraits or copies of Chinese-style landscapes, the Fujiwara era witnessed an outburst of secular painting, both landscapes and scenes of daily court life, painted on folding screens (*byōbu* 屏風) and on paper doors (*fusuma* 襖絵). We know them only by description since none survives.

Perhaps the finest examples of Fujiwara painting are the narrative scrolls (*emakimono* 絵巻物) that came into vogue in the 11th and 12th centuries. Some dealt with famous historical incidents—the Hōgen Rebellion 保元の 乱, for example, or the fate of the wronged courtier Sugawara no Michizane 菅原道真—while some were more religious in nature, depicting the horrors of Buddhist hell or the origins of a temple. Perhaps the most celebrated is the 12th-century *Genji monogatari emaki* 「源氏物語絵巻」, which depicts in elegant color the world of Murasaki's great novel.

Freed from the constraints of religion, painting developed in many directions, and the *yamato-e* influenced the development of a singularly Japanese form of decorative art. Even though new Chinese forms of painting, such as ink painting 水墨画, continued to be introduced, Japanese painters continued to produce new forms of quite distinct character by going back to the *yamato-e* style.

Kamakura period 鎌倉時代

(1185–1333; Kamakura *jidai*). The Kamakura period corresponds roughly to the span of the Kamakura shogunate 鎌倉幕府 (1192–1333) and is named after the city of Kamakura (located in what is now Kanagawa Prefecture), the seat of the government. Distinguishing characteristics of the period are the rise to political power of the provincial warrior class (*bushi*) and the establishment of a military government 武家政権; the emergence of new and strongly proselytizing sects of Buddhism and the spread of Buddhism from the aristocracy to the common people; and a new vitality in literature and the fine arts. These developments also reflect the continued diminution of Chinese cultural influence, a process that had begun in the late 9th century.

Historians agree that the terminal year of the Kamakura shogunate is 1333, when it was destroyed; however, opinions diverge concerning the year of its inception. Some historians hold that the period begins in 1192, the year in which Emperor Go-Toba 後鳥羽天皇 (r 1183–98) recognized the de facto military rule of Minamoto no Yoritomo 源頼朝 by conferring on him the title of shōgun. Others have proposed 1180, when Yoritomo established his base in Kamakura. In this book, however, the period's beginning is understood as 1185, the year in which Yoritomo destroyed the Taira family 平氏 and established his military government through the appointment of *shugo* 守護 (constables; later, military governors) to provinces and *jitō* 地頭 (stewards) to *shōen* 荘園 (private estates) and *kokugaryō* 国衙領 (lands administered by provincial governments).

Background 背景

In 1185 Minamoto forces defeated their old rivals, the Taira family, in the Battle of Dannoura 壇ノ浦の戦い at the western end of the Inland Sea 瀬戸内海, finally bringing to a close the Taira-Minamoto War 源平の争乱, which had lasted for five years and which had been fought over a wide area from eastern to western Japan, including Kyōto. Earlier, as a result of the Hōgen

Disturbance 保元の乱 (1156) and the Heiji Disturbance 平治
の乱 (1159) the Taira had gained control of the imperial
court 朝廷 and had driven the Minamoto out of Kyōto.
The small headquarters that Yoritomo, the leader of
the Minamoto, set up in 1180 to prosecute the Taira-
Minamoto War had grown by 1184 into a formidable
organization of three boards: the Samurai-dokoro 侍所,
or Board of Retainers, which disciplined and controlled
vassals; the Kumonjo 公文所, or Public Documents Office,
which was later absorbed into the Mandokoro 政所, or
Administrative Board; and the Monchūjo 問注所, or
Board of Inquiry, which heard and reviewed claims
and lawsuits. Moreover, within a few months after
Dannoura, Yoritomo was given the authority by the
imperial court to appoint and post two types of officials
throughout the country; a *shugo* 守護 to each province to
maintain law and order, and *jitō* 地頭 to private estates
and provincial government lands to oversee the fulfillment of obligations, such as the submission of taxes. In
addition the Kamakura government was empowered to
levy a tax to help defray the expense of keeping the
peace. The delegation of such broad powers to
Yoritomo, coupled with the conferral on him in 1192 of
the title *seii tai shōgun* 征夷大将軍 ("barbarian-subduing

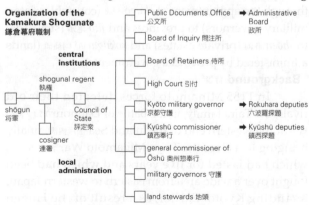

**Organization of the
Kamakura Shogunate
鎌倉幕府職制**

**central
institutions**

Public Documents Office
公文所 → Administrative Board
政所

Board of Inquiry 問注所

Board of Retainers 侍所

High Court 引付

shogunal regent
執権

shōgun
将軍

Council of
State
評定衆

cosigner
連署

**local
administration**

Kyōto military governor
京都守護 → Rokuhara deputies
六波羅探題

Kyūshū commissioner
鎮西奉行 → Kyūshū deputies
鎮西探題

general commissioner of
Ōshū 奥州惣奉行

military governors 守護

land stewards 地頭

generalissimo") by the imperial court following his conquest of northern Honshū, the only remaining enclave of resistance to his rule, amounted to a formal recognition of the Kamakura government by the imperial government at Kyōto. After 1192 Yoritomo's government may properly be termed a shogunate 幕府, and it was the first of a succession of military governments, or shogunates, that ruled Japan for much of the ensuing seven centuries. It was also the beginning of a system of dual rule characterized by the coexistence of a *de jure* sovereign, the emperor, and a de facto ruler, the shōgun.

Structure of Warrior Society 武家社会の構造

Although the majority of Yoritomo's followers were of humble origin and from the remote and backward region of eastern Honshū, the warrior society that he headed was in outlook and structure a distinct military aristocracy. Its leadershp consisted for the most part of descendants of former governors, holders of military commissions, and managers of private estates who had been sent out to the provinces from Kyōto. A few, like Yoritomo, were descendants of emperors.

Kamakura society was strictly ranked into three classes. At the top were the shōgun's vassals (*gokenin* 御家人). Comparatively few in number, they were men of proven loyalty who commanded followings of subvassals. To assure their continued support, Yoritomo accorded them privileged status, assigning special places to them in processions and at state functions, and bestowed on them letters of confirmation (*andojō* 安堵状) that recognized their proprietorship and governance of their lands.

Below them were the *samurai* 侍. In later periods the term came to denote any and all warriors, but in the Kamakura period it referred to a definite rank. The rigid hierarchical relationship that obtained between samurai and *gokenin* is apparent in a passage from a contemporary chronicle: "If a man is made a samurai, he will forget his status and want to be a *gokenin*." Like the *gokenin*, the samurai was mounted and well equipped, and he had a following of subvassals. That both had been elevated to the top of the military aristocracy from lesser origins is apparent in their titles of rank—*gokenin* means "houseman" or "retainer"; samurai, "one who waits on (another)."

At the bottom of warrior society were the foot soldiers. Lightly armed and, early in the period, not especially numerous, they grew considerably in number toward the period's close when the shogunate weakened and warfare increased. The hierarchy was strictly observed at Kamakura, for the leadership felt that once laxity was admitted, greater laxity would ensue.

Life in Kamakura contrasted sharply with that of the court at Kyōto. The *bushi* 武士 was dedicated to the martial arts 武術, such as swordsmanship 剣術, archery 弓道, and horsemanship 馬術, while the courtier, who eschewed violence, devoted his time to poetry and other genteel pursuits. Kamakura society exalted loyalty, honor, and frugality—ideals that were later to inspire the cult of the warrior, or *bushidō* 武士道.

The Hōjō Regency 北条氏の執権政治

The power that Yoritomo wielded did not remain in his family for long. When he died in 1199, there were no Minamoto of any importance to succeed him except two young sons, for in the process of defeating the Taira and establishing Minamoto rule he had eliminated all potential rivals, including his younger brother Minamoto no Yoshitsune 源義経, who had emerged as the hero of the Taira-Minamoto War 源平の争乱. Real power passed to the Hōjō family 北条氏, the family of Yoritomo's widow, Hōjō Masako 北条政子, and for the remainder of the Kamakura period they ruled the country as regents (*shikken* 執権) to Minamoto shōguns, none of whom was more than a figurehead.

On the whole, Hōjō rule was firm and efficient. For example, when the retired emperor Go-Toba 後鳥羽上皇 attempted to take back the reins of government in the Jōkyū Disturbance 承久の乱 of 1221, Hōjō Yoshitoki 北条義時, the second *shikken*, quelled the uprising within a month and sent Go-Toba and two other former emperors into exile, summarily deposed the reigning emperor and designated his successor, and seized lands of court nobles who had supported Go-Toba and awarded them to Hōjō vassals. Finally, he stationed in Kyōto two shogunal deputies (Rokuhara *tandai* 六波羅探題), to watch over the court.

The most resourceful and politically astute of the Hōjō leaders was Hōjō Yasutoki 北条泰時, the third *shikken*. In 1224, at the outset of his regency, he created a new office called *rensho* 連署, or cosigner, and appointed his uncle to the post. The *rensho* cosigned with the regent all decrees and important documents and was, in effect, an associate regent. By sharing the authority of his office with another prominent Hōjō, Yasutoki was able to minimize factionalism and succession disputes within the family.

In 1225 Yasutoki also established the Hyōjōshū 評定衆 (Council of State), which was the chief advisory, administrative, and judicial body of the Kamakura government. Its comparatively large membership of 11 (later 15) allowed broader participation—especially of non-Hōjō families—in the decision-making process than was the case under Minamoto no Yoritomo, who had ruled autocratically. Under Hōjō Tokiyori 北条時頼, the fifth regent, yet another body, the Hikitsuke 引付 (High Court), was created in 1249 to assist the Council of State by passing swift judgment on the increasing number of suits and claims pertaining to land.

An outstanding accomplishment of Yasutoki's

regency was the promulgation in 1232 of a legal code for the warrior class, the Goseibai Shikimoku (the Formulary of Adjudications) 御成敗式目. Drawn up by the Hyōjōshū and consisting of 51 articles, the code embodied customary law 慣習法 of the warrior class and judicial precedents 判例 established by the Kamakura government. It enunciated the rights not only of the warriors but also of women, who were allowed to adopt heirs if they were widows and to inherit and perpetuate fiefs. It clarified the duties and responsibilities of Kamakura-appointed officials, such as the *shugo* 守護 and the *jitō* 地頭, and acted as a restraint on warriors by exhorting them, for example, to respect the rights of shrines and temples and of *shōen* proprietors. The code also reflected the practical nature of justice of the period and the reliance of Kamakura officials on *dōri*, or "common sense," rather than on the laws of earlier times that had been modeled on Chinese laws and institutions. In fact, with the promulgation of the Goseibai Shikimoku, the entire *ritsuryō* system 律令制度, which had been established in the late 7th century, was swept away and replaced by laws that arose from the structure and requirements of warrior society.

The Mongol Invasions 蒙古襲来

Among the most dramatic of events of the Kamakura period were the Mongol invasions of Japan during the regency of Hōjō Tokimune 北条時宗, the eighth *shikken*. The first was launched in 1274 after the Japanese brusquely rejected a Mongol demand that they acknowledge the suzerainty of Khubilai Khan フビライ=ハン (1215–94). Fortunately for the defenders, only a day after the invading force of about 40,000 men landed near Hakata in northern Kyūshū, a storm suddenly arose, destroying a good part of the fleet and causing many of the invaders to drown.

Seven years later, after the Japanese had rejected

his demands once again and, moreover, beheaded his envoys, Khubilai dispatched a huge invasion force of between 140,000 and 150,000 men to Hakata Bay 博多湾. Again, after nearly two months of fighting, a fierce typhoon arose, forcing the invaders to retreat. Until the end of the century the Japanese remained apprehensive. Fortifications that had been built on the shore of the bay following the first invasion were extended and a series of Hōjō family members were appointed special deputies (Chinzei *tandai* 鎮西探題) to resolve disputes between shogunal vassals in Kyūshū and to lead them in battle in the event of another attack.

The repulse of the invasions nourished a certain amount of national pride and temporarily raised the prestige of the Hōjō regency; however, the regency could not make good on promises of reward to warriors and the consequence was increased domestic strife. Because the invaders had come from overseas, the Hōjō took no war booty in the form of land to grant to its victorious vassals. Furthermore, Shintō and Buddhist priests also pressed for rewards, insisting that their prayers had generated the *kamikaze* 神風 ("divine wind") that decimated the invaders. The expediencies that the shogunate resorted to, such as referring the claims of vassal and priest to the Hikitsuke, which delayed judgment, served only to erode confidence in the judicial system and ultimately in the Hōjō regency itself. In an attempt to prevent the increasing impoverishment of its retainers the shogunate issued decrees forbidding the sale or foreclosure of lands held by its retainers. Called *tokusei* 徳政, or "acts of virtuous government," they pleased some but alienated the creditors, whose support the shogunate could ill afford to lose.

The Kamakura-Period Economy 鎌倉時代の経済

Two economic institutions that arose early in and continued through the Kamakura period were the *toimaru* 問丸 and the *za* 座. The former were shipping agents who took rice and other products of the *shōen* on consignment and distributed them over a wide market. The latter were trade guilds 同業組合 that often engaged in monopolistic practices. Both institutions developed more fully in the succeeding Muromachi period 室町時代 (1333–1568).

▮ Popularization of Buddhism 仏教の大衆化

In the Kamakura period Buddhism, which had been chiefly an ornament of the ruling class, turned its attention to the common people. A major role was played in this movement by the tradition of Amida, the Buddha who, doctrine holds, enables believers to be reborn in the Western Pure Land (Saihō Jōdo 西方浄土) in answer to the sincere invocation of his name, *nembutsu*. Hōnen 法然, founder of the Jōdo sect 浄土宗, taught that reliance on the grace of Amida was more efficacious than personal effort toward enlightenment. His disciple Shinran 親鸞, founder of the Jōdo Shin sect 浄土真宗, held that faith, not acts, was the one essential qualification for salvation, which could be achieved by a single invocation of Amida's name. Shinran was also the first Japanese Buddhist priest to take a wife. Although marriage eventually became normal practice in all sects of Japanese Buddhism, the immediate consequence for both Shinran and Hōnen was their exile.

An equally controversial religious figure was Nichiren 日蓮, founder of the Nichiren sect 日蓮宗, who stressed the importance of personal effort toward enlightenment and insisted that the essential teachings of Buddhism were contained in the Lotus Sutra 法華経. He was intolerant of all other forms of Buddhism and of the Kamakura government for patronizing them.

Another form of Buddhism that flourished in this period was Zen 禅. Its simplicity and emphasis on self-discipline and meditation 坐禅 as the means to enlightenment 悟り particularly appealed to the warrior class. Unlike the founders of the other major new Buddhist sects of the period, both Eisai 栄西, who introduced the Rinzai sect 臨済宗, and Dōgen 道元, who introduced the Sōtō sect 曹洞宗, considered themselves disciples of Chinese Zen masters from whom they received teachings, ritual, and even the names of their sects.

▌Literature and the Fine Arts 文学と美術

Although deprived of its political role, the court remained the center of Japanese culture. The *Shin kokin wakashū* 「新古今和歌集」, a poetry anthology that many scholars consider to be the crowning achievement of courtly *waka* 和歌 (chiefly 31-syllable verse), appeared in 1205. Kamo no Chōmei 鴨長明, who in 1204 became a Buddhist monk, had witnessed the terrible events that accompanied the transfer of power from the court to the provinces, and in the Hōjōki 「方丈記」 (1212; tr *The Ten Foot Square Hut* 1928), he dwells upon the impermanence of all human endeavor (*mujō* 無常).

The characteristic form of Kamakura prose literature, however, was the *gunki monogatari* 軍記物語, or war tale. The most famous of these was the chronicle of the Taira-Minamoto wars, *Heike monogatari* 「平家物語」 (13th century; tr *The Tale of the Heike* 1988). Recited to the accompaniment of the *biwa* 琵琶 a plucked string instrument, the story recounts, the rise and fall of the Taira in the context of the Buddhist philosophy of impermanence 無常観. The priest Jien 慈円, whose writing was also deeply influenced by Buddhist philosophy, produced the first interpretive history of Japan, *Gukanshō* 「愚管抄」 (1220; tr *The Future and the Past* 1978). In 1275 Hōjō Sanetoki 北条実時, nephew of the regent Hōjō Yasutoki, established a library and learning center, whose collection of Chinese and Japanese manuscripts became the nucleus of the still-extant Kanazawa Bunko 金沢文庫 (also known as the Kanesawa [or Kanezawa] Bunko.)

Among accomplishments in the fine arts during the Kamakura period the wood sculptures of Unkei 運慶 and Kaikei 快慶, who collaborated on the two huge guardian deities of the great south gate (*nandaimon* 南大門) at Tōdaiji 東大寺, are of particular note. Painters of the era showed a great interest and skill in portraiture, a particularly renowned example of which is the portrait of Minamoto no Yoritomo 源頼朝像 done in the *yamato-e* style and attributed to Fijiwara no Takanobu 藤原隆信. Another important genre was *emakimono* (picture scrolls) 絵巻物. Although the genre arose in the Heian period, it continued to flourish in the Kamakura period. Though much reduced in scale in comparison to earlier eras, the influence of Chinese artistic traditions can yet be seen in ink painting 水墨画 and in the style of temple architecture known as *karayō* (Chinese style) 唐様, both of which were introduced by Zen monks.

Decline and Fall of the Shogunate 幕府の衰退と崩壊

The Kamakura shogunate came to a sudden end in 1333 when two important vassals 武将 turned against their leader. Ashikaga Takauji 足利尊氏 had been sent on a punitive expedition against the retired emperor Go-Daigo 後醍醐天皇, who had recently escaped from the island of Oki to which he had been banished for having defied the shogunate, but Takauji chose instead to support Go-Daigo (Kemmu Restoration 建武の中興[新政]). Another vassal of the shogunate, Nitta Yoshisada 新田義貞, was ordered to proceed against Takauji, but he too turned against his superiors and forced Hōjō Takatoki 北条高時, the 14th regent, to take his own life. Thus ended the 150-year rule of the country's first military regime 軍事政権.

There had been signs of a deterioration of the power of the shogunate in the 1280s, when it had been unable to fulfill its obligation to reward its worthy vassals following the Mongol invasions 蒙古襲来. Equally significant was the fact that Takatoki, the last Hōjō regent, had neither the inclination nor the skills necessary to administer the government, and spent much of his time dancing and watching dogfights. A further contributing factor was the mounting resentment of senior vassals against the virtual monopolization of shogunal offices by the Hōjō. Thus the fall of the Kamakura shogunate in 1333 was not as unexpected as it appeared to be.

Muromachi period 室町時代

(1333–1568; Muromachi *jidai*). A period of cultural achievement and social disorder, lasting from 1333, when forces led by Ashikaga Takauji 足利尊氏 destroyed the Kamakura shōgunate 鎌倉幕府, until 1568, when the hegemon 覇者 Oda Nobunaga 織田信長 captured the capital of Kyōto. Named for the district of Kyōto in which the shogunal residence was situated, it is also commonly known as the Ashikaga period 足利時代, after the family that held the position of shōgun 将軍 from 1338 to 1573.

The dates for the Muromachi period adopted by this book are, however, open to dispute. Some historians date both the founding of the Muromachi shogunate 室町幕府 and the period itself from 1336, when Takauji captured Kyōto, ending the short-lived Kemmu Restoration 建武の中興[新政] of Emperor Go-Daigo 後醍醐天皇. Other scholars contend that Takauji's assumption in 1338 of the title *seii tai shōgun* 征夷大将軍—following the precedent set by Minamoto no Yoritomo 源頼朝 and thus providing himself with rank and office to cloak his usurpation of power—marks the beginning of the period. Similarly, some scholars assign the termination of the period to 1573, when Nobunaga expelled the 15th shōgun, Ashikaga Yoshiaki 足利義昭, from Kyōto, and others to 1588, when the exiled Yoshiaki resigned and thus ended the legal existence of his family's shogunate. Furthermore, some scholars view the years 1337–92, during which Go-Daigo and his scions maintained a separate court in Yoshino 吉野 south of Kyōto to rival the court of the child emperor Kōmyō 光明天皇 (1322–80; r 1336–48) set up by Takauji, as constituting a distinct period (Northern and Southern Courts 南北朝); and many historians argue that the authority of the shogunate had so declined after the Ōnin War 応仁の乱 (1467–77) that the succeeding century, the Warring States or Sengoku period 戦国時代, should be considered a distinct historical era.

Political Developments: Central Government
政治の展開：中央政府

In establishing the Muromachi shogunate 室町幕府, Ashikaga Takauji 足利尊氏 borrowed personnel and institutions from the Kamakura shogunate. He and the warriors who helped him draft the statement of legal and political principles known as the Kemmu Shikimoku 建武式目 (1336) had been vassals of the Hōjō family 北条家, the regents who effectively ruled the Kamakura shogunate, and the Kemmu Shikimoku was a reaffirmation of the principles of the Kamakura warrior code, the Goseibai Shikimoku 御成敗式目 (1232). The chief offices of central and local warrior government, the Board of Retainers (Samurai-dokoro 侍所), the Administrative Board (Mandokoro 政所), the Board of Inquiry (Monchūjo 問注所), and the provincial posts of military governor (shugo 守護) and military land steward (jitō 地頭), had all been developed under the Kamakura shogunate and were now staffed by Ashikaga vassals.

However, unlike the Kamakura regime, under which the Hōjō regents had kept their vassals tightly in rein until the aftermath of the Mongol invasions of Japan 蒙古襲来 (1274 and 1281), Ashikaga control over the vassals they appointed as shugo was from the outset weak. *Shugo* families, many of whom were as powerful militarily as the Ashikaga shōguns, were well entrenched in the provinces and able to take advantage of the disturbances of the 13th and 14th centuries to extend their local authority. Moreover, powerful *shugo* families such as the Shiba family 斯波氏, the Hosokawa family 細川氏, and the Hatakeyama family 畠山氏 were able to monopolize the important office of shogunal deputy (*kanrei* 管領) and to dominate the senior councils of the shogunate. Several of the earlier Ashikaga rulers were able to impose their authority, but later shōguns were much less successful in managing the coalition of *shugo*.

The Muromachi shogunate got off to a troubled start. Takauji allowed considerable administrative and judicial responsibility to his younger brother, Ashikaga Tadayoshi 足利直義, while reserving for himself authority over the Samurai-dokoro and Onshō-gata 恩賞方 (Office of Rewards), which together regulated the affairs of vassals and other warriors. The division of authority resolved into a breach between the brothers that hampered both the conduct of campaigns against the Southern Court loyalists 南朝方 and containment of the local aggrandizements of *shugo*. The death of Emperor Go-Daigo and the assassination of Tadayoshi left Takauji in a stronger position, yet Ashikaga control was far from secure at his death in 1358.

His successors Ashikaga Yoshiakira 足利義詮 (1330–67; r 1359–67) and Ashikaga Yoshimitsu 足利義満 were able, with the support of the general Sasaki Dōyo 佐々木道誉 (1306–73) and the shogunal deputies (*kanrei*) Hosokawa Yoriyuki 細川頼之 (1329–92) and Shiba Yoshimasa 斯波義将 (1350–1410), to increase shogunal authority over the country. Appointed shōgun in 1369 at the age of 11, Yoshimitsu, under the secular tutelage of Hosokawa Yoriyuki and the religious and cultural guidance of the Zen monk 禅僧 Gidō Shūshin 義堂周信, grew into a vigorous, cultivated ruler. Although Yoshimitsu relished the life of the courtier—he gave lavish entertainments for emperors and nobles and in 1395 was granted the highest court office, *dajō daijin* 太政大臣 (grand minister of state)—he did not neglect his responsibilities as the warrior ruler of the country. He took the lead in organizing vassals in western Japan to crush uprisings by the Toki family 土岐氏 in 1390, the Yamana family 山名氏 in 1391 (Meitoku Rebellion 明徳の乱), and the Ōuchi family 大内氏 in 1399–1400 (Ōei Rebellion 応永の乱). He commanded sufficient authority to oblige most *shugo* to establish residences in Kyōto and to remain fairly constantly in attendance at court. The only important area of the country that remained outside the full scope of his control was eastern Japan, where the governor-general of the Kantō region (Kantō *kubō* 関東公方), a cadet member of the Ashikaga house, exercised autonomous regional control from Kamakura, the site of the first shogunate.

Yoshimitsu surrounded himself with such arbiters of taste and literary style as the Nō dramatists Kan'ami 観阿弥 and Zeami 世阿弥, the courtier-poet Nijō Yoshimoto 二条良基, and the Zen master Zekkai Chūshin 絶海中津 and patronized Nō, poetry, painting, and garden design. His "Palace of Flowers" (Hana no Gosho 花の御所) and his Kitayama villa 北山第 (Kinkakuji 金閣寺) in northwestern Kyōto became vital cultural and intellectual centers (Kitayama culture 北山文化). Yoshimitsu encouraged the entrance into court of lowborn but talented individuals, resulting in the transformation of elements of popular culture into high culture.

In 1401, in order to obtain Chinese art objects and cash to offset the relative paucity of shogunal landholdings, Yoshimitsu initiated the tally trade 勘合貿易 with Ming dynasty 明朝 (1368–1644) China. During a period of 10 years, eight embassies completed the voyage, and, as a single embassy might yield as much as 10,000 *kam-mon* (10 million coins), they became an important source of revenue.

The power and prestige of the shogunate declined under Yoshimitsu's son Ashikaga Yoshimochi 足利義持 (1386–1428; r 1395–1423). Although he succeeded in putting down the Rebellion of Uesugi Zenshū 上杉禅秀の乱 in 1417, his commitment to government was erratic. Shogunal authority was reasserted briefly by the despotic sixth shōgun, Ashikaga Yoshinori 足利義教, who put down a revolt by Ashikaga Mochiuji 足利持氏 (1398–1439) in the east, and in the west brought the Ōtomo family 大友氏 and the Ōuchi family to heel. He also reopened the China trade, which Yoshimochi had broken off, and worked to offset the influence of the *kanrei* and *shugo* by making greater use of the corps of hereditary bureaucrats, the *bugyōninshū* 奉行人衆, and his palace guards, the *hōkōshū* 奉公衆, both of which were drawn from lower-ranking warrior families close to the Ashikaga. Yoshinori's policies briefly strengthened the shogunate, but his brutal methods antagonized courtiers and *shugo*, and his assassination in 1441 by Akamatsu Mitsusuke 赤松満祐, one of his own vassals, marked the beginning of the disintegration of Ashikaga authority, accompanied by its increasing inability to protect its lands and its gradual exclusion from the Ming trade by the Hosokawa and Ōuchi families.

Under the eighth shōgun, Ashikaga Yoshimasa 足利義政, shogunal influence over the country all but collasped. *Shugo* family succession disputes festered, encouraging warriors to take sides in unstable alliances. Responding to demands by indebted warriors and peasants, Yoshimasa issued "acts of virtuous government" (*tokusei* 徳政), canceling debts owed moneylenders, merchants, and temples. These debt moratoriums threw the markets into confusion and Yoshimasa's vacillating attempts to revoke them provoked riots and pillaging. His construction of an elegant villa, the Ginkakuji 銀閣寺 (Silver Pavilion), depleted already-straitened shogunal coffers, and his change of mind over a successor at the insistence of his consort Hino Tomiko 日野富子 created a dispute that drew into its vortex rival leagues of *shugo* led by the Hosokawa and Yamana, thus commencing the Ōnin War 応仁の乱. When efforts to halt the conflict proved futile, Yoshimasa retreated to his hillside villa, and the contesting armies reduced Kyōto to ashes. The authority of succeeding shōguns was limited to the environs of the capital, and they were appointed and deposed almost at will by the Hosokawa family, which monopolized the post of *kanrei*.

▌Local Government 地方政治

Under the Ashikaga the imperial institutions of local control withered completely. Provinces, with their scattered estates (*shōen*) held by absentee noble proprietors or by temples or shrines, as well as lands held by resident local warriors (*kokujin* 国人), were assigned to the administrative and judicial authority of *shugo*. In the mid-14th century the shogunate was often too weak to control the *shugo*. Making full use of their powers to grant as prizes lands seized in war, to adjudicate disputes, to bestow rights to half the tax yield (*hanzei* 半済) of local estates, and to impose local levies (*hyōrōmai* 兵糧米), the *shugo* invaded private estates (*shōen*) and organized the powerful *kokujin* as their feudal subordinates. *Shugo* who by these means succeeded in aggrandizing themselves are referred to by historians as *shugo daimyō* 守護大名. None was able to convert his territories into fully feudal domains over which he exerted exclusive proprietary control (*ichien chigyō* 一円知行). Some, however, like the Ōuchi and the Hosokawa, exerted tight control over several provinces.

With the consolidation of shogunal authority by

Yoshimitsu, the *shugo* were put on a shorter leash and obliged to reside more or less permanently in Kyōto (or Kamakura in the case of eastern *shugo*). Entrusted to deputies (*shugodai* 守護代), their provinces were racked by power struggles between the *shugodai* and *kokujin*; provincial uprisings led by local landowners 国一揆 increased and tax income often failed to reach the *shugo*. The majority of *shugo* houses, bereft of the support of strong central authority after the mid-15th century, out-maneuvered by their deputies, starved of income, and torn by succession disputes, were toppled in the late 15th century and their regional domains carved up into more compact units under the control of warlords (Sengoku daimyō 戦国大名), most of whom had emerged from the *kokujin*.

The Sengoku daimyō were a very different breed from the *shugo daimyō*. Indifferent to shogunal authority, they lived in their domains, devoting their energies to improving their own military, political, and economic strength. They promulgated law codes (*bunkokuhō* 分国法), built castle towns 城下町, conducted land surveys (*kenchi* 検地), broke up *shōen*, crushed peasant uprisings, and brought villages under close supervision. It was this fragmented political order, free of central guidance or uniformity, that the Portuguese found upon their arrival in Japan in the 1540s.

▌Economy and Society 経済と社会

Warfare and instability in the Muromachi period did not prevent major advances in agriculture, commerce, transportation, village organization, and urban development. The demands of warrior leaders for arms and provisions, the growth of local power centers, dismemberment of *shōen*, and the loosening of the old political order, which had been dominated by the nobility of the capital, spurred the economy and encouraged social mobility and diversification. The Muromachi period witnessed a quantum leap forward in economic activity and the emergence of two powerful social forces, a self-conscious mercantile 商人 group and an increasingly restive and market-oriented peasantry 農民.

Double-cropping of rice and barley, begun in western Japan, had by the Muromachi period spread into the eastern part of the country. Irrigation systems 灌漑 were improved and more extensive use made of draft animals 荷役用動物, contributing to the increasing availability of crops from all parts of Japan. Mines were pushed deeper to satisfy demands for weapons, coins, and gilded decorations, and the building of massive castles 城郭, around which towns developed, stimulated haulage and forestry. Increases in agricultural output, the growth of crafts, and demands for payment of taxes and levies in cash instead of in rice or cloth contributed to the spread of local markets, to greater specialization among merchants, and to more sophisticated exchange facilities. Copper cash 銅銭, imported from China (*eirakusen* 永楽銭) in small quantities during the Kamakura period, came in much greater quantities during the Muromachi, and monetization of the economy increased markedly. In return for the payment of dues (*utokusen* 有徳銭) to the shogunate, warehouse owners (*dosō* 土倉) and sake brewers (*sakaya* 酒屋) were permitted to engage in usury. Shogunal and *shugo* levies on land under cultivation (*tansen* 段銭 and *tammai* 段米) and on households (*munabetsusen* 棟別銭) were collected in cash, and some among the Sengoku daimyō developed a system of administration whereby landholdings, grants of fief, and military service were expressed in cash units (*kandaka* 貫高). The need for peasants to convert part of their crops into cash to pay taxes and levies contributed to the formation of a market economy.

Ichi 市 were held regularly on six days of the month. Produce from villages was bought by traveling merchants, transported by packhorse haulers (*bashaku* 馬借) over an extended system of roads, and sold at market stalls by retailers. Merchants and craftsmen organized themselves in guildlike associations known as *za* 座, some 40 of which were based in Kyōto and more than 80 in Nara. *Za* were sponsored by nobles or temples to which dues were paid for the protection of monopoly rights and exemption from barrier-station fees (*sekisen* 関銭). Although membership in *za* was restricted, some of them, such as the *za* of oil traders in Ōyamazaki, had as many as 300 members, whose activities spread over a dozen provinces. *Za* served to maintain high standards among members, contributed to small-scale accumulation of capital, and brought order to the growing commercial activity. However, they also sought to block participation by provincial merchants and craftsmen, and from the mid-16th century Sengoku daimyō issued a spate of edicts freeing markets (*rakuichi* 楽市 and *rakuza* 楽座).

The growth of commerce, the China trade, the diffusion of Buddhism, a vogue for pilgrimages, and the deliberate policies of the Sengoku daimyō contributed to urbanization and the growth of entirely new types of towns. Castles, which had formerly been built on craggy peaks, were erected on the plains by Sengoku daimyō and quickly grew into urban centers. New towns sprang up at ports, market sites, and transportation nodes. Ōminato 大湊, Obama 小浜, Tsuruga 敦賀, Mikuni 三国, Yodo 淀, Sakamoto 坂本, and Ōtsu 大津 all developed during this period. Sakai 境, Hakata 博多, and Hyōgo 兵庫 grew rich on the overseas trade. Sakamoto developed as the supply point for the temple Enryakuji 延暦寺, Uji-Yamada 宇治山田 benefited from the influx of pilgrims to Ise Shrine 伊勢神宮, and the towns of Ishiyama 石山 and Yoshizaki 吉崎 were the commercial centers for the powerful Honganji Buddhist communities.

Daimyō exercised autocratic control over their castle towns 城下町. In other towns, however, self-governing civic communities emerged. Thirty-six leading citizens in Sakai formed a council known as the *egōshū* 会合衆, which governed the city. A similar council existed in Hakata, and in Kyōto groups of townsmen (*machishū* 町衆) were responsible for governance of the districts (*machi*) in which they resided. Although tightly controlled by Sengoku daimyō, villages also organized councils (*yoriai* 寄合) to regulate common land and irrigation, to enforce village codes, and to resist excessive claims for taxes. Many villages won the right to collect and forward annual taxes (*hyakushōuke* 百姓請) and to mete out justice to local miscreants, thus laying the basis for the village system (*gōson* system 郷村制) of the Edo period (1600–1868).

Religion and Culture 宗教と文化

Zen Buddhism 禅宗, which was introduced from China in the 13th century, developed rapidly under the patronage of the Ashikaga shōguns and their vassals. The Gozan 五山 network of the Rinzai sect 臨済宗, the head temples of which were in Kyōto and Kamakura, covered Japan and gave training in meditation and the arts to the sons of provincial warriors. Chinese priests, such as Yishan (I-shan; J: Issan Ichinei 一山一寧), introduced to Japan not only Zen practices and Buddhist texts, but Neo-Confucian 朱子学 political thought and Chinese poetry 漢詩 and painting. Zen monasteries were centers for the development of new styles of architecture, the design of gardens 庭園, the tea ceremony 茶の湯, and flower arrangement 生け花. By the mid-Muromachi period, arts inspired by Zen were spreading from monasteries into secular society. Song (Sung) dynasty 宋朝 (960–1279) styles of Chinese ink painting 水墨画, mastered by the Japanese monk-painters Minchō 明兆, Josetsu 如拙 and Shūbun 周文, were transformed and carried outside Zen cloisters by Sesshū Tōyō 雪舟等楊. Under the early Kanō school 狩野派 masters Kanō Masanobu 狩野正信 and Kanō Motonobu 狩野元信, the Chinese style of ink painting developed by Shūbun and Sesshū was blended with the techniques of Japanese-style painting (*yamato-e* 大和絵). A similar secularization and diffusion took place in the development of the tea ceremony, in garden design, and in the art of flower arrangment.

The influence of other sects of Buddhism also spread widely during the Muromachi period. The Nichiren sect 日蓮宗 attracted many samurai followers in the Kantō region and put down deep roots among the townspeople of Kyōto. Adherents of the Jōdo Shin sect 浄土真宗, organized under the leadership of the temple Honganji 本願寺 by Rennyo 蓮如 in the 15th century, included samurai and peasants, and their devotion and militancy enabled them to mount large-scale uprisings (Ikkō *ikki* 一向一揆) against the Sengoku daimyō. With the arrival of Francis Xavier フランシスコ゠ザビエル in 1549, Christianity キリスト教 was also introduced to Japan.

Muromachi culture was an intricate blending of elite and popular elements to which all sectors of society contributed and from which all derived stimulus and enjoyment. Emperors and courtiers shared with high-ranking warriors an interest in Nō 能 and *kyōgen* 狂言 and in the historical chronicles and war tales 軍記物語 of the age, *Jinnō shōtō ki* 「神皇正統記」, *Baishōron* 「梅松論」, *Masukagami* 「増鏡」, and *Taiheiki* 「太平記」, and both shared with commoners a passion for the short tales known as *otogi-zōshi* 御伽草子, dance and mime (*dengaku* 田楽), and linked verse (*renga* 連歌). Sōgi 宗祇 and Sōchō 宗長, two of the finest *renga* poets of the age, were of low birth but through their mastery of their art were able to mix with the highest in the land. Indeed some of the most characteristic arts of the period, including Nō and *kyōgen*, had their origins among the common people before being elevated through the genius of artists such as Zeami 世阿弥 into entertainments for the elite.

Azuchi-Momoyama period 安土桃山時代

(1568–1600; Azuchi-Momoyama *jidai*). During the Azuchi-Momoyama period, a short but spectacular epoch, Japanese society and culture underwent the transition from the medieval 中世 to the early modern era 近世. The political order was transformed, and there was an unprecedented efflorescence of the arts. The activities of European traders and Catholic missionaries 宣教師 in Japan, no less than Japanese ventures overseas, gave the period a cosmopolitan flavor rare in the country's premodern history.

Azuchi-Momoyama witnessed Japan's unification after a century of civil war, the Sengoku period 戦国時代 (1467–1568). The country was reunited by three hegemons, Oda Nobunaga 織田信長 (1534–82), Toyotomi Hideyoshi 豊臣秀吉 (1537–98), and Tokugawa Ieyasu 徳川家康 (1543–1616). The first of these "Three Heroes" founded, and the second developed, the so-called Shokuhō regime 織豊体制, which reconstituted Japan's body politic. The third, Ieyasu, won the hegemony at the Battle of Sekigahara 関ヶ原の戦い in 1600 and three years later established the Tokugawa shogunate 徳川幕府 (1603–1867), thereby starting a new regime and a new epoch, the Edo period 江戸時代 (1600–1868). Institutional historians accordingly set the dates of the Azuchi-Momoyama period from 1568, the year of Nobunaga's emergence as a power in national politics, to 1600, the year of Ieyasu's great victory. The epoch's radiance continued after those events, however, and its terminal date is advanced into the Kan'ei era 寛永時代 (1624–44) by cultural historians focusing on artists such as Hon'ami Kōetsu 本阿弥光悦 and Tawaraya Sōtatsu 俵屋宗達, whose work brought the aesthetic traditions of the Azuchi-

Momoyama period to a brilliant culmination.

The period is named after the sites of two castles, Nobunaga's palatial fortress at Azuchi 安土 to the east of Kyōto and Hideyoshi's headquarters at Momoyama 桃山 in Fushimi 伏見 to the immediate south of Kyōto. Indeed, castles are the best symbols of this age. They were meant not only for military defense but for the glorification of their builders. They glittered with gold and dazzled the viewer with refined luxury, displaying the lords' wealth and overwhelming the vassals with a pictorial profusion of emblems of authority.

Institutional Developments 支配体制の発展

The central governmental system that developed in Japan during the Azuchi-Momoyama period is called the Shokuhō regime after alternative readings of the initial characters of its founders' names, Oda and Toyotomi. Oda Nobunaga and Toyotomi Hideyoshi not only reunified Japan militarily; they devised new measures to regulate society on a nationwide basis.

Nobunaga's march on Kyōto in 1568 initiated the regime. His ostensible purpose was to install the "legitimate" claimant, Ashikaga Yoshiaki 足利義昭, in the Muromachi shogunate 室町幕府, but restoration of legitimacy in the old governing order was not Nobunaga's true objective. Instead, he wanted to enhance his own prestige and power by playing the lead role on the central stage of politics. From the beginning, Nobunaga sought to dominate Yoshiaki and dictated policy to the shogunate. Far from subordinating himself to his protégé, Nobunaga posited a supervening polity, the *tenka* 天下 or "realm," a commonweal over which he himself presided.

Nobunaga did not remain unchallenged; throughout his career, formidable enemies confronted him. The most prominent of these were the *daimyō* Asai Nagamasa 浅井長政 of northern Ōmi Province 近江国 (now

Shiga Prefecture) and Asakura Yoshikage 朝倉義景 of Echizen 越前 (now part of Fukui Prefecture); the pontiff of the Buddhist "religious monarchy" of the Honganji 本願寺, Kennyo Kōsa 顕如光佐 (1543–92); and the great eastern house of Takeda, rulers of Kai 甲斐 (now Yamanashi Prefecture) and its neighboring provinces. Of all these major powers of the Sengoku period, none proved a match for Nobunaga in the end.

Their early successes, however, in 1573 enticed the shōgun Yoshiaki into opening hostilities against Nobunaga. The hegemon responded by burning the greater part of Kyōto, the national capital, but the shōgun remained belligerent. In August 1573 Nobunaga drove Yoshiaki from Kyōto. Yoshiaki would refuse to abdicate until 1588, and the Muromachi shogunate therefore retained a shadowy legal identity; as a functioning political entity, however, it was finished. The regime of unification led by Nobunaga had replaced it at the central fulcrum of politics.

In that same year of 1573, Nobunaga crushed Asakura Yoshikage and Asai Nagamasa. At the crucial Battle of Nagashino in 1575 長篠の戦い, his modern musketry tactics 鉄砲隊戦術 swept the medieval chivalry of Takeda Katsuyori 武田勝頼 from the battlefield. Also in 1575, Nobunaga conquered Echizen Province 越前国 from the armed adherents (Ikkō *ikki* 一向一揆) of the Honganji 本願寺. In 1580, the Honganji itself surrendered and its provincial domain in Kaga 加賀 (now part of Ishikawa Prefecture) was conquered. In 1582, Nobunaga destroyed Katsuyori and distributed the Takeda domains 所領 among his own victorious generals.

As Nobunaga's power and stature increased, his military command structure turned into a public administration with the potential for national governance. Nobunaga achieved mastery over his "realm" by ruthlessly eliminating his daimyō opponents and the armed leagues (*ikki*) of the populace. He maintained it by a new type of command relationship with his vassals, demanding total respect and obedience from them "for the sake of the realm" and binding them with formal regulations even as he assigned them their domains. He moved them and their subordinate *samurai* from one fief to another at will and disenfeoffed those he found lacking in fighting zeal and organizational talent. In order to bring the indigenous gentry of conquered areas to heel, Nobunaga's regime set about destroying their forts and instituted provincewide land surveys (*kenchi* 検地). In 1575–76, the regime followed up the conquest of Echizen by conducting a sword hunt (*katanagari* 刀狩; confiscation of weapons from the populace) in that province, ordering peasants to confine themselves to agriculture, and prohibiting them from changing their status. These measures represented an early attempt at the separation of the military from the farming class (*heinō bunri* 兵農分離), later identified as one of the Shokuhō regime's cardinal policies. Villagers in Echizen were moreover forced to abjure their allegiance to the Honganji and affiliate themselves with temples approved by the regime, foreshadowing the religious inquisition (*shūmon aratame* 宗門改) of the Edo period.

When Nobunaga was killed in the Honnōji Incident 本能寺の変 of 1582, the "realm 天下" governed by his regime covered no less than 30 of Japan's 68 provinces. Central Japan had been reunited under one political authority. Great areas of the country, however, remained unsubdued. The task of national unification was far from over.

That task was completed by Nobunaga's erstwhile subordinate Toyotomi Hideyoshi 豊臣秀吉. Hideyoshi did not inherit Nobunaga's base of power effortlessly. First he destroyed Nobunaga's assassin, Akechi Mitsuhide 明智光秀, at the Battle of Yamazaki

山崎の戦い, a mere 11 days after the Honnōji Incident. The next year, Hideyoshi defeated Shibata Katsuie 柴田勝家, the ruler of Echizen and Kaga, at the Battle of Shizugatake 賤ヶ岳の戦い. By 1583, Hideyoshi had reached an accommodation with Mōri Terumoto 毛利輝元 (1553–1625), the lord of vast territories in westernmost Honshū. Early in 1585, Tokugawa Ieyasu 徳川家康 too agreed to subordinate himself to Hideyoshi, after fighting him to a standoff in the Komaki Nagakute Campaign 小牧長久手の戦い the previous year. In 1585, Hideyoshi conquered Shikoku; in 1587, he overran Kyūshū, bringing the Shimazu 島津 to heel. Three years later, he led the armies of his vassal daimyō against the Hōjō 北条 of Odawara and subjugated the Kantō region.

The northern provinces Mutsu 陸奥 and Dewa 出羽 remained an arena of internecine struggle. Immediately after the surrender of the Hōjō in August 1590, Hideyoshi sent armies under his principal generals to sweep this giant region; by the end of October 1591, after a second campaign, they had wiped out all traces of resistance. When he finally subjugated Mutsu and Dewa, Hideyoshi could for the first time truly claim that he had extended his regime nationwide.

The local barons of Mutsu and Dewa whom Hideyoshi confirmed in their domains were ordered to observe three conditions: to send their wives and children to reside in Kyōto, Hideyoshi's capital (a measure prefiguring the *sankin kōtai* 参勤交代 system of the Edo period); to destroy all forts in their territories save for the lord's residential castle and to have their retainers' wives and children move to the castle town 城下町; and to undertake a cadastral survey (*kenchi* 検地) of their fiefs. These conditions ensured that the provincial lords would be integrated into Hideyoshi's national regime. Insofar as Hideyoshi recognized their autonomous existence, petty barons who had never been secure in their possessions were transformed into daimyō with full authority over their vassals and the populace of their domains. The price they paid was the surrender of their independence to him. Removed from the countryside to the castle town, the military men were destined to turn into a class of bureaucratic administrators.

The samurai were not the only social group given a new identity by the Shokuhō regime. Hideyoshi's national sword-hunt decree 刀狩令 of 1588 disarmed the countrymen, thereby in effect eliminating the village samurai (*jizamurai* 地侍) stratum that had been so turbulent in the Sengoku period and setting the distinction between samurai and farmer. In 1591, Hideyoshi prohibited the change of status among samurai, farmer, and merchant, thereby laying the foundation for the class system of the Edo period.

By the time of Hideyoshi's death in 1598, the great wave of cadastral surveys ordained by him had covered the entire country. All the arable land was measured and assessed by these surveys; its putative agricultural yield was entered on cadastral registers (*kenchichō* 検地帳) prepared village by village for submission to Hideyoshi and his daimyō vassals. Being listed in these registers gave the villagers an unprecedented security of tenure, which served as an incentive to increase production. A uniform system of taxation had replaced the multiple accretion of taxes and dues characteristic of the medieval *shōen* form of landholding.

The Oda-Toyotomi regime displaced the long-established medieval political order, but it lacked its own, clearly formulated justification in political theory. Nobunaga had not been granted the time to develop an ideology for his own political creation, the *tenka* 天下. The parvenu Hideyoshi sought to mystify his obscure origins, to aristocratize himself, and to bind the daimyō to allegiance by identifying himself with the ideal model of political authority in Japanese history, the imperial institution. No matter how powerful he became, he could not hope to obtain the throne himself, but he drew his legitimation from the use of the traditional symbols of authority associated with it. These included most prominently the lofty aristocratic offices of *kampaku* 関白 (imperial regent), with which he had the emperor invest him in 1585, and of *dajō daijin* 太政大臣 (grand minister of state), which he obtained in January 1587.

Hideyoshi failed, however, to safeguard the perpetuity of his house and his regime. Upon his death, the regime was rent by the competing ambitions of his vassals, among whom Tokugawa Ieyasu proved to be the most powerful. After the great succession struggle, the Shokuhō regime was followed in 1603 by the Tokugawa shogunate 徳川幕府, which built upon the framework of its policies. In order to safeguard its own perpetuity, however, the shogunate in 1614 attacked Hideyoshi's son and heir, Hideyori 秀頼 (1593–1615), in his stronghold, Ōsaka Castle 大坂城, and the next year succeeded in destroying the Toyotomi family.

The Culture of the Period 文化

Opulence and ostentation coexisted with restraint and studied rusticity in the epoch's dominant modes of artistic expression. The greatest symbol of Azuchi-Momoyama is the castle—a representation of power, built on a grand scale, decorated lavishly, and meant to overawe the viewer. A nearly coequal symbol is the teahouse 茶室—an evocation of aestheticism 美意識, content with a space nine feet square, eschewing ornamental decor, and designed to permit the visitor to withdraw into solitude from the world of affairs.

Nothing illustrates the ambivalence of Azuchi-Momoyama culture better than Hideyoshi's "Mountain Village Tearoom," a small rustic hut he had built within the precincts of Ōsaka Castle, and his portable "Golden

Tearoom," in which every conceivable surface was gilded and almost all the utensils were golden. The interior decorator, Sen no Rikyū 千利休, a rich merchant often described as the very incarnation of the ideals of *wabicha* ("poverty tea"; a type of tea ceremony supposedly governed by restraint) 侘茶, served the powerful aspirant to cultural accomplishment, Hideyoshi, as his tea master in both these contradictory settings.

The decorative arts flourished in Azuchi-Momoyama. The period's most important artistic commissions were large scale wall paintings 障壁画 and paintings on folding screens 屏風絵 produced for the new warrior aristocracy's residences or the religious shrines they patronized. Richly colored and gilded decorative paintings are the period's representative works of art. Their grand conception and sumptuous execution distinguish the newly blossoming Azuchi-Momoyama culture from the previously dominant aesthetic heritage of the Higashiyama culture 東山文化 (1449–90), which was characterized by monochromatic restraint.

The most renowned master of the grandiose Azuchi-Momoyama style of painting was Kanō Eitoku 狩野永徳, who decorated several palatial residences, including Hideyoshi's Ōsaka Castle 大坂城 and his Jurakudai 聚楽第 in Kyōto. He made his career, however, with the magnificent project he undertook for Nobunaga in the donjon 天守閣 of Azuchi Castle 安土城. In this great tower, the axial edifice of Nobunaga's "realm," Eitoku's art was made to reinforce Nobunaga's statecraft: the lavish decorative program bore a clear political message, made explicit by the edifying themes of the paintings and emphasized by the abundance of gold in their execution. None of these paintings survived when Azuchi Castle was burned after Nobunaga's assassination, however, and few of Eitoku's works remain in existence.

Of the Azuchi-Momoyama period's major painters, only Unkoku Tōgan 雲谷等顔 remained essentially a conservative, rarely infusing color into his work and dealing with his traditional topics in a severe style. Eitoku's other great contemporaries, Kaihō Yūshō 海北友松 and Hasegawa Tōhaku 長谷川等伯, who were specialists in ink painting 水墨画, adapted themselves more readily to the tastes of the times and produced undoubted masterpieces in rich, gilded polychrome.

Another type of versatility was that displayed by Hon'ami Kōetsu 本阿弥光悦, an accomplished calligrapher, potter, and designer of elegant colored paper (*shikishi*) and lacquer ware 漆器. Kōetsu's social position in the high bourgeoisie, no less than his reputation as a creative connoisseur of the arts, enabled him to associate with some of the period's most powerful personages, including Hideyoshi and Ieyasu. In addition, he was on close terms with important members of the Kyōto aristocracy and shared their interest in reviving the classical culture associated with the golden age of the imperial court in the Heian period (794–1185). In his art, Kōetsu accordingly referred consciously to Heian tastes, seeking to evoke the effect of courtliness (*miyabi*), which was that period's prime aesthetic category.

Kōetsu's approach to art expressed itself perfectly in the luxury editions of Japanese classical literature which he began to publish in the first decade of the 17th century at Saga to the northwest of Kyōto. Kōetsu also collaborated with Tawaraya Sōtatsu 俵屋宗達 in a set of handscrolls of Japanese court poetry (*waka* 和歌), another extraordinary example of artistic integration. The classical texts appear in masterful calligraphy on paper decorated in gold and silver wash with motifs derived from the *yamato-e* 大和絵 tradition of Japanese painting; those motifs, familiar since the Heian period, were transformed by Kōetsu and Sōtatsu into stylized if not archetypal patterns, resulting in one of the most elegant products not only of their own epoch but of all of Japanese art history. Sōtatsu was expert at ink painting in the Chinese manner as well. His multiple accomplishment crowns the art history of the Azuchi-Momoyama period.

In the history of literature, Azuchi-Momoyama cannot boast a similar richness. The most important classical and medieval genres, including *waka* and linked verse (*renga* 連歌), continued throughout the period, but their vital force was expiring, while new traditions, such as *jōruri* 浄瑠璃 and *kabuki* 歌舞伎 drama, were barely beginning.

Some of the most interesting literary works to appear during the Azuchi-Momoyama period were produced for the Christian mission and printed by the Jesuit mission press 切支丹版. It is doubtful, however, that these books reached a substantial audience before the Tokugawa shogunate in 1614 initiated the nationwide persecution of Christianity キリシタン, which put a stop to the activities of the mission press and thereby ended a cosmopolitan trend in Japanese literature before it had really had a chance to start.

The International Dimension of the Period
時代の国際的側面

The pronounced international flavor of Azuchi-Momoyama was brought about largely by the novel presence of European traders and Catholic missionaries 宣教師. For the first time, Japan came directly in contact with European civilization, and Europe, through the missionaries' widely published reports, was made familiar with events in Japan in great and dramatic detail.

A full view of this relatively cosmopolitan epoch takes in portions of the Sengoku and Edo periods and spans the years from 1543, when the first recorded Portuguese traders ポルトガル商人 arrived in Japan, to

1639, when the Tokugawa shogunate's final National Seclusion (Sakoku 鎖国) directive put an end to the Portuguese trade and proscribed all Japanese traffic with Catholic lands. A closer but narrower view extends from 1563—the year when the Kyūshū baron Ōmura Sumitada 大村純忠, seeking to cement his ties with the Portuguese traders, accepted baptism from the Jesuit missionaries イエズス会 whom they supported, thus becoming the first of the Christian daimyō キリシタン大名—to 1597, when the Twenty-Six Martyrs 二十六聖人 of Japan were crucified on Hideyoshi's orders in the first bloody persecution of Christianity キリシタン迫害.

To be sure, the period's international history is not circumscribed solely by the compass of the Portuguese merchants and the Catholic priests who came to Japan. The war that Toyotomi Hideyoshi fought in Korea between 1592 and 1598 文禄・慶長の役, a brutal but unsuccessful aggression, is an inexpungible part of that history. Its most distinctive element, however, was contributed by the commercial and religious activities of the Europeans and the growth of a substantial body of Japanese believers in Christianity, who numbered as many as 300,000 in the first decade of the 17th century.

Between 1543 and 1639 the history of Japanese initiatives toward foreign lands described a full circle, from strictly defined and limited contacts to booming expansiveness, and back again to rigidly limited contacts. The tributary relationship with Ming China 明, established in the form of the so-called tally trade 勘合貿易 in the first years of the 15th century, continued until the return of the last official mission in 1549, coincidentally the year when the first Christian missionary, the Jesuit Francis Xavier フランシスコ=ザビエル, landed in Japan. Although pirates (*wakō* 倭寇) and illicit traders remained active even after that date, maintaining a flow of contraband between Japan and China, and although commercial intercourse continued with the Ryūkyū Islands and with Korea, in the 1550s Portuguese traders became the most important source of overseas products, and they maintained that role throughout the Azuchi-Momoyama period. The end of the 16th century, however, saw the beginning of an extraordinary burst of Japanese activities directed toward mainland East Asia and the littoral of the South China Sea 南シナ海. The 1590s witnessed Hideyoshi's abortive military adventure in Korea, which began with bombastic plans to conquer and divide up not only that country but also Ming China, and which ended, after much of Korea was devastated, with the ignominious withdrawal of the beleaguered Japanese troops upon Hideyoshi's death. Japanese ambitions for overseas ventures were thereupon redirected into a more peaceful channel with the systematization of the vermilion seal ship trade (*shuinsen bōeki* 朱印船貿易) under Tokugawa Ieyasu in the first years of the 17th century.

As the Azuchi-Momoyama epoch blended with the Edo period, Spanish, Dutch, and English merchants had joined the Portuguese in Japan, and Japanese traders were ranging as far as Indochina, Siam シャム, and the Spice Islands 香料諸島 in search of profits. In the 1620s and 1630s, however, the Tokugawa shogunate applied ever stricter controls both on foreigners resident in Japan and on Japanese voyaging abroad. From 1639, Japan maintained only a highly restricted form of diplomatic and commercial relations with a few foreign nations, namely the Koreans, the Chinese, and the Protestant Dutch. Merchants from Catholic countries were excluded under the laws of National Seclusion, and Christianity was proscribed as the "pernicious doctrine" (*jahō* 邪法).

The receptivity to contacts with Europeans and the encouragement of Christian missions that had been characteristic of Japan during most of the Azuchi-Momoyama period were replaced at the Edo period's beginning by the execration of everything Christian and by suspiciousness toward Europeans as the potential bearers of the Christian contagion. Azuchi-Momoyama, an extroverted period 外向の時代 of history, was followed by a long era of introversion 内向の時代.

Edo period 江戸時代

(1600–1868; Edo *jidai*). The Edo period, also called the Tokugawa period 徳川時代, is often dated from 1603, when Tokugawa Ieyasu 徳川家康 received the title of shōgun 将軍 and established the Tokugawa shogunate 徳川幕府 in the town of Edo 江戸 (now Tōkyō), until 1867, when the last Tokugawa shōgun resigned. It is alternatively dated from 1600, when Ieyasu defeated his principal rivals in the Battle of Sekigahara 関ヶ原の戦い, to 1868, the year of the Meiji Restoration 明治維新. This book has adopted the latter dates.

One of the major epochs of Japanese history, the Edo period is distinguished by the fact that for more than two centuries (from 1638 to 1864) Japan enjoyed freedom from warfare at home and abroad. Despite authoritarian administration and a policy of National Seclusion 鎖国, Japan experienced significant political, social, economic, and cultural change during this period.

The Edo period witnessed the stabilization of the system of local rule by military lords (*daimyō* 大名) under strong shogunal authority, vested in this case in the Tokugawa family. A self-conscious ruling class of *samurai* monopolized all functions of government above the level of village and town. Under them, the Tokugawa shogunate defined separate classes of commoners, the farmer 農民 and the townsman 町人 being the most important. Since almost the entire samurai class left the countryside to reside in the castle towns 城下町 of their daimyō lords 藩主, they stimulated a rapid and widespread growth of cities.

Establishment of the Tokugawa Power Structure
徳川権力構造の確立

Tokugawa Ieyasu received the title of shōgun from the emperor in 1603, three years after achieving military supremacy over all the daimyō of Japan in the decisive Battle of Sekigahara. The political system created by Ieyasu is now generally referred to as the *bakuhan* system 幕藩体制, under which government functioned through two political mechanisms: the shogunate 幕府 and the daimyō domain 藩. Ieyasu had achieved his hegemony as the head of a coalition of vassals and allied daimyō. He did not eliminate the daimyō; instead he used the daimyō system, seeking only to establish a favorable balance of power under his own authority.

Ieyasu set out some of his loyal retainers as daimyō, creating a class known as *fudai* 譜代 (hereditary vassals), a group that eventually numbered 145 houses. A second category of daimyō were the *shimpan* 親藩 (collateral or cadet daimyō), made up of lineages related to the Tokugawa house, of whom 23 eventually survived. The remaining daimyō were men who had either survived Sekigahara by joining the Tokugawa side before the battle or who had been spared extinction by Ieyasu despite having fought on the losing side. These daimyō, known as *tozama* 外様 (outside lords), numbered some 98 at the end of the 18th century. The Tokugawa house itself constituted a major power bloc. Of Japan's estimated total of 30 million *koku* 石 of land, the shōgun directly held granary lands (known as *tenryō* 天領) assessed at some 4 million *koku*, while another 3 million *koku* were held by the shōgun's enfeoffed *hatamoto* 旗本 (bannermen). The balance of power as measured in landholdings was thus weighted in favor of Tokugawa interests.

Tokugawa Regime: The Authority Structure
徳川政権：支配構造

Tokugawa Ieyasu used the office of shōgun as his prime means of legitimation. In theory the shōgun was the delegate of the emperor, and Ieyasu fully exploited the symbolism of imperial appointment. At the same time, he and his successors made every effort to limit the emperor's political influence. The court nobility (*kuge* 公家) were physically confined to the palace enclosure in Kyōto, watched over by the shōgun's deputy (Kyōto *shoshidai* 京都所司代) and his garrison at Nijō Castle 二条城, and placed under the restraints of a set of regulations known as the Kinchū Narabi ni Kuge Shohatto 禁中並公家諸法度 (Laws Governing the Imperial Court and Nobility). This document excluded the emperor from participation in affairs of state and made his awarding of court honors to the military aristocracy subject to shogunal approval.

As chief of the military estate, the Tokugawa shōgun exercised broad national authority, regulating affairs among the daimyō and religious bodies and setting national military and fiscal policy. In foreign affairs, too, the shōgun assumed the rights to negotiate with other states, stamp out Christianity, control trade, and restrict travel by Japanese. The most important of the shōgun's powers was that of ultimate proprietorship of the country's land. The shōgun held suzerainty over the daimyō, who were his sworn vassals and held their domains as grants from him.

The shōgun's most effective control device was the *sankin kōtai* 参勤交代, or alternate attendance requirement. From the 1630s this practice obliged all daimyō and their families to establish residences near Edo Castle 江戸城 and pay regular homage to the shōgun. Most daimyō were permitted to return home in alternate years, leaving their wives, children, and ranking officials in Edo as hostages. The *sankin kōtai* system continually affirmed the political centrality of Edo.

The shōgun rarely interfered directly in the internal affairs of the domains, giving the daimyō considerable freedom in their administration. However, he did insist upon strict conformity to certain basic policies and regulations. This was made clear in the Buke Shohatto 武家諸法度, as amended in 1635, which stated that "throughout the country all matters are to be carried out in accordance with the laws of Edo." The shōgun did not regularly tax the daimyō, but the daimyō were obliged to keep their domains in order, provide military support, and contribute funds, manpower, and materials for the maintenance of shogunal castles, imperial palaces, and public works.

The shōgun exercised the right to regulate religious bodies as well. In earlier centuries Buddhist communities had played a large role in the political and economic life of the country, but the late-16th-century hegemons Oda Nobunaga and Toyotomi Hideyoshi had succeeded in destroying the political and military power of these religious groups. Under the Tokugawa, religious bodies were reduced in landholdings and the priesthood strictly regulated through numerous edicts. Nonetheless, the Buddhist establishment continued to prosper during the Edo period, in part because of the service it performed for the shogunate in the eradication of Christianity キリシタン禁教.

The Bakuhan System: Central and Local Administration 幕藩体制：中央と地方の行政

The administrative map of Japan during the Edo period was extremely complex. To start with, lands under direct control of the Tokugawa house were distributed unevenly throughout Japan. Then there were some 270 daimyō jurisdictions, plus the holdings of the 5,000 bannermen 旗本, the imperial court, and numerous temples and shrines. Yet all of this somehow was pulled together under the shōgun's overlordship.

The organs of shogunal administration (*bakufu*) emerged from the government that Ieyasu had established when he was still a daimyō in the Kantō region. Consequently, even after Tokugawa authority extended over the entire country, office in the *bakufu* was entrusted only to the hereditary-vassal (*fudai* 譜代) class of daimyō, bannermen, and lesser shogunal retainers (*gokenin* 御家人).

Principal Officials of the Tokugawa Shogunate
徳川幕府の主な役職

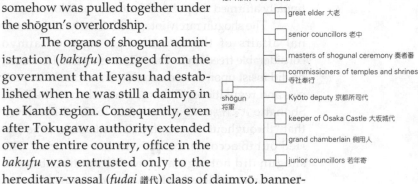

- shōgun 将軍
  - great elder 大老
  - senior councillors 老中
  - masters of shogunal ceremony 奏者番
  - commissioners of temples and shrines 寺社奉行
  - Kyōto deputy 京都所司代
  - keeper of Ōsaka Castle 大坂城代
  - grand chamberlain 側用人
  - junior councillors 若年寄

The shōgun worked through two boards of retainers. A group of five or six senior councillors (*rōjū* 老中) appointed from among mid-ranking *fudai* daimyō made up a high administrative council with authority over matters of nationwide scope. A second board, consisting of three to five junior councillors (*wakadoshiyori* 若年寄), had charge of the shogunate's internal affairs.

The most important functional officers of the shogunate were placed under the senior councillors. These included the commissioners of major cities (*machi bugyō* 町奉行), the commissioners of finance (*kanjō bugyō* 勘定奉行), the keeper (*jōdai* 城代) of Ōsaka Castle, the Kyōto deputy (Kyōto *shoshidai* 京都所司代), the inspectors general (*ōmetsuke* 大目付), and lesser officers. All were either *fudai* daimyō or bannermen.

Villages 村 functioned as basic units of rural control and taxation. They were composed of taxpaying farmers (*hyakushō* 百姓) and their tenants 小作人 and dependent workers. It was left to the *hyakushō* to maintain village self-management. Each village had its headman (*nanushi* 名主 or *shōya* 庄屋), assistant headman (*kumigashira* 組頭), and *hyakushō* representative (*hyakushōdai* 百姓代). Village families were obliged to form into neighborhood groups (*goningumi* 五人組), which promoted mutual assistance and responsibility. In both the shogunal and daimyō domains, government above the level of headman was monopolized by the samurai class. The headman enforced the numerous restrictions on the farmers and mediated between villagers and superior authority.

The Bakuhan System: Social Structure and Class Policy 幕藩体制：社会構造と身分制

The early Tokugawa shōguns inherited a society that already had begun to differentiate into separate functional classes. Most notable was the sharply defined separation of the warrior elite from the farming class—a phenomenon referred to as *heinō bunri*. The land surveys 検地 carried out by Hideyoshi consolidated this separation of the samurai and farmer classes by creating cadastral registers (*kenchichō* 検地帳) in each village. Samurai were defined as persons enrolled on the daimyō or shogunal retainer rosters, while *hyakushō* were those listed on the *kenchichō*. Use of the *kokudaka* 石高 system also meant that samurai not only were detached from the land but could be paid from the lord's storehouse without reference to any specific fief.

Hideyoshi's domestic measures thus brought into being a new samurai class, urban in residence and bureaucratic in function; a class that neither owned agricultural land nor had the legal right to acquire land by purchase. The daimyō had the right to tax their domains, but held them not as private owners but as delegates of the shōgun. Their powers were political, not proprietary. By the same token, the *hyakushō*, by being recorded in the cadastral register, were made more secure in their occupancy of the lands on which they paid taxes.

Class separation took a major step forward under Hideyoshi. The sword hunt 刀狩 order of 1588 aimed at disarming the rural populace, thereby giving samurai a monopoly in arms-bearing. Thereafter samurai assumed as a badge of class distinction the wearing of two swords, long and short. Hideyoshi's edict of 1591 prohibiting changes in status among samurai, farmers, and merchants, although hard to enforce, furthered the codification of the class structure.

Tokugawa legislation refined *shi-nō-kō-shō* 士農工商 class structure by adopting for official purposes a four-class concept that had originated in China. These classes, in order of importance, were warriors 武士, farmers 農民, artisans 職人, and merchants 商人. In actual practice, since artisans and merchants tended to congregate in the cities, they generally were lumped together under the term *chōnin* 町人 (townspeople). Functionally, therefore, Edo society is better conceived of as having had three main classes. In addition, Tokugawa law recognized a number of other social groups, such as the court aristocracy (*kuge* 公家), priests and nuns (*sō* 僧 and *ni* 尼), and outcasts. Each class or group was given a separate identity under law and was treated differently with respect to land rights, tax burden, criminal procedure, and political authority.

The legal separation of classes gave rise to quite different expectations and styles of life for each segment of society. Most samurai lived in towns, within the walled and moated enclosures surrounding their lords' castles, and were restricted to military and civil-bureaucratic service. *Chōnin* were confined to certain sections of town and were expected to provide services for the samurai while maintaining a posture befitting their low status. Farmers by definition lived in villages where they were admonished to work hard and live frugally. Much Tokugawa law dealt with externals—the regulation of housing, clothing, food, and conduct appropriate to each class or group.

Tokugawa law relied heavily on the social concepts of Confucianism 儒教. At the start of the Edo period, shōgun and daimyō faced acute problems of social engineering—in legitimizing their rule and in institutionalizing their social controls. Confucianism, with its heavy emphasis on ethical principles and social harmony, proved relevant to their needs. The official reliance on Confucianism was symbolized by the employment of Hayashi Razan 林羅山 as Confucian adviser to the shōgun in 1607. The basic moral concepts advocated by Confucianism—loyalty (chū 忠) and filial piety (kō 孝)—were conservative and supportive of the existing social and political order.

Restriction of Foreign Contact 海外交流の制限

The basic rationale of the *bakuhan* system did not lead necessarily to the adoption of a policy of National Seclusion 鎖国. But that policy, once adopted, had a profound effect on life in Edo Japan. Ieyasu had tried to develop Edo as a port for trade with the Dutch and English. The failure of this effort, together with a growing suspicion that Christianity was politically dangerous to his regime, prompted him to issue his first anti-Christian edict キリシタン禁教 in 1612. His two immediate successors, Tokugawa Hidetada 徳川秀忠 (r 1605–23) and Tokugawa Iemitsu 徳川家光 (r 1623–51), intensified this policy, and the Shimabara Uprising 島原の乱 of 1637–38 pushed the shogunate to its most extreme anti-Christian measures. From the 1630s the shogunate introduced the *terauke* 寺請 (temple register) and *shūmon aratame* 宗門改 (religious investigation) requirements. All Japanese families had to register at a local temple (*dannadera* 檀那寺) and give evidence annually that they were not contaminated by Christianity.

Meanwhile, regulation of foreign trade moved in parallel. Efforts were made to convert the trade with Korea into a tributary relationship, using the Sō family 宗氏 (daimyō of Tsushima 対馬藩主) as intermediaries. The same was attempted with respect to the Ryūkyūs 琉球, using the Shimazu family 島津氏 (daimyō of Satsuma 薩摩 藩主). At Nagasaki 長崎, which served as the official Tokugawa door to the outside world, elaborate restrictions were placed on trade and foreign contact. In 1635 Japanese nationals were forbidden to travel abroad or return home from overseas (Kaigai Tokō Kinshi Rei 海外 渡航禁止令). In 1639 Portuguese ships ポルトガル船 were excluded from Japanese ports, and only the Dutch オラン ダ and Chinese were allowed to trade at Nagasaki. Trade volume stabilized, but dropped sharply from late in the century, giving Japan minimal contact with the outside world until the 19th century.

Evolution of the Bakuhan State 幕藩体制の変遷

The pattern of Japanese society and culture under Tokugawa rule retained its general contours from the 17th century until the mid-19th century. But isolation and domestic tranquility did not bring social and political change to a standstill.

The first three shōguns perfected the control mechanisms and the administrative machinery of their regimes and made strenuous efforts to increase the balance of power in favor of the shogunate. However, in 1651 Iemitsu was succeeded by his son Tokugawa Ietsuna 徳川家綱 (r 1651–80), a fragile youth of 10. Under him, policy largely was made by the senior councillors 老中, resulting in a style of shogunal rule that reflected the interests of the *fudai* daimyō 譜代大名 more than the central interests of the shōgun.

The fifth shōgun, Tokugawa Tsunayoshi 徳川綱吉 (r 1680–1709), was both colorful and controversial. A mature man when he became shōgun, he put his personal imprint on shogunate policy from the start, in part by relying heavily on his private officials to circumvent the senior councillors. Tsunayoshi's reliance on his favorite, Yanagisawa Yoshiyasu 柳沢吉保, set an example

of rule through the grand chamberlain (*sobayōnin* 側用人).
Tsunayoshi's two successors, Tokugawa Ienobu 徳川家宣
(r 1709–12) and Tokugawa Ietsugu 徳川家継 (r 1713–16),
stayed for a total of only seven years in office. Their
years were marked by the influence of the remarkable
Arai Hakuseki 新井白石, Confucian scholar 儒教 and personal adviser to both shōguns.

In 1716 the main (Tokugawa Hidetada 徳川秀忠)
line of the Tokugawa house failed, so that the eighth
shōgun had to be found in one of the collateral houses.
The choice fell on Tokugawa Yoshimune 徳川吉宗
(r 1716–45), daimyō of Kii 紀伊藩主. Mature and experienced, Yoshimune embarked on a strenuous program
of bureaucratic and financial reforms. Known as the
Kyōhō Reforms 享保の改革, these were the first of three
major reform attempts made during the period. The
main ingredients of these reforms were agrarianism,
hard money, fiscal retrenchment, protection of indebted
samurai, sumptuary regulation, and control of the commercial economy.

Yoshimune's son and grandson, the shōguns
Tokugawa Ieshige 徳川家重 (r 1745–60) and Ieharu 家治
(r 1760–86), are said to have been manipulated by
favorites: Ieshige by Ōoka Tadamitsu 大岡忠光 and Ieharu
by Tanuma Okitsugu 田沼意次. Both of these officials rose
to power from low status; Tanuma in particular has
gone down in history as an extreme example of the corrupt favorite. He was driven from office in 1786.

The country faced many critical domestic problems by the 1780s. Rural unrest was widespread, many
samurai were in debt, and the shogunate and most
daimyō were in financial trouble. Between 1782 and
1787, crop failures caused famine conditions in much of
Japan (Temmei Famine 天明の飢饉). Edo was shaken by
urban riots 打ちこわし, the largest lasting for three days,
and Tanuma was an easy scapegoat. The new shōgun,

Tokugawa Ienari 徳川家斉 (r 1787–1837), being a minor, was placed under the guidance of a new chief shogunate officer 老中首座, Matsudaira Sadanobu 松平定信, who immediately moved to eliminate the influence of Tanuma in government. Sadanobu is credited with carrying out the second of the conservative reform programs, the Kansei Reforms 寛政の改革. His slogan "back to Yoshimune" is indicative of the general thrust of his policies. The results were no more positive or long-lasting than those of the Kyōhō era had been.

Up to the 1790s the shogunate's problems had been mainly domestic, but by the beginning of the 19th century, with the appearance of Russian and British ships in Japanese waters, Japan faced an external threat as well. In the following decades the shogunate was caught in a double crisis, domestic and foreign. In the 1830s the regime experienced one of its worst famines and in 1837 an attempted rebellion in Ōsaka led by Ōshio Heihachirō 大塩平八郎 (a minor Tokugawa official) shook shogunate officialdom.

In 1841, upon the death of Ienari, Mizuno Tadakuni 水野忠邦, chief of the senior councillors, initiated the Tempō Reforms 天保の改革, the last and most drastic of the three reforms. Mizuno's program was intended to improve the economic and political positions of the shogunate, but he managed to antagonize a wide array of people and was soon forced to resign. His successor as head of the senior councillors, Abe Masahiro 阿部正弘, rescinded most of his initiatives.

It was Abe, however, who had to face the crisis created by Commodore Matthew Perry マシュー=ペリー提督 in 1853. Finding himself in an impossible situation, Abe did two things that signaled the end of Tokugawa power. By soliciting all daimyō, including tozama, for opinions on how to handle the American request for the opening of Japanese ports 開港, he abandoned the shogunal prerogative of determining foreign policy unilaterally. By encouraging daimyō to build up their own coastal defenses, he weakened the shōgun's power to control their military strength. With the end of Japan's isolation and the advance of military technology, the shogunate lost its ability to assert national authority, ultimately bringing the Tokugawa regime to an end.

Economic and Cultural Developments of the Period 江戸時代の経済と文化の発展

The Japan "opened" by Perry was vastly different from the Japan that had "closed its doors" in 1639. The greatest achievement of the Tokugawa shogunate was surely the long period of peace and stability it gave to Japan. As a result, the country had prospered both economically and culturally. Along with an increase in population, there is evidence of a general improvement in housing, food, clothing, and education over most of the Edo period.

The most dramatic change to affect Edo society was without question the spread of city life. With the appearance in the mid-16th century of the unified daimyō domains and the movement of the samurai off the land, regional castle towns 城下町 sprang up rapidly throughout Japan. Each daimyō built at the center of his domain a castle headquarters in which he housed his samurai retainers, necessitating the assembling of service groups, merchants, carpenters, artisans, and the like to meet the needs of the assembled samurai. By the end of the 18th century, Edo, the greatest of the castle towns, had nearly 1 million in population, while Ōsaka and Kyōto each had some 300,000 inhabitants.

The samurai, who by tradition considered themselves rural aristocrats, made the transition from military duty to civil-bureaucratic service, becoming literate, cultured, and urbanized. Stress was placed on spiritual training and the cultivation of *bushidō* 武士道, or the Way of the samurai. However, it was in the field of secular scholarship that the samurai of the Edo period made their truly original contribution. The main body of such scholarship was rooted in the Confucian tradition 儒教の伝統. The turn toward Neo-Confucianism 朱子学 and the concurrent rejection of Buddhism began following the establishment of the Tokugawa shogunate. The precedent set by the Tokugawa shōguns in adding the office of Confucian adviser (*jusha* 儒者) to the official bureaucracy and in funding schools, such as the one established by Hayashi Razan 林羅山 in 1630 (forerunner of the Shōheikō 昌平黌), was soon followed by the daimyō.

In the early years, Confucian-based scholarship tended to be derivative, as scholars such as Hayashi Razan sought to assimilate the Confucian tradition to conditions in Japan. One product of this effort was the formulation of the principles of *bushidō* as pioneered by Yamaga Sokō 山鹿素行. As the Edo period advanced, scholars were at work in many domains compiling domainal histories and making collections of laws and precedents. They also pioneered in the recovery of ancient Japanese texts such as the *Kojiki* 「古事記」, *Man'yōshū* 「万葉集」, and *Tale of Genji* 「源氏物語」.

The maturation of urbanized samurai life was accompanied by the rise of an urbanized commercial and service class, the *chōnin* 町人. Confucian theory and Tokugawa law did not serve this class well. For while the *chōnin* were absolutely essential to the samurai in their urban environment, and although many became wealthy by serving the samurai, government policy operated on the premise that merchants were at the bottom of the social scale. The merchant class was denied access to foreign markets and subject to all manner of domestic controls. The small amount of trade permitted at Nagasaki was handled as a shogunal monopoly, and daimyō commonly used domainal monopoly organizations (*han'ei sembai* 藩営専売) to sell special local products. Merchants were protected as merchants, to be sure, particularly after 1721 when merchant guilds and monopoly associations (*kabunakama* 株仲間) were permitted. Also, because they lacked political influence, they were largely left alone, free to accumulate wealth.

Commercial wealth and a growing *chōnin* population gave rise to a bourgeois society with its own cultural style. The *chōnin* had their merchant princes in the great shogunal cities of Edo, Ōsaka, and Kyōto, and to a lesser degree in the provincial castle towns. The greatest of the merchant houses, the Mitsui 三井, Sumitomo 住友, and Kōnoike 鴻池, continued into modern times.

The main elements of the emerging bourgeois culture (*chōnin bunka* 町人文化) were brought to their first flowering in Kyōto and Ōsaka during the Genroku era 元禄時代 (1688–1704). Such were the *jōruri* (puppet) 浄瑠璃 and *kabuki* 歌舞伎 plays of Chikamatsu Monzaemon 近松門左衛門, the popular short stories of Ihara Saikaku 井原西鶴, *ukiyo-e* 浮世絵 of Hishikawa Moronobu 菱川師宣, and the poetic essays and *haiku* 俳句 of Matsuo Bashō 松尾芭蕉. In following decades urban culture continued to develop, and fiction, poetry, drama, and the pictorial arts enjoyed a new burst of vitality in the early 19th century.

The special cultural life of the cities did not extend directly to rural areas. Yet village life did not remain unchanged during the Edo period. From the beginning of this period, agriculture received the particular attention of samurai government. The emphasis was at first on increased production of rice, but eventually such commercial crops as cotton, silk, tobacco, tea, and sugar were stressed.

Commercialization of the rural economy exerted more fundamental, although less visible, influences on village social structure. In the early Edo period, village life generally was dominated by large *hyakushō* families whose extended kinship organization included hereditarily subservient, or servant, households. These dependent family members did much of the work on the main family's large landholdings. More and more, however, large families broke up into smaller units in which the smaller independent families cultivated their own fields while also working portions of other holdings as tenants. The basis of intravillage relations shifted from kinship to economic ties.

The Sense of Crisis 危機意識

By the late Edo period a perceptible sense of unease characterized the national mood, the result of a growing realization that the country faced deep social and economic problems as well as new challenges from abroad. Unease did not translate into a widespread feeling of crisis until well into the 19th century, but it did stimulate social and intellectual movements, all of which responded in one way or another to these new problems.

The main line of Confucian influence on education and political-economic thought remained largely scholastic and conservative. However, scholars such as Dazai Shundai 太宰春台 struggled with questions of government efficiency and how to select officials for merit in a system based on heredity.

Despite the National Seclusion 鎖国 policy, knowledge of Western scholarship and scientific inquiry managed to filter into Japan, particularly after 1720 when Yoshimune lifted the ban on the importation of foreign books and made it possible for persons other than official interpreters to learn Dutch. By the early 19th century, Dutch studies (Rangaku 蘭学) or Western studies (Yōgaku 洋学) had become fairly widespread and their utility sufficiently recognized so that a number of daimyō began to train specialists in Western medicine and other practical sciences. The shogunate, recognizing the importance of keeping abreast of developments in the West, established in 1811 a center for the translation of Western books. But on the whole, specialists in Western studies in Japan did not become a political force agitating for the eventual reopening of their country to foreign intercourse.

After 1800 many Japanese of all walks of life were attracted to an emerging school of National Learning (Kokugaku 国学) that rejected Confucianism and Buddhism as foreign, corruptive influences. This interest in Japanese tradition took on both nationalistic and religious dimensions, especially in the work of Hirata Atsutane 平田篤胤, who called for a return to Shintō tradition and asserted Japan's innate superiority to China for having retained an "unbroken line of deified sovereigns." Members of the Mito school 水戸学, such as Aizawa Seishisai 会沢正志斎, went even further in their rejection of "foreign beliefs" and in their insistence upon Japan's superiority as a "land of the gods (kami)." Revival of the ideological features of Shintō 神道 provided many Japanese with a sense of cultural security in their moment of crisis. It laid the basis for the powerful conservative reaction to the foreign threat under the slogan Revere the Emperor, Expel the Barbarians (sonnō jōi 尊皇攘夷).

Bakumatsu: The End of the Tokugawa Regime
幕末：徳川政権の終わり

Between 1853 and 1860, the shogunate, unable to resist foreign pressures, abandoned its traditional policy and opened a number of ports to foreign ships 外国船. In 1858, by signing trade agreements (Ansei Commercial Treaties 安政の5か国条約) with the foreign powers despite imperial disapproval, it resigned itself to free foreign intercourse. But the country was not ready to go along. The assassination in 1860 of Ii Naosuke 井伊直弼 (Sakuradamongai Incident 桜田門外の変), the shogunate's strongman, brought this phase to an end. There followed an effort to create a coalition government in which the shogunate and daimyō would work together with court nobles under the emperor 公武合体, who would serve as the symbol of national unity. In a final effort at conciliation, the last shōgun, Tokugawa Yoshinobu 徳川慶喜 (r 1867), offered to resign in late 1867 to make way for a coalition government. (Taisei Hōkan 大政奉還).

Already, however, an anti-Tokugawa movement 倒幕運動 was gathering momentum. The two large *tozama* domains of Satsuma 薩摩 and Chōshū 長州 were drawn into alliance by young activist samurai and allied with key figures at the imperial court. In January 1868 this group captured the emperor and declared in his name a restoration of imperial rule (Ōsei Fukko 王政復古). The shōgun had been outmaneuvered. Tokugawa forces made an attempt to resist this turn of events, but troops from the domains of Satsuma 薩摩藩, Chōshū 長州藩, and Tosa 土佐藩 proclaimed themselves an imperial army and routed the Tokugawa forces near Kyōto. The former shōgun was declared a rebel and his lands confiscated. Within a year the new government and the emperor had moved into Edo, where in quick succession the main pillars of the *bakuhan* system were pulled down. In 1871 the daimyō domain system was converted into a centralized prefecture system 廃藩置県. In 1872, with the declaration of class equality, the samurai class was abolished. In 1873 the *kokudaka* system of land registration and taxation was converted to a modern property tax system 地租改正. Between 1853 and 1873 a revolution had taken place.

Meiji period 明治時代

(1868–1912; Meiji *jidai*). The reign of Emperor Meiji 明治天皇 and the beginning of Japan's modern period. It started on 23 October 1868, when the 16-year-old emperor Mutsuhito 天皇睦仁 selected the era name Meiji ("Enlightened Rule") for his reign; the emperor himself is therefore posthumously known as Meiji. Extended retroactively to 3 January, when the restoration of direct imperial rule (Ōsei Fukko 王政復古) had been proclaimed, it ended with the emperor's death on 30 July 1912. The period commenced with the collapse of the Tokugawa shogunate 徳川幕府 and the sweeping reforms attendant upon the Meiji Restoretion 明治維新; it was followed by the Taishō period 大正時代 (1912–26). The Meiji period saw Japan's transformation from a feudal polity 封建国家 into a modern industrial state 近代的工業国, along with its emergence from isolation into the ranks of major world powers.

The Abolition of Feudalism 封建制度の廃止

The Meiji regime began as an alliance between Satsuma 薩摩 (now Kagoshima Prefecture) and Chōshū 長州 (now Yamaguchi Prefecture), two domains behind the overthrow of the Tokugawa shogunate, supported by Tosa 土佐 (now Kōchi Prefecture) and Hizen 肥前 (now Saga Prefecture). Though their dominance was legitimized by alliance with the emperor, Satsuma and Chōshū faced a difficult task in imposing and maintaining national unity. From January 1868 to June 1869, the nascent Meiji state fought the Boshin Civil War 戊辰戦争 against fragmented Tokugawa forces and dissident domains. Even before the Tokugawa finally surrendered, the former shogunal capital, Edo, was renamed Tōkyō and designated as the new national capital.

As it attempted to assert control and restore order, the Meiji government sought to reassure its subjects that this new order would be one of justice and opportunity, aspirations embodied in the Charter Oath 五箇条の御誓文 issued by the emperor on 6 April 1868. The Charter Oath promised, among other things, that deliberative assemblies would be established and all matters decided by public discussion and that evil customs of the past would be abandoned, this last implying a commitment to abolish feudalism. Japan's crises in the 1850s and 1860s had shown the need for a single center of power and decision making; only by controlling an integrated polity could the government build up the nation to face the West.

There were early attempts to implement the "assemblies" and "public discussion" mentioned in the Charter Oath, notably in the Constitution of 1868 (Seitaisho 政体書), but before long the regime reverted to a more authoritarian structure dominated by the Grand Council of State (Dajōkan 太政官). Thereafter reform and innovation proceeded from the initiative of key Restoration leaders from Satsuma, Chōshū, Tosa, and Saga, younger *samurai* who gradually replaced the high-ranking lords and nobles who had initially filled imperial offices.

In 1869 four major *daimyō* were persuaded to relinquish their domain registers to the court (*hanseki hōkan* 版籍奉還) and to urge that henceforth the conduct of all state affairs should repose in the imperial government. Other daimyō followed suit. All were appointed governors 知事 of their former domains by the court, but two years later the court dismissed its daimyō governors and consolidated their domains into more rationally structured prefectures 廃藩置県.

For 18 months from 1871 to 1873, a large part of the Meiji leadership toured America and Europe as part of the Iwakura mission 岩倉遣外使節, in fulfillment of the regime's pledge to seek wisdom throughout the world. Exposure to the West changed the priorities of many, resulting in divisions among the leadership later. The government had already combined former daimyō and court nobles into a new aristocratic elite called the *kazoku* 華族, while also dividing samurai into gentry (*shizoku* 士族) and soldiers (*sotsu* 卒) and improving the status of commoners (*heimin* 平民). Further reform merged *sotsu* into *shizoku* and abolished the outcaste categories by merging them with commoners. In the mission's absence, Tōkyō implemented other planned changes involving release from feudal restrictions and opportunity for commoners to participate in the new society.

Abolishing feudal domains and feudal dues necessitated a new system of taxation. After land surveys in 1873, average productivity was capitalized to produce an estimated market value of land, and the new national land tax was set at 3 percent of this assessment. The sweeping changes of the Land Tax Reform of 1873–1881 地租改正, often poorly understood and brusquely implemented, aroused resistance in the countryside.

The central government now had to shoulder full responsibility for education and defense, matters previously left to the individual domains. The Education Order of 1872 学制 set as its goal universal literacy, dividing the country into higher-school districts with supporting networks of middle and lower schools, all reflecting Western influence.

Samurai no longer provided an acceptable base for military strength: the social base that supported them was changing, their attachments were too often local rather than national, and their adherence to a complex system of social gradations ill-suited them for the large-scale formations of modern warfare. Observation of Western armies and experience with commoner militias (Kiheitai 奇兵隊) during the Restoration convinced the government of the importance of a mass army. In 1872, the government announced a system of military conscription devised by Yamagata Aritomo 山県有朋, a Chōshū loyalist who had visited Europe earlier. The Conscription Ordinance of 1873 徴兵令 called for three years of active service 兵役 and four years in the reserves 予備役 but provided for liberal exceptions.

Deprived of its reason for being, the samurai class was phased out. Most domains had already reduced samurai stipends 家禄 considerably, some to as little as one-tenth of their former amount, yet stipend payments were still viewed as a drain on the nation's resources. After the Iwakura mission's return in 1873, the government decided to begin taxing samurai stipends and ultimately to eliminate them (*chitsuroku shobun* 秩禄処分). A progressive scale of taxation was announced; commutation for lump-sum payments was offered later. Commutation payments were made to 310,000 family heads, but inflation seriously eroded their value.

Samurai from the Restoration domains, where expectations had been highest, were bitterly disappointed. Unhappy with modernization and the government's policy toward Korea, samurai staged a series of revolts across the country from 1874 to 1876 (Saga Rebellion 佐賀の乱; Jimpūren Rebellion 神風連の乱; Akizuki Rebellion of 1876 秋月の乱; Hagi Rebellion 萩の乱). The hardest test for the new government, however, came with the Satsuma Rebellion of 1877 西南戦争, led by the widely admired Saigō Takamori 西郷隆盛.

Victory over Satsuma, though it strained governmental capacities to the utmost, firmly established the Meiji regime. But revolt, assassination, and premature death had cost it some of its early leaders, men like Saigō, Ōkubo Toshimichi 大久保利通, and Kido Takayoshi 木戸孝允. Henceforth, the Meiji leadership would come from such younger Chōshū men as Itō Hirobumi 伊藤博文 and Yamagata Aritomo, the Satsuma finance expert Matsukata Masayoshi 松方正義, and the court nobles Iwakura Tomomi 岩倉具視 and Saionji Kimmochi 西園寺公望. Though many positions were open to outsiders from other domains and even to Tokugawa veterans, the senior statesmen (*genrō* 元老) came from Satsuma and Chōshū.

Faced with runaway inflation incurred by printing money to cover samurai pensions, to assume debts of the old domains, and to finance military campaigns against rebels, the new government was still in a precarious position. A campaign of retrenchment began under the direction of Matsukata Masayoshi, who devoted more than 16 years of his career to Meiji finances. A new land tax and the campaign of industrialization (*shokusan kōgyō* 殖産興業), management of the currency, establishment of the Bank of Japan 日本銀行, and adherence to the gold standard 金本位制 were all carried out under his direction. To help put an end to inflation, Matsukata abandoned some of the government's pilot industrial projects, selling those not of strategic importance to private bidders (*kan'ei jigyō haraisage* 官営事業払下げ). Close to government leaders and sharing their goals, these men emerged as leaders of the future *zaibatsu* 財閥 industrial and financial conglomerates.

In 1884 Matsukata sponsored a study on manufactures (*Kōgyō iken* 興業意見) that set forth a plan for increasing Japan's exports and production by intensified effort in selected markets and commodities. The Matsukata Fiscal Policy 松方財政, particularly of deflation, proved hard on the agrarian sector, which saw crop and land values decline in a depression that often led to forced sales and tenancies. This caused a quickening pace of protest, which contributed to the radicalization of political dissent and, in turn, to the intensification of political repression.

During the Satsuma Rebellion 西南戦争 and the later Takebashi Insurrection of 1878 竹橋騒動, the new conscript army had shown signs of disaffection. Every effort was now bent on making the military a loyal and dependable instrument of the government's will by prohibiting military men from political participation and establishing military police to monitor political activity. But Yamagata Aritomo 山県有朋 also introduced measures that separated the military command function (*tōsuiken* 統帥権) from routine administration, thereby strengthening the military's independent access to the throne. His protégé Katsura Tarō 桂太郎 mapped out the General Staff system 参謀本部制 based on observations of the German military.

Samurai virtues of loyalty and unquestioning obedience were stressed in a campaign culminating in the Imperial Rescript to Soldiers and Sailors 軍人勅諭, which was presented by the emperor in 1882. In 1900 the army minister 陸軍大臣 was required to be a general and the navy minister 海軍大臣 an admiral on the active list (*gumbu daijin gen'eki bukan sei* 軍部大臣現役武官制). Even while civilian control 文民統制 of the military was thus being undermined, military men, as loyal and presumably nonpartisan servants, were considered eligible for nonmilitary office. Yamagata served as home minister 内務大臣 from 1888 to 1890, overseeing the reorganization of local government 地方政治 under central control along German lines. To mobilize the population in the national interest, Yamagata helped develop a system of reserve units (the Imperial Military Reservists' Association 帝国在郷軍人会) that attempted to integrate former soldiers, rural elites, and rural governance into a single patriotic network.

Convinced of the importance of formal constitutional structures in modern Western countries, the government in 1875 established the Genrōin 元老院 as an experimental deliberative body. But when its recommendations seemed likely to lead to a parliament with excessive powers, the regime turned to its principal leaders for alternatives. In 1881, in response to a political crisis, the emperor made a public promise of a constitution to be completed within eight years.

The 1889 Constitution of the Empire of Japan 大日

本帝国憲法 (or Meiji Constitution 明治憲法) was largely the work of Itō Hirobumi 伊藤博文, a Chōshū man who had studied abroad and accompanied the Iwakura mission. For research, Itō returned to Europe, where he was strongly influenced by German constitutional theorists, such as Rudolf Gneist R=グナイスト and Albert Mosse A=モッセ, who argued that the parliament's powers should be limited; that the electorate should be restricted to the wealthier, therefore more responsible, sectors of society; and that the monarch should be given broad powers to ensure continuity and stability. Itō agreed. He saw the imperial house 皇室 as the only possible fulcrum for a new society, believing nothing else could play the moderating and integrative role filled by religion in the West.

Itō completed his draft in 1888. Four years earlier, the government had created a new peerage 華族 whose members would form an upper house 上院 that would balance the expected radicalism of the lower house 下院. The peerage comprised former court nobles, daimyō, and government leaders; it was augmented by life peerages granted to meritorious citizens and leading taxpayers. Thus the old elite, the new plutocracy, and the new meritocracy were enlisted in support of the new order. To review and guard the constitution, a Privy Council 枢密院 was set up.

Itō and his associates regarded their countrymen as backward and ill prepared for the exercise of political rights. They also shared the conviction that radical currents in Japan must be quickly checked by a carefully weighted charter, lest they lead to civil war, a view given substance by the burgeoning Freedom and People's Rights Movement 自由民権運動. Back in 1874, when the government made an unpopular decision against a punitive attack on Korea, many Tosa and Saga leaders had withdrawn from the Meiji regime to issue a call for an elective assembly. The government's decisions, they argued, were arbitrary and capricious: national strength required greater popular participation. Leaders of the Risshisha 立志社, a Tosa samurai organization, were instrumental in forming the more broadly based Aikokusha 愛国者, which in 1881 became the Jiyūtō 自由党, Japan's first national political party. The next year the Rikken Kaishintō 立憲改進党, a similar political organization, was founded.

Government leaders saw these groups as self-willed and irresponsible, but they could not ignore their rising popularity. The early 1880s saw a surge of interest in politics, with hundreds of discussion groups springing up across the country. Many of these prepared private draft constitutions, not a few of which were considerably more liberal than the draft produced by the government. In the countryside, agitation for political rights coincided with economic distress created by the government's policy of deflation.

In the mid-1880s, there were several unsuccessful but alarming rural outbreaks (Chichibu Incident 秩父事件; Iida Incident 飯田事件; Kabasan Incident 加波山事件). By the middle of the decade, with parties temporarily disbanded, the government further restrained political activity with laws regulating the press and freedom of assembly. It also hoped that the new constitution would co-opt the dissidents permanently by granting them limited participation in government through membership in the lower house 衆議院 of the new Imperial Diet 帝国議会.

The Meiji Constitution 明治憲法 was finally promulgated in 1889 as a gift from the sovereign. The constitution invested the emperor with full sovereignty, declaring him "sacred and inviolable 神聖かつ不可侵": he commanded the armed forces 軍の統帥, made peace 講和 and declared war 宣戦, and dissolved 解散 the lower house to call elections. Effective power lay with the executive 行政府, but executive authority was vaguely defined lest it seem to interfere with the imperial prerogative. Since the armed forces had direct and independent access to the throne, the prime minister was first among equals rather than a true head of government.

Yet the constitution marked a genuine step toward popular participation. It recognized private property as inviolate and made provision for a large number of basic rights, all circumscribed "within the limits of the law." The lower house of the Diet, elected by the approximately half-million voters who met tax qualifications, could initiate legislation, though in practice most legislation was prepared by the bureaucracy. Diet approval, however, was required to pass the budget. Should approval be denied, the previous year's budget could be used, but since the government's needs grew constantly, the Diet's budgetary control was real.

The emperor's power of appointment made the Imperial Household Ministry 宮内省 and lord keeper of the privy seal (*naidaijin* 内大臣) important bastions of power. The emperor himself reigned 君臨 rather than ruled 統治. The traditional Japanese method of indirect decision making by groups working in the emperor's name had supplanted German recommendations for an active ruler.

Although a cabinet had replaced the Dajōkan in 1885, the Yamagata cabinet, which took power after elections in 1890, was the first to experience the realities of constitutional government. From the start the lower house, dominated by the reorganized political parties 政党, proved troublesome, taking offense at the high-handed tone of government statements and refusing to approve the government's budget. The highly collegial Meiji leadership saw itself as an embattled elite besieged by office-hungry malcontents. Yet the government was determined to make these new institutions work, for national pride, foreign approval, and political stability all depended upon their successful implementation. The first cabinets used cajolery, bribery, coercion, and imperial rescripts to try to bring the lower house into line.

From the morass of domestic politics, Meiji Japan was suddenly called to the higher ground of national unity through war with China. Although the Tianjin (Tientsin) Convention 天津条約 of 1885 supposedly governed Japanese and Chinese involvement in Korea, the two countries came to blows over Korean requests to China for help against rebels. The Japanese seized the Korean king and forced him to "request" Japan's assistance, allowing them to portray the resulting Sino-Japanese War of 1894–1895 日清戦争 as an altruistic action against a "backward" China on behalf of a Korea in need of "modernization."

Japan's armies were uniformly victorious, destroying Chinese military capability in Korea and seizing the Liaodong (Liaotung) Peninsula 遼東半島 in southern Manchuria 満州. At the peace conference in Shimonoseki 下関講和会議, Japan demanded the island of Taiwan, a large indemnity of 200 million taels, and the Liaodong Peninsula. But the Tripartite Intervention 三国干渉 by Germany, France, and Russia forced retrocession of Liaodong in return for an additional 30 million taels in indemnification. By the Treaty of Shimonoseki 下関条約 Japan also became heir to all privileges extracted by the West from China and gained certain additional concessions, such as the right to manufacture in treaty ports 条約港.

In yielding to the Tripartite Intervention, the Meiji government persuaded many Japanese that their country was still unequal to the West and that greater national strength was essential. This growing unanimity allowed Meiji leaders to enlist prominent party politicians in their cabinets to forge more viable parliamentary tactics. In 1898 two party leaders were even invited to form their own cabinet during a short-lived union of their parties (Ōkuma Cabinet 大隈内閣). When this failed, Itō Hirobumi 伊藤博文 formed his own political party, the Rikken Seiyūkai 立憲政友会, having come to the realization that parties could no longer be excluded from the executive process. Itō's oligarchic colleagues deplored his "surrender" to political self-interest and removed him from the field by having him appointed head of the Privy Council 枢密院, an imperial post theoretically above politics.

The Russo-Japanese War and the Rise to Great Power Status 日露戦争と大国への道

Japan had chafed under the restrictions imposed by the unequal treaties 不平等条約 since the 1850s. The Aoki-Kimberly treaty of 1894 with Great Britain (Anglo-Japanese Commercial Treaty 日英通商航海条約) provided for an end to extraterritoriality 治外法権 and the most-favored-nation clause 最恵国条項 by 1899 and for Japan's right to set its own tariffs by 1911. Similar treaties with other powers soon followed. However, the acquisition of Taiwan and the assumption of privileges in China following the Sino-Japanese War 日清戦争 gave Japan only limited membership in the circle of Western imperialists.

The years following the Sino-Japanese War contained further reminders of Japan's second-class status. During the period of European concession grabbing in China at the end of the century, Russia appropriated the Liaodong Peninsula it had forced Japan to relinquish, while France and Germany secured ports in the south and in Shandong (Shantung 山東半島), respectively. During the Boxer Rebellion 義和団の乱 of 1900, Japanese troops took part in the allied rescue of Beijing (Peking 北京), while Russia utilized the conflict to occupy Manchuria 満州 and respond to Korean pleas for protection. With the Trans-Siberian Railway シベリア横断鉄道 nearing completion, permanent Russian control of southern Manchuria and northern Korea seemed likely.

Britain's search for an ally in the Far East 極東 coincided with Japan's need to offset Russian power. The Anglo-Japanese Alliance 日英同盟 of 1902 gave Japan the protection of the British fleet. Prime Minister Katsura Tarō's 桂太郎 government now entered on a course of hard bargaining and eventual collision with the Russians. Early in 1904, the Japanese fleet launched an attack on the Russian Pacific squadron 太平洋艦隊 at Port Arthur 旅順. The ensuing Russo-Japanese War 日露戦争 proved immensely costly to Japan in men and money, but Japan's proximity to the fronts and indecisiveness among the Russian command brought victories at Port Arthur and in the Battle of Mukden 奉天会戦, culminating in the destruction of the Russian Baltic fleet in the Battle of Tsushima 日本海海戦 in 1905.

At the 1905 peace conference in Portsmouth ポーツマス, Japan gained recognition of its paramount interests in Korea, took back the southern Manchurian leases 租借権 and rights it had been denied 10 years earlier, and acquired the southern half of Sakhalin (Karafuto 樺太). The treaty, however, still disappointed the Japanese people, for they had expected more, in particular a large indemnity.

The last decade of the Meiji period was dominated by Japan's efforts to assume the role of a major imperialist power. Korea, already in Japan's orbit, was formally annexed in 1910 after a Korean patriot assassinated Itō Hirobumi 伊藤博文 (Annexation of Korea 日韓併合). The Franco-Japanese Agreement of 1907 日仏協約, the Russo-Japanese Agreements of 1907–1916 日露協約, and the Takahira-Root Agreement 高平・ルート協定 with the United States in 1908 brought implied or explicit recognition of Japan's sphere of hegemony in Northeast Asia. Domestic politics saw the once-troublesome political party movement drawn into the establishment, with the Seiyūkai 政友会 providing parliamentary support in return for patronage.

Japan's economy was growing rapidly. By 1900 agriculture provided less than half the national product as the share of manufacturing, especially textiles, increased steadily. Industrialization concentrated labor in the cities, bringing fears of urban unrest. Worried about inroads by Western liberalism and radicalism, Meiji leaders focused on upholding Japan's traditional institutions. Emperor Meiji 明治天皇, now associated with success in war and always the symbol of modernization, was raised to new heights of reverence. Textbooks in the compulsory public school course in ethics (*shūshin* 修身) increasingly emphasized national and military heroes as models. The family system 家制度, formally established by an 1898 supplement to the Civil Code 民法, took the samurai family as the norm for the entire nation. The commonwealth was now described as a "family state" in which political and familial loyalties reinforced rather than competed with each other.

The Home Ministry 内務省 undertook to place the native cult of Shintō 神道 at the service of the government by establishing State Shintō 国家神道 shrines within administrative units. Fears of subversion strengthened police surveillance and resulted in the High Treason Incident of 1910 大逆事件, in which an anarchist group accused of plotting against the emperor's life was arrested and executed.

The Meiji period thus left succeeding generations of Japanese with an ambiguous heritage. By the time of the emperor's death (of natural causes) in 1912, Japan stood as a model of rapid and largely successful modernization. In less than half a century it had developed from an isolated, semifeudal society into a modern state that had secured for itself a prominent place in the world community. At the same time, the rapidity of this change had left a number of difficult social problems unresolved and a tendency toward authoritarian solutions that threatened its fledgling constitutional order. Historians' interpretations of the Meiji period vary according to their assessment of the conflicting elements of the Meiji legacy; they are unanimous, however, in seeing in it the foundations of Japan's modern experience.

▌Literature and Art 文学と美術

An imported Western ideology began to affect traditional aesthetics and brought sweeping changes to its literature and art. The usage of colloquial speech was fully achieved for the first time in *Ukigumo* 「浮雲」 (Drifting Clouds) by Futabatei Shimei 二葉亭四迷. Early stylistic influences on the literature were romanticism ロマン主義, introduced in the 1890s by Mori Ōgai 森鷗外, and naturalism 自然主義, out of which developed the genre of the I-novel 私小説. Natsume Sōseki 夏目漱石, along with Ōgai, are considered among the greatest writers of this period.

The initial enthusiasms for Western art soon yielded to renewed appreciation of traditional art, promoted by Okakura Kakuzō 岡倉覚三 (Tenshin 天心) and Ernest Fenollosa アーネスト=フェノロサ. Yet Western-style painting (*yōga* 洋画) soon reasserted itself. In 1893, Kuroda Seiki 黒田清輝 returned from studies in France to become the leader of Western-style painting.

Taishō period 大正時代

(1912–26; Taishō *jidai*). The reign of Emperor Taishō 大正天皇, which one Japanese historian has characterized as "an era of great possibilities." Some historians, employing the term Taishō Democracy 大正デモクラシー, associate the period with the emergence of political and social trends that ultimately made possible the post-1945 democratization of Japan. Looking at a different set of trends, others have found it equally plausible to see in the Taishō period the roots of the radical nationalism ナショナリズム, expansionism 拡張主義, and antiliberalism 反自由主義 that later marked the 1930s and early 1940s.

The ambiguity of the Taishō period may be especially pronounced because historians have trouble discovering a defining event, such as the Meiji Restration 明治維新 (1868) or World War II, that provides an obvious interpretive perspective. For that reason it makes more sense to abandon the entirely arbitrary boundaries set by the accession and death of a monarch and to think instead of "World War I Japan" and "Japan in the 1920s," a distinction that not only situates Japan in the context of world history but also suggests a chronological break that many Japanese sensed at the time.

The Impact of World War I 第一次世界大戦の衝撃

The outbreak of World War I had a profound social and economic impact on Japan. The withdrawal of European business interests from Asian markets after the war began provided a boost to the industrial sector. The rupture of trade with Germany stimulated the chemical, dye, and drug industries; military orders prompted the expansion of the iron, steel, and machine-tool industries; the output of cotton-spinning and textile factories grew to meet Asian demand no longer satisfied by British mills; the shipping industry expanded precipitously to handle expanded trade; and the hydroelectric power industry grew in response to the demand of industrial growth.

The wartime boom brought with it a quick and easy prosperity. Between 1912 and 1919 the national income 国民所得 more than tripled in nominal terms, from ¥4.2 billion to ¥13.3 billion. Astute investors and speculators made quick fortunes, and the newly wealthy (called *narikin*) indulged in ostentatious consumption. The wages of factory workers rose sharply, and farm households enjoyed good times as the demand for rice and other food products rose and the expanding industrial sector provided jobs for their offspring.

The boom had other social effects as well. The factory labor force nearly doubled in size, and the proportion of male workers in heavy industry rose significantly. Male workers, many with families to support, were more likely to express labor militance than the young, unmarried female textile workers who had dominated the factory labor force before the war. Not surprisingly, the number of labor disputes 労働争議 increased. In 1914 there were only 50 recorded labor disputes, but by 1918 there were 417. Workers demanded not only better compensation but recognition of their place in Japanese society as well.

If any single event symbolized the wartime changes, it was the nationwide disturbance known as the Rice Riots of 1918 米騒動. Demonstrations against an exorbitant rise in rice prices began in Toyama Prefecture in late July and spread to most major cities and towns, and many villages as well, during August and September. Crowds milled through the streets, attacking and looting the shops of rice brokers, moneylenders, and other merchants. Nationwide, between 1 million and 2 million people may have participated in the rioting.

To many observers the rice riots marked the beginning of a "popular awakening 大衆の目覚め" that would lead Japan along the path of "democracy 民主主義." And when the war ended in the victory of the Western democracies over the central European monarchies, many journalists, intellectuals, and politicians concluded that the future held the promise for "emancipation" of the masses the world over.

The Postwar Years: The Seeds of Democracy
大戦後：民主主義の芽生え

When the war came to an end, so did the economic boom 好況. Although the economy continued to grow, it did so at a much slower rate. The collapse of overseas markets brought about a recession in 1920. Prices fell, exports dropped, and stock prices tumbled. Many firms found themselves saddled with debt and unable to raise new capital. Workers faced wage cuts and discharges, and the import of colonial rice brought about a sudden end to wartime prosperity in the countryside.

Against this background there emerged new and vocal movements for democratic reform. Intellectuals such as Yoshino Sakuzō 吉野作造 argued that even though sovereignty was formally vested in the emperor it was possible to have Japanese-style democracy—what Yoshino called *mimpon shugi* 民本主義 (literally, "people-as-the-foundation-ism"). In 1919 and 1920 intellectuals, students, and workers took to the streets to demonstrate for universal manhood suffrage 普通選挙運動. They saw the extension of voting rights as a way to break the hold of the "privileged classes" on politics. Although the opposition parties in the Diet favored an end to tax qualifications for voting, the party cabinet 政党内閣 of Hara Takashi 原敬 defeated a universal suffrage bill introduced into the 1920 Diet.

Frustrated by this failure, urban intellectuals and popular movements took a radical turn in the early 1920s. Attracted by the apparent success of the new "socialist experiment" in the Soviet Union, they shifted their focus from political reform to demands for major structural changes in the capitalist socioeconomic system. The labor movement 労働運動, dominated by the Japan Federation of Labor 日本労働総同盟, organized in 1921, came under the influence of leaders committed to anarcho-syndicalism アナルコ=サンジカリスム；労働組合至上主義, democratic socialism 民主社会主義, or Marxism マルクス主義. Student associations became radicalized as well. Worker and student activists took to the countryside to organize tenant unions 小作人組合 and rent strikes against landlord oppression. To confirm the worst fears of the conservative political establishment, the Japan Communist Party 日本共産党 was organized in 1922.

This inescapable evidence of popular and intellectual discontent prompted Diet politicians and concerned bureaucrats to devise ways of accommodating the demands for greater social and political democracy. The Diet passed moderate reform legislation such as a labor exchange bill 労働争議調停法, a tenancy dispute arbitration law 小作調停法, and a minimum wage law 最低賃金法. Most dramatically, in 1925 it passed a universal manhood suffrage law 普通選挙法 that gave the vote to adult males over 25. To attract the newly enfranchised electorate 有権者, a number of small "proletarian parties プロレタリア政党" such as the Labor-Farmer Party (Rōdō Nōmintō 労働農民党) and the Japan Labor-Farmer Party (Nihon Rōnōtō 日本労農党) were organized in 1926. The activists in these parties were drawn from the ranks of the student and labor union movements.

The Seeds of Reaction 反動の種子

The call for democratization and reform was centered mainly in large cities. Most of the votes cast for the proletarian parties in the 1928 election were cast in urban constituencies. The cities fostered intellectual ferment. The educated urban middle classes 中流階級 and even some workers avidly read the latest translations of Western books and provided the audience for new experiments in literature, art, and music. New kinds of mass media マスメディア—largecirculation newspapers, general monthlies 月刊総合誌 such as *Chūō kōron* 「中央公論」 and *Kaizō* 「改造」, and inexpensive paperback books—propagated cultural fads and the latest ideas from the West.

But the trend toward democracy, reform, and change rested on a narrow base. The vast majority of the population still lived in rural communities where traditional folkways and values remained strong. The primary school system 初等教育制度, with its emphasis on inculcating patriotic ideas 愛国精神 and loyalty to the emperor, reinforced conservative tendencies in the countryside. Newfangled middle-class reform ideas, whether about labor unions or love marriages 恋愛結婚, were deeply threatening to rural villagers. A profound cultural gap separated city and country.

The postwar years also saw the emergence of a new right wing 右翼. Alarmed by the growth of popular unrest, the increase in labor disputes, the spread of alien ideas, and leftist militance, right-wing activists organized to counter what they regarded as a deplorable weakening of the traditional social order. Fearing that the country was on the brink of social revolution, they called for a renewal of patriotism, devotion to the emperor, respect for parents and elders, and other traditional values.

While the right wing did not use the tactics of popular protest or street demonstrations, its ideas appealed to a broad spectrum of Japanese society. In rural communities and provincial towns organizations such as the Reservists Associations 在郷軍人会 and Youth Associations 青年団 provided forums for patriotic activities. In the universities conservative students organized themselves to counter the influence of student radicals. And organizations such as the Kokuhonsha (National Foundations Society) 国本社, founded in 1924 by Minister of Justice Hiranuma Kiichirō 平沼騏一郎, included in their numbers high-ranking bureaucrats, military and naval officers, and university professors.

If the passage of the universal suffrage bill 普通選挙法 in 1925 marked the emergence of democratic trends, the Peace Preservation Law of 1925 治安維持法, passed by the same Diet, marked countervailing conservative and right-wing tendencies. Intended to control the spread of "dangerous thoughts," the latter law made it illegal to criticize either the Kokutai 国体 (the "national polity" or state structure of Japan as embodied in the imperial institution) or the system of private property. In 1925 and 1926 the law was invoked to crack down on student radicalism in the universities, and in March 1928 it was used to carry out a national roundup of communists and other "subversive elements" shortly after the first election was held under the new manhood suffrage law. In the late 1920s the forces of the Special Higher Police 特別高等警察, a secret political police organization (also known as the "thought police"), were expanded, and in the 1930s they were the principal instrument for controlling not only radicalism but all kinds of political dissent.

The Legacy of the Taishō Period 大正時代の遺産

The historical legacy of the Taishō period is an ambiguous one. If the 1920s saw the emergence of a nascent democratic movement, they also saw the revival of an older traditionalism and conservatism. Since historians are more often drawn to examine new trends or new developments than old ones, it is easy to understand why many of them were attracted to the concept of "Taishō Democracy 大正デモクラシー." But it is clear that one as readily can find "Taishō Conservatism 大正保守主義" or "Taishō Authoritarianism 大正権力主義." When severe economic crisis struck in the late 1920s, particularly in the countryside, it was these older and more persistent tendencies that overwhelmed the movement for democratization.

Taishō Literature and Painting 大正時代の文学と絵画

The first significant development in Taishō-period literature was the emergence of the Shirakaba school 白樺派. Critical of the earlier trends of naturalism 自然主義 and aestheticism, members of the group were united by their upper-class backgrounds, and also by their basic humanism. Mushanokōji Saneatsu 武者小路実篤, the group's leader, expressed his free-spirited ideas in straightforward prose. Other writers in the group included Shiga Naoya 志賀直哉 and Arishima Takeo 有島武郎.

Other prominent writers of the period were affiliated with the literary magazines *Shinshichō* 「新思潮」 and *Mita bungaku* 「三田文学」. Akutagawa Ryūnosuke 芥川龍之介 was the foremost writer for the first. Other writers for *Shinshichō* included Kikuchi Kan 菊池寛 and Yamamoto Yūzō 山本有三. The leftist journal *Tane maku hito* 「種蒔く人」 began publication in 1921, marking the beginning of the proletarian literature movement プロレタリア文学運動.

In the field of *tanka* poetry, the journal *Araragi* 「アララギ」 fostered such poets as Itō Sachio 伊藤左千夫 and Saitō Mokichi 斎藤茂吉.

The Taishō period saw burgeoning Western influence in the arts. Yasui Sōtarō 安井曾太郎 and Umehara Ryūzaburō 梅原龍三郎 returned to promote the styles of Camille Pissarro C=ピサロ, Paul Cézanne P=セザンヌ, and Pierre Auguste Renoir P=A=ルノワール.

Although on a limited scale, Japanese-style painting too was affected by European styles, especially neoclassicism and, later, postimpressionism. Yokoyama Taikan 横山大観, Shimomura Kanzan 下村観山, and Hishida Shunsō 菱田春草, all to some degree adopted Western-style atmospheric treatment of space and light.

Shōwa period 昭和時代

(1926–89; Shōwa *jidai*). The reign of Emperor Shōwa 昭和天皇 (Hirohito 裕仁), from 25 December 1926 to 7 January 1989, was the longest imperial reign in Japanese history, and one of the most tumultous and controversial. In the course of this 62-year period Japan traversed a complex and often contradictory course that led it from parliamentary democracy and peaceful international cooperation into militarism 軍国主義 and global war, and then from defeat 敗戦 and occupation 占領 by foreign troops to recovery and a level of prosperity that has astonished the Japanese themselves as much as the rest of the world.

Parliamentarianism and International Cooperation
議会政治と国際協力

When Emperor Shōwa ascended the throne, Japan appeared to be moving toward convergence with the Western democracies. Universal manhood suffrage 普通選挙 had been instituted in 1925, and the *genrō* 元老 or elder statesmen, the oligarchic group that had been the moving force behind Japan's establishment as a modern state, were gradually withdrawing from the scene. In their place, political parties 政党 vied for power within Japan's fractious yet vital parliamentary system, and progress was being made in passing legislation to address some of Japan's more acute problems in the areas of tenant farming, labor, and health. Internationally, Japan had committed itself at the Washington Conference ワシントン会議 (1921–22) to a policy of naval arms limitation and cooperation with the United States, Great Britain, and other nations in the effort to preserve peace through international diplomacy. During most of the 1920s the Japanese economy grew at a respectable 3.2 percent a year, and there were signs of the development of a mass consumer culture increasingly integrated in a global system of trade.

Grave problems, however, were concealed in the background of these generally positive developments. Economic growth seemed to primarily benefit the burgeoning financial conglomerates (*zaibatsu* 財閥) and the urban areas of the country; smaller businesses and the rural population were largely left behind to face increasingly difficult times. Then, in the Financial Crisis of 1927 金融恐慌 and the Shōwa Depression 昭和恐慌 touched off by the New York stock market ニューヨーク株式市場 crash of 1929, even the leading sectors of the Japanese economy were thrown into confusion, shaking public confidence in the government. The deflationary policies and the various military and bureaucratic budget cuts attempted by Prime Minister Hamaguchi Osachi 浜口雄幸 did little to restore faith in the political system or in party rule. Fearful of a growing Marxist movement, government officials used the Peace Presevation Law of 1925 治安維持法, which had been passed in conjunction with universal manhood suffrage, to suppress dissent in the name of eradicating communism.

Militarism 軍国主義

During the course of the 1930s a squabbling, constantly shifting antidemocratic coalition of ultranationalist ideologues, disgruntled army officers, "reform" bureaucrats, and ambitious politicians gradually pushed Japan away from the parliamentarianism 議会政治 and internationalism 国際協調主義 of the 1920s toward militarism, authoritarianism, and a "go-it-alone" policy in Asia. The Hamaguchi cabinet's efforts to continue a policy of international arms control at the London Naval Conference ロンドン軍縮会議 of 1930 were met with deep displeasure by an increasingly restive military, and Hamaguchi himself was shot by a right-wing 右翼 assailant, ushering in an era of political assassinations and coup attempts. The situation worsened in September 1931 when insubordinate army officers staged the Manchurian Incident 満州事変, initiating a course of military expansionism in continental Asia that led to increasing friction with the Western powers, the creation of the puppet state 傀儡国 of Manchukuo 満州国 in 1932, and Japan's withdrawal from the League of Nations 国際連盟 in 1933.

This was followed in 1936 by a shocking full-fledged military revolt in Tōkyō (February 26th Incident 二・二六事件) that shook the very foundations of civilian government in Japan. The revolt was suppressed, but as the government tried to deal with these and other acts of lawlessness and insubordination, power increasingly slipped from the hands of party politicians into those of men who, it was hoped, might better be able to control the militarists. Foremost among these new leaders was Prince Konoe Fumimaro 近衛文麿, who served as prime minister from June 1937 to January 1939, and again from July 1940 to October 1941.

Konoe was an ambiguous figure. Though he no doubt desired an end to conflict and chaos, he was weak and indecisive, and was enough of a nationalist that he did little to thwart those calling for a "Shōwa Restoratio 昭和維新," the slogan of the reactionary right. Moreover, in 1937 he permitted the Marco Polo Bridge Incident 盧溝橋事件 to escalate into a full-scale war between China and Japan (Sino-Japanese War of 1937–1945 日中戦争), a bitter and protracted conflict that, despite military victories, only deepened Japan's problems. During his second term of office, Konoe committed Japan to the fateful Tripartite Pact 三国同盟 (1940) with Italy and Germany. This decision to join the Axis alliance 枢軸国, as well as the neutrality pact signed with the Soviet Union 日ソ中立条約 in April 1941, reflected Foreign Minister Matsuoka Yōsuke's 松岡洋右 conviction that a firm stand and new allies would persuade the United States and Great Britain to give Japan a free hand in Asia and the Pacific—especially given their preoccupation with the stunning German victories in the early phases of World War II in Europe.

War in the Pacific 太平洋戦争

Far from discouraging the United States, however, Japan's actions merely served to increase tensions. As early as 1931, the United States had said that it would not recognize further Japanese conquests in Asia (nonrecognition policy 不承認政策). When Japanese forces occupied northern French Indochina フランス領インドシナ in September 1940, the United States stopped iron and steel exports to Japan. Undeterred, the Japanese moved into southern Indochina in July 1941, and the United States responded by organizing an international embargo on oil exports to Japan 対日石油輸出停止. This had a more serious impact, and, faced with dwindling oil reserves and confusion over how to resolve the dilemma, the Konoe cabinet resigned in October 1941, to be succeeded by a government formed by General Tōjō Hideki 東条英機陸軍 大将. After attempts at negotiation between Japan and the United States foundered over the issue of whether or not Japan should be permitted to maintain its military presence in China, Japan struck at Pearl Harbor on 7 December 1941 真珠湾攻撃 and quickly occupied a vast area of Southeast Asia and the Pacific that it designated as the Greater East Asia Coprosperity Sphere 大東亜共栄圏.

Initially, the war went well for the Japanese, as they overran British Malaya and Singapore, took Hong Kong and Burma, and defeated the US forces in the Philippines. However, by the time of the Battle of Midway ミッドウェー海戦 (June 1942) and the bloody campaign for Guadalcanal ガダルカナルの戦い (August 1942–February 1943), it was clear that Japan did not have the forces necessary to control such far-flung territories, nor the material and logistic resources to sustain its war effort. US submarine warfare cut off the Japanese home islands from the resources of Southeast Asia, and the island-hopping campaign across the Pacific brought US long-range bombers within striking range of Japan's urban and industrial heartland.

By 1945 Japan's situation was desperate. Japan turned to the USSR in the hope of finding an intermediary that could help in negotiating some sort of compromise peace, but this hope was shattered by the firmly worded call for "unconditional surrender 無条件降伏" enunciated by the United States, Great Britain, and China in the Potsdam Declaration ポツダム宣言 of July

1945. As Japan hesitated, atomic bombs 原子爆弾 were dropped on Hiroshima 広島 (August 6) and Nagasaki 長崎 (August 9), and the Soviet Union declared war 宣戦布告 on Japan (August 8). Still unable to decide whether to fight on or to accept the Potsdam Declaration, the dead-locked cabinet of Prime Minister Suzuki Kantarō 鈴木貫太郎, in an unprecedented move, appealed to Emperor Shōwa for guidance. The emperor responded that Japan would have to "bear the unbearable 耐え難きを耐えなければならない" and accept its defeat. On 15 August 1945, World War II 第2次世界大戦 came to an end.

▌Occupation 占領

As a result of its defeat, Japan was subjected to the Allied Occupation 連合国軍占領, which lasted from August 1945 to April 1952. During this period the Japanese government was subject to the authority of the supreme commander for the Allied powers 連合国軍最高司令官 (SCAP), a term that referred both to the commander himself (General Douglas MacArthur ダグラス=マッカーサー将軍 until 1951 and then General Matthew B. Ridgway マシュウ=B=リッジウェイ将軍) and to the supporting bureaucracy of several thousand officials, most of them Americans. During the early years of the Occupation, these officials pushed through a sweeping series of reforms that included a new constitution (Constitution of Japan 日本国憲法), the Land Reforms of 1946 農地改革, a revamping of the educational system 教育改革, curtailment of the economic activities of the *zaibatsu* (*zaibatsu* dissolution 財閥解体), and major changes in the legal codes to support equality of the sexes 男女同権 and lessen the authority of Japan's traditional patriarchal family system 家制度. Underlying these and other Occupation actions, including the war crimes trials 戦争犯罪に関する裁判, was an American belief that a small clique of military and civilian leaders had led the great majority of Japan's overly compliant but basically innocent citizenry into an immoral war. Democratic reforms, it was hoped, would create a more peaceful and stable Japan.

The many sudden changes instituted under the Occupation shocked Japan's conservatives. Particularly galling were the constitution's reduction of the emperor to purely symbolic status 象徴, the renunciation of a military establishment 軍備の放棄 contained in article 9, the decentralization of the police and educational system, and the banning from public life of thousands of prewar political and business leaders (Occupation Purge 公職追放). At the same time, Japanese leftists and progressives were disappointed that even more fundamental structural reforms had not been carried out, and in the later years of the Occupation they were dismayed by what they saw as a "reverse course 逆行" in Occupation policy, reflecting cold war 冷戦 tensions. In this later period the scheduled General Strike of 1947 二・一スト was banned, strikes by government employees were outlawed, a Red Purge レッドパージ of suspected communists was initiated, the police and school system were recentralized, and, after the outbreak of the Korean War in 1950, the National Police Reserve 警察予備隊 (which later evolved into the present Self Defense Force 自衛隊) was created. Women, although they had received the right to vote and made important legal and social gains, also found that they did not achieve the degree of equality their most vigorous representatives desired.

The Occupation officially ended in April 1952 with the implementation of the San Francisco Peace Treaty サンフランシスコ平和条約, which Japan had signed with 48 noncommunist nations in September 1951. At the same time, Japan concluded a security treaty with the United States 日米安全保障条約 that permitted US military bases 在日米軍基地 to remain on Japanese soil in return for an American commitment to protect Japan from foreign aggression.

Toward Prosperity 繁栄への道

Japan's economy was still in the arduous process of recovery from the war, but US aid, a stable ¥360-to-$1 exchange rate, a rush of special military procurements (*tokuju* 特需) to support the US and United Nations forces 国連軍 in the Korean War 朝鮮戦争 (1950–53), and hard work by Japanese business and labor combined to push the average annual growth of Japan's gross national product 国民総生産 (GNP) to 8.6 percent in 1951–55, and over 9.1 percent in 1955–60.

The political scene was more turbulent. Attempts by the ruling Liberal Democratic Party 自由民主党 (LDP; established in 1955 by a merger of two existing conservative parties) to alter or roll back a number of the Occupation reforms, including article 9 of the constitution 憲法第9条, were met with fierce protests by the Japan Socialist Party 日本社会党 (JSP; now Social Democratic 社会民主党) and the Japan Communist Party 日本共産党 (JCP). Tension reached a fever pitch in June 1960, when Prime Minister Kishi Nobusuke 岸信介 rammed a revised United States–Japan Security Treaty 日米安全保障条約 through the Diet in the hope of resolving the controversy over the US bases in Japan before President Dwight D. Eisenhower ドワイト=D=アイゼンハワー大統領 arrived for a scheduled official visit. After massive rioting, the revised treaty went into effect, but the turmoil forced Eisenhower to cancel his visit and Kishi to resign. The new prime minister, Ikeda Hayato 池田勇人, and his successor, Satō Eisaku 佐藤栄作, now concentrated on an "income-doubling 所得倍増" policy of high economic growth, and some of the ideological tensions associated with the immediate post-Occupation period began to subside.

Rapid economic growth provided the dominant theme of the last 20 years of Emperor Shōwa's reign. During this time annual growth in GNP rose from the 8–9 percent that characterized the 1950s to 9.7 percent between 1960 and 1965, and 13.1 percent between 1965 and 1970, declining to roughly 7 percent throughout the 1970s. By the early 1970s Japan was the world's largest producer of ships, radios, and televisions, the second largest manufacturer of cars and rubber products, and the third largest producer of cement and iron. By the 1980s, Japan had become the leading manufacturer of cars in the world, and the dominant producer of such high-technology electronic products as videocassette recorders, computer chips, video games, televisions, and audio equipment. Despite pressures from abroad for voluntary restraints on exports 輸出自主規制, and despite vigorous efforts to correct the imbalance in the yen-dollar exchange rate 円・ドル換算相場, Japanese goods remained attractive to consumers in the United States and other countries, and Japan's favorable trade balances 貿易収支, especially with the United States, remained large. Japanese purchases of US bonds, securities, and property also worried some Americans, while many others competed to draw Japanese investment to their regions.

There were many reasons for Japan's high rate of growth during this period. First, Japan's demographic growth from a population of 72 million in 1945 to more than 120 million in 1989 made it the seventh most populous nation in the world. Roughly 60 percent of this population, which was characterized by both a stable birth rate 出生率 (since 1956) and a relatively small number of elderly people 高齢者, was able and willing to work. Second, Japan's low military expenditures 防衛費 (usually below 1 percent of GNP), relatively low investment in social services, and generally high rate of savings 貯蓄率 contributed to heavy capital investment in the latest technology and innovative plants and equipment. Aided by the comparatively easy international access to technology and markets that characterized the 1960s, given generous support by conservative governments, and guided by the policy planning of agencies such as the Ministry of International Trade and Industry 通商産業省 (MITI), the Japanese business community made use of a well-educated and hardworking labor force to turn out a stream of highly successful products. Although this led to unfavorable stereotypes of government-business collusion—as represented by the phrase Japan Incorporated 日本株式会社—it was clear that the Japanese way of doing business and the unprecedented level of prosperity it was generating were rooted in a much more complex and diverse set of economic and social factors.

Japanese Society at the End of the Shōwa Period
昭和時代末期の日本の社会

By the 1980s, Japan's rapid industrialization had brought more than 80 percent of the Japanese population into urban areas, and there was a shift from the traditional extended-family 大家族 ideal to the more modern nuclear family 核家族. The divorce rate 離婚率 rose slightly but remained one-fifth that of the United States, both because opportunities for women were improving and because there was strong social pressure to make marriage work. Few families professed to be very religious, yet the established Buddhist and Shintō sects prospered, while the so-called new religions 新宗教 such as Sōka Gakkai 創価学会, Tenrikyō 天理教, and PL Kyōdan PL教団 kept the adherents they had won during their explosive growth in the 1960s. Marxism in Japan, on the other hand, lost much of its vitality, as it was doing in the rest of the world. Criminal gangs 暴力団 (known as *yakuza*) provided lurid copy for the media, and yet the level of crime and the proliferation of illegal drugs 麻薬 remained surprisingly low in comparison to other advanced industrial nations. Some progress was also made in dealing with the problem of prejudice toward minority groups 少数者集団 and the status of women also slowly improved.

Nonetheless, difficult problems remained. Early in the 1970s, for example, various outbreaks of pollution-related diseases 公害病 demonstrated to a shocked nation some of the environmental costs of high growth. The oil crisis of 1973 石油危機 and a series of unilateral actions by US president Richard M. Nixon リチャード=M=ニクソン大統領 (Nixon Shocks ニクソン=ショック) during the 1970s also reinforced a sense of the Japanese economy's vulnerability to external events and pressures, a sense that many Japanese continue to hold today, amid the mounting chorus of foreign protests against Japan's massive trade surpluses 貿易黒字. By the end of the 1980s, a steep rise in land prices had created a rapidly widening gap between owners and nonowners, young people were worrying about whether they could ever afford to purchase a home, and income distribution in Japan was becoming increasingly unequal. Meanwhile, government efforts to control budget deficits 財政赤字 led to a tightening of expenditures, to the privatization 民営化 of various government-run corporations such as the Japanese National Railways 国鉄, and, in 1988, to the imposition of an unpopular 3 percent consumptiopn tax 消費税, intended in part to help finance improved social services for Japan's rapidly aging population 高齢化社会.

A series of political scandals beginning in the 1970s has also provoked continuing criticism of the nature of party politics in Japan. Prime Minister Tanaka Kakuei 田中角栄 was initially praised for his energetic approach to national issues, but was soon forced to resign after he was implicated in the Lockheed Scandal ロッキード事件. Resentment flared up once again after the 1988 passage of the consumption tax, not only because the tax itself was an irritant, but also because its passage coincided with the disclosure that the Recruit Company had involved a host of leading politicians in illegal stock deals (Recruit Scandal リクルート事件). The ruling LDP managed to stay in power throughout this period, largely because the opposition (including the JSP 日本社会党, JCP 日本共産党, and Kōmeitō 公明党) were too weak and divided among themselves to form an effective coalition 連立政権, but also because the LDP itself has been relatively skillful in polishing its periodically tarnished image and in adapting its political program to meet new popular demands.

The literary giants Mishima Yukio 三島由紀夫 and Kawabata Yasunari 川端康成 committed suicide, radical students fought bitter battles over New Tōkyō International Airport 新東京国際空港建設, and other intellectuals such as Ōe Kenzaburō 大江健三郎 spoke bitterly of present-day absurdities; many people wondered if the best years of the post-war period had passed.

The Shōwa period thus drew to a close on a rather ambiguous note. Pessimists could look at various of the problems outlined above and offer a negative assessment of the state of Japanese society and politics as the nation moved into the last decade of the 20th century; optimists, pointing to the remarkable story of Japan's recovery from war and defeat and its subsequent economic "miracle," could argue that it contained lessons for the rest of the world in management techniques, fiscal restraint, macroeconomic policy, and simple hard work. Whether given to optimism or pessimism, the Japanese themselves felt a sense of uncertainty at the end of the longest period of their modern history, and saw it as a time to begin a renewed questioning of their country's present state and of its future role within the world community.

Heisei period 平成時代

(1989– ; Heisei *jidai*). The reign of the present emperor, Akihito 天皇明仁, who ascended the throne at the death of his father, Emperor Shōwa 昭和天皇, on 7

January 1989. The era name 元号 Heisei is based on two quotations from the Chinese classics *Shi ji* (*Shih chi*; Book of History) 「史記」 and *Shu jing* (*Shu ching*; Book of Documents) 「書経」 that signify the attainment of peace in heaven and on earth, at home and abroad. It is the first era name to be selected and given official recognition under the Gengō Law 元号法 of 1979.

Politics 政治

Public anger over political corruption in the Liberal Democratic Party (LDP) has continued. The LDP's repeated failure to carry out political reforms 政治改革 led to the breakaway of dissidents who formed the Shinseitō (New Life Party) 新生党 and the Shintō Sakigake (New Party Sakigake) 新党さきがけ in 1993. The 1993 election resulted in an unprecedented defeat for the LDP and an equally unexpected setback for the Japan Socialist Party 日本社会党 (JSP). The electoral defeats suffered by these two political parties marked the end of the 1995 status quo 55年体制. A coalition government was formed in August 1993 under Prime Minister Hosokawa Morihiro 細川護熙 by seven parties, including the JSP, the Nihon Shintō (Japan New Party) 日本新党, the Shinseitō, and the Shintō Sakigake. Hosokawa finally succeeded in passing a political reform package 政治改革法案 in January 1994. The legislation called for a fundamental change in the electoral system of the House of Representatives 衆議院, introducing the single-seat constituency 小選挙区 and proportional representation system 比例代表制.

Selected by the same group of coalition parties, Hata Tsutomu 羽田孜 replaced Hosokawa in April 1994. Almost immediately, however, the JSP and the Shintō Sakigake left that coalition and joined with the LDP to form a new coalition government, with JSP member Murayama Tomiichi 村山富市 as prime minister. The alliance between the LDP and the JSP, which had fought bitterly throughout the many years of the 1955 status quo, surprised not only the public but the politicians involved as well.

In December 1994, six opposition parties that had been represented in the Hosokawa cabinet joined together to form the Shinshintō 新進党 (New Frontier Party).

Fearing increasing irrelevancy as politics focused on the rivalry between the two large conservative parties (LDP and Shinshintō), in late 1995 the JSP tried to rally other non-conservative forces to join it in forming a new party. Although it failed in this effort, it changed its name to the Social Democratic Party 社会民主党 (SDP) in January 1996. In September 1996 a large number of younger Diet members from the Shintō Sakigake and the SDP left their parties to establish the Minshutō 民主党 (Democratic Party).

In the 1996 general election the Shinshintō failed to gain political power, and the party was ultimately disbanded in December 1997. This resulted in the formation of the new Jiyūtō (Liberal Party) 自由党, and in November 1998 the Jiyūtō reached an agreement with the LDP to form a coalition government under LDP prime minister Obuchi Keizō 小渕恵三.

Economy 経済

Japan's so-called "bubble economy" バブル経済 began in 1986, and, following a plunge in stock values, burst in the early 1990s. By 1993, the price of land in Tōkyō had fallen 50 percent from its 1990 speculative peak, and the average closing price of the Nikkei stock market index 日経平均株価指数 in 1993 was less than half that recorded at the end of 1989.

Isolated signs of recovery were evident in the spring of 1993, but these were short-lived and did not extend to the economy as a whole, which remained sluggish. The yen showed a marked increase in strength beginning in the summer of 1993 and exceeded ¥90 per U.S. dollar in March 1995. The rise of the yen 円高 was a strong blow to the Japanese economy. Industry, already stagnant at the time, was soon forced to undertake large-scale restructuring リストラ and many companies made unprecedented personnel reductions. Observers warned of a possible hollowing-out of industry 産業の空洞化, as one major manufacturer after another moved its manufacturing operations overseas. Finally, financial institutions continued to labor under a heavy burden of bad debts 不良債権 taken on during the bubble economy.

In 1996 the government decided to use tax money to finance the liquidation of seven housing loan companies (*jūsen* 住専) which had failed due to bad debt. The bankruptcies of the Hokkaidō Takushoku Bank 北海道拓殖銀行 and Yamaichi Securities 山一證券 and the temporary nationalization of the Long-Term Credit Bank of Japan 日本長期信用銀行 and the Nippon Credit Bank 日本債券信用銀行 have both justified and spurred fears over the state of the financial system as the overall economy continues to retrench. In 1998 the government was still trying to come up with a coherent policy for helping financial institutions deal with their bad debt.

The extended stagnation of the economy is evidence both of problems in the structure of Japan's 50-year-old postwar economic system and of an increasing inability to respond flexibly to internal and external changes. In order to promote economic recovery and facilitate growth in the 21st century, the government is trying to reform administrative practices, deregulate the economy, and liberalize the financial system (Japanese Big Bang 日本版ビッグバン).

Society 社会

Japan observed the fiftieth anniversary of the end of World War II on August 15, 1995. In various public opinion polls on Japan's postwar achievements, citizens expressed their overall satisfaction with the country's economic growth, high standard of living, and successful maintenance of peace.

On the other hand, society has recently begun to grapple with such new problems as a lower birth rate 出生率 and a rapidly aging population 高齢化.

In January 1995, the Great Hanshin Awaji Earthquake 阪神・淡路大震災—with its magnitude of 7.2 and epicenter 震源地 in the northern tip of the island of Awajishima—destroyed much of the Hanshin area, including a substantial portion of the city of Kōbe, leaving a total of 6,430 dead and 43,773 injured. This was the largest natural disaster in Japan's post-war history.

In March 1995, the deadly nerve gas sarin was released into Tōkyō's subways in an attack perpetrated by members of the new religion Aum Shinrikyō オウム真理教 (Subway Sarin Gas Incident 地下鉄サリン事件). Japan's first experience with an attack against society-at-large by a cult organization sent deep shock waves through a public already reeling from the destructiveness of the Hanshin earthquake.

Japan has continued its slow but steady efforts to achieve greater diversity in its social fabric and shoulder international responsibility consistent with its economic power. In 1992, the Diet enacted the Law on Cooperation in United Nations Peacekeeping Operations 国連平和維持活動協力法 (PKO), and Japanese Self Defense Forces 自衛隊 personnel were sent to Cambodia in October of that year. Japan's ODA 政府開発援助 was US $9.4 billion in 1996.

GOVERNMENT and DIPLOMACY

Constitution of Japan (Nihonkoku Kempō)
日本国憲法

The Constitution of Japan, successor to the Constitution of the Empire of Japan 大日本帝国憲法 (1889; also known as the Meiji Constitution 明治憲法), became effective on 3 May 1947. Consisting of 11 chapters with a total of 103 articles, it is notable for its declaration that sovereignty resides with the people 国民主権, its assertion of fundamental human rights 基本的人権の尊重, and its renunciation of war and arms 戦争と軍備の放棄. A thoroughly democratic document, it revolutionized the political system, which under the Meiji Constitution had been based on the principle that sovereignty resided with the emperor. For the text of the Constitution, see Appendix.

Enactment 制定

The Japanese surrender in World War II took the form of acceptance of the terms of the Potsdam Declaration ポツダム宣言, which called for the removal of obstacles to democratic tendencies and the establishment of a peace-loving government in accordance with the freely expressed will of the Japanese people. In October 1945 Prime Minister Shidehara Kijūrō 幣原喜重郎 appointed Matsumoto Jōji 松本烝治 (legal scholar and minister of state 国務大臣) to head a committee to investigate the question of constitutional revision. The following February the staff of US General Douglas MacArthur ダグラス=マッカーサー, the supreme commander for the Allied powers (SCAP) 連合国最高司令官, became convinced that the Matsumoto committee was incapable of adequately democratizing the constitution and that the Far Eastern Commission 極東委員会 (representing the Allied powers) might soon intervene in the matter. MacArthur directed his Government Section 民政局

to formulate a model constitution for Japan. The Government Section's hastily drafted constitution was based in part on a policy paper of the American State-War-Navy Coordinating Committee (SWNCC) スウィンク(国務・陸軍・海軍三省調整委員会). On 13 February 1946 Government Section officials delivered their draft to the Japanese cabinet.

After difficult negotiations the SCAP and Japanese officials agreed on a draft constitution 憲法草案 based on the SCAP model. On 6 March 1946 the Shidehara cabinet published the text as its own handiwork.

To ensure legal continuity with the imperial constitution, the proposed new constitution was passed in the form of a constitutional amendment almost unanimously by both houses of the Imperial Diet 帝国議会, and on 3 November 1946 it was promulgated 公布 by the emperor, to become effective 施行 3 May 1947.

Provisions 条項

The Emperor 天皇 Chapter 1, article 1, 第1章第1条 of the Constitution of Japan declares that "the Emperor shall be the symbol of the State 日本国の象徴 and of the unity of the people, deriving his position from the will of the people with whom resides sovereign power." All acts of the emperor in matters of state require the advice and approval of the cabinet, and the emperor has no "powers related to government." The emperor appoints as prime minister the person selected by the Diet and appoints as chief judge of the Supreme Court 最高裁判所 the appointee of the cabinet.

Renunciation of War 戦争の放棄 The most famous provision of the Constitution is article 9, 第9条 which states that the Japanese people "forever renounce war" and that "land, sea, and air forces as well as other war potential will never be maintained." See RENUNCIATION OF WAR.

Rights and Duties of the People 国民の権利及び義務
The Constitution of Japan enumerates the rights and duties of the people, such as freedom of speech 言論の自由. Discrimination "in political, economic or social relations because of race, creed, sex, social status or family origin" is forbidden. The people have the right to maintain "minimum standards of wholesome and cultured living ," and the state is expected to promote social welfare and security 社会福祉：社会保障 and public health 公衆衛生. The right to own property is declared inviolable.

Parliamentary–Cabinet System 議院内閣制 The majority of the Ministers of State 国務大臣 must be chosen from among the members of the Diet. If the House of Representatives 衆議院 (lower house) passes a resolution of no confidence 不信任決議 in the cabinet, the cabinet must resign 総辞職 or the lower house must be dissolved 解散 within 10 days. Thus the new constitution established the parliamentary-cabinet system of democracy. The two houses of the Diet designate the prime minister, but if the two houses are unable to agree, the choice of the lower house prevails. The defeat of a bill by the House of Councillors 参議院 (upper house) may be overridden by a two-thirds majority vote of the lower house, except that a lower-house simple majority may prevail where the budget 予算, a treaty 条約, or the designation of the prime minister is involved.

The Courts 裁判所 The judiciary is described in chapter 6 of the Constitution. The Japanese Supreme Court 最高裁判所 is the court of last resort 終審裁判所 with power to determine the constitutionality 合憲性 of legislation and government acts.

The New Constitution in Practice 新憲法の運用

Shortly before and after the new constitution became effective, the Diet passed 45 laws to implement its provisions. This legislation included the new Imperial Household Law 皇室典範, the Cabinet Law 内閣法,

the Diet Law 国会法, the Local Autonomy Law 地方自治法, electoral laws 選挙法, and amendments to the Civil Code 民法 and the Code of Civil Procedure 民事訴訟法.

Over the years, the constitutionality of the Self Defense Forces 自衛隊 has been frequently challenged in the courts, but the Supreme Court has avoided ruling definitively on this issue. Although conservatives have advocated amendments that would clarify the right to maintain military forces, the Japanese people have thus far not altered a word of their democratic constitution.

Renunciation of war (*sensō no hōki*) 戦争の放棄

Doctrine arising out of article 9 第9条, the most famous and most controversial article, of the Constitution of Japan 日本国憲法 (1947). Article 9 reads as follows:

"Aspiring sincerely to an international peace based on justice and order, the Japanese people forever renounce war as a sovereign right of the nation and the threat or use of force as a means of settling international disputes 国際紛争."

"In order to accomplish the aim of the preceding paragraph, land, sea, and air forces, as well as other war potential, will never be maintained. The right of belligerency of the state 国の交戦権 will not be recognized."

The San Francisco Peace Treaty サンフランシスコ平和条約 of 1951 specifically stated that the Allied powers 連合国 "recognize that Japan as a sovereign nation possesses the inherent right of individual or collective self-defense." With that provision as the basis, the Diet in 1954 passed a law creating the Self Defense Forces (SDF) 自衛隊. The twin questions of the development of the SDF and the possible violation of article 9 have been highly controversial issues in Japanese politics.

The Supreme Court 最高裁判所 of Japan has not dealt directly with the constitutionality of the SDF, only on the constitutionality of the United States-Japan security treaties 日米安全保障条約 that permit US military bases 米軍基地 in Japan. The court has refused to declare such bases unconstitutional, arguing that matters relating to national security 国家安全保障 are by their nature political and must therefore be decided by the sovereign people, who can express political judgments on security matters by exercising their suffrage in free elections.

Democracy (*minshu shugi*) 民主主義

Japan has a functioning democratic system, that is, a system in which sovereignty resides in the people 主権在民, who exercise it through elected representatives and who are guaranteed the civil liberties essential to its exercise.

History 歴史

Japan's democratic tradition stretches back to the early Meiji period 明治時代 (1868–1912). In the 1870s dissatisfied former *samurai* and landowners who were not represented in the new government launched a movement for representative institutions, or "popular rights 民権." Led by such people as Itagaki Taisuke 板垣退助 (1837–1919), they formed several political parties 政党. Ideologically, Itagaki and his followers were influenced by the ideals of French radicalism, while Ōkuma Shigenobu 大隈重信 (1839–1922), based his platform on the ideas of English liberalism and parliamentary government 議会政治.

In 1889 the Japanese government adopted a constitution that permitted a weak House of Representatives 衆議院 and a limited franchise. Political parties gradually became accepted in government after the first party cabinet 政党内閣 was formed in 1898, reaching a peak of power during the Taishō period 大正時代 (1912–26).

The end of World War I 第1次世界大戦, with the apparent victory of democracy in the West and of Marxism in Russia, coupled with a postwar recession in

Japan, stimulated a movement for social, economic, and political reform in Japan among many students, writers, intellectuals, journalists, politicians, and labor leaders. They called for reforms ranging from the introduction of socialism and Marxism and the formation of labor unions 労働組合 to the development of true liberal democracy. The Sōdōmei (Japan Federation of Labor 日本労働総同盟) was formed in 1919 and a communist and several socialist parties 社会主義政党 were formed in the 1920s.

The Japanese government responded to demands for reform with a series of both conciliatory and repressive acts. Some progressive factory and labor laws were adopted and the Universal Manhood Suffrage Law 普通選挙法 was passed in May 1925, but these acts were coupled with the repressive Peace Preservation Law 治安維持法 of 1925 and a series of police raids that destroyed many left-wing groups 左翼団体 or drove them underground by the early 1930s.

From 1930 on army and navy officers involved themselves in a series of incidents that indicated their ability to intervene in civilian affairs. Key events included the Manchurian Incident 満州事変 in 1931, the assassination of Prime Minister Inukai Tsuyoshi 犬養 毅 (1855–1932) in 1932 (May 15th Incident 5・15事件), and a full-fledged military insurrection in 1936 (February 26th Incident 2・26事件). Political parties lost their power and prestige and the military held sway over Japan politically, economically, and socially until the end of World War II.

Postwar Development 第2次世界大戦後の発達

Japan's present democratic system centers on the primary authority of a bicameral Diet 2院国会 (parliament) of representatives elected by the people. Executive power 行政権 is exercised by a prime minister 総理大臣 (chosen by the Diet) and by a cabinet he appoints. Judicial power 行政権 resides in the Supreme Court 最高裁判所 and lower courts 下級裁判所. Popular control over local government 地方政治 is exercised through a system of local and prefectural assemblies 県議会 and executives elected by the people. A system of checks and balances distributes power among the executive, legislative, and judicial branches and assures the people of a voice in government.

However, public confidence in democracy has been severely tested in postwar Japan. A series of scandals from the 1970s to 1990s, including the Lockheed Scandal ロッキード事件 and the Recruit Scandal リクルート事件, and other corrupt practices have occasioned a certain amount of disillusionment and discontent with the actual workings of Japan's political system.

The infrequency with which elected legislative bodies initiate legislation has also been a problem. Representation rarely means the introduction of bills, since at all levels of government most bills are introduced by the executive branch after limited consultation with parties and interest groups 利益団体. The subsequent process of negotiating a consensus occurs behind closed doors, and even the legislative committee "hearings" 公聴会 are not really open either to the public or to interest groups. A predictable consequence of this situation has been a general loss of public confidence in government and increasing feelings of apathy and detachment from the political process. Politicians have sensed this trend and responded to public demands for more democratic practices. Evidence of this can be found in the 1994 election district system 選挙区制度 reform; the first significant change since 1945 (see POLITICAL REFORMS OF 1994).

EMPEROR 天皇

Emperor (*tennō*) 天皇

The title *tennō* was first assumed by Japanese rulers in the 6th or 7th century and has been used by all

Dates of the First 28 Sovereigns according to the *Nihon Shoki*
「日本書紀」の天皇 (第1代〜28代)

Number in the traditional count	Sovereign	Reign dates
1	Jimmu	660 BC–585 BC
2	Suizei	581 BC–549 BC
3	Annei	549 BC–511 BC
4	Itoku	510 BC–477 BC
5	Kōshō	475 BC–393 BC
6	Kōan	392 BC–291 BC
7	Kōrei	290 BC–215 BC
8	Kōgen	214 BC–158 BC
9	Kaika	158 BC– 98 BC
10	Sujin	97 BC– 30 BC
11	Suinin	29 BC– AD 70
12	Keikō	71–130
13	Seimu	131–190
14	Chūai	192–200
15	Ōjin	270–310
16	Nintoku	313–399
17	Richū	400–405
18	Hanzei	406–410
19	Ingyō	412–453
20	Ankō	453–456
21	Yūryaku	456–479
22	Seinei	480–484
23	Kenzō	485–487
24	Ninken	488–498
25	Buretsu	498–506
26	Keitai	507–531
27	Ankan	531(4)–535
28	Senka	535–539

Note: The first 14 sovereigns are considered legendary.

subsequent Japanese sovereigns 君主.

Japan's imperial institution, the oldest hereditary monarchy 世襲君主制 in the world, was already in existence when Japan emerged into recorded history and has since been perpetuated in a predominantly male line of descent, though there has been female *tennō* 女帝. Although the emperor has almost always been regarded as the titular head of the national government, the most striking feature of the office through most of Japanese history has been the tendency to emphasize instead the emperor's role as chief priest in the indigenous Japanese religion, Shintō 神道, and to delegate most of the effective powers of government to others.

From Early Historical Times to the Mid-12th Century
古代から12世紀中頃まで

The emperor figures centrally in a mythology preserved in the historical chronicles *Kojiki* (712, Record of Ancient Matters) 「古事記」 and *Nihon shoki* (720, Chronicle of Japan) 「日本書紀」. According to these, the sun goddess 太陽神 Amaterasu Ōmikami 天照大神, chief divinity of the Shintō pantheon, bequeathed to her grandson Ninigi no Mikoto 瓊瓊杵尊 a mirror, jewels, and a sword (imperial regalia 三種の神器), which he in turn passed on to his descendants, the emperors of Japan, the first of whom was the emperor Jimmu 神武天皇.

The emperor was thought to possess magical powers to propitiate or intercede with divinities. But because of the awe surrounding his person, it was also considered inappropriate for the emperor to concern himself with the secular business of government. That business, including both the making and execution of policies, belonged to ministers serving the emperor, and there was a tendency from very early historical times for those ministers to form political dynasties of their own.

The only extended period of Japanese history in which the emperor combined the roles of both high priest and functioning head of government was from the reign of Tenji 天智天皇 (r 661–672; enthroned in 668), in the latter half of the 7th century, through the reign of Kammu 桓武天皇 (r 781–806) at the end of the 8th century and the beginning of the 9th. It was Tenji who, in the Taika Reform 大化の改新 of 645, made the first major attempt to bring the powerful provincial clans (*uji* 氏) under the control of a strong central regime.

This period of direct imperial rule was characterized by the effort to establish a centralized bureaucratic state in Japan patterned on the example offered by Tang dynasty 唐朝 China. The key instrument in this process was the adoption of law codes, known collectively as the *ritsuryō* (legal codes) system 律令制度, that established an elaborate hierarchy of offices headed by the emperor.

However, in the 9th century several efforts to personalize imperial rule by freeing it from the entrenched bureaucracy backfired, beginning a process in which the emperor was increasingly isolated from the machinery of government. This tendency was exacerbated by the creation or revival of *sesshō* (imperial regent for a minor emperor) 摂政 and *kampaku* (imperial regent for an adult emperor) 関白. From

Reigning and Retired Emperors under the *Insei* System
院政下における天皇と上皇

Reigning emperor	Reign dates	Retired emperor
Go-Sanjō	1068–1073	–
Shirakawa	1073–1087	–
Horikawa	1087–1107	Shirakawa
Toba	1107–1123	Shirakawa
Sutoku	1123–1129	Shirakawa
Sutoku	1129–1142	Toba
Konoe	1142–1155	Toba
Go-Shirakawa	1155–1156	Toba
Go-Shirakawa	1156–1158	–
Nijō	1158–1165	Go-Shirakawa
Rokujō	1165–1168	Go-Shirakawa
Takakura	1168–1180	Go-Shirakawa
Antoku	1180–1181	Takakura
Antoku	1181–1185	Go-Shirakawa
Go-Toba	1183–1192	Go-Shirakawa
Go-Toba	1192–1198	–

Source: Adapted from George Sansom, *A History of Japan to 1334* (1958).

the late 9th century onward, both posts were dominated by members of the powerful Fujiwara family 藤原氏, who ruled in the emperor's name (regency government 摂関政治).

The last century of the Heian period 平安時代 (794–1185) saw a waning of the power of the Fujiwara regents and a brief return of power to the imperial house. The leading figures through most of this period, however, were not reigning emperors but retired sovereigns 上皇.

Medieval Period (mid-12th–16th centuries)
中世(12世紀中頃～16世紀)

Three more families, again nonimperial, held sway over the national government and the imperial institution from the closing years of the Heian period to the end of the Kamakura period 鎌倉時代 (1185–1333), ushering in the age of warrior rule 武家政権時代 that was to last until the Meiji Restoration 明治維新 of 1868.

The first of these, the Taira family 平氏, ruled from Kyōto and legitimated themselves by occupying high offices within the imperial court. The second, the Minamoto family 源氏, destroyed the Taira in 1185 and established the Kamakura shogunate 鎌倉幕府. The emperor remained in Kyōto and continued to preside over the imperial government, but these institutions were now reduced to almost complete impotence, real power devolving on the shogunate. Imperial legitimation for this situation took the form of the naming of the head of the Minamoto family to the office of *seii tai shōgun* 征夷大将軍.

The third family to dominate the national government in this period was the Hōjō family 北条氏, whose members ruled from 1203 as shogunal regents 執権. This initiated a complex and many-tiered delegation of power. The emperor in Kyōto reigned, but the imperial government was controlled by a Fujiwara regent 摂政. The effective national government was in Kamakura, nominally headed by a *shōgun* 将軍, but in fact controlled by the Hōjō regent. To complicate matters further, from the mid-13th century the shogunate began to interfere actively in the imperial succession 皇位継承, creating schisms within the imperial house that further decreased its power.

A clean sweep of this meaningless institutional complexity was undertaken by Emperor Go-Daigo 後醍醐天皇 (r 1318–1339), who in 1333 became head of a reinvigorated imperial government (Kemmu Restoration 建武の中興［新政］). This revival of imperial authority was, however, pathetically brief. In 1336 Ashikaga Takauji 足利尊氏 (1305–1358) deposed him, and set up in his place a puppet from a different branch of the imperial house, the Northern Court 北朝. The latter then appointed Takauji *shōgun*, initiating the 240-year Muromachi shogunate 室町幕府.

Go-Daigo established a rival court, the Southern Court 南朝, that maintained a precarious existence until 1392, when the rivalry between the two Courts was finally resolved by the third Muromachi *shōgun*, Ashikaga Yoshimitsu 足利義満 (1358–1408). The material circumstances of the imperial house reached their nadir in the course of the Muromachi period 室町時代 (1333–1568) and the Imperial Palace was destroyed in the Ōnin War 応仁の乱 (1466–1477).

Early Modern Period (mid-16th–mid-19th centuries) 近世 (16世紀中頃～19世紀中頃)

The restoration of the court's fortunes awaited the reunification of Japan, accomplished between 1568 and 1603 by three men, Oda Nobunaga 織田信長 (1534–1582), Toyotomi Hideyoshi 豊臣秀吉 (1537–1598), and Tokugawa Ieyasu 徳川家康 (1543–1616)—each of whom derived sanction for his rule from the imperial institution. After the collapse of rule by Nobunaga and

Hideyoshi, Ieyasu followed long precedent in having himself named *seii tai shōgun* 征夷大将軍 in 1603, commencing more than 250 years of rule by the Tokugawa shogunate 徳川幕府.

The shogunate devoted great attention to the maintenance and control of the imperial institution. The Imperial Palace 皇居 was restored to its former grandeur and in the surrounding area residences for the entire court nobility (*kuge* 公家) were provided. Income from designated lands was earmarked for the imperial treasury. Yet at the same time rigorous restraints on the freedom of the imperial family and court nobility were drawn up in the Laws Governing the Imperial Court and Nobility 禁中並公家諸法度.

Quite apart from this, however, the imperial institution came to play a new symbolic role in Japanese political thought, constructed in the course of the Edo period 江戸時代 (1600–1868) by writers and thinkers known as *kinnōka*, or "imperial loyalists." 勤皇家 Their stress on the centrality of the imperial house within the Japanese polity proved to be an explosive concept in the mid-19th century, when it combined with the crisis touched off by Western pressure to "open" Japan 開国 to foreign trade and diplomacy. The result was a political movement aimed at fending off the foreign threat, abolishing the shogunate, and replacing it with a new national government under direct imperial rule (*sonnō jōi* ; Revere the Emperor, Expel the Barbarians 尊皇攘夷). This upsurge of imperial loyalism proved a key factor in the toppling of the Tokugawa regime 徳川政権 and the initiation of the Meiji Restoration 明治維新 of 1868.

Modern Period (1868–1945) 近現代(1868年〜1945年)

The leaders of Meiji Japan engaged in 20 years of pragmatic political experimentation to redefine the imperial institution. With the proclamation of the Constitution of the Empire of Japan 大日本帝国憲法 on 11

February 1889, the emperor became a constitutional monarch 立憲君主 in a centralized and unitary state that was to exercise greater political power than any previous form of government in Japan's history.

According to the constitution, the emperor was "sacred and inviolable," 「神聖ニシテ侵スヘカラス」and sovereignty 主権 rested with him as the head of the Japanese empire.

Paradoxically, however, the supreme authority 大権 accorded the emperor in the constitution, and the other efforts made to bolster his centrality to the Japanese polity, were not accompanied by real political power. In fact, the system was designed instead to preserve the emperor's political immunity 政治的免責 while he served as the sacrosanct basis for rule by others, namely, the ministers of state and the chiefs of the armed forces.

Contemporary Monarchy (1945–)
現在の天皇制(1945年以降)

Japan's defeat in World War II 第2次世界大戦 and the subsequent Allied Occupation 連合国占領 wrought momentous changes in the imperial institution and its place in Japanese politics and society. The 1947 CONSTITUTION OF JAPAN 日本国憲法 retained the emperor, though in a drastically altered relation to the state and made the emperor "the symbol of the State 日本国の象徴 and of the unity of the people, deriving his position from the will of the people with whom resides sovereign power." He was to have no political powers. All acts by the emperor in matters of state were reduced to merely formal and ceremonial functions, requiring the advice and approval of the cabinet. Emperor Shōwa 昭和天皇 (Hirohito, r 1926–1989) himself declared on New Year's Day 1946 that he was "not divine"(renunciation of divinity by emperor 天皇人間宣言). Thus the prewar Japanese state with its theory of imperial prerogative was thoroughly dismantled.

Along with these fundamental changes in the legal and institutional relationship of the emperor to the political system, efforts were made to "popularize" the imperial family as the nation's first family. The vast majority of Japanese citizens favor the status quo. This was confirmed when, in January 1989, Emperor Akihito 天皇明仁 (r 1989–) became the first emperor to succeed to the throne under the present constitution. Despite dissenting voices, it seems clear that the consensus in Japan continues to support the retention of the imperial house, within a carefully defined legal framework.

Emperor Akihito 天皇明仁

The present emperor and the 125th sovereign (*tennō*) in the traditional count (which includes several legendary emperors). Born in 1933 as the eldest son of Emperor Shōwa 昭和天皇 (1901–1989) and Empress Nagako 皇后良子 (1903–), the present empress dowager 皇太后. From 1946 to 1950 he was privately tutored in the English language and Western culture by Elizabeth Gray Vining エリザベス=バイニング女史, an American teacher known for her authorship of children's books. In 1952 he entered the Department of Politics at Gakushūin University 学習院大学, and in November of that year the Ceremony of Coming-of-Age 成年式 and the Ceremony of Investiture 立太式 were conducted. While still a college student, he left Japan in the spring of 1953 for a state visit 公式訪問 to the United Kingdom to act as his father's representative at the coronation 戴冠式 of Queen Elizabeth II エリザベス女王. On his tour, he visited 13 countries in Europe and North America before returning to Japan in October. He completed his course of studies at Gakushūin University in March 1956.

In April 1959 Crown Prince 皇太子 Akihito married Shōda Michiko 正田美智子, eldest daughter of Shōda Hidesaburō 正田英三郎, then president of the Nisshin Flour Milling Co., Ltd. 日清製粉株式会社, breaking with the long-established tradition that the wife of the crown prince should be chosen from among the ranks of the imperial family 皇族 or the former peerage 旧華族.

While still crown prince, Akihito represented Emperor Shōwa on a number of state visits overseas, visiting 37 countries in the course of 22 separate trips. He also served as the honorary president of Universiade 1967 ユニバーシアード大会 in Tōkyō and of Expo '70 万国博覧会 in Ōsaka. During Emperor Shōwa's tour of Europe in September 1971 and his tour of the United States in 1975, Crown Prince Akihito conducted affairs of state 国事行為 in his absence. In 1975 he was the first member of the imperial family to officially visit Okinawa after its reversion to Japan in 1972.

On 7 January 1989 he became Emperor Akihito, succeeding to the throne after his father's death. The following day he adopted the formal reign title 元号 Heisei ("Establishing Peace").

Like his father, Emperor Akihito is known as a scholar of marine biology and ichthyology 海洋生物学 and for his research into the fishes of the family Gobiidae. He also enjoys sports and is a lover of music, playing cello in impromptu performances with other members of the royal family. He and Empress Michiko have three children: Crown Prince Naruhito 皇太子徳仁親王, Prince Akishino 秋篠宮文仁親王, and Princess Sayako 紀宮清子内親王.

Empress Michiko 皇后美智子

Wife of emperor Akihito. Born in 1934 as the eldest daughter of Shōda Hidesaburō 正田英三郎, the president of the Nisshin Flour Milling Co., Ltd. 日清製粉株式会社, and his wife Fumiko 富美子. She is a graduate of the University of the Sacred Heart 聖心女子大学 in Tōkyō. In April 1959 she married then crown prince Akihito 皇太子明仁親王. As the first imperial bride to be selected from outside the circle of the imperial family 皇族 and the former peerage 旧華族, her marriage to Crown Prince

Akihito was broadly welcomed by the Japanese people as a symbol of the democratization of the imperial house. On 7 January 1989 she became empress upon her husband's ascension to the throne 即位 as Emperor Akihito. Empress Michiko maintains a lively interest in literature, arts , and music and serves as honorary president of the Japan Red Cross Society 日本赤十字社.

Crown Prince Naruhito 皇太子徳仁親王

Princely title Hiro no Miya 浩宮. Born in 1960 as the eldest son of EMPEROR AKIHITO and EMPRESS MICHIKO. The crown prince graduated from Gakushūin University 学習院大学 in 1982 and completed his initial coursework for the doctorate in history there in 1988. From 1983 to 1985 he studied at Merton College, Oxford University オックスフォード大学メルトンカレッジ, where he conducted research into the sea trade routes and port cities of medieval Europe. He celebrated the Ceremony of Investiture 立太式 on 23 February 1991. In June 1993 Crown Prince Naruhito married Owada Masako 小和田雅子 (b 1963).

Imperial Palace (Kōkyo) 皇居

Official residence of the emperor. Situated in Chiyoda Ward 千代田区, Tōkyō, occupying 1.15 square kilometers (0.44 sq mi). Japanese emperors and their families have resided here since after the Meiji Restoration 明治維新 of 1868, when Edo Castle 江戸城 was designated the official imperial residence (before the Meiji Restoration, emperors resided in Kyōto). A new palace was completed in 1888, but this was destroyed in air raids 空襲 in 1945. The present palace complex, the Kyūden 宮殿, was completed in 1968. Its individual buildings include the Omote Gozasho 表御座所, the emperor's office for affairs of state; the Seiden 正殿, for official ceremonies; the Hōmeiden 豊明殿, for banquets entertaining guests of state 国賓; and the Chōwaden 長和殿, for evening receptions. These buildings are connected by corridors surrounding a large central court-yard. To the northwest is the Fukiage Gosho 吹上御所, formerly the private residence of Emperor Shōwa, now occupied by his widow. A new palace 新御所 residence for EMPEROR AKIHITO was completed in May 1993. Higashi Gyoen 東御苑, part of the palace grounds, is open to the public.

National anthem (*kokka*) 国歌

The de facto Japanese national anthem is "Kimigayo" (His Majesty's Reign)「君が代」. Basil H. Chamberlain バジル=H=チェンバレン (1850–1935), author of *Things Japanese*「日本事物誌」(1890), translated the anthem as follows:

Kimi ga yo wa	君が代は
Chiyo ni yachiyo ni	千代に八千代に
Sazare ishi no	さざれ石の
Iwao to nari te	巌となりて
Koke no musu made :	苔のむすまで

Thousands of years of happy reign be thine
Rule on, my lord, till what are pebbles now
By age united to mighty rocks shall grow
Whose venerable sides the moss doth line

The words of the song are from the 10th-century anthology *Kokin wakashū*「古今和歌集」. The author is unknown. The tune was composed by Hayashi Hiromori 林広守 (1831–96) in 1880. In 1893 the Ministry of Education 文部省 made it the ceremonial song to be sung in elementary schools on national holidays. Soon it was sung at state cer-emonies and sports events. Although popularly identified as the national anthem for many years, "Kimigayo" has never been officially adopted as such.

"Kimigayo"
「君が代」

Words: Anonymous
Music: Hayashi Hiromori

♩ = 69

ki mi ga - yo - wa chi yo ni - - ya chi yo ni

sa za re i shi no i wa o to na ri te

ko ke no mu - su - ma - - de

National flag (*kokki*) 国旗

Hinomaru
日の丸

The national flag of Japan has a crimson disc, symbolizing the sun, in the center of a white field. It is popularly known as the Hinomaru (literally, "sun disc") 日の丸. The Tokugawa shogunate 徳川幕府 (1603–1867) adopted the flag for its ships in the early 1600s. In the mid-19th century the shogunate decreed that all Japanese ships fly flags with the sun on a white field. In 1870 the Meiji government 明治政府 officially designated it for use on Japanese merchant and naval ships and fixed the design. The vertical to horizontal ratio was set at 2:3, the disk was to be placed at the exact center, and the diameter of the disk was to equal three-fifths of the vertical measurement of the flag. It has never been officially designated as the national flag; however, it has become so by customary use.

MAJOR COMPONENTS OF THE GOVERNMENT
立法・行政・司法

Diet (Kokkai) 国会

The legislative branch 立法機関 of the Japanese government. According to the CONSTITUTION OF JAPAN 日本国憲法, the Diet is "the highest organ of state power 国権" and the "sole law-making organ of the State 立法機関." The Diet consists of two chambers: the House of Representatives 衆議院, or lower house, and the House of Councillors 参議院, or upper house. All Diet members are selected in popular elections 普通選挙.

History 歴史

The Imperial Diet 帝国議会, the direct predecessor of the present Diet, was established in 1890 through provisions in the Constitution of the Empire of Japan 大日本帝国憲法 (1889) and consisted of a House of Peers 貴族院 and a House of Representatives. Constitutionally, the Imperial Diet was weak, primarily because the power of legislation 立法権 was vested in the emperor and because the cabinet was responsible to the emperor rather than to the Diet. Initially, the House of Representatives reflected the opinions of a highly restricted segment of the public, representing only the 1.5 percent of the population who paid an annual tax of ¥15 or more. Not until the passage of the Universal Manhood Suffrage Law 普通選挙法 in 1925 did all male citizens over the age of 25 obtain the right to vote for the House of Representatives and thus the possibility of influencing their legislative representatives.

During the Taishō period 大正時代 (1912–1926), substantial changes occurred in Japan's body politic, including its national assembly: Sovereignty might be constitutionally vested in the emperor, but legislative power was exercised by him and his advisers with the consent of the Diet. Members formally organized themselves into parliamentary parties and articulated alternative policies that were covered by the newspapers and thus helped shape public attitudes.

Possibly the best indication of the Diet's growing powers in the 1920s was the energy that its opponents devoted to circumscribing them. Members were accused of being the corrupt tools of vested corporate interests and incapable of protecting the "national polity" 国体. Terrorist groups plotted assassinations, some of which were successful. By the end of the 1930s, parliamentarianism was a flame that flickered uncertainly. Parliamentary parties were forced to serve the interests of the nation's predominantly military rulers. The Diet became a rubber stamp, but those in power did not take the final step of abolishing it altogether.

The transformation of the Imperial Diet into the present Diet 国会 was set forth initially in the postwar constitution 日本国憲法 (effective in May 1947). Unlike the previous constitution, the new constitution gave supreme legislative power to the Diet and made it the most important organ of the government.

Organization 組織

Bicameralism 2院制の was retained at the insistence of Japanese authorities when a model constitution was formulated for Japan, but the hereditary and appointive House of Peers 貴族院 was replaced by the elected House of Councillors 参議院, which consists of 252 members who serve six-year terms.The entire membership of the Diet was to be publicly elected. The prime minister 首相 and a majority of his cabinet ministers were required to be members of the Diet and, "in the exercise of executive power 行政権, shall be collectively responsible to the Diet". The doctrine of parliamentary supremacy had supplanted that of imperial prerogative 天皇大権.

At the same time, the new constitution altered the relationship between the two chambers. The House of Representatives and the House of Councillors share legislative power 立法権: "A bill becomes a law on passage by both Houses..." However, the 500 representatives of the lower house, whose term of office is four years unless the house is dissolved, have authority in three important areas. First, in the designation of the prime minister, if there is disagreement between the two chambers, "the decision of the House of Representatives shall be the decision of the Diet." Second, the national budget 国家予算 must first be submitted to the House of Representatives. Furthermore, if the two houses fail to reach agreement on the budget, and if joint committees 両院協議会 fail to resolve the matter or no decision is made by the House of Councillors within 30 days, the will of the lower house prevails. Third, while international treaties 国際条約 may first be introduced for approval in either chamber, the decision of the lower house prevails over a contrary judgment by the upper house if joint committees fail to resolve the matter or no decision is made by the House of Councillors within 30 days. Also, in all fields of legislation, the House of Representatives can override the House of Councillors by a two-thirds vote. Thus the Diet is bicameral 2院制, but the House of Representatives is predominant in certain crucial spheres.

The Workings of the Diet 国会の活動

A Diet session convening after an election for the House of Representatives or House of Councillors entails the following sequence of five events. First, the presiding officers are elected. Normally, each party nominates its own candidates, with those of the majority party being elected.

Second, the prime minister is elected. When a single party is unable to obtain an absolute majority in both chambers, two or more parties agree to a coalition 連立 to support the election of a prime minister. See PRIME MINISTER AND CABINET.

Third, the emperor appears at an opening ceremony to read an imperial edict 詔書 formally convening the Diet.

Fourth, the prime minister and selected members of his cabinet—normally including at least the minister of finance 大蔵大臣 and minister of foreign affairs 外務大臣—read their statements of basic policy 施政方針 to each of the chambers.

Fifth, each of the parliamentary parties states its own legislative program. Challenge and response occurs frequently at meetings of the Budget Committee 予算委員会 or of a subject-matter committee that is conducting hearings on a particular legislative bill or government policy.

Legally, the presiding officers in each chamber have the responsibility and power to "maintain order in the house." They are assisted by a secretary-general 事務総長 who has the dual responsibility of supervising the secretariat of each chamber and acting as its chief parliamentarian.

If an item of legislation is not controversial, the system usually works smoothly. Legislation is drafted mainly by government bureaucrats 官僚 in various ministries.

House of Councillors 参議院

One of the two elective bodies that make up the Diet. Under Japan's post–World War II constitution, the House of Councillors 参議院 replaced the hereditary, appointive House of Peers 貴族院, which had been established under the Meiji Constitution 明治憲法. Although the House of Councillors and the House of Representatives share power, the latter predominates in decisions on legislation, designation of the prime minister, budgetary matters, and international treaties. Every three years, half of the 252 representatives in the House of Councillors are elected by popular vote to a six-year term of office that is not terminated in the event of dissolution of the House of Representatives. One hundred of the seats are filled on a proportional representation system 比例代表制; the remaining 152 seats are filled on a system of prefectural districts 地方選挙区制.

House of Representatives 衆議院

The lower house 下院 of the Diet. According to the provisions of the Constitution of Japan, the House of Representatives and its collective decisions take precedence over the upper house 上院 (the House of Councillors) in the areas of legislation, the budget, treaty ratification, and the selection of the prime minister. The representatives, who have numbered 500 since December 1994, are elected by popular vote. Their term of office is four years, unless the House has been dissolved 解散 before their term has elapsed.

Prime minister and cabinet (*shushō to naikaku*)
首相と内閣

The chief executive officer of the Japanese

government and his cabinet. The cabinet system 内閣制度 was adopted in Japan in 1885 and has continued without interruption until the present. There have, however, been a number of fundamental changes in the powers, functions, and composition of the cabinet, particularly when the prewar cabinet system under the Meiji Constitution 明治憲法 is compared with the postwar cabinet system under the 1947 constitution. In the postwar system the constitution vests supreme executive authority in the cabinet, which is responsible to the legislature 立法府. In the prewar system the cabinet was not responsible to the legislature and the legislature had no power either to select a prime minister or dissolve a cabinet.

The Prewar Cabinet System 第2次世界大戦前の内閣制度

Following the Meiji Restoration 明治維新 (1868), a Grand Council of State 太政官 was established in 1868 as the supreme political authority. This evolved into a central deliberative body consisting of three state ministers who had direct access to the emperor and seven councillors, or *sangi* 参議. *Sangi* often served as heads of the various government ministries as well.

In 1885 the Dajōkan was abolished and replaced by the cabinet system. The prime minister and the various cabinet ministers were made responsible only to the emperor, not to the Diet. Moreover, upon the promulgation of the constitution in 1889, the oligarchs 藩閥政治家 announced their intention to remain aloof from party politics by adhering to the principle of nonparty or "transcendental" cabinets 超然内閣.

For the seven cabinets between 1885 and 1898 the prime ministership was rotated among the oligarchs. As the oligarchs retired from the cabinet affairs they assumed the role of elder statesmen 元老.

The prewar prime minister enjoyed extensive appointment powers, including the appointment of cabinet ministers and vice-ministers, judges, prosecutors, and prefectural governors 知事. Nevertheless, the prime minister was not a strong chief executive but rather had to share the right to advise the throne with the *genrō*, the officers of the imperial household 宮中官, the privy councillors 枢密院顧問官, and the military chiefs of staff 軍参謀総長.

Until the Taishō Political Crisis 大正の政変 of 1912–1913, the oligarchs coordinated the decision-making process behind the scenes through the vehicle of the informal, extraconstitutional *genrō* council and through their position on the Privy Council 枢密院. Following World War I, this single dominant coordinating oligarchy was gradually replaced by a much larger and more diverse set of institutional elites, composed of the parties, the military, the bureaucracy, the peerage 華族, and the court 皇室. Much of the political history of the 1918–1945 period can be viewed as a competition among these institutional elites for control of the government. From the mid-1930s the military dominated the cabinet until Japan's defeat in World War II.

Postwar Changes in the Cabinet System
戦後の内閣制度の変遷

The postwar constitution introduced two major kinds of change in the cabinet system. First, executive power 行政権 was vested solely in the prime minister and his cabinet. All real executive authority was removed from the emperor, and the throne became a purely symbolic and ceremonial institution. The prime minister is now empowered to appoint and remove all cabinet members at his own discretion. Moreover, to ensure civilian control 文民統制 of the military, the Defense Agency 防衛庁 has formally been made a subordinate part of the Prime Minister's Office 総理府.

The second major change was the clear establishment of cabinet responsibility to the elected representatives of the people. The prime minister is elected by the

DIET 国会, and either house of the Diet may adopt a resolution of impeachment 弾劾決議 against any individual cabinet member. Moreover, if the lower house passes a nonconfidence resolution 不信任決議 or rejects a confidence resolution 信任決議, the cabinet must resign en masse within 10 days or dissolve the lower house, call an election, and resign following the opening of the new Diet. Finally, the constitution requires that the prime minister and the majority of all cabinet members be elected members of the Diet.

The Making of the Prime Minister and His Cabinet 首相の誕生と組閣

The prime minister is selected by a majority vote 議決(多数決) in each House of the Diet and is formally appointed by the emperor. If the two Houses disagree on their selection or the upper house fails to act within 10 days after the lower house has voted, the choice of the lower house stands as the decision of the Diet. New official cabinets come into being following the selection of a new prime minister and after each election of the House of Representatives 総選挙. In practice, cabinet posts are reshuffled much more frequently, with virtually annual major reconstructions of the cabinet 内閣改造 in which over half its personnel are changed. The reasons for this frequent turnover are based on factional politics 派閥政治.

Cabinet Powers and Organizations 内閣の権限と組織

The prime minister and his cabinet have important judicial and legislative powers as well as executive responsibilities. In the judicial area they are empowered to select the chief justice 裁判長 and to appoint the other judges of the Supreme Court 最高裁判所 and to appoint lower-court 下級裁判所 judges from a list nominated by the Supreme Court. In the legislative area the cabinet determines the convocation of extraordinary sessions of the Diet 臨時国会, enacts cabinet orders 政令 to execute the provisions of the constitution and Diet laws, and, most important, prepares and submits bills to the Diet. The various cabinet staff offices 内閣官房 and government ministries and agencies 中央省庁 assist the cabinet in the exercise of this extensive concentration of powers.

As of 1999 the cabinet was composed of the prime minister and the heads of the 12 ministries: Justice 法務省; Foreign Affairs 外務省; Finance 大蔵省; Education 文部省; Health and Welfare 厚生省; Agriculture, Forestry, and Fisheries 農林水産省; International Trade and Industry 通商産業省; Transport 運輸省; Posts and Telecommunications 郵政省; Labor 労働省; Construction 建設省; and Home Affairs 自治省. Another 8 ministers of state without portfolios head other important executive offices and agencies such as the Cabinet Secretariat 内閣官房, the Defense Agency 防衛庁, and the Economic Planning Agency 経済企画庁.

Elections (*senkyo seido*) 選挙制度

Japan has had a national election system since the promulgation of the Constitution of the Empire of Japan 大日本帝国憲法 on 11 February 1889. The extension of the franchise, limited at first to a small proportion of the adult male population, took place gradually, culminating in the adoption of universal suffrage 普通選挙 shortly after the end of World War II.

The Prewar System 第2次世界大戦前の制度

The first national election for the House of Representatives 衆議院 took place in 1890, but the right to vote was restricted to males 25 years of age or older who paid annual taxes of ¥15 or more. Over the next three decades the number of enfranchised voters grew from fewer than 500,000 to about 3 million. The Universal Manhood Suffrage Law 普通選挙法 of 1925 expanded the electorate to about 12 million by granting the vote to all male citizens 25 years of age or older, though women were not enfranchised until December 1945.

Before 1945 there were fewer opportunities for popular participation in Japanese government. Members of the House of Representatives were elected, but seats in the House of Peers 貴族院 were either appointive or hereditary. Local government 地方自治体 was directly subordinate to the central government. Local assemblies were popularly elected, but prefectural governors were appointed by the national government. City mayors 市長 were appointed by prefectural governors 都道府県知事 from a list of names submitted by city assemblies. Headmen and mayors of villages and towns were elected by their respective local assemblies.

Current Practices 現在の制度

The election system was given its present form by the Public Office Election Law 公職選挙法 of April 1950. All Japanese citizens are eligible to vote if they have reached the age of 20 and have met a three-month residency requirement (for voting in local elections 地方選挙). Candidates for political office must meet the stated age requirement for each office. Members of the House of Representatives and of prefectural and local assemblies must be at least 25 years old. Members of the House of Councillors 参議院 and prefectural governors must be at least 30.

Japan has had a comprehensive election system incorporating all levels of government since the end of World War II. Under current election laws, members of all legislative bodies, including both houses of the Diet

House of Representatives Elections and Electoral Systems after World War II
第2次世界大戦後の衆議院選挙と選挙制度

Election number	Date	Number of constituencies	Number of seats
(Medium constituencies; single-entry secret ballot)			
22	1946.4.10	53	466
23	1947.4.25		
24	1949.1.23	117	466
25	1952.10.1		
26	1953.4.19		
27	1955.2.27		
28	1958.5.22	118	467
29	1960.11.20		
30	1963.11.21		
31	1967.1.29	123	486
32	1969.12.27		
33	1972.12.10	124	491
34	1976.12.5		
35	1979.10.7	130	511
36	1980.6.22		
37	1983.12.18		
38	1986.7.6	130	512
39	1990.2.18		
40	1993.7.18	129	511
(Single-seat constituencies and regional blocs of proportional representation; single-entry secret ballot)			
41	1996.10.20	Single-seat constituencies 300	300
		Regional blocs of proportional representation 11	200

Source: Prime Minister's Office.

and prefectural, city, town, and village assemblies, are selected by popular vote 一般投票. Political executives, including prefectural governors and mayors or other chief officials of local governments, are also chosen in popular elections. The prime minister, who is elected by the Diet, is the only political executive not chosen by direct popular vote. Today elections for half of the 252 members of the House of Councillors are held every three years with a combination of proportional-representation 比例代表 and prefectural-district seats 地方選挙区. In the House of Representatives, 500 members are elected for four-year terms, typically in elections held irregularly after the dissolution 解散 of the House. Of these 500, 300 are elected from single-seat constituencies (小選挙区)1人区, and 200 are elected under a proportional representation system 比例代表制. Elections are held every four years for most prefectural and local executive offices and assemblies.

Administration 選挙管理

Japan's electoral system is overseen by election administration committees 選挙管理委員会 within each administrative division of the country, i.e., prefectures, cities, towns, and villages. Administrators in local-government election sections assist the election committees in carrying out the day-to-day tasks of managing the system. The Ministry of Home Affairs 自治省 regulates the system as a whole.

Laws specifying acceptable campaign 選挙運動 practices are extremely detailed and strict in Japan. The period within which campaigns can be conducted, campaign funding and expenditures, and such matters as the number of posters permitted are precisely spelled out. Such practices as sponsorship of parties for constituents, door-to-door visits 戸別訪問 to solicit voter support, and gift-giving by candidates and their supporters are prohibited.

Political Reforms of 1994 (Seiji Kaikaku)
政治改革

Public anger over political corruption in the Liberal Democratic Party (LDP) 自由民主党 has continued since the Lockheed Scandal ロッキード事件 (1976) and reached a new peak with the Recruit Scandal リクルート事件 (1988). At the beginning of the 1990s reform-minded members of the LDP were putting most of the blame for the ongoing corruption on the medium-sized constituency system 中選挙区制 in which each district sends between three and five representatives to the lower house. Claiming this system makes it difficult for power to change hands, they began serious deliberations over reform measures that would introduce proportional representation 比例代表 and smaller election districts 小選挙区 into elections for the House of Representatives 衆議院.

The LDP failed twice in its efforts to carry out political reforms—under Prime Ministers Kaifu Toshiki 海部俊樹 (1931–) and Miyazawa Kiichi 宮沢喜一 (1919–). This resulted in the LDP's ouster in 1993 after four decades as the governing party 与党. In 1993, a coalition 連立 of opposition parties formed a government under Prime Minister Hosokawa Morihiro 細川護煕 (1938–), and the LDP became an opposition party. In early 1994, the Hosokawa cabinet finally succeeded in passing a political reform package through the Diet, but only after negotiating a major compromise with the LDP. The legislation called for a fundamental change in the electoral system 選挙制度 of the House of Representatives. The major parts of the political reform bills are as follows:

The Electoral System 選挙制度 The number of seats in the House of Representatives was reduced from 511 seats to 500. These consist of:

(1) Single-Seat Constituencies 小選挙区: The nation was divided into 300 electoral districts, each of which elect, and are represented in the House of Representa-

tives by, a single seat.

(2) Proportional Representation 比例代表: Separately, the entire nation was divided into 11 regional blocs, and the remaining 200 members of the House are elected from these multi-seat blocs on a proportional representation basis. A party must win at least 2 percent of the proportional representation votes to win a seat.

Fund Raising 政治資金 After a 5-year period all fund raising 資金調達 by individual candidates will be prohibited. During this transitional period each candidate is permitted to set up one fund-raising body. This body can then accept annual contributions of up to ¥500,000 from any single company or organization.

State Subsidies for Political Parties 政党公費助成 Political parties 政党 that include five or more Diet members or that receive at least two percent of the vote in a national Diet election are eligible to receive state subsidies. These subsidies are based on the number of Diet members in the party and the percentage of votes it received. The total amount allocated for these subsidies is determined by multiplying the total population (from the national census) times ¥250. In 1996 this total was ¥30.9 billion (US $284 million).

Expansion of the Election Law Violation Accountability System 公職選挙法違反責任制の拡大 If a candidate or a person in a position of responsibility in the candidate's campaign organization is convicted of an election law violation such as bribery, the candidate's election is invalidated and the person is prohibited from candidacy in the same electoral district for a period of five years. Political reform has resulted in expansion of the scope of the positions covered by these rules to include the candidate's secretary and the man-

Political Fund Income for Major Political Parties (1996)
主な政党の政治資金収入

(in billions of yen)

Political party	Political fund income	(State subsidy) (政党助成金)
Japan Communist Party	30.4	(0.0)
Liberal Democratic Party	26.0	(13.7)
Kōmei	13.1	(0.4)
New Frontier Party	12.2	(9.8)
Social Democratic Party of Japan	9.7	(4.7)
New Party Sakigake	1.3	(0.9)

Note: The state subsidy is the portion of total income that was received from the government under the party subsidy system.

Source: Ministry of Home Affairs.

agers of companies and organizations supporting the candidate.

Six Reforms of the Hashimoto Cabinet
橋本内閣6つの改革

Inaugurated in November 1996, the second cabinet of Prime Minister Hashimoto Ryūtarō 橋本龍太郎 announced reforms would be sought in six key areas: administration 行政, budget 財政構造, social security 社会保障構造, the economy 経済構造, the financial system 金融システム, and education 教育. Underlying these reform efforts is the increasingly widespread belief that the huge public sector and numerous government regulations which supported Japanese economic growth in the 50-year postwar period are today perpetuating a high-cost economic system that cannot respond to the needs of the growing global economy. With Japan facing a rapidly aging population 高齢化 and an increasingly interdependent and competitive global community, extensive reform and deregulation 規制緩和 are seen as a crucial strategy for maintaining the vital private sector economy needed to insure international competitiveness and a prosperous society as Japan enters the 21st century. There is considerable interest in the proposed reforms among the general public as they will have a significant impact on the lives of most citizens.

The Six Reforms and Their Objectives
6つの改革とその目的

(1) ***Administrative reform*** 行政改革: Reduce the size of the central government bureaucracy through deregulation and the transfer of responsibility to local government 地方自治体. A key element of this effort is the reorganization of the central government ministries and agencies. The Administrative Reform Council 行政改革会議 was established in November 1996. Chaired by the prime minister, this council is to prepare a reform

proposal by December 1997.

(2) **Fiscal structural reform** 財政構造: Reduce outlays, eliminate the issue of government bonds for deficit financing, and, by 2003, reduce the fiscal deficit 財政赤字 to less than 3 percent of GDP.

In January 1997 the Conference on Fiscal Structural Reform 財政構造改革会議 was established with the prime minister serving as chairman.

(3) **Structural reform of social security** 社会保障構造: Establish a nursing care insurance system and strive to balance the benefits and burdens of the medical care, pension, and welfare systems. The Ministry of Health and Welfare 厚生省 has primary responsibility for this reform.

(4) **Economic structural reform** 経済構造: Create a business environment that will support the development of new industries and that is attractive from an international perspective. The Ministry of International Trade and Industry 通産省 is to take the lead in this reform.

(5) **Financial system reform** 金融システム: Restore Tōkyō's position alongside New York and London as an international financial center by 2001. Reforms in this area, some of which are referred to as the Japanese "Big Bang," 日本版ビッグバン are to be led by the Ministry of Finance 大蔵省 and the Ministry of Justice 法務省.

(6) **Educational reform** 教育: To encourage creativity and nurture people able to thrive in a global society, rebuild both the content of education and the system used to teach it. In January 1997 the Ministry of Education 文部省 formulated the Education Reform Program 教育改革プログラム to promote the reform effort.

Political parties (*seitō*) 政党

Political parties emerged in Japan after the Meiji Restoration 明治維新 (1868), gained increasing influence with the opening of the Imperial Diet 帝国議会 (1890), and attained temporary political ascendancy following World War I. Outmaneuvered by the military, they declined in the 1930s and were dissolved and absorbed by the Imperial Rule Assistance Association 大政翼賛会 in 1940. Political parties were revived under the Allied Occupation 連合国占領 in the wake of World War II, and since 1952, when Japan regained its independence, they have been the primary force in national and local politics.

Parties in the Making 政党の誕生

The two major party builders of the early Meiji period 明治時代 (1868–1912) were Itagaki Taisuke 板垣退助 (1837–1919) and Ōkuma Shigenobu 大隈重信 (1838–1922). Itagaki had joined the government in 1871 but resigned in 1873 and in the following year founded the first pro-toparty, the Aikoku Kōtō (Public Party of Patriots 愛国公党), which memorialized the government on the need to institute an elected assembly. Itagaki and his compatriots also established a regional group in Ōsaka called the Aikokusha (Society of Patriots) 愛国社, which was the basis for the founding in 1881 of Japan's first national party, the Jiyūtō (Liberal Party) 自由党.

Ōkuma, who had served the new government since 1868, was forced to resign in 1881 and in 1882 formed the Rikken Kaishintō (Constitutional Reform Party) 立憲改進党, which drew its membership mainly from the fledgling urban intelligentsia. It remained active until 1896. More conservative parties, such as the Rikken Teiseitō (Constitutional Imperial Rule Party; 1882) 立憲帝政党, represented themselves as defenders of the oligarchic government 藩閥政府.

Parties in the Diet 帝国議会と政党

Parliamentary politics in the Diet 帝国議会, which opened in November 1890, was marked by an intense rivalry between the oligarchic government, which reserved the right to appoint cabinets, and the Liberal 自

由党 and Constitutional Reform parties 立憲改進党. The Constitutional Reform Party was reconstituted as the Shimpotō (Progressive Party) 進歩党 in 1896 and consolidated its position as the second party. In common parlance the Liberal and Progressive parties were termed *mintō* (popular parties) 民党, while groups of supporters of the oligarchic bureaucracy were referred to as *ritō* (bureaucrats' parties) 吏党. Neither of the popular parties had representation in the hereditary and appointive House of Peers 貴族院, nor did they control local politics, for key local officials were appointed by the central government.

The Politics of Compromise 妥協の政治

Rapprochement between parties and oligarchs 藩閥 was spurred in 1898 when Prime Minister Itō Hirobumi 伊藤博文 (1841–1909), who was a *genrō*, dissolved the Diet due to opposition by the popular parties to his proposal for extra land taxes. The Liberal and Progressive parties merged to form the Kenseitō (Constitutional Party) 憲政党, which won a majority in the Diet in the succeeding election. Ito resigned and invited Ōkuma and Itagaki to form a cabinet, Japan's first party cabinet 政党内閣, which was led by Ōkuma as prime minister and Itagaki as home minister 内務大臣 (内相). The alliance collapsed within months and the Progressive Party faction reorganized as the Kensei Hontō (True Constitutional Party; 1898) 憲政本党 and later as the Rikken Kokumintō (Constitutional Nationalist Party; 1910) 立憲国民党. However, in 1900 Itō formed the Rikken Seiyūkai (Friends of Constitutional Government Party; commonly called Seiyūkai) 立憲政友会(政友会), a coalition of former Jiyūtō members and bureaucrats that won a majority in the Diet, marking the forthright entrance of oligarchs and bureaucrats into party politics. In 1913 General Katsura Tarō 桂太郎 (1847–1913), protégé of the authoritarian oligarch Yamagata

Aritomo 山県有朋 (1838–1922), formed the Rikken Dōshikai (Constitutional Association of Friends) 立憲同志会, absorbing the wealthier half of the Rikken Kokumintō; in 1916 it was reconstituted as the Kenseikai (Constitutional Association) 憲政会. From 1922 onward, rivalry between the Kenseikai and the Seiyūkai became the dominant pattern.

In the late 19th and early 20th centuries a number of proletarian parties プロレタリア政党 appeared but many were banned soon after their formation by the invocation of such repressive laws as the Public Order and Police Law of 1900 治安警察法. Following the Bolshevik Revolution ボルシェヴィキ革命 of 1917 and the emergence of labor unions 労働組合, the Nihon Shakai Shugi Dōmei (Japan Socialist League) 日本社会主義同盟 was established in 1920 and the Japan Communist Party (JCP) 日本共産党 in 1922. The chief threat to the major parties was not the proletarian parties, popular support of which was limited, but the military. The political power of the military was made clear in 1912 when the army minister 陸軍大臣(陸相) Uehara Yūsaku 上原勇作 (1856–1933) resigned to protest the government's decision not to provide funds for two new army divisions. The army's refusal to name a successor to Uehara brought down the cabinet.

Ascendancy of Parties and the Military Takeover
政党の優位と軍の支配

The cabinet formed in 1918 by Hara Takashi 原敬 (1856–1921), largely made up of members of the Seiyūkai 政友会, was the first viable party cabinet 政党内閣, and from then until 1932 the premiership was almost always held by the leaders of major parties.

The two major parties, the Kenseikai 憲政会 (reorganized in 1927 as the Rikken Minseitō 立憲民政党; Constitutional Democratic Party) and the Seiyūkai, alternated in power until the assassination in 1932 of

Inukai Tsuyoshi 犬養毅 (1855–1932), Seiyūkai president and prime minister. Although prime ministers throughout the period were nominally designated by Saionji Kimmochi 西園寺公望 (1849–1940), protégé of Itō Hirobumi, the real cabinet-making power was held by the leaders of the two major parties. It was the influence of parties that distinguished this brief era of Taishō Democracy 大正デモクラシー in the early-20th century.

By the early 1930s there had emerged two legal noncommunist proletarian parties, which united in 1932 to form the Shakai Taishūtō (Socialist Masses Party) 社会大衆党. The JCP 日本共産党, which had been dissolved under govern-ment pressure in 1924, was reestablished underground in 1926 and remained active until about 1935.

The number of voters quadrupled with passage of the Universal Manhood Suffrage Law 普通選挙法 in 1925 and political campaigns became vastly more expensive. The industrial and financial combines Mitsui 三井 and Mitsubishi 三菱, the two largest *zaibatsu* 財閥, funded the Seiyūkai and the Rikken Minseitō, respectively. It was Inukai's death in 1932 at the hands of young naval officers (May 15th Incident 5·15事件) that signaled the end of party cabinets. From that point until the end of World War II, there was a succession of "national unity" cabinets 挙国一致内閣 led by military men or their collaborators. In 1940 all political parties were absorbed by the Imperial Rule Assistance Association 大政翼賛会.

The Postwar Period 戦後期

As soon as the war ended in August 1945, there were efforts to reestablish the prewar parties, and by November all had reappeared, most under new names. The abolition of the military and the replacement of the House of Peers 貴族院 with an elected House of Councillors 参議院 left the civil bureaucracy as the only major institutional rival of the parties, while the new CONSTITUTION OF JAPAN 日本国憲法 made the National DIET

国会 the "highest organ of government" and provided for control of the cabinet by the Diet.

The Occupation Purge 公職追放, which began in 1946, had a debilitating effect on the postwar conservative parties 保守政党 and also removed many local leaders from positions of influence, requiring all of the parties to rebuild their bases of local power. Revision of the election laws lowered the voting age, granted suffrage to women 女子の参政権, and increased the number of members elected from constituencies. This encouraged the participation of independents and minor parties and provoked fierce competition among the major parties, leading to unstable cabinets and frequent stalemates until February 1949, when Yoshida Shigeru 吉田茂 (1878–1967) of the Minshu Jiyūtō 民主自由党 (Democratic Liberal Party reorganized in 1950 as the Liberal Party; Jiyūtō 自由党) formed a stable cabinet that endured until October 1952.

The 1955 Status Quo 55年体制

Following the restoration of Japan's independence in 1952, division among the conservatives made it impossible for either the Liberal Party or the Nihon

Seats Won in House of Representatives Elections under the 1955 Status Quo
55年体制下の衆議院議員選党派別当選者数

Election Day	LDP[2]	JSP[3]	JCP[4]	CGP[5]	DSP[6]	Other	Total
May 22, 1958	287	166	1	–	–	13	467
November 20, 1960	296	145	3	–	17	6	467
November 21, 1963	283	144	5	–	23	12	467
January 29, 1967	277	140	5	25	30	9	486
December 27, 1969	288	90	14	47	31	16	486
December 10, 1972	271	118	38	29	19	16	491
December 5, 1976	249	123	17	55	29	38	511
October 7, 1979	248	107	39	57	35	25	511
June 22, 1980	284	107	29	33	32	26	511
December 18, 1983	250	112	26	58	38	27	511
July 6, 1986	300	85	26	56	26	19	512
February 18, 1990	275	136	16	45	14	26	512
July 18, 1993[1]	223	70	15	51	15	137	511

[1] First election after the downfall of the 1955 Status Quo. [2] Liberal Democratic Party 自由民主党
[3] Japan Socialist Party 日本社会党 [4] Japan Communist Party 日本共産党
[5] Clean Government Party 公明党 [6] Democratic Socialist Party 民社党
Source: House of Representatives.

Minshutō (Japan Democratic Party 日本民主党; successor of the prewar Rikken Minseitō 立憲民政党) to form a stable majority in the Diet, while the Japan Socialist Party (JSP) 日本社会党 had split in 1951 into parties of the Left 左派 and the Right 右派. In 1955, however, the JSP reunited and a month later the conservatives merged to form the Liberal Democratic Party (LDP) 自由民主党, thus giving birth to the "1955 status quo" 55年体制, with the LDP controlling both Houses, the JSP holding roughly half the number of LDP seats in each, and the LDP mounting a series of one-party cabinets. From then on, antagonism between the two parties became a dominant pattern in the Diet over almost all major political programs.

During the late 1950s the LDP took controversial stands in favor of the revision of the new constitution, the augmentation of police powers, and the revision of the United States-Japan Security Treaty 日米安全保障条約. When the last of these was settled in 1960 after considerable turmoil, the government turned to the problems of economic growth 経済成長 and foreign trade 貿易, and in these areas its policies were in general popular.

By the late 1960s, however, the 1955 status quo was showing strain. LDP popularity waned due to a series of political scandals 政治汚職事件 and the party's failure to deal satisfactorily with social and economic issues, such as a housing shortage, environmental pollution 公害, and rising land prices. With the JSP racked by factionalism, the power vacuum was filled by splinter groups, such as the Democratic Socialist Party (DSP) 民主社会党, founded in 1960 by right-wing members of the JSP, and newcomers such as the Kōmeitō (Clean Government Party) 公明党, which, with the support of members of the religious organization Sōka Gakkai 創価学会, gained an increasing number of seats in the Diet in the 1960s. Continuing corruption and factionalism contributed to diminishing popular support of the LDP, and in the periods 1976-80 and 1983-86 the party failed to win a majority of seats in the House of Representatives, while the JSP found its share reduced to 20 percent in the 1970s and 1980s.

In the 1990 elections the LDP did well, retaining a solid majority in the House of Representatives. The JSP also gained a sizable number of new seats in this election; the losers were the other opposition parties such as the Kōmeitō, JCP, and DSP.

The Downfall of the 1955 Status Quo 55年体制の崩壊

The LDP's repeated failure to carry out political reforms 政治改革 led to the breakaway of dissidents who formed the Shinseitō (New Life Party) 新生党 and the Shintō Sakigake (New Party Sakigake) 新党さきがけ in 1993. This, in turn, paved the way for breaking the LDP's grip on the government. The LDP cabinet under Prime Minister Miyazawa Kiichi 宮沢喜一 (1919–) made an outright promise to institute reforms. Its failure to do so opened the way for an overwhelming defeat on a non-confidence vote 内閣不信任案 in the Diet and dissolution 解散, followed by a call for national elections in July 1993. The election resulted in an unprecedented defeat for the LDP and an equally unexpected setback for the JSP which found its seats reduced almost by half. The electoral defeats suffered by these two political parties marked the end of the 1955 status quo. After political maneuvering among the opposition parties, a coalition government 連立政権 was formed in August 1993 under Prime Minister Hosokawa Morihiro 細川護熙 (1938–), the head of the Nihon Shintō (Japan New Party, established in 1992) 日本新党, with the Shinseitō holding the key posts and the remaining posts going to the other seven coalition parties 連立政党, including the JSP.

Despite its relatively high popularity, the Hosokawa government lasted only eight months with Hosokawa resigning in April 1994 after being attacked by the LDP concerning questionable loans he had received. Selected by the same group of coalition parties, Shinseitō member Hata Tsutomu 羽田孜 (1935–) replaced Hosokawa as prime minister. Almost immediately, however, the JSP and the Shintō Sakigake left the coalition, turning it into a minority government and forcing a general resignation in June 1994. The LDP immediately joined with the JSP and the Shintō Sakigake to form a coalition government with JSP member Murayama Tomiichi 村山富市 (1924–) as prime minister. The alliance between the LDP and the JSP, two parties which had fought bitterly up until one year before, surprised not only the public but the politicians involved as well.

In December 1994 six opposition parties, including the Shinseitō, the Kōmeitō, the Nihon Shintō, and the DSP, joined together to form the Shinshintō (New Frontier Party) 新進党. This action left two large conservative parties, the LDP and the Shinshintō, with 200 and 178 House of Representatives seats, respectively, followed by the JSP with 72 seats.

▌Political Reorganization Continues 政界再編成

Public support for the LDP, JSP, and Shintō Sakigake coalition government was low, and opposition Shinshintō candidates made a strong showing in the July 1995 House of Councillors election.

Fearing increasing irrelevancy as politics focused on the rivalry between the two conservative parties (LDP and Shinshintō), in late 1995 the JSP tried to rally liberal forces to form a new party. Failing in this effort, however, it simply changed its name to the Social Democratic Party of Japan (SDP) 社会民主党 in January 1996. The same month, Prime Minister Murayama resigned suddenly, but the LDP, SDP (former JSP), and Shintō Sakigake coalition remained in place, selecting Hashimoto Ryūtarō 橋本龍太郎 (1937-) of the LDP as the next prime minister.

Responding to public dissatisfaction with the unstable ruling coalition, in September 1996 Prime Minister Hashimoto dissolved the House of Representatives and scheduled a national election for the following month. Also in September, 52 relatively young Diet members broke away from both the Shintō Sakigake and the SDP to form a new party, called the Democratic Party 民主党, in an effort to establish themselves as the third major force in the upcoming general election.

While the LDP achieved strong gains in this election, the first held under the new system combining single seat constituencies and proportional representation 小選挙区比例代表並立制, it fell short of a majority. The Shinshintō suffered an overall loss of seats in the same election, and the party was ultimately disbanded in December 1997. Some former Shinshintō members created a new Jiyūtō (Liberal Party) 自由党, and many others subsequently joined the Minshutō, which became Japan's second largest party following the LDP. In January 1999 the Jiyūtō and the LDP formed a coalition government 連立政権 under LDP prime minister Obuchi Keizō 小渕恵三 (1937–). There appears to be no end in sight to the ongoing political party reshuffle.

Bureaucracy (*kanryōsei*) 官僚制

Japanese public bureaucracy comprises a national government bureaucracy, various local government 地方自治体 bureaucracies, and the bureaucracies of public and semipublic corporations 公共事業体.

Under the CONSTITUTION OF JAPAN 日本国憲法 (1947), bureaucrats are responsible to the PRIME MINISTER AND CABINET 首相と内閣. Most public employees are prohibited from striking or even engaging in collective bargaining. Taken together, national government, local government, and public corporations have about 4 million full-time employees.

Meiji Period 明治時代

During the Meiji period (1868–1912) creation of a cabinet system and promulgation of Imperial Ordinance No. 37 官吏服務紀律 in 1887 and the Constitution of the Empire of Japan 大日本帝国憲法 in 1889 established the outlines of a national bureaucracy modeled on that of Prussia プロイセン. Civilian and military bureaucracies were separated, both having direct responsibility to the emperor. Service was to the emperor and the nation, rather than to region or class. Architects of the Meiji regime viewed a powerful parliament 議会, local autonomy 地方自治, and party government 政党政治 as threats to national cohesion and the development of urban-based industrialization. They made efforts to ensure the autonomy and power of the state bureaucracy to protect efficient administration from the perceived dangers of localism and politics. Virtually essential to a high-level bureaucratic career was graduation from an elite state university, such as Tōkyō or Kyōto Imperial University 東京帝国大学：京都帝国大学, with these two schools providing the vast majority of senior civil servants 高級官僚.

Under the Meiji regime, each minister was appointed by—and was directly responsible to—the emperor. Collective cabinet responsibility was further diminished by the emperor's right of supreme command 統帥権, which meant that the emperor, rather than the prime minister or any other civilian authority, had control over the military. This resulted in two national bureaucracies, one civil, the other military, with the latter manipulating its privileged access to control cabinet composition and government policy making.

After World War II 第2次世界大戦後

National government bureaucracies 中央政府の官僚制 The National Government Organization Law 国家行政組織法 of 1948, the basic outline for the country's civil service 行政事務, provides for four types of administrative organs: ministries 省, offices on the ministerial level, agencies 庁, and commissions 委員会. The first two are the primary administrative organs of national government, with the Prime Minister's Office 総理府 being the only actual "office on the ministerial level." The latter two oversee areas of administration different from the main work of a ministry. Unable to submit proposed legislation or cabinet orders 政令 directly to the Diet, or to issue ministerial orders 省令, these hold less formal power than the ministries.

As of 1999, there were 12 main ministries in the Japanese government, each headed by a minister who is

Organization of the Executive Branch of the Government (March 1997)
行政府組織図

Cabinet 内閣
— Cabinet Secretariat 内閣官房 *2
— Cabinet Legislation Bureau 内閣法制局
— Security Council of Japan 安全保障会議
— National Personnel Authority 人事院 *1

*1 auxiliary organ
*2 headed by cabinet ministers
*3 considered an agency

Prime Minister's Office 総理府
— Fair Trade Commission 公正取引委員会
— National Public Safety Commission 国家公安委員会 *2
— Environmental Disputes Coordination Commission 公害等調整委員会
— Imperial Household Agency 宮内庁
— Management and Coordination Agency 総務庁 *2
— Hokkaidō Development Agency 北海道開発庁 *2
— Defense Agency 防衛庁 *2
— Defense Facilities Administration Agency 防衛施設庁
— Economic Planning Agency 経済企画庁 *2
— Science and Technology Agency 科学技術庁 *2
— Environment Agency 環境庁 *2
— Okinawa Development Agency 沖縄開発庁 *2
— National Land Agency 国土庁 *2

Ministry of Foreign Affairs 外務省

Ministry of Construction 建設省

Ministry of Posts and Telecommunications 郵政省

Ministry of Justice 法務省
— Public Security Investigation Agency 公安調査庁
— National Bar Examination Administration Commission 司法試験管理委員会
— Public Security Examination Commission 公安審査委員会

Ministry of Finance 大蔵省
— National Tax Administration 国税庁 *3

Ministry of Education 文部省
— Agency for Cultural Affairs 文化庁

Ministry of Health and Welfare 厚生省
— Social Insurance Agency 社会保険庁

Ministry of Agriculture, Forestry, and Fisheries 農林水産省
— Food Agency 食糧庁
— Forestry Agency 林野庁
— Fisheries Agency 水産庁

Ministry of International Trade and Industry 通商産業省
— Agency for Natural Resources and Energy 資源エネルギー庁
— Patent Office 特許庁 *3
— Small and Medium Enterprise Agency 中小企業庁

Ministry of Transport 運輸省
— Central Labor Relations Commission for Seafarers 船員労働委員会
— Maritime Safety Agency 海上保安庁
— High Marine Accidents Inquiry Agency 海難審判庁
— Meteorological Agency 気象庁

Ministry of Labor 労働省
— Central Labor Relations Commission 中央労働委員会

Ministry of Home Affairs 自治省
— Fire Defense Agency 消防庁

Board of Audit 会計検査院

almost invariably a member of parliament. Each minister is assisted by one or two parliamentary vice-ministers 政務次官, usually members of parliament who serve as liaison between their ministry and the Diet. The remainder of the ministry is composed of members of the appointed civil service. They are headed by an administrative vice-minister 事務次官 who oversees all administrative matters within the ministry. Each ministry is typically divided into 6 to 12 functional bureaus 局, headed by bureau chiefs 局長, plus a secretariat 官房 responsible for ministerial records, statistics, personnel, public relations, and financial accounts. Each ministry has deliberative councils 審議会 composed of representatives of private interest groups and individual experts to provide advice on matters under ministry jurisdiction.

The responsibilities of the Prime Minister's Office include overall coordination of government policies and the awarding of official government decorations. The office consists of 12 external agencies, including the Management and Coordination Agency 総務庁, Imperial Household Agency 宮内庁, and Economic Planning Agency 経済企画庁.

Local government 地方自治体 LOCAL GOVERNMENT is a two-tiered system comprising 47 larger units, known as prefectures 都道府県, and their approximately 3,250 cities and smaller units 市町村. Almost 2.85 million (1996) local public officials are local civil service personnel, appointed and paid by local public bodies.

In principle, local government entities are autonomously governed and administratively independent of the national government. In fact, a good deal of national governmental work is often delegated 委任 to local government agencies, and their actions are often directly overseen by the central government. Relying heavily on central financing, local government accounts for about two-thirds of total government disbursements

Number of Local Government Employees (1996)
地方公務員の数

Category	
education 教育関係	(1,268,768) 44.6%
general administration 一般行政関係	(1,171,659) 41.2%
police 警察関係	(255,295) 9.0%
fire fighting 消防関係	(149,632) 5.3%
Total: 2,845,354	

Source: Ministry of Home Affairs.

歳出, yet collects only about one-third of the nation's tax receipts 税収.

Public corporations 公企業・公団 There are approximately 100 public corporations in Japan, each legally independent but supervised by a national government agency and subject to Diet budgetary control. Performing wide-ranging functions in such diverse fields as transportation, public broadcasting 公共放送, cultural exchange 文化交流, energy development, etc., these public corporations employ some 620,000 individuals. About half of their top officials are retired senior civil servants.

National civil service 国家公務員 National civil service 国家公務員 is overseen by the Management and Coordination Agency 総務庁, which handles organizational issues, and the National Personnel Authority (NPA) 人事院, which is responsible for enforcement of the National Civil Service Law 国家公務員法. Entrance is based primarily on written and oral examinations administered by the NPA.

Once appointed to a post, an individual typically remains with the same agency throughout his career. Advancement is primarily a function of seniority: members of an entering class move upward as a cluster through a variety of positions within an agency. The most senior positions are held for only two or three years before early retirement at age 51 to 55. In a practice called *amakudari* ("descent from heaven") 天下り, many retired bureaucrats find second careers in private industry or public corporations overseen by the agencies for which they worked. A small proportion go on to politics. Approximately 20 percent of Japan's postwar cabinet ministers

Number of National Government Employees (1996)
国家公務員の数

Category	
special services (prime minister, ministers of state, justices, and personnel of the Defense Agency and courts) 特別職	(327,937) 28.3%
regular service 一般職	(831,924) 71.7%
employees under National Personnel Authority pay schemes 給与法適用職員	(508,760) 43.8%
employees of government corporations (post office, forestry, mint, and printing) 郵政・林野・造幣・印刷の4現業職員	(321,037) 27.7%
prosecutors 検察官	(2,127) 0.2%
Total: 1,159,861	

Note: The number is that authorized by the fiscal 1996 budget.
Source: National Personnel Authority.

National Government Personnel by Ministry (1996)
一般職国家公務員省庁別在職者数 (persons)

1	Ministry of Education	134,030
2	Ministry of Health and Welfare	75,761
3	Ministry of Finance	71,914
4	Ministry of Justice	48,600
5	Ministry of Transport	37,349
6	Ministry of Agriculture, Forestry, and Fisheries	36,620
7	Prime Minister's Office	26,987
8	Ministry of Labor	24,905
9	Ministry of Construction	23,916
10	Ministry of International Trade and Industry	12,230
11	Ministry of Foreign Affairs	4,776
12	Ministry of Posts and Telecommunications	2,748
13	Board of Audit	1,227
14	National Personnel Authority	694
15	Ministry of Home Affairs	465
16	Cabinet	245
Total		502,467

Note: Numbers are for employees under National Personnel Authority pay schemes.
Source: National Personnel Authority.

have been former bureaucrats, and the prime ministership has been held by more ex-civil servants than professional politicians.

Because service in a single ministry is the rule and lateral entry rare, loyalty to one's agency or section runs deep. Even sections within the same agency frequently resist cooperation, each seeking to maximize its sphere of influence.

The technical expertise of Japan's bureaucrats allows them to exercise substantial power in public policy formulation: approximately 90 percent of all legislation passed by the Diet since 1955 was drafted within the bureaucracy. Individual agencies have the power to issue ministerial ordinances 省令, and the cabinet can issue a cabinet order 政令, both of which provide powerful extralegislative instruments that can supplement and occasionally bypass the legislative process. Although deliberative councils 審議会 theoretically provide agencies with outside expertise, the ministerial staff defines the problem being investigated, oversees the investigation, and generally writes up the final report.

Administrative reform 行政改革 The Administrative Reform Council 行政改革会議 was established in 1996, with Prime Minister Hashimoto Ryūtarō 橋本龍太郎 (1937–) as chairman. In 1997 this council proposed reforms centering on the reorganization of central government ministries and agencies. In keeping with the recommendations of this report, the Basic Bill for the Reform of Central Ministries and Agencies 中央省庁等改革基本法 was enacted in June 1998. The current 21 ministries and agencies 省庁 are to be reduced to 12 in 2000.

Local government (*chihō seiji*) 地方政治

The general trend in local government since the Meiji Restoration 明治維新 (1868) has been for the expansion of local decision-making authority in areas of local concern and the fuller participation of citizens in the local political process. The World War II years were an exception to this trend.

Establishment of the Prefectural System 廃藩置県

Following the Meiji Restoration, the government began replacing the approximately 260 domains (*han* 藩) of the *bakuhan* (shogunate and domain) system 幕藩体制 with a centralized administrative structure consisting primarily of prefectures (*ken* 県) and urban prefectures (*fu* 府). In 1871 the government instituted a nationwide administrative system consisting of 72 prefectures with prefectural governors 府知事・県知事 appointed by the central government. The central government established the Home Ministry 内務省 in 1873 and vested it with supervisory power over local affairs.

Amalgamations reduced the number of prefectures to 47 (3 *fu*, 43 *ken*, and 1 administrative province or *dō*) by 1888, further promoting uniformity in subnational governance.

In 1888 the Municipal Code (Shisei 市政) and Town and Village Code (Chōsonsei 町村制) were established and declared that the units of local government should administer their own affairs "subject to the supreme control of the central government." The codes provided for the establishment of a mayorship and elected assemblies and specified that male citizens who met certain criteria of age, family, and taxpaying status could vote or hold elective office. In 1890 the Prefectural Code (Fukensei 府県制) and District Code (Gunsei 郡制) made further revisions to the structure of local government.

Universal male suffrage 男子普通選挙, adopted in 1925, expanded citizen participation in local government.

Local Government Expenditures (1891–1944)
地方自治体の歳出

	Local expenditures (millions of yen)	Index
1891	45	100
1906	174	387
1920	963	2,140
1925	1,429	3,176
1930	1,775	3,944
1935	2,229	4,953
1940	3,123	6,940
1944	4,232	9,404

Source: Fujita Takeo, *Gendai Nihon chihō zaisei shi* (1976

In 1929 local self-government powers were strengthened when the home minister 内務大臣 lost the authority to make peremptory cuts in prefectural budgets and local and prefectural assemblies were given more legislative authority.

Wartime Centralization of Government Authority
戦中の中央集権化

Following the outbreak of conflict with China in 1937, the central government required localities to take on more and more war-related duties. In 1940 the Home Ministry 内務省 ordered that community councils 町内会 be organized in city block areas and villages, with mayors 市長 and town and village chiefs 町村長 as heads These councils were made up of neighborhood associations 隣組 responsible for the policing and welfare of their areas. Prefectural laws 府県制 revised in 1943 reduced the powers of prefectural assemblies and enlarged the power of the governorship. The last modification in the local government system before the end of World War II came in July 1943 when the government created nine Regional Administrative Councils 地方行政協議会 to coordinate the action of local bodies and further strengthen central authority.

Postwar Local Government System
戦後期の地方政治制度

Decentralization of governmental authority and the strengthening of local government emerged early as a goal of the Allied Occupation 連合国占領. The new system of local government was intended to break up concentrated bureaucratic power revolving around Home Ministry-appointed governors, increase citizen participation and control, assure fairness in the conduct of local affairs, and expand the scope of autonomous local jurisdiction. In December 1947 educational and police affairs were placed largely in local hands. The new CONSTITUTION OF JAPAN 日本国憲法 (1947) in essence guaranteed the

Number of Local Government Bodies
地方公共団体数

	1871*[1]	1889*[2]	1922	1945	1953*[3]	1956*[4]	1972*[5]	1980	1996
Prefectures	75	46	46	46	46	46	47	47	47
Cities	–	39	91	205	286	498	643	646	666
Towns	–	–	1,242	1,797	1,966	1,903	1,967	1,991	1,993
Villages	–	15,820*[6]	10,982	8,518	7,616	1,574	677	618	573
Total	–	15,905	12,361	10,566	9,914	4,021	3,334	3,302	3,279

*[1] Prefectural system was established.
*[2] Municipal Code and Town and Village Code were issued.
*[3] Law for the Promotion of the Amalgamation of Towns and Villages was enforced.
*[4] Law for the Promotion of Construction of New Cities, Towns, and Villages was enforced.
*[5] Okinawa was returned.
*[6] Total of towns and villages.   Source: Ministry of Home Affairs.

decentralization of political authority by confirming the "principle of local autonomy" 「地方自治の原則」 and by establishing such basic features of the new system as the separation of local from national administration and the direct popular election of prefectural governors and of mayors, as well as local assemblies 地方議会. In 1949 the Local Autonomy Agency 地方自治庁 was created as a successor to the Home Ministry, which had supported prewar centralization. It became the Ministry of Home Affairs 自治省 in 1960.

Post-Occupation Evolution 占領終了後の発展

Recentralization of the police and educational systems, completed by 1956, stirred strong opposition from socialists, unionists, and intellectuals fearful of a reversion to prewar authoritarianism. On the other hand, central government elites encouraged amalgamations of municipalities, upgraded the overall quality of public administration, and facilitated the implementation of economic plans and national functions delegated to local authorities.

Beginning in the mid-1950s, local governments became participants in the national drive for economic growth 経済成長. New national laws for regional development 地域開発 were established in the early 1960s. In response, local authorities competed with each other to receive national government designation as target areas for development, thereby furthering the nationwide spread of the petrochemical, steel, machinery, and other heavy and chemical industries.

By the late 1960s and early 1970s, many local governments began reordering their priorities. Economic growth encouraged a rapid urbanization of the population 人口の都市化 and urban land prices spiraled, making the provision of an adequate social infrastructure 社会基盤 difficult. At the same time, new urban problems such as pollution-related diseases 公害病, traffic congestion 交通渋滞, and uncontrolled urban sprawl proliferated.

The intensity of such problems resulted in substantial grass-roots protests 草の根抵抗運動 and efforts by citizens to seek ameliorative policies from local government. Opposition representation in assemblies increased and coalitions of opposition parties formed around new urban issues 都市問題 succeeded in electing reformist local heads in major areas. Under these circumstances, local authorities began to pioneer new forms of communication with residents, pollution-control measures 公害対策, and social welfare programs 社会福祉計画. As a result, local priorities diverged significantly from national ones and contributed to the eventual shift in national priorities from unrestricted economic growth to establishing a higher quality of life.

Moreover, government reform efforts of the late 1970s and early 1980s led to an increased reliance on local authorities for the implementation of national social and environmental programs. There emerged, in effect, a broad recognition that local governments had matured in their administrative competence, had a unique role in setting local priorities and coordinating public programs, and were necessary partners of the national government in creating livable communities.

The Decentralization Promotion Law 地方分権推進法, which went into effect in May 1995, mandated the establishment of a committee for studying and promoting the decentralization of authority from the national to the local level for a wide range of governmental functions. Based on the recommendations of this committee, the plan for Promoting Decentralization 地方分権推進計画 was created by the cabinet in 1998.

Judicial system (*shihō seido*) 司法制度

The 1947 constitution (art. 76) 日本国憲法第76条 provides that "the whole judicial power is vested in a Supreme Court 最高裁判所 and in such inferior courts 下級裁判所 as are established by law." All courts on all levels are parts of a single system under the sole and complete administration of the Supreme Court. A jury system 陪審制度 does not exist.

The structure of the judicial system is as follows: the Supreme Court (Saikō Saibansho); 8 high courts 高等裁判所 in the eight principal geographical subdivisions of the country; 50 district courts 地方裁判所 in the principal administrative units; 50 family courts 家庭裁判所; and 438 summary courts 簡易裁判所 located throughout the country. The DIET 国会 as the sole law-making organ can change the organization of the courts by passing the necessary legislation, but the administration of the court system remains constitutionally vested in the Supreme Court.

The Supreme Court is headed by the chief justice, who is appointed by the emperor after designation by the cabinet. The other 14 justices are appointed by the cabinet. The court is organized into a grand bench 大法廷 consisting of all 15 justices and three petty benches 小法廷 of 5 justices each. All cases before the Supreme Court

Japan's Court System (1997)
裁判制度

Supreme Court 最高裁判所

8 high courts (6 branches) 高等裁判所

50 district courts (203 branches) 地方裁判所

50 family courts (203 branches) 家庭裁判所

438 summary courts 簡易裁判所

domestic and juvenile cases

serious offenses and civil cases involving ¥900,000 or more in claims

civil cases involving less than ¥900,000 in claims

minor offenses punishable by fine or light sentence

are appeals 上告; it possesses original jurisdiction 一審裁判権 over no cases. The constitution (art. 81) 憲法第81条 also provides that the Supreme Court is the court of last resort 終審裁判所 "with power to determine the constitutionality of any law, order, regulation or official act."

The high courts are essentially appellate courts 控訴裁判所. They are courts of first instance for the crimes of insurrection, preparation for or plotting of insurrection, and of assistance in the acts enumerated.

District courts have original jurisdiction over most cases with the exception of offenses carrying minor punishment and a few others reserved for other courts. In addition, they are courts of appeal for actions taken by the summary courts. Family courts came into existence in 1949. They have jurisdiction over such matters as juvenile crime 少年犯罪 (the age of majority being 20), problems of minors, divorce, and disputes over family property. Summary courts have jurisdiction over minor cases involving less than ¥900,000 in claims or fines or offenses carrying lighter punishments.

Police system (*keisatsu seido*) 警察制度

Japan's approximately 260,000 (1994) police officers are organized into prefectural forces coordinated and partially controlled by the National Police Agency 警察庁 in Tōkyō. They enjoy wide community support and respect.

Historical Development 歴史

Premodern 前近代 Until 1600, social control was performed essentially by the military and by groups of citizens organized for mutual defense. During the Edo period (1600–1868), the Tokugawa shogunate 徳川幕府 developed an elaborate police system based on town magistrates 町奉行, who held *samurai* status and served as chiefs of police, prosecutors, and criminal judges. The shogunate's social control mechanism was augmented by citizens' groups such as the *goningumi* (five-family associations) 五人組, composed of neighbors collectively liable to the government for the activities of their membership.

Establishment of a modern police system 近代的警察制度の成立 After the Meiji Restoration 明治維新 (1868), the Home Ministry 内務省 was established in 1873. With jurisdiction over the Police Bureau 警保局, it effectively controlled the police. This new, centralized police system had wide-ranging responsibilities far beyond the essential police duties, including the authority to issue ordinances 制令 and handle quasi-judicial functions. It also regulated public health 公衆衛生, factories, construction, and businesses and issued permits, licenses, and orders. To help control proscribed political activities, the Special Higher Police 特別高等警察(特高) were established in 1911 in Tōkyō and in 1928 in all prefectures. With the outbreak of the Sino-Japanese War of 1937–1945 日中戦争, the police were given the added responsibilities of regulating business activities for the war effort, mobilizing labor 動員, and controlling transportation. Even fire fighting came under police direction, as did the regulation of publications, motion pictures, political meetings, and election campaigns.

Postwar period 戦後期 After World War II, leaders of the Allied Occupation 連合国占領 required the Diet to enact a new Police Law 警察法. This 1947 law abolished the Home Ministry 内務省. It also decentralized the system by establishing about 1,600 independent municipal police forces 自治体警察 in all cities and towns with populations of over 5,000. Smaller communities would be served by the National Rural Police 国家地方警察. Popular control of the police was to be ensured by the establishment of politically neutral, civilian public safety commissions 公安委員会.

This attempt at decentralization was unsuccessful. In June 1951, the Police Law was amended to allow smaller communities to merge their police forces with the National Rural Police. Eighty percent of the communities with autonomous forces did so. The system was further centralized with passage of a new Police Law in 1954.

Present Structure 現在の組織

Today the Japanese police system is based on prefectural units that are autonomous in daily operations yet are linked nationwide under the National Police Agency 警察庁.

Prefectural police headquarters 県警本部, including the Tōkyō Metro-politan Police Department 警視庁, control everyday police operations in each prefecture. In effect, the prefectures pay for the patrolman on the beat, traffic control, criminal investigation, and other routine functions but have little control over domestic security units, which are funded by the national government, as are the salaries of senior national and prefectural police officials.

Prefectures are divided into districts 管区, each with its own police station 警察署 under direct control of prefectural police headquarters. There are about 1,250 of these police stations nationwide. Districts are further subdivided into jurisdictions of urban *kōban* (police boxes) 交番 and rural *chūzaisho* (residential police boxes) 駐在所.

The mainstay of the Japanese police system is the uniformed patrol officer おまわりさん. The patrol officers man the police boxes and patrol cars and comprise 40 percent of all officers. They are the generalists who usually respond first to all incidents and crimes and then funnel them to the specialized units for further investigation.

The Prefectural Police System
都道府県警察制度

Prefectural Governor 都道府県知事

Prefectural Public Safety Commission
都道府県公安委員会

Prefectural police departments
prefectural police headquarters
都道府県警察本部

police stations
警察署

prefectural police school
(都道府県)警察学校

police boxes
交番

ce: National Police Agency.

The scope of police responsibilities remains broad, though considerably narrowed from the prewar period. Besides solving ordinary crimes, criminal investigators establish the causes of fires and industrial accidents. Crime prevention police bear added responsibility for juveniles, businesses such as bars and Mah-Jongg parlors, and the enforcement of "special laws" regulating gun and sword ownership, drugs, smuggling, prostitution, pornography, and industrial pollution. Public safety commissions 公安委員会 usually defer to police decisions.

Contact with the community is augmented by the requirement that *kōban*-based police visit every home in their jurisdiction to gather information, pass on suggestions regarding crime prevention, and hear complaints. Neighborhood crime prevention and traffic safety associations 防犯協会：交通安全協会 provide another link between police and community, further promoting extensive public involvement in law and order.

Taxes (*sozei seido*) 租税制度

Direct tax 直接税 The most significant tax by far is the national income tax 所得税, producing some 65.4 percent of the ¥54.5 trillion in total national tax revenue 国の税収 for fiscal year 1996. This tax can be classified into two categories. The first is the individual income tax 個人所得税 defined in the Income Tax Law 所得税法 and its supporting enforcement orders and regulations. This tax produced 35.5 percent of fiscal 1996 national tax

Criminal Offenses and Arrests (1995)
刑法犯の主要罪名別認知・検挙件数

Type of crime 罪名	Offenses 認知件数	Arrests 検挙件数	Arrest percentages 検挙率
Theft 窃盗	1,570,492	587,266	37.4
Embezzlement 横領	61,144	60,881	99.6
Fraud 詐欺	45,923	42,940	93.5
Vandalism 器物損壊	31,231	4,041	12.9
Infliction of bodily injury 傷害	17,482	15,209	87.0
Intrusion into a habitation 住居侵入	11,009	3,724	33.8
Extortion 恐喝	11,207	7,295	65.1
Forgery 偽造	9,159	9,054	98.9
Assault 暴行	6,190	5,034	81.3
Sexual assault and child molestation 強制・公然猥褻	4,752	4.312	90.7
Robbery 強盗	2,277	1,882	82.7
Arson 放火	1,710	1,645	96.2
Rape 強姦	1,500	1,410	94.0
Receiving stolen goods 贓物	1,353	1,342	99.2
Murder 殺人	1,281	1,236	96.5
Gambling 賭博・富くじ	702	702	100.0
Other その他	5,532	5,201	94.0
Total all types	1,782,944	753,174	42.2

Note: Traffic offenses and offenses by minors under age 14 are not included.
Source: Ministry of Justice.

revenue. The second category of national income tax is the corporate income tax 法人税 imposed on all legal entities (known as *hōjin* or juristic persons). This tax is defined in the Corporation Tax Law 法人税法 and its supporting enforcement orders and regulations; it provided some 24.9 percent of fiscal 1996 national income tax revenue.

Income taxation in Japan is based on self-assessment 自己申告, and therefore, all corporate taxpayers must file a final corporate tax return with the tax office 税務署 within two months of the end of their business year. However, most individual taxpayers need not file a tax return provided that they have received only remuneration income and all or almost all of that income is from one employer. Their employer calculates their tax amount, which is withheld at source 源泉, and makes a year-end adjustment 年末調整, either collecting additional tax or refunding tax to the taxpayer. Individual taxpayers who have significant renumeration income from two or more sources or who have other types of income are required to file a final income tax return by 15 March of the year following the calendar year for which they are being taxed.

Consumption tax 消費税 Although historically the major emphasis of the Japanese tax system had been on direct rather than indirect taxation, six tax reform bills were enacted in December 1988 that, among other things, introduced a new major indirect tax 間接税, the national consumption tax 消費税. The consumption tax provided 10.9 percent of national tax revenue in 1996.

Administration 徴税行政 The national Japanese domestic tax system is administered by the National Tax Administration 国税庁, a semi-independent agency of the Ministry of Finance 大蔵省. This body oversees 12 regional taxation bureaus 国税局 and 517 local tax offices 税務署. Tax policy and international tax negotiations are handled by an internal bureau of the Ministry of Finance called the Tax Bureau 主税局. Customs matters come under the Customs and Tariff Bureau 関税局 of the Ministry of Finance.

Local tax 地方税 For local tax 地方税 matters, a general framework is established by the Local Tax Law 地方税法, which is overseen by the Local Tax Bureau 税務局 of the Ministry of Home Affairs 自治省. The type of local taxes that can be imposed and their rates are regulated by the national government.

National Tax Tribunal 国税不服審判所 A formal procedure exists for settling tax disputes with the government. Protests must first be filed with the chief of the tax office or the director of the regional taxation bureau. If this proves unsatisfactory, the taxpayer may claim review by the tax court called the National Tax Tribunal. A ruling by the tax court may then be appealed to the regular judicial courts.

INTERNATIONAL RELATIONS 国際関係

History of international relations
(*kokusai kankei shi*) 国際関係史

Japan's relations with foreign nations, following abandonment of the shogunal policy of National Seclusion 鎖国 in 1854, can be divided into the period before and the period after the close of World War II. The earlier period includes the entrance of Japan into the community of nations, its participation as an equal in international affairs, and the creation and collapse of the Greater East Asia Coprosperity Sphere 大東亜共栄圏. The later period embraces the Allied Occupation 連合国占領 (1945–1952), the San Francisco Peace Treaty サンフランシスコ平和条約 (1951), admission to the United Nations 国際連合 (1956), and the gradual reestablishment of an independent diplomatic policy.

Japanese Diplomatic Units Abroad (1996)
日本の在外公館

Embassies	186
Consulates-general	71
Consulates	1
Permanent missions or delegations	6
Total	264

Source: Ministry of Foreign Affairs.

The Opening of Japan and the "Unequal Treaties"
日本の開国と不平等条約

The arrival in Japan of Commodore Matthew Perry ペリー司令長官 and his "black ships" 黒船 in 1853 led to the signing by representatives of the United States and the Tokugawa shogunate of the Kanagawa Treaty of 1854 (Treaty of Peace and Amity between the United States and the Empire of Japan 日米和親条約), which effected the opening of Japan 開国. Formal diplomatic relations were soon established with the United Kingdom, Russia, the Netherlands, and other Western countries. Japan concluded the Ansei commercial treaties 安政5ヵ国条約 with these countries, which provided for broad grants of extraterritoriality 治外法権 and restrictions on Japan's right to levy customs duties 関税. Those were the means by which Japan was forcibly incorporated into a system of international relations developed by the Western powers. Following the formation of the Meiji government in 1868, Japan embarked on a program of forthright Westernization, with the goal of establishing Japan as a great power. Revision of the Unequal Treaties 不平等条約 became a crucial concern, and the issue was raised by a succession of foreign ministers 外務大臣, but the nations of the West were disinclined to relinquish their vested privileges. It was not until the signing of the Anglo-Japanese Commercial Treaty of 1894 日英通商航海条約 that the extraterritorial rights of a foreign power were first abolished. Japan did not fully recover autonomous customs rights 関税自主権 or attain equal status with Western nations until 1911.

Expansion on the Asian Mainland アジア大陸への進出

In 1876 Japan compelled Korea to sign the Treaty of Kanghwa (Kōkatō) 日朝修好条規(江華島条約), gaining for itself access to three Korean ports, extraterritorial rights 治外法権, and full exemption from customs duties. Japan

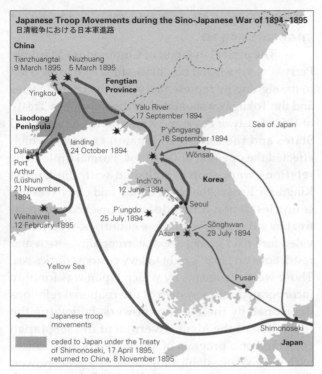

thus succeeded in concluding an unequal treaty with Korea ahead of the Western powers. China, however, held considerable influence over Korean diplomatic and domestic affairs, and rivalry with Japan was inevitable. After a series of political coups inside Korea in 1884, Japan and China agreed to withdraw their troops from Korea; however, in the spring of 1894 the Tonghak Rebellion 東学党の乱 broke out, and the Korean government called on the Chinese for military assistance. Japan too sent an expeditionary force, which clashed with the Chinese in July 1894, leading to the Sino-Japanese War of 1894–1895 日清戦争. The Treaty of Shimonoseki 下関条約 (1895), which ended hostilities, provided for the cession by China of Taiwan and the Pescadores 澎湖列島. Reparation money 賠償金 received from China played a significant role in the industrialization of Japan, while the opening of numerous Chinese ports and cities to Japanese commerce and industry enabled entrance into the Chinese domestic market. The Tripartite Intervention 3国干渉 by Russia, Germany, and France, however, forced Japan to relinquish the Liaodong Peninsula 遼東半島, which it had also obtained from China.

Following the severance of China's interest in Korea, a new rivalry developed between Russia and Japan. After 1900 Russia stationed troops in Manchuria, which Japan considered a grave threat to its position on the Korean peninsula. It was under these circumstances that Japan signed with Britain the Anglo-Japanese Alliance 日英同盟 (1902), the first military treaty concluded by Japan with a foreign country. Renewed in 1905 and 1911, for 20 years it remained the pillar of Japanese foreign policy.

On 6 February 1904 Japan broke off diplomatic relations with Russia over the issues of China and Korea and on 10 February declared war (Russo-Japanese War 日露戦争 of 1904–1905). The terms of the Treaty of Portsmouth ポーツマス条約 (1905), which ended hostilities, gave to Japan the southern half of Sakhalin 樺太 and the Russian lease concessions 租借権 in China, including the Liaodong Peninsula; the latter provided a foothold for eventual Japanese political domination of southern Manchuria 満州. Russia also agreed not to intervene in Korean affairs, and in 1910 Korea became a Japanese colony (annexation of Korea 日韓併合).

In a series of agreements with Russia 日露協約 in 1907, 1910, and 1912, Japan established a sphere of influence in southern Manchuria and the eastern part of Inner Mongolia 内蒙古. By means of the South Manchuria Railway 南満州鉄道, Japan strengthened its position in the area. This activity, however, was in conflict with the Open Door Policy 門戸開放政策 of the United States, which was based on the principle of equal access to Chinese markets, and led to a dispute between Japan and the United States over the issues of railway rights and interests in Manchuria. Friction was exacerbated by restrictions placed by the United States on immigration 移民 from Japan, as well as by rivalry between the US and Japanese navies in the Pacific Ocean.

World War I and Its Aftermath 第1次世界大戦とその結果

Following World War I, Japan was one of the five victorious nations at the Paris Peace Conference パリ平和会議 in 1919; it received confirmation of its occupation of the Shandong Peninsula 山東半島 and the mandate for the Pacific Islands 南洋諸島委任統治権取得 formerly held by Germany. However, because of Japan's strong pressure on China, confrontation between Japan and China increased. Following the Bolshevik revolution in Russia ロシア革命 in November 1917, Japan joined the Allied Siberian Intervention シベリア出兵 (1918–1922).

At the Washington Conference ワシントン会議 of 1921–1922 a plan for international cooperation in East Asia, the so-called Washington System ワシントン体制, was formulated. Japan agreed to remove its military forces from the Shandong Peninsula, and during the 1920s, while also working to develop its established interests, Japan made an effort not to disturb the political equilibrium in Asia. However, when the Chinese Nationalist Party 中国国民党 (Guomindang) extended its sphere of activity to Manchuria and Inner Mongolia, Japan replied with extreme measures such as the assassination of Zhang Zuolin 張作霖.

Growing Japanese Military Activity in China
中国における軍事活動の拡大

The Manchurian Incident 満州事変 of September 1931 and the establishment of the Japanese-controlled puppet state 傀儡国家 Manchukuo 満州国 in 1932 brought the Japan-United States confrontation in Asia close to the flash point. Japan ignored the Nine-Power Treaty 9ヵ国条約, which it had signed at the Washington Conference in 1922. The United States, which opposed all of Japan's activities in Manchuria, responded with the Stimson Doctrine (nonrecognition policy) スチムソン主義(不承認政策).

The Japanese challenge to the Washington System was denounced by a large majority of the member countries of the League of Nations 国際連盟. Japan responded by leaving the League of Nations in March 1933. Japan's economy suffered due to its estrangement from Britain and the United States, and to compensate for its losses Japan extended its influence from Manchuria into northern China. The military dominance of Japan over the entire area of Manchuria created tension with the Soviet Union and led to the signing of the Anti-Comintern Pact (日独)防共協定 in 1936 by Germany and Japan. Triggered by

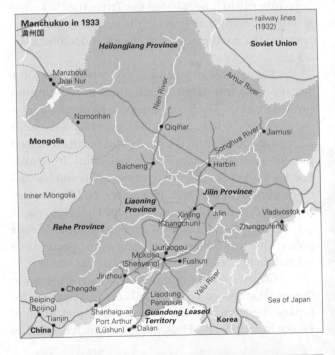

the Marco Polo Bridge Incident 盧溝橋事件 of July 1937, Japan's expansion into northern China escalated into general armed conflict. As the scope of military activity in China increased, the United States reacted by declaring an embargo 通商停止 against Japan.

World War II 第2次世界大戦

The 1938 declaration of the Tōa Shinchitsujo (New Order in East Asia) 東亜新秩序, which encompassed China, Manchukuo, and Japan, and the announcement in August 1940 of the Greater East Asia Coprosperity Sphere 「大東亜共栄圏」, which included Southeast Asia as well, gave notice of Japan's intention to create a new non-Western political order throughout Asia.

The sweeping victories of Germany, following the outbreak of World War II in September 1939, convinced Japan of the value of an alliance, and in September 1940 it negotiated the Tripartite Pact 三国同盟 with Germany and Italy. In the same month, Japan invaded the northern part of French Indochina 仏領インドシナ.

The collapse of Japan-United States relations 日米関係 appeared imminent; negotiations in Washington proved fruitless. The Soviet-Japanese Neutrality Pact 日ソ中立条約, concluded in April 1941, provided assurance against an attack from the north, and Japan advanced into the southern part of French Indochina. In retaliation the United States froze Japanese assets and banned oil exports to Japan. On 26 November the US secretary of state, Cordell Hull, replied with the Hull Note ハル=ノート, which called for radical changes in Japan's Asia policy. This was construed by Japan as an unacceptable ultimatum that left it with no alternative but war.

Overwhelming victories in the Pacific theater in the initial stages of World War II opened the way for Japanese occupation and military administration of French Indochina, the Philippines, the Dutch East Indies

オランダ領東インド, Malaya, and Burma. However, defeat in the Battle of Guadalcanal ガダルカナルの戦い (August 1942–February 1943) put Japan on the defensive, and imperial Japan was on the verge of collapse.

Allied Occupation and Dependence on US Military Strength 連合国占領と米国軍事力への依存

Japan conceded defeat on 15 August 1945 and formally surrendered to the Allied powers 連合国 on 2 September. The right of Japanese to rule their nation was made subject to the authority of the Supreme Commander for the Allied Powers (SCAP) 連合国最高司令官. As supreme commander, Douglas MacArthur ダグラス=マッカーサー presided over General Headquarters (GHQ) 連合国最高司令官総司令部 and set about implementing plans for the demilitarization and democratization of Japan.

Following the victory of the communists in China in 1949 and the establishment of the People's Republic of China (PRC) 中華人民共和国, and the outbreak of the Korean War 朝鮮戦争 in 1950, the United States moved to restore Japan's independence. In September 1951 Japan and the Allied powers (excluding the Soviet Union, China, India, and Burma) signed the San Francisco Peace Treaty サンフランシスコ平和条約, which became effective in April 1952, enabling Japan to reenter the community of independent nations. Prohibited by the new CONSTITUTION OF JAPAN 日本国憲法 from possessing land, sea, or air military forces, Japan was faced with the problem of national security 国家安全保障. The issue was partially resolved when, at the signing of the peace treaty, it concluded the first of the United States-Japan security treaties 日米安全保障条約, bringing Japan under the protective umbrella of the US military. Bases used by the army of occupation remained in the hands of US forces, and during the Korean War 朝鮮戦争 the Japanese economy was stimulated by massive US military procurements. With US backing, Japan was accepted in 1955 as a member of the General Agreement on Tariffs and Trade (GATT) 関税および貿易に関する一般協定 and in 1956 as a member of the United Nations 国際連合. At the end of the 1950s, Japan announced its intention to adhere to "three principles" 「3原則」 in the determination of its foreign policy: membership in the Asian community, diplomacy centered on the United Nations 国際連合, and maintenance of Japan's position in the free world. Throughout the 1960s, however, Japan's foreign policy 外交政策 was strongly influenced by that of the United States. Opponents of this relationship were particularly vocal in 1960, when the United States-Japan Security Treaty was revised, and again following the outbreak of the Vietnam War ベトナム戦争.

Emergence of Japan as an Economic Power
経済大国日本の出現

In the postwar era Japan's expanding foreign trade has played an increasingly influential role in the formation of its diplomacy. In the latter part of the 1960s Japan's economy reached a level competitive with those of the United States and the European Community 欧州共同体 (EC; now European Union 欧州連合 [EU]). Friction over trade issues caused Japan-United States relations to enter a new phase. In the midst of a textile dispute 繊維摩擦 between the two countries in 1969–1971, President Richard Nixon ニクソン大統領 announced in July 1971, without prior consultation with Japan, that he would visit Beijing 北京 to negotiate the establishment of diplomatic relations with China. Out of deference to US anticommunist policy 反共政策 and despite domestic agitation for the normalization of relations with the People's Republic of China 中華人民共和国, Japan had maintained close ties with the Republic of China 中華民国 on

Trade between Japan and the United States
日米貿易

billions of US dollars

exports to the United States from Japan

imports from the United States to Japan

Source: Ministry of Finance.

Taiwan, and this radical shift in policy was construed as a humiliation. On the heels of this "shock" came the announcement by President Nixon, again without consultation, of his New Economic Policy 新経済政策, which resulted in a major appreciation of the yen and the unsettling of Japan's foreign trade.

In the late 1970s friction with the United States, which continued to be Japan's chief trade partner, again grew heated due to several factors: the trade balance 貿易収支 was overwhelmingly in favor of Japan; increasing imports of Japanese steel and electronic products had grave consequences for corresponding US industries; and the United States criticized Japan for not opening domestic markets to US goods. Economic friction 経済摩擦 with the United States persisted through the 1980s and 1990s, and the criticism was voiced in the US Congress 米議会 that Japanese trade practices were "unfair."

A similar trade dispute developed between Japan and the nations of Western Europe. Trade imbalances arising from the enormous export volumes of Japanese steel, electronic products, ships, and automobiles caused friction, which intensified in the 1980s and 1990s and stimulated the formation of a new protectionism and of new economic blocs.

Relations with the Soviet Union and Russia
ソ連・ロシアとの関係

The conclusion of the first United States-Japan Security Treaty in 1952 inevitably brought Japan into confrontation with the Soviet Union. In 1955, during the post-Stalin-era thaw in the cold war 冷戦, the Soviet Union initiated negotiations on the restoration of normal relations with Japan. However, the talks were suspended in mid-1956 due to a dispute over a number of islands off the coast of Hokkaidō that had come under Soviet dominion at the close of World War II and that Japan demanded be returned. Afterward it was decided that an interim agreement terminating the state of war between the two nations would be put into effect, while negotiations continued on a peace treaty 平和条約. The Soviet-Japanese Joint Declaration 日ソ共同宣言 to this effect was signed in October 1956, and diplomatic relations 外交関係 were resumed.

In the 1980s, following the emergence in the Soviet Union of Mikhail Gorbachev M=ゴルバチョフ, international tensions were reduced, bringing an end to the cold war 「冷戦」 that had dominated world politics for more than 40 years. The state visit to Japan by President Gorbachev in April of 1991—the first ever by a Soviet leader—contributed to the amelioration of Soviet-Japanese relations. However, after many twists and turns, such as the dissolution of the Soviet Union and Boris Yeltsin's B=エリツィン succession to the presidency, the issue of the Northern Territories 北方領土問題 has yet to be resolved, and there is scant possibility of conclusion of a peace treaty with Russia any time soon.

Relations with China 中国との関係

When the San Francisco Peace Treaty サンフランシスコ平和条約 was implemented in April 1952, Japan established diplomatic relations with the Nationalist government 国民党政権 on Taiwan, which it recognized as the official government of China. Until 1972 contact with the People's Republic of China was maintained on a largely non-governmental basis, and only limited and intermittent trade was conducted.

In the 1970s dissension within the communist bloc began to grow and the eruption of armed conflict between China and the Soviet Union in 1969 was a factor in the decision of the United States to negotiate with China for the establishment of diplo-

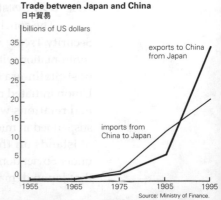

Trade between Japan and China
日中貿易

billions of US dollars

exports to China from Japan

imports from China to Japan

Source: Ministry of Finance.

matic relations. The China-United States rapprochement paved the way for the issuance of the China-Japan Joint Communiqué 日中共同声明 in September 1972 establishing formal diplomatic relations between Japan and the People's Republic of China (of which Japan recognized Taiwan to be a territory) and the signing in 1978 of the China-Japan Peace and Friendship Treaty 日中平和友好条約.

Relations with Korea 朝鮮・韓国との関係

In 1948 the Korean peninsula was divided at the 38th parallel 38度線 between the Democratic People's Republic of Korea (North Korea) 朝鮮民主主義人民共和国 and the Republic of Korea (South Korea) 大韓民国, with which Japan was urged by the United States to establish diplomatic relations. This effort, however, was fraught with difficulties due to the deep resentment felt by Koreans toward the nation that had colonized it. The sentiment culminated in the anti-Japanese policies of the first President Syngman Rhee 李承晩大統領. Following the assumption of power by the government of Pak Chonghui 朴正熙大統領, negotiations were resumed and resulted in the signing of the Korea-Japan Treaty of 1965 日韓基本条約, in which Japan recognized South Korea as the only lawful government on the Korean peninsula. Contacts with North Korea have been largely unofficial, but in 1990 negotiations were initiated to normalize relations.

Relations with Southeast Asia and the Pacific Basin 東南アジア・太平洋地域との関係

Japan's postwar relations with Southeast Asia began with negotiations concerning war reparations 戦時賠償. The first country with which Japan reached an agreement was Burma ビルマ (now Myanmar ミャンマー), followed by the Philippines フィリピン, Indonesia インドネシア, and the Republic of Vietnam ベトナム, all between 1954 and 1959. In the 1960s Japan established close economic relations with many countries in the region, and since then, attaching importance to a special relationship with these nations, Japan has placed particular emphasis on foreign aid (see OFFICIAL DEVELOPMENT ASSISTANCE 政府開発援助). In 1967 Thailand タイ, Malaysia マレーシア, Singapore シンガポール, Indonesia, and the Philippines organized the Association of Southeast Asian Nations (ASEAN) 東南アジア諸国連合 to increase economic cooperation. ASEAN industrial development has been accelerated by Japanese capital funding and technology.

Remarkable advances were made in the early 1980s by South Korea 韓国, Taiwan 台湾, Hong Kong 香港, and Singapore シンガポール, the Asian nations known collectively as the NIEs (Newly Industrializing Economies) 新興工業経済地域. With the ASEAN countries, Japan, and a number of other nations in the East Asia-western Pacific area, they have become the most dynamic regional influence upon the world's economy. As providers of raw materials, Australia オーストラリア, Canada カナダ, New Zealand ニュージーランド, and Mexico メキシコ have become increasingly important to Japan and the other industrialized nations of the region, and growing economic interdependence has lent itself to the idea of a "Pacific Basin Economic Sphere 環太平洋経済圏". In November 1989 government representatives of Canada, the United States, New Zealand, Australia, South Korea, Japan, and the six ASEAN nations (Brunei joined in 1984) met for their first conference, at which they established principles for economic cooperation (APEC; Asia-Pacific Economic Cooperation forum アジア太平洋経済協力会議).

Japan and the Middle East 日本と中東

Japan is almost totally dependent on the import of oil to meet its needs. In the years since the oil crisis 石油危機 of 1973, Japan has established strong economic relations with the countries of the Middle East, not only in regard to the import of oil but also the export of refining plants 精製用プラント and other industrial goods.

During this period Japan chose to support the Arab nations vis-a-vis Israel, but in the wake of the Persian Gulf War 湾岸戦争 of 1990–1991 it is likely that Japan's foreign policy will assume a broader view.

United Nations and Japan (Kokusai Rengō *to* Nihon) 国際連合と日本

Japan was admitted to the United Nations on 18 December 1956, and its foreign policy 外交政策 has since then included "the centrality of the United Nations" 「国連中心外交」 as one of its basic guidelines. Japan has established a permanent mission to the UN headquarters 国連本部 as well as a permanent delegation to the United Nations' European subheadquarters 国連欧州本部 in Geneva ジュネーブ, Switzerland. Since 1958 Japan has been elected to the UN Security Council 国家安全保障理事会 as a nonpermanent (two-year-term) member 非常任理事国 eight times and since 1960 has been a regular member of the Economic and Social Council 経済社会理事会. Tōkyō has been the base of the network of research facilities known as the UN University 国連大学 since its founding in 1974, and in 1996 there were 12 other UN organizations 国連機関 operating in Japan, including the United Nations Information Center 国際連合広報センター, the United Nations Children's Fund (UNICEF) Office in Japan 国際連合児童基金(ユニセフ)駐日事務所, the Japan branch office of the United Nations High Commissioner for Refugees (UNHCR) 国際連合難民高等弁務官, and the United Nations Development Program (UNDP) Tōkyō Liaison Office 国際連合開発計画東京連絡事務所. The nongovernmental organizations registered with the United Nations in Japan include the United Nations Association of Japan 日本国際連合協会 and the National Federation of UNESCO Associations in Japan 日本ユネスコ協会連

Japan's Contribution to the UN Budget
国連の通常予算と日本の分担
(in millions of US dollars)

Years	Japan's contribution	UN budget
1970–71	13.79	363.59
1980–81	103.78	1,339.15
1990–91	194.85	2,134.07
1902–93	254.11	2,389.24
1994–95	279.09	2,608.27

Source: Ministry of Foreign Affairs.

盟. In 1996, Japan's contribution 分担率 to the UN budget was 15.4 percent, second largest behind the United States.

Despite the increasing importance of Japan's role as a member of the United Nations, until 1992 it had not sent troops to participate in UN peacekeeping activities 国連平和維持活動 because of its renunciation of arms 「武力の放棄」 as embodied in article 9 of the Japanese Constitution 日本国憲法第9条. That Japan's contribution was limited to an economic one met with criticism from other countries during the Persian Gulf War 湾岸戦争 of 1990–1991. In 1990 and again in 1991 the ruling Liberal Democratic Party 自由民主党 proposed legislation in the Diet that would enable SELF DEFENSE FORCES 自衛隊 troops to participate in UN peacekeeping activities. In June 1992 the Diet passed the Law on Cooperation in United Nations Peacekeeping Operations 国連平和維持活動(PKO)協力法, and, after a formal request from the United Nations, Japanese troops were sent to Cambodia カンボジア in October of that year. Since then, Self Defense Forces personnel have also participated in UN peacekeeping operations in Mozambique モザンビーク and the Golan Heights ゴラン高原 and, at the request of the UNHCR, have taken part in the refugee relief effort 難民救助活動 in Rwanda ルワンダ.

As its role in overall UN operations expands, there have been increasing calls within Japan for a permanent seat on the UN Security Council. As of the end of 1997 the outcome for Japan of UN deliberations on Security Council membership was uncertain.

Number of UN Secretariat Staff Members (1996)
国連事務局の職員数 (persons)

United States	378
Russia	132
Germany	131
Japan	108
France	96
United Kingdom	78
Italy	66
China	45

Source: United Nations.

International cultural exchange
(*kokusai bunka kōryū*) 国際文化交流

International cultural exchange 文化交流 in the broad sense is the overlap of the two concepts of "cultural exchange," which is exchange between one culture

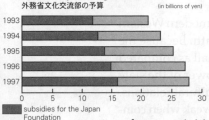

and another culture, and "international exchange," 国際交流 which is the movement of people, goods, money, and information across national borders. In other words, international cultural exchange is the movement of cultures across national borders, but in the narrow sense the term often refers to activities that are organized and intentionally carried out as projects.

Cultural exchange itself is not limited to phenomena that transcend national boundaries, just as international exchange is not limited to things that include the movement of cultures. Further, both concepts are not fundamentally concerned with the intentionality of the activities. Although the definition of international cultural exchange assumes a transcendence of borders and focuses on the movement of various cultural elements along with the movement of people, goods, money, and information over national borders, in the narrow sense it is concerned only with planned activities.

International cultural exchange, in the narrow sense defined above, is an intentional activity to forcefully move culture between sovereign state actors. Therefore, its character evolves in response to qualitative and quantitative changes in modern international relations as well as in the broad-sense reality of international exchange, cultural exchange, and international cultural exchange. The state has long played the major role in managing international exchange so the relationship between the will and power of the state to control international cultural exchange and the resulting quantitative and qualitative changes in the exchange itself is of particular importance. This relationship should be considered as central in the development of international cultural exchange in modern and contemporary Japan.

The First Period: Meiji Restoration (1868) to 1914
第1の時期：明治維新から1914年まで

In this period the importation of modern Western culture was a question of life and death. Because the absolute quantity of exchange was small as compared with later periods, the will and the power of the state extended to almost all international cultural relations. Though Japan's power was extremely weak when compared with that of the Western nations, its will was not. The actors were almost completely limited to either the nation-state or entities operating under state auspices, and, although the content of their activities varied somewhat, the primary aim of improving Japan's international position was almost always the same. The Tōa Dōbunkai (East Asia Common Culture Society; founded in 1898) 東亜同文会, which was concerned with China, and the many bilateral associations founded mainly with Western countries are representative groups from this period.

The Second Period: 1914-1945 第2の時期：1914年～1945年

In this period, which saw the peak of nationalism, the ability of the state to control international cultural relations reached a high point. Although the types of actors increased and the idea spread that it was desirable for international cultural projects, as they were referred to at the time, to be conducted in the private sector, the purpose of these projects was the same. Rather, as the idea of the "fusion of Eastern and Western culture" 「東西文化の融合」 symbolizes, the tendency of insistently trying to prove, and acquire recognition of, Japan's superiority as a cultural entity grew much stronger.

A representative group from this period is the Kokusai Bunka Shinkōkai (KBS; Society for International Cultural Relations) 国際文化振興会, founded in 1934. This group was based on cultural activities concerning China, for which planning began in 1918, and on the Gakugei Kyōiku Kokunai Iinkai (National Committee for

Language Teaching 日本語教育

...eration in overseas Japanese-language edu-
...語教育 has been one of the major pillars of the
...f the Japan Foundation since its founding. A
...nging response has been made to requests
...al overseas educational institutions, including
...patch of specialists to Japanese-language educa-
...nstitutions in numerous foreign countries, the
...ting of aid 補助金交付 for the salaries of local overseas
...ructors, and the conducting of proficiency tests 能力試
...for people whose native language is not Japanese.
...lso, in cities such as Bangkok バンコク, Jakarta ジャカルタ,
and Sydney シドニー, where demand is high, overseas
Japanese-language centers have been established to promote the creation of a comprehensive overseas
Japanese-language education network and to provide
daily-life support to on-site instructors.

Japan Foundation Japanese Language Institute
国際交流基金日本語国際センター

The Japan Foundation Japanese Language
Institute was opened at Urawa in Saitama Prefecture 埼
玉県浦和市 in 1989 as a subsidiary organ of the Japan
Foundation. It is responsible for providing comprehensive support and cooperation for overseas Japanese-
language training. At this institute, training programs
are given for overseas Japanese-language instructors
and diplomats from Asia and the Pacific region アジア・太
平洋地域. The institute also donates Japanese-language
teaching materials appropriate to the conditions of the
country of their destination, develops language teaching materials and teaching methods, carries out surveys
on the present conditions in overseas Japanese-language education, and promotes information exchange.

Introducing Japanese Culture and Arts 日本文化の紹介

One of the foundation's most important activities
is the broad-scale introduction overseas of all fields of

Intellectual Cooperation), which was founded in 1926.
The Nichibei Gakusei Kaigi (Japan-America Student
Conference; JASC) 日米学生会議 was also established in 1934
based on the proposal of a Japanese university student.

During the Pacific War, the role of international
cultural projects declined in inverse proportion to the
increase in budget. "International" cultural exchange,
which presumed a hierarchy of sovereign states, could
not play a major role in a cultural foreign policy based on
ideas like the Greater East Asia Coprosperity Sphere 大東
亜共栄圏. Paradoxically, however, this decline set the stage
for the postwar revival of international cultural exchange.

The Third Period: 1945-1972 第3の時期：1945年〜1972年

Postwar international cultural exchange was
given a special place as part of Japan's program of peace-
oriented diplomacy 平和主義的外交. Regardless of what
type of group, international cultural exchange activities
were encouraged as a means to reconstruct the state and
re-establish Japan's place in the international community. Two events that occurred just before and the after
the end of the Occupation 連合国占領, the founding of the
Kokusai Bunka Kaikan (International House of Japan) 国
際文化会館 in 1952 and the resumption of government
subsidies to KBS in 1953, were proof of Japan's commitment in this area.

During this period, however, Japan's ability to
engage in international activity could not keep up with
its desire to do so. International cultural relations were
only realized in earnest beginning in the 1970s when
strategies for dealing with the cultural conflict accompanying economic growth became an issue.

The Fourth Period: 1972-Present
第4の時期：1972年〜現在

The founding of the Kokusai Kōryū Kikin (JAPAN
FOUNDATION) 国際交流基金 in 1972 was the starting point
for a rapid increase in international cultural exchange.

In addition, this type of activity was not limited to the Ministry of Education 文部省 and the Ministry of Foreign Affairs 外務省, which have jurisdiction over the foundation; many different government agencies began to promote similar endeavors on their own. The activities of corporate foundations, such as the Toyota Foundation トヨタ財団 and the Mitsubishi Bank Foundation 三菱銀行国際財団, and other company activities supporting culture (such as corporate philanthropy) became popular as well. The Japan Forum 国際文化フォーラム founded by Kōdansha also supports exchange activities. International cultural exchange in the private sector has become more and more active, increasing dramatically since the mid-1980s.

There have been two main points of debate concerning international cultural exchange in the last quarter century. The first is whether emphasis should be placed on the sending of one's own culture or on the receiving of another culture. The second is whether activities should be carried out by the government or the private sector. Today, however, with "from exchange to cooperation" as a motto, the debate over the balance of sender and receiver has been surmounted, and pursuing international cultural exchange as a means towards various ends is becoming the norm. A simple comparison of budget size shows that international cultural exchange sponsored by the national gvernment is greatly exceeded by that sponsored by the private sector 民間 and local governments 地方自治体.

In addition, the amount of spontaneous international cultural exchange (in the broad sense of the term) has been increasing exponentially as a result of the globalization that has accompanied the rapid development of media, transportation, and communications. Since the 1970s, international cultural exchange has been expanding tremendously but the ability of the state to control this activity is in relative decline. This trend has been irreversibly a⋯ One is the diversification ⋯ involved in internation⋯ row sense, and the other is ⋯ amount of international exch⋯

Today, the current issues ⋯ the relative position and division ⋯ actor with a breaking away from ⋯ "public" versus "private" categories ⋯ establishment of a method to evaluate inte⋯ tural exchange based on the values of the ⋯ themselves.

Japan Foundation (Kokusai Kōryū Kikin) 国際交流基金

In 1972, the Japan Foundation was established as a special corporation 特殊法人 under the jurisdiction of the Ministry of Foreign Affairs 外務省, and since that time it has served as the pivot point for Japan's international cultural exchange. Throughout its history, it has continued to work toward truly global international cultural exchange through everything from the development of all types of bilateral exchange 2国間文化交流 between Japan and other nations to the promotion of exchange between third nations. Headquarters are in Tōkyō.

Comparison of Selected Cultural Exchange Institutions
世界の主要国際文化交流機関

	Japan Foundation 国際交流基金	Goethe Institute ゲーテ=インスティテュート	British Council ブリティッシュ=カウンシル
Budget (fiscal 1997)	¥19.7 billion* (¥24.3 billion)	DM358 million (¥40.1 billion)	£246 million
Comparative ratio	1	1.23	2.03
Staff (as of March 1997)	317	2,270	5,450
Institution employees	232	352	1,618
Local staff	85	1,515	3,832
Comparative ratio	1	7.2	17.2
Offices (as of March 1997)	22	168	228
Domestic	4	18	31
Overseas	18	150	197
Comparative ratio	1	7.6	10.4

*Designated donations, special expenditures, and the facilities maintenance budget are not included in the Japan Foundation budget figure.
Source: Japan Foundation.

Japanese art, from classical and traditional to contemporary. This includes visual arts 造形芸術 such as painting, sculpture, and calligraphy; performing arts 舞台芸術 such as dance, music, theater, and filmmaking, and life-culture arts 生活文化芸術 such as flower arranging, tea ceremony, *origami*, kites, and fireworks. Also, in recent years there has been an increase in the number of large-scale events held in order to provide a comprehensive introduction to Japanese culture.

Japan Foundation Center for Global Partnership
国際交流基金日米センター

The Center for Global Partnership (CGP) was established in April 1991 in order to administer a ¥50 billion fund for the purpose of deepening and broadening dialogue between Japanese and American people in various fields.

The major work of the CGP is to promote intellectual exchange for global partnership through joint research projects and dialogues on such issues as the environment, north-south problems, and other problems held in common, and to develop better understanding through regional and grass-roots level activities.

Official development assistance
(ODA; *seifu kaihatsu enjo*) 政府開発援助

In Japan ODA is synonymous with foreign aid 海外援助 and includes grants-in-aid 無償資金協力, technical assistance 技術協力, loan aid 政府貸付(円借款), and financial support contributed to international organizations engaged in development and relief work.

Japanese foreign aid following World War II began in the1950s in the form of reparations payments 賠償金支払 to Burma ビルマ (now Myanmar ミャンマー), the Philippines フィリピン, Indonesia インドネシア, and Vietnam ベトナム and grants resembling reparations to several other Asian nations, including South Korea 韓国. This

Official Development Assistance (ODA)
政府開発援助

(billions of US dollars)

1990	9.07
1991	10.95
1992	11.15
1993	11.26
1994	13.24
1995	14.49

Source: OECD Development Cooperation.

was followed by a period in the 1960s when strong export expansion was a principal interest in foreign aid programs. In the late 1960s and early 1970s the provision of aid and investment aimed at securing agricultural and raw material supplies, called "development import" 開発輸入 assistance, became a dominant emphasis.

The marked contrast between the stances taken by Japan at the First United Nations Conference on Trade and Development (UNCTAD I) 国連貿易開発会議, held in Geneva ジュネーブ in 1964, and the fifth conference (UNCTAD V), held in Manila マニラ in 1979, illustrates clearly the significant change in the Japanese approach to economic cooperation 経済協力 with developing countries as a focus in foreign economic policy. The former meeting saw Japan, preoccupied with its own program of heavy industrialization and economic relations with advanced powers, adopting a very negative attitude toward development assistance 開発援助 and the developing countries' case for preferred access to export markets in developed countries. By the time of the 1979 meeting, however, development issues were at the forefront of Japan's foreign policy interests; Japan had become the fourth or fifth largest aid donor, with ODA spending of about US $2.6 billion.

With an ODA outlay of US $9.3 billion in 1997, Japan became the world's largest aid donor, as measured by the disbursement of official development assistance by the industrial countries represented in the Development Assistance Committee (DAC) 開発援助委員会 of the Organization for Economic Cooperation and Development (OECD) 経済協力開発機構. However, measured as a percentage of gross national product (GNP) 国民総生産, at 0.22 percent Japanese aid ranked 19th among DAC nations, which was the DAC average value. Japanese aid in 1997 was 19.7 percent of the total disbursed by all DAC nations.

Ratio of Official Development Assistance to GNP
政府開発援助の対GNP比

(in percentages)

	Japan	United States
1990	0.31	0.19
1991	0.32	0.17
1992	0.30	0.18
1993	0.27	0.15
1994	0.29	0.15
1995	0.28	0.10

Source: OECD Development Cooperation.

ODA of Each DAC Country (1997)
DAC各国のODA

Value of ODA		Ratio to GNP	
(net disbursements in millions of US dollars)		(in percentages)	
1 Japan	9,350	1 Denmark	0.97
2 France	6,348	2 Norway	0.86
3 United States	6,168	3 Netherlands	0.81
4 Germany	5,913	4 Sweden	0.76
5 United Kingdom	3,371	5 Luxembourg	0.50
6 Netherlands	2,946	6 France	0.45
7 Canada	2,140	7 Canada	0.36
8 Sweden	1,672	8 Finland	0.33
9 Denmark	1,635	9 Switzerland	0.32
10 Norway	1,306	10 Belgium	0.31
11 Italy	1,231	10 Ireland	0.31
12 Spain	1,227	12 Australia	0.28
13 Australia	1,076	12 Germany	0.28
14 Switzerland	839	14 Austria	0.26
15 Belgium	764	14 United Kingdom	0.26
16 Austria	531	16 Portugal	0.25
17 Finland	379	16 New Zealand	0.25
18 Portugal	251	18 Spain	0.23
19 Ireland	187	19 Japan	0.22
20 New Zealand	145	20 Italy	0.11
21 Luxembourg	87	21 United States	0.18

Source: Ministry of Foreign Affairs.

The government has emphasized that a priority will be increasing the grant aid 無償資金協力 component of ODA in accordance with the international view that grants ought to be the principal form of aid, and also in response to requests from poorer countries that are in urgent need of this form of aid. Reflecting Japan's increasing worldwide economic impact, the government has gradually moved beyond narrow economic objectives in an effort to shoulder greater responsibility in the international economy.

Aid Administration 援助機関

The administration of official Japanese aid programs and policies rests with a number of government ministries and agencies, in particular the Ministry of Foreign Affairs 外務省, the Ministry of Finance 大蔵省, the Ministry of International Trade and Industry (MITI) 通商産業省, and the Economic Planning Agency 経済企画庁. They are backed up by three government-funded institutions, the Overseas Economic Cooperation Fund (OECF) 海外経済協力基金, the Export-Import Bank of Japan 日本輸出入銀行, and the JAPAN INTERNATIONAL COOPERATION AGENCY (JICA) 国際協力事業団, which respectively oversee the disbursement of soft loans 譲許的借款(条件のゆるやかな円借款), export credits 輸出信用, and technical assistance 技術協力 and grant aid. There is no central aid agency as in some other donor countries.

Japan International Cooperation Agency
(JICA; Kokusai Kyōryoku Jigyōdan) 国際協力事業団

Special public corporation established to promote international cooperation through the provision of overseas development assistance. It was founded in 1974 in accordance with the International Cooperation Agency Law 国際協力事業団法.

JICA's main activities include (1) the strengthening of technical assistance programs to developing countries provided by the Japanese government by bringing technical trainees to Japan and by dispatching specialists and providing needed equipment and materials for projects overseas, (2) the facilitation and promotion of grant assistance programs, (3) the extension of loans and equity investment related to development projects, (4) the training and dispatching of Japan Overseas Cooperation Volunteers (JOCV) 青年海外協力隊.

JICA's activities are administered by the Ministry of Foreign Affairs 外務省; the Ministry of Agriculture, Forestry, and Fisheries 農林水産省; and the Ministry of International Trade and Industry (MITI) 通産省. Its head office is in Tōkyō, with subsidiary agencies, such as the International Center, spread throughout the country. As of March 1998 JICA maintains 55 offices overseas, and its staff numbered 1,213, of whom 300 worked abroad.

Japan Overseas Cooperation Volunteers

青年海外協力隊

Program founded in 1965 to provide technical services and instruction to developing countries. Financed exclusively by the Japanese government, the JOCV sent out 15,966 volunteers 隊員 between 1965 and 1996.

The volunteers, all young people, serve a term of two years and receive a monthly living allowance; their housing is provided by the host country, and they work as members of that country's government. The JOCV places strong emphasis on technical qualifications and experience, and nearly half of its volunteers have been in agriculture, forestry, and fishing and in education and information services.

Fields of Service of Japan Overseas Cooperation Volunteers through September 1997
青年海外協力隊の部門別派遣者数 (in percentages)

education and information services	26.8
agriculture, forestry, and fishery	23.5
maintenance and operation	16.3
health and welfare	12.2
civil engineering and architecture	8.0
sports	7.5
manufacturing	3.1
other	2.6
Total Participants: 15,966	

Source: Japan Overseas Cooperation Volunteers.

Northern Territories issue
(Hoppō Ryōdo *mondai*) 北方領土問題

Dispute concerning Japan's Northern Territories, which consist of Kunashiri 国後島, Etorofu 択捉島, Shikotan 色丹島, and the Habomai Islands 歯舞諸島, occupied by the Soviet Union ソビエト連邦 since 1945 and still occupied by the Russian Federation ロシア連邦 in 1995. The Japanese government maintains that the Russian occupation is illegal and demands the return of these islands.

After Japan's defeat in World War II, it signed the San Francisco Peace Treaty サンフランシスコ平和条約 with 48 Allied nations 連合国 (but not the Soviet Union) in September 1951. In the treaty Japan renounced all rights and title to the Kuril Islands 千島列島, but the text did not stipulate which islands made up the Kuril chain nor which government was to exercise sovereignty over them.

Asserting that Kunashiri, Etorofu, Shikotan, and the Habomai Islands are not included in the term "Kuril Islands" as used in the San Francisco treaty and that they have historically constituted an integral part of the territory of Japan, the Japanese government sought their return. The Soviet Union refused, contending that the territorial issue had already been resolved. Then during

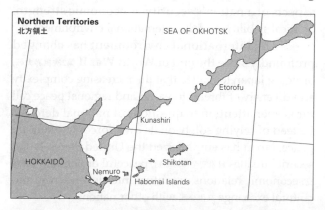

Northern Territories
北方領土

SEA OF OKHOTSK

Etorofu

Kunashiri

HOKKAIDŌ

Nemuro

Shikotan

Habomai Islands

Soviet president Mikhail Gorbachev's ゴルバチョフ大統領 visit to Tōkyō in 1991, both sides confirmed in a joint communiqué 共同宣言 that final resolution of the issue would be carried out as a part of a future peace treaty 平和条約 between the two countries. However, the Soviet Union was dissolved at the end of that year.

At the summit meeting 首脳会談 held in November 1997, Japanese Prime Minister Ryūtarō Hashimoto 橋本龍太郎首相 and Russian President Boris Yeltsin ボリス=エリツィン大統領 agreed to make utmost efforts to sign a peace treaty by the end of 2000 and to discuss the issue of the return of the disputed islands as part of the treaty negotiations. In 1998 Prime Minister Obuchi Keizō 小渕恵三 met with Yeltsin in Moscow, where they signed Moscow Declaration モスクワ宣言. In this declaration, both government referred to the Northern Territories issue with the phrase "demarcating the international boundaries 国境線 of the four islands."

NATIONAL DEFENSE 国防

National defense (*kokubō*) 国防

The Japanese term *kokubō* encompasses the maintenance of military forces as well as such nonmilitary aspects of a nation's security as economic strength, political stability, and the international environment.

The international environment has changed profoundly since the end of World War II 第2次世界大戦, bringing Japan to realize that the increasing complexity and diversity of threats to world and regional peace call for keener attention to questions of national defense. Instead of relying solely on its own forces to maintain peace, Japan has emphasized the United States-Japan security treaties 日米安全保障条約, peaceful diplomacy 平和外交, economic relations of mutual interdependence, and cultural exchange 文化交流 with other nations.

Establishment of the Self Defense Forces
自衛隊の成立

It is said that General Douglas MacArthur 最高司令官ダグラス=マッカーサー, the supreme commander of the Allied forces 連合国 occupying Japan after World War II, intended to dismantle completely the old military forces and military industries 軍需産業 and to transform Japan into "the Switzerland of the Far East." 「極東のスイス」 But in 1950, after the outbreak of war in Korea 朝鮮戦争 and hardening of the cold war 冷戦, a National Police Reserve 警察予備隊 of 75,000 men was formed. In the early days of the cold war, as the United States requested a considerable degree of Japanese rearmament, Prime Minister Yoshida Shigeru 吉田茂首相 resisted on grounds that such action would "suppress the economy and make for domestic instability." In 1952, with Japan's independence restored, the National Police Reserve, adding maritime and air branches, became the National Safety Forces 保安隊, later reorganized as the SELF DEFENSE FORCES (SDF) 自衛隊.

This combination of the relatively small Self Defense Forces with a bilateral security treaty with the United States remains the core of Japan's national defense. Japan has pursued Yoshida's policy of "inexpensive defense" and achieved economic development by favoring peaceful coexistence and promoting an international environment favorable to free trade.

International Military Strength
主要国の兵力

Country	Ground forces (thousands of personnel)	Naval forces (number of vessels)	(displacement in thousands of tons)	Air forces (number of combat aircraft)
United States	501	1,050	5,069	4,200
Russia	670	1,700	4,240	3,440
China	2,200	940	1,045	6,010
United Kingdom	—	300	826	600
Germany	—	210	199	560
France	241	330	460	790
Japan	153	160	346	520

Note: The figures for Japan are for 1995. The figures for ground and air forces for other countries are from *Military Balance* (1995–1996) and those for naval forces are from *Japan's Fighting Ships* (1996–1997). Combat aircraft statistics other than those for Japan include aircraft belonging to air, naval, and marine forces.

Source: Defense Agency.

National Defense Policy 国防政策

The Japanese government's basic policy for national defense, enunciated by its National Defense Council 国防会議 (now Security Council) 安全保障会議 in 1957, sets forth the objectives of preserving Japan's peace and independence, deterring direct or indirect aggression, and repelling any assaults. International cooperation 国際協力, stabilization of public welfare 公共福祉, a gradual increase in defense capabilities 国防能力, and reliance on the security treaties were among the original means to achieving those objectives. Since then, a few new principles have been added. These include the Hikaku Sangensoku (the three nonnuclear principles 非核3原則 of not manufacturing, possessing, or introducing 「作らず」・「持たず」・「持ち込ませず」 into Japanese territory nuclear weapons, as approved by the Diet in 1971), a prohibition on the dispatch of troops overseas 海外派兵, a prohibition against conscription 徴兵制度, the three principles regarding the export of arms 武器輸出3原則, and the maintenance of a "strictly defensive posture" 専守防衛, signifying a passive defense strategy. The strategy centered on the concept of keeping military capabilities to a minimum level necessary for self-defense. The National Defense Program Outline 防衛計画の大綱 adopted in 1976 called for a limited attack into Japanese territory to be repelled by Japan's own defensive forces, with assistance from the United States should these prove to be inadequate. When this outline was adopted, the Miki Takeo cabinet 三木武夫内閣 also enunciated a policy of limiting defense spending 防衛支出 to 1 percent or less of Japan's gross national product 国民総生産 (one-percent defense ceiling 防衛費GNP 1%枠), a precedent followed by almost all succeeding governments.

In November 1995 the government announced a new National Defense Program Outline. In response to changes in the post-cold war world, the new outline specifies lower personnel and armament levels in some categories. At the same time, it reiterates Japan's policy of maintaining a basic defense capability, and it supports continuing Japan-United States security ties. New guidelines cover the use of the Self Defense Forces in natural disasters 災害, United Nations peacekeeping operations 国連平和維持活動, and fighting terrorism.

Self Defense Forces (SDF; Jieitai) 自衛隊

Armed forces 軍隊 responsible for the ground, sea, and air defense of Japan. The term "Self Defense" is used in the official title because the 1947 Constitution of Japan 日本国憲法 prohibits the nation from possessing military forces (see RENUNCIATION OF WAR 戦争の放棄), but, according to the government, does not prohibit the nation from maintaining the ability to defend itself.

Historical Development 成立

After World War II, Japan's army, navy, and air force were dismantled, but, with the outbreak of the Korean War 朝鮮戦争 in 1950, General Douglas MacArthur 連合国最高司令官ダグラス=マッカーサー, commander of the Allied Occupation of Japan, ordered the establishment of a National Police Reserve 警察予備隊 of 75,000 men to fill the gap created by the dispatch of Occupation forces to Korea. From its inception, this force was recognized as possessing greater firepower and mobility than the regular police force. In 1952 its name was changed to National Safety Forces 保安隊 and, together with the Maritime Guard 海上警備隊, it was administered by the newly established National Safety Agency 保安庁.

With the passage of the Self Defense Forces Law 自衛隊法 in 1954, the Safety Agency became the Defense Agency 防衛庁, and the existing forces were reorganized as the Self Defense Forces, with three services: the Ground Self Defense Force (GSDF; J: Rikujō Jieitai) 陸上自衛隊, the Maritime Self Defense Force (MSDF; J: Kaijō

Jieitai) 海上自衛隊, and the Air Self Defense Force (ASDF; J: Kōkū Jieitai) 航空自衛隊.

Organization and Command 組織

Supreme command 最高指揮権 rests with the prime minister, who represents the cabinet. The director-general 長官 of the Defense Agency 防衛庁, a member of the cabinet, receives his orders from the prime minister and is assisted by civilian and military personnel and by the Joint Staff Council 統合幕僚会議. The chiefs of staff 幕僚長 of the three forces carry out within their commands the orders of the director-general and supervise the activities of their respective branches.

Personnel 自衛官

Self Defense Forces personnel enlist between the ages of 18 and 25 for voluntary two- or three-year terms. In 1970 the SDF formed a reserve corps of volunteers on inactive status 予備自衛官制, and in 1974 it began recruiting women. Officers 幹部自衛官 are selected from among graduates of the National Defense Academy 防衛大学校, graduates of regular universities who have passed a qualifying examination, and noncommissioned officers 下士官 who score high on the qualifying examination. Each service has its own officer candidate school, but there is also a National Institute for Defense Studies 防衛研究所 for higher study by selected officers.

Defense Budget 防衛予算

Defense appropriations totaled approximately ¥4.8 trillion (US $45.7 billion) in 1996, or 0.96 percent of the estimated gross national product 国民総生産(GNP). In 1996 the breakdown of expenditures by organization was GSDF 陸上自衛隊, 37.0 percent; MSDF 海上自衛隊, 23.1 percent; ASDF 航空自衛隊, 23.5 percent; Defense Facilities Administration Agency 防衛施設庁, 11.8 percent; and others, 4.7 percent. Of the overall defense budget, 42.8 percent went for personnel expenses 人件費 and 57.2 percent for non-personnel-related expenses (equipment,

Defense-Related Expenditures
防衛関係費 (in trillions of yen)

1955	1,349
1965	3,014
1975	13,273
1985	31,371
1990	41,593
1995	47,236

Source: Defense Agency.

training, bases, research and development, etc).

▌Units and Their Deployment 部隊と装備

The GSDF is divided into 12 infantry divisions 師団 and 1 armored division 機甲(戦車)師団, which are grouped into 5 regional armies 方面隊. The greatest emphasis has been placed on the defense of Hokkaidō. In 1996 GSDF personnel numbered about 152,000. The force is equipped with 1,130 medium tanks 戦車 and helicopters.

The MSDF comprises the Self Defense Fleet 自衛艦隊 and five district units 地方隊. It regards antisubmarine warfare as its most important mission. In 1996 personnel numbered about 44,000 and the MSDF deployed 60 destroyers 駆逐艦 and destroyer escorts 護衛艦, 16 nonnuclear submarines 非核潜水艦, and about 200 antisubmarine aircraft and helicopters 対潜ヘリコプター.

The men and equipment of the ASDF are divided into four air zones 航空方面隊. Operational emphasis is placed on the swift identification of aircraft encroaching on Japanese airspace and on quick response to a possible consolidated air attack. In 1996 personnel numbered some 46,000, and the ASDF possessed some 374 fighter planes 戦闘機 as well as Patriot surface-to-air missiles 地対空ミサイル.

▌The Constitution and the SDF 憲法と自衛隊

Since its inception the SDF has faced the charge that its existence is a violation of article 9 of the constitution 憲法第9条. To this, the government has responded that although the constitution forbids war as a means of resolving international disputes, it does not negate the right of self-defense 自衛権. Although criticism continues, the SDF has won general acceptance from the Japanese public, and the voices calling for abolition are fewer.

With the end of the cold war, there have been increasing calls in Japan for a reduction in the size, and a rethinking of the role, of the SDF. The deployment of forces overseas had been prohibited since its founding, but with the June 1992 enactment of the Law on Cooperation in United Nations Peacekeeping Operations 国連平和維持活動協力法, the SDF is now able to participate in UN peacekeeping activities 国連平和維持活動 and humanitarian relief efforts abroad. The SDF has taken part in peacekeeping operations in Cambodia カンボジア (1992–1993), Mozambique モザンビーク (1993–1995), and the Golan Heights ゴラン高原 (1996–) and refugee relief operations 難民救助活動 in Rwanda ルワンダ (1994).

The new National Defense Program Outline 防衛計画の大綱 announced in November 1995 states that Japan will continue to follow the principle of maintaining a minimum necessary basic defence capability, and it specifies lower authorized personnel levels for the GSDF as well as somewhat smaller numbers for certain armaments. The outline also includes new guidelines for the use of the Self Defense Forces in natural disasters 自然災害, United Nations peacekeeping operations, and fighting terrorism. See also NATIONAL DEFENSE.

ECONOMY

Contemporary economy (*gendai* Nihon *keizai*)
現代日本経済

The Japanese economy is the world's second largest market economy 市場経済, with a gross domestic product (GDP) 国内総生産 of US $4.12 trillion in fiscal 1997. In 1996 Japan's per capita national income, at US $28,470, was fourth in the world behind Luxembourg, Switzerland, and Norway. Recovery from the recession

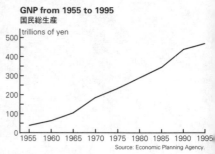

GNP from 1955 to 1995
国民総生産

trillions of yen

Source: Economic Planning Agency.

that followed the collapse of the bubble economy バブル経済 of the late 1980s was slow. After 1993 some signs of recovery were seen, but tight fiscal policies and an increase in the consumption tax 消費税 rate pushed the economy back into recession in 1997. In fiscal 1997 the GDP growth rate was a negative 0.4 percent. The extended economic downturn experienced in the 1990s, known as the Heisei Recession 平成不況, is considered the worst recession since World War II.

A high level of both import and export activity has continued in the 1990s, and in fiscal 1997 the fluctuating trade surplus 貿易黒字 stood at US $93.2 billion.

The High-Growth Era 高度成長期

At the end of the Allied Occupation 連合国占領 in 1952, Japan ranked as a less-developed country 低開発国, with per capita consumption a mere one-fifth that of the United States. During the period 1953–1973, the economy grew with unprecedented rapidity (average growth was 8.0% per annum overall and 10.6% during the 1960s) and Japan became the first less-developed country in the postwar era to graduate to developed status. Real output per person in 1970 was 2.5 times higher than in 1960, and by 1968 Japan had surpassed West

Germany to become the world's second largest economy. This rapid growth resulted in significant changes to Japan's INDUSTRIAL STRUCTURE 産業構造. First, production shifted from a heavy reliance on AGRICULTURE and light manufacturing 軽工業 to a focus on heavy industry 重工業 and, increasingly, services. In 1954, when recovery from World War II was largely complete, the primary sector 第1次産業 (agriculture, fisheries, and mining) still accounted for 24.5 percent of output and 37.9 percent of the labor force 就業人口; in contrast, manufacturing (the secondary sector 第2次産業) accounted for only 23.8 percent of output and 19.5 percent of employment. By 1970, agriculture and mining had fallen to 8.3 percent of output and 17.8 percent of the labor force, while manufacturing had risen to 30.2 percent of output and 27.0 percent of employment. In 1985, 9 percent of the labor force was in primary sector occupations, 33 percent in secondary, and 58 percent in tertiary 第3次産業. Urbanization also progressed rapidly, with the proportion of people living in cities escalating from 38 to 72 percent of the population between 1950 and 1970.

Until 1952 economic policy was dictated by the Occupation. Reforms in 1949 under the Shoup mission シャウプ使節団 and Dodge line ドッジ＝ライン put in place the postwar tax system, balanced the government budget, normalized the financial system, and brought Japan into the world trade system at a fixed exchange rate 固定為替レート of ¥360 per US dollar. These reforms cured the postwar hyperinflation but at the cost of a sharp recession. While profits generated by the large number of special orders (*tokuju* 特需)

Economically Active Population by Industry
業種別就業人口

(in percentages)

	Japan (1970)	Japan (1995)	United States (1970)	United States (1995)
Agriculture, hunting, forestry and fishing 農林水産業	19.3	5.7	3.5	2.9
Mining and quarrying 鉱業	0.4	0.1	0.8	0.5
Manufacturing 製造業	26.2	22.5	24.2	16.4
Electricity, gas, and water supplies 電気・ガス・水道業	0.5	0.7	—	1.2
Construction 建設業	7.5	10.3	5.6	6.1
Trade, restaurants, and hotels 卸・小売業	19.3	22.4	20.1	20.9
Transport, storage, and communication 運輸・通信業	6.2	6.2	4.8	5.8
Financing, insurance, real estate, and business services 金融・保険・不動産業	4.3	8.6	6.3	11.0
Community, social, and personal services サービス業	16.3	23.1	30.7	35.3
Activities not adequately defined 分類不能	0.1	0.4	4.3	—

Source: Bank of Japan, *Kokusai hikaku tōkei.*

for goods and services in Japan to support United Nations forces during the Korean War 朝鮮戦争 helped end the recession, the economy continued to alternate between periods of prosperity and recession.

The first major expansion—the Iwato Boom 岩戸景気 (1959–1961, average growth 12.2%), spurred by Prime Minister Ikeda Hayato's 1960 Income-Doubling Plan 国民所得倍増計画—touched off an investment spree. Growth reached 14.5 percent in 1961, but as in the 1950s this led to increased imports, and the government was forced to slow growth during 1962 because of the resulting balance-of-payments 国際収支 crisis. Further expansions occurred in 1963–1964 (average growth 11.8%), 1967–1970 (the Izanagi Boom, average growth 11.2%), and 1972–1973 (the Tanaka expansion, average growth 8.9%).

Many factors contributed to rapid growth, including the shift in employment from low-productivity primary sector pursuits to manufacturing and the entry of an increasingly skilled and better-educated postwar-baby-boom generation into the labor force. In addition, macroeconomic policies were conducive to growth, the international environment was blessed with stable commodity prices and expanding trade, and investment was high. Together with the introduction of better technology, productivity increased rapidly.

The contribution of government industrial policy to economic growth 経済成長 is less clear, and on net was probably not large. The government was heavily interventionist during the early years of the Occupation, but direct controls were eased after 1949 and largely eliminated by 1955. Industrial policy was implemented via indirect controls, requiring licenses for imports and technology transfer. Japan became a member of the International Monetary Fund (IMF) 国際通貨基金 in 1952 and the General Agreement on Tariffs and Trade (GATT)

Per Capita National Income (1996)
1人当たり国民所得 (in US dollars)

Luxembourg	38,392
Switzerland	36,247
Norway	30,014
Japan	28,470
Denmark	27,696
United States	24,901
Germany	24,762
Austria	24,488
Belgium	24,184
Sweden	23,580

Source: Economic Planning Agency.

関税と貿易に関する一般協定 in 1955. Around 1960, Japan committed itself to TRADE LIBERALIZATION 貿易の自由化 by seeking IMF article 8 status and deciding to join the OECD 経済協力開発機構, both of which were realized in 1964. Tariffs and quantitative controls on most goods were removed by 1970, and, with the exception of agriculture and some high-technology products, most nontariff barriers were eliminated by the 1980s. Nevertheless, the overall bias was for a greater degree of protection of domestic producers than in the United States.

Indirect government assistance also came in the form of tax breaks, treasury investment and loans, and the Ministry of International Trade and Industry's 通産省 policy of administrative guidance 行政指導. An important example is the Machinery Industries Promotion Law 機械工業振興臨時措置法 of 1956, which supported the machine tool industry 工作機械産業 as well as automotive parts and other metalworking sectors. Ultimately, most industries obtained some government favors, and it is unclear that any industry was effectively promoted relative to its rivals. However, domestic policies did result in a minimal presence by foreign firms in most sectors, and permitted some industries to survive that would otherwise have succumbed to foreign competition.

Financial assets were wiped out by the 1945–1949 hyperinflation, but from the 1950s the banking system 銀行制度 was gradually rebuilt, largely along pre-World War II lines. In 1949 the stock exchange was reopened, but it did not develop into a major source of new funds until the 1980s, and a bond market was not allowed to develop. Banks sought customers in emerging industries, encouraging the entry of new firms into the market and hence the presence of vigorous interfirm competition. Corporate finance depended on bank financing as the major source of outside funds, giving rise to a capital structure dominated by debt. To prevent takeovers, enterprise groups 企業グループ, or *keiretsu* 系列, actively sought cross-shareholdings with a variety of firms, including major financial institutions (banks in Japan are permitted to purchase up to 5% of the shares of a client firm). Small and medium enterprises remained relatively important during this period, employing nearly three-quarters of the labor force. However, unlike the larger enterprise groups, small and medium-sized firms were tied to local banks, employed less-skilled or older workers (or temporary and female workers), and paid lower wages. In manufacturing, they often functioned as subcontractors (*shitauke* 下請け) to larger firms.

During the 1950s the major exporters—and thus the leading firms—were in textiles and other light industries, whose products were marketed by general trading companies; government promotion, however, focused on heavy manufacturing located in major coastal industrial complexes. During the 1960s the iron and steel industry 鉄鋼業 and the shipbuilding industry 造船業 came to the fore, followed by the chemical industry 化学工業 and in the early 1970s the electronics industry; the automotive industry 自動車産業 rose to prominence in the late 1970s. Exports were important, especially for textiles and shipbuilding, which were aided by a rapid increase in world trade throughout the 1960s.

But growth was fueled above all by investment based on increased consumer spending. As incomes grew, consumption shifted from basic products such as radios, fans, and scooters to more expensive and luxurious items such as color televisions, air conditioners, and cars. In the case of manufacturing, a mature industrial base made it feasible to purchase new machinery and to concentrate on improving managerial performance. New machinery meant

Ownership Rate of Consumer Durables
耐久消費財の普及率
(percentage of households)

	1970	1980	1990
Electric washing machine	91.4	98.8	99.5
Electric refrigerator	89.1	99.1	98.2
Vacuum cleaner	68.3	95.8	98.8
Color TV set	26.3	98.2	99.4
Air conditioner	5.9	39.2	63.7
Piano	6.8	15.8	22.7
Car	22.1	57.2	77.3

Source: Economic Planning Agency.

Household Expenditures
家計支出

(in percentages)

	1970	1980	1990	1995
Food	34.1	29.0	25.4	23.7
Housing	4.9	4.6	4.8	6.5
Utilities	4.4	5.7	5.5	6.1
Furniture & household goods	5.0	4.3	4.0	3.8
Clothing	9.5	7.9	7.4	6.1
Medical care & health expenses	2.7	2.5	2.8	3.0
Transportation & communication	5.2	8.0	9.5	10.0
Education	2.7	3.6	4.7	4.7
Recreation & entertainment	9.6	8.5	9.7	9.6
Other	22.6	25.8	26.3	26.6

Source: Management and Coordination Agency.

new technology, which meant lower costs and higher profits. Furthermore, in the case of many industries, no firm could afford to lag behind its rivals in installing new equipment. Growth fueled investment, which in turn fueled further growth.

To facilitate the adoption of new technology, after 1955 large firms adopted the modern employment system and trained their "lifetime" employees 終身雇用 in new skills. Labor unions based on an enterprise rather than an industry or a craft cooperated in this, since new skills led to higher incomes and assured future jobs. Labor disputes were of minor importance after 1960, and annual contract negotiations occurring during the spring wage offensive 春闘 helped to keep workers aware of the link between wages and productivity. As a consequence, inflationary hikes within the wage system were generally avoided.

Rapid growth was not without its problems. Until the late 1960s, Japan faced chronic balance-of-payments difficulties, due variously to surging imports when the economy grew too fast, or poor exports when foreign markets were in recession. The government therefore used monetary policy to slow the economy in 1953–1954, 1957, 1961, 1963, and again in 1967. Inflation and price stability also proved to be problematic, at least comparatively: during the 1960s, consumer prices rose at an average annual rate of 5.8 percent in Japan, versus 2.7 percent in the United States. The spread of pollution 公害 and pollution-related diseases 公害病 went unchecked until the late 1960s, when abysmal air quality in Tōkyō and multiple fatalities from mercury and cadmium poisoning prompted more stringent pollution control laws (see ENVIRONMENTAL QUALITY). Government provision for social welfare 社会福祉 also lagged; only from about 1970 did social security 社会保障 coverage become universal, so until then workers had to rely entirely upon private savings. Only in the late 1980s did corporate and national pensions reach a level sufficient to help the average retiree. On the other hand, income distribution remained remarkably even; no underclass emerged (see SOCIAL SECURITY PROGRAMS).

Mature Economy 経済の成熟

By 1973, many of the factors that supported rapid growth lost their strength. First, Japanese industry had caught up with the best practices abroad; improving productivity required more resources than in the past. This in turn lowered the profitability of new investment, which fell to a permanently lower level after 1974. By 1973, the growth of the now urban and better-educated labor force had peaked. Finally, the international environment became less favorable, due mainly to the revaluation of the yen and trade friction with the United States. The Japan-United States textile talks 日米繊維交渉 of 1969, the Nixon Shocks ニクソン=ショック of 1971, a worldwide commodity price boom that culminated in the quadrupling of oil prices during the oil crisis 石油危機 of 1973, and the movement of the yen to a floating rate 変動相場制 in 1973 all worked to slow growth.

Domestic macroeconomic policy was also less conductive to growth. The government made a major policy blunder in 1971–1972, when it permitted exporters to convert their dollars to yen, which rapidly increased the money supply. This was magnified by Prime Minister Tanaka Kakuei's 田中角栄 plan to rebuild the Japanese archipelago (Nihon Rettō Kaizō Ron) 日本列島改造論, which interacted with easy money and rising international commodity prices to touch off a speculative binge in real estate and domestic commodity markets. Japan was thus already suffering from double-digit inflation by October 1973, when the first oil crisis 石油危機 touched off sharp price increases and hoarding.

Even before the October 1973 oil crisis, the government had started to slow the economy in response to rising inflation; combined with the impact of a quadrupling of oil prices, gross national product (GNP) 国民総生産 fell 1.4 percent in 1974, the first actual decline since the 1950s. More significant, the oil shock and recession lowered expectations of future growth: private investment fell from 31 percent of GNP in 1973–1974 to under 25 percent of GNP from 1977 on. Growth slowed from the 10 percent level to an average of 3.6 percent during 1974–1979 and 4.4 percent during 1980–1990. Consumer prices stabilized after 1975, and Japan experienced comparatively low inflation following the second oil crisis in 1978. Furthermore, unemployment never surpassed 3 percent.

Gross fixed investment, public and private, rose to a peak of 37 percent of GNP in 1973 before receding to 31–33 percent in the late 1970s. The economy was threatened with recession, particularly since consumption failed to increase and savings remained high. Tax cuts in 1974, 1975, and 1977, however, served to stimulate the economy, while increases in central government expenditures continued at a steady pace. The central government budget deficit 財政赤字 ballooned to 6.1 percent of GNP in 1979, which kept the economy out of recession. The overall government deficit, however, peaked in 1978 at 5.5 percent of GNP, as local and provincial surpluses partially offset the central government deficit.

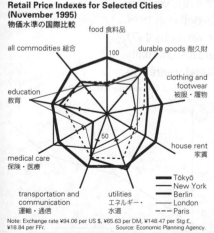

Retail Price Indexes for Selected Cities (November 1995)
物価水準の国際比較

food 食料品
all commodities 総合
100
durable goods 耐久財
clothing and footwear 被服・履物
education 教育
50
house rent 家賃
medical care 保険・医療
transportation and communication 運輸・通信
utilities エネルギー・水道

━━━ Tōkyō
──── New York
━━━ Berlin
──── London
- - - Paris

Note: Exchange rate ¥94.06 per US $, ¥65.63 per DM, ¥148.47 per Stg £, ¥18.84 per FFr.
Source: Economic Planning Agency.

The deficit was held in check from 1979; in addition, monetary policy turned restrictive, with the Bank of Japan 日本銀行 raising the discount rate 公定歩合 in stages from 4.25 percent to 9 percent. Indeed, continued concerns about large deficits led to a succession of tight budgets throughout the 1980s, though tax increases were held in abeyance until 1987 and 1988. The primary exceptions granted in the tight budgets in the 1980s were for social security, NATIONAL DEFENSE 国防, and foreign aid. By 1985 the consolidated government deficit shrank to 0.8 percent of GNP, and turned into a surplus from 1987. Again, a decline in fiscal stimulus by 6 percent of GNP might be expected to drag the economy into a recession. This time shifts in international trade offset the decline in domestic demand. The trade balance remained relatively stable during the 1970s, and in 1980 actually showed a slight deficit. But by 1985, the current account surplus 経常収支の黒字 in Japan's balance of payments 国際収支 reached 3.7 percent of GNP. While the economy was weak in 1981–1983, exports increased sharply during 1983–1985, due in part to the strengthening of the US dollar.

After the 1985 Plaza Accord プラザ合意, the yen rose sharply in value, reaching ¥120 to the US dollar in 1988, twice its average 1984 value and three times its 1971 value. As a result, after 1986 the trade surplus gradually shrank. But this time around, domestic demand increased to pick up the slack. Monetary policy was eased four times during 1986, as the Bank of Japan lowered the discount rate from 5.0 percent to 2.5 percent, the lowest level since World War II. Consumption began increasing in 1986, and investment took over during 1987–1990; in fact, corporate investment rose to 19.6 percent of

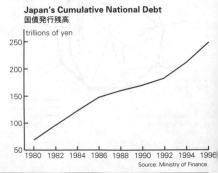

Japan's Cumulative National Debt
国債発行残高

trillions of yen

Source: Ministry of Finance.

GNP in 1988 and 21.7 percent in 1989, far above the 15.3–17.5 percent that had prevailed during 1980–1987, and exceeding total investment in plant and equipment in 1989 for the entire United States in both percentage and value.

With higher stock prices, new equity issues sky-rocketed to ¥16.8 trillion (US $116 billion) in 1987 and ¥24.8 trillion (US $177 billion) in 1989, becoming a significant source of finance for corporations for the first time since the crash of the Tōkyō market in 1961. Banks found a new outlet for funds in real estate development. In turn, corporations attempted to maximize the productivity of their assets using real estate holdings as collateral for stock market speculation in a method referred to as *zaitech* ("financial technology") 財テク. In the ensuing speculative binge (1986–1989), land prices doubled and the Tōkyō Nikkei stock market index 東証日経株価指数 rose 2.7 times.

Japan tightened monetary policy beginning in May 1989, and higher interest rates touched off a collapse of stock prices. By the end of 1990, the Tōkyō stock market had fallen 38 percent from its peak, wiping out ¥300 trillion (US $2.3 trillion) in value in the space of a few months.

By 1993 land prices 地価 in Tōkyō had fallen 49.3 percent from the 1990 speculative peak, leaving major Japanese banks saddled with a large volume of bad debt 不良債権 as borrowers are unable to pay back loans on real estate purchased at inflated prices.

According to the Economic Planning Agency 経済企画庁, the recession which began in April 1991 bottomed out in October 1993. The economic recovery since then, however, has been extremely slow. There are many factors involved in this stagnation. First, there is the huge volume of bad debt born by Japan's financial institutions. In 1996 the government decided to use tax money

The Yen-Dollar Exchange Rate
為替レート

Year	Yen per US dollar
1970	360.00
1975	296.79
1980	226.74
1985	238.54
1990	144.79
1991	134.71
1992	126.65
1993	111.20
1994	102.21
1995	94.06
1996	108.78
1997	121.00

Note: From 1949 to 1970, the fixed rate of exchange was ¥360 per US dollar.
Source: Bank of Japan.

to finance the liquidation of seven housing loan companies (*jūsen* 住専) which had failed due to bad debt. To an extent this clarified the policy to be followed for resolving the bad debt problem; however, little progress has been made in improving bank balance sheets, and this is becoming an obstacle to investment activity.

A second factor in the stagnation has been the sharp rise in the value of the yen 円高. The exchange rate, which averaged ¥145 per dollar in 1990, passed the ¥100 yen per dollar mark in June 1994 and recorded an all-time high of ¥79.75 in April 1995. This rise pushed companies to move aggressively in shifting production overseas, a phenomenon which has incited fears of a hollowing out of Japanese industry. At the same time, finished goods imports 製品輸入 have increased, further affecting domestic production. Since the 1995 high, a fall in Japan's current account balance 経常収支 surplus as well as dollar purchases resulting from the increasing gap between Japanese and US interest rates have brought the yen back down somewhat. In 1997 it fluctuated primarily in the ¥110 to ¥130 per dollar range. The weaker yen has helped exporting companies and some recovery in facility investment activity has been seen. The key to economic recovery, however, is individual consumption, and that has remained at a low level, partly because of an increase in the consumption tax 消費税 rate and a decrease in the portion of medical bills covered by national health insurance. The bankruptcies of the Hokkaidō Takushoku Bank 北海道拓殖銀行 and Yamaichi Securities 山一證券 in 1997 and the temporary nationalization of the Long-Term Credit Bank of Japan, Ltd. (株)日本長期信用銀行, and the Nippon Credit Bank, Ltd. (株)日本債券信用銀行, in 1998 have both justified and spurred fears over the state of the financial system as the overall economy continues to retrench.

Japan has had a general government financial

balance deficit 財政赤字 since 1993, and in 1996 this deficit reached 4.8 percent of GDP, the second worst, behind Italy, among developed nations 先進国. Improving government finances has become a major issue, but reforms in this area received a setback in late 1997 when the government announced it was implementing a special income tax cut and a special government bond issue as part of its efforts to increase consumer spending and stabilize the financial system.

The extended stagnation of the economy is evidence both of problems in the structure of Japan's 50-year-old post-war economic system and of an increasing inability to respond flexibly to internal and external changes. In order to promote economic recovery and facilitate growth in the 21st century, the government is trying to reform administrative practices 行政改革, deregulate the economy 規制緩和, and liberalize the financial system 金融自由化 through a series of reforms known as the Japanese Big Bang 日本版ビッグバン. In addition, supervisory authority over Japan's private financial institutions, which had long been in the hands of the Ministry of Finance 大蔵省, was shifted to the newly established Financial Supervisory Agency 金融監督庁 in 1998. See also FOREIGN TRADE.

Economic history (Nihon *keizaishi*) 日本経済史
Economic History before 1600 1600年まで

Jōmon culture, which flourished from around 10,000 BC to around 300 BC, provides the first evidence of economic activity. Early Jōmon people formed a hunting and gathering society that left behind shell mounds containing pottery, tools, and other artifacts. Agriculture entered Japan in the 3rd century BC, and a new culture emerged, Yayoi culture 弥生文化, marking a transition to a settled agricultural society.

Around AD 250 a powerful elite group, known for its great tomb mounds (*kofun* 古墳) and an advanced material culture, appeared within Yayoi society. Social differentiation was first visible during the Kofun period (ca 300–710). The ruling clans (*uji* 氏) controlled support groups (*be* 部 or *tomo* 伴) composed of craftsmen, warriors, ceremonial personnel, or cultivators. By the mid-5th century the Yamato *uji* 大和氏, forerunner of the imperial house, which claimed descent from the sun goddess, was dominant in western Japan. The emergent Yamato Court 大和朝廷, centered in the Yamato Basin, showed evidence of barter and foreign trade.

The 6th and 7th centuries saw new tensions in Yamato society as the Soga family attempted to usurp political leadership. The coup in 645 against the Soga family, which resulted in the Taika Reform 大化改新, however, reasserted the authority of the sovereign. A new *ritsuryō* (legal codes) system 律令制 of government, modeled after that of Tang China 唐 (618–907), was eventually developed. The state took title to all agricultural land. An elaborate system of land management (the *handen shūju* system 班田収授の法) rationalized field boundaries and assigned rights to income and cultivation.

In 723 the government offered tenure for three generations to those who reclaimed lands. Later this was extended to perpetual tenure rights as an incentive for reclamation. These policies undermined state control over agricultural land and contributed to the eventual breakdown of the *handen shūju* system. Economic expansion in the 8th century is indicated by the issuance of coins by the central government in 708. Japan was not yet a monetary society, and coins circulated largely in the Kinai or capital region. Official missions to and from China encouraged the growth of foreign trade.

Private control of land spread in response to government efforts to develop new farmland. Many elite houses and major shrines and temples exceeded their allotments and reclaimed vast tracts of land for private use. While these lands were subject to taxes, permanent tenure was the first step toward the creation of private landed estates 荘園, in which the proprietor assumed the duties of governance. By the 12th century 5,000 *shōen* existed, comprising most of the agricultural land in Japan.

The use of coins for transactions became more common during the 13th century. *Shōen* tax goods were increasingly sold at local markets for cash. Members of the *samurai* (warrior) class were also increasingly dependent on cash in the Kamakura period (1185–1333), obtaining cash loans from moneylenders. Market towns appeared in the period. Retail shops emerged, and wholesalers (*toimaru* 問丸), who began as merchant-officials charged with marketing and storing *shōen* tax goods, appeared to supply them with goods.

The 14th century saw the diffusion of intensive cultivation methods in agriculture, resulting in more monetary transactions in the economically advanced Kinai 畿内 region. As commerce and the monetary economy grew, the *sake* brewers and pawnbrokers (*dosō* 土倉) became tax collectors for the shogunate and provincial warlords 守護大名. They loaned funds to both *daimyō* and the urban nobility and amassed great economic power. By the time of the Ōnin War 応仁の乱 (1467–1477), wealthy urban residents (*machishū* 町衆) administered much of Kyōto, and their authority increased as the power of the Muromachi shogunate 室町幕府 declined.

The Ōnin War destroyed the *shōen* system and the authority of the Muromachi shogunate. *Shugo daimyō* were replaced by local military leaders (Sengoku *daimyō* 戦国大名). Sengoku *daimyō* domains were autonomous and independent of central authority. They instituted a new tax system that replaced *shōen* revenues. All taxing authority was in their hands, and local and absentee power holders were eliminated.

Main Destinations of the Vermilion Seal Ships
主な朱印船渡航地

Destination	Number of voyages
Central Vietnam (Nguyen domain)	87
Siam (Thailand)	56
Luzon (northern Philippines)	56
Cambodia	44
North Vietnam (Trinh domain)	37
Taiwan	36

Source: Adapted by Robert Innes from Iwao Seiichi, *Nan'yō nihommachi no kenkyū* (1966).

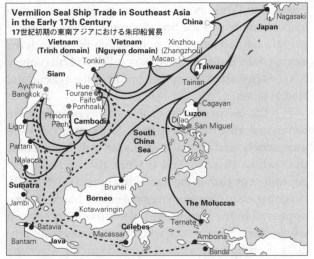

Vermilion Seal Ship Trade in Southeast Asia in the Early 17th Century
17世紀初期の東南アジアにおける朱印船貿易

——— major sea-routes of the vermilion seal ship trade
– – – minor sea-routes
● *nihommachi*
● other areas with Japanese residents

The 16th century was a period of major urbanization. Trade and handicraft production were concentrated in the castle towns 城下町 of the *daimyō*. *Samurai* were assembled in the castle towns, leaving village administration in the hands of the farmers. The castle towns became political, economic, and transportation centers of the domains. *Daimyō* eliminated trade barriers and broke up the monopolistic powers of the guilds , which encouraged trade expansion and accelerated commercial activity. In the 1540s European traders entered Japanese waters bringing new commodities such as European luxury goods and firearms.

By the late 16th century, Oda Nobunaga 織田信長 (1534–1582) and his successor, Toyotomi Hideyoshi 豊臣秀吉 (1537–1598) surveyed all land under their control and replaced the *kandaka* system 貫高制 of taxes computed in cash with the *kokudaka* system 石高制, in which productivity was measured in rice as the tax base. After Nobunaga's death in 1582 and unification of the country by Hideyoshi in 1590, the *kokudaka* system was extended to the entire country.

Edo-Period (1600–1868) Economy
江戸時代(1600年〜1868年)の経済

Following the death of Hideyoshi 秀吉 in 1598, Tokugawa Ieyasu 徳川家康 (1543–1616) emerged as the most powerful warlord in the country. In 1603 his shogunate was headquartered in Edo (now Tōkyō), which soon developed into the largest city in Japan. In order to secure allegiance of the other *daimyō*, the Tokugawa instituted the *sankin kōtai* system 参勤交代制, whereby *daimyō* were required to spend alternate years in Edo to attend on the *shōgun*. This political measure was to have profound economic effects. Edo became the center of a new economic network as all kinds of commodities were shipped to the city for consumption by the *daimyō*, their *samurai* retainers, and other service personnel. By the mid-18th century, Edo had a population of over 1 million. Ōsaka, with its easy access to waterborne transport, became the primary commodity market in the central Kinai region. *Daimyō* from western Japan shipped tax rice 年貢米 to Ōsaka for sale to obtain the cash necessary to support their Edo residences and their travels to and from the capital. In time Ōsaka merchants hired by the *daimyō* as warehouse managers 蔵元 or account agents 掛屋 also provided the *daimyō* with long-term credit as well.

Urbanization progressed during the Edo period, and population growth continued from the early 17th through the mid-18th century. Demands for food, textiles, utensils, housing, and other essentials led to a rapid expansion in commercial activity. This in turn required increases in the volume of currency and banking facilities. The Ōsaka money changers 両替商 organized an official association, and, by 1670, 10 moneylenders 十人両替 supervised financial activity in the city. Bills of exchange and certificates of deposit circulated like paper money within and between cities, and *daimyō* domains issued domainal paper currency 藩札 はんさつ for circulation within domain boundaries.

Foreign trade during the Edo period was subject to new controls imposed by the shogunate. The shogunate in the early 17th century prohibited foreign voyages by Japanese, and concentrated foreign trade in Nagasaki. There was trade with Korea through the *daimyō* of Tsushima 対馬藩主, and the Satsuma domain 薩摩藩 also traded with the Ryūkyū Islands, but all other trade was monopolized by the shogunate at Nagasaki where limited trade with Holland was carried on through Dutch traders.

Enterprise size ranged from large merchant houses such as the Mitsui 三井 and the Sumitomo 住友, with hundreds of employees and family members, to small retail or craft shops. A wide range of artisans and entertainers made urban life possible and attractive, and many village residents derived their incomes exclusively from wage labor or nonagricultural employment. Trade and craft production were clearly separated from farming. This separation of economic roles, which was the foundation of the Edo-period class system, increasingly became a legal fiction.

Until the late 16th century, there had been few large towns outside the Kyōto-Ōsaka region, but by the mid-18th century the urbanized population had increased to over 10 percent. Urban life, however, proved difficult for the *daimyō* and *samurai* as revenues and incomes failed to keep pace with the costs of city existence. *Daimyō* were forced to borrow from their retainers, further reducing *samurai* disposable income. The incomes of both the *daimyō* and the *samurai* were based on land taxes paid in kind, while their expenditures were in cash. As tax receipts proved inadequate, the best sources of credit were the merchants who managed their rice warehouses. Merchants thus became major creditors to *daimyō* and *samurai*.

By the mid-19th century Japan, which had entered the Edo period as an agrarian society, had become a highly monetized and commercialized economy. The economic policies of the shogunate, however, were out of step with economic realities. Land taxes no longer supported the needs of the shogunate or the domain governments. Currency debasement, forced loans, debt abrogations, and temporary levies helped defray immediate crises, but no long-term solutions existed. The stage was set for dramatic changes; the demand of foreigners for trade would totally transform the social and economic order of Tokugawa Japan, forcibly thrusting it into a growing world economy.

Early Modern Economy 近代初期の経済

At the time of the Meiji Restoration 明治維新 (1868), a number of conditions that had coalesced over time during the Edo period provided a favorable base for industrialization. Among these were the growth of a large educated population; a surplus of labor in the agricultural sector; a highly monetized economy controlled by a wealthy and capable merchant class; and the large *samurai* class, capable of filling leadership and administrative positions.

The opening of Japanese ports to foreign trade in 1859 exposed the still-underdeveloped economy to the

Foreign Employees of the Meiji Period (1874)
明治政府の御雇外国人

Ministry	Total	United States	Britain	France	Germany	Other
Foreign Affairs 外交	14	6	2	1	1	4
Finance 財政	27	7	16	–	–	4
Army 陸軍	38	–	–	36	–	2
Navy 海軍	66	–	29	36	–	1
Education 教育	77	14	25	10	24	4
Public Works 土木	228	7	185	13	6	17
Hokkaidō Colonization Office 開拓使	11	7	1	–	3	–
Other その他	42	6	11	12	3	10
Total	503	47	269	108	37	42

Source: Umetani Noboru, *Oyatoi gaikokujin* (1968).

threat of colonial domination by the West. In an effort to avoid the fate of other Asian nations colonialized by Western powers, the Meiji-period (1868–1912) government imposed a number of controls on the economic activities of foreigners in Japan, including travel restrictions and bans on land ownership.

Industrialization and Economic Modernization
工業化と経済の近代化

In preparation for the rapid development of Japanese industry, much of the socioeconomic system of the Edo period, including the complex *shi-nō-kō-shō* class system 士農工商制 was dismantled. The *sekisho* (barrier stations) 関所 were abolished, and other restrictions on transportation and communication were lifted. Land ownership rights for farmers were established; and restrictions on the planting of crops other than rice were abolished. These reforms led to the modernization of agricultural management. The government also implemented land tax reform, under which land taxes, which had been paid chiefly in rice since the early Edo period, were made payable in currency. In 1876 the stipends of former *samurai* (*shizoku* 士族) were converted into government bonds and hereditary pensions were paid off on a sliding scale.

In addition, the Meiji government first abolished the old, complex currency system and established a new, unified national currency system with decimal denominations and standardized units. It also introduced new systems of banking and company organization. The banking system was modeled on the US system of national banks, and in 1882 a central bank, the Bank of Japan 日本銀行, was founded.

Private Sector Development Efforts 民間企業の努力

The private sector leadership played a key role in the modernization of the economy. Among these entrepreneurs were a number of members of such wealthy merchant families from the Edo period as the Mitsui and the Sumitomo. Most of them, however, came from the ranks of the former *samurai*, peasant, or merchant classes and became modern businessmen amid the turmoil of the early Meiji period.

The Development of the Factors of Production
生産要因の充実

Large amounts of capital accumulated in the hands of merchants and landowners in the late Edo and early Meiji periods. This capital was invested in new companies and business ventures, primarily in factories, machinery, and other fixed assets. A large surplus of workers developed during the depression that accompanied the unification of the currency system from 1881 to 1885. These people, chiefly former farmers, provided a portion of the industrial labor force; low-ranking former *samurai* and small businessmen also experienced a high rate of bankruptcy, and many then became workers.

Growth Industries 成長産業

The centerpiece of Japan's expanding industrial development was the textile industry. The Meiji government strongly promoted the modernization of this industry in order to reduce dependence on imports, employing foreign technicians to supply technical know-how and assistance. In 1897 cotton yarn 綿糸 exports exceeded imports for the first time. By 1918 six giant spinning firms had been formed.

The first major production facility in the IRON AND STEEL INDUSTRY 鉄鋼業 began operation around 1890 at Kamaishi, Iwate Prefecture. The government-run Yawata Iron and Steel Works 八幡製鉄所 began operation in 1901 and became Japan's leading ironworks after the Russo-Japanese War 日露戦争 of 1904–1905. The ship-

Merchant Vessels Launched by Country
国別商船進水量比率 (in percentage of world total gross tons)

	Japan	United Kingdom	West Germany	Sweden	Other countries
1913	2.0	58.0	14.0	0.6	25.4
1921	5.2	35.4	11.7	1.5	46.2
1924	3.2	64.1	7.8	1.4	23.5
1927	1.9	54.6	12.9	3.0	27.6
1930	5.3	51.9	8.7	4.6	29.5
1933	15.4	27.3	8.8	12.7	35.8
1936	14.1	40.9	18.3	7.4	19.3
1939	13.1	25.3	12.1	8.5	41.0
1950	7.8	29.5	3.5	7.8	51.4

Source: For 1913–30: League of Nations, *International Statistical Yearbook.* For 1933–50: United Nations, *Statistical Yearbook* (annual).

building industry 造船業 grew rapidly at the turn of the century, fostered by supportive government policies and the efforts of such firms as Mitsubishi Shipbuilding 三菱造船所 (now Mitsubishi Heavy Industries, Ltd. 三菱重工業[株]), Kawasaki Shipyard Co. 川崎造船所 (now Kawasaki Heavy Industries, Ltd. 川崎重工業[株]), and Ōsaka Iron 大阪鉄工所.

A number of special banks were established after 1897, including the Nippon Kangyō Bank 日本勧業銀行 (now Dai-Ichi Kangyō Bank, Ltd. (株)第一勧業銀行); the Industrial Bank of Japan, Ltd. (株)日本興業銀行; the Bank of Taiwan 台湾銀行; and the Bank of Korea 朝鮮銀行. Bank deposits increased, and, with the cancellation of excess loans, five giant banking concerns had come to dominate by 1917: the Dai-Ichi Bank 第一銀行; the Mitsui Bank 三井銀行 (now Sakura Bank, Ltd. (株)さくら銀行); the Mitsubishi Bank, Ltd. 三菱銀行 (now the Bank of Tōkyō-Mitsubishi Ltd. (株)東京三菱銀行); the Sumitomo Bank, Ltd. (株)住友銀行; and the Yasuda Bank 安田銀行 (now Fuji Bank, Ltd. (株)富士銀行).

The Problems of Growth 成長の問題点

Behind the rapid growth in the industrial sector was the sluggish development of agriculture, which continued to be characterized by a premodern tenancy system with small farms averaging less than 1 hectare (2.47 acres). In commerce and industry, alongside the emerging large modern enterprises, numerous small enterprises and cottage industries continued to exist. (This dual structure has continued to be a central feature of the Japanese economy.) Despite the modernization of important industries, the income level of the common people remained low.

In the West, as industrialization spread, so too did the socialist and labor movements. In Japan this was not the case, as the government took active steps to suppress them at home. The Public Order and Police Law of 1900 治安警察法 was largely effective in suppressing organized union activity by government surveillance before World War I. Its replacement, the Peace Preservation Law of 1925 治安維持法, which was directed against communists and anarchists, suppressed the more radical elements within the labor movement.

Economic growth came to a halt in 1920, when the Japanese economy fell into a severe depression following its rapid expansion during World War I. A tolerable recovery had been achieved when, on 1 September 1923, a massive earthquake struck the greater Tōkyō region. In 1927 an unprecedented financial crisis occurred when a number of important banks failed. Then in 1930–1931 the Japanese economy was engulfed by the worldwide depression 世界恐慌 that followed the 1929 crash of the US stock market.

Throughout this period of crisis, bankruptcies of small and medium-sized enterprises 中小企業 were common in almost all economic activities. There was also a push for the concentration of capital, resulting in a striking growth in the power of the industrial and financial combines known as *zaibatsu* 財閥. The Mitsui 三井, Mitsubishi 三菱, Sumitomo 住友, and Yasuda 安田 *zaibatsu* developed into conglomerates between 1909 and 1920, and in the following decade they expanded their affiliated enterprises and established positions of firm dominance over the Japanese economy.

The farm economy also suffered. The depression gave independent farmers, as well as tenant farmers a severe level of debt. Tenant farmer disputes increased in number, and there was an overall growth in social unrest. Against this background the Manchurian Incident 満州事変 occurred in September 1931, and the government soon embarked on a program of increasing military expenditures. Military demand contributed to the recovery of strategic industries, employment, and the farm economy.

On the other hand, the Manchurian Incident was the first in a series of Sino-Japanese conflicts leading to the outbreak of the Sino-Japanese War of 1937–1945 日中戦争 and then Japan's entry into World War II in 1941. Throughout the war the government strengthened its control over the economy and promoted the development of strategic industries, but production in important manufacturing industries dropped, especially after 1943, until it collapsed under aerial bombardment in 1944 and 1945. The wartime economy itself collapsed with Japan's surrender on 15 August 1945. Overall production at the end of 1945 was only one-sixth of prewar (1935–1937 average) levels. At the war's end more than 25 percent of Japan's physical capital stock and 45 percent of the prewar empire had been lost.

▋ The Reform Period 改革の時代

After World War II, the Allied Occupation 連合国軍占領 of Japan lasted 80 months, from 15 August 1945, when Japan accepted the Potsdam Declaration ポツダム宣言, to 28 April 1952. It is often divided into four periods: reform (August 1945–February 1947), reverse course (February 1947–December 1948), Dodge Line ドッジ=ライン (December 1948–June 1950), and Korean War 朝鮮戦争 (June 1950–April 1952). In the reform period economic recovery was left largely in Japanese hands, and the activities of SCAP (Supreme Commander for the Allied Powers) 連合国軍最高司令官総司令部(GHQ) during 1945–1947 were concentrated upon a series of reforms. The most important of these reforms concerned agriculture (the land reforms of 1946 農地改革, encouragement of agricultural cooperative associations 農業協同組合, and rice price 米価 controls), labor (legalization of trade unions and collective bargaining 団体交渉, and enforcement of labor standards), and industry (passage of an Antimonopoly

GNP During and After World War II
第2次大戦前後のGNP

	1944	1946	1950	1955
GNP (nominal; in billion yen)	74.5	474	3,946.7	8,235.5
GNP per capita (in yen)	1,010	6,293	47,455	92,292
Per capita GNP index (1955=100)	1.1	6.8	51.4	100

Source: Economic Planning Agency.

Law 独占禁止法の制定, *zaibatsu* dissolution 財閥解体, and deconcentration of economic power 経済力の分散).

As a simple matter of avoiding famine, massive aid was essential to Japan, with the United States the almost exclusive source. The aid program included a wide range of industrial raw materials and paid for more than half of Japan's total imports through 1949.

Although the occupation purge 公職追放 was directed primarily at political and military leaders of the Japanese war effort, an "economic purge" was extended to cover industrial, commercial, and financial leaders judged to have cooperated actively with the Japanese military. The effect of the purge on economic recovery was questionable, and over 200,000 of those purged were later officially depurged by appeals boards and administrative action.

Because Japan financed its political and economic reforms largely by printing new money, the country experienced accelerating inflation in 1945–1949. An initial Occupation effort to check this inflation in February 1946 took the form of an abortive "new yen" 新円 currency reform. All pre-1946 currency was invalidated, with new notes issued yen-for-yen but only for limited amounts. Both demand and savings deposits were also frozen. However, budgetary deficits 財政赤字 of the Japanese government and credit creation by the Bank of Japan 日本銀行 were both financed by the printing of currency in sufficient volume to restore the February level by September.

Two important agencies of economic recovery and expansion were set up by the Japanese in late 1946, after the failure of the "new yen" experiment. These were the Keizai Antei Hombu, or Economic Stabilization Board 経済安定本部 (ESB; the present Economic Planning Agency 経済企画庁), and the Fukkō Kin'yū Kinko, or Reconstruction Finance Bank (RFB) 復興金融金庫. The ESB planned and supervised a revived system of price controls and rationing and also subsidized increased production. The RFB made longer-term loans to public and private institutions to increase their productive capacities. A characteristic of Japanese planning was to select particular industries as keys to the next stage of economic expansion, and to concentrate assistance on such industries with little regard for short-term market forces 傾斜生産方式. Priorities shifted from coal and food in 1946 to iron, steel, and fertilizer production in 1948.

The Reverse Course Period 逆行の時代

The reverse course may be dated from 1 February 1947, the scheduled date for a general strike by a united front of government workers' unions. SCAP decided to forbid the strike, and a pattern of hostility between SCAP and the Japanese Left crystallized and continued for the remainder of the Occupation. Whereas SCAP had been antimilitarist, antinationalist, and antifascist before February 1947, anticommunism and antiunionism came to overshadow these earlier ideologies after that date.

With partial revival of Japanese production by 1948, international trade became increasingly important, but under SCAP's supervision all commercial imports as well as exports required licensed approval by the Japanese authorities. Only in 1948 did SCAP begin to permit the entry, and then the permanent residence, of foreign private traders.

The Dodge Line Period ドッジ=ラインの時代

In the fall of 1948 a Detroit banker Joseph M. Dodge ジョセフ=M=ドッジ was appointed a special adviser to SCAP on economic matters. The measures undertaken during this period were known collectively as the Dodge line. Under the Dodge program, the price control system, production subsidies, and the RFB loans were terminated. Dodge advocated free-market economics, balanced budgets, lower taxes, stabilization of the exchange value

Annual Value of Japan's Exports and Imports (1948–65)
年間輸出入額

(in millions of US dollars)

Calendar year	Exports (FOB values)	Imports (CIF values)	Trade balance
1948	258	684	−426
1950	820	974	−154
1955	2,011	2,471	−461
1960	4,055	4,491	−437
1965	8,452	8,169	283

Source: Japan Tariff Association.

of the yen (at ¥360 to the US dollar), and strict regulation of the money supply. His drastic anti-inflationary measures, combined with a recession in world markets for Japanese exports, brought on a severe decline in aggregate demand; the results were business failures and unemployment. By the spring of 1950 the short-term outlook for the Japanese economy was bleak.

The Korean War Period 朝鮮戦争の時代

The outbreak of the Korean War 朝鮮戦争 caught both SCAP and the Japanese authorities by surprise. After the war began on 25 June 1950 the semimilitary economy that Japan almost immediately became was dominated by *tokuju* (special procurement demand) 特別調達需要(特需) for the United Nations forces 国連軍 in Korea; the Japanese economy thus returned to full capacity, boom conditions, and high growth. The money supply was freed from its Dodge line fetters. As for the Dodge line as a whole, three main pillars remained in place: an annually balanced budget, a stable yen-dollar exchange rate, and the dissolution of the price-control and rationing machinery. See also CONTEMPORARY ECONOMY.

National budget (*kokka yosan*) 国家予算

The general account budget 一般会計予算 of the national government's revenues and expenditures 国の歳入歳出 is usually regarded as the most important of all government budgets. In addition to this budget, there are also individual budgets for a group of special accounts 特別会計予算 created to implement government policies. Thirty-eight special accounts were operative in 1998.

Social Security 社会保障関係費

Various outlays for public assistance programs 生活保護制度, social welfare programs 社会福祉制度, social insurance programs 社会保険制度, public health services 保健衛生対策, and unemployment measures 失業対策 are included in this category, which represented 18.8 percent of the 1997 general account budget. Public assistance provides support to individuals who are unable to meet the cost of living. The national government provides 75 percent of this assistance and local governments 25 percent. Social welfare programs are intended to support those people for whom care is necessary, such as children, the aged, and the physically and mentally disabled.

Social insurance can be classified into health insurance, pensions, employment insurance, and workers' compensation insurance. The medical and health insurance system 医療保険制度 consists of employee insurance 健康保険 and national health insurance 国民健康保険. The pension system, similarly, has two classes. National pension insurance provides basic, mandatory coverage for all citizens, while other programs provide additional benefits for private- and public-sector employees. While these programs depend mainly on contributions made by employers and employees, subsidies from the general account are also substantial. Measures to combat tuberculosis and public sanitation are carried out by the public health service. To cope with unemployment, there are employment insurance and special measures to promote employment. See also SOCIAL SECURITY PROGRAMS.

Public Works 公共事業関係費

One of the features of Japanese public expendi-

General Account Budget, Fiscal 1997
一般会計予算（平成9年度予算）

Revenues 歳入	Amount (in billions of yen)	Percentage
Tax and stamp receipts 租税及び印紙収入	57,802	74.7
Revenue other than tax その他の収入	2,881	3.7
Public bonds 公債金	16,707	21.6
Total	77,390	

Expenditures 歳出	Amount (in billions of yen)	Percentage
Social security 社会保障関係費	14,550	18.8
Education and science 文教及び科学振興費	6,344	8.2
National debt 国債費	16,802	21.7
Pensions 恩給関係費	1,597	2.1
Local allocation tax 地方交付税交付金	15,481	20.0
National defense 防衛関係費	4,947	6.4
Public works 公共事業関係費	9,745	12.6
Economic cooperation 経済協力費	1,088	1.4
Measures for small businesses 中小企業対策費	187	0.2
Measures for energy エネルギー対策費	686	0.9
Staple food 主要食糧関係費	269	0.3
Transfers to the Industrial Investment Special Account 産業投資特別会計への繰入	172	0.2
Miscellaneous その他の事項経費	5,172	6.7
Contingency 予備費	350	0.5
Total	77,390	

Source: Ministry of Finance.

ture is a relatively high level of government investment (12.6 percent of the 1997 general account budget). The main emphasis since the late 1960s has been on public works 公共事業 aimed at increasing social overhead capital. Social capital includes erosion and flood-control projects 洪水対策; road construction 道路工事; port, harbor, and airport facilities; housing; public service facilities; improvement of conditions for agricultural production; forest roads; and water supply for industrial use. Of these, the heaviest investment is in road construction, which is managed primarily through the Road Improvement Special Account 道路整備特別会計. The expenditures in this special account consist of expenses for projects under the direct control of the national government, subsidies to local governments, and investments in public expressway corporations. The main sources of revenue for these expenditures are transfers from the general account.

Education and Science 文教及び科学振興費

Expenditures in this category were 8.2 percent of the 1997 general account budget. Schools for compulsory education 義務教育 (elementary schools and middle schools) are operated by local authorities; the national government is required by law to provide one-half of the teachers' salaries in these schools. Other government outlays are expenses for public school facilities, school education assistance, transfers to the National Schools Special Account 国立学校特別会計, loans to students, and the promotion of science and technology. The revenue and expenditures of national universities and hospitals attached to national schools are managed through the National Schools Special Account.

Staple Food (Transfers to the Foodstuff Control Special Account) 主要食糧関係費(食糧管理特別会計への繰入)

The Foodstuff Control Special Account 食糧管理特別会計 was originally created to stabilize the prices of agricultural products by controlling the purchase and sale of rice, wheat, barley, and other commodities. However, sale prices of domestic rice and some other crops are not high enough to cover the government's purchase price and overhead expenses. As a result, a large deficit has developed in this special account, and funds are transferred from the general account each year to cover the deficit. Expenditures for the support of conversion from rice to other crops are also included.

Economic Cooperation 経済協力費

In fiscal 1997 the government expenditure for economic cooperation was estimated at ¥1.0885 trillion (1.4 percent of the general account budget). Government economic assistance to developing countries has increased rapidly. See also OFFICIAL DEVELOPMENT ASSISTANCE.

Local Allocation Tax Grants 地方交付税交付金

This expenditure—which equals 30 percent of income, corporation, liquor, and consumption taxes and which represented 20.0 percent of the 1997 general account budget—is distributed by the national government to assist local governments 地方自治体 through a special account for allotment of the local allocation tax and transferred tax 交付税及び譲与税配付金特別会計. Local governments can use these grants at their discretion. The national government allocates these grants according to the financial needs of each local government.

Budget Cutting 歳出削減

In June 1997 the Cabinet approved a proposal to cut the budget deficit in half over a six-year period and bring it to within 3 percent of the GDP by about 2003. Under the spending curbs proposed, the general expenditures in the initial fiscal 1998 budget are 0.5 percent less than in 1997. Compared to 1997, fiscal 1998 target expenditures are 0.7 percent less for public works and 10 percent less for overseas economic cooperation. Defense spending is also to be cut. Social security spending is to be limited to a ¥300 billion increase instead of the ¥800 billion projected, and education expenditures are to be held to less than the previous year; however, spending on the promotion of science and technology is to increase 5 percent.

National income (*kokumin shotoku*) 国民所得

The national income measures used in international comparisons are gross national product (GNP) 国民総生産 and gross domestic product (GDP) 国内総生産. Japan's GDP in 1995 was ¥459 trillion (US $4.89 trillion), making it the second largest market economy in the world. In the same year per capita income was US $31,885, comparable with that of Western nations after adjusting for Japan's high cost of housing and other goods. This high economic scale was achieved largely due to high economic growth 経済成長 from 1955 to the late 1960s, during which period the nation's average annual growth rate was around 10 percent, about double that of Western nations. Although this rate declined, it still remained higher than that of most other industrialized nations in the 1970s and 1980s. After the end of the 1986 to 1991 boom period known as the "bubble economy," バブル経済 growth slowed drastically, with the GDP growth rate falling to 0.5 percent in 1994 and 0.9 percent in 1995. New corporate investment stagnated as a result of both the economic slowdown and a sharp rise in the value of the Japanese yen. As of the end of 1997, prospects for recovery were uncertain.

Structure of National Income 国民所得の構造

The Japanese economy can be understood by examining three aspects of the national income: production, distribution, and disposition. Regarding production, primary industry (agriculture, forestry, and fishing), which accounted for 26.0 percent of the GDP in 1950, fell to 2.1 percent in 1992, while the share of secondary industry (manufacturing) rose from 31.8 percent to 36.7 percent, and tertiary industry (services) rose from 42.3 percent to 61.2 percent in the same years. In recent years, the share of secondary industry appears to have reached a ceiling, and that of tertiary industry has continued to develop, creating a service-oriented economy (see INDUSTRIAL STRUCTURE).

As for distribution, the proportion of employee compensation has increased, whereas that of income from private corporations and private unincorporated entrepreneurial income has decreased. In 1950, employee compensation 雇用者所得 stood at 41.8 percent, while private unincorporated entrepreneurial income was 45.6 percent. In 1995, these figures were 73.4 percent and 11.2 percent, respectively.

When expenditures, or disposition of national income, are broken down into consumption and savings, the share of savings in national disposable income steadily increased from about 20 percent in the 1950s, peaking at 30.3 percent in 1970. It then fell to an average of 22.8 percent in the 1990–1992 period. Even now, however, this figure is higher than that of other advanced nations.

Income distribution (*shotoku bumpu*) 所得分布

Household income differentials in Japan narrowed sharply after World War II, especially in the high-growth period of the 1960s and 1970s. However, income differentials have started to widen in recent years. There are a number of factors accounting for this trend. First, wage levels of workers in large corporations often differ markedly from those of their counterparts in smaller firms. In the 1950s this situation was referred to

Distribution of National Income at Factor Cost (1995)
分配国民所得

(in percentages)

	Japan	United States
Compensation of employees 雇用者所得	73.4	72.4
Property income of households & private non-profit institutions 家計・民間非営利団体の財産所得	7.8	15.6
Private unincorporated entrepreneurial income 個人企業所得	11.2	8.3
Incorporated entrepreneurial income 法人企業所得	8.4	6.5
General government property income 一般政府の財産所得	−0.8	−2.9
Total of national income distributed.	375,075 (in billions of yen)	5,829 (in billions of US dollars)

Source: Bank of Japan, *Kokusai hikaku tōkei.*

Monthly Wages by Industry, 1995
産業別月間賃金

(in thousands of yen)

Industry	Men	Women
Service industries サービス業	358.5	240.3
Utilities 電気・ガス・熱供給・水道業	440.9	267.4
Transportation and communications 運輸・通信業	359.2	241.1
Real estate 不動産業	389.5	222.3
Finance and insurance 金融・保険業	466.6	248.0
Wholesale and retail sales and restaurants 卸売・小売業、飲食店	351.3	210.8
Construction 建設業	361.7	207.9
Mining 鉱業	346.2	198.8
Manufacturing (management, office, and technical staff) 製造業(管理・事務・技術労働者)	401.4	214.7
Manufacturing (production) 製造業(生産労働者)	318.9	169.3

Note: Monthly wages listed here include basic salary, supplementary payments, and overtime pay.
Source: Ministry of Labor.

Monthly Wages by Employee Age and Company Size, 1995
年齢・会社規模別月間賃金

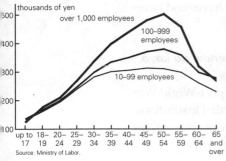

Source: Ministry of Labor.

as the dual structure of the economy, which was more or less eliminated in the high-growth period. In the 1980s, however, wage differentials based on corporate size began to expand again. The considerably higher levels of non-monetary compensation provided by large corporations, including expense accounts 必要経費 and housing and other benefits, further exacerbate the effects of the dual structure.

A second feature of wage differentials in Japan is that they are far greater among different age groups than in other developed countries. This is primarily due to the seniority system 年功序列制度 followed by most Japanese corporations.

The third factor concerns women in the workplace. In previous decades an increasing number of Japanese women in households with lower incomes sought employment in order to supplement their husbands' limited incomes. This development originally served to equalize Japanese family incomes. Recently, however, supplementary incomes earned by working women have tended to widen income differences between families, as many women in high-income-bracket households are now also gainfully employed.

The wage gap between the sexes remains conspicuous in Japan. In 1993 the average monthly salary of a female worker amounted to only 62 percent of the salary of her male counterpart. This is primarily because the average working woman's career is only about 60 percent as long as the average man's, a definite disadvantage in a wage system based on seniority; women are more often employed in comparatively low-paying industries and smaller firms; and many women are part-time workers パートタイム労働者.

Although income distribution in Japan is still relatively equal in terms of employment income, the gap between rich and poor is seen as much wider when considered in terms of asset ownership. The gaps in asset ownership widened markedly in the second half of the 1980s because of skyrocketing land prices. While falling land prices in the early 1990s have narrowed the disparity somewhat, there continues to be a big prosperity gap between property haves and have-nots.

Modern employment system (gendai no koyō seido) 現代の雇用制度

The employment system in the post-World War II period has been based on three essential institutions: lifetime employment 終身雇用, the seniority system 年功序列, and enterprise unionism 企業別労働組合.

Lifetime Employment 終身雇用

In the characteristic Japanese employment system, companies recruit workers immediately upon graduation from a school or university, and these workers continue in the same company until retirement. This is considered to be the ideal employment relationship, but it is mostly limited to larger firms.

Regular employees can expect

Retirement Pay (Males, 1993)
男子定年退職金

(in millions of yen)

	University graduates	Senior high graduates	Junior high graduates
Company Size			
30–99 employees	10.48	9.19	6.24
100–999	18.54	9.54	10.00
1000–	27.78	14.39	15.29
Length of service			
20–24 years	12.85	6.01	6.23
25–29	16.93	9.70	9.54
30–34	25.04	13.33	12.39
35–	28.48	16.82	16.02

Note: "University graduates": administration, office work, and engineering. "Senior high graduates" and "Junior high graduates": blue-collar work.
Source: Ministry of Labor.

Weekly Working Hours by Country (manufacturing)
週当りの労働時間(製造業)

	Japan	United States	United Kingdom	Germany*[1]	France
1985	43.0	41.3	43.7	42.2	38.6
1987	42.9	42.2	43.8	41.7	38.7
1989	42.7	42.2	44.5	41.4	38.8
1991	41.3	41.7	42.9	40.9	38.7
1993	39.0	42.4	43.1	39.4	38.7
1995	39.2	42.7	43.4[2]	39.6[2]	38.7*[2]

Note: Figures are for production workers in manufacturing industries.
*1 1985–1989 figures for West Germany.
*2 1994.
Source: Bank of Japan, Kokusai hikaku tōkei.

Unemployment Rate
失業率

(in percentages)

	Japan	United States	United Kingdom	Germany	France
1990	2.1	5.6	5.8	6.4	8.9
1991	2.1	6.8	8.0	5.7	9.4
1992	2.2	7.5	9.8	7.8	10.4
1993	2.5	6.9	10.3	8.9	11.7
1994	2.9	6.1	9.4	9.6	12.2
1995	3.2	5.6	8.3	9.4	11.6
1996	3.4	5.4	7.6	10.4	12.4

Source: Bank of Japan, *Kokusai hikaku tōkei.*

to be employed until retirement unless they violate any of the rules of employment. When business is depressed, regular employees are dismissed only as a last resort. In return for this job security, employees are expected to accept transfers to other departments or to subsidiaries when business is bad and to respond positively by working overtime when the company is doing well. As long as employees maintain such a commitment, it is commonly understood to be the employer's responsibility to maintain stability of employment.

In many small companies working conditions do not improve with increasing length of service. As a result, labor mobility among small firms is high and many workers are hired in mid-career. Lifetime employment, therefore, is a system operating mainly in large private companies and the public sector 公共セクター.

■ Seniority System 年功序列

System of employment in Japan in which an employee's rank, salary, and qualifications within a firm are based on the length of service in the company. Workers, upon hire, are expected to stay with the company until their retirement. Starting wages are determined by educational background, age, sex, and type of job, while wage increases are primarily governed by age and length of service; retirement pay is based on length of employment, position, and wage level at the time of retirement. Seniority is also an important factor in promotions. This system can be traced to a period of serious labor shortages during World War I when the Yokosuka Naval Shipyard adopted it as a means of securing enough technical and skilled workers.

The seniority system enables employees to benefit from stability of employment. Employers can benefit from strong worker loyalty and stability and the resultant ease with which they can formulate personnel plans. They suffer, however, from the necessity of carrying along surplus workers and growing inflexibility within their organizations.

With the steady increase in the number of employees in higher age brackets, the pyramidal personnel structure has started to crumble as Japanese corporations begin to suffer from skyrocketing labor costs. The problem will only get worse as the average age of Japan's population continues to grow, putting increasing pressure on companies to place more emphasis on employee ability and less on seniority.

Enterprise Unionism 企業別労働組合

The third basic feature of the Japanese employment system is the prevalence of enterprise unions. This form of unionism was established after World War II because of the following factors: (1) strong paternalism among postwar employers of all sizes and types; (2) a wide variety of working conditions, which prevented the development of a unitary wage structure based on technical qualifications and competence; and (3) the interest of union members in secure jobs and income, owing to the inadequacy of government social security. These factors led Japanese union members to prefer to bargain with management at the level of the individual enterprise. Paternalistic management and enterprise unionism have both supported lifetime employment and promoted labor-management harmony.

Temporary Employees 臨時雇

The Japanese employment system is dependent on a variety of temporary employees. Because the number of regular workers is limited,

Labor Union Memberships, 1996 労働組合員数	(in percentages)
Japanese Trade Union Confederation 連合	61.5
National Confederation of Trade Unions 全労連	6.9
National Trade Union Council 全労協	2.3
other その他	29.3
Total number of memberships in 1996: 12,451,149	

Source: Ministry of Labor.

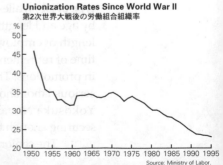

Unionization Rates Since World War II
第2次世界大戦後の労働組合組織率

Source: Ministry of Labor.

Part-Time Workers (Nonagricultural Sector)
パートタイム労働者 (非農林業)

	Total		Female	
	Part-time workers (million)	Share of employed population (%)	Part-time workers (million)	Share of employed population (%)
1970	2.2	6.7	1.3	12.2
1975	3.5	9.9	2.0	17.4
1980	3.9	10.0	2.6	19.3
1985	4.7	11.1	3.3	22.0
1990	7.2	15.2	5.0	27.9
1995	9.0	17.4	6.3	31.6

Source: Ministry of Labor.

companies take on temporary workers for a fixed period in response to business upturns. If the situation deteriorates, the companies simply release the temporary workers. In addition to temporary employees who work the same hours as regular employees, there are part-time workers パートタイム労働者, students, and those on loan from employment agencies 派遣会社, who work a limited number of hours only. When regular employees reach retirement age, some are retained with the special status of "nonregular staff" (*shokutaku*), but they are regarded as temporary employees. There is a strict demarcation between regular and temporary employees in terms of working conditions, job status, wages, and benefits.

CORPORATIONS 企業

Corporations (*kigyō*) 企業

In 1994 Japan had 2,407,278 corporations, of which slightly more than 99 percent were medium and small enterprises with less than 300 employees. There were 1,735 corporations listed on the Tōkyō Stock Exchange 東京証券取引所 as of the end of 1996.

Financial Characteristics 資金調達の特徴

The huge capital requirements of many corporations during the period of rapid economic growth, which began in the 1950s, led to a dependence on debt financing. Since Japan's capital markets 資本市場 were still undeveloped at that time, companies were forced to rely on the banks for financing. Banks were then able to exert considerable influence over management decisions, while holders of common shares exerted little control over corporate decision making 企業の意思決定.

Because banks, in turn, had to rely on the Bank of Japan 日本銀行, the country's central bank, for additional funds, the government was able to exercise a major influence on important corporate decisions using direct credit expansion controls known as *madoguchi shidō* ("window guidance").

In the 1980s, however, development of the capital markets and substantial liquidity in the total economy led to a reduction in dependence on debt financing. With deregulation, companies became better able to raise funds on their own utilizing financial instruments such as convertible bonds 転換社債.

Enterprise Groups and Subsidiaries 企業グループと子会社

Following World War II, the *zaibatsu* (financial and industrial combines) 財閥 were dissolved by Occupation fiat. Many groups later recombined, however, because of traditional ties and an urgent need for the capital that could be obtained from the banks of the group. Although mutual shareholding reinforces the connections, there is no central ownership, and group coordination is much looser than in prewar *zaibatsu*.

Of more importance to the operations of the corporation than its connections with other large companies is the pattern of subsidiaries and subcontracting firms that has developed. These smaller firms not only pay lower wages, but also provide a smaller package of benefits. Hence, there is a considerable eco-

Top 30 Companies in Declared Income (1995)
1995年度法人所得上位30社 (in millions of yen)

	Company	Declared income
1	Nippon Telegraph and Telephone Corporation	384,801
2	Toyota Motor Corporation	366,398
3	Tōkyō Electric Power, Inc.	274,053
4	Dai-Ichi Kangyō Bank, Ltd.	250,299
5	Bank of Tōkyō, Ltd. (now Bank of Tōkyō-Mitsubishi, Ltd.)	198,725
6	Mitsubishi Bank, Ltd. (now Bank of Tōkyō-Mitsubishi, Ltd.)	177,976
7	Mitsubishi Heavy Industries, Ltd.	171,202
8	Tokio Marine & Fire Insurance Co., Ltd.	158,062
9	Tōshiba Corporation	146,609
10	Kansai Electric Power Co., Inc.	146,168
11	Nippon Life Insurance Co.	138,640
12	Kyōcera Corporation	133,927
13	Nintendō Co., Ltd.	124,974
14	NEC Corporation	121,989
15	Japan Tobacco, Inc.	120,680
16	Mitsubishi Electric Corporation	120,011
17	Takefuji Corporation	119,223
18	Tōkai Bank, Ltd.	118,371
19	Meiji Mutual Life Insurance Co.	118,075
20	Takeda Chemical Industries, Ltd.	116,030
21	Chiba Bank, Ltd.	114,402
22	Fuji Photo Film Co., Ltd.	106,127
23	Chūbu Electric Power Co., Inc.	105,405
24	Nomura Securities Co., Ltd.	104,600
25	East Japan Railway Co.	101,887
26	Hitachi, Ltd.	101,639
27	Sankyō Co., Ltd.	99,754
28	Yasuda Mutual Life Insurance Co.	99,079
29	Seven-Eleven Japan Co., Ltd.	97,904
30	Tōhoku Electric Power Co., Inc.	92,142

Source: National Tax Administration.

nomic advantage to using smaller firms as suppliers of those components or subassemblies that require less-skilled labor. The subsidiary or subcontractor relationship also gives the parent company flexibility in scheduling and allows cyclic downturns in demand to be displaced onto the smaller firms.

Employment Practices 雇用形態

The pattern of Japanese employment has as its basis a mutual commitment by the corporation and the employee. The corporation undertakes to retain each person that it selects until retirement, despite later temptations to terminate employment. Employees undertake to remain in the employ of the corporation once they make their choice, however attractive alternative positions might appear. Large corporations recruit employees directly from school, and hiring is not for a particular skill or job. Each assumes that over time the individual will fill a range of positions. Compensation is based on seniority, with rank, performance, and other special conditions as additional considerations.

The effect of this pattern is to establish an unusual identity between the interests of the individual employee and the interests of the corporation itself. The employee's security and assurance of continued improvement in income depend directly on the success of the firm. Midcareer moves from one firm to another for more money are relatively rare. The enterprise union system also tends to reinforce rather than dilute employee identification with the company.

It should be noted that this employment pattern applies primarily to the regular employees of large corporations, never to temporary workers and seldom to employees in small firms (see MODERN EMPLOYMENT SYSTEM). Changes in the pattern are occurring. Many companies have tried to shift the emphasis from seniority to performance when determining promotions and raises. The recession in the 1990s has put additional pressure for change on the traditional pattern, and under the label "restructuring" some corporations are trying to reduce their population of high-paid older employees. Finally, the bankruptcies of major Japanese financial institutions have made it clear that lifetime employment can be terminated by the failure of the company as well as by the retirement of the employee.

Corporate history (*kigyō no rekishi*) 企業の歴史

An analysis of the development of Japanese business from the Meiji period (1868–1912) to the eve of World War II.

The Legacy of the Edo-Period Merchants
江戸時代の町人の遺産

The activities of the merchants of the Edo period (1600–1868) facilitated the use of money throughout Japan and resulted in an increasingly unified market. Ōsaka became the commercial and financial center of the country, and developed highly advanced trading and financial techniques. Central to the commercial activities of the period was the concept of the household (*ie*), composed of the owner-family and all those employed by it, who, in exchange for absolute loyalty, were guaranteed permanent employment. Within the household each member had his place in a strictly ordered hierarchical system.

The Leaders of the Meiji Government as Modernizers 近代化を進めた明治時代の指導者

The leaders of the Meiji Restoration 明治維新 of 1868 superimposed selected Western-style institutions on traditional Japanese society. Class privileges and class restrictions were abolished, and former *samurai* were helped toward gainful employment; merchant guilds were prohibited; freedoms of enterprise and migration were proclaimed. In 1871 a unified currency, based on the yen, was established. The Ministry of Public Works 工部省, established in 1870, planned the importation of technology and the promotion of industry; it employed more than 500 foreign experts as technicians and instructors.

After 1884, most government enterprises were sold to private concerns—such as Mitsui, Sumitomo, and Mitsubishi—which would later develop into *zaibatsu* (financial cliques). Western-style businesses, notably factories and banks, were hailed as part of the new era of "Civilization and Enlightenment" 文明開化. The government, however, saw modern business primarily in terms of strengthening the state rather than in terms of satisfying consumer demands.

The Growth of Modern Business (1868–1937)
近代的ビジネスの成長(1868年～1937年)

The overall growth of modern business passed through four major stages in Japan. There was a pioneering period from 1868 to 1884, when sound financial conditions were restored after the government initiated deflationary policies in 1881 (Matsukata fiscal policy) 松方財政. Many firms collapsed during the period of deflation. The second period, from 1884 to 1919, was one of accelerated growth that was stimulated by Japan's policy of imperial expansion, notably after the Sino-Japanese War of 1894–1895 日清戦争 and the Russo-Japanese War of 1904–1905 日露戦争. The latter gave a particular impetus to the shipbuilding industry and to heavy industry in general. Industrial paid-up capital tripled during World War I, when the Asian market was left totally open to Japanese trade. Worldwide economic dislocation following World War I led to the prolonged depression that was the major feature of the third period, which ended in 1931. There were waves of bankruptcies, mass unemployment, and a growing concentration of capital in the hands of the *zaibatsu*. After 1931, the fourth period saw a reflation under the influence of war preparations. Exports were strongly promoted, and the economy reflated toward full employment.

Modern banks were launched in 1876 in the form of private banking facilities established in accordance with the National Bank Ordinance 日本銀行条例. The Bank of Japan 日本銀行, established in 1882, acted as the central bank, and a few government-run banks granted long-term loans for foreign trade, industry, and agriculture. The main weakness of Japan's banking system was the large number of small banks that were tied to individual firms by continued extension of large loans. In periods of crisis, many such banks failed, and this in turn led to a heavy concentration of banking capital. Between 1926 and 1929 the number of banks decreased from 1,417 to 897, and, by 1935, 40 percent of all deposits were held by the "Big Five" (Dai-Ichi 第一銀行 [now Dai-Ichi Kangyō Bank, Ltd. (株)第一勧業銀行], Mitsui 三井銀行 [now Sakura Bank, Ltd. (株)さくら銀行], Mitsubishi 三菱銀行 [now the Bank of Tōkyō-Mitsubishi Ltd. (株)東京三菱銀行], Yasuda 安田銀行 [now Fuji Bank, Ltd. (株)富士銀行], and Sumitomo 住友銀行).

During the 1920s and 1930s general trading companies 総合商社, notably those of the *zaibatsu*, played the key role in expanding Japan's international trade. The Mitsubishi, Kawasaki, Ishikawajima, and Hitachi shipyards grew and integrated vertically into large industrial enterprises that produced heavy machinery, railway engines and coaches, electric cables, and other heavy iron and steel products. Shipping received some subsidy but was left to private initiative. Nippon Yūsen Kaisha 日本郵船会社 (controlled by Mitsubishi), Ōsaka Shōsen 大阪商船, and Tōyō Kisen 東洋汽船 emerged as the three major shipping companies.

By 1886 a total of 32 railway companies had come into existence, and by 1905, 67 percent of some 7,800 kilometers (4,846 mi) of railway lines were oper-

Sales and Profits of Three Major Shipping Companies
三大海運会社の売上高と利益

(in thousands of yen)

| | Nippon Yūsen Kaisha | | Ōsaka Shōsen | | Tōyō Kisen | |
	Sales	Profit	Sales	Profit	Sales	Profit
1913	34,030	5,880	20,180	3,240	9,010	800
1914	34,190	4,840	19,350	2,460	7,870	−40
1915	42,100	7,730	23,600	4,020	10,610	1,800
1916	68,190	26,860	43,670	15,120	17,590	5,910
1917	116,040	48,500	72,460	29,040	44,030	17,890
1918	222,910	86,310	167,870	42,210	42,490	13,460
1919	216,760	50,180	127,170	20,820	28,050	2,510
1920	153,550	26,390	89,720	11,050	23,180	1,190

Source: *Meiji Taishō kokusei yōran.*

ated by private companies. Nationalization of all but 9 percent of the lines was carried out in 1906–1907.

Forms of Business 企業の形態

In 1893 the parts of the Commercial Code 商法 dealing with companies were put into force and three types of company were distinguished: joint-stock company 株式会社, limited partnership company 合資会社, and unlimited partnership company 合名会社. The *zaibatsu* holding companies 持株会社, which preferred the last two company types, controlled the expanding network of financial and industrial companies through a system of direct and interlocking stockholdings and through the appointment of loyal top managers. The limited liability company 有限会社 was added by the Limited Liability Company Law of 1938.

There were four main reasons for the growth of Japan's *zaibatsu*. First, they had large initial capital resources. Second, the holding-company system itself gave them ready access to financial resources (banks), raw materials (mines), and direct lines of foreign trade. Third, they were led by able individuals who were entrepreneurs and who actively secured new managerial talent. Fourth, they were family-based organizations that applied the concept of the household (*ie*) to the new business environment. They delegated decision making but demanded the unswerving loyalty of their managers and employees.

Corporate culture (*kigyō bunka*) 企業文化

Japanese corporate cultures tend to share certain basic understandings and managerial ideologies that differ from those of Western corporations, including conceptions of such crucial matters as profits, dividends, contractual obligations, and company personnel practices. These features reflect the values and characteristics of Japan's social and economic systems.

Background 背景

In the early Meiji period 明治時代 (1868–1912) there was considerable foreign influence on the Japanese business community, but it was only a part of larger and more complex developments, in which the legacies of premodern Japan and particular processes and markets played significant roles in shaping the character of emerging companies. Two sources of indigenous organizational influence were the official *han* (domain) 藩 and Tokugawa shogunate 徳川幕府 bureaucracies and the successful merchant houses 商家. The supreme ideal of serving political authority and thus society was espoused by merchants as well as bureaucrats.

Confucian thought 儒教思想—with its conception of the social order as one of many parts working together for the common good, its acceptance of hierarchy, and its emphasis on social identity—was easily adapted as an ideology for modern organizations. The close-knit agricultural hamlet and the work-oriented forms of the patron-client (*oyabun-kobun*) relationship 親分子分の関係 are two elemental social institutions influencing Japanese corporate consciousness.

Typical Corporate Ideology 典型的な企業意識

The contemporary Japanese company generally possesses an official company ideology expressed in the company song, in essays by company elders, in catechismlike lists of primary goals and values, and in annual celebrations and public events. Each company's leader seeks to create an distinct ideology and company spirit (*shafū*). The company is portrayed as a big family, or in terms that underline the common interest, comradeship, and long-term relationships involved. Harmony, cooperation, and hard work will bring prosperity and growth despite a fiercely competitive and changing environment. The company is clearly the highest priority, and the morality of membership is judged in terms of loyal service to the company.

It is also common for company ideologies to contain lofty pronouncements stressing that business success must be honestly won with the best interests of society in mind. The company's work is seen as contributing to the glory and prosperity of Japan. The money, the people, the company's history, and the results of business are all seen as merged into one organic social entity.

Reinforcement 企業文化の浸透

Japanese have little trouble accepting that companies will try to mold their members to fit a particular ethos and style. The worker's character, attitudes, and values are properly subjects of company concern. Therefore, new employees usually undergo intensive corporate education and training programs 企業内教育制度.

Training represents a conscious effort on the part of management to reinforce corporate culture. Most employees are willing to participate in informal company-sponsored activities. Relations within small work groups are expected to be personal, warm, and actively developed outside working hours. The ideal boss is one who will aid subordinates in personal problems, give advice, and enter into a close association.

Corporate culture is reinforced by routine behavior. A prime example is the simple matter of morning greetings among workers. Typically company policy calls for a brief ceremony to begin the day in each office or workshop and, however seemingly mundane it may become, its absence can create difficulties.

One of the most characteristic qualities of Japanese corporate culture, in fact, is the degree to which it is managed. Japanese of all ages and stations in life tend to defer to the group, particularly its leaders. Due to the general absence of strong personal religious beliefs and concomitant ideological commitment, the governance of daily social conduct has typically become a matter of rather particularistic group and institutional norms. Japanese companies fulfill this role through the sponsorship of their own lively subculture.

Management (*keiei kanri*) 経営管理

In Japan, the origins of the professional manager go back to the pre-World War II period. As the *zaibatsu* expanded and diversified, the families owning them began to turn over the operation of these vast enterprises to professional managers, and by the 1930s professional managers had come to assume the major management responsibilities. This trend became firmly established in the postwar era, as the *zaibatsu* were dissolved (*zaibatsu* dissolution) 財閥解体 and stock ownership became widely disbursed. With few exceptions, large Japanese enterprises are now managed by professional managers.

Organizational Structure and Decision Making
組織の構造と意思決定

In Japan the individual, at least historically, existed only as a member of a group and not as a strong, clearly identifiable, and distinct entity. The basic unit of Japanese organizations remains the group. A task is assigned to and performed by a group rather than by individuals. The task is defined on the basis of the group, the assignment is carried out by the group, and the responsibility is shared by all. Under such an organizational arrangement, a leader must first create and then maintain a climate in which every member of the organization can work together harmoniously.

The decision-making process commonly followed in large bureaucratic organizations is known as the *ringi* system 稟議制度, which has often been described as an approval-seeking process. In it a proposal, known as a *ringisho* 稟議書, is prepared by a lower functionary. The *ringisho* works its way up through the organizational hierarchy in a highly circuitous manner, often at a snail's pace, and at each step is examined by the proper officials, whose approval is indicated by affixing a seal (see NEMAWASHI). Out of this process a decision emerges. The dynamic but informal interaction that characterizes every stage of decision making is the essence of the *ringi* system. From the very stage during which a decision is first being shaped, various ideas and alternatives are explored, albeit very informally. Different interests are accommodated, and compromises are sought. At the same time, a process of education, persuasion, and coordination among various groups takes place.

An elusive element in the *ringi* system is the role of the formal leader. In this system the formal leader is not a decision maker in the classical sense. In the Japanese organization, while the status of a leader is meticulously defined, his role in the decision-making process is little differentiated from that of other members of the organization. In other words, the leader participates with his subordinates in the decision-making process. Thus, the degree to which the leader's view is incorporated into a decision depends largely on how well he is accepted and respected by his subordinates and on the kind of relationships he enjoys with them.

Another basic condition for making the *ringi* system effective is the need for a high degree of shared understanding and values among the participants. In large Japanese companies, the development of such shared understanding and organizational commitment begins with the recruiting system and is reinforced through subsequent personnel practices. Young men are carefully selected from among the graduates of the best universities and have thus already survived a series of rigorous screening processes and are highly homogeneous in ability, training, background, and values. Once they have been recruited by a company, they go through an intensive socialization process during which they are indoctrinated with the values of a particular firm and through which, after a number of years, they develop a high degree of shared understanding and commitment. Japanese practices are undergoing gradual change, but the patterns outlined here are found today in almost every large Japanese corporation.

Corporate decision making (*kigyō no ishi kettei*)
企業の意思決定

The *ringi* system, a process of decision making through the use of circular letters, is known as a system unique to Japanese enterprises. More formal decisions, however, often are made in a meeting of company executives, as is the case in other countries. Top management decides fundamental managerial policy; proposals for and research on actual measures to be followed are assigned to each responsible division. Middle management takes a leading part in planning a measure, and after informal negotiations with other related departments the plan is formally presented in the form of a *ringisho*, a letter bearing the proposal that is circulated among the various departments of the organization. Since information is reported to the top level, upper management, including the CEO (chief executive officer) 経営最高責任者, is well acquainted with the plan when it is finally submitted at a board of directors' meeting.

Consequently the support of the plan in such a meeting is, in principle, unanimous.

As a company increases in size and the business diversifies, decision-making authority is passed down to each responsible division. However, at the very least fundamental plans for the corporate group and decisions on important matters are made at meetings of the parent company's 親会社 top-level management. In addition, the CEO of the parent company controls the whole group by retaining control over important personnel appointments and budget allocations to each division or subsidiary. In Japan it is the company's main bank, its principal customer, and its employees' union, rather than its stockholders, that exercise outside influence on the decision-making process.

TRADE 貿易

Foreign trade (*bōeki*) 貿易

Narrowly defined, foreign trade refers to the export and import of goods and services from and to Japan. However, in the sense of international commerce, it can be considered to include financial or capital flows as well.

The Opening of Japan 日本の開国

Japan's modern foreign trade officially began in 1859. The Tokugawa shogunate 徳川幕府 (1603–1867) until then had maintained a policy of National Seclusion. However, with the signing of the Harris Treaty (United States–Japan Treaty of Amity and Commerce) 日米修好通商条約 in July 1858, Japan opened its doors to Western commerce. At the outset the most important Japanese export was raw silk, which was welcomed in the

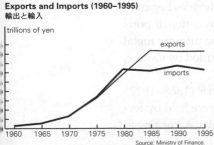

Exports and Imports (1960–1995)
輸出と輸入

trillions of yen

exports

imports

1960 1965 1970 1975 1980 1985 1990 1995

Source: Ministry of Finance.

European market. Other exports were primarily raw material goods, semimanufactures, and foodstuffs; these included tea, copper ware, marine products, medicine, oil, and lacquer ware. Key imports were cotton thread, cotton and wool textiles, ironware, sugar, medicinal herbs, military ships, and guns. Approximately 80 percent of Japan's trade was with the United Kingdom, the next largest trading partners being the United States and the Netherlands.

Initially Japan maintained a continual surplus balance of trade 貿易収支. However, after lowering import tariffs by the signing of the Tariff Convention 改税約書 of 1866, imports of manufactured goods increased, and Japan entered a period of deficit trade balances. Trade treaties concluded during this period did not recognize Japan's right to set its own customs duties, and Japan did not obtain tariff autonomy until 1911.

From the Meiji Restoration (1868) to World War I
明治維新(1868年)から第1次世界大戦まで

After the Meiji Restoration 明治維新, Japanese foreign trade increased dramatically every year. As part of its efforts to increase production and modernize Japanese industry, the government actively worked to further foreign trade and promoted overseas such products as raw silk, tea, hemp, tobacco, camphor, and soy. Considering individual products, raw silk's percentage of total exports gradually declined from the level of more than 70 percent in 1863. Manufactured goods such as matches, silk products, and cotton textiles began to be exported around 1890. After 1900, raw cotton imports replaced cotton thread, iron became the primary metal import, and ship imports were supplanted by various types of machinery.

In the early Meiji period 明治時代 (1868–1912) almost all commercial trading rights were held by foreign merchants, primarily English traders. According to an 1877 study, 94 percent of all exports were handled by foreign firms.

Japan's trade volume, which in 1870 had been less than ¥30 million (US $84,000), exceeded ¥500 million (US $1.4 million) by World War I. During the 47 years from 1868 to 1915, there were only 12 years in which Japan had a surplus balance of trade.

From World War I Prosperity to a Wartime Trading System 第1次世界大戦による好景気から戦時貿易体制へ

World War I provided the opportunity for a major increase in export business. The war caused a sharp decrease in exports of European and US products and an increase in demand for Japanese products. There was also an increase in exports of military supplies to the countries at war. As a result, the structure of Japanese exports changed, with a decrease in the percentage of raw materials and semimanufactures and an increase in the percentage of finished goods. Compared to prewar statistics, Japan's exports doubled by 1916, and in 1918, the last year of the war, exports were three times prewar levels. The cumulative trade surplus during the four years of the war was ¥1.4 billion (US $3.9 million).

After the war, however, because of an increase in Japan's domestic demand, the foreign trade balance changed from a surplus to a deficit. The worldwide Great Depression 大恐慌, which began with the New York stock market crash of 1929, dealt a serious blow to Japan's foreign trade. The adverse effect was heightened by a steep increase in the value of Japanese currency resulting from Japan's ill-timed return to the gold standard 金本位制 in January 1930. Japan's 1930 exports declined 31.6 percent compared to the previous year, and 1931 exports declined another 46.6 percent compared to 1930. Import levels also

Exports and Imports (1912–1921)
大正時代の貿易額
millions of yen

exports

imports

1912 1913 1914 1915 1916 1917 1918 1919 1920 1921

Source: Tōyō Keizai Shimpō Sha, *Meiji Taishō kokusei sōran.*

dropped severely. Imports in 1930 declined 30.2 percent compared to the previous year, and 1931 imports declined 40.3 percent compared to 1930.

Following the Manchurian Incident 満州事変 (1931) Japan adopted foreign trade and exchange controls in the course of organizing its war economy. With the development of trading blocs within the world trading system, the 1930s were marked by a great expansion of Japan's trade with its colonies. After the outbreak of the Sino-Japanese War of 1937–1945 日中戦争, Japan's foreign trade began increasingly to take on a wartime character. Imports became a means of obtaining military materials, and exports were promoted in order to acquire the foreign currency needed for imports.

Japan became heavily dependent on trade within the "yen bloc," which included its colonies, and trade with countries outside this bloc was cut drastically. Japan had a trade surplus with respect to yen bloc countries and a large trade deficit with other countries.

Foreign Trade after World War II
第2次世界大戦後の貿易

Immediately following World War II, the devastation of Japan caused a continuing foreign trade deficit as well as a chronic lack of foreign currency. It was not until the high-growth period of the late 1950s and early 1960s that export power increased significantly because of dramatic advances in manufacturing capacity and technology. Japan's trade balance began to show a surplus starting in the second half of the 1960s, although oil crises in 1973 and 1979 caused a temporary balance-of-trade deficit. After 1983 Japan's trade surplus grew rapidly, reaching US $106.8 billion in 1995. Factors behind this success include both the competitive strength of the Japanese company and the nature of the Japanese economy, which tends to encourage exports and discourage imports.

Postwar Exports 第2次世界大戦後の輸出

In the 1960s, Japan's average dollar-base export increase of 18.4 percent per year was 2.3 times the overall rate of increase in world trade. The makeup of Japan's exports continued to shift to the heavy-industry fields of steel, machinery, and chemical products and away from textiles and light-industry products. In the 1970s, exports of machinery and electronics jumped as increasing emphasis was placed on high-value-added products. As a result, the focus of TRADE FRICTION 貿易摩擦 shifted from textiles and steel to products such as color televisions and automobiles.

In the 1980s, exports of advanced-technology-intensive products including computers, semiconductors, videocassette recorders, machine tools, and facsimile machines continued to increase sharply, and trade friction over these products began to occur. Many Japanese companies, the most conspicuous being the automobile manufacturers, established local production facilities in the United States and Europe, partly in response to growing protectionist sentiments there. This caused a partial shift in the makeup of Japanese exports from finished goods to parts and subassemblies. In an effort to maintain price competitiveness after the sharp rise in the value of the yen which began in 1985, many Japanese companies also moved the manufacturing of labor-intensive and technically less-complex parts and products to China and other Asian countries in order to take advantage of the low labor costs there. In 1997, 29.3 percent of Japanese exports went to North America, 17.1% to the EU, and 44.9 percent to Asia.

Japanese Exports by Type, 1960-1995
商品別輸出構造 (in percentages)

	1960	1970	1980	1990	1995
Foodstuffs	6.6	3.5	1.2	0.6	0.5
Textiles	30.2	12.5	4.8	2.5	2.0
Chemicals	4.2	6.4	5.2	5.5	6.8
Metal products	13.8	19.7	16.4	6.8	6.5
Machinery and transport equipment	25.3	46.3	62.8	75.0	74.7
Other	19.9	11.6	9.6	9.6	9.5

Source: Ministry of International Trade and Industry.

Japanese Imports by Type, 1960–1995
商品別輸入構造 (in percentages)

	1960	1970	1980	1990	1995
Foodstuffs	12.2	13.6	10.4	13.4	15.2
Raw materials	49.1	35.4	16.9	12.1	9.8
Mineral fuels	16.5	20.7	49.8	24.2	15.9
Manufactured goods	21.9	29.8	21.8	47.6	56.9
Other	0.3	0.5	1.1	2.7	2.2

Source: Ministry of International Trade and Industry.

Postwar Imports 第2次世界大戦後の輸入

In the period immediately following World War II, raw fuels and textile raw materials made up the bulk of the imports. The relative importance of textile raw material imports decreased and that of mineral fuel and metal raw materials increased along with the development of Japanese heavy industry. As a result of the 1973 and 1979 oil crises, crude oil prices soared, and in 1980 mineral fuels were approximately 50 percent of total imports. By 1990 mineral fuels had fallen to 24.2 percent of imports due to lower oil prices and the successful energy-conservation efforts of Japanese industry.

At the beginning of the 1980s, manufactured goods represented only 25 percent of Japanese imports. This share increased rapidly during the second half of the decade, exceeding 50 percent in 1990. Part of the increase was due to large-volume imports from the production facilities that Japanese companies established in Asia in response to the rising value of the yen. In 1993 color television imports exceeded exports for the first time. In the 1990s, there have also been cases of Japanese automobile companies "re-importing" 逆輸入 into Japan vehicles manufactured in the United States and elsewhere.

Government policy on foreign trade
(bōeki seisaku) 貿易政策

Japan's modern trade policy began in the Meiji period (1868–1912), and its first major objective was the achievement of parity with the West. Until the end of the Unequal Treaties 不平等条約, tariffs and trade were in the hands of the Western powers, so the Japanese government was limited in the measures it could take to improve the nation's trade position. The government promoted industrialization and economic development through subsidies, loans, and technical assistance. This necessitated the import of equipment, ships, steel, and other commodities that Japan itself did not make and that had to be paid for by exports. Thus evolved what has remained a fundamental part of Japan's trade policy: Japan exports in order to import.

After 1899 tariff protection of specific industries was undertaken. At the same time, tariffs on raw materials were kept low, increasing the effective protection and further stimulating manufacturing. Protection of the home market was later extended to colonies and occupied territories. The need to secure raw material and markets in a hostile international trading environment led to efforts to form the so-called Greater East Asia Coprosperity Sphere 大東亜共栄圏 in the years immediately preceding World War II.

Following the war there was an immediate need to resuscitate the economy, especially trade. Priorities for imports were set by the government. There were protective tariffs on manufactured goods, while raw materials were allowed in essentially duty-free. Specific assistance was given or removed as industries developed or gained strength. Thus steel was given priority first, then automobiles in the 1950s, and computers in the 1960s and 1970s. Industries with either export potential or strategic economic importance were favored, and the government encouraged exports via special tax and credit incentives.

Fundamental economic policies have had as much of an impact on trade as trade-specific policies. The government's push to industrialize placed a premium on investment and growth. Financial resources were channeled through the city banks, the government development banks, the tax structure, and the government's expenditure patterns to such areas as steel, chemicals, shipping, and shipbuilding. The primary architect of the plan was the Heavy Industry Bureau of the Ministry of International Trade and Industry (MITI) 通商産業省, along with the Ministry of Finance 大蔵省. The

Japan's Imports and Exports by Area (1995)
地域別輸出入割合 (in percentages)

	Exports	Imports
Asia	43.6	36.6
Middle East	2.2	9.5
EU	16.7	16.1
North America	28.6	25.7
Latin America	4.4	3.5
Oceania	2.4	5.5
other	2.1	3.1

Source: Ministry of International Trade and Industry.

focus on growth and industrialization in turn led to rapid increases in manufacturing investment and productivity, which enhanced Japanese competitiveness.

Import liberalization 輸出の自由化 continued slowly through the 1960s and 1970s as Japan's industrial strength and export surplus developed further. After 1968, Japan's export surplus developed rapidly due to the Vietnam War, rising US inflation, and Japan's improving productivity. In turn, external pressures, especially from the United States, for real and substantive liberalization increased markedly. But the government still did not embrace full liberalization quickly.

Since the 1980s the major trade issue has been the growing trade surplus, and Japan's current trade policies are thus increasingly oriented toward encouraging imports while keeping the volume of exports down. This has created the need for major institutional reversals. Some obvious policy steps have been taken to encourage imports, including unilateral tariff cuts, removal of import restrictions 輸入制限, reform of the system for standards certification 基準認可制度, and import promotion campaigns. In addition, there have been periodic voluntary export restrictions 輸出自主規制 on items such as automobiles to specific markets. Liberalization of agricultural imports, particularly rice, has continued to be a politically sensitive issue, since almost all political parties owe a considerable part of their support to agriculture. The coalition government 連立政府 of Prime Minister Hosokawa Morihiro (1938–) finally decided at the end of 1993 that it would partially open the rice market to imports. The decision was part of the last-minute agreement reached at the Uruguay Round ウルグアイ=ラウンド as well as an emergency measure to make up for a poor rice crop that year.

Much remains to be done to change ingrained procedures. Many of the gains in import liberalization have come only as a result of direct foreign pressure. See also FOREIGN TRADE.

Trade friction (*bōeki masatsu*) 貿易摩擦

Trade friction has been a recurring issue in Japan's relationships with other nations since the mid-1950s. Until the early 1980s, friction primarily involved efforts to control rising Japanese exports and to prevent alleged dumping of Japanese products. In contrast, during most of the 1980s Japan's trade disputes with the United States typically involved attempts to gain greater access to the Japanese market. The Structural Impediments Initiative talks 日米構造協議, which began in 1989, marked a new phase by addressing so-called nontariff obstacles 非関税障壁 to trade between the United States and Japan.

The history of Japan's trade friction is both lengthy and broad in scope. For example, Japan has placed voluntary limits on exports 輸出自主規制 to the United States of cotton goods (1957), steel (1969), wood and synthetic fibers (1972), color televisions (1977), and automobiles (1981). Japan also agreed to restrain its steel exports to Europe in 1972. To counter dumping, the United States instituted a formula to trigger penalties on steel and machine tools imported at unfairly low prices (1978).

Through the late 1970s and the 1980s, as a result of the US objective of improving access to the Japanese market, the following accommodations were reached: increases in Japanese import quotas in beef and oranges, revision of Japanese import standards and certification procedures, the Japanese government's Action Program to Improve Market Access 市場開放のためのアクション=プログラ ム, the Japan-United States Semicon-

Trade Surplus
貿易黒字の推移
billions of US dollars

1965 1970 1975 1980 1985 1990 1995
Source: Bank of Japan.

ductor Agreement 日米半導体協定, and the Market-Oriented Sector Selective agreement 市場重視型個別協議 covering Japanese markets for telecommunications equipment, electronics, pharmaceuticals, medical equipment, forest products, and transportation equipment. Similarly, the "Super 301"

Export Ratio of Selected Products
主要商品の輸出比率 (in percentages)

	1992	1993	1994	1995	1996
Iron and steel	21.1	25.6	25.5	24.4	21.9
Magnetic disk units	67.3	70.5	69.1	80.7	89.9
Machine tools	33.2	39.3	44.9	47.5	45.7
IC	54.1	62.0	66.0	68.6	71.6
Automobiles	47.0	46.0	43.1	38.1	36.4
Motorcycles	52.2	56.9	51.7	48.2	52.5
Copy machines	77.6	68.8	66.0	65.1	61.4

Source: Ministry of International Trade and Industry.

スーパー301条 clause of the US Omnibus Trade and Competitiveness Act 米国包括通商競争力法 (1988) was applied to improve access to Japan's supercomputer, satellite, and wood product markets (1988). In contrast with the market-opening approach adopted by the United States, Japan has had a number of disputes with the EU countries and Australia concerning Japanese exports of videocassette recorders and semiconductors.

As Japan's huge trade surplus 貿易黒字 with the United States continued to grow in the 1990s, the emphasis in talks between the two countries expanded from specific products to include comprehensive negotiations on macroeconomic policies. Under the Structural Impediments Initiative agreement of 1990, Japan and the United States established a wide-ranging basis on which each country will address structural issues affecting bilateral trade. A new series of negotiations, called The Japan-United States Framework Talks for a New Economic Partnership 日米包括経済協議, began in July 1993. These talks have covered three areas: macroeconomic policies such as Japanese tax rates and public investment and the US budget deficit, specific industries such as computers and automobiles, and cooperation on global problems such as the environment and AIDS. Progress, however, was slowed by a dispute over the issue of numerical targets 数値的目標. After both countries agreed in February 1994 that numerical targets would not be set, the negotiations proceeded and agreements were reached that year concerning government procurement in the telecommunications industry and deregulation in the insurance industry. In 1996 the US-Japan Semiconductor Agreement, which did contain numerical targets, was discontinued. Efforts to solve trade friction between the United States and Japan are gradually shifting to international arenas, such as the World Trade Organization 世界貿易機関 (WTO), where many countries are involved in the negotiations.

Disagreement among the nations of the European Union, the United States, and Japan over agricultural trade has stalled General Agreement on Tariffs and Trade (GATT) 関税および貿易に関する一般協定 talks since the start of the so-called Uruguay Round ウルグアイ・ラウンド of 1986. In particular, since the mid-1980s the United States has been strongly urging Japan to liberalize its rice market 米市場. Despite continued opposition from farmers, the Japanese government partially opened the rice market as part of a last-minute agreement reached at Uruguay Round talks held in 1993.

The series of negotiated settlements covering Japan's trade friction has in turn spawned a number of significant economic developments. For example, Japan responded to US import restrictions by starting automobile production in the United States in the mid 1980s. Japanese companies also increased the number of automobiles and copy machines manufactured in Europe.

Balance of payments (*kokusai shūshi*) 国際収支

A statistical record of all economic transactions between residents of the reporting country and residents of all other countries. In 1993 the International Monetary Fund (IMF) 国際通貨基金 issued a new manual covering international balance of payments statistics, and in January 1996 Japan converted to this new method. As a result of this change, current account balance 経常収支,

which was previously divided into trade balance 貿易収支, balance on services and income, and balance on unrequited transfers, is now divided into balance on goods and services 貿易・サービス収支, balance on income 所得収支, and current transfers 経常移転収支. In addition, for the capital account balance 資本収支, the previous long-term 長期収支 and short-term 短期収支 categories were combined in the new financial account category 投資収支, which comprises direct investment 直接投資, portfolio investment 証券投資, and other investment. In the past official statistics were stated in both US dollars and Japanese yen, but now only yen will be used, with US dollar information provided for reference only.

Balance on Goods and Services 貿易・サービス収支

Balance on goods is defined as the difference between exports and imports; this is one of the most frequently used measures of a country's balance-of-payments performance. Japan ran a deficit in merchandise trade in the early postwar years through the mid-1950s, a time when the national economy underwent gradual recovery. By the mid-1960s Japan had increased its international competitiveness to the point where it began consistently to run a surplus in its merchandise trade balance.

Balance on services includes expenditures and receipts for transportation, business travel and tourism, and royalties and license fees. Data on Japan's balance on services since 1961 show a consistent trend toward larger and larger deficits. A number of factors account for the deficits. First, because of Japan's imports of raw materials, transportation payments

Japan's International Balance of Payments
国際収支
(in millions of US dollars)

	1993	1994	1995	1996
Current Account 経常収支	131,915	130,540	110,421	65,802
Balance on Goods and Services 貿易・サービス収支	96,235	96,219	73,937	21,304
Balance on Goods 貿易収支	139,223	144,137	131,241	83,624
Balance on Services サービス収支	−42,988	−47,917	−57,302	−62,320
Balance on Income 所得収支	40,763	40,414	44,198	53,484
Current Transfers 経常移転収支	−5,802	−6,090	−7,711	−8,986
Capital and Financial Account 資本収支	−105,247	−87,980	−66,717	−30,770
Financial Account 投資収支	−103,765	−86,101	−64,437	−27,518
Capital Account その他資本収支	−1,484	−1,878	−2,279	−3,252

Source: Ministry of Finance.

tend to be high. Second, for years Japan has paid a considerable amount in licensing arrangements for technology to foreign firms. In the second half of the 1980s, Japan's deficit in services increased rapidly because of the rise in the yen's value and increases in overseas tourism. Japan's deficit in current transfers also grew quickly during this period because of increases in official development assistance (ODA) 政府開発援助.

Current Account Balance 経常収支

This balance combines net merchandise trade, income payment, and current transfer payments. Japan's current account fluctuated between deficit and surplus in the mid-1950s and mid-1960s, reflecting the business cycle 景気変動. It has since maintained a consistent current account surplus except for a few years of deficit caused by the two oil crises in the 1970s. In the first half of the 1980s the current account surplus grew due to a drop in oil prices and to increases in exports. After peaking in 1993, however, the current account surplus declined in each of the next three years because of a falling surplus in the balance on goods and a rising deficit in the balance on services.

Net External Assets
日本の対外純資産

(billions of US dollars)

1975	70
1980	115
1985	1,298
1990	3,281
1991	3,831
1992	5,160
1993	6,108
1994	6,890
1995	7,481

Source: Economic Planning Agency.

INDUSTRIES 産業

Industrial history (*sangyōshi*) 産業史

Japan's modern industrial history can be roughly divided into two periods: first, the early modern era from the Meiji Restoration 明治維新 (1868) to the end of World War II, during which capitalism was established, and second, the contemporary period which has seen reconstruction and rapid economic growth.

Early Modern Industry (1868–1945)
近代の産業(1868年～1945年)

Japan's industrial revolution began in the late

1880s. Light industry 軽工業, notably the textile industry 繊維産業, grew rapidly between 1887 and 1896, while a second wave of industrialization between 1897 and 1906 led to the establishment of many heavy industries 重工業. The Meiji government took the lead in developing such basic industries as railroads and mining, as well as a number of manufacturing industries such as shipbuilding 造船業, iron and steel 鉄鋼業, and machine tools 工作機械業. Most of these enterprises were later turned over to the private sector.

During World War I Japanese industry experienced significant growth, as it benefited greatly from the inability of European suppliers, preoccupied with the war, to trade in Asian markets. Japan provided the Allies with military supplies, and there was great demand for Japanese shipping. An industrial boom took place during the period of the war as the values of Japanese exports rose threefold, and there was a rapid accumulation of capital. Industrial production overtook agricultural production during the war; capitalism in Japan had become fully entrenched.

Despite economic hardships caused by a depression in 1920, the Tōkyō Earthquake of 1923 関東大震災, and the Shōwa Depression 昭和恐慌 of the 1930s, the productivity of Japanese industry continued to increase as a result of technological progress, greater efficiency in production techniques, and the development of managerial techniques designed to secure employee loyalty. Japan's heavy industries, such as iron and steel and shipbuilding, grew rapidly in the 1930s. The output of the chemical, machine tool, electric machinery, and ceramics industries all increased greatly during this period. Exports rose sharply, led by shipments of textile products and sundry goods. In the precision machinery industry 精密機械工業, which became the foundation for Japan's munitions industry, domestic products were almost meeting domestic demand.

Throughout this period there was no antimonopoly policy in Japan. Since the Meiji Restoration the overriding concern of the nation's leaders had been Japan's national survival in the face of the political and economic threat of Western domination. Therefore, in the period before Japan's defeat in World War II it is not clear that the government placed a premium on economic competition in itself. Administrations considered rather that the national interest would best be served by supporting the interests of large, powerful, and well-established companies such as Mitsui, Mitsubishi, and Sumitomo—the *zaibatsu* (financial cliques)—that had the resources to lead the nation's industrial progress. The *zaibatsu* dominated industry in this period, exercising an oligopolistic control over a wide range of industries such as manufacturing, mining, and transportation, as well as finance and overseas trade.

Meanwhile, a dual structure 二重構造 had developed within the manufacturing industry itself, between, on the one hand, the relatively small number of firms with capital-intensive production methods, and, on the other hand, vast numbers of low-capital, labor-intensive small firms and family concerns, many of which were more or less wholly dependent on the business of a single larger firm. In 1930, 60 percent of the nation's manufacturing labor force was employed by firms with fewer than 10 workers. Although this figure had fallen to just 9 percent by 1986, the "dual structure"—the high proportion of smaller-scale businesses in dependency relationships with larger firms—has continued to be a key characteristic of the Japanese economy in the post-World War II period.

A great many new industries emerged in the years between the world wars. For instance, the development of the electric power industry 電力産業 gave a great boost to the domestic aluminum-smelting industry アルミニウム精錬産業. The development of the radio led to the beginning of vacuum tube 真空管 production. Many new businesses entered this area, including the companies now known as Tōshiba Corporation (株)東芝 and Victor Co., of Japan, Ltd. 日本ビクター(株). Many other major Japanese manufacturing companies of the present day were founded at this time, such as Toyota Motor Corporation トヨタ自動車(株), Nissan Motor Co., Ltd. 日産自動車(株), and Mitsubishi Heavy Industries, Ltd. 三菱重工業(株).

Merchant Vessels Launched by Major Country
国別商船竣工比率 (in percentage of world total gross tons)

	Japan	Korea	Germany	Total production
1970	48.1	0.01	7.8	20.980
1975	49.7	1.2	8.3	34.202
1980	46.5	4.0	5.5	13.101
1985	52.3	14.4	5.1	18.157
1990	43.0	21.8	5.4	15.885
1994	46.8	22.2	5.8	17.907

Source: Shipbuilder's Association of Japan.

Subsidies supported the production of military vehicles and the substitution of domestic production for the import of cargo ships. The birth of Nippon Seitetsu (Nippon Steel Co.) 日本製鉄会社 was the result of government guidance. Industrial growth was also fostered by laws enacted for individual industries, with emphasis placed on automobiles, petrochemicals, iron and steel, machine tools, and aircraft. For example, the infant automotive industry was promoted by the Automotive Manufacturing Industries Law 自動車製造事業法 of 1935.

Contemporary Industrial History (from 1945)
現代(1945年以降)

During the reconstruction period following World War II, the recovery of key industries was aided by an industrial policy known as the Priority Production Program 傾斜生産方式. Underdeveloped capacity in certain areas was seen as a bottleneck limiting overall growth, so the electric power, iron and steel, marine transportation, and coal industries were targeted for rapid reconstruction.

The Korean War 朝鮮戦争 (1950–1953) enabled Japanese industry to climb out of the stagnation in which it was mired at the end of the 1940s. By supplying the United Nations forces 国連軍 serving in Korea with vast quantities of matériel, Japan was able to earn the foreign exchange necessary to pay for vital imports; the war thus provided the stimulus for the economic recovery of the 1950s.

During the rapid-growth period from the late 1950s to the early 1970s, industries such as iron and steel, construction 建設産業, and pharmaceuticals 製薬産業 grew quickly, and the household electrical products industry 家電業界 and the petrochemical industry 石油化学工業 developed. The international economic environment at this time was favorable for Japanese exports; in the 1960s, Japan's average export increase of 18.4 percent per year was 2.5 times the overall increase in world trade. This period saw the establishment of an industrial structure based on imported raw materials that were domestically processed for export.

In the wake of the export successes of the iron and steel and shipbuilding industries, other industries such as precision machinery 精密機器産業 and electronic 電

Selected Japanese Production Indexes
戦後復興期主要生産指数

General, 1945–1952					
	Agriculture and fisheries (1933–35=100)	Mining and manufacturing	Mining	Manufacturing	Public utilities
			(1934–36=100)		
1945	60	60	73	59	88
1946	77	31	52	29	109
1947	75	37	67	35	124
1948	86	55	80	53	138
1949	93	71	92	69	155
1950	99	84	97	82	168
1951	99	114	111	115	185
1952	111	126	114	128	201
Specific, 1946-1948					
	Rice (1933–35=100)	Fish	Coal	Iron and steel	Chemicals	Textiles
				(1934–36=100)	
1946	102	53	58	12	28	14
1947	98	84	76	18	36	18
1948	104	105	90	37	55	24

Source: G.C.Allen, *Japan's Economic Expansion* (1965). Uchino Tatsurō, "Shōwa kōki (Sengo fukkō to kōdo seichō)" in Nakayama Ichirō and Shinohara Miyohei, ed. *Nihon keizai jiten* (1973).

子機器産業 and optical equipment 工学機器産業 also turned to export-led growth. Huge investments were made in production facilities for heavy industry, located in the Tōkaidō megalopolis 東海道メガロポリス that stretches along the Pacific coast from Tōkyō to Ōsaka and Kōbe. Total plant and equipment investments exceeded profits, and the ratio of borrowed capital increased.

Aggressive management created an increasing demand for funds, which banks satisfied using their large volumes of household savings deposits 家計貯蓄. Relationships between corporations and their main banks became closer, and industrial groups of affiliated companies formed around major banks. This aggressive corporate capitalism and strong reliance on indirect financing were characteristic of the Japanese industrial structure and were the basic mechanisms responsible for the strong economic growth. Japan's national income 国民所得 more than doubled in the 1960s, and in 1968 its gross national product 国民総生産 became the second largest among the world's market economies. The spring labor offensive 春闘 became in the 1960s the established mechanism by which labor bargained for more equitable income distribution.

Efforts to reduce costs and increase efficiency in response to the oil crisis 石油ショック of 1973 strengthened the competitiveness of major export industries. Successful conservation efforts were made by both management and labor; as a result, energy demand fell by 37 percent in the chemical industry and by more than 20 percent in the iron and steel industry. In the automobile industry energy-saving efforts led to lighter automobiles and increased fuel economy, which further increased export competitiveness.

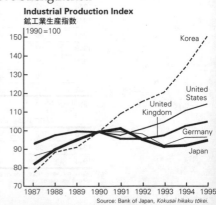

Industrial Production Index
鉱工業生産指数

Source: Bank of Japan, *Kokusai hikaku tōkei.*

Industries

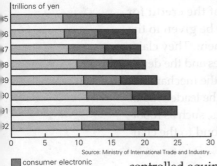

Electronics Industry Growth
エレクトロニクス産業の成長

trillions of yen

85
86
87
88
89
90
91
92

0   5   10   15   20   25   30

Source: Ministry of International Trade and Industry.

- consumer electronic products
- electronic components
- industrial electronic equipment

The oil crisis of 1979 also caused distinctive changes in the country's industrial structure. The heavy industries, which had supported rapid economic growth, stagnated, and the emphasis shifted to industries that utilize high technology and sophisticated machinery. Productivity increased through innovations such as the mounting of small computers on machine tools to develop numerically controlled equipment. It was also during the late 1970s that the computer industry コンピューター産業 and the semiconductor industry 半導体産業 began to grow rapidly.

In response to growing trade friction 貿易摩擦 with the United States and Europe, in the 1980s many Japanese companies in key export industries, such as electronics and automobiles, set up local manufacturing facilities overseas. The rapid rise in the value of the yen 円の急騰 after 1985 has also forced some companies to move part of their manufacturing operations to China and Southeast Asia in order to maintain price competitiveness. Although export levels remain high in the 1990s, the shift of manufacturing jobs overseas has provoked fear of the hollowing out of Japanese industry 産業の空洞化.

Many outside observers tend to emphasize the role of the intimate relationship between business and government in increasing the industrial competitiveness of Japan. Since the Meiji Restoration, Japanese administrations have indeed worked closely with industry to develop Japan's economy. It is argued that, particularly since World War II, the government has identified key industrial sectors for development and then actively encouraged major corporations to undertake the necessary research, investment, and development. Recent examples were the official encouragements in the early 1980s to Japanese manufacturers to overtake the US computer giant IBM. However, other observers have insisted that much of the credit for Japan's rapid economic growth must be given to the private sector rather than the government. They claim that the introduction of new technologies and the development of new products owe more to the mechanisms of market competition than they do to the leadership of government, and that in many key areas, such as robotics, the government was slow to respond to the challenge of the new technology.

Industrial structure (*sangyō kōzō*) 産業構造

National economies 国民経済 are conventionally divided into three sectors: primary industries 第1次産業 (agriculture 農業, forestry 林業, and fisheries 水産業), secondary industries 第2次産業 (mining 鉱業, manufacturing 製造業, and construction 建設業), and tertiary industries 第3 次産業 (transportation 運輸, communications 通信, retail and wholesale trade 商業, banking 銀行, finance 金融 and real estate 不動産, business services 公務, personal services その他のサービス, and public administration 公共行政). In general, national economies in the early stages of development are dominated by primary production related to land. As the economy develops and income rises, the primary sector shares of output, capital, and labor tend to fall, and those of the secondary sector tend to rise. In late stages of development, the primary sector accounts for only a small fraction of total economic activities, the secondary sector begins to decline in relative terms, and the tertiary sector comes to the fore.

Historical Experience of Japan 日本の歴史的経験

Japan's economic development since the Meiji Restoration (1868) is an excellent illustration of these patterns. In the distribution of the labor force between agriculture and nonagriculture, changes were slow until the early 1900s, considerably accelerated from then up to World War II, and very rapid during the decades following the war. After 1960 the agricultural labor force began to contract in absolute terms, and even those who remained on farms worked only part-time as farmers.

In the secondary sector, statistics show a continued relative expansion in employment and production until the mid-1970s. The tertiary sector maintained a relatively stable share in net domestic product before World War II, although its share of the national labor force expanded. After World War II, its share of employment continued to increase, while its share of gross domestic product (GDP) 国内総生産 remained stable until the early 1960s when it, too, started to rise.

Changes in Manufacturing 製造業の変遷

A broad comparison of light and heavy manufacturing 重工業 reveals that light manufacturing 軽工業 accounted for as much as 85 percent of total production until 1900. From then on, the share steadily declined, and after 100 years the relative positions of light and heavy manufacturing were reversed. The textile industry 繊維産業 was the dynamic catalyst in Japan's industrialization. Textile output was less than 10 percent of the total in the 1870s but jumped above 25 percent in the 1890s and stayed close to 30 percent until World War II. Its continued expansion through the prewar period provided significant employment opportunities, especially for surplus female labor in agriculture. This temporary migration was a salient feature of prewar labor mobility. After World War II, the textile industry began to decline, and by 1990 it accounted for only 3.1 percent of the national labor force.

In heavy manufacturing, the

Composition of Manufacturing Production
製造業の産業別生産高比較 (in percentages)

	light manufacturing	heavy manufacturing
1874–1879	84.5	15.4
1880–1889	85.0	15.0
1890–1899	86.7	13.3
1900–1909	81.8	18.2
1910–1919	72.4	27.5
1920–1929	68.8	31.9
1930–1939	55.7	44.3
1950–1959	42.8	57.3
1960–1969	31.5	68.5
1970–1978	22.4	77.5

Source: For 1874–1939: Miyohei Shinohara, *Mining and Manufacturing* (1972). For 1950–69: Kazushi Ohkawa and Miyohei Shinohara, *Patterns of Japanese Economic Development* (1979). For 1970–78: extrapolated by the author from Ministry of International Trade and Industry production indexes.

iron and steel industry 鉄鋼業 began to expand in the decade beginning in 1910, but government protection was necessary to shield it from international competition. After World War II, basic metals maintained a stable share of manufacturing output. On the other hand, the machine tool industry 工作機械産業, after making relatively slow progress in the pre-World War II period, experienced a spectacular expansion in the three decades after 1945; its share of manufacturing output exceeded 40 percent by 1972. Japan is now one of the world's leading exporters of machinery. The chemical industry 化学工業 maintained a comparatively stable 10 percent share before World War II and rose to 20 percent after the war.

The most recent stage in the development of national economies has been called postindustrialism, which is marked by a decrease in the employment share of the secondary sector and a shift from production of goods to services. This "service revolution" サービス革命 brings the continuing growth of tertiary industries; it seems to have begun in Japan in the mid-1970s, when manufacturing employment started to decline. In 1990 the tertiary sector accounted for 60.8 percent of total output and employed 59.0 percent of the national labor force.

Relationship to the Foreign Trade Structure
外国貿易との関連

The composition of a nation's exports and imports closely reflects its stage of industrialization.

Gross Domestic Product by Industry
GDPの産業別内訳

(in percentages)

	1970	1980	1985	1990	1994
Primary industries	5.9	3.6	3.1	2.4	2.0
Secondary industries	43.1	37.8	36.3	36.9	34.0
Manufacturing	34.9	28.2	28.4	27.4	23.5
Mining and construction	8.3	9.5	7.9	9.6	10.5
Tertiary industries	51.0	58.6	60.7	60.7	63.9
Wholesale and retail	13.9	14.8	12.8	12.1	12.2

Source: Economic Planning Agency.

Japan's main exports were tea and raw silk when the country opened its doors to foreign powers in the 1860s, and raw silk remained the most important export item until 1929. In the 1930s, cotton replaced raw silk as the most important category of Japanese exports. In the early postwar period, more than half of exports were in light manufacturing, but with the expansion of heavy industries Japanese exports continued to shift to heavy manufactured goods, which came to account for more than 87 percent of the total value of exports by 1990.

Japan's imports consisted almost entirely of manufactured products in the early Meiji period. Industrialization in the subsequent decades enabled Japan to increase imports of crude materials. Thus, in the 1930s, Japan's imports consisted of light manufactures (12 percent), heavy manufactures (30 percent), food-stuffs (18 percent), raw materials (33 percent), and fuels (7 percent). Comparable figures in 1988–1990 were 16, 31, 14, 14, and 22 percent (others 3 percent), respectively.

Agriculture (nōgyō) 農業

Prior to the Meiji Restoration 明治維新 of 1868, as much as 80 percent of the population of Japan was engaged in farming. Rice 米 has been overwhelmingly dominant as the main crop. The emphasis has always been on improving productivity per unit of land area in rice and other plant crops. Highly labor-intensive farming methods were developed as a result of the limited acreage allotted to each farm household. These agricultural characteristics gave rise to farming practices and folk customs 民俗風習 that in turn profoundly affected the nature of Japanese culture as a whole. Since the Meiji Restoration, industrialization and urbanization have had a significant impact on Japanese agriculture. The proportion of farmers to the total population, the proportion of cultivated acreage to the total area of the country, and the relative importance of agriculture in the total economy have all declined, while the importation of foodstuffs has increased. With these tendencies, many of the events and customs of Japanese rural life have begun to lose their importance.

Premodern Agriculture 前近代の農業

Japanese agriculture began about 2,000 years ago with the cultivation of rice. Other crops cultivated in Japan since ancient times include wheat, barley, *awa* (Italian millet) 粟, *hie* (barnyard millet) 稗, soybeans 大豆, *azuki* beans 小豆, *daikon* (radish) 大根, and cucurbits.

The oldest farm tools were made of wood or stone. When technology from the continent brought the manufacture of iron tools, rapid progress in agriculture was made and much wasteland was brought under cultivation.

From the end of the Heian period (794–1185) influential families emerged in the provinces and accumulated wealth through agricultural production. Taking control of the government in the Kamakura period (1185–1333), they showed greater concern about agriculture than did former rulers and encouraged improvements. With the emergence of a large number of cities and towns in the Edo period (1600–1868), the percentage of the population not engaged in agriculture increased, and farmers were required to produce more and more. However, more than half of the rice produced was collected as land tax, and farmers were frequently left with insufficient amounts for their own needs. They made do with wheat, barley, or millet. Agricultural output 農業生産高 was increased with endeavors in three major areas: reclaimed lands, fertilizers, and plant breeding.

During Japan's drive toward modernization after the Meiji Restoration, Western practices in agriculture were studied closely. However, since the natural

Traditional Farming Tools
伝統的な農具
Kama (sickles) 鎌
kuwakirigama   kamisorigama

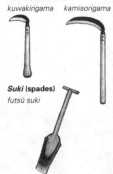

Suki (spades)
futsū suki

Kuwa (hoes) 鍬
itaguwa   bitchūguwa

Production of Selected Crops
農産物生産高
(in metric tons)

Crop	Production (1970)	(1994)
Grains		
Rice イネ	12,689,000	11,981,000
Wheat ムギ	1,046,000	790,000
Vegetables		
White potato バレイショ	3,611,000	3,377,000
Japanese white radish ダイコン	2,778,000	2,154,000
Cabbage キャベツ	1,433,000	1,511,000
Sweet potato カンショ	2,564,000	1,264,000
Chinese cabbage ハクサイ	1,744,000	1,118,000
Onion タマネギ	973,000	1,109,000
Cucumber キュウリ	965,000	866,000
Tomato トマト	793,000	758,000
Carrot ニンジン	497,000	658,000
Eggplant ナス	722,000	510,000
Welsh onion ネギ	614,000	525,000
Lettuce レタス	165,000	528,000
Spinach ホウレンソウ	363,000	367,000
Pumpkin カボチャ	306,000	265,000
Burdock ゴボウ	293,000	244,000
Fruits		
Mandarin orange ミカン	2,552,000	1,247,000
Apple リンゴ	1,021,000	989,000
Watermelon スイカ	1,004,000	655,000
Japanese pear ニホンナシ	445,000	417,000
Melon メロン	191,000	397,000
Grape ブドウ	234,000	245,000
Persimmon カキ	343,000	302,000
Strawberry イチゴ	134,000	198,000
Peach モモ	279,000	174,000
Japanese plum ウメ	68,000	113,000

Source: Ministry of Agriculture, Forestry, and Fisheries.

condition of the land in Japan is quite different from the West, mere transplantation of foreign technology often did not work well. Emphasis was shifted, therefore, back to rice as the main crop and to the development of intensive farming methods 集約的な農法. Agriculture experimental stations 農業試験場 were built by the state to conduct most of the plant breeding 品種改良 of important crops.

Agricultural Modernization
農業の近代化

Of all the reform programs that followed World War II, the Land Reforms of 1946 1946年の農地改革 were perhaps the most successful in bringing about basic and far-reaching changes in Japan. A sweeping redistribution of land largely eliminated tenancy by 1949 and resulted in about 90 percent of cultivated land being farmed by owners. Postwar food shortages, high prices, a black market in rice, and general inflation all worked to the advantage of Japan's farmers. In most cases they were able to pay off the debts on their new land with relative ease and to begin investing the capital that was needed for the rationalization of agriculture. The government aided farmers by establishing price support programs, especially for rice. It also gave strong support to agricultural technical schools, experimental stations, and extension programs. Agricultural cooperative associations 農業協同組合 enhanced these government initiatives by extending low-interest loans and developing group marketing at the village level. The end result was a relatively affluent farming population with the education, incentive, and access to capital needed to purchase the new crop strains and fertilizers to increase yields, as well as the machinery to ease labor demand.

Number of Agricultural Workers
農業就業人口

(in thousands of persons)

	1975	1980	1985	1990	1994
60 years old and over 60歳以上	2,499	2,499	2,767	2,437	2,538
16 to 59 years old 16~59歳	5,408	4,474	3,596	2,382	1,758
Total	7,907	6,973	6,363	4,819	4,296

Source: Ministry of Agriculture, Forestry, and Fisheries.

Japan began to experience labor shortages by the late 1950s after the beginning of rapid economic growth. The demand for labor in the urban-industrial centers resulted in a growing exodus of people from rural areas. Part-time farmers are numerous, and well over half the labor force is female.

It seems unlikely that Japanese agriculture could have succeeded without the spread of machines, chemicals, and other labor-saving devices. Virtually all land is now cultivated by machine. Traditional methods of farming were replaced with power cultivators, tractors, and other machines. Due to all of these factors Japan's total rice crop increased from about 9.5 million metric tons (10.5 million short tons) in 1950 to over 13 million metric tons (14.3 million short tons) in 1975. Per capita rice consumption, however, has declined, and the government is now concerned with problems of overproduction and surplus storage. Farmers have been encouraged, and in some cases subsidized, to convert their rice fields to other crops. This governmental policy of production adjustment 生産調整 exacerbated the shortage caused by the extremely poor rice crop in 1993. Changes in Japanese eating habits 食習慣 since around 1960 have resulted in increased production of meat, dairy products 乳製品, fruits, and vegetables. In the 1990s, however, stagnating consumption and expanding import volumes have led to decreases in the production of these farm products. See also RICE.

Japan's traditional labor-intensive agriculture has

Self-Sufficiency Rates for Major Farm Products
主要食用農産物の自給率

(in percentages)

	1960	1970	1980	1990	1994
Staple food grains* 主食用穀物	89	74	69	67	74
Rice 米	102	106	100	100	120
Wheat 小麦	39	9	10	15	9
Pulses 豆類	44	13	7	8	5
Vegetables 野菜	100	99	97	91	86
Fruits and Nuts 果実	100	84	81	63	47
Meat 肉類	93	89	80	70	60
Beef 牛肉	96	90	72	51	42
Pork 豚肉	96	98	87	74	66
Chicken 鶏肉	100	98	94	82	73
Hen eggs 鶏卵	101	97	98	98	96
Milk and milk products 牛乳・乳製品	89	89	82	78	73
Overall fishery products 食用水産物総合	111	104	89	67	60
Overall farm products 食用農産物総合	91	81	75	67	62
Total foodstuffs 食料総合	90	88	80	67	62

Note: The self-sufficiency rate equals domestic production divided by total consumption, multiplied by 100.
*Rice, wheat, barley, and naked barley.

Source: Ministry of Agriculture, Forestry, and Fisheries.

been transformed into a highly mechanized and capital-intensive system in less than a generation and much of its new technology serves as a model for developing Asian nations. Yet some problems and questions remain for the future. Production costs, especially for rice, are very high, and Japanese agriculture requires heavy subsidies. Most farms are too small in scale for maximum utilization of land and capital. The loss of vitality in farming communities is also a significant problem, with the average age of farm workers exceeding 60 in 1995. As part of the agreement concerning agricultural products that was reached at the Uruguay Round ウルグアイ・ラウンド talks in 1993, Japan decided to convert remaining quotas, except for rice, to tariffs and reduce tariff rates. It also agreed to partially open the rice market. Major changes are taking place in both the international and domestic agricultural landscape, one such change being the liberalization of rice distribution that went into effect with the implementation of the Law for Stabilization of Supply and Demand and Prices of

Staple Food 主要食糧の需給及び価格の安定に関する法律 in 1995. Japanese agriculture must find ways to respond flexibly to these changes.

Fishing industry (*gyogyō*) 漁業

The modern Japanese fishing industry operates boats worldwide, though the principal Japanese fisheries are in the North Pacific, including the Bering Sea ベーリング海 and the Sea of Okhotsk オホーツク海. Industry production for 1996—7.3 million metric tons (8.03 million short tons) of fish and other seafood—was the fourth largest in the world after China, Peru, and Chile.

Traditional Japanese Fishing 伝統的漁法

Although modern commercial fishing methods are responsible for the bulk of Japan's fish production, traditional techniques are still in use. Long "fish corrals," up to 1,000 meters (3,281 ft) in length and made of bamboo or net hurdles, are used in lakes, and weirs are built into streams to catch river fish. The Japanese catch octopuses in ceramic or concrete pots suspended from lines. Japanese divers collect abalone, oysters, and sea plants. Cormorant fishing 鵜飼い, an ancient technique for catching river fish, has survived to the present day as a tourist attraction.

The State of the Industry 漁業の現状

In 1996 there were 60,000 fishing concerns in Japan, of which 72 percent were family-run operations using boats of less than 10 tons, and 19 percent were family-run aquiculture firms, including seaweed cultivation 海藻養殖 and fish and shellfish farming 魚介養殖 businesses. Large and medium-sized fishing companies made up only 9 percent. All large Japanese fishing companies (except for setnet fisheries) are licensed by the national or prefectural governments.

Modern Commercial Fishing 現代の商業漁業

The Japanese fishing industry has adopted a host

Seafood Production
漁業部門別生産高

(in thousands of metric tons)

Type of production	1960	1965	1970	1975	1980	1985	1990	1994
Open-sea fishing	1,410	1,733	3,429	3,168	2,167	2,111	1,496	1,063
Offshore fishing	2,515	2,788	3,279	4,469	5,705	6,498	6,081	3,720
Coastal fishing	1,893	1,861	1,889	1,935	2,037	2,268	1,992	1,807
Marine aquiculture	285	380	549	773	992	1,088	1,273	1,344
Inland fishing and aquiculture	90	146	168	199	221	206	209	169
Total	6,193	6,908	9,315	10,545	11,122	12,171	11,052	8,103

Source: Ministry of Agriculture, Forestry, and Fisheries.

of new fishing devices and techniques to reduce operating hours and compensate for the shrinking labor force. Highly automated fishing vessels are now common, and various types of ultrasonic devices that monitor the movement of fish around boats, warn of fish entering a net, and provide information on the condition of the net are widely used. Remote-control meters show the height of a net in relation to fish movements, allowing a boat to adjust its speed accordingly, and seine net depth meters are widely used to help boats place nets in the path of oncoming fish.

In 1996 the total catch from coastal fisheries was slightly under 2.0 million metric tons (2.2 million short tons). Although the coastal fishing 沿岸漁業 catch has been dropping since the early 1980s, the shortfall has been made up by aquiculture harvests, which amounted to nearly 1.3 million metric tons (1.4 million short tons) of products in 1996.

Offshore fishing 沖合漁業 within about 200 miles of shore is carried out by boats of more than 10 tons using purse seines, trawls, drift nets, and hook and line. Most fish caught offshore are migrating species, so catches vary widely from year to year. In 1996 the offshore catch totaled approximately 3.2 million metric tons (3.5 million short tons), of which sardines and mackerel accounted for about half.

Open-sea (pelagic) fishing 外洋漁業, conducted

with large factory ships equipped with freezing and processing equipment, also uses such methods as purse seining, trawling, and drift netting, along with longline angling. Annual catches were large throughout the late 1960s and early 1970s. Around the mid-1970s, however, the industry initiated self-imposed restrictions on the size of open-sea catches in anticipation of changes in international fishing zones 漁業水域. In 1976 the United States adopted a 200-mile fishery zone, as did Canada, the Soviet Union (now the Russian Federation), and various European countries. This put many fishing grounds off limits to Japanese boats. The government launched a long-term program to increase the amount of fish and sea life in Japan's own 200-mile fishing zone, but in the meantime increasing demand for fish, combined with shrinking catches, boosted Japan's imports of marine products. By 1996 Japan's open-sea catch had fallen to 800,000 metric tons (880,000 short tons), and imports of marine products had soared to 3.5 million metric tons (3.85 million short tons), making Japan the world's leading importer of marine products.

Fresh and Frozen Fish Imports (1987–1996)
生鮮魚類の輸入

billions of US dollars

Source: Ministry of International Trade and Industry.

Configuration of Seafood Imports (1996)
輸入魚介類の品目別構成

(in percentages)

fresh and frozen fish	42.7
shellfish	40.1
processed seafood	14.5
salted seafood	2.7

Source: Ministry of International Trade and Industry.

Forestry (*ringyō*) 林業

About 70 percent of Japan's total area is wooded. Forests play a particularly important role in land conservation 土地保全 in Japan, as steep mountain ranges run along the midline of the islands from north to south and the rivers are short and torrential. Japan is a great consumer of wood as well as the world's greatest importer of logs and wood chips (accounting for about 20 percent of the world's wood trade). It is also notable for its exceptionally high proportion of planted forests 植樹林, which occupy about 40 percent of the nation's total forest area.

Supply of Domestic and Imported Timber Material
国産・外材別消費需要量

(in millions of cubic meters)

	domestic	imported
1975	35	62
1980	35	74
1985	33	60
1990	29	82
1994	24	85

Note: Timber material includes logs, sawlogs, pulp and chips, and plywoods.
Source: Forest Agency.

Forest Conditions in Japan 日本の森林

A great variety of trees grow in Japan because of the marked temperature differences from north to south and a high level of humidity brought about by warm ocean currents. Trees can be classified as evergreen broad-leaved types 常緑広葉樹 such as camellias and *kusunoki* (camphor tree), deciduous broad-leaved types 落葉広葉樹 such as *buna* (beech) and *tochinoki* (Japanese horse chestnut), and conifers 針葉樹 such as *sugi* (cedar) and *hinoki* (cypress). Of the total forest area of about 24.7 million hectares (61.0 million acres), about 9.9 million hectares (24.5 million acres) support planted forests consisting mainly of cedar, cypress, and pines.

Forestry Operations 森林の運営

In the 18th century, exploitive forestry aiming at simply gathering wood from natural forests was replaced by sustained-yield forestry with artificial planting 人工植林 and cultivation of trees. After the Meiji Restoration of 1868 forestland was divided into privately owned and government-owned areas. National forests 国有林 account for about 7.3 million hectares (18.0 million acres) of the total wooded area of Japan, private forests 私有林 for 14.0 million hectares (34.6 million acres), and forests owned by local governments 公有林 for the remainder. Private forests occupy 56 percent of Japan's entire forest area. The continued migration of young farm workers to urban areas and factories has greatly reduced the number of forestry workers.

History of Wood Utilization 木材利用の歴史

Wood has been used for construction and fuel in Japan since early times, but the use of lumber for construction increased rapidly starting in the 8th century as wooden palaces and temples such as Tōdaiji and Tōji were built. Kyōto became Japan's center of wood consumption.

The flourishing of urban culture in the Edo

Forest Area (1990)
森林面積 (in percentages)

privately-owned forest	56.0
national forest	29.7
public forest	12.5
other	1.8
Total: 24,621,000 ha	

Source: Forest Agency.

period (1600–1868) accelerated an increasing demand for wood products for furniture, building, and fuel. Starting in the late 18th century, regional lumber markets developed along the lower reaches of the large rivers; these markets continued to grow in the 19th century. With the modernization of the Japanese economy following the Meiji Restoration, the demand for wood grew rapidly. Following the Tōkyō Earthquake of 1923 関東大震災, imports, particularly from the United States, became an important factor in Japan's wood supply.

After World War II, the need for building materials escalated, as did the demand for such wood products as paper pulp and plywood. However, domestic production was on the decline. In recent years emphasis has been increasingly placed on forests as places of recreation and as natural environments in need of conservation. Thus Japan has had to rely more and more on outside sources of wood. In 1996 Japan's total wood supply was 112 million cubic meters (3.95 billion cu ft), of which only 20 percent was domestically produced. Lumber made up 52.2 percent of the total, pulp and wood chips 34 percent, and plywood 13.8 percent.

Iron and steel industry (tekkōgyō) 鉄鋼業

Modern iron-making techniques and steel production began in Japan in 1901 with the opening of the state-owned Yawata Iron and Steel Works 八幡製鉄所, an integrated steel plant.

In the first decade of the 20th century many steel-using industries started to develop in Japan, and private capital moved into the production of steel. By 1912 four major private steelmakers had been established: Nippon Kōkan 日本鋼管(株), Kawasaki Shipyard Co. 川崎造船所 (now Kawasaki Steel Corporation 川崎製鉄 (株)), Sumitomo Metal Industries, Ltd. 住友金属工業(株), and Kōbe Steel, Ltd. (株)神戸製鋼所.

Lumber Imports by Country of Origin (1995)
原産地別木材輸入先

(in percentages)

United States	27.0
Canada	18.1
Russia	17.3
Malaysia	14.0
New Zealand	6.4
Papua New Guinea	4.6
Finland	2.2
Chile	2.0
other	8.4

Total: 33.8 million cubic meters

Note: Total of logs and sawlogs.
Source: Japan Tariff Association.

Crude Steel Production for Selected Countries
世界の粗鋼生産高の推移 (in thousands of metric tons)

	Japan	United States	USSR	Germany	United Kingdom	China	Korea
1900	1	10,351	2,214	6,646	4,979	—	—
1910	250	26,512	3,444	13,699	6,476	—	—
1920	845	42,807	162	8,538	9,212	—	—
1930	2,289	41,351	5,761	11,511	7,443	—	—
1940	7,528	60,765	19,000	19,141	13,183	—	—
1950	4,839	87,848	27,300	12,121	16,553	61	—
1960	22,138	91,920	65,292	34,100	24,695	1,866	—
1970	93,322	119,310	115,886	45,041	28,314	1,779	—
1980	111,395	101,457	148,000	43,838	11,278	3,712	8,558
1990	110,339	89,276	154,414	44,022	17,896	6,535	23,125
1995	101,640	96,191	51,323	42,051	17,655	92,968	36,772

Note: Pre-World War II figures for Japan include Korea and Manchuria.
Pre-1917 and 1995 figures for USSR are for Russia. Figures from 1950 to 1990 for Germany are for West Germany.
Source: Japan Iron and Steel Federation.

The industry suffered in the worldwide depression beginning in 1929. Japan's leaders sought to strengthen the steel industry. One measure was the 1934 formation of Nippon Steel. Nippon Steel was an amalgamation of the state-owned Yawata with five private firms. The strongest private firms, Nippon Kōkan, Kawasaki, Sumitomo, and Kōbe, remained independent. Japan's maximum yearly production of crude steel prior to the end of World War II was 7.7 million tons in 1943; this was 9.5 percent of US production for the same year.

After World War II 第2次世界大戦後

Following the war, Nippon Steel was broken up into Yawata Steel and Fuji Steel 富士製鉄, and intense competition developed within the industry. Supported by rapid economic growth, production facilities were expanded, and Japan became the world's largest steel-exporting nation.

A new Nippon Steel Corporation 新日本製鐵(株) was created in 1970 through the merger of Yawata Steel and Fuji Steel, and today the five major Japanese steel producers are Nippon Steel Corporation, Kawasaki Steel Corporation, NKK Corporation, Sumitomo Metal

Industries, Ltd., and Kōbe Steel. The product break-down for fiscal 1997 production was pig iron 銑鉄, 78.3 million tons; crude steel 粗鋼, 102.8 million tons; ordinary steel products 普通鋼, 79.2 million tons; special steel products 特殊鋼, 15.9 million tons; and ferro-alloy 合金鉄, 1.0 million tons.

The Japanese steel industry is totally dependent on imports of iron ore and coal, but it has maintained its international competitiveness through a high-quality labor force and the implementation of new production facilities and technology. In 1997 Nippon Steel was the largest producer of crude steel in the world.

Although Japan remains a key steel-exporting country, voluntary export restrictions 輸出自主規制 to the United States (begun in 1969), the rise in value of the yen, and the increase in steel production by China and South Korea have led to decreases in the quantity and monetary value of Japan's steel exports. In response to this trend many of the steel companies have been restructuring and reducing personnel levels in the 1990s.

Automotive industry (*jidōsha sangyō*) 自動車産業

The Japanese automotive industry got its start in 1902, when a small company called the Ōtomobiru Shōkai オートモビル商会 produced a trial car with a 12-hp American engine. Trial models by many other makers followed, but domestic makes, produced in small quantity, could not compete with the imported cars (mostly from the United States) that flooded Japan just after the Tōkyō Earthquake of 1923 関東大震災. Ford and General Motors, with their superior production techniques, marketing, and service systems, established subsidiary companies 子会社 in Japan in 1925–26 and started assembling trucks and passenger cars from imported parts. Soon after, foreign automobiles completely took over the Japanese market.

Steel Exports and Imports
鉄鋼の輸出入量

(in millions of metric tons)

	Exports	Imports
1980	30.3	2.4
1985	33.3	4.5
1990	17.0	11.7
1995	23.0	11.7

Source: Japan Iron and Steel Federation.

Destination of Vehicle Exports (1995)
4輪車・2輪車地域別輸出割合
(in percentages)

Four-wheeled vehicles	
North America	34.3
Europe	24.2
Asia	16.6
Central and South America	8.7
Oceania	7.0
Middle East	5.4
Africa	3.6
other	0.2
Total: 3,790,778	

Motorcycles	
Asia	35.1
Europe	25.7
North America	20.2
Central and South America	13.4
Oceania	2.4
Africa	2.0
Middle East	1.2
Total: 1,407,856	

Source: Japan Automobile Manufacturers Association, Inc.

Before World War II, the Japanese automotive industry, under government direction, concentrated on producing trucks for the military. Nissan Motor Co., Ltd. 日産自動車(株), Toyota Motor Corporation トヨタ自動車(株) and later the forerunner of Isuzu Motors, Ltd. いすゞ自動車(株), were licensed under the Automotive Manufacturing Industries Law 自動車製造事業法 of 1935. This act was aimed at protecting and promoting domestic automobile production by providing tax breaks for domestic manufacturers and by imposing restrictions on (and in 1940 eliminating altogether) the activities of foreign automobile makers. After the beginning of World War II, the domestic makers, including the newly added Mitsubishi Heavy Industries, Ltd. 三菱自動車工業(株), and Hino Motors, Ltd. 日野自動車工業(株), were involved in wartime production. After the war, Occupation authorities allowed Japanese manufacturers to continue some production, mostly of trucks, but total production in 1946 was only 20,000 vehicles. Passenger car 乗用車 production began again in 1952, with most of the demand for passenger cars coming from the taxi business. From around this time, the government, led by the Ministry of International Trade and Industry (MITI), began its support and protection of the domestic auto industry.

After 1960 the domestic production of passenger cars increased at an unprecedented rate. Companies that began manufacturing passenger cars around this time included the Tōyō Kōgyō Co., Ltd. 東洋工業(株) (now Mazda Motor Corporation マツダ[株]); Fuji Heavy Industries, Ltd. 富士重工業(株); Daihatsu Motor Co., Ltd. ダイハツ工業(株); and Honda Motor Co., Ltd. 本田技研工業(株) Many large new factories were built, the parts industry 部品産業 was integrated and concentrated (facilitating the development of an organized subcontracting system 下請け制度), and nationwide sales networks were strengthened.

Around 1968 Toyota and Nissan increased their exports of automobiles and light trucks. By 1975 they were joined by Honda and other Japanese manufacturers. In the wake of the oil crisis 石油危機 of the 1970s, demand in the American automobile market shifted from the large, high-powered, gas-guzzling models to the smaller, more fuel-efficient makes for which Japanese manufacturers were known, bringing their share of the North American automobile market to 23 percent by the late 1970s. Pressure from American domestic manufacturers led to voluntary export restrictions 輸出自主規制 on Japanese auto manufacturers (1981–1994). After 1985, increasing US-Japan trade friction 貿易摩擦 and a drop in export profits led more and more Japanese auto manufacturers to set up production plants in Canada and the United States. As of August 1996, eight Japanese auto companies had established 10 plants (4 of which are US-Japan joint ventures) in North America, with total annual output approaching 2.4 million vehicles; in Europe, Japan's second largest automotive export market, Japanese automobile assembly plants had also started production (in the United Kingdom); and in Southeast Asia, Japanese manufacturers were either cooperating with domestic automobile producers or setting up multinational diversified assembly operations. Japanese parts suppliers followed the major auto manufacturers abroad, expanding their overseas production capacity and building up technology transfer 技術移転 and cooperation networks. In 1997 the Japanese automobile industry produced 10.98 million vehicles, of which 4.6 million were exported.

Computer industry (*kompyūtā sangyō*)
コンピューター産業

Japan has the second largest data-processing industry データ処理産業 in the world after that of the

Production of Passenger Cars by Manufacturer (1995) 乗用車のメーカー別生産台数 (in percentages)	
Toyota Motor Corporation	33.6
Nissan MotorCo., Ltd.	19.8
Mitsubishi Motors Corporation	11.9
Honda Motor Co., Ltd.	10.7
Mazda Motor Corporation	8.0
Suzuki Motor Corporation	7.9
Fuji Heavy Industries, Ltd.	3.9
Daihatsu Motor Co., Ltd.	3.5
Isuzu Motors, Ltd.	0.7
Total: 7,610,533	

Source: Japan Automobile Manufacturers Association.

Computer Production
コンピューター生産台数
(in thousands)

	1970	1980	1990	1995
Mainframe computers	4.4	15.2	13.9	8.9
Office computers	–	–	240.1	101.5
Personal computers	–	–	3,018.3	6,382.2
Control computers (minicomputers)	0.3	2.5	20.0	154.7
Total	4.6	17.2	3,292.3	6,647.3

Source: Ministry of International Trade and Industry.

Computer Exports and Imports (1995)
コンピューター輸出入の国別割合
(in percentages)

Export destination	
United States	47.1
Germany	9.2
Netherlands	7.7
United Kingdom	5.8
Singapore	5.3
other	24.9
Total: 2.77 trillion yen	

Import source	
United States	31.6
Singapore	17.7
Taiwan	14.5
United Kingdom	5.5
South Korea	3.2
other	27.5
Total: 1.44 trillion yen	

Note: The statistics include the main computer unit, output/input devices, and memory units as well as other peripheral equipment, components, and shipments.

Source: JECC, *Computer Notes* (1996).

United States, with large-scale subsectors producing mainframe computers 大型コンピューター, minicomputers, personal computers パーソナルコンピューター, peripheral equipment 周辺機器, and software. Total domestic hardware, software, and data processing production in 1994 reached ¥11.0 trillion (US $107.6 billion) , and exports of computers amounted to ¥1.6 trillion (US $16.0 billion). In 1994 the top five computer makers in Japan were Fujitsū, Ltd. 富士通(株), NEC Corporation NEC(日本電気[株]), IBM Japan, Ltd. 日本IBM(株), Hitachi, Ltd. (株)日立製作所, and Tōshiba Corporation (株)東芝.

Japan's computer market is the second largest in the world after the United States. The personal computer's share of the hardware market is increasing every year as a result of expanding home computer use spurred by falling prices and the growing popularity of computer networks such as the Internet. Of the total of 6,650,000 computers produced in 1995, 96 percent were personal computers. With the increase in personal computer processing power and the downsizing (shift to smaller hardware) trend among corporations, the demand for mainframes and workstations is falling sharply.

History 歴史

Although Ōsaka University launched Japan's first computer development program in 1947, the first electronic digital computer was not constructed until 1956, 10 years after ENIAC, the first electronic computer, was developed in the United States. Following the first exports of US computers to Japan in 1954, the Ministry of International Trade and Industry (MITI) 通産省 organized the Research Committee on the Computer to coordinate computer industry development, but computers did not attain urgent priority in Japanese industrial policy until the mid-1960s.

In 1960 IBM was granted permission to manufacture in Japan in return for licensing basic patents to all interested Japanese manufacturers; 13 Japanese companies immediately entered cross-licensing agreements 見返り特許権契約 with IBM. By 1964 RCA, TRW, Honeywell, General Electric, and Sperry Rand had all entered technical assistance agreements with Japanese makers.

The Japanese government's vigorous promotion of the computer industry dates from 1964. In that year IBM's introduction of its System 360 and its success at the Tōkyō Olympic Games graphically demonstrated to Japanese political and business circles the strategic potential of computers.

To achieve rapid advancement in domestic computer technologies, MITI launched several national priority projects. The FONTAC project (1962–1964), undertaken by Fujitsū, Oki Electric Industry Co., Ltd. 沖電気工業(株), and NEC, was the first prototype manufacturing project of a general-purpose large-scale computer system in Japan. Another project, aimed at prototype manufacture of a super-high-performance computer system, was undertaken from 1966 to 1972. As a result of the success of these domestic projects, the Japanese computer industry made rapid strides in the late 1960s.

In the early 1970s, prior to liberalizing the Japanese computer market, MITI organized the six mainframe makers into three specialized research and development (R&D) 研究開発 groups with the aim of developing a computer to match IBM's 370 series; the groups were provided with government R&D subsidies. When IBM brought out its fourth-generation computer 第4世代のコンピューター utilizing VLSI (very large scale integration) 超大規模集積回路 technology, MITI responded by organizing another "national project." By the early 1980s

Personal Computer Market Share (1995)
パソコンの国内シェア

(in percentages)

NEC	43.3
Fujitsū	20.8
Apple Computer	12.5
IBMJapan	10.3
Tōshiba	5.5
other	7.6
Total: 6,382,200	

Note: On a units shipped basis.
Source: *Nikkei sangyō shimbun.*

the Japanese computer industry had in many respects closed the 10-year gap in hardware sophistication that had existed in relation to IBM in the 1950s, although its software remained inferior in most applications. IBM was in Japan by the early 1990s no more than one among several major manufacturers; in 1990 it had to yield its leading position in the mainframe market to Fujitsū.

Structure of the Industry 産業の構造

In contrast to US and European patterns, there are virtually no specialized major computer makers in Japan. Except for Fujitsū, there is not a single major Japanese computer maker for which computers provide over 35 percent of total sales. Three of the six major producers, Fujitsū, NEC, and Oki, are telecommunications firms that diversified into computers. The other three, Hitachi, Mitsubishi Electric, and Tōshiba, are general electronics firms that diversified into computers in the early 1960s.

The fact that computers are only one of the many products sold by Japanese computer makers gives these companies a stable base to operate from, but it also reduces the pressure they feel to move forward aggressively with the introduction of new technology and the development of new and innovative products and techniques. As a result Japanese manufacturers lagged considerably behind their U.S. competitors in taking advantage of the shift from mainframes to personal computers that occurred in the 1990s. A major recent development in the computer industry in Japan has been the rapid increase in use of the Internet computer network since commercial access providers appeared in 1993. At the end of 1997 Japan was estimated to have over 10 million Internet users and 1.2 million computers connected. Personal computer demand continues to grow, spurred by the increasing popularity of the Internet インターネット, electronic mail 電子メール, computer games, etc.

Energy sources (*enerugī shigen*) エネルギー資源

Japan's energy options are seriously limited by its lack of domestic energy sources coupled with the huge energy demands of its industries. Japan's dependence on imports for its primary energy supply rose from 43.4 percent in 1960 to 80 percent in 1996.

Oil 石油

From 1965 to 1974 the rapid growth of the Japanese economy led to a 10.2 percent average annual increase in energy demand, more than twice the world average of 4.8 percent. During the same period there was a shift from coal to oil as an energy source because of the depletion of domestic coal mines and the relative efficiency of oil; as a result the increased energy demand had to be met almost entirely by imported oil.

The fourfold increase in oil prices brought on by the oil crisis of 1973 石油危機 led to profound changes in Japanese energy policy エネルギー政策. In 1973 Japan was importing 99 percent of its crude oil 原油, and the imported oil represented 77 percent of the total energy supply. Eighty-five percent of the imported oil originated in the Middle East and northern Africa. Because of its overdependence on imported oil, the impact of the "oil shock," オイルショック as it was commonly called, was felt even more strongly in Japan than in many other

Crude Oil Imports
日本の原油輸入量

(millions of kiloliters)

1970	205
1975	261
1980	248
1985	195
1990	240
1995	262

Source: Ministry of Finance.

Oil Consumption in Selected Countries (1994)
世界の石油消費量

(millions of kiloliters)

United States	1028.26
Japan	329.29
Russia	184.48
China	182.29
Germany	167.08
South Korea	107.71
Italy	106.84
United Kingdom	106.61
France	106.38
Canada	100.23

Source: Japan Petrochemical Industry Association.

Energy Consumption by Source
種類別1次エネルギー消費

(in 10^{12} kcal)

	1960	1970	1980	1990	1995
Coal	415.2	635.7	673.3	807.5	899.0
Oil	379.3	2,298.9	2,624.4	2,835.6	3,035.8
Natural gas	9.4	39.7	241.6	492.8	589.3
Hydroelectric power	157.8	178.9	204.8	205.1	188.9
Nuclear power	—	10.5	185.8	455.1	655.3
Other	—	33.3	42.1	66.9	70.8
Total	1,008.1	3,197.1	3,972.0	4,863.1	5,439.1
Dependence on imports (%)	—	84.4	89.8	92.6	94.0

Source: Ministry of International Trade and Industry.

countries. It affected all sectors of the economy, causing aggravated inflation, prolonged recession, rising unemployment, and business failures. Facing the threat of disruption in the oil supply, the government announced an oil emergency policy in November 1973 aimed at reducing dependence on oil, increasing geographical diversification of oil sources, and conserving energy. At the same time a new policy more sympathetic toward Arab countries was also announced, with a view to improving Japan's relationship with key oil-producing nations.

Although Japan remains heavily dependent on imported oil, as a result of conservation efforts and development of alternative energy sources oil's share of the country's total energy supply dropped to 55.8 percent by 1995.

Coal 石炭

Coal provided 16.5 percent of Japan's energy in 1995. Production in the 1995 was 6.3 million metric tons (6.9 million short tons). In 1997 the decision was made to close the 108-year-old Miike Coal Mines 三池炭鉱 within the year. This will leave only two active coal mines in Japan, and the future of these two mines is in doubt. With coal imports in 1995 reaching 124 million metric tons (136 million short tons), the focus of government policy has shifted to securing a stable supply of foreign coal.

Natural Gas 天然ガス

The share of natural gas in Japan's total energy supply was 10.8 percent in 1995. The domestic production of natural gas, like that of oil, is very limited, and if natural gas is to play a significant role in the future as an alternative energy source it will have to be in the form of imports of liquefied natural gas (LNG) 液化天然ガス. In 1995 Japan imported 44 million metric tons (48.4 million short tons) of LNG, compared to 17 million metric tons

Nuclear Energy as a Percentage of Overall Fuel Consumption (1993)
各国のエネルギー消費に占める
原子力比率 (in percentages)

France	40.0
Japan	14.2
Germany	11.8
United Kingdom	9.0
United States	8.2

Source: British Petroleum Company, *BP Statistical Review of World Energy.*

(18.7 million short tons) in 1980. Liquefied gas 液化ガス has various advantages as an energy source, including cleanness and convenience. Its areas of production are more evenly distributed around the world than is the case with oil.

Nuclear Energy 原子力エネルギー

In Japan, because of its lack of domestic energy resources, nuclear energy has received the highest priority in the search for alternatives to oil. Japan's first nuclear power plant 原子力発電所 was built in 1963. As in other countries, the antinuclear movement, with its concerns over the location, safety, and waste products of nuclear power plants, has many supporters in Japan. See also ELECTRIC POWER.

Other Energy Sources and Conservation
その他のエネルギー資源と省エネ

Hydroelectric power 水力発電 accounted for 3.5 percent of the total energy supply in 1995. New energy 新エネルギー sources such as geothermal energy 地熱発電, solar power 太陽発電, and wind hold promise for the future, but, while they may be technically feasible and research is proceeding, they are not yet economically practical. These new energy sources provided only 1.3 percent of the total power supply in 1995.

Energy conservation 省エネ constitutes one of the pillars of Japan's energy policy and many efforts are being made to increase efficiency in energy use. However, great conservation efforts have already been made in industry, which is the major energy-consuming sector in Japan, and most industries will find it extremely difficult to raise efficiency further. Per capita energy consumption in Japan in 1993 was at the relatively low level of about 2.5 metric tons (2.8 short tons) oil equivalent, as

Energy Consumption in Selected Countries (1994)
エネルギー消費国際比較 (in percentages)

| | Total | Breakdown of total consumption | | | |
		Solids	Liquids	Gas	Electricity
United States	2,078.1	26.9	36.9	26.1	10.1
China	764.8	80.2	15.4	2.1	2.3
Russia	618.5	22.5	20.8	50.4	6.3
Japan	434.9	19.2	49.7	13.1	18.0
Germany	311.5	27.7	37.4	21.6	13.3
India	240.6	66.1	24.1	6.6	3.2

Note: The units for the totals are millions of metric tons of oil equivalent.
Source: United Nations.

against 5.5 metric tons (6.1 short tons) oil equivalent in the United States, which alone indicates that there is limited potential for major benefits from conservation in the future.

Electric power (*denryoku*) 電力

Electric power was introduced to Japan in the form of thermal power 火力発電 in 1887; hydroelectric power 水力発電 followed in 1890. From 1887 to 1911, thermal power predominated. Most hydroelectric power plants were located far from cities, and electricity could be transmitted only over short distances, making hydroelectric power unsuitable for city use. From about 1900, transmission voltage increased, resulting in power transmission over longer distances. Gradually more hydroelectric power plants were established, finally overtaking thermal power in 1912. Hydroelectric power continued to predominate during an almost 50-year period (1912–1965) that spanned the two world wars. In the 1920s, electric utilities began selling surplus electricity inexpensively, encouraging the expansion of electrochemical and other industries.

During the reconstruction period that followed World War II, development of new power generating sites, both thermal and hydroelectric, rapidly increased. Large dam power plants began to be used in the development of hydroelectric power. In spite of these innovations, thermal power generating facilities took on more importance because construction of hydroelectric generating facilities required a good deal of time and capital.

After 1960, a period of high economic growth in Japan, iron and steel, chemical, machinery, and other heavy industries 重工業 expanded rapidly. With the resulting rise in indi-

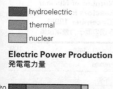

■ hydroelectric
■ thermal
□ nuclear

Electric Power Production
発電電力量

(in billion kwh)

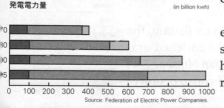

Source: Federation of Electric Power Companies.

vidual incomes, electric appliances 電化製品 became common household items and demand for electricity rose accordingly. Japan's first nuclear power plant 原子力発電所 for commercial use began operating in July 1966, and after the 1973 oil shock there was an upsurge in the development of nuclear power.

In 1994 total power generated for commercial use amounted to 849.3 billion kilowatt hours, of which thermal power plants (oil, LNG, and coal) supplied 60 percent; nuclear power plants, 31.6 percent; hydroelectric power plants, 8.2 percent; and alternative energy sources such as geothermal power, 0.2 percent.

In Japan maximum transmission voltage has been 500 kilovolts since 1974 because of the increase in the number of nuclear and other generating facilities built far from cities. Increasingly, safer underground transmission lines have replaced overhead power lines close to urban areas.

Nuclear power plants 原子力発電所

As of July 1997 there were 52 commercial reactors in operation at 17 power plants in Japan. These 52 consist of 1 gas-cooled reactor ガス冷却炉, 26 boiling-water reactors 沸騰水型原子炉, 23 pressurized-water reactors 加圧水型軽水炉, and 2 advanced boiling-water reactors 新型転換炉; their total electric power generation capacity is 45,083,000 kilowatts. There is also the "Fugen" 「ふげん」 advanced thermal reactor with a capacity of 165,000 kilowatts. Japan's nuclear power plant capacity is the world's third largest, behind the United States and France. Standing at 34 percent in 1995, the percentage of Japan's electric power produced by nuclear power plants is increasing every year.

Although Japan has depended on Britain, the United States, and France for all of the enriched uranium 濃縮ウラン used as fuel, in 1991 Japan Nuclear Fuel Industries, Inc. 日本原燃(株), completed construction of

Number of Nuclear Reactors in Operation (December 1995)
各国の原子力発電設備

United States	109
France	56
Japan	50
United Kingdom	35
Russia	26
Germany	21
World total: 432	

Source: Atomic Energy Commission.

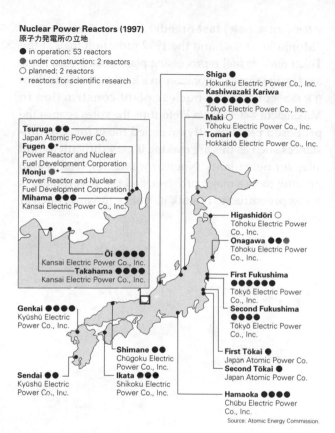

Nuclear Power Reactors (1997)
原子力発電所の立地

● in operation: 53 reactors
● under construction: 2 reactors
○ planned: 2 reactors
* reactors for scientific research

Tsuruga ●●
Japan Atomic Power Co.
Fugen ●*
Power Reactor and Nuclear
Fuel Development Corporation
Monju ●*
Power Reactor and Nuclear
Fuel Development Corporation
Mihama ●●●
Kansai Electric Power Co., Inc.

Ōi ●●●●
Kansai Electric Power Co., Inc.
Takahama ●●●●
Kansai Electric Power Co., Inc.

Genkai ●●●●
Kyūshū Electric
Power Co., Inc.

Sendai ●●
Kyūshū Electric
Power Co., Inc.

Shimane ●●
Chūgoku Electric
Power Co., Inc.
Ikata ●●●
Shikoku Electric
Power Co., Inc.

Shiga ●
Hokuriku Electric Power Co., Inc.
Kashiwazaki Kariwa
●●●●●●●
Tōkyō Electric Power Co., Inc.
Maki ○
Tōhoku Electric Power Co., Inc.
Tomari ●●
Hokkaidō Electric Power Co., Inc.

Higashidōri ○
Tōhoku Electric Power
Co., Inc.
Onagawa ●●●
Tōhoku Electric Power
Co., Inc.

First Fukushima
●●●●●●
Tōkyō Electric Power
Co., Inc.
Second Fukushima
●●●●
Tōkyō Electric Power
Co., Inc.

First Tōkai ●
Japan Atomic Power Co.
Second Tōkai ●
Japan Atomic Power Co.

Hamaoka ●●●●
Chūbu Electric Power
Co., Inc.
Source: Atomic Energy Commission.

Japan's first nuclear fuel plant in the village of Rokkasho 六ヶ所村, Aomori Prefecture. The plant began operation in 1992, meeting a portion of Japan's demand for enriched uranium.

Following the catastrophe at the Chernobyl nuclear power plant チェルノブイリ原子力発電所 in the Soviet Union in 1986, many Japanese expressed concern over the safety of such facilities. Opposition to nuclear power has grown nationwide in recent years following the 1995 sodium leak at the Power Reactor and Nuclear Fuel Development Corporation's 動力炉・核燃料開発事業団 (now the Japan Nuclear Cycle Development Institute 核

燃料サイクル開発機構) fast breeder reactor 高速増殖炉原型炉 "Monju"「もんじゅ」and the 1997 radiation leak at the Tōkai nuclear fuel reprocessing plant 東海再処理工場 operated by the same corporation. In a local 1996 referendum 住民投票 concerning nuclear plant construction in Makimachi 巻町, Niigata Prefecture, the votes against the proposed plant greatly exceeded those for. Circumstances such as this are making it very difficult to find sites for new plants. Nuclear waste disposal is also proving to be a major problem, and the government is being pressured to rethink its policy towards nuclear power.

SOCIETY

社会環境	Social Environment
教育	Education
交通	Transportation
マスコミ	Mass Communications

Social security programs (*shakai hoshō seido*)
社会保障制度

Social security programs in Japan are designed to guarantee a minimum standard of living and to protect citizens from certain types of social and economic risk. Japan's social security programs consists of four major components: public assistance, social insurance, social welfare services, and public health maintenance. In 1996 social security-related expenses 社会保障関係費 accounted for 19.0 percent of the general account expenditure of the national budget.

Development of Social Security 社会保障の発達

Modern social security in Japan began in the early Meiji period (1868–1912), when a system of disability and retirement allowances for military personnel and public officials was instituted. The Poor Relief Regulation 恤救規則 of 1874, a government reaction to popular unrest, provided limited support to poor people, but it was not until the passage of the Health Insurance Law 健康保険法 of 1922 (implemented in 1927) that Japan had its first true social security legislation for workers. In 1938 the National Health Insurance 国民健康保険 system was established to cover those excluded by the 1922 law. Though these steps were important in the development of social security in Japan, they were largely conciliatory gestures by the government to appease labor during a period of social unrest caused by rapid industrialization and modernization.

Post-World War II Reforms
第2次世界大戦後の改革

After World War II, the Allied Occupation 連合国占領軍 established new legal and philosophical bases for social security in Japan and extensively

Social Security and related systems
社会保障関係費

(in billions of yen)

	1965	1990	1994	1995
Social insurance	1,228	42,137	54,421	58,213
Social welfare	65	2,428	3,483	3,916
Public assistance	138	1,352	1,428	1,541
Health and sanitation	194	2,819	4,796	4,807
Unemployment measures	63	85	64	64
Others	261	5,050	6,072	6,499
Total	1,949	53,871	70,264	75,040

Source: Ministry of Health and Welfare.

Social Security Benefits and Medical Expenses
社会保障給付金と国民医療費の対GNP比

	Social security benefits Per capita (US$)	Share of GNP (%)	Medical expenses Share of GNP (%)
France	4,087	19.0	8.7 *[1]
Germany	2,455	11.6	7.4 *[1]
Italy	3,358	19.7	8.2
Japan *[2]	4,115	10.9	6.5
South Korea	130	1.7	3.6
United Kingdom	1,047	6.5	6.7 *[2]
United States	1,955	8.0	11.1 *[3]

*[1] 1990.
*[2] 1994.
*[3] 1989.
Source: Bank of Japan, *Kokusai hikaku tōkei.*

reformed the administration of the existing social security system. The philosophy of this time is set forth in the Constitution of Japan 日本国憲法, which states that "All people shall have the right to maintain the minimum standards of wholesome and cultured living," and is further codified in the Livelihood Protection Law 生活保護法 of 1946. Although the initial social security programs established were small-scale, the postwar legal reforms clearly established the responsibility of the government to promote and improve social security. Through subsequent legislation, mainly in the 1950s and 1960s, and through a series of reforms in the 1980s, Japan has established a comprehensive social security system. In order to help provide care for the country's rapidly growing population of elderly, a long-term care insurance 介護保険 system will be implemented in 2000.

Categories of Social Security 社会保障の種類

Public assistance 生活保護 Programs designed to assure a minimum level of security to those who are unable to generate subsistence-level income are classed as public assistance. In recent years the number of people receiving public assistance has decreased steadily, with only 0.71 percent of the population receiving such assistance in 1994.

Social insurance 社会保険 This covers four main areas: health and medical insurance, public pensions 公的年金, employment insurance 雇用保険, and workers' compensation 労働者災害補償.

Medical and health insurance 医療保険: All citizens are entitled to coverage under one of Japan's basic medical health insurance programs, depending on employment status or place of residence. The main program, based on the Health Insurance Law 健康保険法 of

1922, automatically covers all employees in firms with more than five workers. The National Health Insurance 国民健康保険 program covers many of the remaining noninsured, including the self-employed, the elderly, and

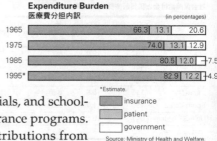

Distribution of the Medical Care Expenditure Burden
医療費分担内訳

(in percentages)

	insurance	patient	government
1965	66.3	13.1	20.6
1975	74.0	13.1	12.9
1985	80.5	12.0	7.5
1995*	82.9	12.2	4.9

*Estimate.

Source: Ministry of Health and Welfare.

foreign residents. Seamen, public officials, and schoolteachers are covered by separate insurance programs. Health insurance is financed by contributions from employers and employees, as well as by subsidies from the national treasury. See also MEDICAL AND HEALTH INSURANCE.

Long-term care insurance 介護保険: An insurance program covering long-term medical care and rehabilitation services received at home or in an institution 施設. Managed by the local municipality, all citizens aged 40 and over must belong and pay premiums 保険料 determined based on the individual's income level. The person who receives the service is responsible for paying 10 percent of the cost.

Pensions 年金: Since 1961 all Japanese of working age have been legally required to be covered by one of the public pension 公的年金 programs, all of which provide old-age, disability, and survivor benefits. In 1986 public pensions were organized into a two-tiered system. At one level, the National Pension 国民年金 provides mandatory basic pensions for all citizens. Aside from this basic pension, a second level of support that includes the Employees' Pension Insurance 厚生年金保険 program and mutual aid association pensions 共済年金 provides additional coverage and benefits for private- and public-sector employees. See also PENSIONS.

Employment insurance 雇用保険: Legislation protecting workers against unemployment began when the government passed the Employment Security Law 職業安定法 of 1947, which set up a network of public employment security offices 公共職業安定所. In the same year the Unemployment Insurance Law 失業保険法 was passed. After playing a vital role in the nation's unemployment relief program, the law was finally repealed in 1974 and replaced by the Employment Insurance Law 雇用保険法. Employment Insurance pays unemployment benefits and conducts programs such as employment assurance and worker skill development. Programs are funded by employees and employers and with funds from the national treasury.

Workers' compensation 労働者災害補償: Current workers' compensation programs, based on the Factory Law 工場法 of 1911 and two postwar laws, the Labor Standards Law 労働基準法 and the Workers' Compensation Law 労働者災害補償保険法, assign liability to employers to provide compensation for workers in the event of injury or death resulting from work-related accidents.

Social welfare services 福祉サービス The three major types are: services for the handicapped, services for the aged, and services for children, which include aid to fatherless families. Government programs for the handicapped include pensions, institutional care, rehabilitation programs, special education, and cash subsidies. Emphasis is given to services for the handicapped outside of institutional settings, including medical counseling and "home helper" programs. Programs for vocational guidance and employment opportunities are offered by the Ministry of Labor 労働省.

Japan's rapidly aging population has made welfare services for the elderly a pressing social problem. The Old-Age Welfare Law 老人福祉法 of 1963 introduced nursing homes, free annual health examinations, a system of home helpers, and local welfare

Welfare Institutions for the Aged
老人福祉施設

(number of institutions)

	1985	1990	1994
Nursing homes for the aged 養護老人ホーム	944	950	947
Special nursing homes for the aged 特別養護老人ホーム	1,619	2,260	2,982
Low-cost homes for the aged 軽費老人ホーム	280	295	436
Welfare centers for the aged 老人福祉センター	1,767	2,024	2,190
Daily service centers for the aged 老人デイサービスセンター	–	977	3,261
Total	4,610	6,506	9,816

Source: Ministry of Health and Welfare.

centers for the aged. In 1973 the government introduced free medical care for all persons 70 years or older. However, the 1983 Law concerning Health and Medical Services for the Aged 老人保健法 reintroduced the requirement that certain health-care fees be paid by the individual.

Welfare services are also offered to needy families with children. The Child Welfare Law 児童福祉法 of 1947 established the government's responsibility to protect children in need. The 1964 Law for the Welfare of Mothers, Children, and Widows 母子及び寡婦福祉法 provides financial assistance and such services as vocational counseling and homes for fatherless families.

Activities of Health Centers (1994)
保健所の活動 *(in thousands)*

Medical Examination 健康診断	
Total recipients	9,677
Tuberculosis control 結核	3,201
Adults (age 40 and over) 成人	2,984
Babies and infants 乳幼児	2,195
Other その他	1,297
Prevention of Parasites 寄生虫病予防	
Total persons examined	128
Maternal and Infant Health Guidance 母子衛生	
Total recipients	3,132
Pregnant women 妊婦	187
Puerperal women 産婦	248
Babies 乳児	1,083
Infants 幼児	1,614
Prevention of Epidemics 防疫	
Bacillary dysentery examination 細菌性赤痢検査	4,429
Dental Hygiene Examination 歯科衛生	
Total recipients	2,822
Nutrition Guidance 栄養指導	
Total recipients	4,349

Source: Ministry of Health and Welfare.

Public health 公衆衛生 The fourth component of the social security system, public health, includes public sanitation and the prevention and treatment of infectious diseases, including pollution-related diseases. Rapid economic growth has brought about considerable progress in all aspects of public health in Japan. See also ENVIRONMENTAL QUALITY.

Administration 運営管理

Most social security-related activities are administered by the Ministry of Health and Welfare 厚生省, although the ministries of labor and education also fulfill important social security functions. The Social Insurance Agency 社会保険庁 administers the key public pension programs. However, implementation of most programs is left to local governments: independent bureaus for health and welfare services operate at prefectural, city, town, and village government levels. In addition, welfare offices 福祉事務所 at the city and district level administer public assistance and engage in other welfare activities. At the private level, social welfare councils have served as focal points for community social welfare activities, fostering citizen volunteers and senior citizens' clubs 老人クラブ. Volunteer welfare commissioners 民生委員 designated by the welfare minister provide help to those who need it in cooperation with welfare offices.

Pensions (*nenkin*) 年金

The Japanese pension system centers on public pensions administered by the national government, providing old-age, disability, and survivor benefits. Public pensions are supplemented by individual pension plans and pensions provided by private enterprises. By law, all Japanese citizens of working age must subscribe to a public pension plan.

Japanese pensions started in 1875 with the *onkyū* system 恩給制度 for retired army and navy servicemen. This system was later expanded to cover government officials, schoolteachers, and policemen. In 1939 the first pension program for private-sector employees, the Seamen's Insurance Law 船員保険法, was enacted. From 1942 Laborers' Pension Insurance 労働者年金保険 provided coverage for general workers; this was the precursor to the current Employees' Pension Insurance 厚生年金保険. In 1959 the National Pension Law 国民年金法 was passed; it covers farmers, the self-employed, housewives, and other categories of people who had been excluded from employees' pensions.

In 1986 the pension system was greatly simplified and was reorganized into a two-tiered system. The National Pension was extended to provide basic, mandatory pension coverage to all Japanese citizens. Spouses of employees' pension subscribers are now required to enroll in the National Pension program. As of March 1997, 70.2 million citizens were enrolled in this program. Two supplemental programs provide additional coverage and benefits. The Employees' Pension Insurance program provides coverage for 33 million private-sector employees. Mutual aid association pensions 共済年金 enroll an additional 5.8 million public employees and teachers. A declining number still receive *onkyū* pensions. Additional coverage for employees of certain companies is provided by privately funded corporate pensions.

The National Pension and Employees' Pension Insurance are administered by the Ministry of Health and Welfare 厚生省. The mutual-aid-association programs are under the jurisdiction of various ministries. One-third of the costs of contributory National Pension benefits are provided by the national treasury, with the rest supplied by contributions from the insured and from other pension plans. The costs of employee insurance are usually covered by equal contributions of employer and employee proportionate to the employee's wage rate.

Since reform of the pension system in 1986, joining the National Pension program is mandatory for all Japanese citizens between the ages of 20 and 60. Employed persons also receive additional benefits from Employees' Pension Insurance or mutual aid association pensions.

In 1997 the monthly payment required of all individual contributors to the National Pension system was ¥12,800. The minimum contributory period to receive benefits is 25 years; the full benefit of ¥65,458 per month (as of April 1995) is received for 40 years of contributions.

Medical and health insurance (*iryō hoken*) 医療保険

Central component of Japan's medical care security system, designed to provide nationwide health care coverage. The cornerstone of the present system of public health insurance is the 1922 Health Insurance Law,

Monthly Full Pension Benefit (April 1997)
年金額(月額)一覧 (in yen)

National Pension	
Old-age pension	65,458
Disability pension	
1st class	81,825
2nd class	65,458
Survivors' pension (with one child)	84,292
Old-age welfare pension	33,533
Employees' Pension Insurance	215,800*

*Average monthly benefit for employee.
Source: Ministry of Health and Welfare.

National Medical Expenditures and Medical Expenditures for the Aged
国民医療費と老人医療費
(in trillions of yen)

Year	National cost	Cost for aged
1985	16.02	4.07 (25.4%)*
1986	17.07	4.44 (26.0%)
1987	18.08	4.83 (26.7%)
1988	18.76	5.16 (27.5%)
1989	19.73	5.56 (28.2%)
1990	20.61	5.93 (28.8%)
1991	21.83	6.41 (29.4%)
1992	23.48	6.94 (29.6%)
1993	24.36	7.45 (30.6%)
1994	25.79	8.16 (31.6%)

*Percent of national cost.
Source: Ministry of Health and Welfare.

Social Environment

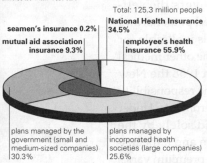

Health Insurance Coverage (March 1996)
医療保険の加入者内訳

Total: 125.3 million people

seamen's insurance 0.2%

National Health Insurance 34.5%

mutual aid association insurance 9.3%

employee's health insurance 55.9%

plans managed by the government (small and medium-sized companies) 30.3%

plans managed by incorporated health societies (large companies) 25.6%

Source: Ministry of Health and Welfare.

providing coverage primarily for factory workers and miners. By the enforcement in 1961 of an amended Health Insurance Law all Japanese citizens and aliens resident in Japan have been entitled to coverage under one of six alternative health insurance plans. Chief among them are employees' health insurance 被用者保険, which covers most private-sector employees, and National Health Insurance 国民健康保険, for people ineligible for employee health insurance. Other plans provide coverage for seamen, national public-service employees, local public-service employees, and private-school teachers and employees. The 1982 Law concerning Health and Medical Services for the Aged 老人保健法 provides for medical care for citizens aged 70 and over. By 1980, 99.3 percent of the total population was covered under one of the six plans; the remaining 0.7 percent was covered by the medical assistance program. Under most Japanese medical insurance plans, members are required to pay 10 to 30 percent of their medical expenses, depending on the type of treatment provided; the insurance carrier then remunerates the doctor, hospital, clinic, or other medical care provider directly for the remainder on a fee-for-service basis determined by the Ministry of Health and Welfare.

The nationwide cost of health care has been rising faster than national income 国民所得, with medical costs accounting for 3.1 percent of national income in 1960 and 6.8 percent in 1993. Increased costs incurred by the aged accounted for the majority of this growth. The rapid expansion of Japan's aged population since the 1970s and its effects on medical care and costs is one of the major issues that the medical and health insurance system must face in coming decades.

National Health Insurance 国民健康保険

National Health Insurance covers the self-employed and their dependents, retired persons, and various other categories of individuals ineligible for employees' health insurance or any of the other medical and health insurance 医療保険 plans. In 1958 the New National Health Insurance Law gave the responsibility of overseeing the insurance to local governments. Under the present system premiums are paid solely by the insured; they consist of a fixed portion and a means-proportional portion. The amount of the premium varies from one municipality to another. The system also receives financial assistance from the national treasury. The insurance covers 70 percent of medical costs incurred by the principal insured or the principal's dependents (the rate is 80 percent for an insured retiree). As of 1996 there were 43.24 million people enrolled in National Health Insurance plans.

Aging population (*kōreika*) 高齢化

The Japanese population is aging faster than any other in the world, a situation which is causing serious problems for society. The percentage of Japan's population aged 65 or over was only at the 7 percent level in 1970, but just 25 years later in 1995 it reached 14.5 percent. A falling birth rate 出生率 and rising average life expectancy 平均余命 will continue to push this trend forward, and it is projected that in 2050 one of every three Japanese alive will be 65 or older.

The aging population is placing an increasingly heavy burden on the medical care 医療 and pension systems 年金制度. In 1983 the existing system of free health care for the elderly was replaced by the Law concerning Health and Medical Services for the Aged 老人保健法. Under this law health care expenses for people aged 70 and over are paid for by fixed-rate contributions from

Japan's Projected Life Expectancy at Birth
日本人の平均余命

Year	Male (years)	Female (years)
1935-36	46.9	49.6
1947	50.1	54.0
1955	63.6	67.8
1965	67.7	72.9
1975	71.7	76.9
1985	74.8	80.5
1993	76.3	82.5
1994	76.6	83.0
1995	76.4	82.8

Source: Ministry of Health and Welfare.

Social Environment

Ratio of the Population Age 65 and Older in Major Countries
主要国65歳以上人口割合 (in percentages)

	1990	1995	2000	2005	2010	2015	2020	2025
Japan	12.0	14.5	17.0	19.1	21.3	24.1	25.5	25.8
United States	12.5	12.6	12.4	12.3	12.9	14.3	16.1	18.1
France	15.7	15.5	15.3	15.2	15.7	17.1	18.0	19.0
Germany	15.0	15.2	16.0	18.1	19.2	19.7	20.9	22.9
United Kingdom	14.0	14.9	15.7	16.0	16.2	17.9	19.7	21.3
Sweden	17.8	17.3	16.7	16.6	17.9	19.8	20.7	21.2

Note: Figures for 1995 and after are projections.
Source: Ministry of Health and Welfare.

Projected Life Expectancy in Selected Countries
主要国の平均余命

	Year or Period	Male (years)	Female (years)
Japan	1990	75.9	81.9
Sweden	1990	74.8	80.4
France	1990	72.8	80.9
United States	1990	71.9	78.9
China	1985-90	68.0	70.9
South Korea	1989	66.9	75.0

Source: United Nations.

local governments, the National Health Insurance program, employee insurance plans, and the individual receiving treatment. A 1986 amendment further increased the costs borne by the elderly themselves. Since then expenses have continued to increase, and in 1995 31.5 percent of national medical care expenditure 国民医療費 was devoted to caring for the elderly. Also in 1986, the revision of various pension laws created a more unified pension system and raised the uniform starting age for public pensions from 60 to 65.

As the average age increases, the population of bedridden and senile elderly is growing rapidly. To help care for them, a system of elderly nursing care insurance 介護保険 was established in 1997. Under this component of Japan's social insurance system, all citizens of age 40 or older are to pay an insurance premium to fund the services provided.

In the years ahead a shrinking working population 労働人口 will have to shoulder the burden of expanding pension and medical care expenses. The government is now attempting to restructure the social security system so that it does not push the total of all taxes and social insurance fees 社会保険料 paid by Japanese citizens up to over 50 percent of NATIONAL INCOME 国民所得 when the average age of society reaches a peak. Taxes and social insurance fees were 38.2 percent of national income in 1997.

Life cycle (*raifu saikuru*) ライフサイクル

Society's schedule of stages for an individual's life. The cycle is generally thought to extend from birth to death, although an individual is considered a social entity before birth, and many religions posit continuing life for the soul after death. Stages of the cycle mark a person's readiness to participate in social roles and institutions. The schedule has evolved over time and has been altered radically by the institutions of 20th-century mass society 大衆社会 and by the greater longevity of modern populations.

Age Reckoning 年齢認識

For social purposes age is reckoned in both relative and absolute terms. Relative age is set by order of birth: one is senior, peer, or junior to someone else. Japanese often claim that theirs is a uniquely "vertical" society タテ社会, pervaded by rules of seniority. Seniority rules, however, are common to modern institutions such as schools, corporations, and bureaucracies in all societies. Premodern Japanese custom counted age by calendar years 数え年. That is, a child was one in the year of his or her birth, and on 1 January a year was added to every person's age. Since World War II, Japanese most often reckon age from the day of one's birth, and it is common to celebrate birthday anniversaries.

Certain ages traditionally have been considered favorable, others dangerous. The most favorable years—61, 70, 77, and 88—mark successful aging. The danger years 厄年 occur earlier: 19 and 33 for women, 25 and 42 for men. Although most Japanese scorn the danger years as superstition, many continue to observe them. To ward off danger, people obtain protective amulets and purifications at Shinto shrines and avoid new ventures during the year.

The following outline depicts life stages as a typical individual might pass through them.

Infancy 幼児期

In Japan it is common for an expectant mother to don an abdominal sash 腹帯 in the fifth month of pregnancy (*obiiwai*): this is society's first overt recognition of a new individual. One month after birth the infant is taken to a local Shinto shrine to be introduced to the guardian gods and symbolically to all of society (*miya-mairi*). Annual celebrations for children occur on 3 March for girls (Doll Festival) 雛祭, 5 May for boys (Children's Day) 子供の日, and on 15 November for girls aged seven and three and boys aged five (Shichigosan).

Childhood (about 7–13 years) 幼年期

In the past, when children reached the age of seven they were expected to help their parents with household tasks and to assume community duties as members of the children's group (*kodomo-gumi*). Today, however, a child's first duty is to study. Under the modern school system in Japan the most important rites of passage 通過儀礼 are matriculation and graduation. During this stage of life one's "age" is reckoned more by years-in-school than by years-since-birth.

Youth (about 13–25 years) 青年期

Although only nine years of schooling are required, more than 90 percent of Japanese young people complete high school, and more than 40 percent enter college. In middle school and high school many students also attend special tutoring academies (*juku*) or cram schools (*yobikō*) to prepare for entrance examinations for the next level of schooling. The demands of this "examination hell" have had a great impact on the daily lives not only of students but of their families and friends as well.

Today one attains legal maturity at age 20, and municipal governments celebrate Coming-of-Age Day 成人の日 for 20-year-olds on 15 January.

Maturity (about 26–60 years) 成熟期

A man's pace of life and focus of ambition are caught up in promotions, raises, and occupational skills, and less in the family dynamics. Most women find paid work after leaving school and an increasing number of women are able to sustain long-term occupational careers. In contrast to a century ago, the typical woman today gives birth to only two or three children, spaced closely together, so that she has completed the period of intensive child care within about a decade after marriage. Many women then find jobs, though they are at a disadvantage in the labor market.

Old Age (about 61 and over) 老齢期

The 60th birthday, when the zodiac signs complete a full cycle (*kanreki*), was the traditional beginning of old age; today many Japanese celebrate this birthday with family and friends. In some organizations, retirement (*teinen*) occurs before age 60, and long-term employees receive pension benefits.

After Death 死後

In Buddhist tradition, at death an individual is given a posthumous name by the priest of the family temple. This is inscribed on the tombstone and on a personal memorial tablet (*ihai*) kept in the *butsudan*. In the early weeks and months after death, frequent rites are held to comfort the soul. Thereafter, deathday anniversaries 法事 are honored for up to 50 years. After that, one's individuality dissolves into the collective body of the household ancestors, and, except for the famous or notorious, social recognition ceases.

Change 変遷

Under the impact of modernization different parts of the life-cycle schedule have changed in ways that may often be contradictory. Legal maturity is granted at age 20, but popular opinion regards anyone as immature until married or embarked on a working career. Family versus work is a serious issue for many men and women. Retirement before 60 seems unduly early when life expectancy 平均余命 is now 80 years. Options have widened at some stages of the cycle and narrowed at others. There are now no legal barriers to the choice of spouse or occupation, but schooling and retirement have become compulsory at fixed times. Japanese social critics in the 1970s began calling on individuals and the state to build into all institutions and programs a life-cycle perspective relevant to the changes in modern society.

Family (*kazoku*) 家族

The most common Japanese terms for family are *ie*, *kazoku*, and *setai*; although these words are often used interchangeably today, in the past they had different meanings. *Ie* (often translated as "household") has come to be used by scholars for Japan's traditional type of family, especially as it existed during the Edo period (1600–1868); it means a united or corporate group of people who share residence and economic and social life and who regard themselves as a continuing unit of kin. The term *kazoku* appears to be more recent than *ie*. When used distinctively, it means a corporate domestic group consisting only of genetic and affinal kin or in-laws. *Setai* denotes a residential group or household, regardless of the relationships of its members, although these are most commonly kin. Neither *kazoku* nor *setai* carries the connotation of continuity of the term *ie*. See also MARRIAGE.

The Traditional Family 伝統的な家

The family was organized as a hierarchy with the male household head 家長 at the apex, theoretically in a position of absolute authority over others. Until after World War II, this authority was supported by law. The authority of the wife of the family head related to domestic matters. Seniority in age conferred prestige, but sex and specific position of authority strongly affected status. A retired household head was respected but had little or no authority. Generally, when the head retired, his eldest son succeeded him, remaining with his parents after marriage and maintaining the continuity of the family line. The future household head held a

Average Number of Household Members
平均世帯人員

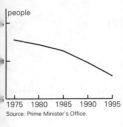

people

1975 1980 1985 1990 1995
Source: Prime Minister's Office.

(in percentages)

	1975	1980	1985	1990	1995
Nuclear families	58.7	60.3	61.1	60.0	58.9
Married couples without dependents	11.8	13.1	14.6	16.6	18.4
Married couples with children	42.7	43.1	41.9	38.2	35.3
Single parents with children	4.2	4.2	4.6	5.1	5.2
Three-generation households	16.9	16.2	15.2	13.5	12.5
Single-person households	18.2	18.1	18.4	21.0	22.6
Other	6.2	5.4	5.3	5.6	6.1
Number of households (in thousands)	32,877	35,338	37,226	40,273	40,770

Source: Ministry of Health and Welfare.

status much superior to that of his younger siblings. A bride, who traditionally held the lowest status in the family, might be divorced if she failed to please her in-laws or produce a child.

Authority meant responsibility as well as privilege. The family head was responsible for the economic welfare and also the deportment of other members. He exercised control over family property and the conduct of farming or other occupations, and he was also responsible for the welfare of deceased ancestors, seeing that proper ceremonies were conducted in their honor.

The welfare of the family ideally took precedence over the needs of any individual member. Confucian views on relations between husband and wife and between parent and child were explicitly taught. Religion, whether Shinto or Buddhism, with its emphasis on reverence for ancestors, also gave support to the traditional family organization. The functions of the family related to almost every aspect of life. Close emotional bonds have continued to characterize the Japanese family and Japanese society in general.

The Contemporary Family 現代の家族

The typical Japanese family today is a nuclear family 核家族, with a mother, father, and two children, in a two- or three-bedroom apartment or house in an urban area. Most typically, the father commutes by train

Number of Divorces
離婚数

Year	Number of divorces	Per 1,000 population
1950	83,689	1.01
1955	75,267	0.84
1960	69,410	0.74
1965	77,195	0.79
1970	95,937	0.93
1975	119,135	1.07
1980	141,689	1.22
1985	166,640	1.39
1990	157,608	1.28
1995	199,032	1.60

Source: Ministry of Health and Welfare.

to his job in the city, while the wife cares for the children and the house, creating a nurturing environment for the whole family.

Western culture and values have had a large influence, inspiring postwar legal reforms and general social change. The ancient distinctions between eldest and younger sons, and between sons and daughters have disappeared. Eldest sons are no longer universally expected to live with and take care of their parents, and daughters-in-law 嫁 have been freed from the absolute authority of their mothers-in-law 姑. Women, less restricted to the home, are freer to pursue education, jobs, and hobbies, and to initiate divorce.

Despite such rapid change, however, the Japanese family is characterized by stability and continuity. Growing individualism still gives way to the needs of the group, and roles within the family remain clearly differentiated. The divorce rate remains low compared to that of the United States. Children often care for their parents in their old age.

As a result of Japan's postwar prosperity, almost all families consider themselves middle class and, in fact, the urban middle-class family is the dominant type and model for all Japan. Middle-class ideals and standards of living 生活水準 have penetrated rural areas as well.

Husband-wife relationships 夫と妻の関係 In contrast to the past, today a woman's relationship with her husband is much more important than her relationship with any of his relatives. Most young people, influenced by the West, want to have a more companionable and romantic marriage 恋愛結婚 than their parents had. Nevertheless, after a year or two of marriage, most couples settle into a pattern of separate social worlds and a clear-cut division of labor. The husband's life is absorbed in his company; he works long hours and socializes with his work group. The wife becomes absorbed in her mothering role as soon as she becomes pregnant. Her social life revolves around her children but may include female relatives and friends.

The husband nominally heads the family and bears clear responsibility for financial support. However, far from being a strong authority figure, he is more likely to let his wife take effective charge of everything concerning the house and children. Though the custom is on the decline, the husband often turns his salary over to his wife, and she controls the finances, including the allocation of her husband's spending money. Among households where the husband is a salaried worker, in 1996 the number of wives who worked exceeded the number who were full-time housewives.

Though some couples are quite close and companionable, emotional intimacy is less important than in the West. Fulfillment of one's duties as a parent takes precedence over affective needs. The continuity of the family is thought to be more important than marital gratification. Accordingly the divorce rate 離婚率 in Japan has remained rather low (around 1.6 per 1,000 persons in 1995), although the number fluctuates slightly.

Child rearing and education 育児と教育 Not only is the rearing and education of children the responsibility of the mother, but it is a task that does not allow for substitutes. Motherhood and the careful nurturing of children are valued as supremely important in Japan. The number of women continuing to work while raising children is increasing, but the mother-child relationship continues to be the strongest and closest within the family. Even so, in recent years many fathers have been taking a more active role in their children's lives, and there is a growing feeling that the burden and rewards of child rearing have fallen too exclusively on the mother.

In order to assure a child's success in the Japan of

today, whether the child is a boy or a girl, the mother must spend much time and thought on education. Though Japanese complain about the examination system and often make fun of the so-called education mother 教育ママ who single-mindedly drives her children toward educational achievement, most middle-class mothers feel they have no choice but to be one. See ENTRANCE EXAMINATIONS.

Grandparents 祖父母 Filial piety 親孝行 is no longer the cornerstone of Japanese morality. Still, most Japanese consider it "natural" to take care of their parents in their old age. Elderly parents ideally live with or near one grown child, and while there remains some tendency to choose an elder son, many parents now prefer to live with a daughter. With the overall aging of the population, however, care for the elderly is a growing social problem.

Marriage (*kon'in*) 婚姻

Marriage in Japan has been characterized as centering on arranged marriage 見合い結婚, in which a man, a woman, and their families are formally introduced to each other by a go-between, or *nakōdo*. Allied to this is the traditional Japanese concept of marriage as the creation of links between two households rather than the joining of two individuals. Put simply, marriage has traditionally been more of a family affair in Japan than it has in most Western cultures.

However, the Japanese attitudes to marriage have changed in response to a host of new social situations, some of which are the result of influence from the West. While traditional ideas concerning the mechanics of making a match in Japan have not been completely abandoned, marriage in contempo-

Number of Marriages
婚姻件数

	1970	1980	1990	1995
Number of marriages	1,029,405	774,702	722,138	791,888
1st marriage for both (in percentages)	88.9	84.9	81.7	81.6
Remarriage for both (in percentages)	3.2	5.1	6.8	6.5

Source: Ministry of Health and Welfare.

rary Japan is a private decision between two people. Households, in particular the parents of a couple contemplating marriage, do not have as final a say in the matter as they did 50 years ago; and the function of the *nakōdo* 仲人 has in many cases shrunk to a largely ceremonial role.

Marriage in the Premodern Period 近代以前の婚姻

During the Nara and Heian periods (710–1185), among the court aristocracy marriage was essentially matrilocal, with a man moving into his wife's house after they were married 妻問婚. Men of rank and importance could divide their time between two or three different houses, and marriage practices among the ruling elite are thought to have been largely polygynous.

An aristocratic woman usually conducted herself with discretion, since her pregnancies needed recognition by a man for her children to have any importance in society. Children might be confirmed to the rank of their father, or they could be adopted into other households to achieve rank.

It was much more difficult for lower classes to follow the marriage practices of the elite. Farmers, artisans, and low-ranking warriors had a better chance of maintaining their status through permanent marriage with one wife.

By the late 12th century the *samurai* class had become the ruling elite. The political imbalances, warring factions, and military reprisals that had brought the *samurai* to power frequently involved households related through marriage. It was during this politically unsettled time that marriage, that is, *seiryaku kekkon* (marriage of convenience) 政略結婚 began to assume importance as a means of ceremonially establishing military alliances between families.

Among *samurai* families the practice of maintaining multiple wives became less common. *Samurai*

Average Age of People Getting Married for the First Time
夫婦の平均初婚年齢

Year	Men	Women
1950	25.9	23.0
1955	26.6	23.8
1960	27.2	24.4
1965	27.2	24.5
1970	26.9	24.2
1975	27.0	24.7
1980	27.8	25.2
1985	28.2	25.5
1990	28.4	25.9
1995	28.5	26.3

Source: Ministry of Health and Welfare.

Social Environment

marriage customs also stressed the immediate transfer of the wife from her parents' home to her husband's residence. Family concerns became important in the selection of a spouse, intensifying the need for professional *nakōdo* to ensure an appropriate match.

The marriage practices of rural commoners were less affected by the rise of the military elite. Practices that lent a more casual air to marriage customs, such as night visiting 夜這い and multiple liaisons, continued in the provinces.

With the establishment of the Tokugawa shogunate in 1603 and the return of political stability, the *samurai* emphasis on arranged marriage continued throughout the Edo period (1600–1868) and urban commoners 町人 increasingly emulated *samurai* custom. The *miai*, a formal meeting of prospective marriage partners and their families, became popular. The *yuinō*, a ceremonial exchange of engagement gifts 結納 between families, also became an important part of marriage practice among urban commoners.

Marriage and Industrialization 婚姻と工業化

After the Meiji Restoration of 1868, Japan began an all-out effort to industrialize and catch up with the West.

The increased mobility of the population during the Meiji period (1868–1912) was a key factor in changing attitudes toward marriage in many rural areas. As in urban centers, the *miai*, *yuinō*, the use of *nakōdo*, and other practices that had originated with the *samurai* became more common in rural areas. Parental arrangement of and authority over marriages increased.

In the Meiji period, under the Civil Code 民法 of 1898 marriage was legally conducted under the so-called *ie* (household) system, which necessitated the agreement of the heads of the two households involved in a marriage. Under Meiji civil law husband and wife were far from equal: through marriage, the wife lost her legal capacity to engage in property transactions; management of her own property came under her husband's control; and only the wife had the duty of chastity. After World War II, the new Civil Code of 1947 abolished the *ie* system and eliminated the legal inequality of husband and wife.

Post-World War II Japan 第2次世界大戦後

Though the legal requirements of marriage in Japan changed radically after the war, marriage practices were slower to respond to outside influence. The traditional marriage pattern continued relatively unchanged, especially in high-status families. Very few Japanese of the mid-20th century expected to find a spouse through casual meeting or dating.

More Japanese now say they prefer a *ren'ai kekkon*, or "love marriage," 恋愛結婚 over the traditional arranged marriage. Individual choice has in many cases become the deciding factor in settling on a marriage partner, and the level of familial involvement in the marriage process has come to resemble that found in Western countries.

Women in the labor force (*joshi rōdō*) 女子労働

Women were traditionally an important part of Japan's agrarian labor force, but the industrialization that followed the Meiji Restoration 明治維新 of 1868 initiated the flow of female workers into the textile industry 繊維産業. Most received very low wages; some even were indentured by their families in return for a lump-sum payment. In an environment of growing nationalism, their working conditions deteriorated while their numbers increased.

The Factory Law 工場法 of 1911, implemented in 1916, limited workdays for women to 12 hours, forbade night work between 10 pm and 4 am, and required a minimum of 2 days off per month.

Although concentrated in the textile industry,

women outnumbered men in the total labor force until about 1930. Women also moved into other manufacturing jobs and skilled occupations as growing numbers of men joined the military.

After World War II, with many women left single and impoverished by the war, women's participation in the labor force remained necessarily high. Before World War II, most working Japanese women were young and single, but with rapid economic growth many companies began to offer part-time employment, and the number of married women employees rose considerably. Since 1955 the percentage of married women in the female labor force has almost tripled, rising to 64.9 percent in 1990.

Until about 1950, over 60 percent of working women were "family workers," 家内労働者 mainly in agriculture. By 1990, family workers had declined to 16.7 percent. Recently women's entry into "prestige professions" such as law and medicine has been increasing rapidly but only 1 percent of female employees occupy managerial posts 管理職.

In 1996 clerical and related jobs accounted for the largest percentage of female employees (34.4 percent), followed by craft and production workers (17.6 percent), professional and technical workers (15.1 percent), sales workers (12.3 percent), service workers (12.2 percent), and other occupations (8.4 percent). The order of distribution has not changed for some time, although the number of women in each occupation has varied, increasing in professional and technical fields while decreasing in manual labor.

The treatment of women in Japan's labor force resembles their treatment in other industrialized countries. In both Japan and the West, female workers make up more than one-third of the total labor force and earn lower wages than men. Residual prejudice against women, however, has resulted in somewhat more discrimination against them in Japan than in the West. Tradition holds that women should devote themselves to the home after marriage, a view that causes the length of uninterrupted employment at the same firm to be rather short. Japanese court decisions have ruled against forcing women to retire upon marriage or upon having passed the "appropriate" age for marriage 結婚適齢期.

Japan's Labor Standards Law 労働基準法 of 1947 stipulates equal pay for equal work, but this is rare in practice because of continuing tendencies to channel women into dead-end jobs and favor men at promotion time. According to one survey, the average monthly wage paid to female employees in 1994 was 62 percent of that paid to male employees. The difference in Japan between men's and women's wages is still the greatest in the industrialized world, although it has narrowed slightly.

This disparity is due largely to the seniority system 年功序列 that presupposes lifetime employment 終身雇用 of men, whereas the length of uninterrupted employment, average age, and educational level of women have tended to be lower than those of men. Very few women attain positions of high responsibility in business, although the number is increasing.

Enacted in 1986, the Equal Employment Opportunity Law for Men and Women 男女雇用機会均等法 was designed to eliminate discrimination against women in the workplace. As the law lacks binding force, however, it has done little to end discrimination. After reviewing the law, the Women's and Young Workers' Problems Council 婦人少年問題審議会 in December 1996 submitted a report proposing revisions to ban discrimination against female workers in job advertisements, hiring, placement, and promotion. The revisions suggested in the report

Women's Wages as a Percentage of Men's
男女間賃金格差 (in percentages)

	1965	1970	1975	1980	1982	1990	1995
Basic salary or wage	55.4	55.6	58.4	58.9	59.6	60.2	62.5
Basic salary or wage and overtime	51.9	51.3	56.0	55.3	56.1	57.1	60.2
Bonus	42.7	44.2	47.7	48.1	49.5	49.1	54.1

Source: Ministry of Labor.

were approved in 1997 and implemented in April 1999 along with regulations prohibiting sexual harassment. Also in 1997, Labor Standards Law restrictions on over-time and late-night work by women were lifted (except in the case of protection of motherhood).

Foreigners in Japan (*zainichi gaikokujin*)
在日外国人

The number of foreign nationals resident in Japan has steadily increased and exceeded 1,400,000 in 1996. This figure includes only foreigners registered in accordance with the Alien Registration Law 外国人登録法; tourists in Japan for less than 90 days, children under the age of two months, and members of foreign diplo-matic services are not included. The largest national group, accounting for 46.4 percent of the total, is com-posed of North and South Koreans, followed by citizens of China and Taiwan (16.6 percent), Brazil (14.3 per-cent), the Philippines (6.0 percent), and the United States (3.1 percent).

Since the revision of the Immigration Control Law in 1990, regulations governing employment of foreigners have been more strictly enforced; however, the revised law also makes foreign nationals of Japanese descent eligible for long-term resident status 定住者在留資格, and their numbers have suddenly increased. For example, the number of Brazilians of Japanese descent residing in Japan increased almost 29 times between 1985 and 1990.

About fifty percent of all foreigners in Japan live in the four prefectures of Tōkyō, Ōsaka, Hyōgo, and Aichi, with the highest concentration in Tōkyō. Some 50 percent of registered aliens in Japan are permanent resi-dents 永住者; the rest are temporary residents 短期滞在者, drawn to Japan by increasing foreign direct investment 直接投資, by employment opportunities offered by the growing demand of Japanese firms for foreign workers,

Foreign Residents in Japan (1996)
国籍別外国人登録者数

Nationality	Number
North and South Korea	657,159
China	234,264
Brazil	201,795
Philippines	84,509
United States	44,168
Peru	37,099
Thailand	18,187
United Kingdom	13,328
Vietnam	10,228
Indonesia	8,742
Other	105,657
Total	1,415,136

Source: Ministry of Justice.

International Marriages by Japanese
国際結婚

	1970 Foreign bride	Foreign groom	1990 Foreign bride	Foreign groom	1995 Foreign bride	Foreign groom
Korea	1,536	1,386	8,940	2,721	4,521	2,842
China	280	195	3,614	708	5,174	769
United States	75	1,571	260	1,091	198	1,303
Other	217	286	7,212	1,080	10,894	2,026
Total	2,108	3,438	20,026	5,600	20,787	6,940

Source: Ministry of Health and Welfare.

and by the chance to study in Japan. The influx of workers from South America, South and Southeast Asia, and the Middle East, a significant number of whom are employed illegally, has become a much-discussed trend.

The number of international marriages 国際結婚 increased 4.6 times between 1970 and 1990. From 1975 onward, the number of marriages involving Japanese men and foreign women, many from China, Korea, or the Philippines, surpassed the number of Japanese women marrying foreign men.

A number of Japanese local governments have begun to implement new services to respond to the needs of foreign residents, such as the publication of information pamphlets in English, Chinese, and Portuguese and the assignment of English-speaking personnel to provide assistance. Since many foreign nationals of Japanese descent bring their families with them to Japan, special courses are being set up in elementary schools in areas where their numbers are especially concentrated. See also FOREIGN STUDENTS IN JAPAN; FOREIGN WORKERS.

Alien registration (*gaikokujin tōroku*) 外国人登録

The Alien Registration Law (外国人登録法, 1952) requires all foreigners residing in Japan for more than one year to apply for registration to the mayor or headman of the village, town, or city where they live and to present a passport and copies of a photograph within 90

Japanese Living Abroad by Region
地域別海外在留邦人

Region	1985	1995
Asia	68,274	136,581
North America	170,547	289,077
South America	154,503	116,859
Europe	69,384	128,239
Africa	7,662	7,866
Oceania	9,538	33,701
Other	831	15,945
Total	480,739	728,268

Note: Includes long-term residents and permanent residents.
Source: Ministry of Foreign Affairs.

days from the date of entry into Japan. The information required on the application form includes the applicant's name, date and place of birth, sex, nationality, occupation, date of entry, passport number, and address while in Japan.

Upon registration by the local government official, registrants are issued a Certificate of Alien Registration 外国人登録証明書 that must be renewed every five years or whenever visa status changes. Each registrant, excluding children under the age of 16, is required to carry this certificate at all times and to present it upon demand to police officers, maritime safety officials 海上保安官, immigration inspectors, immigration control officers 入国警備官, or other public officials.

A growing number of noncitizens in Japan have objected strongly to the requirement that fingerprints be taken as part of the registration procedure, arguing that fingerprinting is the treatment given to criminals. By December 1991, 156 people had refused to be fingerprinted, and several prosecutions had resulted in guilty verdicts and fines. In response to growing protests the Ministry of Justice 法務省 abolished the fingerprinting requirement 指紋押捺 for persons with permanent resident status, effective January 1993.

Emigration and immigration control (*shutsunyūkoku kanri*) 出入国管理

Immigration into and emigration from Japan are both regulated by the Immigration Control and Refugee Recognition Law 出入国管理及び難民認定法 which was originally enacted as the Immigration Control Order of 1951. The order was revised and renamed to its present name in 1982 to meet changes in the international environment. In regard to foreigners' entry into Japan, it states that no alien shall enter Japan without a valid passport or crewman's pocket ledger 乗員手帳 (art. 3). The Ministry of Justice grants visas, often renewable, of no more than three years' duration; only those in special categories such as diplomats and government officials may receive longer visas. Permanent residence 永住権 is rarely granted. Entry is denied to aliens judged unsuitable by the authorities, and certain undesirable aliens may be deported. All Japanese nationals may emigrate from Japan to any other country. Japanese nationals with a known police record have difficulty obtaining a passport.

Foreigners Entering Japan Legally by Region (1995)
地域別正規入国外国人数

South America 3.1%
Europe 13.8%
Oceania 2.5%
Africa 0.4%
North America 17.4%
Asia 62.8%
Total: 3,732,450
Source: Ministry of Justice.

Foreign students in Japan (*gaikokujin ryūgakusei*) 外国人留学生

In 1949 the Japanese government began granting scholarships to students from Asian countries. In 1954 Japanese government scholarships for foreign students (the so-called Mombushō scholarships) 文部省奨学金 were established. At present Japan accepts foreign students in three categories: those receiving Japanese government scholarships, those receiving government support from their own countries, and those at private expense. Students receiving Japanese government scholarships are themselves divided into two categories: research students, who pursue graduate-level studies, and undergraduate students, who enroll in university departments, technical colleges 高等専門学校, or special training schools 専修学校. Japanese government scholarship students 国費留学生 in 1997 numbered 8,250, of whom more than 90 percent were Asians. Students not on Japanese or foreign government scholarships numbered 42,797 in 1997.

Since 1980 the total number of foreign students in Japan has grown each year, increasing from 6,572 in 1980

Nationality of Foreign Students (1997)
国籍別外国人留学生

Nationality	Students	(%)
China	22,323	43.7
Korea	11,785	23.1
Taiwan	4,323	8.5
Malaysia	2,128	4.2
Indonesia	1,070	2.1
United States	999	2.0
Other	8,419	16.4
Total	51,047	100.0

Source: Ministry of Education.

to 51,047 in 1997. However, these figures are still small when compared with the 457,984 foreign students in the United States in 1996. The Ministry of Education 文部省 has set a goal of admitting 100,000 foreign students into Japan by the year 2000. Even though the number of students is increasing, however, the rate of increase has slowed since a 1990 peak so the Ministry's goal will be difficult to meet.

Foreign workers (*gaikokujin rōdōsha*)
外国人労働者

Paid employment of workers who are citizens of foreign countries is strictly regulated by the Immigration Control and Refugee Recognition Law 出入国管理及び難民認定法, which was extensively revised in 1989. Except for permanent residents, spouses of permanent residents, spouses of Japanese nationals, and people of Japanese descent, permission to work is granted to foreigners only in 21 categories such as specialized positions in education, medicine, and finance. In principle, manual workers 単純労働者 are not allowed entry, and students from overseas who work part-time are also subject to restrictions.

The majority of illegal foreign workers in the early 1980s were women who had entered the country with tourist visas and worked in bars and entertainment districts. However, severe shortages of labor triggered by the economic boom of the late 1980s attracted a large influx of male foreign workers, mostly from Asian countries such as the Philippines, Bangladesh, and Iran. In recent years Japanese have been avoiding the so-called "3K" jobs (those that are *kitsui, kitanai, kiken;* "difficult, dirty, dangerous"), and there has been a significant increase in the number of construction and small engineering firms that are prepared to employ foreign manual laborers illegally.

The revision of the Immigration Control and

Foreigners Entering Japan for the First Time for the Purpose of Work
就労目的の新規入国外国人数

(in thousands of persons)

1990	94.9
1991	113.5
1992	108.1
1993	97.1
1994	111.7
1995	81.5

Source: Ministry of Justice.

Refugee Recognition Law extended the right of long-term residence (three years) to descendants of Japanese emigrants and removed restrictions on their ability to work in Japan. Due to high inflation in Brazil, many Brazilians of Japanese descent have sought to take advantage of this change in the law; twice as many were working in Japan in 1990 as in the previous year. However, the recession in the Japanese economy in the early 1990s has resulted in fewer jobs for foreign workers.

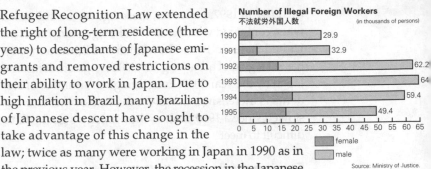

Number of Illegal Foreign Workers
不法就労外国人数 (in thousands of persons)

Year	Value
1990	29.9
1991	32.9
1992	62.2
1993	64
1994	59.4
1995	49.4

female
male

Source: Ministry of Justice.

Environmental quality (*kankyō mondai*) 環境問題

Environmental pollution in Japan has accompanied industrialization since the Meiji period (1868–1912). One of the earliest and well known cases was the copper poisoning caused by drainage from the Ashio Copper Mine 足尾銅山 in Tochigi Prefecture, beginning as early as 1878. The subsequent development of the textile and paper and pulp industries led to water pollution, and the use of coal as the major fuel for industry in general contributed to widespread but still localized air pollution. In the period of rapid growth following World War II, however, the isolated cases coalesced into a national crisis, with Japan becoming one of the most polluted countries in the world. The strict environmental protection measures that were subsequently implemented have reduced pollution caused by industrial drainage and air pollutant emissions. On the other hand, pollution from chemical substances such as asbestos アスベスト and dioxin ダイオキシン and problems with processing nuclear, industrial, and household wastes are becoming increasingly serious. Worldwide environmental issues like the destruction of the ozone layer and global warming cannot be resolved by a single country, so it is clear that the cooperation of all countries is increasingly necessary to protect the environment. Japan is trying to play an active role in this global effort.

Pollution-related diseases 公害病 Although the pollution-related Minamata disease 水俣病 was first reported in May 1956, the existence of the disease had been concealed and patients secretly hospitalized in municipal isolation wards. A Kumamoto University research team identified mercury from the Chisso Corporation plant as the cause of the disease in 1959, but the government did not officially recognize this as the cause until 1967. By the late 1960s, however, the degradation of the environment had deeply struck the national consciousness, and a series of strict environmental protection measures were taken.

In four major lawsuits involving *itai-itai* disease イタイイタイ病 (1971), Niigata Minamata disease 新潟水俣病 (1971), Yokkaichi asthma 四日市喘息 (1972), and Kumamoto Minamata disease 熊本水俣病 (1973) the right of the officially designated victims 認定患者 to compensation was established. The decisions in these cases clarified the responsibility of the companies to ensure that their activities were nonpolluting and to prevent pollution from actually taking place. Subsequently, Minamata disease victims who had not been officially designated as such (未認定患者) also sued the government demanding compensation. The government in 1995 issued a proposal for a final solution in which it offered to provide government support to these victims. The groups involved accepted this offer and in 1996 the claims against the government were settled. This brought to an end 40 years of struggle by the Minamata disease victims to obtain redress.

Water pollution 水質汚染 From the 1960s to 1970s, four major factors especially contributed to the emergence in Japan of water-pollution problems: rapid industrialization, rapid urbanization, the lag in constructing such social overhead capital 社会資本 facilities as sewage systems 下水道, and a public policy that heavily favored economic growth over public health 公衆衛生 and a clean environment.

As a consequence of the increased concern with pollution problems, there has been an overall improvement in water quality 水質, but the progress has been uneven. Strict emission controls on waste industrial waters have reduced cases of toxic-substance pollution to a very small number. On the other hand, rivers and coastal waters within metropolitan districts continue to suffer considerable pollution from organic substances. The problem is even more severe in bays, inland seas, lakes, and other water areas, including Tōkyō, Ise, and Ōsaka bays and Lakes Biwa, Kasumigaura, and Suwa.

Another water-pollution problem is that of thermal pollution. As an increasing number of power plants are being built on an ever-larger scale, their heating of surrounding waters poses a threat to marine life and the fishing industry.

A number of measures have been taken to improve the quality of the water in Japan. These include the setting of national standards for toxic substances and of variable standards for the living environment and the establishing of strict effluent controls and of a comprehensive surveillance and monitoring system. Also, many laws fixing responsibility for pollution damages have been passed, and these have been reinforced by court decisions favorable to the victims.

Air pollution 大気汚染 Japan's efforts to control air pollution have also met with mixed results. The greatest success has been attained in limiting pollution by sulfur oxides (SO_2) and carbon monoxide (CO). The relatively successful control of sulfur oxides reflects a long-term commitment on the part of the government to reduce

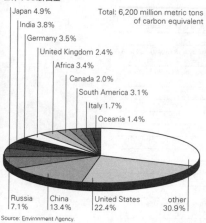

Composition of World CO₂ Emissions (1994)
世界のCO₂排出量

Japan 4.9%
India 3.8%
Germany 3.5%
United Kingdom 2.4%
Africa 3.4%
Canada 2.0%
South America 3.1%
Italy 1.7%
Oceania 1.4%

Total: 6,200 million metric tons of carbon equivalent

Russia 7.1%
China 13.4%
United States 22.4%
other 30.9%

Source: Environment Agency.

Japan's CO₂ Emissions
日本のCO₂排出量

(million metric tons of carbon equivalent)

1985	275
1986	269
1987	281
1988	297
1989	308
1990	320
1991	326
1992	330
1993	324
1994	330
1995	332

Source: Environment Agency.

their concentrations. In the case of nitrogen oxides (NO₂), the overall relaxation of standards in 1978 caused a delay in reducing nitrogen oxide concentrations in the air. Photochemical smog 光化学スモッグ, to which nitrogen oxides are a principal contributor, first appeared in Tōkyō in July 1970; since then it has appeared regularly in different parts of Japan. The increasing concentrations in the air of the nitrogen oxides (NOx) emitted by motor vehicles continue to be a serious problem, and in 1992 a law was passed that attempts to reduce pollution levels by restricting the types of vehicles registered in the Tōkyō and Ōsaka areas.

Ozonosphere protection オゾン層保護 In the late 1980s a growing body of scientific evidence suggested that the ozone layer of the atmosphere is being destroyed by chlorofluorocarbons. Concern over these findings in Japan led to the passing of the Ozonosphere Protection Law オゾン層保護法 of 1988. Progress is being made on restricting the manufacture of chlorofluorocarbons and on introducing substitute materials.

Other pollution その他の公害 The government has taken measures to cope with a variety of other forms of pollution or environmental disruption, including noise, vibration, waste disposal, ground subsidence, offensive odors, soil pollution, and pollution by agricultural chemicals. The number of complaints about noise is greater than for any other type of pollution. The greatest number of complaints concerns noise from factories, but construction, traffic, airport, and railroad (especially the high-speed Shinkansen line) noise have all generated a considerable number of complaints.

1878	Drainage from the Ashio Copper Mine, Tochigi Prefecture, contaminates nearby rivers.
1893	Air pollution from the Besshi Mine Field, Ehime Prefecture, is first noticed.
1953	Minamata disease appears in Kumamoto Prefecture.
1955	First public reports of *itai-itai* disease, previously diagnosed by a doctor in Toyama Prefecture.
1963	Marked increase in the number of cases of asthma in Yokkaichi, Mie Prefecture, is first connected to air pollution from an industrial complex.
1964	Minamata disease appears in Niigata Prefecture.
1967	Pollution Countermeasures Basic Law is passed.
1968	Air Pollution Control Law is passed.
1970	Photochemical smog appears in Tōkyō.
1971	Environment Agency is established.
1972	Nature Conservation Law is passed.
1974	National Institute for Environmental Study is established.
1980	Research begins on acid rain.
1983	Dioxin is found in emissions from trash incineration.
1988	Ozonosphere Protection Law is passed, with provisions to reduce the use of chlorofluorocarbons.
1989	Air Pollution Control Law is amended to control the use of asbestos.
1993	Basic Environmental Law is enacted.
1995	Minamata disease victim organizations accept a government offer to provide support to the victims. Sodium leak occurs at the Power Reactor and Nuclear Fuel Development Corporation's fast breeder reactor "Monju."
1997	Oil spill from the Russian tanker *Nakhodka* pollutes Sea of Japan coastal waters. Radiation leak occurs at the Tōkai nuclear fuel reprocessing plant operated by the Power Reactor and Nuclear Fuel Development Corporation.

In the 1990s damage to Japan's forests, presumably caused by acid rain 酸性雨, was recognized as a problem, and the Environment Agency 環境庁 has held international conferences with neighboring countries, including China and South Korea, to address the issue.

Conservation 自然保護 In response to the sharp deterioration in the natural environment caused by the postwar period of rapid economic growth, the Nature Conservation Law 自然環境保全法 was passed in 1972 to serve as the basis for all legal measures to protect the natural environment. To protect nature and promote recreation, an extensive system of national parks 国立公園, quasi-national parks 国定公園, and prefectural natural parks was established.

As part of its nature conservation efforts, in 1980 Japan joined the Ramsar Convention ラムサール条約 for preserving important wetlands, especially waterfowl habitats, and in 1992 it joined the World Heritage Convention 世界遺産条約 for protecting the world's cultural and natural heritage. In 1991 the Environment Agency issued a *Red Data Book* 「レッドデータブック」 edition on the habitat and population of animals in danger of extinction, and in 1997 it announced an edition on plants. The animal edition is currently being revised based on new International Union for Conservation of Nature and Natural Resources (IUCN) 国際自然保護連合 categories.

In recent years there has also been increasing activity by citizens' groups working to protect the local environment, and conservation organizations from across the country joined together in 1992 to create the Association of National Trust in Japan 日本ナショナルトラスト協会.

Antipollution and environmental preservation policies 公害および環境保護政策 The Pollution Countermeasures Basic Law 公害対策基本法 in 1967 sought to create common principles and policies for pollution control in all government agencies and to promote an integrated effort to clean up the environment. The Basic Law indicates the responsibilities of the central government, local governments, and business firms with regard to controlling pollution. In addition, the Basic Law laid the framework for establishing environmental quality standards, drafting pollution-control programs 公害規制計画, and aiding victims of diseases caused by pollution.

The Pollution Countermeasures Basic Law, however, applies only to certain types of pollution, and so it has become increasingly difficult to address new global environmental problems using its provisions. For this reason, in 1993 the government enacted the Basic Environmental Law 環境基本法 to facilitate implementation of comprehensive and systematic measures to protect the environment, and it is actively working to promote environmental preservation worldwide through international cooperation and a rethinking of high-volume consumption practices in society. In 1997 the Environmental Impact Assessment Law 環境影響評価法(環境アセスメント法) was enacted. This law defines requirements for assessment of the environmental impact of large-scale projects.

Housing problems (*jūtaku mondai*) 住宅問題

Urban housing problems in Japan arose as the country entered the stage of industrialization and urbanization around 1900. Before the end of World War II no public measures were taken, but in the 1950s three major pieces of legislation established a general framework for Japanese housing policy. The Government Housing Loan Corporation 住宅金融公庫 founded in 1950 was a means of channeling public funds for low-interest, long-term loans for owner-occupied housing. Under the Public Housing Law 公営住宅法 of 1951 local authorities were empowered to build public housing for rental to low-income households with subsidies from the central government. Finally, the Japan Housing Corporation 日本住宅公団 was founded in 1955 as a public nonprofit developer to supply housing units for urban dwellers.

In 1966 the Housing Construction Planning Law 住宅建設計画法 was enacted to coordinate public policy measures for housing. The act mandated that the central government formulate five-year comprehensive housing construction plans at five-year intervals starting in 1966.

Housing Units in Selected Prefectures (1993)
住宅数と面積

Prefecture	Number of housing units	Ownership ratio(%)	Average size of housing unit Number of rooms	Total area(m²)
Tōkyō	4,660,300	39.6	3.52	62.05
Ōsaka	3,062,600	47.9	4.21	71.37
Toyama	317,700	79.8*	6.90*	154.85*
Nationwide	40,773,300	59.8	4.85	91.92

*Largest in Japan.   Source: Ministry of Construction.

Social Environment

The first Five-Year Housing Construction Plan aimed at constructing a total of 6.7 million housing units.

The second Housing Construction Plan, initiated in 1971, aimed at achieving "one room for each member of the household." Although the plan was to construct 9.6 million housing units in five years, only 8.26 million units were actually built.

The third Housing Construction Plan, approved in 1976, stated explicitly that the main priority of housing policy should be shifted from an emphasis on quantity to the improvement of quality. The purpose of the fourth Housing Construction Plan, begun in 1981, was to continue to improve housing quality, especially in urban areas.

High prices for land have forced many people to buy housing at a considerable distance from their workplaces, particularly in the Tōkyō metropolitan region 首都圏. In all of Japan's intensely crowded urban areas it is becoming increasingly difficult for the average "sarariman" (middle-class workers) to purchase a single-family dwelling. Multistory buildings with individual units for sale, similar to condominiums in the United States, have become the standard form of urban housing.

The fifth Housing Construction Plan (1986–1990) set forth a number of guidelines, including new standards for residential housing floor space and facilities. The sixth Housing Construction Plan (1991–1995) was again concerned with housing quality and also gave special attention to the promotion of a housing environment in which the elderly can continue living in areas they are familiar with. The seventh Housing Construction Plan (1996–2000) focuses on the providing of public rental housing to the elderly and the promotion of housing tailored to

One-Way Commuting Time in Japan (1993)
片道通勤時間

(in percentages)

	National Average	Greater Tōkyō	Greater Nagoya	Greater Ōsaka
None	1.7	1.5	1.5	1.4
Up to 30 min.	53.3	31.3	56.2	39.3
30-59 min.	28.9	34.6	31.4	37.7
60-89 min.	12.5	25.0	9.2	17.6
90-119 min.	2.9	6.5	1.5	3.3
More than 120 min.	0.7	1.1	0.2	0.7

Source: Ministry of Construction.

the special physical needs of the elderly. The plan also sets higher goals for residential housing floor space. Many issues remain, in addition to the challenge of housing the growing number of elderly, there are also the problems of the nearly 10 percent of all Japanese families who live in substandard private rental housing, as well as the obstacles faced by the handicapped and other socially disadvantaged members of Japanese society in securing adequate housing.

International Comparison of Per Capita Housing Area
主要国の1人あたり床面積

(in square meters)

Japan	30.6 (1993)
United States	62.6 (1991)
United Kingdom	40.2 (1991)
West Germany	35.5 (1987)
France	34.6 (1992)

Source: Bank of Japan, *Kokusai hikaku tōkei.*

EDUCATION 教育

History of education (*kyōikushi*) 教育史

Education in the sense of reading and writing began in Japan after the introduction of the Chinese writing system in the 6th century or before. The aristocracy was educated in Confucian thought and Buddhism in the Nara (710–794) and Heian (794–1185) periods. Buddhist priests were the first teachers in ancient Japan, and temples became centers of learning. Education spread to the military class during the Kamakura period (1185–1333); at the same time, through the growth of popular forms of Buddhism, the peasantry was also increasingly exposed to education. During the Edo period (1600–1868) both the shogunal and domainal governments established schools; the official systems were supplemented by private schools at shrines and temples. Education was widely diffused by the time of the Meiji Restoration 明治維新 of 1868.

Nationalism and the drive toward modernization were strong influences on education during the late 19th century. The nationalist influence was predominant after Japan militarized in the 1930s, while the post-World War II period brought decentralization and

Ratio of Advancement to Institutions of Higher Education
主要国の高等教育進学率

(in percentages)

	Japan (1995)	United States (1992)	United Kingdom (1993)	Germany (1993)
Female	47.8	52.4	55.3	29.7
Male	43.9	44.9	57.7	35.6
Total	45.8	48.6	56.4	32.7

Source: Ministry of Education.

new democratic influences to education. The postwar system provides nine years of compulsory schooling, and high school education is also nearly universal. Some 40 percent of Japanese students continue their education in universities. The schools are administered by local autonomous bodies 地方自治体 under the broad supervision of the Ministry of Education 文部省.

Education before 1600 1600年以前の教育

Education in ancient Japan was fostered by the imperial family. Prince Shōtoku 聖徳太子 (574–622) constructed Hōryūji, a temple in Nara, as a place of learning. The emperor Shōmu 聖武天皇 (701–756; r 724–749) constructed temples in each province; monks were sent to these temples by the government as instructors. Of particular importance in the period was the education of clergy, who were among the leaders of society.

With the establishment of the Chinese-inspired *ritsuryō* (legal codes) system 律令制度 of centralized government in the late 7th century, two types of schools for the nobility were established: the Daigakuryō, to educate the children of the nobility in the capital, and the *kokugaku*, to educate the children of the provincial nobility.

During the Kamakura period (1185–1333) when political power shifted to the provincial military class, *samurai* drew up *kakun* (house laws) 家訓 to educate their children and ensure family solidarity.

The Christian missionaries who came to Japan in the 16th century founded schools where both general and vocational education 職業教育 were conducted. By this time the Daigakuryō 大学寮 and the provincial *kokugaku* 国学 had declined. The most representative educational institution of this period was the Ashikaga Gakkō 足利学校, where monks made up a large part of the students body and the curriculum concentrated on Confucian learning. The school flourished during the late 1500s, when enrollment reached 3,000.

Edo-Period Education 江戸時代の教育

The civilizing effect of two and a half centuries of peace and modest economic growth during the Edo period (1600–1868) was nowhere more apparent than in the field of formal education. At the beginning of the period the literacy rate 識字率 was very low. Tutors, mostly priests, could be found for the children of noble families, but there were virtually no schools.

The contrast at the end of the period was great. Large schools organized by the domainal authorities (*hankō* 藩校) gave a graded instruction in the Chinese classics to almost every *samurai* child, and local *terakoya* 寺子屋, the schools for commoners, taught reading and writing to villagers as well as townsmen. Other private schools and academies called *shijuku* 私塾 provided more advanced instruction in a variety of disciplines and schools of thought to both *samurai* and commoners. Books abounded. Japan had almost certainly reached the 40 percent literacy threshold that some consider a prerequisite for modern growth.

Schools were also established that specialized in Dutch, later Western, learnings 蘭学：洋学. From the first spurt of interest in Dutch science—particularly medical science—in the 1770s until the mid-1850s, these exotic studies were largely carried on by individual doctors and low-ranking *samurai*. A number of special schools for Western studies were begun in the 1850s, notably the shogunate's Bansho Shirabesho (Institute for the Investigation of Barbarian Books) 蕃書調所, which rapidly developed into a flourishing school that admitted pupils from all over Japan.

For the Japanese of the Edo period the Chinese classics were the repository of wisdom and knowledge. Learning painfully to "construe" these classics was the central business of the domain schools 藩校. The Buddhist temples yielded authority in the moral sphere to Neo-

Confucianism 朱子学. The school during the Edo period thus came to combine the functions shared in Western society between school and church, with continuing consequences for the educational system of modern Japan.

Modern Education 近現代の教育

The Education Order of 1872 学制 established the foundation for a modern public education system. Many Edo-period schools were incorporated into the new educational system. *Terakoya*, schools for the common people, became primary schools; the shogunate-controlled, elite school called Kaiseijo (expanded from the Yōsho Shirabesho, formerly the Bansho Shirabesho) developed into a university that later became Tōkyō University, while many domain schools became public middle schools, which eventually developed into universities. Most of the schools of Western Learning developed into private *semmon gakkō* (professional schools) 専門学校.

The educational reform effort based on the Gakusei was overambitious and was thus revised two times, in 1879 and 1880. A significant development was the 1879 issuance of the Kyōgaku Taishi (Outline of Learning) 教学大旨, which emphasized Confucian values of humanity, justice, loyalty, and filial piety 親孝行. In 1880 education in *shūshin* ("moral" training) 修身 took on new importance. The utmost priority came to be placed on nationalistic moral education. This formed the basis for national educational policy until the end of World War II.

In 1885 the cabinet system was created, and Mori Arinori (1847–1889) became the first minister of education. In 1886 he issued in quick succession the Elementary School Order 小学校令, the Middle School Order 中学校令, the Imperial University Order 帝国大学令, and the Normal School Order 師範学校令. The imperial universities were intended to be the institutions that would create capable leaders who would absorb advanced Western Learning necessary for the modernization of the nation.

Elementary School Attendance Rate during the Meiji Period
明治時代の小学校就学率 (in percentages)

	1873	1875	1880	1885	1890	1895	1900	1905	1910
Boys	39.9	50.6	58.2	65.8	65.1	76.7	90.4	97.7	98.8
Girls	15.1	18.7	22.6	32.1	31.1	43.9	71.7	93.3	97.4
Total	28.1	35.4	41.2	49.6	48.9	61.2	81.5	95.6	98.1

Source: *Dai Nihon Teikoku tōkei nenkan.*

In these ways a comprehensive school system was established for the purpose of modernization on one hand and the spiritual unification of the people on the other. In 1890 the Imperial Rescript on Education 教育勅語 was issued in the name of Emperor Meiji. The rescript served as a powerful instrument of political indoctrination and remained in effect until the end of World War II. In 1898 the attendance rate 就学率 for compulsory education reached 69 percent. Compulsory education 義務教育 was extended to six years in 1907.

Stimulated by the Russo-Japanese War (1904–1905) and World War I, capitalism developed rapidly in Japan. During this period the governmental Rinji Kyōiku Kaigi (Extraordinary Council on Education) 臨時教育会議 issued several reports that formed the basis for the expansion of the education system over the next decade or so. Until 1918 universities had been limited to the imperial universities 帝国大学, but the reforms contained in the University Order of 1918 大学令 extended recognition to colleges and private universities. In accordance with this order many national, public, and private *semmon gakkō* were raised to the status of university.

After the Manchurian Incident 満州事変 of 1931, educational policy soon became ultranationalistic; after the beginning of the Sino-Japanese War of 1937–1945, it became militaristic. Elementary schools were changed to *kokumin gakkō* (national people's schools) 国民学校, which were to train subjects for the empire, and *seinen gakkō* (youth schools, for vocational education) 青年学校 became obligatory for graduates of elementary schools.

Normal schools 師範学校 were raised in status to *semmon gakkō*. After Japan entered World War II, militaristic education became even stronger.

Post-World War II Education 第2次世界大戦後の教育

After defeat in 1945 Japan was placed under the Occupation of the Allied forces until the San Francisco Peace Treaty サンフランシスコ平和条約 of 1952. Reports of the United States education missions to Japan アメリカ教育使節団, which came to Japan in 1946 and 1950, became the blueprints for educational reform. The core of the reform was the Fundamental Law of Education 教育基本法 (1947), which took the place of the Imperial Rescript on Education as the basic philosophy of education. Based on this law, the School Education Law 学校教育法 of 1947 was promulgated in the same year, and a new school system was established. The essential elements of the new system were the replacement of the existing dual-track (popular and elite) system with a single-track 6-3-3-4 system (six years of elementary school, three years of middle school, three years of high school, and four years of university), compulsory education in elementary and middle schools, the establishment of the principle of coeducation, and the creation of the board of education 教育委員会 system. There have been calls for further educational reforms in response to the social and economic changes that have occurred in Japan since the late 1940s, and in 1984 the Nakasone cabinet established its own advisory council, the Provisional Council on Educational Reform (Rinji Kyōiku Shingikai 臨時教育審議会; also called Rinkyōshin), which presented a final report in 1987. It stressed the principle of respect for and encouragement of individuality as a fundamental goal.

There is growing concern that the 50-year-old postwar education system does not have the flexibility needed to respond either to problems already occurring because of rapid changes taking place in society or to future challenges that will result from an aging population and internationalization. In the year 2000 Japan's entire public school system, from kindergarten through high school is scheduled to begin operating five days per week instead of six. This change is to be accompanied by a revision of the school curriculum, resulting in a 30-percent reduction in content. Looking ahead to education in the 21st century, in 1997–98 the Central Council for Education (Chūō Kyōiku Shingikai; also called Chūkyōshin), which serves as a decision-making body for government education policy, issued a report that includes recommendations for a system of unified middle and high schools and a proposal to allow exceptions to university entrant age restrictions. Proposals such as these are being seen as the first step toward reforms that could effect great changes in postwar Japanese education.

School system (*kyōiku seido*) 教育制度

The first modern school system in Japan was established by the Education Order of 1872 学制. Curricula for pre-World War II schools were established by the government, and textbooks for elementary and middle schools were either compiled or authorized by the government. Employees of public schools were considered government officials, and even private schools were required to conduct their educational activities according to government guidelines. The Japanese school system has undergone substantial change since World War II. The Educational Reforms of 1947, carried out under the direction of the Allied Occupation 連合国占領, decentralized control of education, authorized autonomous private schools, and encouraged the development of community education 社会教育. Textbooks for elementary, middle, and high schools are now compiled under the sponsorship of private publishing houses; however, authorization by the Ministry of Education is still required (see also SCHOOL TEXTBOOKS).

The nucleus of the school system is the system of six-year elementary schools, three-year middle schools, three-year high schools, and four-year universities. In addition there are kindergartens, five-year technical colleges 高等専門学校 for graduates of middle school, and schools for the handicapped. Universities include undergraduate colleges, junior colleges, and graduate schools. Aside from these regular schools there are miscellaneous schools 各種学校, most of which are vocational or technical training schools. Education is compulsory through middle school, and over 95 percent of elementary and middle schools are public; private schools play a larger role at the secondary and university level (24 percent of Japan's high schools and 73 percent of its universities are private institutions).

School curriculum (*kyōiku katei*) 教育課程

The modern Japanese educational system was established in the early Meiji period (1868–1912) with the assistance of such American advisers as David Murray and Marion Scott. In 1886 the government set up the first regular curriculum. Under Japan's system of compulsory education 義務教育 (initially four years of elementary school), the required subjects were *shūshin* (courses instilling patriotism), arithmetic, reading and writing, composition, penmanship, and physical education. Drawing and singing were sometimes included.

In 1890 the government issued the Imperial Rescript on Education 教育勅語. This document, based on traditional Confucian tenets, articulated the guiding principles of education in Japan; it remained in effect until the end of World War II. After the Sino-Japanese War of 1894–1895, the government consolidated the school system and introduced more up-to-date subject matter into the curriculum. After 1907 compulsory education was increased to six years and the courses taught were *shūshin* 修身, Japanese, arithmetic, physical education, Japanese history, geography, science, drawing, singing, and, for girls, sewing. This curriculum continued basically unchanged until 1941, when elementary schools were reorganized as *kokumin gakkō* (national people's schools) 国民学校, and the curriculum was drastically revised to meet the objective of "training loyal subjects of the emperor." Such courses as *shūshin* and history were infused with a strong militaristic and nationalistic tone, and almost every aspect of schooling stressed absolute loyalty to the emperor.

After Japan's defeat in 1945, Occupation authorities suspended the teaching of *shūshin*, Japanese history, and geography and forbade the formal reading of the Imperial Rescript on Education. In 1946 a team of American education specialists visited Japan and made a number of recommendations for the reorganization of the school system. Following this visit a new curriculum was developed, and the school system was decentralized and revised to accord with regional differences and individual needs. The educational reforms of 1947 教育改革(1947) established social studies 社会科 as a part of the curriculum and emphasized educating students to be responsible members of society. The School Education Law of 1947 学校教育法 provided for the basic framework and organization of the postwar Japanese school system, while school course guidelines 学習指導要領, first issued in 1947, stated the aim of each subject taught and the contents of teaching in each grade.

Under the contemporary system, compulsory education consists of six years of elementary school and three years of middle school; three years of high school are optional. The elementary school curriculum is uniform: all students in the same year study the same topics;

no special classes or groups based on different attainment levels are formed; and students are not allowed to skip grades. Middle school curriculums, unlike those in elementary school, are under the direction of the teacher in charge of the course. Foreign language is an elective subject, but most middle schools offer only English, so English is, in effect, a required course. High schools stress matching electives to each student's abilities, aptitudes, and future course of study. Both primary and middle school curricula include one hour of moral education 道徳教育 per week, and additional guidance is provided in all educational activities. Religious education 宗教教育 is not included in the public school curriculum. Extracurricular activities 課外活動 receive strong emphasis. Curriculum standards are reviewed by the Curriculum Council 教育課程審議会 of the Ministry of Education and are usually revised every 10 years, most recently in 1989.

The Structure of Education 教育科目

Elementary schools teach Japanese language, social studies, arithmetic, science, music, arts and crafts, physical education, and homemaking. The 1989 school course guidelines mandate life environmental studies 生活科, rather than social studies and science, to teach first- and second-graders about society and nature through activities and experiences geared to their immediate environment. In middle school, Japanese language, social studies, mathematics, science, and industrial arts 技術 and homemaking are required subjects 必修科目; music, art, and health and physical education are partly required and partly elective. Foreign language is an elective 選択科目, but nearly all middle school students study English; a few schools offer other languages (generally French or German). In high school, Japanese language, geography and history, civics, mathematics, science, health and physical education, the arts, and home economics are common required courses. Foreign language, usually English, is an elective taken by the majority of students; far fewer students take French or German, although more high schools than middle schools offer these languages. Specialized vocational courses are available, and extracurricular activities are required in all grades. The contents of the principal courses are as follows:

Japanese language 国語 Reading and writing is stressed. By the time students complete their elementary and middle school education, they are expected to have learned the 1,945 characters known as the *jōyō kanji* (Chinese characters for common use) 常用漢字. In middle and high schools the reading and appreciation of classical Japanese 古文 and *kambun* (classical Chinese) 漢文 are included. Composition is taught from first grade; calligraphy, using a brush, begins in third grade.

Social studies 社会 Social studies was included in the postwar curriculum to teach democracy and pacifism, but the subject is now divided into geography, history, and civics. In elementary school, third- to sixth-graders learn about their community, their nation, and Japanese history in a combined course. In middle school children study geography and history concurrently in the first and second years; in the third year they study civics (politics, economics, and society). Social studies in high school was divided into two subjects in 1989: geography and history (taught as one course) and civics. The initial focus of geography education is on one's own community (as in the life environmental studies course for first- and second-graders) and then gradually expands to cover a larger sphere. In middle and high school students begin with a view of the world as a whole and then study Japan and their own city in the geography and history and civics courses.

Mathematics 算数・数学 Elementary school programs cover four areas: numbers and calculation, quantity and measurement, geometry, and quantity relationships. In middle school numbers and formulas, functions, geometry, and qualitative relationships including probability and statistics are taught. High schools offer general math, algebra, geometry, basic analysis, differentiation and integration, and probability and statistics.

Science 理科 To learn about the world around them, third- to sixth-graders study living things and their environment, matter and energy, the earth and the universe. In middle school, science comprises physics, chemistry, biology, and earth science. High school students must take two of the following: comprehensive science, basic science, physics, chemistry, biology, or earth science.

Music and art 音楽・美術 Singing, instrumental music 器楽, composition, and appreciation of both Western and traditional Japanese music are taught. Elementary school students learn to play the harmonica in the lower grades and later the recorder. Elementary and middle school students are taught to appreciate and express themselves through drawing, sculpture, design, and handicrafts. High-schoolers choose two from among music, art (painting, drawing, sculpture, graphic design), calligraphy, and crafts.

Health and physical education 保健・体育 In physical education 体育 students may take gymnastics, track and field, swimming, various kinds of ball games, *kendō*, *sumō*, *jūdō*, and dancing. In health classes, students study the functions and development of the body and mind, the prevention of accidents and illness, and, at the middle school level, the effects of smoking, alcohol, and recreational drug use on health.

Home economics 家庭科 Students acquire basic knowledge and skills relating to food, clothing, shelter, child care 育児, and welfare for the aged. Both boys and girls must take home economics from the fifth grade through high school. Classes in industrial arts and home-making teach middle school students the rudiments of cooking and sewing, the child-parent relationship 親子関係, consumer life, and computer use.

Foreign language 外国語 English is taught in middle and high school, and German and French are offered in some middle and high schools. See ENGLISH LANGUAGE TRAINING.

Extracurricular activities 特別活動 Additional student activities include class assemblies, club activities, ceremonies, athletic meets (*undōkai*), school plays and concerts (*gakugeikai*), excursions (*shūgaku ryokō*) and field trips (*ensoku*), and educational guidance relating to student life, such as traffic safety guidance and training in the use of the school library.

School textbooks (*kyōkasho*) 教科書

In Japan all elementary, middle, and high schools are obliged to use government-approved textbooks. Textbooks are compiled by private publishers, who are given a certain amount of freedom in the style of presentation, but are also required to conform to government-issued school course guidelines 学習指導要領. Authorization is given only after evaluation of the texts by Ministry of Education 文部省 specialists and appointed examiners and a final review by the Textbook Authorization and Research Council 教科用図書検定調査審議会, an advisory organ of the ministry.

A system of free distribution of textbooks for compulsory education 義務教育 was established in 1963. The textbooks used in each school district are chosen by the local board of education 教育委員会 from among those authorized by the central government; in the case of private schools the responsibility lies with the school principal.

The purpose of the official authorization of textbooks, a system that has been in effect in Japan since 1886, is the standardization of education and the maintenance of objectivity and neutrality on political and religious issues. The textbook approval process has engendered considerable controversy and has led to one famous court case, a suit brought against the government by historian Ienaga Saburō 家永三郎 (1913–) in 1965, charging that the authorization process was both illegal and unconstitutional 違憲.

English language training (*eigo kyōiku*) 英語教育

English is the most widely studied foreign language in Japan. During the Meiji period (1868–1912), the study of English was considered essential for importing the Western technology necessary for modernization. Language training was chiefly based on reading ability and not on conversation.

Because the written entrance examinations for universities and high schools test for English ability, grammar and reading comprehension are stressed in the English classes offered by most high schools and middle schools. However, there is a growing awareness that neglecting speaking and listening during the first six years of English language training leads to problems. The school course guidelines for 1989 stress spoken communication, and the Ministry of Education has brought in native English speakers as assistant teachers of middle and high school English classes. In 1996 there were 4,574 such assistant teachers invited to Japan.

English conversation schools, courses on television and on radio, and company-run classes for employees offer further training in English. In 1995, some 3.5 million people took the Test in Practical English Proficiency 実用英語技能検定試験(英検) (approved by the Ministry of Education since 1963).

Foreign Language Teaching Assistants under the JET Program (1994)
語学指導等を行う外国青年招致事業(JETプログラム)による外国語指導助手(ALT)

Country	Number of assistants
United States	2,025
United Kingdom	705
Australia	215
New Zealand	193
Canada	663
Ireland	53
France	8
Germany	3
Total	3,865*

*English 3,854, French 8, and German 3.
Source: Ministry of Education.

Entrance examinations (*nyūgaku shiken*)
入学試験

Entrance examinations are given great weight in Japan's educational system. Although nursery, primary, and middle schools also conduct such tests, Japanese society attaches the most importance to entrance exams for high schools and universities.

High school is attended by 97 percent of middle school graduates, so the function of high school entrance tests is not to weed out unqualified applicants, but to determine which school a student may attend. Private high schools design their own tests and conduct applicant interviews to select students, while public high school entrance standards are determined by the local school system. Generally, achievement test results in five categories (English, mathematics, Japanese, social studies, and science) are evaluated, along with the student's junior high school records.

Objective achievement-test performance is the key factor in university applicant selection, but certain universities may include essay-writing tests 論述テスト, or performance tests 実技試験 for applicants in music or physical education, in their evaluation process. All national and other public universities (and a few private ones) require prospective applicants to take the University Entrance Examination Center Tests 大学入試センター試験—a series of standardized multiple-choice examinations 多項式選択テスト measuring competence in the Japanese language, social studies, mathematics, science, and foreign languages. Based on the results, students may then make a more informed choice as to which schools to apply to. Ultimately, admission is based on the combined results of the general test plus the independent examination offered by the university in question. Entrance examinations for both high schools and universities are administered each year during the period from January through March. Students may apply to more than one high school or university.

The Japanese entrance examination system does not establish in advance a target score that, if achieved, assures admission; those applying at the same time compete for a limited number of openings. In Japanese society it is generally accepted that the school one attends will decisively influence the course of one's life and career (*gakureki shakai*). Entrance tests are therefore regarded as major events in determining one's fate, and the battle to qualify for the best schools is waged with fierce intensity. The competition is seen as having assumed excessive proportions in the 1980s. This has not only led to enormous prosperity for the operators of *juku* (private tutoring schools) 塾 and cram schools 予備校, but is also thought to have helped precipitate many education-related problems. However, the population of 18-year-olds, which peaked in 1990, has continued to shrink ever since. The excesses that were seen in Japan's high-school and college entrance examination system during the 1980s and early 1990s are beginning to disappear.

Hensachi (deviation) 偏差値

Statistical term frequently used in Japanese education to express a student's performance on a standardized examination relative to a mean average score. Since the early 1960s *hensachi* figures have been used in Japan to calculate an individual's percentile ranking for practice ENTRANCE EXAMINATIONS. Guidance counselors often base their assessment of how likely a student is to gain admission to certain schools by comparing the student's *hensachi* with the average *hensachi* of other students applying to the same schools. The industry of private tutoring schools (*juku*) and cram schools (*yobikō*) also calculates *hensachi* figures for students, based on

the results of large-scale practice examinations 模擬試験,
to advise them on test-taking strategies.

Transportation (*kōtsū*) 交通

Japan has a highly developed domestic and
international transportation network. The system as it
now exists was developed in the century following the
Meiji Restoration 明治維新 of 1868, but even earlier the
transportation system was relatively sophisticated for a
preindustrial society.

Premodern Transportation 前近代の交通

The establishment of a rice tax system and legal
codes system 律令制度 in the late 7th century was accompanied by the construction of the first major roads. The
Inland Sea 瀬戸内海 was a major transportation route
between settlements in Japan from early times.

After the establishment of the Tokugawa shogunate 徳川幕府 (1603–1867), international transportation
activity was halted by the National Seclusion 鎖国 policy,
which was in force from 1639 to 1854. Domestic trans-

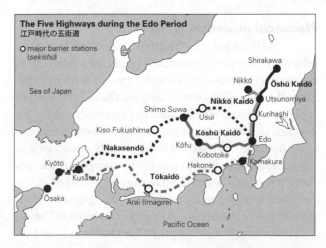

The Five Highways during the Edo Period
江戸時代の五街道

○ major barrier stations (*sekisho*)

Sea of Japan

Shirakawa
Nikkō
Ōshū Kaidō
Utsunomiya
Nikkō Kaidō
Kurihashi
Shimo Suwa
Usui
Kiso Fukushima
Kōshū Kaidō
Edo
Nakasendō
Kōfu
Kobotoke
Kamakura
Kyōto
Hakone
Tōkaidō
Kusatsu
Ōsaka
Arai (Imagire)
Pacific Ocean

Passenger Transportation
国内旅客輸送量 　　　　　　　(in billions of passenger-kilometers)

	1970	1975	1980	1985	1990	1995
Automobile and buses	284.2	360.9	431.7	489.3	853.1	917.4
Rail	288.8	323.8	314.5	330.1	387.5	400.1
Ship	4.8	6.9	6.1	5.8	6.3	5.5
Air	9.3	19.1	29.7	33.1	51.6	65.0
Total	587.2	710.7	782.0	858.2	1298.4	1388.0

Source: Ministry of Transport.

portation, on the other hand, grew and improved greatly during the Edo period (1600–1868). Coastal shipping routes were extended to support the expanding commodity trade, and the road network was also improved.

Meiji Period (1868–1912) to World War II 明治時代から第2次世界大戦まで

Following the Meiji Restoration of 1868, Japan absorbed Western technology at a rapid pace. The first steam-powered train ran on a narrow-gauge track between Shimbashi and Yokohama in 1872, the first automobile was imported in 1899. Western-type vessels quickly replaced most traditional Japanese sailing ships as the government subsidized the ship-building industry 造船業. From the 1880s onward the rail network 鉄道網 expanded rapidly and in 1906 major portions of it were nationalized. In 1927 the first subway in Tōkyō began operation. Bus service and trucking companies began in the 1910s, with rapid expansion after the Tōkyō Earthquake of 1923 関東大震災. During the 1930s taxis developed into an important means of urban transportation.

By the 1940s the mainstay of the passenger transportation 旅客輸送 system was the railroads, while freight transportation 貨物輸送 was conducted primarily through coastal shipping and the railroads.

Postwar Transportation Network
第2次世界大戦後の交通ネットワーク

The postwar era was characterized by an explosive growth in the number of automobiles, trucks, and airlines. By 1990 the rail share of total domestic passenger transportation had fallen to 30 percent, with automobiles increasing from less than 1 percent in 1950 to 66 percent in 1990. Buses also compete with the railroads to some extent, but they mainly provide feeder service to train stations or operate in rural areas where there is no rail service. SUBWAYS are an important means of urban transportation.

Scheduled domestic airlines 定期国内便 have grown rapidly but still occupy a small share of total passenger transportation. International air travel has also grown at a tremendous pace: the number of passengers carried by scheduled Japanese airlines was only 112,000 in 1955 but exceeded 10 million in 1990.

For freight transportation, the rail share of total ton-kilometers fell to 5 percent by 1990, while trucks expanded from 8 percent in 1950 to 50 percent in 1990, and coastal shipping went from 39 percent to 45 percent.

Coordination of the transportation system has been a problem because different modes of transportation are governed by separate laws and represented by different bureaus within the Ministry of Transport 運輸省.

Railroads 鉄道 The network of RAILWAYS consists of the JR (Japan Railways) group and a number of private railways 私鉄. The JR group is made up of six passenger railway companies, a freight railway company, and several other affiliated companies, all of which were created when long-term financial difficulties led to the privatization of the Japanese National Railways (JNR) 日本国有鉄道 in 1987. In 1990 the rail system comprised 26,895 operation-kilometers (16,710 mi), of which JR companies operated 20,175 or 75 percent of the total. JR passenger service includes intercity trunk lines, urban feeder service, and a large number of rural lines. It also operates Japan's fastest passenger trains on the SHINKANSEN "bullet train" 弾丸列車(新幹線) lines of standard gauge 標準軌間. In 1950 the JNR alone generated 59 percent of all passenger-kilometers 旅客輸送人キロ, but this figure had fallen to 18 percent for the JR in 1990. The JR

Freight Transportation
国内貨物輸送量 (in billions of ton-kilometers)

	1970	1975	1980	1985	1990	1995
Motorvehcles	135.9	129.7	178.9	205.9	274.2	294.6
Rail freight	63.0	47.1	37.4	21.9	27.2	25.1
Freight ship	151.2	183.6	222.2	205.8	244.5	238.3
Air	0.1	0.2	0.3	0.5	0.8	0.9
Total	350.3	360.5	438.8	434.2	546.8	559.0

Source: Ministry of Transport.

group's Japan Freight Railway Co 日本貨物鉄道会社. provides almost all of the rail freight service in Japan, but railroads can no longer effectively compete with trucks for most freight business.

In addition to the JR group companies, there are 16 large railway companies and 58 smaller railways. Unlike the JR, the other large railway companies have evolved into conglomerates of related activities, operating sports stadiums, baseball teams, department stores, amusement parks, and real estate. More of their profits often come from these related businesses than from railway businesses.

Motor vehicles 自動車 Private automobiles have been one of the fastest growing segments of passenger transportation because of three factors that became conspicuous in the 1960s: the rapid growth of income to a point where families could afford automobiles, the development of a domestic automotive industry geared to the specific needs of the domestic market (small-sized vehicles) 小型車, and the improvement of roads. The number of registered motor vehicles increased from only about 1.5 million in 1960 to over 43 million in 1990. Paving on national highways 国道 was extended from 29 percent in 1960 to 98 percent in 1991. Japan had also developed a total of 5,930 kilometers (3,684 mi) of EXPRESSWAYS 高速道路 by 1996. Even as late as 1960, 20 percent of all automobiles were business vehicles, but by 1990 private automobiles were 97 percent of total registrations.

As roads have improved, trucks have increased in size. Whereas most commercial trucks did not exceed a 5-ton capacity in the mid-1950s, 18-ton trucks are now common and the number of trailer trucks is also increasing.

Highway safety continues to be a major problem. Although major

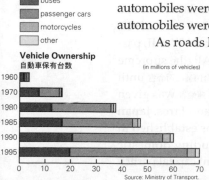

trucks
buses
passenger cars
motorcycles
other

Vehicle Ownership
自動車保有台数

(in millions of vehicles)

1960
1970
1980
1985
1990
1995

0　10　20　30　40　50　60　70
Source: Ministry of Transport.

Merchant Ship Tonnage
商船船腹量

(in thousands of gross tons)

| | Freighters 貨物船 | | Passenger ships 客船 | | Oil tankers タンカー | | Total | |
	Ships	Gross tons	Ships	Gross tons	Ships	Gross tons	Ships	Gross tons
1960	1,328	4,406	184	174	407	1,422	1,919	6,002
1970	5,282	14,563	472	269	2,113	8,883	7,867	23,715
1980	5,546	20,632	1,551	1,284	1,728	17,099	8,825	39,015
1990	4,769	16,037	1,690	1,563	1,209	7,586	7,668	25,186
1994	4,334	13,320	1,771	1,800	1,120	6,768	7,165	21,888

Note: Steel ships with gross tonnage of 100 tons or more.

Source: Japanese Shipowners' Association.

safety campaigns led to a steady decline in traffic deaths between 1970 and 1980, since then the trend has reversed, and after 1988 highway fatalities exceeded 10,000 in each year.

Marine transportation 海運　Seaborne freight is the primary means of transporting Japan's huge volume of raw-materials imports and finished-goods exports. Total tonnage handled by Japanese ports grew at an annual rate of 15 percent from 1980 to 1990. The most important of Japan's 121 international ports are the Tōkyō Bay area (Tōkyō, Yokohama, Kawasaki, and Chiba), Nagoya, the Ōsaka Bay area (Ōsaka and Kōbe), Kita Kyūshū, and Wakayama Shimotsu (a major oil port).

Since the oil crisis of 1973 an oversupply of ships worldwide has hurt the shipping industry as a whole. Japanese shipping companies have lost international competitiveness because of rising wages and the continuing high value of the yen 円高 since 1985. By 1990 the total gross tons of vessels flying the Japanese flag had fallen about 42 percent from its peak of 35 million tons in 1982.

Air transportation 空運　After World War II, passenger airlines were prohibited by SCAP (the supreme commander for the Allied powers) 連合国最高司令官 until 1951, when the Ministry of Transport 運輸省 was given control over licensing airline routes and fares. Japan Airlines Co., Ltd. (JAL) 日本航空(株), was established in 1953 as an international airline (including domestic trunk lines) with 50 percent government capital participation. At the same time approval was also given to two private regional firms, which later merged to become All Nippon Airways Co., Ltd. (ANA) 全日本空輸 (株). JAL became a private company in 1987.

As of September 1998 there were 6 scheduled international airlines in Japan, including JAL and ANA, as well as 10 scheduled domestic airlines. In 1998 Skymark Airlines Co., Ltd., became the first scheduled airline to enter the market in 35 years when it initiated service between Tōkyō and Fukuoka. To handle the increased air traffic, AIRPORTS have also expanded. In the spring of 1978, the New Tōkyō International Airport (Narita) 新東京国際空港(成田空港) replaced Tōkyō International Airport (Haneda) 東京国際空港(羽田空港) as the main international airport for Tōkyō. Kansai International Airport 関西国際空港 opened in 1994 in Ōsaka.

Railways (*tetsudō*) 鉄道

Railways in Japan date from 1872, only four years into the country's modern period, but almost four decades from the time that railways first appeared in Europe and the United States. Progress was rapid after the late start, however, and in the 20th century Japan's railways have compared favorably with those of any other nation in the world. In the post-World War II period, and especially since the development of the SHINKANSEN "bullet train," Japan has been at the forefront of railway technology.

Early Development 草創期

The first line, begun in 1870 and completed in 1872, was of modest proportions, running 28 kilometers (17.4 mi) from Shimbashi in Tōkyō to Yokohama on narrow gauge track 狭軌. Following initial government plans calling for a trunk line 幹線 between Tōkyō and Kyōto, running through a coastal route, the Tōkaidō was first spanned by rails in 1893. Two years later the nation's first electric railway began operating in Kyōto. By 1901 tracks had been laid the entire length of the main island of Honshū, and each of the other three main islands also had some trackage by this time. A nationwide network was in place by the eve of nationalization in 1906–1907.

Volume of Railway Passengers in Selected Countries
主要国の鉄道旅客輸送量 (in billions of passenger-kilometers)

	1960	1970	1980	1990
Japan	180.9	288.1	313.3	383.7
France	31.7	41.1	54.5	63.6
Italy	30.7	32.5	39.6	45.5
United Kingdom	34.7	35.6	31.7	34.1
United States	34.3	17.3	17.7	9.9*

*1990 US figures exclude commuter railroads.
Source: United Nations.

Nationalization 国有化

Although the earliest lines had been constructed by the government, after about 1885 the apparent profitability of railways was sufficient to attract a flood of private entrepreneurs into the field. The wars with China (1894–1895) and Russia (1904–1905), however, raised the question of the desirability of private control of such a key national resource. The importance of foreign loans in financing railway development was thought to raise the specter of foreign control of the private lines, and this possibility was a key element in arguments in favor of nationalization, which went into effect in 1906–1907 under the Railway Nationalization Law 鉄道国有法 of 1906. The system was known as the Japanese National Railways (JNR) 日本国有鉄道, a public corporation 公共企業体, from 1949 until denationalization took place in 1987.

Postwar Developments 第2次世界大戦後の発達

The extension of urban commuter systems, including subways, has been a major accomplishment of the postwar period, but the most spectacular development has been the routes of the world-famed Shinkansen "bullet trains". The original section of the Shinkansen was opened in 1964 as a route between Tōkyō and Ōsaka.

Overnight trains with sleeping car service are available on non-Shinkansen routes. Many limited express and ordinary express trains operate on principal lines every day, along with local trains 普通列車.

Railway Freight Traffic Volume
JR・私鉄鉄道貨物輸送分担量
(in millions of freight ton-kilometers)

Fiscal year	JR	Private	Total
1950	33,309	540	33,849
1955	42,564	690	43,254
1960	53,592	923	54,515
1965	56,408	890	57,299
1970	62,435	988	63,423
1975	46,577	770	47,347
1980	36,961	740	37,701
1985	21,626	509	22,135
1990	26,728	468	27,196
1995	24,702	399	25,101

Source: Ministry of Transport.

Railway Passenger Traffic Volume
JR・私鉄鉄道旅客輸送分担量 (in millions of passenger-kilometers)

Fiscal year	JR	Private	Total
1950	69,004	36,464	105,468
1955	91,239	44,873	136,112
1960	123,983	60,357	184,340
1965	174,014	81,370	255,384
1970	189,726	99,090	288,816
1975	215,289	108,511	323,800
1980	193,143	121,399	314,542
1985	197,463	132,620	330,083
1990	237,657	149,821	387,478
1995	248,998	151,059	400,056

Source: Ministry of Transport.

Denationalization 民営化

The basic form of the railway system remained the same from nationalization in 1906–1907 until 1987, when the Japanese National Railways was privatized and broken up into six regional private passenger services and one rail freight company, known collectively as the JR (Japan Railways) group. The JNR had been suffering an increasing burden of debt and operating deficits since the 1960s. Most of the new JR companies returned to profitability within two to three years of privatization by cutting staff, by reducing services on loss-making lines or abolishing them altogether, and by buying into service industries such as restaurants and hotels.

In addition to the main JR network—20,022 kilometers (12,444 mi) of track—and the private local lines, subway systems serve the main cities of Japan. As crowding of the aboveground rail lines increases even further, subways should become an even more important component of the urban transportation system.

Shinkansen (New Trunk Line) 新幹線

The Shinkansen is a high-speed passenger railroad system consisting of five lines operated by three companies of the JR group. Central Japan Railway Co. JR 東海 is responsible for the Tōkaidō line, West Japan Railway Co. JR西日本 for the San'yō line, and East Japan Railway Co. JR東日本 for the Tōhoku, Jōetsu, and Hokuriku (Nagano) lines. Often called the "bullet train" because of its shape and speed, the Shinkansen provides first-class, or "Green Car," service as well as reserved and unreserved ordinary-car service. There are no sleeping facilities and few dining facilities on Shinkansen trains, since most runs can be made in a few hours.

Tōkaidō-San'yō Shinkansen 東海道・山陽新幹線

The railroad that serves the 500-kilometer (311-mi) corridor between Tōkyō and Ōsaka has always been considered the main artery of Japan. Located on the Pacific coast of central Honshū, this zone is the industrial and socioeconomic nucleus of the country; almost half the population and two-thirds of the nation's industry are concentrated there.

In the 1950s innovations on the conventional Tōkaidō rail line, which served this district, were given priority over other lines in an effort to meet steadily increasing demand. The eventual solution was to construct a high-speed railroad on a separate double track of standard gauge 標準軌間—the Shinkansen. Ground was broken for the project in April 1959, and construction was completed in July 1964. Service was begun on 1 October 1964, 9 days before the opening of the Tōkyō Olympic Games, with initial daily service of 60 trains with 12 cars each. The total construction cost was ¥380.0 billion (US $1.1 billion), double the original estimate.

The Shinkansen reduced the minimum trip time between Tōkyō and Ōsaka from 6 hours and 30 minutes to 3 hours and 10 minutes. The Shinkansen was enthusiastically welcomed by the public because of its high speed, short trip time, good ride comfort, and superb on-time operation. The image of the Shinkansen speeding past a snowcapped Mt. Fuji was seen as a symbol of modern Japan.

The line's popularity and the rapid growth in traffic volume brought about a need for the westward extension of the Shinkansen system. The San'yō Shinkansen opened for service

Passenger-Kilometers Traveled on the Shinkansen Lines
新幹線旅客輸送量の推移 (in millions of passenger-kilometers)

	1990	1991	1992	1993	1994	1995
Tōkaidō	41,341	41,841	40,655	40,504	38,907	39,817
San'yō	16,064	16,277	16,161	16,026	13,310	14,759
Tōhoku	10,678	11,689	11,837	11,695	11,763	11,956
Jōetsu	4,089	4,413	4,408	4,339	4,267	4,295
Total	72,172	74,220	73,061	72,564	68,247	70,827

Source: Ministry of Transport.

The Shinkansen Lines
新幹線網

Line	Termini	Route length (km)	Travel time of fastest train	Maximum speed (km/h)
Tōkaidō	Tōkyō-Ōsaka	552.6	2 hrs 30 min	270
San'yō	Ōsaka-Hakata	623.3	2 hrs 17 min	300
Tōhoku	Tōkyō-Morioka	535.3	2 hrs 21 min	275
Jōetsu	Tōkyō-Niigata	333.9	1 hrs 40 min	275
Hokuriku (Nagano)	Tōkyō-Nagano	222.4	1 hrs 20 min	260

Source: Ministry of Transport.

The Shinkansen Railroad System
新幹線網

— in operation (······ mini Shinkansen)
— under construction
······ scheduled for construction

Sapporo
Oshamambe
Hachinohe
Aomori
Akita
Morioka
Niigata
Yamagata
Itoigawa
Okayama
Uozu
Sendai
Toyama
Fukushima
Hiroshima
Kanazawa
Takasaki
Shimonoseki
Ōmiya
Fukuoka (Hakata)
Tōkyō
Nagasaki
Karuizawa
Yatsushiro
Nagano
Nagoya
Tsuruga
Kumamoto
Ōsaka
Kagoshima

Source: Ministry of Transport.

with a 160.9 kilometer (100-mi) stretch between Ōsaka and Okayama in March 1972. The project had taken five years to complete at a cost of ¥224.0 billion (US $739.0 million). The line was extended to Hakata in Kyūshū through the Kammon undersea tunnel 関門トンネル in March 1975. The construction for this stretch of 392.8 kilometers (244 mi) also took five years, and the cost was ¥729.0 billion (US $2.4 billion). The combined route, with a total length of 1,069 kilometers (664 mi), is known as the Tōkaidō-San'yō Shinkansen. The Tōkaidō Shinkansen has a maximum speed of 270 kilometers per hour (168 mph), and the minimum trip time between Tōkyō and Ōsaka is 2 hours 30 minutes. The San'yō Shinkansen has a maximum speed of 300 kilometers per hour (186 mph) and the minimum trip time between Ōsaka and Hakata is 2 hours 17 minutes. A Shinkansen train departs Tōkyō for Ōsaka or some point further west about every seven minutes throughout most day-time schedules, lasting from approximately 6 AM to 12 PM. In 1997, 280 trains were scheduled on the route per day, each with 16 cars. Between the inauguration of service on the line in 1964 and early 1996, the Tōkaidō-San'yō Shinkansen carried 3.5 billion passengers.

Tōhoku, Jōetsu, Hokuriku, Yamagata, and Akita Shinkansen 東北・上越・北陸・山形・秋田新幹線

The Tōhoku Shinkansen and Jōetsu Shinkansen commenced service in 1982. The former connects Tōkyō and Morioka in northern Japan, with a route length of 535.3 kilometers (332.6 mi) and a minimum trip time of 2 hours 21 minutes. On average 144 trains are scheduled daily and passengers number over 50 million per year. The latter connects Tōkyō and Niigata on the coast of the Sea of Japan, with a route length of 333.9 kilometers (207.5 mi) and a minimum trip time of 1 hour 40 minutes. On average 88 trains are scheduled daily and passengers number 27 million per year. From the inauguration of service to 1996, the two lines carried over 800 million passengers.

The 117-kilometer (73-mi) Takasaki-Nagano section of the Hokuriku Shinkansen began operation in October 1997. Construction of this section (which is also called the Nagano Shinkansen) was scheduled so that it would be ready in time for the 1998 Nagano Winter Olympic Games 長野冬季オリンピック. Twenty-eight-car trains operate daily, and the trip from Tōkyō to Nagano can be made in as little as 1 hour 19 minutes. When complete, the Hokuriku Shinkansen will run from Takasaki to Kanazawa to Ōsaka. The Yamagata and Akita Shinkansen lines are called mini-Shinkansen because the trains must use standard local tracks for part of the run. The Yamagata line, which began operation in 1992, runs from Tōkyō to Fukushima on Shinkansen tracks and from there to Yamagata on standard tracks. The newest Shinkansen, the Akita line, began operation in 1997 and runs from Tōkyō to Morioka on Shinkansen tracks and from there to Akita on standard tracks.

▌Technical Aspects 技術

The Shinkansen track is a conventional ballasted track バラスト軌道 between Tōkyō and Ōsaka. This track structure, however, requires a great deal of time and labor to maintain the track geometry. Consequently, concrete slab track コンクリート製スラブ軌道, which is maintenance free, was adopted for further line extensions. The Shinkansen has a DC series traction motor installed on each single-wheel axle, allowing dynamic brakes to be applied to all axles at once, and uses electric multiple-unit trains fed by AC 25 kilowatts. Automatic Train Control (ATC) 自動列車制御装置 is used to prevent collisions by maintaining a safety distance between trains and to prevent excess speeds by applying brakes automatically. All trains are continuously monitored and controlled from computer-aided traffic control systems (CTC) コムトラック in two central control rooms in Tōkyō. Electric power supply to the trains is also monitored and controlled from the same rooms by electric power dispatchers. In case of accidents or other problems, the dispatchers act promptly to secure alternative power to restore the failure.

Since it was inaugurated in 1964, the Shinkansen has had a remarkable record of high-speed operation, safety, volume of transport, and punctuality. The success of the Shinkansen revolutionized thinking about high-speed trains. It has been described as the "savior of the declining railroad industry" since its example has stimulated many other countries to take on the new construction or the modernization of railroads as national projects, among which are the French TGV, the English HST, and the Northeast Corridor Rail Improvement Project in the United States.

Subways (*chikatetsu*) 地下鉄

Japan's first underground rail service started

operating in December 1927 over a 2.2-kilometer (1.4-mi) route between Ueno and Asakusa stations in Tōkyō under the management of the Tōkyō Underground Railway Co. The line later became part of the present Ginza Line, operated by the Teito Rapid Transit Authority 帝都高速度交通営団. The rapid concentrations of population in large cities since World War II and the resulting transport congestion have led to successive subway-network-building programs in Tōkyō, Ōsaka, Nagoya, Kōbe, Sapporo, Yokohama, Kyōto, Fukuoka, and Sendai. In 1997 there were some 35 lines totaling 573.9 kilometers (356.7 mi) operating in nine cities. More than 8 million passengers a day travel on the 12 Tōkyō lines (239.6 km; 148.9 mi) and 2.6 million on the 7 Ōsaka subway lines (115.6 km; 71.8 mi). Many of the subway lines currently under construction are designed to connect directly with existing suburban surface rail networks, the intention being to ease congestion at terminus stations and to improve convenience for passengers.

Airports (*kūkō*) 空港

Commercial airports in Japan are classified by the government into three categories based on size and use. As of 1994, class 1 consisted of Japan's 4 major international airports: Tōkyō International Airport (Haneda) 東京国際空港(羽田), New Tōkyō International Airport (Narita) 新東京国際空港(成田), Ōsaka International Airport 大阪国際空港, and Kansai International Airport 関西国際空港. Class 2 comprised 25 major domestic airports (some with international service), and class 3 was composed of 48 smaller domestic airports. Besides these, there were 12 unclassified airports used jointly by commercial and military aircraft or for other purposes. Of these 89 commer-

Passenger Transport by Scheduled Flight
定期航空旅客輸送量   (in millions of persons)

Year	Domestic	International	Total
1960	1.3	0.1	1.4
1965	5.1	0.5	5.6
1970	15.4	1.7	17.1
1975	25.4	2.6	28.0
1980	40.4	4.9	45.3
1985	43.8	6.5	50.3
1990	64.5	10.9	75.4
1994	74.5	12.7	87.2

Source: Ministry of Transport.

Year	Domestic	International	Total
1960	9.0	3.2	12.2
1965	33.3	11.9	45.2
1970	116.4	51.0	167.4
1975	190.4	125.9	316.3
1980	328.7	238.2	566.9
1985	538.0	379.6	917.6
1990	684.7	619.8	1,304.5
1994	745.9	808.9	1,554.8

Source: Ministry of Transport.

cial and semicommercial airports, 53 had facilities for jet passenger aircraft.

Airport operations are regulated by the Airport Improvement Law 空港整備法 of 1956, and facilities are maintained by the government's Special Account for Airport Improvement 空港整備特別会計. Landing fees and a tax on aircraft fuel are the chief sources of revenue for airports.

Tōkyō International Airport 東京国際空港

Commonly referred to as Haneda Airport. Located on the shore of Tōkyō Bay in Ōta Ward, Tōkyō, Haneda Airport services 40 million passengers per year and is the hub of Japan's domestic air-traffic network 航空交通網. It is linked to 42 airports nationwide by approximately 520 incoming and outgoing flights 発着陸 per day. The airport began operations in 1931 as Japan's first commercial airpor 民間空港. The US military requisitioned the facility following World War II; however, from 1952, when it was restored to Japanese control, until 1978, when the New Tōkyō International Airport was opened, it was the chief gateway to Japan.

In order to expand capacity and reduce complaints about noise, Haneda Airport has undertaken a three-stage project of land reclamation and construction in Tōkyō Bay. With the completion of the second stage in 1993, a new passenger terminal 旅客ターミナル opened and the airport grew from two runways to three and from 408 hectares (1,008 acres) to 894 hectares (2,209 acres). The Tōkyō Monorail runs between Haneda Airport and Hamamatsuchō Station on the JR line.

New Tōkyō International Airport 新東京国際空港

Also known as Narita Airport. International airport located some 66 kilometers (41 mi) east of Tōkyō in the city of Narita, Chiba Prefecture. It opened in May

1978 and replaced Tōkyō International Airport as Japan's chief international airport. Construction work on the airport at Narita began in 1969, but its completion was delayed from 1971 to 1975 and its opening until 1978 because of fierce opposition from a coalition of local inhabitants and radical students.

The New Tōkyō International Airport is served by two railways, the JR line and the Keisei line. Check-in procedures for most flights can be performed at Tōkyō City Air Terminal 東京シティ=エア=ターミナル, located in Hakozaki, Chūō Ward.

The New Tōkyō International Airport's main runway measures 4,000 meters (13,120 ft) in length. Under a

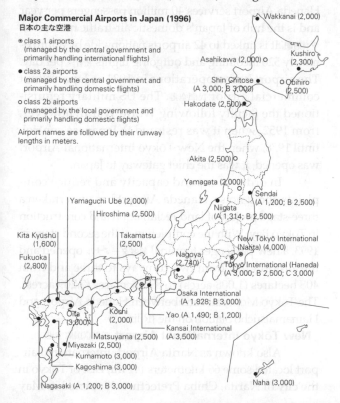

Major Commercial Airports in Japan (1996)
日本の主な空港

⊛ class 1 airports
(managed by the central government and primarily handling international flights)

● class 2a airports
(managed by the central government and primarily handling domestic flights)

○ class 2b airports
(managed by the local government and primarily handling domestic flights)

Airport names are followed by their runway lengths in meters.

Wakkanai (2,000)

Kushiro (2,300)

Asahikawa (2,000)

Shin Chitose (A 3,000; B 3,000)

Obihiro (2,500)

Hakodate (2,500)

Akita (2,500)

Yamagata (2,000)

Sendai (A 1,200; B 2,500)

Niigata (A 1,314; B 2,500)

Yamaguchi Ube (2,000)

Hiroshima (2,500)

Takamatsu (2,500)

Kita Kyūshū (1,600)

Fukuoka (2,800)

Nagoya (2,740)

New Tōkyō International (Narita) (4,000)

Tōkyō International (Haneda) (A 3,000; B 2,500; C 3,000)

Osaka International (A 1,828; B 3,000)

Ōita (3,000)

Kōchi (2,000)

Yao (A 1,490; B 1,200)

Matsuyama (2,500)

Kansai International (A 3,500)

Miyazaki (2,500)

Kumamoto (3,000)

Kagoshima (3,000)

Nagasaki (A 1,200; B 3,000)

Naha (3,000)

second-stage construction program, begun in 1987, a 2,500-meter (8,200-ft) parallel runway 平行滑走路 is being built. Upon completion, which has been delayed by continuing opposition, the area of the airport will double in size to 1,065 hectares (2,631 acres). As of January 1997, 50 airlines of 38 countries utilized the airport, with approximately 340 flights landing and departing daily. The airport annually handles some 25.4 million passengers and 1.6 million metric tons (1.8 million short tons) of air freight.

Kansai International Airport 関西国際空港

Located on an artificial island built 5 kilometers (3.1 mi) from shore in Ōsaka Bay, this airport opened in September 1994. Because of the limited size of Ōsaka International Airport 大阪国際空港 and the continuing noise complaints from surrounding residents which resulted in restrictions on operating hours, construction of a new international airport to serve the KANSAI REGION began in 1987. The Kansai International Airport has one 3,500-meter (11,483-ft) runway and is 510 hectares (1,260 acres) in size. In addition to expressway access, the airport has rail connections to Ōsaka (Nankai and JR lines) and Kyōto (JR line) and high-speed passenger boat service to Kōbe.

Expressways (*kōsoku dōro*) 高速道路

Construction of expressways in Japan began in the 1960s. Intercity expressways 都市間高速道路 are designed for a maximum speed of 120 kilometers (75 mi) per hour, although legal speed limits are usually lower. These four-lane, limited-access, divided highways have a 3.6-meter (11.8-ft) lane width.

Since the opening in 1965 of the Meishin Expressway 名神高速 between Nagoya and Kōbe, the first part of the expressway system, 5,930 kilometers (3,684 mi) had been completed by March 1996, and construction of the projected 11,520-kilometer (7,157-mi) network is expected to be finished early in the 21st century. Because of the nature of the terrain and the high concentration of housing, cultivated land, and factories along the routes, the cost of highway construction has been high in Japan relative to that in other countries, and expressway tolls are also proportionately high. However, expressways are used extensively; in fiscal 1997 average daily traffic between Tōkyō and Komaki in Aichi Prefecture was 408,000 automobiles. Of the total traffic in that year, 76 percent consisted of passenger cars and 24 percent of other vehicles. Measures are being taken to protect residents along routes against highway noise and exhaust fumes. Expressways are administered by the Japan Highway Public Corporation 日本道路公団.

Japan's Expressways (1994)
日本の高速道路

Expressway	Length (kilometers)	Vehicles per day
Dōou Expressway	270.2	89,795
Tōhoku Expressway	679.5	258,191
Kan'etsu Expressway	246.3	176,426
Jōban Expressway	175.5	171,030
Higashi Kantō Expressway	74.5	194,423
Chūō Expressway	366.8	253,319
Hokuriku Expressway	481.1	134,522
Tōmei Expressway	346.7	398,097
Meishin Expressway	189.3	235,499
Chūgoku Expressway	543.1	145,907
San'yō Expressway	358.2	162,238
Kyūshū Expressway	323.0	181,287
Other (29 expressways)	1,622.9	1,275,882
Total	5,677.1	3,676,616

Source: Japan Highway Public Corporation.

MASS COMMUNICATIONS マスコミ

Mass communications (*masukomi*) マスコミ

The Edo period (1600–1868) left Japan with a superb social base for modern mass communications in its geographically compact, culturally homogeneous, politically centralized, education-oriented, and increasingly urbanized population. The spread of democratic institutions, university education, and urban lifestyle in the 20th century created enormous markets for newspapers, magazines, and books and for the electronic media.

Structures and Functions 構造と機能

In organization, scale, and allocation of functions, the Japanese mass media have developed uniquely out of the indigenous economic and social structure and philosophical bent.

Newspapers 新聞 Competitive pressures in a basically unitary national newspaper market have led to a striking uniformity of format, content, editorial viewpoint, and reportorial style for the prefectural newspapers and the three regional "bloc" newspapers ブロック紙 as well as the five nationwide newspapers 全国紙 (the *Yomiuri shimbun* 読売新聞, *Asahi shimbun* 朝日新聞, *Mainichi shimbun* 毎日新聞, *Sankei shimbun* 産経新聞, and *Nihon keizai shimbun* 日本経済新聞). With the nationwide newspapers relying mainly on their own domestic and foreign news bureaus, Japan's two news agencies, Kyōdō News Service 共同通信社 and Jiji Press 時事通信社, play a supplementary role except for the local press. With a total monthly publication of 73 million, Japan ranked first in the world in per capita circulation of newspapers in 1996.

Broadcasting 放送 In 1926 the Japan Broadcasting Corporation (NHK) 日本放送協会(NHK) was granted a radio broadcasting monopoly under the firm control of the Ministry of Communications 逓信省. In 1950 the Broadcasting Law 放送法 made provision for a commercial sector and reorganized NHK as a strictly public service organization. Since television broadcasting started in 1953, there has been much competition between the public and private sectors of Japan's dual system. NHK is the most popular news source and provides lavish cultural and informational programming on both its general and educational channels. The five commercial chains are Nippon Television Network Corporation (NTV) 日本テレビ放送網(株); Tokyo Broadcasting System, Inc. (TBS) (株)東京放送; Television Tōkyō Channel 12, Ltd. (株)テレビ東京; Fuji Telecasting Co., Ltd. (株)フジテレビジョン; and Asahi National Broadcasting Co., Ltd. 全国朝日放送(株). These five have been strengthened by tie-ups with the five nationwide newspapers. The introduction of digital technology will greatly transform the broadcasting industry. As of 1998 digital broadcasting in Japan was being done only by two satellite broadcasting services, using communications satellites (CS). Terrestrial television stations are to begin digital broadcasts by 2000.

Advertising Expenditures by Medium (1996)
メディア別広告費 (in billions of yen)

	1985	1990	1994	1995	1996
Newspapers	8,887	13,592	11,211	11,657	12,379
Magazines	2,230	3,741	3,473	3,743	4,073
Radio	1,612	2,335	2,029	2,082	2,181
Television	10,633	16,046	16,435	17,553	19,162
Sales promotions	11,657	19,815	18,409	19,070	19,730

Source: Dentsū, Inc.

Journalists ジャーナリスト

The journalists in Japan's major media firms enjoy high professional status. Japan's highly literate public, deferential toward intellectual authority and eager for information, sustains an extensive high-grade sector of "mass quality" newspapers. The surprising homogeneity, especially in news coverage, derives from the unique organization of news gathering in Japan. The typical reporter writes not so much independent stories as raw material for reprocessing at the departmental desk, and the correspondents themselves are organized into exclusive press clubs (*kisha kurabu*) attached to all major government institutions and public figures.

Censorship and Freedom of the Press
検閲と報道の自由

The Japanese press was under constant regulation and periodic suppression from the time of the Press Ordinance of 1875 新聞紙条例 through the militaristic regime of the 1930s, the war years, and then the censorship of the Allied Occupation authorities. Democratization during the Occupation nevertheless left the press in 1952 in a far more liberated state than it had ever before experienced. Today, Japanese journalism continues to enjoy great freedom from statutory restraint, but the press has often failed to attack government and business promptly and head-on over major evils such as graft or pollution. The collaborative ties between the

Foreign News Organs and Reporters in Japan (January 1997)
日本における外国の報道機関と特派員

	News organs	Reporters
United States	69	295
United Kingdom	29	160
South Korea	24	54
France	19	43
Germany	18	37
China	16	23
Hong Kong	10	18
Russia	7	15
Australia	6	15
Italy	6	9

Source: Foreign Press Center.

Mass Communication

press and its sources in the press clubs, among club members, and between media management and big business have all joined with general group psychology to produce a more comfortable relation between journalism and established power than would be deduced from their formal adversarial relationship.

Publishing (*shuppan*) 出版
Development of Modern Publishing
近現代の出版の発達

Newspapers, magazines, and books underwent a process of Westernization after the Meiji Restoration 明治維新. Following the practice in Europe and the United States at that time, the Japanese press and newspapers formed their own unique sphere from the beginning. The rest of the printed media, such as books and magazines, formed a separate world of publishing. This division has exercised a great influence on the formation of the character of Japanese journalism.

Before World War II, freedom of the press was greatly restricted by the Publication Law of 1893 出版法, the Press Law of 1909 新聞紙法, the Peace Preservation Law of 1925 治安維持法, and other repressive laws and regulations. A large number of publishers, editors, scholars, and writers were punished and imprisoned under these laws. After World War II, however, article 21 of the 1947 constitution guaranteed freedom of speech and the press 言論の自由：出版の自由, prohibited censorship 検閲, and abolished all the laws and regulations that had controlled the press. In 1994 Japan published 48,824 new book titles.

Until 1955 weeklies had been put out by newspaper companies, but beginning with *Shūkan shinchō* (1956), publishing companies began to issue their own weeklies. With government, scholarly, and corporate publications included, the total number of magazine titles in Japan is estimated to be over 10,000. Sales of monthly and weekly magazines for 1997 totaled ¥1.57 trillion (US $13.0 billion).

The Publishing Industry 出版産業

As in the publishing industry throughout the world, the majority of Japanese publishers operate on a small scale. According to the 1998 edition of *The Almanac of Publishing* 出版年鑑, the total number of publishers in Japan was 4,612, of which publishers with capital of less than ¥5 million—or whose capital was not known—numbered 2,056 (44.6%) and those with 10 employees or fewer (or with unknown numbers) totaled 3,080 (66.8%). According to the same source, 80 percent of the new titles in Japan were published by 300 publishers.

The basic route of distribution for publications in Japan is from publisher to agent to bookstore. The basis of the sales system is fixed-price sales and consignment sales, by which the majority of publications are traded.

As of 1997, 10,233 bookstores belonged to the Japan Federation of Commercial Cooperatives of Bookstores 日本書店商業組合連合会; when nonmember stores are added, the total number exceeds 25,000. A distribution agent 取次店 connects a bookstore with a publisher and handles the distribution and return of books. Books and magazines traded by this route are considered to account for 68 percent of the total; about 70 percent are handled by the two major agencies, Tōhan Corporation and Nippon Shuppan Hambai, Inc. (abbreviated Nippan).

The buying and selling of published material by the so-called regular route has been characterized since the 1920s by strict observance of fixed

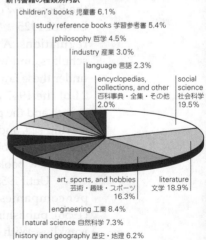

New Book Titles by Category (1995)
新刊書籍の種類別内訳

children's books 児童書 6.1%
study reference books 学習参考書 5.4%
philosophy 哲学 4.5%
industry 産業 3.0%
language 言語 2.3%
encyclopedias, collections, and other 百科事典・全集・その他 2.0%
social science 社会科学 19.5%
literature 文学 18.9%
art, sports, and hobbies 芸術・趣味・スポーツ 16.3%
engineering 工業 8.4%
natural science 自然科学 7.3%
history and geography 歴史・地理 6.2%
Total: 58,310 titles

Source: Research Institute for Publications.

retail prices and consignment sales. An antitrust law 独占禁止法 prohibits producers from compelling agents or retailers to sell at fixed prices. From its inception, however, this law exempted so-called cultural items and daily necessities and in 1953 extended exemptions to include published material as well. As a result, published materials in Japan have been sold according to price maintenance agreements 価格維持協定. The Japanese Fair Trade Commission 公正取引委員会 has begun reviewing the price maintenance system because of growing consumer pressure.

▮Postwar Reforms 第2次世界大戦後の変革

In prewar Japanese publishing circles, a clear line was drawn between publications for intellectuals and those for the masses. Since the end of the war, however, the movement toward a mass society has been symbolized by television, as well as the numerous weekly magazines created by publishing companies, and the so-called masses are no longer distinguished from the intellectual elite in the prewar sense. After 1950 best-seller fiction consisted of books of quality intended for the masses. Equality of the sexes, improvement of labor conditions, and an increase and leveling in income also stimulated the creation of a new class of readers.

What played the decisive role for the postwar publishing boom, however, was the spread of secondary-school and university education. Only 3 percent of all youths attended universities in 1940, while in 1975, 30 percent attended a university or junior college.

The 1990s has seen increasing activity in electronic publishing utilizing computer media such as CD-ROMs, IC cards, and diskettes. As of 1997 electronic publishing 電子出版 has concentrated mostly on encyclopedias and dictionaries as they are especially suited to the large volume storage and extensive search capabilities provided by computers.

Newspapers (*shimbun*) 新聞

In the vanguard of Japan's newspaper industry are several colossal national newspaper organizations that publish both morning and evening editions 朝刊：夕刊. In addition to these major national media companies, there is a host of local and special-interest newspapers 地方紙：専門紙 that also help cater to the diverse interests of the world's most literate readership.

History 歴史

The first modern newspaper was the *Nagasaki Shipping List and Advertiser*, an English paper, published twice a week beginning in 1861 by the Englishman A. W. Hansard in Nagasaki. In 1862 the Tokugawa shogunate (1603–1867) began publishing the *Kampan Batabiya shimbun*, a translated and re-edited edition of *Javasche Courant*, the organ of the Dutch government in Indonesia. These two papers contained only foreign news. Newspapers covering domestic news were first started by the Japanese in Edo (now Tōkyō), Ōsaka, Kyōto, and Nagasaki in 1868. Yanagawa Shunsan's 柳河春三 *Chūgai shimbun* 「中外新聞」, typical of these early papers and a model for later papers, carried domestic news as well as abridged translations from foreign papers. The first Japanese daily paper 日刊紙, the *Yokohama mainichi shimbun* 「横浜毎日新聞」, was launched in 1871. The *Tōkyō nichinichi shimbun* 「東京日日新聞」 (predecessor of the *Mainichi shimbun*), the *Yūbin hōchi shimbun* 「郵便報知新聞」 (predecessor of the *Hōchi shimbun*), and the oldest existing local newspaper, the *Kōchū shimbun* 「峡中新聞」 (predecessor of the *Yamanashi nichinichi shimbun*), were all begun in 1872.

Most papers published at this time were referred to as "political forums" because they demanded the establishment of a national Diet and printed political opinions at the time of the Freedom and People's Rights Movement 自由民権運動. However, after the establishment

Circulation of the Five Major National Newspapers (1996)
全国紙発行部数

(in millions of copies)

Newspapers	Morning edition	Evening edition
Yomiuri shimbun	10.15	4.40
Asahi shimbun	8.35	4.35
Mainichi shimbun	3.95	1.89
Nihon keizai shimbun	2.97	1.66
Sankei shimbun	1.94	0.96

Note: Circulation figures are for the period July-December 1996.
Source: Japan Newspaper Publishers and Editors Association.

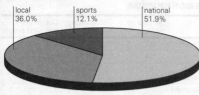

Types of Japanese Daily Newspapers (1994)
日刊紙の種類別内訳

local 36.0%　sports 12.1%　national 51.9%

Total: 52,600,000 copies per day

Note: Papers that publish both a morning and an evening edition are counted as one.

Source: Japan Newspaper Publishers and Editors Association.

of the Diet, the newspapers virtually became organs of the newly formed political parties. These newspapers were called *ōshimbun* 大新聞 (large newspapers). *Koshimbun* 小新聞 (small newspapers) were popular newspapers containing local news, human interest stories, and light fiction. The *Yomiuri shimbun*「読売新聞」, which began publishing in 1874, is a typical example. Partially because strong government pressure caused the *ōshimbun* to fail, new newspapers printing impartial news started springing up around 1880. The *Asahi shimbun*「朝日新聞」was launched in 1879 in Ōsaka, and the *Jiji shimpō*「時事新報」in 1882 in Tōkyō. The sudden increase in circulation made possible in the 1890s by the widespread use of rotary presses and the growth of advertising turned Japanese newspapers into large business enterprises.

When the Tōkyō Earthquake of 1923 関東大震災 destroyed much of Tōkyō, the Ōsaka-based *Asahi* and *Mainichi* became the two largest national newspapers 全国紙 overnight, virtually dominating the Japanese newspaper industry. The opinion-shaping activity of Japanese newspapers gradually declined as the papers became interested in profits and had to respond to a broader readership. The heavy pressures from the government and the military authorities also weakened the papers' capacity for strong editorial policy.

The press was placed under complete government control from the outbreak of the Sino-Japanese War 日中戦争 in 1937 until the end of World War II in 1945. Newsprint was rationed, and many newspapers were forced to merge. The number of newspapers dropped from 848 in 1939 to 54 in 1942.

Free competition among newspapers revived after the abolition of wartime regulations and the lifting of controls on newsprint in 1951. The system of morning and evening editions of the same paper, which had been suspended, also revived, and major papers started printing local editions 地方版. When weekly magazines 週刊誌, comic magazines 漫画雑誌, and television became popular, most general newspapers 一般紙 began to concentrate on news and advertising. In the late 1970s and 1980s Japanese newspapers greatly increased the efficiency of their operations by full computerization of all aspects of their work—reporting, editing, typesetting, and printing—and by utilizing satellite communications.

Circulation of Daily Newspapers in Selected Countries (1992)
各国の日刊紙発行部数

	Number of dailies	Circulation in thousands	Copies per thousand people
Japan*	121	72,047	574
China	74	50,520	43
South Korea	63	18,000	412
Germany	357	25,952	323
United Kingdom	101	22,100	383
France	77	11,695	205
Russia	339	57,367	387
United States	1,570	60,164	236

Note: Morning and evening editions are counted separately.
*1995.   Source: UNESCO.

▌Circulation 発行部数

According to statistics of the Japan Newspaper Publishers and Editors Association 日本新聞協会, the total circulation of daily papers as of 1997 was 53,765,803 (a morning and an evening edition are counted as one) or an average of 1.18 newspapers per household.

The five major daily general papers in order of their circulation are: *Yomiuri shimbun*, *Asahi shimbun*, *Mainichi shimbun* 「毎日新聞」, *Nihon keizai shimbun* 「日本経済新聞」, and *Sankei shimbun* 「産経新聞」. Maintaining their own nationwide home-delivery networks, they account for more than 50 percent of the entire circulation of daily general papers. The two leading newspapers, the *Yomiuri* and the *Asahi*, had circulations of 10.17 million and 8.38 million respectively, in 1997 (morning editions).

Circulation of Daily Newspapers
日刊紙発行部数

Year	Circulation (in millions)	Copies per household
1960	24.44	1.18
1970	36.30	1.24
1980	46.39	1.29
1990	51.91	1.26
1995	52.85	1.19

Source: Japan Newspaper Publishers and Editors Association.

▌Home Delivery System 宅配制度

At first, newspapers were sold on consignment to bookstores, but the *Tōkyō nichinichi shimbun* 「東京日日新聞」 initiated a home delivery system that was soon followed by other papers. The *Hōchi shimbun* 「報知新聞」 started exclusive dealerships in 1903 to distribute only its own papers nationwide. The dealers not only were responsible for delivery but also acted as subscription salesmen. News of the increase in circulation for the *Hōchi* prompted other papers to set up their own news dealerships, and the system of monopoly newspaper dealerships peculiar to Japan was created in 1930.

Broadcasting (*hōsō*) 放送

Broadcasting is defined in Japan's Broadcasting Law (放送法, 1950) and Radio Law (電波法, 1950) as "wireless communication intended for direct reception by the general public."

History of Broadcasting 放送の歴史

On 20 August 1926 the Ministry of Communications (Teishinshō 逓信者; now the Ministry of Posts and Telecommunications 郵政省) established the Nippon Hōsō Kyōkai (NHK; Japan Broadcasting Corporation 日本放送協会[NHK]). NHK monopolized the country's broadcasting industry until after World War II, but it was placed under the strict supervision of the Ministry of Communications.

After World War II all legislation suppressing freedom of speech and the press was abolished in an effort to further Japan's democratization. When the Broadcasting Law came into effect in June 1950, NHK was reorganized, and a new corporation was formed. This law also paved the way for private commercial broadcast stations 民間放送局. In April 1950 preliminary licenses were issued to a total of 16 private broadcast stations in 14 districts of the country. Despite early pessimism about their commercial viability, these ventures soon showed large profits. The way was opened for television broadcasting with the granting of a preliminary license to Nippon Television Network Corporation (NTV) 日本テレビ放送網(株) on 31 July 1952. The first actual telecast in Japan was made by NHK's Tōkyō station on

1 February 1953. In 1964 experimental telecasts from Japan to the United States were conducted via satellite.

Present-Day Broadcasting 今日の放送

Terrestrial broadcasting 地上放送 NHK operates a nationwide broadcasting network. Private broadcasting stations licensed in their respective local regions also have their own networks. In 1998 commercial television broadcasting consisted of five networks (key station and number of stations in parenthesis): JNN (Tōkyō Broadcasting System, Inc. [TBS]; 28 stations) (株)東京放送, NNN (Nippon Television Network Corporation [NTV]; 30 stations) 日本テレビ放送網(株), FNN (Fuji Telecasting Co., Ltd.; 28 stations) (株)フジテレビジョン, ANN (Asahi National Broadcasting Co., Ltd.; 26 stations) 全国朝日放送(株), and TXN (Television Tōkyō Channel 12, Ltd.; 6 stations) (株)テレビ東京. At the center of each of these networks is a news network. General programming other than news is also distributed through these networks. In 1997 there were 126 commercial television stations, 47 commercial AM radio stations, 142 commercial FM stations, and 1 shortwave station.

There are two major commercial radio broadcasting networks: the Japan Radio Network ジャパンラジオネットワーク and the National Radio Network ナショナルラジオネットワーク, both established in 1965. Commercial FM broadcasting is dominated by the Japan FM Broadcasting Association 日本FM放送協議会, which operates a nationwide network with FM Tōkyō as its key station.

The Ministry of Posts and Telecommunications 郵政省 announced the year 2000 as its target for the start of digital television transmissions by cable television ケーブルテレビ services and terrestrial television stations now using conventional analog signals. The implementation of digital broadcasting will require huge broadcasting infrastructure investments in equipment to handle the transmission and receipt of digital signals. In conjunc-

Cable and Satellite TV Subscribers
ケーブルテレビと衛星テレビの加入者数

(in thousands of subscribers)

	Cable television 1991	1995	Satellite 1994
France	891	1,497	1,010
Germany	9,899	15,808	8,320
Japan	730	2,817	5,863
United Kingdom	267	1,420	3,390
United States	52,600	65,957	3,800

Source: OECD.

tion with broadcast digitization, the government is also proceeding with deregulation 規制緩和 of the broadcast industry. This has resulted in the entry into the market of both foreign companies and Japanese companies from other industries (trading companies, electrical product companies, etc.).

Satellite broadcasting 衛星放送 In an effort to provide television service to remote areas, NHK began direct broadcasting satellite (BS) test broadcasts in 1984. Full-scale NHK BS broadcasts began in 1989 with two channels. In 1991 Japan Satellite Broadcasting, Inc. 日本衛星放送, introduced Japan's first commercial satellite broadcasting channel, called WOWOW ワウワウ. These three channels plus a channel used for experimental high-definition television (Hi-Vision) broadcasts comprise the four current BS channels. Japan's first digital audio broadcasts were begun in 1991 using part of the WOWOW signal and employing pulse code modulation (PCM) technology. The start of BS digital broadcasting is planned for 2000.

Commercial analog format communications satellite (CS) broadcasts 通信衛星放送 began in 1992. Digital CS broadcasts were started by PerfecTV パーフェクティービー (now SKY PerfecTV スカイパーフェクティービー) in 1996, and the following year a second digital CS broadcast service, called DirecTV ディレクティービー, entered the market.

Financing 財政 The ordinary operating revenues of NHK are obtained from viewer fees 受信料, government subsidies, and miscellaneous revenues from other sources, with some 98 percent of the entire revenue represented by viewer fees. The distribution of television sets, however, has almost reached the saturation point, so that it is difficult to foresee any large increase in revenue from future fees. In 1997, 36 million households were paying reception fees to NHK.

Private television broadcasting companies 民放 are showing large profits with the tremendous increase in revenue from television advertising. Advertisement expenditures 広告費 paid to television firms exceeded those paid to newspapers in 1975, and television has been the top advertising medium ever since. Subscribers to the private satellite broadcasting services pay a monthly fee.

CULTURE

Religion (*shūkyō*) 日本の宗教

Religious life in Japan is rich and varied, with a long history of interaction among a number of religious traditions. Most of the individual features of Japanese religion are not unique; the distinctiveness of Japanese religion lies in the total pattern of interacting traditions.

Many traditional Japanese beliefs and practices hark back to prehistoric customs, and most of these form the core of SHINTŌ, the only major religion indigenous to Japan. Indian BUDDHISM, the Chinese contributions of Confucianism 儒教 and Taoism 道教 (transmitted first through the cultural bridge of Korea), and, much later, Christianity キリスト教 were introduced to Japan from outside. All these foreign traditions have undergone significant transformations in a process of mutual influence with the native tradition.

The Historical Formation of Japanese Religion
日本の宗教の沿革

In Japanese religion there are not one but many deities; there is no one sacred book, but many religious scriptures; rather than emphasis on sin as disobedience to the deity there is a concern with ritual impurity 穢れ and purification 禊; one person usually participates in more than one religious tradition; there is no regular worship day but many seasonal FESTIVALS; and ethical codes are more closely related to family life and philosophy than to organized religion, while ethical shortcomings are not linked directly to divine will but are considered in terms of human imperfection.

In early Japan religious life was closely related to rice agriculture 稲作農業. Religious rites focused on seasonal celebrations anticipating and giving thanks for agricultural fertility and on venerating ancestral spirits who were considered directly responsible for fertility.

Ratio of Believers (1995)
宗教別信者内訳

Shintoism 神道系	54.1%
Buddhism 仏教系	40.5%
Christianity キリスト教系	0.7%
other religions 諸教	4.7%

Note: Percentages are based on the number of members reported by the religious organization.
Source: Agency for Cultural Affairs.

From about AD 400, Japan was developing into a centralized kingdom headed by an imperial family. From about AD 500, the high culture of China entered Japan and immediately became a major influence upon the elite class and eventually upon the common people. The tendency in Japanese history has not been "either-or" exclusivity, but rather "both-and" inclusivity, in adopting foreign cultural elements. Therefore, instead of rejecting Buddhism, the Japanese eventually incorporated it into the life of the family, making Buddhist memorial rites central to the veneration of family ancestors and directly linking Buddhist divinities to Shintō gods. Confucian notions were adopted to encourage loyalty to the emperor.

By the 8th century, local myths and traditions were largely unified around one account of creation and the descent of the emperor from the gods as seen in the *Kojiki* (712, Record of Ancient Matters) 「古事記」 and *Nihon shoki* (720, Chronicles of Japan) 「日本書紀」. Partly in reaction to the highly organized Buddhist religion, Japanese rituals and practice came to be organized as Shintō, "the Way of the gods." 神道 From this time on, Buddhism and Shintō were the major organized religions and gradually penetrated more into the lives of ordinary people. Many Shintō shrines that originated as family institutions developed into territorial shrines and eventually expanded to include branch shrines 分社 in other locales. Buddhist temples for the common people also gradually arose to fulfill the need for funerary and memorial services. From about 800 to 1400, various Buddhist sects 宗派 and Shintō schools developed. In the Edo period (1600–1868) Buddhist temples became closely allied with the power of the state, and families were required to belong to a specific temple; at about the same time, Confucian thought became important for providing the rationale for the state. With the Meiji

Restoration of 1868 明治維新, however, Shintō became prominent in justifying and maintaining the new nation-state under its emperor and was influential even in education.

The Major Features of Traditional Japanese Religion
日本の宗教の特徴

The seven major features that characterized Japanese religion until about 1900 overlapped and interlocked to form the general pattern of what is now considered traditional Japanese religion. These features can be identified briefly as follows:

Mutual interaction among several religious traditions 多様な宗教的伝統の相互作用 Typical of religious history in Japan is both a plurality of religious traditions and simultaneous or alternate participation by one person (or family). In recent times a person might be married in a Shintō shrine or Christian church, live his life according to Confucian social teachings, hold some Taoistic beliefs about "lucky" and "unlucky" 吉凶 phenomena, participate in folk festivals, and have his funeral conducted by a Buddhist temple.

Intimate relationship between man and the gods and the sacredness of nature 人と神の密接な関係と神聖なる自然 In Japan the relationship between man and the sacred 神 is very close. In addition to the specific deities represented in mythology 神話, natural phenomena and emperors and other special human beings were also considered to be sacred or *kami*. The spirits of the dead of each family, as revered ancestors, were termed either *hotoke* (Buddhas) 仏 or *kami*. In Japanese religion *kami* and Buddhas are not conceived as being in another world so much as they are thought to exist within the world of nature and in the lives of human beings. Natural phenomena such as mountains, streams, and trees were seen as expressing extraordinary power and were considered to be sacred or *kami*.

The religious significance of the family and ancestors 家と先祖の宗教的重要性 The ancient Japanese emphasis on lineage or family carried with it devotion to clan *kami* 氏神, and Confucianism, with its insistence on filial piety 孝養 and social harmony, provided a philosophical rationale for strong family ties. The home was always a center of religious practice, and this became more formalized during the Edo period, when it became customary for most homes to possess both Shintō family altars 神棚 and Buddhist altars 仏壇 for venerating ancestors. Traditional Japanese religious life was conducted by family participation rather than by individual choice.

Purification as a basic principle of religious life 宗教生活の原則としての清め Notions of purity and impurity (*kegare*) 「穢れ」 and procedures of ritual purification (*harae; misogi*) 「祓」:「禊」 in Japan have assumed an extraordinary importance and have pervaded the culture as a whole. The Japanese people have not conceptualized sin (*tsumi*) as a violation of divine commandments, but they have had a clear sense of the impurity or defilement that separates one from one's fellowmen and especially from the *kami*. The traditional observance at a Shintō shrine is to rinse the hands and mouth ceremonially as a symbolic act of purification before coming into contact with the *kami*. In Japan no one tradition dominates ethical concerns; rather each tradition contributes its concepts of ideal behavior: for Shintō, ritual purity and sincerity; for Buddhism, compassion and liberation from desire; for Confucianism, loyalty to superiors and benevolence toward inferiors.

Festivals as the major means of religious celebration 宗教的祝典としての祭り The pattern of religious activities was determined by each religious institution observing its own special festival days, in addition to annual festivals 年中行事 celebrated by families and the nation as a whole. Festivals at shrines and temples often celebrate the particular *kami* or Buddhist divinities enshrined there, but more often festivals are part of a seasonal drama reenacted every year. Shrines usually have both a spring festival and fall festival roughly coinciding with the transplanting and harvesting of rice. The time surrounding the NEW YEAR 正月 is a long festival period marked by large crowds visiting both Shintō shrines and Buddhist temples. The summer Bon Festival 盂蘭盆会 in honor of the returning spirits of the dead is observed in most Japanese homes.

Religion in daily life 日常生活における宗教 In traditional Japan, religion was not an organization apart from everyday life but closely related to every aspect of economic and social life. Rituals followed a person throughout life, from birth to marriage and death. Aesthetic pursuits such as the TEA CEREMONY 茶の湯 and FLOWER ARRANGEMENT 華道 also embodied religious notions concerning veneration of the forces of nature.

Close relationship between religion and state 宗教と国家の密接な関係 In Japan the general rule has been for religious authority to be subservient to political power. From the beginnings of Japanese history, myth has sanctioned the unity of ritual and government 祭政一致 through the notion that the *kami* created the Japanese islands as a sacred land to be ruled by a sacred emperor who was a descendant of the supreme *kami*, the sun goddess Amaterasu Ōmikami 天照大神. Cultural influence from China, especially Confucianism and Buddhism, strengthened and modified this basic pattern.

Religion in Modern Japan 現代日本の宗教

After the remarkable changes in national life of the late 19th and early 20th centuries, religion changed drastically.

In the 19th century, popular movements formed around pilgrimage associations 講 and charismatic leaders. Such groups often expanded to form the so-called new religions 新宗教. Until 1945 the government controlled religion closely, but new religious movements continued to arise and expand, and after 1945 they became the most conspicuous development of the religious scene. With urbanization and centralization, folk customs generally and folk religion 民間信仰 in particular declined. Social mobility, especially immigration to cities, tended to weaken both local ties and family relationships, in turn impinging upon organized religion.

Buddhism in Japan (Nihon *no* Bukkyō) 日本の仏教

According to the *Nihon shoki* (720, Chronicles of Japan) 「日本書紀」, Buddhism was officially introduced into Japan from Korea in 552, when the king of Paekche 百済 sent a mission to the emperor of Japan bearing presents including "an image of Śākyamuni in gold and copper" and "a number of sutras." 経典 However, current scholarship favors another traditional date for this event, 538.

The Soga family 蘇我氏 argued that Japan should accept Buddhism. Others, particularly the Mononobe family 物部氏 and the Nakatomi family 中臣氏, claimed that the native gods would be offended by the respect shown to a foreign deity. Buddhism was publicly accepted after the Soga family's political and military defeat of the Mononobe (587) and became prominent in the 7th-century reign of the empress Suiko 推古天皇 (r 593–628). Her regent, the devout Prince Shōtoku 聖徳太子 (574–622), is considered the real founder and first great patron of Buddhism in Japan. He established a number of important monasteries, among them Hōryūji 法隆寺 and Shitennōji 四天王寺.

Studies of Buddhist teachings began in earnest as six prominent schools were introduced from China during the 7th and the early 8th centuries. These were the Ritsu sect 律宗, the Kusha school 倶舎宗, the Jōjitsu school

成実宗, the Sanron school 三論宗, the Hossō sect 法相宗, and the Kegon sect 華厳宗. In the Nara period 奈良時代 (710–794), especially under the aegis of Emperor Shōmu 聖武天皇 (r 724–749), Buddhism was promoted as the state religion. Official provincial temples 国分寺 were established in each province. At Tōdaiji, the head temple, an enormous image of the Buddha was erected.

Early in the Heian period (794–1185), the Tendai sect 天台宗 and Shingon sect 真言宗 were introduced to Japan by Saichō 最澄 (767–822) and Kūkai 空海 (774–835), respectively. They received support principally from the ruling aristocratic class. At the beginning of the Kamakura period (1185–1333), ZEN Buddhism 禅宗 was introduced from China and was especially favored by the dominant military class. The Zen Buddhism Eisai 栄西 (1141–1215) introduced is called the Rinzai sect 臨済宗. The form introduced by Dōgen 道元 (1200–1253) is known as the Sōtō sect 曹洞宗. The popular Nichiren sect 日蓮宗 founded by Nichiren 日蓮 (1222–1282) and the many schools of Pure Land Buddhism 浄土教, such as the Jōdo sect 浄土宗 by Hōnen 法然 (1133–1212), the Jōdo Shin sect 浄土真宗 by Shinran 親鸞 (1173–1263) and the Ji sect 時宗 by Ippen 一遍 (1239–1289), emerged around the same time. Thus, by the 13th century, all the major sects of Japanese Buddhism still active today had emerged.

Under the Tokugawa shogunate 徳川幕府 (1603–1867), Buddhism and its network of temples were used to eradicate Christianity (*shūmon aratame*, religious inquisition 宗門改め), but Buddhism also came under the strict regulatory power of the shogunate. After the Meiji Restoration (1868), the government sought to establish Shintō as the national religion, and many Buddhist temples were disestablished (*haibutsu kishaku*, abolish the Buddha; destroy Śākyamuni 廃仏毀釈). Since then, Buddhist organizations have survived by adjusting to the developments of the modern age.

Gorintō
五輪塔

— emptiness 空
— wind 風
— fire 火
— water 水
— earth 地

A kind of small stupa that came into use about the middle of the Heian period (794-1185). A *gorintō* is composed of five distinct tiers of different shapes, each representing one of the five elements believed in esoteric Buddhism to make up the universe.

After World War II, many religious groups among the so-called *shin shūkyō* (new religions) 新宗教 were organized as lay Buddhist movements. Several of the largest of these groups (Sōka Gakkai 創価学会, Risshō Kōseikai 立正佼成会, Reiyūkai 霊友会, etc.) draw upon Nichiren's teachings and the Lotus Sutra 法華経.

Several characteristic tendencies can be seen in the history of Japanese Buddhism: (1) an emphasis on the importance of human institutions; (2) a nonrational, symbolic orientation; (3) an acceptance of the phenomenal world; (4) an openness to accommodation with ancient shamanistic practices and Shintō; and (5) the development of lay leadership.

In Tōkyō and Kyōto there are several universities established by the Buddhist sects and institutes chiefly dedicated to the study of Buddhist theology. Buddhism in Japan maintains some 77,000 temples with nearly 300,000 priests.

Zen 禅

School of East Asian Buddhism that emphasizes the practice of meditation 坐禅. The Zen (Chan in China) school arose in China out of the encounter between Buddhism and indigenous Taoist thought and was held in high regard for several centuries after having survived the persecution of Buddhism there in 845. Zen blossomed again after being brought to Japan, where it underwent further development during the Kamakura period 鎌倉時代 (1185–1333). The two major sects of Japanese Zen are the Sōtō sect (Ch: Caodong) 曹洞宗 and the Rinzai sect (Ch: Linji) 臨済宗. Though they vary in teaching and methods, both schools assign a central role to meditation as the foundation of their spiritual practice.

History 歴史

According to legend, the meditative practices that characterize Zen Buddhism were introduced to

China by an Indian monk named Bodhidharma 達磨 (d ca 532). Huineng 慧能 (638–713), the sixth patriarch of the Chan movement of the Tang dynasty 唐 (618–907), is considered to be the actual establisher of Zen in China. *The Platform Sutra* 「六祖壇経」, ascribed to Huineng, clarified the essential traits of the Chan school of Buddhism. The so-called five houses of the Chan tradition were established toward the end of the Tang dynasty and during the period of the Five Dynasties (907–960). Two of these schools, the Linji and Caodong, endured and were transplanted to Japan.

The introduction of the Chan school to Japan was one of the most important events in Japanese religious history. Together with the proclamation of faith in the Buddha Amida 阿弥陀 and the rise of the Nichiren sect 日蓮宗, it marked a renewal of Buddhism during the Kamakura period. Although Chinese Zen masters came to Japan and attempted to propagate the Chan tradition, it did not develop into a major branch of Japanese Buddhism until the time of Eisai 栄西 (1141–1215) and Dōgen 道元 (1200–1253). Both of them studied the way of Zen in China. Upon their return to Japan, Eisai founded the Rinzai sect in Japan and Dōgen founded the Sōtō sect 曹洞宗.

The achievements of the Rinzai school were conspicuous in the nation's imperial capital, Kyōto, and the shogunal capital, Kamakura. These cities saw the rise of the Five Great Temples 五山, which were active cultural centers as well as sites of religious practice. Abbots of these monasteries were often granted the title "national teacher" 国師 by the imperial court. Eisai, after founding Japan's first Rinzai temple, Shōfukuji 聖福寺, in Hakata (now in Fukuoka Prefecture) in 1195, became the first abbot of Jufukuji 寿福寺 in Kamakura and then of Kenninji 建仁寺 in Kyōto, both of which were to become part of the Gozan system 五山.

The most outstanding Japanese figure in Rinzai Zen during this early period was Enni Bennen 円爾弁円 (1202–1280), who returned from a stay in China with the seal 印可 of enlightenment of the Linji (Rinzai) school. He served as head of the Kyōto temple Tōfukuji and at the same time undertook reform measures at Kenninji. A characteristic of this phase of Rinzai Zen in Japan was the activity of both Chinese and Japanese monks. In the shogunal capital of Kamakura, the Chinese masters Rankei Dōryū 蘭渓道隆 (1213–1278) and Mugaku Sogen 無学祖元 (1226–1286) founded Kenchōji and Engakuji 円覚寺, respectively, and in Kyōto temples such as Daitokuji 大徳寺, Nanzenji 南禅寺, and Tenryūji 天竜寺 became influential centers of Japanese culture.

It was in China that Dōgen attained enlightenment and the seal of approval to succeed his master Rujing 如浄 (1163–1228) in the Sōtō lineage. After his sojourn in China, Dōgen was first active in small temples near Kyōto. He built the first completely independent Zen temple and meditation hall, Kōshō Hōrinji 興聖宝林寺, in 1233. Later, distraught by the hostility and political intrigues of the Tendai sect, he established Eiheiji 永平寺 in 1243 in the mountains of Echizen Province (now Fukui Prefecture), which became the center of the Sōtō school. Another important temple of the Sōtō school was Sōjiji 総持寺, founded by Keizan Jōkin 瑩山紹瑾 (1268–1325) in 1321 in Noto Province (now Ishikawa Prefecture).

During the Muromachi period (1333–1568) Chinese cultural influence on Japan reached its highest level. Zen displayed extraordinary vitality and spread broadly. The temple Myōshinji 妙心寺, established in 1337 in Kyōto, became a model for the strict discipline espoused by its first abbot, Kanzan Egen 関山慧玄 (1277–1360). The most famous monk of the time was Musō Soseki 夢窓疎石 (1275–1351). He was spiritual mentor to emperors and military rulers. Soseki was instrumental in the establishment of the Gozan system and, aided by his political associations, contributed to the spread of Rinzai-sect Zen throughout Japan.

During the Muromachi period Zen exerted a formative influence on the arts of ink painting 水墨画, NŌ drama, the TEA CEREMONY 茶の湯, FLOWER ARRANGEMENT 華道, and landscaping. Gozan literature 五山文学 (secular writings in both poetry and prose), cultivated by monks of the Gozan temples, had a profound influence on the culture of the ruling class.

The Edo period (1600–1868) afforded peace and an environment beneficial to the popularization of Zen. A third branch of Zen, the Ōbaku sect 黄檗宗, was introduced to Japan during the Edo period by the Chinese master Yinyuan (J: Ingen 隠元; 1592–1673). Its practice, developed during the Ming dynasty (1368–1644), is a combination of Zen and *nembutsu*. The Chinese architecture and ornamentation of the Ōbaku sect's central temple, Mampukuji in Uji attracted much interest.

Outstanding among Rinzai monks at the beginning of the Edo period were Takuan Sōhō 沢庵宗彭 (1573–1645) and Bankei Yōtaku 盤珪永琢 (1622–1693). Takuan taught the affinity between Zen and swordsmanship; Bankei was responsible for making Zen accessible to the simplest of the unlettered. Hakuin 白隠 (1686–1769), one of the greatest Japanese Rinzai monks, was also renowned as an artist of exceptional achievement. His life represents a pinnacle in the history of Zen mysticism, and no other Zen master is thought to have articulated such a wealth of inner experience.

After the Meiji Restoration of 1868, the Meiji government favored the Shintō religion and ordered that all syncretic associations with Buddhism be dissolved. Though adversely affected by this decree, Buddhism was already deeply rooted in Japan and soon regained a position of importance. The most prominent Rinzai fig-

full lotus position

half lotus position

Burmese position

using a *seiza* bench

seiza position

an alternative approach

ure of this period was Imakita Kōsen 今北洪川 (1816–1892), who became the abbot of Engakuji 円覚寺 in Kamakura in 1875. His successor, Shaku Sōen 釈宗演 (1859–1919), is known as the teacher of Daisetz T. Suzuki 鈴木大拙 (1870–1966), Zen's principal exponent in the West.

Practice and Enlightenment 修行と悟り

Zen practice primarily consists of meditation in the lotus posture 蓮華坐, known in Japanese as *zazen*, and the study of *kōan*. Practice within the Sōtō school emphasizes the sitting meditation of *zazen*. The Rinzai school also acknowledges the value of *zazen*; however, it encourages its practitioners to exhaust their thinking in the contemplation of riddlelike *kōan* to progress in meditation.

Meditation in the lotus posture 蓮華坐の瞑想

Zazen is not entirely of Zen origin. Its basic form is taken from the Indian tradition of yoga. The practitioner sits with legs crossed and drawn in, and back perfectly upright. Zen recommends breathing in a natural, rhythmical way with a prolonged exhalation. By shutting out all sense impressions and conscious thinking, the Zen practitioner seeks to attain the highest possible state of mental concentration.

Zazen can also be said to represent the enlightened state of mind itself. This conception is found particularly in the teachings of Dōgen and his school. The lotus posture is the external sign of enlightenment 悟り, just as the Buddha Śākyamuni 釈迦 and all Buddhas sitting in this posture reveal the enlightened Buddha-nature.

Kōan study 公案

The study of questions for meditation, *kōan*, began in China. The grotesque events, bizarre scenes, exchanges 問答 between master and disciple, paradoxical expressions, and words of wisdom that make up the content of the *kōan* stem from the early period of Chinese Zen.

A *kōan* cannot be solved rationally. The practitioner is obliged to "hold" the *kōan* constantly in mind, day and night. Concentration increases until the tension causes rational thinking to give way under the pressure and a breakthrough occurs. This is the "turn back to the roots of consciousness" that opens the mind to a new way of seeing. Concentration, confrontation with an inescapable situation, and a breakthrough compose the psychological progression in this practice. Because this practice can be traumatic and requires careful monitoring to advance, *kōan* practice cannot be undertaken without the personal guidance of the master in private interviews.

It was the Japanese master Hakuin who perfected the *kōan* system. His famous *kōan* "What is the sound of one hand clapping?" 「隻手(片手)の音声」 uniquely displays the paradoxical character of the enlightenment experience: "When you clap your hands together a sound arises. Listen to the sound of one hand."

Enlightenment 悟り *Satori* is a mystical experience that does not lend itself to definition. The inner experience can only be described and interpreted. Certain characteristics are clearly evident in descriptions of *satori*, and the suddenness of the experience has been set down as one mark of Zen enlightenment. Many accounts of *satori* describe it as a merging or becoming one with the whole universe. Feelings of ecstasy accompany the experience of total unity or oneness. A surging joy—what Buddhists call "dharma rapture" 法悦—overcomes the enlightened person who, completely forgetting the self, feels at one with everything. One who experiences enlightenment is thought to go beyond the trivial self of usual consciousness.

The Zen Movement in the West 西洋における禅

The numerous writings and lectures in North America and Europe of D. T. Suzuki introduced Zen

Buddhism to the Western public and awakened much interest and appreciation for it. Today, scholars in a variety of disciplines carry on the research he began on Zen Buddhism, but perhaps his influence is most strongly felt in the meditation movement of our day.

There are various schools and lineages within Zen Buddhism, and consequently a wide variation in practices. Different forms of Zen meditation have found their way to the West, and Zen centers 禅センター have been established in North America and European countries, especially in Britain, France, and Germany.

Nourished within the great Asian cultures of India and China and reaching maturity in Japan, Zen has found a deep resonance in the West.

Shintō 神道

Japan's indigenous religion. The term Shintō first appears in the historical chronicle *Nihon shoki* (720, Chronicles of Japan) 「日本書紀」, where it refers to religious observance, the divinities, and shrines, but not until the late 12th century was it used to denote a body of religious doctrines. The worship of *kami* slowly emerged at the dawn of Japanese history, crystallized as an imperial religious system during the Nara (710–794) and Heian (794–1185) periods, and subsequently was in constant interaction with Buddhism 仏教 and Confucianism 儒教. This interaction gave birth to various syncretic cults that combined the worship of *kami* with the imported religions. In the Muromachi (1333–1568) and Edo (1600–1868) periods, however, there was a revival of Shintō as the "Ancient Way," and an attempt was made to pare away all foreign influences. This expurgated system became the state religion 国家宗教 of Japan during the Meiji period (1868–1912), but in 1945 Shintō was disestablished and again became one among other forms of worship.

Shintō can be regarded as a two-sided phenomenon. On the one hand it is a loosely structured set of practices, creeds, and attitudes rooted in local communities, and on the other it is a strictly defined and organized religion at the level of the imperial line and the state.

Origins and Formative Period 起源と形成期

Artifacts of the Yayoi period 弥生時代 (ca 300 BC–ca AD 300), during which important population movements occurred and contacts with the continent intensified, show that religious life was becoming complex. Wetland agriculture necessitated stable communities, and agricultural rites 農耕儀礼 that later played an important role in Shintō were developed.

The Kofun period 古墳時代 (ca 300–710) was marked by influences from the continent and by the emergence of Japan as a nation. The 100 or so Japanese "kingdoms" mentioned in the late-3rd-century Chinese chronicle *Wei zhi* 「魏志」 were gradually unified as relationships of clientage and allegiance were formed around the leaders of the powerful Yamato clan 氏, from which developed the imperial line. Not only the Yamato kings, but also the chiefs of major clans (*uji*)—each worshiping its own tutelary divinity 氏神—were buried in stone chambers covered by earthen mounds (*kofun*) and accompanied by swords, curved gemstones 勾玉, and mirrors, suggestive of the myth of the three imperial regalia 三種の神器 (three sacred objects that are the symbols of the legitimacy and authority of the emperor). It was during this period that the Ise Shrine 伊勢神宮 and Izumo Shrine 出雲大社, the most important shrines of the imperial tradition of Shintō, were established.

Imperial legitimacy, based on mythical, ritual, and religious coherence, was established through the compilation of the histories *Kojiki* (712, Record of Ancient Matters) 「古事記」 and *Nihon shoki*. The centrality of religious practices to the *ritsuryō* (legal codes) system

律令制 of government, created after the Taika Reform 大化の改新 (645) and under which all the lands and people of Japan belonged to the emperor, is reflected in the fact that the Office of Shintō Worship 神祇官 was in form, if not in practice, preeminent over the Grand Council of State 太政官. The Shintō rituals surrounding the imperial family and its satellite clans were codified in the early 10th century in the Engi Shiki (Procedures of the Engi Era) 延喜式. Imperial Shintō thus achieved the status of a coherent religion, with a system of myths, rituals, sacerdotal lineages, and shrines.

The official recognition of Buddhism by Empress Suiko 推古天皇 (r 593–628) in 594 and its acceptance by the upper strata of society not only contributed to the systematization of the traditions that later came to be known as Shintō, but also initiated a process of syncretism that was formalized in the medieval period (mid-12th–16th centuries). At the beginning of the 8th century, Buddhist temples were already being built on or next to the grounds of Shintō shrines and were called *jingūji* (literally, "shrine-temples") 神宮寺. Buddhist monks considered the Shintō divinities 神 to be in need of salvation and read and lectured on the Buddhist sutras in front of Shintō shrines.

Crucial developments in the interaction between Shintō and Buddhism occurred during the Heian period, following the introduction from China of the Tendai sect 天台宗 by Saichō (767–822) and esoteric Shingon teachings by Kūkai (774–835), founder of the Shingon sect 真言宗. The Tendai sect was permeated by Shingon doctrines after Saicho died, and the two sects established a close relationship with Shintō, resulting in the development of syncretic ritual and philosophical systems in the medieval period.

The Medieval Period 中世

Of several pivotal theories of amalgamation

introduced by Buddhism, the *honji suijaku* ("original prototype and local manifestation") 本地垂迹 theory played a key role in the evolution of Shintō-Buddhist relationships. At its core lies the notion that Shintō divinities are manifestations of Buddhas and bodhisattvas. Hence worship of a *kami* was worship of a Buddha in its *kami* form. Associations between Shintō divinities and Buddhas, such as that which obtained between Amaterasu Ōmikami, chief divinity of the Ise Shrine, and Dainichi, were established at the level of particular shrines and temples, and each devised its own system of rituals and practices surrounding its syncretic pantheon. Legends explaining the origin of these associations and descriptions of ritual systems were recorded in illustrated handscrolls 絵巻物. There also developed between the 13th and 19th centuries a vast body of mythicohistorical and philosophical treatises composed by scholarly monks and priests. Its major categories are treatises based on schools of Buddhism, especially the Tendai and Shingon sects; treatises based on shrine traditions; and treatises written by Shintō priests. Examples of the first category are works dealing with Sannō Shintō 山王神道 and Sannō Ichijitsu Shintō 山王一実神道, which arose from the Tendai sect, and Ryōbu Shintō 両部神道, which arose from the Shingon sect. The second category includes works of cults that originated at major shrines, such as the Kumano Sanzan Shrines 熊野三山神社, Iwashimizu Hachiman Shrine 石清水八幡宮, and Kasuga Shrine 春日大社. The third category is represented by works of the imperial tradition of Shintō, such as Watarai Shintō 度会神道 at the Ise Shrine and Yuiitsu Shintō 唯一神道 at the Yoshida Shrine 吉田神社, that evince a reaction to Buddhist influence.

The Edo Period 江戸時代

There developed in the Edo period a shift of Shintō away from Buddhism and a rapprochement

Shintō Architecture
神道建築

Sumiyoshi style 住吉造
Sumiyoshi Shrine, Ōsaka

Ōtori style 大鳥造
Ōtori Shrine, Ōsaka

shimmei style 神明造
Ise Inner Shrine, Mie Prefecture

Izumo Taisha style 大社造
Kamosu Shrine, Shimane Prefecture

nagare style 流造
Kamo Mioya Shrine, Kyōto

Kasuga style 春日造
Kasuga Shrine, Nara

Hachiman style 八幡造
Usa Hachiman Shrine, Ōita
Prefecture

gongen style 権現造
Tōshōgū, Tochigi Prefecture

with Neo-Confucianism. At the same time scholars of the Kokugaku (National Learning) 国学 movement attempted, through rigorous philological study of old texts, to gain new insights into the culture and religious beliefs of ancient Japan as they had existed before the introduction of Confucianism and Buddhism.

The Meiji Period and After 明治時代から現代まで

The 19th century was a crucial turning point in Shintō history: on the one hand a number of religious movements emerged to form Sect Shintō 教派神道, and on the other the expurgated imperial tradition of Shintō became the state religion, giving to the Meiji Restoration of 1868 the superficial appearance of a return to the Age of the Gods. The system of national shrines was reinstated, as well as the classical Office of Shintō Worship 神祇官. Shrines were supported by the government, and Shintō, whose doctrines were taught in schools, took on an increasingly nationalistic coloration. After Japan's defeat in World War II, State Shintō 国家神道 was disestablished and replaced by shrine Shintō 神社神道, which represents the bulk of Shintō shrines at the regional and local levels.

Industrialization and fundamental social changes are now confronting Shintō with what may be its greatest challenge.

Shintō Worship and Ritual 神道と儀式

Shintō practice is circumscribed within the context of sacred space and sacred time. The oldest known form of sacred space is a rectangular area covered with pebbles, surrounded by stones, and marked off by a rope linking four corner pillars; in the middle of this area is a stone (*iwasaka* 磐境 or *iwakura* 磐座), a pillar, or a tree (*himorogi* 神籬). This ritually purified place where divinities were invoked (*kanjō* 勧請) was located in the midst of a sacred grove. The typical shrine (*jinja* 神社) is located near the source of a river at the foot of a mountain. Surrounded by a fence (*tamagaki* 玉垣), its entrance is marked by a wooden gate (*torii* 鳥居) of simple style, on which a rope (*shimenawa* 注連縄) has been fixed.

The etymology of the term *kami* 神, which is often rendered as "deity" or "god" but is translated here as "divinity," is unclear. The Shintō pantheon consists of the *yaoyorozu no kami* (literally, "800 myriads of divinities") 八百万の神. Natural phenomena—wind, sun, moon, water, mountains, trees—are *kami*. Certain *kami* are divinized ancestors or great figures of the past, and until 1945 the emperor was regarded as divine.

Each *kami* is endowed with an efficient force called *tama*, which is the object of religious activity and may be seen as violent (*aramitama* 荒御霊) or peaceful (*nigimitama* 和御霊). *Tama*, the force that supports all life, dwells in human beings as *tamashii* 魂 and departs at the time of death. The *tama* of a *kami* is called upon at the outset of a ceremony to listen to the praise of the community and to its wishes. It is then offered food, praised again, and sent back. During ceremonies the *tama* of a divinity is thought to invest itself in the sacred tree or stone described above, or, more commonly, in a stone, root, branch, sword, mirror, or other object that is kept out of sight in a shrine.

Rituals and ceremonies are performed at each shrine by priests or by a rotating group of community members, on a cyclical and yearly basis.

The other central aspect of Shintō ritual is purification 清め. Grounded in mythology, it takes two forms: *misogi* 「禊」, purification from contact with sullying elements 穢れ such as disease or death, and *harae* 「祓」, the restoration of proper relationships after wrongdoing, through the offering of compensation.

Ritual implements, such as the folded paper strips 紙垂 that are affixed to ropes, gates, and sacred trees, and offerings of hemp, ramie, salt, and rice derive from the tradition of *harae* and serve the function of *mis-*

ogi. The emphasis on purity in Shintō worship is also manifested in the custom of undergoing a period of interdiction 忌み：潔斎 of as long as 30 days, which requires avoidance of contact with death, disease, menstruating women, and disfigured persons and abstention from sexual activity and the eating of meat, as well as adherence to conventions in food preparation, clothing, and bathing.

Shintō and the Arts 神道と美術

Important objects of Shintō art are the artifacts found in archaeological sites, such as polished gemstones 玉：勾玉, mirrors, swords, earthenware statuettes 土偶, and other ritual implements. It has been suggested that wooden sculptures representing anthropomorphic divinities owed their appearance to the introduction of Buddhism, or, perhaps, to Chinese influence in general. In any case, a number of statues that have been preserved are of extreme beauty, characterized by august simplicity (those in the Matsunoo Shrine 松尾大社 and Kumano Hayatama Shrine 熊野速玉大社), or by stern but refined elegance (Tamayori Hime 玉依姫命像 of the Yoshino Mikumari Shrine 吉野水分神社). A type of painting used in syncretic ritual is the shrine mandala 神道曼荼羅. Depicting shrine-temple complexes, such mandalas served as maps for mental pilgrimages and as objects of meditation. Famous examples are the Fuji mandala 富士曼荼羅 of the Fuji Hongū Sengen Shrine 富士山本宮浅間神社, the Kasuga Honjibutsu mandala 春日本地仏曼荼羅 of the Tōkyō National Museum, and the Kumano Nachi mandala 熊野那智曼荼羅 of the Tōkei Shrine 闘鶏神社.

Shrines 神社

A Shintō shrine is an enclosed area containing a wooden sanctuary and several auxiliary buildings where Shintō rites 神道儀式 are performed and prayers offered. The shrine is the focal point of organized Shintō religious practice, including annual festivals 年祭 and

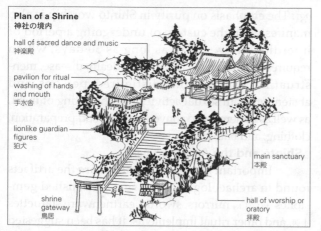

Plan of a Shrine
神社の境内

hall of sacred dance and music
神楽殿

pavilion for ritual washing of hands and mouth
手水舎

lionlike guardian figures
狛犬

main sanctuary
本殿

shrine gateway
鳥居

hall of worship or oratory
拝殿

kagura (sacred dance and music) 神楽. In urban areas it provides a sense of community to those living within its parish. In rural areas it tends to create a feeling of kinship among villagers by stressing the common tie that all have to the shrine deity.

A typical medium-size shrine might be laid out as follows: Toward the rear of the shrine precinct 境内, which is often rectangular and surrounded by a fence marking it off as a sanctified area, stands the *honden* (main sanctuary) 本殿, which houses the *shintai*, a sacred object in which the spirit of the deity (*kami*) is believed to reside. Usually more than one deity is enshrined. Directly in front of the *honden* is the *haiden* (hall of worship or oratory) 拝殿, where the priests conduct their rituals and individuals make their offerings. Worshipers announce their presence to the deity or deities enshrined in the *honden* by clapping their hands and tugging on a heavy bell rope hanging from the eaves of the *haiden*. A wooden box stands in front of the *haiden* to receive money offerings. The interior of the *haiden* may be entered by laymen only on special ritual occasions, and the *honden* only by priests on rare occasions. At the entrance to the shrine stands a *torii*, the characteristic shrine gateway 鳥

The Four Main Styles of Torii
鳥居の様式

kasagi 笠木

nuki 貫

shimmei style 神明鳥居

Ise style 伊勢鳥居

shimagi 島木

gakuzuka 額束

myōjin style 明神鳥居

ryōbu style 両部鳥居

居. A pair of highly stylized stone lions called *komainu* 狛犬 stand guard in front of the gate or *haiden*.

Christianity (Kirisutokyō) キリスト教

Christianity was introduced into Japan in the middle of the 16th century. The religion was generally tolerated until the beginning of the 17th century, but the Tokugawa shogunate 徳川幕府 (1603–1867) eventually proscribed it and persecuted its adherents. When relations with the West were restored in the middle of the 19th century, Christianity was reintroduced and has continued to exist in Japan with varying fortunes. In premodern Japan Christianity and Christians were called Kirishitan, from the Portuguese "Christão." キリシタン

Introduction to Japan 日本伝来

Portuguese traders first reached Japan in 1543, to be followed by the Jesuit イエズス会 missionary 宣教師 Francis Xavier, who arrived in 1549 with two companions. Xavier's preaching met with some success, although his efforts were hampered by the language barrier. Reinforcements arrived to continue his work and were in general well received by local rulers, who often associated them with the lucrative Portuguese trade. Activity was concentrated in Kyūshū, especially Nagasaki. In 1563 Ōmura Sumitada 大村純忠 became the first *daimyō* 大名 to receive baptism 洗礼, and by 1579 no fewer than six *daimyō* had been converted (Christian *daimyō*) キリシタン大名. In 1579 the Jesuit Alessandro Valignano arrived to conduct the first of three inspection tours of the mission. When he left in 1582, he was accompanied by four boys who formed an embassy to Rome on behalf of the Christian *daimyō* of Kyūshū (Mission to Europe of 1582) 天正遣欧使節.

By this time Christianity had attracted the attention of national figures. The national unifier Oda Nobunaga 織田信長 favored the missionaries and granted them generous concessions. His successor, Toyotomi Hideyoshi 豊臣秀吉, continued this policy until 1587, when, on realizing the extent of Christian influence in Kyūshū, he abruptly ordered missionaries to leave the country. The Jesuits were eventually joined by Spanish Franciscan フランシスコ会 friars; while the new influx added impetus to evangelization, national rivalries gave rise to unseemly quarrels among the religious orders.

Martyrdoms 殉教

In 1596 the Spanish ship *San Felipe* foundered off Shikoku and the Japanese confiscated its rich cargo (San Felipe Incident) サン=フェリペ号事件. A controversy among Japanese, Jesuits, and friars resulted; Toyotomi Hideyoshi once more turned anti-Christian and condemned to death the Franciscans and their parishioners in Kyōto. Twenty-six Christians (Twenty-Six Martyrs) 二十六聖人—both foreigners and Japanese—were crucified at Nagasaki in 1597. No further hostile action was taken, and missionary work continued unobtrusively. By this time the Church had reached its greatest expansion, with the number of Christians being estimated at about 300,000. Tokugawa Ieyasu 徳川家康, who became the de facto ruler in 1600, was at first willing to tolerate the missionaries' presence for the sake of the profitable Portuguese trade, but the arrival of Protestant プロテスタント Dutch and English merchants allowed him to act more freely against the Catholic missionaries. As the final showdown between Ieyasu and Toyotomi Hideyori, son of the late Hideyoshi, approached, Ieyasu turned against the Church, knowing that his rival commanded considerable support in western Japan, where Christian influence was strongest. Ieyasu was victorious, and in 1614 the Tokugawa shogunate ordered missionaries to leave the country; most of them departed, but some 40, including a few Japanese priests, remained to continue their work under cover.

Persecution and Suppression 迫害と禁教

Within a few years organized persecution commenced. In 1622, 55 Christians were executed at Nagasaki, and two years later 50 were burned alive in Edo (now Tōkyō). A total of 3,000 believers are estimated to have been martyred; this figure does not include the many who died as a result of sufferings in prison or in exile. In 1633 some 30 missionaries were executed, and by 1637 only 5 were left at liberty. The Shimabara Uprising 島原の乱 of 1637–1638, which was seen as a Christian-inspired rebellion, prompted the government to sever contacts with the West, except for some merchants of the Dutch East India Company オランダ東インド会社, confined to Dejima, an artificial island constructed in Nagasaki Harbor. Subsequent missionary attempts to enter and work in the country were unsuccessful.

The Japanese are noted for their religious tolerance, and the persecution was occasioned by social and political rather than purely religious factors. The shogunate was on the alert for any coalition of disaffected elements that might threaten its hegemony, and Christianity was viewed as a possible catalyst.

Reintroduction 再伝来

Japan's period of isolation ended in the mid-19th century, when Westerners were again allowed to enter the country. In 1859 a Catholic priest took up an appointment as interpreter for the French consulate in Edo, and in the same year representatives of three Protestant churches reached Japan. Ostensibly these ministers came to serve foreign residents, but their true aim was to begin direct work among the Japanese.

Social Activity 社会活動

At the beginning of the 20th century Christians made a notable contribution to the foundation of the socialist and trade union movements in an effort to solve the grave social problems caused by rapid industrialization. Many of the founding members of the Social Democratic Party (社会民主党; 1901) were active Christians. A Christian, Suzuki Bunji, founded the Yūaikai or Friendship Association 友愛会, in 1912; this later developed into the Nihon Rōdō Sōdōmei, or Japan Federation of Labor 日本労働総同盟. Despite this contribution at the time of their foundation, many of these movements were later split by disputes and much of the initial Christian influence was weakened or lost.

War and Recovery 第2次世界大戦と復興

The growing spirit of nationalism in the 1930s raised problems of conscience for Christians, especially when the authorities urged attendance at Shintō shrines as "a civil manifestation of loyalty." Foreign missionaries of all churches were interned or repatriated at the outbreak of World War II or at best allowed limited freedom. In 1941 government pressure led to the formation of the Nihon Kirisuto Kyōdan, or United Church of Christ in Japan 日本基督教団, a union of some 30 Protestant churches. After the war some churches withdrew from the union, but it is still regarded as the most influential Protestant body today.

Christianity Today 今日のキリスト教

Christianity in Japan is characterized by unobtrusive activity, with emphasis still placed on education as a means of spreading the gospel message. In 1990 Christians numbered some 1,075,000, or less than 1 percent of the population. There were 436,000 Catholics カソリック with some 800 parishes in 16 dioceses, while Protestants プロテスタント numbered 639,000 with nearly 7,000 churches.

AESTHETICS 美学

Fūryū 風流

This term refers to the refined taste of a cultivated, sophisticated person and to works of art and other things associated with such persons. The word was derived from the Chinese term *fengliu*, which literally meant "good deportment and manner." After reaching Japan around the 8th century, it was employed in a more aesthetic sense, referring to the refined manners of an urbane person and later to all things regarded as elegant, tasteful, or artistic. The term *fūga* 風雅 is sometimes employed in the same sense as *fūryū*, but, in general, *fūryū* is a more inclusive term, referring not just to poetry but to all the arts.

In the 12th century *fūryū* began to follow two separate lines of semantic evolution. In one, *fūryū* was applied to the more earthy, showy beauty manifest in popular arts. In the other, men attempted to discover *fūryū* in the beauty of landscape GARDENS, FLOWER ARRANGEMENT 生け花, ARCHITECTURE, and Chinese nature poetry. This latter trend gave birth to the TEA CEREMONY 茶の湯 in the Muromachi period (1333–1568).

In the modern era Kōda Rohan 幸田露伴 endeavored to achieve a union of love, art, and religion in the name of *fūryū* in the short story "Fūryūbutsu"「風流仏」(1889). In *Kusamakura* (1906; tr *The Three-Cornered World*, 1965)「草枕」the novelist Natsume Sōseki 夏目漱石 attempted to revitalize the concept by injecting it with compassion and humanism.

Wabi 侘

An aesthetic and moral principle advocating the enjoyment of a quiet, leisurely life free from worldly concerns. Originating in the medieval eremitic tradition, it emphasizes a simple, austere type of beauty and a serene, transcendental frame of mind. It is a central concept in the aesthetics of the tea ceremony and is also manifest in some works of WAKA 和歌, *renga* 連歌, and HAIKU 俳句. Its implications partly coincide with those of SABI 寂 and FŪRYŪ 風流.

The word *wabi* was derived from the verb *wabu* (to languish) 佗ぶ and the adjective *wabishi* (lonely, comfortless) 佗びし, which initially denoted the pain of a person who fell into adverse circumstances. But ascetic literati of the Kamakura (1185–1333) and Muromachi (1333–1568) periods developed it into a more positive concept by making poverty and loneliness synonymous with liberation from material and emotional worries and by turning the absence of apparent beauty into a new and higher beauty. These new connotations of *wabi* were cultivated especially by masters of the TEA CEREMONY, such as Sen no Rikyū 千利休 (1522–1591), who sought to elevate their art by associating it with the spirit of ZEN and stressed the importance of seeking richness in poverty and beauty in simplicity.

Sabi 寂

Poetic ideal fostered by Bashō 芭蕉 (1644–1694) and his followers in *haikai* 俳諧 (HAIKU), though the germ of the concept and the term existed long before them. *Sabi* points toward a medieval aesthetic combining elements of old age, loneliness, resignation, and tranquillity, yet the colorful and plebeian qualities of Edo-period (1600–1868) culture are also present. At times *sabi* is used synonymously or in conjunction with WABI, an aesthetic ideal of the TEA CEREMONY.

Fujiwara no Toshinari 藤原俊成 (1114–1204), the first major poet to employ a *sabi*-related word (the verb *sabu*) in literary criticism, stressed its connotations of loneliness and desolation, pointing to such images as frost-withered reeds on the seashore. With later medieval artists such as Zeami 世阿弥 (1363–1443), Zenchiku 禅竹 (1405–1468), and Shinkei 心敬 (1406–1475), the implications of *sabi* focused so heavily on desolation that the emerging beauty seemed almost cold. Underlying this aesthetic was the cosmic view typical of medieval Buddhists, who recognized the existential loneliness of all men and tried to resign themselves to, or even find beauty in, that loneliness.

Iki and sui (iki to sui) 粋と粋(いきとすい)

Aesthetic and moral ideals of urban commoners in the Edo period 江戸時代 (1600–1868). The concept of *sui* was cultivated initially in the Ōsaka area during the late 17th century, while *iki* prevailed mostly in Edo (now Tōkyō) during the early 19th century. Aesthetically both pointed toward an urbane, chic, bourgeois type of beauty with undertones of sensuality. Morally they envisioned the tasteful life of a person who was wealthy but not attached to money, who enjoyed sensual pleasure but was never carried away by carnal desires, and who knew all the intricacies of earthly life but was capable of disengaging himself from them. In their insistence on sympathetic understanding of human feelings, *sui* and *iki* resembled the Heian courtiers' ideal of *aware* (see MONO NO AWARE), yet they differed from it in their inclusion of the more plebeian aspects of life.

In modern Japanese *sui* is usually written with a Chinese character meaning "pure essence" but other characters like "sour" 酸, "to infer" 推, "water" 水, and "leader" 帥 were also used for transcribing the word. *Sui* comprised all these meanings: it described the language and deportment of a person who fully knew the sour taste of this life and was able to infer other people's suffering, adapt himself to various human situations with the shapelessness of water, and become a leader in taste and fashion for his contemporaries.

Iki originally denoted "spirit" or "heart." 意気 Later it came to mean "high spirit" 威勢のいい or "high heart" 元気のいい and referred also to the way in which a high-spirited person talked, behaved, or dressed. As it became expressive of the Edo commoners' ideal, its connotations were affected by the Ōsaka concept of *sui* and moved closer to the latter. Indeed, *iki* was sometimes used as an equivalent of *sui*. Yet usually it carried a slightly different shade of meaning. As an aesthetic concept *iki* leaned toward a beauty somewhat less colorful than *sui*. Also, *iki* seems to have had a slightly more sensual connotation than *sui*. It was often applied to the description of a woman, especially a professional entertainer who knew exactly how much display of eroticism was desirable by the highest standard of taste.

Mono no aware もののあわれ

A literary and aesthetic ideal cultivated during the Heian period (794–1185). At its core is a deep, empathetic appreciation of the ephemeral beauty manifest in nature and human life, and it is therefore usually tinged with a hint of sadness; under certain circumstances it can be accompanied by admiration, awe, or even joy. The word was revived as part of the vocabulary of Japanese literary criticism through the writings of Motoori Norinaga 本居宣長 (1730–1801).

In Norinaga's view, *mono no aware* is a purified and exalted feeling, close to the innermost heart of man and nature. Theoretically the meaning of *mono no aware* is as comprehensive as the whole range of human emotions and can be viewed as a humanistic value, but in its actual usage it tends to focus on the beauty of impermanence and on the sensitive heart capable of appreciating that beauty.

Mujō (impermanence, transience, mutability) 無常

Originally a Buddhist term expressing the doctrine that everything that is born must die and that nothing remains unchanged. The phrase *shogyō mujō* (all the various realms of being are transient) 諸行無常 is the first of the Three Laws of Buddhism 三法印. Japanese have traditionally been keenly aware of the impermanence of things, and the sense of *mujō* has been a major theme in literature.

Concept of nature (*shizenkan*) 自然観

The basic, etymological meaning of the Japanese word *shizen*, which is used to translate the English word "nature," is the power of spontaneous self-development and what results from that power. The Chinese characters for the Japanese term *shizen* literally mean "from itself thus it is," expressing a mode of being rather than the existence of a natural order.

The term *shizen* as a general expression for nature is not found in ancient Japanese. The ancient Japanese people recognized every phenomenon as a manifestation of the *kami* (god or gods). Such terms as *ametsuchi* (heaven and earth) あめつち and *ikitoshi ikerumono* (living things) 生きとし生けるもの were the closest to a comprehensive word for nature in their literature.

In the mythology of the *Nihon shoki* 「日本書紀」 (720) the first offspring of the primordial couple Izanagi and Izanami were neither *kami* nor human but islands and landmasses. Thus human beings were not considered to be superior or opposed to nature, as in Western thought, but related as if in one family.

SOCIAL CONCEPTS 社会概念

Giri and *ninjō* 義理と人情

Social obligation 義理 and human feelings 人情. *Giri* refers to the obligation to act according to the dictates of society in relation to other persons. It applies, however, only to particular persons with whom one has certain social relations and is therefore a particular rather than a universal norm. *Ninjō* broadly refers to universal human feelings of love, affection, pity, sympathy, sorrow, and the like, which one "naturally" feels toward others, as in relations between parent and child or between lovers.

Giri is a norm that obliges the observance of reciprocal relations—to help those who have helped one, to do favors 恩 for those from whom one has received favors, and so forth. The concept implies a moral force that compels members of society to engage in socially expected reciprocal activities even when their natural inclination (*ninjō*) may be to do otherwise. To feudal warriors, *giri* referred foremost to their obligation to serve their lord, even at the cost of their lives, and to repay *on* (favor) received from the lord. In Japan, to be observant of *giri* is an indication of high moral worth. To neglect the obligation to reciprocate is to lose the trust of others expecting reciprocation and eventually to lose their support.

Generally human feelings do not conflict with social norms 社会規範, and observance of *giri* does not contradict *ninjō*. However, occasions sometimes arise where one is caught between social obligation and natural inclination. Though *giri* and *ninjō* as terms have outmoded connotations in modern Japan, the concepts are still important in guiding the conduct of the Japanese.

Sempai-kōhai (senior-junior) 先輩・後輩

An informal relationship ubiquitous in Japanese organizations, schools, and associations, in which older, experienced members offer friendship, assistance, and advice to inexperienced members, who reciprocate with gratitude, respect, and, often, personal loyalty.

The *sempai-kōhai* tie is determined by the date of entrance into a particular organization. The *sempai*, perhaps a graduate of the same school or a senior in the work group, acts as a friend and patron, disciplining and teaching the neophyte appropriate conduct. *Sempai-kōhai* ties permeate Japanese society.

Nemawashi (prior consultation) 根回し

A technique used in Japan to avoid conflicts and obtain a consensus in decision making 意思決定. The literal meaning of *nemawashi* is to dig around the roots of a tree prior to transplanting, thus making the uprooting and movement much easier. But the term is used much more widely in a figurative sense to describe maneuvering behind the scenes to reach a consensus and obtain certain objectives, especially in politics and business. When various interests are potentially in conflict, reaching a consensus and attaining political objectives are very difficult through direct, public confrontation. Instead, in Japanese politics and business the practice is to discuss decisions in advance with various interested parties and to incorporate their views, wherever possible, into any final proposals. Much of the groundwork for decisions is therefore laid well in advance of meetings where final decisions are made, and, if the *nemawashi* is successful, conflicts can be avoided in public discussion.

Etiquette (*reigi sahō*) 礼儀作法

"Etiquette" refers to conventional rules of behavior concerning interpersonal relationships. It differs from morality or ethics in that it concerns specific rules as applied to concrete situations rather than generalities and states requirements of outward conduct rather than inner beliefs or convictions. This distinction is important, because although at one level of consciousness Japanese recognize that etiquette and morality should go hand in hand, they also recognize that in reality the two may be discrepant.

Formalized Ideal and Real Behavior
形式的規範と実際の行動

Since Japanese society is based on the notion that one's existence is dependent upon those around one, it is essential to maintain smoothly operating human relations. Society thus demands the suppression of any antagonistic feelings one may have toward another and requires an outward behavior that reflects social harmony. This dichotomy is expressed in the Japanese concept of *tatemae*, or pro forma aspects of social relationships 建前, versus *honne*, or one's inner feelings and intentions 本音. The two are not expected to coincide in all cases, but socially proper conduct always takes precedence. Accordingly, Japanese strive to be aware of a possible discrepancy between outward conduct and true feeling and must be able to guess the latter, while interacting as if there were no discrepancy. This is often easier said than done—a reason why intermediaries are so often used in sensitive negotiations.

Although the discrepancy between expected conduct and inner feelings exists in all societies, in Japan it is openly condoned as natural. As a corollary to this, the rules of etiquette are more fully elaborated, and the social expectation to learn and conform to rules of etiquette is very strong.

Social Organization 社会秩序

By specifying rules of behavior appropriate for each status, etiquette helps to define social organization. Japanese etiquette specifies, for example, that the younger show deference to the older. The level of formality in speech such as *keigo* 敬語 is one of the more obvious ways in which status difference is manifested. Characteristically, Japanese wear clothes, such as uniforms, that readily manifest their social status, allowing others to interact with them in a socially appropriate manner. Seating arrangement 席次 is another way of defining status: those of higher social

Seating Arrangement 席次

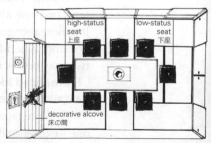

high-status seat 上座

low-status seat 下座

decorative alcove 床の間

status are seated at a more honored place, closest to the *tokonoma* (decorative alcove) 床の間 in a Japanese-style living room.

Festivals (*matsuri*) 祭

Japanese festivals, holidays, and other ceremonial occasions fall into two main categories: *matsuri* (festivals) and *nenchū gyōji* (annual events; also pronounced *nenjū gyōji*) 年中行事. *Matsuri* are essentially native Japanese festivals of Shintō origin, held annually on established dates. *Nenchū gyōji* is a larger category of annual and seasonal observances, many of which are of Chinese or Buddhist origin. *Nenchū gyōji* are arranged seasonally to form an annual calendar of events. *Matsuri* are often included in this calendar, and there is some overlapping between the two categories.

Matsuri are chiefly of sacred origin, related (at least originally) to the cultivation of rice and the spiritual well-being of local communities. They derive ultimately from ancient Shintō rites for the propitiation of the gods and the spirits of the dead, and for the fulfillment of the agricultural round. Some of these Shintō rites were incorporated, along with Buddhist and Confucian rites and ceremonies imported from China, into the imperial calendar of annual observances.

The word *matsuri* includes the rites and festivals practiced in both Folk Shintō 土着神道 and institutionalized Shintō. A *matsuri* is basically a symbolic act whereby participants enter a state of active communication with the gods (*kami*); it is accompanied by communion among participants in the form of feast and festival. In a broad sense, *matsuri* may also include festivals in which the playful element and commercial interests have all but obliterated the original sacramental context.

The Matsuri and the Seasons 祭と季節

Matsuri are in origin and tradition closely related to rice-centered agriculture, especially the growing cycle of rice. Among annual rites, spring and autumn *matsuri* are the most important. The spring festivals invoke a rich harvest or celebrate an anticipated good harvest; the autumn festivals are held in thanksgiving for a plentiful harvest.

Besides spring and autumn fetes, there are summer festivals (*natsu matsuri*) and winter festivals (*fuyu matsuri*). In farming areas the summer *matsuri* have the role of driving away natural disasters that might threaten the crops. In the cities, especially since the medieval period (mid-12th–16th centuries), the role of such festivals has been to ward off plague and pestilence. The winter *matsuri*, held between the harvest and spring seeding, have elements of both the autumn and spring *matsuri*. Thus, Japanese *matsuri* are synchronized with seasonal changes and are classified according to the four seasons.

Essentials of the *Matsuri* 祭の本質

Monoimi, or purificatory asceticism 物忌(清めのための禁欲生活) *Monoimi* serves as the symbolic gate by which the participants in a festival leave the everyday world 俗世(ケ) to enter into the special realm 聖域(ハレ) of the *matsuri*. The purification rites have been greatly simplified in recent years. In premodern Japan, however, people were not allowed to participate in the *matsuri* unless they had undergone the purification process.

Offerings 供物 Another essential element of the *matsuri* is the offerings made to the gods. Typical items include regular and glutinous (*mochi*) rice, *sake* (rice wine), seaweed, vegetables, and fruits. In Japan there are no sacrifices of living creatures いけにえ during *matsuri*.

Communion 直会 The *naorai*, in which participants in the *matsuri* partake of the food offerings at the place of celebration together with the gods, is another essential element of the *matsuri*.

The *Matsuri* and the Group 祭と集団

The *matsuri* presupposes the existence of a definite group of people to act it out. Generally speaking, in both the cities and villages of Japan every local community has a shrine that is its religious symbol. The members of a community, and thus of a certain shrine, are known as *ujiko*, and they in turn refer to their shrine as the *ujigami* (local Shintō deity) 氏神.

Most *matsuri* are conducted by a ceremonial organization consisting of Shintō priests and a small group of laymen selected from the *ujiko* community.

The *Matsuri* and Modern Society 祭と現代社会

After World War II, Japan underwent rapid changes in population distribution and the structure of traditional communities. These changes had direct and indirect effects on the *matsuri*. Although many of the traditional patterns are still evident on closer scrutiny, human interaction has become the framework of new events, showing a move from the closed and vertical order of communion between man and god to the more open and horizontal order of interpersonal relationship.

New Year (Shōgatsu) 正月

New Year observances are the most important and most elaborate of Japan's annual events 年中行事. Although local customs differ, at this time homes are decorated and the holidays are celebrated by family gatherings, visits to shrines or temples, and formal calls on relatives and friends. The New Year festivities have been officially observed from 1 January through 3 January, during which time all government offices and most companies are closed.

Preparations for seeing in the New Year were originally undertaken to greet the *toshigami*, or deity of the incoming year 年神. These began on 13 December, when the house was given a thorough cleaning; the date is usually nearer the end of the month now. The house is then decorated in the traditional fashion: A sacred rope of straw 注連縄 with dangling white paper strips 紙垂 is hung over the front door to demarcate the temporary abode of the *toshigami* and to prevent malevolent spirits from entering. It is also customary to place *kadomatsu*, an arrangement of tree sprigs, beside the entrance way to serve as a dwelling place for the god who brings good luck. A special altar, known as a *toshidana* (literally, "year shelf") 年棚, is piled high with *kagamimochi* (flat, round rice cakes) 鏡餅, *sake* (rice wine), persimmons, and other foods in honor of the *toshigami*. The night before New Year's is called Ōmisoka 大晦日. Many people visit Buddhist temples to hear the temple bells rung 108 times at midnight (*joya no kane*; New Year's Eve bells 除夜の鐘) to dispel the evils of the past year. It is also customary to eat *toshikoshi soba* (literally, "year-crossing noodles") 年越しそば in the hope that one's family fortunes will extend like the long noodles.

New Year's Days 正月三箇日

The first day of the year 元日 is usually spent with members of the family. People also throng to Buddhist temples and Shintō shrines (see HATSUMŌDE). In the Imperial Palace at dawn or early on the morning of 1 January, the emperor performs the rite of *shihōhai* (worship of the four quarters) 四方拝, in which he does reverence in the directions of various shrines and imperial tombs and offers prayers for the well-being of the nation. On 2 January the public is allowed to enter the inner palace grounds. On the second and third days of the New Year holidays, friends and business acquaintances visit one another to extend greetings (*nenshi* 年始) and sip *toso*, a spiced rice wine とそ.

Ōshōgatsu and Koshōgatsu 大正月と小正月

Shōgatsu refers to the first month of the year as

well as to the period of the New Year's holidays. The events described above concern what is commonly referred to as Ōshōgatsu (literally, "Big New Year") 大正月. There is, however, another traditional New Year called Koshōgatsu (literally, "Small New Year") 小正月. The former follows the date calculated by the Gregorian calendar グレゴリウス暦, and the latter is set according to the lunar calendar 太陰暦. Koshōgatsu thus starts with the first full moon of the year or more commonly on about 15 January and is largely observed in the rural areas of Japan, where the *toshigami* 年神 have been traditionally considered as agricultural deities.

Hatsumōde ("first shrine or temple visit") 初詣

Word used to refer to a person's first visit to a Shintō shrine or Buddhist temple during the New Year. Prayers are offered for the good fortune of the family. Because it was customary to visit the shrine or temple located in the direction from one's home considered to be the most auspicious that year (*ehō* 恵方), this practice was also called *ehōmairi* 恵方詣. Today, however, it has become more common to visit well-known shrines and temples, regardless of their location. These visits, which begin at midnight on New Year's Eve 大晦日, are made annually by large numbers of Japanese.

Bon Festival (Urabon'e) 盂蘭盆会

Buddhist observance honoring the spirits of ancestors; traditionally observed from 13 to 15 July (August in some areas). Also called Urabon or Obon お盆.

Typically at Bon, a "spirit altar" 精霊棚 is set up in front of the *butsudan* (Buddhist family altar) 仏壇 to welcome the ancestors' souls; then a priest is requested to come and read a sutra. Among the traditional preparations for the ancestors' return are the cleaning of grave sites and preparing a path from them to the house and the provision of straw horses or oxen for the ancestors' transportation. The welcoming fire 迎え火, built on the 13th, and the send-off fire 送り火, built on the 16th, are intended to illuminate the path.

Bon and the NEW YEAR are the two high points of the Japanese festival calendar. On both occasions, custom strongly urges all members of a family, no matter how scattered, to gather together to honor their ancestors.

National holidays (*kokumin no shukujitsu*)
国民の祝日

As of 1997, there were 14 national holidays authorized under the Law concerning National Holidays 国民の祝日に関する法律. In addition, in 1985 May 4 was designated as a principal holiday; along with 3 national holidays, it is part of the period from April 29 to May 5 that is popularly known as Golden Week ゴールデンウィーク. Beginning in 2000, Seijin no Hi and Taiiku no Hi will be celebrated on the second Monday of their respective months. The 14 national holidays are as follows:

Ganjitsu (*New Year's Day*) 元日. 1 January.

Seijin no Hi (*Coming-of-Age Day*) 成人の日. 15 January. This holiday honors people who attain the age of 20 years.

Kenkoku Kinen no Hi (*National Foundation Day*) 建国記念の日. 11 February. Nationalistic commemoration of the legendary enthronement of Japan's first emperor, Jimmu.

Shumbun no Hi (*Vernal Equinox Day*) 春分の日. Around 21 March. Visits to family graves and family reunions occur on this day, the central day of a seven-day Buddhist memorial service 彼岸会.

Midori no Hi (*Greenery Day*) みどりの日. 29 April. In 1989 this was designated as a day for nature appreciation. Prior to that the birthday of Emperor Shōwa was celebrated on this day.

Kempō Kinembi (*Constitution Memorial Day*) 憲法記念日. 3 May. Commemoration of the day the Constitution of Japan 日本国憲法 became effective in 1947.

Kodomo no Hi (*Children's Day*) こどもの日. 5 May. Day set aside for praying for the health and happiness of Japan's children. Traditionally cerebrated as the Tango Festival 端午の節句.

Umi no Hi (*Marine Day*) 海の日. 20 July. Day for people to express gratitude for the gifts of the sea and pray for the prosperity of Japan as a maritime nation.

Keirō no Hi (*Respect-for-the-Aged Day*) 敬老の日. 15 September. Day honoring Japan's elderly and celebrating their longevity. Established to commemorate the enactment of the Law concerning Welfare for the Aged 老人福祉法 in 1966.

Shūbun no Hi (*Autumnal Equinox Day*) 秋分の日. Around 23 September. Visits to family graves and family reunions occur on this day, the central day of a seven-day Buddhist memorial service (*higan'e* 彼岸会).

Taiiku no Hi (*Sports Day*) 体育の日. 10 October. Day on which good physical and mental health are fostered through physical activity. Established to commemorate the Tōkyō Olympic Games, which were held 10–24 October 1964.

Bunka no Hi (*Culture Day*) 文化の日. 3 November. Day on which the ideals articulated in Japan's postwar constitution—the love of peace and freedom—are fostered through cultural activities.

Kinrō Kansha no Hi (*Labor Thanksgiving Day*) 勤労感謝の日. 23 November. Day on which people express gratitude to each other for their labors throughout the year and for the fruits of those labors.

Tennō Tanjōbi (*Emperor's Birthday*) 天皇誕生日. 23 December. Celebration of the birthday of Japan's present emperor, Akihito.

Setsubun 節分

Traditional ceremony to dispel demons, now observed on 3 or 4 February. The practice of scattering beans 豆まき to drive away demons is one of a number of magical rites performed to ward off evil.

On *Setsubun*, beans (usually soybeans) are scattered inside and outside the house or building to the common chant of *oni wa soto, fuku wa uchi* ("Out with demons! In with good luck!"). It is customary for family members to eat the same number of beans as their age.

Doll Festival (Hina Matsuri) 雛祭

Festival for girls held on 3 March. Tiered platforms for *hina* dolls 雛人形 (a set of dolls representing emperor, empress, attendants, and musicians in ancient court dress) are set up in the home, and the family celebrates with a meal, eating diamond-shaped *hishimochi* 菱餅 and drinking *shirozake* (made with rice malt and *sake*) 白酒. The *hina* dolls of the modern festival are thought to be a combination of the *katashiro* 形代 (a scapegoat in the exorcism of ritual impurities) and the paper *hina* dolls with which Heian-period girls played. Also called Jōshi no Sekku 上巳の節句, Momo no Sekku 桃の節句, and Sangatsu Sekku 三月節句.

Hanami (literally, "flower viewing"; generally, cherry-blossom viewing) 花見

Excursions and picnics for enjoying flowers, particularly cherry blossoms; one of the most popular events of the spring. In some places flower-viewing par-

Annual Events
年中行事

MONTH/DATE		EVENT
1	7	Seven Herb Festival 七草の節句
	15	Little New Year 小正月
2	3 or 4	Bean-Scattering Ceremony 節分
	4 or 5	Beginning of spring; Old Solar New Year 立春
	8	Needle memorial service 針供養
3	3	Doll Festival 雛祭
	17-24	Spring *higan* 彼岸
4	8	Flower Festival 花祭
5	2 or 3	"88th Night" 八十八夜
6	21 or 22	Summer solstice 夏至
7	7	Tanabata Festival 七夕祭
	13-15	Bon Festival お盆
9	1	"210th Day" 二百十日
	9	Chrysanthemum Festival 菊の節句
	17-20	Autumn *higan* 秋彼岸
	23 or 24	Autumnal Equinox Day 秋分の日
	Night of the full moon	"15th Night" 十五夜
11	15	"Seven-Five-Three" Festival 七五三
12	21 or 22	Winter solstice 冬至
	late part of month	Year-end fairs 年の市
	31	New Year's Eve 大晦日

ties are held on traditionally fixed dates according to the old lunar calendar. The subject of flower viewing has long held an important place in literature, dance, and the fine arts.

Today radio and television stations regularly broadcast reports on the blossoming of local cherry trees. Popular viewing spots include Yoshinoyama 吉野山 in Nara Prefecture and Ueno 上野 in Tōkyō.

CEREMONIES 儀式

Weddings (*kekkonshiki*) 結婚式

Weddings, perhaps the most important of the Japanese rites of passage 通過儀礼, are one of the four major ceremonial occasions referred to as *kankon sōsai* (coming-of-age, marriage, funerals, ancestor worship) 冠婚葬祭. For a MARRIAGE 婚姻 to be official, a new family register 戸籍 must be compiled for the couple at the local administrative office. However, social and public recognition of a marriage in Japan is still often sought through the holding of extravagant weddings with elaborate formal costumes and large receptions.

Traditional Weddings 伝統的な結婚式

The "traditional" wedding of today was established as a pattern during the Meiji period (1868–1912). Although the marriage procedure varied a great deal with locality, most weddings included the customs described here. The day of the wedding was chosen carefully to avoid inauspicious days as determined by Chinese and Japanese astrological traditions. Traditional wedding rituals began the day before the wedding, when the bride prayed at the family shrine or temple or had a parting banquet with neighbors and parents. The

Wedding Reception Venues
披露宴会場の推移

Source: Sanwa Bank Home Consultant.

wedding-day rituals primarily took place at the household of the groom, or at the household of the bride if the groom was adopted into her family in the kind of marriage called *mukoirikon* 婿入り婚. In cases where the bride entered the groom's household, she dressed in white as she took formal leave of her parents. The white was symbolic of the death of her natal ties to them. At the household of the groom she appeared wearing a colorful *furisode*-style *kimono* and a cotton or silk head covering called *tsunokakushi* (literally, "horn-hiding") 角隠し, which was supposed to suppress and hide the feminine "horns of jealousy." The groom wore a *kimono* with family crests 家紋 and the loose trousers called *hakama* 袴.

Modern Weddings 現代の結婚式

Traditional weddings were basically secular rites decided upon by local customs and personal preference. Weddings today are still determined by these considerations but are more likely to include a religious ceremony, even when the couple has no particular belief or religious affiliation. Shintō weddings 神前結婚式, which became popular after the Shintō marriage ceremony held for the crown prince in 1900, are more common than Buddhist weddings 仏式結婚式, although Christian ceremonies have become increasingly fashionable. The trend has shifted from weddings at home to weddings in shrines, temples, and (since World War II) hotels, restaurants, churches, or special wedding halls 結婚式場, which are often furnished with special wedding chambers of Shintō or Christian design. Although the custom of *satogaeri* 里帰り (the wife returned to her family home, bringing gifts for relatives and friends) might still be observed by some, most Japanese try to take a honeymoon of at least a week. Although large-scale, expensive weddings directed and financed by the parents are still common, there are also an increasing number of weddings that more closely reflect the personal wishes of the couple.

Funerals (*sōgi*) 葬儀

About 90 percent of the funerals in Japan are conducted according to Buddhist rites. Upon death the body is washed with hot water (*yukan*) 湯灌, then dressed by family members in white garments (*kyōkatabira*) 経帷子 or in his favorite clothes. More recently it has become the practice for physicians and nurses to cleanse the body and for morticians to dress it. In many cases the entire process of funeral rites is entrusted to a mortuary.

The body is laid out with the head toward the north without a pillow and is covered with a sheet of white cloth. A priest from the Buddhist parish temple recites sutras at the bedside and gives a posthumous Buddhist name 戒名 to the deceased. The body is then placed in an unpainted wooden coffin.

A notice of mourning, written on a piece of white paper with a black frame, is posted on the front door or gate of the house throughout the mourning period 忌中. An all-night wake 通夜 or a briefer "half wake" 半通夜 is held. Refreshments are served and mourners present gifts of "incense money" 香典. The day after the wake the funeral service is held at home, the parish temple, or a funeral hall. There are both Buddhist and Shintō forms of service.

After cremation pieces of the bones of the deceased are gathered, placed in a small jar (*kotsutsubo*) 骨壷, and brought home for later burial. Every 7th day until the 49th day, rites are held around the altar where the *kotsutsubo* is kept. The family members of the deceased express their gratitude to mourners by sending acknowledgment notes and return gifts (*kōdengaeshi*) valued at about half of the *kōden*. The *kotsutsubo* is buried at the grave site during this period.

Literature (Nihon *bungaku*) 日本文学

Japanese literary art has received foreign influences since its beginning in the 6th century. Before the middle of the 19th century, the sources of influence were the culture of China. After the middle of the 19th century, the impact of modern Western culture became predominant.

Early and Heian Literature 古代と平安時代の文学

Official embassies to Sui (589–618) and Tang (618–907) 遣隋使：遣唐使 dynasty China, initiated in 600, were the chief means by which Chinese culture, technology, and methods of government were introduced on a comprehensive basis in Japan. The *Kojiki* (712, Record of Ancient Matters)「古事記」 and the *Nihon shoki* (720, Chronicles of Japan)「日本書紀」, the former written in hybrid Sino-Japanese and the latter in classical Chinese, were compiled under the sponsorship of the government for the purpose of authenticating the legiti-

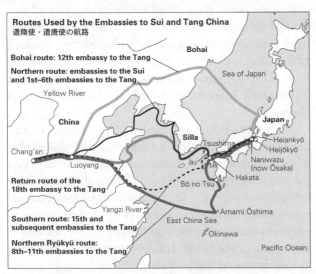

Routes Used by the Embassies to Sui and Tang China
遣隋使・遣唐使の航路

Bohai route: 12th embassy to the Tang

Northern route: embassies to the Sui and 1st–6th embassies to the Tang

Bohai

Sea of Japan

Yellow River

China

Japan

Silla

Chang'an

Luoyang

Tsushima

Iki

Heiankyō
Heijōkyō

Naniwazu
(now Ōsaka)

Hakata

Return route of the 18th embassy to the Tang

Bō no Tsu

Yangzi River

Amami Ōshima

Southern route: 15th and subsequent embassies to the Tang

East China Sea

Okinawa

Northern Ryūkyū route: 8th–11th embassies to the Tang

Pacific Ocean

macy of its polity. However, among these collections of myths, genealogies, legends of folk heroes, and historical records there appear a number of songs—largely irregular in meter and written with Chinese characters representing Japanese words or syllables—that offer insight into the nature of preliterate Japanese verse.

The first major collection of native poetry, again written with Chinese characters, was the *Man'yōshū* (late 8th century; tr *The Ten Thousand Leaves*) 「万葉集」, which contains verses, chiefly the 31-syllable WAKA, that were composed in large part between the mid-7th and mid-8th centuries. The earlier poems in the collection are characterized by the direct expression of strong emotion but those of later provenance show the emergence of the rhetorical conventions and expressive subtlety that dominated the subsequent tradition of court poetry.

A revolutionary achievement of the mid-9th century was the development of a native orthography (*kana*) for the phonetic representation of Japanese. Employing radically abbreviated Chinese characters to denote Japanese sounds, the system contributed to a deepening consciousness of a native literary tradition distinct from that of China. Poets compiled collections 私家集 of their verses, and, drawing in part on these, the *Kokin wakashū* (905; Collection from Ancient and Modern Times) 「古今和歌集」, the first of 21 imperial anthologies of native poetry, was assembled in the early 10th century.

The introduction of *kana* also led to the development of a prose literature in the vernacular, early examples of which are the *Utsubo monogatari* (late 10th century; Tale of the Hollow Tree) 「宇津保物語」, a work of fiction; the *Ise monogatari* (mid-10th century; Tales of Ise) 「伊勢物語」, a collection of vignettes centered on poems; and the diary *Tosa nikki* (935; tr *The Tosa Diary*) 「土佐日記」. From the late 10th century the ascendancy of the Fujiwara regents 藤原氏の摂政, whose power over emperors depended on the reception of their daughters as imperial consorts, resulted in the formation of literary coteries of women in the courts of empresses, and it was these women who produced the great prose classics of the 11th century. Such works as *Genji monogatari* (early 11th century; tr *The Tale of Genji*)「源氏物語」, a fictional narrative by Murasaki Shikibu 紫式部, and the *Makura no sōshi* (996–1012; tr *The Pillow Book of Sei Shōnagon*)「枕草子」, a collection of essays by Sei Shōnagon 清少納言, are considered by Japanese to be a watershed in the development of the native literary tradition.

Medieval Literature 中世の文学

The chief development in poetry during the medieval period (mid-12th–16th centuries) was linked verse 連歌. Arising from the court tradition of *waka*, *renga* was cultivated by the warrior class as well as by courtiers, and some among the best *renga* poets, such as Sōgi, were commoners. A major development in prose literature of the medieval era was the war tale 軍記物語. The *Heike monogatari* (tr *The Tale of the Heike*)「平家物語」relates the events of the war between the Taira and Minamoto families that brought an end to imperial rule; it was disseminated among all levels of society by itinerant priests who chanted the story to the accompaniment of a lutelike instrument, the *biwa* 琵琶. The social upheaval of the early years of the era led to the appearance of works deeply influenced by the Buddhist notion of the inconstancy of worldly affairs 無常. Not only does the theme of *mujō* provide the ground note of the *Heike monogatari* and the essay collections *Hōjōki* (1212; tr *The Ten Foot Square Hut*)「方丈記」by Kamo no Chōmei 鴨長明 and *Tsurezuregusa* (ca 1330; tr *Essays in Idleness*)「徒然草」by Yoshida Kenkō 吉田兼好, it is also an element of the theoretical framework of the historical work *Gukanshō* (ca 1220; Notes on Foolish Views)「愚管抄」by the Buddhist priest Jien 慈円.

Edo Literature 江戸時代の文学

The formation of a stable central government in Edo (now Tōkyō), after some 100 years of turmoil, and the growth of a market economy based on the widespread use of a standardized currency led to the development in the Edo period (1600–1868) of a class of wealthy townsmen. General prosperity contributed to an increase in literacy, and literary works became marketable commodities, giving rise to a publishing industry. Humorous fictional studies of contemporary society such as *Kōshoku ichidai otoko* (1682; tr *The Life of an Amorous Man*)「好色一代男」by Ihara Saikaku 井原西鶴 were huge commercial successes, and prose works, often elaborately illustrated, that were directed toward a mass audience became a staple of Edo-period literature. Commercial playhouses were established for the performance of puppet plays (*jōruri* 人形浄瑠璃) and *kabuki*, whose plots often centered on conflicts arising from the rigidly hierarchical social order that was instituted by the Tokugawa shogunate.

The 17-syllable form of light verse known as *haikai* 俳諧 (later known as HAIKU 俳句), whose subject matter was drawn from nature and the lives of ordinary people, was raised to the level of great poetry by Matsuo Bashō 松尾芭蕉. A number of philologists, among them Keichū 契沖, Kamo no Mabuchi 賀茂真淵, and Motoori Norinaga 本居宣長, wrote scholarly studies on early literary texts, such as the *Kojiki*「古事記」, the *Man'yōshū*「万葉集」, and *The Tale of Genji*「源氏物語」, in which they attempted to elucidate the native Japanese world view.

Modern Literature 近現代の文学

The imperial restoration of 1868 was followed by the wholesale introduction of Western technology and culture, which largely displaced Chinese culture. As a result the novel became established as a serious and respected genre of the literature of Japan. A related development was the gradual abandonment of the literary language 文語 in favor of the usages of colloquial speech, fully achieved for the first time in *Ukigumo* (1887–1889; Drifting Clouds) 「浮雲」 by Futabatei Shimei 二葉亭四迷. Although the *tanka* and the *haiku* remained viable poetic forms, notably in the hands of Ishikawa Takuboku 石川啄木, Yosano Akiko 与謝野晶子, Masaoka Shiki 正岡子規, and Takahama Kyoshi 高浜虚子, there developed under the influence of Western poetry a genre of free verse, the first great achievement of which was the collection *Wakanashū* (1897; Collection of Young Herbs) 「若菜集」 by Shimazaki Tōson 島崎藤村. Early stylistic influences on Japanese literature were romanticism ロマン主義, introduced in the 1890s by Mori Ōgai 森鴎外; symbolism 象徴主義, introduced in Ueda Bin's 上田敏 *Kaichōon* 「海潮音」 (1905), a collection of translations of French poems; and naturalism 自然主義, which reigned supreme from 1905 to 1910 and out of which developed the enduring genre of the confessional novel (I-novel or *watakushi shōsetsu* 私小説).

Until the 1950s a distinctive feature of the Japanese literary community was the publication of coterie magazines 同人誌 by writers of like mind. The humanist Shirakaba school 白樺派 of writers, including Mushanokōji Saneatsu 武者小路実篤 and Shiga Naoya 志賀直哉, published the journal *Shirakaba* (1910–1923; White Birch) 「白樺」, and works of the proletarian writers プロレタリア作家 Kobayashi Takiji 小林多喜二 and Sata Ineko 佐多稲子 were published in *Senki* (1928–1931; Battle Flag) 「戦旗」, a Marxist-oriented periodical. The serial publication of novels in newspapers has also been a common practice, and some of the best Japanese novelists, from Natsume Sōseki 夏目漱石 to Nagai Kafū 永井荷風, Tanizaki Jun'ichirō 谷崎潤一郎, and Kawabata Yasunari 川端康成, have written for the newspapers. Translations of Japanese literary works have appeared in rapidly increasing numbers since the 1970s, and the best creations of Sōseki 漱石,

Ōgai 鴎外, Kafū 荷風, Akutagawa Ryūnosuke 芥川龍之介, Shiga 志賀, Tanizaki 谷崎, Kawabata 川端, Ibuse Masuji 井伏鱒二, Dazai Osamu 太宰治, Enchi Fumiko 円地文子, and Mishima Yukio 三島由紀夫 are available in English versions. Among the foremost writers of fiction in the 1990s were Ōe Kenzaburō 大江健三郎, Abe Kōbō 安部公房, Endō Shūsaku 遠藤周作, Tsushima Yūko 津島佑子, Murakami Ryū 村上龍, Nakagami Kenji 中上健次, and Murakami Haruki 村上春樹. See also MODERN FICTION.

Waka ("Japanese poetry") 和歌

A genre of verse of various prosodic types that began to take form in the hands of the court aristocracy in the mid-6th century. By the late 8th century the term was used synonymously with *tanka* ("short poem") 短歌, a type of verse that consists of five lines in 31 syllables in the pattern 5-7-5-7-7 and that is still composed today.

Prosody and Rhetorical Devices 韻律と修辞的技巧

The primary sources of our knowledge of early Japanese poetry are the annals *Kojiki* (712, Record of Ancient Matters) 「古事記」 and *Nihon shoki* (720, Chronicles of Japan) 「日本書紀」 and the late-8th-century anthology of poetry *Man'yōshū* (Collection of Ten Thousand Leaves or Collection for Ten Thousand Generations) 「万葉集」, most of the more than 4,000 poems in which were culled from earlier anthologies that are no longer extant. The oldest poems display little prosodic regularity, although there was a tendency to alternate longer and shorter lines. In the 7th century, however, possibly arising from the influence of the five-character and seven-character lines of Chinese verse, the number of syllables per line became standardized at five and seven. From the mid-7th century the *tanka* form appears to have been paramount, but until the middle of the 8th century it was rivaled by the *chōka* ("long poem") 長歌, consisting of an indefinite number of pairs of five- and seven-syllable lines with an extra seven-syllable line at the end. Other forms were the *katauta* ("half poem") 片歌, of 3 lines of five, seven, and five syllables, to which another poet replied to form a set; the *sedōka* ("head-repeated poem") 旋頭歌, of 6 lines in the syllable pattern 5-7-7-5-7-7; and the *bussokuseki no uta*, or "Buddha's foot-stone poem," 仏足石の歌 also of 6 lines but in the syllable pattern 5-7-5-7-7-7, the chief examples of which are inscribed on an ancient stela erected beside a stone on which the Buddha's footprints are incised.

Until the mid-8th century the dominant cadence of *waka* was 5-7, but thereafter the 7-5 cadence gained the ascendancy. It also became common for the cadence to be broken, usually at the end of the third line, by a caesura. In the following 12th-century poem by the priest Jakuren, the third line terminates with a conclusive verb inflection and is followed by a noun phrase:

Sabishisa wa	さびしさは	To be alone—
Sono iro to shi mo	その色としも	It is of a color that
Nakarikeri	なかりけり	Cannot be named:
Maki tatsu yama no	槇立つ山の	This mountain where cedars rise
Aki no yūgure	秋の夕ぐれ	Into the autumn dusk.

Imagery and Subject Matter 比喩と題材

Classical *waka* employed a high proportion of images drawn from nature, personification of which led increasingly to allegory. The conventions of *waka* militated against the innovative use of natural images—the stock of which, in the case of insects, included the cicada and the cricket, but not the butterfly, the bee, or the firefly—and a consequence of this narrowing of content was that a new poem inevitably alluded to earlier poems in the tradition.

Waka poets concentrated on a handful of subjects, primarily human affairs (celebration, separation, grief, and especially love) and nature (natural beauty and the changing aspects of the seasons), avoiding war, physical suffering, death, and all that was ugly or low. With the growing influence of a Buddhist world view nature poetry came typically to express a lyric melancholy, while poetry of love expressed a poignant consciousness of the impermanence of personal ties.

Historical Development 歴史

Following the *Man'yōshū*, the next major collection of *waka* was the *Kokin wakashū* (905, Collection from Ancient and Modern Times) 「古今和歌集」, the first of 21 imperial anthologies 勅撰和歌集. These anthologies varied considerably in size and quality, but each was considered the most important literary enterprise of its day. Among the chief sources from which poems were drawn for inclusion in the imperial anthologies were the *shikashū*, collections of poetry written and compiled by individual poets. Other important repositories of classical *waka*—and of critical judgments—are the records of poetry matches 歌合.

Waka of the *Kokin wakashū* was much influenced by the mannered elegance and precious conceits of Chinese poetry of the late Six Dynasties period 六朝時代 (222–589), in particular the monumental *Wen xuan* (J: *Monzen*) 「文選」. Nevertheless, the *Kokin wakashū* also displays in its verse, as well as in the vernacular preface written by one of its compilers, Ki no Tsurayuki, a strong consciousness of a native poetics.

The eighth imperial anthology, *Shin kokin wakashū* (1205, New Collection from Ancient and Modern Times) 「新古今和歌集」, one of whose editors was Fujiwara no Teika 藤原定家, brought to fulfillment the organizational concepts, already apparent in the *Kokin wakashū*, of association and progression. Adjacent poems were linked by such devices as similarity of image or common allusion to an older poem, while all of the poems of the major divisions of the anthology, such as those devoted to individual seasons or to love, were ordered on the basis of the appearance of seasonal phenomena or the progress of a love affair.

The last imperial anthology, *Shin shoku kokin wakashū* (New Collection from Ancient and Modern Times, Continued) 「新続古今和歌集」 was completed in 1439. Following the *Shin kokin wakashū*, imperial anthologies displayed an increasingly sterile style, marked by a slavish veneration of the conventions of the Heian period, and by the Edo period (1600–1868) the center of *waka* composition had passed from the court to society at large.

Early in the Meiji period (1868–1912), the influential poet-critics Yosano Tekkan 与謝野鉄幹 and Masaoka Shiki 正岡子規 called for a break with the past and, following their practice, the custom arose of referring to the art of 31-syllable poetry as *tanka*, rather than *waka*. In 1899, with other young *tanka* poets, Tekkan founded the Shinshisha (New Poetry Society) 新詩社, which in 1900 initiated the publication of the literary magazine *Myōjō* (Bright Star) 「明星」. One of the leading contributors was Yosano Akiko 与謝野晶子, whose passionate lyricism brought a new vigor to the genre.

Tanka continues in the post-World War II period to be a widely practiced form of verse; nevertheless, though today hundreds of societies and millions of practitioners carry on the tradition, the best Japanese poets have increasingly chosen to work in the genre of free verse 自由詩.

Haiku 俳句

A 17-syllable verse form consisting of three metrical units of 5, 7, and 5 syllables, respectively. One of the most important forms of traditional Japanese poetry, *haiku* remains popular in modern Japan, and in recent years its popularity has spread to other countries.

Haiku, Hokku, and Haikai 俳句・発句・俳諧

Loose usage by students, translators, and even poets themselves has led to much confusion about the distinction between the three related terms *haiku*, *hokku*, and *haikai*. The term *hokku* literally means "starting verse." 発句 A *hokku* was the first or "starting" link of a much longer chain of verses known as a *haikai no renga*, or simply *haikai*, in which alternating sets of 5-7-5 syllables and 7-7 syllables were joined. *Hokku* gradually took on an independent character. Largely through the efforts of Masaoka Shiki 正岡子規 (1867–1902), this independence was formally established in the 1890s through the creation of the term "*haiku*." *Haiku* was a new type of verse, in form quite similar to the traditional *hokku* but different in that it was to be written, read, and understood as an independent poem, complete in itself, rather than as part of a longer chain.

Development of Haikai 俳諧の発展

Renga, or linked verse 連歌, was originally considered a diversion by which poets could relax from the serious business of composing WAKA poetry. By the time of the *renga* master Sōgi 宗祇 (1421–1502), however, it had become a serious art with complex rules and high aesthetic standards. *Haikai no renga*, or simply *haikai*, was conceived as a lighthearted amusement in which poets could indulge after the solemn refinements of serious *renga*.

In the 17th century Matsunaga Teitoku 松永貞徳 (1571–1653) succeeded in establishing a conservative and formalistic approach to *haikai*. He established strict rules concerning the composition of *haikai* and sought to endow the form with the elegance and aesthetic elevation of *waka* and serious *renga*.

After Teitoku's death his formalistic approach

was challenged by the more freewheeling Danrin school of *haikai* 談林俳諧 led by Nishiyama Sōin 西山宗因 (1605–1682). Sōin emphasized the comic aspects of *haikai*. Characteristic of the Danrin style of poetry was the practice of *yakazu haikai* 矢数俳諧, in which a single poet would reel off verse after verse as quickly as possible in a sort of exercise in free association.

Matsuo Bashō 松尾芭蕉 (1644–1694) was not only the greatest of *haikai* poets, he was also primarily responsible for establishing *haikai* as a true art form. Having received instruction in both the Teitoku and Danrin styles of *haikai*, he gradually developed in the late 17th century a new style that, through its artistic sincerity, transcended the conflict between serious *renga* and comic *haikai* and could express humor, humanity, and profound religious insight all within the space of a single *hokku*. His representative works include *Oku no hosomichi* (1694; tr *The Narrow Road to the Deep North*) 「奥の細道」. Bashō also had a great number of disciples. Of these, the so-called Ten Philosophers 蕉門の十哲 are particularly well known.

In the late 18th century, there arose a movement of poets who sought to restore the high aesthetic standards of Bashō. The principal figure in this *haikai* reform was the talented painter-poet Yosa Buson (1716–1784), and the main cry of the movement was "Return to Bashō!" 蕉風への復古 Buson possessed great imagination and culture and a painter's eye for vivid pictorial scenes.

The number of composers of *haikai* grew rapidly in the early 19th century. This popularization, however, was accompanied by a general decline in quality. The most notable exception was Kobayashi Issa 小林一茶 (1763–1827). Issa's poems about his poverty and about his love for small animals and insects are particularly memorable. His best known work is *Oraga haru* (1820; tr

① This rude hermit cell
Will be different now,
knowing Doll's
Festival as well.
草の戸も住替る代ぞ雛の家

② (Senju)
Loath to let spring go,
Birds cry, and even fishes'
Eyes are wet with tears.
行く春や鳥啼き魚の目は泪

③ (Nikkō)
O holy, hallowed shrine!
How green all the fresh
young leaves
In thy bright sun shine!
あらたふと青葉若葉の日の光

④ (Sukagawa)
For verse, it did suffice
To hear the northern
peasants sing
As they planted rice.
風流の初めや奥の田植えうた

⑤ (Hiraizumi)
A mound of summer grass;
Are warriors' heroic deeds
Only dreams that pass?
夏草や兵どもが夢の跡

⑥ (Risshakuji)
In this hush profound,
Into the very rocks it
seeps–
The cicada sound.
閑さや岩にしみ入る蝉の声

⑦ (Mogamigawa)
Gathering as it goes
All the rains of June, how
swiftly
The Mogami Flows!
五月雨をあつめて早し最上川

⑧ (Izumozaki)
O'er wild ocean spray,
All the way to Sado Isle
Spreads the Milky Way!
荒海や佐渡によこたふ天河

⑨ (Ōgaki)
Sadly, I part from you;
Like a clam torn from its
shell,
I go, and autumn too.
蛤のふたみにわかれ行く秋ぞ

Bashō's Route in *Oku no Hosomichi*
「奥の細道」芭蕉の足跡

The Year of My Life)「おらが春」.

Modern *Haiku* 現代の俳句

The history of modern *haiku* dates from Masaoka Shiki's reform, begun in 1892, which established *haiku* as a new independent poetic form. Basic to the modernization of *haiku* was Shiki's most important concept, *shasei* 写生, or sketching from life 写生. The magazine that Shiki began in 1897, *Hototogisu*「ホトトギス」, became the *haiku* world's most important publication.

In 1912 Takahama Kyoshi 高浜虚子 began in the pages of *Hototogisu* (which he had edited since 1898) his lifelong defense of the traditional 17-syllable form, the seasonal theme, and the descriptive realism of Shiki.

By 1920 a second generation of poets clustered about *Hototogisu*, including Mizuhara Shūōshi 水原秋桜子, Awano Seiho 阿波野青畝, Yamaguchi Seishi 山口誓子, and Takano Sujū 高野素十.

Mizuhara Shūōshi broke away from *Hototogisu* in 1931, two years after having assumed the editorship of the magazine *Ashibi*「馬酔木」(1928–).

During the military-dominated prewar and World War II period, *haiku* was controlled by government censorship.

After the war, the effort to unite all poets was stimulated by a widely discussed 1946 article entitled "Daini geijutsuron" (On a Second-Class Art) 「第二芸術論」, in which the critic Kuwabara Takeo 桑原武夫 maintained that modern *haiku* was not a serious literary genre but only a pleasant pastime. A number of efforts to "modernize *haiku*"—to make it relevant to contemporary experience—were stimulated by the publicity given Kuwabara's article.

One such effort was *Tenrō* 「天狼」 (1948–1994), a magazine begun in 1948 under Yamaguchi Seishi's editorship. *Tenrō* and the prewar *Ashibi* were the two most important vehicles of the nontraditional *haiku*.

Haiku Abroad 海外における俳句

The West's first introduction to *haiku* came in Basil Hall Chamberlain's pioneer work, *Japanese Poetry* (1910), in a chapter entitled "Bashō and the Japanese Epigram." William Porter's early anthology of translations was entitled *A Year of Japanese Epigrams* (1911). *Haiku* was first introduced to France by Paul-Louis Couchoud at the time of the Russo-Japanese War. The title of his introduction to *haiku* was *Les Epigrammes Lyriques du Japon*. The use of the term "epigram" in these titles is indicative of how *haiku* was first interpreted abroad.

Ezra Pound quickly noticed and appropriated the *haiku* technique of cutting up the poem into two independent yet associated images. In France Paul Eluard wrote poems in the *haiku* style. *Haiku* has rapidly become naturalized both in Europe and in the United States, and magazines of original *haiku* are published. *Haiku* magazines in the United States include *Modern Haiku*, *byways*, and *Tweed*.

Modern fiction (*kingendai no shōsetsu*)
近現代の小説

Modern fiction in Japan has its origins in the Meiji period (1868–1912), when a flood of translations of Western literature collided with a vigorous native tradition of imaginative writing. The *gesaku* fiction 戯作 of the Edo period (1600–1868) continued to have a powerful influence upon the style and content of the early Meiji fiction, and it was in reaction to this influence that Tsubouchi Shōyō 坪内逍遥 produced the first critical treatise in Japanese regarding the theory and aims of the modern novel, *Shōsetsu shinzui* (1885–1886, The Essence of the Novel) 「小説神髄」.

Fiction had been traditionally regarded as a form of vulgar entertainment, and Tsubouchi, after examining recently imported Western models of writing, sensed the need for a new kind of imaginative writing capable of depicting the realities of modern life and establishing the novel as a serious form of artistic expression. He argued the merits of realistic fiction 写実主義小説 as a medium for expressing the perceptions and aspirations of contemporary society, and discussed the need for novelists to create a written language with the vigor and comprehensibility of the spoken language, as well as the versatility and precision essential to a serious literature 純文学.

Relying upon Tsubouchi's theories and personal guidance, Futabatei Shimei 二葉亭四迷 produced what has been called Japan's first modern novel, *Ukigumo* (1887–1889, Drifting Clouds; tr *Ukigumo*, 1967) 「浮雲」. The plot concerns an unremarkable government clerk whose tenacious adherence to old-fashioned virtues renders him a pathetic figure in the eyes of both his more opportunistic colleagues and his female cousin, who is also his presumed fiancee. What is strikingly fresh about the novel is the colloquial style of the language, Futabatei's conception of his hero's plight within the context of a quickly changing society, and his subtle psychological examination of his protagonist.

For over a decade after *Ukigumo*, few writers shared Futabatei's interest in or understanding of the modern psychological novel. But in the 1890s this quest was continued by several young writers who are usually associated with the romantic movement centering on the famous literary journal *Bungakukai* (1893–1898, The Literary World) 「文学界」. The most impressive work of fiction published in *Bungakukai* was the story "Takekurabe" (1895–1896; tr "Growing Up," 1956) 「たけくらべ」 by Higuchi Ichiyō 樋口一葉. Ichiyō's language is still heavily classical in diction and imagery, but the content of the story is extraordinarily modern. In this tale of children living in the shadow of the Yoshiwara pleasure quarter 吉原遊郭, Ichiyō describes the loneliness of adolescence, the confusion that attends a growing awareness of sex, and the callousness of the adult world, which must soon be theirs. The subtlety and seriousness of her handling of youthful psychology betokens something very new in her vision.

But Ichiyō died too young, and it was another of her colleagues from *Bungakukai* 「文学界」, Shimazaki Tōson 島崎藤村, who set the pattern for one stream of modern writers by moving gradually from romantic poetry to the writing of realistic fiction to assert the authenticity of the individual personality. His first novel, *Hakai* (1906; tr *The Broken Commandment*, 1974) 「破戒」, relates the story of a *burakumin* schoolteacher who hides his origins in the outcaste community until he realizes his only salvation as a human being lies in divulging his secret. In this powerful work, themes of bigotry, guilt, and isolation are treated with a psychological sophistication and social awareness that were new in Japanese literature. After *Hakai*, however, Tōson followed the direction set by Tayama Katai's 田山花袋 confessional novel *Futon* (1907; tr *The Quilt*, 1981)「蒲団」and retreated into his own private world to write in the genre of autobiographical or semiautobiographical novel known as the I-novel 私小説.

Thus it was not through Tōson but through Natsume Sōseki 夏目漱石 that the modern Japanese realistic novel was brought to full maturity. Sōseki wrote a series of novels that are still among the most probing fictional accounts of the vicissitudes of modern middle-class life in Japan. His heroes are usually university-educated men made vulnerable by the new "egoism" and a too-keen perception of their separation from the rest of the world. In *Kokoro* (1914, The Heart; tr *Kokoro*, 1957), the most popular of his later novels, the hero, lonely and unable to overcome his guilt for having driven a friend to suicide because of their love of the same woman, finally kills himself. Guilt, betrayal, and isolation are for Sōseki the inevitable consequences of the liberation of the self and all the uncertainties that have come with the advent of Western culture. These motifs are also explored in his novels *Mon* (1910, The Gate; tr *Mon*, 1972) and *Kōjin* (1912–1913; tr *The Wayfarer*, 1967)「行人」.

Doctor, head of the army medical corps, German scholar, translator, master stylist, critic, historian, and novelist, Mori Ōgai 森鴎外 was the versatile intellectual par excellence of his time.

Ōgai first won acclaim with three romantic short stories set in Germany, each with a central Japanese character. The most popular, "Maihime" (1890; tr "The Dancing Girl," 1975)「舞姫」, deals with the doomed love affair of a young Japanese student in Berlin with a German dancer of humble circumstances. Ōgai's major novels with contemporary settings are not as dramatic as Sōseki's, nor are they as rich in explicit social commentary. Yet in such works as *Gan* (1911–1913; tr *The Wild Geese*, 1959) 「雁」, about a usurer's mistress who falls in love with a student, we find a new complexity in the psychological delineation of the characters. His most representative late works are essentially fictionalized studies in history and biography, such as the short story "Sakai jiken" (1914; tr "The Incident at Sakai," 1977) 「堺事件」 and the meticulously researched life of an Edo-period doctor presented in *Shibue Chūsai* 「渋江抽斎」 (1916).

Akutagawa Ryūnosuke 芥川龍之介, a younger contemporary of Ōgai's and one of Japan's most famous short-story writers 短編作家, also sought an outlet for his sly and supple imagination by setting many stories in the past. For Akutagawa, the past offered through its very remoteness a freedom that the present could not. Such stories as "Rashōmon" (1915; tr "Rashōmon," 1930) 「羅生門」, and "Yabu no naka" (1922; tr "In a Grove," 1952) 「藪の中」 are brilliantly told, combining psychological subtlety and modern cynicism with a fanciful delight in the grotesque.

Nagai Kafū 永井荷風 was another of the major figures in modern Japanese fiction who reflected the tension between modernity and a yearning for an older Japan. His life as a writer began with travels to America and France. He is best known, however, for his elegiac works—notably *Bokutō kitan* (1937; tr *A Strange Tale from East of the River*, 1958) 「濹東綺譚」—depicting the fading demimonde of Tōkyō with a richness of attention to place and mood that has won him a lasting place in literary history.

Shiga Naoya 志賀直哉, who established his reputation with a body of brilliantly crafted short stories, went on to cap his accomplishments with a single full-length psychological novel, *An'ya kōro* (1921–1937; tr *A Dark Night's Passing*, 1976) 「暗夜行路」. The search for identity in the modern world is the theme of this masterwork, as the hero, born of an incestuous liaison between his mother and her father-in-law, learns this ugly fact and suddenly finds his sense of self challenged at its very foundations.

It was Tanizaki Jun'ichirō 谷崎潤一郎 who took modern Japanese writing a step further into a realm of pure and playful fictionality. In early novels such as *Chijin no ai* (1924–1925; tr *Naomi*, 1985) 「痴人の愛」 and *Manji* (1928–1930) 「卍」, Tanizaki went far beyond the conventions of earlier realistic fiction. Both works are tales of sexual infidelity, abandon, obsession, and fantasy in which the deceptions engaged in by the characters are metaphors for the deceptiveness of fiction itself. He possessed a rare capacity to articulate through allegory the cultural confusions of modern Japan. In novels such as *Tade kuu mushi* (1928–1929; tr *Some Prefer Nettles*, 1955) 「蓼食ふ虫」, Tanizaki sought a sense of continuity amid contemporary uneasiness by turning to the past.

Japan's plunge into World War II and the shattering defeat that ensued, were sufficiently powerful to obliterate communion with the past. The writer who most clearly reflected the sense of loss and confusion following the war, both in his writing and his tragic life, was Dazai Osamu 太宰治. Dazai's early work focused upon his own dissipation and debauchery, but the chaos is intensified to the breaking point in *Shayō* (1947; tr *The Setting Sun*, 1956) 「斜陽」 and the novel published just before his suicide, *Ningen shikkaku* (1948; tr *No Longer Human*, 1958) 「人間失格」.

Not every writer after the war accepted Dazai's utterly negative response to the defeat. Ibuse Masuji 井伏鱒二 was one who clung to a sense of geographical place as a mooring, but his focus was on the struggle to maintain that identification in the face of forces that threaten to obliterate it. This is clear in his finest work, *Kuroi ame* (1965–1966; tr *Black Rain*, 1969) 「黒い雨」, about the atomic bombing of Hiroshima. The greatness of the novel, which is narrated through the diaries of ordinary people, lies in its ability to depict all of the horrifying details of the event and yet conclude with an affirmation of humanity.

Not long after the defeat, Tanizaki Jun'ichirō also published his masterpiece, the massive novel *Sasameyuki* (1943–1948; tr *The Makioka Sisters*, 1957) 「細雪」, serial publication of which had been suppressed during the war. A chronicle of the lives of the daughters of a patrician merchant family in its last stages of decline before the outbreak of the war, it is a beautiful elegy to the final passing of all that remained of an older and more elegant world.

Writers such as Enchi Fumiko 円地文子 also sought to reestablish the severed links with the cultural past by calling upon such classical texts as the *Tale of Genji* 「源氏物語」 and transporting them into a very different modern setting. Her novels *Onnazaka* (1949–1957; tr *The Waiting Years*, 1971) 「女坂」 and *Onnamen* (1958; tr *Masks*, 1983) 「女面」 describe the continuing struggle of women confined within traditional social roles.

The link between people and place has grown painfully fragile in the fiction of Nobel laureate, Kawabata Yasunari 川端康成. In novels such as *Yukiguni* (1935–1948; tr *Snow Country*, 1956) 「雪国」, Kawabata creates enormous distances between his characters, suggesting a dread of intimacy that threatens even the most promising of human relationships. After the war, Kawabata took to writing what he called "elegies to the lost Japan" in such works as *Yama no oto* (1949–1954; tr *The Sound of the Mountain*, 1970) 「山の音」, in which the aging protagonist, Shingo 信吾, unable to endure the frustrating losses that surround him, opens a gulf between himself and his family by retreating into his memories of the irretrievable past.

Yet Japanese writing in the early postwar years could not be characterized solely in terms of the shock and dislocation of defeat. There was, in fact, a vigorous renascence of literary activity after 1945, and a new group of writers who debuted at this time came to be known as the "first generation" of postwar authors. They had been attracted to Marxist philosophy マルクス主義 before the war, and returned from the war to assert the need for a type of fiction that would examine all the political, philosophical, and moral aspects of their experience. Members of this group include Noma Hiroshi 野間宏, whose novel *Shinkū chitai* (1952; tr *Zone of Emptiness*, 1956)「真空地帯」depicts the military in wartime as an extension of the oppressive prewar Japanese social order, and Ōoka Shōhei 大岡昇平, who in *Nobi* (1951; tr *Fires on the Plain*, 1957)「野火」, a novel set in the last days of the fighting in the Philippines, depicts a solitary Japanese soldier who is reduced to the lowest level of humanity by his wartime experiences.

The "second generation" of postwar writers includes Abe Kōbō 安部公房 and Mishima Yukio 三島由紀夫, both of whom debuted in the late 1940s. Abe would eventually create a distinctive type of Kafkaesque existential allegory in novels such as *Suna no onna* (1962; tr *The Woman in the Dunes*, 1964)「砂の女」, while Mishima attracted an international readership with his opulent aestheticism, his vision of a postwar Japan clinging to external forms but hollow within, and his complex psychological examination of character and motivation in such works as *Kinkakuji* (1956; tr *The Temple of the Golden Pavilion*, 1959)「金閣寺」.

Critics have posited a turning point in the 1950s, after which Japanese fiction can no longer be easily characterized in terms of the early postwar consciousness. Beginning about this time, a revival and restructuring of the I-novel form was achieved by a "third generation" of postwar writers—Kojima Nobuo 小島信夫, who examined the collapse of the family system in *Hōyō kazoku* (1965, Embracing Family) 「抱擁家族」; Yasuoka Shōtarō 安岡章太郎, who brought a new sense of ironic perspective to the personal narrative in *Umibe no kōkei* (1959; tr *A View by the Sea*, 1984) 「海辺の光景」; and Shimao Toshio 島尾敏雄, whose fiction, culminating in *Shi no toge* (1960; tr *The Sting of Death*, 1985) 「死の棘」, transposes the agony and anxiety of his war experience onto his postwar marital relationship. Also included in this group is Endō Shūsaku 遠藤周作, a Catholic convert who examines the issues of betrayal, cowardice, and martyrdom in novels such as *Chimmoku* (1966; tr *Silence*, 1969) 「沈黙」, set during the Christian persecutions of early-17th-century Japan.

From the 1960s onward, writers have sought to synthesize various approaches to fiction or to experiment with new modes of representation. Ōe Kenzaburō 大江健三郎, who received the Nobel Prize for literature in 1994, has been a prodigiously inventive force in contemporary fiction, continuously experimenting with form and mode of presentation in dealing with both political and personal issues in such novels as *Kojinteki na taiken* (1964; tr *A Personal Matter*, 1968) 「個人的な体験」 and *Man'en gannen no futtobōru* (1967; tr *The Silent Cry*, 1974) 「万延元年のフットボール」. Kōno Taeko 河野多恵子 has examined the repressed psychology of women in *Fui no koe* (1968, Sudden Voice) 「不意の声」 and other works, while Tsushima Yūko 津島佑子, the daughter of Dazai Osamu, has explored the lives of women who are single parents in *Chōji* (1978; tr *Child of Fortune*, 1983) 「寵児」. And finally, the generation raised on the rebellious, rock-and-roll international culture of the last decades has found its voice in writers such as Murakami Ryū 村上龍, author of *Kagirinaku tōmei ni chikai burū* (1976; tr *Almost Transparent Blue*, 1977) 「限りなく透明に近いブルー」, and

Murakami Haruki 村上春樹, whose *Noruuē no mori* (1987; tr *Norwegian Wood*, 1989) 「ノルウェイの森」 sold more than 3 million copies. In Japan, as in the West, critics have periodically proclaimed the death of fiction and bemoaned the decline in the audience for serious literature, but this news has apparently not reached the Japanese public, which is buying and reading a greater number and variety of books than ever before.

Folktales (*minwa*) 民話

Narrative literature of the people, handed down orally from generation to generation. Some tales can be traced back even before writing was introduced to Japan.

Outside of the oral tradition, there is rich documentation of folk material throughout the ages. The 8th century saw the first written records of the imperial history with the *Kojiki* (712, Record of Ancient Matters) 「古事記」 and *Nihon shoki* (720, Chronicles of Japan) 「日本書紀」, which contain many tale motifs. The *Nihon ryōiki* (tr *Miracle Stories of Japan*) 「日本霊異記」, *Konjaku monogatari* (tr *Tales of Times Now Past*) 「今昔物語」, and *Uji shūi monogatari* (tr *A Collection of Tales from Uji*) 「宇治拾遺物語」 of the following centuries are collections of traditional narratives, Buddhist and secular, totaling well over 1,000 in number. Also, the classic dramas of the 15th century, the NŌ 能 and *kyōgen* 狂言, as well as KABUKI 歌舞伎, which originated in the early 17th century, are examples of how dramatists based their plots and themes on folk material, resulting in the preservation of tale motifs today.

Collecting Folktales 民話の採集

Systematic collecting of folktales was started in the 1930s. To encourage local collecting of folktale material, Yanagita Kunio 柳田国男 (1875–1962), founder of Japanese folklore studies, published a handbook entitled *Mukashi-banashi saishū techō* (1936, Manual for Collecting Folktales) 「昔話採集手帖」. One hundred representative Japanese tale types were selected and arranged according to his own system.

Nippon mukashi-banashi meii 「日本昔話名彙」 (1948, A List of Japanese Folktales) was compiled by Yanagita Kunio; it classified his vast notes into an organized list of Japanese tale types. It is useful as a checklist and is still being used for field collecting.

In 1958 Seki Keigo 関敬吾 published *Nippon mukashi-banashi shūsei* 「日本昔話集成」, a six-volume anthology of 8,600 folktales. He classified the material into 700 types using his own system of classification.

Diffusion Routes to Japan 日本への伝来ルート

In prehistoric times Japan seems to have had closer contact with the Eurasian continent than is commonly thought. It was an era of dynamic migration from east to west along many routes. One that intimately concerns Japan was the circumpolar route that eventually populated the Americas. Situated adjacent to this route, Japan shares many cultural features with the races along this grand migration route.

The warm tides washing the shores of Japan suggest another far-reaching route of diffusion. Because many Japanese myths and legends correspond to those of ancient Greece, there is a strong possibility of an overseas route that connected the two areas by way of ports of call dotting the southern fringe of the Eurasian continent.

Again there are Japanese tales and legends that are shared by cultures on the perimeter of the Pacific Ocean. This circumpacific diffusion route follows the Japan Current, which circulates clockwise about the Pacific, north from Taiwan along the east coast of Japan, then across to the western shores of North and South America, and returns west through the Southern Pacific Ocean.

With the advent of the Yayoi period 弥生時代 (ca 300 BC–ca AD 300), an entirely new sort of culture complex came into Japan from the southern part of Korea. From about the 3rd to the 5th centuries, the present emperor's ancestors consolidated their power in central Honshu. The *Kojiki* and *Nihon shoki* trace the imperial family history back to the mythical era and incorporate many preexistent tale motifs.

With the introduction of writing and Buddhism to Japan, first from Korea and then directly from China, Japanese folk literature 民俗文学 gained yet another overland route to sources in Central Asia and down to India through Tibet. Tales recorded in the *Nihon ryōiki* 「日本霊異記」 and *Konjaku monogatari* 「今昔物語」 belong to this group.

Momotarō (Peach Boy) 「桃太郎」

Popular folktale recounting the adventures of the boy Momotarō. Born from a peach found by an elderly woman washing clothes on a riverbank, Momotarō is adopted by the woman and her husband. Maturing quickly, he goes off with a dog, a pheasant, and a monkey to conquer Ogre Island and returns home with treasures for his foster parents. The tale exists in many versions; its present form has been widely popular since the late Edo period 江戸時代 (1600–1868).

Shitakiri suzume (The Tongue-Cut Sparrow) 「舌きり雀」

A sparrow owned by an honest old man eats some rice paste prepared by a greedy old woman (in some versions the man's wife). Enraged, the woman cuts out the tongue of the sparrow and drives it away. The grieving old man goes in search of his sparrow and is well treated by the sparrow's family. On leaving them, he is offered a choice of two boxes; he takes the lighter one, which turns out to be full of treasure. The greedy woman then pays a visit to the sparrows and demands the heavier box, from which emerge goblins and serpents; the woman dies of shock. The archetype of this story is found in the 13th-century collection of tales *Uji shūi monogatari* 「宇治拾遺物語」.

Art (Nihon *bijutsu*) 日本美術

Over the centuries, a wide variety of social, economic, political, cultural, and environmental factors have had an influence on the development of Japanese art. The temperate climate and four distinct seasons provided an abundance of seasonal symbols and motifs, such as the plum, the cherry, the maple, and the chrysanthemum, which appear again and again in Japanese art. The Japanese love of nature is reflected in the use of such raw materials as lacquer, wood, bamboo, and paper throughout Japanese architecture. The high humidity and frequent earthquakes and typhoons common to Japan discouraged the use of more permanent materials such as stone in architecture and ensured the preference for the more readily mendable and available materials that dominate the Japanese aesthetic.

At the same time, the influence of China, whose culture rests at the heart of East Asian creativity, was particularly felt in Japan; Chinese artistic styles and larger segments of Chinese culture, including the great international tradition of Buddhist art 仏教美術, reached Japan either directly or filtered through the Korean peninsula. Even the famous secular style of the Heian court (794–1185) received notable inspiration from continental shores.

Despite Japan's contact with and absorption of foreign aesthetics from prehistoric times to the present, Japanese art had little, if any, influence on outside cultures, especially Western cultures, until the last half of the 19th century, when European artists discovered its beauties and developed a passion for *japonaiserie* ジャポニズム. Exposure to and consciousness of Japanese art through, for example, Japanese ceramics and woodblock prints played a major role in the development of a

Classic Design Motifs (1)
日本の伝統デザイン

Stylized clouds between curved vertical lines.

Eddies mark this pattern, known as *kanzemizu*, which also features a chrysanthemum motif.

Four elliptical flower petals set inside interlocking circles—a popular pattern known as *shippōtsunagi*.

Many wave patterns depict a sea rough with breakers.

modern European painting aesthetic, as well as influencing the aesthetic course of the decorative arts. Present-day Japanese artists are making an increasingly active contribution to the development of contemporary international art.

Buddhist art (Bukkyō *bijutsu*) 仏教美術

Like Japanese Buddhism itself, Japanese Buddhist art was a national variant of an international tradition. In Japan the Buddhist art forms that were periodically introduced from China and Korea were tempered in the crucible of local custom and usage, to yield a rich tradition of religious art and architecture.

Early Buddhist Art 初期の仏教美術

Buddhism was formally transmitted to Japan from China and Korea in the 6th century. The forms of Buddhism and Buddhist art that first arrived in Japan were chiefly those of the Mahāyāna (J: Daijō Bukkyō 大乗仏教) tradition, a theistic and catholic system of belief that stressed universal salvation and that was to remain the underlying framework of most sects of Buddhist belief and practice in Japan through the modern era.

From its inception Buddhism in Japan engaged the concern and patronage of ruling interests and became virtually a state creed. Temples and monastic compounds usually consisted of at least seven typical structures, including a *tō* (pagoda) 塔, a main hall called the *kondō* ("golden hall") 金堂, a lecture hall 講堂 called the *kōdō*, and a *kyōzō* or sutra repository 経蔵. In the first wave of such construction, numerous temples were erected from the late 6th to the early 7th century in what is now the Kyōto-Ōsaka region, most notably Asukadera 飛鳥寺, Shitennōji 四天王寺, and Hōryūji 法隆寺. After Heijōkyō (Nara) was designated the national capital in 710, a new wave of temple construction in the early 8th century produced the great Nara-period (710–794) metropolitan

Classic Design Motifs (2)
日本の伝統デザイン

Arrow feathers alternating positive and negative.

A *shidarezakura*, or weeping cherry. The cherry blossom is Japan's national flower.

In this pattern, six diamonds combine to form a six-pointed star that resembles the leaf of the hemp plant.

This design, called *ichimatsu*, was popularized by a famous Edo-period *kabuki* actor.

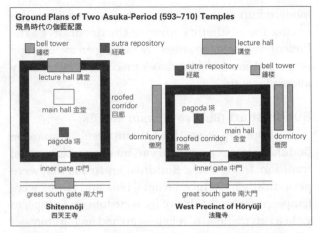

Ground Plans of Two Asuka-Period (593–710) Temples
飛鳥時代の伽藍配置

bell tower
鐘楼

sutra repository
経蔵

lecture hall
講堂

lecture hall 講堂

main hall 金堂

roofed
corridor
回廊

pagoda 塔

dormitory
僧房

inner gate 中門

great south gate 南大門

Shitennōji
四天王寺

sutra repository
経蔵

bell tower
鐘楼

pagoda 塔

main hall
金堂

roofed corridor
回廊

dormitory
僧房

inner gate 中門

great south gate 南大門

West Precinct of Hōryūji
法隆寺

monasteries, among them Kōfukuji 興福寺, Daianji 大安寺, and Yakushiji 薬師寺.

A tremendous amount of Buddhist art was commissioned for the halls and chapels of these temple complexes. Paintings and sculptures representing various Buddhas, bodhisattvas, and guardian deities were the icons to which worship and ritual were directed. A corollary art form, that of the illustrated handscroll (*emakimono* 絵巻物), was developed for Buddhist narrative instruction. The oldest in this genre is the 8th-century biography of Shaka 釈迦 called the *E inga kyō* (Illustrated Sutra of Cause and Effect) 「絵因果経」.

The construction of Tōdaiji from 747 marked the apex of classical Buddhist art and architecture in Japan. The temple's *honzon*, or principal object of worship 本尊, is a colossal gilt-bronze image —measuring some 15 meters (49 ft) in height— of the cosmic Buddha 毘盧遮那 called Birushana (Skt: Vairocana). A technical feat, this giant sculpture—called the Nara Daibutsu ("Great Buddha of Nara") 奈良大仏—came to symbolize the power, wealth, and intrusiveness of state-sanctioned Buddhism.

▍Esoteric Buddhism 密教

In part as a reaction to the state Buddhism symbolized by Tōdaiji and the Nara Daibutsu, a new regime moved the capital to Heiankyō (now Kyōto) in 794. Largely coincidental with this move was the emergence into prominence of *mikkyō*, "the secret teachings," 密教 a system of esoteric Buddhist belief and practice that was to be articulated in the Shingon sect 真言宗 and the Tendai sect 天台宗.

The Buddha Dainichi 大日如来 (Skt: Mahāvairocana) became the organizing principle of esoteric Buddhism and the focus of worship.

Key to Shingon and Tendai practice were the paired mandalas of the Diamond or Thunderbolt Realm 金剛界曼荼羅 and the Matrix or Womb Realm 胎蔵界曼荼羅, together referred to as the "Two Mandalas." 両部曼荼羅.

The paintings and sculptures that filled Shingon and Tendai temples displayed an aesthetic and stylistic tenor appropriate to the mystery of ritual and meditation at a remote temple in mountain setting. An important example of this tendency is seen in the 9th-century set of five statues of the Bodhisattvas of the Void (Godai Kokūzō Bosatsu 五大虚空蔵菩薩像), each in painted wood, at Jingoji. Also coincidental with the development of esotericism was a trend in sculpture toward the carving of votive statues out of single blocks of wood, their surfaces left unadorned with paint or lacquer in deference to the inherent sanctity of the sacred tree 神木. The principal examples of this "plain wood" style are the Yakushi figures at Gangōji 元興寺 (early 9th century) and at Jingoji 神護寺 (early 9th century).

Pure Land Buddhism 浄土教

Even though esotericism remained a major element in Japanese religious life, by the close of the 10th century it had begun to give way as a system of popular belief to Pure Land faith and practice. In the Pure Land 浄土 tradition worship focused on the Buddha Amida

(Skt: Amitābha) 阿弥陀仏 and on rebirth in his Western Paradise 極楽, or Pure Land, called Gokuraku (Skt: Sukhāvatī).

A celebrated example of Pure Land art and aesthetics is the *amidadō* (Amida hall) 阿弥陀堂, now called the Phoenix Hall 鳳凰堂, at Byōdōin in Uji, which was constructed in 1053 by Fujiwara no Yorimichi 藤原頼通 (992–1074), who, with his father, Fujiwara no Michinaga 藤原道長 (966–1028), was one of the great patrons of Pure Land Buddhism 浄土教 and art.

One of the principal treatises of Japanese Pure Land Buddhism—one that had a major impact on art production—was a work by the Tendai monk Genshin 源信 (Eshin Sōzu 恵心僧都; 942–1017) called *Ōjōyōshū* (985, The Essentials of Pure Land Rebirth) 「往生要集」, in which was set forth an exhaustive account of Amida's nine sectors of paradise and the nine degrees of rebirth 九品往生 therein.

In painting, a key Pure Land genre was the so-called *raigōzu* ("welcoming pictures") 来迎図, in which Amida and his heavenly entourage are shown arriving to welcome and guide the dying to paradise. The *raigōzu* genre was heavily influenced by Genshin's work. An important example is the mid-12th-century triptych *Amida shōju raigōzu* 阿弥陀聖衆迎図 (Descent of Amida and the Heavenly Multitude) at Mt. Kōya 高野山.

In *Ōjōyōshū* Genshin did not limit his discussion to paradise; the first part of this treatise provides a horrific vision of the six realms of existence 六道, and especially various hells. By the 12th century an imagery of hell and karmic retribution was fully developed. Celebrated examples of this genre are the *Gaki-zōshi* (Scrolls of Hungry Ghosts) 餓鬼草紙 and *Jigoku-zōshi* (Scrolls of Hells) 地獄草紙. Another *emakimono* genre, that of temple histories 縁起 and biographies of saints and monks, was also developed. An example of this popular genre is *Shigisan engi emaki* (The Legends of Mt. Shigi) 「信貴山縁起絵巻」.

Zen Buddhism 禅宗

In the 13th century the Zen (Ch: Chan) sect, disseminated by Japanese and Chinese monks, took hold among the ruling military elites and introduced new currents in art.

Zen temples were strongly continental in flavor and differed significantly from the architectural models used in other sects. Layout, nomenclature, furnishings, and even structural details were derived from the Buddhist architecture of south central China. The typical Zen monastic compound, especially the semiautonomous subtemple 塔頭 known as *tatchū,* usually incorporated a carefully composed small garden. In keeping with the austerity of Zen taste, some of these gardens, in a format called "rock and sand garden" 枯山水, were landscaped without the standard pond or stream.

The private halls and quarters at a Zen compound accomodated the painted portrait of a teacher 頂相.

The impact of Zen aesthetics and doctrine was by no means limited to the monastic compound. The development of a pure landscape painting genre in Japan (*sansuiga* 山水画), as well as the emergence of a mature *suibokuga* (ink painting) 水墨画 tradition, owes much to the influence of Zen and Zen monk-painters.

Buddhism under the Tokugawa Shogunate
徳川幕府と仏教

The spread of Neo-Confucian orthodoxy in China and Korea also affected Japan, where the unifying ideology of the Tokugawa shogunate (1603–1867) and its widespread educational system constituted an official state Confucianism. As Buddhism lost its centrality to politics and culture, Buddhist art gave way to secular forms, although Buddhist values remained visible in much of Japanese taste and aesthetics.

Painting (*kaiga*) 絵画

Japanese painting is characterized by a wide range of styles in a wide array of formats, from horizontal and hanging scrolls to album leaves 草紙, fans, walls, and free-standing and sliding screens 屏風：襖. Like the history of Japanese art in general, Japanese painting has been dominated by two components, continental and indigenous, in the development of style and technique. Until the 19th century, China was the principal source of innovation. Much of the history of painting in premodern Japan can be described as a dialogue between Chinese and native styles.

Painting through the Nara Period (710–794)
奈良時代(710年～794年)までの絵画

With the introduction of Buddhism and Buddhist culture from Korea and China in the 6th century, painting began to flourish as the production of Buddhist art and architecture became a major concern of the ruling class.

A number of paintings from the late 7th and early 8th centuries are preserved at the temple Hōryūji. In Hōryūji Great Treasure House 法隆寺大宝蔵殿 a votive shrine called the Tamamushi Shrine, or "Beetle-Wing Shrine," 「玉虫厨子」 bears a series of 7th-century paintings on its panels, whose bronze filigree frames were backed originally by the iridescent wings of the *tamamushi* beetle. These paintings illustrate episodes from the life of the Buddha as well as depicting figures of bodhisattvas and other deities.

Painting of the Heian (794–1185) and Kamakura (1185–1333) Periods
平安(794年～1185年)・鎌倉(1185年～1333年)時代の絵画

With the rise in the early 9th century of esoteric Buddhism as developed by the Shingon sect and the Tendai sect, the painted mandala 曼荼羅 emerged into prominence. Important examples of this genre are the Diamond Realm (Kongōkai) and Womb Realm

(Taizōkai) mandalas 金剛界曼荼羅：胎蔵界曼荼羅, dated 824–833, at the temple Jingoji, and the 11th-century *Kojima Mandala* 「子島曼荼羅」 at Kojimadera 子島寺 in Nara. The five-story pagoda 五重塔 at Daigoji 醍醐寺, constructed in 952, contains a number of murals depicting various esoteric deities in a mandala format.

After the 10th century, the influence of Pure Land Buddhism 浄土教—popularized by the Jōdo sect 浄土宗 and its predecessors—became increasingly apparent in painting. An important new genre was the *raigōzu*, a depiction of the Buddha Amida arriving to welcome the dying to paradise.

By the mid-Heian period, Chinese modes of painting 唐絵 had begun to give way to a distinctly indigenous style known as *yamato-e* 大和絵. The earliest paintings in this style were sliding screens and folding screens. Two new painting formats evolved as the native style was developed: the album leaf (*sōshi* 草紙) and the illustrated handscroll 絵巻物.

Painting of the Muromachi Period (1333–1568)

室町時代(1333年～1568年)の絵画

During the 14th century, scroll painting declined as *suibokuga*, or ink painting 水墨画, took hold in the great Zen monasteries of Kamakura and Kyōto. An austere monochrome style, introduced from Song (960–1279) and Yuan (1279–1368) China, was favored by Zen painters and their patrons. The styles of the Chinese monk-painters Muqi (J: Mokkei 牧谿; fl ca 1250) and Liang Kai (1140?–1210?) were particularly influential.

During the 15th century, Tenshō Shūbun 天章周文 (d ca 1460) and Sesshū Tōyō 雪舟等楊 (1420–1506) developed the Chinese-inspired monochrome landscape style into a fully Japanese format. A key work by Sesshū is *Amanohashidate* 「天橋立図」 (ca 1501, Kyōto National Museum), which depicts the famous scenic spot of that name.

In the last years of Ashikaga rule, a new genre of ink painting was developed largely outside the Zen community by artists of the Ami school 阿弥派 and the Kanō school 狩野派. The Kanō school was initiated by Kanō Masanobu 狩野正信 (1434–1530), the official painter of the Muromachi shogunate, and continued by his son Kanō Motonobu 狩野元信 (1476–1559). Although Chinese styles and themes remained their model, Kanō-school artists introduced a more decorative and plastic sensibility that would come to dominate the landscape painting of the succeeding centuries.

Painting of the Azuchi-Momoyama (1568–1600) and Edo (1600–1868) Periods

安土桃山(1568年～1600年)・江戸(1600年～1868年)時代の絵画

The Kanō school, promoted by Oda Nobunaga 織田信長 (1534–1582), Toyotomi Hideyoshi 豊臣秀吉 (1537–1598), and other powerful patrons, dominated painting in the late 16th century and developed a grandiose polychromed style for screen and wall painting 障屏画. Kanō Eitoku 狩野永徳 (1543–1590) was commissioned by Nobunaga to decorate Azuchi Castle 安土城 (1576–1579; destroyed 1582) near Lake Biwa 琵琶湖 and by Hideyoshi to decorate Jurakudai Palace 聚楽第 (1587; destroyed 1595) in Kyōto. Eitoku is believed to be the first painter to have introduced the dramatic use of fields of gold leaf in large mural compositions. By the time that Eitoku's grandson Kanō Tan'yū 狩野探幽 (1602–1674) was active, the Kanō school was firmly established as the painting academy of the Tokugawa shogunate (1603–1867).

Another genre, one belonging to the *yamato-e* tradition, was developed by painters of the Tosa school 土佐派, whose small-scale works often illustrated the literary classics of earlier generations. The *yamato-e* tradition also gave rise to the decorative painters of the group called Rimpa 琳派. The principal artists of this school were Tawaraya Sōtatsu 俵屋宗達 (d 1643?) and Ogata Kōrin 尾形光琳 (1658–1716), whose works—taking classical styles and themes and presenting them in a new, boldly decorative format—have come to symbolize the lavish tastes of Edo (now Tōkyō) society in the 17th and 18th centuries.

Fūzokuga, or genre paintings 風俗画, became popular in the late 16th century and gave rise to UKIYO-E, "paintings of the floating world," 浮世絵 which captured the transient experiences of the pleasure quarters of Edo and other urban centers. The woodblock print 木版画 as a significant Edo-period medium emerged out of this tradition.

The late Edo period was one of eclecticism in painting. The influence of European painting was increasingly apparent. Major artists of this period include Maruyama Ōkyo 円山応挙 (1733–1795) and Matsumura Goshun 松村呉春 (1752–1811), founders of the Maruyama-Shijō school 円山四条派, and Itō Jakuchū 伊藤若冲 (1716–1800).

Another major trend in late-Edo-period painting was that of *bunjinga*, "literati painting." 文人画 This style entered Japan in the 18th century via Nagasaki, where it was introduced by Chinese immigrant painters.

Painting of the Meiji Period (1868–1912)
明治時代(1868年～1912年)の絵画

During the Meiji period, political and social change was effected in the course of a modernization campaign by the new government. Western-style painting 洋画 was promoted officially, and a number of painters such as Harada Naojirō 原田直次郎 (1863–1899), Yamamoto Hōsui 山本芳翠 (1850–1906), and Asai Chū 浅井忠 (1856–1907) traveled abroad for study under government auspices. However, the initial burst of enthusiasm for Western art soon yielded to renewed appreciation of traditional Japanese art, promoted by the art critic

Okakura Kakuzō 岡倉覚三 (1862–1913) and the American educator Ernest Fenollosa (1853–1908). Japanese-style painting 日本画 rose to prominence as its conservative advocates gained control of art institutions. By the 1880s, Western-style painters were barred from exhibitions and widely criticized.

Confronted by the resurgence of traditionalism, Western-style painters formed the Meiji Bijutsukai (Meiji Fine Arts Society) 明治美術会 and began to hold their own exhibitions. Prominent among these painters was Kuroda Seiki 黒田清輝 (also known as Kuroda Kiyoteru; 1866–1924), who introduced pleinairism 戸外主義 and established the influential White Horse Society 白馬会.

Painting of the Taishō Period (1912–1926)
大正時代(1912年～1926年)の絵画

The Taishō period saw burgeoning Western influence in the arts. After long stays in Europe the painters Yamashita Shintarō 山下新太郎 (1881–1966), Saitō Yori 斎藤与里 (1885–1959), and Arishima Ikuma 有島生馬 (1882–1974) introduced impressionism 印象主義 and early features of the postimpressionist movement 後期印象主義運動 to Japan; Yasui Sōtarō 安井曾太郎 (1888–1955) and Umehara Ryūzaburō 梅原龍三郎 (1888–1986), whose careers would span the modern period, returned to promote the styles of Camille Pissarro, Paul Cézanne, and Pierre Auguste Renoir. The eclecticism that informed Taishō-period painting came as a direct result of the rapid infusion of the full range of contemporary European styles.

Although on a limited scale, Japanese-style painting too was affected by European styles, especially neoclassicism 新古典主義 and, later, postimpressionism. Yokoyama Taikan 横山大観 (1868–1958), Shimomura Kanzan 下村観山 (1873–1930), and Hishida Shunsō 菱田春草 (1874–1911), all to some degree adopted Western-style atmospheric treatment of space and light.

Painting of the Shōwa Period (1926–1989)
昭和時代(1926年～1989年)の絵画

The painters Yasui Sōtarō and Umehara Ryūzaburō stood at the forefront of pre-World War II Shōwa painting. The period 1925–1940 is termed the "Yasui-Umehara era." While incorporating notions of pure art and abstraction, both succeeded in surmounting the heretofore largely derivative character of Western-style painting in Japan. Umehara in particular brought aspects of the *nihonga* tradition to his work and launched Western-style painting on a more interpretative path.

However, neither artist completely dominated Western-style painting of the 1930s. A far more international contemporary of Yasui and Umehara was Fujita Tsuguharu 藤田嗣治 (also known as Fujita Tsuguji, Léonard Foujita; 1886–1968). The Nika Society 二科会 widened its sphere of influence by absorbing surrealism 超現実主義 and abstractionism 抽象主義, and the essentially fauvist Dokuritsu Bijutsu Kyōkai (Independent Art Association) 独立美術協会 was formed in 1931.

Japan Art Academy 日本芸術院 was formed in 1947 and contains both *yōga* and *nihonga* divisions. Government-sponsored art exhibitions like the Bunten have disappeared. The Nitten (Nihon Bijutsu Tenrankai; Japan Art Exhibition) 日展 in particular has functioned as the modern counterpart of the Bunten.

Today Japanese artists are active members of a worldwide artistic community. By the 1960s, avant-garde notions of art had been embraced, and an internationalization of Japanese art followed. Postwar trends in the West have been taken up rapidly in Japan, from the abstract expressionism 抽象表現主義 of the 1950s to later developments such as the antiart movement 反芸術運動, assemblage, pop and op art, primary structure, minimal art, and kinetic art. After a largely derivative past, modern Japanese painters have emerged as significant contributors to international movements in art.

Ukiyo-e 浮世絵

A genre of art, chiefly in the medium of the woodblock print 木版画, that arose early in the Edo period (1600–1868) and built up a broad popular market among the middle classes. Subject matter tended to focus on the brothel districts and the *kabuki* 歌舞伎 theaters, and formats ranged from single-sheet prints to albums and book illustrations. *Ukiyo-e* flourished throughout Japan, attaining their most characteristic form in the prints produced in Edo (now Tōkyō) from about 1680 to the 1850s.

Early *Ukiyo-e* 初期の浮世絵

The distinctive milieu from which *ukiyo-e* would emerge was flourishing as early as the Kan'ei era 寛永年間 (1624–1644). Genre paintings 風俗画 of the time depict pleasure seekers of every social class thronging the entertainment district beside the river Kamogawa 鴨川 in Kyōto. It was in such districts, in Kyōto, Ōsaka, and Edo, that there developed the freewheeling way of life of the *ukiyo*, or "floating world," 浮世 and the genre of art, *ukiyo-e*, that glorified it.

Sex manuals (*shunga*; literally, "spring pictures" 春画) and courtesan critiques 遊女評判記 were among the earliest types of printed *ukiyo-e*. Hishikawa Moronobu 菱川師宣 (?–1694) is the first recorded artist of *shunga* to whom individual works can be assigned. Thereafter *shunga* remained a genre at which most *ukiyo-e* artists tried their hand. The critiques of courtesans, essentially picture books with commentary, contained stylized portraits of the leading courtesans of the day, engaged in some casual activity such as reading or adjusting their hair. The interest of such scenes is chiefly in the poses and the draping of *kimono*. A similar type of picture was the *bijin-e* ("beautiful-woman picture") 美人絵, in which courtesans of the highest rank (*tayū*) were depicted. Pictures of courtesans remained popular throughout the history of *ukiyo-e*; the Kaigetsudō school 懐月堂派 (early 18th century) of *ukiyo-e* painters rarely turned to any other subject.

Edo *Ukiyo-e* 江戸の浮世絵

By the late 17th century, the center of *ukiyo-e* had shifted from Kamigata (the Kyōto-Ōsaka area) to Edo, where the single-sheet print 一枚刷り, probably initially intended for mounting on scrolls (*kakemono-e*), seems to have become a specialty in the closing years of the Genroku era (1688–1704).

It was the development of the single-sheet print, that marked a turning point in the history of *ukiyo-e*, the coming of age of which was closely joined to that of *kabuki*. Portrayals of actors 役者絵 in popular roles had already become standard subject matter of *ukiyo-e*, but it was the Torii school 鳥居派 that achieved the greatest success in rendering the pyrotechnics of an *aragoto* performance 荒事 in graphic terms. Torii Kiyonobu I 鳥居清信1世 (1664?–1729) and Torii Kiyomasu I 鳥居清倍1世 (fl 1697–1720s) perfected a style that, with its vigorous use of line and robust forms, was particularly appropriate for theatrical subjects, and their school soon acquired a virtual monopoly over commissions in Edo for painted theatrical posters 看板絵 and illustrated program notes 絵番付.

Color Prints 色刷り

In about 1745, a technique was conceived for registering successive blocks, each printing a different color on a single sheet. The resulting prints, called *benizuri-e* (pictures printed in red) 紅摺絵 because the most striking color was a red derived from the petals of the safflower (*benibana*), were produced only in two or three colors. It was not until 1764 that the first full-color prints appeared, a development that is closely associated with the sudden popularity of the work of Suzuki Harunobu 鈴木春信 (1725?–1770). By 1766 almost every *ukiyo-e* artist was working in Harunobu's style. These new prints, called *nishiki-e* (brocade pictures) 錦絵 or *edo-e* (Edo pictures) 江戸絵, represented the final stage of technical advancement in color printing achieved in the Edo period.

The Golden Age of *Ukiyo-e* 浮世絵の黄金時代

The late 18th century was largely a period of consolidation rather than innovation; however, development of the more generous *ōban* format and the introduction of diptychs and triptychs led to more complex composition. After 1790, *ukiyo-e* images acquired a new intensity and styles began to succeed one another with greater rapidity. Kitagawa Utamaro 喜多川歌麿 (1753–1806) and Sharaku 写楽 (active mid-1794–early 1795) brought a new sense of realism and achieved a heightened closeness to their subjects by using the format of the *ōkubi-e* or bust portrait 大首絵. Utamaro's women are often sensuous, even sensual, to an extreme.

After 1800, there appears to have been a radical change in taste, accompanied by a faltering of inspiration in design and a deterioration in the quality of printing. Short figures with hunched shoulders and sharp features replaced the tall, elegant figures of the 1770s and 1780s, *kimono* patterns became coarser and more strident, and pictures of actors tended toward the exaggerated and grotesque. One reason for this was change in the print-buying public, which had grown larger and presumably less discriminating, resulting in prints that were produced hastily and in great numbers.

Landscape 風景画

The emergence of the landscape print 風景版画 was a relatively late phenomenon in the history of *ukiyo-e*. Prior to Katsushika Hokusai's 葛飾北斎 (1760–1849)

Fugaku sanjūrokkei (1823, Thirty-Six Views of Mount Fuji) 「富嶽三十六景」, landscape as independent subject matter for *ukiyo-e* was largely unknown. Active as an artist for some 60 years, Hokusai developed a style that was highly individual, combining Chinese and Western influences with elements drawn from the native Kanō school 狩野派, the Tosa school 土佐派, and the Rimpa 琳派 tradition. He was also a prolific draftsman who employed a variety of techniques to create the astounding array of images in his famous 13-volume *Hokusai manga* (1814–1849, Hokusai's Sketches) 北斎漫画.

Hokusai's only true rival in landscape was Andō Hiroshige 安藤広重 (1797–1858), whose great *Tōkaidō gojūsantsugi* (1833–1834, The Fifty-Three Stations of the Tōkaidō Road) 「東海道五十三次」 brought him fame and a host of imitators. Hiroshige displays in this and other works a greater concern than Hokusai with atmosphere, light, and weather.

As an integral element of the Edo-period culture that it mirrored, *ukiyo-e* was unable to survive that society's demise in the wake of the radical Westernization that transformed Japan during the Meiji period (1868–1912).

Ceramics (*tōjiki*) 陶磁器

Ceramics in Japan has a long history, stretching over 12,000 years. The Japanese archipelago is abundantly supplied with the raw material for ceramics, and an appreciation for clay and its multitude of possible uses has been a steady force in Japanese culture for millennia.

In the development of ceramic materials, China was the great innovator, and all of Japan's advanced technology came directly or indirectly from there; more often than not, China also set the style. Yet also typical of Japan's attitude toward ceramics was the fact that, while newer wares representing advanced technology might be accorded a position of highest status, they by no means obliterated existing wares and techniques, which for the most part continued unaffected. As a result, Japanese ceramics became steadily richer in variety, and the ceramic articles produced in Japan today cover the full range from earthenware directly descended from neolithic precedents to the most demanding Chinese-style glazed wares.

Glazed Ceramics 釉薬をかけた陶磁器

By the Nara period (710–794) continental ceramic technology had been introduced: intentional glazing of high-fired wares.

Production of lead-glazed wares began at kilns in or around the modern city of Nara. Plain green-glazed pieces were being made by the late 7th century, and polychrome glazes were added by the early 8th century. These early Nara wares, produced under government control, include three-color wares 三彩陶器 —usually green, white, and yellowish brown—called *sansai tōki*.

Duplication of the celadon technology occurred with the development at the Sanage kilns 猿投陶窯 (in the vicinity of modern Nagoya) of a feldspathic glaze applied to a high-fired gray or white body. Sanage received direct support from the Heian court.

By the end of the 12th century, however, most central Sanage kilns were making only the unglazed, popular tablewares. A movement from eastern Sanage toward better sources of white, kaolin-like clay led to the establishment of a new center for glazed ware in Seto 瀬戸 (Aichi Prefecture).

Medieval Ceramics 中世の陶磁器

Under the patronage of the Kamakura shogunate (1192–1333) and Zen temples, Seto began by copying newly introduced Southern Song 南宋 (1127–1279)

Chinese forms—four-eared jars, flasks, ewers—with amber or green ash glaze applied over carved, stamped, or sprigged designs. By the 14th century Seto had also perfected use of the iron-brown *temmoku* glaze 天目釉 inspired by brown-glazed teabowls brought back from China.

Seto kilns 瀬戸窯 reached their peak in the mid-15th century. The center for glazed wares shifted to Mino 美濃 (now part of Gifu Prefecture). Efforts to imitate porcelains from Ming 明 (1368–1644) China led to the development of the opaque, white feldspathic glaze with underglaze iron decoration that became popular as Shino ware 志野焼 late in the 16th century.

Although glazed as well as unglazed wares continued to be produced at Seto, Mino, and other medieval kilns, from the 12th through the 16th century the principal Japanese ceramic product was a sturdy, unglazed stoneware, called *yakishime* 焼締 or *sekki* 炻器, that was made in a limited set of shapes primarily for utilitarian storage. The most important kilns to produce this type of stoneware were those at Tokoname 常滑焼.

With the growing commercial significance of ceramics in the Muromachi period (1333–1568), when unglazed stonewares in particular emerged as valuable sources of cash income, potters became more professional as output increased. Beginning with tea jars, everyday wares began to be glazed, resulting in further improvements in kiln structure. Mino potters were most influential in dispersing glazing technology to stoneware kilns.

Nevertheless, the same kilns that were striving to develop glazes were also influenced by the interest of the tea masters in unglazed pieces (particularly in ceramics imported from Southeast Asia, known as *namban* ware 南蛮焼) for use as tea ceremony 茶の湯 vessels. This interest reflected an increasing appreciation of simplicity and rusticity, aesthetic values that came to a peak in the tea ceremony school founded by Sen no Rikyū 千利休 (1522–1591). Bizen 備前 produced the outstanding early pieces in this mode. Around 1600 the conscious manipulation at the Iga kilns 伊賀窯 of the features of unglazed medieval stonewares, including "natural" ash glaze, represented the epitome of the artificial naturalism espoused by many tea ceremony adherents.

▋Edo-Period Ceramics 江戸時代の陶磁器

The Edo period (1600–1868) saw a continuation of innovative stylistic and technological developments in stonewares and in glazed and unglazed ceramics.

Japan's invasions of Korea in 1592 and 1597 文禄・慶長の役 gave military leaders the opportunity to bring Korean potters, with their superior skills of throwing and glazing, to Japan to work in their domains. The introduction from Korea of the *noborigama* ("climbing kiln") 登り窯 revolutionized the firing of stonewares and made possible the successful firing of porcelain after suitable clays were discovered in the Arita area of northern Kyūshū by Korean potters in the early 17th century.

By the mid-17th century a crucial influence was added in the form of the European market. The Dutch East India Company オランダ東インド会社 not only placed enormous orders but also provided models and directions for what was wanted in Europe. Special preference was accorded an Arita-produced decorated ware called Kakiemon ware 柿右衛門, which was characterized by application of polychrome enamels and underglaze cobalt to a milk-white porcelain body.

The second half of the 17th century saw the full flowering of such decorated wares. Colorful Imari ware 伊万里焼 and Kakiemon ware were shipped to Europe from Kyūshū in great quantities; the finer Kakiemon and Nabeshima ware 鍋島焼 porcelains were reserved for local rulers. In Kyōto, a popular form of decorated earthenware or stoneware known as *kyō-yaki* 京焼 was developed by such potter-decorators as Nonomura Ninsei 野々村仁清 (fl mid-17th century) and Ogata Kenzan 尾形乾山 (1663–1743). Only isolated ventures, such as Kutani ware 九谷焼, attempted the production of porcelain in competition with the dominant kilns in Arita.

Modern Ceramics 現代の陶磁器

The opening of Japan to the West brought new opportunities for ceramics export and the development of porcelain centers at Kyōto and Yokohama. Through the work of the German technician Gottfried Wagener (1831–1892) in Arita 有田, Kyōto, and Tōkyō, and through Japanese participation in international expositions in Europe and the United States, Western ceramic technology and taste were introduced.

Contemporary Japanese ceramics may be said to have begun shortly after 1900 with the emergence of the "studio potter" アトリエ陶芸家 with an individual name and style. The studio potter of the 20th century came to ceramics by choice rather than by birth, and the typical eclectic style was based on a strong knowledge of Japanese ceramic history. Itaya Hazan 板谷波山 (1872–1963), for example, was trained as a sculptor, and Kitaōji Rosanjin 北大路魯山人 (1883–1959) began making pottery to supply his own gourmet restaurant.

From 1926, the FOLK CRAFTS movement 民芸運動 led by Yanagi Muneyoshi 柳宗悦 (1889–1961) began to foster interest in the aesthetic value of traditional craftwork and skillfully made simple objects of daily use—among them ceramics. The potters Kawai Kanjirō 河井寛次郎 (1890–1966) and Hamada Shōji 浜田庄司 (1894–1978) participated in this movement, and it was through the latter, who established his workshop in Mashiko 益子 (Tochigi Prefecture), that the town became famous as a center of folk-style pottery 民芸陶器. Many foreign potters have studied in the town.

Swords (*nihontō*) 日本刀

The origins of the Japanese sword go back to the 8th century. Japanese swords are particularly impressive because of the early technical mastery achieved in Japanese steelmaking and because of the elegant shape, lines, texture, and shades of color of the steel fabric. For more than 12 centuries the sword has had a spiritual significance for the Japanese; along with the mirror and jewels, it is one of the three Imperial Regalia 三種の神器.

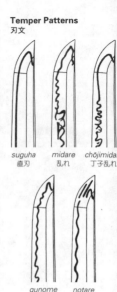

Temper Patterns
刃文

suguha
直刃

midare
乱れ

chōjimidare
丁子乱れ

gunome
互の目

notare
濩れ

Swordsmiths 刀工

The Japanese swordsmith was traditionally held in high regard. The earliest swordsmiths were often *yamabushi* 山伏, members of the Shugendō sect 修験道派, who with their apprentices lived an austere and religiously dedicated life. The approximately 200 schools of Japanese swordsmith-artists were scattered throughout Japan, each with its own history and its own identifiable and surprisingly consistent blade characteristics that can be traced down through the centuries.

Forging 鍛造

As early as the 8th to 10th century, sword blades of high-quality steel were being made in Japan. After the steel was forged, the "skin steel" 皮金 was some 10 to 20 times hammered into plates, which were then hardened, broken into coin-sized pieces, stacked, and welded. This hardened steel was later welded onto the surface of the less brittle inner steel 心金. This repeated folding and welding gave the Japanese blade one of its unique qualities—a texture 地肌 like that of the grain of wood.

Tempering and Polishing 焼入れと研磨

The *hamon*, or temper pattern 刃文 of the blade, is one of the most noticeable and beautiful features of the sword and also an important means of identifying its origin. By the early Kamakura period (1185–1333), this *hamon* was made to exhibit many shapes and forms. Generally a specific type of temper or group of types

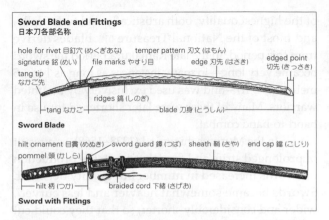

Sword Blade and Fittings
日本刀各部名称

hole for rivet 目釘穴 (めくぎあな)　temper pattern 刃文 (はもん)
signature 銘 (めい)　file marks やすり目　edge 刃先 (はさき)　edged point 切先 (きっさき)
tang tip なかご先
ridges 鎬 (しのぎ)　blade 刀身 (とうしん)
tang なかご

Sword Blade

hilt ornament 目貫 (めぬき)　sword guard 鐔 (つば)　sheath 鞘 (さや)　end cap 鐺 (こじり)
pommel 頭 (かしら)
hilt 柄 (つか)　braided cord 下緒 (さげお)

Sword with Fittings

was employed by an individual school or smith. The final polishing and sharpening were done by a sword polisher, who set the sword to a series of stones of increasing fineness that were lubricated with water.

Jōkotō (Ancient Sword) Period 上古刀時代

Jōkotō, or ancient swords 上古刀, have come down to us almost exclusively from the ancient burial mounds of the Kofun period (ca 300–710) and are badly rusted. These ancient blades were nearly always straight, with a very small and sharply angled slanted point (*bōshi* 帽子). Swords of the Nara period (710–794) and the early Heian period (794–1185) were similar to those found in the mounds. Being rather short and lightweight, they were probably used for thrusting rather than slashing. From approximately the 9th and 10th centuries, blades were made longer with a slightly curved shape and with ridge lines on both sides, a far more efficient weapon for mounted warriors.

Kotō (Old Sword) Period 古刀時代

The quality of the sword greatly improved in the middle Heian and early Kamakura periods, or from approximately the 10th to the early 13th century, when its use markedly increased, especially by mounted warriors. The swords of the Kamakura period (*tachi* 太刀) are of the highest quality, both artistically and technically, and most of the National Treasure 国宝 blades derive from this period. In the late Kamakura period the sword became very long—in many instances as long as 1 to 1.5 meters (3–5 ft)—and was used exclusively by mounted warriors. Many of these were later shortened for use in hand-to-hand combat.

In the Muromachi period (1333–1568), as a result of prolonged strife and feudal combat, the production of swords increased in number but quality declined. Swords became somewhat heavier and less curved, wider and considerably shorter, so that they could cut through the heavier armor then coming into use. This new blade was called *katana* and was upward of 60 centimeters (2 ft) in length. It was soon accompanied by a somewhat shorter blade, *wakizashi* 脇差. The *katana* and *wakizashi* were worn thrust through the sash and these swords were called *daishō*, "long and short." 大小

Shintō (New Sword) Period 新刀時代

During the Azuchi-Momoyama (1568–1600) and Edo (1600–1868) periods individual swordsmiths founded new schools. Many swords had extraordinarily brilliant tempering patterns, a substantial structure of well-hammered and well-tempered steel, and beautiful chiseled engravings (*horimono* 彫物) and grooves. Sword guards 鍔 and other fittings (*koshirae* 拵え) for swords and for daggers became highly ornate.

The years from 1800 to the close of the Edo period are known in sword history as the Shinshintō (New, New Sword) 新・新刀 period. It was a brief renaissance marked by a final effort to revive the beauty and quality of the ancient sword.

Modern Period 現代

The emperor Meiji promulgated regulations forbidding the making or wearing of swords but permitted a small number of smiths to continue their work in order to keep the art alive.

After World War II, the Allied Occupation forces ordered all swords destroyed, but the order was modified to exclude swords of artistic, religious, or spiritual significance belonging to museums, shrines, or private collections.

There has been a gradual renewal of interest in the art of the ancient sword, and a number of smiths are currently attempting to restore the ancient skills.

Folk crafts (*mingei*) 民芸

The term *mingei* refers to objects handcrafted for daily use, as well as to the movement begun by Yanagi Muneyoshi 柳宗悦 (1889–1961), who coined the term in 1926. Yanagi himself preferred to translate *mingei* as "folk crafts," which emphasizes the utilitarian aspect, rather than "folk arts," although both terms have been used.

The Folk Craft Movement 民芸運動

Collecting examples of folk crafts from the Korean Yi dynasty 李朝 (1392–1910) led Yanagi to realize that the most beautiful objects were the products not of individual artists but of the collective genius of the Korean people. He concluded that the approach of modern European art history, which emphasized the creativity of individual artists, was inadequate in understanding *mingei*.

Instead, Yanagi turned his attention to the work of a Japanese priest, Mokujiki Gogyō 木食五行 (1718–1810), who had carved tens of thousands of rough Buddhist images while traveling throughout Japan. To Yanagi these figures, created in response to the hopes and aspirations of the masses, were more beautiful than the Buddhist images by famous sculptors displayed by great temples. Around this time Yanagi also discovered Tamba ware, with its rich patterns of glaze formed during firing from wood ash randomly falling and fusing with the ceramic surface. Reflecting on this process, he concluded that beauty was not the result of any conscious intent but was born of chance and the cumulative skill of generations of unknown artists. Yanagi saw this process as akin to the Buddhist concept of *tariki* 他力.

Based on these theories Yanagi coined the term *mingei* to differentiate between *bijutsu*, or fine art, which he saw as created for aesthetic appreciation alone, and *kōgei* 工芸, or utilitarian craftwork made for practical use. Yanagi saw *kōgei* as a broader term than *mingei*: *kōgei* included objects made by machine and by individual artists, as well as "aristocratic" works. But he also claimed that the best of *kōgei* belonged to the category of *mingei*. According to Yanagi, the character of *kōgei* was defined, first, by *yō* (use or function): *kōgei* objects must be simple and sturdy to function effectively. Second, *kōgei* objects must be produced on a large scale at low prices. Third, the beauty of authentic *kōgei* is created by anonymous laborers who have honed their skill by turning out large numbers of articles without thought of self-expression. Fourth, handcrafted *kōgei* objects are superior to those made by machine.

History of Japanese Folk Crafts 日本における民芸の歴史

Most of what is today considered *mingei* survives from the Muromachi period (1333–1568). This is doubtless partly because the traditional Japanese style of living, as presently understood, became widely established at that time: the *shoin-zukuri* type of residential architecture was perfected, and techniques for making lacquer ware 漆器 and pottery were highly developed. This, along with increased production, led to wider distribution of articles. The popularization of the tea ceremony 茶の湯 from the Muromachi period through the Azuchi-Momoyama period (1568–1600) was another important factor. Local pottery and textile producers flourished in the latter half of the Edo period (1600–1868). Many examples from this period can still be found, and they set the standards of beauty in Japanese folk crafts. By the early 20th century, however, with the introduction of synthetics and increasing reliance on machinery, folk crafts began to decline. Folk crafts in Yanagi's sense of the term have nearly become extinct in Japan.

However, folk traditions in a broader sense are thriving. Under the Cultural Properties Law 文化財保護法 of 1950 the concept of cultural assets was revised and broadened, encouraging governmental participation in the preservation of folk knowledge 民間知識, folk performing arts 民俗芸能, games, and folk utensils used for making clothing, food, and shelter and in trade or communal life.

Classification of Folk Crafts 主な民芸

Folk crafts are generally classified in the categories of ceramics; wood and bamboo articles; metal and leather objects; dyeing and weaving; paper; and painting, sculpture, and calligraphy.

Ceramics 陶磁器 The kilns of Okinawa produce various types of ceramics called Tsuboya ware 壺屋焼. In Kyūshū, such ceramics as Karatsu ware, Agano ware 上野焼, and Takatori ware 高取焼 are produced by techniques learned from Korean potters. Imari ware 伊万里焼 (Arita ware 有田焼) is also famous for its excellent quality. Other superior ceramics are Koishiwara ware and Onta ware 小鹿田焼. In the Shikoku region, the only well-known ceramic ware is Tobe ware 砥部焼. In the Chūgoku region, some of the most ancient Japanese kilns are found in Fushina 布志名, Ushinoto 牛ノ戸, and Bizen 備前. The Kinki region is noted for Tamba ware 丹波焼, Kyōto ceramics 京焼, Shigaraki ware 信楽焼, and Iga ware. The Chūbu region, largest of Japan's ceramics centers, is famous for Seto ware 瀬戸焼 and Mino 美濃焼 ware. The

Kantō region produced unglazed pottery such as Imado ware 今戸焼. Mashiko, the center of the folk crafts movement, is famous for its Mashiko ware 益子焼.

Wood and Bamboo Craftworks 漆器・木工・竹細工 These categories include *ryūkyū-nuri* 琉球漆器 (lacquer work inlaid with gold) from Okinawa; lacquer ware and *ikkambari uchiwa* (fans made by painting lacquer over a paper frame) 一閑張団扇 from Shikoku; *yanagi-gōri* (wicker trunks made of willow branches) 柳行李 from the San'in region; *funadansu* (ship trunks) 船箪笥 from Niigata Prefecture used on ships (*kaisen*) traveling between Ōsaka and northern Japan during the Edo period; *shunkei-nuri* 春慶塗 from Takayama (Gifu Prefecture); *wakasa-nuri* 若狭塗 and *wajima-nuri* 輪島塗 from Fukui and Ishikawa Prefectures; woodcrafts from Hida 飛騨 (Gifu Prefecture) and Matsumoto (Nagano Prefecture); *kokeshi* こけし dolls and other woodcrafts, including *kago* (woven baskets) 籠, *magemono* (round containers) 曲物, and *kabazaiku* (birch woodcrafts) 樺細工, from the Tōhoku region; lacquer ware such as *aizu-nuri* 会津塗 (Fukushima Prefecture) and *tsugaru-nuri* 津軽塗 (Aomori Prefecture); and Ainu woodcrafts from Hokkaidō.

Metalwork 金属製品 Metalwork includes hardware and carpentry tools from Miki 三木 (Hyōgō Prefecture); razors and other cutting instruments from Seki 関 (Gifu Prefecture); metal fittings made in Sendai 仙台 (Miyagi Prefecture); and Nambu cast-iron ware 南部鉄器 from Morioka (Iwate Prefecture).

Dyeing, Weaving, and Quilting 染め物・織物・刺子 Textiles include *bingata* 紅型 (surface-dyed textile) and *bashō* (abaca) cloth 芭蕉布 from Okinawa; Satsuma *jōfu* 薩摩上布 (linen cloth) Kagoshima Prefecture; *kurume-gasuri* (Kurume ikat cloth) 久留米絣 from Fukuoka Prefecture and *iyo-gasuri* (Iyo ikat cloth) 伊予絣 from Ehime Prefecture; indigo (*ai* 藍) from Tokushima Prefecture, which was once valued throughout the country as *awa-ai* 阿波藍, a natural dye; cotton cloth from Tamba (Hyōgo and Kyōto prefectures); *saki-ori* 裂織 (woven from strips made from old clothes) from the Hokuriku and Tōhoku regions; *habutae* silk 羽二重 from Fukui Prefecture and *chijimi* 縮 (crepe) from Niigata Prefecture; Mikawa *momen* (Mikawa cotton) 三河木綿 from Aichi Prefecture and *kaiki* 甲斐絹 (Kai silk) from Yamanashi Prefecture; silk weaving 絹織物 from the Kantō region at Kiryū (Gumma Prefecture), Ashikaga (Tochigi Prefecture), and Hachiōji (Tōkyō Prefecture); *kogin* こぎん from the Tsugaru region; *hishizashi* 菱刺 from Aomori and Iwate prefectures; and *sashiko* (quiltings) 刺子 made by the Ainu in Hokkaidō.

Paper 和紙 *Washi* (Japanese paper) 和紙, once produced throughout the country, is now rarely used in everyday life. Japanese papers still produced today are *tosa-gami* from Kōchi Prefecture and Sekishū *hanshi* 石州半紙 and *izumo-gami* from Shimane Prefecture. *Washi* made in Kyōto and Nara has been famous for centuries. Ise *katagami* (dyed pattern paper) 伊勢型紙 is still produced in Suzuka (Mie Prefecture). Echizen *hōsho* 越前奉書 and *tori-noko-gami* 鳥の子紙 from Fukui Prefecture are well known, as is Yatsuo paper 八尾和紙 made in Toyama Prefecture. Surviving *washi* products include kites from Nagasaki Prefecture and *shibuuchiwa* (fans) from Kutami 来民 in Kumamoto Prefecture.

Painting and Sculpture 絵画・彫刻 Numerous types of paintings and religious sculptures are considered representative of Japanese folk crafts, although in these categories there are different opinions about what is and what is not folk craft. (According to Yanagi's somewhat personal and subjective criteria, *ōtsu-e* 大津絵 are included among folk arts whereas *ukiyo-e* are not.) Present designations of what can be considered *mingei* should not be accepted as final, since scholars may develop a more comprehensive method of categorization in the future.

Modern architecture (*kingendai no kenchiku*)
近現代の建築

Following the Meiji Restoration 明治維新 of 1868, the government invited foreign engineers and experts to train Japanese and oversee initial construction projects. At first, Western methods and designs were incorporated into traditional Japanese methods of wood construction.

In 1877 Josiah Conder of Britain arrived in Japan to teach at the Industrial College (forerunner of the Department of Engineering at Tōkyō University); he trained many architects, including Tatsuno Kingo 辰野金吾 and Katayama Tōkuma 片山東熊. The Akasaka Detached Palace 赤坂離宮 (1909) by Katayama and the main office of the Bank of Japan 日本銀行 (1896) and Tōkyō Station 東京駅 (1914) by Tatsuno are typical of the kind of Western-style buildings designed by Japanese at this time.

In the 1880s there was a general reaction against excessive Westernization in many fields, including architecture. Architect and art historian Itō Chūta 伊東忠太 was among the first to advocate Asian models for Japanese architecture. After World War I architects like Frank Lloyd Wright フランク゠ロイド゠ライト and Antonin Raymond アントニン゠レイモンド of the United States and Bruno Taut ブルーノ゠タウト of Germany came to Japan, contributing to the reevaluation of traditional Japanese architecture. The renewed interest in tradition led to the development by Yoshida Isoya 吉田五十八 of a new style in residential architecture that assimilated traditional *sukiya-zukuri* 数寄屋造り techniques.

One of the best-known and most influential modern Japanese architects is Tange Kenzō 丹下健三 (1913–). He developed a methodology linking Japanese traditional elements with the achievements of science and technology in architectural form and established his reputation with a number of dramatic buildings in the 1950s and 1960s such as the Yoyogi National Stadium 国立代々木競技場 (1963), built for the 1964 Tōkyō Olympics, and the Dentsū head office building (1967). The 1960s were a period both of pioneering work by individual architects and of the industrialization and depersonalization of architecture, as fast-working design and construction companies specializing in building groups of standardized, characterless structures came to dominate the field. Cities in Japan as in many other countries were rapidly filled with boxlike buildings.

The reevaluation of architectural priorities was led by Isozaki Arata 磯崎新 (1931–). Rejecting the tendency toward the total commercialization of architecture and construction, Isozaki argued that architecture had to regain its independence from commercial and technological imperatives. Examples of his work such as the Museum of Modern Art in Gumma Prefecture 群馬県立近代美術館 (1975) and his many critical writings had an immense impact on the rising younger generation of architects in the 1970s. It was about this time that architects who regarded themselves primarily as artists began to make their appearance, among the most distinguished being Andō Tadao 安藤忠雄 (1941–), Shinohara Kazuo 篠原一男 (1925–), and Kurokawa Kishō 黒川紀章 (1934–). During this period Japanese architects were preoccupied with reassessing the functional and utilitarian aspects of postwar Japanese architecture and its relationship to Japanese traditions.

In the 1980s, however, the economy once again began to boom, and this was reflected in architectural circles by a union between new commercial imperatives, prompted by government deregulation of the construction industry, and the emphasis on pure design. The demand of business for imposing buildings—which had led to the construction of the first skyscrapers 超高層ビル in the Shinjuku area in the early 1970s—reasserted itself in the 1980s, but now architects responded with buildings that incorporated more artistic design features. Tange Kenzō's Tōkyō Metropolitan Government Offices 東京都庁舎 (1991) are a good example of the monumental style that resulted.

The 1980s and early 1990s also saw a rapid increase in the number of works by Japanese architects being built in other countries. Works like Isozaki's Museum of Contemporary Art in Los Angeles (1986) and Tange Kenzō's OUB Center in Singapore (1986) marked the advent of active two-way international exchange in the field of architecture.

Traditional domestic architecture
(*dentōteki* Nihon *kenchiku*) 伝統的日本建築

Traditional residential architecture in Japan is perhaps best viewed as a response to the natural environment. Traditional Japan was a primarily agricultural society 農耕社会, centering on activities associated with rice planting 稲作. A feeling of cooperation, rather than an antagonistic relationship, developed between the Japanese and their natural surroundings. Instead of resistance or defense, accommodation and adaptation became the basic stance. Traditional Japanese architecture is characterized by the same attitude toward the natural environment, responding in particular to climatic and geographical conditions.

Japan's climate is distinguished by long, hot, humid summers and relatively short, cold, dry winters, and the Japanese house has evolved accordingly to make the summers more bearable. The traditional Japanese house was raised slightly off the ground and the interior opened up to allow for unrestricted movement of air around and below the living spaces. Associated with the heat and humidity of summer were sun and frequent rain. This necessitated a substantial roof structure with long, low overhangs to protect the interior.

The development of the individual spaces within the house was a gradual process of breaking down the larger open space that was available into smaller, more human-scaled spaces. Individual rooms were later defined by *shōji* and *fusuma*, "sliding doors" 障子、襖 that could still be removed to form a single large space.

Materials and Construction 建材と構造

The choice of building materials 建材 has been determined by the climate, wood being preferred to stone. Wood responds more sensitively to the climate, being much cooler and absorbing moisture in summer and not as cold to the touch in winter. Wood is also more suited to withstand earthquakes, almost daily occurrences in Japan.

The choice of wood and an open structure allows for flexibility in living arrangements according to seasonal changes and the needs of the family. Inner partitions such as *shōji* and *fusuma* can be removed to open up the interior, and, except for the roof's supporting columns, a clear space can be exposed.

Apart from the use of wood, the apparently little consideration given to earthquake protection in the structure itself is striking. Rigidity, however, is not the only way of protecting a structure against earthquakes. Wood is flexible and can take more shear and torque for its weight than most other materials. The joinery makes use of the strengths of wood. The walls, consisting essentially of bamboo lattices 竹格子 heavily plastered with clay, are not at all substantial by Western standards but are surprisingly resistant to earthquakes. One room of the traditional house is plastered heavily on four walls in this way, with only a minimal entrance in one. This is directly connected to some of the main supports and helps to strengthen the building. In older structures the joint between a foundation stone and the support post or column was not fixed, so that when the earth moved, the column sometimes simply slid off its foundation stone. After the earthquake, the house could be lifted up and the support placed on another stone with no real damage to the structure.

Engawa 縁側

An important aspect of traditional design is the relationship of the house to its specific environment, particularly the GARDEN; the two are continuous. The Japanese do not see exterior and interior as two separate entities; in other words, there is no definite point at which exterior ends and interior begins. The Japanese veranda 縁側 plays an important role between the house and the garden, serving as a transition space from inside to outside. Its function is further expressed by the materials used in its construction. Whereas the floors of the interior of the house are covered with *tatami* mats 畳 and the exterior is made of earth and rock, the *engawa* is made of unfinished wood planks, belonging neither to the soft and accommodating interior nor to the harsh and more primitive materials on the outside.

Gardens (*teien*) 庭園

Japanese gardens possess a unique beauty derived from the combination and synthesis of various elements. There is a compositional beauty derived from a blending of natural plantings, sand, water, and rock, made unique by the natural beauty of Japan's landscape and seasonal change, and a symbolic beauty arising from the expression of Shintō beliefs and Buddhist intellectual conventions.

History 歴史

It has been said that the use of groupings of rocks is a distinguishing feature of the Japanese garden and provides its basic framework. The ancestors of the modern Japanese referred to places surrounded by natural rock as *amatsu iwasaka* ("heavenly barrier") 天津磐境 or *amatsu iwakura* ("heavenly seat") 天津磐座, believing that gods lived there. Dense clusters of trees were also thought to be the dwelling places of gods and were called *himorogi* ("divine hedge") 神籬. Moats or streams that enclosed sacred ground were called *mizugaki* ("water fences") 瑞垣.

The first gardens amidst the mountains of Yamato imitated ocean scenes with large ponds rimmed by wild "seashores" and dotted with islands. During this period Buddhism was transmitted to Japan, and immigrants from Paekche 百済 contributed continental influences to the Japanese garden.

In 794 the capital was moved from Nara to Kyoto. Here several rivers converged, and channels were dug to carry water through the city. Narrow streams 遣水 were made to pass between buildings and flow through the gardens of the *shinden-zukuri* 寝殿造り mansions. The ponds were of simple shape yet were large enough for boating, and at their edges, jutting out over the water, were erected *tsuridono* 釣殿 connected by roofed corridors to the other structures of the mansion. The large area between the main buildings and the pond was covered with white sand and used for formal ceremonies.

With the rise of the cult of the Buddha Amida 阿弥陀仏 in the 10th century, the *shinden* style of garden, modeled on the image of the Pure Land (Jōdo 浄土) as described in scripture and religious tracts, was developed. A good example of this is the garden of the Byōdōin 平等院.

The Muromachi period (1333–1568) has been called the golden age of Japanese gardens. Skilled groups of craftsmen known as *senzui kawaramono* 山水河原者 were active, and the new *karesansui* style 枯山水 of garden appeared. Waterless rock and sand gardens arose under the influence of Zen Buddhist doctrine, *shoin*-style architecture 書院造, and Chinese ink painting, together with potted dwarf trees 盆栽 and tray landscapes 盆景.

The TEA CEREMONY 茶の湯 as taught by Sen no Rikyū 千利休 emphasized a quiescent spirituality. The approach to a teahouse was through a tea garden 露地(茶庭), the ideal of which Rikyū sought in the desolate tranquility of a mountain trail. Among the contributions of the tea garden to the contemporary Japanese garden are stepping-stones 飛び石, stone lanterns 石灯籠, and groves of trees, as well as stone washbasins 手水鉢 and simply constructed gazebos for guests being served tea (*machiai* 待合).

During the Edo period (1600–1868) a synthesis of preceding forms took place. The garden of the Katsura Detached Palace 桂離宮 in Kyōto, which achieved considerable renown through the writings of the German architect Bruno Taut, is made up of a number of tea gardens. This is an example of the *kaiyū* or "many-pleasure" 廻遊式 style, which became fully established in the mid-Edo period. A representative garden designer 作庭家 of this period was Kobori Enshū 小堀遠州, whose work included the gardens of the Sentō Palace 仙洞御所 in Kyōto.

Castles (*shiro*) 城

Japanese castles were originally military fortifications 軍事要塞 designed to provide protection against enemy attack. With the rise of feudalism, however, they became distinctive architectural forms serving as both palatial residence and seat of military and political power of feudal barons.

Medieval Castles 中世の城

Internal wars were frequent in Japan during the medieval period (mid-12th–16th centuries). From the period of the Northern and Southern Courts 南北朝時代 (1337–1392) to the Sengoku period 戦国時代 (1467–1568),

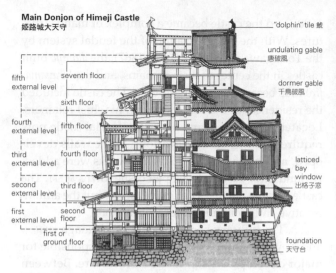

Main Donjon of Himeji Castle
姫路城大天守

"dolphin" tile 鯱

undulating gable
唐破風

dormer gable
千鳥破風

fifth
external level

seventh floor

sixth floor

fourth
external level

fifth floor

third
external level

fourth floor

latticed
bay
window
出格子窓

second
external level

third floor

first
external level

second
floor

first or
ground floor

foundation
天守台

territorial warlords repeatedly fought each other, and
castles were constructed throughout the country. Their
forms varied, but many were small, semipermanent fortifications built at the tip of steep mountain ridges.

By the Sengoku period, constant warfare made it
necessary to build permanent structures. Military chieftains built fortifications similar to their own residences,
with the addition of raised watchtowers on the roof.
This was the beginning of castle architecture in Japan.
Most castles of the medieval period were of the mountain castle type and were used only in times of war.
Ordinarily the warrior chieftain lived in a fortified residence located on a plain or low plateau. This was the
origin of the plain castle 平城 and the so-called hill-on-
the-plain castle 平山城. An example of the *hirajiro* is Edo
Castle in Tōkyō. The *hirayamajiro* was generally sited on
a low-lying plateau set in a plain.

Azuchi-Momoyama and Edo Period Castles
安土桃山・江戸時代の城

There was great development in the building of
castles during the Azuchi-Momoyama period (1568–

1600), and the castle became a complex of many structures. With the reorganization of the feudal system by the Tokugawa shogunate (1603–1867), the *daimyō* built castles in the center of their domains, and the *hirayama-jiro* thus became the standard type. The castle included the residences of the castle lord and his chief retainers. Located as it was, near a plain, the feudal castle now required additional fortifications. Stone walls developed, moats 濠 were dug, and earthworks were added. Around these castles developed castle towns 城下町. The castle became not just a defensive facility but the administrative and economic center of its region.

The military hegemons Oda Nobunaga 織田信長 and Toyotomi Hideyoshi 豊臣秀吉 were responsible for major developments in castle architecture. Between 1576 and 1579 Nobunaga constructed the central part of an enormous castle project at Azuchi in what is now Shiga Prefecture. Azuchi Castle 安土城 was destroyed after the death of Oda Nobunaga in 1582. It established a tradition of large-scale, sumptuous castles that was continued in Fushimi Castle 伏見城 (1594) and Ōsaka Castle 大坂城 (1583), both built by Hideyoshi and no longer extant. After the Battle of Sekigahara 関ヶ原の戦い (1600), through the Keichō era 慶長年間 (1596–1615), there was a surge of castle construction by *daimyō* throughout the country.

By 1615 the Tokugawa shogunate 徳川幕府, seeking to secure complete control over the country, ordered that there could be only one castle to each domain. The art of castle architecture went into a gradual decline during the Edo period (1600–1868).

Castle-Building Techniques and Design
築城技術とデザイン

The most important step in building a castle was the site planning 縄張り, in which the building's outline was fixed on the prospective site by stretching ropes.

Ideally, a castle was composed of a main compound or ward (*hommaru* 本丸) centered around the donjon 天守閣 or main tower (*tenshu* or *tenshukaku*) surrounded by or connected with minor compounds or enclosures. The most important feature of castle architecture from the late Muromachi period 室町時代 (1333–1568) through the Edo period, the donjon originated in the watchtower built atop a warrior's residence. There were several entrances to the castle, but the important ones were called the *ōte* 大手 and *karamete* 搦手. The former was the main entrance and the latter the rear entrance. In case the castle was overrun, the *karamete* could be used as an avenue of escape. A moat (*hori*) or system of moats, ponds, waterways, and trenches surrounded the castle, and natural features of the land were also employed in its fortifications. In order to reach the donjon it was necessary to traverse a mazelike route.

Stone foundation walls 石垣 were built vertically in earlier times on sites with foundation soil, but where the ground was not stable, walls with a concave profile came to be used both for structural and decorative reasons. The early donjon had exposed wood members, but at the height of the castle-building era most surfaces came to be plastered.

THEATER 芸能

Traditional theater (*koten geinō*) 古典芸能

The five major genres of Japanese traditional theater, all still in performance, are *bugaku* 舞楽, NŌ 能, *kyōgen* 狂言, BUNRAKU 文楽, and KABUKI 歌舞伎. Although different in content and style, they are linked by strong aesthetic relationships, derived from a confluence of sources both inside and outside Japan. The evolution of performing arts 舞台芸術 throughout Asia has been governed by an integral relationship among dance, music, and lyrical narrative. The synthesis of the disparate elements of speech, music, and dance led to highly developed styles, of which the five Japanese genres represent supreme examples.

Among the five Japanese genres, *bugaku* stands apart as a ceremonial dance associated only with court ritual, in which the theatrical element is minimal and music predominates. *Bugaku* incorporates aesthetic and structural principles current in the 8th century—admixtures of Central Asian, Indian, and Korean elements assimilated by China and adopted by Japan during a period of cultural borrowing.

Nō, *kyōgen*, *bunraku*, and *kabuki*, by contrast, are indigenous forms representing successive periods of political and social change in Japan. The first two belong to an age when Chinese influences were still potent; the latter two come from a time when Japan was politically isolated. But all adhere to Asian dramatic principles emphasizing symbolism and allusive imagery, as opposed to the Aristotelian concept of mimesis, the imitation of reality, which dominates Western dramatic theory.

Nō drama seeks to reveal the ephemeral nature of reality through stage techniques stressing imagery, metaphor, and symbolism. Medieval Buddhist thought, which profoundly influenced Nō, rejected factual reality as illusory: in Buddhist theory it is only at the moment of perception that anything exists; thus, all existence is fleeting.

Kyōgen, the comic interludes that are an integral part of Nō performance, poke fun at human frailties as did the traditional Asian storytellers, jesting at social pretensions, marital discord, quackery, and so forth. The comic actor becomes a catalyzing agent, relieving tension through the arrangement of his appearance between the serious plays.

Bunraku has a unique place in the theater world of Japan, where puppet performance has been accepted as the equal of orthodox drama. Indeed, it is impossible to speak of *bunraku* without mentioning *kabuki*, since a sizable part of the latter's repertoire consists of plays originally written for puppet drama, which has also greatly influenced the style of *kabuki* acting. In turn, *bunraku* has taken much from the sophisticated technical presentation of *kabuki* and has incorporated some of its popular dance dramas into its own repertoire.

Kabuki carries even further the deployment of speech, sound, movement, and space as equal contributory forces. Stylization conditions every level of performance in *kabuki*. Narrative musical forms are used constantly to convey mood, emphasize emotional tensions, and provide exposition.

Nō 能

The oldest extant professional theater; a form of musical dance-drama originating in the 14th century. Nō preserves what all other important contemporary theater has lost: its origin in ritual, reflecting an essentially Buddhist view of existence. The performance looks and sounds more like solemn observance than life. The actors are hieratic, playing their ancient roles of intermediaries between the worlds of gods and men. To the bare stage come soberly dressed instrumentalists, the six-or-eight-member chorus 地謡, then the supporting character ワキ, handsomely robed, often as a priest. Finally, out of the darkness at the end of the long passageway leading to the stage proper, evoked by drums and flute, the resplendently caparisoned (usually masked) leading character シテ materializes. In strict rhythms, out of music, voice, and movement rather than the artifice of stagecraft, time and space are created and destroyed. Language is largely poetic. Costumes are rich and heavy, movement, even in dance, deliberate. The *shite* seeks intercession by the *waki* and, having attained it at the end, returns to the darkness freed of karma.

Origins 起源

At the middle of the 14th century professional theater was based in Kyōto and Nara, and the actors organized into troupes under the patronage of Shintō shrines and Buddhist temples. They raised money, piously and commercially, with subscription Nō 勧進能.

Some troupes presented *dengaku* 田楽 Nō, others *sarugaku* 猿楽 Nō. At this time little distinguished the two kinds, for both had a common theatrical inheritance.

The transformation of *sarugaku* into Nō, in basically the same form it has today, was accomplished by Kan'ami 観阿弥 and his son Zeami 世阿弥, both prodigious actor-dancers and playwrights of the Muromachi period (1333–1568).

In 1374 Kan'ami and Zeami performed before the *shōgun* Ashikaga Yoshimitsu 足利義満, who, greatly taken by the performance and by Zeami, thereafter sponsored the troupe. Kan'ami's troupe, the Kanze school 観世流, was preeminent, and three other troupes that now survive, the Komparu school 金春流, the Hōshō school 宝生流, and the Kongō school 金剛流, adopted the Kanze style of performance. It was on the Zen artistic principles of restraint, economy of expression, and suggestion rather than statement that Zeami fashioned his 40 or so plays, his acting, and his productions. His ideas on every aspect of the theater were set down in a series of essays that remain the essential documents of the Nō.

Evolution 発展

Nō found its most enthusiastic support when Toyotomi Hideyoshi 豊臣秀吉 came to power in 1582. Hideyoshi bolstered his soldiers' morale by having all four troupes perform for them, and he commissioned 10 plays written about himself, in which he played the lead. When Tokugawa Ieyasu became *seii tai shōgun* in 1603 he celebrated the occasion with Nō performances, and in 1609 he employed all of Hideyoshi's performers and established them in Edo (now Tōkyō). The Kita school 喜多流, which still exists today, was added to the original four in 1618. Nō became the official property and ceremonial art of the Tokugawa line. Over more than two centuries Nō became more and more codified, even surpassing Zeami's refined art in solemnity.

When the shogunate fell in 1867 and government subsidy of Nō stopped, some of the nobility kept Nō alive. Their support ended with the end of World War II, however, and the public became Nō's sole sponsor. Today Nō has a small but dedicated following.

Stage 舞台

Tokugawa formalization of Nō also standardized the stage, and today that architecture is requisite for the correct performance of the plays. The elaborate, carved, cypress-bark-covered roof ひわだ葺きの屋根 of Shintō shrine architecture extends over the main stage 舞台, which measures 6 by 6 meters (19.7 by 19.7 ft), as well as the side stage 脇座, the rear stage 後座, and the bridge (*hashigakari* 橋懸り). The bridge joins the main stage at an oblique angle, connecting it with the "mirror room" 鏡の間, the actors' dressing room. Musicians (*hayashikata* 囃子方) and

The Nō Stage
能舞台

① main stage 舞台 ② side stage 脇座 ③ rear stage 後座 ④ bridge 橋懸り ⑤ mirror room 鏡の間 ⑥ strip of pebbles 白洲 ⑦ first pine 一の松 ⑧ second pine 二の松 ⑨ third pine 三の松 ⑩ mirror board, acoustic 鏡板 ⑪ sliding door 切り戸 ⑫ three steps 階 (きざはし) ⑬ comedian's pillar 狂言柱 ⑭ principal actor's pillar シテ柱 ⑮ eye-fixing pillar 目付柱 ⑯ subordinate actor's pillar ワキ柱 ⑰ flute pillar 笛柱 ⑱ curtain 揚げ幕

actors enter and exit on the bridge. The only other entrance to the stage is a 1 meter (39 in) high sliding door 切り戸, upstage left on the main stage, used by stage assistants 後見 and the members of the chorus (*jiutai* 地謡).

Along the front of the entire structure, at audience level, is a strip of pebbles. In front of the bridge in this area are three equidistantly placed pine trees. A stylized pine tree, the only scenic background, is painted on the back wall (*kagamiita* 鏡板) of the main stage. The entire structure is built of polished Japanese cypress (*hinoki* 檜).

Performers 演者

All performers are male, and their organization is that established in the Edo period. Each of the five schools of Nō, mentioned earlier, trains its own *shite*, his "companion" ツレ, the child actor 子方, the chorus 地謡, and the stage assistants. The *waki* and his "companion" have their own separate schools, such as Fukuō 福王流 and Takayasu 高安流. Each instrument—the flute, small and large hand drums, and the large drum standing on the floor—is taught in a number of different schools.

Properties, Masks, and Costumes 小道具・面・装束

The actor's expressiveness is enhanced by hand properties, among them letters, umbrellas, rosaries, and the bamboo branch signifying derangement, but most of all by the folding fan 中啓. Closed, partly closed, or open, it may represent any object suggested by its shape and handling—dagger, lantern, rising moon. In other *kata* it represents not objects but actions—listening, moon viewing, sleeping. The abstract or pictorial design painted on the fan is conventionally associated with a type of character such as a ghost, old woman, or demon. Only the *shite* and *waki* use them. The other actors and the chorus carry fans (*ōgi*) bearing the crest of the school. The chorus place their fans, always closed, on the floor in front of them and pick them up to signal the beginning of a chant.

Only the *shite* and his companions wear masks, carved of wood and painted, though not in plays in which the characters they portray are living men. Masks are traditionally placed in seven categories such as old men, old women, gods, demons or spirits, blind people, men, and women and in many plays the *shite* changes masks midway through the play, the second mask revealing the character's true being.

Many of the costumes (*shōzoku* 装束) used today were constructed in the 18th and 19th centuries when the patterns, colors, and materials to be worn by a given character were systematized. Nō costumes 能装束 are worn in layers— generally a soft underkimono covered by a stiff brocade *kosode kimono* (*atsuita* 厚板 for male roles and *kara-ori* 唐織 for female roles). In addition, divided skirts 大口、半切 and cloaks of brocade or gauze (*happi* 法被, *kariginu* 狩衣, *chōken* 長絹), often with double width sleeves, may be worn. The stiffness of the fabric gives the costumed figure a well-defined outline and larger-than-life appearance.

Plays 演目

Okina 「翁」, the oldest item in the repertory, consists principally of three dances extant in the 10th century that are prayers for peace, fertility (the basis of Shintō), and longevity. Scarcely a play, it is performed only on ceremonial occasions and always first on the program. The usual program today consists of two or three Nō plays with *kyōgen* between them.

The other 240 or so plays now performed, most dating from the 15th century, are grouped into five categories, corresponding to the five parts of the traditional Nō program called *goban-date* 五番立. *Shobamme-mono* (part-one plays) 初番目物 are sometimes called *wakinō-mono* 脇能物 or *kami* (god) plays 神能. *Nibamme-mono* (part-two plays) 二番目物, or *shura-mono* 修羅物, are often about men or warriors. *Sambamme-mono* (part-three plays) 三番目物 are also called *katsura-mono* ("wig" plays) 鬘物 and are usually about women. *Yobamme-mono* (part-four plays) 四番目物 are also called *zō-mono* ("miscellaneous Nō") 雑物 or "madwoman" plays. Some of these are referred to as "present-day" plays 現在物. *Gobamme-mono* 五番目物 (part-five plays) are also called "demon" plays 鬼物, or *kirinō-mono* ("final Nō") 切能物.

Kabuki 歌舞伎

One of the three major classical theaters of Japan, together with the N Ō and the BUNRAKU puppet theater. *Kabuki* began in the early 17th century as a kind of variety show performed by troupes of itinerant entertainers. By the Genroku era 元禄時代 (1688–1704), it had achieved its first flowering as a mature theater, and it continued, through much of the Edo period (1600–1868), to be the most popular form of stage entertainment 舞台芸能. *Kabuki* reached its artistic pinnacle with the brilliant plays of Tsuruya Namboku IV 四世鶴屋南北 (1755–1829) and Kawatake Mokuami 河竹黙阿弥 (1816–1893). Through a magnificent blend of playacting, dance, and music, *kabuki* today offers an extraordinary spectacle combining form, color, and sound and is recognized as one of the world's great theatrical traditions.

Origin of *Kabuki* 歌舞伎の起源

The creation of *kabuki* is ascribed to Okuni 阿国, a female attendant at the Izumo Shrine 出雲大社, who, documents record, led her company of mostly women in a light theatrical performance featuring dancing and comic sketches on the dry bed of the river Kamogawa in Kyōto in 1603. Her troupe gained nationwide recognition and her dramas became identified as "*kabuki*," a term connoting its "out-of-the-ordinary" and "shocking" character.

The strong attraction of *onna* (women's) *kabuki* 女歌舞伎, which Okuni had popularized, was largely due to its sensual dances and erotic scenes. Because fights frequently broke out among the spectators over these entertainers, who also practiced prostitution, in 1629 the Tokugawa shogunate (1603–1867) banned women from appearing in *kabuki* performances. Thereafter, *wakashu* (young men's) *kabuki* 若衆歌舞伎 achieved a striking success, but, as in the case of *onna kabuki*, the authorities strongly disapproved of the shows, which continued to be the cause of public disturbances because the adolescent actors also sold their favors.

Edo-Period *Kabuki* 江戸時代の歌舞伎

In 1652 *wakashu kabuki* was forbidden, and the shogunate required that *kabuki* performances undergo a basic reform to be allowed to continue. The performers of *yarō* (men's) *kabuki* 野郎歌舞伎, who now began to replace the younger males, were compelled to shave off their forelocks, as was the custom at the time for men, to signify that they had come of age. They also had to make representations to the authorities that their performances did not rely on the provocative display of their bodies and that they were serious artists who would not engage in prostitution. By the mid-17th century, the major cities, Kyōto, Ōsaka, and Edo, were permitted to build permanent *kabuki* playhouses 歌舞伎小屋.

By the beginning of the Genroku era in 1688 there had developed three distinct types of *kabuki* performance: *jidai-mono* (historical plays) 時代物, often with elaborate sets and a large cast; *sewa-mono* (domestic plays) 世話物, which generally portrayed the lives of the townspeople and which, in comparison to *jidai-mono*, were presented in a realistic manner; and *shosagoto* (dance pieces) 所作事, consisting of dance performances and pantomime. In the Kyōto-Ōsaka 上方 area, Sakata Tōjūrō I 初代坂田藤十郎 (1647–1709), whose realistic style of acting was called *wagoto* 和事, was enormously popular for his portrayal of romantic young men, and his contemporary Yoshizawa Ayame I 初代芳沢あやめ (1673–1729)

consolidated the role of the *onnagata* (female imperson-ator) 女形 and established its importance in the *kabuki* tradition. For a period of some 10 years until about 1703, when he returned to the puppet theater, Chikamatsu Monzaemon 近松門左衛門 (1653–1724) wrote a number of *kabuki* plays, many of them for Tōjūrō I 初代藤十郎, which gained public recognition for the craft of the playwright. The commanding stage presence and powerful acting of Ichikawa Danjūrō I 初代市川団十郎 made him the pre-mier *kabuki* performer in Edo, and as a playwright, under the name Mimasuya Hyōgo 三升屋兵庫, he was once considered the rival of the great Chikamatsu.

During the first half of the 18th century, one of the more notable *kabuki* playwrights was Namiki Shōzō I 初世並木正三 (1730–1773), best known as the inventor of the revolving stage 回り舞台. It was a pupil of Shōzō I, the dramatist Namiki Gohei I 初世並木五瓶 (1747–1808), along with Sakurada Jisuke I 初世桜田治助 (1734–1806), who was instrumental in transmitting the realism traditionally associated with the *sewa-mono* (domestic plays) of the Kyōto-Ōsaka area to Edo. Their plays laid the founda-tion for the development of the realistic *kizewa-mono* ("bare" domestic plays) 生世話物 written by Tsuruya Namboku IV 四世鶴屋南北, Segawa Jokō III 三世瀬川如皐 (1806–1881), and Kawatake Mokuami 河竹黙阿弥. Mokuami created the *shiranami-mono* (thief plays) 白浪物, which had robbers, murderers, confidence men, and cunningly vicious women in the leading roles.

Modern *Kabuki* 現代の歌舞伎

After the Meiji Restoration actors such as Ichikawa Danjūrō IX 9代目市川団十郎 (1838–1903) and Onoe Kikugorō V 5代目尾上菊五郎 (1844–1903) urged the preservation of classical *kabuki*, and in the later years of their careers agitated for the continued staging of the great plays of the *kabuki* tradition and trained a younger generation of actors in the art that they would inherit.

In the postwar era the popularity of *kabuki* has been maintained and the great plays of the Edo period, as well as a number of the modern classics, continue to be performed in Tōkyō at the Kabukiza 歌舞伎座 and the National Theater 国立劇場. However, offerings have become considerably shortened and, particularly at the Kabukiza, limited for the most part to favorite acts and scenes presented together with a dance piece. The National Theater continues to present full-length plays. The average length of a *kabuki* performance is about five hours, including intermissions. The roles once played by the great postwar actors Morita Kan'ya XIV 14代目守田勘弥 (1907–1975), Ichikawa Danjūrō XI 11代目市川団十郎 (1909– 1965), Nakamura Kanzaburō XVII 17代目中村勘三郎 (1909– 1988), Onoe Shōroku II 2代目尾上松緑 (1913–1989), Onoe Baikō VII 7代目尾上梅幸 (1915–1995), and Nakamura Utaemon VI 6代目中村歌右衛門 (1917–) are now performed by Ichikawa Danjūrō XII 12代目市川団十郎 (1946–), Ichikawa Ennosuke III 3代目市川猿之助 (1939–), Matsumoto Kōshirō IX 9代目松本幸四郎 (1942–), Nakamura Kichiemon II 2代目中村吉右衛門 (1944–), Onoe Kikugorō VII 7代目尾上菊五郎 (1942–), Bandō Tamasaburō V 5代目坂東玉三郎 (1950–), Kataoka Nizaemon XV 15代目片岡仁左衛門(片山孝夫) (formerly Kataoka Takao; 1944–), and Nakamura Kankurō V 5代目中村勘九郎 (1955–). Dramas in which Tamasaburō V appears in the role of the *onnagata* and Nizaemon XV that of the leading man, or *tachiyaku*, are always well attended.

▌ The *Kabuki* Stage 歌舞伎舞台

The *kabuki* stage uses a draw curtain 引き幕. It has broad black, green, and orange vertical stripes and is normally drawn open from stage right to stage left accompanied by the striking of wooden clappers 拍子木. The curtain may also serve as a backdrop for brief scenes given before or after the performance on the main part of the stage. *Kamite* (stage left) 上手 is regarded

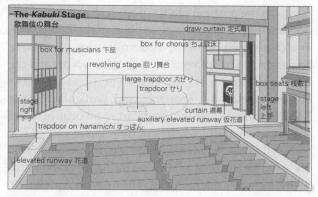

The *Kabuki* Stage
歌舞伎の舞台

draw curtain 定式幕

box for chorus ちよぼ床

box for musicians 下座

revolving stage 回り舞台

large trapdoor 大ぜり
trapdoor せり

box seats 桟敷

stage right 下手

stage left 上手

curtain 揚幕
auxiliary elevated runway 仮花道

trapdoor on *hanamichi* すっぽん

elevated runway 花道

as the place of honor and is occupied by characters of high rank, guests, and important messengers or official representatives. *Shimote* (stage right) 下手 is occupied by characters of low rank and members of a household; most entrances and exits take place on this side, usually by way of the *hanamichi* 花道. A unique feature of the *kabuki* stage is the *mawaributai*, a circular platform that can be rotated to permit a second scene to be performed simultaneously with the scene already in progress or to dramatize a flashback.

Acting Forms 型

The powerful influence of a long theatrical tradition is graphically illustrated by *kata* (forms) 型, the stylized gestures and movements of *kabuki* performers. Since *kata* are not subject to rejection at the whim of the actor, they have helped to maintain the artistic integrity of *kabuki*. *Tate* (stylized fighting) 殺陣, *roppō* (dramatic exit accompanied by exaggerated gestures) 六法, *mie* (striking an attitude) 見得, and *dammari* (silent scene) だんまり all belong to this category.

Costumes 衣装

Costume, wig, and makeup are carefully matched with the nature of a role. In general, the costumes in *jidai-mono* are more stlyized and elegant, befitting members of the nobility and the samurai class. By contrast,

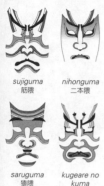

sujiguma
筋隈

nihonguma
二本隈

saruguma
猿隈

kugeare no
kuma
公家荒の隈

the prevailing fashions of society at large during the Edo period are portrayed quite realistically in *sewamono* plays. The costumes used in *shosagoto* dance pieces are especially noted for their color, design, and workmanship. Wigs are classified according to age of characters, historical period, social status, occupation, and other considerations. Makeup varies widely depending on the role. The most striking example is *kumadori*, an established set of masklike makeup styles 隈取 numbering about 100 and used in *jidai-mono*.

Shūmei (Stage Names) 襲名

Each performer belongs to an acting family by whose name he is known. Professionally, he is part of a closely knit hierarchical organization, headed by one of the leading actors, and must spend many years as an apprentice. An actor may eventually receive a new name (*shūmei*) as a mark of his elevation to a higher position within the professional organization. It is awarded at a *shūmei* ceremony, and in the company of his colleagues the actor delivers from the stage an address (*kōjō*) in which he requests the continued patronage of the audience. The name Ichikawa Danjūrō, which can be traced back to the formative years of *kabuki*, is regarded even today as the most illustrious of honors a *kabuki* actor can receive.

Bunraku 文楽

The professional puppet theater 人形劇 of Japan. Like the KABUKI theater, *bunraku* is an enduring form of art developed by city-dwelling commoners of the Edo period (1600–1868).

The term *bunraku* is of relatively recent origin. A puppet troupe organized in the early 19th century by Uemura Bunrakuken 植村文楽軒 (d 1810) in Ōsaka was named as Bunrakuza 文楽座 in 1872. Because Bunrakuza is the only "professional puppet theater" to have endured commercially in modern Japan, *bunraku* came to mean "professional puppet theater." The more precise term, *ayatsuri jōruri* 操浄瑠璃, denotes the component elements of the theater: *ayatsuri* means "puppetry," and *jōruri* refers to the dramatic text and the art of chanting it. Historically, it was the fortuitous joining of two independent art forms, puppetry and *jōruri*, that gave birth to *bunraku*.

Conventions of the Theater 文楽の仕掛

The *bunraku* theater presents dramas both serious and entertaining, as well as beautifully choreographed dances, for an audience primarily of adults with cultivated sensibilities. The performance is a composite of four elements: the puppets, which are approximately two-thirds to full life size; the movement given to the puppets by their operators; the vocal delivery by the *tayū* (chanter) 太夫; and the rhythmical musical accompaniment provided by the player of the three-stringed *shamisen*. To add to the complexity of the performance, each puppet portraying a major character is operated jointly by three men.

Bunraku puppets are not operated by strings. With his left arm and hand the *omozukai* (principal operator) 主遣い supports the puppet and manipulates the mechanisms that control the movable eyelids, eyeballs, eyebrows, and mouth; with his right hand he operates the puppet's right arm. The *hidarizukai* (first assistant) 左遣い functions solely to operate the puppet's left arm, and the *ashizukai* (second assistant) 足遣い operates the puppet's legs. Most female puppets do not have legs. The movements of a female puppet's legs are simulated through manipulating and shaping the lower part of the *kimono*.

The puppeteers 人形遣い are usually dressed in black robes; the assistants wear black hoods over their heads to become "invisible" in the audience's eyes. Although the *omozukai* may be similarly hooded—usually in scenes that require the utmost delicacy in the expression of emotions—he is most often seen full face by the audience, for he is a celebrity in the theatrical world. At times bedecked in a robe of lustrous white silk and ceremonial vest of brilliant hue, he becomes an important part of the total visual spectacle.

A single *tayū* speaks on behalf of all puppets on the stage—men, women, and children—and so his voice must cover an extremely broad range, from a raspy bass to a silky falsetto. Several *tayū* may perform simultaneously, as in the Gion Ichiriki Teahouse scene of the best known of all *bunraku* plays, *Kanadehon chūshingura* (1748; tr *Chūshingura: The Treasury of Loyal Retainers*, 1971) 「仮名手本忠臣蔵」.

A distinguishing aural feature of *bunraku* is the melodious, deep-toned thrumming of the solo *shamisen*. In *bunraku*, the puppets' movements must be synchronized with the *tayū*'s chanting and the *shamisen* accompaniment. Seldom is there visual contact between the puppeteers onstage and the *tayū* and *shamisen* player, who face the audience from the *yuka*, an elevated platform projecting from the stage. The *shamisen* player, by his strumming, normally dictates the pace of the narrative and the timing of the action.

Early History 黎明期

The earliest extant written reference to puppetry in Japan dates from the 11th century. During the 15th and 16th centuries, blind bards 琵琶法師 garbed in Buddhist robes were chanting the *Heike monogatari* (13th century; tr *The Tale of the Heike*, 1975, 1988) 「平家物語」.

The chanting style of medieval narratives changed remarkably in the 16th century with the evolution of a style of chanting called *jōruri*. Also around that time the *shamisen* was imported into Japan from Okinawa and came to be preferred over the lute by chanters of *jōruri*. *Shamisen* players composed new melodies that, in turn, influenced the style of *jōruri* chanting. This collaboration was the beginning of *bunraku*, which caught the fancy of the townspeople.

Stages of Development 発展期

By the mid-17th century the puppet theater was flourishing in Ōsaka and Kyōto, where puppeteers and chanters of *jōruri* were reaching new heights of artistry. *Bunraku* became the rage in 1685, when the *tayū* Takemoto Gidayū I 初代竹本義太夫 (1651–1714) of Ōsaka garnered accolades for the virile beauty of his chanting style. It was his collaboration, however, with the greatest playwright of the Edo period, Chikamatsu Monzaemon 近松門左衛門 (1653–1742), that led to the transformation of *bunraku* from popular entertainment to artistic theater.

Chikamatsu employed the imagery, diction, and literary techniques of classical prose, drama, and poetry in writing plays that focused on both historical and contemporary subjects and that emphasized prevalent codes of morality and ethics as thematic material. The success of his *Sonezaki shinjū* (tr *Love Suicides at Sonezaki*, 1961) 「曾根崎心中」 in 1703 started a vogue for dramas treating love affairs between merchants and prostitutes.

Many of the techniques, such as movable eyelids and mouths, used in *bunraku* today were developed after Chikamatsu's death.

Kabuki actors were influenced by the style of the *bunraku tayū* and even imitated the stylized gestures of the puppets.

Contemporary *Bunraku* 現代の文楽

With the Japanese welcoming Western forms of theatrical art and developing their own "modern" theater, *bunraku* fared poorly in the competition to attract audiences. After Japan's defeat in World War II, *bunraku* languished as many Japanese turned away from the traditional aspects of their own culture, and in the early

1960s it tottered on the verge of commercial extinction. It has survived largely with government support and the establishment of the National Theater 国立劇場 in Tōkyō and the National Bunraku Theater 国立文楽劇場 in Ōsaka. *Bunraku* may enjoy a mild revival because of a new appreciation of tradition among younger Japanese, but its future is uncertain.

Traditional music (*hōgaku*) 邦楽

Term applied to the varieties of music performed in Japan in premodern times and to forms of such music that are played today. The traditional history of Japanese music normally starts with the Nara period (710–794). Japanese music had its roots in the music of Buddhism and the vibrant traditions of Tang dynasty (618–907) China.

History 歴史

Buddhism was established as an official court religion by the 6th century, and its sounds and music theories became influential in Japan. Chinese and Korean courts or monasteries were the sources and models of most of the music in courts and temples but, because of the international dynamism of continental Asia from the 7th through the 10th century, influences from South and Southeast Asia can be found as well. The fact that Japan seemed to be "at the end of the line" in this cultural diffusion is of particular interest, for many traditions remained in Japan long after they had disappeared in the lands of their origins. The instrumental and dance repertoires of the court, generically known as GAGAKU, reflect such origins in their classification into two categories: *tōgaku* 唐楽, pieces derived from Chinese or Indian sources, and *komagaku* 高麗楽, music from Korea and Manchuria.

During the turbulent change from a court-dominated to a military-dominated culture at the end of the

12th century, more theatrical genres of music became popular. The *biwa* (lute) 琵琶 of the court became the accompaniment not only of itinerant priests and evangelists but also of chanters who recited long historical tales, particularly the *Heike monogatari*. The 13-stringed *koto* (zither) 琴 was used for ancient courtly solo and chamber music 室内楽 and continued to develop in the 16th century, primarily in the mansions of the rich or in temples. By the 17th century quite different *koto* pieces appeared, particularly in the new Ikuta school 生田流. The founding of the Yamada school 山田流 in the 18th century further enriched the repertoire. Both these schools have continued to the present day, and their solo and chamber music form the basis of what most Japanese would consider to be their "classical" music. The end-blown *shakuhachi* (bamboo flute) 尺八 also developed new schools of performance and repertory during this period, but it is the three-stringed plucked lute 三味線 that best represents the new musical styles and new audiences of the 16th through the 19th century. By the 18th century the narrative tradition of the puppet theater 文楽 had become a major source of literature, which was performed by skilled chanters 太夫 with *shamisen* accompaniment. The KABUKI theater adopted some of this material for its own plays, but it also developed a combination of other genres of *shamisen* music plus the percussion and flute ensemble 囃子 of the N Ō. In the 19th century, compositions using theatrical genres and instruments but intended for dance recital or purely concert performances had appeared. The *shamisen* genre called *nagauta* was particularly active in this new field.

Musical Characteristics 音楽的特徴

Most Japanese music shares with its East Asian counterparts a general tendency to be word-oriented. Except for the variation (*dammono* 段物) pieces for the *koto*, Japanese traditional music has either a vocal part with text or a title that evokes some image. No matter how large or small an ensemble may be, the tone color of the instruments combined is such that the sounds do not "melt" into a single experience as they do in some Western orchestral music.

Perhaps the most difficult aspect of traditional music for the inexperienced listener is that it is generally through-composed. It does not state a theme and then develop it as in the standard Western classical tradition. Instead it moves on to new musical ideas. What gives it a sense of logical progression is its conventions of form, which are stated most generally by the terms *jo, ha,* and *kyū* (introduction, scattering, rushing toward the finale) 「序・破・急」. After becoming used to the music's reduced volume and activity, it is possible to begin to appreciate the artistry of "less action—more meaning". The challenge is to the flexibility of the listener, not the composer or performer.

Gagaku 雅楽

Traditional music of the Japanese imperial court. *Gagaku* comprises three main bodies of music: *tōgaku* 唐楽, music said to be in the style of Tang dynasty (618–907) China; *komagaku* 高麗楽, a music style said to have been introduced from ancient Korea; and, finally, all of the many forms of native Japanese music associated with rituals of the Shintō religion.

The oldest and most carefully preserved of the various forms of Shintō ritual music and dance used in the imperial court is the *kagura* 神楽, formally called *mikagura* (court *kagura*) 御神楽 in order to distinguish it from the various folk forms of Shintō music that are also called *kagura*. Also included in the *gagaku* repertoire are *saibara* 催馬楽 (regional Japanese folk songs reset in an elegant court style), though only a small number of *saibara* compositions continue to be performed by court musicians.

History 歴史

In the early Heian period (794–1185), the various styles of foreign music were combined into the *tōgaku* and *komagaku* categories and were performed both by the court nobles and by hereditary guilds of professional musicians. With the fall of the noble classes in the early part of the Kamakura period (1185–1333), the popularity of *gagaku* waned. It was maintained by guilds and the remaining nobles, each in relative isolation from the other. The guild musicians were divided into three groups and were in service in Kyōto, Nara, and Ōsaka.

After the Meiji Restoration of 1868 and the relocation of the Imperial Palace to Tōkyō, the three groups were brought together as the official musicians of the newly established state. The musicians of the present-day Imperial Palace Music Department 宮内庁式部職楽部 are still largely the direct descendants of the members of the first musicians' guilds that performed *gagaku* in Japan during the 8th century. They perform all the ritual music and dances required by the court and also give regular public *gagaku* concerts.

Instruments 楽器

The instruments used in performances of *gagaku* are Japanese modifications of those used in the Tang court ensembles. The instrumentation is determined by the type of music being performed. A small double-reed pipe similar to an oboe or shawm, called the *hichiriki* 篳篥, is used in all the instrumental ensembles. Three different types of flute are used, the *kagurabue* 神楽笛 generally for the Shintō rituals, the *komabue* 高麗笛 for *komagaku*, and the *ryūteki* or dragon flute 竜笛 for *tōgaku*. In addition to these wind instruments 管楽器, *tōgaku* uses a small mouth organ of 17 bamboo pipes called the *shō* 笙, which plays tone clusters of 5 or 6 notes. *Tōgaku* and *komagaku* each use three percussion instruments, two of which are common to both types of music. These are a hanging *ōdaiko*, or large drum 大太鼓, and the *shōko*, a small bronze gong 鉦鼓. In *komagaku* there is also a small hourglass drum called *san no tsuzumi*, played with a single stick; the *kakko* 羯鼓, a small drum played with two sticks, is used in *tōgaku*. In Shintō vocal music, the only percussion instrument is a pair of wooden clappers (*shakubyōshi* 笏拍子). Stringed instruments are no longer used in the *tōgaku* dance repertoire or in *komagaku*, but two have been retained in the *kangen*, or chamber music setting of *tōgaku*: the *gakusō* 楽箏, which is usually called by its common name, *koto*, and the *biwa*. Only one stringed instrument, the *wagon* 和琴, is used in Shintō music. The repertoire of *gagaku* music is played at tempos that, although varied, seem very slow when compared to Western music or even to other forms of Japanese music.

Rakugo 落語

Popular form of comic monologue in which a storyteller (*rakugoka* 落語家) creates an imaginary drama through episodic narration and skillful use of vocal and facial expressions to portray various characters. Typically, the storyteller uses no scenery; the only musical accompaniment is the *debayashi* 出囃子, a brief flourish of drum, *shamisen*, and bamboo flute that marks his entrance and exit. The storyteller, dressed in a plain *kimono*, crosses to stage center and seats himself on a cushion before his audience, with a hand towel and a fan as his only props. There he remains until he has delivered his final line, usually a punning punch line オチ. This is the characteristic ending from which the term *rakugo* was coined.

In a *rakugo* performance the interplay between performer and audience is extremely important. Since the repertory of classic *rakugo* is small, aficionados have heard the basic story many times. They delight in the storyteller's particular version, his arrangement of familiar episodes, and appreciate his timing and the verisimilitude of the details he adds, such as the sound of *sake* as he pours it into his imaginary cup. The introduction to the story proper must be completely original. The plots of the stories are never as important as the characterizations in them, for *rakugo* pokes fun at all manner of human foibles.

By the early 1670s professional performers called *hanashika* had emerged. Tsuyu no Gorobei 露の五郎兵衛 (1643–1703) from Kyōto and Yonezawa Hikohachi (d 1714) from Ōsaka are regarded as the forefathers of Kamigata (Kyōto-Ōsaka) *rakugo* 上方落語, while Shikano Buzaemon 鹿野武左衛門 (1649–1699) is credited with founding the Edo *rakugo* 江戸落語 tradition, later perfected by San'yūtei Enchō 三遊亭圓朝.

A regular entertainment feature at roadside shows, private banquets, and makeshift stages set up at restaurants during off-hours, this vagabond art found a home in 1791 when the first permanent Japanese-style vaudeville theater, or *yose* 寄席, was opened in Edo (now Tōkyō). Soon afterward the popularity of *yose* spread to Kyōto and Ōsaka.

After surviving the challenge of cinema in the 1920s and 1930s, which significantly reduced *yose* attendance, *rakugo* performers met with increasing official disapproval during World War II, because they did not adapt their material to complement national ideology.

With the resumption of civilian broadcasting at the end of World War II, *rakugo* recovered its popularity. Although the proliferation of new entertainment media has greatly reduced the number of *yose*, the adaptability of *rakugo* to both radio and television has ensured its survival. There are still four traditional *yose* in Tōkyō. In many universities there are *rakugo* clubs 落語研究会 whose members study and perform *rakugo* for their own entertainment.

Manzai 漫才

Performing art in which a comic dialogue is carried on by two comedians. Said to have had its beginnings in the Nara period (710–794), *manzai* spread throughout Japan in the Edo period (1600–1868).

Toward the close of the Edo period, *manzai* was performed in makeshift theaters, and by the first decade of the 20th century its popularity, especially in Ōsaka, increased rapidly. After World War II, passing from the age of radio to that of television, *manzai* has continued to flourish. Today the repartee of *manzai* performers—the wit is now called *tsukkomi* つっこみ and the straight man *boke* ぼけ—is distinguished by its fast pace, its use of current events, and its swift shifts, often by bizarre association, from topic to topic.

Japanese film (Nihon *eiga*) 日本映画

The Japanese first imported motion pictures in 1896. By 1899 they were filming their own. Until the coming of talkies トーキー, movies in Japan were accompanied by a *benshi*, a live performer 弁士 who sat by the side of the screen and orally interpreted the images of the film. Because *benshi* supplied expository connections and full dialogue, the first filmmakers replicated Japanese stage plays and generally ignored film techniques being developed in the West by such film directors as D. W. Griffith (1875–1948).

▎Early History 草創期

Makino Shōzō 牧野省三 (1878–1929), the father of the Japanese cinema, began to direct movies in 1907. He gradually dropped KABUKI elements from his costume dramas to concentrate on stories from juvenile literature and *kōdan* (oral storytelling). Films with contemporary stories drew on the *shimpa* theatrical repertoire throughout the early 1900s. After World War I, would-be filmmakers, influenced by the ideals of *shingeki* ("new theater") 新劇 and by the flood of movies from abroad, cried for "modernization and realism."

The early 1920s marked the emergence of *jidaigeki* (period films) 時代劇. In 1924 Makino Shōzō collaborated with the Shinkokugeki drama troupe in a movie version of its swashbuckling hit *Kunisada Chūji* 「国定忠治」. *Jidaigeki* subsequently evolved over 70 years through a symbiotic relationship among literary, theater, and film works focused on swords and solitary heroes.

Gendaigeki, the other genre of the post-1920 Japanese cinema, encompasses all stories with modern settings. Mizoguchi Kenji 溝口健二 (1898–1956), the most eclectic of early *gendaigeki* directors, drew on sources ranging from the German film *The Cabinet of Dr. Caligari* 「カリガリ博士」 (1919) to traditional *shimpa* drama.

The Late 1920s and Early 1930s
1920年代後半から1930年代前半まで

The economic depression that hit Japan before 1929 engendered left-wing tendencies in literature, *shingeki*, and films. After the invasion of Manchuria in 1931, more stringent government censorship ended these tendencies. The *jidaigeki* moved to satire and comedy after Itami Mansaku's 伊丹万作 (1900–1946) *Kokushi musō* (1932, Peerless Patriot) 「国士無双」. The most important new direction for *jidaigeki* was initiated by Yamanaka Sadao 山中貞雄 (1909–1938) and Inagaki Hiroshi 稲垣浩 (1905–1980), who brought the slice-of-life, lower-class urban milieu of many *gendaigeki* to the period film. In *gendaigeki*, Shimazu Yasujirō 島津保次郎 (1897–1945), with his *Tonari no Yae-chan* (1934, Our Neighbor Miss Yae) 「隣の八重ちゃん」, focused on the small joys and passive endurance of the world. The works of Ozu Yasujirō 小津安二郎 (1903–1963) best reflected the continuing development of the *shōshimin geki*, "dramas about the petite bourgeoisie." 小市民劇 For three years in a row, critics chose his stories of imperfect fathers—

Umarete wa mita keredo (1932, I Was Born, But ...)「生まれて
は見たけれど」, *Dekigokoro* (1933, Passing Fancy)「出来ごころ」,
and *Ukigusa monogatari* (1934, A Story of Floating
Weeds)「浮草物語」—as the best pictures of their respective years.

The Talkies トーキー

Gosho Heinosuke's 五所平之助 (1902–1981) family
comedy *Madamu to nyōbō* (The Neighbor's Wife and
Mine)「マダムと女房」was Japan's first technically successful talkie as well as the critical and popular success of
1931. Talkies did not become the major portion of production until 1936.

The bulk of *jidaigeki* continued to be nihilistic
chambara adventures. Several small studios survived
throughout the 1930s by turning out cheap, silent
jidaigeki for the surviving *benshi* market. Although feature production had risen to a steady average of 650 per
year by the mid-1920s, the average annual output stabilized at 550 throughout the 1930s. Under wartime
restraints this number suddenly decreased to 232 in 1941
and fell to 26 in 1945.

Censorship, the War, and the Postwar Era
検閲および第2次世界大戦から終戦直後まで

Film censorship was consolidated under the control of the national Police Bureau 警保局 of the Home
Ministry 内務省 in 1925 and gradually tightened during
the 1930s. In 1939 the Home Ministry ordered filmmakers to follow its list of essential "national policy" 国策
subjects, which accented patriotic home life and sacrifice
for the nation. Despite strong official encouragement,
fewer than one-fifth of all wartime features complied
with government guidelines.

The Allied Occupation abolished Home Ministry
censorship and set up its own office to supervise film
content. In 1949 Occupation authorities eased their controls in return for the industry's establishment of a

self-regulatory body, the Motion Picture Code Committee 映画倫理規定管理委員会(映倫).

The six major studios—Tōhō 東宝, Shin Tōhō 新東宝, Shōchiku 松竹, Nikkatsu 日活, Daiei 大映, and Tōei 東映—controlled the industry through a cartel-like hold on film distribution and exhibition. The number of movie theaters reached an all-time high of 7,457 in 1960. This was 8.8 times as many as when the war ended. Two men whose directing careers had begun during the war came to the forefront during the early Occupation era: Kurosawa Akira 黒沢明 (1910–1998) and Kinoshita Keisuke 木下恵介 (1912–1998). Along with two other directors of their generation, Imai Tadashi 今井正 (1912–1991) and Yoshimura Kōzaburō 吉村公三郎 (1911–), they dominated the 1947–1950 period with films about postwar life.

The 1950s 1950年代

The decade of the 1950s, apart from being the most prosperous in the history of the Japanese cinema, is considered by many to be its creative Golden Age. Five times during this decade critics voted a film by Imai the best of the year, a streak that began with *Mata au hi made* (1950, Until the Day We Meet Again) 「また逢う日まで」. When Kurosawa's innovative *jidaigeki Rashōmon* 「羅生門」 (1950) won the top prize at the Venice Film Festival ベネチア映画祭 in 1951, it opened the Japanese cinema to international audiences. Kurosawa's style alternated between such social issue–oriented *gendaigeki* as *Ikiru* (1952, To Live) 「生きる」 and such seminal *jidaigeki* epics as *Shichinin no samurai* (1954, *Seven Samurai*) 「七人の侍」.

Mizoguchi abandoned his early postwar love stories to refashion the historical film with such exquisite works as *Saikaku ichidai onna* (1952, The Life of a Woman by Saikaku; shown abroad as *The Life of Oharu*) 「西鶴一代女」 and *Ugetsu monogatari* (1953, *Ugetsu*) 「雨月物語」. In *Banshun* (1949, Late Spring), and *Tōkyō monogatari*

(1953, Tōkyō Story)「東京物語」Ozu Yasujirō and his scenarist Noda Kōgo 野田高梧 (1893–1968) concentrated on the emotional complexities of middle-class family life, while Naruse Mikio 成瀬巳喜男 (1905–1969) and Gosho Heinosuke continued the prewar *shōshimin geki* tradition. Naruse later turned to a new major interest: portraits of women fighting the domination of men in such films as *Ukigumo* (1955, Floating Clouds)「浮雲」. Gosho's major work was *Entotsu no mieru basho* (1953, Where Chimneys Are Seen)「煙突の見える場所」.

Comedy grew in sophistication. Shibuya Minoru (1907–1980) perfected the farce in *Honjitsu kyūshin* (1952, Clinic Closed Today)「本日休診」, Kawashima Yūzō 川島雄三 (1918–1963) created the definitive postwar *jidaigeki* comedy in *Bakumatsu taiyō den* (1957, A Tale of the Sun during the Last Days of the Shogunate)「幕末太陽伝」, and Ichikawa Kon 市川崑 (1915–) pioneered black humor in *Kagi* (1959, The Key; shown abroad as *Odd Obsession*)「鍵」. The new Tōei company captured a large new audience for *jidaigeki* by creating young *chambara* stars, and it also backed *jidaigeki* old masters: Itō Daisuke 伊藤大輔 (1898–1981), Uchida Tomu 内田吐夢 (1898–1970), and Makino Masahiro マキノ雅裕 (1908–1993). To strengthen its principal market among urban, middle-class audiences, Tōhō made pop musicals and dozens of comedies about middle-aged white-collar workers. In 1954 Tōhō created Japan's first film monster in *Godzilla*「ゴジラ」by Tsuburaya Eiji 円谷英二 (1901–1970). A horde of Tōhō and Daiei monsters followed for two decades. Kinoshita's *Karumen kokyō ni kaeru* (Carmen Comes Home)「カルメン故郷に帰る」inaugurated a decade of technical innovation in 1951 with the first Japanese color feature. Three years later Kinugasa Teinosuke's 衣笠貞之介 (1896–1982) *Jigokumon* (1953, Gate of Hell)「地獄門」won the highest international acclaim for innovative use of color. In the late 1950s, *taiyōzoku* (sun tribe) 太陽族 films exploited the hedonism of affluent postwar youth. This accelerated interest in movie sex and violence.

Television and a New Wave テレビとニューウェーブ

In 1958, five years after television broadcasting had begun, there were 1.6 million television sets throughout the country. By 1969 there were 21.9 million sets, a figure almost equal to the number of households. Attendance at the movies fell from the all-time high of 1.1 billion in 1958 to 300 million in 1968. The Shin Tōhō studios went bankrupt in 1961. Half of the movie theaters in the country closed during the 1960s.

In 1958 Masumura Yasuzō 増村保造 (1924–1986) called for the destruction of the established Japanese cinema and soon was joined by other young directors. Ōshima Nagisa 大島渚 (1932–) demanded an end to lyricism, heaviness, naturalism, and *mono no aware*. Ōshima and two tradition-breaking fellow directors at Shōchiku, Shinoda Masahiro 篠田正浩 (1931–) and Yoshida Yoshishige 吉田喜重 (1933–), were dubbed the "Shōchiku Nūberu Bāgu" (*nouvelle vague*, or new wave) 松竹ヌーベルバーグ. Ōshima's Brechtian *Kōshikei* (1968, Death by Hanging) 「絞死刑」 and *Shinjuku dorobō nikki* (1969, Diary of a Shinjuku Thief) 「新宿泥棒日記」 established him as the principal new film maker of the cosmopolitan 1960s. Imamura Shōhei 今村昌平 (1926–) rivaled Ōshima with a call to destroy the illusionistic pretensions of fiction and documentary films. Imamura searched for clues to Japanese national identity in the pseudobiography *Nippon konchūki* (1963, Story of a Japanese Insect; shown abroad as *The Insect Woman*) 「にっぽん昆虫記」 and the modern primitive myth *Kamigami no fukaki yokubō* (1968, The Profound Desire of the Gods; shown abroad as *Kuragejima: Tales from a Southern Island*) 「神々の深き欲望」.

In *jidaigeki*, major directors looked occasionally to the classical theater. Kurosawa adapted elements from the Nō theater to his syncretic version of Macbeth,

Kumonosujō (1957, Throne of Blood)「蜘蛛巣城」. Uchida Tomu in *Naniwa no koi no monogatari* (1959, Naniwa Love Story)「浪花の恋の物語」and Shinoda Masahiro in *Shinjū Ten no Amijima* (1969, Love Suicide at Amijima; Double Suicide)「心中天網島」used plays by Chikamatsu Monzaemon (1653–1724) and borrowed respectively from *kabuki* and *bunraku* drama. In 1963 Tōei originated the *yakuza* (gangster) genre. The immediate popularity of Tōei *yakuza* pictures 東映ヤクザ映画 soon wiped out *jidaigeki* as the main arena for *chambara*.

Since the 1970s 1970年代以降

The dominant director of the 1970s was a major-studio man, Yamada Yōji 山田洋次 (1931–) of Shōchiku. Although his principal works were prize-winning portraits of lower-class family life such as *Kazoku* (1970, shown abroad as *Where Spring Comes Late*)「家族」, his overwhelmingly popular success was the *Tora san* series (formal series title *Otoko wa tsurai yo*; It's Tough Being a Man「男はつらいよ」). Yamada wrote and directed 48 films in this series, which began in 1969 and ended in 1996 with the death of series star Atsumi Kiyoshi. These films fused the two bedrock motifs of Japanese film: the everyday collective life of a family and the adventures of a lonely wanderer.

The satires of director Itami Jūzō 伊丹十三 (1933–1997), including *Tampopo* (1985, Dandelion)「タンポポ」and *Marusa no onna* (1987, A Taxing Woman)「マルサの女」were some of the most popular movies of the 1980s. In the 1990s Japanese films are again attracting attention abroad. *Shi no toge* (1990, The Sting of Death)「死の棘」and *Nemuru otoko* (1996, Sleeping Man)「眠る男」by director Oguri Kōhei 小栗康平 (1945–) won prizes at the Cannes and Montreal film festivals カンヌ国際映画祭：モントリオール映画祭, respectively. In 1997 *Unagi* (1997, Eel)「うなぎ」by Imamura Shōhei became the second film by that director to win the Cannes Film Festival Grand

Prize, the first being *Narayama-bushi kō* (1983, The Ballad of Narayama)「楢山節考」. In the same year *HANA-BI* (1997, Flower and Fire)「HANA-BI」by Kitano Takeshi 北野武 (1947–) won the Venice Film Festival ベネチア国際映画祭 Grand Prize. In the second half of the 1990s a changing of the guard appears to be taking place in Japanese cinema with the appearance of new directors such as Iwai Shunji 岩井俊二 (1963–), who directed *Love Letter* (1995), and Suō Masayuki 周防正行 (1956–), who directed *Shall We Dance?* (1996).

In 1994 the number of theaters in Japan grew for the first time in 18 years because of the construction of new multiple-screen cinema complexes シネコン. Japan had 1,826 theaters in 1996, an increase of 50 over the previous year.

LANGUAGE 言語

Japanese language (*nihongo*) 日本語

The native language of the overwhelming majority of the more than 100 million inhabitants of the Japanese archipelago.

Although the Japanese and Chinese languages are entirely unrelated genetically, the Japanese writing system derives from that of Chinese. Chinese characters 漢字 were introduced sometime in the 6th century, if not before, and the modern writing system is a complex one in which Chinese characters are used in conjunction with two separate phonetic scripts developed from them in Japan. Japanese has also absorbed LOANWORDS 外来語 freely from other languages, especially Chinese and English, the former chiefly from the 8th to the 19th century and the latter in the 20th century.

There seems to be a growing consensus among Japanese scholars that syntactically Japanese shows an Altaic affinity アルタイ語系, but that at some time in its prehistory it received an influence in vocabulary and morphology from the Malayo-Polynesian languages マライ・ポリネシア語 to the south.

The Japanese Dialects and the Speech of Tōkyō
方言と東京ことば

Modern Japanese language has a large number of local dialects, existing alongside, but gradually being overwhelmed by, the officially recognized standard language 標準語, which is based on the speech of the capital, Tōkyō.

Two important urban dialects that flourish alongside the standard language of Tōkyō are those of the cities of Kyōto and Ōsaka. Kyōto was the imperial capital for more than 1,000 years, and, though it was not always the seat of real political or economic power, both it and its language continued to have the highest prestige. During the Edo period (1600–1868), Edo (now Tōkyō), which was the seat of the Tokugawa Shogunate, grew into an important commercial and administrative city. Both it and the older commercial city of Ōsaka became thriving centers of the culture and language of the merchant classes 町人, and the language of Edo in particular—the locus of political power and the home of the *samurai* bureaucracy—gradually developed a prestige of its own. When Edo was renamed Tōkyō and made the new imperial capital, the language of its educated elite was gradually systematized and transformed. Incorporated into this language were a number of expressions from the language of the nobility from Kyōto. The resulting mixture became what is now the standard language 標準語, sometimes loosely referred to as "the Tōkyō dialect." 東京語

The Phonology of the Standard Language
標準語の音韻

The short or unit vowels 短母音 of standard Japanese, *a, i, u, e,* and *o,* are pronounced more or less as in Spanish or Italian. (In this description the phonemes of Japanese will be written in the standard Hepburn romanization ヘボン式ローマ字, phonetic symbols being added only when necessary for clarity.) The long vowels 長母音, *ā, ii, ū, ei,* and *ō,* are pronounced double the length of the short vowels (*a:, i:, u:, e:,* and *o:*), except that *ei* is

The Japanese Syllabaries
五十音図

n ン	wa ワ	ra ラ	ya ヤ	ma マ	ha ハ	na ナ	ta タ	sa サ	ka カ	a ア
	ゐ ヰ	ri リ		mi ミ	hi ヒ	ni ニ	chi チ	shi シ	ki キ	i イ
	う ウ	ru ル	yu ユ	mu ム	fu フ	nu ヌ	tsu ツ	su ス	ku ク	u ウ
	ゑ ヱ	re レ	e エ	me メ	he ヘ	ne ネ	te テ	se セ	ke ケ	e エ
	o ヲ	ro ロ	yo ヨ	mo モ	ho ホ	no ノ	to ト	so ソ	ko コ	o オ

often pronounced as a sequence of two separate vowels. The distinction between long and short vowels is essential for meaning. Aside from *ei,* sequences of vowels such as *ai, au, ae, oi, ue,* and so forth are so pronounced that the individual vowels retain their identity, although a glide often occurs; they are treated as separate syllables.

The consonants are *k, s, sh, t, ch, ts, n, h, f, m, y, r, w, g, j, z, d, b,* and *p.* The fricative *sh* (as in English "shoe") and the affricates *ch, ts,* and *j* (as in English "church," "patsy," and "judge," respectively) are treated as single consonants. *G* is always pronounced as in English "good" (never as in "genetics"). The rest are pronounced more or less as in English except that *f* is a bilabial rather than labiodental fricative 両唇音, *r* is flapped, and *t, d,* and *n* are dental. When *n* is used at the end of a syllable as opposed to the beginning, it expresses a uvular syllabic nasal [N]; this changes to one of three different types of nasals when followed by certain consonants: *n* (dental) before *t, d,* or *n;* (velar, as in English "thank") before *k* or *g;* and *m* (bilabial) before *p, b,* or *m.*

Japanese has no stress accent 強弱アクセント like that of English. Each syllable is given equal stress, successions of syllables being pronounced with metronomic regularity. Standard Japanese and a number of the dialects do have, however, a high-low pitch accent 高低アクセント system, accent in a word or sequence of words being marked by the syllable after which the pitch drops. The way in which the same word (or the same set of contrasting homophones) is accented can differ significantly among those dialects that have pitch accents.

Another characteristic of standard Japanese is the strong tendency to devoice the vowels *i* and *u* when they fall between two voiceless consonants 無声子音, so that *shitakusa* (undergrowth) becomes *sh'tak'sa*. The vowels are not always dropped entirely, however: often they are sounded faintly, or at least their metronomic beat preserved. The vowel *u* at the end of a word after a voiceless consonant is also often devoiced or dropped, most notably in *desu*, the polite form of the copula, and in the polite verb ending -*masu*, which are often pronounced *des'* and *mas'*, respectively.

The Grammar of Modern Japanese
現代日本語の文法

Nouns: 名詞 Japanese nouns are uninflected words that have neither number nor gender and do not influence the inflection of the adjectives modifying them.

There do exist a number of pluralizing suffixes as in *hitobito* from *hito*; however, such devices are not used as a matter of course, and in most cases there is no explicit indication of plurality.

In Japanese the grammatical function of nouns within a sentence is not indicated by word order 語順 as in English; neither are nouns inflected for grammatical case as in some languages. Instead grammatical function is indicated by grammatical particles 格助詞 (sometimes called postpositions), which follow the noun. Among the more important of these are *ga, o, ni,* and *no*, which function as case markers, *ga* indicating subject of verb, *o* direct object of verb, *ni* dative or indirect object, and *no* genitive. A particularly important particle is *wa*. This is not a case marker but rather marks the topic or theme of the sentence. All of these particles also have various other functions and meanings depending on grammatical structure and context. There are a number of other postpositions that function much as prepositions do in English.

Verbs 動詞 Japanese verbal inflections do not indicate person or number. The dictionary forms of all verbs in the modern language end in the vowel -*u*. When citing the dictionary form of Japanese verbs in English, it is conventional to refer to them by the English infinitive; thus *kaku* is often cited as "to write," although this form is actually the present (more precisely the non-past) tense, which means "write/writes" or "will write." Other inflectional forms include *kakanai* (negative: "does not/will not write"), *kakō* (tentative or hortatory: "someone may write"; "let's write"), *kakitai* (often called "desiderative": "wants to write"), *kaita* (past: "wrote"), *kakeba* (provisional or conditional: "if someone writes"), and *kake* (nonpolite imperative: "write!"). Verbs can be used not only to form the predicate of a sentence or clause but also attributively to modify nouns (e.g., *kaku hito*, "the person who writes").

Verb conjugations 動詞活用 are classified in two main types. One of these consists of the consonant-stem verbs 子音語幹動詞 (verbs whose stems end in consonants), including verbs such as *kaku* (write), *hanasu* (talk), and *utsu* (hit), whose stems are *kak-*, *hanas-*, and *uts-*, respectively. The other type comprises the vowel-stem verbs, which are themselves of two types, with stems ending in either the vowel *i* or the vowel *e*; e.g., *miru* (see) and *taberu* (eat), whose stems are *mi-* and *tabe-*, respectively. (The dictionary forms of vowel-stem verbs 母音語幹動詞 all end in -*iru* or -*eru*; however, not all verbs so ending are vowel-stem verbs. Some are consonant-stem verbs with stems ending in *r*; e.g., *kiru* "cut"). In modern Japanese there are two fully conjugated irregular verbs, *kuru* (come) and *suru* (do), bringing the total number of standard verb conjugations to five.

The copula 繋辞 The Japanese copula or linking verb 連結動詞 (plain form *da*; polite form *desu*) is used to link two nouns (or nominal phrases) in the pattern A *wa* B *da* or A *wa* B *desu* (A is B). The literal meaning of this pattern is "as for A, it is B" or "as for A, it is in the category of B," e.g., *neko wa dōbutsu da* (cats are animals; literally, "as for cats, they are animals"). For this reason the Japanese copula cannot always be translated by the English "to be." For example, *watakushi wa bīru desu* does not mean "I am beer" but "I am having beer" (literally, "as for me, it is beer").

Adjectives 形容詞 Japanese adjectives are inflected in some ways like verbs, and like verbs they can function either attributively, coming before the nouns they modify (*shiroi hana*; a white flower), or as the predicates of sentences or clauses, in the latter case appearing at the end of the sentence or clause (*hana wa shiroi*; the flower is white). The dictionary forms of all adjectives end in one of four vowels (*a, i, u,* or *o*) followed by a final *i*. The stem of the adjective is obtained by dropping the final *i*; e.g., *takai* (high; stem *taka*), *utsukushii* (beautiful; stem *utsukushi*), *samui* (cold; stem *samu*), and *shiroi* (white; stem *shiro*).

Levels of speech 談話の位相 Japanese expresses a consciousness of social relationships by various grammatical means. Plain versus polite verb forms distinguish between easy informality and abruptness on the one hand and a correct, neutral politeness on the other. In the system of levels known as HONORIFIC LANGUAGE 敬語, the speaker chooses among a number of alternative ways of saying the same thing, the choice being determined by such factors as relative age, sex, and social status.

The sentence 文型 The typical Japanese sentence is built on the pattern of subject-object-verb (SOV), as in *neko ga nezumi o tsukamaeta* (the cat caught the mouse). However, since the particle *ga* marks *neko* (cat) as the subject, and the particle *o* marks *nezumi* (mouse) as the object of the verb *tsukamaeta*, a certain amount of inversion, as for stylistic purposes, is possible; *nezumi o neko ga tsukamaeta* (OSV) would have virtually the same meaning as the SOV sentence, whereas in English such inversion of subject and object would change the meaning entirely. To return to the basic SOV sentence, if an adverbial modifier, for instance *subayaku* (swiftly), is inserted, it may come before the subject, the object, or the verb, with slight differences of emphasis.

There are no relative pronouns 関係代名詞 in Japanese as in the English "the cat that caught the mouse died." In Japanese the entire subordinate clause is placed directly in front of the noun as a modifier: *nezumi o tsukamaeta neko ga shinda* (literally, "the caught-the-mouse cat died"). A sentence can also be made into a subordinate clause in another sentence by inserting either the nominalizing particle *no* (not to be confused with the genitive particle *no* mentioned earlier) or the function word *koto* (thing; matter) after the final verb of the sentence, which then modifies the particle, forming a noun clause.

Vocabulary 語彙

Japanese has an extremely rich and varied vocabulary, not only its large stock of native words, which are felt to be particularly expressive and sonorous, but also a great quantity of words of Chinese origin. To these are added the many loanwards 外来語 from English and other European languages that have come into Japanese, especially during the 20th century. Many of the loanwords from Chinese have been so thoroughly absorbed into the daily vocabulary that their foreign origin is no longer felt. Much of the intellectual and philosophical vocabulary is of Chinese origin, but not all of this is due entirely to Chinese cultural influence; an important part of the modern intellectual vocabulary consists of words coined in Japan in the late 19th and early 20th centuries by devising new combinations of Chinese characters as translations of concepts then being introduced from the West. This process of coinage still continues, but there is a growing tendency, particularly in the sciences, to use Western words intact. Aside from the sciences, words are often used with meanings quite different from those of their original languages, and new Japanese words are sometimes coined by combining parts of Western language words in startling ways. One particularly interesting feature of the native Japanese vocabulary is the large number of established onomatopoeic words 擬声語 it contains. These include not only words imitating sounds but also words expressing abstract qualities or subjective feelings.

Writing System 文字

The Japanese writing system uses Chinese characters 漢字 in combination with two separate forms of the phonetic syllabic script 仮名 known as KANA: *hiragana* and *katakana*. Some words are written entirely in *kana*, others entirely in Chinese characters, and others in a combination of the two. In the latter case the stem of the word is written with a Chinese character, or characters, and inflectional endings or other suffixes with *kana*. Grammatical particles and function words (such as demonstratives and auxiliary verbs) are written in *kana*. The resulting text is sometimes sprinkled with Roman letters ローマ字 (e.g., acronyms such as PTA, model numbers, and occasionally entire foreign words), so that the number of scripts needed to write modern Japanese actually comes to four.

Kana 仮名

General term for a number of syllabic writing systems 表音文字 developed in Japan, all based on Chinese characters 漢字, used to express the sounds of Japanese rather than the meanings of individual words.

Two sets of *kana* are used in the present-day Japanese writing system: *hiragana*, a cursive form (and the one commonly used for native words and any words of Chinese origin not to be written in characters), and *katakana*, a noncursive form. *Katakana* is most typically used to write loanwords 借用語 from other languages, for emphasis, or for representation of onomatopoeic words, thus performing functions similar to the use of italics in Western orthography. Both *katakana* and *hiragana* derive from an earlier set of *kana* known as *man'yōgana* 万葉仮名, and *hiragana* in particular derives from the cursive form of *man'yōgana* known as *sōgana* 草仮名.

Man'yōgana 万葉仮名

Man'yōgana are a set of unmodified Chinese characters that were once used as phonetic symbols to represent Japanese syllables. As the name suggests, *man'yōgana* was the writing system used in the *Man'yōshū*, an 8th-century poetry anthology. Most attempts to write Japanese prior to the Heian period (794–1185) fall into the category of *man'yōgana*.

The *man'yōgana* differs from the two currently used *kana* systems in at least three important aspects. First, there is no one-to-one relationship between syllables and characters. There were 87 syllable types in 8th-century Japanese, but more than 970 Chinese characters were used to write them. Second, the Chinese characters were used as written in Chinese, without modification or simplification. For this reason a text written in *man'yōgana* superficially resembles a text in Chinese; however, because many of the characters are used only for their pronunciation and not for their meaning and because the language represented is Japanese, the text is likely to be unintelligible to a

Chinese reader. Third, the types of character pronunciation represented in *man'yōgana* are more varied than in *hiragana* and *katakana*, including the *on* reading 音読み and *kun* reading 訓読み of the character.

Katakana 片仮名

In its modern, standard form, *katakana* is a system of 48 syllabic writing units for writing non-Chinese loanwords, onomatopoeia, emphasized words, and the names of flora and fauna. The *kata* in *katakana* means "partial," "not whole," "fragmentary." It is so named because many of the *katakana* are a part and not the whole of a Chinese character. In its earlier stages, *katakana* was used as a mnemonic device for pronouncing (*kambun kunten*) Buddhist texts written in Chinese. Next appeared Japanese texts written in a mixture of Chinese characters and *katakana*. This writing system is called *kanamajiri bun* (sentences mixing *kana* and characters) 仮名混じり文. By the middle of the 10th century, anthologies of Japanese verse (WAKA) came to be written in *katakana* and by the 12th century collections of folktales came to be written in a mixture of Chinese characters and *katakana*.

Hiragana 平仮名

In its modern, standard form, *hiragana* is a system of 48 syllabic writing units for writing indigenous Japanese words and often for Chinese loanwords that cannot be written with the 1,945 characters officially approved for general use. *Hira* means "commonly used," "easy," "rounded." *Hiragana* is so named because the letters are considered rounded and easy to write compared with the full forms of the original Chinese characters. In its early forms *hiragana* was used by women, while the unsimplified Chinese characters were used by men; for this reason, the earliest *hiragana* was also called *onnade* (women's hand) 女手. By the end of the 9th century *onnade* ceased to be a system limited to women and became an accepted device for recording poems. *Hiragana* gained full acceptance when the imperial poetic anthology *Kokin wakashū* 「古今和歌集」(905) was written in *onnade*.

Kanji (Chinese characters) 漢字

Ideographs 表意文字 of ancient Chinese origin that are still used in China, Korea, and Japan and were formerly used in other areas influenced by Chinese culture such as Vietnam. Chinese characters are ideographs in that essentially each character or graph symbolizes a single idea and, by extension, the sound (i.e., spoken word or morpheme) associated with that idea. For example, the Chinese character 犬 is "dog" in English, *quan* in modern standard Chinese, and *ken* or *inu* in Japanese.

On and *Kun* Readings 音読みと訓読み

Since in the Japanese writing system Chinese characters can be used to write either words of Chinese origin or native Japanese words, the pronunciations that can be assigned to them in reading fall naturally into two categories: (1) the Japanese imitations or approximations of the sound of the original Chinese syllable and (2) the native Japanese word that translates the meaning of the character. The former are called *on* readings (*on yomi*), *on* being written with a character that means "sound" (i.e., the original Chinese sound); these are often referred to as "Sino-Japanese" readings in English. The latter are called *kun* readings (*kun yomi*), *kun* being written with a character that originally meant "to interpret the meaning" (i.e., the meaning of the character as expressed by the Japanese word).

Number of Characters in Use 一般に使われている漢字の数

The number of Chinese characters currently used in Japan is limited to a small percentage of the 40,000 to 50,000 contained in the larger dictionaries. A list of characters called *tōyō kanji* (Chinese characters for daily use) 当用漢字 was selected by the Ministry of

Character Styles
漢字の書体

modern printed form

woman | heart | music, pleasure

"oracle bone" characters
甲骨文字

bronze inscriptions
金文

tadpole characters
蝌蚪文字

greater seal script
大篆

lesser seal script
小篆

clerical style
隷書

standard style
楷書

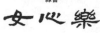

semicursive style
行書

cursive style or "grass writing"
草書

Education 文部省 in 1946, limiting the number of characters for official, educational, and general public use to 1,850. In 1981 this list was superseded by a similar but larger one (the *jōyō kanji*; Chinese characters for common use 常用漢字) containing 1,945 characters.

Honorific language (*keigo*) 敬語

Often referred to in English as "polite speech" or "honorifics." The Japanese language has an extensive system of honorific language to show respect by the speaker to the addressee. *Keigo* in the broad sense refers to the entire system of speech levels. In its narrow sense *keigo* means "terms of respect" and refers to honorific words and expressions. In speaking, a choice is made as to the degree of politeness to be expressed. Depending on the status of the speaker relative to the addressee and on the context of the conversation, a simple question can be phrased in as many as two dozen different ways.

Choice of Speech Style 話法の選択

The speech style 話法 is basically determined by the status of the speaker and the addressee and the degree of intimacy between them. The general rule is that when the addressee is of higher status than the speaker, or when the two are not very intimate, the polite style 丁寧語 (with *desu-masu* verb forms) is to be used. Relative status is determined by a combination of factors, such as age, sex, rank, or social status and favors done or owed. In the reverse case, where the speaker is of higher status in an in-group situation, the speaker has a choice of plain (with *da* verb forms) 平常語 or polite style. When two individuals who do not belong to the same group meet for the first time, both individuals will use the polite style unless there are some obvious differences in age or social status as reflected in dress, manner, or occupation.

The speech style chosen by women is often a

step politer than that selected by men. Women are not as likely to speak in the plain style to a junior-ranking adult as men are. They tend to use the polite style much more widely and indiscriminately, restricting the use of the plain style to immediate family members, close friends, and children.

Types of Honorifics 敬語の種類

The final verb phrase of the sentence that differentiates the speech styles is only one aspect of *keigo*. There are innumerable other honorifics to be found in various parts of speech, including nouns, pronouns, verbs, adjectives, adverbs, and conjunctions. These honorifics, also referred to as *keigo*, are normally classified into three groups: *sonkeigo* (exalted terms) 尊敬語, *kenjōgo* (humble terms) 謙譲語, and *teineigo* (polite terms) 丁寧語. Exalted terms are used to refer to the addressee and anything directly associated with the addressee, such as kin, house, or possessions, while humble terms are used to refer to the speaker and anything associated with the speaker. By elevating the addressee through exalted terms and lowering the speaker through humble terms, a greater distance is created between the two, thereby expressing deeper respect for the addressee. Exalted terms are also used to refer to a third person of higher status if he is not a member of the speaker's in-group. *Teineigo* or polite terms are used without reference to the addressee or speaker and are found in increasing numbers as the speech level goes up.

The give-receive verbs play an important role in the *keigo* system. These verbs are used as main verbs in describing the giving and receiving of gifts and as auxiliary verbs in compound verb 複合動詞 phrases to express the giving and receiving of actions done as a favor. The rules in using the give-receive verbs are complex, and group membership becomes an important factor.

In comparison with verbs, honorific nouns are

relatively simple. There are underived exalted and humble nouns, but the majority of these are used in writing. Most exalted nouns are created through grammatical rules. In general, the prefix *o-* is attached to neutral nouns of Japanese origin, such as *oniwa* (garden), *otegami* (letter); and the prefix *go-* to Chinese compounds, such as *gobyōki* (illness), *goiken* (opinion). In the case of nouns referring to people, *-san* is suffixed in addition to the prefix *o-*, such as *otetsudaisan* (maid), *oishasan* (doctor).

Rules exist for the use of *keigo* in referring to a third person, as well as for first- and second-person pronouns. The result is an all-pervasive system that allows for fine gradations in the level of politeness within each speech style.

Loanwords (*gairaigo*) 外来語

Foreign loanwords and phrases that are extensively used in Japanese and normally written in the *katakana* syllabary are called *gairaigo*. Loanwords from China are not normally treated as *gairaigo*, since they are not only numerous but written in Chinese characters and hence are not easily distinguishable from native words. The most important *gairaigo* are American and European loanwords.

Foreign words were introduced along with new things and new ideas from foreign cultures; many of these, such as the large number of technical terms, had no adequate Japanese equivalent. Even when Japanese had equivalent expressions, foreign words were in many cases employed for their novelty or the sense of prestige they gave the speaker. A foreign word is often substituted as a euphemism for a Japanese word, as in the case of "WC" and *toire* (from "toilet").

After the arrival of the Portuguese in 1543, Christian and commercial terms were borrowed from Portuguese. In the late Edo period (1600–1868), English,

French, and Russian words began to arrive. At present English loanwords outnumber all others; among the countless examples are *sutoraiki* (labor strike), *depāto* (department store), and *karē raisu* (curried rice). French words are especially numerous in fashion, cooking, foreign affairs, and politics. German words are most numerous in medicine and the humanities and among mountaineering and skiing terms. Italian words are used especially for music and food.

Names (*namae*) 名前

Two years after the Meiji Restoration 明治維新 of 1868, everyone was allowed to take a family name, and in 1875 family names 苗字 were made compulsory.

At the present time, the names Satō and Suzuki each account for more than 1.5 percent of the population, and other common family names are Tanaka, Yamamoto, Watanabe, Kobayashi, Saitō, Tamura, Itō, and Takahashi. Proper names in Japan present a problem since virtually all Chinese characters used in names have a multiplicity of readings—both *on* readings 音読み, based on Chinese pronunciation, and *kun* readings 訓読み, based on native Japanese words. Moreover, since most names are written with two or more characters, it is often impossible to be sure of the combination of readings needed in any particular case without having personal knowledge. Conversely, the same name element usually can be found written with a number of different characters.

People's Names 呼称

In Japanese usage the family name comes before the personal name 名前, but otherwise the treatment of names is much the same as in the West. A Japanese has a family name and an official personal name; artistic or professional names 号：芸名 also are often used. Suffixes equivalent to titles such as Mr. or Mrs. (*san*) or Dr (*sensei*)

The Top 50 Japanese Family Names
日本の苗字ベスト50

1.	佐藤	Satō
2.	鈴木	Suzuk
3.	高橋	Takahashi
4.	田中	Tanaka
5.	渡辺	Watanabe
6.	伊藤	Itō
7.	小林	Kobayashi
8.	中村	Nakamura
9.	山本	Yamamoto
10.	加藤	Katō
11.	吉田	Yoshida
12.	山田	Yamada
13.	斎藤	Saitō
14.	佐々木	Sasaki
15.	山口	Yamaguchi
16.	松本	Matsumoto
17.	木村	Kimura
18.	井上	Inoue
19.	清水	Shimizu
20.	林	Hayashi
21.	阿部	Abe
22.	山崎	Yamazaki
23.	池田	Ikeda
24.	中島	Nakajima
25.	森	Mori
26.	石川	Ishikawa
27.	橋本	Hashimoto
28.	小川	Ogawa
29.	石井	Ishii
30.	長谷川	Hasegawa
31.	後藤	Gotō
32.	斉藤	Saitō
33.	山下	Yamashita
34.	藤田	Fujita
35.	遠藤	Endō
36.	前田	Maeda
37.	岡田	Okada
38.	近藤	Kondō
39.	青木	Aoki
40.	村上	Murakami
41.	金子	Kaneko
42.	三浦	Miura
43.	坂本	Sakamoto
44.	福田	Fukuda
45.	太田	Ōta
46.	田村	Tamura
47.	小野	Ono
48.	藤井	Fujii
49.	竹内	Takeuchi
50.	中川	Nakagawa

Source: Asahi Mutual Life Insurance Co.

are used after the family name and within the family or among intimates the familiar ending *chan* is used after personal names, often in abbreviated form, very much as -y is used in diminutives such as Willy or Lizzy.

Group (Clan and Family) Names 集団名

Up to the end of the 8th century, the two main types of group names within society were *uji*, to indicate lineage groups or clans氏, and *kabane*, hereditary titles 姓 indicating the social rank of *uji*. The *kabane* was used between the name of the *uji* and the personal name; for example, Nakatomi no Muraji Kamako 中臣連鎌子 indicates one Kamako of the Nakatomi clan who had the rank of *muraji* 連.

During the Heian period (794–1185), clans such as the Ariwara, Minamoto, and Taira, which were related to the imperial line and had been granted their names by the court, increased in size so much that subdivisions became necessary. These smaller groups usually were distinguished by their locations.

From the 13th century on, military families in rural areas distinguished themselves from others of the same clan by using as their standard family name the name of their locality, and all types of group names had become wholly fixed by the early 17th century. With a few exceptions, the use of family names remained limited to the upper classes of society, with the lower orders generally being referred to only by their personal names or, where necessary, by prefixes indicative of their trade or location.

Personal Names 人名

Various considerations may apply in the naming of children in modern Japan—seniority in the case of brothers, for example, or the advice of fortune-tellers in choosing characters deemed appropriate to the family name. In nearly all cases, though, names and characters are chosen primarily for their auspicious meanings and happy associations, that is, as talismans of good fortune.

The choice of characters permitted for use in personal names was first limited in 1948 and was restricted as of 1990 to the 1,945 *jōyō kanji* (Chinese characters for common use) 常用漢字 and the 284 characters selected for use only in personal names.

Men's Names 男子名

In premodern Japan men of the upper ranks of society could have a variety of personal names. The main categories were as follows: (1) *Yōmyō* 幼名. Often ending in -*waka*, -*maru*, or -*maro*, a name of this type was customarily given to a boy on or by the seventh day after birth 七夜 and generally was used until superseded by other names at *gempuku* (coming-of-age ceremony) 元服 when he was about 15. Men of the lower classes normally used these child names throughout their lives. (2) *Tsūshō* or *yobina*, *zokumyō*, *kemyō* (current name) 通称、呼名、俗名、仮名. This name was given to a male at *gempuku* together with his *jitsumyō* and was the one by which he generally was known (e.g., Tarō). (3) *Jitsumyō* or *nanori* (true name) 実名、名乗. This was a formal adult name used in association with the clan name. Upon the death of a dignitary, his *jitsumyō* would be used as his *imina* (posthumous name) 諱(戒名).

Many other types of name were, and still are, used in special circumstances. Nicknames あだ名 were not uncommon, used either alone or in conjunction with a *tsūshō*—for example, Nossori Jūbei ("Plodder" Jūbei). More current are the *yagō* (house names) 屋号 traditionally associated with *kabuki* actors and families, which are shouted out by members of the audience during performances.

Women's Names 女子名

Before the 9th century most women's names seem to have ended in -*me*, -*iratsume*, or -*toji*, as in Shima-me. From then on, high-ranking court ladies had

The Top 20 Boy's Names of Recent Years
最近の男児名ベスト20

1.	翔太	Shōta
2.	健太	Kenta
3.	大輝	Hiroki, Daiki
4.	翼	Tsubasa
5.	大樹	Hiroki, Daiki
6.	拓海	Takumi
7.	直人	Naoto
8.	達也	Tatsuya
9.	翔	Shō, Kakeru
10.	康平	Kōhei
11.	雄大	Takehiro, Yūdai
12.	亮太	Ryōta
13.	直樹	Naoki
14.	大貴	Hirotaka, Daiki
15.	大地	Daichi
16.	匠	Shō, Takumi
17.	凌	Ryō
18.	諒	Ryō
19.	涼	Ryō
20.	駿	Shun

Source: Meiji Mutual Life Insurance Co.

formal personal names consisting of one character followed by the suffix *-ko*—for example, Sadako—but the taboos against the general use of such *jitsumyō* led also to the wide use of *yōmyō, tsūshō* (e.g., Murasaki Shikibu), and, later, to the use of various elegant names, many of them derived from *The Tale of Genji* 「源氏物語」. Among humbler women the *-ko* suffix was never used, but the 16th century saw the introduction of the prefix *o-*, as in Oichi. This practice spread during the Edo period (1600–1868), when most women had two-syllable names, often written in *kana* and a woman's status was immediately evident from her name.

The changes brought about by the Meiji Restoration 明治維新 (1868), however, led to a vast increase in the use of Chinese characters. The employment of the formerly aristocratic suffix *-ko* grew steadily from about 3 percent in the mid-1880s to 80 percent in 1935. Today the number of women's names having two-syllables plus *-ko* is decreasing and elegant two or three-syllable names, such as Risa or Ayaka, with no suffix are becoming the norm.

Place Names 地名

Accounts of the origins of place names are a common feature of the earliest written works in Japan, especially those known as *fudoki* (regional chronicles) 風土記, but many of their etymologies are still uncertain. In general, though, they can be said to derive from natural features 自然地形 or historical causes.

The names of geographical origin generally refer to obvious features of the land and are combined with prefixes describing such aspects as size, length, depth, or direction, such as Nagasaki (long cape), Yokohama (side beach), or Hiroshima (broad island).

History-based names include some derived from the Ainu, most typically those ending in *-betsu* or *-nai* in northern parts of Japan. Names such as Shinden (new rice fields) indicate the development of an area, while others show religious associations by the use of such components as *kami* (god) 「神」, *miya* (shrine) 「宮(神社)」, and *tera* (temple) 「寺(寺院)」. Also, Edo was renamed Tōkyō (eastern capital) in 1868 in contrast to its predecessor Kyōto (capital metropolis).

LIFE

生活

衣・食・住	**Daily Life**
レジャー	**Leisure**
スポーツ	**Sports**

Clothing (*ifuku*) 衣服

Clothing in Japan is broadly categorized as either *wafuku* (Japanese style) 和服 or *yōfuku* (Western style) 洋服. KIMONO 着物 is the modern designation for the traditional Japanese robelike garment but this garment was historically called a *kosode* 小袖. The history of Japanese clothing is in large part the history of the evolution of the *kosode* and the Japanization of imported styles and textiles.

Ancient Clothing (to ad 794) 古代(794年まで)

With the Yayoi period 弥生時代 (ca 300 BC–ca AD 300) came the rise of sericulture (silkworm breeding) and weaving techniques.

Influenced by the importation of Buddhism and the Chinese government system, Prince Shōtoku 聖徳太子 (574–622) followed the practice of the Sui court 隋王朝 (589–618), establishing rules of dress for aristocrats and court officials. Figures depicted in paintings and embroideries wear long, loose clothing that shows the influence of Han-dynasty 漢王朝 (25–220) fashion. The Taihō Code 大宝律令 (701) and Yōrō Code 養老律令 (718; effective 757) reformed clothing styles, following the system used in Tang China 唐王朝 (618–907). Garments were divided into three categories: ceremonial dress, court dress, and working clothes.

Heian Period (794–1185) 平安時代(794年～1185年)

As Japan drew away from continental influence, clothing became simpler in cut but more elaborate in layers. For formal occasions the male aristocrat's layered outfit (*sokutai* 束帯) included loose trousers stiffened by divided skirts (*ōguchi* 大口), worn underneath, and many layers of long, loose upper garments (*hō* 袍).

The formal costume of the Heian lady-in-waiting was the *karaginumo* 唐衣裳, often referred to after the 16th century as the 12-layered garment 十二単衣. Its most

Styles of Japanese Clothing through History (1)
日本の衣服の移り変わり

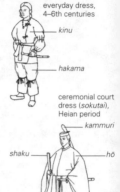

everyday dress, 4–6th centuries
— *kinu*
— *hakama*

ceremonial court dress (*sokutai*), Heian period
— *kammuri*
shaku — — *hō*
hirao —
train of *shitagasane*

ceremonial court dress (*karaginumo* or *jūnihitoe*), Heian and Kamakura periods

— *karaginu*
— *hikigoshi*
— *mo*
uchiki

everyday dress of court nobles, Heian period
— *eboshi*
nōshi —
sashinuki —

samurai dress,
Kamakura and
Muromachi periods

— hitatare

— hakama

court winter dress,
Muromachi and Azuchi-
Momoyama periods

kosode —

uchikake
or kaidori —

samurai court dress,
Azuchi-Momoyama
and Edo periods

— kataginu

— hakama

formal dress of
married women,
Edo period

obi —

edozuma —

everyday dress of
samurai, Edo period

— haori

— obi

— kosode

important element was the *uchiki* 袿, the layers of lined robes (5, 10, or more) also called *kasane-uchiki* 重袿 or *kasane* (layers) 重ね. Great consideration was given to the combination of colors in the layers of *uchiki*. Each layer was longer than the one over it, so that the edge of each color showed, creating a striking effect.

Kamakura (1185–1333) and Muromachi (1333–1568) Periods 鎌倉(1185年〜1333年)・室町(1333年〜1568年)時代

With the establishment of the Kamakura shogunate and the decline of the prestige of the imperial court, stiffened military garments replaced luxurious silk. The highest officials wore the formal *sokutai* 束帯 of the Heian period, but the informal hunting jacket (*kariginu* 狩衣) became the standard uniform of the *samurai* 侍, along with a stiffened cloak (*suikan* 水干).

At the beginning of the Kamakura period, women wore a combination of *uchiki* 袿 robes and *hakama* 袴 skirt-trousers as the formal outfit. Later these were replaced by the small-sleeved undergarment, the *kosode*, worn with *hakama*. In the Muromachi period an extra jacket (*uchikake* 打掛 or *kaidori* 掻取) was worn over the *kosode* to complete the formal dress; today it is part of the bridal outfit 花嫁衣装.

Azuchi-Momoyama Period (1568–1600)
安土・桃山時代(1568年〜1600年)

In the late 16th century the powerful generals Oda Nobunaga and Toyotomi Hideyoshi, great patrons of the arts, encouraged a wave of bold, decorative brilliance. The *samurai* continued to wear matched upper and lower garments 裃. The upper garment was sleeveless. Gradually the material was made stiffer and the shoulders more flared; together with trailing pleated trousers (*nagabakama* 長袴), this continued as formal wear 正装 for *samurai* throughout the Edo period.

Edo Period (1600–1868) 江戸時代(1600年〜1868年)

During the 250 peaceful years of Tokugawa government, the wealthy merchant community (*chōnin* 町人) supported new forms of artistic expression. The KABUKI theater and the entertainment quarters led fashion. The *kosode*, the basic garment for both men and women, was more brilliantly decorated after the development of *yūzen* dyeing 友禅染 and tie-dyeing 絞り染め patterns.

Over the *kosode* the Edo man often wore a *haori* 羽織 jacket, a loose garment with a straight collar. The Tokugawa shogunate reformed clothing regulations for the military class toward the close of the period. The standard uniform became a *kosode*, ankle-length *hakama*, and *haori*. A number of early-Edo-period fashions reflected Portuguese influence. From the Portuguese large cape came the *kappa* 合羽 raincoat.

▌Modern Developments 現代

After the Meiji Restoration of 1868 the Japanese slowly changed over to Western clothing. The process began with a government decree that civil servants, such as soldiers, police, and postmen, should wear Western dress. Soon students were also wearing Western uniforms. By World War I, almost all men dressed in trousers, shirts, and jackets.

Women were generally slower in adopting Western styles. The aristocracy, however, sported imported Western gowns and accessories at the European-style balls held at the Rokumeikan 鹿鳴館 from 1883 to 1889, and after World War I professional and educated women began to adopt Western clothing as their daily wear. It was not until after World War II that the habit of wearing Western clothing became the norm for all classes.

Kimono 着物

The word *kimono* is usually used in the narrow sense for the traditional Japanese wrap-around garment. The word is occasionally used in the broad sense as a

Styles of Japanese Clothing through History (2)
日本の衣服の移り変わり

formal dress of unmarried women, Edo period

obi

furisode

everyday dress, Meiji and early Taishō periods

bowler hat

haori

hakama

student dress, Meiji and early Taishō periods

kimono

hakama

boots

term for clothing or for the native dress in general as opposed to Western-style clothing (*yōfuku* 洋服). The predecessor of the *kimono* is the *kosode* ("small sleeves") 小袖, which was worn as an undergarment from about the Nara period (710–794) and as the everyday outer garment from about the mid-16th century. The term *kimono* gained favor over *kosode* only in the 18th century (see also CLOTHING).

Today most women wear *kimono* mainly for social and ceremonial events or when performing certain traditional arts. Children and young men and women may wear *kimono* for such occasions as New Year, the Shichigosan festival 七五三, Coming-of-Age Day 成人の日, graduations, and weddings.

Kimono may be unlined (*hitoe* 単), lined (*awase* 袷), or cotton-quilted (*wataire* 綿入れ). Unlined *kimono* are worn from June through September; for everyday wear, stencil-dyed 型染め cotton *yukata* 浴衣 are most common. For street or formal wear, materials such as silk gauze 絽、紗 or fine linen 上布 are used. Lined *kimono* 袷 are worn from October through May and are mainly made of silk

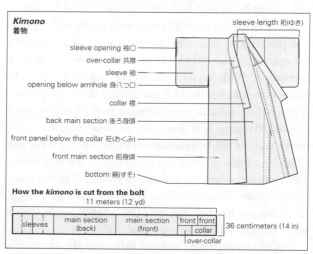

Kimono
着物

sleeve length 裄(ゆき)

sleeve opening 袖口
over-collar 共襟
sleeve 袖
opening below armhole 身八つ口
collar 襟
back main section 後ろ身頃
front panel below the collar 衽(おくみ)
front main section 前身頃
bottom 裾(すそ)

How the *kimono* is cut from the bolt
11 meters (12 yd)

sleeves	main section (back)	main section (front)	front	front	36 centimeters (14 in)
				collar	
			over-collar		

or wool. Cotton quilted *kimono*, or cotton-quilted robes called *tanzen* 丹前 worn over *kimono*, are for midwinter at home.

The ceremonial *kimono* for men is made of black *habutae* 羽二重 silk and decorated in several places with the family crest 家紋 in white. Women wear different types of formal *kimono*. The dazzling wedding costume 花嫁衣裳 consists of a white or red silk *kimono* with embroidery or brocade 錦. Married women wear dark-colored silk, with a lighter design, for festive occasions and black silk, without a design, for funerals.

Generally when dressing one first dons *tabi* (socks) 足袋; top undergarment and wrap-around under-skirt; and then the underkimono 長襦袢, which is tied tightly with a wide belt (*datemaki* 伊達巻). The *nagajuban* 長襦袢 has a collar (*han'eri* 半襟), usually white, which should show about 2 centimeters (1 in) above the collar of the *kimono* that is worn over it. The left side of the *kimono* is lapped over the right in front.

Obi 帯

The long sash worn with traditional Japanese KIMONO. Until the early 8th century people wore loose, one-piece robes or upper garments with wide trousers for men and pleated skirts for women, secured by a narrow *obi*. With the introduction of new weaving tech-niques from Korea and China during the Nara period (710–794), *obi* became more elegant. In the Heian period (794–1185) gems and other stones were used to adorn men's leather *obi*, but the court ladies did not wear *obi*. Clothing styles did not call for *obi* until the end of the 15th century, when the *kosode* 小袖 emerged as the basic style of dress. The *obi* became an article of major impor-tance during the Edo period (1600–1868), since *kosode* worn without *hakama* 袴 require an *obi*.

Men's *obi* have changed little over the centuries.

otaiko   fukurasuzume

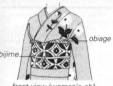

obiage

bijime

front view (woman's *obi*)

kainokuchi   front view
(man's *obi*)

The *obi* worn by men today are either stiff, about 9 centimeters (3.5 in) wide (*kakuobi* 角帯), and tied in a half-bow 貝の口, or of soft gray or black silk that is often tie-dyed (*hekoobi* へこ帯). The latter is at least 50 centimeters (20 in) wide; when folded over it forms a narrow band that is worn tied or tucked in just under the waist.

Early in the Edo period women's *obi* measured approximately 30 centimeters (1 ft) in width and 2 meters (6.6 ft) in length, eventually reaching their present length of about 3–4 meters (10–13 ft). Women's *obi* were usually made of silk. Girls and unmarried women tied their *obi* at the back, while married women tied them in front.

Today most women, married or single, wear their *obi* tied in back in a square-shaped bow おたいこ. The season of the year and the nature of the occasion usually determine what kind of *obi* a woman wears. Formal *obi* are made of brocade (*nishiki* 錦) or figured brocade 綴織; daily-wear *obi* are made of figured satin 繻子(サテン) or *habutae* 羽二重 silk. The *obi* is often considered a more important element of dress than the *kimono*, and a good one may cost several times as much as a *kimono*.

Modern housing (*gendai no sumai*) 現代の住まい

Housing in Japan has changed dramatically in the past century as a result of rapid urbanization, population pressures, changes in family and social relationships, and the influence of Western architecture. Especially in large cities, multiunit dwellings 集合住宅 have become the norm, although the majority of people still aspire to own their homes.

The Modern Japanese House 現代の日本の住居

There has been a progressive shrinking of the living space available to the middle-class household, from an average total floor space 床面積 of 165 square meters (1,776 sq ft) at the turn of the century to 100 square meters

(1,076 sq ft) by the beginning of the Shōwa period (1926–1989), and by 1993 average total floor space had shrunk to 88 square meters (947 sq ft). In the 1980s this trend was exacerbated by the rapid rise in the cost of land, which forced would-be homeowners into the suburbs and into the market for small *tateuri jūtaku* (developer-built houses) 建て売り住宅. Large tracts of *tateuri jūtaku* housing have become a common sight within a two-hour commuting distance of major urban centers such as Tōkyō, Ōsaka, and Nagoya.

Whether built by the owner on his or her own property or by a developer, the two-story detached house 戸建て住宅 with a tiled roof 瓦屋根, a small (sometimes tiny) ornamental garden enclosed by a high stone wall or hedge, and garage space for the family automobile remains the ideal for the majority of Japanese. Such houses are basically wooden structures with overlaid plaster walls モルタル塗り. The average total floor area in a house built by a salaried worker about 40 years of age is about 115.48 square meters (1,242 sq ft). There is a dining room-kitchen, two or three Japanese-style rooms 和室 with TATAMI 畳 mats, and one or two Western-style rooms 洋間 with carpeted or wooden floors.

Passage through traditional houses was from room to room rather than along a corridor. Rooms were separated by sliding screens 障子 and sliding doors 襖, which allowed for a more flexible multipurpose use of the rooms than is possible in Western houses, in which rooms tend to have fixed functions. The introduction of Western features such as corridors, hinged rather than sliding doors, Western-style furniture, and

Trends in Japanese Housing
日本の住宅の種類   (percentage of all households)

Type of dwelling	1968	1973	1978	1983	1988	1993
Detached houses	66.5	64.8	65.1	64.3	62.3	59.2
Town houses[*1]	14.7	12.3	9.6	8.3	6.7	5.3
Apartments in buildings less than three stories high	13.7	14.1	13.1	11.6	11.5	12.2
Apartments in buildings three stories and higher	4.7	8.4	11.7	15.3	18.9	22.8
Other[*2]	0.4	0.4	0.5	0.5	0.5	0.5

[*1] Rows of dwellings that share at least one wall with their neighbors.
[*2] Includes dwellings that are part of factories or office buildings.
   Source: Management and Coordination Agency.

Number of Housing Units and Average Floor Space
住宅戸数と平均床面積

		Average size of housing unit	
	Total number of housing units (millions)	Number of rooms*	Total area (square meters)
1963	21.09	3.82	72.52
1968	25.59	3.84	73.86
1973	31.06	4.15	77.14
1978	35.45	4.52	80.28
1983	38.61	4.73	85.92
1988	42.01	4.86	89.29
1993	45.88	4.85	91.92

*Does not include bathrooms. Kitchens are included only when their total floor space, excluding sink, is 5 square meters or more.
   Source: Management and Coordination Agency.

beds has tended to make many modern Japanese houses more compartmentalized and somewhat more private than traditional houses. Eighty percent of all newly constructed single-family dwellings have Western-style toilets 洋式トイレ and living or dining rooms; the entry 玄関 of 60 percent has Western-style doors rather than sliding doors. However, since almost 90 percent of these new houses also have a traditional Japanese *tokonoma* (alcove) 床の間, it is clear that many Japanese prefer a blend of Japanese and Western styles.

Multiunit Dwellings 集合住宅

In 1955 the Japan Housing Corporation 日本住宅公団 (JHC; now Housing and Urban Development Corporation 住宅・都市整備公団; HUDC) was established, and apartment buildings and housing projects (*danchi* 団地) became a familiar sight in Japan. The JHC standardized apartment layouts, introducing the concept of the dining room-kitchen ("dining-kitchen"; DK), a space of about 8 square meters (86 sq ft) used for both cooking and dining. This soon became a popular feature.

The most common unit in early JHC housing was the 2DK, or two rooms and the dining-kitchen area; in such apartments one of the rooms would serve as a living room during the day. An enlarged DK is called an LDK, or living room-dining-kitchen area. The emphasis in recent HUDC housing has been on 3DK and 3LDK units.

In addition to the publicly subsidized *danchi* apartments, there are a great number of mid- to high-rise buildings 高層住宅 constructed by private developers since the 1960s; these have individual units for sale or rent and are known as *manshon* (the English word "mansion" was borrowed to distinguish them from the more spartan 1960s public *danchi* apartment buildings). See also MODERN ARCHITECTURE; TRADITIONAL DOMESTIC ARCHITECTURE; HOUSING PROBLEMS.

Tatami 畳

Mat used as a flooring material in traditional Japanese-style rooms 日本間. Even today, most Japanese houses have at least one room done in the traditional style, with *tatami* and sliding doors 襖・障子.

Since the Muromachi period *tatami* have been made of a thick baseof straw covered with a soft surface of woven rush (*igusa* 藺草). The size of *tatami* was gradually standardized within each region of Japan, and today *tatami* continue to be used as a unit of measure (pronounced *jō*) for Japanese and sometimes even for Western-style rooms. For example, a room with floor space for six mats is called a *rokujōma* ("six-mat room") 6畳間. A *tatami* generally measures 1.91 by 0.95 meters (6.3 by 3.1 ft) in the Kyōto area, 1.82 by 0.91 meters (6.0 by 3.0 ft) in the Nagoya area, and 1.76 by 0.88 meters(5.8 by 2.9 ft) in the Tōkyō area. The thickness is on the average 6 centimeters (2.4 in).

Shōji 障子

Sliding screen, used since the Heian period (794–1185) to set off a room from a hallway or another room. The present *fusuma* 襖, a wooden sliding door frame with cloth or paper applied on both sides, was initially called *fusuma shōji*, but now the term *shōji* refers only to screens comprising a wooden frame on one side of which translucent paper 障子紙 is applied. Since *shōji* admit light, they are also used for window fixtures and ornamentation. With the contemporary trend toward Western-style interiors, *shōji* are becoming less common as fittings 建具 in modern buildings.

Bath (*furo*) 風呂

The typical Japanese bath consists of a tub deep enough for the bather to immerse the body up to the neck when sitting. Water is piped to the tub from a water heater or heated in the tub by a gas burner at one end. There is a drain in the floor of the bathroom, and the bather washes and rinses the body completely before entering the tub to soak, thus keeping the bathwater as clean as possible for other bathers.

Modern public baths 銭湯 now have separate entrances, dressing rooms 脱衣場, and bathing rooms 浴場 for men and women. Plastic stools and basins are provided for the use of customers, who sit in rows before sets of hot- and cold-water faucets where they wash before entering one of the large tubs to soak. However, because people increasingly have baths in their own homes, many *sentō* are going out of business. In 1964 there were 23,016 public baths in Japan, but in 1994 there were only 9,586.

Modern-day baths in the home are in small rooms, usually separate from the toilet. The room is usually tiled. Although traditionally made of wood, tile, or, more rarely, metal, tubs are now often made of polypropylene reinforced with fiberglass. On Children's Day こどもの日 (5 May) many people still put the fragrant leaves of the *shōbu* plant 菖蒲 in the bathwater. Several customs of the *furo* have entered other aspects of Japanese life. For example, the square cloth known as *furoshiki* ("bath spread") 風呂敷, used since the Edo period (1600–1868) to carry toilet articles into the *sentō* and to stand on while dressing, is now a common article used to wrap gifts or to carry many other items.

Japanese cooking (Nihon *ryōri*) 日本料理

There are three fundamental types of traditional full-course Japanese cuisine: *honzen ryōri* 本膳料理, an assembly of dishes served on legged trays at formal banquets; *chakaiseki ryōri* 茶懐石料理, a series of dishes sometimes served before the TEA CEREMONY; and KAISEKI RYŌRI 会席料理, a series of dishes for parties, often served at restaurants specializing in Japanese cuisine (*ryōtei* 料亭). Other types are *osechi ryōri* お節料理, dishes traditionally served on important holidays such as NEW YEAR'S, and *shōjin ryōri*, Buddhist vegetarian dishes 精進料理.

Ingredients 材料 The main ingredients in Japanese cooking are seafood, vegetables, and rice. The consumption of raw seafood has long been a distinguishing feature of native cuisine, and its preparation requires that fish be very fresh and that it be skillfully cut with a very sharp knife (*hōchō* 包丁). Because of the abundance of foods supplied by the seas surrounding Japan and the influence of Buddhism, which militated against the killing of animals, Japanese cooking formerly made little use of the flesh of animals and fowl, dairy products, and oils and fat. Principal seasonings are fermented products 発酵製品 of soybeans, such as SOY SAUCE 醤油 and *MISO* (soybean paste) 味噌, or of RICE, such as *SAKE*, vinegar, and *mirin* (sweet *sake*) みりん. To preserve the natural flavors of ingredients, strong spices are avoided in favor of milder herbs and spices, such as *kinome* 木の芽 (aromatic sprigs of the tree known as *sanshō* 山椒), *yuzu* (citron) 柚, *wasabi* (Japanese horseradish) わさび, ginger 生姜, *myōga* 茗荷 (a plant of the same genus as ginger), and dried and ground *sanshō* seeds.

Tableware 食器 In preparing foods for serving one arranges them in a manner that harmonizes colors and textures, on plates or in bowls that accord with the season of the year; for example, glass and bamboo are considered appropriate for summer. Dishes of contrasting shapes, sizes, and patterns are used during the course of a meal to achieve an aesthetic balance between food and receptacle that pleases the eye and stimulates the appetite.

▌Dashi だし

The basis of all Japanese cooking is stock だし, the standard form of which is made with the type of seaweed known as sea tangle コンブ and dried bonito-fillet 鰹節 shavings.

Shirumono 汁物

Shirumono (soups) can be roughly divided into two types, *sumashijiru* (clear soup) すまし汁 and *misoshiru* (*miso* soup) 味噌汁. Ingredients may include white-fleshed fish 白身魚, prawns 海老, shellfish 貝, *tōfu* 豆腐, fowl 鶏肉, seaweed 海藻, and seasonal vegetables 季節の野菜; one or two ingredients that accord with the remainder of the menu are selected from among these. To add more zest and aroma, *yuzu*, *kinome*, *sanshō*, ginger, or *mitsuba* (a tri-foliolate herb of the same genus as honewort) may be added.

For *sumashijiru* すまし汁, or clear soup, *dashi*, to which salt and soy sauce have been added, is customarily used.

Yakimono 焼き物

The principal ingredients of *yakimono* (grilled foods) 焼き物 are fish, shellfish, meat, and vegetables. Foods are pierced with a skewer or placed on a wire net and grilled over an open fire. One may also make *yakimono* using an iron skillet or oven broiler. The basic type of *yakimono* is *shioyaki* 塩焼き, in which salt is sprinkled over the food before grilling. The distinctive flavor of fish is best enjoyed in this way. For *tsukeyaki* つけ焼き the food is first marinated for about an hour in *awase-jōyu*, a mixture of soy sauce and *sake* or *mirin*. Teriyaki 照り焼き is a *yakimono* prepared with a stronger-flavored *awase-jōyu*. For *misozukeyaki*, the food is marinated in *miso* flavored with *sake* or *mirin*. In arranging a grilled whole fish on a plate, the head of the fish is positioned to the left with the belly facing the diner.

Nimono 煮物

Nimono are simmered dishes 煮物 seasoned with salt, soy sauce, *sake*, *mirin*, sugar, vinegar, or other condiments. The most common *nimono* is *nitsuke*—fish or shellfish cooked briefly in a relatively thick mixture of *sake*, soy sauce, *mirin*, and sugar. In the case of the white-fleshed fish *tai*, the fillets are cooked with a relatively light mixture of water, *sake, mirin,* and soy sauce. Bluefish, such as mackerel, sardines, and saurel, are cooked in a mixture of water, *sake*, *miso*, and *mirin*. This is called *misoni* 味噌煮.

Agemono 揚げ物

Agemono, or deep-fried foods 揚げ物, are of three basic types. *Suage* 素揚げ, in which foods are fried without a coating of flour or batter, is appropriate for freshwater fish, eggplant, green peppers, and other vegetables whose color and shape can be utilized to good effect. *Karaage* frying 唐揚げ, in which food is first dredged in flour or arrowroot starch, preserves the natural water content of the food and crispens the outer surface. In *tatsutaage* 竜田揚げ, a variant of *karaage*, pieces of chicken are marinated in a mixture of *sake*, soy sauce, and sugar, lightly covered with arrowroot starch, and deep-fried. *Tempura* belongs to a third type of *agemono*, in which foods are coated with batter.

Mushimono 蒸し物

Mushimono are steamed foods 蒸し物. With this method, natural flavors do not escape and the taste is very light. Foods may be sprinkled with salt and steamed (*shiomushi* 塩蒸し) or sprinkled with salt and *sake* (*sakamushi* 酒蒸し). The latter method is particularly appropriate for clams or abalone. *Mushimono* are served with seasoned *dashi* thickened with arrowroot starch and sprinkled with grated ginger, *yuzu* rind, or chopped scallion. The foundation of *chawan mushi* 茶碗蒸し is a mixture of beaten eggs and *dashi* (about three times the volume of the eggs). Ingredients such as shrimp, mushrooms, and chicken are placed in individual bowls. The egg mixture is poured in and the bowls covered and steamed over medium heat.

Sunomono and Aemono 酢の物・和え物

Sunomono are vinegared fish or vegetables; *aemono* are fish or vegetables with a dressing, the basic ingredient of which is ground sesame seed すり胡麻, *miso*, or mashed *tōfu*. Fish and shellfish are sometimes broiled or steamed, or they may be sliced, sprinkled with salt, and marinated in vinegar or sea-tangle stock. Vegetables are either blanched, rubbed with salt, boiled, or steamed. Excess water should be eliminated.

Yosemono and Nerimono 寄せ物・練り物

Yosemono are molded dishes 寄せ物 made with agar-agar or gelatin. Foods such as rock trout, flounder, and chicken that have a relatively high gelatin content are used. *Nerimono* are foods that have been mashed into a paste. For one such dish, fish or shellfish is chopped into small pieces and mashed in a mortar with a pinch of salt. The paste is mixed with beaten eggs, grated *yamanoimo* (a type of yam) 山芋, and *dashi* and divided into portions for boiling, deep-frying, or steaming. It is eaten with soy sauce and grated ginger.

Gohammono 御飯物

Gohammono are dishes consisting of rice combined with other ingredients. *Sekihan* (red rice) 赤飯, or *okowa*, is prepared by mixing parboiled *azuki* beans in *mochigome* (glutinous rice) もち米 and steaming it. *Sekihan* is served on auspicious occasions. *Takikomigohan* 炊き込み御飯 is made by cooking rice and another ingredient—in spring, green peas or pieces of bamboo shoot; in autumn, *matsutake* mushrooms or chestnuts—in seasoned water or *dashi*. *Gomokumeshi* 五目飯 (also known as *kayakugohan*) is prepared by adding finely diced chicken, carrot, fried *tōfu*, *shiitake* mushroom, and burdock to rice and cooking it in *dashi* seasoned with soy sauce, *sake*, and sugar. *Domburimono* 丼物 are dishes in which cooked rice is placed in a bowl (*domburi*) and then topped with various prepared ingredients.

Menrui 麺類

Menrui is a category of dishes, served hot or cold, whose chief ingredient is noodles. The most common types of noodles are *udon*, *sōmen*, and *soba*. The first two are made with wheat flour, and *soba* with buckwheat flour. *Sōmen* is always dried; *soba* and *udon* may be either fresh or dried.

Nabemono 鍋物

Nabemono are dishes cooked in a pot of simmering broth at the table. Ingredients are arranged on platters so that each person may cook what he or she likes. The chief types of *nabemono* 鍋物 are *mizutaki* 水炊き, *yudōfu* 湯豆腐, *udonsuki* うどんすき, *kanisuki* 蟹すき, *dotenabe* 土手鍋, *shabushabu* しゃぶしゃぶ, and *sukiyaki* すき焼き. *Mizutaki* is prepared by cooking fillets of white-fleshed fish 白身魚 with vegetables, *tōfu*, and *harusame* (thin potato-starch noodles) in a pot of *kombu* stock, or chicken and vegetables in chicken broth. Grated white radish, red pepper, and chopped onion are used as condiments, and the food is dipped in *ponzu*, a sauce made from citron and soy sauce.

Kaiseki ryōri 会席料理

One of the three basic styles of traditional JAPANESE COOKING. *Kaiseki ryōri* is a type of cuisine served at *sake* parties 宴会 and developed in its present form as restaurants became popular in Japan in the early 19th century. Although the basic features of *kaiseki ryōri* can be traced to the more formal styles of Japanese cooking—*honzen ryōri* 本膳料理 and *chakaiseki ryōri* 茶懐石料理—in *kaiseki ryōri* diners are able to enjoy their meal in a relaxed mood, unrestricted by elaborate rules of etiquette. Today this type of cooking can be found in its most complex form at first-class Japanese-style restaurants 料亭. *Sake* is drunk during the meal, and, because the Japanese customarily do not eat rice while drinking *sake,* rice is served at the end. Appetizers 先付け、お通し, *sashimi* (sliced raw fish; also called *tsukuri*) 刺身, *suimono* (clear soup) 吸い物, *yakimono* (grilled foods) 焼き物, *mushimono* (steamed foods) 蒸し物, *nimono* (simmered foods) 煮物, and *aemono* (dressed saladlike foods) 和え物 are served first, followed by *miso* soup 味噌汁, *tsukemono* (pickles), rice, Japanese sweets, and fruit. Tea concludes the meal. The types and order of foods served in *kaiseki ryōri* are the basis for the contemporary full-course Japanese meal.

Sushi 鮨

Vinegared rice 酢飯 topped or combined with such items as raw fish, shellfish, or cooked egg. Served in restaurants and sold at supermarkets and take-out shops, *sushi* can also be prepared at home. It is enjoyed in many regional varieties all over Japan and is one of a handful of Japanese foods, along with TEMPURA, that have become popular internationally.

Sushi cuisine originated in ancient China as a method of preserving fish. After packing the fish in rice and salt, the mixture was left to ferment for anywhere from two months to one year. After fermentation the rice was discarded and the pickled fish was eaten. This method probably came to Japan with the introduction of wet rice culture 稲作文化 sometime in the Yayoi period 弥生時代 (ca 300 BC–ca AD 300). Variations on the fermentation process reduced the waiting time and introduced vinegar as a flavoring agent, and after a time the rice came to be eaten along with the pickled fish. It was not until the early 19th century, however, in Edo 江戸 (now Tōkyō), that the pickling process was dropped and fresh raw fish was served on freshly cooked vinegared rice. The *sushi* of this period was sold from stalls as a snack food; the stalls were the precursors of today's *sushi* restaurants 寿司屋.

Today *sushi* can be divided into four broad categories:

Nigirizushi (hand-pressed *sushi*) 握り鮨 is the *sushi* developed in Edo in the 1800s. It is also known as *edo-maezushi*. It consists of a bite-sized portion of vinegared rice topped with a small slice of raw fish or shellfish (cooked shellfish is also used) and seasoned with a dab of *wasabi* (Japanese horseradish) わさび between the rice and the topping. Some of the most popular fish used in *nigirizushi* are tuna (*maguro*) and sea bream (*tai*). Also used are shrimp (*ebi*), salmon roe (*ikura*), octopus (*tako*), and squid (*ika*). *Nigirizushi* is dipped lightly in soy sauce before eating.

For *makizushi* (rolled *sushi*) 巻き鮨, vinegared rice is spread over a sheet of lightly toasted seaweed (*nori*) and various types of seafood and/or vegetables are arranged along the center; a thin bamboo mat まきす placed beneath the seaweed beforehand is used to roll the *makizushi* into a cylinder, which is sliced crosswise into bite-sized pieces. Some of the most popular types of *makizushi* are *tekkamaki* (tuna roll) 鉄火巻, *kappamaki* (cucumber roll) かっぱ巻, *kampyōmaki* (gourd roll) かんぴょう巻, and *futomaki* (a thick roll of omelet, gourd, bits of vegetables, and otheringredients) 太巻. For *temakizushi* the seaweed and other ingredients are loosely rolled by hand (without the bamboo mat) into a conelike shape that is not cut into pieces. The various types of *makizushi* may also be dipped in soy sauce for eating.

The category of *chirashizushi* ("scattered" *sushi*) ちらし鮨 is divided into two regional varieties. In the Tōkyō variety cooked and uncooked seafood, vegetables, and sliced omelet are arranged over a bowl of vinegared rice. Soy sauce is served on the side for dipping. In the Ōsaka version cooked seafood and vegetables are chopped and mixed into the vinegared rice, and the whole is topped with thin strips of omelet.

Oshizushi (pressed *sushi*) 押し鮨 is a specialty of the KANSAI REGION (Kyōto-Ōsaka-Kōbe) made by pressing marinated seafood and vinegared rice in a small, boxlike wooden mold. It is sliced into bite-sized pieces and eaten dipped in soy sauce. *Battera* is *oshizushi* topped with marinated mackerel. *Inarizushi* consists of a pocket of deep-fried bean curd 油揚げ filled with vinegared rice mixed with roasted poppy or sesame seeds.

Tempura 天ぷら

Fresh fish, shellfish, or vegetables dipped in a batter (天ぷらなどの)衣 of flour mixed with egg and water and then deep-fried. *Tempura* tastes best eaten right after frying, accompanied by a side dish of special *tempura* dipping sauce and grated radish. The sauce is a mixture of SOY SAUCE, *mirin* (sweet *sake*), and *dashi* (stock).

The origins of *tempura* date to the mid-16th century, a time when many items of Portuguese and Spanish culture, including methods of frying game, were brought to Japan (the word *tempura* is generally thought to be a corruption of the Portuguese *tempero* or cooking). Open-air *tempura* stalls became popular in early-19th-century Edo (now Tōkyō), and many of these stalls developed into full-scale *tempura* restaurants 天ぷら屋.

A wide variety of foods can be used as ingredients for *tempura*. Low-fat fish such as smelt (*kisu*), a kind of whitebait (*shirauo*), conger eel (*anago*), cuttlefish (*ika*), shrimp, and such shellfish as scallops are commonly used. Vegetables used include lotus root, mushrooms, ginkgo nuts, beefsteak plant (*shiso*), and green peppers. Shrimp *tempura* is commonly served in a bowl atop a bed of rice in a dish known as *tendon*, or atop noodles as *tempura soba* or *tempura udon*.

Sukiyaki すき焼き

Thinly sliced beef, vegetables, *tōfu*, and other

ingredients cooked at the table in a large skillet or iron pot in a broth of SOY SAUCE, *mirin* (sweet SAKE), and sugar.

Although meat dishes such as *sukiyaki* are now popular among the Japanese, traditional Buddhist injunctions against the consumption of the flesh of four-legged animals effectively prevented the widespread eating of meat in Japan for much of its history. The word *sukiyaki* first appeared in documents from the beginning of the 19th century as a name given to a dish prepared from the meat of wild geese or ducks that was broiled on top of a spade (*suki*) and basted with *tamari* soy sauce. *Sukiyaki* as it is known today was created during the Meiji period (1868–1912), after Western influence helped make the consumption of beef and other types of meat common among large segments of the Japanese population. "Western-style" restaurants began by serving a dish of thinly sliced beef with coarsely cut scallions. Flavoring the meat with soy sauce, *mirin*, and sugar soon became popular.

Today, the most typical recipe for *sukiyaki*, among many regional and personal variations, calls for beef (usually a high-quality, well-marbled variety), spring onions (*negi*), a type of thin, gelatinous noodle known as *shirataki*, *tōfu*, chrysanthemum leaves 春菊, and a type of mushroom (*shiitake*). After first browning the sliced beef, the soy-sauce-based broth and other ingredients are added, and the resulting stewlike mixture is brought to a boil. The cooked meat is dipped in beaten raw egg before eating.

Traditional confections (*wagashi*) 和菓子

The development of what are now considered "traditional" Japanese confections was affected by a series of stimuli from abroad, beginning in the Nara period (710–794) with the introduction of Chinese confections by Japanese scholars studying in China, then the spread of ZEN Buddhism 禅宗 (also from the continent, where *wagashi* were an integral part of the priests' vegetarian diet 菜食) during the Kamakura period (1185–1333), and later by such *namban-gashi* ("southern barbarian" confections) 南蛮菓子 as *kasutera*, brought to Japan by Portuguese missionaries during the Muromachi period 室町時代 (1333–1568).

The popularization of the tea ceremony 茶の湯 during the Edo period (1600–1868), especially in the Genroku era 元禄時代 (1688–1704), saw a dramatic increase in *wagashi* varieties, many of which have remained unchanged into the present. Around this time the first stores specializing in confections (*kashiya*) began to appear in Edo (now Tōkyō), in Ōsaka, and particularly in Kyōto, where confections called *kyōgashi* 京菓子 were developed as religious offerings and to be presented to the imperial household.

Among the defining characteristics of *wagashi* are their distinctive ingredients. The principal ingredient is *an*, a sweet paste made of red *azuki* beans or white bush beans, sugar, and water, which was first developed in the Kamakura period. Wheat and rice flours are also used, but dairy products and vegetable oils are not. Instead, sparing use is made of such ingredients as walnuts, peanuts, or sesame seeds, which have their own natural oils. Artificial flavoring is not added, and even natural flavorings with strong aromas are avoided. Another characteristic is the way seasonal change is incorporated in the shapes and colors of *wagashi*, as well as in the names chosen for each variety. For instance, *sakuramochi* ("cherry" confections) 桜餅 are the color of cherry blossoms (white or light pink) and are wrapped in pickled cherry leaves.

Rice (*kome*) 米

Principal Japanese staple crop 主食; an annual

marshland plant of tropical origin; introduced into Japan in the Yayoi period (ca 300 BC–ca AD 300), either from China or the Korean peninsula. Rice cultivation was traditionally regarded as a religious act—an invoking of the *inadama* or spirit of the rice plant 稲魂. Supplications to the deity survive today in various forms of folk performing arts 民俗芸能. Many festivals in honor of tutelary deities 氏神 are also harvest festivals 収穫祭り. It is generally agreed that the Japanese extended family (*ie*) system 家制度 evolved within the context of the rice culture 米文化. In this sense rice may be said to have determined the very contours of Japanese society.

Production and Consumption of Rice
米の生産と消費

Year	Production		Consumption	
	Tonnage (1,000 metric tons)	Area (1,000 ha)	Total (1,000 metric tons)	Per capita(kg)
1960	12,858	3,308	12,618	114.9
1965	12,409	3,255	12,993	111.7
1970	12,689	2,923	11,948	95.1
1975	13,165	2,764	11,964	88.0
1980	9,751	2,377	11,209	78.9
1985	11,662	2,342	10,849	74.6
1990	10,499	2,074	10,484	70.0
1995	10,748	2,118	10,485	67.8

Note: Production and total consumption figures refer to unpolished rice. Per capita consumption figures refer to white rice.
Source: Ministry of Agriculture, Forestry, and Fisheries.

More than 100,000 varieties of rice are grown in more than 100 countries, with several thousand in Japan alone. In Japan, improvement of rice plants on an institutionalized and modern scientific basis was started in 1904 with hybridization experiments 交配実験; pure line selection 純系選抜 and, later, radiation breeding 放射線育種 have also been utilized. These experiments have resulted in improved productivity, early maturity, and resistance to disease, cold weather, and lodging (stalk collapse). Since World War II, with land improvement, breeding of varieties responsive to fertilizers, improvement of fertilizing techniques, and the development of chemical fertilizers 化学肥料, herbicides, and insecticides, average yields have increased to more than 4.0 metric tons per hectare (1.8 short tons per acre). Since the beginning of the 1960s agricultural machinery 農機具 has largely replaced human and animal labor, and threshing and hulling as well as transplanting of seedlings 田植え are now done by machines. At the same time, because of herbicides, there has been a reduction in the work load.

Rice consumption 米の消費 has decreased dramatically in Japan since the early 1960s. This phenomenon may be explained by the increased consumption of bread and animal food products. Rice contains somewhat less protein than wheat, but the quality of the protein is superior. Although customarily boiled and eaten plain, rice can be processed in many ways. Cooked glutinous rice もち米 is pounded into a kind of dough called *mochi*. Rice confections, such as *dango*, are made from rice flour, as are the type of rice crackers known as *sembei*. Rice is also brewed as rice wine (SAKE), rice vinegar, and cooking wine (*mirin*), and by adding *kōji*, a fermenting agent, is made into a sweet, fermented rice drink (*amazake*) or used as a pickling base.

From 1942 to 1995 the pricing and distribution of rice was strictly controlled by the government under the Foodstuff Control Law 食糧管理法. However, the Law for Stabilization of Supply and Demand and Prices of Staple Food 主要食糧需給価格安定法, which went into effect in November 1995, reduced the government's buying and selling of rice to two categories: rice stores for emergency use and imported rice.

The Japanese rice market 米市場 had, with the exception of the early postwar era, long been closed to rice imports when, under pressure from the United States and other countries, the government announced a partial opening in 1993. The percentage of the domestic market open to imported rice is to increase gradually from 4 percent in 1995 to 8 percent in 2000.

Sake 酒

A brewed alcoholic beverage アルコール飲料 made from fermented RICE. *Sake* is also used as a generic term for all alcoholic drinks. The formal name for refined *sake*, the kind most commonly drunk in Japan, is *seishu*; it is often referred to as *nihonshu* 日本酒 to distinguish it from Western liquors 洋酒. The other traditional Japanese alcoholic beverage is a distilled spirit 蒸留酒 called *shōchū*. Malted rice 麹 is the fermenting agent in both refined *sake* and *shōchū*.

Today there are about 3,000 manufacturers of refined *sake* in Japan. The chief producing districts are Kyōto and Hyōgo prefectures. A few national brands are also produced in places such as Akita and Hiroshima prefectures. *Jizake* (local brands) 地酒 are numerous and are produced all over Japan.

Sake is made with steamed rice, a yeast of rice 酵母, malted rice, and water. This is placed in a vat, additional amounts of these ingredients are added in three cycles, and the mixture is left to ferment for 20 days. After fermentation the mixture is ready for pressing, filtration, and blending. The *sake* is then pasteurized, bottled, and stored. The alcohol content of crude *sake* 原酒 is about 40 proof; *sake* on the market is about 32 proof. A good-quality *sake* has a subtle blend of the so-called five flavors 五味 (sweetness, sourness, pungency, bitterness, and astringency) and a mellow fragrance. Older *sake* has a soft, mellow taste, but *sake* is rarely stored for more than a year. Unrefined *sake* 濁酒 is called *nigorizake*. A sweet *sake* called *mirin* is made especially for cooking.

Soy sauce (*shōyu*) 醤油

Basic flavoring agent 調味料 used in Japanese cuisine; made by fermenting water, salt, and a yeast of soybean and wheat—a process that may take over a year. Its prototype, a pasty substance called *hishio* 醤, made by adding fish to salt, is known to have been made in the Yayoi period 弥生時代 (ca 300 BC–ca AD 300). *Shōyu* as it is known today was first made in Japan in the Muromachi period (1333–1568).

Shōyu is distinguished according to the ingredients used in its preparation and the length of fermentation 発酵. *Koikuchi shōyu*, widely used, is fermented for a longer time and is thick; *usukuchi shōyu* is fermented for a shorter period. The addition of *mirin* (sweet *sake*) gives the latter a delicate color, flavor, and aroma, making it suitable for seasoning vegetables, white-fleshed fish, and clear soups. Both types are now produced mainly in Chiba and Hyōgo prefectures. There are also local variations: the sweeter *tamari*, made in central Honshū; the pale yellow *shottsuru* 塩汁 of Akita Prefecture, made with fish; and the white *shiroshōyu* 白醬油 of the Nagoya area.

Miso (bean paste) 味噌

 Miso is made by mixing steamed soybeans with salt and a fermenting agent (*kōji* 麹) made of rice, wheat, or soybeans; together with SOY SAUCE (*shōyu*), it is the basic flavoring of Japanese cuisine. *Miso* is a good source of protein, especially the amino acids lysine and threonine, but it also contains a large amount of salt, as much as 8 to 15 percent. Introduced from China in the 7th century, it became popular during the Muromachi period 室町時代 (1333–1568). The color, aroma, and taste of *miso* differ according to the combination of ingredients, which vary from place to place.

 Miso is most commonly used for making *miso* soup 味噌汁, which along with rice is an indispensable part of a Japanese-style meal 和食. Because of its strong flavor *miso* is often used for marinating or cooking fish. It is also used as a preservative.

Tableware (*shokki*) 食器

 Almost contemporaneous with the perfection of what is now considered "traditional" Japanese cuisine, the development of Japanese tableware 和食器 culminated during the Edo period (1600–1868) in nearly the same form that it has today. The use of *hashi* (CHOPSTICKS) 箸 as eating utensils was a shaping force in that development. Unlike metal knives and forks, *hashi* are usually made of softer materials such as wood or lacquered wood, so dishes could be made of similar materials as well as ceramics. Also, because *hashi* can be maneuvered in smaller areas, dishes could be made in a variety of shapes and sizes. The *wan* (bowl) 椀 was developed so that, in the case of soup for example, one could alternately drink the broth and use *hashi* to pick up the solid ingredients. Since *hashi* cannot readily be used for slicing, food is usually cut into small pieces beforehand and served in individual dishes. The amount of tableware needed for a Japanese meal, therefore, is much greater than that for a Western meal.

Characteristic of Japanese cuisine is the emphasis placed on seasonal awareness 季節感, and tableware plays an important role in conveying this sense. There are fixed designs and patterns that distinguish seasonal tableware, and the way in which chefs select and combine tableware from various regions, made of diverse materials, is a measure of their skill.

Traditional forms of Japanese cuisine include KAISEKI RYŌRI 会席料理, *honzen ryōri* 本膳料理, and *chakaiseki ryōri* 茶懐石料理. The fundamental rule governing the menu for all of these is formulated as "one soup and three side dishes." 一汁三菜 For example, a meal of *kaiseki ryōri* (the typical cuisine for banquets and gatherings) corresponding to a Western dinner would consist of the following: *shirumono* (soups), *sashimi* (raw fish), *yakimono* (grilled foods), and *nimono* (simmered foods). At the conclusion of the meal, rice and pickles are served. The kind of tableware necessary for such a meal includes individual place settings of *hashi*, lacquer soup bowls 汁椀, plates for *sashimi* as well as tiny dipping bowls for soy sauce, plates for *yakimono*, bowls for *nimono*, rice bowls 御飯茶碗, and small dishes for pickles. Also, if SAKE is served, *sakazuki* (*sake* cups) 杯 and *tokkuri* (*sake* decanters) 徳利 might be added. Depending on the menu, the number of side dishes for *kaiseki ryōri* can be increased to 5, 7, or as many as 11. Noodles (such as *udon* and *soba*), SUSHI, and foods for formal ceremonies all have their own specialized tableware.

With increasing availability of Western food, Western tableware 洋食器 has come to play a prominent role in Japan. Recently tableware that can be used for both Japanese and Western foods has become prevalent. However, almost every home is supplied with *chawan*, soup bowls, and *hashi*, since these are the basic eating utensils for Japanese food. Most tableware come in sets of five, but generally all members of a family have their own individual *chawan* and *hashi* for daily use.

Chopsticks (*hashi*) 箸

All Japanese dishes are eaten with *hashi*; in the case of soups, the solid ingredients are eaten with *hashi* and the stock sipped directly from the soup bowl. *Hashi* are commonly made of light but strong wood, such as cypress or willow, and then lacquered; they are also made of bamboo or, increasingly, of plastic. It is customary in the Japanese household for each person to have a pair of *hashi* reserved for his or her exclusive use. Disposable plain-wood chopsticks 割り箸, which the diner splits apart before using, are common in restaurants. Long chopsticks made of bamboo and used for cooking are called *saibashi* 菜箸. Long metal chopsticks with wooden handles are used for deep-frying. When not in use during a meal, *hashi* are rested upon small ceramic, wooden, or glass stands called *hashioki* 箸置き.

Restaurants (*inshokuten*) 飲食店

Today among the more than 1 million restaurants in Japan there are many that offer foreign cuisines. Chief among these are restaurants that specialize in

Chinese, Korean, French, or Italian cooking, and recently Southeast Asian cuisines, such as Thailand's, have enjoyed particular popularity.

Restaurants serving Japanese cooking range from elegant *ryōtei*, which provide elaborate multicourse meals, to simple eating houses. Many restaurants specialize in one type of Japanese food, such as SUSHI, TEMPURA, SUKIYAKI, broiled eel (*unagi*), deep-fried pork cutlets (*tonkatsu*), grilled chicken (*yakitori*), simmered foods (*oden*), pancakes containing vegetables (*okonomiyaki*), or *tōfu*. There are also restaurants that serve regional cuisine 郷土料理, such as that of OKINAWA Prefecture or Akita Prefecture, as well as locally brewed brands of SAKE.

Number of Restaurants and Sales by Type (1992)
飲食店の店舗数と年間売上高

Type	Number	Annual sales (billions of yen)
Restaurants	241,028	8,334
General	94,108	2,053
Japanese	41,368	2,254
Western	27,150	1,832
Chinese and Oriental	78,402	2,195
Chinese noodle	34,434	666
Chinese	24,360	914
Korean barbecue	17,307	534
Oriental	2,301	80
Soba and *udon* restaurants	37,564	981
Sushi restaurants	44,974	1,508
Coffee shops	115,143	1,445
Other restaurants	35,339	867
Hamburger	3,526	366
Okonomi-yaki	22,970	212
Other	8,843	288
Total	474,048	13,135

Note: Sales figures do not add up to total because of rounding.
Source: Ministry of International Trade and Industry.

One of the more popular noon meals consists of Japanese noodles (*soba*; *udon*), which are served at restaurants known as *sobaya*. Many such restaurants also serve *domburimono*, a bowl of rice topped with any of a variety of ingredients. *Rāmen*, a Japanese version of Chinese-style noodles, is also a common lunchtime repast. *Rāmen'ya*, the Chinese restaurants that specialize in it, serve other simple Chinese dishes as well, such as fried rice (*chāhan*) and fried or steamed pork dumplings (*gyōza*). *Yōshokuya*, which specialize in Japanese variations of Western dishes, offer such foods as pork cutlets, spaghetti, and beef stew.

On their way home office workers often stop at drinking houses 飲み屋、居酒屋 that serve a variety of foods such as *yakitori*, grilled fish (*yakizakana*), raw fish (*sashimi*), chilled *tōfu*, and pickles (*tsukemono*) to go along with beer, *sake*, or the distilled liquor known as *shōchū*. Young people in particular have acquired a taste for Western-style fast foods ファーストフード, and a number of franchise chains have established restaurants throughout the country. There is also a type of large restaurant known as a family restaurant ファミリーレストラン that serves a wide range of Western foods from club sandwiches to steak and to which parents often take their children.

Tea ceremony (*chanoyu*) 茶の湯

Also called chadō or sadō. A highly structured method of preparing powdered green tea 抹茶 in the company of guests. The tea ceremony incorporates the preparation and service of food as well as the study and utilization of architecture, gardening, ceramics, calligraphy, history, and religion. It is the culmination of a union of artistic creativity, sensitivity to nature, religious thought, and social interchange.

History of Tea in Japan 日本における茶の歴史

During the Nara period (710–794), the influence of Chinese culture included the introduction of tea in conjunction with Buddhism. Early in the Kamakura period (1185–1333), the Japanese priest Eisai (1141–1215) returned from Buddhist studies in China, bringing the tea ritual practiced in Chinese Buddhist temples during the Song dynasty (960–1279). Eisai also brought tea seeds from the plant that was to become the source of much of the tea grown in Japan today.

In Sakai, south of Ōsaka, there was a group of wealthy merchants 豪商 called the *nayashū* ("warehouse school") 納屋衆, which espoused a modest manner of tea drinking. Out of this tradition came Takeno Jōō 武野紹鷗 (1502–1555), who taught the use of the *daisu* (the stand for the tea utensils), as it had been handed down from Murata Jukō 村田珠光 (1422–1502, tea master to shōgun Ashikaga Yoshimasa 足利義政), as well as a sensitive connoisseurship and the aesthetic sensibility known as WABI. His influence was widely felt but was most important in his instruction of his student Sen no Rikyū 千利休 (1522–1591).

Rikyū transformed the tea ceremony, perfected the use of the *daisu*, and substituted common Japanese-made objects for the rare and expensive Chinese tea utensils used previously. Tea was no longer made in one room and served to guests in another, but rather was made in their midst.

Rikyū's successor, Furuta Oribe 古田織部 (1544–1615), introduced a decorative style that some considered superficial. Oribe's pupil Kobori Enshū 小堀遠州 (1579–1647) continued the grand style and was teacher to the Tokugawa *shōgun*, moving freely among the nobility, while also designing gardens and teahouses.

There were many masters of tea 茶人, with heirs and followers who eventually gathered into schools. Ura Senke 裏千家 and Omote Senke 表千家 are the leading schools in Japan today.

Practice of the Tea Ceremony 茶事・茶会

The manner of preparing powdered green tea may be influenced by many styles and techniques, depending on the practices of the various schools. The following procedure is adapted from the Ura Senke way of preparation. A full tea presentation with a meal 茶事 is called a *chaji*, while the actual making of the tea is called *temae* 点前. A simple gathering for the service of tea may be called a *chakai*. The selection of utensils (*dōgu* 道具) is determined by time of year, season, and time of day or night, as well as special occasions such as welcoming someone, bidding farewell, a memorial, a wedding, flower viewing, and so on.

The tea is prepared in a specially designated and designed room, the *chashitsu* (tearoom) 茶室. It is devoid of decoration with the exceptions of a hanging scroll 掛け

物 and flowers in a vase (*hanaire* 花入れ). The scroll provides the appropriate spiritual atmosphere for serving tea. Flowers for tea 茶花 are simple, seasonal, and seemingly "unarranged," unlike those in *ikebana* (FLOWER ARRANGEMENT).

Chaji 茶事 The following are some of the highlights of a *chaji*: The guests assemble in a waiting room where they sample the hot water to be used in making the tea. Once the host has received them, the guests enter the tea garden 茶庭(露地) where they may rest briefly on a waiting bench. After replenishing the water in the stone basin つくばい and purifying his hands and mouth, the host proceeds through the *chūmon* (middle gate) 中門 to welcome the guests with a silent bow. The guests purify their hands and mouths and enter the tearoom by crawling though a small door, or *nijiriguchi*. Individually they look at the scroll in the *tokonoma* (alcove) 床の間, the kettle, and the hearth and take their seats.

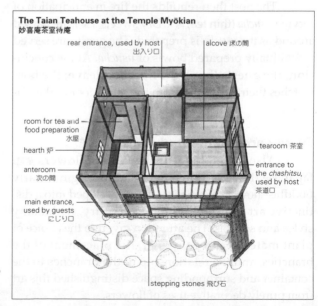

The Taian Teahouse at the Temple Myōkian
妙喜庵茶室待庵

rear entrance, used by host 出入り口

alcove 床の間

room for tea and food preparation 水屋

hearth 炉

anteroom 次の間

main entrance, used by guests にじり口

tearoom 茶室

entrance to the *chashitsu*, used by host 茶道口

stepping stones 飛び石

Designed by tea master Sen no Rikyū, the 16th-century Taian Teahouse has been designated a National Treasure.

After greeting the guests, the host serves the tea meal which is called *kaiseki* 懐石 or *chakaiseki* 茶懐石 and consists of fresh, seasonal, and carefully prepared foods. The meal concludes with a sweet. The guests then retire to the garden while the host makes preparations for serving the tea.

Alone, the host removes the scroll and replaces it with flowers, sweeps the room, and sets out tea utensils for preparing *koicha* (thick tea) 濃茶, which is the focal point of the gathering. When the guests reenter, they take turns admiring the flowers and displayed utensils.

The *koicha*, made by adding a very small amount of hot water to the powdered tea, is prepared by the host in a single bowl from which all guests drink. After savoring it, each wipes the rim of the bowl before passing it to the next guest. The bowl is then returned and rinsed, and the guests inspect the tea container, its wrapper, and the tea scoop 茶杓.

The host then rebuilds the fire in anticipation of serving *usucha* (thin tea) 薄茶. Dry sweets 干菓子 are passed around as the *usucha* is prepared. The guests are served individually prepared bowls of *usucha*. At the conclusion, the guests thank the host and leave; the host watches their departure from the open door of the tearoom.

Flower arrangement (*ikebana*) 生け花

Also called *kadō*, or the Way of flowers 華道. Japanese flower arrangement had its origin in early Buddhist flower offerings 献花 and developed into a distinctive art form from the 15th century, with many styles and schools. The attention given to the choice of plant material and container, the placement of the branches, and the relationship of the branches to the container and surrounding space distinguished this art from purely decorative uses of flowers.

moribana

frontal view

overhead view

nageire

frontal view

overhead view

Traditional _Ikebana_ 伝統的生け花

Buddhist ritual flower offerings 供華 were introduced to Japan from China early in the 7th century by Ono no Imoko, from whom the Ikenobō school of arranging claims descent. The important "three-element" (_mitsugusoku_ 三具足) offering placed in front of a Buddhist image consisted of an incense burner 香炉 flanked by a candlestick 燭台 and a vase of flowers 華瓶. From the _mitsugusoku_ tradition developed the style known as _rikka_ ("standing flowers") 立花, a more sophisticated arrangement that sought to reflect the majesty of nature and from which all later schools of Japanese flower arrangement derive.

In the late 16th century, a new form of flower arrangement called _nageire_ ("to throw or fling into") 抛入 emerged for use in the tea ceremony. An austere and simple form was required for _chabana_ 茶花, a general term for flower arrangements used in the TEA CEREMONY, in which a single vase might hold only one flower disposed with deceptively simple elegance.

The late 17th century saw the emergence of a thriving merchant class and a shift away from aristocratic and priestly forms of flower arrangement. A growing demand for simplification of the increasingly contrived _rikka_ styles gave rise to a new form of arrangement called _shōka_ or _seika_ (living flowers) 生花, basically consisting of three main branches arranged in an asymmetrical triangle. The ideal in _shōka_ was to convey the plant's essence. _Shōka_ combined the dignity of _rikka_ with the simplicity of _nageire_, and by the end of the 18th century it had become the most popular style.

Modern _Ikebana_ 現代の生け花

After the Meiji Restoration of 1868, traditional Japanese arts, including _ikebana_, were temporarily overwhelmed by enthusiasm for Western culture. In the late 19th century, however, there was a revival of _ikebana_ when Ohara Unshin 小原雲心 (1861–1916), founder of the Ohara school 小原流, introduced his *moribana* (piled-up flowers) 盛花 style.

In the late Taishō (1912–1926) and early Shōwa (1926–1989) periods, the foundations of modern *ikebana* were laid in the work of Ohara Kōun 小原光雲 (1880–1938) and Adachi Chōka 安達潮花 (1887–1969), among others. Up until about 1930, *ikebana* was taught exclusively by private instructors in upper-class homes, but now masters began to concentrate on developing *ikebana* schools that could attract large numbers of students from all social classes.

In the postwar era, avant-garde *ikebana* 前衛生け花, spearheaded by Sōgetsu school 草月流 founder Teshigahara Sōfū 勅使河原蒼風 (1900–1979), Ohara Hōun 小原豊雲 (1908–1995), and Nakayama Bumpo 中山文甫 (1899–1986), revolutionized the materials considered acceptable. These artists used not only live flowers and grasses but also plastic, plaster, and steel to express surrealistic and abstract concepts in their arrangements.

Today, there are approximately 3,000 *ikebana* schools in Japan. The most popular styles are the Ikenobō 池坊, Ohara 小原流, and Sōgetsu 草月流.

Before World War II, foreign interest in, and knowledge of, *ikebana* was scant. After the war, however, *ikebana* became popular with the wives of Allied military officers stationed in Japan, and many returned home as certified teachers, bringing the influence of *ikebana* to untold numbers of students abroad.

Calligraphy (*sho*) 書

In Japan, as in other countries in the Chinese cultural sphere, calligraphy is considered one of the fine arts 美術.

The history of Japanese calligraphy begins with the introduction into Japan of the Chinese writing sys-

① *Kaisho* (noncursive style).
② *Gyōsho* (semicursive style).
③ *Sōsho* (cursive style).
④ *Tensho* (seal script style).
⑤ *Reisho* (clerical script style).

tem in about the 5th century AD. Initially the Japanese wrote in Chinese, but they soon began using Chinese characters 漢字, or KANJI, in new ways to suit the requirements of their native language. The poetry anthology *Man'yōshū* 「万葉集」 (mid-8th century), for example, was written using Chinese characters to convey either Japanese words or syllables. The latter phonetic method of writing is now known as *man'yōgana* 万葉仮名. This practice ultimately led to the creation in the early 9th century of Japanese syllabaries, or KANA 仮名. For a long time the Chinese language retained its status as the literary language of the elite.

Scripts 書体

Various types of Chinese-character scripts, or *shotai* 書体, representing the historical development of writing in China, are practiced. *Tensho* 篆書, or archaic script, is traditionally used for carving official seals. *Reisho* 隷書, or clerical script, was once used for official documents. These are very ancient Chinese scripts and did not come into extensive use in Japan until the Edo period (1600–1868), when Chinese historical studies received much attention. More common is *kaisho* 楷書, or block-style script, perhaps the most popular style since the characters are easily recognizable. *Gyōsho* 行書, or "running-style" script, is created by a faster movement of the brush and some consequent abbreviation of the character. *Sōsho* 草書, or "grass-writing," is a true cursive style that abbreviates and links parts of a character, resulting in fluid and curvilinear writing.

Implements 道具

Compared to writing styles, calligraphy implements have changed very little since the early days of the art. There are two basic kinds of brush: *futofude* (thick brush) 太筆 and *hosofude* (slender brush) 細筆. *Sumi*

墨, or Chinese ink, is usually made of soot from burned wood or oil mixed with fishbone or hide glue. To make liquid ink the stick is rubbed on an inkstone, or *suzuri* 硯. The *suiteki* 水滴, or small water dropper, which is either ceramic or metal, completes the basic paraphernalia. When not in use, writing equipment is kept in a box called a *suzuribako* 硯箱, which is usually lacquer ware and often elaborately decorated.

▌Early History 初期の歴史

With the introduction of BUDDHISM and Confucianism to Japan around the 6th century, numerous examples of Chinese writing entered Japan, mostly sutras and Buddhist commentaries 仏教注釈書 written in brush and ink on paper in varied script styles. The earliest extant handwritten text by a Japanese is thought to be the *Commentary on the Lotus Sutra* 「法華義疏」, which is purported to have been written by Prince Shōtoku 聖徳太子 (574–622). It is written in a typical clerical-cursive style that was current in China from the late 4th century to the late 6th century.

From the late 7th century through the 8th century, early Tang 唐代 (618–907) dynasty calligraphic styles were rapidly mastered in Japan, notably through increased sutra-copying 写経 activities that began in earnest with the establishment of the Shakyōjo, or Sutra-Copying Bureau 写経所, in the capital city of Nara.

An early influence upon the development of Japanese calligraphy was the monk Kūkai 空海 (774–835), who promoted an awareness of calligraphy as an aesthetic form. Kūkai and his contemporaries, Emperor Saga 嵯峨天皇 (786–842) and the courtier Tachibana no Hayanari 橘逸勢 (d 842), were known to later generations as the Sampitsu (the "Three Brushes") 「三筆」.

A major transformation in calligraphy from a rigid emulation of Chinese styles to creative assimilation occurred in the 10th and 11th centuries. This was the time of the Sanseki (Three Brush Traces) 「三蹟」: Ono no Tōfū (894–966), Fujiwara no Sukemasa (944–998), and Fujiwara no Yukinari (or Fujiwara no Kōzei; 972–1028).

Kamakura (1185–1333) and Muromachi (1333–1568) Periods 鎌倉(1185年〜1333年)・室町時代(1333年〜1568年)

Chinese Song (960–1279) calligraphy had a great impact on Japanese practitioners, especially through ZEN monks. No calligrapher was so artistically aware of the expressive potential of Song calligraphy as Shūhō Myōchō 宗峰妙超 (1282–1337). His powerful style follows in the Song tradition, particularly that of Huang Tingjian (1045–1105). Lanqi Daolong (J: Rankei Dōryū 蘭渓道隆; 1213–1278), one of a number of Chinese monks who came to Japan, wrote in the style of the Song calligrapher Zhang Jizhi 張即之 (1186–1266), best known for his regular script.

Works of calligraphy by Zen monks came to be known as *bokuseki* ("ink traces") 墨蹟 and were prized by monastic communities, which treated them as icons symbolizing spiritual transmission from master to master.

Edo (1600–1868) Period 江戸時代(1600年〜1868年)

The establishment in 1661, largely by Chinese monks, of the Ōbaku sect 黄檗宗 of Zen in Uji 宇治, south of Kyōto, contributed to an influx of Ming-dynasty 明代 (1368–1644) styles of calligraphy. They were enthusiastically received by Japanese men of letters 文人, who created a new orthodoxy called *karayō* (Chinese mode) 唐様, which eventually overshadowed the *wayō* tradition. Hosoi Kōtaku 細井広沢 (1658–1735), Rai San'yō 頼山陽 (1781–1832), and Sakuma Shōzan 佐久間象山 (1811–1864) are among the more famous calligraphers who wrote in this mode.

Contemporary Calligraphy 現代の書

In the modern era, calligraphy has continued to thrive, and it is represented, along with painting and sculpture, at the annual Nitten exhibitions. In post-

World War II Japan, avant-garde calligraphy 前衛書道 was born—a genre in itself. This recent trend in calligraphy asserts new artistic forms of pure abstraction, coming close to some aspects of 20th-century Western pictorial art and deviating sharply from the traditional script styles and emulative aspects of the age-old art of calligraphy.

Bonsai 盆栽

The art of dwarfing trees or plants by growing and training them in containers according to prescribed techniques. The word *bonsai* also refers to the miniature potted trees 盆栽 themselves. *Bonsai*, which first appeared in China more than 1,000 years ago, was introduced to Japan in the Kamakura period (1185–1333).

Bonsai can be developed from seeds or cuttings, from young trees, or from naturally occurring stunted trees transplanted into containers. Most *bonsai* range in height from 5 centimeters (2 in) to 1 meter (approximately 3 ft). *Bonsai* are kept small and trained by pruning branches 剪定 and roots, by periodic repotting, by pinching off new growth, and by wiring the branches and trunk so that they grow into the desired shape.

Grown in special containers, *bonsai* are usually kept outdoors, although they are often displayed on special occasions in the *tokonoma* 床の間. As a rule, oval containers complement deciduous trees; rectangular ones, evergreens.

Growing *Bonsai* 仕立て方

Given proper care, *bonsai* can live for hundreds of years, with prized specimens being passed from generation to generation, admired for their age. Venerable *bonsai* are generally more respected than young ones, but age is not essential. It is more important that the tree produce the artistic effect desired, that it be in proper proportion to the appropriate container, and that it be in

***Bonsai* Styles (1)**
盆栽の形

twisting-trunk style
蟠幹(ばんかん)

upright style
直幹(ちょっかん)

cascading style
懸崖(けいがん)

clumped style
根連り

forest style
寄せ植え

rock planting
石付(いしつき)

slanting style
斜幹(しゃかん)

good health. The two basic styles of *bonsai* are the classic (*koten*) and the informal or comic (*bunjin*). In the former, the trunk of the tree is wider at the base and tapers off toward the top; it is just the opposite in the *bunjin*, a style more difficult to master.

Bonsai are ordinary trees or plants, not special hybrid dwarfs. Small-leaved varieties are most suitable. In Japan varieties of pine, bamboo, and plum are most often used. The artist never merely duplicates nature but rather expresses a personal aesthetic or sensibility by manipulating it. The *bonsai* must look natural and never show the intervention of human hands.

Aesthetics and Philosophy 美学と哲学

The *bonsai* with its container and soil, physically independent of the earth since its roots are not planted in it, is a separate entity, complete in itself, yet part of nature. This is what is meant by the expression "heaven and earth in one container." A *bonsai* tree should always be positioned off-center in its container, for not only is asymmetry vital to the visual effect, but the center point is symbolically where heaven and earth meet, and nothing should occupy this place. Another aesthetic principle is the triangular pattern necessary for visual balance and for expression of the relationship shared by a universal principle (life-giving energy or deity), the artist, and the tree itself.

Origami 折紙

Folded paper; also the art of folding paper 折紙 to form shaped figures and ornamental objects. *Origami* ranges from a simple form of child's play to a complex art form. It is used in certain Japanese ceremonies and rituals, as well as for practical, educational, and entertainment purposes.

Background 背景

Origami as a form of entertainment probably

began during the Heian period 平安時代 (794–1185). *Origami* with only folding and no cutting developed first in the Muromachi period 室町時代 (1333–1568). In the Edo period 江戸時代 (1600–1868) other techniques of folding, cutting, and dyeing paper were developed. By the Taishō period 大正時代 (1912–1926) patterns for some 150 different kinds of *origami* figures had been established. The new art of creative *origami* does not, generally speaking, use cutting or coloring techniques, and the main pattern of expression is cubic.

Uses for *Origami* 折紙の利用

The oldest known use of *origami* in Japan is found in the *katashiro* 形代, used from ancient times in Shintō ceremonies at the Ise Shrine. The *katashiro* is a symbolic representation of a deity. Vestiges of *katashiro* can still be found in the paper cutouts of human figures currently used in various purification ceremonies 祓い and in the paper dolls displayed on the occasion of the DOLL FESTIVAL 雛祭 in March.

Origami also plays an important part in formal etiquette. There are many different ways to fold wrap-

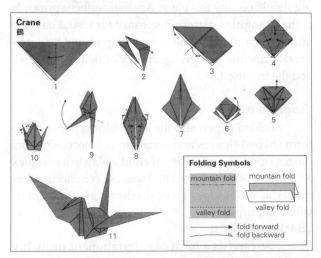

Crane
鶴

Folding Symbols

mountain fold
valley fold

mountain fold
valley fold

→ fold forward
fold backward

ping paper 包み紙 for gifts presented on ceremonial occasions or on special days in the cycle of annual events 年中行事. Weddings and funerals, in particular, require elaborate folded paper ornaments such as the male and female butterflies that adorn SAKE bottles. Paper folding has been an important part of Japanese folk ritual 民間儀礼 as well; for example, it is used in making *noshi*, a kind of traditional ornament attached to gifts.

Go 碁

Also called *igo* 囲碁. A game for two players in which black and white stones 碁石 are alternately placed at the intersections of lines on a board with the object of capturing the opponent's stones and securing control over open spaces on the board.

Its rules are simple and few, yet the number of possible play sequences is staggering; it is calculated to be 10^{750} or 1 followed by 750 zeros.

Basic Rules ルール

Modern *go* is played on a wooden board, the surface of which is engraved with 19 vertical and 19 horizontal lines, thus producing 361 intersections. Nine of the intersections are specially marked with a small dot and called *hoshi* (star) 星; these serve to orient the players and are also used as positions for handicap stones in official matches 対局.

Only four basic rules are necessary to describe *go*, the second of which contains the central premise of the game: (1) Two players (Black and White) alternate in placing their stones on unoccupied intersections of the board, Black being the first to play. A stone cannot be moved once it is played, except when it is captured. (2) If a stone or a group of stones is completely surrounded by the opponent's stones with no empty points within the surrounding area, it is captured, removed from the board, and retained by the opponent. (3) Each captured stone or surrounded intersection counts as one point. (In China the stones on the board are also counted.) (4) If a move would result in the reversal of the previous move by the opponent, the player is required to abstain from that move until other plays have been made; this is called *kō* and is meant to prevent stalemates through perpetual repetition.

The game ends when all stones have been placed or the possibilities for gaining territory or capturing the opponent's stones have been exhausted. At this point all captured stones are placed in the opponent's vacant spaces, and the player with the most remaining vacant spaces under his control wins.

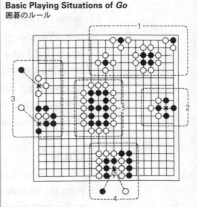

Basic Playing Situations of *Go*
囲碁のルール

1. CAPTURE (THE BLACK STONES ARE CAPTURED).
2. *Kō* (a white stone played at X captures the black stone to its left; black could recapture on the next move, but since white could retaliate, leading to perpetual repetition, immediate recapture is prohibited).
3. Disallowed placement because completely surrounded.
4. *Seki* (a move by either player at X would lead to capture of his stones by a play at Y).
5. *Nimoku* (black's territory contains two eyes and is impregnable).

Ranks 段位

There are millions of *go* fans in Japan but only about 400 professionals. Amateurs are ranked from the ninth *kyū* 級 or degree, the lowest, to the first *kyū*; from there the rankings advance to *shodan* (first grade) 初段, with *rokudan* (sixth grade) usually the highest amateur ranking. A small number of *nanadan* (seventh grade) amateurs are as strong as professionals of the professional first grade; the top of the professional rankings is *kudan* (ninth grade). The ranks are used to decide handicaps for official matches; each rank represents a one-stone handicap for amateurs and a one-third-stone handicap for professionals. Promotions are granted on the basis of official games 大手合. Newspapers sponsor regular competitions; professionals make their living through prize money offered in these matches.

History 歴史

Legend attributes the invention of *go* to a vassal

Leisure

named Wu in ancient China, perhaps 4,000 years ago, although some accounts state that the game developed in India. From China *go* was brought to Korea and later to Japan by Chinese missionaries in the 5th or 6th century. The oldest *go* board 碁盤 in Japan is displayed at the Shōsōin in Nara, and the game is mentioned in the 11th-century *Tale of Genji*「源氏物語」.

Modern *go* history begins in 1612, when the Tokugawa shogunate set up four *go* schools 碁の家元, called Hon'imbō, Hayashi, Inoue, and Yasui. Intense competitions were held to determine the best player of the game, who was installed in the position of *godokoro*. Annual official games were held in the presence of the *shōgun* at his castle in Edo (now Tōkyō); these were called *oshirogo*. Dōsaku, Hon'imbō IV (1645–1702), was the most outstanding player of the early modern period and is referred to as the "saint of *go*." 碁聖

Professional *go* players met hard times after the Meiji Restoration (1868) when their stipends were discontinued by the government. Top professionals formed a study group called Hoensha in 1879, and the Japan Go Association 日本棋院 was formed in 1924. In 1939 Shūsai, Hon'imbō XXI (1874–1940), gave the title Hon'imbō to the association to be awarded in regular competition thereafter.

Go is slowly but steadily spreading in the Western world. The International Go Federation 国際囲碁協会, based in Tōkyō, was organized in 1982. As of 1999 there were *go* associations in 60 countries, with an estimated combined membership of 30 million.

Shōgi 将棋

A board game involving two players and 40 pieces 駒; commonly referred to in the West as "Japanese chess." The object of the game is to checkmate the opponent's king. There are many similarities to chess in the way the pieces move, but what is different is that a captured piece can be used again as one's own piece. There are an estimated 20 million *shōgi* players in Japan. The present-day Japan Shōgi Federation 日本将棋連盟 was founded in 1947.

The prototype of *shōgi* is believed to have originated in India. From there it made its way to Europe via Persia, becoming what is known today as Western chess. It also moved east, to China, where it became known as *xiangqi* (Japanese pronunciation *shōgi*). *Shōgi* may have been introduced to Japan in the Nara period (710–794) by Japanese envoys who were sent to Tang dynasty (618–907) China. In the Heian period (794–1185) several forms of *shōgi* were popular among the nobility, but by the Muromachi period 室町時代 (1333–1568) the rules of the game had been modified, and the game had become very much like present-day *shōgi*.

In 1607 the Tokugawa shogunate established an office for *shōgi* and GO 碁将棋所, under the jurisdiction of the commissioner of shrines and temples 寺社奉行; a monk named Hon'imbō Sansa 本因坊算砂 (1558–1623) was made its head. Later the office was turned over to Ōhashi Sōkei 大橋宗桂 (1555–1634), who was installed as its first lifetime *meijin* ("master") 名人. The *meijin* rank was inherited within a *shōgi* "family"; a *meijin* remained one for life, with no alteration of status despite any change in his actual ability. The lifetime *meijin* system was abolished in 1935, and annual contests for the title of *meijin* were begun. Kimura Yoshio 木村義雄 (1905–1986) was the first to win the title. Championship matches 選手権戦, usually sponsored by newspaper companies, are held regularly, and game moves in such matches are featured daily in newspaper columns.

The Game ルール

The *shōgi* board 将棋盤 is a square wooden block with a grid of 81 squares. Each player uses 20 flat wooden pieces of an elongated, irregular pentagon shape. Each piece is placed on the grid with its apex pointing toward the opponent. The pieces are distinguished by characters written on each side. Captured pieces are placed to the player's right and returned ("dropped") to the board at the discretion of the player who captured the piece, for his or her own use.

The *ōshō* 王将 (king; *ō* for short) and *gyokushō* 玉将 (jewel; *gyoku* for short) are in essence the same piece, i.e., a king. Making one king a "jewel" (by adding one stroke to the character for "king") avoided having two kings on the same board, a custom that supposedly originated on the request of an emperor in ancient times. The better player has the king and the other player has the jewel. The *ōsho* or *gyokushō* can move one square in any direction, like a king in chess.

The other pieces are the *hisha* 飛車 (rook; abbreviated, only in writing, as *hi*), which moves like a rook in chess; the *kakugyō* (bishop; *kaku* for short) 角行, which corresponds to the chess bishop; the *kinshō* 金将 (*kin* for short), or "gold," which can move one square in any direction except diagonally backward; the *ginshō* 銀将 (*gin* for short), or "silver," which moves one square in any direction except sideways or straight backward; the *keima*

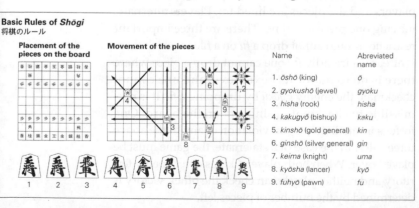

Basic Rules of *Shōgi*
将棋のルール

Placement of the pieces on the board

Movement of the pieces

Name	Abreviated name
1. *ōshō* (king)	*ō*
2. *gyokushō* (jewel)	*gyoku*
3. *hisha* (rook)	*hisha*
4. *kakugyō* (bishop)	*kaku*
5. *kinshō* (gold general)	*kin*
6. *ginshō* (silver general)	*gin*
7. *keima* (knight)	*uma*
8. *kyōsha* (lancer)	*kyō*
9. *fuhyō* (pawn)	*fu*

桂馬 (knight; *kei* for short), which is similar to the knight in chess except that it may jump only to one of two squares two ranks ahead and one file to the left or right; the *kyōsha* 香車 (*kyō* for short), or "lance," which moves any number of squares straight forward only; and the *fuhyō* 歩兵 (pawn; *fu* for short), which corresponds to the chess pawn except that it captures forward, not diagonally.

The pieces can take enemy pieces that are in range of their movements. The two aspects of *shōgi* that distinguish it from chess are *utsu*, the use of captured pieces, and *naru*, the promotion of one's own pieces. All the pieces except the *ō* or *gyoku* and *kin* can be promoted after penetrating enemy territory. The piece is turned over to show its new name. The *hisha* becomes a *ryūō* (*ryū* for short), which has the combined powers of a rook and a king. The *kaku* becomes a *ryūme* (*uma* for short), which has the combined powers of a bishop and a king. The *ginshō* becomes the *narigin*, which has the same powers as the *kin*. The *kei*, *kyō*, and *fu* can all be promoted to the powers of a *kin*. Their names after promotion are, respectively, *narikei*, *narikyō*, and *tokin*. To promote or not is a matter of choice. A promoted piece returns to its original status when captured.

To begin play, the board is placed between two players and the pieces are lined up. Players alternate, moving one piece at a time. There are three important restrictions: one cannot drop a *fu* on a file in which there is already a friendly *fu*, one cannot drop a piece where there is no room for its next move, and one cannot checkmate the enemy *gyoku* by dropping a *fu*. It is permissible to checkmate using a *fu* on the board. One forfeits immediately upon violation of any of the above three rules. In the case of a stalemate, the game must be played over. When both players' kings enter enemy territory and neither player can check the other, victory is determined by the number of pieces left.

Mah-Jongg (J: *mājan*) 麻雀

Game of Chinese origin usually played by four persons with 136 pieces called tiles 牌. The two Chinese characters for Mah-Jongg literally mean "house sparrow," and the name is said to derive from the way the shuffling of the tiles sounds like the twittering of sparrows. It is thought that the game itself derives from tarot cards introduced to China from Europe. Mah-Jongg is similar to the Western card game of rummy in that the object is to collect combinations of sequences and sets of identical tiles.

Mah-Jongg was introduced to Japan early in the 20th century. By the 1920s it had become especially popular in urban areas, and it achieved an unprecedented level of popularity after World War II. Today there are more than 25,000 Mah-Jongg parlors 雀荘 in the country and more than 14 million players. In Japan Mah-Jongg has traditionally been a man's game, frequently played for money.

Pachinko パチンコ

Japan's most popular arcade game アーケードゲーム; a variety of pinball. First played commercially in Nagoya in 1948, it rapidly became popular throughout the country. *Pachinko* is played in brightly lit, gaudy parlors. A player buys a number of steel balls, loads them into a *pachinko* machine, and (in one of the original mechanical models) flips a lever in order to propel a ball to the top of the machine. The ball then bounces down through a maze of pegs, either falling into a winning hole on the way down or becoming lost in a hole at the bottom of the machine. When the ball enters a winning hole, the machine discharges additional balls, which can be fed back into the machine or redeemed for prizes (which are sometimes illegally exchanged for cash). Today, mechanical *pachinko* machines have been completely replaced by computer-controlled machines in which a knob is turned and the balls are propelled automatically. Some newer types of *pachinko* machines have number displays similar to those of slot machines. A winning combination earns the player bonus points. The illegal use of certain types of these machines for gambling has led to their regulation.

Karaoke カラオケ

Prerecorded musical accompaniment, usually on compact or laser disc. An essential part of one of the most popular leisure-time activities in Japan: the singing of songs backed by *karaoke* musical accompaniment at bars and pubs, at parties, or at home. Recording studios and radio stations started using music-only *karaoke* tapes in the mid-1960s, and in the 1970s bar owners hit upon the idea of outfitting their establishments with *karaoke* sound systems so that patrons could sing along (today's systems display the song lyrics on a separate video monitor, and smaller systems are available for home use). Most *karaoke* establishments have a large and eclectic catalog of songs; the sentimental songs known as *enka* and contemporary music are among the most popular selections.

Comic magazines (*komikku zasshi*) コミック雑誌

The flourishing of a "comic culture" (*manga bunka*) is one of the significant features of mass culture 大衆文化 in present-day Japan. Comic magazines fall into four categories: boys' comics, girls' comics, youth comics, and adult comics. Comic magazines are published weekly, biweekly, and monthly.

Boys' and girls' comics average around 400 pages, and a given issue usually contains some 15 serialized stories. Especially popular serials may continue for 10 years. Total combined circulation of the major weekly boys' comic magazines is about 10 million, and it is estimated that two-thirds of all boys aged 5 to 18 read these magazines on a regular basis. More than one-sixth of Japanese girls in the same age group are regular readers of girls' comics. Youth and adult comics average about 250 pages and contain about 10 serialized "story cartoons" and 5 "nonsense cartoons" in each issue. Including the so-called vulgar comics, 40 to 50 different youth and adult comic magazines are published.

Hot springs (*onsen*) 温泉

Hot springs are numerous in Japan, and for centuries the Japanese people have enjoyed hot spring bathing. Visits to hot spring resorts were hailed not only as a means of relaxation but also for the beneficial medicinal properties attributed to thermal spring water. Hot springs are still major attractions for vacationing Japanese, and many have been modernized and developed into large-scale resort complexes. Under the 1948 Hot Spring Law 温泉法, the Japanese government recognizes as *onsen* only those hot springs that reach certain standards regarding temperature and mineral composition; the number of these as of 1990 was about 2,300.

History of Utilization 利用の歴史

Dōgo Hot Spring 道後温泉 in Ehime Prefecture is reputedly the oldest hot spring in Japan. It was the site, according to tradition, of therapeutic bathing 湯治 by several legendary or early historical emperors.

Gotō Konzan 後藤艮山, a doctor in Edo (now Tōkyō), noticed the effectiveness of hot spring bathing as a cure for certain disorders and in 1709 initiated the first medical study of hot springs, advocating the use of baths as therapy for various ailments. After World War II, national hot spring hospitals 温泉病院 were created, making hot springs for medical treatment available around the country. Hot springs are utilized in the treatment of chronic rheumatism リューマチ; neuralgia 神経痛; chronic diseases of the stomach 胃, intestines 腸, liver 肝臓, and gallbladder 胆嚢; hypertension 高血圧; hemiplegia 半身不随; glucosuria 糖尿病; and gout 痛風. They are also used for treating external injuries and for postoperative treatment and rehabilitation.

Martial arts (*bujutsu*) 武術

Also called *bugei*; now usually called *budō* 武道 or "the martial Way." The Japanese terms encompass such martial arts as KENDŌ (fencing) 剣道, JŪDŌ, and KYŪDŌ (archery) 弓道. The old expression *bugei jūhappan* (the 18 martial arts) 武芸十八般 refers to the arts of archery, horsemanship, spearmanship (*sōjutsu*), fencing, swimming, *iai* (sword drawing) 居合術, the short sword, the truncheon 十手術, dagger throwing 手裏剣術, needle spitting 含針術, the halberd 薙刀術, gunnery 砲術, roping 捕手術, *yawara* (present-day *jūdō*), *ninjutsu* (spying) 忍術, the staff 棒術, *mojiri* (a staff with numerous barbs on one end), and the chained sickle 鎖鎌術. KARATE is not considered one of the traditional Japanese martial arts, although it is sometimes referred to as such outside of Japan. In the Edo period (1600–1868), in addition to academic subjects, warriors were required to learn six martial arts: fencing, spearmanship, archery, horseback riding, *jūjutsu* (now known as jūdō), and firearms. These six, together with military strategy, were called the seven martial arts 七芸. These were taught under the name *bushidō* (the Way of the warrior) 武士道.

After the Meiji Restoration (1868) the content of martial arts changed greatly, reflecting the fact that they were no longer meant to be used in combat and were no longer exclusive attainments of the warrior class. Reflecting this new circumstance, *bujutsu* was replaced by the term *budō*, implying that one would be trained in spiritual principles rather than for combat.

Modern *budō* seeks the development of skills through physical exercise and, by establishing objective standards of skills, provides opportunities for competition. In this sense it can be considered a form of sport. Yet behind the martial arts lie the philosophies of Confucianism, Buddhism, and Taoism. Japanese martial arts started with *waza* (skills) for killing and fighting and, through searches for *kokoro* (or *shin*, heart), the heart that transcends victory and defeat, were led to the Buddhist view of life and death and the Confucian way of natural harmony, *yawara* (pliancy) 柔.

Jūdō 柔道

One of the martial arts 武道; a form of unarmed combat that stresses agile motions, astute mental judgment, and rigorous form rather than sheer physical strength. The Chinese character for *jū* derives from a passage in the ancient Chinese military treatise *Sanlüe* 「三略」, which states, "softness (*jū*; Ch: rou) controls hardness well." 柔よく剛を制す *Jūdō* techniques 技 include throwing 投げ技, grappling 固め技, and attacking vital points 当て身技. The first two techniques are used in competition, but the *atemiwaza* is used only in practice. Developed as a sport by Kanō Jigorō (1860–1938) from *jūjutsu*, *jūdō* has been valued as a method of exercise, moral training, and self-defense.

History 歴史

Jūjutsu began with *sechie-zumō* (court banquet wrestling) 節会相撲, a court event popular in the Nara (710–794) and Heian (794–1185) periods. During the Edo period (1600–1868) *jūjutsu* developed as a self-defense martial art and was used in making arrests. *Jūjutsu* schools proliferated during this period but declined with the collapse of the *samurai* class after the Meiji Restoration of 1868. In 1882 Kanō Jigorō organized the

Kōdōkan *jūdō* school at Eishōji, a temple in Tōkyō.

Kanō arranged a system of training in the techniques and fostered a great number of accomplished disciples. He was the first to organize *jūdō* matches. In 1911, *jūdō* became a requirement in middle school physical education programs. Immediately after World War II, school *jūdō* was prohibited by the Allied Occupation. In 1949, however, the All-Japan Jūdō Federation 全日本柔道連盟 was organized and in 1951, school *jūdō* was revived. *Jūdō* was made a formal entry in the Olympics for the first time in 1964 at the Tōkyō games.

The System of Ranks 段級制度

Kanō Jigorō set up a system of ranks 段 and classes 級 as an encouragement for his disciples. These designations have been recognized internationally. There are ranks from 1 to 10, with 10 the highest. Those in ranks 1 to 5 wear a black belt 黒帯, ranks 6 to 8 have a scarlet and white striped belt, and those in ranks 9 to 10 have a scarlet belt. The classes are below the ranks and range from the fifth class to the first and highest class. Adults in the first to third class wear a brown belt; children in the first to third class wear a purple belt. Those in the fourth and fifth class wear a white belt.

Kendō 剣道

Japanese fencing 剣道 based on the techniques of

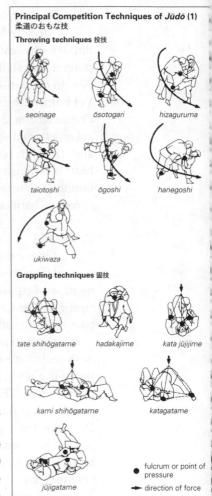

Principal Competition Techniques of *Jūdō* (1)
柔道のおもな技

Throwing techniques 投技

seoinage

ōsotogari

hizaguruma

taiotoshi

ōgoshi

hanegoshi

ukiwaza

Grappling techniques 固技

tate shihōgatame

hadakajime

kata jūjijime

kami shihōgatame

katagatame

jūjigatame

● fulcrum or point of pressure
→ direction of force

the two-handed sword of the *samurai*. Before the Shōwa period (1926–1989) it was customarily referred to as *kenjutsu* 剣術 or *gekken* 撃剣. *Kendō* is a relatively recent term that implies spiritual discipline as well as fencing technique.

Fencing with the single-edged, straight-blade sword was probably introduced from Sui (589–618) or early Tang (618–907) China. The cultivation of sword skills flourished during the Kamakura shogunate (1192–1333). With the establishment of nationwide peace by the Tokugawa shogunate in the early 17th century, *kenjutsu* went into a decline. The moral and spiritual element became prominent, drawing on Confucianism, SHINTŌ, and BUDDHISM, especially ZEN. *Kenjutsu* became an element for training the mind and body. In the late 18th century protective equipment 防具 and bamboo training swords 竹刀 were introduced.

The weapon is a hollow cylinder made of four shafts of split bamboo. It is bound with a leather grip and cap connected by a silk or nylon cord and a leather thong wound three times around the bamboo cylinder and knotted. The length varies for different age groups. Fencers' faces are protected by the *men* (face mask) 面; the trunk of the body is protected by the *dō* (chest protector) 胴. The thighs are protected with five overlapping

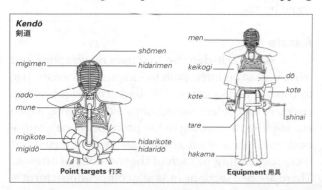

Kendō
剣道

shōmen
migimen
hidarimen
nodo
mune
migikote
migidō
hidarikote
hidaridō

Point targets 打突

men
keikogi
dō
kote
kote
tare
shinai
hakama

Equipment 用具

quilted panels (*tare*), and the hands with padded mittens 小手. Training is based on a variety of movements of attack and defense known as *waza*. Most fundamental are stance, footwork, cuts, thrusts, feints, and parries.

Kyūdō (Japanese archery) 弓道

Kyūjutsu, the technique of the bow, was the term more commonly used until well into the 19th century. Under the influence of Chinese culture from the 6th century, Japanese archery was divided into military and civil archery. Military archery was primarily mounted archery, while civil archery was shooting in the standing position, with emphasis on form and etiquette. Over the centuries the rules of archery became systematized, and schools began to proliferate. Those of the Ogasawara school 小笠原流, the Heki school 日置流, and the Honda school 本多流 dominate modern *kyūdō*.

The bow is usually 2 meters 21 centimeters (7 ft 3 in) in length. It is an eccentric bow; that is, two-thirds of its length is above the grip and one-third below. Two target distances are used in modern *kyūdō* competition. Usually the archer stands 28 meters (92 ft) from a circular target 36 centimeters (14 in) in diameter. In contrast to Western archery, in *kyūdō* the emphasis is on form rather than accuracy. Certain schools are strongly influenced by ZEN.

Karate 空手

Art of self-defense that uses no weapons and relies instead on three main techniques: arm strikes 打ち, thrusts 突き, and kicks 蹴り. A distinction is made between offensive and defensive techniques 攻め技 : 受け技, which are modified according to the position of one's opponent. For defense, there are various parrying methods 受け corresponding to each of the methods of offense. There are two sections in *karate* competitions: form 型

competition and sparring 組み手 matches.

Karate was historically most widely practiced in China and Okinawa and thus is not considered one of the traditional Japanese martial arts. Current forms of *karate* developed from a style of Chinese boxing called *quanfa* (known as kung fu カンフー in the West; J: *kempō*), which is thought to have been transmitted by the Indian Buddhist monk Bodhidharma 達磨 (d ca 532) along with ZEN Buddhist teachings to Chinese disciples at Shaolin temple (J: Shōrinji) 少林寺 in Henan. The method of self-defense traced to these beginnings is called Shōrinji *kempō* in Japan; it had spread widely through China by the time of the medieval Ming dynasty 明朝 (1368–1644), but it was suppressed in the Qing period 清代 (1644–1912) because it was used by a secret society aspiring to reestablish Ming rule. The subsequent development of *karate* took place primarily in Okinawa. Chinese fighting techniques (referred to in Japanese as *tōde* 唐手) merged with indigenous techniques (called *te*) to produce the *karate* style. A *karate* club was established at a middle school in Okinawa in 1905 after the islands had become a prefecture of modern Japan, and the sport thereafter began to emerge from obscurity. It became known throughout mainland Japan in 1922, when Funakoshi Gichin 船越義珍 (1868–1957), an Okinawan master, performed a demonstration in Tōkyō.

After World War II, *karate* and the other martial arts experienced a decline that lasted until around 1955. After that the sport increased in popularity, and it is more widespread now than ever.

Sumō 相撲

A 2,000-year-old form of wrestling that is considered by many to be the national sport 国技 of Japan. *Sumō* became a professional sport in the early Edo period (1600–1868), and although it is practiced today by clubs

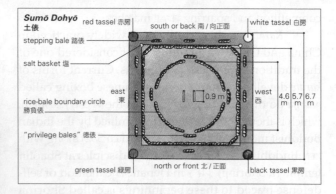

Sumō Dohyō 土俵
red tassel 赤房
white tassel 白房
south or back 南 / 向正面
stepping bale 踏俵
salt basket 塩
east 東
rice-bale boundary circle 勝負俵
"privilege bales" 徳俵
west 西
0.9 m
4.6 m | 5.7 m | 6.7 m
green tassel 緑房
north or front 北 / 正面
black tassel 黒房

in high schools, colleges, and amateur associations, it has its greatest appeal as a professional spectator sport.

The object of this sport is for a wrestler to force his opponent out of the *dohyō* (center circle of the elevated cement-hard clay ring) 土俵 or cause him to touch the surface of the *dohyō* with any part of his body other than the soles of his feet. The *sumō* wrestlers 力士 may spend as much as the first four minutes in the ring in a ritual of stamping, squatting, puffing, glowering, and tossing salt in the air, but the actual conflict is only a matter of seconds. To decide who has stepped out or touched down first is often extremely difficult and requires the closest attention of a referee 行司, dressed in the court costume of a 14th-century nobleman, on the *dohyō* and judges (*shimpan*) sitting around the *dohyō* at floor level.

The Japan Sumō Association 日本相撲協会, the governing body of professional *sumō*, officially lists 70 winning techniques 決まり手 consisting of assorted throws, trips, lifts, thrusts, shoves, and pulls. Of these, 48 are considered the "classic" techniques but the number in actual daily use is probably half that. Of primary concern in *sumō* are ring decorum and sportsmanship.

Unique to *sumō* is the use of a belly band or belt まわし called a *mawashi*. Most *sumō* matches center on the wrestlers' attempts to get a firm, two-handed grip on

Winning Techniques in
Sumō (1)
相撲の決まり手

yorikiri

tsukiotoshi

oshidashi

uwatenage

hikiotoshi

sukuinage

shitatenage

okuridashi

tsukidashi

kotenage

tottari

kubinage

utchari

kimedashi

sotogake

their opponent's *mawashi* while blocking him from getting a similar grip on theirs. During tournaments, a string apron さがり is also worn tucked into the front folds of the *mawashi*, whence it falls frequently in the heat of the match.

The Wrestlers 力士

Traditionally *sumō* has drawn the majority of its recruits from rural communities. Most wrestlers start in their mid-teens and retire from this rigorous sport in their early thirties. Top-ranking wrestlers have an average height of 185 centimeters (6 ft) and an average weight of 148 kilograms (326 lb).

The wrestlers in professional *sumō* are organized into a pyramid. Progress from the ranks of beginners at the bottom to the grand champion's 横綱 pinnacle at the top depends entirely on ability. The speed with which a wrestler rises or falls depends entirely on his win-loss record at the end of each tournament. Based on this, his ranking is calculated for the next tournament and then written with his name and those of other wrestlers in Chinese characters on a graded list called the *banzuke* 番付. The only permanent rank is that of *yokozuna*, "grand champion," but a *yokozuna* who cannot maintain a certain level of championship performance is expected to retire.

Only wrestlers in the top two divisions, *jūryō* and *makuuchi*, receive regular salaries. They also enjoy the title *sekitori* 関取, "top-ranking wrestler," and the right to have their long, oiled hair combed into the elegant *ōichōmage* (ginkgo-leaf knot) 大銀杏髷 during tournaments.

Annual Tournaments 本場所

Traditionally only two tournaments were held each year, but by 1958 this number had grown to six, where it stood in the 1990s. The big six are held every other month in four different cities.

In 1949 the length of a tournament increased from the traditional 10 days to 15 days. A tournament day starts with the apprentices of *maezumō* (pre-*sumō*) 前相撲 fighting, then the long march of the four lower divisions. The boy-men in these divisions—*jonokuchi*, *jonidan*, *sandamme*, and *makushita*—wrestle on 7 of the 15 days of the tournament. For them a winning record 勝ち越し begins with 4 wins against 3 losses, which ensures promotion.

Sekitori in the *jūryō* and *makuuchi* divisions wrestle once a day for 15 days. *Sekitori* must win 8 of their 15 bouts for a *kachikoshi* record. The entire tournament is won by the *makuuchi* wrestler with the most wins.

The Stable System 部屋制度

The *sumō* stable 相撲部屋 system has as its purpose the training of young wrestlers into senior champions while inculcating them with the strict etiquette, discipline, and special values of *sumō*.

Physically, a stable (*heya*) is a self-contained unit complete with all living-training facilities. Every professional *sumō* wrestler belongs to one, making it his home throughout his ring career and often even into retirement. The only exceptions to the live-in rule are the married *sekitori*, who may live outside with their wives and commute to daily practice at the *heya*. As of December 1997 there were 50 active *heya*.

A stable is managed under the absolute control of a single boss (*oyakata*). All *oyakata* are former senior wrestlers and members of the Japan Sumō Association. The stable they run is usually the stable where they wrestled. *Oyakata* are generally married and live in special quarters with their wives, known by the title of *okamisan*, the only women to live in *heya*. *Heya* expenses are paid for by regular allowances from the Japan Sumō Association and gifts from the *heya* fan club 後援会.

Sumō Practice 稽古

Keiko, "practice," is a sacred word in *sumō*. The day begins at 4:00 or 5:00 AM for the youngest, lowest-ranked wrestlers, who ready the ring and begin their

Winning Techniques in
Sumō (2)
相撲の決まり手

katasukashi

uwate dashinage

kirikaeshi

abisetaoshi

tsuridashi

shitatehineri

hatakikomi

watashikomi

makiotoshi

exercises. The higher a wrestler's rank, the longer he may sleep. *Makushita* are up at 6:30 and in the ring at 7:00. *Jūryō* wrestlers enter the ring around 8:00 and *makuuchi* shortly after.

At 11:00 AM the wrestlers head for the baths, seniors first, followed by the lower ranks. Next is *chankonabe* brunch, the first and largest *sumō* meal of the day.

▌The Japan Sumō Association 日本相撲協会

Every aspect of professional *sumō* is controlled by the Japan Sumō Association, composed of 105 retired wrestlers known as elders 年寄りand including representation from *sumō*'s "working ranks," i.e., active wrestlers, referees, and ring stewards 呼出し.

Professional baseball (*puro yakyū*) プロ野球

The first professional baseball team was organized in Japan in 1934, when the mass media entrepreneur and politician Shōriki Matsutarō 正力松太郎 formed the core of the team that is known today as the Yomiuri Giants. Six additional teams had been established by 1936, when the first professional baseball league was organized. Since 1950 there have been two professional leagues: the Central League セントラル゠リーグ and the Pacific League パシフィック゠リーグ. In 1999 the following teams constituted the Central League: the Yomiuri Giants, the Chūnichi Dragons, the Hanshin Tigers, the Hiroshima Tōyō Carp, the Yakult Swallows, and the Yokohama BayStars. In the same year, the Pacific League comprised the following teams: the Kintetsu Buffaloes, the Seibu Lions, the Fukuoka Daiei Hawks, the Nippon-Ham Fighters, the Orix BlueWave, and the Chiba Lotte Marines. Each team plays the five other teams in its league 27 times each season for a total of 135 games. The teams with the highest winning percentage in each league face each other in the Japan

Series 日本シリーズ to decide that year's championship team. Approximately 20 million fans attend baseball games annually in Japan, and millions more watch it on television, making baseball one of the nation's most popular professional sports.

Japan Professional Football League
(Nihon Puro Sakkā Rīgu) 日本プロサッカーリーグ

The first professional soccer league in Japan. Commonly referred to as the "J. League," the Japan Professional Football League was founded in February 1991. It held its first professional tournament, the Cup Matches, in the fall of 1992. Games for the regular season, known as the League Matches, began in May 1993. The 10 original member teams are: the Kashima Antlers 鹿島アントラーズ, JEF United Ichihara ジェフユナイテッド市原, Urawa Red Diamonds 浦和レッズ, Verdy Kawasaki ヴェルディ川崎 (now FC Nippon), Yokohama Flügels 横浜フリューゲルズ, Yokohama Marinos 横浜マリノス, Shimizu S-Pulse 清水エスパルス, Nagoya Grampus Eight 名古屋グランパスエイト, Gamba Ōsaka ガンバ大阪, and Sanfrecce Hiroshima サンフレッチェ広島. seven new teams, Júbilo Iwata ジュビロ磐田, Bellmare Hiratsuka ベルマーレ平塚, Cerezo Ōsaka セレッソ大阪, Kashiwa Reysol 柏レイソル, Kyōto Purple Sanga 京都パープルサンガ, Avispa Fukuoka アビスパ福岡, and Vissel Kōbe ヴィッセル神戸 joined the league, bringing the total membership to 17 teams in 1997.

In 1999 the Yokohama Marinos and the Yokohama Flügels merged to create the Yokohama F Marinos 横浜F・マリノス, leaving 16 teams in the league. These 16 became division 1 (J1) 1部 teams when the new two-division system 2部制 was implemented in March 1999. Division 2 (J2) 2部 has 10 teams: Consadole Sapporo コンサドーレ札幌, Vegalta Sendai ベガルタ仙台, Montedio Yamagata モンテディオ山形, Ōmiya Ardija 大宮アルディージャ, F.C. Tōkyō FC東京, Kawasaki Frontale 川崎フロ

ンターレ, Ventforet-Kōfu ヴァンフォーレ甲府, Albirex Niigata アルビレックス新潟, Sangan Tosu サガン鳥栖, and Ōita Trinita 大分トリニータ.

To gain membership in the league, teams are required to meet four conditions. Each team must: 1) be a legally incorporated body; 2) have the official local support of a designated "hometown"; 3) have access to a home stadium with a seating capacity of over 15,000; and 4) foster the development of future soccer players by maintaining its own youth division.

Golf (*gorufu*) ゴルフ

Golf was introduced to Japan by Arthur H. Groom, an English merchant, in the early 20th century. Since World War II, the popularity of golf has increased tremendously, even though golf is one of Japan's most costly sports. Many corporations buy company memberships in golf clubs for entertaining and other business purposes; however, the number of college-student and women golfers is on the increase. As of 1998 the number of professional golfers was 3,863, including 561 women. The same year there were approximately 2,000 golf courses, which were being used by some 10 million golfers.

Ekiden kyōsō 駅伝競走

Long-distance relay race in which the distance to be run is divided into sections and a cloth sash たすき is passed among the runners on a team and worn by each member as they run their section. The word *ekiden* derives from the name of an ancient Japanese relay system of transportation using horses. The average number of team members ranges from 5 to 10. The distance run per section by men ranges from 5 to 20 kilometers (3–12 mi); women runners run from 2 to 10 kilometers (1–6 mi) per section. The first *ekiden kyōsō* was run in 1917 between

Kyōto and Tōkyō. Today a wide variety of *ekiden kyōsō* are held in Japan, one of the oldest of which is the Tōkyō-Hakone Ōfuku Daigaku Ekiden 東京-箱根間往復駅伝, a competition for male college students. There are also international competitions to which foreign teams are invited.

A P P E N D I X 　付録

Promulgated on November 3, 1946;
Put into effect on May 3, 1947

1946年(昭和21)11月3日公布
1947年(昭和22)5月3日施行

We, the Japanese people, acting through our duly elected representatives in the National Diet, determined that we shall secure for ourselves and our posterity the fruits of peaceful cooperation with all nations and the blessings of liberty throughout this land, and resolved that never again shall we be visited with the horrors of war through the action of government, do proclaim that sovereign power resides with the people and do firmly establish this Constitution. Government is a sacred trust of the people, the authority for which is derived from the people, the powers of which are exercised by the representatives of the people, and the benefits of which are enjoyed by the people. This is a universal principle of mankind upon which this Constitution is founded. We reject and revoke all constitu-tions, laws, ordinances, and rescripts in conflict herewith.

日本国民は、正当に選挙された国会における代表者を通じて行動し、われらとわれらの子孫のために、諸国民との協和による成果と、わが国全土にわたつて自由のもたらす恵沢を確保し、政府の行為によつて再び戦争の惨禍が起ることのないやうにすることを決意し、ここに主権が国民に存することを宣言し、この憲法を確定する。そもそも国政は、国民の厳粛な信託によるものであつて、その権威は国民に由来し、その権力は国民の代表者がこれを行使し、その福利は国民がこれを享受する。これは人類普遍の原理であり、この憲法は、かかる原理に基くものである。われらは、これに反する一切の憲法、法令及び詔勅を排除する。

We, the Japanese people, desire peace for all time and are deeply conscious of the high ideals controlling human relationship, and we have determined to preserve our security and existence, trusting in the justice and faith of the peace-loving peoples of the world. We desire to occupy an honored place in an international society striving for the preservation of peace, and the banishment of tyranny and slavery, oppression and intolerance for all time from the earth. We recognize that all peoples of the world have the right to live in peace, free from fear and want.

日本国民は恒久の平和を念願し、人間相互の関係を支配する崇高な理想を深く自覚するのであつて、平和を愛する諸国民の公正と信義に信頼して、われらの安全と生存を保持しようと決意した。われらは、平和を維持し、専制と隷従、圧迫と偏狭を地上から永遠に除去しようと努めてゐる国際社会において、名誉ある地位を占めたいと思ふ。われらは、全世界の国民が、ひとしく恐怖と欠乏から免かれ、平和のうちに生存する権利を有することを確認する。

We believe that no nation is responsible to itself alone, but that laws of political morality are universal; and that obedience to such laws

われらは、いづれの国家も、自国のことのみに専念して他国を無視してはならないのであつて、政治道徳の法則は、普遍的なものであり、

is incumbent upon all nations who would sustain their own sovereignty and justify their sovereign relationship with other nations.

We, the Japanese people, pledge our national honor to accomplish these high ideals and purposes with all our resources.

Chapter I. The Emperor
Article 1.

The Emperor shall be the symbol of the State and of the unity of the people, deriving his position from the will of the people with whom resides sovereign power.

Article 2.

The Imperial Throne shall be dynastic and succeeded to in accordance with the Imperial House Law passed by the Diet.

Article 3.

The advice and approval of the Cabinet shall be required for all acts of the Emperor in matters of state, and the Cabinet shall be responsible therefor.

Article 4.

The Emperor shall perform only such acts in matters of state as are provided for in this Constitution and he shall not have powers related to government.
The Emperor may delegate the performance of his acts in matters of state as may be provided by law.

Article 5.

When, in accordance with the Imperial House Law, a Regency is established, the Regent shall perform his acts in matters of state in the Emperor's name. In this case, paragraph one of the preceding article will be applicable.

この法則に従ふことは、自国の主権を維持し、他国と対等関係に立たうとする各国の責務であると信ずる。

日本国民は、国家の名誉にかけ、全力をあげてこの崇高な理想と目的を達成することを誓ふ。

第1章　天皇
第1条

天皇は、日本国の象徴であり日本国民統合の象徴であつて、この地位は、主権の存する日本国民の総意に基く。

第2条

皇位は、世襲のものであつて、国会の議決した皇室典範の定めるところにより、これを継承する。

第3条

天皇の国事に関するすべての行為には、内閣の助言と承認を必要とし、内閣が、その責任を負ふ。

第4条

天皇は、この憲法の定める国事に関する行為のみを行ひ、国政に関する権能を有しない。

天皇は、法律の定めるところにより、その国事に関する行為を委任することができる。

第5条

皇室典範の定めるところにより摂政を置くときは、摂政は、天皇の名でその国事に関する行為を行ふ。この場合には、前条第1項の規定を準用する。

Article 6.

The Emperor shall appoint the Prime Minister as designated by the Diet.

The Emperor shall appoint the Chief Judge of the Supreme Court as designated by the Cabinet.

Article 7.

The Emperor, with the advice and approval of the Cabinet, shall perform the following acts in matters of state on behalf of the people:

1. Promulgation of amendments of the constitution, laws, cabinet orders and treaties;
2. Convocation of the Diet;
3. Dissolution of the House of Representatives;
4. Proclamation of general election of members of the Diet;
5. Attestation of the appointment and dismissal of Ministers of State and other officials as provided for by law, and of full powers and credentials of Ambassadors and Ministers;
6. Attestation of general and special amnesty, commutation of punishment, reprieve, and restoration of rights;
7. Awarding of honors;
8. Attestation of instruments of ratification and other diplomatic documents as provided for by law;
9. Receiving foreign ambassadors and ministers;
10. Performance of ceremonial functions.

Article 8.

No property can be given to, or received by, the Imperial House, nor can any gifts be made therefrom, without the authorization of the Diet.

第6条

天皇は、国会の指名に基いて、内閣総理大臣を任命する。

天皇は、内閣の指名に基いて、最高裁判所の長たる裁判官を任命する。

第7条

天皇は、内閣の助言と承認により、国民のために、左の国事に関する行為を行ふ。

1. 憲法改正、法律、政令及び条約を公布すること。
2. 国会を召集すること。
3. 衆議院を解散すること。
4. 国会議員の総選挙の施行を公示すること。
5. 国務大臣及び法律の定めるその他の官吏の任免並びに全権委任状及び大使及び公使の信任状を認証すること。
6. 大赦、特赦、減刑、刑の執行の免除及び復権を認証すること。
7. 栄典を授与すること。
8. 批准書及び法律の定めるその他の外交文書を認証すること。
9. 外国の大使及び公使を接受すること。
10. 儀式を行ふこと。

第8条

皇室に財産を譲り渡し、又は皇室が、財産を譲り受け、若しくは賜与することは、国会の議決に基かなければならない。

Chapter II. Renunciation of War
Article 9.

Aspiring sincerely to an international peace based on justice and order, the Japanese people forever renounce war as a sovereign right of the nation and the threat or use of force as means of settling international disputes.

In order to accomplish the aim of the preceding paragraph, land, sea, and air forces, as well as other war potential, will never be maintained. The right of belligerency of the state will not be recognized.

Chapter III. Rights and Duties of the People
Article 10.

The conditions necessary for being a Japanese national shall be determined by law.

Article 11.

The people shall not be prevented from enjoying any of the fundamental human rights. These fundamental human rights guaranteed to the people by this Constitution shall be conferred upon the people of this and future generations as eternal and inviolate rights.

Article 12.

The freedoms and rights guaranteed to the people by this Constitution shall be maintained by the constant endeavor of the people, who shall refrain from any abuse of these freedoms and rights and shall always be responsible for utilizing them for the public welfare.

Article 13.

All of the people shall be respected as individuals. Their right to life, liberty, and the

第2章　戦争の放棄
第9条

日本国民は、正義と秩序を基調とする国際平和を誠実に希求し、国権の発動たる戦争と、武力による威嚇又は武力の行使は、国際紛争を解決する手段としては、永久にこれを放棄する。

前項の目的を達するため、陸海空軍その他の戦力は、これを保持しない。国の交戦権は、これを認めない。

第3章　国民の権利及び義務
第10条

日本国民たる要件は、法律でこれを定める。

第11条

国民は、すべての基本的人権の享有を妨げられない。この憲法が国民に保障する基本的人権は、侵すことのできない永久の権利として、現在及び将来の国民に与へられる。

第12条

この憲法が国民に保障する自由及び権利は、国民の不断の努力によつて、これを保持しなければならない。又、国民は、これを濫用してはならないのであつて、常に公共の福祉のためにこれを利用する責任を負ふ。

第13条

すべて国民は、個人として尊重される。生命、自由及び幸福追及に対する国民の権利について

pursuit of happiness shall, to the extent that it does not interfere with the public welfare, be the supreme consideration in legislation and in other governmental affairs.

は、公共の福祉に反しない限り、立法その他の国政の上で、最大の尊重を必要とする。

Article 14.

All of the people are equal under the law and there shall be no discrimination in political, economic or social relations because of race, creed, sex, social status or family origin. Peers and peerage shall not be recognized.

No privilege shall accompany any award of honor, decoration or any distinction, nor shall any such award be valid beyond the lifetime of the individual who now holds or hereafter may receive it.

第14条

すべて国民は、法の下に平等であつて、人種、信条、性別、社会的身分又は門地により、政治的、経済的又は社会的関係において、差別されない。

華族その他の貴族の制度は、これを認めない。栄誉、勲章その他の栄典の授与は、いかなる特権も伴はない。栄典の授与は、現にこれを有し、又は将来これを受ける者の一代に限り、その効力を有する。

Article 15.

The people have the inalienable right to choose their public officials and to dismiss them.

All public officials are servants of the whole community and not of any group thereof.

Universal adult suffrage is guaranteed with regard to the election of public officials.

In all elections, secrecy of the ballot shall not be violated. A voter shall not be answerable, publicly or privately, for the choice he has made.

第15条

公務員を選定し、及びこれを罷免することは、国民固有の権利である。

すべて公務員は、全体の奉仕者であつて、一部の奉仕者ではない。

公務員の選挙については、成年者による普通選挙を保障する。

すべて選挙における投票の秘密は、これを侵してはならない。選挙人は、その選択に関し公的にも私的にも責任を問はれない。

Article 16.

Every person shall have the right of peaceful petition for the redress of damage, for the removal of public officials, for the enactment, repeal or amendment of laws, ordinances or regulations and for other matters, nor shall any person be in any way discriminated against for sponsoring such a petition.

第16条

何人も、損害の救済、公務員の罷免、法律、命令又は規則の制定、廃止又は改正その他の事項に関し、平穏に請願する権利を有し、何人も、かかる請願をしたためにいかなる差別待遇も受けない。

Article 17.

Every person may sue for redress as provided by law from the State or a public entity, in case he has suffered damage through illegal act of any public official.

Article 18.

No person shall be held in bondage of any kind. Involuntary servitude, except as punishment for crime, is prohibited.

Article 19.

Freedom of thought and conscience shall not be violated.

Article 20.

Freedom of religion is guaranteed to all. No religious organization shall receive any privileges from the State nor exercise any political authority.

No person shall be compelled to take part in any religious acts, celebration, rite or practice.

The State and its organs shall refrain from religious education or any other religious activity.

Article 21.

Freedom of assembly and association as well as speech, press and all other forms of expression are guaranteed.

No censorship shall be maintained, nor shall the secrecy of any means of communication be violated.

Article 22.

Every person shall have freedom to choose and change his residence and to choose his occupation to the extent that it does not interfere with the public welfare.

Freedom of all persons to move to a

第17条

何人も、公務員の不法行為により、損害を受けたときは、法律の定めるところにより、国又は公共団体に、その賠償を求めることができる。

第18条

何人も、いかなる奴隷的拘束も受けない。又、犯罪に因る処罰の場合を除いては、その意に反する苦役に服させられない。

第19条

思想及び良心の自由は、これを侵してはならない。

第20条

信教の自由は、何人に対してもこれを保障する。いかなる宗教団体も、国から特権を受け、又は政治上の権力を行使してはならない。

何人も、宗教上の行為、祝典、儀式又は行事に参加することを強制されない。

国及びその機関は、宗教教育その他いかなる宗教的活動もしてはならない。

第21条

集会、結社及び言論、出版その他一切の表現の自由は、これを保障する。

検閲は、これをしてはならない。通信の秘密は、これを侵してはならない。

第22条

何人も、公共の福祉に反しない限り、居住、移転及び職業選択の自由を有する。

何人も、外国に移住し、又は国籍を離脱する

foreign country and to divest themselves of their nationality shall be inviolate.

自由を侵されない。

Article 23.

Academic freedom is guaranteed.

第23条

学問の自由は、これを保障する。

Article 24.

Marriage shall be based only on the mutual consent of both sexes and it shall be maintained through mutual cooperation with the equal rights of husband and wife as a basis.

With regard to choice of spouse, property rights, inheritance, choice of domicile, divorce and other matters pertaining to marriage and the family, laws shall be enacted from the standpoint of individual dignity and the essential equality of the sexes.

第24条

婚姻は、両性の合意のみに基いて成立し、夫婦が同等の権利を有することを基本として、相互の協力により、維持されなければならない。

配偶者の選択、財産権、相続、住居の選定、離婚並びに婚姻及び家族に関するその他の事項に関しては、法律は、個人の尊厳と両性の本質的平等に立脚して、制定されなければならない。

Article 25.

All people shall have the right to maintain the minimum standards of wholesome and cultured living.

In all spheres of life, the State shall use its endeavors for the promotion and extension of social welfare and security, and of public health.

第25条

すべて国民は、健康で文化的な最低限度の生活を営む権利を有する。

国は、すべての生活部面について、社会福祉、社会保障及び公衆衛生の向上及び増進に努めなければならない。

Article 26.

All people shall have the right to receive an equal education correspondent to their ability, as provided by law.

All people shall be obligated to have all boys and girls under their protection receive ordinary educations as provided for by law. Such compulsory education shall be free.

第26条

すべて国民は、法律の定めるところにより、その能力に応じて、ひとしく教育を受ける権利を有する。

すべて国民は、法律の定めるところにより、その保護する子女に普通教育を受けさせる義務を負ふ。義務教育は、これを無償とする。

Article 27.

All people shall have the right and the obligation to work.

第27条

すべて国民は、勤労の権利を有し、義務を負ふ。

Standards for wages, hours, rest and other working conditions shall be fixed by law.

Children shall not be exploited.

賃金、就業時間、休息その他の勤労条件に関する基準は、法律でこれを定める。

児童は、これを酷使してはならない。

Article 28.

The right of workers to organize and to bargain and act collectively is guaranteed.

第28条

勤労者の団結する権利及び団体交渉その他の団体行動をする権利は、これを保障する。

Article 29.

The right to own or to hold property is inviolable.

Property rights shall be defined by law, in conformity with the public welfare.

Private property may be taken for public use upon just compensation therefor.

第29条

財産権は、これを侵してはならない。

財産権の内容は、公共の福祉に適合するやうに、法律でこれを定める。

私有財産は、正当な補償の下に、これを公共のために用ひることができる。

Article 30.

The people shall be liable to taxations as provided by law.

第30条

国民は、法律の定めるところにより、納税の義務を負ふ。

Article 31.

No person shall be deprived of life or liberty, nor shall any other criminal penalty be imposed, except according to procedure established by law.

第31条

何人も、法律の定める手続によらなければ、その生命若しくは自由を奪はれ、又はその他の刑罰を科せられない。

Article 32.

No person shall be denied the right of access to the courts.

第32条

何人も、裁判所において裁判を受ける権利を奪はれない。

Article 33.

No person shall be apprehended except upon warrant issued by a competent judicial officer which specifies the offense with which the person is charged, unless he is apprehended, the offense being committed.

第33条

何人も、現行犯として逮捕される場合を除いては、権限を有する司法官憲が発し、且つ理由となつてゐる犯罪を明示する令状によらなければ、逮捕されない。

Article 34.

No person shall be arrested or detained without being at once informed of the

第34条

何人も、理由を直ちに告げられ、且つ、直ちに弁護人に依頼する権利を与へられなければ、

charges against him or without the immediate privilege of counsel; nor shall he be detained without adequate cause; and upon demand of any person such cause must be immediately shown in open court in his presence and the presence of his counsel.

抑留又は拘禁されない。又、何人も、正当な理由がなければ、拘禁されず、要求があれば、その理由は直ちに本人及びその弁護人の出席する公開の法廷で示されなければならない。

Article 35.

The right of all persons to be secure in their homes, papers and effects against entries, searches and seizures shall not be impaired except upon warrant issued for adequate cause and particularly describing the place to be searched and things to be seized, or except as provided by Article 33.

Each search or seizure shall be made upon separate warrant issued by a competent judicial officer.

第35条

何人も、その住居、書類及び所持品について、侵入、捜索及び押収を受けることのない権利は、第33条の場合を除いては、正当な理由に基いて発せられ、且つ捜索する場所及び押収する物を明示する令状がなければ、侵されない。

捜索又は押収は、権限を有する司法官憲が発する各別の令状により、これを行ふ。

Article 36.

The infliction of torture by any public officer and cruel punishments are absolutely forbidden.

第36条

公務員による拷問及び残虐な刑罰は、絶対にこれを禁ずる。

Article 37.

In all criminal cases the accused shall enjoy the right to a speedy and public trial by an impartial tribunal.

He shall be permitted full opportunity to examine all witnesses, and he shall have the right of compulsory process for obtaining witnesses on his behalf at public expense.

At all times the accused shall have the assistance of competent counsel who shall, if the accused is unable to secure the same by his own efforts, be assigned to his use by the State.

第37条

すべて刑事事件においては、被告人は、公平な裁判所の迅速な公開裁判を受ける権利を有する。

刑事被告人は、すべての証人に対して審問する機会を充分に与へられ、又、公費で自己のために強制的手続により証人を求める権利を有する。

刑事被告人は、いかなる場合にも、資格を有する弁護人を依頼することができる。被告人が自らこれを依頼することができないときは、国でこれを附する。

Article 38.

No person shall be compelled to testify against himself.

第38条

何人も、自己に不利益な供述を強要されない。

Confession made under compulsion, torture or threat, or after prolonged arrest or detention shall not be admitted in evidence.

No person shall be convicted or punished in cases where the only proof against him is his own confession.

Article 39.

No person shall be held criminally liable for an act which was lawful at the time it was committed, or of which he has been acquitted, nor shall he be placed in double jeopardy.

Article 40.

Any person, in case he is acquitted after he has been arrested or detained, may sue the State for redress as provided by law.

Chapter IV. The Diet
Article 41.

The Diet shall be the highest organ of state power, and shall be the sole law-making organ of the State.

Article 42.

The Diet shall consist of two Houses, namely the House of Representatives and the House of Councillors.

Article 43.

Both Houses shall consist of elected members, representative of all the people.

The number of members of each House shall be fixed by law.

Article 44.

The qualifications of members of both Houses and their electors shall be fixed by law. However, there shall be no discrimination because of race, creed, sex, social status, family origin, education, property or income.

強制、拷問若しくは脅迫による自白又は不当に長く抑留若しくは拘禁された後の自白は、これを証拠とすることができない。

何人も、自己に不利益な唯一の証拠が本人の自白である場合には、有罪とされ、又は刑罰を科せられない。

第39条

何人も、実行の時に適法であつた行為又は既に無罪とされた行為については、刑事上の責任を問はれない。又、同一の犯罪について、重ねて刑事上の責任を問はれない。

第40条

何人も、抑留又は拘禁された後、無罪の裁判を受けたときは、法律の定めるところにより、国にその補償を求めることができる。

第4章　国会
第41条

国会は、国権の最高機関であつて、国の唯一の立法機関である。

第42条

国会は、衆議院及び参議院の両議院でこれを構成する。

第43条

両議院は、全国民を代表する選挙された議員でこれを組織する。

両議院の議員の定数は法律でこれを定める。

第44条

両議院の議員及びその選挙人の資格は、法律でこれを定める。但し、人種、信条、性別、社会的身分、門地、教育、財産又は収入によつて差別してはならない。

Article 45.

The term of office of members of the House of Representatives shall be four years. However, the term shall be terminated before the full term is up in case the House of Representatives is dissolved.

Article 46.

The term of office of members of the House of Councillors shall be six years, and election for half the members shall take place every three years.

Article 47.

Electoral districts, method of voting and other matters pertaining to the method of election of members of both Houses shall be fixed by law.

Article 48.

No person shall be permitted to be a member of both Houses simultaneously.

Article 49.

Members of both Houses shall receive appropriate annual payment from the national treasury in accordance with law.

Article 50.

Except in cases provided by law, members of both Houses shall be exempt from apprehension while the Diet is in session, and any members apprehended before the opening of the session shall be freed during the term of the session upon demand of the House.

Article 51.

Members of both Houses shall not be held liable outside the House for speeches, debates or votes cast inside the House.

第45条

衆議院議員の任期は、4年とする。但し、衆議院解散の場合には、その期間満了前に終了する。

第46条

参議院議員の任期は、6年とし、3年ごとに議員の半数を改選する。

第47条

選挙区、投票の方法その他両議院の議員の選挙に関する事項は、法律でこれを定める。

第48条

何人も、同時に両議院の議員たることはできない。

第49条

両議院の議員は、法律の定めるところにより、国庫から相当額の歳費を受ける。

第50条

両議院の議員は、法律の定める場合を除いては、国会の会期中逮捕されず、会期前に逮捕された議員は、その議院の要求があれば、会期中これを釈放しなければならない。

第51条

両議院の議員は、議院で行つた演説、討論又は表決について、院外で責任を問はれない。

Article 52.

An ordinary session of the Diet shall be convoked once per year.

Article 53.

The Cabinet may determine to convoke extraordinary sessions of the Diet. When a quarter or more of the total members of either House makes the demand, the Cabinet must determine on such convocation.

Article 54.

When the House of Representatives is dissolved, there must be a general election of members of the House of Representatives within forty (40) days from the date of dissolution, and the Diet must be convoked within thirty (30) days from the date of election.

When the House of Representatives is dissolved, the House of Councillors is closed at the same time. However, the Cabinet may in time of national emergency convoke the House of Councillors in emergency session.

Measures taken at such session as mentioned in the proviso of the preceding paragraph shall be provisional and shall become null and void unless agreed to by the House of Representatives within a period of ten (10) days after the opening of the next session of the Diet.

Article 55.

Each House shall judge disputes related to qualifications of its members. However, in order to deny a seat to any member, it is necessary to pass a resolution by a majority of two-thirds or more of the members present.

Article 56.

Business cannot be transacted in either

第52条

国会の常会は、毎年1回これを召集する。

第53条

内閣は、国会の臨時会の召集を決定することができる。いづれかの議院の総議員の4分の1以上の要求があれば、内閣は、その召集を決定しなければならない。

第54条

衆議院が解散されたときは、解散の日から40日以内に、衆議院議員の総選挙を行ひ、その選挙の日から30日以内に、国会を召集しなければならない。

衆議院が解散されたときは、参議院は、同時に閉会となる。但し、内閣は、国に緊急の必要があるときは、参議院の緊急集会を求めることができる。

前項但書の緊急集会において採られた措置は、臨時のものであつて、次の国会開会の後10日以内に、衆議院の同意がない場合には、その効力を失ふ。

第55条

両議院は、各々その議員の資格に関する争訟を裁判する。但し、議員の議席を失はせるには、出席議員の3分の2以上の多数による議決を必要とする。

第56条

両議院は、各々その総議員の3分の1以上の出

House unless one-third or more of total membership is present.

All matters shall be decided, in each House, by a majority of those present, except as elsewhere provided in the Constitution, and in case of a tie, the presiding officer shall decide the issue.

Article 57.

Deliberation in each House shall be public. However, a secret meeting may be held where a majority of two-thirds or more of those members present passes a resolution therefor.

Each House shall keep a record of proceedings. This record shall be published and given general circulation, excepting such parts of proceedings of secret session as may be deemed to require secrecy.

Upon demand of one-fifth or more of the members present, votes of the members on any matter shall be recorded in the minutes.

Article 58.

Each House shall select its own president and other officials.

Each House shall establish its rules pertaining to meetings, proceedings and internal discipline, and may punish members for disorderly conduct. However, in order to expel a member, a majority of two-thirds or more of those members present must pass a resolution thereon.

Article 59.

A bill becomes a law on passage by both Houses, except as otherwise provided by the Constitution.

A bill which is passed by the House of Representa-tives, and upon which the

席がなければ、議事を開き議決することができない。

両議院の議事は、この憲法に特別の定のある場合を除いては、出席議員の過半数でこれを決し、可否同数のときは、議長の決するところによる。

第57条

両議院の会議は、公開とする。但し、出席議員の3分の2以上の多数で議決したときは、秘密会を開くことができる。

両議院は、各々その会議の記録を保存し、秘密会の記録の中で特に秘密を要すると認められるもの以外は、これを公表し、且つ一般に頒布しなければならない。

出席議員の5分の1以上の要求があれば、各議員の表決は、これを会議録に記載しなければならない。

第58条

両議院は、各々その議長その他の役員を選任する。

両議院は、各々その会議その他の手続及び内部の規律に関する規則を定め、又、院内の秩序をみだした議員を懲罰することができる。但し、議員を除名するには、出席議員の3分の2以上の多数による議決を必要とする。

第59条

法律案は、この憲法に特別の定のある場合を除いては、両議院で可決したとき法律となる。

衆議院で可決し、参議院でこれと異なった議決をした法律案は、衆議院で出席議員の3分の2

House of Councillors makes a decision different from that of the House of Representatives, becomes a law when passed a second time by the House of Representatives by a majority of two-thirds or more of the members present.

The provision of the preceding paragraph does not preclude the House of Representatives from calling for the meeting of a joint committee of both Houses, provided for by law.

Failure by the House of Councillors to take final action within sixty (60) days after receipt of a bill passed by the House of Representatives, time in recess excepted, may be determined by the House of Representatives to constitute a rejection of the said bill by the House of Councillors.

以上の多数で再び可決したときは、法律となる。

前項の規定は、法律の定めるところにより、衆議院が、両議院の協議会を開くことを求めることを妨げない。

参議院が、衆議院の可決した法律案を受け取つた後、国会休会中の期間を除いて60日以内に、議決しないときは、衆議院は、参議院がその法律案を否決したものとみなすことができる。

Article 60.

The Budget must first be submitted to the House of Representatives.

Upon consideration of the budget, when the House of Councillors makes a decision different from that of the House of Representatives, and when no agreement can be reached even through a joint committee of both Houses, provided for by law, or in the case of failure by the House of Councillors to take final action within thirty (30) days, the period of recess excluded, after the receipt of the budget passed by the House of Representatives, the decision of the House of Representatives shall be the decision of the Diet.

第60条

予算は、さきに衆議院に提出しなければならない。

予算について、参議院で衆議院と異なつた議決をした場合に、法律の定めるところにより、両議院の協議会を開いても意見が一致しないとき、又は参議院が、衆議院の可決した予算を受け取つた後、国会休会中の期間を除いて30日以内に、議決しないときは、衆議院の議決を国会の議決とする。

Article 61.

The second paragraph of the preceding article applies also to the Diet approval required for the conclusion of treaties.

第61条

条約の締結に必要な国会の承認については、前条第2項の規定を準用する。

Article 62.

Each House may conduct investigations in relation to government, and may demand the presence and testimony of witnesses, and the production of records.

Article 63.

The Prime Minister and other Ministers of State may, at any time, appear in either House for the purpose of speaking on bills, regardless of whether they are members of the House or not. They must appear when their presence is required in order to give answers or explanations.

Article 64.

The Diet shall set up an impeachment court from among the members of both Houses for the purpose of trying those judges against whom removal proceedings have been instituted.

Matters relating to impeachment shall be provided by law.

Chapter V. The Cabinet
Article 65.

Executive power shall be vested in the Cabinet.

Article 66.

The Cabinet shall consist of the Prime Minister, who shall be its head, and other Ministers of State, as provided for by law.

The Prime Minister and other Ministers of State must be civilians.

The Cabinet, in the exercise of executive power, shall be collectively responsible to the Diet.

Article 67.

The Prime Minister shall be designated

第62条

両議院は、各々国政に関する調査を行ひ、これに関して、証人の出頭及び証言並びに記録の提出を要求することができる。

第63条

内閣総理大臣その他の国務大臣は、両議院の一に議席を有すると有しないとにかかはらず、何時でも議案について発言するため議院に出席することができる。又、答弁又は説明のため出席を求められたときは、出席しなければならない。

第64条

国会は、罷免の訴追を受けた裁判官を裁判するため、両議院の議員で組織する弾劾裁判所を設ける。

弾劾に関する事項は、法律でこれを定める。

第5章　内閣
第65条

行政権は、内閣に属する。

第66条

内閣は、法律の定めるところにより、その首長たる内閣総理大臣及びその他の国務大臣でこれを組織する。

内閣総理大臣その他の国務大臣は、文民でなければならない。

内閣は、行政権の行使について、国会に対し連帯して責任を負ふ。

第67条

内閣総理大臣は、国会議員の中から国会の議

from among the members of the Diet by a resolution of the Diet. This designation shall precede all other business.

If the House of Representatives and the House of Councillors disagrees and if no agreement can be reached even through a joint committee of both Houses, provided for by law, or the House of Councillors fails to make designation within ten (10) days, exclusive of the period of recess, after the House of Representatives has made designation, the decision of the House of Representatives shall be the decision of the Diet.

Article 68.

The Prime Minister shall appoint the Ministers of State. However, a majority of their number must be chosen from among the members of the Diet.

The Prime Minister may remove the Ministers of State as he chooses.

Article 69.

If the House of Representatives passes a non-confidence resolution, or rejects a confidence resolution, the Cabinet shall resign en masse, unless the House of Representatives is dissolved within ten (10) days.

Article 70.

When there is a vacancy in the post of Prime Minister, or upon the first convocation of the Diet after a general election of members of the House of Representa-tives, the Cabinet shall resign en masse.

Article 71.

In the cases mentioned in the two preceding articles, the Cabinet shall continue its functions until the time when a new Prime Minister is appointed.

決で、これを指名する。この指名は、他のすべての案件に先だつて、これを行ふ。

衆議院と参議院とが異なつた指名の議決をした場合に、法律の定めるところにより、両議院の協議会を開いても意見が一致しないとき、又は衆議院が指名の議決をした後、国会休会中の期間を除いて10日以内に、参議院が、指名の議決をしないときは、衆議院の議決を国会の議決とする。

第68条

内閣総理大臣は、国務大臣を任命する。但し、その過半数は、国会議員の中から選ばれなければならない。

内閣総理大臣は、任意に国務大臣を罷免することができる。

第69条

内閣は、衆議院で不信任の決議案を可決し、又は信任の決議案を否決したときは、10日以内に衆議院が解散されない限り、総辞職をしなければならない。

第70条

内閣総理大臣が欠けたとき、又は衆議院議員総選挙の後に初めて国会の召集があつたときは、内閣は、総辞職をしなければならない。

第71条

前2条の場合には、内閣は、あらたに内閣総理大臣が任命されるまで引き続きその職務を行ふ。

Article 72.

The Prime Minister, representing the Cabinet, submits bills, reports on general national affairs and foreign relations to the Diet and exercises control and supervision over various administrative branches.

Article 73.

The Cabinet, in addition to other general administrative functions, shall perform the following functions:

1. Administer the law faithfully; conduct affairs of state;

2. Manage foreign affairs;

3. Conclude treaties. However, it shall obtain prior or, depending on circumstances, subsequent approval of the Diet;

4. Administer the civil service, in accordance with standards established by law;

5. Prepare the budget, and present it to the Diet;

6. Enact cabinet orders in order to execute the provisions of this Constitution and of the law. However, it cannot include penal provisions in such cabinet orders unless authorized by such law.

7. Decide on general amnesty, special amnesty, commutation of punishment, reprieve, and restoration of rights.

Article 74.

All laws and cabinet orders shall be signed by the competent Minister of State and countersigned by the Prime Minister.

Article 75.

The Ministers of State, during their tenure of office, shall not be subject to legal action without the consent of the Prime Minister. However, the right to take that action is not impaired hereby.

第72条

内閣総理大臣は、内閣を代表して議案を国会に提出し、一般国務及び外交関係について国会に報告し、並びに行政各部を指揮監督する。

第73条

内閣は、他の一般行政事務の外、左の事務を行ふ。

1. 法律を誠実に執行し、国務を総理すること。

2. 外交関係を処理すること。

3. 条約を締結すること。但し、事前に、時宜によつては事後に、国会の承認を経ることを必要とする。

4. 法律の定める基準に従ひ、官吏に関する事務を掌理すること。

5. 予算を作成して国会に提出すること。

6. この憲法及び法律の規定を実施するために、政令を制定すること。但し、政令には、特にその法律の委任がある場合を除いては、罰則を設けることができない。

7. 大赦、特赦、減刑、刑の執行の免除及び復権を決定すること。

第74条

法律及び政令には、すべて主任の国務大臣が署名し、内閣総理大臣が連署することを必要とする。

第75条

国務大臣は、その在任中、内閣総理大臣の同意がなければ、訴追されない。但し、これがため、訴追の権利は、害されない。

Chapter VI. Judiciary

Article 76.

The whole judicial power is vested in a Supreme Court and in such inferior courts as are established by law.

No extraordinary tribunal shall be established, nor shall any organ or agency of the Executive be given final judicial power.

All judges shall be independent in the exercise of their conscience and shall be bound only by this Constitution and the laws.

Article 77.

The Supreme Court is vested with the rule-making power under which it determines the rules of procedure and of practice, and of matters relating to attorneys, the internal discipline of the courts and the administration of judicial affairs.

Public procurators shall be subject to the rule-making power of the Supreme Court. The Supreme Court may delegate the power to make rules for inferior courts to such courts.

Article 78.

Judges shall not be removed except by public impeachment unless judicially declared mentally or physically incompetent to perform official duties. No disciplinary action against judges shall be administered by any executive organ or agency.

Article 79.

The Supreme Court shall consist of a Chief Judge and such number of judges as may be determined by law; all such judges excepting the Chief Judge shall be appointed by the Cabinet.

The appointment of the judges of the Supreme Court shall be reviewed by the

第6章　司法

第76条

すべて司法権は、最高裁判所及び法律の定めるところにより設置する下級裁判所に属する。

特別裁判所は、これを設置することができない。行政機関は、終審として裁判を行ふことができない。

すべて裁判官は、その良心に従ひ独立してその職権を行ひ、この憲法及び法律にのみ拘束される。

第77条

最高裁判所は、訴訟に関する手続、弁護士、裁判所の内部規律及び司法事務処理に関する事項について、規則を定める権限を有する。

検察官は、最高裁判所の定める規則に従はなければならない。

最高裁判所は、下級裁判所に関する規則を定める権限を、下級裁判所に委任することができる。

第78条

裁判官は、裁判により、心身の故障のために職務を執ることができないと決定された場合を除いては、公の弾劾によらなければ罷免されない。裁判官の懲戒処分は、行政機関がこれを行ふことはできない。

第79条

最高裁判所は、その長たる裁判官及び法律の定める員数のその他の裁判官でこれを構成し、その長たる裁判官以外の裁判官は、内閣でこれを任命する。

最高裁判所の裁判官の任命は、その任命後初めて行はれる衆議院議員総選挙の際国民の審査

people at the first general election of members of the House of Representatives following their appointment, and shall be reviewed again at the first general election of members of the House of Representatives after a lapse of ten (10) years, and in the same manner thereafter.

In cases mentioned in the foregoing paragraph, when the majority of the voters favors the dismissal of a judge, he shall be dismissed.

Matters pertaining to review shall be prescribed by law.

The judges of the Supreme Court shall be retired upon the attainment of the age as fixed by law.

All such judges shall receive, at regular stated intervals, adequate compensation which shall not be decreased during their terms of office.

に付し、その後10年を経過した後初めて行はれる衆議院議員総選挙の際更に審査に付し、その後も同様とする。

前項の場合において、投票者の多数が裁判官の罷免を可とするときは、その裁判官は、罷免される。

審査に関する事項は、法律でこれを定める。

最高裁判所の裁判官は、法律の定める年齢に達した時に退官する。

最高裁判所の裁判官は、すべて定期に相当額の報酬を受ける。この報酬は、在任中、これを減額することができない。

Article 80.

第80条

The judges of the inferior courts shall be appointed by the cabinet from a list of persons nominated by the Supreme Court. All such judges shall hold office for a term of ten (10) years with privilege of reappointment, provided that they shall be retired upon the attainment of the age as fixed by law.

The judges of the inferior courts shall receive, at regular stated intervals, adequate compensation which shall not be decreased during their terms of office.

下級裁判所の裁判官は、最高裁判所の指名した者の名簿によつて、内閣でこれを任命する。その裁判官は、任期を10年とし、再任されることができる。但し、法律の定める年齢に達した時には退官する。

下級裁判所の裁判官は、すべて定期に相当額の報酬を受ける。この報酬は、在任中、これを減額することができない。

Article 81.

第81条

The Supreme Court is the court of last resort with power to determine the constitutionality of any law, order, regulation or official act.

最高裁判所は、一切の法律、命令、規則又は処分が憲法に適合するかしないかを決定する権限を有する終審裁判所である。

Article 82.

Trials shall be conducted and judgment declared publicly.

Where a court unanimously determines publicity to be dangerous to public order or morals, a trial may be conducted privately, but trials of political offenses, offenses involving the press or cases wherein the rights of people as guaranteed in Chapter III of this Constitution are in question shall always be conducted publicly.

Chapter VII. Finance
Article 83.

The power to administer national finances shall be exercised as the Diet shall determine.

Article 84.

No new taxes shall be imposed or existing ones modified except by law or under such conditions as law may prescribe.

Article 85.

No money shall be expended, nor shall the State obligate itself, except as authorized by the Diet.

Article 86.

The Cabinet shall prepare and submit to the Diet for its consideration and decision a budget for each fiscal year.

Article 87.

In order to provide for unforeseen deficiencies in the budget, a reserve fund may be authorized by the Diet to be expended upon the responsibility of the Cabinet.

The Cabinet must get subsequent approval of the Diet for all payments from the reserve fund.

第82条

裁判の対審及び判決は、公開法廷でこれを行ふ。

裁判所が、裁判官の全員一致で、公の秩序又は善良の風俗を害する虞があると決した場合には、対審は、公開しないでこれを行ふことができる。但し、政治犯罪、出版に関する犯罪又はこの憲法第3章で保障する国民の権利が問題となつてゐる事件の対審は、常にこれを公開しなければならない。

第7章 財政
第83条

国の財政を処理する権限は、国会の議決に基いて、これを行使しなければならない。

第84条

あらたに租税を課し、又は現行の租税を変更するには、法律又は法律の定める条件によることを必要とする。

第85条

国費を支出し、又は国が債務を負担するには、国会の議決に基くことを必要とする。

第86条

内閣は、毎会計年度の予算を作成し、国会に提出して、その審議を受け議決を経なければならない。

第87条

予見し難い予算の不足に充てるため、国会の議決に基いて予備費を設け、内閣の責任でこれを支出することができる。

すべて予備費の支出については、内閣は、事後に国会の承諾を得なければならない。

Article 88.

All property of the Imperial Household shall belong to the State. All expenses of the Imperial Household shall be appropriated by the Diet in the budget.

Article 89.

No public money or other property shall be expended or appropriated for the use, benefit or maintenance of any religious institution or association, or for any charitable, educational or benevolent enterprises not under the control of public authority.

Article 90.

Final accounts of the expenditures and revenues of the State shall be audited annually by a Board of Audit and submitted by the Cabinet to the Diet, together with the statement of audit, during the fiscal year immediately following the period covered.

The organization and competency of the Board of Audit shall be determined by law.

Article 91.

At regular intervals and at least annually the Cabinet shall report to the Diet and the people on the state of national finances.

Chapter VIII. Local Self-Government
Article 92.

Regulations concerning organization and operations of local public entities shall be fixed by law in accordance with the principle of local autonomy.

Article 93.

The local public entities shall establish assemblies as their deliberative organs, in

第88条

すべて皇室財産は、国に属する。すべて皇室の費用は、予算に計上して国会の議決を経なければならない。

第89条

公金その他の公の財産は、宗教上の組織若しくは団体の使用、便益若しくは維持のため、又は公の支配に属しない慈善、教育若しくは博愛の事業に対し、これを支出し、又はその利用に供してはならない。

第90条

国の収入支出の決算は、すべて毎年会計検査院がこれを検査し、内閣は、次の年度に、その検査報告とともに、これを国会に提出しなければならない。

会計検査院の組織及び権限は、法律でこれを定める。

第91条

内閣は、国会及び国民に対し、定期に、少くとも毎年1回、国の財政状況について報告しなければならない。

第8章　地方自治
第92条

地方公共団体の組織及び運営に関する事項は、地方自治の本旨に基いて、法律でこれを定める。

第93条

地方公共団体には、法律の定めるところにより、その議事機関として議会を設置する。

accordance with law.

The chief executive officers of all local public entities, the members of their assemblies, and such other local officials as may be determined by law shall be elected by direct popular vote within their several communities.

Article 94.

Local public entities shall have the right to manage their property, affairs and administration and to enact their own regulations within law.

Article 95.

A special law, applicable only to one local public entity, cannot be enacted by the Diet without the consent of the majority of the voters of the local public entity concerned, obtained in accordance with law.

Chapter IX. Amendments
Article 96.

Amendments to this Constitution shall be initiated by the Diet, through a concurring vote of two-thirds or more of all the members of each House and shall thereupon be submitted to the people for ratification, which shall require the affirmative vote of a majority of all votes cast thereon, at a special referendum or at such election as the Diet shall specify.

Amendments when so ratified shall immediately be promulgated by the Emperor in the name of the people, as an integral part of this Constitution.

Chapter X. Supreme Law
Article 97.

The fundamental human rights by this Constitution guaranteed to the people of

地方公共団体の長、その議会の議員及び法律の定めるその他の吏員は、その地方公共団体の住民が、直接これを選挙する。

第94条

地方公共団体は、その財産を管理し、事務を処理し、及び行政を執行する権能を有し、法律の範囲内で条例を制定することができる。

第95条

一の地方公共団体のみに適用される特別法は、法律の定めるところにより、その地方公共団体の住民の投票においてその過半数の同意を得なければ、国会は、これを制定することができない。

第9章　改正
第96条

この憲法の改正は、各議院の総議員の3分の2以上の賛成で、国会が、これを発議し、国民に提案してその承認を経なければならない。この承認には、特別の国民投票又は国会の定める選挙の際行はれる投票において、その過半数の賛成を必要とする。

憲法改正について前項の承認を経たときは、天皇は、国民の名で、この憲法と一体を成すものとして、直ちにこれを公布する。

第10章　最高法規
第97条

この憲法が日本国民に保障する基本的人権は、人類の多年にわたる自由獲得の努力の成果

Japan are fruits of the age-old struggle of man to be free; they have survived the many exacting tests for durability and are conferred upon this and future generations in trust, to be held for all time inviolate.

であつて、これらの権利は、過去幾多の試練に堪へ、現在及び将来の国民に対し、侵すことのできない永久の権利として信託されたものである。

Article 98.

This Constitution shall be the supreme law of the nation and no law, ordinance, imperial rescript or other act of government, or part thereof, contrary to the provisions hereof, shall have legal force or validity.

The treaties concluded by Japan and established laws of nations shall be faithfully observed.

第98条

この憲法は、国の最高法規であつて、その条項に反する法律、命令、詔勅及び国務に関するその他の行為の全部又は一部は、その効力を有しない。

日本国が締結した条約及び確立された国際法規は、これを誠実に遵守することを必要とする。

Article 99.

The Emperor or the Regent as well as Ministers of State, members of the Diet, judges, and all other public officials have the obligation to respect and uphold this Constitution.

第99条

天皇又は摂政及び国務大臣、国会議員、裁判官その他の公務員は、この憲法を尊重し擁護する義務を負ふ。

Chapter XI. Supplementary Provisions
Article 100.

This Constitution shall be enforced as from the day when the period of six months will have elapsed counting from the day of its promulgation.

The enactment of laws necessary for the enforcement of this Constitution, the election of members of the House of Councillors and the procedure for the convocation of the Diet and other preparatory procedures for the enforcement of this Constitution may be executed before the day prescribed in the preceding paragraph.

第11章　補則
第100条

この憲法は、公布の日から起算して6箇月を経過した日から、これを施行する。

この憲法を施行するために必要な法律の制定、参議院議員の選挙及び国会召集の手続並びにこの憲法を施行するために必要な準備手続は、前項の期日よりも前に、これを行ふことができる。

Article 101.

If the House of Councillors is not constituted before the effective date of this

第101条

この憲法施行の際、参議院がまだ成立してゐないときは、その成立するまでの間、衆議院は、

Constitution, the House of Representatives shall function as the Diet until such time as the House of Councillors shall be constituted.

国会としての権限を行ふ。

Article 102.

The term of office for half the members of the House of Councillors serving in the first term under this Constitution shall be three years. Members falling under this category shall be determined in accordance with law.

第102条

この憲法による第1期の参議院議員のうち、その半数の者の任期は、これを3年とする。その議員は、法律の定めるところにより、これを定める。

Article 103.

The Ministers of State, members of the House of Representatives, and judges in office on the effective date of this Constitution, and all other public officials, who occupy positions corresponding to such positions as are recognized by this Constitution shall not forfeit their positions automatically on account of the enforcement of this Constitution unless otherwise specified by law. When, however, successors are elected or appointed under the provisions of this Constitution, they shall forfeit their positions as a matter of course.

第103条

この憲法施行の際現に在職する国務大臣、衆議院議員及び裁判官並びにその他の公務員で、その地位に相応する地位がこの憲法で認められてゐる者は、法律で特別の定をした場合を除いては、この憲法施行のため、当然にはその地位を失ふことはない。但し、この憲法によつて、後任者が選挙又は任命されたときは、当然その地位を失ふ。

Cairo Declaration Signed 27 November 1943

Statement Issued Following the Conference of President Roosevelt, Generalissimo Chiang Kai-shek and Prime Minister Churchill

「ローズヴェルト」大統領、蔣介石大元帥及「チアーチル」総理大臣ハ各自ノ軍事及外交顧問ト共ニ「北アフリカ」ニ於テ会議ヲ終了シ左ノ一般的声明発セラレタリ

The several military missions have agreed upon future military operations against Japan. The Three Great Allies expressed their resolve to bring unrelenting pressure against their brutal enemies by sea, land, and air. This pressure is already rising.

各軍事使節ハ日本国ニ対スル将来ノ軍事行動ヲ協定セリ三大同盟国ハ海路、陸路及空路ニ依リ其ノ野蛮ナル敵国ニ対シ仮借ナキ弾圧ヲ加フルノ決意ヲ表明セリ右弾圧ハ既ニ増大シツツアリ

The Three Great Allies are fighting this war to restrain and punish the aggression of Japan. They covet no gain for themselves and have no thought of territorial expansion. It is their purpose that Japan shall be stripped of all the islands in the Pacific which she has seized or occupied since the beginning of the first World War in 1914, and that all the territories Japan has stolen from the Chinese, such as Manchuria, Formosa, and the Pescadores, shall be restored to the Republic of China. Japan will also be expelled from all other territories which she has taken by violence and greed. The aforesaid three great powers, mindful of the enslavement of the people of Korea, are determined that in due course Korea shall become free and independent.

三大同盟国ハ日本国ノ侵略ヲ制止シ且之ヲ罰スル為今次ノ戦争ヲ為シツツアルモノナリ右同盟国ハ自国ノ為ニ何等ノ利得ヲモ欲求スルモノニ非ズ又領土拡張ノ何等ノ念ヲモ有スルモノニ非ズ
右同盟国国ノ目的ハ日本国ヨリ千九百十四年ノ第一次世界戦争ノ開始以後ニ於テ日本国ガ奪取シ又ハ占領シタル太平洋ニ於ケル一切ノ島嶼ヲ剥奪スルコト並ニ満州、台湾及澎湖島ノ如キ日本国ガ中国人ヨリ盗取シタル一切ノ地域ヲ中華民国ニ返還スルコトニ在リ
日本国ハ又暴力及貪欲ニ依リ日本国ガ略取シタル他ノ一切ノ地域ヨリ駆逐セラルベシ

With these objects in view the three Allies, in harmony with those of the United Nations at war with Japan, will continue to persevere in the serious and prolonged operations necessary to procure the unconditional surrender of Japan.

前記三大国ハ朝鮮ノ人民ノ奴隷状態ニ留意シ軈テ朝鮮ヲ自由且独立ノモノタラシムルノ決意ヲ有ス右ノ目的ヲ以テ右三同盟国ハ同盟諸国中日本国ト交戦中ナル諸国ト協調シ日本国ノ無条件降伏ヲ斎スニ必要ナル重大且長期ノ行動ヲ続行スベシ

Proclamation Defining Terms for Japanese Surrender

日本の降伏条件に関する宣言

1. We — The President of the United States, the President of the National Government of the Republic of China, and the Prime Minister of Great Britain, representing the hundreds of millions of our countrymen, have conferred and agree that Japan shall be given an opportunity to end this war.

1. 吾等合衆国大統領、中華民国主席及「グレート、ブリテン」国総理大臣ハ吾等ノ数億ノ国民ヲ代表シ協議ノ上日本国ニ対シ今次ノ戦争ヲ終結スルノ機会ヲ与フルコトニ意見一致セリ

2. The prodigious land, sea and air forces of the United States, the British Empire and of China, many times reinforced by their armies and air fleets from the west, are poised to strike the final blows upon Japan. This military power is sustained and inspired by the determination of all the Allied Nations to prosecute the war against Japan until she ceases to resist.

2. 合衆国、英帝国及中華民国ノ巨大ナル陸、海、空軍ハ西方ヨリ自国ノ陸軍及空軍ニ依ル数倍ノ増強ヲ受ケ日本国ニ対シ最後ノ打撃ヲ加フルノ態勢ヲ整ヘタリ右軍事力ハ日本国ガ抵抗ヲ終止スルニ至ル迄同国ニ対シ戦争ヲ遂行スルノ一切ノ連合国ノ決意ニ依リ支持セラレ且鼓舞セラレ居ルモノナリ

3. The result of the futile and senseless German resistance to the might of the aroused free peoples of the world stands forth in awful clarity as an example to the people of Japan. The might that now converges on Japan is immeasurably greater than that which, when applied to the resisting Nazis, necessarily laid waste to the lands, the industry and the method of life of the whole German people. The full application of our military power, backed by our resolve, will mean the inevitable and complete destruction of the Japanese armed forces and just as inevitably the utter devastation of the Japanese homeland.

3. 蹶起セル世界ノ自由ナル人民ノ力ニ対スル「ドイツ」国ノ無益且無意義ナル抵抗ノ結果ハ日本国国民ニ対スル先例ヲ極メテ明白ニ示スモノナリ現在日本国ニ対シ集結シツツアルカハ抵抗スル「ナチス」ニ対シ適用セラレタル場合ニ於テ全「ドイツ」国人民ノ土地、産業及生活様式ヲ必然的ニ荒廃ニ帰セシメタルカニ比シ測リ知レザル程更ニ強大ナルモノナリ吾等ノ決意ニ支持セラルル吾等ノ軍事力ノ最高度ノ使用ハ日本国軍隊ノ不可避且完全ナル壊滅ヲ意味スベク又同様必然的ニ日本国本土ノ完全ナル破壊ヲ意味スベシ

4. The time has come for Japan to decide whether she will continue to be controlled by those self-willed militaristic advisers whose unintelligent calculations have brought the Empire of Japan to the threshold of

4. 無分別ナル打算ニ依リ日本帝国ヲ滅亡ノ淵ニ陥レタル我儘ナル軍国主義的助言者ニ依リ日本国ガ引続キ統御セラルベキカ又ハ理性ノ経路ヲ日本国履ムベキカヲ日本国ガ決定スベキ時期ハ到来セリ

annihilation, or whether she will follow the path of reason.

5. Following are our terms. We will not deviate from them. There are no alternatives. We shall brook no delay.

6. There must be eliminated for all time the authority and influence of those who have deceived and misled the people of Japan into embarking on world conquest, for we insist that a new order of peace, security and justice will be impossible until irresponsible militarism is driven from the world.

7. Until such a new order is established and until there is convincing proof that Japan's war-making power is destroyed, points in Japanese territory to be designated by the Allies shall be occupied to secure the achievement of the basic objectives we are here setting forth.

8. The terms of the Cairo Declaration shall be carried out and Japanese sovereignty shall be limited to the islands of Honshu, Hokkaido, Kyushu, Shikoku and such minor islands as we determine.

9. The Japanese military forces, after being completely disarmed, shall be permitted to return to their homes with the opportunity to lead peaceful and productive lives.

10. We do not intend that the Japanese shall be enslaved as a race or destroyed as a nation, but stern justice shall be meted out to all war criminals, including those who have visited cruelties upon our prisoners. The Japanese Government shall remove all obstacles to the revival and strengthening of democratic tendencies among the Japanese people. Freedom of speech, of religion, and of thought, as well as respect for the fundamental human rights shall be established.

11. Japan shall be permitted to maintain such industries as will sustain her economy

5.　吾等ノ条件ハ左ノ如シ
吾等ハ右条件ヨリ離脱スルコトハナカルベシ右ニ代ル条件存在セズ吾等ハ遅延ヲ認ムルヲ得ズ

6.　吾等ハ無責任ナル軍国主義ガ世界ヨリ駆逐セラルルニ至ル迄ハ平和、安全及正義ノ新秩序ガ生ジ得ザルコトヲ主張スルモノナルヲ以テ日本国国民ヲ欺瞞シ之ヲシテ世界征服ノ挙ニ出ヅルノ過誤ヲ犯サシメタル者ノ権力及勢力ハ永久ニ除去セラレザルベカラズ

7.　右ノ如キ新秩序ガ建設セラレ且日本国ノ戦争遂行能力ガ破砕セラレタルコトノ確証アルニ至ル迄ハ連合国ノ指定スベキ日本国域内ノ諸地点ハ吾等ノ茲ニ指示スル基本的目的ノ達成ヲ確保スル為占領セラルベシ

8.　「カイロ」宣言ノ条項ハ履行セラルベク又日本国ノ主権ハ本州、北海道、九州及四国並ニ吾等ノ決定スル諸小島ニ局限セラルベシ

9.　日本国軍隊ハ完全ニ武装ヲ解除セラレタル後各自ノ家庭ニ復帰シ平和的且生産的ノ生活ヲ営ムノ機会ヲ得シメラルベシ

10.　吾等ハ日本人ヲ民族トシテ奴隷化セントシ又ハ国民トシテ滅亡セシメントスルノ意図ヲ有スルモノニ非ザルモ吾等ノ俘虜ヲ虐待セル者ヲ含ム一切ノ戦争犯罪人ニ対シテハ厳重ナル処罰加ヘラルベシ日本国政府ハ日本国国民ノ間ニ於ケル民主主義的傾向ノ復活強化ニ対スル一切ノ障礙ヲ除去スベシ言論、宗教及思想ノ自由並ニ基本的人権ノ尊重ハ確立セラルベシ

11.　日本国ハ其ノ経済ヲ支持シ且公正ナル実物賠償ノ取立ヲ可能ナラシムルガ如キ産業ヲ維持

and permit the exaction of just reparations in kind, but not those industries which would enable her to re-arm for war. To this end, access to, as distinguished from control of, raw materials shall be permitted. Eventual Japanese participation in world trade relations shall be permitted.

12. The occupying forces of the Allies shall be withdrawn from Japan as soon as these objectives have been accomplished and there has been established in accordance with the freely expressed will of the Japanese people a peacefully inclined and responsible government.

13. We call upon the government of Japan to proclaim now the unconditional surrender of all Japanese armed forces, and to provide proper and adequate assurances of their good faith in such action. The alternative for Japan is prompt and utter destruction.

スルコトヲ許サルベシ但シ日本国ヲシテ戦争ノ為再軍備ヲ為スコトヲ得シムルガ如キ産業ハ此ノ限ニ在ラズ右目的ノ為原料ノ入手(其ノ支配トハ之ヲ区別ス)ヲ許サルベシ日本国ハ将来世界貿易関係ヘノ参加ヲ許サルベシ

12. 前記諸目的ガ達成セラレ且日本国国民ノ自由ニ表明セル意思ニ従ヒ平和的傾向ヲ有シ且責任アル政府ガ樹立セラルルニ於テハ連合国ノ占領軍ハ直ニ日本国ヨリ撤収セラルベシ

13. 吾等ハ日本国政府ガ直ニ全日本国軍隊ノ無条件降伏ヲ宣言シ且右行動ニ於ケル同政府ノ誠意ニ付適当且充分ナル保障ヲ提供センコトヲ同政府ニ対シ要求ス右以外ノ日本国ノ選択ハ迅速且完全ナル壊滅アルノミトス

| **San Francisco Peace Treaty** | Signed 8 September 1951 Implemented 28 April 1952 |

| **サンフランシスコ 平和条約** | 調印：1951年9月8日 発効：1952年4月28日 |

Treaty of Peace with Japan

Whereas the Allied Powers and Japan are resolved that henceforth their relations shall be those of nations which, as sovereign equals, cooperate in friendly association to promote their common welfare and to maintain international peace and security, and are therefore desirous of concluding a Treaty of Peace which will settle questions still outstanding as a result of the existence of a state of war between them;

Whereas Japan for its part declares its intention to apply for membership in the United Nations and in all circumstances to conform to the principles of the Charter of the United Nations; to strive to realize the

日本国との平和条約

連合国及び日本国は、両者の関係が、今後、共通の福祉を増進し且つ国際の平和及び安全を維持するために主権を有する対等のものとして友好的な連携の下に協力する国家の間の関係でなければならないことを決意し、よって、両者の間の戦争状態の存在の結果として今なお未決である問題を解決する平和条約を締結することを希望するので、

日本国としては、国際連合への加盟を申請し且つあらゆる場合に国際連合憲章の原則を遵守し、世界人権宣言の目的を実現するために努力し、国際連合憲章第55条及び第56条に定められ且つ既に降伏後の日本国の法制によって作られ

objectives of the Universal Declaration of Human Rights; to seek to create within Japan conditions of stability and well-being as defined in Articles 55 and 56 of the Charter of the United Nations and already initiated by post-surrender Japanese legislation; and in public and private trade and commerce to conform to internationally accepted fair practices;

Whereas the Allied Powers welcome the intentions of Japan set out in the foregoing paragraph;

The Allied Powers and Japan have therefore determined to conclude the present Treaty of Peace, and have accordingly appointed the undersigned Plenipotentiaries, who, after presentation of their full powers, found in good and due form, have agreed on the following provisions;

Chapter I. Peace
Article 1.
(a)   The state of war between Japan and each of the Allied Powers is terminated as from the date on which the present Treaty comes into force between Japan and the Allied Power concerned as provided for in Article 23.

(b)   The Allied Powers recognize the full sovereignty of the Japanese people over Japan and its territorial waters.

Chapter II. Territory
Article 2.
(a)   Japan, recognizing the independence of Korea, renounces all right, title and claim to Korea, including the islands of Quelpart, Port Hamilton and Dagelet.

(b)   Japan renounces all right, title and claim to Formosa and the Pescadores.

(c)   Japan renounces all right, title and claim

はじめた安定及び福祉の条件を日本国内に創造するために努力し、並びに公私の貿易及び通商において国際的に承認された公正な慣行に従う意思を宣言するので、

連合国は、前項に掲げた日本国の意思を歓迎するので、

よって連合国及び日本国は、この平和条約を締結することに決定し、これに応じて下名の全権委員を任命した。これらの全権委員は、その全権委任状を示し、それが良好妥当であると認められた後、次の規定を協定した。

第1章　平和
第1条
(a)　日本国と各連合国との間の戦争状態は、第23条の定めるところによりこの条約が日本国と当該連合国との間に効力を生ずる日に終了する。

(b)　連合国は、日本国及びその領水に対する日本国民の完全な主権を承認する。

第2章　領域
第2条
(a)　日本国は、朝鮮の独立を承認して、済州島、巨文島及び鬱陵島を含む朝鮮に対するすべての権利、権原及び請求権を放棄する。

(b)　日本国は、台湾及び澎湖諸島に対するすべての権利、権原及び請求権を放棄する。

(c)　日本国は、千島列島並びに日本国が1905年

to the Kurile Islands, and to that portion of Sakhalin and the islands adjacent to it over which Japan acquired sovereignty as a consequence of the Treaty of Portsmouth of September 5, 1905.

(d) Japan renounces all right, title and claim in connection with the League of Nations Mandate System, and accepts the action of the United Nations Security Council of April 2, 1947, extending the trusteeship system to the Pacific Islands formerly under mandate to Japan.

(e) Japan renounces all claim to any right or title to or interest in connection with any part of the Antarctic area, whether deriving from the activities of Japanese nationals or otherwise.

(f) Japan renounces all right, title and claim to the Spratly Islands and to the Paracel Islands.

Article 3.

Japan will concur in any proposal of the United States to the United Nations to place under its trusteeship system, with the United States as the sole administering authority, Nansei Shoto south of 29° north latitude (including the Ryukyu Islands and the Daito Islands), Nanpo Shoto south of Sofu Gan (including the Bonin Islands, Rosario Island and the Volcano Islands) and Parece Vela and Marcus Island. Pending the making of such a proposal and affirmative action thereon, the United States will have the right to exercise all and any powers of administration, legislation and jurisdiction over the territory and inhabitants of these islands, including their territorial waters.

Article 4.

(a) Subject to the provisions of paragraph

9月5日のポーツマス条約の結果として主権を獲得した樺太の一部及びこれに近接する諸島に対するすべての権利、権原及び請求権を放棄する。

(d) 日本国は、国際連盟の委任統治制度に関連するすべての権利、権原及び請求権を放棄し、且つ、以前に日本国の委任統治の下にあった太平洋の諸島に信託統治制度を及ぼす1947年4月2日の国際連合安全保障理事会の行動を受諾する。

(e) 日本国は、日本国民の活動に由来するか又は他に由来するかを問わず、南極地域のいずれの部分に対する権利若しくは権原又はいずれの部分に関する利益についても、すべての請求権を放棄する。

(f) 日本国は、新南群島及び西沙群島に対するすべての権利、権原及び請求権を放棄する。

第3条

日本国は、北緯29度以南の南西諸島(琉球諸島及び大東諸島を含む。)、孀婦岩の南の南方諸島(小笠原群島、西之島及び火山列島を含む。)並びに沖の鳥島及び南鳥島を合衆国を唯一の施政権者とする信託統治制度の下におくこととする国際連合に対する合衆国のいかなる提案にも同意する。このような提案が行われ且つ可決されるまで、合衆国は、領水を含むこれらの諸島の領域及び住民に対して、行政、立法及び司法上の権力の全部及び一部を行使する権利を有するものとする。

第4条

(a) この条の(b)の規定を留保して、日本国及

(b) of this Article, the disposition of property of Japan and of its nationals in the areas referred to in Article 2, and their claims, including debts, against the authorities presently administering such areas and the residents (including juridical persons) thereof, and the disposition in Japan of property of such authorities and residents, and of claims, including debts, of such authorities and residents against Japan and its nationals, shall be the subject of special arrangements between Japan and such authorities. The property of any of the Allied Powers or its nationals in the areas referred to in Article 2 shall, insofar as this has not already been done, be returned by the administering authority in the condition in which it now exists, (The term nationals whenever used in the present Treaty includes juridical persons.)

(b)   Japan recognizes the validity of dispositions of property of Japan and Japanese nationals made by or pursuant to directives of the United States Military Government in any of the areas referred to in Articles 2 and 3.

(c)   Japanese owned submarine cables connecting Japan with territory removed from Japanese control pursuant to the present Treaty shall be equally divided, Japan retaining the Japanese terminal and adjoining half of the cable, and the detached territory the remainder of the cable and connecting terminal facilities.

Chapter III. Security

Article 5.

(a)   Japan accepts the obligations set forth in Article 2 of the Charter of the United Nations, and in particular the obligations.

 (i)   to settle its international disputes by peaceful means is such a manner that

びその国民の財産で第2条に掲げる地域にあるもの並びに日本国及びその国民の請求権(債権を含む。)で現にこれらの地域の施政を行っている当局及びそこの住民(法人を含む。)に対するものの処理並びに日本国におけるこれらの当局及び住民の財産並びに日本国及びその国民に対するこれらの当局及び住民の請求権(債権を含む。)の処理は、日本国とこれらの当局との間の特別取極の主題とする。第2条に掲げる地域にある連合国又はその国民の財産は、まだ返還されていない限り、施政を行っている当局が現状で返還しなければならない。(国民という語は、この条約で用いるときはいつでも、法人を含む。)

(b)   日本国は、第2条及び第3条に掲げる地域のいずれかにある合衆国軍政府により、又はその指令に従って行われた日本国及びその国民の財産の処理の効力を承認する。

(c)   日本国とこの条約に従って日本国の支配から除かれる領域とを結ぶ日本所有の海底電線は、二等分され、日本国は、日本の終点施設及びこれに連なる電線の半分を保有し、分離される領域は、残りの電線及びその終点施設を保有する。

第3章　安全

第5条

(a)   日本国は、国際連合憲章第2条に掲げる義務、特に次の義務を受諾する。

 (i)   その国際紛争を、平和的手段によって国際の平和及び安全並びに正義を危うくしないよう

international peace and security, and justice, are not endangered;

(ii) to refrain in its international relations from the threat or use of force against the territorial integrity or political independence of any State or in any other manner inconsistent with the Purposes of the United Nations;

(iii) to give the United Nations every assistance in any action it takes in accordance with the Charter and to refrain from giving assistance to any State against which the United Nations may take preventive or enforcement action.

(b) The Allied Powers confirm that they will be guided by the principles of Article 2 of the Charter of the United Nations in their relations with Japan.

(c) The Allied Powers for their part recognize that Japan as a sovereign nation possesses the inherent right of individual or collective self-defense referred to in Article 51 of the Charter of the United Nations and that Japan may voluntarily enter into collective security arrangements.

に解決すること。

(ii) その国際関係において、武力による威嚇又は武力の行使は、いかなる国の領土保全又は政治的独立に対するものも、また、国際連合の目的と両立しない他のいかなる方法によるものも慎むこと。

(iii) 国際連合が憲章に従ってとるいかなる行動についても国際連合にあらゆる援助を与え、且つ、国際連合が防止行動又は強制行動をとるいかなる国に対しても援助の供与を慎むこと。

(b) 連合国は、日本国との関係において国際連合憲章第2条の原則を指針とすべきことを確認する。

(c) 連合国としては、日本国が主権国として国際連合憲章第51条に掲げる個別的又は集団的自衛の固有の権利を有すること及び日本国が集団的安全保障取極を自発的に締結することができることを承認する。

Article 6.

(a) All occupation forces of the Allied Powers shall be withdrawn from Japan as soon as possible after the coming into force of the present Treaty, and in any case not later than 90 days thereafter. Nothing in this provision shall, however, prevent the stationing or retention of foreign armed forces in Japanese territory under or in consequence of any bilateral or multilateral agreements which have been or may be made between one or more of the Allied Powers, on the one hand, and Japan on the other.

(b) The provisions of Article 9 of the Potsdam Proclamation of July 26, 1945,

第6条

(a) 連合国のすべての占領軍は、この条約の効力発生の後なるべくすみやかに、且つ、いかなる場合にもその後90日以内に、日本国から撤退しなければならない。但し、この規定は、1又は2以上の連合国を一方とし、日本国を他方として双方の間に締結された若しくは締結される二国間若しくは多数国間の協定に基く、又はその結果としての外国軍隊の日本国の領域における駐とん又は駐留を妨げるものではない。

(b) 日本国軍隊の各自の家庭への復帰に関する1945年7月26日のポツダム宣言の第9項の規定は、

dealing with the return of Japanese military forces to their homes, to the extent not already completed, will be carried out.

(c)   All Japanese property for which compensation has not already been paid, which was supplied for the use of the occupation forces and which remains in the possession of those forces at the time of the coming into force of the present Treaty, shall be returned to the Japanese Government within the same 90 days unless other arrangements are made by mutual agreement.

Chapter IV. Political and Economic Clauses
Article 7.

(a)   Each of the Allied Powers, within one year after the present Treaty has come into force between it and Japan, will notify Japan which of its prewar bilateral treaties or conventions with Japan it wishes to continue in force or revive, and any treaties or conventions so notified shall continue in force or be revived subject only to such amendments as may be necessary to ensure conformity with the present Treaty. The treaties and conventions so notified shall be considered as having been continued in force or revived three months after the date of notification and shall be registered with the Secretariat of the United Nations. All such treaties and conventions as to which Japan is not so notified shall be regarded as abrogated.

(b)   Any notification made under paragraph (a) of this Article may except from the operation or revival of a treaty or convention any territory for the international relations of which the notifying Power is responsible, until three months after the date on which notice is given to Japan that such exception shall cease to apply.

まだその実施が完了されていない限り、実行されるものとする。

(c)   まだ代貨が支払われていないすべての日本財産で、占領軍の使用に供され、且つ、この条約の効力発生の時に占領軍が占有しているものは、相互の合意によって別段の取極が行われない限り、前記の90日以内に日本国政府に返還しなければならない。

第4章   政治及び経済条項
第7条

(a)   各連合国は、自国と日本国との間にこの条約が効力を生じた後1年以内に、日本国との戦前のいずれの二国間の条約又は協約を引き続いて有効とし又は復活させることを希望するかを日本国に通告するものとする。こうして通告された条約又は協約は、この条約に適合することを確保するための必要な修正を受けるだけで、引き続いて有効とされ、又は復活される。こうして通告された条約及び協約は、通告の日の後3箇月で、引き続いて有効なものとみなされ、又は復活され、且つ、国際連合事務局に登録されなければならない。日本国にこうして通告されないすべての条約及び協約は、廃棄されたものとみなす。

(b)   この条の(a)に基いて行う通告においては、条約又は協約の実施又は復活に関し、国際関係について通告国が責任をもつ地域を除外することができる。この除外は、除外の適用を終止することが日本国に通告される日の3箇月後まで行われるものとする。

Article 8.

(a)   Japan will recognize the full force of all treaties now or hereafter concluded by the Allied Powers for terminating the state of war initiated on September 1, 1939, as well as any other arrangements by the Allied Powers for or in connection with the restoration of peace. Japan also accepts the arrangements made for terminating the former League of Nations and Permanent Court of International Justice.

(b)   Japan renounces all such rights and interests as it may derive from being a signatory power of the Conventions of St. Germain-en-Laye of September 10, 1919, and the Straits Agreement of Montreux of July 20, 1936, and from Article 16 of the Treaty of Peace with Turkey signed at Lausanne on July 24, 1923.

(c)   Japan renounces all rights, title and interests acquired under, and is discharged from all obligations resulting from, the Agreement between Germany and the Creditor Powers of January 20, 1930, and its Annexes, including the Trust Agreement, dated May 17, 1930; the Convention of January 20, 1930, respecting the Bank for International Settlements; and the Statutes of the Bank for International Settlements. Japan will notify to the Ministry of Foreign Affairs in Paris within six months of the first coming into force of the present Treaty its renunciation of the rights, title and interests referred to in this paragraph.

Article 9.

Japan will enter promptly into negotiations with the Allied Powers so desiring for the conclusion of bilateral and multilateral agreements providing for the regulation or limitation of fishing and the conservation and development of fisheries on the high seas.

第8条

(a)   日本国は、連合国が1939年9月1日に開始された戦争状態を終了するために現に締結し又は今後締結するすべての条約及び連合国が平和の回復のため又はこれに関連して行う他の取極の完全な効力を承認する。日本国は、また、従前の国際連盟及び常設国際司法裁判所を終止するために行われた取極を受諾する。

(b)   日本国は1919年9月10日のサン・ジェルマン＝アン＝レイの諸条約及び1936年7月20日のモントルーの海峡条約の署名国であることに由来し、並びに1923年7月24日にローザンヌで署名されたトルコとの平和条約の第16条に由来するすべての権利及び利益を放棄する。

(c)   日本国は、1930年1月20日のドイツと債権国との間の協定及び1930年5月17日の信託協定を含むその附属書並びに1930年1月20日の国際決済銀行に関する条約及び国際決済銀行の定款に基いて得たすべての権利、権原及び利益を放棄し、且つ、それらから生ずるすべての義務を免かれる。日本国は、この条約の最初の効力発生の後6箇月以内に、この項に掲げる権利、権原及び利益の放棄をパリの外務省に通告するものとする。

第9条

日本国は、公海における漁猟の規制又は制限並びに漁業の保存及び発展を規定する二国間及び多数国間の協定を締結するために、希望する連合国とすみやかに交渉を開始するものとする。

Article 10.

Japan renounces all special rights and interests in China, including all benefits and privileges resulting from the provisions of final Protocol signed at Peking on September 7, 1901, and all annexes, notes and documents supplementary thereto, and agrees to the abrogation in respect to Japan of the said protocol, annexes, notes and documents.

Article 11.

Japan accepts the judgments of the International Military Tribunal for the Far East and other Allied War Crimes Courts both within and outside Japan, and will carry out the sentences imposed thereby upon Japanese nationals imprisoned in Japan. The power to grant clemency, to reduce sentences and to parole with respect to such prisoners may not be exercised except on the decision of the Government or Governments which imposed the sentence in each instance, and on the recommendation of Japan. In the case of persons sentenced by the International Military Tribunal for the Far East, such power may not be exercised except on the decision of a majority of the Governments represented on the Tribunal, and on the recommendation of Japan.

Article 12.

(a)　Japan declares its readiness promptly to enter into negotiations for the conclusion with each of the Allied Powers of treaties or agreements to place their trading, maritime and other commercial relations on a stable and friendly basis.

(b)　Pending the conclusion of the relevant treaty or agreement, Japan will, during a period of four years from the first coming into force of the present Treaty.

第10条

日本国は、1901年9月7日に北京で署名された最終議定書並びにこれを補足するすべての附属書、書簡及び文書の規定から生ずるすべての利得及び特権を含む中国におけるすべての特殊の権利及び利益を放棄し、且つ、前記の議定書、附属書、書簡及び文書を日本国に関して廃棄することに同意する。

第11条

日本国は、極東国際軍事裁判所並びに日本国内及び国外の他の連合国戦争犯罪法廷の裁判を受諾し、且つ、日本国で拘禁されている日本国民にこれらの法廷が課した刑を執行するものとする。これらの拘禁されている者を赦免し、減刑し、及び仮出獄させる権限は、各事件について刑を課した1又は2以上の政府の決定及び日本国の勧告に基く場合の外、行使することができない。極東国際軍事裁判所が刑を宣告した者については、この権限は、裁判所に代表者を出した政府の過半数の決定及び日本国の勧告に基く場合の外、行使することができない。

第12条

(a)　日本国は、各連合国と、貿易、海運その他の通商の関係を安定した且つ友好的な基礎の上におくために、条約又は協定を締結するための交渉をすみやかに開始する用意があることを宣言する。

(b)　該当する条約又は協定が締結されるまで、日本国は、この条約の最初の効力発生の後4年間、

1. accord to each of the Allied Powers, its nationals, products and vessels

(i) most-favored-nation treatment with respect to customs duties, charges, restrictions and other regulations on or in connection with the importation and exportation of goods;

(ii) national treatment with respect to shipping, navigation and imported goods, and with respect to natural and juridical persons and their interests-such treatment to include all matters pertaining to the levying and collection of taxes, access to the courts, the making and performance of contracts, rights to property (tangible and intangible), participation in juridical entities constituted under Japanese law, and generally the conduct of all kinds of business and professional activities;

2. ensure that external purchases and sales of Japanese state trading enterprises shall be based solely on commercial considerations.

(c) In respect to any matter, however, Japan shall be obliged to accord to an Allied Power national treatment, or most-favored-nation treatment, only to the extent that the Allied Power concerned accords Japan national treatment or most-favored nation treatment, as the case may be, in respect of the same matter. The reciprocity envisaged in the foregoing sentence shall be determined, in the case of products, vessels and juridical entities of, and persons domiciled in, any non-metropolitan territory of an Allied Power, and in the case of juridical entities of, and persons domiciled in, any state or province of an Allied Power having a federal government, by reference to the treatment accorded to Japan in such territory, state or province.

1. 各連合国並びにその国民、産品及び船舶に次の待遇を与える。

(i) 貨物の輸出入に対する、又はこれに関連する関税、課金、制限その他の規制に関する最恵国待遇

(ii) 海運、航海及び輸入貨物に関する内国民待遇並びに自然人、法人及びその利益に関する内国民待遇。この待遇は、税金の賦課及び徴収、裁判を受けること、契約の締結及び履行、財産権(有体財産及び無体財産に関するもの)、日本国の法律に基いて組織された法人への参加並びに一般にあらゆる種類の事業活動及び職業活動の遂行に関するすべての事項を含むものとする。

2. 日本国の国営商企業の国外における売買が商業的考慮にのみ基くことを確保する。

(c) もっとも、いずれの事項に関しても、日本国は、連合国が当該事項についてそれぞれ内国民待遇又は最恵国待遇を日本国に与える限度においてのみ、当該連合国に内国民待遇又は最恵国待遇を与える義務を負うものとする。前段に定める相互主義は、連合国の非本土地域の産品、船舶、法人及びそこに住所を有する人の場合並びに連邦政府をもつ連合国の邦又は州の法人及びそこに住所を有する人の場合には、その地域、邦又は州において日本国に与えられる待遇に照らして決定される。

(d)   In the application of this Article, a discriminatory measure shall not be considered to derogate from the grant of national or most-favored-nation treatment, as the case may be, if such measure is based on an exception customarily provided for in the commercial treaties of the party applying it, or on the need to safeguard that party's external financial position or balance of payments (except in respect to shipping and navigation), or on the need to maintain its essential security interests, and provided such measure is proportionate to the circumstances and not applied in an arbitrary or unreasonable manner.

(e)   Japan's obligations under this Article shall not be affected by the exercise of any Allied rights under Article 14 of the present Treaty; nor shall the provisions of this Article be understood as limiting the undertakings assumed by Japan by virtue of Article 15 of the Treaty.

(d)   この条の適用上、差別的措置であって、それを適用する当事国の通商条約に通常規定されている例外に基くもの、その当事国の対外的財政状態若しくは国際収支を保護する必要に基くもの(海運及び航海に関するものを除く。)又は重大な安全上の利益を維持する必要に基くものは、事態に相応しており、且つ、ほしいままな又は不合理な方法で適用されない限り、それぞれ内国民待遇又は最恵国待遇の許与を害するものと認めてはならない。

(e)   この条に基く日本国の義務は、この条約の第14条に基く連合国の権利の行使によって影響されるものではない。また、この条の規定は、この条約の第15条によって日本国が引き受ける約束を制限するものと了解してはならない。

Article 13.

(a)   Japan will enter into negotiations with any of the Allied Powers, promptly upon the request of such Power or Powers, for the conclusion of bilateral or multilateral agreements relating to international civil air transport.

(b)   Pending the conclusion of such agreement or agreements, Japan will, during a period of four years from the first coming into force of the present Treaty, extend to such Power treatment not less favorable with respect to air-traffic rights and privileges than those exercised by any such Powers at the date of such coming into force, and will accord complete equality of opportunity in respect to the operation and development of air services.

第13条

(a)   日本国は、国際民間航空運送に関する二国間又は多数国間の協定を締結するため、1又は2以上の連合国の要請があったときはすみやかに、当該連合国と交渉を開始するものとする。

(b)   1又は2以上の前記の協定が締結されるまで、日本国は、この条約の最初の効力発生の時から4年間、この効力発生の日にいずれかの連合国が行使しているところよりも不利でない航空交通の権利及び特権に関する待遇を当該連合国に与え、且つ、航空業務の運営及び発達に関する完全な機会均等を与えるものとする。

(c) Pending its becoming a party to the Convention on International Civil Aviation in accordance with Article 93 thereof, Japan will give effect to the provisions of that Convention applicable to the international navigation of aircraft, and will give effect to the standards, practices and procedures adopted as annexes to the Convention in accordance with the terms of the Convention.

Chapter V. Claims and Property
Article 14.

(a) It is recognized that Japan should pay reparations to the Allied Powers for the damage and suffering caused by it during the war. Nevertheless it is also recognized that the resources of Japan are not presently sufficient, if it is to maintain a viable economy, to make complete reparation for all such damage and suffering and at the same time meet its other obligations.

Therefore,

1. Japan will promptly enter into negotiations with Allied Powers so desiring, whose present territories were occupied by Japanese forces and damaged by Japan, with a view to assisting to compensate those countries for the cost of repairing the damage done, by making available the services of the Japanese people in production, salvaging and other work for the Allied Powers in question. Such arrangements shall avoid the imposition of additional liabilities on other Allied Powers, and, where the manufacturing of raw materials is called for, they shall be supplied by the Allied Powers in question, so as not to throw any foreign exchange burden upon Japan.

2.(I) Subject to the provisions of sub-paragraph (II) below, each of the Allied Powers shall have the right to seize, retain,

(c) 日本国は、国際民間航空条約第93条に従って同条約の当事国となるまで、航空機の国際航空に適用すべきこの条約の規定を実施し、且つ、同条約の条項に従って同条約の附属書として採択された標準、方式及び手続きを実施するものとする。

第5章 請求権及び財産
第14条

(a) 日本国は、戦争中に生じさせた損害及び苦痛に対して、連合国に賠償を支払うべきことが承認される。しかし、また、存立可能な経済を維持すべきものとすれば、日本国の資源は、日本国がすべての前記の損害及び苦痛に対して完全な賠償を行い且つ同時に他の債務を履行するためには現在充分でないことが承認される。

よって

1. 日本国は、現在の領域が日本国軍隊によって占領され、且つ、日本国によって損害を与えられた連合国が希望するときは、生産、沈船引揚げその他の作業における日本人の役務を当該連合国の利用に供することによって、与えた損害を修復する費用をこれらの国に補償することに資するために、当該連合国とすみやかに交渉を開始するものとする。その取極は、他の連合国に追加負担を課することを避けなければならない。また、原材料からの製造が必要とされる場合には、外国為替上の負担を日本国に課さないために、原材料は、当該連合国が供給しなければならない。

2.(I) 次の(II)の規定を留保して、各連合国は、次に掲げるもののすべての財産、権利及び利益でこの条約の最初の効力発生の時にその管轄の

liquidate or otherwise dispose of all property, rights and interests of

(a) Japan and Japanese nationals,

(b) persons acting for or on behalf of Japan or Japanese nationals, and

(c) entities owned or controlled by Japan or Japanese nationals,

which on the first coming into force of the present Treaty were subject to its jurisdiction. The property, rights and interests specified in this sub-paragraph shall include those now blocked, vested or in the possession or under the control of enemy property authorities of Allied Powers, which belonged to, or were held or managed on behalf of, any of the persons or entities mentioned in (a), (b) or (c) above at the time such assets came under the controls of such authorities.

(II) The following shall be excepted from the right specified in sub-paragraph (I) above:

(i) property of Japanese natural persons who during the war resided with the permission of the Government concerned in the territory of one of the Allied Powers, other than territory occupied by Japan, except property subjected to restrictions during the war and not released from such restrictions as of the date of the first coming into force of the present Treaty;

(ii) all real property, furniture and fixtures owned by the Government of Japan and used for diplomatic or consular purposes, and all personal furniture and furnishings and other private property not of an investment nature which was normally necessary for the carrying out of diplomatic and consular functions, owned by Japanese diplomatic and consular personnel;

(iii) property belonging to religious bodies or private charitable institutions and used exclusively for religious or charitable purposes;

下にあるものを差し押え、留置し、清算し、その他何らかの方法で処分する権利を有する。

(a) 日本国及び日本国民

(b) 日本国又は日本国民の代理者又は代行者並びに

(c) 日本国又は日本国民が所有し、又は支配した団体

この(I)に明記する財産、権利及び利益は、現に、封鎖され、若しくは所属を変じており、又は連合国の敵産管理当局の占有若しくは管理に係るもので、これらの資産が当該当局の管理の下におかれた時に前記の(a)、(b)又は(c)に掲げるいずれかの人又は団体に属し、又はこれらのために保有され、若しくは管理されていたものを含む。

(II) 次のものは、前記の(I)に明記する権利から除く。

(i) 日本国が占領した領域以外の連合国の一国の領域に当該政府の許可を得て戦争中に居住した日本の自然人の財産。但し、戦争中に制限を課され、且つ、この条約の最初の効力発生の日にこの制限を解除されない財産を除く。

(ii) 日本国政府が所有し、且つ、外交目的又は領事目的に使用されたすべての不動産、家具及び備品並びに日本国の外交職員又は領事職員が所有したすべての個人の家具及び用具類その他の投資的性質をもたない私有財産で外交機能又は領事機能の遂行に通常必要であったもの。

(iii) 宗教団体又は私的慈善団体に属し、且つ、もっぱら宗教又は慈善の目的に使用した財産。

(iv) property, rights and interests which have come within its jurisdiction in consequence of the resumption of trade and financial relations subsequent to September 2, 1945, between the country concerned and Japan, except such as have resulted from transactions contrary to the laws of the Allied Power concerned;

(v) obligations of Japan or Japanese nationals, any right, title or interest in tangible property located in Japan, interests in enterprises organized under the laws of Japan, or any paper evidence thereof; provided that this exception shall only apply to obligations of Japan and its nationals expressed in Japanese currency.

(III) property referred to in exceptions (i) through (v) above shall be returned subject to reasonable expenses for its preservation and administration. If any such property has been liquidated the proceeds shall be returned instead.

(IV) The right to seize, retain, liquidate or otherwise dispose of property as provided in sub-paragraph (I) above shall be exercised in accordance with the laws of the Allied Power concerned, and the owner shall have only such rights as may be given him by those laws.

(V) The Allied Powers agree to deal with Japanese trademarks and literary and artistic property rights on a basis as favorable to Japan as circumstances ruling in each country will permit.

(b) Except as otherwise provided in the present Treaty, the Allied Powers waive all reparations claims of the Allied Powers, other claims of the Allied Powers and their nationals arising out of any actions taken by Japan and its nationals in the course of the prosecution of the war, and claims of the Allied Powers for direct military costs of occupation.

(iv)関係国と日本国との間における1945年9月2日後の貿易及び金融の関係の再開の結果として日本国の管轄内にはいった財産、権利及び利益。但し、当該連合国の法律に反する取引から生じたものを除く。

(v) 日本国若しくは日本国民の債務、日本国に所在する有体財産に関する権利、権原若しくは利益、日本国の法律に基いて組織された企業に関する利益又はこれらについての証書。但し、この例外は、日本国の通貨で表示された日本国及びその国民の債務にのみ適用する。

(III)前記の例外(i)から(v)までに掲げる財産は、その保存及び管理のために要した合理的な費用が支払われることを条件として、返還しなければならない。これらの財産が清算されているときは、代りに売得金を返還しなければならない。

(IV)前記の(I)に規定する日本財産を差し押さえ、留置し、清算し、その他何らかの方法で処分する権利は、当該連合国の法律に従って行使され、所有者は、これらの法律によって与えられる権利のみを有する。

(V) 連合国は日本の商標並びに文学的及び美術的著作権を各国の一般的事情が許す限り日本国に有利に取り扱うことに同意する。

(b) この条約に別段の定がある場合を除き、連合国は、連合国のすべての賠償請求権、戦争の遂行中に日本国及びその国民がとった行動から生じた連合国及びその国民の他の請求権並びに占領の直接軍事費に関する連合国の請求権を放棄する。

Article 15.

(a) Upon application made within nine months of the coming into force of the present Treaty between Japan and the Allied Power concerned, Japan will, within six months of the date of such application, return the property, tangible and intangible, and all rights or interests of any kind in Japan of each Allied Power and its nationals which was within Japan at any time between December 7, 1941, and September 2, 1945, unless the owner has freely disposed thereof without duress or fraud. Such property shall be returned free of all encumbrances and charges to which it may have become subject because of the war, and without any charges for its return. Property whose return is not applied for by or on behalf of the owner or by his Government within the prescribed period may be disposed of by the Japanese Government as it may determine. In cases where such property was within Japan on December 7, 1941, and cannot be returned or has suffered injury or damage as a result of the war, compensation will be made on terms not less favorable than the terms provided in the draft Allied Powers Property Compensation Law approved by the Japanese Cabinet on July 13, 1951.

(b) With respect to industrial property rights impaired during the war, Japan will continue to accord to the Allied Powers and their nationals benefits no less than those heretofore accorded by Cabinet Orders No. 309 effective September 1, 1949, No. 12 effective January 28, 1950, and No. 9 effective February 1, 1950, all as now amended, provided such nationals have applied for such benefits within the time limits prescribed therein.

(c)(i) Japan acknowledges that the literary

第15条

(a) この条約が日本国と当該連合国との間に効力を生じた後9箇月以内に申請があったときは、日本国は、申請の日から6箇月以内に、日本国にある各連合国及びその国民の有体財産及び無体財産並びに種類のいかんを問わずすべての権利又は利益で、1941年12月7日から1945年9月2日までの間のいずれかの時に日本国内にあったものを返還する。但し、所有者が強迫又は詐欺によることなく自由にこれらを処分した場合は、この限りでない。この財産は、戦争があったために課せられたすべての負担及び課金を免除して、その返還のための課金を課さずに返還しなければならない。所有者により若しくは所有者のために又は所有者の政府により所定の期間内に返還が申請されない財産は、日本国政府がその定めるところに従って処分することができる。この財産が1941年12月7日に日本国に所在し、且つ、返還することができず、又は戦争の結果として損傷若しくは損害を受けている場合には、日本国内閣が1951年7月13日に決定した連合国財産補償法案の定める条件よりも不利でない条件で補償される。

(b) 戦争中に侵害された工業所有権については、日本国は、1949年9月1日施行の政令第309号、1950年1月28日施行の政令第12号及び1950年2月1日施行の政令第9号(いずれも改正された現行のものとする。)によりこれまで与えられたところよりも不利でない利益を引き続いて連合国及びその国民に与えるものとする。但し、前記の国民がこれらの政令に定められた期限までにこの利益の許与を申請した場合に限る。

(c)(i) 日本国は、公にされ及び公にされなかった

and artistic property rights which existed in Japan on December 6, 1941, in respect to the published and unpublished works of the Allied Powers and their nationals have continued in force since that date, and recognizes those rights which have arisen, or but for the war would have arisen, in Japan since that date, by the operation of any conventions and agreements to which Japan was a party on that date, irrespective of whether or not such conventions or agreements were abrogated or suspended upon or since the outbreak of war by the domestic law of Japan or of the Allied Power concerned.

(ii) Without the need for application by the proprietor of the right and without the payment of any fee or compliance with any other formality, the period from December 7, 1941, until the coming into force of the present Treaty between Japan and the Allied Power concerned shall be excluded from the running of the normal term of such rights; and such period, with an additional period of six months, shall be excluded from the time within which a literary work must be translated into Japanese in order to obtain translating rights in Japan.

Article 16.

As an expression of its desire to indemnify those members of the armed forces of the Allied Powers who suffered undue hardships while prisoners of war of Japan, Japan will transfer its assets and those of its nationals in countries which were neutral during the war, or which were at war with any of the Allied Powers, or, at its option, the equivalent of such assets, to the International Committee of the Red Cross which shall liquidate such assets and

連合国及びその国民の著作物に関して1941年12月6日に日本国に存在した文学的及び美術的著作権がその日以後引き続いて効力を有することを認め、且つ、その日に日本国が当事者であった条約又は協定が戦争の発生の時又はその時以後日本国又は当該連合国の国内法によって廃棄され又は停止されたかどうかを問わず、これらの条約及び協定の実施によりその日以後日本国において生じ、又は戦争がなかったならば生ずるはずであった権利を承認する。

(ii) 権利者による申請を必要とすることなく、且つ、いかなる手数料の支払又は他のいかなる手段もすることなく、1941年12月7日から日本国と当該連合国との間にこの条約が効力を生ずるまでの期間は、これらの権利の通常期間から除算し、また、日本国において翻訳権を取得するために文学的著作物が日本語に翻訳されるべき期間からは、6箇月の期間を追加して除算しなければならない。

第16条

日本国の捕虜であった間に不当な苦難を被った連合国軍隊の構成員に償いをする願望の表現として、日本国は、戦争中中立であった国にある又は連合国のいずれかと戦争していた国にある日本国及びその国民の資産又は、日本国が選択するときは、これらの資産と等価のものを赤十字国際委員会に引き渡すものとし、同委員会は、これらの資産を清算し、且つ、その結果生ずる資金を、同委員会が衡平であると決定する基礎において、捕虜であった者及びその家族のために、適当な国内機関に対して分配しなけれ

distribute the resultant fund to appropriate national agencies, for the benefit of former prisoners of war and their families on such basis as it may determine to be equitable. The categories of assets described in Article 14 (a) 2 (II) (ii) through (v) of the present Treaty shall be excepted from transfer, as well as assets of Japanese natural persons not residents of Japan on the first coming into force of the Treaty. It is equally understood that the transfer provision of this Article has no application to the 19,770 shares in the Bank for International Settlements presently owned by Japanese financial institutions.

ばならない。この条約の第14条(a)2(II)の(ii)から(v)までに掲げる種類の資産は、条約の最初の効力発生の時に日本国に居住しない日本の自然人の資産とともに、引渡しから除外する。またこの条の引渡規定は、日本国の金融機関が現に所有する1万9770株の国際決済銀行の株式には適用がないものと了解する。

Article 17.

(a)   Upon the request of any of the Allied Powers, the Japanese Government shall review and revise in conformity with international law any decision or order of the Japanese Prize Courts in cases involving ownership rights of nationals of that Allied Power and shall supply copies of all documents comprising the records of these cases, including the decisions taken and orders issued. In any case in which such review or revision shows that restoration is due, the provisions of Article 15 shall apply to the property concerned.

(b)   The Japanese Government shall take the necessary measures to enable nationals of any of the Allied Powers at any time within one year from the coming into force of the present Treaty between Japan and the Allied Power concerned to submit to the appropriate Japanese authorities for review any judgment given by a Japanese court between December 7, 1941, and such coming into force, in any proceedings in which any such national was unable to make adequate presentation of his case either as plaintiff or defendant. The

第17条

(a)   いずれかの連合国の要請があったときは、日本国政府は、当該連合国の国民の所有権に関係のある事件に関する日本国の捕獲審検所の決定又は命令を国際法に従い再審査して修正し、且つ、行われた決定及び発せられた命令を含めて、これらの事件の記録を構成するすべての文書の写を提供しなければならない。この再審査又は修正の結果、返還すべきことが明らかになった場合には、第15条の規定を当該財産に適用する。

(b)   日本国政府は、いずれかの連合国の国民が原告又は被告として事件について充分な陳述ができなかった訴訟手続きにおいて、1941年12月7日から日本国と当該連合国との間にこの条約が効力を生ずるまでの期間に日本国の裁判所が行った裁判を、当該国民が前記の効力発生の後1年以内にいつでも適当な日本国の機関に再審査のため提出することができるようにするために、必要な措置をとらなければならない。日本国政府は、当該国民が前記の裁判の結果損害を受けた場合には、その者をその裁判が行われる前の地位に回復するようにし、又はその者にそれぞ

Japanese Government shall provide that, where the national has suffered injury by reason of any such judgment, he shall be restored in the position in which he was before the judgment was given or shall be afforded such relief as may be just and equitable in the circumstances.

れの事情の下において公正且つ衡平な救済が与えられるようにしなければならない。

Article 18.

(a) It is recognized that the intervention of the state of war has not affected the obligation to pay pecuniary debts arising out of obligations and contracts (including those in respect of bonds) which existed and rights which were acquired before the existence of a state of war, and which are due by the Government or nationals of Japan to the Government or nationals of one of the Allied Powers, or are due by the Government or nationals of one of the Allied Powers to the Government or nationals of Japan. The intervention of a state of war shall equally not be regarded as affecting the obligation to consider on their merits claims for loss or damage to property or for personal injury or death which arose before the existence of a state of war, and which may be presented or re-presented by the Government of one of the Allied Powers to the Government of Japan, or by the Government of Japan to any of the Governments of the Allied Powers. The provisions of this paragraph are without prejudice to the rights conferred by Article 14.

(b) Japan affirms its liability for the prewar external debt of the Japanese State and for debts of corporate bodies subsequently declared to be liabilities of the Japanese State, and expresses its intention to enter into negotiations at an early date with its creditors with respect to the resumption of payments on those debts; to encourage negotiations in

第18条

(a) 戦争状態の介在は、戦争状態の存在前に存在した債務及び契約(債権に関するものを含む。)並びに戦争状態の存在前に取得された権利から生ずる金銭債務で、日本国の政府若しくは国民が連合国の一国の政府若しくは国民に対して、又は連合国の一国の政府若しくは国民が日本国の政府若しくは国民に対して負っているものを支払う義務に影響を及ぼさなかったものと認める。戦争状態の介在は、また、戦争状態の存在前に財産の滅失若しくは損害又は身体障害若しくは死亡に関して生じた請求権で、連合国の一国の政府が日本国政府に対して、又は日本国政府が連合国政府のいずれかに対して提起し又は再提起するものの当否を審議する義務に影響を及ぼすものとみなしてはならない。この項の規定は、第14条によって与えられる権利を害するものではない。

(b) 日本国は、日本国の戦前の対外債務に関する責任と日本国が責任を負うと後に宣言された団体の債務に関する責任とを確認する。また、日本国は、これらの債務の支払再開に関して債権者とすみやかに交渉を開始し、他の戦前の請求権及び債務に関する交渉を促進し、且つ、これに応じて金額の支払を容易にする意図を表明する。

respect to other prewar claims and
obligations; and to facilitate the transfer of
sums accordingly.

Article 19.

(a)   Japan waives all claims of Japan and its
national against the Allied Powers and their
nationals arising out of the war or out of
actions taken because of the existence of a
state of war, and waives all claims arising
from the presence, operations or actions of
forces or authorities of any of the Allied
Powers in Japanese territory prior to the
coming into force of the present Treaty.

(b)   The foregoing waiver includes any
claims arising out of actions taken by any of
the Allied Powers with respect to Japanese
ships between September 1, 1939, and the
coming into force of the present Treaty, as
well as any claims and debts arising in
respect to Japanese prisoners of war and
civilian internees in the hands of the Allied
Powers, but does not include Japanese claims
specifically recognized in the laws of any
Allied Power enacted since September 2, 1945.

(c)   Subject to reciprocal renunciation, the
Japanese Government also renounces all
claims (including debts) against Germany
and German nationals on behalf of the
Japanese Government and Japanese
nationals, including intergovernmental
claims and claims for loss or damage
sustained during the war, but excepting (a)
claims in respect of contracts entered into and
rights acquired before September 1, 1939 and
(b) claims arising out of trade and financial
relations between Japan and Germany after
September 2, 1945. Such renunciation shall
not prejudice actions taken in accordance
with Articles 16 and 20 of the present Treaty.

(d)   Japan recognizes the validity of all acts

第19条

(a)   日本国は、戦争から生じ、又は戦争状態が
存在したためにとられた行動から生じた連合国
及びその国民に対する日本国及びその国民のす
べての請求権を放棄し、且つ、この条約の効力
発生の前に日本国領域におけるいずれかの連合
国の軍隊又は当局の存在、職務遂行又は行動か
ら生じたすべての請求権を放棄する。

(b)   前記の放棄には、1939年9月1日からこの条
約の効力発生までの間に日本国の船舶に関して
いずれかの連合国がとった行動から生じた請求
権並びに連合国の手中にある日本人捕虜及び被
抑留者に関して生じた請求権及び債権が含まれ
る。但し、1945年9月2日以後いずれかの連合国
が制定した法律で特に認められた日本人の請求
権を含まない。

(c)   相互放棄を条件として、日本国政府は、ま
た、政府間の請求権及び戦争中に受けた滅失又
は損害に関する請求権を含むドイツ及びドイツ
国民に対するすべての請求権(債権を含む。)を日
本国政府及び日本国民のために放棄する。但し、
(a)1939年9月1日前に締結された契約及び取得さ
れた権利に関する請求権並びに(b)1945年9月2日
後に日本国とドイツとの間の貿易及び金融の関
係から生じた請求権を除く。この放棄は、この
条約の第16条及び第20条に従ってとられる行動
を害するものではない。

(d)   日本国は、占領期間中に占領当局の指令に

and omissions done during the period of occupation under or in consequence of directives of the occupation authorities or authorized by Japanese law at that time, and will take no action subjecting Allied nationals to civil or criminal liability arising out of such acts or omissions.

基いて若しくはその結果として行われ、又は当時の日本国の法律によって許可されたすべての作為又は不作為の効力を承認し、連合国民をこの作為又は不作為から生ずる民事又は掲示の責任に問ういかなる行動もとらないものとする。

Article 20.

Japan will take all necessary measures to ensure such disposition of German assets in Japan as has been or may be determined by those powers entitled under the Protocol of the proceedings of the Berlin Conference of 1945 to dispose of those assets, and pending the final disposition of such assets will be responsible for the conservation and administration thereof.

第20条

日本国は、1945年のベルリン会議の議事の議定書に基いてドイツ財産を処分する権利を有する諸国が決定した又は決定する日本国にあるドイツ財産の処分を確実にするために、すべての必要な措置をとり、これらの財産の最終的処分が行われるまで、その保存及び管理について責任を負うものとする。

Article 21.

Notwithstanding the provisions of Article 25 of the present Treaty, China shall be entitled to the benefits of Articles 10 and 14 (a) 2; and Korea to the benefits of Articles 2, 4, 9 and 12 of the present Treaty.

第21条

この条約の第25条の規定にかかわらず、中国は、第10条及び第14条(a)2の利益を受ける権利を有し、朝鮮は、この条約の第2条、第4条、第9条及び第12条の利益を受ける権利を有する。

Chapter VI. Settlement of Disputes
Article 22.

If in the opinion of any Party to the present Treaty there has arisen a dispute concerning the interpretation or execution of the Treaty, which is not settled by reference to a special claims tribunal or by other agreed means, the dispute shall, at the request of any party thereto, be referred for decision to the International Court of Justice. Japan and those Allied Powers which are not already parties to the Statute of the International Court of Justice will deposit with the Registrar of the Court, at the time of their respective ratifications of the present Treaty,

第6章　紛争の解決
第22条

この条約のいずれかの当事国が特別請求裁判所への付託又は他の合意された方法で解決されない条約の解釈又は実施に関する紛争が生じたと認めるときは、紛争は、いずれかの紛争当事国の要請により、国際司法裁判所に決定のため付託しなければならない。日本国及びまだ国際司法裁判所規程の当事国でない連合国は、それぞれがこの条約を批准する時に、且つ、1946年10月15日の国際連合安全保障理事会の決議に従って、この条に掲げた性質をもつすべての紛争に関して一般的に同裁判所の管轄権を特別の合意なしに受諾する一般的宣言書を同裁判所書記に寄託するものとする。

and in conformity with the resolution of the United Nations Security Council, dated October 15, 1946, a general declaration accepting the jurisdiction, without special agreement, of the Court generally in respect to all disputes of the character referred to in this Article.

Chapter VII. Final Clauses
Article 23.

(a)   The present Treaty shall be ratified by the States which sign it, including Japan, and will come into force for all the States which have then ratified it, when instruments of ratification have been deposited by Japan and by a majority, including the United States of America as the principal occupying Power, of the following States, namely Australia, Canada, Ceylon, France, Indonesia, the Kingdom of the Netherlands, New Zealand, Pakistan, the Republic of the Philippines, the United Kingdom of Great Britain and Northern Ireland, and the United States of America. The present Treaty shall come into force for each State which subsequently ratifies it, on the date of the deposit of its instrument of ratification.

(b)   If the Treaty has not come into force within nine months after the date of the deposit of Japan's ratification, any State which has ratified it may bring the Treaty into force between itself and Japan by a notification to that effect given to the Governments of Japan and the United States of America not later than three years after the date of deposit of Japan's ratification.

Article 24.

All instruments of ratification shall be deposited with the Government of the United States of America which will notify all the

第7章　最終条項
第23条

(a)　この条約は、日本国を含めて、これに署名する国によって批准されなければならない。この条約は、批准書が日本国により、且つ、主たる占領国としてのアメリカ合衆国を含めて、次の諸国、すなわちオーストラリア、カナダ、セイロン、フランス、インドネシア、オランダ、ニュー・ジーランド、パキスタン、フィリピン、グレート・ブリテン及び北部アイルランド連合王国及びアメリカ合衆国の過半数により寄託された時に、その時に批准しているすべての国に関して効力を生ずる。この条約は、その後これを批准する各国に関しては、その批准書の寄託の日に効力を生ずる。

(b)　この条約が日本国の批准書の寄託の日の後9箇月以内に効力を生じなかったときは、これを批准した国は、日本国の批准書の寄託の日の後3年以内に日本国政府及びアメリカ合衆国政府にその旨を通告して、自国と日本国との間にこの条約の効力を生じさせることができる。

第24条

すべての批准書は、アメリカ合衆国政府に寄託しなければならない。同政府は、この寄託、第23条(a)に基くこの条約の効力発生の日及びこ

signatory States of each such deposit, of the date of the coming into force of the Treaty under paragraph (a) of Article 23, and of any notifications made under paragraph (b) of Article 23.

の条約の第23条(b)に基いて行われる通告をすべての署名国に通告する。

Article 25.

For the purposes of the present Treaty the Allied Powers shall be the States at war with Japan, or any State which previously formed a part of the territory of a State named in Article 23, provided that in each case the State concerned has signed and ratified the Treaty. Subject to the provisions of Article 21, the present Treaty shall not confer any rights, titles or benefits on any State which is not an Allied Power as herein defined; nor shall any right, title or interest of Japan be deemed to be diminished or prejudiced by any provision of the Treaty in favor of a State which is not an Allied Power as so defined.

第25条

この条約の適用上、連合国とは、日本国と戦争していた国又は以前に第23条に列記する国の領域の一部をなしていたものをいう。但し、各場合に当該国がこの条約に署名し且つこれを批准したことを条件とする。第21条の規定を留保して、この条約は、ここに定義された連合国の一国でないいずれの国に対しても、いかなる権利、権原又は利益も与えるものではない。また、日本国のいかなる権利、権原又は利益も、この条約のいかなる規定によっても前記のとおり定義された連合国の一国でない国のために減損され、又は害されるものとみなしてはならない。

Article 26.

Japan will be prepared to conclude with any State which signed or adhered to the United Nations Declaration of January 1, 1942, and which is at war with Japan, or with any State which previously formed a part of the territory of a State named in Article 23, which is not a signatory of the present Treaty, a bilateral Treaty of Peace on the same or substantially the same terms as are provided for in the present Treaty, but this obligation on the part of Japan will expire three years after the first coming into force of the present Treaty. Should Japan make a peace settlement or war claims settlement with any State granting that State greater advantages than those provided by the present Treaty, those same advantages shall be extended to the parties to the present Treaty.

第26条

日本国は、1942年1月1日の連合国宣言に署名し若しくは加入しており且つ日本国に対して戦争状態にある国又は以前に第23条に列記する国の領域の一部をなしていた国で、この条約の署名国でないものと、この条約に定めるところと同一の又は実質的に同一の条件で二国間の平和条約を締結する用意を有すべきものとする。但し、この日本国の義務は、この条約の最初の効力発生の後3年で満了する。日本国が、いずれかの国との間で、この条約で定めるところよりも大きな利益をその国に与える平和処理又は戦争請求権処理を行ったときは、これと同一の利益は、この条約の当事国にも及ぼさなければならない。

Article 27.

The present Treaty shall be deposited in the archives of the Government of the United States of America which shall furnish each signatory State with a certified copy thereof.

In faith whereof the undersigned Plenipotentiaries have signed the present Treaty.

Done at the city of San Francisco this eighth day of September 1951, in the English, French, and Spanish languages, all being equally authentic, and in the Japanese language.

United States-Japan Security Treaty	Signed 8 September 1951 Implemented 28 April 1952

Security Treaty between Japan and the United States of America

Japan has this day signed a Treaty of Peace with the Allied Powers. On the coming into force of that Treaty, Japan will not have the effective means to exercise its inherent right of self-defense because it has been disarmed.

There is danger to Japan in this situation because irresponsible militarism has not yet been driven from the world. Therefore Japan desires a Security Treaty with the United States of America to come into force simultaneously with the Treaty of Peace between Japan and the United States of America.

The Treaty of Peace recognizes that Japan as a sovereign nation has the right to enter into collective security arrangements, and further, the Charter of the United Nations recognizes that all nations possess an inherent right of individual and collective self-defense.

第27条

この条約は、アメリカ合衆国政府の記録に寄託する。同政府は、その認証謄本を各署名国に交付する。

以上の証拠として、下名の全権委員は、この条約に署名した。

1951年9月8日にサン・フランシスコ市で、ひとしく正文である英語、フランス語及びスペイン語により、並びに日本語により作成した。

(署名欄省略)

旧・日米安全保障条約	調印：1951年9月8日 発効：1952年4月28日

日本国とアメリカ合衆国との間の安全保障条約

日本国は、本日連合国との平和条約に署名した。日本国は、武装を解除されているので、平和条約の効力発生の時において固有の自衛権を行使する有効な手段をもたない。

無責任な軍国主義がまだ世界から駆逐されていないので、前記の状態にある日本国には危険がある。よつて、日本国は、平和条約が日本国とアメリカ合衆国の間に効力を生ずるのと同時に効力を生ずべきアメリカ合衆国との安全保障条約を希望する。

平和条約は、日本国が主権国として集団的安全保障取極を締結する権利を有することを承認し、さらに、国際連合憲章は、すべての国が個別的及び集団的自衛の固有の権利を有することを承認している。

In exercise of these rights, Japan desires, as a provisional arrangement for its defense, that the United States of America should maintain armed forces of its own in and about Japan so as to deter armed attack upon Japan.

The United States of America, in the interest of peace and security, is presently willing to maintain certain of its armed forces in and about Japan, in the expectation, however, that Japan will itself increasingly assume responsibility for its own defense against direct and indirect aggression, always avoiding any armament which could be an offensive threat or serve other than to promote peace and security in accordance with the purposes and principles of the United Nations Charter.

Accordingly, the two countries have agreed as follows:

Article 1.

Japan grants, and the United States of America accepts, the right, upon the coming into force of the Treaty of Peace and of this Treaty, to dispose United States land, air and sea forces in and about Japan. Such forces may be utilized to contribute to the maintenance of international peace and security in the Far East and to the security of Japan against armed attack from without, including assistance given at the express request of the Japanese Government to put down large-scale internal riots and disturbances in Japan, caused through instigation or intervention by an outside power or powers.

Article 2.

During the exercise of the right referred to in Article 1, Japan will not grant, without

これらの権利の行使として、日本国は、その防衛のための暫定措置として、日本国に対する武力攻撃を阻止するため日本国内及びその附近にアメリカ合衆国がその軍隊を維持することを希望する。

アメリカ合衆国は、平和と安全のために、現在、若干の自国軍隊を日本国内及びその附近に維持する意思がある。但し、アメリカ合衆国は、日本国が、攻撃的な脅威となり又は国際連合憲章の目的及び原則に従つて平和と安全を増進すること以外に用いられうべき軍備をもつことを常に避けつつ、直接及び間接の侵略に対する自国の防衛のため漸増的に自ら責任を負うことを期待する。

よつて、両国は、次のとおり協定した。

第1条

平和条約及びこの条約の効力発生と同時に、アメリカ合衆国の陸軍、空軍及び海軍を日本国内及びその附近に配備する権利を、日本国は、許与し、アメリカ合衆国は、これを受諾する。この軍隊は、極東における国際の平和と安全の維持に寄与し、並びに、1又は2以上の外部の国による教唆又は干渉によつて引き起された日本国における大規模の内乱及び騒じょうを鎮圧するため日本国政府の明示の要請に応じて与えられる援助を含めて、外部からの武力攻撃に対する日本国の安全に寄与するために使用することができる。

第2条

第1条に掲げる権利が行使される間は、日本国は、アメリカ合衆国の事前の同意なくして、

the prior consent of the United States of America, any bases or any rights, powers or authority whatsoever, in or relating to bases or the right of garrison or of maneuver, or transit of ground, air or naval forces to any third power.

基地、基地における若しくは基地に関する権利、権力若しくは権能、駐兵若しくは演習の権利又は陸軍、空軍若しくは海軍の通過の権利を第三国に許与しない。

Article 3.

The conditions which shall govern the disposition of armed forces of the United States of America in and about Japan shall be determined by administrative agreements between the two Governments.

第3条

アメリカ合衆国の軍隊の日本国内及びその附近における配備を規律する条件は、両政府間の行政協定で決定する。

Article 4.

This Treaty shall expire whenever in the opinion of the Governments of Japan and the United States of America there shall have come into force such United Nations arrangements or such alternative individual or collective security dispositions as will satisfactorily provide for the maintenance by the United Nations or otherwise of international peace and security in the Japan Area.

第4条

この条約は、国際連合又はその他による日本区域における国際平和と安全の維持のため充分な定をする国際連合の措置又はこれに代る個別的若しくは集団的の安全保障措置が効力を生じたと日本国及びアメリカ合衆国の政府が認めた時はいつでも効力を失うものとする。

Article 5.

This Treaty shall be ratified by Japan and the United States of America and will come into force when instruments of ratification thereof have been exchanged by them at Washington.

In witness whereof the undersigned Plenipotenti-aries have signed this Treaty.

Done in duplicate at the city of San Francisco, in the Japanese and English languages, this eighth day of September, 1951.

    For Japan:
    Shigeru Yoshida
    For the United States of America:
    Dean Acheson

第5条

この条約は、日本国及びアメリカ合衆国によて批准されなければならない。この条約は、批准書が両国によつてワシントンで交換された時に効力を生ずる。

以上の証拠をして、下名の全権委員は、この条約に署名した。

1951年9月8日にサン・フランシスコ市で、日本語及び英語により、本書2通を作成した。

    日本国のために
    吉田茂
    アメリカ合衆国のために
    ディーン・アチソン

John Foster Dulles　　　　　ジョン・フォスター・ダレス
Alexander Wiley　　　　　　アレキサンダー・ワイリー
Styles Bridges　　　　　　　スタイルス・ブリッジス

United States-Japan Security Treaty	Signed 19 November 1960 Implemented 23 June 1960	日米安全保障条約	調印：1960年11月19日 発効：1960年1月23日

Treaty of Mutual Cooperation and Security between Japan and the United States of America

日本国とアメリカ合衆国との間の相互協力及び安全保障条約

Japan and the United States of America,

Desiring to strengthen the bonds of peace and friendship traditionally existing between them, and to uphold the principles of democracy, individual liberty, and the rule of law,

Desiring further to encourage closer economic cooperation between them and to promote conditions of economic stability and well-being in their countries,

Reaffirming their faith in the purposes and principles of the Charter of the United Nations, and their desire to live in peace with all peoples and all governments,

Recognizing that they have the inherent right of individual or collective self-defense as affirmed in the Charter of the United Nations,

Considering that they have a common concern in the maintenance of international peace and security in the Far East,

Having resolved to conclude a treaty of mutual cooperation and security,

Therefore agree as follows:

日本国及びアメリカ合衆国は、

両国の間に伝統的に存在する平和及び友好の関係を強化し、並びに民主主義の諸原則、個人の自由及び法の支配を擁護することを希望し、

また、両国の間の一層緊密な経済的協力を促進し、並びにそれぞれの国における経済的安定及び福祉の条件を助長することを希望し、

国際連合憲章の目的及び原則に対する信念並びにすべての国民及びすべての政府とともに平和のうちに生きようとする願望を再確認し、

両国が国際連合憲章に定める個別的又は集団的自衛の固有の権利を有していることを確認し、

両国が極東における国際の平和及び安全の維持に共通の関心を有することを考慮し、

相互協力及び安全保障条約を締結することを決意し、

よって、次のとおり協定する。

Article l.

The Parties undertake, as set forth in the Charter of the United Nations, to settle any international disputes in which they may be involved by peaceful means in such a manner

第1条

締約国は、国際連合憲章に定めるところに従い、それぞれが関係することのある国際紛争を平和的手段によつて国際の平和及び安全並びに正義を危うくしないように解決し、並びにそれ

that international peace and security and justice are not endangered and to refrain in their international relations from the threat or use of force against the territorial integrity or political independence of any state, or in any other manner inconsistent with the purposes of the United Nations.

The Parties will endeavor in concert with other peace-loving countries to strengthen the United Nations so that its mission of maintaining international peace and security may be discharged more effectively.

Article 2.

The Parties will contribute toward the further development of peaceful and friendly international relations by strengthening their free institutions, by bringing about a better understanding of the principles upon which these institutions are founded, and by promoting conditions of stability and well-being. They will seek to eliminate conflict in their international economic policies and will encourage economic collaboration between them.

Article 3.

The Parties, individually and in cooperation with each other, by means of continuous and effective self-help and mutual aid will maintain and develop, subject to their constitutional provisions, their capacities to resist armed attack.

Article 4.

The Parties will consult together from time to time regarding the implementation of this Treaty, and, at the request of either Party, whenever the security of Japan or international peace and security in the Far East is threatened.

それの国際関係において、武力による威嚇又は武力の行使を、いかなる国の領土保全又は政治的独立に対するものも、また、国際連合の目的と両立しない他のいかなる方法によるものも慎むことを約束する。

締約国は、他の平和愛好国と協同して、国際の平和及び安全を維持する国際連合の任務が一層効果的に遂行されるように国際連合を強化することに努力する。

第2条

締約国は、その自由な諸制度を強化することにより、これらの制度の基礎をなす原則の理解を促進することにより、並びに安定及び福祉の条件を助長することによつて、平和的かつ友好的な国際関係の一層の発展に貢献する。締約国は、その国際経済政策におけるくい違いを除くことに努め、また、両国の間の経済的協力を促進する。

第3条

締約国は、個別的に及び相互に協力して、継続的かつ効果的な自助及び相互援助により、武力攻撃に抵抗するそれぞれの能力を、憲法上の規定に従うことを条件として、維持し発展させる。

第4条

締約国は、この条約の実施に関して随時協議し、また、日本国の安全又は極東における国際の平和及び安全に対する脅威が生じたときはいつでも、いずれか一方の締約国の要請により協議する。

Article 5.

Each Party recognizes that an armed attack against either Party in the territories under the administration of Japan would be dangerous to its own peace and safety and declares that it would act to meet the common danger in accordance with its constitutional provisions and processes.

Any such armed attack and all measures taken as a result thereof shall be immediately reported to the Security Council of the United Nations in accordance with the provisions of Article 51 of the Charter. Such measures shall be terminated when the Security Council has taken the measures necessary to restore and maintain international peace and security.

Article 6.

For the purpose of contributing to the security of Japan and the maintenance of international peace and security in the Far East, the United States of America is granted the use by its land, air and naval forces of facilities and areas in Japan.

The use of these facilities and areas as well as the status of United States armed forces in Japan shall be governed by a separate agreement, replacing the Administrative Agreement under Article 3 of the Security Treaty between Japan and the United States of America, signed at Tokyo on February 28, 1952, as amended, and by such other arrangements as may be agreed upon.

Article 7.

This Treaty does not affect and shall not be interpreted as affecting in any way the rights and obligations of the Parties under the Charter of the United Nations or the responsibility of the United Nations for the maintenance of international peace and security.

第5条

各締約国は、日本国の施政の下にある領域における、いずれか一方に対する武力攻撃が、自国の平和及び安全を危うくするものであることを認め、自国の憲法上の規定及び手続に従つて共通の危険に対処するように行動することを宣言する。

前記の武力攻撃及びその結果として執つたすべての措置は、国際連合憲章第51条の規定に従つて直ちに国際連合安全保障理事会に報告しなければならない。その措置は、安全保障理事会が国際の平和及び安全を回復し及び維持するために必要な措置を執つたときは、終止しなければならない。

第6条

日本国の安全に寄与し、並びに極東における国際の平和及び安全の維持に寄与するため、アメリカ合衆国は、その陸軍、空軍及び海軍が日本国において施設及び区域を使用することを許される。

前記の施設及び区域の使用並びに日本国における合衆国軍隊の地位は、1952年2月28日に東京で署名された日本国とアメリカ合衆国との間の安全保障条約第3条に基く行政協定(改正を含む。)に代わる別個の協定及び合意される他の取極により規律される。

第7条

この条約は、国際連合憲章に基づく締約国の権利及び義務又は国際の平和及び安全を維持する国際連合の責任に対しては、どのような影響も及ぼすものではなく、また、及ぼすものと解釈してはならない。

Article 8.

This Treaty shall be ratified by Japan and the United States of America in accordance with their respective constitutional processes and will enter into force on the date on which the instruments of ratification thereof have been exchanged by them in Tokyo.

Article 9.

The Security Treaty between Japan and the United States of America signed at the city of San Francisco on September 8, 1951 shall expire upon the entering into force of this Treaty.

Article 10.

This Treaty shall remain in force until in the opinion of the Governments of Japan and the United States of America there shall have come into force such United Nations arrangements as will satisfactorily provide for the maintenance of international peace and security in the Japan area.

However, after the Treaty has been in force for ten years, either Party may give notice to the other Party of its intention to terminate the Treaty, in which case the Treaty shall terminate one year after such notice has been given.

In witness whereof the undersigned Plenipoten-tiaries have signed this Treaty.

Done in duplicate at Washington in the Japanese and English languages, both equally authentic, this 19th day of January, 1960.

For Japan:

Nobusuke Kishi

Aiichiro Fujiyama

Mitsujiro Ishii

Tadashi Adachi

Koichiro Asakai

For the United States of America:

第8条

この条約は、日本国及びアメリカ合衆国により各自の憲法上の手続に従つて批准されなければならない。この条約は、両国が東京で批准書を交換した日に効力を生ずる。

第9条

1951年9月8日にサン・フランシスコ市で署名された日本国とアメリカ合衆国との間の安全保障条約は、この条約の効力発生の時に効力を失う。

第10条

この条約は、日本区域における国際の平和及び安全の維持のため十分な定めをする国際連合の措置が効力を生じたと日本政府及びアメリカ合衆国政府が認める時まで効力を有する。

もつとも、この条約が10年間効力を存続した後は、いずれの締約国も、他方の締約国に対しこの条約を終了させる意思を通告することができ、その場合には、この条約は、そのような通告が行なわれた後1年で終了する。

以上の証拠として、下名の全権委員は、この条約に署名した。

1960年1月19日にワシントンで、ひとしく正文である日本語及び英語により本書2通を作成した。

日本国のために

岸　　信介

藤山愛一郎

石井光次郎

足立　　正

朝海浩一郎

アメリカ合衆国のために

Christian A. Herter
Douglas MacArthur 2nd
J. Graham Parsons

クリスチャン・A・ハーター
ダグラス・マックアーサー2世
J・グレイアム・パースンズ

Exchange of Notes

条約第6条の実施に関する交換公文

Washington, January 19, 1960

Excellency:

I have the honour to refer to the Treaty of Mutual Cooperation and Security between Japan and the United States of America signed today, and to inform Your Excellency that the following is the understanding of the Government of Japan concerning the implementation of Article 6 thereof:

Major changes in the deployment into Japan of United States armed forces, major changes in their equipment, and the use of facilities and areas in Japan as bases for military combat operations to be undertaken from Japan other than those conducted under Article 5 of the said Treaty, shall be the subjects of prior consultation with the Government of Japan.

I should be appreciative if Your Excellency would confirm on behalf of your Government that this is also the understanding of the Government of the United States of America.

I avail myself of this opportunity to renew to Your Excellency the assurance of my highest consideration.

Nobusuke Kishi

His Excellency
Christian A. Herter,
Secretary of State of the United States of America.

**

January 19, 1960

Excellency:

I have the honor to acknowledge the

内閣総理大臣から合衆国国務長官にあてた書簡
書簡をもつて啓上いたします。本大臣は、本日署名された日本国とアメリカ合衆国との間の相互協力及び安全保障条約に言及し、次のことが同条約第6条の実施に関する日本国政府の了解であることを閣下に通報する光栄を有します。

合衆国軍隊の日本国への配置における重要な変更、同軍隊の装備における重要な変更並びに日本国から行なわれる戦闘作戦行動(前記の条約第5条の規定に基づいて行なわれるものを除く。)のための基地としての日本国内の施設及び区域の使用は、日本国政府との事前の協議の主題とする。

本大臣は、閣下が、前記のことがアメリカ合衆国政府の了解でもあることを貴国政府に代わつて確認されれば幸いであります。

本大臣は、以上を申し進めるに際し、ここに重ねて閣下に向かつて敬意を表します。

1960年1月19日にワシントンで
岸　信介
アメリカ合衆国国務長官
クリスチャン・A・ハーター閣下

**

合衆国国務長官から内閣総理大臣にあてた書簡
書簡をもつて啓上いたします。本長官は、本

receipt of Your Excellency's Note of today's date, which reads as follows:

"I have the honour to refer to the Treaty of Mutual Cooperation and Security between Japan and the United States of America signed today, and to inform Your Excellency that the following is the understanding of the Government of Japan concerning the implementation of Article 6 thereof:

Major changes in the deployment into Japan of United States armed forces, major changes in their equipment, and the use of facilities and areas in Japan as bases for military combat operations to be undertaken from Japan other than those conducted under Article 5 of the said Treaty, shall be the subjects of prior consultation with the Government of Japan.

"I should be appreciative if Your Excellency would confirm on behalf of your Government that this is also the understanding of the Government of the United States of America.

"I avail myself of this opportunity to renew to Your Excellency the assurance of my highest consideration."

I have the honor to confirm on behalf of my Government that the foregoing is also the understanding of the Government of the United States of America.

Accept, Excellency, the renewed assurances of my highest consideration.

Christian A. Herter
Secretary of State of the United States
of America
His Excellency
Nobusuke Kishi,
Prime Minister of Japan.

日付けの閣下の次の書簡を受領したことを確認する光栄を有します。

書簡をもつて啓上いたします。本大臣は、本日署名された日本国とアメリカ合衆国との間の相互協力及び安全保障条約に言及し、次のことが同条約第6条の実施に関する日本国政府の了解であることを閣下に通報する光栄を有します。

合衆国軍隊の日本国への配置における重要な変更、同軍隊の装備における重要な変更並びに日本国から行なわれる戦闘作戦行動(前記の条約第5条の規定に基づいて行なわれるものを除く。)のための基地としての日本国内の施設及び区域の使用は、日本国政府との事前の協議の主題とする。

本大臣は、閣下が、前記のことがアメリカ合衆国政府の了解でもあることを貴国政府に代わつて確認されれば幸いであります。

本大臣は、以上を申し進めるに際し、ここに重ねて閣下に向かつて敬意を表します。

本長官は、前記のことがアメリカ合衆国政府の了解でもあることを本国政符に代わつて確認する光栄を有します。

本長官は、以上を申し進めるに際し、ここに重ねて閣下に向かつて敬意を表します。
1960年1月19日
アメリカ合衆国国務長官
クリスチャン・A・ハーター
日本国総理大臣
岸　信介閣下

Agreement under Article VI of the Treaty of Mutual Cooperation and Security between Japan and the United States of America, Regarding Facilities and Areas and the Status of United States Armed Forces in Japan

日本国とアメリカ合衆国との間の相互協力及び安全保障条約第6条に基づく施設及び区域並びに日本国における合衆国軍隊の地位に関する協定

Japan and the United States of America, pursuant to Article VI of the Treaty of Mutual Cooperation and Security between Japan and the United States of America signed at Washington on January 19, 1960, have entered into this Agreement in terms as set forth below:

日本国及びアメリカ合衆国は、1960年1月19日にワシントンで署名された日本国とアメリカ合衆国との間の相互協力及び安全保障条約第6条の規定に従い、次に掲げる条項によりこの協定を締結した。

Article l.

In this Agreement the expression—
(a) "members of the United States armed forces" means the personnel on active duty belonging to the land, sea or air armed services of the United States of America when in the territory of Japan.
(b) "civilian component" means the civilian persons of United States nationality who are in the employ of, serving with, or accompanying the United States armed forces in Japan, but excludes persons who are ordinarily resident in Japan or who are mentioned in paragraph 1 of Article 14. For the purposes of this Agreement only, dual nationals, Japanese and United States, who are brought to Japan by the United States shall be considered as United States nationals.
(c) "dependents" means
  (i) Spouse, and children under 21;
  (ii) Parents, and children over 21, if dependent for over half their support upon a member of the United States armed forces or civilian component.

第1条

この協定において、
(a) 「合衆国軍隊の構成員」とは、日本国の領域にある間におけるアメリカ合衆国の陸軍、海軍又は空軍に属する人員で現に服役中のものをいう。
(b) 「軍属」とは、合衆国の国籍を有する文民で日本国にある合衆国軍隊に雇用され、これに勤務し、又はこれに随伴するもの(通常日本国に居住する者及び第14条1に掲げる者を除く。)をいう。この協定のみの適用上、合衆国及び日本国の二重国籍者で合衆国が日本国に入れたものは、合衆国国民とみなす。

(c) 「家族」とは、次のものをいう。
  (i) 配偶者及び21才未満の子
  (ii) 父、母及び21才以上の子で、その生計費の半額以上を合衆国軍隊の構成員又は軍属に依存するもの

Article 2.

1.(a) The United States is granted, under Article 6 of the Treaty of Mutual Cooperation and Security, the use of facilities and areas in Japan. Agreements as to specific facilities and areas shall be concluded by the two Governments through the Joint Committee provided for in Article 25 of this Agreement. "Facilities and areas" include existing furnishings, equipment and fixtures necessary to the operation of such facilities and areas.

(b) The facilities and areas of which the United States has the use at the time of expiration of the Administrative Agreement under Article 3 of the Security Treaty between Japan and the United States of America, shall be considered as facilities and areas agreed upon between the two Governments in accordance with sub-paragraph (a) above.

2. At the request of either Government, the Governments of Japan and the United States shall review such arrangements and may agree that such facilities and areas shall be returned to Japan or that additional facilities and areas may be provided.

3. The facilities and areas used by the United States armed forces shall be returned to Japan whenever they are no longer needed for purposes of this Agreement, and the United States agrees to keep the needs for facilities and areas under continual observation with a view toward such return.

4.(a) When facilities and areas are temporarily not being used by the United States armed forces, the Government of Japan may make, or permit Japanese nationals to make, interim use of such facilities and areas provided that it is agreed between the two Governments through the Joint Committee that such use would not be harmful to the purposes for which the facilities and areas

第2条

1.(a) 合衆国は、相互協力及び安全保障条約第6条の規定に基づき、日本国内の施設及び区域の使用を許される。個個の施設及び区域に関する協定は、第25条に定める合同委員会を通じて両政府が締結しなければならない。「施設及び区域」には、当該施設及び区域の運営に必要な現存の設備、備品及び定着物を含む。

(b) 合衆国が日本国とアメリカ合衆国との間の安全保障条約第3条に基く行政協定の終了の時に使用している施設及び区域は、両政府が(a) の規定に従つて合意した施設及び区域とみなす。

2. 日本国政府及び合衆国政府は、いずれか一方の要請があるときは、前記の取極を再検討しなければならず、また、前記の施設及び区域を日本国に返還すべきこと又は新たに施設及び区域を提供することを合意することができる。

3. 合衆国軍隊が使用する施設及び区域は、この協定の目的のため必要でなくなつたときは、いつでも、日本国に返還しなければならない。合衆国は、施設及び区域の必要性を前記の返還を目的としてたえず検討することに合意する。

4.(a) 合衆国軍隊が施設及び区域を一時的に使用していないときは、日本国政府は、臨時にそのような施設及び区域をみずから使用し、又は日本国民に使用させることができる。ただし、この使用が、合衆国軍隊による当該施設及び区域の正規の使用の目的にとつて有害でないことが合同委員会を通じて両政府間に合意された場合に限る。

are normally used by the United States armed forces.

(b) With respect to facilities and areas which are to be used by United States armed forces for limited periods of time, the Joint Committee shall specify in the agreements covering such facilities and areas the extent to which the provisions of this Agreement shall apply.

(b) 合衆国軍隊が一定の期間を限つて使用すべき施設及び区域に関しては、合同委員会は、当該施設及び区域に関する協定中に、適用があるこの協定の規定の範囲を明記しなければならない。

Article 3.

1. Within the facilities and areas, the United States may take all the measures necessary for their establishment, operation, safeguarding and control. In order to provide access for the United States armed forces to the facilities and areas for their support, safeguarding and control, the Government of Japan shall, at the request of the United States armed forces and upon consultation between the two Governments through the Joint Committee, take necessary measures within the scope of applicable laws and regulations over land, territorial waters and airspace adjacent to, or in the vicinities of the facilities and areas. The United States may also take necessary measures for such purposes upon consultation between the two Governments through the Joint Committee.

2. The United States agrees not to take the measures referred to in paragraph 1 in such a manner as to interfere unnecessarily with navigation, aviation, communication, or land travel to or from or within the territories of Japan. All questions relating to frequencies, power and like matters used by apparatus employed by the United States designed to emit electric radiation shall be settled by arrangement between the appropriate authorities of the two Governments. The Government of Japan shall, within the scope

第3条

1. 合衆国は、施設及び区域内において、それらの設定、運営、警護及び管理のため必要なすべての措置を執ることができる。日本国政府は、施設及び区域の支持、警護及び管理のための合衆国軍隊の施設及び区域への出入の便を図るため、合衆国軍隊の要請があつたときは、合同委員会を通ずる両政府間の協議の上で、それらの施設及び区域に隣接し又はそれらの近傍の土地、領水及び空間において、関係法令の範囲内で必要な措置を執るものとする。合衆国も、また、合同委員会を通ずる両政府間の協議の上で前記の目的のため必要な措置を執ることができる。

2. 合衆国は、1に定める措置を、日本国の領域への、領域からの又は領域内の航海、航空、通信又は陸上交通を不必要に妨げるような方法によつては執らないことに同意する。合衆国が使用する電波放射の装置が用いる周波数、電力及びこれらに類する事項に関するすべての問題は、両政府の当局間の取極により解決しなければならない。日本国政府は、合衆国軍隊が必要とする電気通信用電子装置に対する妨害を防止し又は除去するためのすべての合理的な措置を関係法令の範囲内で執るものとする。

of applicable laws and regulations, take all reasonable measures to avoid or eliminate interference with telecommunications electronics required by the United States armed forces.

3. Operations in the facilities and areas in use by the United States armed forces shall be carried on with due regard for the public safety.

Article 4.

1. The United States is not obliged, when it returns facilities and areas to Japan on the expiration of this Agreement or at an earlier date, to restore the facilities and areas to the condition in which they were at the time they became available to the United States armed forces, or to compensate Japan in lieu of such restoration.

2. Japan is not obliged to make any compensation to the United States for any improvements made in the facilities and areas or for the buildings or structures left thereon on the expiration of this Agreement or the earlier return of the facilities and areas.

3. The foregoing provisions shall not apply to any construction which the Government of the United States may undertake under special arrangements with the Government of Japan.

Article 5.

1. United States and foreign vessels and aircraft operated by, for, or under the control of the United States for official purposes shall be accorded access to any port or airport of Japan free from toll or landing charges. When cargo or passengers not accorded the exemptions of this Agreement are carried on such vessels and aircraft, notification shall be given to the appropriate Japanese authorities,

3. 合衆国軍隊が使用している施設及び区域における作業は、公共の安全に妥当な考慮を払つて行なわれなければならない。

第4条

1. 合衆国は、この協定の終了の際又はその前に日本国に施設及び区域を返還するに当たつて、当該施設及び区域をそれらが合衆国軍隊に提供された時の状態に回復し、又はその回復の代りに日本国に補償する義務を負わない。

2. 日本国は、この協定の終了の際又はその前における施設及び区域の返還の際、当該施設及び区域に加えられている改良又はそこに残される建物若しくはその他の工作物について、合衆国にいかなる補償をする義務も負わない。

3. 前記の規定は、合衆国政府が日本国政府との特別取極に基づいて行なう建設には適用しない。

第5条

1. 合衆国及び合衆国以外の国の船舶及び航空機で、合衆国によつて、合衆国のために又は合衆国の管理の下に公の目的で運航されるものは、入港料又は着陸料を課されないで日本国の港又は飛行場に出入することができる。この協定による免除を与えられない貨物又は旅客がそれらの船舶又は航空機で運送されるときは、日本国の当局にその旨の通告を与えなければならず、その貨物又は旅客の日本国への入国及び同国か

and their entry into and departure from Japan shall be according to the laws and regulations of Japan.

2.　The vessels and aircraft mentioned in paragraph 1, United States Government-owned vehicles including armor, and members of the United States armed forces, the civilian component, and their dependents shall be accorded access to and movement between facilities and areas in use by the United States armed forces and between such facilities and areas and the ports or airports of Japan. Such access to and movement between facilities and areas by United States military vehicles shall be free from toll and other charges.

3.　When the vessels mentioned in paragraph 1 enter Japanese ports, appropriate notification shall, under normal conditions, be made to the proper Japanese authorities. Such vessels shall have freedom from compulsory pilotage, but if a pilot is taken pilotage shall be paid for at appropriate rates.

らの出国は、日本国の法令による。

2.　1に掲げる船舶及び航空機、合衆国政府所有の車両(機甲車両を含む。)並びに合衆国軍隊の構成員及び軍属並びにそれらの家族は、合衆国軍隊が使用している施設及び区域に出入し、これらのものの間を移動し、及びこれらのものと日本国の港又は飛行場との間を移動することができる。合衆国の軍用車両の施設及び区域への出入並びにこれらのものの間の移動には、道路使用料その他の課徴金を課さない。

3.　1に掲げる船舶が日本国の港に入る場合には、通常の状態においては、日本国の当局に適当な通告をしなければならない。その船舶は、強制水先を免除される。もつとも、水先人を使用したときは、応当する料率で水先料を支払わなければならない。

Article 6.

1.　All civil and military air traffic control and communi-cations systems shall be developed in close coordination and shall be integrated to the extent necessary for fulfillment of collective security interests. Procedures, and any subsequent changes thereto, necessary to effect this coordination and integration will be established by arrangement between the appropriate authorities of the two Governments.

2.　Lights and other aids to navigation of vessels and aircraft placed or established in the facilities and areas in use by United States armed forces and in territorial waters adjacent thereto or in the vicinity thereof

第6条

1.　すべての非軍用及び軍用の航空交通管理及び通信の体系は、緊密に協調して発達を図るものとし、かつ、集団安全保障の利益を達成するため必要な程度に整合するものとする。この協調及び整合を図るため必要な手続及びそれに対するその後の変更は、両政府の当局間の取極によつて定める。

2.　合衆国軍隊が使用している施設及び区域並びにそれらに隣接し又はそれらの近傍の領水に置かれ、又は設置される燈火その他の航行補助施設及び航空保安施設は、日本国で使用されている様式に合致しなければならない。これらの

shall conform to the system in use in Japan. The Japanese and United States authorities which have established such navigation aids shall notify each other of their positions and characteristics and shall give advance notification before making any changes in them or establishing additional navigation aids.

施設を設置した日本国及び合衆国の当局は、その位置及び特徴を相互に通告しなければならず、かつ、それらの施設を変更し、又は新たに設置する前に予告をしなければならない。

Article 7.

The United States armed forces shall have the use of all public utilities and services belonging to, or controlled or regulated by the Government of Japan, and shall enjoy priorities in such use, under conditions no less favorable than those that may be applicable from time to time to the ministries and agencies of the Government of Japan.

第7条

合衆国軍隊は、日本国政府の各省その他の機関に当該時に適用されている条件よりも不利でない条件で、日本国政府が有し、管理し、又は規制するすべての公益事業及び公共の役務を利用することができ、並びにその利用における優先権を享有するものとする。

Article 8.

The Government of Japan undertakes to furnish the United States armed forces with the following meteorological services in accordance with arrangements between the appropriate authorities of the two Governments:

(a)   Meteorological observations from land and ocean areas including observations from weather ships.

(b)   Climatological information including periodic summaries and the historical data of the Meteorological Agency.

(c)   Telecommunications service to disseminate meteorological information required for the safe and regular operation of aircraft.

(d)   Seismographic data including forecasts of the estimated size of tidal waves resulting from earthquakes and areas that might be affected thereby.

第8条

日本国政府は、両政府の当局間の取極に従い、次の気象業務を合衆国軍隊に提供することを約束する。

(a)   地上及び海上からの気象観測(気象観測船からの観測を含む。)

(b)   気象資料(気象庁の定期的概報及び過去の資料を含む。)

(c)   航空機の安全かつ正確な運航のため必要な気象情報を報ずる電気通信業務

(d)   地震観測の資料(地震から生ずる津波の予想される程度及びその津波の影響を受ける区域の予報を含む。)

Article 9.

1.　The United States may bring into Japan persons who are members of the United States armed forces, the civilian component, and their dependents, subject to the provisions of this Article.

2.　Members of the United States armed forces shall be exempt from Japanese passport and visa laws and regulations. Members of the United States armed forces, the civilian component, and their dependents shall be exempt from Japanese laws and regulations on the registration and control of aliens, but shall not be considered as acquiring any right to permanent residence or domicile in the territories of Japan.

3.　Upon entry into or departure from Japan members of the United States armed forces shall be in possession of the following documents:

(a)　personal identity card showing name, date of birth, rank and number, service, and photograph; and

(b)　individual or collective travel order certifying to the status of individual or group as a member or members of the United States armed forces and to the travel ordered. For purposes of their identification while in Japan, members of the United States armed forces shall be in possession of the foregoing personal identity card which must be presented on request to the appropriate Japanese authorities.

4.　Members of the civilian component, their dependents, and the dependents of members of the United States armed forces shall be in possession of appropriate documentation issued by the United States authorities so that their status may be verified by Japanese authorities upon their entry into or departure from Japan, or while in Japan.

第9条

1.　この条の規定に従うことを条件として、合衆国は、合衆国軍隊の構成員及び軍属並びにそれらの家族である者を日本国に入れることができる。

2.　合衆国軍隊の構成員は、旅券及び査証に関する日本国の法令の適用から除外される。合衆国軍隊の構成員及び軍属並びにそれらの家族は、外国人の登録及び管理に関する日本国の法令の適用から除外される。ただし、日本国の領域における永久的な居所又は住所を要求する権利を取得するものとみなされない。

3.　合衆国軍隊の構成員は、日本国への入国又は日本国からの出国に当たつて、次の文書を携帯しなければならない。

(a)　氏名、生年月日、階級及び番号、軍の区分並びに写真を掲げる身分証明書

(b)　その個人又は集団が合衆国軍隊の構成員として有する地位及び命令された旅行の証明となる個別的又は集団的旅行の命令書

合衆国軍隊の構成員は、日本国にある間の身分証明のため、前記の身分証明書を携帯していなければならない。身分証明書は、要請があるときは日本国の当局に提示しなければならない。

4.　軍属、その家族及び合衆国軍隊の構成員の家族は、合衆国の当局が発給した適当な文書を携帯し、日本国への入国若しくは日本国からの出国に当たつて又は日本国にある間その身分を日本国の当局が確認することができるようにしなければならない。

5. If the status of any person brought into Japan under paragraph 1 of this Article is altered so that he would no longer be entitled to such admission, the United States authorities shall notify the Japanese authorities and shall, if such person be required by the Japanese authorities to leave Japan, assure that transportation from Japan will be provided within a reasonable time at no cost to the Government of Japan.

6. If the Government of Japan has requested the removal from its territory of a member of the United States armed forces or civilian component or has made an expulsion order against an ex-member of the United States armed forces or the civilian component or against a dependent of a member or ex-member, the authorities of the United States shall be responsible for receiving the person concerned within its own territory or otherwise disposing of him outside Japan. This paragraph shall apply only to persons who are not nationals of Japan and have entered Japan as members of the United States armed forces or civilian component or for the purpose of becoming such members, and to the dependents of such persons.

Article 10.

1. Japan shall accept as valid, without a driving test or fee, the driving permit or license or military driving permit issued by the United States to a member of the United States armed forces, the civilian component, and their dependents.

2. Official vehicles of the United States armed forces and the civilian component shall carry distinctive numbered plates or individual markings which will readily identify them.

3. Privately owned vehicles of members

5. 1の規定に基づいて日本国に入国した者の身分に変更があつてその者がそのような入国の資格を有しなくなつた場合には、合衆国の当局は、日本国の当局にその旨を通告するものとし、また、その者が日本国から退去することを日本国の当局によつて要求されたときは、日本国政府の負担によらないで相当の期間内に日本国から輸送することを確保しなければならない。

6. 日本国政府が合衆国軍隊の構成員若しくは軍属の日本国の領域からの送出を要請し、又は合衆国軍隊の旧構成員若しくは旧軍属に対し若しくは合衆国軍隊の構成員、軍属、旧構成員若しくは旧軍属の家族に対し退去命令を出したときは、合衆国の当局は、それらの者を自国の領域内に受け入れ、その他日本国外に送出することにつき責任を負う。この項の規定は、日本国民でない者で合衆国軍隊の構成員若しくは軍属として又は合衆国軍隊の構成員若しくは軍属となるために日本国に入国したもの及びそれらの者の家族に対してのみ適用する。

第10条

1. 日本国は、合衆国が合衆国軍隊の構成員及び軍属並びにそれらの家族に対して発給した運転許可証若しくは運転免許証又は軍の運転許可証を、運転者試験又は手数料を課さないで、有効なものとして承認する。

2. 合衆国軍隊及び軍用の公用車両は、それを容易に識別させる明確な番号標又は個別の記号を付けていなければならない。

3. 合衆国軍隊の構成員及び軍属並びにそれら

of the United States armed forces, the civilian component, and their dependents shall carry Japanese number plates to be acquired under the same conditions as those applicable to Japanese nationals.

の家族の私有車両は、日本国民に適用される条件と同一の条件で取得する日本国の登録番号標を付けていなければならない。

Article 11.

1. Save as provided in this Agreement, members of the United States armed forces, the civilian component, and their dependents shall be subject to the laws and regulations administered by the customs authorities of Japan.

2. All materials, supplies and equipment imported by the United States armed forces, the authorized procurement agencies of the United States armed forces, or by the organizations provided for in Article 15, for the official use of the United States armed forces or for the use of the members of the United States armed forces, the civilian component, and their dependents, and materials, supplies and equipment which are to be used exclusively by the United States armed forces or are ultimately to be incorporated into articles or facilities used by such forces, shall be permitted entry into Japan; such entry shall be free from customs duties and other such charges. Appropriate certification shall be made that such materials, supplies and equipment are being imported by the United States armed forces, the authorized procurement agencies of the United States armed forces, or by the organi-zations provided for in Article 15, or, in the case of materials, supplies and equipment to be used exclusively by the United States armed forces or ultimately to be incorporated into articles or facilities used by such forces, that delivery thereof is to be taken by the United States armed forces for the purposes specified above.

第11条

1. 合衆国軍隊の構成員及び軍属並びにそれらの家族は、この協定中に規定がある場合を除くほか、日本国の税関当局が執行する法令に服さなければならない。

2. 合衆国軍隊、合衆国軍隊の公認調達機関又は第15条に定める諸機関が合衆国軍隊の公用のため又は合衆国軍隊の構成員及び軍属並びにそれらの家族の使用のため輸入するすべての資材、需品及び備品並びに合衆国軍隊が専用すべき資材、需品及び備品又は合衆国軍隊が使用する物品若しくは施設に最終的には合体されるべき資材、需品及び備品は、日本国に入れることを許される。この輸入には、関税その他の課徴金を課さない。前記の資材、需品及び備品は、合衆国軍隊、合衆国軍隊の公認調達機関又は第15条に定める諸機関が輸入するものである旨の適当な証明書(合衆国軍隊が専用すべき資材、需品及び備品又は合衆国軍隊が使用する物品若しくは施設に最終的には合体されるべき資材、需品及び備品にあつては、合衆国軍隊が前記の目的のために受領すべき旨の適当な証明書)を必要とする。

3.   Property consigned to and for the personal use of members of the United States armed forces, the civilian component, and their dependents, shall be subject to customs duties and other such charges, except that no duties or charges shall be paid with respect to:

(a) Furniture and household goods for their private use imported by the members of the United States armed forces or civilian component when they first arrive to serve in Japan or by their dependents when they first arrive for reunion with members of such forces or civilian component, and personal effects for private use brought by the said persons upon entrance.

(b) Vehicles and parts imported by members of the United States armed forces or civilian component for the private use of themselves or their dependents.

(c) Reasonable quantities of clothing and household goods of a type which would ordinarily be purchased in the United States for everyday use for the private use of members of the United States armed forces, civilian component, and their dependents, which are mailed into Japan through United States military post offices.

4.   The exemptions granted in paragraphs 2 and 3 shall apply only to cases of importation of goods and shall not be interpreted as refunding customs duties and domestic excises collected by the customs authorities at the time of entry in cases of purchases of goods on which such duties and excises have already been collected.

5.   Customs examination shall not be made in the following cases:

(a) Units of the United States armed forces under orders entering or leaving Japan;

(b) Official documents under official seal and official mail in United States military

3.   合衆国軍隊の構成員及び軍属並びにそれらの家族に仕向けられ、かつ、これらの者の私用に供される財産には、関税その他の課徴金を課する。ただし、次のものについては、関税その他の課徴金を課さない。

(a) 合衆国軍隊の構成員若しくは軍属が日本国で勤務するため最初に到着した時に輸入し、又はそれらの家族が当該合衆国軍隊の構成員若しくは軍属と同居するため最初に到着した時に輸入するこれらの者の私用のための家具及び家庭用品並びにこれらの者が入国の際持ち込む私用のための身回品

(b) 合衆国軍隊の構成員又は軍属が自己又はその家族の私用のため輸入する車両及び部品

(c) 合衆国軍隊の構成員及び軍属並びにそれらの家族の私用のため合衆国において通常日常用として購入される種類の合理的な数量の衣類及び家庭用品で、合衆国軍事郵便局を通じて日本国に郵送されるもの

4.   2及び3で与える免除は、物の輸入の場合のみに適用するものとし、関税及び内国消費税がすでに徴収された物を購入する場合に、当該物の輸入の際関税関当局が徴収したその関税及び内国消費税を払いもどすものと解してはならない。

5.   税関検査は、次のものの場合には行なわないものとする。

(a) 命令により日本国に入国し、又は日本国から出国する合衆国軍隊の部隊

(b) 公用の封印がある公文書及び合衆国軍事郵便路線上にある公用郵便物

postal channels;

(c) Military cargo shipped on a United States Government bill of lading

6. Except as such disposal may be authorized by the Japanese and United States authorities in accordance with mutually agreed conditions, goods imported into Japan free of duty shall not be disposed of in Japan to persons not entitled to import such goods free of duty.

7. Goods imported into Japan free from customs duties and other such charges pursuant to paragraphs 2 and 3, may be re-exported free from customs duties and other such charges.

8. The United States armed forces, in cooperation with Japanese authorities, shall take such steps as are necessary to prevent abuse of privileges granted to the United States armed forces, members of such forces, the civilian component, and their dependents in accordance with this Article.

9.(a) In order to prevent offenses against laws and regulations administered by the customs authorities of the Government of Japan, the Japanese authorities and the United States armed forces shall assist each other in the conduct of inquiries and the collection of evidence.

(b) The United States armed forces shall render all assistance within their power to ensure that articles liable to seizure by, or on behalf of, the customs authorities of the Government of Japan are handed to those authorities.

(c) The United States armed forces shall render all assistance within their power to ensure the payment of duties, taxes, and penalties payable by members of such forces or of the civilian component, or their dependents.

(c) 合衆国政府の船荷証券により船積みされる軍事貨物

6. 関税の免除を受けて日本国に輸入された物は、日本国及び合衆国の当局が相互間で合意する条件に従つて処分を認める場合を除くほか、関税の免除を受けて当該物を輸入する権利を有しない者に対して日本国内で処分してはならない。

7. 2及び3の規定に基づき関税その他の課徴金の免除を受けて日本国に輸入された物は、関税その他の課徴金の免除を受けて再輸出することができる。

8. 合衆国軍隊は、日本国の当局と協力して、この条の規定に従つて合衆国軍隊、合衆国軍隊の構成員及び軍属並びにそれらの家族に与えられる特権の濫用を防止するため必要な措置を執らなければならない。

9.(a) 日本国の当局及び合衆国軍隊は、日本国政府の税関当局が執行する法令に違反する行為を防止するため、調査の実施及び証拠の収集について相互に援助しなければならない。

(b) 合衆国軍隊は、日本国政府の税関当局によつて又はこれに代わつて行なわれる差押えを受けるべき物件がその税関当局に引き渡されることを確保するため、可能なすべての援助を与えなければならない。

(c) 合衆国軍隊は、合衆国軍隊の構成員若しくは軍属又はそれらの家族が納付すべき関税、租税及び罰金の納付を確保するため、可能なすべての援助を与えなければならない。

(d) Vehicles and articles belonging to the United States armed forces seized by the customs authorities of the Government of Japan in connection with an offense against its customs or fiscal laws or regulations shall be handed over to the appropriate authorities of the force concerned.

Article 12.

1.   The United States may contract for any supplies or construction work to be furnished or undertaken in Japan for purposes of, or authorized by, this Agreement, without restriction as to choice of supplier or person who does the construction work. Such supplies or construction work may, upon agreement between the appropriate authorities of the two Governments, also be procured through the Government of Japan.

2.   Materials, supplies, equipment and services which are required from local sources for the maintenance of the United States armed forces and the procurement of which may have an adverse effect on the economy of Japan shall be procured in coordination with, and, when desirable, through or with the assistance of, the competent authorities of Japan.

3.   Materials, supplies, equipment and services procured for official purposes in Japan by the United States armed forces, or by authorized procurement agencies of the United States armed forces upon appropriate certification shall be exempt from the following Japanese taxes:

  (a) Commodity tax
  (b) Travelling tax
  (c) Gasoline tax
  (d) Electricity and gas tax.

aterials, supplies, equipment and services ocured for ultimate use by the United

(d) 合衆国軍隊に属する車両及び物件で、日本国政府の関税又は財務に関する法令に違反する行為に関連して日本国政府の税関当局が差し押えたものは、関係部隊の当局に引き渡さなければならない。

第12条

1.   合衆国は、この協定の目的のため又はこの協定で認められるところにより日本国で供給されるべき需品又は行なわれるべき工事のため、供給者又は工事を行なう者の選択に関して制度を受けないで契約することができる。そのような需品又は工事は、また、両政府の当局間で合意されるときは、日本国政府を通じて調達することができる。

2.   現地で供給される合衆国軍隊の維持のため必要な資材、需品、備品及び役務でその調達が日本国の経済に不利な影響を及ぼすおそれがあるものは、日本国の権限のある当局との調整の下に、また、望ましいときは日本国の権限のある当局を通じて又はその援助を得て、調達しなければならない。

3.   合衆国軍隊又は合衆国軍隊の公認調達機関が適当な証明書を附して日本国で公用のため調達する資材、需品、備品及び役務は、日本の次の租税を免除される。

  (a) 物品税
  (b) 通行税
  (c) 揮発油税
  (d) 電気ガス税

  最終的には合衆国軍隊が使用するため調達される資材、需品、備品及び役務は、合衆国軍隊

States armed forces shall be exempt from commodity and gasoline taxes upon appropriate certification by the United States armed forces. With respect to any present or future Japanese taxes not specifically referred to in this Article which might be found to constitute a significant and readily identifiable part of the gross purchase price of materials, supplies, equipment and services procured by the United States armed forces, or for ultimate use by such forces, the two Governments will agree upon a procedure for granting such exemption or relief therefrom as is consistent with the purposes of this Article.

4.　Local labor requirements of United States armed forces and of the organizations provided for in Article 15 shall be satisfied with the assistance of the Japanese authorities.

5.　The obligations for the withholding and payment of income tax, local inhabitant tax and social security contributions, and, except as may otherwise be mutually agreed, the conditions of employment and work, such as those relating to wages and supplementary payments, the conditions for the protection of workers, and the rights of workers concerning labor relations shall be those laid down by the legislation of Japan.

6.　Should the United States armed forces or as appropriate an organization provided for in Article 15 dismiss a worker and a decision of a court or a Labor Relations Commission of Japan to the effect that the contract of employment has not terminated become final, the following procedures shall apply:

　(a) The United States armed forces or the said organization shall be informed by the Government of Japan of the decision of the court or Commission;

の適当な証明書があれば、物品税及び揮発油税を免除される。両政府は、この条に明示してない日本の現在の又は将来の租税で、合衆国軍隊によつて調達され、又は最終的には合衆国軍隊が使用するため調達される資材、需品、備品及び役務の購入価格の重要なかつ容易に判別することができる部分をなすと認められるものに関しては、この条の目的に合致する免税又は税の軽減を認めるための手続について合意するものとする。

4.　現地の労務に対する合衆国軍隊及び第15条に定める諸機関の需要は、日本国の当局の援助を得て充足される。

5.　所得税、地方住民税及び社会保障のための納付金を源泉徴収して納付するための義務並びに、相互間で別段の合意をする場合を除くほか、賃金及び諸手当に関する条件その他の雇用及び労働の条件、労働者の保護のための条件並びに労働関係に関する労働者の権利は、日本国の法令で定めるところによらなければならない。

6.　合衆国軍隊又は、適当な場合には、第15条に定める機関により労働者が解職され、かつ、雇用契約が終了していない旨の日本国の裁判所又は労働委員会の決定が最終的のものとなつた場合には、次の手続が適用される。

　(a) 日本国政府は、合衆国軍隊又は前記の機関に対し、裁判所又は労働委員会の決定を通報する。

(b) Should the United States armed forces or the said organization not desire to return the worker to duty, they shall so notify the Government of Japan within seven days after being informed by the latter of the decision of the court or Commission, and may temporarily withhold the worker from duty;

(c) Upon such notification, the Government of Japan and the United States armed forces or the said organization shall consult together without delay with a view to finding a practical solution of the case;

(d) Should such a solution not be reached within a period of thirty days from the date of commencement of the consultations under (c) above, the worker will not be entitled to return to duty. In such case, the Government of the United States shall pay to the Government of Japan an amount equal to the cost of employment of the worker for a period of time to be agreed between the two Governments.

7. Members of the civilian component shall not be subject to Japanese laws or regulations with respect to terms and conditions of employment.

8. Neither members of the United States armed forces, the civilian component, nor their dependents, shall by reason of this Article enjoy any exemption from taxes or similar charges relating to personal purchases of goods and services in Japan chargeable under Japanese legislation.

9. Except as such disposal may be authorized by the Japanese and United States authorities in accordance with mutually agreed conditions, goods purchased in Japan exempt from the taxes referred to in ,paragraph 3, shall not be disposed of in Japan • persons not entitled to purchase such ,ods exempt from such tax.

(b) 合衆国軍隊又は前記の機関が当該労働者を就労させることを希望しないときは、合衆国軍隊又は前記の機関は、日本国政府から裁判所又は労働委員会の決定について通報を受けた後7日以内に、その旨を日本国政府に通告しなければならず、暫定的にその労働者を就労させないことができる。

(c) 前記の通告が行なわれたときは、日本国政府及び合衆国軍隊又は前記の機関は、事件の実際的な解決方法を見出すため遅滞なく協議しなければならない。

(d) (c)の規定に基づく協議の開始の日から30日の期間内にそのような解決に到達しなかつたときは、当該労働者は、就労することができない。このような場合には、合衆国政府は、日本国政府に対し、両政府間で合意される期間の当該労働者の雇用の費用に等しい額を支払わなければならない。

7. 軍属は、雇用の条件に関して日本国の法令に服さない。

8. 合衆国軍隊の構成員及び軍属並びにそれらの家族は、日本国における物品及び役務の個人的購入について日本国の法令に基づいて課される租税又は類似の公課の免税をこの条の規定を理由として享有することはない。

9. 3に掲げる租税の免除を受けて日本国で購入した物は、日本国及び合衆国の当局が相互間で合意する条件に従つて処分を認める場合を除くほか、当該租税の免除を受けて当該物を購入する権利を有しない者に対して日本国内で処分してはならない。

Article 13.

1. The United States armed forces shall not be subject to taxes or similar charges on property held, used or transferred by such forces in Japan.

2. Members of the United States armed forces, the civilian component, and their dependents shall not be liable to pay any Japanese taxes to the Government of Japan or to any other taxing agency in Japan on income received as a result of their service with or employment by the United States armed forces, or by the organizations provided for in Article 15. The provisions of this Article do not exempt such persons from payment of Japanese taxes on income derived from Japanese sources, nor do they exempt United States citizens who for United States income tax purposes claim Japanese residence from payment of Japanese taxes on income. Periods during which such persons are in Japan solely by reason of being members of the United States armed forces, the civilian component, or their dependents shall not be considered as periods of residence or domicile in Japan for the purpose of Japanese taxation.

3. Members of the United States armed forces, the civilian component, and their dependents shall be exempt from taxation in Japan on the holding, use, transfer *inter se*, or transfer by death of movable property, tangible or intangible, the presence of which in Japan is due solely to the temporary presence of these persons in Japan, provided that such exemption shall not apply to property held for the purpose of investment or the conduct of business in Japan or to any intangible property registered in Japan. There is no obligation under this Article to grant exemption from taxes payable in respect of the use of roads by private vehicles.

第13条

1. 合衆国軍隊は、合衆国軍隊が日本国において保有し、使用し、又は移転する財産について租税又は類似の公課を課されない。

2. 合衆国軍隊の構成員及び軍属並びにそれらの家族は、これらの者が合衆国軍隊に勤務し、又は合衆国軍隊若しくは第15条に定める諸機関に雇用された結果受ける所得について、日本国政府又は日本国にあるその他の課税権者に日本の租税を納付する義務を負わない。この条の規定は、これらの者に対し、日本国の源泉から生ずる所得についての日本の租税の納付を免除するものではなく、また、合衆国の所得税のために日本国に居所を有することを申し立てる合衆国市民に対し、所得についての日本の租税の納付を免除するものではない。これらの者が合衆国軍隊の構成員若しくは軍属又はそれらの家族であるという理由のみによつて日本国にある期間は、日本の租税の賦課上、日本国に居所又は住所を有する期間とは認めない。

3. 合衆国軍隊の構成員及び軍属並びにそれらの家族は、これらの者が一時的に日本国にあることのみに基づいて日本国に所在する有体又は無体の動産の保有、使用、これらの者相互間の移転又は死亡による移転についての日本国における租税を免除される。ただし、この免除は、投資若しくは事業を行なうため日本国において保有される財産又は日本国において登録された無体財産権には適用しない。この条の規定は、私有車両による道路の使用について納付すべき租税の免除を与える義務を定めるものではない。

Article 14.

1.   Persons, including corporations organized under the laws of the United States, and their employees who are ordinarily resident in the United States and whose presence in Japan is solely for the purpose of executing contracts with the United States for the benefit of the United States armed forces, and who are designated by the Government of the United States in accordance with the provisions of paragraph 2 below, shall, except as provided in this Article, be subject to the laws and regulations of Japan.

2.   The designation referred to in paragraph 1 above shall be made upon consultation with the Government of Japan and shall be restricted to cases where open competitive bidding is not practicable due to security considerations, to the technical qualifications of the contractors involved, or to the unavailability of materials or services required by United States standards, or to limitations of United States law.

The designation shall be withdrawn by the Government of the United States:

(a) upon completion of contracts with the United States for the United States armed forces;

(b) upon proof that such persons are engaged in business activities in Japan other than those pertaining to the United States armed forces; or

(c) when such persons are engaged in practices illegal in Japan.

3.   Upon certification by appropriate United States authorities as to their identity, such persons and their employees shall be accorded the following benefits of this Agreement:

(a) Rights of accession and movement, as provided for in Article 5, paragraph 2;

第14条

1.   通常合衆国に居住する人(合衆国の法律に基づいて組織された法人を含む。)及びその被用者で、合衆国軍隊のための合衆国との契約の履行のみを目的として日本国にあり、かつ、合衆国政府が2の規定に従い指定するものは、この条に規定がある場合を除くほか、日本国の法令に服さなければならない。

2.   1にいう指定は、日本国政府との協議の上で行なわれるものとし、かつ、安全上の考慮、関係業者の技術上の適格要件、合衆国の標準に合致する資材若しくは役務の欠如又は合衆国の法令上の制限のため競争入札を実施することができない場合に限り行なわれるものとする。

前記の指定は、次のいずれかの場合には、合衆国政府が取り消すものとする。

(a) 合衆国軍隊のための合衆国との契約の履行が終わつたとき。

(b) それらの者が日本国において合衆国軍隊関係の事業活動以外の事業活動に従事していることが立証されたとき。

(c) それらの者が日本国で違法とされる活動を行なつているとき。

3.   前記の人及びその被用者は、その身分に関する合衆国の当局の証明があるときは、この協定による次の利益を与えられる。

(a) 第5条2に定める出入及び移動の権利

(b) Entry into Japan in accordance with the provisions of Article 9;

(c) The exemption from customs duties, and other such charges provided for in Article 11, paragraph 3, for members of the United States armed forces, the civilian component, and their dependents;

(d) If authorized by the Government of the United States, the right to use the services of the organizations provided for in Article 15;

(e) Those provided for in Article 19, paragraph 2, for members of the armed forces of the United States, the civilian component, and their dependents;

(f) If authorized by the Government of the United States, the right to use military payment certificates, as provided for in Article 20;

(g) The use of postal facilities provided for in Article 21;

(h) Exemption from the laws and regulations of Japan with respect to terms and conditions of employment.

4. Such persons and their employees shall be so described in their passports and their arrival, departure and their residence while in Japan shall from time to time be notified by the United States armed forces to the Japanese authorities.

5. Upon certification by an authorized officer of the United States armed forces, depreciable assets except houses, held, used, or transferred, by such persons and their employees exclusively for the execution of contracts referred to in paragraph 1 shall not be subject to taxes or similar charges of Japan.

6. Upon certification by an authorized officer of the United States armed forces, such persons and their employees shall be exempt from taxation in Japan on the holding, use, transfer by death, or transfer to persons or

(b) 第9条の規定による日本国への入国

(c) 合衆国軍隊の構成員及び軍属並びにそれらの家族について第11条3に定める関税その他の課徴金の免除

(d) 合衆国政府により認められたときは、第15条に定める諸機関の役務を利用する権利

(e) 合衆国軍隊の構成員及び軍属並びにそれらの家族について第19条2に定めるもの

(f) 合衆国政府により認められたときは、第20条に定めるところにより軍票を使用する権利

(g) 第21条に定める郵便施設の利用

(h) 雇用の条件に関する日本国の法令の適用からの除外

4. 前記の人及びその被用者は、その身分の者であることが旅券に記載されていなければならず、その到着、出発及び日本国にある間の居所は、合衆国軍隊が日本国の当局に随時に通告しなければならない。

5. 前記の人及びその被用者が1に掲げる契約の履行のためにのみ保有し、使用し、又は移転する減価償却資産(家屋を除く。)については、合衆国軍隊の権限のある官憲の証明があるときは、日本の租税又は類似の公課を課されない。

6. 前記の人及びその被用者は、合衆国軍隊の権限のある官憲の証明があるときは、これらの者が一時的に日本国にあることのみに基づいて日本国に所在する有体又は無体の動産の保有、使用、死亡による移転又はこの協定に基づいて

agencies entitled to tax exemption under this Agreement, of movable property, tangible or intangible, the presence of which in Japan is due solely to the temporary presence of these persons in Japan, provided that such exemption shall not apply to property held for the purpose of investment or the conduct of other business in Japan or to any intangible property registered in Japan. There is no obligation under this Article to grant exemption from taxes payable in respect of the use of roads by private vehicles.

7. The persons and their employees referred to in paragraph 1 shall not be liable to pay income or corporation taxes to the Government of Japan or to any other taxing agency in Japan on any income derived under a contract made in the United States with the Government of the United States in connection with the construction, maintenance or operation of any of the facilities or areas covered by this Agreement. The provisions of this paragraph do not exempt such persons from payment of income or corporation taxes on income derived from Japanese sources, nor do they exempt such persons and their employees who, for United States income tax purposes, claim Japanese residence, from payment of Japanese taxes on income. Periods during which such persons are in Japan solely in connection with the execution of a contract with the Government of the United States shall not be considered periods of residence or domicile in Japan for the purposes of such taxation.

8. Japanese authorities shall have the primary right to exercise jurisdiction over the persons and their employees referred to in paragraph 1 of this Article in relation to offenses committed in Japan and punishable

租税の免除を受ける権利を有する人若しくは機関への移転についての日本国における租税を免除される。ただし、この免除は、投資のため若しくは他の事業を行なうため日本国において保有される財産又は日本国において登録された無体財産権には適用しない。この条の規定は、私有車両による道路の使用について納付すべき租税の免除を与える義務を定めるものではない。

7. 1に掲げる人及びその被用者は、この協定に定めるいずれかの施設又は区域の建設、維持又は運営に関して合衆国政府と合衆国において結んだ契約に基づいて発生する所得について、日本国政府又は日本国にあるその他の課税権者に所得税又は法人税を納付する義務を負わない。この項の規定は、これらの者に対し、日本国の源泉から生ずる所得についての所得税又は法人税の納付を免除するものではなく、また、合衆国の所得税のために日本国に居所を有することを申し立てる前記の人及びその被用者に対し、所得についての日本の租税の納付を免除するものではない。これらの者が合衆国政府との契約の履行に関してのみ日本国にある期間は、前記の租税の賦課上、日本国に居所又は住所を有する期間とは認めない。

8. 日本国の当局は、1に掲げる人及びその被用者に対し、日本国において犯す罪で日本国の法令によつて罰することができるものについて裁判権を行使する第一次の権利を有する。日本国の当局が前記の裁判権を行使しないことに決

by the law of Japan. In those cases in which the Japanese authorities decide not to exercise such jurisdiction they shall notify the military authorities of the United States as soon as possible. Upon such notification the military authorities of the United States shall have the right to exercise such jurisdiction over the persons referred to as is conferred on them by the law of the United States.

定した場合には、日本国の当局は、できる限りすみやかに合衆国の軍当局にその旨を通告しなければならない。この通告があつたときには、合衆国の軍当局は、これらの者に対し、合衆国の法令により与えられた裁判権を行使する権利を有する。

Article 15.

1.(a) Navy exchanges, post exchanges, messes, social clubs, theaters, newspapers and other non-appropriated fund organizations authorized and regulated by the United States military authorities may be established in the facilities and areas in use by the United States armed forces for the use of members of such forces, the civilian component, and their dependents. Except as otherwise provided in this Agreement, such organizations shall not be subject to Japanese regulations, license, fees, taxes or similar controls.

(b) When a newspaper authorized and regulated by the United States military authorities is sold to the general public, it shall be subject to Japanese regulations, license, fees, taxes or similar controls so far as such circulation is concerned.

2. No Japanese tax shall be imposed on sales of merchandise and services by such organizations, except as provided in paragraph 1 (b), but purchases within Japan of merchandise and supplies by such organizations shall be subject to Japanese taxes.

3. Except as such disposal may be authorized by the Japanese and United States authorities in accordance with mutually agreed conditions, goods which are sold by

第15条

1.(a) 合衆国の軍当局が公認し、かつ、規制する海軍販売所、ピー・エックス、食堂、社交クラブ、劇場、新聞その他の歳出外資金による諸機関は、合衆国軍隊の構成員及び軍属並びにそれらの家族の利用に供するため、合衆国軍隊が使用している施設及び区域内に設置することができる。これらの諸機関は、この協定に別段の定めがある場合を除くほか、日本の規制、免許、手数料、租税又は類似の管理に服さない。

(b) 合衆国の軍当局が公認し、かつ、規制する新聞が一般の公衆に販売されるときは、当該新聞は、その頒布に関する限り、日本の規制、免許、手数料、租税又は類似の管理に服する。

2. これらの諸機関による商品及び役務の販売には、1(b)に定める場合を除くほか、日本の租税を課さず、これらの諸機関による商品及び需品の日本国内における購入には、日本の租税を課する。

3. これらの諸機関が販売する物品は、日本国及び合衆国の当局が相互間で合意する条件に従つて処分を認める場合を除くほか、これらの諸機関から購入することを認められない者に対し

such organizations shall not be disposed of in Japan to persons not authorized to make purchases from such organizations.

4.   The organizations referred to in this Article shall provide such information to the Japanese authorities as is required by Japanese tax legislation.

Article 16.

It is the duty of members of the United States armed forces, the civilian component, and their dependents to respect the law of Japan and to abstain from any activity inconsistent with the spirit of this Agreement, and, in particular, from any political activity in Japan.

Article 17.

1.   Subject to the provisions of this Article,

(a) the military authorities of the United States shall have the right to exercise within Japan all criminal and disciplinary jurisdiction conferred on them by the law of the United States over all persons subject to the military law of the United States;

(b) the authorities of Japan shall have jurisdiction over the members of the United States armed forces, the civilian component, and their dependents with respect to offenses committed within the territory of Japan and punishable by the law of Japan.

2.(a) The military authorities of the United States shall have the right to exercise exclusive jurisdiction over persons subject to the military law of the United States with respect to offenses, including offenses relating to its security, punishable by the law of the United States, but not by the law of Japan.

(b) The authorities of Japan shall have the right to exercise exclusive jurisdiction over members of the United States armed forces,

---

て日本国内で処分してはならない。

4.   この条に掲げる諸機関は、日本国の当局に対し、日本国の税法が要求するところにより資料を提供するものとする。

第16条

日本国において、日本国の法令を尊重し、及びこの協定の精神に反する活動、特に政治的活動を慎むことは、合衆国軍隊の構成員及び軍属並びにそれらの家族の義務である。

第17条

1.   この条の規定に従うことを条件として、

(a) 合衆国の軍当局は、合衆国の軍法に服するすべての者に対し、合衆国の法令により与えられたすべての刑事及び懲戒の裁判権を日本国において行使する権利を有する。

(b) 日本国の当局は、合衆国軍隊の構成員及び軍属並びにそれらの家族に対し、日本国の領域内で犯す罪で日本国の法令によつて罰することができるものについて、裁判権を有する。

2.(a) 合衆国の軍当局は、合衆国の軍法に服する者に対し、合衆国の法令によつて罰することができる罪で日本国の法令によつては罰することができないもの(合衆国の安全に関する罪を含む。)について、専属的裁判権を行使する権利を有する。

(b) 日本国の当局は、合衆国軍隊の構成員及び軍属並びにそれらの家族に対し、日本国の法令によつて罰することができる罪で合衆国の法令

the civilian component, and their dependents with respect to offenses, including offenses relating to the security of Japan, punishable by its law but not by the law of the United States.

(c) For the purposes of this paragraph and of paragraph 3 of this Article a security offense against a State shall include

(i) treason against the State;

(ii) sabotage, espionage or violation of any law relating to official secrets of that State, or secrets relating to the national defense of that State.

3. In cases where the right to exercise jurisdiction is concurrent the following rules shall apply:

(a) The military authorities of the United States shall have the primary right to exercise jurisdiction over members of the United States armed forces or the civilian component in relation to

(i) offenses solely against the property or security of the United States, or offenses solely against the person or property of another member of the United States armed forces or the civilian component or of a dependent;

(ii) offenses arising out of any act or omission done in the performance of official duty.

(b) In the case of any other offense the authorities of Japan shall have the primary right to exercise jurisdiction.

(c) If the State having the primary right decides not to exercise jurisdiction, it shall notify the authorities of the other State as soon as practicable. The authorities of the State having the primary right shall give sympathetic consideration to a request from the authorities of the other State for a waiver of its right in cases where that other State

によつては罰することができないもの(日本国の安全に関する罪を含む。)について、専属的裁判権を行使する権利を有する。

(c) 2及び3の規定の適用上、国の安全に関する罪は、次のものを含む。

(i) 当該国に対する反逆

(ii) 妨害行為(サボタージュ)、諜報行為又は当該国の公務上若しくは国防上の秘密に関する法令の違反

3. 裁判権を行使する権利が競合する場合には、次の規定が適用される。

(a) 合衆国の軍当局は、次の罪については、合衆国軍隊の構成員又は軍属に対して裁判権を行使する第一次の権利を有する。

(i) もつぱら合衆国の財産若しくは安全のみに対する罪又はもつぱら合衆国軍隊の他の構成員若しくは軍属若しくは合衆国軍隊の構成員若しくは軍属の家族の身体若しくは財産のみに対する罪

(ii) 公務執行中の作為又は不作為から生ずる罪

(b) その他の罪については、日本国の当局が、裁判権を行使する第一次の権利を有する。

(c) 第一次の権利を有する国は、裁判権を行使しないことに決定したときは、できる限りすみやかに他方の国の当局にその旨を通告しなければならない。第一次の権利を有する国の当局は、他方の国がその権利の放棄を特に重要であると認めた場合において、その他方の国の当局から要請があつたときは、その要請に好意的考慮を払わなければならない。

considers such waiver to be of particular importance.

4. The foregoing provisions of this Article shall not imply any right for the military authorities of the United States to exercise jurisdiction over persons who are nationals of or ordinarily resident in Japan, unless they are members of the United States armed forces.

5.(a) The authorities of Japan and the military authorities of the United States shall assist each other in the arrest of members of the United States armed forces, the civilian component, or their dependents in the territory of Japan and in handing them over to the authority which is to exercise jurisdiction in accordance with the above provisions.

(b) The authorities of Japan shall notify promptly the military authorities of the United States of the arrest of any member of the United States armed forces, the civilian component, or a dependent.

(c) The custody of an accused member of the United States armed forces or the civilian component over whom Japan is to exercise jurisdiction shall, if he is in the hands of the United States, remain with the United States until he is charged by Japan.

6.(a) The authorities of Japan and the military authorities of the United States shall assist each other in the carrying out of all necessary investigations into offenses, and in the collection and production of evidence, including the seizure and, in proper cases, the handing over of objects connected with an offense. The handing over of such objects may, however, be made subject to their return within the time specified by the authority delivering them.

(b) The authorities of Japan and the

4. 前諸項の規定は、合衆国の軍当局が日本国民又は日本国に通常居住する者に対し裁判権を行使する権利を有することを意味するものではない。ただし、それらの者が合衆国軍隊の構成員であるときは、この限りでない。

5.(a) 日本国の当局及び合衆国の軍当局は、日本国の領域内における合衆国軍隊の構成員若しくは軍属又はそれらの家族の逮捕及び前諸項の規定に従つて裁判権を行使すべき当局へのそれらの者の引渡しについて、相互に援助しなければならない。

(b) 日本国の当局は、合衆国の軍当局に対し、合衆国軍隊の構成員若しくは軍属又はそれらの家族の逮捕についてすみやかに通告しなければならない。

(c) 日本国が裁判権を行使すべき合衆国軍隊の構成員又は軍属たる被疑者の拘禁は、その者の身柄が合衆国の手中にあるときは、日本国により公訴が提起されるまでの間、合衆国が引き続き行なうものとする。

6.(a) 日本国の当局及び合衆国の軍当局は、犯罪についてのすべての必要な捜査の実施並びに証拠の収集及び提出(犯罪に関連する物件の押収及び相当な場合にはその引渡しを含む。)について、相互に援助しなければならない。ただし、それらの物件の引渡しは、引渡しを行なう当局が定める期間内に還付されることを条件として行なうことができる。

(b) 日本国の当局及び合衆国の軍当局は、裁判

military authorities of the United States shall notify each other of the disposition of all cases in which there are concurrent rights to exercise jurisdiction.

7.(a) A death sentence shall not be carried out in Japan by the military authorities of the United States if the legislation of Japan does not provide for such punishment in a similar case.

(b) The authorities of Japan shall give sympathetic consideration to a request from the military authorities of the United States for assistance in carrying out a sentence of imprisonment pronounced by the military authorities of the United States under the provisions of this Article within the territory of Japan.

8.　Where an accused has been tried in accordance with the provisions of this Article either by the authorities of Japan or the military authorities of the United States and has been acquitted, or has been convicted and is serving, or has served, his sentence or has been pardoned, he may not be tried again for the same offense within the territory of Japan by the authorities of the other State. However, nothing in this paragraph shall prevent the military authorities of the United States from trying a member of its armed forces for any violation of rules of discipline arising from an act or omission which constituted an offense for which he was tried by the authorities of Japan.

9. Whenever a member of the United States armed forces, the civilian component or a dependent is prosecuted under the jurisdiction of Japan he shall be entitled:

(a) to a prompt and speedy trial;

(b) to be informed, in advance of trial, of the specific charge or charges made against him;

権を行使する権利が競合するすべての事件の処理について、相互に通告しなければならない。

7.(a) 死刑の判決は、日本国の法制が同様の場合に死刑を規定していない場合には、合衆国の軍当局が日本国内で執行してはならない。

(b) 日本国の当局は、合衆国の軍当局がこの条の規定に基づいて日本国の領域内で言い渡した自由刑の執行について合衆国の軍当局から援助の要請があつたときは、その要請に好意的考慮を払わなければならない。

8.　被告人がこの条の規定に従つて日本国の当局又は合衆国の軍当局のいずれかにより裁判を受けた場合において、無罪の判決を受けたとき、又は有罪の判決を受けて服役しているとき、服役したとき、若しくは赦免されたときは、他方の国の当局は、日本国の領域内において同一の犯罪について重ねてその者を裁判してはならない。ただし、この項の規定は、合衆国の軍当局が合衆国軍隊の構成員を、その者が日本国の当局により裁判を受けた犯罪を構成した作為又は不作為から生ずる軍紀違反について、裁判することを妨げるものではない。

9.　合衆国軍隊の構成員若しくは軍属又はそれらの家族は、日本国の裁判権に基づいて公訴を提起された場合には、いつでも、次の権利を有する。

(a) 遅滞なく迅速な裁判を受ける権利

(b) 公判前に自己に対する具体的な訴因の通知を受ける権利

(c) to be confronted with the witnesses against him;

(d) to have compulsory process for obtaining witnesses in his favor, if they are within the jurisdiction of Japan;

(e) to have legal representation of his own choice for his defense or to have free or assisted legal representation under the conditions prevailing for the time being in Japan;

(f) if he considers it necessary, to have the services of a competent interpreter; and

(g) to communicate with a representative of the Government of the United States and to have such a representative present at his trial.

10.(a)Regularly constituted military units or formations of the United States armed forces shall have the right to police any facilities or areas which they use under Article 2 of this Agreement. The military police of such forces may take all appropriate measures to ensure the maintenance of order and security within such facilities and areas.

(b) Outside these facilities and areas, such military police shall be employed only subject to arrangements with the authorities of Japan and in liaison with those authorities, and in so far as such employment is necessary to maintain discipline and order among the members of the United States armed forces.

11. In the event of hostilities to which the provisions of Article 5 of the Treaty of Mutual Cooperation and Security apply, either the Government of Japan or the Government of the United States shall have the right, by giving sixty days' notice to the other, to suspend the application of any of the provisions of this Article. If this right is exercised, the Governments of Japan and

(c) 自己に不利な証人と対決する権利

(d) 証人が日本国の管轄内にあるときは、自己のために強制的手続により証人を求める権利

(e) 自己の弁護のため自己の選択する弁護人をもつ権利又は日本国でその当時通常行なわれている条件に基づき費用を要しないで若しくは費用の補助を受けて弁護人をもつ権利

(f) 必要と認めたときは、有能な通訳を用いる権利

(g) 合衆国の政府の代表者と連絡する権利及び自己の裁判にその代表者を立ち会わせる権利

10.(a)合衆国軍隊の正規に構成された部隊又は編成隊は、第2条の規定に基づき使用する施設及び区域において警察権を行なう権利を有する。合衆国軍隊の軍事警察は、それらの施設及び区域において、秩序及び安全の維持を確保するためすべての適当な措置を執ることができる。

(b) 前記の施設及び区域の外部においては、前記の軍事警察は、必ず日本国の当局との取極に従うことを条件とし、かつ、日本国の当局と連絡して使用されるものとし、その使用は、合衆国軍隊の構成員の間の規律及び秩序の維持のため必要な範囲内に限るものとする。

11. 相互協力及び安全保障条約第5条の規定が適用される敵対行為が生じた場合には、日本国政府及び合衆国政府のいずれの一方も、他方の政府に対し60日前に予告を与えることによつて、この条のいずれの規定の適用も停止させる権利を有する。この権利が行使されたときは、日本国政府及び合衆国政府は、適用を停止される規定に代わるべき適当な規定を合意する目的をもつて直ちに協議しなければならない。

the United States shall immediately consult with a view to agreeing on suitable provisions to replace the provisions suspended.

12. The provisions of this Article shall not apply to any offences committed before the entry into force of this Agreement. Such cases shall be governed by the provisions of Article 17 of the Administrative Agreement under Article 3 of the Security Treaty between Japan and the United States of America, as it existed at the relevant time.

Article 18.

1. Each Party waives all its claims against the other Party for damage to any property owned by it and used by its land, sea or air defense services, if such damage

 (a) was caused by a member or an employee of the defense services of the other Party in the performance of his official duties; or

 (b) arose from the use of any vehicle, vessel or aircraft owned by the other Party and used by its defense services, provided either that the vehicle, vessel or aircraft causing the damage was being used for official purposes, or that the damage was caused to property being so used.

　　Claims for maritime salvage by one Party against the other Party shall be waived, provided that the vessel or cargo salved was owned by a Party and being used by its defense services for official purposes.

2.(a) In the case of damage caused or arising as stated in paragraph 1 to other property owned by either Party and located in Japan, the issue of the liability of the other Party shall be determined and the amount of damage shall be assessed, unless the two Governments agree otherwise, by a sole

12.　この条の規定は、この協定の効力発生前に犯したいかなる罪にも適用しない。それらの事件に対しては、日本国とアメリカ合衆国との間の安全保障条約第3条に基く行政協定第17条の当該時に存在した規定を適用する。

第18条

1.　各当事国は、自国が所有し、かつ、自国の陸上、海上又は航空の防衛隊が使用する財産に対する損害については、次の場合には、他方の当事国に対するすべての請求権を放棄する。

 (a) 損害が他方の当事国の防衛隊の構成員又は被用者によりその者の公務の執行中に生じた場合

 (b) 損害が他方の当事国が所有する車両、船舶又は航空機でその防衛隊が使用するものの使用から生じた場合。ただし、損害を与えた車両、船舶若しくは航空機が公用のため使用されていたとき、又は損害が公用のため使用されている財産に生じたときに限る。

　　海難救助についての一方の当事国の他方の当事国に対する請求権は、放棄する。ただし、救助された船舶又は積荷が、一方の当事国が所有し、かつ、その防衛隊が公用のため使用しているものであつた場合に限る。

2.(a) いずれか一方の当事国が所有するその他の財産で日本国内にあるものに対して1 に掲げるようにして損害が生じた場合には、両政府が別段の合意をしない限り、(b)の規定に従つて選定される一人の仲裁人が、他方の当事国の責任の問題を決定し、及び損害の額を査定する。仲裁人は、また、同一の事件から生ずる反対の請求

arbitrator selected in accordance with subparagraph (b) of this paragraph. The arbitrator shall also decide any counterclaims arising out of the same incident.

(b) The arbitrator referred to in subparagraph (a) above shall be selected by agreement between the two Governments from amongst the nationals of Japan who hold or have held high judicial office.

(c) Any decision taken by the arbitrator shall be binding and conclusive upon the Parties.

(d) The amount of any compensation awarded by the arbitrator shall be distributed in accordance with the provisions of paragraph 5 (e) (i), (ii) and (iii) of this Article.

(e) The compensation of the arbitrator shall be fixed by agreement between the two Governments and shall, together with the necessary expenses incidental to the performance of his duties, be defrayed in equal proportions by them.

(f) Nevertheless, each Party waives its claim in any such case up to the amount of l,400 United States dollars or 504,000 yen. In the case of considerable variation in the rate of exchange between these currencies the two Governments shall agree on the appropriate adjustments of these amounts.

3.   For the purposes of paragraphs 1 and 2 of this Article the expression "owned by a Party" in the case of a vessel includes a vessel on bare boat charter to that Party or requisitioned by it on bare boat terms or seized by it in prize (except to the extent that the risk of loss or liability is borne by some person other than such Party).

4.   Each Party waives all its claims against the other Party for injury or death suffered by any member of its defense services while such member was engaged in the

を裁定する。

(b) (a)に掲げる仲裁人は、両政府間の合意によつて、司法関係の上級の地位を現に有し、又は有したことがある日本国民の中から選定する。

(c) 仲裁人が行なつた裁定は、両当事国に対して拘束力を有する最終的のものとする。

(d) 仲裁人が裁定した賠償の額は、5(e) (i)、(ii)及び(iii)の規定に従つて分担される。

(e) 仲裁人の報酬は、両政府間の合意によつて定め、両政府が、仲裁人の任務の遂行に伴う必要な費用とともに、均等の割合で支払う。

(f) もつとも、各当事国は、いかなる場合においても1400合衆国ドル又は50万4千円までの額については、その請求権を放棄する。これらの通貨の間の為替相場に著しい変動があつた場合には、両政府は、前記の額の適当な調整について合意するものとする。

3.   1及び2の規定の適用上、船舶について「当事国が所有する」というときは、その当事国が裸用船した船舶、裸の条件で徴発した船舶又は拿捕した船舶を含む。ただし、損失の危険又は責任が当該当事国以外の者によつて負担される範囲については、この限りでない。

4.   各当事国は、自国の防衛隊の構成員がその公務の執行に従事している間に被つた負傷又は死亡については、他方の当事国に対するすべての請求権を放棄する。

performance of his official duties.

5.　Claims (other than contractual claims and those to which paragraphs 6 or 7 of this Article apply) arising out of acts or omissions of members or employees of the United States armed forces done in the performance of official duty, or out of any other act, omission or occurrence for which the United States armed forces are legally responsible, and causing damage in Japan to third parties, other than the Government of Japan, shall be dealt with by Japan in accordance with the following provisions:

　(a) Claims shall be filed, considered and settled or adjudicated in accordance with the laws and regulations of Japan with respect to claims arising from the activities of its Self-Defense Forces.

　(b) Japan may settle any such claims, and payment of the amount agreed upon or determined by adjudication shall be made by Japan in yen.

　(c) Such payment, whether made pursuant to a settlement or to adjudication of the case by a competent tribunal of Japan, or the final adjudication by such a tribunal denying payment, shall be binding and conclusive upon the Parties.

　(d) Every claim paid by Japan shall be communicated to the appropriate United States authorities together with full particulars and a proposed distribution in conformity with subparagraphs (e) (i) and (ii) below. In default of a reply within two months, the proposed distribution shall be regarded as accepted.

　(e) The cost incurred in satisfying claims pursuant to the preceding subparagraphs and paragraph 2 of this Article shall be distributed between the Parties as follows:

　(i)　Where the United States alone is

5.　公務執行中の合衆国軍隊の構成員若しくは被用者の作為若しくは不作為又は合衆国軍隊が法律上責任を有するその他の作為、不作為若しくは事故で、日本国において日本国政府以外の第三者に損害を与えたものから生ずる請求権(契約による請求権及び6又は7の規定の適用を受ける請求権を除く。)は、日本国が次の規定に従つて処理する。

　(a) 請求は、日本国の自衛隊の行動から生ずる請求権に関する日本国の法令に従つて、提起し、審査し、かつ、解決し、又は裁判する。

　(b) 日本国は、前記のいかなる請求をも解決することができるものとし、合意され、又は裁判により決定された額の支払を日本円で行なう。

　(c) 前記の支払(合意による解決に従つてされたものであると日本国の権限のある裁判所による裁判に従つてされたものであるとを問わない。)又は支払を認めない旨の日本国の権限のある裁判所による確定した裁判は、両当事国に対し拘束力を有する最終的のものとする。

　(d) 日本国が支払をした各請求は、その明細並びに(e) (i)及び(ii)の規定による分担案とともに、合衆国の当局に通知しなければならない。2箇月以内に回答がなかつたときは、その分担案は、受諾されたものとみなす。

　(e) (a)から(d)まで及び2の規定に従い請求を満たすために要した費用は、両当事国が次のとおり分担する。

　(i) 合衆国のみが責任を有する場合には、

responsible, the amount awarded or adjudged shall be distributed in the proportion of 25 percent chargeable to Japan and 75 percent chargeable to the United States.

(ii) Where Japan and the United States are responsible for the damage, the amount awarded or adjudged shall be distributed equally between them. Where the damage was caused by the defense services of Japan or the United States and it is not possible to attribute it specifically to one or both of those defense services, the amount awarded or adjudged shall be distributed equally between Japan and the United States.

(iii) Every half-year, a statement of the sums paid by Japan in the course of the half-yearly period in respect of every case regarding which the proposed distribution on a percentage basis has been accepted, shall be sent to the appropriate United States authorities, together with a request for reimbursement. Such reimbursement shall be made, in yen, within the shortest possible time.

(f) Members or employees of the United States armed forces, excluding those employees who have only Japanese nationality, shall not be subject to any proceedings for the enforcement of any judgment given against them in Japan in a matter arising from the performance of their official duties.

(g) Except in so far as subparagraph (e) of this paragraph applies to claims covered by paragraph 2 of this Article, the provisions of this paragraph shall not apply to any claim arising out of or in connection with the navigation or operation of a ship or the loading, carriage, or discharge of a cargo, other than claims for death or personal injury to which paragraph 4 of this Article is not apply.

され、合意され、又は裁判により決定された額は、その25パーセントを日本国が、その75パーセントを合衆国が分担する。

(ii) 日本国及び合衆国が損害について責任を有する場合には、裁定され、合意され、又は裁判により決定された額は、両当事国が均等に分担する。損害が日本国又は合衆国の防衛隊によつて生じ、かつ、その損害をこれらの防衛隊のいずれか一方又は双方の責任として特定することができない場合には、裁定され、合意され、又は裁判により決定された額は、日本国及び合衆国が均等に分担する。

(iii) 比率に基づく分担案が受諾された各事件について日本国が6箇月の期間内に支払つた額の明細書は、支払要請書とともに、6箇月ごとに合衆国の当局に送付する。その支払は、できる限りすみやかに日本円で行なわなければならない。

(f) 合衆国軍隊の構成員又は被用者(日本の国籍のみを有する被用者を除く。)は、その公務の執行から生ずる事項については、日本国においてその者に対して与えられた判決の執行手続に服さない。

(g) この項の規定は、(e)の規定が2に定める請求権に適用される範囲を除くほか、船舶の航行若しくは運用又は貨物の船積み、運送若しくは陸揚げから生じ、又はそれらに関連して生ずる請求権には適用しない。ただし、4の規定の適用を受けない死亡又は負傷に対する請求権については、この限りでない。

6. Claims against members or employees of the United States armed forces (except employees who are nationals of or ordinarily resident in Japan) arising out of tortious acts or omissions in Japan not done in the performance of official duty shall be dealt with in the following manner:

(a) The authorities of Japan shall consider the claim and assess compensation to the claimant in a fair and just manner, taking into account all the circumstances of the case, including the conduct of the injured person, and shall prepare a report on the matter.

(b) The report shall be delivered to the appropriate United States authorities, who shall then decide without delay whether they will offer an ex gratia payment, and if so, of what amount.

(c) If an offer of ex gratia payment is made, and accepted by the claimant in full satisfaction of his claim, the United States authorities shall make the payment themselves and inform the authorities of Japan of their decision and of the sum paid.

(d) Nothing in this paragraph shall affect the jurisdiction of the courts of Japan to entertain an action against a member or an employee of the United States armed forces unless and until there has been payment in full satisfaction of the claim.

7. Claims arising out of the unauthorized use of any vehicle of the United States armed forces shall be dealt with in accordance with paragraph 6 of this Article, except in so far as the United States armed forces are legally responsible.

8. If a dispute arises as to whether a tortious act or omission of a member or an employee of the United States armed forces was done in the performance of official duty

6. 日本国内における不法の作為又は不作為で公務執行中に行なわれたものでないものから生ずる合衆国軍隊の構成員又は被用者(日本国民である被用者又は通常日本国に居住する被用者を除く。)に対する請求権は、次の方法で処理する。

(a) 日本国の当局は、当該事件に関するすべての事情(損害を受けた者の行動を含む。)を考慮して、公平かつ公正に請求を審査し、及び請求人に対する補償金を査定し、並びにその事件に関する報告書を作成する。

(b) その報告書は、合衆国の当局に交付するものとし、合衆国の当局は、遅滞なく、慰謝料の支払を申し出るかどうかを決定し、かつ、申し出る場合には、その額を決定する。

(c) 慰謝料の支払の申出があつた場合において、請求人がその請求を完全に満たすものとしてこれを受諾したときは、合衆国の当局は、みずから支払をしなければならず、かつ、その決定及び支払つた額を日本国の当局に通知する。

(d) この項の規定は、支払が請求を完全に満たすものとして行なわれたものでない限り、合衆国軍隊の構成員又は被用者に対する訴えを受理する日本国の裁判所の裁判権に影響を及ぼすものではない。

7. 合衆国軍隊の車両の許容されていない使用から生ずる請求権は、合衆国軍隊が法律上責任を有する場合を除くほか、6の規定に従つて処理する。

8. 合衆国軍隊の構成員又は被用者の不法の為又は不作為が公務執行中にされたものでかどうか、また、合衆国軍隊の車両の使容されていたものであるかどうかについ

or as to whether the use of any vehicle of the United States armed forces was unauthorized, the question shall be submitted to an arbitrator appointed in accordance with paragraph 2 (b) of this Article, whose decision on this point shall be final and conclusive.

9.(a) The United States shall not claim immunity from the jurisdiction of the courts of Japan for members or employees of the United States armed forces in respect of the civil jurisdiction of the courts of Japan except to the extent provided in paragraph 5 (f) of this Article.

(b) In case any private movable property, excluding that in use by the United States armed forces, which is subject to compulsory execution under Japanese law, is within the facilities and areas in use by the United States armed forces, the United States authorities shall, upon the request of Japanese courts, possess and turn over such property to the Japanese authorities.

(c) The authorities of Japan and the United States shall cooperate in the procurement of evidence for a fair hearing and disposal of claims under this Article.

10. Disputes arising out of contracts concerning the procurement of materials, supplies, equipment, services and labor by or for the United States armed forces, which are not resolved by the parties to the contract concerned, may be submitted to the Joint Committee for conciliation, provided that the provisions of this paragraph shall not prejudice any right which the parties to the contract may have to file a civil suit.

The term "defense services" used in this Article is understood to mean for Japan its Defense Forces and for the United States its armed forces.

が生じたときは、その問題は、2(b)の規定に従つて選任された仲裁人に付託するものとし、この点に関する仲裁人の裁定は、最終的のものとする。

9.(a) 合衆国は、日本国の裁判所の民事裁判権に関しては、5(f)に定める範囲を除くほか、合衆国軍隊の構成員又は被用者に対する日本国の裁判所の裁判権からの免除を請求してはならない。

(b) 合衆国軍隊が使用している施設及び区域内に日本国の法律に基づき強制執行を行なうべき私有の動産(合衆国軍隊が使用している動産を除く。)があるときは、合衆国の当局は、日本国の裁判所の要請に基づき、その財産を差し押えて日本国の当局に引き渡さなければならない。

(c) 日本国及び合衆国の当局は、この条の規定に基づく請求の公平な審理及び処理のための証拠の入手について協力するものとする。

10. 合衆国軍隊による又は合衆国軍隊のための資材、需品、備品、役務及び労務の調達に関する契約から生ずる紛争でその契約の当事者によつて解決されないものは、調停のため合同委員会に付託することができる。ただし、この項の規定は、契約の当事者が有することのある民事の訴えを提起する権利を害するものではない。

11. この条にいう「防衛隊」とは、日本国についてはその自衛隊をいい、合衆国についてはその軍隊をいうものと了解される。

12. Paragraphs 2 and 5 of this Article shall apply only to claims arising incident to non-combat activities.

13. The provisions of this Article shall not apply to any claims which arose before the entry into force of this Agreement. Such claims shall be dealt with by the provisions of Article 18 of the Administrative Agreement under Article 3 of the Security Treaty between Japan and the United States of America.

Article 19.

1. Members of the United States armed forces, the civilian component, and their dependents, shall be subject to the foreign exchange controls of the Government of Japan.

2. The preceding paragraph shall not be construed to preclude the transmission into or outside of Japan of United States dollars or dollar instruments representing the official funds of the United States or realized as a result of service or employment in connection with this Agreement by members of the United States armed forces and the civilian component, or realized by such persons and their dependents from sources outside of Japan.

3. The United States authorities shall take suitable measures to preclude the abuse of the privileges stipulated in the preceding paragraph or circumvention of the Japanese foreign exchange controls.

Article 20.

1.(a) United States military payment certificates denominated in dollars may be used by persons authorized by the United States for internal transactions within the facilities and areas in use by the United States

12. 2及び5の規定は、非戦闘行為に伴つて生じた請求権についてのみ適用する。

13. この条の規定は、この協定の効力発生前に生じた請求権には適用しない。それらの請求権は、日本国とアメリカ合衆国との間の安全保障条約第3条に基く行政協定第18条の規定によつて処理する。

第19条

1. 合衆国軍隊の構成員及び軍属並びにそれらの家族は、日本国政府の外国為替管理に服さなければならない。

2. 1の規定は、合衆国ドル若しくはドル証券で、合衆国の公金であるもの、合衆国軍隊の構成員及び軍属がこの協定に関連して勤務し、若しくは雇用された結果取得したもの又はこれらの者及びそれらの家族が日本国外の源泉から取得したものの日本国内又は日本国外への移転を妨げるものと解してはならない。

3. 合衆国の当局は、2に定める特権の濫用又は日本国の外国為替管理の回避を防止するため適当な措置を執らなければならない。

第20条

1.(a) ドルをもつて表示される合衆国軍票は衆国によつて認可された者が、合衆国軍用している施設及び区域内における相互引のため使用することができる。合衆国合衆国の規則が許す場合を除くほか、

armed forces. The Government of the United States will take appropriate action to insure that authorized personnel are prohibited from engaging in transactions involving military payment certificates except as authorized by United States regulations. The Government of Japan will take necessary action to prohibit unauthorized persons from engaging in transactions involving military payment certificates and with the aid of United States authorities will undertake to apprehend and punish any person or persons under its jurisdiction involved in the counterfeiting or uttering of counterfeit military payment certificates.

(b) It is agreed that the United States authorities will apprehend and punish members of the United States armed forces, the civilian component, or their dependents, who tender military payment certificates to unauthorized persons and that no obligation will be due to such unauthorized persons or to the Government of Japan or its agencies from the United States or any of its agencies as a result of any unauthorized use of military payment certificates within Japan.

2. In order to exercise control of military payment certificates the United States may designate certain American financial institutions to maintain and operate, under United States supervision, facilities for the use of persons authorized by the United States to use military payment certificates. Institutions authorized to maintain military ~~nking facilities will establish and maintain ~~h facilities physically separated from their ~~nese commercial banking business, with ~~nnel whose sole duty is to maintain and ~~ such facilities. Such facilities shall be ~~d to maintain United States currency ~~unts and to perform all financial

た者が軍票を用いる取引に従事することを禁止するよう適当な措置を執るものとする。日本国政府は、認可されない者が軍票を用いる取引に従事することを禁止するため必要な措置を執るものとし、また、合衆国の当局の援助を得て、軍票の偽造又は偽造軍票の使用に関与する者で日本国の当局の裁判権に服すべきものを逮捕し、及び処罰するものとする。

(b) 合衆国の当局が認可されない者に対し軍票を行使する合衆国軍隊の構成員及び軍属並びにそれらの家族を逮捕し、及び処罰すること並びに、日本国における軍票の許されない使用の結果として、合衆国又はその機関が、その認可されない者又は日本国政府若しくはその機関に対していかなる義務をも負うことはないことが合意される。

2. 軍票の管理を行なうため、合衆国は、その監督の下に、合衆国が軍票の使用を認可した者の用に供する施設を維持し、及び運営する一定のアメリカの金融機関を指定することができる。軍用銀行施設を維持することを認められた金融機関は、その施設を当該機関の日本国における商業金融業務から場所的に分離して設置し、及び維持するものとし、これに、この施設を維持し、かつ、運営することを唯一の任務とする職員を置く。この施設は、合衆国通貨による銀行勘定を維持し、かつ、この勘定に関するすべての金融取引(第19条2に定める範囲内における資金の受領及び送付を含む。)を行なうことを許される。

transaction in connection therewith including receipt and remission of funds to the extent provided by Article 19, paragraph 2, of this Agreement.

Article 21.

The United States may establish and operate, within the facilities and areas in use by the United States armed forces, United States military post offices, for the use of members of the United States armed forces, the civilian component, and their dependents, for the transmission of mail between United States military post offices in Japan and between such military post offices and other United States post offices.

Article 22.

The United States may enroll and train eligible United States citizens residing in Japan, who apply for such enrollment, in the reserve organizations of the armed forces of the United States.

Article 23.

Japan and the United States will cooperate in taking such steps as may from time to time be necessary to ensure the security of the United States armed forces, the members thereof, the civilian component, their dependents, and their property. The Government of Japan agrees to seek such legislation and to take such other action as may be necessary to ensure the adequate security and protection within its territory of installations, equipment, property, records and official information of the United States, and for the punishment of offenders under the applicable laws of Japan.

第21条

合衆国は、合衆国軍隊の構成員及び軍属並びにそれらの家族が利用する合衆国軍事郵便局を、日本国にある合衆国軍事郵便局間及びこれらの軍事郵便局と他の合衆国郵便局との間における郵便物の送達のため、合衆国軍隊が使用している施設及び区域内に設置し、及び運営することができる。

第22条

合衆国は、日本国に在留する適格の合衆国市民で合衆国軍隊の予備役団体への編入の申請を行なうものを同団体に編入し、及び訓練することができる。

第23条

日本国及び合衆国は、合衆国軍隊、合衆国軍隊の構成員及び軍属並びにそれらの家族並びにこれらのものの財産の安全を確保するため随時に必要となるべき措置を執ることについて協力するものとする。日本国政府は、その領域において合衆国の設備、備品、財産、記録及び公務上の情報の十分な安全及び保護を確保するため、並びに適用されるべき日本国の法令に基づいて犯人を罰するため、必要な立法を求め、及び必要なその他の措置を執ることに同意する。

Article 24.

1. It is agreed that the United States will bear for the duration of this Agreement without cost to Japan all expenditures incident to the maintenance of the United States armed forces in Japan except those to be borne by Japan as provided in paragraph 2.

2. It is agreed that Japan will furnish for the duration of this Agreement without cost to the United States and make compensation where appropriate to the owners and suppliers thereof all facilities and areas and rights of way, including facilities and areas jointly used such as those at airfields and ports, as provided in Articles 2 and 3.

3. It is agreed that arrangements will be effected between the Governments of Japan and the United States for accounting applicable to financial transactions arising out of this Agreement.

Article 25.

1. A Joint Committee shall be established as the means for consultation between the Government of Japan and the Government of the United States on all matters requiring mutual consultation regarding the implementation of this Agreement. In particular, the Joint Committee shall serve as the means for consultation in determining the facilities and areas in Japan which are required for the use of the United States in carrying out the purposes of the Treaty of Mutual Cooperation and Security.

　　　The Joint Committee shall be composed
　represen-tative of the Government of
　n and a representative of the
　　nment of the United States, each of
　　　shall have one or more deputies and a
　　e Joint Committee shall determine its
　　　edures, and arrange for such

第24条

1.　日本国に合衆国軍隊を維持することに伴うすべての経費は、2に規定するところにより日本国が負担すべきものを除くほか、この協定の存続期間中日本国に負担をかけないで合衆国が負担することが合意される。

2.　日本国は、第2条及び第3条に定めるすべての施設及び区域並びに路線権(飛行場及び港における施設及び区域のように共同に使用される施設及び区域を含む。)をこの協定の存続期間中合衆国に負担をかけないで提供し、かつ、相当の場合には、施設及び区域並びに路線権の所有者及び提供者に補償を行なうことが合意される。

3.　この協定に基づいて生ずる資金上の取引に適用すべき経理のため、日本国政府と合衆国政府との間に取極を行なうことが合意される。

第25条

1.　この協定の実施に関して相互間の協議を必要とするすべての事項に関する日本国政府と合衆国政府との間の協議機関として、合同委員会を設置する。合同委員会は、特に、合衆国が相互協力及び安全保障条約の目的の遂行に当たつて使用するため必要とされる日本国内の施設及び区域を決定する協議機関として、任務を行なう。

2.　合同委員会は、日本国政府の代表者一人及び合衆国政府の代表者一人で組織し、各代表者は、一人又は二人以上の代理及び職員団を有するものとする。合同委員会は、その手続規則を定め、並びに必要な補助機関及び事務機関を設ける。合同委員会は、日本国政府又は合衆国政府のいずれか一方の代表者の要請があるときは

auxiliary organs and administrative services as may be required. The Joint Committee shall be so organized that it may meet immediately at any time at the request of the representative of either the Government of Japan or the Government of the United States.

3.   If the Joint Committee is unable to resolve any matter, it shall refer that matter to the respective Governments for further consideration through appropriate channels.

Article 26.

1.   This Agreement shall be approved by Japan and the United States in accordance with their legal procedures, and notes indicating such approval shall be exchanged.

2.   After the procedure set forth in the preceding paragraph has been followed, this Agreement will enter into force on the date of coming into force of the Treaty of Mutual Cooperation and Security, at which time the Administrative Agreement under Article 3 of the Security Treaty between Japan and the United States of America, signed at Tokyo on February 28, 1952, as amended, shall expire.

3.   The Government of each Party to this Agreement undertakes to seek from its legislature necessary budgetary and legislative action with respect to provisions of this Agreement which require such action for their execution.

Article 27.

Either Government may at any time request the revision of any Article of this Agreement, in which case the two Governments shall enter into negotiation through appropriate channels.

いつでも直ちに会合することができるように組織する。

3.   合同委員会は、問題を解決することができないときは、適当な経路を通じて、その問題をそれぞれの政府にさらに考慮されるように移すものとする。

第26条

1.   この協定は、日本国及び合衆国によりそれぞれの国内法上の手続に従つて承認されなければならず、その承認を通知する公文が交換されるものとする。

2.   この協定は、1に定める手続が完了した後、相互協力及び安全保障条約の効力発生の日に効力を生じ、1952年2月28日に東京で署名された日本国とアメリカ合衆国との間の安全保障条約第3条に基く行政協定(改正を含む。)は、その時に終了する。

3.   この協定の各当事国の政府は、この協定の規定中その実施のため予算上及び立法上の措置を必要とするものについて、必要なその措置を立法機関に求めることを約束する。

第27条

いずれの政府も、この協定のいずれの条についてもその改正をいつでも要請することができる。その場合には、両政府は、適当な経路を通じて交渉するものとする。

Article 28.

This Agreement, and agreed revisions thereof, shall remain in force while the Treaty of Mutual Cooperation and Security remains in force unless earlier terminated by agreement between the two Governments.

In witness whereof the undersigned Plenipotentiaries have signed this Agreement.

Done at Washington, in duplicate, in the Japanese and English languages, both texts equally authentic, this 19th day of January, 1960.

For Japan:
Nobusuke Kishi
Aiichiro Fujiyama
Mitsujiro Ishii
Tadashi Adachi
Koichiro Asakai
For the United States of America:
Christian A. Herter
Douglas MacArthur 2nd
J. Graham Parsons

第28条

この協定及びその合意された改正は、相互協力及び安全保障条約が有効である間、有効とする。ただし、それ以前に両政府間の合意によつて終了させたときは、この限りでない。

以上の証拠として、下名の全権委員は、この協定に署名した。

1960年1月19日にワシントンで、ひとしく正文である日本語及び英語により本書2通を作成した。

日本国のために
岸　　信介
藤山愛一郎
石井光次郎
足立　　正
朝海浩一郎
アメリカ合衆国のために
クリスチャン・A・ハーター
ダグラス・マックアーサー2世
J・グレイアム・パースンズ

U.S.-Japan Security Consultative Committee
New York, New York
September 23, 1997

日米安全保障協議委員会
於　ニュー・ヨーク
1997年9月23日

The U.S.-Japan alliance is indispensable for ensuring the security of Japan and continues to play a key role in maintaining peace and stability in the Asia-Pacific region. It also facilitates the positive engagement of the United States in the region. The alliance reflects such common values as respect for freedom, democracy, and human rights, and serves as a political basis for wide-ranging bilateral cooperation, including efforts to build a more stable international security environment. The success of such efforts benefits all in the region.

The "Guidelines for U.S.-Japan Defense Cooperation" (the Guidelines), approved by the 17th Security Consultative Committee (SCC) on November 27, 1978, resulted from studies and consultations on a comprehensive framework for cooperation in the area of defense. Significant achievements for closer defense cooperation under the Guidelines have increased the credibility of bilateral security arrangements.

Although the Cold War has ended, the potential for instability and uncertainty persists in the Asia-Pacific region. Accordingly, the maintenance of peace and stability in this region has assumed greater importance for the security of Japan.

The "U.S.-Japan Joint Declaration on Security" issued by President Clinton and Prime Minister Hashimoto in April 1996, reconfirmed that the U.S.-Japan security relationship remains the cornerstone for achieving common security objectives, and

日米同盟関係は、日本の安全の確保にとって必要不可欠なものであり、また、アジア太平洋地域における平和と安定を維持するために引き続き重要な役割を果たしている。日米同盟関係は、この地域における米国の肯定的な関与を促進するものである。この同盟関係は、自由、民主主義及び人権の尊重等の共通の価値観を反映するとともに、より安定した国際的な安全保障環境の構築のための努力を始めとする広範な日米間の協力の政治的な基礎となっている。このような努力が成果を挙げることは、この地域のすべての者の利益となる。

1978年11月27日の第17回日米安全保障協議委員会(SCC)で了承された「日米防衛協力のための指針」(「指針」)は、防衛の分野における包括的な協力態勢に関する研究・協議の結果として策定された。指針の下で行われたより緊密な防衛協力のための作業の成果には顕著なものがあり、これは、日米安全保障体制の信頼性を増進させた。

冷戦の終結にもかかわらず、アジア太平洋地域には潜在的な不安定性と不確実性が依然として存在しており、この地域における平和と安定の維持は、日本の安全のために一層重要になっている。

1996年4月に橋本総理大臣とクリントン大統領により発表された「日米安全保障共同宣言」は、日米安全保障関係が、共通の安全保障上の目標を達成するとともに、21世紀に向けてアジア太平洋地域において安定的で繁栄した情勢を維持するための基礎であり続けることを再確認した

for maintaining a stable and prosperous environment in the Asia-Pacific region as we enter the twenty-first century. The President and the Prime Minister agreed to initiate a review of the 1978 Guidelines to build upon the close working relationship already established between the United States and Japan.

In June 1996, the two Governments reconstituted the Subcommittee for Defense Cooperation (SDC) under the auspices of the SCC, to conduct the review of the Guidelines (the Review) on the basis of Japan's "National Defense Program Outline" of November 1995, and the "U.S.-Japan Joint Declaration on Security." In view of the changes in the post-Cold War environment, and based on the achievements made under the Guidelines, the SDC has considered:

—cooperation under normal circumstances;
—actions in response to an armed attack against Japan; and
—cooperation in situations in areas surrounding Japan that will have an important influence on Japan's peace and security (situations in areas surrounding Japan).

These considerations aimed at providing a general framework and policy direction for the roles and missions of the two countries and ways of cooperation and coordination, both under normal circumstances and during contingencies. The Review did not address situations in specific areas.

The SDC has conducted the Review with the objective of identifying ideas and specific items that would contribute to more effective bilateral cooperation with the intention to complete the Review by autumn of 1997, as instructed by the SCC in September 1996. The discussions at the SDC the course of the Review are summarized

また、総理大臣と大統領は、日本と米国の間に既に構築されている緊密な協力関係を増進するため、1978年の指針の見直しを開始することで意見が一致した。

1996年6月、日米両国政府は、1995年11月の日本の「防衛計画の大綱」及び「日米安全保障共同宣言」を踏まえて指針の見直し（「見直し」）を行うため、日米安全保障協議委員会の下にある防衛協力小委員会(SDC)を改組した。防衛協力小委員会は、冷戦後の情勢の変化にかんがみ、指針の下での成果を基礎として、以下の分野について検討を行ってきた。

—平素から行う協力
—日本に対する武力攻撃に際しての対処行動等

—日本周辺地域における事態で日本の平和と安全に重要な影響を与える場合（「周辺事態」）の協力

これらの検討は、平素からの及び緊急事態における日米両国の役割並びに協力及び調整の在り方について、一般的な大枠及び方向性を示すことを目的としたものである。見直しは、特定の地域における事態を議論して行ったものではない。

防衛協力小委員会は、1996年9月の日米安全保障協議委員会による指示を受け、1997年秋に終了することを目途に、より効果的な日米協力に資するような考え方及び具体的な項目を洗い出すことを目標として見直しを行った。見直しの過程で防衛協力小委員会において行われた議論は、1996年9月の「日米防衛協力のための指針の見直しの進捗状況報告」及び1997年6月の「日米

in the "Progress Report on the Guidelines Review for U.S.-Japan Defense Cooperation" of September 1996, and in the "Interim Report on the Review of the Guidelines for U.S.-Japan Defense Cooperation" of June 1997.

防衛協力のための指針の見直しに関する中間とりまとめ」に整理されている。

The SDC prepared and submitted to the SCC new "Guidelines for U.S.-Japan Defense Cooperation." The SCC approved and issued the following Guidelines, which supersede the 1978 Guidelines.

防衛協力小委員会は、新たな「日米防衛協力のための指針」を作成し、これを日米安全保障協議委員会に報告した。日米安全保障協議委員会は、以下に示す指針を了承し、公表した。この指針は、1978年の指針に代わるものである。

The Guidelines for U.S.-Japan Defense Cooperation

日米防衛協力のための指針

I. The Aim of the Guidelines

I. 指針の目的

The aim of these Guidelines is to create a solid basis for more effective and credible U.S.-Japan cooperation under normal circumstances, in case of an armed attack against Japan, and in situations in areas surrounding Japan. The Guidelines also provide a general framework and policy direction for the roles and missions of the two countries and ways of cooperation and coordination, both under normal circumstances and during contingencies.

この指針の目的は、平素から並びに日本に対する武力攻撃及び周辺事態に際してより効果的かつ信頼性のある日米協力を行うための、堅固な基礎を構築することである。また、指針は、平素からの及び緊急事態における日米両国の役割並びに協力及び調整の在り方について、一般的な大枠及び方向性を示すものである。

II. Basic Premises and Principles

II. 基本的な前提及び考え方

The Guidelines and programs under the Guidelines are consistent with the following basic premises and principles.

指針及びその下で行われる取組みは、以下の基本的な前提及び考え方に従う。

1. The rights and obligations under the Treaty of Mutual Cooperation and Security between the United States of America and Japan (the U.S.-Japan Security Treaty) and its related arrangements, as well as the fundamental framework of the U.S.-Japan alliance, will remain unchanged.

1. 日米安全保障条約及びその関連取極に基づく権利及び義務並びに日米同盟関係の基本的な枠組みは、変更されない。

2. Japan will conduct all its actions within

2. 日本のすべての行為は、日本の憲法上の制

the limitations of its Constitution and in accordance with such basic positions as the maintenance of its exclusively defense-oriented policy and its three non-nuclear principles.

3.   All actions taken by the United States and Japan will be consistent with basic principles of international law, including the peaceful settlement of disputes and sovereign equality, and relevant international agreements such as the Charter of the United Nations.

4.   The Guidelines and programs under the Guidelines will not obligate either Government to take legislative, budgetary or administrative measures. However, since the objective of the Guidelines and programs under the Guidelines is to establish an effective framework for bilateral cooperation, the two Governments are expected to reflect in an appropriate way the results of these efforts, based on their own judgements, in their specific policies and measures. All actions taken by Japan will be consistent with its laws and regulations then in effect.

III. Cooperation under Normal Circumstances

Both Governments will firmly maintain existing U.S.-Japan security arrangements. Each Government will make efforts to maintain required defense postures. Japan will possess defense capability within the scope necessary for self-defense on the basis of the "National Defense Program Outline." In order to meet its commitments, the United States will maintain its nuclear deterrent capability, its forward deployed forces in the Asia-Pacific region, and other forces capable of reinforcing those forward deployed forces.

Both Governments, based on their

約の範囲内において、専守防衛、非核三原則等の日本の基本的な方針に従って行われる。

3.   日米両国のすべての行為は、紛争の平和的解決及び主権平等を含む国際法の基本原則並びに国際連合憲章を始めとする関連する国際約束に合致するものである。

4.   指針及びその下で行われる取組みは、いずれの政府にも、立法上、予算上又は行政上の措置をとることを義務づけるものではない。しかしながら、日米協力のための効果的な態勢の構築が指針及びその下で行われる取組みの目標であることから、日米両国政府が、各々の判断に従い、このような努力の結果を各々の具体的な政策や措置に適切な形で反映することが期待される。日本のすべての行為は、その時々において適用のある国内法令に従う。

III. 平素から行う協力

日米両国政府は、現在の日米安全保障体制を堅持し、また、各々所要の防衛態勢の維持に努める。日本は、「防衛計画の大綱」にのっとり、自衛のために必要な範囲内で防衛力を保持する。米国は、そのコミットメントを達成するため、核抑止力を保持するとともに、アジア太平洋地域における前方展開兵力を維持し、かつ、来援し得るその他の兵力を保持する。

日米両国政府は、各々の政策を基礎としつつ、

espective policies, under normal
ircumstances will maintain close
cooperation for the defense of Japan as well
as for the creation of a more stable
international security environment.

Both Governments will under normal
circumstances enhance cooperation in a
variety of areas. Examples include mutual
support activities under the Agreement
between the Government of Japan and the
Government of the United States of America
concerning Reciprocal Provision of Logistic
Support, Supplies and Services between the
Self-Defense Forces of Japan and the Armed
Forces of the United States of America; the
Mutual Defense Assistance Agreement
between the Unites States of America and
Japan; and their related arrangements.

**1. Information Sharing and Policy
Consultations**

Recognizing that accurate information
and sound analysis are at the foundation of
security, the two Governments will increase
information and intelligence sharing and the
exchange of views on international situations
of mutual interest, especially in the Asia-
Pacific region. They will also continue close
consultations on defense policies and military
postures.

Such information sharing and policy
consultations will be conducted at as many
levels as possible and on the broadest range
of subjects. This will be accomplished by
taking advantage of all available
opportunities, such as SCC and Security Sub-
Committee (SSC) meetings.

2. Various Types of Security Cooperation

Bilateral cooperation to promote
regional and global activities in the field of
security contributes to the creation of a more
stable international security environment.

日本の防衛及びより安定した国際的な安全保障
環境の構築のため、平素から密接な協力を維持
する。

日米両国政府は、平素から様々な分野での協
力を充実する。この協力には、日米物品役務相
互提供協定及び日米相互防衛援助協定並びにこ
れらの関連取決めに基づく相互支援活動が含ま
れる。

1. 情報交換及び政策協議

日米両国政府は、正確な情報及び的確な分析
が安全保障の基礎であると認識し、アジア太平
洋地域の情勢を中心として、双方が関心を有す
る国際情勢についての情報及び意見の交換を強
化するとともに、防衛政策及び軍事態勢につい
ての緊密な協議を継続する。

このような情報交換及び政策協議は、日米安
全保障協議委員会及び日米安全保障高級事務レ
ベル協議(SSC)を含むあらゆる機会をとらえ、
できる限り広範なレベル及び分野において行わ
れる。

2. 安全保障面での種々の協力

安全保障面での地域的な及び地球的規模の諸
活動を促進するための日米協力は、より安定し
た国際的な安全保障環境の構築に寄与する。

Recognizing the importance and significance of security dialogues and defense exchanges in the region, as well as international arms control and disarmament, the two Governments will promote such activities and cooperate as necessary.

When either or both Governments participate in United Nations peacekeeping operations or international humanitarian relief operations, the two sides will cooperate closely for mutual support as necessary. They will prepare procedures for cooperation in such areas as transportation, medical services, information sharing, and education and training.

When either or both Governments conduct emergency relief operations in response to requests from governments concerned or international organizations in the wake of large-scale disasters, they will cooperate closely with each other as necessary.

3. Bilateral Programs

Both Governments will conduct bilateral work, including bilateral defense planning in case of an armed attack against Japan, and mutual cooperation planning in situations in areas surrounding Japan. Such efforts will be made in a comprehensive mechanism involving relevant agencies of the respective Governments, and establish the foundation for bilateral cooperation.

Bilateral exercises and training will be enhanced in order not only to validate such bilateral work but also to enable smooth and effective responses by public and private entities of both countries, starting with U.S. Forces and the Self-Defense Forces. The two Governments will under normal circumstances establish a bilateral coordination mechanism involving relevant agencies to be operated during contingencies.

日米両国政府は、この地域における安全保障対話・防衛交流及び国際的な軍備管理・軍縮の意義と重要性を認識し、これらの活動を促進するとともに、必要に応じて協力する。

日米いずれかの政府又は両国政府が国際連合平和維持活動又は人道的な国際救援活動に参加する場合には、日米両国政府は、必要に応じて、相互支援のために密接に協力する。日米両国政府は、輸送、衛生、情報交換、教育訓練等の分野における協力の要領を準備する。

大規模災害の発生を受け、日米いずれかの政府又は両国政府が関係政府又は国際機関の要請に応じて緊急援助活動を行う場合には、日米両国政府は、必要に応じて密接に協力する。

3. 日米共同の取組み

日米両国政府は、日本に対する武力攻撃に際しての共同作戦計画についての検討及び周辺事態に際しての相互協力計画についての検討を含む共同作業を行う。このような努力は、双方の関係機関の関与を得た包括的なメカニズムにおいて行われ、日米協力の基礎を構築する。

日米両国政府は、このような共同作業を検証するとともに、自衛隊及び米軍を始めとする日米両国の公的機関及び民間の機関による円滑かつ効果的な対応を可能とするため、共同演習・訓練を強化する。また、日米両国政府は、緊急事態において関係機関の関与を得て運用される日米間の調整メカニズムを平素から構築しておく。

IV. Actions in Response to an Armed Attack against Japan

Bilateral actions in response to an armed attack against Japan remain a core aspect of U.S.-Japan defense cooperation.

When an armed attack against Japan is imminent, the two Governments will take steps to prevent further deterioration of the situation and make preparations necessary for the defense of Japan. When an armed attack against Japan takes place, the two Governments will conduct appropriate bilateral actions to repel it at the earliest possible stage.

1. When an Armed Attack against Japan is Imminent

The two Governments will intensify information and intelligence sharing and policy consultations, and initiate at an early stage the operation of a bilateral coordination mechanism. Cooperating as appropriate, they will make preparations necessary for ensuring coordinated responses according to the readiness stage selected by mutual agreement. Japan will establish and maintain the basis for U.S. reinforcements. As circumstances change, the two Governments will also increase intelligence gathering and surveillance, and will prepare to respond to activities which could develop into an armed attack against Japan.

The two Governments will make every effort, including diplomatic efforts, to prevent further deterioration of the situation.

Recognizing that a situation in areas surrounding Japan may develop into an armed attack against Japan, the two Governments will be mindful of the close interrelationship of the two requirements: preparations for the defense of Japan and responses to or preparations

IV. 日本に対する武力攻撃に際しての対処行動等

日本に対する武力攻撃に際しての共同対処行動等は、引き続き日米防衛協力の中核の要素である。

日本に対する武力攻撃が差し迫っている場合には、日米両国政府は、事態の拡大を抑制するための措置をとるとともに、日本の防衛のために必要な準備を行う。日本に対する武力攻撃がなされた場合には、日米両国政府は、適切に共同して対処し、極力早期にこれを排除する。

1. 日本に対する武力攻撃が差し迫っている場合

日米両国政府は、情報交換及び政策協議を強化するとともに、日米間の調整メカニズムの運用を早期に開始する。日米両国政府は、適切に協力しつつ、合意によって選択された準備段階に従い、整合のとれた対応を確保するために必要な準備を行う。日本は、米軍の来援基盤を構築し、維持する。また、日米両国政府は、情勢の変化に応じ、情報収集及び警戒監視を強化するとともに、日本に対する武力攻撃に発展し得る行為に対応するための準備を行う。

日米両国政府は、事態の拡大を抑制するため、外交上のものを含むあらゆる努力を払う。

なお、日米両国政府は、周辺事態の推移によっては日本に対する武力攻撃が差し迫ったものとなるような場合もあり得ることを念頭に置きつつ、日本の防衛のための準備と周辺事態への対応又はそのための準備との間の密接な相互関係に留意する。

for situations in areas surrounding Japan.

2. When an Armed Attack against Japan Takes Place

(1) Principles for Coordinated Bilateral Actions

(a) Japan will have primary responsibility immediately to take action and to repel an armed attack against Japan as soon as possible. The United States will provide appropriate support to Japan. Such bilateral cooperation may vary according to the scale, type, phase, and other factors of the armed attack. This cooperation may include preparations for and execution of coordinated bilateral operations, steps to prevent further deterioration of the situation, surveillance, and intelligence sharing.

(b) In conducting bilateral operations, U.S. Forces and the Self-Defense Forces will employ their respective defense capabilities in a coordinated, timely, and effective manner. In doing this, they will conduct effective joint operations of their respective Forces' ground, maritime and air services. The Self-Defense Forces will primarily conduct defensive operations in Japanese territory and its surrounding waters and airspace, while U.S. Forces support Self-Defense Forces' operations. U.S. Forces will also conduct operations to supplement the capabilities of the Self-Defense Forces.

(c) The United States will introduce reinforcements in a timely manner, and Japan will establish and maintain the basis to facilitate these deployments.

(2) Concept of Operations

(a) Operations to Counter Air Attack against Japan

U.S. Forces and the Self-Defense Forces will bilaterally conduct operations to counter

2. 日本に対する武力攻撃がなされた場合

(1) 整合のとれた共同対処行動のための基本的な考え方

(a) 日本は、日本に対する武力攻撃に即応して主体的に行動し、極力早期にこれを排除する。その際、米国は、日本に対して適切に協力する。このような日米協力の在り方は、武力攻撃の規模、態様、事態の推移その他の要素により異なるが、これには、整合のとれた共同の作戦の実施及びそのための準備、事態の拡大を抑制するための措置、警戒監視並びに情報交換についての協力が含まれ得る。

(b) 自衛隊及び米軍が作戦を共同して実施する場合には、双方は、整合性を確保しつつ、適時かつ適切な形で、各々の防衛力を運用する。その際、双方は、各々の陸・海・空部隊の効果的な統合運用を行う。自衛隊は、主として日本の領域及びその周辺海空域において防勢作戦を行い、米軍は、自衛隊の行う作戦を支援する。米軍は、また、自衛隊の能力を補完するための作戦を実施する。

(c) 米国は、兵力を適時に来援させ、日本は、これを促進するための基盤を構築し、維持する。

(2) 作戦構想

(a) 日本に対する航空侵攻に対処するための作戦

自衛隊及び米軍は、日本に対する航空侵攻に対処するための作戦を共同して実施する。

air attack against Japan.

The Self-Defense Forces will have primary responsibility for conducting operations for air defense.

自衛隊は、防空のための作戦を主体的に実施する。

U.S. Forces will support Self-Defense Forces' operations and conduct operations, including those which may involve the use of strike power, to supplement the capabilities of the Self-Defense Forces.

米軍は、自衛隊の行う作戦を支援するとともに、打撃力の使用を伴うような作戦を含め、自衛隊の能力を補完するための作戦を実施する。

(b) Operations to Defend Surrounding Waters and to Protect Sea Lines of Communication

(b) 日本周辺海域の防衛及び海上交通の保護のための作戦

U.S. Forces and the Self-Defense Forces will bilaterally conduct operations for the defense of surrounding waters and for the protection of sea lines of communication.

自衛隊及び米軍は、日本周辺海域の防衛のための作戦及び海上交通の保護のための作戦を共同して実施する。

The Self-Defense Forces will have primary responsibility for the protection of major ports and straits in Japan, for the protection of ships in surrounding waters, and for other operations.

自衛隊は、日本の重要な港湾及び海峡の防備、日本周辺海域における船舶の保護並びにその他の作戦を主体的に実施する。

U.S. Forces will support Self-Defense Forces' operations and conduct operations, including those which may provide additional mobility and strike power, to supplement the capabilities of the Self-Defense Forces.

米軍は、自衛隊の行う作戦を支援するとともに、機動打撃力の使用を伴うような作戦を含め、自衛隊の能力を補完するための作戦を実施する。

(c) Operations to Counter Airborne and Seaborne Invasions of Japan

(c) 日本に対する着上陸侵攻に対処するための作戦

U.S. Forces and the Self-Defense Forces will bilaterally conduct operations to counter airborne and seaborne invasions of Japan.

自衛隊及び米軍は、日本に対する着上陸侵攻に対処するための作戦を共同して実施する。

The Self-Defense Forces will have primary responsibility for conducting operations to check and repel such invasions.

自衛隊は、日本に対する着上陸侵攻を阻止し排除するための作戦を主体的に実施する。

U.S. Forces will primarily conduct operations to supplement the capabilities of the Self-Defense Forces. The Unites States will introduce reinforcements at the earliest possible stage, according to the scale, type, and other factors of the invasion, and will support Self-Defense Forces' operations.

米軍は、主として自衛隊の能力を補完するための作戦を実施する。その際、米国は、侵攻の規模、態様その他の要素に応じ、極力早期に兵力を来援させ、自衛隊の行う作戦を支援する。

(d) Responses to Other Threats

(i) The Self-Defense Forces will have primary responsibility to check and repel guerilla-commando type attacks or any other unconventional attacks involving military infiltration in Japanese territory at the earliest possible stage. They will cooperate and coordinate closely with relevant agencies, and will be supported in appropriate ways by U.S. Forces depending on the situation.

(ii) U.S. Forces and the Self-Defense Forces will cooperate and coordinate closely to respond to a ballistic missile attack. U.S. Forces will provide Japan with necessary intelligence, and consider, as necessary, the use of forces providing additional strike power.

(3) Activities and Requirements for Operations

(a) Command and Coordination

U.S. Forces and the Self-Defense Forces, in close cooperation, will take action through their respective command-and-control channels. To conduct effective bilateral operations, the two Forces will establish, in advance, procedures which include those to determine the division of roles and missions and to synchronize their operations.

(b) Bilateral Coordination Mechanism

Necessary coordination among the relevant agencies of the two Governments will be conducted through a bilateral coordination mechanism. In order to conduct effective bilateral operations, U.S. Forces and the Self-Defense Forces will closely coordinate operations, intelligence activities, and logistics support through this coordination mechanism including use of a bilateral coordination center.

(c) Communications and Electronics

The two Governments will provide mutual support to ensure effective use of communications and electronics capabilities.

(d) その他の脅威への対応

(i) 自衛隊は、ゲリラ・コマンドウ攻撃等日本領域に軍事力を潜入させて行う不正規型の攻撃を極力早期に阻止し排除するための作戦を主体的に実施する。その際、関係機関と密接に協力し調整するとともに、事態に応じて米軍の適切な支援を得る。

(ii) 自衛隊及び米軍は、弾道ミサイル攻撃に対応するために密接に協力し調整する。米軍は、日本に対し必要な情報を提供するとともに、必要に応じ、打撃力を有する部隊の使用を考慮する。

(3) 作戦に係る諸活動及びそれに必要な事項

(a) 指揮及び調整

自衛隊及び米軍は、緊密な協力の下、各々の指揮系統に従って行動する。自衛隊及び米軍は、効果的な作戦を共同して実施するため、役割分担の決定、作戦行動の整合性の確保等についての手続をあらかじめ定めておく。

(b) 日米間の調整メカニズム

日米両国の関係機関の間における必要な調整は、日米間の調整メカニズムを通じて行われる。自衛隊及び米軍は、効果的な作戦を共同して実施するため、作戦、情報活動及び後方支援について、日米共同調整所の活用を含め、この調整メカニズムを通じて相互に緊密に調整する。

(c) 通信電子活動

日米両国政府は、通信電子能力の効果的な活用を確保するため、相互に支援する。

(d) Intelligence Activities

The two Governments will cooperate in intelligence activities in order to ensure effective bilateral operations. This will include coordination of requirements, collection, production, and dissemination of intelligence products. Each Government will be responsible for the security of shared intelligence.

(e) Logistics Support Activities

U.S. Forces and the Self-Defense Forces will conduct logistics support activities efficiently and properly in accordance with appropriate bilateral arrangements.

To improve the effectiveness of logistics and to alleviate functional shortfalls, the two Governments will undertake mutual support activities, making appropriate use of authorities and assets of central and local government agencies, as well as private sector assets. Particular attention will be paid to the following points in conducting such activities:

(i) Supply

The United States will support the acquisition of supplies for systems of U.S. origin while Japan will support the acquisition of supplies in Japan.

(ii) Transportation

The two Governments will closely cooperate in transportation operations, including airlift and sealift of supplies from the United States to Japan.

(iii) Maintenance

Japan will support the maintenance of U.S. Forces' equipment in Japan; the United States will support the maintenance of items of U.S. origin which are beyond Japanese maintenance capabilities. Maintenance support will include the technical training of maintenance personnel as required. Japan will also support U.S. Forces' requirement

(d) 情報活動

日米両国政府は、効果的な作戦を共同して実施するため、情報活動について協力する。これには、情報の要求、収集、処理及び配布についての調整が含まれる。その際、日米両国政府は、共有した情報の保全に関し各々責任を負う。

(e) 後方支援活動

自衛隊及び米軍は、日米間の適切な取決めに従い、効率的かつ適切に後方支援活動を実施する。

日米両国政府は、後方支援の効率性を向上させ、かつ、各々の能力不足を軽減するよう、中央政府及び地方公共団体が有する権限及び能力並びに民間が有する能力を適切に活用しつつ、相互支援活動を実施する。その際、特に次の事項に配慮する。

(i) 補給

米国は、米国製の装備品等の補給品の取得を支援し、日本は、日本国内における補給品の取得を支援する。

(ii) 輸送

日米両国政府は、米国から日本への補給品の航空輸送及び海上輸送を含む輸送活動について、緊密に協力する。

(iii)整備

日本は、日本国内において米軍の装備品の整備を支援し、米国は、米国製の品目の整備であって日本の整備能力が及ばないものについて支援を行う。整備の支援には、必要に応じ、整備要員の技術指導を含む。また、日本は、サルベージ及び回収に関する米軍の需要についても支援を行う。

for salvage and recovery.

(iv) Facilities

Japan will, in case of need, provide additional facilities and areas in accordance with the U.S.-Japan Security Treaty and its related arrangements. If necessary for effective and efficient operations, U.S. Forces and the Self-Defense Forces will make joint use of Self-Defense Forces facilities and U.S. facilities and areas in accordance with the Treaty and its related arrangements.

(v) Medical Services

The two Governments will support each other in the area of medical services such as medical treatment and transportation of casualties.

V. Cooperation in Situations in Areas Surrounding Japan That Will Have an Important Influence on Japan's Peace and Security (Situations in Areas Surrounding Japan)

Situations in areas surrounding Japan will have an important influence on Japan's peace and security. The concept, situations in areas surrounding Japan, is not geographical but situational. The two Governments will make every effort, including diplomatic efforts, to prevent such situations from occurring. When the two Governments reach a common assessment of the state of each situation, they will effectively coordinate their activities. In responding to such situations, measures taken may differ depending on circumstances.

1. When a Situation in Areas Surrounding Japan is Anticipated

When a situation in areas surrounding Japan is anticipated, the two Governments will intensify information and intelligence sharing and policy consultations, including efforts to reach a common assessment of the situation.

(iv) 施設

日本は、必要に応じ、日米安全保障条約及びその関連取極に従って新たな施設・区域を提供する。また、作戦を効果的かつ効率的に実施するために必要な場合には、自衛隊及び米軍は同条約及びその関連取極に従って、自衛隊の施設及び米軍の施設・区域の共同使用を実施する。

(v) 衛生

日米両国政府は、衛生の分野において、傷病者の治療及び後送等の相互支援を行う。

V. 日本周辺地域における事態で日本の平和と安全に重要な影響を与える場合(周辺事態)の協力

周辺事態は、日本の平和と安全に重要な影響を与える事態である。周辺事態の概念は、地理的なものではなく、事態の性質に着目したものである。日米両国政府は、周辺事態が発生することのないよう、外交上のものを含むあらゆる努力を払う。日米両国政府は、個々の事態の状況について共通の認識に到達した場合に、各々の行う活動を効果的に調整する。なお、周辺事態に対応する際にとられる措置は、情勢に応じて異なり得るものである。

1. 周辺事態が予想される場合

周辺事態が予想される場合には、日米両国政府は、その事態について共通の認識に到達するための努力を含め、情報交換及び政策協議を強化する。

At the same time, they will make every effort, including diplomatic efforts, to prevent further deterioration of the situation, while initiating at an early stage the operation of a bilateral coordination mechanism, including use of a bilateral coordination center. Cooperating as appropriate, they will make preparations necessary for ensuring coordinated responses according to the readiness stage selected by mutual agreement. As circumstances change, they will also increase intelligence gathering and surveillance, and enhance their readiness to respond to the circumstances.

2. **Responses to Situations in Areas Surrounding Japan**

The two Governments will take appropriate measures, to include preventing further deterioration of situations, in response to situations in areas surrounding Japan. This will be done in accordance with the basic premises and principles listed in Section II above and based on their respective decisions. They will support each other as necessary in accordance with appropriate arrangements.

Functions and fields of cooperation and examples of items of cooperation are outlined below, and listed in the Annex.

(1) Cooperation in Activities Initiated by Either Government

Although either Government may conduct the following activities at its own discretion, bilateral cooperation will enhance their effectiveness.

(a) Relief Activities and Measures to Deal with Refugees

Each Government will conduct relief activities with the consent and cooperation of the authorities in the affected area. The two Governments will cooperate as necessary, taking into account their respective capabilities.

同時に、日米両国政府は、事態の拡大を抑制するため、外交上のものを含むあらゆる努力を払うとともに、日米共同調整所の活用を含め、日米間の調整メカニズムの運用を早期に開始する。また、日米両国政府は、適切に協力しつつ、合意によって選択された準備段階に従い、整合のとれた対応を確保するために必要な準備を行う。更に、日米両国政府は、情勢の変化に応じ、情報収集及び警戒監視を強化するとともに、情勢に対応するための即応態勢を強化する。

2. **周辺事態への対応**

周辺事態への対応に際しては、日米両国政府は、事態の拡大の抑制のためのものを含む適切な措置をとる。これらの措置は、上記Ⅱに掲げられた基本的な前提及び考え方に従い、かつ、各々の判断に基づいてとられる。日米両国政府は、適切な取決めに従って、必要に応じて相互支援を行う。

協力の対象となる機能及び分野並びに協力項目例は、以下に整理し、別表に示すとおりである。

(1) 日米両国政府が各々主体的に行う活動における協力

日米両国政府は、以下の活動を各々の判断の下に実施することができるが、日米間の協力は、その実効性を高めることとなる。

(a) 救援活動及び避難民への対応のための措置

日米両国政府は、被災地の現地当局の同意と協力を得つつ、救援活動を行う。日米両国政府は、各々の能力を勘案しつつ、必要に応じて協力する。

The two Governments will cooperate in dealing with refugees as necessary. When there is a flow of refugees into Japanese territory, Japan will decide how to respond and will have primary responsibility for dealing with the flow; the United States will provide appropriate support.

(b) Search and Rescue

The two Governments will cooperate in search and rescue operations. Japan will conduct search and rescue operations in Japanese territory; and at sea around Japan, as distinguished from areas where combat operations are being conducted. When U.S. Forces are conducting operations, the United States will conduct search and rescue operations in and near the operational areas.

(c) Noncombatant Evacuation Operations

When the need arises for U.S. and Japanese noncombatants to be evacuated from a third country to a safe haven, each Government is responsible for evacuating its own nationals as well as for dealing with the authorities of the affected area. In instances in which each decides it is appropriate, the two Governments will coordinate in planning and cooperate in carrying out their evacuations, including for the securing of transportation means, transportation and the use of facilities, using their respective capabilities in a mutually supplementary manner. If similar need arises for noncombatants other than of U.S. or Japanese nationality, the respective countries may consider extending, on their respective terms, evacuation assistance to third country nationals.

(d) Activities for Ensuring the Effectiveness of Economic Sanctions for the Maintenance of International Peace and Stability

Each Government will contribute to activities for ensuring the effectiveness of

日米両国政府は、避難民の取扱いについて、必要に応じて協力する。避難民が日本の領域に流入してくる場合については、日本がその対応の在り方を決定するとともに、主として日本が責任を持ってこれに対応し、米国は適切な支援を行う。

(b) 捜索・救難

日米両国政府は、捜索・救難活動について協力する。日本は、日本領域及び戦闘行動が行われている地域とは一線を画される日本の周囲の海域において捜索・救難活動を実施する。米国は、米軍が活動している際には、活動区域内及びその付近での捜索・救難活動を実施する。

(c) 非戦闘員を退避させるための活動

日本国民又は米国国民である非戦闘員を第三国から安全な地域に退避させる必要が生じる場合には、日米両国政府は、自国の国民の退避及び現地当局との関係について各々責任を有する。日米両国政府は、各々が適切であると判断する場合には、各々の有する能力を相互補完的に使用しつつ、輸送手段の確保、輸送及び施設の使用に係るものを含め、これらの非戦闘員の退避に関して、計画に際して調整し、また、実施に際して協力する。日本国民又は米国国民以外の非戦闘員について同様の必要が生じる場合には、日米両国が、各々の基準に従って、第三国の国民に対して退避に係る援助を行うことを検討することもある。

(d) 国際の平和と安定の維持を目的とする経済制裁の実効性を確保するための活動

日米両国政府は、国際の平和と安定の維持を目的とする経済制裁の実効性を確保するための

economic sanctions for the maintenance of international peace and stability. Such contributions will be made in accordance with each Government's own criteria.

Additionally, the two Governments will cooperate with each other as appropriate, taking into account their respective capabilities. Such cooperation includes information sharing, and cooperation in inspection of ships based on United Nations Security Council resolutions.

(2) Japan's Support for U.S. Forces Activities
  (a) Use of Facilities

Based on the U.S.-Japan Security Treaty and its related arrangements, Japan will, in case of need, provide additional facilities and areas in a timely and appropriate manner, and ensure the temporary use by U.S. Forces of Self-Defense Forces facilities and civilian airports and ports.

  (b) Rear Area Support

Japan will provide rear area support to those U.S. Forces that are conducting operations for the purpose of achieving the objectives of the U.S.-Japan Security Treaty. The primary aim of this rear area support is to enable U.S. Forces to use facilities and conduct operations in an effective manner. By its very nature, Japan's rear area support will be provided primarily in Japanese territory. It may also be provided on the high seas and international airspace around Japan which are distinguished from areas where combat operations are being conducted.

In providing rear area support, Japan will make appropriate use of authorities and assets of the central and local government agencies, as well as private sector assets. The Self-Defense Forces, as appropriate, will provide such support consistent with their mission for the defense

活動に対し、各々の基準に従って寄与する。

また、日米両国政府は、各々の能力を勘案しつつ、適切に協力する。そのような協力には、情報交換、及び国際連合安全保障理事会決議に基づく船舶の検査に際しての協力が含まれる。

(2) 米軍の活動に対する日本の支援
  (a) 施設の使用

日米安全保障条約及びその関連取極に基づき、日本は、必要に応じ、新たな施設・区域の提供を適時かつ適切に行うとともに、米軍による自衛隊施設及び民間空港・港湾の一時的使用を確保する。

  (b) 後方地域支援

日本は、日米安全保障条約の目的の達成のため活動する米軍に対して、後方地域支援を行う。この後方地域支援は、米軍が施設の使用及び種々の活動を効果的に行うことを可能とすることを主眼とするものである。そのような性質から、後方地域支援は、主として日本の領域において行われるが、戦闘行動が行われている地域とは一線を画される日本の周囲の公海及びその上空において行われることもあると考えられる。

後方地域支援を行うに当たって、日本は、中央政府及び地方公共団体が有する権限及び能力並びに民間が有する能力を適切に活用する。自衛隊は、日本の防衛及び公共の秩序維持のための任務の遂行と整合を図りつつ、適切にこのような支援を行う。

of Japan and the maintenance of public order.

(3) U.S.-Japan Operational Cooperation

As situations in areas surrounding Japan have an important influence on Japan's peace and security, the Self-Defense Forces will conduct such activities as intelligence gathering, surveillance and minesweeping, to protect lives and property and to ensure navigational safety. U.S. Forces will conduct operations to restore the peace and security affected by situations in areas surrounding Japan.

With the involvement of relevant agencies, cooperation and coordination will significantly enhance the effectiveness of both forces' activities.

VI. Bilateral Programs for Effective Defense Cooperation under the Guidelines

Effective bilateral defense cooperation under the Guidelines will require the United States and Japan to conduct consultative dialogue throughout the spectrum of security conditions: normal circumstances, an armed attack against Japan, and situations in areas surrounding Japan. Both sides must be well informed and coordinate at multiple levels to ensure successful bilateral defense cooperation. To accomplish this, the two Governments will strengthen their information and intelligence sharing and policy consultations by taking advantage of all available opportunities, including SCC and SSC meetings, and they will establish the following two mechanisms to facilitate consultations, coordinate policies, and coordinate operational functions.

First, the two Governments will develop a comprehensive mechanism for bilateral planning and the establishment of common standards and procedures, involving not only

(3) 運用面における日米協力

周辺事態は、日本の平和と安全に重要な影響を与えることから、自衛隊は、生命・財産の保護及び航行の安全確保を目的として、情報収集、警戒監視、機雷の除去等の活動を行う。米軍は、周辺事態により影響を受けた平和と安全の回復のための活動を行う。

自衛隊及び米軍の双方の活動の実効性は、関係機関の関与を得た協力及び調整により、大きく高められる。

VI. 指針の下で行われる効果的な防衛協力のための日米共同の取組み

指針の下での日米防衛協力を効果的に進めるためには、平素、日本に対する武力攻撃及び周辺事態という安全保障上の種々の状況を通じ、日米両国が協議を行うことが必要である。日米防衛協力が確実に成果を挙げていくためには、双方が様々なレベルにおいて十分な情報の提供を受けつつ、調整を行うことが不可欠である。このため、日米両国政府は、日米安全保障協議委員会及び日米安全保障高級事務レベル協議を含むあらゆる機会をとらえて情報交換及び政策協議を充実させていくほか、協議の促進、政策調整及び作戦・活動分野の調整のための以下の2つのメカニズムを構築する。

第一に、日米両国政府は、計画についての検討を行うとともに共通の基準及び実施要領等を確立するため、包括的なメカニズムを構築する。これには、自衛隊及び米軍のみならず、各々の

U.S. Forces and the Self-Defense Forces but also other relevant agencies of their respective Governments.

The two Governments will, as necessary, improve this comprehensive mechanism. The SCC will continue to play an important role for presenting policy direction to the work to be conducted by this mechanism. The SCC will be responsible for presenting directions, validating the progress of work, and issuing directives as necessary. The SDC will assist the SCC in bilateral work.

Second, the two Governments will also establish, under normal circumstances, a bilateral coordination mechanism that will include relevant agencies of the two countries for coordinating respective activities during contingencies.

1. **Bilateral Work for Planning and the Establishment of Common Standards and Procedures**

Bilateral work listed below will be conducted in a comprehensive mechanism involving relevant agencies of the respective Governments in a deliberate and efficient manner. Progress and results of such work will be reported at significant milestones to the SCC and the SDC.

(1) **Bilateral Defense Planning and Mutual Cooperation Planning**

U.S. Forces and the Self-Defense Forces will conduct bilateral defense planning under normal circumstances to take coordinated actions smoothly and effectively in case of an armed attack against Japan. The two Governments will conduct mutual cooperation planning under normal circumstances to be able to respond smoothly and effectively to situations in areas surrounding Japan.

Bilateral defense planning and mutual cooperation planning will assume various

政府のその他の関係機関が関与する。

日米両国政府は、この包括的なメカニズムの在り方を必要に応じて改善する。日米安全保障協議委員会は、このメカニズムの行う作業に関する政策的な方向性を示す上で引き続き重要な役割を有する。日米安全保障協議委員会は、方針を提示し、作業の進捗を確認し、必要に応じて指示を発出する責任を有する。防衛協力小委員会は、共同作業において、日米安全保障協議委員会を補佐する。

第二に、日米両国政府は、緊急事態において各々の活動に関する調整を行うため、両国の関係機関を含む日米間の調整メカニズムを平素から構築しておく。

1. 計画についての検討並びに共通の基準及び実施要領等の確立のための共同作業

双方の関係機関の関与を得て構築される包括的なメカニズムにおいては、以下に掲げる共同作業を計画的かつ効率的に進める。これらの作業の進捗及び結果は、節目節目に日米安全保障協議委員会及び防衛協力小委員会に対して報告される。

(1) 共同作戦計画についての検討及び相互協力計画についての検討

自衛隊及び米軍は、日本に対する武力攻撃に際して整合のとれた行動を円滑かつ効果的に実施し得るよう、平素から共同作戦計画についての検討を行う。また、日米両国政府は、周辺事態に円滑かつ効果的に対応し得るよう、平素から相互協力計画についての検討を行う。

共同作戦計画についての検討及び相互協力計画についての検討は、その結果が日米両国政府

possible situations, with the expectation that results of these efforts will be appropriately reflected in the plans of the two Governments. The two Governments will coordinate and adjust their plans in light of actual circumstances. The two Governments will be mindful that bilateral defense planning and mutual cooperation planning must be consistent so that appropriate responses will be ensured when a situation in areas surrounding Japan threatens to develop into an armed attack against Japan or when such a situation and an armed attack against Japan occur simultaneously.

(2) Establishment of Common Standards for Preparations

The two Governments will establish under normal circumstances common standards for preparations for the defense of Japan. These standards will address such matters as intelligence activities, unit activities, movements and logistics support in each readiness stage. When an armed attack against Japan is imminent, both Governments will agree to select a common readiness stage that will be reflected in the level of preparations for the defense of Japan by U.S. Forces, the Self-Defense Forces and other relevant agencies.

The two Governments will similarly establish common standards for preparations of cooperative measures in situations in areas surrounding Japan so that they may select a common readiness stage by mutual agreement.

(3) Establishment of Common Procedures

The two Governments will prepare in advance common procedures to ensure smooth and effective execution of coordinated U.S. Forces and Self-Defense Forces operations for the defense of Japan.

の各々の計画に適切に反映されることが期待されるという前提の下で、種々の状況を想定しつつ行われる。日米両国政府は、実際の状況に照らして、日米両国各々の計画を調整する。日米両国政府は、共同作戦計画についての検討と相互協力計画についての検討との間の整合を図るよう留意することにより、周辺事態が日本に対する武力攻撃に波及する可能性のある場合又は両者が同時に生起する場合に適切に対応し得るようにする。

(2) 準備のための共通の基準の確立

日米両国政府は、日本の防衛のための準備に関し、共通の基準を平素から確立する。この基準は、各々の準備段階における情報活動、部隊の活動、移動、後方支援その他の事項を明らかにするものである。日本に対する武力攻撃が差し迫っている場合には、日米両国政府の合意により共通の準備段階が選択され、これが、自衛隊、米軍その他の関係機関による日本の防衛のための準備のレベルに反映される。

同様に、日米両国政府は、周辺事態における協力措置の準備に関しても、合意により共通の準備段階を選択し得るよう、共通の基準を確立する。

(3) 共通の実施要領等の確立

日米両国政府は、自衛隊及び米軍が日本の防衛のための整合のとれた作戦を円滑かつ効果的に実施できるよう、共通の実施要領等をあらかじめ準備しておく。これには、通信、目標位置の伝達、情報活動及び後方支援並びに相撃防止

These will include procedures for communications, transmission of target information, intelligence activities and logistics support, and prevention of fratricide. Common procedures will also include criteria for properly controlling respective unit operations. The two forces will take into account the importance of communications and electronics interoperability, and will determine in advance their mutual requirements.

2. Bilateral Coordination Mechanism

The two Governments will establish under normal circumstances a bilateral coordination mechanism involving relevant agencies of the two countries to coordinate respective activities in case of an armed attack against Japan and in situations in areas surrounding Japan.

Procedures for coordination will vary depending upon items to be coordinated and agencies to be involved. They may include coordination committee meetings, mutual dispatch of liaison officers, and designation of points of contacts. As part of such a bilateral coordination mechanism, U.S. Forces and the Self-Defense Forces will prepare under normal circumstances a bilateral coordination center with the necessary hardware and software in order to coordinate their respective activities.

VII. Timely and Appropriate Review of the Guidelines

The two Governments will review the Guidelines in a timely and appropriate manner when changes in situations relevant to the U.S.-Japan security relationship occur and if deemed necessary in view of the circumstances at that time.

のための要領とともに、各々の部隊の活動を適切に律するための基準が含まれる。また、自衛隊及び米軍は、通信電子活動等に関する相互運用性の重要性を考慮し、相互に必要な事項をあらかじめ定めておく。

2. 日米間の調整メカニズム

日米両国政府は、日米両国の関係機関の関与を得て、日米間の調整メカニズムを平素から構築し、日本に対する武力攻撃及び周辺事態に際して各々が行う活動の間の調整を行う。

調整の要領は、調整すべき事項及び関与する関係機関に応じて異なる。調整の要領には、調整会議の開催、連絡員の相互派遣及び連絡窓口の指定が含まれる。自衛隊及び米軍は、この調整メカニズムの一環として、双方の活動について調整するため、必要なハードウェア及びソフトウェアを備えた日米共同調整所を平素から準備しておく。

VII. 指針の適時かつ適切な見直し

日米安全保障関係に関連する諸情勢に変化が生じ、その時の状況に照らして必要と判断される場合には、日米両国政府は、適時かつ適切な形でこの指針を見直す。

Functions and Fields	Examples of Items of Cooperation	
Cooperation in activities initiatedby either Government	Relief activities and measures to deal with refugees	●Transportation of personnel and supplies to the affected area ●Medical services, communications and transportation in the affected area ●Relief and transfer operations for refugees, and provision of emergency materials to refugees
	Search and rescue	●Search and rescue operations in Japanese territory and at sea around Japan and information sharing related to such operations
	Noncombatant evacuation operations	●Information sharing, and communication with and assembly and transportation of noncombatants ●Use of Self-Defense Forces facilities and civilian airports and ports by U.S. aircraft and vessels for transportation of noncombatants ●Customs, immigration and quarantine of noncombatants upon entry into Japan ●Assistance to noncombatants in such matters as temporary accommodations, transportation and medical services in Japan
	Activities for ensuring the effectiveness of economic sanctions for the maintenance of international peace and stability	●Inspection of ships based on United Nations Security Council resolutions for ensuring the effectiveness of economic sanctions and activities related to such inspections ●Information sharing

Functions and Fields		Examples of Items of Cooperation
Japan's support for U.S. Forces activities	Use of facilities	●Use of Self-Defense Forces facilities and civilian airports and ports for supplies and other purposes by U.S. aircraft and vessels ●Reservation of spaces for loading/unloading of personnel and materials by the United States and of storage areas at Self-Defense Forces facilities and civilian airports and ports

周辺事態における協力の対象となる機能及び分野並びに協力項目例

機能及び分野	協力項目名
米両国政府が各々主体的に行う活動における協力	救援活動及び避難民への対応のための措置	●被災地への人員及び補給品の輸送 ●被災地における衛生、通信及び輸送 ●避難民の救援及び輸送のための活動並びに避難民に対する応急物資の支給
	捜索・救難	●日本領域及び日本の周囲の海域における捜索・救難活動並びにこれに関する情報の交換
	非戦闘員を退避させるための活動	●情報の交換並びに非戦闘員との連絡及び非戦闘員の集結・輸送 ●非戦闘員の輸送のための米航空機・船舶による自衛隊施設及び民間空港・港湾の使用 ●非戦闘員の日本入国時の通関、出入国管理及び検疫 ●日本国内における一時的な宿泊，輸送及び衛生に係る非戦闘員への援助
	国際の平和と安定の維持を目的とする経済制裁の実効性を確保するための活動	●経済制裁の実効性を確保するために国際連合安全保障理事会決議に基づいて行われる船舶の検査及びこのような検査に関連する活動 ●情報の交換

機能及び分野	協力項目名
米軍の活動に対する日本の支援	施設の使用	●補給等を目的とする米航空機・船舶による自衛隊施設及び民間空港・港湾の使用 ●自衛隊施設及び民間空港・港湾における米国による人員及び物資の積卸しに必要な場所及び保管施設の確保

		●Extension of operating hours for Self-Defense Forces facilities and civilian airports and ports for the use by U.S. aircraft and vessels ●Use of Self-Defense Forces airfields by U.S. aircraft ●Provision of training and exercise areas ●Construction of offices, accommodations, etc., inside U.S. facilities and areas
Rear area support	Supply	●Provision of materials (except weapons and ammunition) and POL (petroleum, oil and lubricants) to U.S. aircraft and vessels at Self-Defense Forces facilities and civilian airports and ports ●Provision of materials (except weapons and ammunition) and POL to U.S. facilities and areas
	Transportation	●Land, sea and air transportation inside Japan of personnel, materials and POL ●Sea transportation to U.S. vessels on the high seas of personnel, materials and POL ●Use of vehicles and cranes for transportation of personnel, materials and POL
	Maintenance	●Repair and maintenance of U.S. aircraft, vessels and vehicles ●Provision of repair parts ●Temporary provision of tools and materials for maintenance
	Medical services	●Medical treatment of casualties inside Japan ●Transportation of casualties inside Japan ●Provision of medical supply
	Security	●Security of U.S. facilities and areas ●Sea surveillance around U.S. facilities and areas ●Security of transportation routes inside Japan ●Information and intelligence sharing

●米航空機・船舶による使用のための自衛隊施設及び民間空港・港湾の運用時間の延長

●米航空機による自衛隊の飛行場の使用

●訓練・演習区域の提供
●米軍施設・区域内における事務所・宿泊所等の建設

後方地域支援	補給	●自衛隊施設及び民間空港・港湾における米航空機・船舶に対する物資(武器・弾薬を除く。)及び燃料・油脂・潤滑油の提供
		●米軍施設・区域に対する物資(武器・弾薬を除く。)及び燃料・油脂・潤滑油の提供
	輸送	●人員、物資及び燃料・油脂・潤滑油の日本国内における陸上・海上・航空輸送 ●公海上の米船舶に対する人員、物資及び燃料・油脂・潤滑油の海上輸送 ●人員、物資及び燃料・油脂・潤滑油の輸送のための車両及びクレーンの使用
	整備	●米航空機・船舶・車両の修理・整備 ●修理部品の提供 ●整備用資器材の一時提供
	衛生	●日本国内における傷病者の治療 ●日本国内における傷病者の輸送 ●医薬品及び衛生機具の提供
	警備	●米軍施設・区域の警備 ●米軍施設・区域の周囲の海域の警戒監視 ●日本国内の輸送経路上の警備 ●情報の交換

	Communications	●Provision of frequencies (including for satellite communications) and equipment for communications among relevant U.S. and Japanese agencies
	Others	●Support for port entry/exit by U.S. vessels ●Loading/unloading of materials at Self-Defense Forces facilities and civilian airports and ports ●Sewage disposal, water supply, and electricity inside U.S. facilities and areas ●Temporary increase of workers at U.S. facilities and areas
U.S.-Japan operational cooperation	Surveillance	●Intelligence sharing
	Minesweeping	●Minesweeping operations in Japanese territory and on the high seas around Japan, and information and intelligence sharing on mines
	Sea and Airspace management	●Maritime traffic coordination in and around Japan in response to increased sea traffic ●Air traffic control and airspace management in and around Japan

	通信	●日米両国の関係機関の間の通信のための周波数(衛星通信用を含む。)の確保及び器材の提供
	その他	●米船舶の出入港に対する支援 ●自衛隊施設及び民間空港・港湾における物資の積卸し ●米軍施設・区域内における汚水処理、給水、給電等 ●米軍施設・区域従業員の一時増員
運用面における日米協力	警戒監視	●情報の交換
	機雷除去	●日本領域及び日本の周囲の公海における機雷の除去並びに機雷に関する情報の交換
	海・空域調整	●日本領域及び周囲の海域における交通量の増大に対応した海上運航調整 ●日本領域及び周囲の空域における航空交通管制及び空域調整

Japanese History	World History

Prehistory

Before 30,000 BC ●Paleolithic culture (kyūsekki bunka); crude stone tools produced by a preceramic hunting and gathering society.

Ca 10,000 BC ●Manufacture of Jōmon pottery and polished stone tools marks the beginning of the Jomon period.

Ca 300 BC ●Yayoi culture emerges in northern Kyūshū with the introduction of wet-rice cultivation from the Korean peninsula.
    334 BC●Alexander the Great begins his conquest of the East.

Ca 1 AD ●Japan mentioned in Chinese historical records as the land of Wa, composed of a number of states.

57 ●King of the state of Na (Nakoku) in Wa offers tribute to Emperor Guangwu of the Chinese Later Han dynasty (25–220) and is awarded a seal in return (Kan no Wa no Na no Kokuō no In).

239 ●Himiko, queen of Yamatai, sends an envoy to the kingdom of Wei in China, receiving from Emperor Ming a gold seal and the title *qin wei wowang* (J: *shingi waō*; Wa ruler friendly to Wei).

Kofun period 300–710

The Kofun period was characterized by the construction of large tomb mounds (*kofun*), indicating the stratification of the agricultural society inherited from the Yayoi period. The Kofun period witnessed the introduction of Buddhism and the Chinese writing system from the Asian continent and the rise of the Yamato court. The last period of the Kofun period is called the Asuka period (593–710), which is generally considered Japan's first historical age.

350 ●By this time the Yamato court has been established in what is now Nara Prefecture.

552 ●Traditional date of introduction of Buddhism to Japan, when Buddhist images and sutras are sent from Korea by King Song of Paekche. An earlier date, 538, is assigned to this event by many scholars.
    589●Beginning of the Sui dynasty (589–618) in China.

600 ●First embassy to Sui-dynasty (589–618) China (*kenzuishi*) dispatched.

604 ●*Kan'i jūnikai* system of court ranks instituted. Prince Shōtoku promulgates Seventeen-Article Constitution.

607 ●Ono no Imoko appointed leader of the second embassy to Sui China.
●Construction of the Buddhist temple Hōryūji completed.
    622●Prophet Muhammad arrives in Medina; the Islamic Era begins.

630 ●First embassy to Tang-dynasty (618–907) China (*kentōshi*) dispatched.
    624●China unified under the Tang dynasty (618–907).

645 ●Prince Naka no Ōe (later Emperor Tenji) and Nakatomi no Kamatari (later Fujiwara no Kamatari) destroy the Soga family and initiate the Taika Reform.

667 ●Imperial palace Ōtsu no Miya established by Prince Naka no Ōe on the southwestern shore of Lake Biwa. Capital until 672.
    668●Silla unifies Korea.

672 ●Prince Ōama (later Emperor Temmu) usurps the throne from his nephew and designated heir Prince Ōtomo (Jinshin Disturbance).

684 ●System of eight cognomens (*yakusa no kabane*)

日本史	世界史

先史時代

紀元前30,000 ●旧石器文化：前土器の狩猟採集社会。打製石器をつくる。

紀元前10,000 ●縄文土器と磨製石器を製造。縄文時代始まる。

紀元前300 ●朝鮮半島から稲作が伝わり北九州で弥生文化がはじまる。　**紀元前334**●アレクサンダー大王の
　　　　　　　　　　　　　　　　　　　　　　　　　　　　　　　　東征はじまる。

....

1 ●倭(日本)が中国の歴史書に百余国に分立と記される。

57 ●倭の奴国王中国後漢(25年～220年)の光武帝に貢を献上し、「漢委奴
　　国王」の印綬を授けられる。

....

239 ●邪馬台国女王卑弥呼中国の魏に使者を送り、明帝から金印と「親魏
　　倭王」(魏と友好的な倭の支配者)の称号をおくられる。

古墳時代　古墳(盛り土をした巨大な墳墓)が造られたのが特徴で、弥生時代以来の農業社会で階層分化が進んだことを
300–710　示している。大陸から仏教と漢字が伝来し、大和朝廷が確立した。古墳時代の末期は飛鳥時代(593年～710
　　　　　　年)とよばれ、日本における最初の歴史時代と考えられている。

....

350 ●この時期までに現在の奈良県に大和朝廷成立。

....

552 ●百済の聖明王から仏像と経典を贈られる。これをもって仏教公伝と　**589**●中国に隋王朝(589年～618年)
　　するが伝教伝来538年説をとる学者が多い。　　　　　　　　　　　　はじまる。

....

600 ●隋王朝(589年～618年)へ最初の遣隋使派遣。

604 ●「冠位十二階」制定。聖徳太子「十七条憲法」を公布。

607 ●小野妹子を第2回遣隋使に任命。

　　　●法隆寺完成。　　　　　　　　　　　　　　　　　　　　　　　**622**●予言者マホメット、メディナ
630 ●唐王朝(618年～907年)へ第1回遣唐使派遣。　　　　　　　　　　到着。イスラム暦元年。

　　　　　　　　　　　　　　　　　　　　　　　　　　　　　　　　624●唐王朝(618年～907年)中国統
645 ●中大兄皇子(後の天智天皇)と中臣鎌足(後の藤原鎌足)、蘇我氏を滅　　一。
　　ぼし大化の改新始まる。

667 ●中大兄皇子、琵琶湖の南西岸に大津宮を造営。672年まで都となる。　**668**●新羅朝鮮統一。

672 ●大海人皇子(後の天武天皇)、甥の大友皇子を滅ぼし皇位継承を宣言
　　(壬申の乱)。

684 ●八色の姓制定。氏に姓を授与し、天皇を頂点とするピラミッド型の

	instituted, under which members of lineage groups (*uji*) are assigned titles of rank, forming a social pyramid with the emperor at its apex.	
694	●Capital city Fujiwarakyō established. Capital until 710.	
701	●Compilation of the Taihō Code of penal and administrative laws completed; becomes effective the following year.	
708	●Minting of the Wadō *kaihō* initiated; it is one of the first coinage minted in Japan along with the *fuhonsen*.	

Nara period 710–794

The establishment of the capital city Heijōkyō (Nara) marked the beginning of the Nara period, which was characterized by the maturation of the Chinese-inspired *ritsuryō* system of government and the active adoption of Chinese culture and technology. Buddhism gained official recognition as the state religion, and temples were constructed throughout Japan.

710	●Capital city Heijōkyō (Nara) established. Capital until 784.
712	●Compilation of the historical narrative *Kojiki*, Japan's oldest extant chronicle, is completed by Ō no Yasumaro.
720	●Historical narrative *Nihon shoki* completed.
733	●Regional gazetteer *Izumo no kuni fudoki* completed.
743	●Konden Einen Shizai Hō promulgated; this law lays the legal basis for the emergence of the landed estates called *shōen*.
	●Construction of a huge Buddha image (*daibutsu*) at the temple Tōdaiji initiated by imperial decree; it is completed in 752.
751	●*Kaifūsō* compiled; it is the oldest extant collection of Chinese poetry by Japanese poets.
759	●Ganjin founds the temple Tōshōdaiji.
	●The *Man'yōshū* is completed around this time.
784	●Capital moved to Nagaokakyō. Capital until 794.
788	●Saichō, founder of the Tendai sect of Buddhism, establishes the temple Enryakuji.

Heian period 794–1185

The Heian period, which began with the establishment of the imperial capital at Heiankyō (Kyōto), saw the full assimilation of Chinese influences and the flowering of an indigenous aristocratic culture. The development of the Japanese *kana* syllabary gave birth to a truly native literary tradition. Politically, the Heian period was characterized by the domination of the imperial court by regents of the Fujiwara family.

794	●Capital moved to Heiankyō (Kyōto).

905	●The *Kokin wakashū*, the first imperial anthology of *waka* verse, is completed.	
985	●The Buddhist monk Genshin completes the religious tract *Ōjōyōshū*; the work contributes to the spread of Pure Land Buddhism among the aristocracy.	**960**●Beginning of the Northern Song dynasty (960–1126) in China.
995	●Fujiwara no Michinaga becomes head of the Fujiwara family; golden age of its domination of the imperial court begins.	
996	●A portion of Sei Shōnagon's *Makura no sōshi* is now in circulation.	

1008	●Entry in Murasaki Shikibu's diary indicates that a substantial part of the *Tale of Genji*, has now been written.
1087	●Emperor Shirakawa abdicates, establishes the system of "cloister government" (*insei*).

　　　　●階層制を形成。

694　●藤原京を都とする。710年まで都となる。
701　●大宝律令の編纂完了；翌年施行。

708　●「和同開珎」の鋳造開始；富本銭と共に日本最古の鋳造貨幣の1つ。

奈良時代
710–794　平城京(奈良)に都がおかれた時代。中国の影響で始まった律令政治が成熟期を迎え、中国の文化や技術を積極的に採り入れた。仏教が国教として認められ、日本全国に寺院が建設された。

710　●平城京(奈良)を都とする。784年まで都となる。
712　●太安万侶が歴史物語「古事記」(現存する日本最古の年代記)を撰上。

720　●歴史物語「日本書紀」完成。
733　●「出雲国風土記」完成。
743　●墾田永年私財法公布；荘園の法的根拠となる。

　　　　●詔勅により東大寺巨大仏像(大仏)の造立始まる；752年完成。

751　●「懐風藻」成立；日本人の手による現存最古の漢詩集。

759　●鑑真が唐招提寺創建。
　　　　●「万葉集」この頃完成。
784　●長岡京に遷都。794年まで都がおかれる。
788　●天台宗開祖最澄、延暦寺を建立。

平安時代
794–1185　平安京(京都)遷都とともにはじまる平安時代は中国伝来の文化が十分に消化吸収されて、国風の貴族文化が花開いた。また仮名文字が発展して、日本固有の文学の伝統が生まれた。この時代の政治は藤原氏一族の摂政・関白による朝廷支配によって特徴づけられる。

794　●平安京(京都)遷都。

905　●第一代勅撰和歌集「古今和歌集」成立。

985　●僧源信が経論集「往生要集」を完成；貴族の間に浄土教が広まる。

　　　　　　　　　　　　　　　　　　　　　　　　　960●中国に北宋(960年〜1126年)
　　　　　　　　　　　　　　　　　　　　　　　　　はじまる。
995　●藤原道長、藤原氏の氏長者となる；藤原氏による朝廷支配の黄金時代はじまる。

996　●清少納言「枕草子」の一部が流布する。

1008　●「紫式部日記」の記載によると「源氏物語」主要部分、この頃までに完成。
1087　●白河天皇退位、院政開始。

1156	●Hōgen Disturbance: rivalry between the Taira family and the Minamoto family for political power at court begins.	1127●Beginning of the Southern Song dynasty (1127–1279) in China.
1160	●Heiji Disturbance (Heiji 1.12): influence of the Taira family over the imperial court established.	
1175	●Hōnen begins to preach in Kyōto and founds the Jōdo sect of Buddhism.	

Kamakura period 1185–1333

Minamoto no Yoritomo's victory in the Taira-Minamoto War (Gempei no Sōran) heralded the beginning of the Kamakura period and the rise to political power of the provincial warrior class. His appointment of provincial governors (*shugo*) and estate stewards (*jitō*) established the foundations of the Kamakura shogunate.

1192	●Minamoto no Yoritomo appointed *seii tai shōgun* by Emperor Go-Toba.	

1203	●Hōjō Tokimasa assumes the office of shogunal regent (*shikken*).	
1205	●The *Shin kokin wakashū* is submitted to the throne.	
1219	●Minamoto no Sanetomo assassinated, ending the line of Minamoto shoguns. Members of the Hōjō family continue to rule as regents.	1215●Magna Carta issued, under duress, by King John of England.
1221	●Jōkyū Disturbance: abdicated emperors Go-Toba and Juntoku sent into exile by the shogunate.	
1224	●Shinran establishes the Jōdo Shin sect of Buddhism.	
1227	●Dōgen establishes the Sōtō sect of Zen Buddhism.	
1232	●Goseibai Shikimoku promulgated; it is the first codification of warrior house law.	
1253	●Nichiren establishes the Nichiren sect of Buddhism.	
1274	●First of the Mongol Invasions of Japan.	1271●Marco Polo sets out on his journey to the court of the Mongol emperor Kublai Khan.
1281	●Second of the Mongol Invasions of Japan.	

1330	●Yoshida Kenkō completes *Tsurezuregusa* around this time.	

Muromachi period 1333–1568

The destruction of the Kamakura shogunate by Ashikaga Takauji signified the beginning of the Muromachi period, an era of great cultural achievement and persistent social instability. The first decades of the Muromachi shogunate were disrupted by conflict between the Northern and Southern Courts. The shogunate was unable to restrain the provincial governors (*shugo daimyō*) and collapsed entirely after the Ōnin War, which ushered in a century of civil strife known as the Sengoku period (1467–1568).

1333	●Kamakura shogunate collapses; power restored to Emperor Go-Daigo (Kemmu Restoration).	
1336	●The Kemmu Shikimoku, a code of governmental principles, is promulgated by Ashikaga Takauji.	1337●Hundred Years' War, waged by England against France, begins.
1337	●Emperor Go-Daigo escapes to Yoshino and establishes the Southern Court.	1368●Zhu Yuanzhang founds the Ming dynasty (1368–1644) in China.
1338	●Ashikaga Takauji receives the title of *seii tai shōgun* from the Northern Court, founds the Muromachi shogunate.	
1392	●Northern and Southern Courts reconciled.	1392●Yi Song-gye declares himself king of Korea, founds the Yi dynasty (1392–1910).
1397	●Shōgun Ashikaga Yoshimitsu begins construction of the temple Kinkakuji in Kyōto.	

1400	●Zeami completes the first three chapters of his *Fūshi kaden*.	1445●Johannes Gutenberg completes the Forty-Two Line Bible, the earliest book printed in Europe from movable type.
1404	●Tally trade initiated with Ming-dynasty (1368–1644) China.	
1467	●Ōnin War begins (1467–1477); Kyōto laid waste.	

	日本史	世界史

1156 ●保元の乱：朝廷における平氏と源氏の政治権力をめぐる対立はじまる。

1127●中国に南宋(1127年～1279年)はじまる。

1160 ●平治の乱(平治1年 12月)：平氏、朝廷において権力を確立する。

1175 ●法然が京都で説法をはじめ浄土宗を開く。

鎌倉時代 1185–1333

源平の争乱における源頼朝の勝利は鎌倉時代の幕開けを告げ、地方武士階級の政治的進出のはじまりでもあった。頼朝による守護・地頭の任命は鎌倉幕府の基礎を固めた。

1192 ●源頼朝、後鳥羽天皇により征夷大将軍に任命される。

1203 ●北条時政執権となる。

1205 ●「新古今和歌集」撰進。

1219 ●源実朝暗殺され源氏の将軍絶える。北条氏の執権支配が続く。

1215 ●英王ジョン「マグナカルタ」を承認。

1221 ●承久の乱：後鳥羽上皇、順徳上皇、幕府によって流罪に処せられる。

1224 ●親鸞浄土真宗を開く。

1227 ●道元禅宗の一派曹洞宗を開く。

1232 ●御成敗式目制定；最初の武家法典。

1253 ●日蓮日蓮宗を開く。

1274 ●第1回蒙古襲来(文永の役)。

1281 ●第2回蒙古襲来(弘安の役)。

1271●マルコ=ポーロ、フビライ=ハーンのモンゴル(元)へ旅立つ。

1330 ●この頃吉田兼好「徒然草」完成。

室町時代 1333–1568

足利尊氏が鎌倉幕府を滅ぼし、室町時代がはじまる。文化は大いに発展したが、社会的には不安定な時代であった。室町時代に入って数十年間、幕府は南北朝の抗争で混乱した。また幕府は守護大名を制御することが出来ず、応仁の乱以後は完全に衰退し、戦国時代(1467年～1568年)と呼ばれる内乱の100年へと突入していく。

1333 ●鎌倉幕府滅亡；後醍醐天皇復権、建武の中興(建武の新政)。

1336 ●幕府の施政方針を定めた建武式目が足利尊氏によって公布される。

1337●英仏百年戦争はじまる。

1337 ●後醍醐天皇吉野にのがれ南朝を設立。

1368●朱元璋、中国に明(1368年～1644年)を建国する。

1338 ●足利尊氏、北朝より征夷大将軍に任じられ室町幕府はじまる。

1392 ●南北朝合一。

1397 ●将軍足利義満、京都に金閣寺の造営はじめる。

1392●朝鮮で李成桂、王を称し李王朝(1392年～1910年)をたてる。

1400 ●世阿弥「風姿花伝」第1編～3編を完成。

1445●グーテンベルグ「四十二行聖書」完成：ヨーロッパにおける最初の活版印刷本。

1404 ●明(1368年～1644年)との勘合貿易はじまる。

1467 ●応仁の乱(1467年～1477年)はじまる；京都荒廃。

Japanese History	World History

	1483	●Retired shōgun Ashikaga Yoshimasa settles at the villa that later becomes the temple Ginkakuji.	*1492*●Christopher Columbus lands in the Bahamas.
	1488	●Adherents of the Jōdo Shin sect of Buddhism vanquish the army of the governor (*shugo*) of Kaga Province and establish autonomous rule there (Ikkō Ikki).	*1498*●Vasco da Gama, after a voyage around the Cape of Good Hope, reaches Calicut in India.

	1543	●Matchlock muskets (*hinawajū*) are introduced to Japan by the Portuguese on the island of Tanegashima.	*1517*●Martin Luther nails the Ninety-Five Theses to the church door at Wittenberg.
	1549	●Francis Xavier establishes Japan's first Christian mission at Kagoshima.	*1534*●Founding of the Society of Jesus (Jesuits) by Ignatius of Loyola.

Azuchi-Momoyama period
1568–1600

The Azuchi-Momoyama period was defined by the rise of three successive hegemons, Oda Nobunaga, Toyotomi Hideyoshi, and Tokugawa Ieyasu, who brought about the political unification of Japan following a century of civil war. During this brief period, Japan was exposed to Western (*namban*) culture through contact with European traders and missionaries.

	1568	●Oda Nobunaga enters Kyōto, installs Ashikaga Yoshiaki as shōgun.	*1571*●Spain founds Manila.
	1575	●Battle of Nagashino: 3,000 musketeers are deployed by Oda Nobunaga in his victory over Takeda Katsuyori.	
	1576	●Oda Nobunaga begins construction of Azuchi Castle.	
	1582	●Honnōji Incident: Oda Nobunaga commits suicide after a surprise attack by his vassal Akechi Mitsuhide.	
		●Toyotomi Hideyoshi initiates the Taikō *kenchi*, a national survey of lands and their productive capacity.	
	1587	●Toyotomi Hideyoshi issues an edict expelling all Christian missionaries from Japan.	
	1588	●Toyotomi Hideyoshi issues an edict prohibiting possession of weapons by peasants (*katanagari*).	
	1590	●Toyotomi Hideyoshi destroys the Later Hōjō family (Odawara Campaign), pacifies all of Japan.	
	1592	●Toyotomi Hideyoshi launches the first of the invasions of Korea.	

Edo period
1600–1868

Victory in the Battle of Sekigahara established Tokugawa Ieyasu's hegemony over Japan, commencing the Edo period. Over two centuries of peace followed under the rule of the Tokugawa shogunate, which isolated Japan through its policy of National Seclusion (Sakoku). In the turbulent period following Commodore Matthew Perry's arrival in 1853, the shogunate lost its ability to assert national authority, and the Tokugawa regime collapsed.

	1600	●Battle of Sekigahara: Tokugawa Ieyasu establishes hegemony over Japan.	*1600*●British East India Company incorporated by royal charter.
	1603	●Tokugawa Ieyasu is granted the title of *seii tai shōgun*, founds the Tokugawa shogunate.	*1602*●Dutch government grants the Dutch East India Company a monopoly on trade in the East Indies.
	1609	●Dutch Factory (Oranda Shōkan) established at Hirado; Dutch trade begins.	*1607*●English settlement established in North America at Jamestown, Virginia.
	1612	●Shogunate issues directives aimed at restricting Christianity (anti-Christian edicts; *kinkyōrei*).	
	1635	●Revision of the Buke Shohatto (Laws for the Military Houses); system of mandatory alternate residence in Edo by *daimyō* formalized (*sankin kōtai*).	
	1636	●Buildings on the artificial island of Dejima at Nagasaki completed.	
	1639	●Edicts establishing National Seclusion (Sakoku) are completed: all Westerners except the Dutch are	

日本史	世界史
1483 ●譲位した足利義政別邸を造営。後に銀閣寺となる。	*1492* ●コロンブス、バハマ諸島に上陸。
1488 ●浄土真宗門徒(一向宗徒)加賀の守護勢を打破、自治支配を確立(一向一揆)。	*1498* ●ヴァスコ=ダ=ガマ、喜望峰を廻ってインド、カリカットに到着。
1543 ●ポルトガル人によって種子島に火縄銃が伝えられる。	*1517* ●マルチン=ルター「95箇条の論題」をウィッテンベルグの教会のドアに張り出す。
1549 ●ザビエル、鹿児島において日本最初のキリスト教布教開始。	*1534* ●イグナティウス=ロヨラ、イエズス会設立。

安土桃山時代 1568–1600

安土桃山時代は織田信長、豊臣秀吉、徳川家康の3人の覇者の登場によって特徴づけられる。彼らは100年にわたる内乱を克服し、日本の政治的統一を成し遂げた。この短い期間に日本はヨーロッパの貿易商や宣教師との接触を通じて南蛮文化に触れた。

日本史	世界史
1568 ●織田信長、足利義昭を将軍に擁立して京都に入る。	*1571* ●スペイン、マニラ市建設。
1575 ●長篠の戦い：織田信長、3,000人の鉄砲隊を配置して武田勝頼を破る。	
1576 ●信長安土城築城に着手。	
1582 ●本能寺の変：織田信長、家臣明智光秀の急襲を受け自害。	
●豊臣秀吉、太閤検地(全国的な土地とその生産力の調査)開始。	
1587 ●秀吉キリシタン宣教師の国外追放を布告。	
1588 ●秀吉百姓の武器所有禁止の布告を出す(刀狩)。	
1590 ●秀吉後北条氏を滅ぼし(小田原征伐)天下統一を達成。	
1592 ●秀吉第1回朝鮮侵略を行う(文禄の役)。	

江戸時代 1600–1868

関ヶ原の戦いの勝利によって徳川家康の全国にわたる覇権が確立し、江戸時代がはじまる。徳川幕府の支配の下、2世紀を超える平和が続き、その間鎖国政策により世界から孤立した。1853年のペリー提督来航に続く激動の中で、幕府の国家最高機関としての機能は失われ、徳川体制は崩壊する。

日本史	世界史
1600 ●関ヶ原の戦い：徳川家康、全土に覇権確立。	*1600* ●勅許状によってイギリス東インド会社を設立。
1603 ●徳川家康、征夷大将軍に任じられ徳川幕府はじまる。	*1602* ●オランダ政府、オランダ東インド会社に東インド貿易の独占権を与える。
1609 ●平戸にオランダ商館が開かれる：オランダ貿易はじまる。	
1612 ●幕府キリスト教を禁じる(禁教令)。	*1607* ●北米大陸ヴァージニアにイギリス植民地ジェームズタウン建設。
1635 ●武家諸法度改定：参勤交代制度化される。	
1636 ●長崎に人工島出島完成。	
1639 ●鎖国の諸法令完成：オランダ人を除く全ヨーロッパ人の来航禁止。	

Japanese History	World History
prohibited from entering Japan.	**1644**●Manchus establish the Qing dynasty (1644–1912) in China.
1657 ●Meireki Fire ravages Edo, killing more than 100,000 people.	
1682 ●Ihara Saikaku publishes *Kōshoku ichidai otoko*.	
1688 ●Beginning of the Genroku era (1688–1704), a time of cultural flowering known in particular as the golden age of *kabuki* and *bunraku*.	
1689 ●Matsuo Bashō departs on the journey of *Oku no hosomichi*.	

1703 ●Band of former retainers of the Akō domain, under the leadership of Ōishi Yoshio, carry out a vendetta against Kira Yoshinaka (Forty-Seven Rōnin Incident; Genroku 15.12).	
1707 ●Last eruption of Fujisan.	
1716 ●Tokugawa Yoshimune becomes *shōgun*; Kyōhō Reforms (1716–1745) commence.	
1732 ●Locust plague and unseasonable weather cause Kyōhō Famine in southwestern Japan.	
1774 ●*Kaitai shinsho* published by Sugita Gempaku and Maeno Ryōtaku.	**1776**●Continental Congress issues the US Declaration of Independence.
1782 ●Temmei Famine begins; estimates of the nationwide death toll range from 200,000 to 900,000.	**1789**●George Washington becomes the first president of the United States.
1792 ●Adam Erilovich Laksman arrives at Nemuro with Daikokuya Kōdayū; Laksman negotiates unsuccessfully with shogunal officials for the establishment of trade relations between Japan and Russia.	●French Revolution begins. **1796**●Edward Jenner performs first smallpox inoculation.
1798 ●Motoori Norinaga completes the *Kojiki den*.	

1800 ●Inō Tadataka begins his cartographic survey of all Japan; it is completed in 1816.	
1802 ●Jippensha Ikku publishes the first volume of the *Tōkaidōchū hizakurige*.	
1804 ●Russian envoy Nikolai Petrovich Rezanov reaches Nagasaki, unsuccessfully seeks the establishment of trade relations with Japan.	**1804**●Napoleon crowns himself emperor of France.
1809 ●Mamiya Rinzō discovers the Tatar Strait, proving that Sakhalin is an island.	
1820 ●Kobayashi Issa completes the *Oraga haru*.	
1823 ●Philipp Franz von Siebold arrives in Japan; the following year he opens the Narutakijuku and teaches Western medicine and science.	
1833 ●Tempō Famine (1833–1836) begins; some 200,000 to 300,000 people are thought to have died.	**1837**●Victoria becomes queen of England (1837–1901).
1853 ●Four warships of the US East India Squadron, commanded by Commodore Matthew Perry, call at Uraga.	**1839**●Opium War begins in China (1839–1842).
1854 ●Fleet of seven US naval vessels, led by Commodore Matthew Perry, anchors in Edo Bay. ●Treaty of Peace and Amity between the United States and the Empire of Japan signed.	
1856 ●US consul general Townsend Harris arrives at Shimoda to initiate negotiations with the shogunate on the Harris Treaty (Nichibei Shūkō Tsūshō Jōyaku).	
1858 ●Ansei commercial treaties (Ansei gokakoku jōyaku) are concluded between the shogunate and the United States, the Netherlands, Russia, Great Britain, and France.	
1860 ●Shogunal mission to the United States leaves aboard the American warship Powhatan to ratify the Harris Treaty. It	**1861**●Civil War begins in the United States (1861–1865).

日本史	世界史
1657 ●明暦の大火江戸を焼きつくし死者10万人以上に及ぶ。	**1644** ●中国に満州族による清王朝 (1644年〜1912年)成立。
1682 ●井原西鶴「好色一代男」刊行。	
1688 ●元禄時代(1688年〜1704年)はじまる。歌舞伎、文楽の黄金時代として知られる文化の開花期。	
1689 ●松尾芭蕉「奥の細道」の旅に出立。	

1703 ●赤穂藩浪士大石良雄ら仇敵吉良義央を討つ(赤穂事件；元禄15年12月)。	
1707 ●富士山噴火。	
1716 ●徳川吉宗将軍となる；享保の改革(1716年〜1745年)はじまる。	
1732 ●西南日本に蝗害と天候不順による享保の飢饉。	
1774 ●杉田玄白、前野良沢ら「解体新書」刊行。	**1776** ●アメリカ、大陸会議でアメリカ独立宣言発布。
1782 ●天明の飢饉はじまる；死者は全国で20万人から90万人にのぼると見られる。	**1789** ●ジョージ=ワシントン、アメリカ初代大統領に就任。
1792 ●ラクスマン、大黒屋光太夫を伴って根室に来航；日露貿易開始について幕府出先機関と交渉するが、不調に終る。	●フランス革命はじまる。
1798 ●本居宣長「古事記伝」完成。	**1796** ●エドワード=ジェンナー、初の天然痘予防接種に成功。

1800 ●伊能忠敬日本地図作成のため全国の測量はじめる；1816年完了。	
1802 ●十返舎一九「東海道中膝栗毛」初編刊行。	
1804 ●ロシア使節レザノフ長崎に来航。通商を要求したが容れられず。	**1804** ●ナポレオン、フランス皇帝となる。
1809 ●間宮林蔵タタール海峡(間宮海峡)を発見、樺太が島であることを確認。	
1820 ●小林一茶「おらが春」完成。	
1823 ●シーボルト日本に到着；翌年「鳴滝塾」を開きヨーロッパの医学や科学を教える。	
1833 ●天保の飢饉(1833年〜1836年)はじまる；死者20万人から30万人。	**1837** ●イギリスヴィクトリア女王即位(1837年〜1901年)。
1853 ●ペリー提督率いるアメリカの東インド艦隊の軍艦4隻、浦賀に投錨。	**1839** ●中国でアヘン戦争(1839年〜1842年)はじまる。
1854 ●ペリー提督、7隻の艦隊を率いて江戸湾に停泊。	
●日米和親条約調印。	
1856 ●アメリカ総領事ハリスが下田に着任。幕府とハリス条約(日米修好通商条約)について交渉開始。	
1858 ●安政5ヵ国条約をアメリカ合衆国、オランダ、ロシア、イギリス、フランスと締結。	
1860 ●万延元年遣米使節、ハリス条約批准のためアメリカ軍艦ポーハタンでアメリカに向けて出発。咸臨丸同行。	**1861** ●アメリカで南北戦争(1861年〜1865年)はじまる。

is accompanied by the *Kanrin maru*.
●Assassination of Ii Naosuke (Sakuradamongai Incident).

1862 ●Richardson Affair (Namamugi Jiken): murder of a British merchant by retainers of the Satsuma domain.

1864 ●Shimonoseki Bombardment (Bakan Sensō): naval expedition by the Western powers against the Chōshū domain.

1866 ●Satsuma-Chōshū Alliance (Satchō Dōmei) formed against the Tokugawa shogunate.

1867 ●Formal return of political authority to the emperor by the last shōgun, Tokugawa Yoshinobu (Taisei Hōkan).

1864●The International Workingmen's Association (commonly known as the First International) is founded in London.

Meiji period
1868–1912

The Meiji Restoration of direct imperial rule commenced the Meiji period and began Japan's transformation into a modern industrial society. Restoration leaders welded former feudal domains into a modern nation-state, established a centralized bureaucracy, enacted a new land tax system, and created a modern conscript army.

1868 ●Restoration of imperial rule (Meiji Restoration).
●Charter Oath (Gokajō no Goseimon) pledged by Emperor Meiji; Gobō no Keiji (Five Public Notices) issued by the government.
●The city of Edo is renamed Tōkyō.

1869 ●Formal return of domainal registers to Emperor Meiji (Hanseki Hōkan).

1871 ●Postal Service established.
●Domains dissolved and prefectures established (*haihan chiken*).

1872 ●Railroad begins operation between Shimbashi and Yokohama.
●The Education Order of 1872 (Gakusei) establishes Japan's first modern school system.

1875 ●Treaty of St. Petersburg (Karafuto-Chishima Kōkan Jōyaku) gives Sakhalin to Russia and the Kuril Islands (Chishima Rettō) to Japan.

1876 ●Treaty of Kanghwa (Nitchō Shūkō Jōki), signed with Korea, gains unequal privileges for Japan.

1877 ●Satsuma Rebellion (Seinan Sensō); Saigō Takamori commits suicide.

1883 ●Completion of the Rokumeikan; it is the site for Western-style social events attended by prominent Japanese and foreigners.

1889 ●Constitution of the Empire of Japan promulgated.

1890 ●Imperial Rescript on Education (Kyōiku Chokugo) distributed to all schools.

1894 ●Sino-Japanese War of 1894–1895 (Nisshin Sensō) begins.

1895 ●Tripartite Intervention (Sangoku Kanshō): Japan forced by Russia, France, and Germany to relinquish territory ceded to it by China.

1876●The first successful telephone transmission is achieved by Alexander Graham Bell.

1883●Sino-French War (1883–1885) begins; in 1885 China recognizes Vietnam as a protectorate of France.

1899●US secretary of state John Hay sends his Open Door notes concerning China to Great Britain, Germany, France, Russia, Italy, and Japan.

1902 ●Anglo-Japanese Alliance (Nichiei Dōmei) signed.

1904 ●Russo-Japanese War (1904–1905; Nichiro Sensō) begins.

1910 ●Korea is made a colony of Japan (Annexation of Korea; Nikkan Heigō); Government-General of Korea (Chōsen Sōtoku Fu) established.

1911 ●Treaties signed with the Western powers that restore tariff autonomy to Japan.

1903●Wilbur and Orville Wright achieve the first sustained flight in a power-driven airplane.

	●井伊直弼暗殺される(桜田門外の変)。		
1862	●リチャードソン事件(生麦事件)：薩摩藩士、イギリス商人リチャードソンを殺害。		
1864	●四国艦隊下関砲撃事件(馬関戦争)：欧米艦隊長州藩を海上より攻撃。	1864	●国際労働者協会(通称第1インターナショナル)、ロンドンで結成。
1866	●徳川幕府に対抗し、薩長同盟成立。		
1867	●最後の将軍徳川慶喜が大政奉還。		

明治時代
1868–1912

明治維新によって天皇制国家に転換し明治時代がはじまり、近代産業社会への改革がはじまった。維新の指導者は、封建的藩体制を廃止して近代的国家に統合し、中央集権的官僚制度、新しい土地税制、徴兵による近代的軍隊を実施した。

1868	●明治維新。 ●明治天皇「五箇条の御誓文」を誓約：「五榜の掲示」公布。		
1869	●江戸を東京と改める。 ●藩の領有権を明治天皇に返還(版籍奉還)。		
1871	●郵便制度はじまる。 ●廃藩置県。		
1872	●新橋・横浜間に鉄道開通。 ●「学制」公布：日本初の近代的学校制度発足。		
1875	●樺太千島交換条約によって樺太はロシア領に千島は日本領となる。		
1876	●朝鮮と江華島条約(日朝修好条規)調印、日本は一方的な特権を得る。	1876	●ベル、電話を発明。
1877	●西南戦争；西郷隆盛自害。		
1883	●鹿鳴館完成：日本の上流社会や外国の貴賓による西洋風社交の場となる。	1883	●清仏戦争(1883年～1885年)はじまる；中国、フランスのヴェトナム保護権を認める(1885年)。
1889	●「大日本帝国憲法」発布。		
1890	●教育勅語をすべての学校に配布。		
1894	●日清戦争(1894年～1895年)はじまる。	1899	●アメリカ国務長官ジョン=ヘイ、中国の「門戸開放」覚書をイギリス、ドイツ、フランス、ロシア、イタリア、日本に通告。
1895	●三国干渉：ロシア、フランス、ドイツの干渉により中国から得た領土を返還。		
1902	●日英同盟調印。	1903	●ライト兄弟(ウィルバー、オーヴィル)初めて動力飛行機による飛行に成功。
1904	●日露戦争(1904年～1905年)はじまる。		
1910	●韓国、日本の植民地とされる(日韓併合)；朝鮮総督府を置く。		
1911	●ヨーロッパ列強と関税自主権回復の条約に調印。		

Taishō period
1912–1926

The Taishō period was marked by the advent of true party government, increased popular involvement in politics, the growth of organized labor and left-wing movements, and a domestic economic boom fueled by World War I. Taishō Democracy was supported by the emergence of an educated urban middle class and the rise of new forms of mass media.

....

1914	●Japan enters World War I on the side of Great Britain and its allies.
1915	●Japan presents China with its Twenty-One Demands for territorial and other concessions.
1918	●Commencement of the Siberian Intervention (1918–1922).
1920	●League of Nations established; Japan is granted permanent membership in the League Council.
1921	●Washington Conference (1921–1922) begins; it will result in the signing of the Four-Power Treaty, the Nine-Power Treaty, and the Washington Naval Treaty of 1922.
1923	●Tōkyō Earthquake (Kantō Daishinsai); assigned a magnitude of 7.9, this earthquake resulted in more than 100,000 deaths.
1925	●Enactment of the Peace Preservation Law of 1925 (Chian Iji Hō). ●Universal Manhood Suffrage Law (Futsū Senkyo Hō) passed.

1912●Republic of China established with Sun Yat-sen (Son Issen) as president; Emperor Puyi abdicates. *1914*●Archduke Francis Ferdinand assassinated at Sarajevo; World War I begins. *1917*●October Revolution in Russia. *1922*●Benito Mussolini forms a cabinet of Fascists and Nationalists in Italy.

Shōwa period
1926–1989

The Shōwa period was one of the most turbulent in Japanese history. In its first decades an ultranationalist coalition of right-wing politicians and army officers seized control of the country, setting Japan on a course of militarist expansionism in continental Asia that culminated in the Sino-Japanese War of 1937–1945 and entry into World War II. Japan's defeat ushered in a period of Occupation by Allied military forces and sweeping democratic reforms that included a new Constitution of Japan. The postwar decades saw reentry into the international community and phenomenal economic growth that transformed Japan into the world's second largest economy.

....

1927	●Financial Crisis of 1927 (Kin'yū Kyōkō).
1932	●Guandong Army (Kantōgun) establishes the state of Manchukuo; the last Qing-dynasty (1644–1912) emperor, Puyi (J: Fugi), appointed as head of state. ●May 15th Incident: Prime Minister Inukai Tsuyoshi assassinated.
1933	●Japan withdraws from the League of Nations to express its opposition to a report criticizing it as an aggressor in Manchuria.
1936	●February 26th Incident: 1,400 troops participate in an unsuccessful coup d'état.
1937	●Marco Polo Bridge Incident (Rokōkyō Jiken): Sino-Japanese War of 1937–1945 (Nitchū Sensō) commences.
1938	●Passage of the National Mobilization Law (Kokka Sōdōin Hō).
1939	●Nomonhan Incident: heavy fighting between Japanese and Soviet troops ends in a rout of Japanese forces.
1940	●Tripartite Pact (Nichidokui Sangoku Dōmei) signed by Japan, Germany, and Italy.
1941	●Soviet-Japanese Neutrality Pact signed. ●Japanese attack Pearl Harbor, the Malay Peninsula, and the Philippines; war declared against the United States, Great Britain, and the Netherlands.
1945	●Atomic bomb dropped on Hiroshima and Nagasaki. ●Japan accepts the terms of the Potsdam Declaration.

1927●Chiang Kai-shek (Shō Kaiseki) sets up a Nationalist government in Nanjing. *1929*●US stock market crashes, prolonged depression begins. *1933*●Adolf Hitler becomes chancellor of Germany.

1939●Germany invades Poland; World War II (1939–1945) begins in Europe.

大正時代
1912–1926

大正時代は本格的な政党内閣の出現、民衆の政治参加の拡大、労働運動や左翼運動の発展、第1次世界大戦の刺激による好景気等によって特徴づけられる。大正デモクラシーは都市の中流知識人層の出現と新しいマスメディアの登場に支えられた。

	日本史	世界史
1914	●日本、イギリスなど協商国側に立って第1次世界大戦に参戦。	1912 ●中華民国設立、孫逸仙(孫文)大統領に就任; 皇帝溥儀退位。
1915	●日本、中国に対華21ヵ条要求提出、領土その他の利権を要求する。	
1918	●シベリア出兵(1918年〜1922年)開始。	1914 ●オーストリア皇太子フランツ=フェルディナンド、サラエボで暗殺される; 第1次世界大戦はじまる。
1920	●国際連盟設立; 日本常任理事国となる。	1917 ●ロシアで10月革命。
1921	●ワシントン会議(1921年〜1922年)はじまる; 翌年4ヵ国条約、9ヵ国条約、ワシントン海軍軍縮条約成立。	1922 ●ムソリーニがイタリアにファシストと国家主義者たちの政府を組織。
1923	●関東大震災; マグニチュード7.9を記録。死者10万人以上。	
1925	●治安維持法成立。	
	●普通選挙法成立(男子のみ)。	

昭和時代
1926–1989

昭和時代は日本史上最大の激動期の一つである。最初の20年間は右翼政治家と軍部からなる超国家主義者たちが国の指導権をにぎり、アジア大陸への軍事的膨張路線へ日本を導いた。それは日中戦争(1937年〜1945年)で頂点に達し、遂に第2次世界大戦へ突入した。敗戦により日本は連合国の占領下に置かれ、新しい日本国憲法の制定を含む徹底的な民主改革が行われた。戦後の数十年間で日本は国際社会に復帰し、驚異的な経済成長を成し遂げ、世界第2位の経済大国となった。

	日本史	世界史
1927	●金融恐慌。	1927 ●蒋介石が中国南京に国民政府樹立。
1932	●関東軍満州国を建国。清朝(1644年〜1912年)最後の皇帝溥儀を国家元首(満州国皇帝)にする。	1929 ●アメリカで株式暴落、長期不況はじまる。
	●5・15事件: 犬養毅首相暗殺。	
1933	●日本の満州侵略を批判した国際連盟報告書に反対して、日本は国際連盟を脱退。	1933 ●ヒットラーがドイツ首相となる。
1936	●2・26事件: 1,400名の部隊が参加したが失敗。	
1937	●盧溝橋事件: 日中戦争(1937年〜1945年)はじまる。	
1938	●国家総動員法成立。	
1939	●ノモンハン事件: 日本・ソ連間の激しい軍事衝突、日本軍の大敗に終わる。	1939 ●ドイツがポーランド侵入、ヨーロッパで第2次世界大戦(1939年〜1945年)はじまる。
1940	●日独伊三国同盟調印。	
1941	●日ソ中立条約調印。	
	●日本が真珠湾、マレー半島、フィリピンを攻撃; アメリカ合衆国、イギリス、オランダに宣戦布告。	
1945	●原子爆弾、広島・長崎に投下される。	
	●日本ポツダム宣言受諾。	

Japanese History	World History
●Douglas MacArthur, supreme commander for the Allied powers (SCAP), arrives at Atsugi Airfield.	*1945*●US president Harry Truman, Soviet premier Joseph Stalin, and British prime minister Winston Churchill call for the unconditional surrender of Japan in the Potsdam Declaration.
1946 ●Emperor Shōwa renounces his divinity in New Year's address.	
●Implementation of the Land Reforms of 1946 begins.	
●Constitution of Japan promulgated.	
1949 ●Yukawa Hideki awarded the Nobel Prize for physics; he is the first Japanese to receive a Nobel Prize.	*1948*●Republic of Korea established in the southern part of the Korean peninsula and the Democratic People's Republic of Korea in the north.
1950 ●National Police Reserve created.	
1951 ●San Francisco Peace Treaty and the United States-Japan Security Treaty signed.	
1953 ●Television broadcasting begins in Japan.	*1950*●Korean War begins (1950–1953).
1954 ●Defense Agency and the Self Defense Forces established.	
1955 ●Japan joins GATT (General Agreement on Tariffs and Trade).	
●Liberal Democratic Party formed.	
1956 ●Soviet-Japanese Joint Declaration reestablishes diplomatic relations between the two countries.	
●Japan granted membership in the United Nations.	*1957*●Soviet Union launches the first space satellite, Sputnik 1.
1964 ●High-speed Shinkansen trains begin operations between Tōkyō and Ōsaka.	*1961*●Organization for Economic Cooperation and Development (OECD) organized; Japan joins in 1964.
●Eighteenth Summer Olympic Games held in Tōkyō.	
1965 ●Korea-Japan Treaty of 1965 signed; diplomatic relations between Japan and the Republic of Korea restored.	*1962*●Algeria gains independence from France.
1968 ●University upheavals of 1968–1969 (*daigaku funsō*) begin.	*1965*●US airplanes begin bombing North Vietnam.
1970 ●Expo '70 opens in Ōsaka.	*1966*●Cultural Revolution sweeps across China.
1972 ●Okinawa returned to Japanese sovereignty by the United States.	*1969*●US Apollo 11 spacecraft puts the first man on the moon.
●China-Japan Joint Communiqué of 1972 issued; it announces the establishment of diplomatic relations between Japan and the People's Republic of China.	*1973*●Fourth Arab-Israeli War triggers the oil crisis.
1973 ●Floating exchange rate introduced.	
●Oil crisis of 1973: oil prices spiral.	*1975*●North Vietnam achieves the unification of Vietnam.
1976 ●Lockheed Scandal: Japanese government officials charged with taking bribes from Lockheed Aircraft Corporation.	*1979*●Peace treaty signed by Egypt and Israel.
1978 ●New Tōkyō International Airport (Narita Airport) opens.	
1985 ●Enactment of the Equal Employment Opportunity Law For Men and Women.	*1986*●Nuclear accident at Chernobyl in the Soviet Union.
1988 ●Recruit Scandal diminishes popular support of the LDP.	

Heisei period 1989–

On 15 August 1995 Japan observed the fiftieth anniversary of the end of World War II. Today Japanese society is facing major new challenges, such as a falling birth rate and a rapidly aging population. Japan is also working to transform postwar-era practices in areas such as government, finance, and education so that the country will remain strong in a world where the interdependence of all nations continues to increase.

Japanese History	World History
1989 ●Death of Emperor Shōwa; accession of Emperor Akihito.	*1989*●Tiananmen Square Incident; thousands of demonstrators for democratization in China are killed by government troops.
●Sōhyō disbands and is largely absorbed into Rengō.	
1993 ●Non-LDP coalition government is formed, marking the end of the LDP's 38 years in power.	
1994 ●Political reform bills pass in the Diet.	●Berlin Wall demolished.
●Kansai International Airport opens.	*1990*●Reunification of Germany.
1995 ●Kōbe Earthquake; this magnitude 7.2 earthquake resulted in more than 6,000 deaths.	*1991*●Soviet Union dissolved.
●Subway Sarin Incident.	*1993*●Treaty on European Union (Treaty of Maastricht) enters into force.
1998 ●Yamaichi Securities and Hokkaidō Takushoku Bank go bankrupt.	

日本史	世界史

●連合国最高司令官(SCAP)ダグラス=マッカーサー厚木飛行場に到着。

1945●アメリカ大統領トルーマン、ソ連首相スターリン、イギリス首相チャーチル、ポツダム宣言を発し、日本に無条件降伏を要求。

1946 ●昭和天皇、年頭の挨拶で人間宣言。

●農地改革はじまる。
●日本国憲法成立。

1949 ●湯川秀樹ノーベル物理学賞受賞;日本人初のノーベル賞受賞。

1948●朝鮮半島に大韓民国、朝鮮民主主義人民共和国成立。

1950 ●警察予備隊創設。
1951 ●サンフランシスコ平和条約と日米安全保障条約調印。

1953 ●テレビ放送はじまる。
1954 ●防衛庁と自衛隊発足。

1950● 朝鮮戦争(1950年〜1953年)はじまる。

1955 ●日本、ガット(関税と貿易に関する一般協定)に加盟。
●自由民主党結成。
1956 ●日ソ共同宣言によって両国の国交回復。

●日本、国際連合加盟を認められる。
1964 ●東京・大阪間で高速の新幹線営業開始。

1957●ソ連、初の人工衛星スプートニク1号の打上げに成功。
1961●経済協力開発機構(OECD)結成 (日本は1964年に加盟)。

●第18回夏季オリンピック大会、東京で開催。
1965 ●日韓基本条約調印;日韓国交回復。

1962●アルジェリア、フランスから独立。

1968 ●大学紛争(1968年〜1969年)はじまる。
1970 ●日本万国博覧会大阪で開催。
1972 ●アメリカ、沖縄の施政権を日本に返還。

1965●アメリカ空軍の北ベトナム空爆開始。
1966●中国で文化大革命広がる。

●日中共同声明;日中国交回復。

1969●アメリカの宇宙船アポロ11号飛行士、初の月面着陸に成功。
1973●第4次アラブイスラエル戦争(中東戦争)、オイルショックの引き金となる。

1973 ●円の変動相場制導入。
●石油危機;石油価格高騰。
1976 ●ロッキード事件;日本政府高官ロッキード社からの収賄の疑いで告発される。

1975●北ベトナム、ベトナム全土を統一。
1979●エジプトとイスラエル平和条約に調印。

1978 ●新東京国際空港(成田空港)開港。
1985 ●男女雇用機会均等法成立。

1986● ソ連のチェルノブイリ原子力発電所で事故。

1988 ●リクルート事件;自由民主党の支持率下がる。

平成時代
1989–

1995年8月15日、日本は第2次世界大戦の終戦50周年を迎えた。日本の社会は出生率の低下や人口の急速な高齢化など新しい問題に直面している。国際的な相互依存関係がますます高まるなか、日本は活力を維持するために行政・金融・教育などの分野で戦後制度の改革を進めている。

1989 ●昭和天皇崩御;天皇明仁即位。
●総評が解散し連合に吸収される。
1993 ●非自民連立内閣成立し38年に及ぶ自民党支配終わる。

1989●天安門事件;中国の民主化を求めるデモ隊を軍隊が制圧、死者多数。
●ベルリンの壁崩壊。

1994 ●政治改革関連法案国会通過。
●関西国際空港開港。
1995 ●阪神淡路大震災;マグニチュード7.2、死者6,000人を超える。

●地下鉄サリン事件。
1998 ●山一證券廃業、北海道拓殖銀行業務停止。

1990● 東西ドイツ統一。
1991● ソビエト連邦解体。
1993●欧州連合条約(マーストリヒト条約)発効。

環境庁は、両生類及び爬虫類と植物について、レッドリスト（日本の絶滅のおそれのある野生生物の種のリスト）の見直しを行った。レッドリストは、「レッドデータブック」（絶滅のおそれのある野生生物の個々の種の生息状況等をまとめたもの）の基礎となるものであり、これ自体が法的規制等の強制力を伴うものではなく、絶滅のおそれのある野生生物への理解を広めることを目的としたものである。

1.「レッドデータブック」の見直しについて
(1). 目的・経緯
野生生物を人為的に絶滅させないためには、絶滅のおそれのある種を的確に把握し、一般への理解を広める必要があることから、レッドリストは、昭和61年度より＜緊急に保護を要する動植物の種の選定調査＞を実施し、その結果を「レッドデータブック：日本の絶滅のおそれのある野生生物　脊椎動物篇、無脊椎動物篇」として平成3年に取りまとめた。しかし、IUCN（国際自然保護連合）で採択された新しいカテゴリーの考え方に基づき、また、生息状況や生息環境の変化に関する最新の知見等を踏まえ、「レッドデータブック」の見直しを行う必要が出たため、環境庁では平成7年度より、哺乳類、鳥類といった分類群毎に見直し作業に着手し、このほかの分類群についても、次のスケジュールで見直し作業を進めている。

【動物篇「レッドデータブック」見直しスケジュール】
- 両生・爬虫類、鳥類　　　H7～H9
- 哺乳類、魚類　　　　　　H8～H10
- 無脊椎動物　　　　　　　H9～H11

(2). 調査方法と調査体制
「動物篇：レッドデータブック」の見直しについては、環境庁自然保護局に、＜絶滅のおそれのある野生生物の選定・評価検討会＞を、その下に＜「レッドデータブック」改訂分科会＞、＜両生・爬虫類分科会＞等を設置し、作業を進めた。今回の両生・爬虫類の見直しにおいては、既存知見による評価を基本とし、それを補うために必要に応じ若干の現地調査を行った。

2.「レッドデータブック」のカテゴリーの改訂
平成3年の「動物篇：レッドデータブック」においては、IUCNによる「レッドデータブック」に準じ、定性的要件に基づくカテゴリー区分により評価を行った。今回の見直しでは、1994年(平成6年)にIUCNが採択した、減少率等の数値による客観的な評価基準に基づく新しいカテゴリーに従うが、我が国では数値的に評価が可能となるようなデータが得られない種も多いこと等の理由から、定性的要件と定量的要件を組み合わせたカテゴリーを策定されている。新たなカテゴリーの概要は次のとおり。

- 絶滅(EX)
我が国ではすでに絶滅したと考えられる種。
- 野生絶滅(EW)
飼育・栽培下でのみ存続している種。
- 絶滅危惧
絶滅危惧1類(CR+EN)絶滅の危機に瀕している種。
絶滅危惧1A類(CR)
絶滅危惧1B類(EN)
絶滅危惧2類(VU)絶滅の危険が増大している種。
- 準絶滅危惧(NT)
現時点では絶滅危険度は小さいが、生息条件の変化によっては「絶滅危惧」に移行する可能性のある種。
- 情報不足(DD)
評価するだけの情報が不足している種。
- 付属資料地域個体群(LP)
地域的に孤立しており、地域レベルでの絶滅のおそれが高い個体群。

植物1
(維管束植物：種子植物・シダ植物)

注1)「種」のレベル（亜種・変種を含む）で掲載。

注2)「都道府県別分布」は、今回のメッシュ単位の調査結果に基づき現存する都道府県名を記載。また、メッシュ単位の現存情報は得られなかったが文献等による分布状態にある場合が多い。

注3) 準絶滅危惧(NT)と情報不足(DD)は科ごとに種名を掲載。

植物	絶滅
	EX

コウヨウザンカズラ
Lycopodium cunninghamioides :
ヒカゲノカズラ科

タカナハナワラビ
Botrychium boreale : ハナヤスリ科

イオウジマハナヤスリ
Ophioglossum nudicaule : ハナヤスリ科

オオイワヒメワラビ
Hypolepis tenuifolia :
コバノイシカグマ科

オオアオガネシダ
Asplenium austrochinense :
チャセンシダ科

オオヤグルマシダ
Dryopteris wallichiana : オシダ科

ウスバシダモドキ
Tectaria dissecta : オシダ科

ヒトツバノキシノブ
Pyrrosia angustissimum : ウラボシ科

ホソバノキミズ
Elatostema lineolatum var. majus :
イラクサ科

オオユリワサビ
Eutrema tenuis var. okinosimensis :
アブラナ科

オオミコゴメグサ
Euphrasia insignis var. omiensis :
ゴマノハグサ科

リュウキュウスズカケ
Veronicastrum liukiuense :
ゴマノハグサ科

ムジナノカミソリ
Lycoris sanguinea var. koreana :
ヒガンバナ科

タカノホシクサ
Eriocaulon cauliferum : ホシクサ科

ヒュウガホシクサ
Eriocaulon seticuspe : ホシクサ科

ハツシマラン
Odontochilus hatusimanus : ラン科

ジンヤクラン
Renanthera (=Arachnis) labrosa : ラン科

ヒュウガシケシダ
Deparia minamitanii :
メシダ(イワデンダ)科

コブシモドキ
Magnolia pseudokobus : モクレン科

エッチュウミセバヤ
Hylotelephium sieboldii var. ettyuense :
ベンケイソウ科

リュウキュウベンケイ
Kalanchoe integra : ベンケイソウ科

オオカナメモチ
Photinia serrulata : バラ科

ナルトオウギ
Astragalus sikokianus : マメ科

オリヅルスミレ
Viola stoloniflora : スミレ科

リュウキュウアセビ
Pieris japonica var. koidzumiana :
ツツジ科

タモトユリ
Lilium nobilissimum : ユリ科

サツマオモト
Rohdea japonica var. latifolia : ユリ科

タイワンアオイラン
Acanthephippium striatum : ラン科

キバナコクラン
Liparis nigra var. sootenzanensis :
ラン科

イヌヤチスギラン
Lycopodium carolinianum :
ヒカゲノカズラ科 : 滋賀

ヒモスギラン
Lycopodium fargesii :
ヒカゲノカズラ科 : 鹿児島

ヨウラクヒバ
Lycopodium phlegmaria :
ヒカゲノカズラ科 : 鹿児島、沖縄

ヒメヨウラクヒバ
Lycopodium salvinioides :
ヒカゲノカズラ科 : 沖縄

ヒモラン
Lycopodium sieboldii :
ヒカゲノカズラ科 : 愛媛、高知、熊本、
宮崎、鹿児島、神奈川、静岡、愛知、三重、

和歌山、福岡、佐賀、長崎、大分

リュウキュウヒモラン
*Lycopodium sieboldii var.
christensenianum* : ヒカゲノカズラ科 :
熊本、鹿児島、沖縄、宮崎

イブリハナワラビ
Botrychium microphyllum :
ハナヤスリ科 : 北海道

ミヤコジマハナヤスリ
Helminthostachys zeylanica :
ハナヤスリ科 : 沖縄、鹿児島

トネハナヤスリ
Ophioglossum namegatae :
ハナヤスリ科 : 栃木、千葉、大阪

チャボハナヤスリ
Ophioglossum parvum : ハナヤスリ科 :
東京、静岡、三重

ヒノタニリュウビンタイ
Angiopteris fokienssis :
リュウビンタイ科 : 宮崎、鹿児島

カンザシワラビ
Schizaea dichotoma : フサシダ科 :
沖縄、鹿児島

マルバコケシダ
Trichomanes bimarginatum :
コケシノブ科 : 沖縄

イヌイノモトソウ
Lindsaea ensifolia : ホングウシダ科 :
沖縄、鹿児島

シノブホングウシダ
Lindsaea kawabatae : ホングウシダ科 :
鹿児島

コビトホラシノブ
Sphenomeris minutula :
ホングウシダ科 : 鹿児島

ワラビツナギ
Arthropteris palisotii : ツルシダ科 :
鹿児島、沖縄

イワウラジロ
Cheilanthes krameri :
ミズワラビ科(ホウライシダ)科 : 群馬、東
京、埼玉

シマタキミシダ
Antrophyum formosanum : シシラン科 :
鹿児島

イトシシラン
Vittaria mediosora : シシラン科 : (埼玉、
長野)

ミミモチシダ
Acrostichum aureum : イノモトソウ科 :
沖縄

タイワンアマクサシダ
Pteris formosana : イノモトソウ科 :
鹿児島

アシガタシダ
Pteris grevilleana : イノモトソウ科 :
鹿児島、沖縄

ヒメイノモトソウ
Pteris yamatensis : イノモトソウ科 :
奈良

ヒメタニワタリ
Asplenium cardiophyllum :
チャセンシダ科 : (東京、沖縄)

ホコガタシダ
Asplenium ensiforme : チャセンシダ科 :
熊本、宮崎

マキノシダ
Asplenium loriceum : チャセンシダ科 :
沖縄

イエジマチャセンシダ
*Asplenium oligophlebium var.
iezimaense* : チャセンシダ科 : 沖縄

ウスイロホウビシダ
Asplenium subnormale :
チャセンシダ科 : (鹿児島、沖縄)

オオギミシダ
Woodwardia harlandii : シシガシラ科 :
沖縄

オキナワアツイタ
Elaphoglossum callifolium :
ツルキジノオ科 : 沖縄

シビカナワラビ
Arachniodes hekiana : オシダ科 :
鹿児島、(大分)

ヒュウガカナワラビ
Arachniodes hiugana : オシダ科 : 熊本、
宮崎

コバヤシカナワラビ
Arachniodes sp. : オシダ科 : (宮崎)

コキンモウイノデ
Ctenitis microlepigera : オシダ科 : (東京)

クマヤブソテツ
*Cyrtomium macrophyllum var.
microindusium* : オシダ科 : 熊本

オオミネイワヘゴ
Dryopteris lunanensis : オシダ科 : 奈良、
(三重)

ヤタケイワヘゴ
Dryopteris otomasui : オシダ科 : 熊本

シビイタチシダ
Dryopteris shibipedis : オシダ科 :
鹿児島

ツツイイワヘゴ
Dryopteris tsutsuiana : オシダ科 : 福岡、
熊本

スルガイノデ
*Polystichum fibrilloso-paleaceum var.
marginale* : オシダ科 : (静岡)

マシャイノデ
Polystichum neo-lobatum : オシダ科 :
神奈川、長野、(山梨)

アマミデンダ
Polystichum obai : オシダ科 : 鹿児島

ナクラジマイノデ
Polystichum piceopaleaceum :
オシダ科 : 佐賀、(鹿児島)

シムライノデ
Polystichum shimurae : オシダ科 :
東京、神奈川、静岡

コモチナナバケシダ
Tectaria fauriei : オシダ科 : 鹿児島

タイヨウシダ
Thelypteris erubescens : ヒメシダ科 :
(鹿児島)

タイワンアリサンイヌワラビ
Athyrium arisanense :
メシダ(イワデンダ)科 : 鹿児島

シビイヌワラビ
Athyrium kenzo-satakei :
メシダ(イワデンダ)科 : 鹿児島

コモチイヌワラビ
Athyrium strigillosum :
メシダ(イワデンダ)科 : 熊本

ジャコウシダ
Diplazium heterophlebium :
メシダ(イワデンダ)科 : (鹿児島)

フクレギシダ
Diplazium pin-faense .
メシダ(イワデンダ)科 : 熊本、(鹿児島)

ヒメデンダ
Woodsia subcordata :
メシダ(イワデンダ)科 : 群馬、山梨、長
野、(北海道、静岡)

Aglaomorpha coronans : ウラボシ科 :
沖縄

ヤクシマウラボシ
Crypsinus yakuinsularis : ウラボシ科 :
徳島、(三重、和歌山、高知、鹿児島)

キレハオクボシダ
Ctenopteris sakaguchiana : ウラボシ科 :
奈良、(埼玉、東京、山梨、長野、静岡、熊
本)

オニマメヅタ
Lemmaphyllum pyriforme : ウラボシ科 :
島根、鹿児島

ウロコノキシノブ
Lepisorus oligolepidus : ウラボシ科 :
長野

タイワンアオネカズラ
Polypodium formosanum : ウラボシ科 :
鹿児島、沖縄

ヒトツバハマメヅタ
Pyrrosia adnascens : ウラボシ科 : (沖縄)

ナガバコウラボシ
Grammitis tuyamae : ヒメウラボシ科 :
熊本

ナンゴクデンジソウ
Marsilea crenata : デンジソウ科 :
福岡、鹿児島、沖縄

ヤツガタケトウヒ
Picea koyamae : マツ科 : 長野、(山梨)

ヒメマツハダ
Picea shirasawae : マツ科 : 山梨、長野

ヒダカミネヤナギ
Salix hidaka-montana : ヤナギ科 : 北海道

サキシマエノキ
Celtis biondii var. insularis : ニレ科 :
沖縄

オオヤマイチジク
Ficus iidaiana : クワ科 : (東京)

オガサワラグワ
Morus boninensis : クワ科 : (東京)

ヨナクニトキホコリ
Elatostema yonakuniense : イラクサ科 :
(沖縄)

チョクザキミズ
Lecanthus peduncularis : イラクサ科 :
大分、宮崎

ソハヤキミズ
Pilea sohayakiensis : イラクサ科 :
和歌山、徳島、宮崎

セキモンウライソウ
Procris boninensis : イラクサ科 : (東京)

キュウシュウツチトリモチ
Balanophora kiusiana : ツチトリモチ科 :
熊本、大分、(宮崎)

ナンブトラノオ
Bistorta hayachinensis : タデ科 : 岩手

アラゲタデ
Persicaria lanatum : タデ科 : (沖縄)

キブネダイオウ
Rumex nepalensis var. andreaenus :
タデ科 : 京都、岡山

オキナワマツバボタン
Portulaca pilosa ssp. okinawensis :
スベリヒユ科 : 鹿児島、沖縄

ミツモリミミナグサ
Cerastium arvense var. ovatum :
ナデシコ科 : 北海道、(青森)

オグラセンノウ
Lychnis kiusiana : ナデシコ科 : 岡山、広
島、熊本、大分、(大阪)

チシマツメクサ
Sagina saginoides : ナデシコ科 : 青森、
長野、(富山)

エゾマンテマ
Silene foliosa : ナデシコ科 : 北海道

カムイビランジ
Silene hidaka-alpina : ナデシコ科 :
北海道

チシママンテマ
Silene repens var. latifolia : ナデシコ科 :
(北海道)

スガワラビランジ
Silene stenophylla : ナデシコ科 : 北海道

カンチヤチハコベ
Stellaria calycantha : ナデシコ科 : 静岡、
(群馬、富山、長野)

オオイワツメクサ
Stellaria nipponica var. yezoensis :
ナデシコ科 : 北海道

シナクスモドキ
Cryptocarya chinensis : クスノキ科 :
宮崎

オキナワコウバシ
Lindera communis var. okinawensis :
クスノキ科 : 沖縄

オンタケブシ
Aconitum metajaponicum :
キンポウゲ科 : 群馬、埼玉、長野、(秋田、
山形)

ダイセツトリカブト
Aconitum yamazakii : キンポウゲ科 :
北海道

シコクイチゲ
Anemone sikokiana : キンポウゲ科 :
愛媛

キリギシソウ
*Callianthemum sachallinense var.
kirigishiense* : キンポウゲ科 : (北海道)

オオワクノテ
Clematis serratifolia : キンポウゲ科 :
北海道

キバナサバノオ
Dichocarpum pterigionocaudatum :
キンポウゲ科 : 兵庫、(滋賀、京都、岡山)

カラクサキンポウゲ
Ranunculus gmelinii : キンポウゲ科 :
(北海道)

ヒメバイカモ
Ranunculus kazusensis : キンポウゲ科 :
宮城、福井、福岡、熊本、(福島、茨城、千
葉、大分)

ヒメキツネノボタン
Ranunculus yaegatakensis :
キンポウゲ科 : (鹿児島)

ミョウギカラマツ
Thalictrum minus var. chionophyllum :
キンポウゲ科 : 群馬

ヒレフリカラマツ
Thalictrum toyamae：キンポウゲ科：
佐賀、長崎

ウジカラマツ
Thalictrum ujiensis：キンポウゲ科：
鹿児島

ホウザンツヅラフジ
Cocculus sarmentosus：ツヅラフジ科：
鹿児島

ギフヒメコウホネ
Nuphar sp.：スイレン科：岐阜

タイヨウフウトウカズラ
Piper postelsianum：コショウ科：(東京)

オナガサイシン
Asarum leptophyllum：
ウマノスズクサ科：(沖縄)

シジキカンアオイ
Heterotropa controversa：
ウマノスズクサ科：(長崎)

テンリュウカンアオイ
Heterotropa draconis：
ウマノスズクサ科：静岡

ジュロウカンアオイ
Heterotropa kinoshitae：
ウマノスズクサ科：(三重)

オナガカンアオイ
Heterotropa minamitaniana：
ウマノスズクサ科：宮崎

モノドラカンアオイ
Heterotropa monodraeflora：
ウマノスズクサ科：(沖縄)

シモダカンアオイ
Heterotropa muramatsui var. shimodana：ウマノスズクサ科：静岡

ヒナカンアオイ
Heterotropa okinawensis：
ウマノスズクサ科：(沖縄)

センカクカンアオイ
Heterotropa senkakuinsularis：
ウマノスズクサ科：(沖縄)

クニガミヒサカキ
Eurya zigzag：ツバキ科：沖縄

ツキヌキオトギリ
Hypericum sampsonii：オトギリソウ科：
福岡、佐賀、長崎、熊本、鹿児島、(高知)

センカクオトギリ
Hypericum senkakuinsulare：
オトギリソウ科：(沖縄)

トサオトギリ
Hypericum tosaense：オトギリソウ科：
高知、(岡山、香川)

ダイセツヒナオトギリ
Hypericum yojiroanum：
オトギリソウ科：北海道

ムジナモ
Aldrovanda vesiculosa：
モウセンゴケ科：埼玉、(茨城、群馬、東京、京都)

ハナナズナ
Berteroella maximowiczii：アブラナ科：
長崎、(岡山、広島)

ミヤウチソウ
Cardamine trifida：アブラナ科：(北海道)

ハナハタザオ
Dontostemon dentatus：アブラナ科：
山梨、広島、熊本、(群馬、神奈川、静岡)

シリベシナズナ
Draba igarashii：アブラナ科：北海道

キタダケナズナ
Draba kitadakensis：アブラナ科：山梨、
(長野、静岡)

ソウウンナズナ
Draba nakaiana：アブラナ科：(北海道)

ヤツガタケナズナ
Draba oiana：アブラナ科：山梨、長野、
(埼玉)

ハマタイセイ
Isatis yezoensis：アブラナ科：北海道

タカネグンバイ
Thlaspi japonicum：アブラナ科：北海道

ヒゴミズキ
Corylopsis gotoana var. pubescens：
マンサク科：熊本

トキワマンサク
Loropetalum chinense：マンサク科：
静岡

アマミクサアジサイ
Cardiandra amamiohsimensis：
ユキノシタ科：鹿児島

エチゼンダイモンジソウ
Saxifraga acerifolia：ユキノシタ科：石川

エゾノクモマグサ
Saxifraga nishidae：
ユキノシタ科：北海道

ユウバリクモマグサ
Saxifraga yuparensis：ユキノシタ科：
北海道

オオミトベラ
Pittosporum chichijimense：トベラ科：
(東京)

コバノトベラ
Pittosporum parvifolium：トベラ科：
(東京)

クロミサンザシ
Crataegus chlorosarca：バラ科：北海道

ノカイドウ
Malus spontanea：バラ科：宮崎、(鹿児島)

メアカンキンバイ
Potentilla miyabei：バラ科：北海道

ブコウマメザクラ
Prunus incisa var. bukosanensis：
バラ科：群馬、東京、(埼玉)

マメナシ
Pyrus calleryana：バラ科：愛知、(長野、岐阜、三重)

コバノアマミフユイチゴ
Rubus amamiana var. minor：バラ科：
鹿児島

マヤイチゴ
Rubus tawadanus：バラ科：鹿児島

エゾノトウウチソウ
Sanguisorba japonensis：バラ科：
北海道

ナンブトウウチソウ
Sanguisorba obtusa：バラ科：岩手

エゾモメンヅル
Astragalus japonicus：マメ科：(北海道)

カリバオウギ
Astragalus yamamotoi：マメ科：
(北海道)

タイワンミヤマトベラ
Euchresta formosana：マメ科：(沖縄)

タシロマメ
Intsia bijuga：マメ科：沖縄

レブンソウ
Oxytropis megalantha：マメ科：(北海道)

リシリゲンゲ
Oxytropis rishiriensis：マメ科：北海道

シタン
Pterocarpus indicus：マメ科：(沖縄)

ツクシムレスズメ
Sophora franchetiana：マメ科：宮崎、
(熊本、鹿児島)

オオバフジボクサ
Uraria lagopodioides：マメ科：沖縄

ホソバフジボグサ
Uraria picta：マメ科：沖縄

スナジマメ
Zornia cantoniensis：マメ科：高知

タシロカワゴケソウ
Cladopus austroosumiensis：
カワゴケソウ科：鹿児島

トキワカワゴケソウ
Cladopus austrosatsumensis：
カワゴケソウ科：(鹿児島)

マノセカワゴケソウ
Cladopus doianus：カワゴケソウ科：
(鹿児島)

カワゴケソウ
Cladopus japonicus：カワゴケソウ科：
(鹿児島)

アマミカタバミ
Oxalis exilis：カタバミ科：鹿児島

タイワンヒメコバンノキ
Breynia formosana：トウダイグサ科：
(沖縄)

セキモンノキ
Claoxylon centenarium：
トウダイグサ科：(東京)

エノキフジ
Discocleidion ulmifolium：
トウダイグサ科：(鹿児島、沖縄)

ムサシタイゲキ
Euphorbia sendaica var. musashiensis：
トウダイグサ科：(東京)

ニュウガタイゲキ
Euphorbia sp.：トウダイグサ科：宮崎

コウライタチバナ
Citrus nippokoreana：ミカン科：山口

ムニンゴシュユ
Evodia nishimurae：ミカン科．(東京)

オオバゲッキツ
Murraya koenigii：ミカン科：(鹿児島)

タイワンフシノキ
Rhus javanica：ウルシ科：(沖縄)

ヒメモチ
Ilex beecheyi：モチノキ科：(東京)

アマミヒイラギモチ
Ilex dimorphophylla：モチノキ科：
鹿児島

ヒロハタマミズキ
Ilex macrocarpa：モチノキ科：(鹿児島)

アンドンマユミ
Euonymus oligospermus：ニシキギ科：
(福島)

ナガバヒゼンマユミ
Euonymus sp.：ニシキギ科：大分

クニガミクロウメモドキ
Rhamnus calicicola：クロウメモドキ科：
(沖縄)

ヒメクロウメモドキ
Rhamnus kanagusuki：
クロウメモドキ科：(沖縄)

クマガワブドウ
Vitis quinqueangularis：ブドウ科：宮崎、
鹿児島、(熊本)

アツバウオトリギ
Grewia biloba：シナノキ科：(沖縄)

マンシュウボダイジュ
Tilia mandschurica：シナノキ科：山口

ツクシボダイジュ
Tilia rufo-villosa：シナノキ科：大分、
(熊本)

ツチビノキ
Daphnimorpha capitellata：

ジンチョウゲ科：宮崎

ジンヨウキスミレ
Viola alliariaefolia：スミレ科：北海道

アマミスミレ
Viola amamiana：スミレ科：鹿児島

タニマスミレ
Viola epipsila ssp. repens：スミレ科：
(北海道)

タデスミレ
Viola thibaudieri：スミレ科：長野

シソバキスミレ
Viola yubariana：スミレ科：北海道

ナガバキブシ
Stachyurus macrocarpus：キブシ科：
(東京)

ゴバンノアシ
Barringtonia asiatica：サガリバナ科：
(沖縄)

ムニンノボタン
Melastoma tetramerum：ノボタン科：
(東京)

ヒルギモドキ
Lumnitzera racemosa：シクンシ科：
沖縄

テリハモモタマナ
Terminalia nitens：シクンシ科：(沖縄)

エダウチアカバナ
Epilobium fastigiatoramosum：
アカバナ科：(北海道)

ミズキンバイ
Ludwigia stipulacea：アカバナ科：
千葉、神奈川、高知、宮崎、(群馬、山口、
鹿児島)

ナガバアリノトウグサ
Haloragis chinensis：アリノトウグサ科：
沖縄

クマノダケ
Angelica mayebarana：セリ科：熊本

イシヅチボウフウ
Angelica saxicola：セリ科：高知

レブンサイコ
Bupleurum triraediatum：セリ科：
北海道

アマミイワウチワ
Shortia rotundifolia var. amamiana：
イワウメ科：(鹿児島)

イチゲイチヤクソウ
Moneses uniflora：イチヤクソウ科：
(北海道)

エゾイチヤクソウ
Pyrola minor：イチヤクソウ科：(北海道)

ヤチツツジ
Chamaedaphne calyculata：ツツジ科：
北海道、秋田

ゴヨウザンヨウラク
Menziesia goyozanensis：ツツジ科：
岩手

ムラサキツリガネツツジ
Menziesia multiflora var. purpurea：
ツツジ科：群馬、神奈川、(静岡)

ムニンツツジ
Rhododendron boninense：ツツジ科：
(東京)

ヒダカミツバツツジ
Rhododendron dilatatum var. boreale：
ツツジ科：(北海道)

ハヤトミツバツツジ
*Rhododendron dilatatum var.
satsumense*：ツツジ科：(鹿児島)

センカクツツジ
*Rhododendron eriocarpum var.
tawadae*：ツツジ科：(沖縄)

ウラジロヒカゲツツジ
*Rhododendron keiskei var.
hypoglaucum*：ツツジ科：群馬、東京、
(茨城、栃木、埼玉)

アマクサミツバツツジ
*Rhododendron viscistylum var.
amakusaense*：ツツジ科：熊本

チョウセンヤマツツジ
*Rhododendron yedoense var.
pooukhanense*：ツツジ科：長崎

ヤドリコケモモ
Vaccinium amamianum：ツツジ科：
鹿児島

トチナイソウ
Androsace lehmanniana：
サクラソウ科：岩手

トウサワトラノオ
Lysimachia candida：サクラソウ科：愛
知

ヒメミヤマコナスビ
Lysimachia liukiuensis：サクラソウ科：
鹿児島

カムイコザクラ
Primula hidakana var. kamuiana：
サクラソウ科：北海道

ヒメコザクラ
Primula macrocarpa：サクラソウ科：岩手

ミョウギイワザクラ
Primula reinii var. myogiensis：
サクラソウ科：群馬

ユウバリコザクラ
Primula yuparensis：サクラソウ科：
北海道

センカクハマサジ
Limonium senkakuense：イソマツ科：
(沖縄)

ムニンノキ
Planchonella boninensis：アカテツ科：
（東京）

ウチダシクロキ
Symplocos kawakamii：ハイノキ科：
（東京）

チチジマクロキ
Symplocos pergracilis：ハイノキ科：
（東京）

ヤナギバモクセイ
Osmanthus okinawensis：モクセイ科：
沖縄

タイワンチトセカズラ
Gardneria shimadae：マチン科：沖縄

リシリリンドウ
Gentiana jamesii：リンドウ科：北海道

ヤクシマリンドウ
Gentiana yakushimensis：リンドウ科：
（鹿児島）

チチブリンドウ
Gentianopsis contorta：リンドウ科：
群馬、長野

シマアケボノソウ
Swertia kuroiwai：リンドウ科：沖縄

ソナレセンブリ
Swertia noguchiana：リンドウ科：
静岡、（東京）

ナンゴクカモメヅル
Cynanchum austrokiusianum：
ガガイモ科：宮崎、（鹿児島）

エゾノクサタチバナ
Cynanchum inamoenum：ガガイモ科：
北海道

ヤマワキオゴケ
Cynanchum yamanakae：ガガイモ科：
高知

マメヅタカズラ
Dischidia formosana：ガガイモ科：（沖縄）

ヨナグニカモメヅル
Tylophora yonakuniensis：ガガイモ科：
（沖縄）

シソノミグサ
Knoxia corymbosa：アカネ科：（沖縄）

ヒジハリノキ
Randia sinensis：アカネ科：（沖縄）

ハナシノブ
Polemonium kiushianum：
ハナシノブ科：熊本、宮崎、（大分）

ナガバアサガオ
Aniseia martinicensis：ヒルガオ科：
（沖縄）

クシロネナシカズラ
Cuscuta europaea：ヒルガオ科：北海道

エゾルリムラサキ

Eritrichium nipponicum var. albiflorum：
ムラサキ科：（北海道）

イワムラサキ
Hackelia deflexa：ムラサキ科：長野

エゾルリソウ
Mertensia pterocarpa var. yezoensis：
ムラサキ科：北海道

チョウセンカメバソウ
Trigonotis nakaii：ムラサキ科：熊本

ケルリソウ
Trigonotis radicans：ムラサキ科：熊本

シマムラサキ
Callicarpa glabra：クマツヅラ科：（東京）

タカクマムラサキ
Callicarpa longissima：クマツヅラ科：
（鹿児島）

ウラジロコムラサキ
Callicarpa nishimurae：クマツヅラ科：
（東京）

オオニンジンボク
Vitex quinata：クマツヅラ科：（沖縄）

シマカコソウ
Ajuga boninsimae：シソ科：（東京）

ヒメタツナミソウ
Scutellaria kikaiisularis：シソ科：（鹿児島）

エゾニガクサ
Teucrium veronicoides：シソ科：
青森、宮城、山口、（北海道、茨城、佐賀）

テンジクナスビ
Solanum anguivi：ナス科：（沖縄）

ムニンホオズキ
Solanum biflorum var. glabrum：ナス科：
東京

イラブナスビ
Solanum miyakojimense：ナス科：沖縄

イナコゴメグサ
Euphrasia multifolia var. inaensis：
ゴマノハグサ科：長野

カミガモソウ
Gratiola fluviatilis：ゴマノハグサ科：
兵庫、（京都、長崎、鹿児島）

キタミソウ
Limosella aquatica：ゴマノハグサ科：
北海道、埼玉、熊本

ウスユキクチナシグサ
Monochasma savatieri：
ゴマノハグサ科：熊本

センリゴマ
Rehmannia japonica：ゴマノハグサ科：
静岡、（岐阜）

ツルウリクサ
Torenia concolor var. formosana：
ゴマノハグサ科：沖縄、（鹿児島）

スズカケソウ

Veronicastrum villosulum：
ゴマノハグサ科：岐阜、徳島、（鳥取）

ユウパリソウ
Lagotis takedana：ウルップソウ科：
北海道

ミヤコジマソウ
Hemigraphis reptans：キツネノマゴ科
沖縄

ヒシモドキ
Trapella sinensis：ゴマ(ヒシモドキ)科：
秋田、兵庫、佐賀、（青森、宮城、山形、栃
木、群馬、千葉、新潟、石川、福井、愛知、
京都、岡山、徳島、福岡）

ナガミカズラ
Aeschynanthus acuminatus：
イワタバコ科：（沖縄）

タイワンシシンラン
Lysionotus sp.：イワタバコ科：（沖縄）

フサタヌキモ
Utricularia dimorphantha：タヌキモ科：
岩手、愛知、兵庫、（青森、宮城、秋田、山
形、新潟、静岡、三重、滋賀、京都、和歌
山、岡山）

タイワンツクバネウツギ
Abelia chinensis var. ionandra：
スイカズラ科：鹿児島、（沖縄）

キタカミヒョウタンボク
Lonicera demissa var. borealis：
スイカズラ科：岩手

ヤブヒョウタンボク
Lonicera linderifolia：スイカズラ科：岩手

ホザキツキネキソウ
Triosteum pinnatifidum：スイカズラ科：
山梨

ツキネキソウ
Triosteum sinuatum：スイカズラ科：
長野

ヒロハガマズミ
Viburnum koreanum：スイカズラ科：
北海道

オオベニウツギ
Weigela florida：スイカズラ科：（福岡）

ツクシイワシャジン
Adenophora hatsushimae：キキョウ科：
熊本、宮崎

ヤチシャジン
Adenophora palustris：キキョウ科：
岡山、（岐阜、愛知、広島）

ユウバリシャジン
*Adenophora pereskiaefolia var.
yamadae*：キキョウ科：北海道

ホウオウシャジン
Adenophora takedae var. howozana：
キキョウ科：山梨

タチミゾカクシ
Lobelia hancei：キキョウ科：沖縄、
(宮崎)

ホソバエゾノコギリ
Achillea ptarmica var. yezoensis：
キク科：北海道

エゾノチチコグサ
Antennaria dioica：キク科：北海道

ユキヨモギ
Artemisia momiyamae：キク科：
神奈川、静岡、(東京)

シブカワシロギク
Aster rugulosus var. shibukawaensis：
キク科：静岡

ホソバノギク
Aster sohayakiensis：キク科：和歌山、
(三重)

ヨナグニイソノギク
Aster walkeri：キク科：(沖縄)

ヤクシマギク
Aster yakushimensis：キク科：(鹿児島)

ヤナギタウコギ
Bidens cernua：キク科：(北海道、青森)

タカサゴアザミ
Cirsium japonicum var. australe：
キク科：(沖縄)

ユズリハワダン
Crepidiastrum ameristophyllum：
キク科：(東京)

ヘラナレン
Crepidiastrum linguifolium：キク科：
(東京)

フタマタタンポポ
Crepis hokkaidoensis：キク科：北海道

ミヤマノギク
Erigeron miyabeanus：キク科：北海道

コケセンボンギク
Lagenophora lanata：キク科：
長崎、鹿児島、沖縄、(岡山、広島、熊本)

オオヒラウスユキソウ
Leontopodium miyabeanum：キク科：
北海道

ヤマタバコ
Ligularia angusta：キク科：群馬、神奈
川、長野、静岡、(東京)

ヤクシマコウヤボウキ
Pertya yakushimensis：キク科：(鹿児島)

シマトウヒレン
Saussurea insularis：キク科：長崎

フタナミソウ
Scorzonera rebunensis：キク科：
(北海道)

コウリンギク
Senecio argunensis：キク科：大分

ヤブレガサモドキ
Syneilesis tagawae：キク科：兵庫、高知

タカネタンポポ
Taraxacum yuparense：キク科：北海道

アズミノヘラオモダカ
Alisma canaliculatum var.：オモダカ科：
(長野)

カラフトグワイ
Sagittaria natans：オモダカ科：(北海道)

ガシャモク
Potamogeton dentatus：ヒルムシロ科：
千葉、福岡、(群馬)

イヌイトモ
Potamogeton obtusifolius：
ヒルムシロ科：(北海道)

ツツイトモ
Potamogeton panormitanus：
ヒルムシロ科：青森、徳島、福岡、(秋田、
新潟、長野、鹿児島)

ネジリカワツルモ
Ruppia maritima：ヒルムシロ科：(青森、
新潟)

ムサシモ
Najas ancistocarpa：イバラモ科：
宮城、千葉、徳島、(石川、静岡、岡山)

ヒメイバラモ
Najas tenuicaulis：イバラモ科：(秋田、
神奈川、新潟、山梨、長野、鳥取)

イトイバラモ
Najas yezoensis：イバラモ科：北海道、
秋田、(青森)

タカクマソウ
Sciaphila takakumensis：
ホンゴウソウ科：(鹿児島、沖縄)

ヒメソクシンラン
Aletris makiyataroi：ユリ科：香川

カンカケイニラ
Allium togashii：ユリ科：香川

タマボウキ
Asparagus oligoclonos：ユリ科：熊本、
(大分)

クロカミシライトソウ
Chionographis japonica var.
kurokamiana：ユリ科：佐賀

ミノシライトソウ
Chionographis japonica var. minoensis：
ユリ科：岐阜

カイコバイモ
Fritillaria kaiensis：ユリ科：山梨、静岡、
(東京)

ウラジロギボウシ
Hosta hypoleuca：ユリ科：愛知、(静岡)

セトウチギボウシ
Hosta pycnophylla：ユリ科：山口

ウケユリ
Lilium alexandrae：ユリ科：鹿児島

キバナノヒメユリ
Lilium concolor var. flaviflorum：ユリ科：
沖縄

ジンリョウユリ
Lilium japonicum var. abeanum：
ユリ科：徳島、(静岡)

ミヤマスカシユリ
Lilium maculatum var. bukosanense：
ユリ科：埼玉

タカオワニグチソウ
Polygonatum desoulavyi var. azegamii：
ユリ科：東京、(山梨、長野)

コワニグチソウ
Polygonatum miserum：ユリ科：長野、
(青森、福島)

サクライソウ
Protolirion sakuraii：ユリ科：長野、岐阜、
鹿児島、(石川、福井、京都)

アッカゼキショウ
Tofieldia coccinea var. akkana．ユリ科：
岩手

ゲイビゼキショウ
Tofieldia coccinea var. geibiensis：
ユリ科：岩手

ミヤマゼキショウ
Tofieldia coccinea var. kiusiana：
ユリ科：宮崎

サガミジョウロウホトトギス
Tricyrtis ishiiana：ユリ科：神奈川

スルガジョウロウホトトギス
Tricyrtis ishiiana var. surugensis：
ユリ科：静岡

シラオイエンレイソウ
Trillium x hagae：ユリ科：北海道、(青森)

イズドコロ
Dioscorea izuensis：ヤマノイモ科：静岡

ユワンドコロ
Dioscorea tabatao：ヤマノイモ科：
鹿児島

キリガミネヒオウギアヤメ
Iris setosa var. hondoensis：アヤメ科：
長野

キリシマシャクジョウ
Burmannia liukiuensis：
ヒナノシャクジョウ科：愛媛、熊本、大
分、(東京、高知、長崎、宮崎、鹿児島、沖
縄)

ヒナノボンボリ
Oxygyne hyodoi：
ヒナノシャクジョウ科：愛媛、(兵庫)

ホシザキシャクジョウ
Saionia shinzatoi：

ヒナノシャクジョウ科：宮崎

タヌキノショクダイ
Thismia abei：ヒナノシャクジョウ科：
静岡、徳島、(宮崎、鹿児島)

キリシマタヌキノショヨクダイ
Thismia tuberculata：
ヒナノシャクジョウ科：鹿児島、(宮崎)

ヒゼンコウガイゼキショウ
Juncus hizenensis：イグサ科：長崎

エゾイトイ
Juncus potaninii：イグサ科：長野、(北海道、富山、山梨、静岡)

コシガヤホシクサ
Eriocaulon heleocharioides：
ホシクサ科：(埼玉)

ミカワイヌノヒゲ
Eriocaulon mikawanum：ホシクサ科：
愛知

ザラツキヒナガリヤス
Calamagrostis nana ssp. *hayachinensis*：
イネ科：岩手、(青森、群馬)

ユウバリカニツリ
Deschampsia caespitosa var. *levis*：
イネ科：北海道

タカネエゾムギ
Elymus yubaridakensis：イネ科：北海道

ヤマオオウシノケグサ
Festuca rubra var. *hondoensis*：イネ科：
群馬、長野、(北海道、福井、静岡)

オオヌカキビ
Panicum paludosum：イネ科：沖縄

ムラサキオバナ
Saccharum kanashiroi：イネ科：沖縄

フクロダガヤ
Tripogon japonicus：イネ科：栃木、
(茨城)

キタダケカニツリ
Trisetum spicatum var. *kitadakense*：
イネ科：山梨、静岡、(長野)

ツルギテンナンショウ
Arisaema abei：サトイモ科：徳島、
高知、(愛媛)

ホロテンナンショウ
Arisaema cucullatum：サトイモ科：
(三重、奈良)

オオアマミテンナンショウ
Arisaema heterocephalum ssp. *majus*：
サトイモ科：鹿児島

オキナワテンナンショウ
Arisaema heterocephalum ssp.
okinawaense：サトイモ科：沖縄

イシヅチテンナンショウ
Arisaema ishizuchiense：サトイモ科：
徳島、高知

カミコウチテンナンショウ
Arisaema ishizuchiense var. *brevicollum*：
サトイモ科：長野、岐阜

オモゴウテンナンショウ
Arisaema iyoanum：サトイモ科：山口、
愛媛、高知

トクノシマテンナンショウ
Arisaema kawashimae：サトイモ科：
鹿児島

アマギテンナンショウ
Arisaema kuratae：サトイモ科：静岡

ヒュウガヒロハテンナンショウ
Arisaema minamitanii：サトイモ科：
宮崎、(鹿児島)

ツクシテンナンショウ
Arisaema ogatae：サトイモ科：熊本、
宮崎

イナヒロハテンナンショウ
Arisaema ovale var. *inaense*：
サトイモ科：岐阜、(長野)

セッピコテンナンショウ
Arisaema seppikoense：サトイモ科：
(兵庫)

タカハシテンナンショウ
Arisaema undulatifolium ssp. *nambae*：
サトイモ科：岡山

ヒメハブカズラ
Raphidophora liukiuensis：サトイモ科：
(沖縄)

ヤクシマスゲ
Carex atroviridis：カヤツリグサ科：
(宮崎、鹿児島)

クリイロスゲ
Carex diandra：カヤツリグサ科：
北海道、青森、(長野)

ホソスゲ
Carex disperma：カヤツリグサ科：
(北海道)

カンチスゲ
Carex gynocrates：カヤツリグサ科：
北海道、岩手

センジョウスゲ
Carex lehmannii：カヤツリグサ科：
山梨、長野

マンシュウクロカワスゲ
Carex peiktusanii：カヤツリグサ科：長野

チチブシラスゲ
Carex planiculmis var. *urasawae*：
カヤツリグサ科：埼玉

クグスゲ
Carex pseudo-cyperus：
カヤツリグサ科：北海道、青森、長野

カラフトイワスゲ
Carex rupestris：カヤツリグサ科：

長野、(北海道、山梨、静岡)

ヒメウシオスゲ
Carex subspathacea：カヤツリグサ科：
青森、(北海道)

ツシマスゲ
Carex tsushimensis：カヤツリグサ科：
佐賀、長崎

コウシュンスゲ
Cyperus pedunculatus：
カヤツリグサ科：(沖縄)

イッスンテンツキ
Fimbristylis kadzusana：
カヤツリグサ科：愛知、(千葉、静岡)

チャイロテンツキ
Fimbristylis leptoclada var. *takamineana*：
カヤツリグサ科：沖縄

ハハジマテンツキ
Fimbristylis longispica var. *hahajimensis*：
カヤツリグサ科：(東京)

イワキアブラガヤ
Scirpus georgianus：カヤツリグサ科：
神奈川、福岡、(福島、滋賀)

タイワンショウキラン
Acanthephippium sylhetense：ラン科：
沖縄、(鹿児島)

ミスズラン
Androcorys japonensis：ラン科：長野、
(青森、栃木、群馬、静岡)

コウシュンシュスラン
Anoectochilus koshunensis：ラン科：
沖縄

クスクスラン
Bulbophyllum affine：ラン科：沖縄、(鹿
児島)

タネガシマシコウラン
Bulbophyllum macraei var.
tanegashimense：ラン科：(鹿児島)

ダルマエビネ
Calanthe alismaefolia：ラン科：宮崎、
鹿児島

キリシマエビネ
Calanthe aristulifera：ラン科：和歌山、
徳島、大分、(三重、愛媛、高知、佐賀、長
崎、熊本、宮崎、鹿児島)

アマミエビネ
Calanthe aristulifera var. *amamiana*：
ラン科：鹿児島

タガネラン
Calanthe bungoana：ラン科：大分

タマザキエビネ
Calanthe densiflora：ラン科：(鹿児島、
沖縄)

タイワンエビネ
Calanthe formosana：ラン科：沖縄

アサヒエビネ
Calanthe hattorii：ラン科：(東京)

ホシツルラン
Calanthe hoshii：ラン科：(東京)

オオキリシマエビネ
Calanthe izu-insularis：ラン科：(東京)

ヒロハノカラン
Calanthe japonica：ラン科：宮崎、鹿児島

ユウヅルエビネ
Calanthe matumurana：ラン科：沖縄

サクラジマエビネ
Calanthe oblanceolata：ラン科：(鹿児島)

キソエビネ
Calanthe schlechteri：ラン科：栃木、神奈川、山梨、長野、岐阜、静岡、高知、(岩手、宮城、福島、群馬、徳島、愛媛)

ホテイラン
Calypso bulbosa var. japonica：ラン科：埼玉、東京、山梨、長野、(静岡)

クゲヌマラン
Cephalanthera erecta var. shizuoi：ラン科：青森、宮城、神奈川、徳島、(岩手、茨城、千葉、静岡、愛知、三重、和歌山、香川)

アカバシュスラン
Cheirostylis liukiuensis：ラン科：沖縄

アリサンムヨウラン
Cheirostylis takeoi：ラン科：鹿児島

チクセツラン
Corymborkis subdensa：ラン科：(東京)

オオスズムシラン
Cryptostylis arachnites：ラン科：沖縄

タカオオオスズムシラン
Cryptostylis taiwaniana：ラン科：(沖縄)

ヘツカラン
Cymbidium dayanum：ラン科：(鹿児島)

ツシマニオイシュンラン
Cymbidium goeringii：ラン科：(長崎)

アキザキナギラン
Cymbidium javanicum var. aspidistrifolium：ラン科：熊本、宮崎、沖縄、(佐賀)

カンラン
Cymbidium kanran：ラン科：静岡、和歌山、徳島、高知、熊本、鹿児島、沖縄、(愛知、三重、山口、愛媛、福岡、佐賀、長崎、宮崎)

コラン
Cymbidium koran：ラン科：(熊本)

ホウサイラン
Cymbidium sinense：ラン科：鹿児島、沖縄

カラフトアツモリソウ
Cypripedium calceolus：ラン科：北海道

チョウセンキバナアツモリソウ
Cypripedium guttatum：ラン科：(秋田)

キバナノアツモリソウ
Cypripedium guttatum var. yatabeanum：ラン科：秋田、福井、山梨、長野、(北海道、青森、福島、群馬、石川、静岡、高知、熊本)

オキナワセッコク
Dendrobium okinawense：ラン科：沖縄

コカゲラン
Didymoplexiella siamensis：ラン科：(鹿児島)

ヒメヤツシロラン
Didymoplexis pallens：ラン科：(鹿児島、沖縄)

サガリラン
Diploprora championii：ラン科：鹿児島

ジョウロウラン
Disperis philippinensis：ラン科：沖縄

タカサゴヤガラ
Eulophia taiwanensis：ラン科：沖縄

ツシマラン
Evrardia poilanei：ラン科：(長崎)

マツゲカヤラン
Gastrochilus ciliaris：ラン科：(鹿児島)

ナヨテンマ
Gastrodia gracilis：ラン科：静岡、愛知、岡山、(福島、千葉、東京、広島、高知、宮崎、鹿児島)

ナンゴクヤツシロラン
Gastrodia shimizuana：ラン科：沖縄

トサカメオトラン
Geodorum densiflorum：ラン科：沖縄

ヤブミョウガラン
Goodyera fumata：ラン科：沖縄

ムカゴトンボ
Habenaria flagellifera：ラン科：愛知、高知、長崎、熊本、鹿児島、(岐阜、静岡、徳島、佐賀、宮崎)

ヒゲナガトンボ
Habenaria flagellifera var. yosiei：ラン科：宮崎

イヨトンボ
Habenaria iyoensis：ラン科：高知、(山口、徳島、宮崎)

タコガタサギソウ
Habenaria lacertifera var. triangularis：ラン科：宮崎

ヒメクリソラン
Hancockia japonica：ラン科：鹿児島

クシロチドリ
Herminium monorchis：ラン科：青森

オオキヌラン
Heterozeuxine nervosa：ラン科：沖縄

コハクラン
Kitigorchis itoana：ラン科：山梨、長野

サキシマスケロクラン
Lecanorchis flavicans：ラン科：沖縄

ヤエヤマスケロクラン
Lecanorchis japonica var. tubiformis：ラン科：沖縄

キイムヨウラン
Lecanorchis kiiensis：ラン科：愛知、和歌山、(徳島)

ヤクムヨウラン
Lecanorchis nigricans var. yakusimensis：ラン科：鹿児島

アワムヨウラン
Lecanorchis trachycaula：ラン科：和歌山、徳島、鹿児島

ミドリムヨウラン
Lecanorchis virellus：ラン科：鹿児島

コゴメキノエラン
Liparis elliptica：ラン科：鹿児島

シマクモキリソウ
Liparis hostaefolia：ラン科：(東京)

クモイジガバチ
Liparis truncata：ラン科：(栃木、岐阜、静岡)

キノエササラン
Liparis uchiyamae：ラン科：(鹿児島)

ナンバンカモメラン
Macodes petola：ラン科：沖縄

シマホザキラン
Malaxis boninensis：ラン科：(東京)

ハハジマホザキラン
Malaxis hahajimensis：ラン科：(東京)

ホザキヒメラン
Malaxis latifolia：ラン科：沖縄

マツダヒメラン
Malaxis matsudai：ラン科：(沖縄)

ツクシアリドオシラン
Myrmechis tsukusiana：ラン科：(愛媛、鹿児島)

ツクシサカネラン
Neottia kiusiana：ラン科：(鹿児島)

ムカゴサイシン
Nervilia nipponica：ラン科：神奈川、高知、大分、宮崎、沖縄、(東京、長野、静岡、和歌山、鹿児島)

オオバヨウラクラン
Oberonia makinoi：ラン科：徳島、高知、沖縄、(東京、和歌山、宮崎、鹿児島)

オオギミラン
Odontochilus tashiroi：ラン科：(沖縄)

クロカミラン
Orchis graminifolia var. kurokamiana：ラン科：佐賀

サツマチドリ
Orchis graminifolia var. micropunctata：
ラン科：(鹿児島)

アワチドリ
Orchis graminifolia var. suzukiana：
ラン科：千葉

ガンゼキラン
Phaius flavus：ラン科：静岡、高知、長崎、熊本、大分、宮崎、鹿児島、(東京、三重、和歌山、徳島、愛媛、佐賀、沖縄)

ヒメカクラン
Phaius mishmensis：ラン科：沖縄

カクチョウラン
Phaius tankarvilleae：ラン科：沖縄、(鹿児島)

ハチジョウツレサギ
Platanthera okuboi：ラン科：(東京)

クニガミトンボソウ
Platanthera sonoharai：ラン科：沖縄

ソハヤキトンボソウ
Platanthera stenoglossa subsp.hottae：
ラン科：奈良、大分

イリオモテトンボソウ
Platanthera stenoglossa var. iriomotensis：ラン科：沖縄

ナゴラン
Sedirea japonica：ラン科：佐賀、長崎、大分、鹿児島、(東京、福井、静岡、京都、和歌山、島根、徳島、愛媛、高知、熊本、宮崎、沖縄)

コオロギラン
Stigmatodactylus sikokianus：ラン科：高知、(和歌山、徳島、熊本、宮崎、鹿児島)

ケイタオフウラン
Thrixspermum saruwatarii：ラン科：(鹿児島)

ミゾホシラン
Vrydagzynea albida：ラン科：沖縄

植物	絶滅危惧1B類 EN

チシマヒカゲノカズラ
Lycopodium alpinum：
ヒカゲノカズラ科：青森、宮城、山形、山梨、長野、(北海道、福島、富山、静岡)

ヒモヅル
Lycopodium casuarinoides：
ヒカゲノカズラ科：山口、福岡、長崎、熊本、(三重、和歌山、鹿児島)

スギラン
Lycopodium cryptomerinum：
ヒカゲノカズラ科：青森、岩手、宮城、秋田、福島、東京、神奈川、新潟、富山、石川、福井、山梨、長野、岐阜、静岡、愛知、京都、兵庫、奈良、和歌山、広島、徳島、愛媛、高知、熊本、大分、宮崎、(北海道、山形、茨城、群馬、埼玉、三重、滋賀、大阪、岡山、山口、福岡、鹿児島)

ボウカズラ
Lycopodium laxum：
ヒカゲノカズラ科：沖縄

シナミズニラ
Isoetes sinensis：ミズニラ科：茨城、岡山、広島、山口、高知、福岡、佐賀、長崎、熊本、大分、宮崎

ヒメドクサ
Equisetum scirpoides：トクサ科：北海道

サクラジマハナヤスリ
Ophioglossum kawamurae：
ハナヤスリ科：東京、鹿児島

コブラン
Ophioglossum pendulum：
ハナヤスリ科：東京、鹿児島、沖縄

カネコシダ
Gleichenia laevissima：ウラジロ科：佐賀、長崎、熊本、大分、(鹿児島)

ハハジマホラゴケ
Cephalomanes boninense：
コケシノブ科：東京

ホウライクジャク
Adiantum capillus-junonis：
ミズワラビ(ホウライシダ)科：大分

タキミシダ
Antrophyum obovatum：シシラン科：福井、山梨、静岡、愛知、滋賀、奈良、和歌山、徳島、愛媛、高知、熊本、宮崎、(千葉、神奈川、新潟、富山、岐阜、三重、京都、大阪、兵庫、鳥取、島根、広島、山口、香川、福岡、佐賀、長崎、鹿児島)

オオバシシラン
Vittaria forrestiana：シシラン科：(鹿児島)

クマガワイノモトソウ
Pteris deltodon：イノモトソウ科：熊本、(宮崎)

ヒノタニシダ
Pteris nakasimae：イノモトソウ科：鹿児島

オオタニワタリ
Asplenium antiquum：チャセンシダ科：和歌山、長崎、熊本、宮崎、鹿児島、沖縄、(東京、三重、徳島、高知、福岡)

クロガネシダ
Asplenium coenobiale：
チャセンシダ科：高知

ラハオシダ
Asplenium excisum：チャセンシダ科：東京、鹿児島、沖縄

ヒロハアツイタ
Elaphoglossum tosaense：
ツルキジノオ科：静岡、和歌山、徳島、高知、宮崎、(東京、三重、奈良、熊本、鹿児島)

アツイタ
Elaphoglossum yoshinagae：
ツルキジノオ科：東京、和歌山、徳島、高知、鹿児島、(三重、宮崎)

ツルダカナワラビ
Arachniodes chinensis：オシダ科：佐賀、熊本、(鹿児島)

サツマシダ
Ctenitis sinii：オシダ科：熊本、鹿児島、(三重、宮崎)

イワカゲワラビ
Dryopteris laeta：オシダ科：岩手、宮城、長野、(北海道)

センジョウデンダ
Polystichum gracilipes var. gemmiferum：オシダ科：長野、(山梨、静岡)

キュウシュウイノデ
Polystichum kiusiuense：オシダ科：熊本、鹿児島

タカネシダ
Polystichum lachenense：オシダ科：山梨、長野、静岡、(富山)

ハイミミガタシダ
Thelypteris aurita：ヒメシダ科：福岡、鹿児島

トサノミゾシダモドキ
Thelypteris flexilis：ヒメシダ科：高知

コウライイヌワラビ
Deparia coreana：
メシダ(イワデンダ)科：青森、宮城、秋田、静岡、(大分)

アソシケシダ
Deparia otomasui：
メシダ(イワデンダ)科：熊本、大分、(宮崎)

リュウキュウキンモウワラビ
Hypodematium fordii：
メシダ(イワデンダ)科：沖縄

クラガリシダ
Drymotaenium miyoshianum：
ウラボシ科：福井、長野、岐阜、愛知、滋賀、京都、奈良、和歌山、鳥取、広島、山口、愛媛、(石川、静岡、三重、兵庫、高知、大分)

ハカマウラボシ
Drynaria fortunei：ウラボシ科：沖縄

トヨグチウラボシ
Lepisorus clathratus：ウラボシ科：長野

アマミアオネカズラ
Polypodium amamianum：ウラボシ科：
鹿児島

オオエゾデンダ
Polypodium vulgare：ウラボシ科：
北海道、青森、鳥取

タイワンビロウドシダ
Pyrrosia linearifolia var. *heterolepis*：
ウラボシ科：沖縄

ヒメバラモミ
Picea maximowiczii：マツ科：山梨、長
野、(埼玉、静岡)

ヤクタネゴヨウ
Pinus armandii var. *amamiana*：マツ科：
(鹿児島)

リシリビャクシン
Juniperus sibirica：ヒノキ科：北海道

ユビソヤナギ
Salix hukaoana：ヤナギ科：宮城、群馬

エゾマメヤナギ
Salix nummularia ssp. *pauciflora*：
ヤナギ科：(北海道)

エゾノタカネヤナギ
Salix yezoalpina：ヤナギ科：北海道

チチブミネバリ
Betula chichibuensis：カバノキ科：
岩手、群馬、東京、長野、(埼玉、山梨)

ハナガガシ
Cyclobalanopsis hondae：ブナ科：愛媛、
高知、大分、宮崎、(長崎、熊本、鹿児島)

タチゲヒカゲミズ
Parietaria micrantha var. *coreana*：
イラクサ科：東京、長野、岡山、福岡、
(大分)

ナガバサンショウソウ
Pellionia yosiei：イラクサ科：宮崎

ムニンビャクダン
Santalum boninense：ビャクダン科：
(東京)

ホソバイヌタデ
Persicaria erecto-minor var.
trigonocarpa：タデ科：宮城、栃木、埼玉、
千葉、神奈川、福井、大阪、兵庫、(茨城、
群馬、京都、大分)

サイコクヌカボ
Persicaria foliosa var. *nikaii*：タデ科：
兵庫、岡山、徳島、香川、福岡、宮崎、(三
重、滋賀、京都、大阪、山口、佐賀、大分)

タカネミミナグサ
Cerastium rubescens var. *ovatum*：
ナデシコ科：富山、長野

マツモトセンノウ
Lychnis sieboldii：ナデシコ科：熊本、
宮崎

エンビセンノウ
Lychnis wilfordii：ナデシコ科：北海道、
青森、長野、(埼玉、山梨)

エゾタカネツメクサ
Minuartia arctica：ナデシコ科：北海道

クシロワチガイソウ
Pseudostellaria sylvatica：ナデシコ科：
北海道、青森、岩手

タカネマンテマ
Silene wahlenbergella：ナデシコ科：
山梨、長野、(静岡)

エゾハコベ
Stellaria humifusa：ナデシコ科：北海道

エゾイワツメクサ
Stellaria pterosperma：ナデシコ科：
北海道

アッケシソウ
Salicornia europaea：アカザ科：北海道、
岡山、香川、(宮城、徳島、愛媛)

クロボウモドキ
Polyalthia liukiuensis：バンレイシ科：
(沖縄)

ハナカズラ
Aconitum ciliare：キンポウゲ科：福岡、
熊本、大分、宮崎、鹿児島

キタダケトリカブト
Aconitum kitadakense：キンポウゲ科：
山梨

オオサワトリカブト
Aconitum senanense var. *isidzukae*：
キンポウゲ科：山梨、静岡

タカネトリカブト
Aconitum zigzag：キンポウゲ科：長野、
岐阜

キタダケソウ
Callianthemum insigne var. *hondoense*：
キンポウゲ科：山梨

ヒダカソウ
Callianthemum miyabeanum：
キンポウゲ科：北海道

クロバナハンショウヅル
Clematis fusca：キンポウゲ科：北海道

シコクハンショウヅル
Clematis obvallata var. *shikokiana*：
キンポウゲ科：徳島、愛媛、高知

ツクモグサ
Pulsatilla nipponica：キンポウゲ科：
北海道、富山、長野、(新潟)

シコタンキンポウゲ
Ranunculus grandis var. *austrokurilensis*：
キンポウゲ科：北海道、青森

キタダケキンポウゲ
Ranunculus kitadakeanus：
キンポウゲ科：山梨

オオイチョウバイカモ
Ranunculus nipponicus：キンポウゲ科：
群馬、長野、静岡

イトキンポウゲ
Ranunculus reptans：キンポウゲ科：
福島、栃木、群馬

ヤツガタケキンポウゲ
Ranunculus yatsugatakensis：
キンポウゲ科：長野、(山梨)

チトセバイカモ
Ranunculus yesoensis：キンポウゲ科：
北海道、青森

ナガバカラマツ
Thalictrum integrilobum：
キンポウゲ科：北海道

イワカラマツ
Thalictrum sekimotoanum：
キンポウゲ科：青森、宮城、秋田、栃木、
長野、香川、(山形、群馬)

タマカラマツ
Thalictrum watanabei：キンポウゲ科：
愛知、奈良、徳島、香川、高知、宮崎、(静
岡、三重、大分)

クモイイカリソウ
Epimedium coelestre：メギ科：群馬、
(岩手)

サイコクイカリソウ
Epimedium kitamuranum：メギ科：
兵庫、徳島、香川

マルバウマノスズクサ
Aristolochia contorta：
ウマノスズクサ科：山形、群馬、長野、
岐阜、兵庫、(京都、島根)

カギガタアオイ
Heterotropa curvistigma：
ウマノスズクサ科：山梨、静岡

ハツシマカンアオイ
Heterotropa hatsushimae：
ウマノスズクサ科：(鹿児島)

オニカンアオイ
Heterotropa hirsutisepala：
ウマノスズクサ科：(鹿児島)

アケボノアオイ
Heterotropa kiusiana var. *tubulosa*：
ウマノスズクサ科：佐賀、長崎

クワイバカンアオイ
Heterotropa kumagoana：
ウマノスズクサ科：宮崎、(鹿児島)

イワタカンアオイ
Heterotropa kurosawae：
ウマノスズクサ科：静岡、愛知

サツマアオイ
Heterotropa satsumensis：
ウマノスズクサ科：(熊本、鹿児島)

ホシザキカンアオイ
Heterotropa stellata：
ウマノスズクサ科：高知

マルミカンアオイ
Heterotropa subglobosa：
ウマノスズクサ科：熊本、宮崎

ヤエヤマカンアオイ
Heterotropa yaeyamensis：
ウマノスズクサ科：(沖縄)

ベニバナヤマシャクヤク
Paeonia obovata：ボタン科：北海道、青森、岩手、宮城、山形、福島、栃木、群馬、東京、神奈川、富山、山梨、長野、岐阜、静岡、愛知、兵庫、岡山、広島、山口、徳島、香川、愛媛、高知、熊本、大分、宮崎、(秋田、茨城、埼玉、京都、大阪、奈良、和歌山、島根)

コウライトモエソウ
Hypericum ascyron var. longistylum：
オトギリソウ科：長崎、熊本、大分、(宮崎)

アゼオトギリ
Hypericum oliganthum：
オトギリソウ科：栃木、千葉、石川、岐阜、静岡、愛知、和歌山、岡山、広島、香川、高知、佐賀、長崎、大分、宮崎、(茨城、群馬、埼玉、東京、神奈川、三重、滋賀、京都、大阪、兵庫、奈良、山口、徳島、福岡、熊本)

ナガバノイシモチソウ
Drosera indica：モウセンゴケ科：茨城、栃木、千葉、岐阜、愛知、三重、宮崎、(静岡、大分)

エゾオオケマン
Corydalis curvicalcarata：ケシ科：北海道

ツルキケマン
Corydalis ochotensis：ケシ科：北海道、岩手、栃木、群馬、岐阜、(宮城、秋田、福島、埼玉、山梨、静岡)

ヘラハタザオ
Arabis lignlifolium：アブラナ科：長野

クモイナズナ
Arabis tanakana：アブラナ科：富山、山梨、長野、(静岡)

オオマルバコンロンソウ
Cardamine arakiana：アブラナ科：兵庫、岡山、宮崎、(京都、徳島)

タカチホガラシ
Cardamine kiusiana：アブラナ科：徳島、熊本、宮崎

トモシリソウ
Cochlearia oblongifolia：アブラナ科：北海道

ナンブイヌナズナ
Draba japonica：アブラナ科：北海道、岩手

モイワナズナ
Draba sachalinensis：アブラナ科：北海道、長野

シロウマナズナ
Draba shiroumana：アブラナ科：富山、山梨、長野、(群馬、静岡)

ミセバヤ
Hylotelephium sieboldii：
ベンケイソウ科：群馬、奈良、香川、(埼玉)

ゲンカイイワレンゲ
Orostachys genkaiense：
ベンケイソウ科：福岡、長崎

イワレンゲ
Orostachys iwarenge：
ベンケイソウ科：秋田、山形、岐阜、兵庫、福岡、長崎、(茨城、群馬、山梨、静岡、山口、佐賀)

ナナツガマママンネングサ
Sedum drymarioides：ベンケイソウ科：長崎

ヤハズマンネングサ
Sedum tosaense：ベンケイソウ科：徳島、高知

モミジバショウマ
Astilbe platyphylla：ユキノシタ科：北海道

エゾネコノメソウ
Chrysosplenium alternifolium var. sibiricum：ユキノシタ科：(北海道)

トカラタマアジサイ
Hydrangea involuculata var.takaraensis：ユキノシタ科：鹿児島

マルバチャルメルソウ
Mitella nuda：ユキノシタ科：北海道、長野

トサチャルメルソウ
Mitella yoshinagae：ユキノシタ科：徳島、高知、熊本、宮崎

クモマユキノシタ
Saxifraga laciniata：ユキノシタ科：北海道

チシマイワブキ
Saxifraga punctata ssp. reniformis：ユキノシタ科：富山、長野

アポイヤマブキショウマ
Aruncus dioicus var. subrotundus：バラ科：北海道

シコクシモツケソウ
Filipendula tsuguwoi：バラ科：徳島、高知、宮崎、(愛媛)

シロヤマブキ
Rhodotypos scandens：バラ科：福井、岡山、広島、香川、(長野、島根)

ゴショイチゴ
Rubus chingii：バラ科：山口、高知、(愛媛、大分)

シマバライチゴ
Rubus lambertianus：バラ科：長崎、熊本

エゾシモツケ
Spiraea media var. sericea：バラ科：北海道、青森

リシリオウギ
Astragalus secundus：マメ科：北海道、富山、長野

モダマ
Entada phaseoloides：マメ科：鹿児島、沖縄

ミヤコジマツルマメ
Glycine tabacina：マメ科：沖縄

エゾオヤマノエンドウ
Oxytropis japonica var. sericea：マメ科：(北海道)

ウスカワゴロモ
Hydrobryum floribundum：カワゴケソウ科：(鹿児島)

カワゴロモ
Hydrobryum japonicum：カワゴケソウ科：(宮崎、鹿児島)

アサマフウロ
Geranium soboliferum：フウロソウ科：福島、栃木、山梨、長野、静岡、(群馬)

ツクシフウロ
Geranium soboliferum var. kiusianum：フウロソウ科：東京、熊本、大分

ハマビシ
Tribulus terrestris：ハマビシ科：千葉、大阪、兵庫、岡山、広島、山口、香川、愛媛、長崎、(茨城、神奈川、福井、静岡、愛知、京都、和歌山、島根、福岡、佐賀、熊本)

マルミノウルシ
Euphorbia ebracteolata：トウダイグサ科：北海道、青森、岩手、宮城、群馬、埼玉、東京、(福島、長野、三重)

ハギクソウ
Euphorbia escula var. nakaii：トウダイグサ科：愛知

リュウキュウダイゲキ
Euphorbia liukiuensis：トウダイグサ科：(鹿児島)

センダイタイゲキ
Euphorbia sendaica：トウダイグサ科：岩手、栃木、千葉、(宮城、福島、茨城)

チャンチンモドキ
Choerospondias axillaris var. *japonica* : ウルシ科 : 岐阜、熊本、鹿児島

クロビイタヤ
Acer miyabei : カエデ科 : 北海道、青森、岩手、秋田、福島、長野

シバタカエデ
Acer miyabei var. *shibatai* : カエデ科 : 群馬、長野、(福島)

ヒゼンマユミ
Euonymus chibai : ニシキギ科 : 山口、徳島、長崎、大分、鹿児島、沖縄、(福岡)

オキナワツゲ
Buxus liukiuensis : ツゲ科 : 沖縄

タイワンアサマツゲ
Buxus microphylla var. *sinica* : ツゲ科 : (沖縄)

ハマナツメ
Paliurus ramosissimus : クロウメモドキ科 : 和歌山、徳島、高知、長崎、熊本、大分、宮崎、鹿児島、(静岡)

ヤエヤマネコノチチ
Rhamnella franguloides var. *inaequilatera* : クロウメモドキ科 : 鹿児島、沖縄

ミヤマハンモドキ
Rhamnus ishidae : クロウメモドキ科 : 北海道

タチスミレ
Viola raddeana : スミレ科 : 栃木、群馬、大分、宮崎、鹿児島、(宮城、茨城、千葉、東京、長野)

ミズスギナ
Rotala hippuris : ミソハギ科 : 福岡、佐賀、長崎、宮崎、(群馬、静岡、愛知、三重、愛媛、鹿児島)

ミズキカシグサ
Rotala leptopetala var. *littorea* : ミソハギ科 : 栃木、埼玉、長野、愛知、山口、長崎、熊本、大分、宮崎、鹿児島、(青森、岩手、秋田、山形、群馬、神奈川、富山、福井、山梨、静岡、三重、滋賀、京都、和歌山、岡山、広島、徳島、高知、福岡)

ムニンフトモモ
Metrosideros boninensis : フトモモ科 : (東京)

ヒメノボタン
Osbeckia chinensis : ノボタン科 : 和歌山、高知、長崎、熊本、鹿児島、沖縄、(佐賀、大分)

エゾゴゼンタチバナ
Cornus suecica : ミズキ科 : 北海道

ツクシトウキ
Angelica pseudo-shikokiana : セリ科 :

佐賀

シナノノダケ
Angelica sinanomontana : セリ科 : (長野)

ウバタケニンジン
Angelica ubatakensis : セリ科 : 高知、大分、宮崎

トサボウフウ
Angelica yoshinagae : セリ科 : 徳島、高知

エキサイゼリ
Apodicarpum ikenoi : セリ科 : 栃木、埼玉、千葉、愛知、(茨城、群馬、東京)

ホソバハナウド
Heracleum dulce var. *akasimontanum* : セリ科 : 山梨、長野、静岡

ツクシボウフウ
Pimpinella thellungiana var. *gustavohegiana* : セリ科 : 大分

シムラニンジン
Pterygopleurum neurophyllum : セリ科 : 栃木、千葉、熊本、大分、(茨城、群馬、鹿児島)

ヤマナシウマノミツバ
Sanicula kaiensis : セリ科 : 群馬、山梨、長野、(埼玉、静岡)

ヌマゼリ
Sium suave var. *nipponicum* : セリ科 : 宮城、福島、群馬、千葉、東京、兵庫、山口、徳島、香川、愛媛、高知、大分、宮崎、(青森、岩手、秋田、茨城、埼玉、新潟、静岡、滋賀、京都、大阪、熊本、鹿児島)

カラフトイチヤクソウ
Pyrola faurieana : イチヤクソウ科 : 北海道、岩手、宮城、(青森、福島、山梨)

ヨウラクツツジ
Menziesia purpurea : ツツジ科 : 岐阜、熊本、大分、宮崎

アマギツツジ
Rhododendron amagianum : ツツジ科 : 静岡

アマミセイシカ
Rhododendron amamiense : ツツジ科 : 鹿児島

キョウマルシャクナゲ
Rhododendron degronianum ssp. *metternichii* var. *kyomaruense* : ツツジ科 : 長野、静岡

ジングウツツジ
Rhododendron sanctum : ツツジ科 : 愛知、(静岡、三重)

シブカワツツジ
Rhododendron sanctum var. *lasiogynum* : ツツジ科 : 静岡

トキワバイカツツジ
Rhododendron uwaense : ツツジ科 : 愛媛

オオツルコウジ
Ardisia montana : ヤブコウジ科 : 大分、(静岡、岡山、鹿児島)

マルバタイミンタチバナ
Myrsine okabeana : ヤブコウジ科 : 東京

サクラソウモドキ
Cortusa matthioli var. *yezoensis* : サクラソウ科 : 北海道

ノジトラノオ
Lysimachia barystachys : サクラソウ科 : 栃木、群馬、埼玉、千葉、神奈川、長野、(福島、茨城、東京、山梨、熊本、鹿児島)

サワトラノオ
Lysimachia leucantha : サクラソウ科 : 静岡、熊本、大分、(埼玉、千葉、福岡、佐賀、鹿児島)

オニコナスビ
Lysimachia tashiroi : サクラソウ科 : 福岡、佐賀、熊本、大分

カッコソウ
Primula kisoana : サクラソウ科 : 群馬

シコクカッコソウ
Primula kisoana var. *shikokiana* : サクラソウ科 : 徳島、香川、愛媛

イワザクラ
Primula tosaensis : サクラソウ科 : 岐阜、奈良、徳島、愛媛、高知、熊本、宮崎、鹿児島、(山梨、三重)

ホザキザクラ
Stimpsonia chamaedryoides : サクラソウ科 : 山口、鹿児島、(沖縄)

ショウドシマレンギョウ
Forsythia togashii : モクセイ科 : 香川

ヒメナエ
Mitrasacme indica : マチン科 : 秋田、栃木、千葉、静岡、熊本、宮崎、(青森、岩手、宮城、山形、福島、茨城、群馬、富山、福井、兵庫、佐賀)

サンプクリンドウ
Comastoma pulmonarium ssp. *sectum* : リンドウ科 : 山梨、長野、(静岡)

ヒナリンドウ
Gentiana aquatica : リンドウ科 : 長野、(山梨)

ユウパリリンドウ
Gentianella yuparensis : リンドウ科 : (北海道)

アカイシリンドウ
Gentianopsis furusei : リンドウ科 : 山梨、長野、(静岡)

ホソバツルリンドウ
Pterygocalyx volubilis：リンドウ科：
北海道、青森、岩手、宮城、秋田、山形、
福島、栃木、東京、神奈川、新潟、富山、
山梨、長野、岐阜、愛知、愛媛、(群馬、埼
玉、静岡、高知)

シノノメソウ
Swertia swertopsis：リンドウ科：静岡、
愛媛、高知、熊本、大分、(宮崎)

テングノコヅチ
Tripterospermum involubile：
リンドウ科：富山、長野、岐阜

バシクルモン
*Trachomitum venetum var.
basikururmon*：キョウチクトウ科：
北海道、青森、新潟

ロクオンソウ
Cynanchum amplexicaule：ガガイモ科：
岩手、山口、福岡、長崎、熊本、宮崎、鹿
児島、(佐賀、大分)

ハナムグラ
Galium tokyoense：アカネ科：宮城、栃
木、埼玉、千葉、大分、(岩手、秋田、山形、
福島、茨城、群馬、神奈川、長野、静岡、
広島)

クシロハナシノブ
*Polemonium coeruleum ssp.
campanulatum var. paludosum*：
ハナシノブ科：北海道

リュウキュウチャノキ
Ehretia dichotoma：ムラサキ科：沖縄、
(鹿児島)

ムラサキ
*Lithospermum officinale ssp.
erythrorhizon*：ムラサキ科：北海道、青
森、岩手、宮城、秋田、山形、栃木、群馬、
東京、神奈川、長野、静岡、愛知、兵庫、
岡山、広島、山口、高知、福岡、大分、(福
島、茨城、埼玉、山梨、岐阜、三重、京都、
大阪、奈良、和歌山、徳島、愛媛、長崎、
熊本、宮崎)

オキナワヤブムラサキ
Callicarpa oshimensis var. okinawensis：
クマツヅラ科：(沖縄)

ヒルギダマシ
Avicennia marima：ヒルギダマシ科：
沖縄

カイジンドウ
Ajuga ciliata var. villosior：シソ科：
北海道、青森、岩手、宮城、山梨、長野、
静岡、熊本、大分、(秋田、山形、福島、茨
城、栃木、群馬、東京、神奈川、宮崎)

ヒイラギソウ
Ajuga incisa：シソ科：栃木、群馬、東京、

(茨城、、埼玉)

ムシャリンドウ
Dracocephalum argunense：シソ科：
北海道、青森、岩手、秋田、福島、山梨、
長野、(宮城、山形、茨城、栃木、群馬、石
川、静岡)

ホソバヤマジソ
Mosla chinensis：シソ科：岡山、山口、
長崎、大分、(広島、佐賀)

シナノアキギリ
Salvia koyamae：シソ科：群馬、長野

タジマタムラソウ
Salvia omerocalyx：シソ科：兵庫、鳥取

コナミキ
Scutellaria guilielmii：シソ科：愛知、岡
山、広島、山口、徳島、長崎、熊本、大分、
宮崎、沖縄、(静岡、三重、兵庫、和歌山、
高知、福岡、鹿児島)

ケミヤマナミキ
Scutellaria shikokiana var. pubicaulis：
シソ科：香川、愛媛、大分、宮崎、(徳島、
鹿児島)

エゾナミキソウ
Scutellaria yezoensis：シソ科：北海道、
青森、長野、(岐阜)

ヤマホオズキ
Physalis chamaesaracholdes：ナス科：
栃木、東京、愛知、兵庫、徳島、香川、福
岡、長崎、熊本、大分、(神奈川、静岡、三
重、京都、大阪、奈良、和歌山、岡山、山
口、高知、佐賀、宮崎、鹿児島)

ゴマクサ
Centranthera cochinchinensis var. lutea：
ゴマノハグサ科：栃木、千葉、愛知、兵
庫、岡山、広島、山口、高知、福岡、熊本、
大分、宮崎、鹿児島、沖縄、(茨城、群馬、
神奈川、静岡、三重、滋賀、京都、大阪、
奈良、和歌山、徳島、香川、佐賀、長崎)

マルバノサワトウガラシ
Deinostema adenocaulum：
ゴマノハグサ科：宮城、秋田、山形、福
井、長野、滋賀、徳島、福岡、佐賀、熊本、
宮崎、鹿児島、(青森、岩手、福島、茨城、
栃木、群馬、新潟、富山、静岡、大阪、兵
庫、奈良、和歌山、岡山、広島、香川、高
知、大分)

ハチジョウコゴメグサ
Euphrasia hachijoensis：
ゴマノハグサ科：(東京)

イブキコゴメグサ
Euphrasia insignis ssp. iiunmae：
ゴマノハグサ科：滋賀

イズコゴメグサ
Euphrasia insignis ssp. iiunumai var.

idzuensis：ゴマノハグサ科：神奈川、静
岡、愛知

ナヨナヨヨコグサメグサ
Euphrasia microphylla：
ゴマノハグサ科：徳島、高知

ホソバママコナ
Melampyrum setaceum：
ゴマノハグサ科：山口、佐賀、大分、(広
島、福岡、長崎)

スズメノハコベ
Microcarpaea minima：ゴマノハグサ科：
栃木、岐阜、静岡、愛知、山口、長崎、熊
本、宮崎、鹿児島、(福島、群馬、埼玉、三
重、大阪、和歌山、岡山、徳島、高知、福
岡、佐賀、大分)

キバナシオガマ
Pedicularis oederi var. heteroglossa：
ゴマノハグサ科：北海道

ミカワシオガマ
Pedicularis resupinata var. microphylla：
ゴマノハグサ科：岐阜、愛知、(静岡)

ツクシトラノオ
Pseudolysimachion kiusianum：
ゴマノハグサ科：熊本、宮崎

ツクシクガイソウ
Veronicastrum sibiricum var. zuccarinii：
ゴマノハグサ科：熊本、大分、宮崎

キノクニスズカケ
Veronicastrum tagawae：
ゴマノハグサ科：和歌山

ウルップソウ
Lagotis glauca：ウルップソウ科：
北海道、富山、長野、(新潟)

ホソバウルップソウ
Lagotis yesoensis：ウルップソウ科：
北海道

シシンラン
Lysionotus pauciflorus：イワタバコ科：
静岡、京都、奈良、鳥取、愛媛、高知、福
岡、熊本、宮崎、(三重、和歌山、島根、徳
島、大分、鹿児島)

イワギリソウ
Opithandra primuloides：イワタバコ科：
京都、奈良、和歌山、鳥取、山口、徳島、
香川、愛媛、高知、大分、鹿児島、(三重、
兵庫、島根)

ミカワタヌキモ
Utricularia exoleta：タヌキモ科：愛知、
兵庫、福岡、佐賀、長崎、熊本、大分、宮
崎、鹿児島、沖縄、(静岡、三重、滋賀、京
都、奈良、和歌山)

ヒメミミカキグサ
Utricularia nipponica：タヌキモ科：
愛知、(静岡、三重)

ヤチコタヌキモ
Utricularia ochroleuca：タヌキモ科：
北海道、青森、福島、長野、(群馬)

エゾヒョウタンボク
Lonicera alpigena ssp. *glehnii*：
スイカズラ科：北海道、青森、岩手、宮
城、秋田、新潟、福井、長野、(福島、山梨)

スルガヒョウタンボク
Lonicera alpigena ssp. *glehnii* var.
viridissima：スイカズラ科：山梨、長野、
静岡

ネムロブシダマ
Lonicera chrysantha var. *crassipes*：
スイカズラ科：(北海道)

コゴメヒョウタンボク
Lonicera linderifolia var. *konoi*：
スイカズラ科：長野、(群馬、静岡)

ハナヒョウタンボク
Lonicera maackii：スイカズラ科：岩手、
長野、(青森、群馬)

キンキヒョウタンボク
Lonicera ramosissima var. *kinkiensis*：
スイカズラ科：兵庫、広島、香川、(大阪、
奈良)

オオチョウジガマズミ
Viburnum carlesii：スイカズラ科：長崎

チシマキンレイカ
Patrinia sibirica：オミナエシ科：北海道

ヒナシャジン
Adenophora maximowicziana：
キキョウ科：高知

シマシャジン
Adenophora tashiroi：キキョウ科：
(長崎)

ヤツシロソウ
Campanula glomerata var. *dahurica*：
キキョウ科：熊本、大分

マルバテイショウソウ
Ainsliaea fragrans var. *integrifolia*：
キク科：高知、熊本、宮崎、(鹿児島)

クリヤマハハコ
Anaphalis sinica var. *viscosissima*：
キク科：栃木、群馬、(埼玉)

ワタヨモギ
Artemisia gilvescens：キク科：徳島、
(山口、愛媛)

イソノギク
Aster asa-grayi：キク科：(鹿児島、沖縄)

カワラノギク
Aster kantoensis：キク科：栃木、東京、
神奈川、(長野、静岡)

クルマギク
Aster tenuipes：キク科：和歌山

コモチミミコウモリ

Cacalia auriculata var. bulbifera：
キク科：北海道

モミジコウモリ
Cacalia kiusiana：キク科：熊本、宮崎、
(鹿児島)

アイズヒメアザミ
Cirsium aidzuense：キク科：福島、長野、
(山形、栃木、群馬、新潟)

ミヤマコアザミ
Cirsium japonicum var. *ibukiense*：
キク科：滋賀、佐賀

イナベアザミ
Cirsium magofukui：キク科：岐阜、滋
賀、(静岡、三重)

ウスバアザミ
Cirsium tenue：キク科：岡山、徳島、(島
根、広島)

コヘラナレン
Crepidiastrum grandicollum：キク科：
東京

オオイワインチン
Dendranthema pallasianum：キク科：
群馬、富山、長野

チョウセンノギク
Dendranthema zawadskii var. *latilobum*：
キク科：長崎

ヒゴタイ
Echinops setifer：キク科：岐阜、鳥取、
広島、山口、長崎、熊本、大分、(愛知、三
重、島根、岡山、福岡、宮崎、鹿児島)

ホソバムカシヨモギ
Erigeron acris var. *linearifolius*：キク科：
富山、(福島、新潟、福井)

アポイアズマギク
Erigeron thunbergii var. *angustifolius*：
キク科：北海道

アキノハハコグサ
Gnaphalium hypoleucum：キク科：
岩手、宮城、栃木、群馬、埼玉、千葉、神
奈川、新潟、福井、長野、静岡、愛知、兵
庫、奈良、岡山、香川、愛媛、(秋田、山形、
福島、茨城、東京、石川、山梨、岐阜、三
重、滋賀、京都、大阪、広島、山口、徳島、
高知、福岡、佐賀、長崎、熊本、大分、宮
崎、鹿児島)

チョウセンスイラン
Hololeion maximowiczii：キク科：福岡、
佐賀、長崎、熊本、大分、宮崎、鹿児島

エゾコウゾリナ
Hypochoeris crepidioides：キク科：
北海道

ホソバニガナ
Ixeris makinoana：キク科：栃木、群馬、
岐阜、静岡、福岡、熊本、大分、宮崎、(千

葉、兵庫、和歌山、岡山、山口、徳島、鹿
児島)

エゾウスユキソウ
Leontopodium discolor：キク科：北海道

ハヤチネウスユキソウ
Leontopodium hayachinense：キク科：
岩手

ミコシギク
Leucanthemella linearis：キク科：愛知、
岡山、広島、(茨城、群馬、岐阜、静岡)

ユキバヒゴタイ
Saussurea chionophylla：キク科：北海道

フォーリーアザミ
Saussurea fauriei：キク科：北海道

イナトウヒレン
Saussurea inaensis：キク科：長野

ウスユキトウヒレン
Saussurea yanagisawae：キク科：
北海道

トサトウヒレン
Saussurea yoshinagae：キク科：徳島、
高知

タカネコウリンギク
Senecio flammeus：キク科：熊本、大分

ツクシタンポポ
Taraxacum kiushianum：キク科：長野、
愛媛、高知、福岡、熊本、大分、宮崎、(佐
賀)

クザカイタンポポ
Taraxacum kuzakaiense：キク科：岩手

シコタンタンポポ
Taraxacum shikotanense：キク科：
北海道

クモマタンポポ
Taraxacum trigonolobum：キク科：
北海道

ホソバノシバナ
Triglochin palustre：ホロムイソウ科：
北海道、青森、岩手、秋田、福島、群馬、
(宮城、山形)

コバノヒルムシロ
Potamogeton cristatus：ヒルムシロ科：
宮城、福島、群馬、兵庫、和歌山、愛媛、
熊本、(茨城、栃木、石川、福井、山梨、長
野、静岡、滋賀、京都、大阪、奈良、岡山、
山口、徳島、香川、佐賀、大分、鹿児島)

オオミズヒキモ
Potamogeton kamogawaensis：
ヒルムシロ科：神奈川、(東京、新潟、滋
賀、京都、兵庫、徳島、香川)

ササエビモ
Potamogeton nipponicus：
ヒルムシロ科：青森、群馬、神奈川、(北
海道、福島、茨城、栃木)

ナガバエビモ
Potamogeton praelongus：
ヒルムシロ科：(北海道)

カワツルモ
Ruppia maritima：ヒルムシロ科：青森、
愛知、兵庫、和歌山、鳥取、岡山、香川、
愛媛、福岡、大分、宮城、秋田、福島、千
葉、東京、神奈川、福井、静岡、三重、大
阪、広島、山口、徳島、高知、長崎、熊本、
宮崎、鹿児島)

ヤハズカワツルモ
Ruppia truncatifolia：ヒルムシロ科：
(北海道)

サガミトリゲモ
Najas indica：イバラモ科：宮城、福島、
栃木、神奈川、兵庫、香川、大分、(青森、
茨城、群馬、石川、福井、静岡、滋賀、京
都、大阪、和歌山、島根、岡山、山口、徳
島、愛媛、高知、福岡、長崎、宮崎、鹿児
島、沖縄)

イトトリゲモ
Najas japonica：イバラモ科：宮城、福
島、栃木、群馬、神奈川、愛知、大阪、兵
庫、岡山、香川、福岡、大分、(北海道、青
森、岩手、秋田、山形、茨城、新潟、福井、
長野、岐阜、静岡、滋賀、京都、鳥取、島
根、広島、山口、徳島、高知、長崎、熊本、
宮崎)

トリゲモ
Najas minor：イバラモ科：宮城、栃木、
群馬、埼玉、千葉、神奈川、富山、静岡、
愛知、兵庫、徳島、大分、沖縄、(青森、福
島、茨城、新潟、石川、和歌山、岡山、広
島、山口、香川、愛媛、高知、福岡、長崎、
宮崎、鹿児島)

ホンゴウソウ
Andorius japonica：ホンゴウソウ科：
静岡、京都、兵庫、広島、山口、徳島、香
川、愛媛、高知、長崎、鹿児島、沖縄、(宮
城、栃木、新潟、愛知、三重、大阪、奈良、
和歌山、福岡、佐賀、熊本、大分、宮崎)

イズモサツキ
Allium schoenoprasum var. idzuense：
ユリ科：神奈川、静岡、(東京)

アズマシライトソウ
Chionographis japonica var. hisauchiana：
ユリ科：東京、(埼玉)

チャボシライトソウ
Chionographis koidzumiana：ユリ科：
愛知、和歌山、徳島、高知、宮崎、(静岡、
鹿児島)

アワコバイモ
Fritillaria japonica：ユリ科：岐阜、静岡、
愛知、徳島、香川、愛媛、熊本

トサコバイモ
Fritillaria shikokiana：ユリ科：徳島、香
川、高知、(愛媛)

ヒメアマナ
Gagea japonica：ユリ科：北海道、岩手、
茨城、栃木、山梨、長野、滋賀、(宮城、秋
田、群馬、静岡)

オオシロショウジョウバカマ
Heloniopsis leucantha：ユリ科：
鹿児島、沖縄

ワスレグサ
Hemerocallis major：ユリ科：佐賀、(長
崎、鹿児島)

バランギボウシ
Hosta alismifolia：ユリ科：愛知、高知、
(岐阜)

ウバタケギボウシ
Hosta pulchella：ユリ科：大分、宮崎

ナガサキギボウシ
Hosta tibae：ユリ科：長崎

ヒメユリ
Lilium concolor var. buschianum：
ユリ科：青森、岐阜、大阪、奈良、和歌
山、岡山、徳島、香川、愛媛、高知、熊本、
大分、宮崎、(秋田、三重、京都、兵庫、広
島、山口)

ヒメサユリ
Lilium rubellum：ユリ科：宮城、山形、
福島、新潟

カノコユリ
Lilium speciosum：ユリ科：徳島、熊本、
鹿児島、(長崎)

ウスギワニグチソウ
Polygonatum cryptanthum：ユリ科：
福岡、(長崎)

ジョウロウホトトギス
Tricyrtis macrantha：ユリ科：高知

キバナノツキヌキホトトギス
Tricyrtis perfoliata：ユリ科：宮崎

ヒダカエンレイソウ
Trillium x miyabeanum：ユリ科：
北海道、青森、岩手、宮城

ツクシタチドコロ
Dioscorea asclepiadea：ヤマノイモ科：
熊本、宮崎、鹿児島

エヒメアヤメ
Iris rossii：アヤメ科：岡山、山口、愛媛、
佐賀、熊本、大分、(広島、福岡、宮崎)

セキショウイ
Juncus prominens：イグサ科：青森、
(岩手)

ネムロホシクサ
Eriocaulon glaberrimum：ホシクサ科：
(北海道)

アズミイヌノヒゲ
*Eriocaulon mikawanum ssp.
azumianum*：ホシクサ科：長野

オオムラホシクサ
Eriocaulon omuranum：ホシクサ科：
長野

クロホシクサ
Eriocaulon parvum：ホシクサ科：栃木、
千葉、静岡、和歌山、山口、徳島、高知、
福岡、佐賀、熊本、宮崎、(茨城、群馬、新
潟、富山、福井、長野、三重、滋賀、京都、
兵庫、鹿児島)

ミヤマハルガヤ
Anthoxanthum odoratum var. furumii：
イネ科：山梨、長野、静岡

オニビトノガリヤス
Calamagrostis onibitoana：イネ科：長崎

タシロノガリヤス
Calamagrostis tashiroi：イネ科：愛媛、
高知、大分、宮崎、(徳島)

エゾコウボウ
Hierochloe pluriflora：イネ科：北海道

ナンブソモソモ
Poa hayachinensis：イネ科：岩手

タチイチゴツナギ
Poa nemoralis：イネ科：青森、宮城、福
島、長野、(北海道、秋田、栃木、群馬、山
梨、静岡)

ヒゲナガコメススキ
Ptilagrostis mongholica：イネ科：富山、
山梨

フォーリーガヤ
Schizachne purpurascens：イネ科：
(北海道、長野)

ミヤマカニツリ
Trisetum koidzumianum：イネ科：富山、
山梨、長野、静岡

リシリカニツリ
Trisetum spicatum：イネ科：北海道、富
山、山梨、長野、静岡

ヤマコンニャク
Amorphophalus hirtus var. kiusianus：
サトイモ科：長崎、沖縄、(高知、鹿児島)

シコクテンナンショウ
Arisaema iyoanum ssp. nakaianum：
サトイモ科：徳島、愛媛、高知

シコクヒロハテンナンショウ
Arisaema longipedunculatum：
サトイモ科：徳島、愛媛、高知、熊本、
大分、宮崎、(静岡)

ハリママムシグサ
Arisaema minus：サトイモ科：兵庫

ヒンジモ
Lemna trisulca：ウキクサ科：北海道、

福島、栃木、長野、静岡、(青森、岩手、秋田、茨城、群馬、埼玉、千葉、神奈川、山梨、滋賀、徳島、宮崎)

ウキミクリ
Sparganium gramineum：ミクリ科：新潟、富山

チシマミクリ
Sparganium hyperboreum：ミクリ科：(北海道)

トダスゲ
Carex aequialta：カヤツリグサ科：(福島、茨城、栃木、埼玉、東京、愛知、三重、熊本)

タルマイスゲ
Carex buxbaumii：カヤツリグサ科：(北海道、青森、長野)

タカネシバスゲ
Carex capillaris：カヤツリグサ科：北海道、岩手、長野、(山形)

ジョウロウスゲ
Carex capricornis：カヤツリグサ科：青森、宮城、秋田、山形、栃木、千葉、山梨、(北海道、茨城、埼玉、神奈川)

タイワンスゲ
Carex formosensis：カヤツリグサ科：茨城、栃木、福岡、佐賀、長崎、(熊本)

トナカイスゲ
Carex globularis：カヤツリグサ科：(北海道)

ホウザンスゲ
Carex hoozanensis：カヤツリグサ科：(沖縄)

トクノシマスゲ
Carex kimurae：カヤツリグサ科：鹿児島

ヒメミコシガヤ
Carex laevissima：カヤツリグサ科：兵庫、岡山、(大阪)

イトナルコスゲ
Carex laxa：カヤツリグサ科：北海道、岩手、(青森、栃木)

タカネヒメスゲ
Carex melanocarpa：カヤツリグサ科：北海道

キシュウナキリスゲ
Carex nachiana：カヤツリグサ科：愛知、兵庫、山口、徳島、高知、福岡、(茨城、和歌山、島根、宮崎、鹿児島)

イトヒキスゲ
Carex remotiuscula：カヤツリグサ科：(北海道、長野)

タカネナルコ
Carex siroumensis：カヤツリグサ科：富山、山梨、長野、(静岡)

ツクシオオガヤツリ
Cyperus ohwii：カヤツリグサ科：千葉、福岡、熊本、(茨城)

ミスミイ
Eleocharis fistulosa：カヤツリグサ科：兵庫、和歌山、香川、大分、鹿児島、沖縄、(愛知、大阪、宮崎)

シロミノハリイ
Eleocharis margaritacea：カヤツリグサ科：北海道、岩手

ムニンテンツキ
Fimbristylis longispica var. boninensis：カヤツリグサ科：(東京)

ミクリガヤ
Rhynchospora malasica：カヤツリグサ科：愛知、山口、佐賀、大分、宮崎、(静岡、三重、和歌山、鹿児島)

ビャッコイ
Scirpus crassius：カヤツリグサ科：福島

カガシラ
Scleria caricina：カヤツリグサ科：千葉、岐阜、静岡、愛知、兵庫、宮崎、(三重、大阪、和歌山、岡山、山口、佐賀、熊本、大分、鹿児島、沖縄)

ミカワシンジュガヤ
Scleria mikawana：カヤツリグサ科：千葉、愛知、兵庫、(茨城、静岡、三重、滋賀、京都、大阪、岡山、山口、徳島、福岡、佐賀、熊本、大分、宮崎、鹿児島)

シマクマタケラン
Alpinia boninsimensis：ショウガ科：東京

エンレイショウキラン
Acanthephippium sylhetense var. pictum：ラン科：沖縄

ヒナラン
Amitostigma gracile：ラン科：栃木、新潟、兵庫、鳥取、岡山、徳島、香川、高知、長崎、熊本、大分、鹿児島、(茨城、石川、静岡、愛知、三重、滋賀、京都、大阪、奈良、和歌山、島根、広島、山口、愛媛、福岡、佐賀、宮崎)

イワチドリ
Amitostigma keiskei：ラン科：岐阜、静岡、愛知、和歌山、愛媛、高知、(富山、長野、三重、奈良、徳島)

キバナシュスラン
Anoectochilus formosanus：ラン科：沖縄

シコウラン
Bulbophyllum macraei：ラン科：鹿児島、沖縄

キンセイラン
Calanthe nipponica：ラン科：北海道、青森、岩手、宮城、秋田、山形、栃木、新

潟、富山、山梨、長野、岐阜、静岡、徳島、愛媛、高知、熊本、(福島、茨城、群馬、埼玉、東京、石川、三重、奈良、島根、広島、大分、宮崎)

キエビネ
Calanthe sieboldii：ラン科：福井、兵庫、和歌山、岡山、山口、徳島、香川、愛媛、高知、福岡、長崎、熊本、大分、(静岡、滋賀、島根、広島、鹿児島)

サルメンエビネ
Calanthe tricarinata：ラン科：北海道、岩手、宮城、秋田、山形、栃木、群馬、新潟、富山、福井、山梨、滋賀、京都、兵庫、奈良、岡山、愛媛、高知、熊本、大分、宮崎、鹿児島、(青森、福島、長野、岐阜、静岡、三重、和歌山、島根、広島、山口、徳島、香川、福岡、佐賀)

ヒメホテイラン
Calypso bulbosa：ラン科：北海道、青森

オガサワラシコウラン
Cirrhopetalum boninense：ラン科：(東京)

トケンラン
Cremastra unguiculata：ラン科：北海道、青森、宮城、秋田、山形、栃木、新潟、石川、福井、京都、兵庫、鳥取、岡山、徳島、愛媛、福岡、(岩手、福島、山口、香川、大分)

サガミランモドキ
Cymbidium aberrans：ラン科：東京、神奈川、(群馬)

スルガラン
Cymbidium ensifolium：ラン科：(長崎)

マヤラン
Cymbidium macrorhizon：ラン科：栃木、埼玉、千葉、東京、神奈川、岐阜、愛知、滋賀、兵庫、和歌山、徳島、香川、高知、福岡、長崎、鹿児島、(福井、静岡、三重、大阪、佐賀、宮崎、沖縄)

ホテイアツモリ
Cypripedium macranthum var. hoteiatsumorianum：ラン科：福井、山梨、長野、(石川、静岡)

レブンアツモリソウ
Cypripedium macranthum var. rebunense：ラン科：(北海道)

アツモリソウ
Cypripedium macranthum var. speciosum：ラン科：北海道、青森、岩手、宮城、山形、福島、山梨、長野、岐阜、(秋田、茨城、栃木、群馬、埼玉、東京、神奈川、静岡、京都)

キバナノセッコク
Dendrobium tosaense：ラン科：高知、

長崎、熊本、宮崎、(東京、徳島、愛媛、佐賀、鹿児島、沖縄)

キリガミネアサヒラン
Eleorchis japonica var. conformis：ラン科：群馬、長野、(福島、富山)

ハコネラン
Ephippianthus sawadanus：ラン科：東京、神奈川、静岡、(埼玉、山梨、奈良)

トラキチラン
Epipogium aphyllum：ラン科：北海道、山梨、長野、(福島、栃木、群馬、埼玉、静岡)

アオキラン
Epipogium japonicum：ラン科：山形、長野、(宮城、群馬、山梨)

オオサラン
Eria corneri：ラン科：鹿児島、沖縄

リュウキュウセッコク
Eria ovata：ラン科：沖縄

オサラン
Eria reptans：ラン科：高知、熊本、宮崎、(東京、奈良、和歌山、徳島、鹿児島、沖縄)

イモネヤガラ
Eulophia zollingeri：ラン科：宮崎、鹿児島、沖縄

コンジキヤガラ
Gastrodia javanica：ラン科：沖縄

クロヤツシロラン
Gastrodia pubilabiata：ラン科：神奈川、静岡、愛知、福岡、(石川、福井、徳島、高知、宮崎、鹿児島)

ヒロハツリシュスラン
Goodyera pendula var. brachyphylla：ラン科：青森、岩手、宮城、秋田、群馬、新潟、静岡、(北海道、山形、長野)

キンギンソウ
Goodyera procera：ラン科：鹿児島、沖縄

クニガミシュスラン
Goodyera sonoharae：ラン科：(沖縄)

シマシュスラン
Goodyera viridiflora：ラン科：鹿児島、沖縄

フジチドリ
Gymnadenia fujisanensis：ラン科：青森、秋田、山梨、(岩手、神奈川、静岡)

テツオサギソウ
Habenaria delessertiana：ラン科：(沖縄)

ダイサギソウ
Habenaria dentata：ラン科：千葉、和歌山、高知、長崎、熊本、宮崎、沖縄、(神奈川、静岡、徳島、鹿児島)

オオミズトンボ
Habenaria linearifolia：ラン科：(北海道、青森、千葉、長野)

リュウキュウサギソウ
Habenaria longitentaculata：ラン科：沖縄、(鹿児島)

タカサゴサギソウ
Habenaria tentaculata：ラン科：沖縄、(鹿児島)

ヤクシマアカシュスラン
Hetaeria yakusimensis：ラン科：静岡、愛媛、高知、宮崎、沖縄、(東京、和歌山、鹿児島)

フガクスズムシソウ
Liparis fujisanensis：ラン科：岩手、秋田、山形、神奈川、新潟、山梨、岐阜、奈良、徳島、愛媛、高知、大分、(青森、福島、静岡、三重、宮崎)

チケイラン
Liparis plicata：ラン科：宮崎、鹿児島、沖縄

ヤチラン
Malaxis paludosa：ラン科：北海道、秋田、福島、栃木、群馬、(青森、岩手)

サカネラン
Neottia nidus-avis var. mandshurica：ラン科：北海道、青森、岩手、神奈川、山梨、長野、(宮城、秋田、山形、福島、栃木、群馬、東京、新潟、静岡、宮崎)

イナバラン
Odontochilus inabae：ラン科：沖縄、(鹿児島)

カモメラン
Orchis cyclochila：ラン科：北海道、岩手、宮城、山形、栃木、群馬、新潟、山梨、長野、岐阜、静岡、徳島、高知、(福島、埼玉、東京、神奈川、福井)

ニョホウチドリ
Orchis joo-iokiana：ラン科：福島、栃木、群馬、埼玉、富山、石川、福井、山梨、長野、静岡

ツクシチドリ
Platanthera (brevicalcarata var.) yakumontana：ラン科：大分、(愛媛)

シロウマチドリ
Platanthera hyperborea：ラン科：北海道、富山、長野、(静岡)

オオバナオオヤマサギソウ
Platanthera sachalinensis var.hondoensis：ラン科：埼玉、静岡、滋賀

ムカデラン
Sarcanthus scolopendrifolius：ラン科：群馬、静岡、愛知、徳島、高知、佐賀、長崎、大分、宮崎、(埼玉)

イリオモテムヨウラン

Stereosandra javanica：ラン科：沖縄

ヒメトケンラン
Tainia laxiflora：ラン科：長崎、熊本、鹿児島、沖縄、(高知、宮崎)

ハガクレナガミラン
Thrixspermum fantasticum：ラン科：沖縄

イリオモテラン
Trichoglottis luchuensis：ラン科：沖縄

アコウネッタイラン
Tropidia calcarata：ラン科：沖縄

ヤクシマネッタイラン
Tropidia nipponica：ラン科：高知、宮崎、鹿児島、沖縄

ヒロハトンボソウ
Tulotis fuscescens：ラン科：北海道、福島、山梨、長野、岐阜

イイヌマムカゴ
Tulotis iinumae：ラン科：青森、宮城、秋田、山形、福島、神奈川、愛知、奈良、(栃木、群馬、東京、新潟、石川、福井、静岡、三重、兵庫、和歌山、山口、徳島、香川、高知、大分)

オオハクウンラン
Vexillabium fissum：ラン科：青森、秋田、山形、神奈川、長野、大分、(岩手、宮城、茨城、栃木、群馬、東京)

ヤクシマヒメアリドオシラン
Vexillabium yakushimense：ラン科：長野、鹿児島、沖縄

キバナノショウキラン
Yoania amagiensis：ラン科：埼玉、東京、神奈川、山梨、長野、静岡、徳島、香川、愛媛、熊本、宮崎、(群馬、富山、高知、大分、鹿児島)

アオジクキヌラン
Zeuxine affinis：ラン科：沖縄

植物	絶滅危惧2類
	VU

マツバラン
Psilotum nudum：マツバラン科：福島、栃木、群馬、千葉、東京、神奈川、静岡、愛知、滋賀、京都、兵庫、奈良、和歌山、広島、山口、徳島、香川、愛媛、高知、福岡、佐賀、長崎、熊本、大分、宮崎、鹿児島、沖縄、茨城、埼玉、石川、山梨、三重、大阪、島根)

コスギトウゲシバ
Lycopodium somae：
ヒカゲノカズラ科：鹿児島

イヌカタヒバ
Selaginella moellendorffii：イワヒバ科：山口、(沖縄)

エゾノヒモカズラ
Selaginella sibirica：イワヒバ科：北海道

ヒメミズニラ
Isoetes asiatica：ミズニラ科：北海道、青森、岩手、山形、福島、群馬、長野、(秋田、新潟)

ミズニラ
Isoetes japonica：ミズニラ科：青森、岩手、宮城、秋田、山形、福島、茨城、群馬、埼玉、千葉、東京、神奈川、新潟、石川、福井、長野、岐阜、静岡、愛知、滋賀、大阪、兵庫、奈良、和歌山、鳥取、岡山、広島、山口、香川、(富山、三重、京都、徳島、熊本)

チシマヒメドクサ
Equisetum variegatum：トクサ科：北海道

ヒメハナワラビ
Botrychium lunaria：ハナヤスリ科：北海道、岩手、宮城、栃木、福島、石川、福井、山梨、長野、(山形、福島、神奈川、静岡、鳥取)

リュウビンタイモドキ
Marattia boninensis：リュウビンタイ科：(東京)

キクモバホラゴケ
Cephalomanes apiifolium：コケシノブ科：(鹿児島、沖縄)

キクシノブ
Humata repens：シノブ科：和歌山、徳島、高知、宮崎、鹿児島、沖縄

オトメクジャク
Adiantum edgeworthii：ミズワラビ(ホウライシダ)科：大分

ヒメウラジロ
Cheilanthes argentea：ミズワラビ(ホウライシダ)科：岩手、栃木、群馬、埼玉、東京、神奈川、長野、兵庫、和歌山、岡山、広島、山口、徳島、香川、愛媛、高知、福岡、長崎、熊本、大分、宮崎、(山梨、静岡、佐賀、鹿児島)

キドイノモトソウ
Pteris kidoi：イノモトソウ科：岡山、山口、愛媛、福岡、熊本、大分、(高知)

シマオオタニワタリ
Asplenium nidus：チャセンシダ科：東京、沖縄、(鹿児島)

オトメシダ
Asplenium tenerum：チャセンシダ科：(東京、沖縄)

ツルキジノオ
Lomariopsis spectabilis：ツルキジノオ科：東京、沖縄

ヤクシマカナワラビ

Arachniodes cavalerii：オシダ科：(鹿児島)

コミダケシダ
Ctenitis iriomotensis：オシダ科：(沖縄)

ムカシベニシダ
Dryopteris anadroma：オシダ科：(鹿児島)

ホソバヌカイタチシダ
Dryopteris gymnosora var. angustata：オシダ科：(鹿児島)

ニセヨゴレイタチシダ
Dryopteris hadanoi：オシダ科：山口、高知、長崎、大分、宮崎

ヒメミゾシダ
Stegnogramma gymnocarpa ssp. amabilis：ヒメシダ科：広島、愛媛、長崎、鹿児島、沖縄、(佐賀)

タイワンハシゴシダ
Thelypteris castanea：ヒメシダ科：(沖縄)

ホコザキノコギリシダ
Diplazium yaoshanense：メシダ(イワデンダ)科：沖縄

キンモウワラビ
Hypodematium crenatum ssp. fauriei：メシダ(イワデンダ)科：栃木、群馬、埼玉、京都、山口、長野、高知、熊本、(宮崎)

タカウラボシ
Microsorium rubidum：ウラボシ科：(沖縄)

ヒメウラボシ
Grammitis dorsipila：ヒメウラボシ科：鹿児島、沖縄

デンジソウ
Marsilea quadrifolia：デンジソウ科：青森、岩手、宮城、山形、福島、埼玉、千葉、神奈川、福井、長野、愛知、兵庫、鳥取、岡山、広島、山口、徳島、愛媛、福岡、佐賀、長崎、熊本、大分、鹿児島、(北海道、秋田、茨城、栃木、群馬、東京、新潟、石川、山梨、岐阜、静岡、三重、滋賀、京都、大阪、奈良、和歌山、島根、香川、高知、宮崎)

サンショウモ
Salvinia natans：サンショウモ科：青森、岩手、宮城、秋田、山形、福島、栃木、群馬、埼玉、千葉、東京、神奈川、新潟、富山、石川、福井、山梨、長野、静岡、愛知、三重、滋賀、兵庫、和歌山、岡山、山口、徳島、香川、愛媛、佐賀、大分、(茨城、岐阜、京都、大阪、奈良、広島、高知、福岡、熊本)

アカウキクサ
Azolla imbricata：アカウキクサ科：静岡、愛知、滋賀、和歌山、岡山、広島、

山口、徳島、愛媛、高知、佐賀、長崎、熊本、大分、宮崎、鹿児島、沖縄、(富山、山梨、岐阜、三重、京都、大阪、奈良、香川、福岡)

オオアカウキクサ
Azolla japonica：アカウキクサ科：山形、栃木、埼玉、千葉、東京、神奈川、新潟、富山、石川、福井、長野、静岡、愛知、滋賀、京都、大阪、兵庫、奈良、鳥取、岡山、広島、徳島、愛媛、佐賀、長崎、(宮城、秋田、福島、茨城、群馬、山梨、三重、島根、熊本)

トガサワラ
Pseudotsuga japonica：マツ科：奈良、和歌山、高知、(三重)

ケショウヤナギ
Chosenia arbutifolia：ヤナギ科：北海道、長野

コマイワヤナギ
Salix rupifraga：ヤナギ科：群馬、山梨、長野、静岡

タライカヤナギ
Salix taraikensis：ヤナギ科：(北海道)

ヤエガワカンバ
Betula davurica：カバノキ科：群馬、東京、神奈川、山梨、長野、岐阜、(埼玉)

ヤチカンバ
Betula ovalifolia：カバノキ科：(北海道)

タイワントリアシ
Boehmeria formosana：イラクサ科：沖縄、(鹿児島)

トキホコリ
Elatostema densiflorum：イラクサ科：北海道、群馬、埼玉、千葉、東京、神奈川、(宮城、福島、茨城、栃木、静岡、兵庫)

ランダイミズ
Elatostema edule：イラクサ科：(沖縄)

アマミサンショウソウ
Elatostema oshimensis：イラクサ科：鹿児島

トウカテンソウ
Nanocnide pilosa：イラクサ科：(鹿児島)

アラゲサンショウソウ
Pellionia brevifolia：イラクサ科：(宮崎、鹿児島)

ミヤコミズ
Pilea kiotensis：イラクサ科：京都、兵庫、奈良、和歌山、岡山、山口、福岡、大分、(三重)

ミヤマツチトリモチ
Balanophora nipponica：ツチトリモチ科：青森、岩手、宮城、秋田、山形、福島、栃木、群馬、東京、神奈川、新潟、富山、福井、山梨、長野、岐阜、

静岡、愛知、奈良、和歌山、広島、徳島、愛媛、高知、(石川、滋賀、兵庫、宮崎)

ヤナギヌカボ
Persicaria foliosa var. *paludicola*：
タデ科：青森、宮城、秋田、栃木、埼玉、千葉、福井、長野、岐阜、静岡、愛知、兵庫、和歌山、岡山、山口、佐賀、長崎、熊本、(福島、群馬、神奈川、新潟、滋賀、京都、大阪、徳島、福岡、大分、宮崎、鹿児島)

ヌカボタデ
Persicaria taquetii：タデ科：宮城、秋田、福島、栃木、千葉、新潟、富山、岐阜、静岡、愛知、和歌山、岡山、徳島、香川、佐賀、熊本、大分、宮崎、(青森、山形、茨城、群馬、埼玉、神奈川、石川、長野、三重、滋賀、京都、大阪、兵庫、奈良、高知、福岡、鹿児島)

ノダイオウ
Rumex longifolius：タデ科：北海道、青森、岩手、宮城、秋田、山形、福島、群馬、新潟、富山、福井、長野、岐阜、愛知、(茨城、栃木、神奈川、滋賀、兵庫、奈良、岡山)

コギシギシ
Rumex nipponicus：タデ科：栃木、群馬、埼玉、千葉、神奈川、愛知、和歌山、岡山、山口、徳島、香川、高知、佐賀、熊本、大分、宮崎、沖縄、(福島、茨城、富山、静岡、福岡、長崎)

ヌマハコベ
Montia fontana：スベリヒユ科：北海道、栃木、(岩手、秋田、群馬)

カトウハコベ
Arenaria katoana：ナデシコ科：北海道、岩手、群馬

チョウカイフスマ
Arenaria merckioides var. *chokaiensis*：ナデシコ科：秋田、山形

ゲンカイミミナグサ
Cerastium fischerianum var. *molle*：ナデシコ科：福岡、佐賀、長崎

タガソデソウ
Cerastium pauciflorum var. *amurense*：ナデシコ科：山梨、長野

タチハコベ
Moehringia trinervia：ナデシコ科：北海道、青森、岩手、宮城、広島、愛媛、熊本、(福島、群馬、三重、滋賀、京都、和歌山、岡山、徳島、福岡、大分、鹿児島)

ナンブワチガイソウ
Pseudostellaria japonica：ナデシコ科：岩手、宮城、福島、長野、(茨城)

アオモリマンテマ

シレネ・アオモレンシス
Silene aomorensis：ナデシコ科：秋田、(青森)

オオビランジ
Silene keiskei：ナデシコ科：群馬、神奈川、山梨、長野、静岡、(栃木、埼玉)

テバコマンテマ
Silene yanoei：ナデシコ科：徳島、愛媛、高知

シコタンハコベ
Stellaria ruscifolia：ナデシコ科：北海道、富山、山梨、長野、静岡、(栃木)

シチメンソウ
Suaeda japonica：アカザ科：福岡、佐賀、長崎、(大分)

ヒロハマツナ
Suaeda malacosperma：アカザ科：愛知、兵庫、広島、山口、福岡、佐賀、長崎、(熊本、大分、鹿児島)

シデコブシ
Magnolia tomentosa：モクレン科：岐阜、愛知、(三重)

マルバニッケイ
Cinnamomum daphnoides：クスノキ科：福岡、長崎、鹿児島、沖縄

テングノハナ
Illigera luzonensis：ハスノハギリ科：(沖縄)

イブキレイジンソウ
Aconitum chrysopilum：キンポウゲ科：岐阜、滋賀

センウズモドキ
Aconitum jaluense ssp. *iwatekense*：キンポウゲ科：青森、岩手、宮城、(福島、茨城、群馬、長野)

シレトコトリカブト
Aconitum maximum var. *misaoanum*：キンポウゲ科：(北海道)

ミチノクフクジュソウ
Adonis multiflora：キンポウゲ科：青森、岩手、宮城、千葉、神奈川、福井、長野、岐阜、(熊本、大分、宮崎、鹿児島)

フクジュソウ
Adonis ramosa：キンポウゲ科：青森、岩手、宮城、秋田、山形、福島、群馬、東京、新潟、富山、山梨、長野、岐阜、静岡、滋賀、京都、大阪、奈良、和歌山、岡山、広島、徳島、愛媛、高知、(栃木、埼玉、山口、宮崎)

フタマタイチゲ
Anemone dichotoma：キンポウゲ科：北海道

カザグルマ
Clematis patens：キンポウゲ科：宮城、福島、栃木、群馬、埼玉、千葉、東京、神奈川、新潟、山梨、長野、岐阜、静岡、愛知、滋賀、兵庫、奈良、和歌山、岡山、広島、山口、香川、高知、熊本、大分、宮崎、(岩手、秋田、山形、茨城、石川、三重、大阪、愛媛)

ムニンセンニンソウ
Clematis terniflora var. *boninensis*：キンポウゲ科：(東京)

ハコネシロカネソウ
Dichocarpum hakonense：キンポウゲ科：神奈川、(静岡)

ヒメキンポウゲ
Halerpestes kawakamii：キンポウゲ科：青森、宮城、秋田、(岩手、山形)

オキナグサ
Pulsatilla cernua：キンポウゲ科：青森、岩手、宮城、秋田、山形、福島、栃木、群馬、神奈川、新潟、富山、石川、山梨、長野、静岡、愛知、滋賀、京都、大阪、兵庫、奈良、鳥取、岡山、広島、山口、徳島、香川、愛媛、福岡、佐賀、熊本、大分、宮崎、(茨城、埼玉、千葉、東京、福井、岐阜、三重、和歌山、島根、高知、鹿児島)

コキツネノボタン
Ranunculus chinensis：キンポウゲ科：北海道、岩手、栃木、千葉、山梨、(宮城、秋田、山形、茨城、埼玉、神奈川、佐賀)

ヒキノカサ
Ranunculus extorris：キンポウゲ科：埼玉、静岡、岡山、徳島、香川、(福島、茨城、栃木、群馬、千葉、神奈川、熊本)

クモマキンポウゲ
Ranunculus pygmaeus：キンポウゲ科：(富山、長野)

タカネキンポウゲ
Ranunculus sulphureus：キンポウゲ科：(富山、長野)

セツブンソウ
Shibateranthis pinnatifida：キンポウゲ科：埼玉、山梨、長野、岐阜、静岡、愛知、滋賀、兵庫、岡山、広島、(三重、京都、大阪)

ハルカラマツ
Thalictrum baicalense：キンポウゲ科：栃木、群馬、(北海道、福島、埼玉)

チャボカラマツ
Thalictrum foetidum var. *glabrescens*：キンポウゲ科：北海道、岩手

ヒメミヤマカラマツ
Thalictrum nakamurae：キンポウゲ科：群馬、(山形、新潟)

ノカラマツ
Thalictrum simplex var. *brevipes*：キンポウゲ科：茨城、栃木、千葉、長野、

岡山、熊本、大分、宮崎、(青森、岩手、宮城、福島、群馬、埼玉、神奈川、富山、大阪、福岡、佐賀、鹿児島)

ヤチマタイカリソウ
Epimedium grandiflorum：メギ科：徳島、高知、熊本

トガクシソウ
Ranzania japonica：メギ科：青森、岩手、秋田、山形、福島、群馬、新潟、富山、長野、(宮城)

オニバス
Euryale ferox：スイレン科：茨城、群馬、千葉、新潟、岐阜、静岡、愛知、滋賀、京都、大阪、兵庫、奈良、和歌山、岡山、広島、徳島、香川、福岡、佐賀、熊本、大分、宮崎、鹿児島、(宮城、栃木、埼玉、東京、富山、石川、福井、三重)

オグラコウホネ
Nuphar oguraense：スイレン科：愛知、京都、兵庫、和歌山、広島、徳島、福岡、佐賀、長崎、熊本、宮崎、鹿児島、(大阪)

ネムロコウホネ
Nuphar pumilum：スイレン科：北海道、青森、宮城、秋田、(岩手)

オゼコウホネ
Nuphar pumilum var. ozeense：スイレン科：秋田、山形、福島、群馬

ヒメコウホネ
Nuphar subintegerrimum：スイレン科：栃木、神奈川、福井、岐阜、愛知、滋賀、京都、兵庫、和歌山、岡山、広島、山口、徳島、高知、佐賀、熊本、大分、宮崎、鹿児島、(静岡、三重、長崎)

エゾベニヒツジグサ
Nymphaea tetragona var. erythrostigmatica：スイレン科：(北海道)

シマゴショウ
Peperomia boninsimensis：コショウ科：(東京)

オキナワスナゴショウ
Peperomia okinawensis：コショウ科：(沖縄)

キビヒトリシズカ
Chloranthus fortunei：センリョウ科：兵庫、和歌山、岡山、広島、香川、福岡、長崎、熊本、(愛媛)

コウシュンウマノスズクサ
Aristolochia tubiflora：ウマノスズクサ科：沖縄

クロフネサイシン
Asiasarum dimidiatum：ウマノスズクサ科：奈良、徳島、香川、高知、福岡、熊本、大分、宮崎、(広島)

トリガミネカンアオイ

Heterotropa (=Asarum) pellucidum：ウマノスズクサ科：鹿児島

ミヤビカンアオイ
Heterotropa celsa：ウマノスズクサ科：(鹿児島)

トサノアオイ
Heterotropa costata：ウマノスズクサ科：高知

ナンゴクアオイ
Heterotropa crassa：ウマノスズクサ科：(鹿児島)

ミチノクサイシン
Heterotropa fauriei：ウマノスズクサ科：青森、岩手、秋田、山形、福島、新潟、富山、岐阜、(宮城)

ミヤマアオイ
Heterotropa fauriei var. nakaiana：ウマノスズクサ科：富山、長野、岐阜

フジノカンアオイ
Heterotropa fudsinoi：ウマノスズクサ科：(鹿児島)

グスクカンアオイ
Heterotropa gusuk：ウマノスズクサ科：(鹿児島)

ツクシアオイ
Heterotropa kiusiana：ウマノスズクサ科：佐賀、長崎、熊本、宮崎

ナンカイアオイ
Heterotropa nankaiensis：ウマノスズクサ科：兵庫、徳島、香川、高知

キンチャクアオイ
Heterotropa perfecta：ウマノスズクサ科：熊本、宮崎、鹿児島、(福岡)

サカワサイシン
Heterotropa sakawana：ウマノスズクサ科：徳島、愛媛、高知

オトメアオイ
Heterotropa savatieri：ウマノスズクサ科：神奈川、静岡、(山梨)

ズソウカンアオイ
Heterotropa savatieri var. pseudosavatieri：ウマノスズクサ科：神奈川、(静岡)

トクノシマカンアオイ
Heterotropa similis：ウマノスズクサ科：(鹿児島)

タマノカンアオイ
Heterotropa tamaensis：ウマノスズクサ科：埼玉、東京、神奈川、(静岡)

サンコカンアオイ

Heterotropa trigyna：ウマノスズクサ科：(鹿児島)

カケロマカンアオイ
Heterotropa trinacriformis：ウマノスズクサ科：鹿児島

ウンゼンカンアオイ
Heterotropa unzen：ウマノスズクサ科：福岡、佐賀、長崎、熊本、鹿児島、(大分)

ヤマシャクヤク
Paeonia japonica：ボタン科：青森、岩手、宮城、秋田、山形、福島、栃木、群馬、東京、神奈川、新潟、富山、石川、福井、山梨、長野、岐阜、静岡、愛知、滋賀、京都、兵庫、奈良、和歌山、鳥取、岡山、広島、山口、徳島、香川、高知、福岡、佐賀、熊本、大分、宮崎、鹿児島、(茨城、埼玉、長崎)

マメヒサカキ
Eurya emarginata var. minutissima：ツバキ科：沖縄、(鹿児島)

エゾオトギリ
Hypericum yezoense：オトギリソウ科：北海道、青森、岩手、秋田

ナガバノモウセンゴケ
Drosera anglica：モウセンゴケ科：北海道、福島、群馬

イシモチソウ
Drosera peltata var. nipponica：モウセンゴケ科：千葉、石川、岐阜、静岡、愛知、滋賀、兵庫、奈良、和歌山、岡山、広島、山口、徳島、香川、愛媛、(茨城、神奈川、三重、京都、大阪)

タチスズシロソウ
Arabis kawasakiana：アブラナ科：富山、滋賀、(静岡、愛知、三重、大阪、兵庫、愛媛、高知)

ハナタネツケバナ
Cardamine pratensis：アブラナ科：北海道

エゾノジャニンジン
Cardamine schinziana：アブラナ科：北海道

クモマナズナ
Draba nipponica：アブラナ科：栃木、富山、山梨、長野、静岡、(群馬)

キリシマミズキ
Corylopsis glabrescens：マンサク科：奈良、愛媛、高知、宮崎、鹿児島

トサミズキ
Corylopsis spicata：マンサク科：高知、(埼玉)

ヒダカミセバヤ
Hylotelephium cauticolum：ベンケイソウ科：北海道

チャボツメレンゲ
Meterostachys sikokianus:
ベンケイソウ科：徳島、愛媛、高知、福
岡、長崎、大分、宮崎、(三重、熊本)

コモチレンゲ
Orostachys iwarenge var. *boehmeri*:
ベンケイソウ科：北海道、青森、秋田

ムニンタイトゴメ
Sedum boninense：ベンケイソウ科：
(東京)

マツノハマンネングサ
Sedum hakonense：ベンケイソウ科：
東京、神奈川、山梨、静岡

ウンゼンマンネングサ
Sedum polytrichoides：
ベンケイソウ科：兵庫、岡山、佐賀、長
崎、大分、(福岡)

ヒメキリンソウ
Sedum sikokianum：ベンケイソウ科：
徳島、高知、(愛媛)

ウメウツギ
Deutzia uniflora：ユキノシタ科：東京、
神奈川、山梨、(埼玉、静岡)

リュウキュウコンテリギ
Hydrangea liukiuensis：ユキノシタ科：
沖縄

ヒュウガアジサイ
Hydrangea serrata var. *minamitanii*：
ユキノシタ科：宮崎

キレンゲショウマ
Kirengeshoma palmata：ユキノシタ科：
奈良、広島、徳島、高知、熊本、大分、宮崎

モミジチャルメルソウ
Mitella acerina：ユキノシタ科：滋賀、
(福井、京都)

ツクシチャルメルソウ
Mitella kiusiana：ユキノシタ科：熊本、
大分、宮崎、(愛媛)

タキミチャルメルソウ
Mitella stylosa：ユキノシタ科：岐阜、
滋賀、(三重)

ワタナベソウ
Peltoboykinia watanabei：
ユキノシタ科：奈良、徳島、愛媛、高知、
熊本、大分、宮崎

タコノアシ
Penthorum chinense：ユキノシタ科：
青森、岩手、宮城、山形、福島、茨城、栃
木、群馬、埼玉、千葉、東京、神奈川、新
潟、富山、石川、福井、山梨、岐阜、静岡、
愛知、滋賀、京都、兵庫、和歌山、岡山、
広島、山口、徳島、愛媛、高知、福岡、佐
賀、熊本、大分、宮崎、鹿児島、(長野、三
重、大阪、奈良、島根、長崎)

ヤシャビシャク
Ribes ambiguum：ユキノシタ科：青森、
岩手、宮城、秋田、山形、福島、栃木、群
馬、東京、神奈川、新潟、富山、石川、福
井、山梨、長野、岐阜、静岡、愛知、滋賀、
兵庫、和歌山、鳥取、岡山、広島、山口、
徳島、高知、福岡、熊本、大分、宮崎、(茨
城、埼玉、三重、京都、奈良、島根、愛媛、
鹿児島)

センダイソウ
Saxifraga sendaica：ユキノシタ科：
奈良、和歌山、徳島、高知、福岡、長崎、
熊本、宮崎、(三重、愛媛、大分)

ハハジマトベラ
Pittosporum beecheyi：トベラ科：(東京)

チョウセンキンミズヒキ
Agrimonia coreana：バラ科：宮城、群
馬、千葉、東京、神奈川、長野、滋賀、宮
崎、(岩手、埼玉)

ハゴロモグサ
Alchemilla japonica：バラ科：北海道、
富山、山梨、長野、(静岡)

テンノウメ
Osteomeles anthyllidifolia：バラ科：
鹿児島、沖縄

シマカナメモチ
Photinia wrightiana：バラ科：東京、沖
縄、(鹿児島)

ツチグリ
Potentilla discolor：バラ科：岐阜、兵庫、
山口、香川、福岡、大分、宮崎、(愛知、大
阪、広島、長崎、熊本)

キンロバイ s.l.
Potentilla fruticosa：バラ科：北海道、岩
手、宮城、山形、群馬、山梨、長野、徳島、
(秋田、東京、静岡、三重、奈良)

ユウバリキンバイ
Potentilla matsumurae var. *yuparensis*：
バラ科：北海道

ウラジロキンバイ
Potentilla nivea var. *camtschatica*：
バラ科：北海道、富山、山梨、長野、静岡

サンショウバラ
Rosa hirtula：バラ科：神奈川、山梨、静
岡

キイシモツケ
Spiraea nipponica var. *ogawae*：
バラ科：和歌山

ホザキシモツケ
Spiraea salicifolia：バラ科：北海道、岩
手、栃木、長野

カラフトゲンゲ s.l.
Hedysarum hedysaroides：マメ科：
(北海道)

クロバナキハギ
Lespedeza bicolor var. *melanantha*：
マメ科：愛知、熊本

イヌハギ
Lespedeza tomentosa：マメ科：青森、
岩手、宮城、秋田、山形、福島、埼玉、千
葉、東京、神奈川、新潟、富山、石川、山
梨、長野、静岡、愛知、滋賀、京都、大阪、
兵庫、岡山、広島、山口、徳島、香川、愛
媛、高知、福岡、佐賀、長崎、熊本、宮崎、
(茨城、栃木、群馬、岐阜、和歌山、鹿児
島、沖縄)

ヒダカミヤマノエンドウ
Oxytropis hidaka-montana：マメ科：
(北海道)

イソフジ
Sophora tomentosa：マメ科：鹿児島、
沖縄

ヤクシマカワゴロモ
Hydrobryum puncticulatum：
カワゴケソウ科：(鹿児島)

オオヤマカタバミ
Oxalis obtriangulata：カタバミ科：
栃木、群馬、埼玉、東京、長野、愛知、徳
島、大分、(山梨、愛媛、熊本、宮崎)

カイフウロ
Geranium shikokianum var. *kai-
montanum*：フウロソウ科：群馬、山梨、
長野、(埼玉)

ハツバキ
Drypetes integerrima：トウダイグサ科：
(東京)

ノウルシ
Euphorbia adenochlora：
トウダイグサ科：北海道、青森、岩手、
宮城、秋田、山形、茨城、栃木、群馬、千
葉、新潟、富山、石川、長野、静岡、滋賀、
京都、大阪、兵庫、岡山、佐賀、(福島、埼
玉、東京、神奈川、福井、岐阜、三重、福
岡、熊本)

ボロジノニシキソウ
Euphorbia sparrmanni：
トウダイグサ科：(沖縄)

タチバナ
Citrus tachibana：ミカン科：静岡、愛知、
和歌山、山口、徳島、愛媛、高知、長崎、
熊本、大分、宮崎、鹿児島、(三重、福岡)

クスノハカエデ
Acer oblongum var. *itoanum*：
カエデ科：鹿児島、沖縄

ハナノキ
Acer pycnanthum：カエデ科：長野、岐
阜、愛知

ムニンイヌツゲ

Ilex matanoana：モチノキ科：(東京)

シマモチ
Ilex mertensii：モチノキ科：(東京)

アオツリバナ
Euonymus yakushimensis：
ニシキギ科：宮崎、(鹿児島)

ハリツルマサキ
Maytenus diversifolia：ニシキギ科：
鹿児島、沖縄

コバノクロヅル
Tripterygium doianum：ニシキギ科：
熊本、宮崎、(鹿児島)

チョウセンヒメツゲ
Buxus microphylla var. insularis：
ツゲ科：岡山、広島、徳島

ヤエヤマハマナツメ
Colubrina asiatica：クロウメモドキ科：
沖縄

リュウキュウクロウメモドキ
Rhamnus liukiuensis：
クロウメモドキ科：鹿児島、沖縄

キビノクロウメモドキ
Rhamnus yoshinoi：クロウメモドキ科：
岡山、広島、徳島、高知、福岡、熊本、宮崎

シラガブドウ
Vitis amurensis var. shiragai：ブドウ科：
岡山

チョウセンナニワズ
Daphne pseudo-mezereum var.
koreana：ジンチョウゲ科：群馬、東京、
山梨、長野、静岡、滋賀、徳島、高知、(埼
玉、奈良)

サクラガンピ
Diplomorpha pauciflora：
ジンチョウゲ科：神奈川、静岡

ムニンアオガンピ
Wikstroemia pseudoretusa：
ジンチョウゲ科：(東京)

ハコネグミ
Elaeagnus matsunoana var.
hypostellata：グミ科：神奈川、静岡、
(山梨)

チシマウスバスミレ
Viola blandaeformis var. pilosa：
スミレ科：北海道、福島、群馬、長野、
(岩手)

オオバタチツボスミレ
Viola kamtschadalorum：スミレ科：
北海道、青森、岩手、福島、群馬、新潟、
長野

キスミレ
Viola orientalis：スミレ科：山梨、静岡、
愛知、愛媛、高知、熊本、大分、宮崎、(長
野、島根、広島、佐賀、鹿児島)

アポイタチツボスミレ
Viola sachalinensis var. alpina：
スミレ科：北海道

イシガキスミレ
Viola tashiroi var. tairae：スミレ科：(沖縄)

コウトウシュウカイドウ
Begonia fenicis：シュウカイドウ科：
(沖縄)

シマサルスベリ
Lagerstroemia subcostata：
ミソハギ科：東京、鹿児島

ミズマツバ
Rotala pusilla：ミソハギ科：宮城、秋田、
福島、栃木、群馬、埼玉、千葉、東京、神
奈川、新潟、富山、長野、岐阜、静岡、愛
知、大阪、和歌山、岡山、広島、山口、香
川、愛媛、佐賀、長崎、熊本、大分、宮崎、
鹿児島、(岩手、山形、茨城、福井、奈良、
徳島、福岡、沖縄)

ヒメビシ
Trapa incisa：ヒシ科：宮城、秋田、山形、
福島、茨城、石川、福井、山梨、長野、岐
阜、静岡、愛知、滋賀、奈良、和歌山、岡
山、徳島、香川、高知、福岡、熊本、大分、
(群馬、埼玉、新潟、富山、京都、大阪、兵
庫、鳥取、佐賀、宮崎)

ヒメフトモモ
Syzygium cleyeraefolium：フトモモ科：
(東京)

コバノミヤマノボタン
Bredia okinawensis：ノボタン科：沖縄

ハハジマノボタン
Melastoma pentapetalum：ノボタン科：
(東京)

トダイアカバナ
Epilobium formosanum：アカバナ科：
神奈川、長野、徳島、高知、宮崎、(埼玉、
山梨、滋賀、広島)

オオアカバナ
Epilobium hirsutum var. villosum：
アカバナ科：青森、福島、(新潟、石川)

ウスゲチョウジタデ
Ludwigia greatrexii：アカバナ科：千葉、
神奈川、福井、静岡、長崎、鹿児島、(埼
玉、徳島、香川、沖縄)

オグラノフサモ
Myriophyllum oguraense：
アリノトウグサ科：宮城、兵庫、岡山、
香川、宮崎、(青森、茨城、群馬、新潟、滋
賀、京都、大阪、奈良、島根、広島、山口、
鹿児島)

ヤエヤマヤマボウシ
Cornus hongkongensis：ミズキ科：(沖縄)

ムニンヤツデ

Fatsia oligocarpela：ウコギ科：(東京)

ヒュウガトウキ
Angelica furcijuga：セリ科：大分、宮崎

ホソバトウキ
Angelica stenoloba：セリ科：北海道

ミシマサイコ
Bupleurum scorzoneraefolium var.
stenophyllum：セリ科：宮城、栃木、群
馬、千葉、神奈川、静岡、愛知、大阪、兵
庫、鳥取、岡山、広島、山口、徳島、香川、
愛媛、高知、福岡、熊本、大分、宮崎、鹿
児島、(福島、茨城、東京、富山、石川、山
梨、三重、滋賀、京都、奈良、和歌山、佐
賀、長崎)

ツルギハナウド
Heracleum moellendorffii var.
tsurugisanense：セリ科：徳島、高知

チシマツガザクラ
Bryanthus gmelinii：ツツジ科：北海道、
青森、岩手

ヤクシマヨウラクツツジ
Menziesia yakushimensis：ツツジ科：
鹿児島

エゾムラサキツツジ
Rhododendron dauricum：ツツジ科：
北海道

ナンゴクミツバツツジ
Rhododendron kiyosmense ssp.
mayebarae：ツツジ科：熊本、大分、宮
崎

オオスミミツバツツジ
Rhododendron kiyosmense ssp.
mayebarae var. ohsumiense：ツツジ科：
宮崎、(鹿児島)

アシタカツツジ
Rhododendron komiyamae：ツツジ科：
山梨、静岡

ホソバシャクナゲ
Rhododendron makinoi：ツツジ科：
静岡、愛知

ゲンカイツツジ
Rhododendron mucronulatum var.
ciliatum：ツツジ科：鳥取、岡山、広島、
山口、愛媛、福岡、長崎、熊本、大分、(島
根)

キリシマミツバツツジ
Rhododendron nudipes var.
kirishimense：ツツジ科：宮崎

ウラジロミツバツツジ
Rhododendron osuzuyamense：
ツツジ科：宮崎

サカイツツジ
Rhododendron parvifolium：ツツジ科：
(北海道)

ツクシアケボノツツジ
Rhododendron pentaphyllum var. villosum : ツツジ科 : 熊本、宮崎

ケラマツツジ
Rhododendron scabrum : ツツジ科 : 鹿児島、沖縄

ヤクシマヤマツツジ
Rhododendron yakuinsulare : ツツジ科 : (鹿児島)

ハコネコメツツジ
Tsusiophyllum tanakae : ツツジ科 : 群馬、神奈川、山梨、長野、静岡、(埼玉、東京)

ヒメツルコケモモ
Vaccinium microcarpum : ツツジ科 : 北海道、群馬、長野、(青森、福島)

ナガボナツハゼ
Vaccinium sieboldii : ツツジ科 : 静岡、愛知

ヒダカイワザクラ
Primula hidakana : サクラソウ科 : 北海道

コイワザクラ
Primula reinii : サクラソウ科 : 群馬、神奈川、山梨、長野、静岡、(東京)

クモイコザクラ
Primula reinii var. kitadakensis : サクラソウ科 : 山梨、長野、(埼玉、静岡)

サクラソウ
Primula sieboldii : サクラソウ科 : 北海道、青森、岩手、宮城、福島、栃木、群馬、埼玉、山梨、長野、岐阜、静岡、鳥取、岡山、広島、熊本、大分、宮崎、鹿児島、(山形、茨城、東京、神奈川、石川、福井、三重、滋賀、兵庫、和歌山、島根、岡)

ソラチコザクラ
Primula sorachiana : サクラソウ科 : 北海道

テシオコザクラ
Primula takedana : サクラソウ科 : 北海道

シナノコザクラ
Primula tosaensis var. brachycarpa : サクラソウ科 : 長野、静岡

ハイハマボッス
Samolus parviflorus : サクラソウ科 : 北海道、青森、宮城、秋田、山形、千葉、新潟、長野、山口、(岩手、福井、滋賀、兵庫)

ハマサジ
Limonium tetragonum : イソマツ科 : 宮城、福島、愛知、大阪、兵庫、和歌山、岡山、広島、山口、徳島、香川、愛媛、高

知、福岡、佐賀、長崎、熊本、大分、宮崎、(富山、静岡、三重、鹿児島)

イソマツ
Limonium wrightii : イソマツ科 : 東京、鹿児島、沖縄

キバナイソマツ
Limonium wrightii var. luteum : イソマツ科 : 鹿児島

コバノアカテツ
Planchonella obovata var. dubia : アカテツ科 : (東京、沖縄)

ヤワラケガキ
Diospyros eriantha : カキノキ科 : (沖縄)

ムニンクロキ
Symplocos boninensis : ハイノキ科 : (東京)

ミヤマシロバイ
Symplocos confusa : ハイノキ科 : 鹿児島、沖縄

ヒトツバタゴ
Chionanthus retusus : モクセイ科 : 長野、岐阜、愛知、長崎

オキナワソケイ
Jasminum superfluum : モクセイ科 : 鹿児島、沖縄

トゲイボタ
Ligustrum tamakii : モクセイ科 : (沖縄)

オガサワラモクレイシ
Geniostoma glabra : マチン科 : 東京

コヒナリンドウ
Gentiana aquatica var. laeviuscula : リンドウ科 : 長野、(山梨、静岡)

イイデリンドウ
Gentiana nipponica var. robusta : リンドウ科 : 山形、福島、(新潟)

リュウキュウコケリンドウ
Gentiana squarrosa var. liukiuensis : リンドウ科 : 鹿児島

イヌセンブリ
Swertia diluta var. tosaensis : リンドウ科 : 岩手、宮城、秋田、福島、栃木、千葉、神奈川、新潟、静岡、愛知、滋賀、京都、大阪、兵庫、和歌山、岡山、広島、山口、徳島、香川、高知、福岡、佐賀、長崎、熊本、大分、宮崎、鹿児島、(山形、茨城、群馬、埼玉、東京、富山、石川、長野、三重、奈良、愛媛)

ムラサキセンブリ
Swertia pseudochinensis : リンドウ科 : 栃木、千葉、東京、神奈川、福井、山梨、長野、静岡、岡山、和歌山、岡山、広島、山口、香川、高知、福岡、佐賀、長崎、熊本、大分、宮崎、(青森、岩手、福島、群馬、大阪、奈良、鹿児島)

ヒメシロアサザ
Nymphoides coreana : ミツガシワ科 : 宮城、栃木、埼玉、静岡、愛知、和歌山、岡山、長崎、大分、宮崎、沖縄、(岩手、群馬、三重、奈良、徳島、香川、福岡)

ガガブタ
Nymphoides indica : ミツガシワ科 : 宮城、茨城、千葉、新潟、石川、岐阜、静岡、愛知、滋賀、兵庫、和歌山、岡山、広島、徳島、香川、高知、福岡、熊本、大分、宮崎、(秋田、山形、福島、栃木、群馬、神奈川、富山、福井、三重、京都、大阪、奈良、鳥取、島根、愛媛、鹿児島)

アサザ
Nymphoides peltata : ミツガシワ科 : 青森、宮城、秋田、福島、茨城、埼玉、千葉、長野、静岡、愛知、滋賀、大阪、兵庫、和歌山、岡山、山口、徳島、香川、佐賀、大分、(岩手、山形、栃木、群馬、神奈川、新潟、富山、石川、福井、三重、京都、奈良、鳥取、島根、愛媛、高知、福岡、長崎、熊本、宮崎)

チョウジソウ
Amsonia elliptica : キョウチクトウ科 : 北海道、青森、宮城、秋田、山形、福島、栃木、埼玉、新潟、石川、福井、静岡、兵庫、和歌山、山口、徳島、福岡、大分、宮崎、(岩手、茨城、群馬、神奈川、富山、岐阜、三重、滋賀、大阪、奈良、島根、岡山、広島)

イシダテクサタチバナ
Cynanchum calcareum : ガガイモ科 : 徳島、高知

クサナギオゴケ
Cynanchum katoi : ガガイモ科 : 千葉、岐阜、静岡、愛知、兵庫、徳島、高知、(山梨)

スズサイコ
Cynanchum paniculatum : ガガイモ科 : 北海道、青森、岩手、宮城、秋田、山形、福島、栃木、群馬、千葉、東京、神奈川、新潟、石川、福井、山梨、長野、岐阜、静岡、愛知、滋賀、京都、大阪、兵庫、奈良、和歌山、鳥取、岡山、広島、山口、徳島、香川、高知、福岡、佐賀、長崎、熊本、大分、宮崎、鹿児島、(茨城、埼玉、富山)

エゾキヌタソウ
Galium boreale var. kamtschaticum : アカネ科 : 北海道

植物	準絶滅危惧
	NT

マツバコケシダ コケシノブ科
ヤンバルフモトシダ

コバノイシカグマ科
スキヤクジャク
ミズワラビ(ホウライシダ)科
カワリミフサシダ イノモトソウ科
キリシマイワヘゴ、イナデンダ
オシダ科
エゾミヤマヤナギ、ミヤマヤチヤナギ
ヤナギ科
サクラバハンノキ カバノキ科
ヤエヤマラセイタソウ イラクサ科
ニンドウバノヤドリギ ヤドリギ科
ユワンツチトリモチ ツチトリモチ科
ミスミソウ s.l. キンポウゲ科
オモロカンアオイ、コシノカンアオイ、トカラカンアオイ ウマノスズクサ科
ハコネオトギリ オトギリソウ科
チドリケマン、ナガミノツルキケマン、リシリヒナゲシ ケシ科
コイヌガラシ アブラナ科
アテツマンサク マンサク科
ツメレンゲ、サツママンネングサ
ベンケイソウ科
キバナハナネコノメ、ムカゴネコノメ、ヤエヤマヒメウツギ ユキノシタ科
ヤクシマシロバナヘビイチゴ、リシリトウウチソウ バラ科
ボウコツルマメ、ワニグチモダマ
マメ科
ヤクシマフウロ フウロソウ科
コウシュンカズラ キントラノオ科
ナガバコバンモチ ホルトノキ科
シャクナンガンピ ジンチョウゲ科
ヤクシマグミ グミ科
タカネスミレ スミレ科
マルヤマシュウカイドウ
シュウカイドウ科
ヤクシマサルスベリ ミソハギ科
マヤブシギ ハマザクロ科
タチモ アリノトウグサ科
リュウキュウハナイカダ ミズキ科
ムニンハマウド、ツシマノダケ セリ科
シマイワウチワ イワウメ科
オオウメガサソウ イチヤクソウ科
ヤクシマミツバツツジ ツツジ科
シマギンレイカ サクラソウ科
ヤエヤマコクタン カキノキ科
コニシハイノキ ハイノキ科
ヤマトレンギョウ モクセイ科
ヨコヤマリンドウ、チシマリンドウ、シロウマリンドウ、ハナヤマツルリンドウ、ヤクシマツルリンドウ リンドウ科
ホソバヤロード キョウチクトウ科
ケナシツルモウリンカ ガガイモ科
シマザクラ、ニコゲルリミノキ、シチョウゲ、オオイナモリ アカネ科
マルバアサガオカラクサ ヒルガオ科
ヤエヤマハマゴウ クマツヅラ科
タチカランソウ、コチトウバナ、ミゾコウジュ、ヤクシマシソバツナミ、ムニンタツナミソウ シソ科
カワヂシャ ゴマノハグサ科
チョウジガマズミ スイカズラ科
オオナガバハグマ、ヒロハヤマヨモギ、ヒメカタビラコ、ヤマザトタンポポ、オダサムタンポポ キク科
アギナシ オモダカ科
アマミラッキョウ、ヤクシマシライトソウ、ヒメカラカ、タカクマホトトギス ユリ科
ヒメシャガ アヤメ科
タカネイ、クモマスズメノヒエ、コゴメヌカボシ イグサ科
スイシャホシクサ ホシクサ科
ヒメコヌカグサ、タイワンアシカキ、オガサワラススキ イネ科
オガサワラビロウ、ヤエヤマヤシ ヤシ科
ミクリ、ナガエミクリ ミクリ科
タカネヤガミスゲ、シマタヌキラン、チャイロスゲ、オキナワヒメナキリ、サコスゲ、ヒロハオゼヌマスゲ
カヤツリグサ科
シラン、トクサラン、ユウレイラン、シラヒゲムヨウラン、オキナワムヨウラン、シマササバラン、ボウラン、ヤクシマトンボ、イシガキキヌラン ラン科

植物	情報不足
	DD

ツルカタヒバ、コケカタヒバ
イワヒバ科
ヤチスギナ、フサスギナ トクサ科
ミヤマハナワラビ ハナヤスリ科
ムニンコケシダ、ムニンホラゴケ
コケシノブ科
ムニンエダウチホングウシダ
ホングウシダ科
イワホウライシダ、ホソバイワガネソウ
ミズワラビ(ホウライシダ)科
カワラタハチジョウシダ
イノモトソウ科
ヤマドリトラノオ、ナンカイシダ
チャセンシダ科
オガサワラツルキジノオ
ツルキジノオ科
ムニンベニシダ、ヒイラギデンダ、ナガバウスバシダ オシダ科
オオホシダ ヒメシダ科

ヘイケイヌワラビ、シマクジャク、ムニンミドリシダ メシダ(イワデンダ)科
ホソバクリハラン、オキノクリハラン、ムニンサジラン、シナノキシノブ、ハハジマヌカボシ ウラボシ科
ヒロハヒメウラボシ ヒメウラボシ科
アズサバラモミ マツ科
シマムロ ヒノキ科
サルクラハンノキ、アポイカンバ
カバノキ科
オオトキワイヌビワ クワ科
クニガミサンショウヅル、オトギリマオ、ヤエヤマカテンソウ イラクサ科
タイワンヤマモガシ ヤマモガシ科
ヒメイワタデ、リュウキュウタデ、カラフトノダイオウ タデ科
アオモリミミナグサ、コバノミミナグサ、エゾセンノウ、ヒナワチガイソウ、エゾヤママンテマ、カラフトマンテマ、アポイマンテマ、オオハコベ
ナデシコ科
インドヒモカズラ ヒユ科
オオバナオオガタノキ モクレン科
ケスナヅル、イトスナヅル、ムニンヤブニッケイ、コブガシ、タブガシ
クスノキ科
ヒダカトリカブト、セイヤブシ、コウライブシ、ハクバブシ、キタザワブシ、ミョウコウトリカブト、キタミフクジュソウ、コウヤハンショウヅル、コウヤシロカネソウ、リュウキュウヒキノカサ、エゾキンポウゲ、ダイセンカラマツ、オオミヤマカラマツ、ニオイカラマツ
キンポウゲ科
ホウライツヅラフジ ツヅラフジ科
コウヤカンアオイ、ムラクモアオイ、アマギカンアオイ、キナンカンアオイ、スエヒロアオイ ウマノスズクサ科
ムニンヒサカキ ツバキ科
トガクシナズナ、ミギワガラシ
アブラナ科
アポイミセバヤ、オオチッパベンケイ、ムラサキベンケイソウ、ツガルミセバヤ、ハママンネングサ、オオメノマンネングサ ベンケイソウ科
オオチダケサシ、ミカワショウマ、オキナワヒメウツギ、クロミノハリスグリ、トカチスグリ、キヨシソウ
ユキノシタ科
コヤスノキ、オキナワトベラ トベラ科
エゾサンザシ、オオバサンザシ、ツクシカイドウ、タチテンノウメ、チシマイチゴ、ツクシアキツルイチゴ、チチジマイチゴ、タイワンウラジロイチゴ バラ科

ヤエヤマネムノキ、カラフトモメンヅ
ル、トカチオウギ、ソラハギ、ヤエヤマ
ハギカズラ、チョウセンニワフジ、シロ
ヤマハギ、チョウセンキバギ、サツマハ
ギ、アイラトビカズラ、マシケゲンゲ、
ヒメツルアズキ　マメ科
テリハニシキソウ、アカハダコバンノキ
トウダイグサ科
アツバショウテツ、シロテツ、オオバシロ
テツ　ミカン科
ホザキサルノオ、ササキカズラ
キントラノオ科
シンチクヒメハギ、リュウキュウヒメ
ハギ、ヒナノキンチャク　ヒメハギ科
タイシャクイタヤ　カエデ科
サクノキ　アワブキ (アオカズラ)科
アツバシマモチ　モチノキ科
ヒメマサキ、リュウキュウツルマサキ
ニシキギ科
クサミズキ　クロタキカズラ科
シマホルトノキ　ホルトノキ科
ヒシバウオトリギ、チュウゴクボダイ
ジュ、ケナシハテルマカズラ
シナノキ科
テリハハマボウ　アオイ科
フウセンアカメガシワ　アオギリ科
オオシマガンピ　ジンチョウゲ科
タンゴグミ、カツラギグミ　グミ科
コバノクスドイゲ　イイギリ科
シマジリスミレ、テリハオリヅルスミ
レ、オキナワスミレ　スミレ科
ハザクラキブシ　キブシ科
ムニンカラスウリ、イシガキカラスウリ
ウリ科
ホザキキカシグサ　ミソハギ科
ミヤマハシカンボク、イオウノボタン
ノボタン科
ヤマニタデ　アカバナ科
カワゼンゴ　セリ科
タカクマミツバツツジ、ムニンシャシ
ャンボ、アクシバモドキ　ツツジ科
シナタチバナ、シマタイミンタチバナ
ヤブコウジ科
ヘツカコナスビ、ミチノクコザクラ、レ
ブンコザクラ、チチブイワザクラ
サクラソウ科
オバケエゴノキ　エゴノキ科
ムニンネズミモチ、オオモクセイ、ナン
ゴクモクセイ　モクセイ科
リュウキュウホウライカズラ　マチン科
オノエリンドウ、ヒメセンブリ
リンドウ科
ゴムカズラ、シマソケイ
キョウチクトウ科

サツマビャクゼン、マルバノフナバラ
ソウ、ヒメイヨカズラ、ホソバノロクオ
ンソウ、アキノウサタチバナ、アマミイ
ケマ、ホウライアオカズラ、タイワンキ
ジョラン　ガガイモ科
ヤクシマヤマグラ、ビンゴムグラ、ヤ
ツガタケムグラ、ヤエヤマハシカグサ、
コバンムグラ、ヒロハケニオイグサ、コ
ハナガサノキ、オオシラタマカズラ、ハ
リザクロ、シマギョクシンカ　アカネ科
ヒメノアサガオ　ヒルガオ科
トゲミイヌチャ、シマスナビキソウ、
ハイルリソウ　ムラサキ科
キタダケオドリコソウ、ヒメキセワタ、
オチフジ、オオヤマジソ、タシロタツナ
ミソウ、アツバツナミソウ、テイネニ
ガクサ、イヌニガクサ　シソ科
アオホオズキ、セイバンナスビ　ナス科
マルバコゴメグサ、マツラコゴメグサ、
コケコゴメグサ、エゾノダッタンコゴ
メグサ、シソバウリクサ、ヒメクチバシ
グサ、ヒメサギゴケ、ベニシオガマ、ホ
ザキシオガマ、キタダケトラノオ、ハマ
トラノオ、ゲンジバナ　ゴマノハグサ科
ツシマヒョウタンボク、ヒメスイカズ
ラ、シマガマズミ　スイカズラ科
オオキンレイカ　オミナエシ科
トウシャジン　キキョウ科
ヤクシマウスユキソウ、オオウサギギ
ク、シコタンヨモギ、イズカニコウモリ、
オガサワラアザミ、アポイアザミ、サド
アザミ、トヨシマアザミ、チシマコハマ
ギク、ピレオギク、ドロニガナ、ミヤコ
ジシバリ、カワラウスユキソウ、ヒメウ
スユキソウ、トナカイアザミ、ヒナヒゴ
タイ、キバナウリンカ、タンバヤブレ
ガサ、エゾヨモギギク、イワヤクシソウ
キク科
ヒメウミヒルモ、ウミヒルモ
トチカガミ科
オオアマモ、スゲアマモ、タチアマモ、
コアマモ　アマモ科
スズフリホンゴウソウ　ホンゴウソウ科
イトラッキョウ、イズモコバイモ、コウ
ライワニグチソウ、ドウモンワニグチソ
ウ、アラガタオオサンキライ、キイジョ
ウロウホトトギス、カワユエンレイソウ
ユリ科
ナスヒオウギアヤメ　アヤメ科
ミドリシャクジョウ
ヒナノシャクジョウ科
ミヤマイ、オキナワイ、エゾノミクリゼ
キショウ、ホロムイコウガイ、クロコウ
ガイゼキショウ、ミヤマゼキショウ、セ

イタカヌカボシソウ、チシマスズメノヒ
エ　イグサ科
ナンゴクヤブミョウガ　ツユクサ科
アマノホシクサ、ユキイヌノヒゲ、ヤマ
トホシクサ、クシロホシクサ、オキナワ
ホシクサ、エゾホシクサ、ナスノクロイ
ヌノヒゲ、ハライヌノヒゲ、シロエゾホ
シクサ、エゾイヌノヒゲ、カラフトホシ
クサ、コケヌマイヌノヒゲ、イヌノヒゲ
モドキ、ガリメキイヌノヒゲ、イズノシ
マホシクサ、オクトネホシクサ
ホシクサ科
オニカモジ、タイシャクカモジ、ユキク
ラヌカボ、マツバシバ、オオマツバシバ、
ヒナヨシ、オオミネヒナノガリヤス、イ
リオモテガヤ、オニコメススキ、シマギ
ョウギシバ、イブキトボシガラ、タカネ
ソモソモ、コツブチゴザサ、ケナシハイ
チゴザサ、ヒメハイチゴザサ、ヒメカモ
ノハシ、シマカモノハシ、イネガヤ、コ
ゴメビエ、タカネタチイチゴツナギ、キ
タダケイチゴツナギ　タニイチゴツナギ、
オオバヤダケ、コモロコシガヤ、ヒメネ
ズミノオ、ヒメウシノシッペイ、ホソバ
ドジョウツナギ、ネズミシバ　イネ科
ヒメソルアダン　タコノキ科
アポイタヌキラン、オハグロスゲ、カヤ
ツリスゲ、タデシナヒメスゲ、ハナビス
ゲ、ヒメアゼスゲ、ゲンカイモエギスゲ、
ネムロスゲ、ヒルゼンスゲ、ヤリスゲ、
ムセンスゲ、アカンスゲ、ノルゲスゲ、チ
ャボカワズスゲ、ウスイロスゲ、キビノ
ミノボロスゲ、ヒロハイッポンスゲ、ア
カスゲ、ウシオスゲ、ヌマスゲ、コヌマ
スゲ、マツカゼスゲ、アシボソスゲ、シ
コタンスゲ、ミヤケスゲ、サヤスゲ、イ
ヌノゲヤ、タチガヤツリ、ホウキガヤツ
リ、ニイガタガヤツリ、ホクトガヤツリ、
トサノハマスゲ、チシママツバイ、クロ
ミノハリイ、カヤツリマツバイ、オキナ
ワハリイ、カドハリイ、オキナワイヌシ
カクイ、ウナツキテンツキ、イシガキイ
テンツキ、ハタケテンツキ、ヒゲハリ
スゲ、シマイガクサ、オオサンカクイ、
ヒメワタスゲ、ヒメマツカサススキ、イ
ヌフトイ、ツクシアブラガヤ
カヤツリグサ科
チクリンカ、ツクシハナミョウガ、ハダ
カゲットウ　ショウガ科
アカボシツルラン、ムニンシュスラン、
ヒメミズトンボ、オゼノサワトンボ、シ
ロスジカゲロウラン、オオカゲロウラ
ン、ムニンボウラン、ムニンキヌラン、
ヤンバルキヌラン　ラン科

(維管束植物以外)

注1)「種」のレベル(亜種・変種等を含む)で掲載。

注2) 準絶滅危惧(NT)と情報不足(DD)は分類群ごとに種名又は学名を記載。

蘚苔類

植物	絶滅危惧1類 CR+EN

ノマフデノホゴケ
Acroporium stramineum (Reinw. et Hornsch.) Fl. (= A. suzukii Sak.) (蘚類):九州、沖縄

ニカゲノカヅラモドキ
Aerobryopsis parisii (Card.) Broth. (蘚類):四国、沖縄

和名なし
Aerobryum speciosum (Dozy et Molk.) Dozy et Molk. (蘚類):沖縄

ガッサンクロゴケ
Andreaea nivalis Hook. (蘚類):北海道、本州

和名なし
Anomobryum yasudae Broth. (蘚類):本州、四国

アオシマヒメシワゴケ
Aulacopilum trichophyllum Aongstr. ex C. Muell. (蘚類):本州、九州

キヌシッポゴケモドキ
Brachydontium trichodes (Web.) Milde (蘚類):北海道、本州

サオヒメゴケ
Callicostella papillata (Mont.) Mitt. (蘚類):沖縄

ハセガワカタシロゴケ
Calymperes fasciculatum Dozy et Molk. (= C. hasegawae (Tak. et Iwats.) Iwats.) (蘚類):四国、九州

ヒロハコモチイトゴケ
Clastobryella tenella Fl. (蘚類):四国、九州

オオタマコモチイトゴケ
Clastobryopsis robusta (Broth.) Fl. (= Aptychella robusta (Broth.) Fl.) (蘚類):本州、九州

イトヒバゴケ
Cryphaea obovatocarpa Okam. (蘚類):本州、四国

コキジノオゴケ
Cyathophorella hookeriana (Griff.) Fl. (蘚類):本州、四国、九州、沖縄

キジノオゴケ
Cyathophorella tonkinensis (Broth. et Par.) Broth. (蘚類):本州、四国、九州、沖縄

シノブチョウチンゴケ
Cyrtomnium hymenophylloides (Hueb.) Kop. (蘚類):北海道、本州

フチナシクジャクゴケ
Dendrocyathophorum paradoxum (Broth.) Dix. (蘚類):本州、四国、九州

コシノヤバネゴケ
Dichelyma japonicum Card. (蘚類):北海道、本州

コバノイクビゴケ
Diphyscium perminutum Tak. (蘚類):本州、四国、九州

スズキイクビゴケ
Diphyscium suzukii Iwats. (蘚類):本州、四国

ミギワイクビゴケ
Diphysium unipapillosum Deguchi (蘚類):四国

オクヤマツガゴケ
Distichophyllum carinatum Dix. et Nicols. (蘚類):本州

セイタカヤリカツギ
Encalypta procera Bruch (= 日本産のE. streptocarpa Hedw.) (蘚類):本州、四国

ミヤマヤリカツギ
Encalypta vulgaris var. rhabdocarpa (Schwaegr.) Lawton (蘚類):本州

ダンダンゴケ
Eucladium verticillatum (Brid.) B.S.G. (蘚類):北海道

シワナシチビイタチゴケ
Felipponea esquirolii (Ther.) Akiyama (蘚類):九州

ジョウレンホウオウゴケ
Fissidens geppii Fl. (蘚類):本州、四国、九州

ヒロハシノブイトゴケ
Floribundaria aurea ssp. nipponica (Nog.) Nog. (蘚類):本州、四国、九州

クロカワゴケ
Fontinalis antipyretica Hedw. (蘚類):北海道、本州

カワゴケ
Fontinalis hypnoides C.J.Hartm. (蘚類):北海道、本州

シバゴケ
Garckea flexuosa (Griff.) Marg. et Nork. (蘚類):本州、四国、九州

カクレゴケ
Garovaglia elegans (Dozy et Molk.) Hampe ex Bosch et Lac. (蘚類):九州、沖縄

サジバラッコゴケ
Gollania japonica (Card.) Ando et Higuchi (蘚類):北海道、本州

フガゴケ
Gymnostomiella longinervis Broth. (蘚類):本州、九州、沖縄

カラフトシノブゴケ
Helodium sachalinense (Lindb.) Broth. (蘚類):北海道、本州

ヒメタチヒラゴケ
Homaliadelphus sharpii var. rotundatus (Nog.) Iwats. (蘚類):本州、四国、九州

ヒメハゴロモゴケ
Homaliodendron exiguum (Bosch et Lac.) Fl. (蘚類):本州、四国、九州、沖縄

キサゴゴケ
Hypnodontopsis apiculata Iwats. et Nog. (蘚類):本州、九州

和名なし
Hypnum vaucheri Lesq. (蘚類):本州

ヒナクジャクゴケ
Hypopterygium tenellum C. Muell. (蘚類):本州、四国、九州、沖縄、小笠原諸島

コモチイトゴケ
Isopterygium propaguliferum Toy. (蘚類):四国、九州

ツヤダシタカネイタチゴケ
Leucodon alpinus Akiyama (蘚類):北海道、本州

コマノイタチゴケ
Leucodon coreensis Card. (蘚類):北海道、本州、四国

オオヤマトイタチゴケ
Leucodon giganteus Nog. (蘚類):四国

和名なし
Macromitrium holomitrioides Nog. (蘚類):九州

コシノシンジゴケ
Mielichhoferia sasaokae Broth. (蘚類):本州

カイガラゴケ
Myurella julacea (Schwaegr.) B.S.G. (蘚類):北海道、本州、四国

レイシゴケ
Myurella sibirica (C.Muell.) Reim. (蘚類):北海道、本州、九州

トガリカイガラゴケ
Myurella tenerrima (Brid.) Lindb. (蘚類):本州

トサヒラゴケ
Neckeropsis obtusata (Mont.) Fl. in

Broth. (蘚類):本州、四国、九州、沖縄、小笠原諸島

イヌコクサゴケ
Neobarbella comes (Griff.) Nog. (= incl. var. pilifera (Broth. et Yas.) Nog.) (蘚類):本州

ヤクシマナワゴケ
Oedicladium rufescens var. yakushimense (Sak.) Iwats. (蘚類):本州、九州

イシヅチゴケ
Oedipodium griffithianum (Dicks.) Schwaegr. (蘚類):北海道、本州、四国

タチチョウチンゴケ
Orthomnion dilatatum (Mitt.) Chen (蘚類):本州、四国、九州

タチチョウチンゴケモドキ
Orthomnion loheri Broth. (蘚類):四国、九州

タチミツヤゴケ
Orthothecium rufescens (Brid.) B.S.G. (蘚類):北海道、本州

カトウゴケ
Palisadula katoi (Broth.) Iwats. (蘚類):本州、四国、九州

ハシボソゴケ
Papillidiopsis macrosticta (Broth. et Par.) Buck and Tan (= Rhaphidostichum macrostictum (Broth. et Par.) Broth.) (蘚類):本州、九州、沖縄

キブリハネゴケ
Pinnatella makinoi (Broth.) Broth. (蘚類):本州、四国、九州

テツカチョウチンゴケ
Plagiomnium tezukae (Sak.) Kop. (蘚類):本州

オオサナダゴケ
Plagiothecium neckeroideum B.S.G. (蘚類):北海道、本州、四国

トサノタスキゴケ
Pseudobarbella laosiensis (Broth. et Par.) Nog. (蘚類):本州、四国、九州、沖縄

キブネゴケ
Rhachithecium nipponicum (Toy.) Wijk et Marg. (蘚類):本州

ホソバハシボソゴケ
Rhaphidostichum longicuspidatum Seki (蘚類):沖縄

オオミツヤゴケ
Sakuraia concophylla (Card.) Nog. (蘚類):本州

アオモリカギハイゴケ
Okamuraea aomoriensis (Par.) Kanda (蘚類):本州

ヒカリゴケ
Schistostega pennata (Hedw.) Web. et Mohr (蘚類):北海道、本州

サンカクキヌシッポゴケ
Seligeria austriaca Schauer (蘚類):本州、四国、九州

ハナシキヌシッポゴケ
Seligeria donniana (Sm.) C.Muell. (蘚類):本州

コキヌシッポゴケ
Seligeria pusilla (Hedw.) B.S.G. (蘚類):北海道、本州、四国、九州

オオミズゴケ
Sphagnum palustre L. (蘚類):北海道、本州、四国、九州

フトハイゴケ
Stereodontopsis pseudorevoluta (Reim.) Ando (蘚類):四国、九州

シダレウニゴケ
Symphyodon perrottetii Mont. (蘚類):本州、四国、九州、沖縄

和名なし
Syntrichia gemmascens (Chen) Zand (= Desmatodon gemmascens Chen) (蘚類):本州、四国

ミヤマコネジレゴケ
Syntrichia sinensis (C. Muell.) Ochyra (= Tortula sinensis (C.Muell.) Broth. ex Levier) (蘚類):本州、四国

イサワゴケ
Syrrhopodon tosaensis Card. (蘚類):本州、四国、九州、沖縄

ヤクシマアミゴケ
Syrrhopodon yakushimensis Tak. et Iwats. (蘚類):九州

タイワントラノオゴケ
Taiwanobryum speciosum Nog. (蘚類):本州、四国、九州

ナンジャモンジャゴケ
Takakia lepidozyoides Hatt. et Inoue (蘚類):北海道、本州

キャラハゴケモドキ
Taxiphyllosis iwatsukii Higuchi et Deguchi (蘚類):本州、四国

コウライイチイゴケ
Taxiphyllum alternans (Card.) Iwats. (蘚類):本州、四国、九州

タイワンユリゴケ
Tayloria indica Mitt. (蘚類):九州

コアブラゴケ
Thamniopsis utacamundiana (Mont.) Buck (= Hookeriopsis utacamundiana (Mont.) Broth.) (蘚類):九州

クマノゴケ
Theriotia lorifolia Card. (蘚類):本州、四国、九州

ミヤマクサスギゴケ
Timmia megapolitana Hedw. (蘚類):北海道、本州

シマオバナゴケ
Trematodon semitortidens Sak. (蘚類):本州、九州

リュウキュウナガハシゴケ
Trichosteleum boschii (Dozy et Molk.) Jaeg. (= Rhaphidostichum boschii ssp. thelidictyon (Sull. et Lesq.) Seki) (蘚類):四国、九州

チチブイチョウゴケ
Acrobolbus ciliatus (Mitt.) Schiffn. (苔類):秩父山地、岐阜県、紀伊半島、高知県、愛知県、熊本県、宮崎県、神奈川

ヒメトロイブゴケ
Apotreubia nana (Hatt. et Inoue) Hatt. e Mizut. (苔類):長野県、岩手県、秩父山地

ドクダミサイハイゴケ
Asterella odora Hatt. (苔類):東京都、埼玉県秩父山地

ミヤマミズゼニゴケ
Calycularia crispula Mitt. (苔類):青森県、岩手県、秩父山地、紀伊半島、宮崎県

ヨウジョウゴケ
Cololejeunea goebelii (Schiffn.) Schiffn. (苔類):本州千葉県以西

ナガバムシトリゴケ
Colura tenuicornis (Evans) Steph. (苔類):鹿児島県屋久島、開聞岳、高知県、和歌山県

ヒカリゼニゴケ
Cyathodium smaragdinum Schiffn. (苔類):熊本県

サガリヤスデゴケ
Frullania trichodes Mitt. (苔類):宮崎県、高知県

ケナシオヤコゴケ
Gottschea nuda (Horik.) Grolle et Zijlstra (苔類):鹿児島県奄美大島、徳之島

キレハコマチゴケ
Haplomitrium hookeri (Sm.) Nees (苔類):富山県、長野県

ヤクシマスギバゴケ
Hattoria yakushimensis (Horik.) Schust. (苔類):鹿児島県屋久島、大隅半島、三重県

イイシバヤバネゴケ
Iwatsukia jishibae (Steph.) N. Kitag. (苔類):鹿児島県屋久島、近畿地方、長野県

マクシマスギバゴケ
.epicolea Yakushimensis (Hatt.) Hatt.
苔類）：鹿児島県屋久島

コビゴケ
.eptolejeunea elliptica (Lehm. et
.indenb.) Schiffn. (苔類)：本州福島県以
ち

イギイチョウゴケ
.ophozia igiana Hatt. (苔類)：徳島県、高
知県、岡山県、長野県

イワゼニゴケ
Mannia triandra (Scop.) Grolle (苔類)：
北海道、岩手県

ケハネゴケモドキ
Marsupidium knightii Mitt. (苔類)：
鹿児島県屋久島、奄美大島

ハットリヤスデゴケ
Neohattoria herzogii (Hatt.) Kamim.
苔類）：北海道、岩手県、秩父山地、長野
県

サトミヨツデゴケ
Pseudolepicolea trolii (Herz.) Grolle et
Ando (苔類)：富山県黒部渓谷

ミミケビラゴケ
Radula chinenenis Steph. (苔類)：
岡山県、石川県、岐阜県

ウキゴケ
Riccia fluitans L. (苔類)：北海道、本州全
土、四国、九州、沖縄

イチョウウキゴケ
Ricciocarpos natans (L.) Corda (苔類)：
日本各地

ミジンコゴケ
Zoopsis liukiuensis Horik. (苔類)：
沖縄県、鹿児島県屋久島、大隅半島、東
京都小笠原諸島

キノボリツノゴケ
Dendroceros japonicus Steph.
(ツノゴケ類)：千葉県以西、四国、九州

| 植物 | 絶滅危惧2類 |
| | VU |

トガリバギボウシゴケ
Anomodon acutifolius Mitt.
(蘚類)：本州

フジサンギンゴケモドキ
Aongstroemia julacea (Hook.) Mitt.
(蘚類)：本州

和名なし
Aongstroemia orientalis Mitt. (蘚類)：
本州

ウワバミゴケ
Breutelia arundinifolia (Duby) Fl. (蘚類)：
九州

和名なし
Calymperes lonchophyllum Schwaegr.
(蘚類)：小笠原諸島、沖縄

和名なし
Calyptothecium urvilleanum (C. Muell.)
Broth. (蘚類)：沖縄

マユハケゴケ
Campylopus fragilis (Brid.) B.S.G.
(蘚類)：本州、四国

ヒロスジツリバリゴケ
Campylopus gracilis (Mitt.) Jaeg. (= C.
schwarzii Schimp.) (蘚類)：本州、九州

ミスジヤバネゴケ
Clastobryum glabrescens (Iwats.) Tan
et Iwats. (= Tristichella glabrescens
Iwats.) (蘚類)：九州

和名なし
Desmatodon latifolius (Hedw.) Brid.
(蘚類)：本州

アカネジクチゴケ
Didymodon asperifolius (Mitt.) Crum,
Steere et Anderson (蘚類)：本州

マルバツガゴケ
Distichophyllum obtusifolium Ther.
(蘚類)：本州、四国

フチナシツガゴケ
Distichophyllum osterwardii Fl. (蘚類)：
沖縄

シロウマヤリカツギ
Encalypta alpina Sm. (蘚類)：本州

ヤクシマホウオウゴケ
Fissidens obscurus Mitt. (蘚類)：九州

シライワスズゴケ
Forsstroemia noguchii Stark (蘚類)：
本州、四国

和名なし
Glossadelphus yakoushimae (Card.)
Nog. (蘚類)：九州、沖縄

オオカギイトゴケ
Gollania splendens (Ihs.) Nog. (蘚類)：
本州

ミギワギボウシゴケ
Grimmia mollis Bruch et Schim. in
B.S.G. (蘚類)：本州

ムチエダイトゴケ
Haplohymenium flagelliforme Saviz-
Ljubitskaya (蘚類)：本州、九州

ホウライハゴロモゴケ
Homaliodendron microdendron (Mont.)
Fl. (蘚類)：沖縄

キダチゴケ
Hypnodendron vitiense Mitt. (蘚類)：
沖縄

オニシメリゴケ

Leptodictyum mizushimae (Sak.) Kanda
(蘚類)：北海道、本州

ジャワシラガゴケ
Leucobryum javense (Brid.) Mitt.
(蘚類)：沖縄

ヨコグライタチゴケ
Leucodon sohayakiensis Akiyama
(蘚類)：本州、四国、九州

ニセハプタエゴケ
Leucophanes octoblepharioides Brid.
(蘚類)：沖縄

クロコゴケ
Luisierella barbula (Schwaegr.) Steere
(蘚類)：本州、四国

ホソヒモゴケ
Meteorium papillarioides Nog. (蘚類)：
九州

和名なし
Molendoa hornschuchiana (Hook.)
Lindb. ex Limpr. (蘚類)：本州

カタナワゴケ
Oedicladium fragile Card. (蘚類)：九州、
沖縄

ヤマゴケ
Oreas martiana (Hoppe et Hornsch. ex
Hornsch.) Brid. (蘚類)：本州

和名なし
Orthotrichum laevigatum var.
japonicum (Iwats.) Lewinsky (= O.
macounii ssp. japonicum Iwats.) (蘚類)：
本州

ヌマチゴケ
Paludella squarrosa (Hedw.) Brid.
(蘚類)：北海道

モミノキゴケ
Pinnatella anacamptolepis (C. Muell.)
Broth. (= Porotrichum gracilescens
Nog.) (蘚類)：四国、九州、沖縄

ヒメハミズゴケ
Pogonatum camusii (Ther.) Touw
(蘚類)：沖縄

和名なし
Polytrichum juniperinum ssp. strictum
(Brid.) Nyl. et Sael. (蘚類)：本州

オニゴケ
Pseudospiridentopsis horrida (Card.) Fl.
(蘚類)：九州

和名なし
Radulina elegantissima (Fl.) Buck et Tan
(= Trichosteleum elegantissimurn Fl.)
(蘚類)：九州

カサゴケモドキ
Rhodobryum ontariense (Kindb.) Kindb.
(蘚類)：北海道、本州、四国、九州

キヌシッポゴケ
Seligeria recurvata (Hedw.) Bruch et Schimp. in B. S. G. (蘚類)：本州、九州
マルバユリゴケ
Tayloria hornschuchii (Grev. et Arnott) Broth. (蘚類)：本州
イブキキンモウゴケ
Ulota perbreviseta Dix. et Sak. (蘚類)：本州、四国、九州
ヤクシマキンモウゴケ
Ulota yakushimensis Iwats. (蘚類)：四国、九州
カメゴケモドキ
Zygodon viridissimus (Dicks.) Brid. (蘚類)：本州
ケミドリゼニゴケ
Aneura hirsuta Furuki (苔類)：沖縄県西表島
チチブゼニゴケ
Athalamia nana (Shim. et Hatt.) Hatt. (苔類)：埼玉県秩父山地
カネマルムチゴケ
Bazzania ovistipula (Steph.) Abeyw. (苔類)：鹿児島県屋久島、熊本県、三重県、奈良県
マルバホラゴケモドキ
Calypogeia aeruginosa Mitt. (苔類)：鹿児島県屋久島
ケスジヤバネゴケ
Cephaloziella elachista (Gott. et Rabenh.) Schiffn. (苔類)：青森県、京都府
アマミウロコゴケ
Chiloscyphus aselliformis (Reinw. et al.) Ness (苔類)：鹿児島県奄美大島、沖縄県
ヒメウキヤバネゴケ
Cladopodiella francisci (Hook.) Joerg. (苔類)：北海道
オガサワラキララゴケ
Cololejeunea subminutilobula Mizut. (苔類)：東京都小笠原諸島
エゾヒメソロイゴケ
Cryptocoleopsis imbricata Amak. (苔類)：北海道利尻島、長野県
マルバサンカクゴケ
Drepanolejeunea obtusifolia Yamag. (苔類)：沖縄県石垣島
イリオモテウロコゼニゴケ
Fossombronia mylioides Inoue (苔類)：沖縄県西表島
イリオモテヤスデゴケ
Frullania iriomotensis Hatt. (苔類)：沖縄県西表島、石垣島
ヤエヤマスギバゴケ

Lepidpzia mamillosa Schiffn. (苔類)：沖縄県西表島
オオサワラゴケ
Mastigophora diclados (Brid.) Nees (苔類)：和歌山県、高知県、宮崎県、鹿児島県屋久島
サイシュウホラゴケモドキ
Metacalypogeia querpaertensis Hatt. et Inoue (苔類)：鹿児島県屋久島、三重県
ヤワラゼニゴケ
Monosolenium tenerum Griff. (苔類)：関東地方以西
ムニンハネゴケ
Plagiochila boninensis Inoue (苔類)：東京都小笠原諸島
ウルシハネゴケ
Plagiochila pseudopunctata Inoue (苔類)：埼玉県
シャンハイハネゴケ
Plagiochila shangaica Steph. (苔類)：山口県
オビケビラゴケ
Radula campanigera Mont. subsp. *obiensis* (Hatt.) Yamada (苔類)：鹿児島県屋久島、宮崎県
ジンチョウゴケ
Sauteria alpina (Nees) Nees (苔類)：北海道
ヤツガタケゼニゴケ
Sauteria yatsuensis Hatt. (苔類)：長野県
ムカシヒシャクゴケ
Scapania ornithopodioides (With.) Waddel (苔類)：高知県、埼玉県、長野県、岩手県
ハマグリゼニゴケ
Targionia hypophylla L. (苔類)：埼玉県
テララゴケ
Telaranaea iriomotensis Yamag. (苔類)：沖縄県西表島
ミドリツノゴケ
Folioceros appendiculatus (Steph.) Haseg. (ツノゴケ類)：鹿児島県徳之島

植物	準絶滅危惧 NT

蘚類
ヤマトハクチョウゴケ、カワブチゴケ、マツムラゴケ、セイナンヒラゴケ

植物	情報不足 DD

蘚類
コサナダゴケモドキ、ヒトヨシゴケ、オガサワラカタシロゴケ、オオカタシロ

ゴケ、*Calymperes strictifolium* (Mitt.) Roth、ヘビゴケ、*Clastobryella cuculligera* (Lac.) Fl.、タカサゴツガゴケ、*Distichophyllum nigricaule* Mitt. ex Bosch et Lac.、オオノコギリゴケ、*Exodictyon blumii* (C.Muell.) Fl.、ジャワホウオウゴケ、ヒメスズゴケ、エビスゴケ、ハナシタチヒラゴケ、ヒヨクゴケ、シロシラガゴケ、キタイタチゴケ、*Macromitrium reinwardtii* Schwaegr.、マムシゴケ、オオキヌタゴケ、ヤマタチヒダゴケ、イブキタチヒダゴケ、ヒメハネゴケ、ヒョウタンハリガネゴケ、マツカリタケナガゴケ、*Podperaea krylovii* (Podp.) Iwats. et Glime、*Pohlia drummondii* (C.Muell.) Andrews、カサゴケ、*Schistidium maritimum* (Turn.) Bruch et Schimp. In B.S.G.、エゾキヌシッポゴケ、ホソベリミズゴケ、オオツボゴケ、キイアミゴケ、スルメゴケ、カシミイルクマノゴケ、イボエシノブゴケ、ヒログチキンモウゴケ

苔類
ヒメモミジゴケ、サンカクヨウジョウゴケ、ボウズムシトリゴケ、ハッコウダゴケ、コサキジロゴケ、ユキミイチョウゴケ、ウルシゼニゴケ、イトミゾゴケ、ヤツガタケゼニゴケ、リシリゼニゴケ、ハットリムカイバハネゴケ、ミズゴケモドキ、タカネゼニゴケ、ミゾゴケモドキ、キノボリヤバネゴケ、ヒメゴヘイゴケ

藻類

植物	絶滅 EX

イケダシャジクモ
Chara benthamii var. *brevibracteata* Kasaki (車軸藻類)：
ハコネシャジクモ
Chara globularis Thullier var. *hakonensis* Kasaki (車軸藻類)：
チュウゼンジフラスコモ
Nitella flexilis Agardh var. *bifurcata* Kasaki (車軸藻類)：
テガヌマフラスコモ
Nitella furcata Braun var. *fallosa* Imahori (車軸藻類)：
キザキフラスコモ
Nitella minispora Imahori (車軸藻類)：

植物	野生絶滅 EW

スイゼンジノリ

Aphanothece sacrum (Suringar) Okada
(藍藻類):
ホシツリモ
Vitellopsis obtusa Groves (車軸藻類):

植物	絶滅危惧1類 CR+EN

オオイシソウモドキ
Compsopogonopsis japonica Chihara
(紅藻類):沖縄県石垣島
オキチモズク
Nemalionopsis tortuosa Yoneda et Yagi
(紅藻類):九州
マルバアマノリ
Porphyra kuniedae Kurogi (紅藻類):
東北
アサクサノリ
Porphyra tenera Kjellman (紅藻類):本州
カイガラアマノリ
Porphyra tenuipedalis Miura (紅藻類):
東京湾、伊勢湾、瀬戸内海
シマチスジノリ
Thorea gaudichaudii Agardh (紅藻類):
沖縄県
クビレミドロ
Pseudodichotomosiphon constrictus
(Yamada) Yamada (= Vaucheria
constricta Yamada) (黄緑藻類):沖縄県
ホソエガサ
Acetabularia caliculus Lamouroux
(緑藻類):九州北部、石川県能登半島
マリモ
Cladophora aegagropila (Linnaeus)
Rabenhorst (緑藻類):北海道、本州
ダジクラドゥス
Dasycladus vermicularis Krasser
(緑藻類):南西諸島
ケナガシャジクモ
Chara benthamii Zaneveld var.
benthamii (車軸藻類):日本各地
シャジクモ
Chara braunii Thuillier (車軸藻類):
日本各地
オオシャジクモ
Chara corallina Willdenow (車軸藻類):
青森県以南
カタシャジクモ
Chara globularis Thuillier var. globularis
(車軸藻類):北海道から本州中北部
アメリカシャジクモ
Chara sejuncta Braun (車軸藻類):
関東以南
ハダシャジクモ
Chara zeylanica Willdenow (車軸藻類):

青森県以南
チャボフラスコモ
Nitella acuminata Braun var. capitulifera
Imahori (車軸藻類):日本各地
トガリフラスコモ
Nitella acuminata Braun var.
subglomerata Braun (車軸藻類):
本州中部以南、四国、九州
カワモズクフラスコモ
Nitella batrachosperma (車軸藻類):
ヒメフラスコモ
Nitella flexilis Agardh var. flexilis
(車軸藻類):日本各地
オオフラスコモ
Nitella flexilis Agardh var. longifolia
Braun (車軸藻類):日本各地
フタマタフラスコモ
Nitella furcata Braun var. furcata
(車軸藻類):日本各地
オトメフラスコモ
Nitella hyalina Agardh (車軸藻類):
本州、鹿児島県種子島
フラスコモダマシ
Nitella imahorii Wood (車軸藻類):
日本各地
チリフラスコモ
Nitella microcarpa Braun (車軸藻類):
北海道、本州、四国、九州
イノカシラフラスコモ
Nitella mirabilis Nordstedt
inokasiraensis Kasaki (車軸藻類):
千葉県
ナガホノフラスコモ
Nitella morongii T.F. Allen var.
spiciformis (Morioka) Imahori
(車軸藻類):北海道、本州
キヌフラスコモ
Nitella mucronata Miquel var. gracilens
(Morioka) Imahori (車軸藻類):本州中部
ナガフラスコモ
Nitella orientalis T.F. Allen (車軸藻類):
本州、四国、九州
オオバホンノサフラスコモ
Nitella pseudoflabellata Braun f.
macrophylla (車軸藻類):
ミノフサフラスコモ
Nitella pseudoflabellata Braun var.
mucosa Bailey (車軸藻類):本州、四国、
九州
ホンフサフラスコモ
Nitella pseudoflabellata Braun var.
pseudoflabellata (車軸藻類):本州、四国、
九州
ハデフラスコモ

Nitella pulchella T. F. Allen (車軸藻類):
シラタマモ
Nitellopsis obtusa Groves (車軸藻類):
徳島県

植物	絶滅危惧2類 VU

イバラオオイシソウ
Compsopogon aeruginosus (J. Agardh)
Kuetzing (紅藻類):福島県以南
アツカワオオイシソウ
Compsopogon corticrassus Chihara et
Nakamura (紅藻類):福島県以南
インドオオイシソウ
Compsopogon hookeri Montagne
(紅藻類):福島県以南
オオイシソウ
Compsopogon oishii Okamura
(紅藻類):福島県以南
ムカゴオオイシソウ
Compsopogon prolificus Yadava et
Kumano (紅藻類):福島県以南
チスジノリ
Thorea okadae Yamada (紅藻類):九州、
本州

植物	準絶滅危惧 NT

紅藻類
イシカワモヅク、ヒメカワモヅク、カワ
モヅク、ミドリカワモヅク、アオカワモ
ヅク、ナツノカワモヅク、
Batrachospermum testale Sirodot、
Batrachospermum turfosum Bory、タニ
コケモドキ、アヤギヌ、ササバアヤギヌ、
アマクサキリンサイ、リュウキュウオゴ
ノリ、タンスイベニマダラ、トサカノリ、
ニセカワモヅク、ユタカカワモヅク
褐藻類
アツバミスジコンブ、エナガコンブ、カ
ラフトコンブ、エンドウコンブ
緑藻類
クロキヅタ、チョウチンミドロ、カワノ
リ

地衣類

植物	絶滅 EX

ホソゲジゲジゴケ
Anaptychia angustiloba (Mull. Arg.)
Kurok.:
イトゲジゲジゴケ
Anaptychia leucomelaena (L.) Mass.:

ヌマジリゴケ
Erioderma asahinae Zahlbr. :

タチクリイロトゲキノリ
Cetraria aculeata (Schreb.) Fr.
(=*Cornicularia aculeata* (Schreber) Link.) :
山梨県

ミゾハナゴケモドキ
Cladonia acuminata (Ach.) Norrlin. :
長野県

ヒダカハナゴケ
Cladonia hidakana Kurok. : 北海道

クロウラカワイワタケ
Dermatocarpon moulinsii (Mont.)
Zahlbr. : 北海道、秋田県

ミヤマウロコゴケ
Dermatocarpon tuzibei Sato : 岩手県

オオツブゴケ
Gymnoderma coccocarpum Nyl. :
鹿児島県屋久島

ツブミゴケ
Gymnoderma insulare Yoshim. :
和歌山県、徳島県

ナヨナヨサガリゴケ
Lethariella togashii (Asah.) Krog :
北海道、山梨県

アマギウメノキゴケ
Myelochroa amagiensis (Asah.) Hale :
静岡県

ヤマトパウリア
Paulia japonica Asah. : 高知県

オガサワラトリハダゴケ
Pertusaria boninensis Shib. :
東京都小笠原諸島

和名なし
Phaeographina pseudomontagnearum
M. Nak. : 徳島県

和名なし
Phaeographis flavicans Kashiw. : 山梨県

フジイシガキモジゴケ
Phaeographis fujisanensis Kashiw. &
M. Nak. : 山梨県

ラマロディウムゴケ
Ramalodium japonicum (Asah.) Henss.
(= *Leciophysma japonicum* Asah.) :
愛知県

トゲナシフトネゴケ
Relicina echinocarpa (Kurok.) Hale :
福岡県、宮崎県、熊本県

キフトネゴケモドキ
Relicina sydneyensis (Gyelnik) Hale :
静岡県、紀伊半島、高知県

ニセミヤマキゴケ
Stereocaulon curtatoides Asah. :
鹿児島県開聞岳、屋久島

ヒロハキゴケモドキ
Stereocaulon wrightii Tuck. : 吾妻山

オオバキノリ
Thyrea latissima Asah. : 埼玉県、岡山県、
徳島県

フジカワゴケ
Toninia tristis (Th. Fr.) Th. Fr. ssp.
fujikawae (Sato) Timdal (= *Lecidea
fujikawae* Sato) : 岩手県、群馬県、長野
県、高知県

オオウラヒダイワタケ
Umbilicaria muhlenbergii (Ach.) Tuck. :
青森県

オオサビイボゴケ
Brigantiaea nipponicum (Sato)
Haffellner : 徳島県、高知県

トゲエイランタイ
Cetrariella delisei (Bory ex Shaer.)
Karnef. & Thell : 北海道、本州中部山岳

コウヤハナゴケ
Cladonia koyaensis Asah. : 和歌山県、
島根県隠岐島

オガサワラスミレモモドキ
Coenogonium boninense Sato :
東京都小笠原諸島

コガネエイランタイ
Flavocetraria nivalis (L.) Karnef. : 北海道

ヒメキウメノキゴケ
Flavopuncteria soredica (Nyl.) Hale :
長野県

ニュウガサウメノキゴケ
Hypotrachyna sinuosa (Sm.) Hale :
長野県、埼玉県

テガタアオキノリ
Leptogium palmatum var.
fusidosporum Kurok. : 埼玉県、広島県

コバノカワズゴケ
Lobaria angustifolia (Asah.) Yoshim. :
山梨県

トゲカブトゴケ
Lobaria kazawaensis (Asah.) Yoshim. :
群馬県、新潟県、埼玉県

和名なし
Parmelia erumpens Kurok. : 静岡県、愛
知県

ハナビラツメゴケ
Peltigera lepidophora (Nyl.) Vainio :
長野県

コヒラミツメゴケ
Peltigera nigripunctata Bitt. : 岩手県、長
野県、山梨県、静岡県

ヒメツメゴケ
Peltigera venosa (L.) Baumg. : 北海道、
長野県、山梨県

ハクテンヨロイゴケ
Pseudocyphellaria argyracea (Del.)
Vainio : 九州南部、東京都小笠原諸島

オニサネゴケ
Pyrenula gigas Zahlbr. :
鹿児島県屋久島、徳之島

ヒラミヤイトゴケ
Solorina platycarpa Hue : 埼玉県、長野
県

クボミヤイトゴケ
Solorina saccata (L.) Ach. : 徳島県

エダウチヤイトゴケ
Solorina saccata var. *spongiosa* Nyl. :
長野県

コフキセンスゴケ
Sticta limbata (Sm.) Ach. : 北海道、山梨
県

フクレヘラゴケ
Thysanothecium scutellatum (Fr.)
Galloway : 広島県、静岡県

クロカワアワビゴケ
Tuckermannopsis kurokawae (Shibuichi
& Yoshida) Kurok. (= *Cetraria
kurokawae* Shib. & Yoshida) : 秩父山地、
四国

トゲイワタケ
Umbilicaria deusta (L.) Baumg. : 北海道

カニメゴケ、ヒメミゾナハゴケ、コレマ
カロピスム、コバノイワノリ、ツクシイ
ワノリ、*Collema latzelii* Zahlbr.、アツバ
イワノリ、*Collema polycarpon* Hoffm.
var. *corcyrense* (Arn.) Degel.、コフキザ
クロゴケ、クイシウメノキゴケ、ムニン
サビイボゴケ、シマハナビラゴケ、マッ
トゴケ、タチナミガタウメノキゴケ、コ
ナマツゲゴケ、フィズマゴケ、アカウラ
ヤイトゴケ

チゾメセンニンゴケ、*Buellia atrata*
(Sm.) Anzi、チヂレバカワラゴケ、シオ
バラノリ、*Collema undulatum* Flotow、
ムニンヌカゴケ、*Hyperphyscia
adglutinata* (Florke) Mayrhofter & Poelt、

ecanora muralis (Schreb.) Rabenh.、
obothallia alphoplaca (Wahlbenb. in
ch.) Haffellner、ムニンブソロマゴケ、
オガサワラピルギルス、Pyxine cocooes
w.) Nyl.、Pyxine meissnerina Nyl.、ニ
ムクムクキゴケ、スツリグラニチデ
ラ、アカチクビゴケ、Trypethelium
oninense Kurok.

菌類

植物	絶滅 EX

ハハジマモリノカサ
Agaricus hahashimensis S. Ito & Imai:

和名なし
Allescheriella crocea (Mont.) Hughes:

ニュウガハンチクキン
Astrinella hiugensis Hino & Hidaka.

フタイロコガサタケ
Camarophyllus microbicolor S. Ito:

ハハシマアコウショウロ
Circulocolumella hahashimensis (S. Ito & Imai) S. Ito:

ムニンメサカズキタケ
Clitocybe castaneifloccosa S. Ito & Imai:

ハハノツエ
Collybia miatris S, Ito & Imai:

ムニンヒトヨタケ
Coprinus boninensis S. Ito & Imai:

ハヤカワセミタケ
Cordyceps owariensis Kobayasi:

ムラサキチャヒラタケ
Crepidotus subpurpureus S. Ito & Imai:

カバイロチャダイゴケ
Cyathus badius Kobayasi:

ムニンチャダイゴケ
Cyathus boninensis S. Ito & Imai:

オガワラツムタケ
Gymnopilus noviholocirrhus S. Ito & Imai:

オオミノアカヤマタケ
Hygrocybe macrospora (S. Ito & Imai) S. Ito:

ムニンキヤマタケ
Hygrocybe miniatostriata (S. Ito & Imai) S. Ito:

オガサワラハツタケ
Lactarius ogasawarashimensis S. Ito & Imai:

ムニンヒメカラカサタケ
Lepiota boninensis S. Ito & Imai:

ムニンチヂミタケ
Leptoglossum boninensis S. Ito & Imai:

コメツブホコリタケ
Lycoperdon henningsii Sacc. & Syd.:
埼玉県秩父

ダイドウベニヒダタケ
Pluteus daidoi S. Ito & Imai:

フサベニヒダタケ
Pluteus horridilamellus S. Ito & Imai:

マチダベニヒダタケ
Pluteus machidae S. Ito & Imai:

オカベニヒダタケ
Pluteus okabei S. Ito & Imai:

ムニンシカタケ
Pluteus verruculosus S. Ito & Imai:

オガサワライタチタケ
Psathyrella boninensis S. Ito & Imai:

ムニンチャモミウラタケ
Rhodophyllus brunneolus (S. Ito & Imai) S. Ito:

オガサワラキハツタケ
Russula boninensis S. Ito & Imai:

チチブシメジタケ
Tricholoma boninensis S. Ito & Imai:

植物	野生絶滅 EW

和名なし
Cunninghamella homothallica Kominami & Tubaki:

植物	絶滅危惧1類 CR+EN

ミツエタケ
Arcangeliella mitsueae Imai:
神奈川県横浜市

クチキトサカタケ
Ascoclavulina sakaii Otani: 東北

シンジュタケ
Boninogaster phalloides Kobayasi:
東京都小笠原諸島

キリノミタケ
Chorioactis geaster (Peck) Eckblad:
宮崎県

ミドリクチキムシタケ
Cordyceps atrovirens Kobayasi & Shimizu: 埼玉県秩父

カイガラムシツブタケ
Cordyceps coccidiicola Kobayasi & Shimizu: 中部以西、東北

イリオモテクモタケ
Cordyceps cylindrica Pecth:
沖縄県西表島

オサムシタンポタケ
Cordyceps entomorrhiza (Dicks.: Fr.) Fr.: 宮城県蔵王町

フトクビクチキムシタケ

Cordyceps facis Kobayasi & Shimizu:
埼玉県秩父

クサギムシタケ
Cordyceps hepialidicola Kobayasi & Shimizu: 埼玉県秩父

ハエヤドリトガリツブタケ
Cordyceps iriomoteana Kobayasi & Shimizu: 沖縄県西表島

コヨゴメカマキリムシタケ
Cordyceps mantidicola Kobayasi & Shimizu: 埼玉県秩父

チチブクチキムシタケ
Cordyceps nanatakiensis Kobayasi & Shimizu: 埼玉県秩父

オグラクモタケ
Cordyceps ogurasanensis Kobayasi & Shimizu: 長野県南佐久郡

シロヒメサナギタケ
Cordyceps pallidioliovacea Kobayasi & Shimizu: 沖縄県西表島

ウスキタンポセミタケ
Cordyceps pleuricapitata Kobayasi & Shimizu: 沖縄県西表島

ヒメハルゼミタケ
Cordyceps polycephala Kobayasi & Shimizu: 沖縄県西表島

エダウチタンポタケ
Cordyceps ramosostipitata Kobayasi & Shimizu: 沖縄県西表島

アカエノツトノミタケ
Cordyceps rubiginosostipitata Kobayasi & Shimizu: 沖縄県西表島

スズキセミタケ
Cordyceps ryogamimontana Kobayasi:
埼玉県秩父

サキシマヤドリバエタケ
Cordyceps sakishimensis Kobayasi & Shimizu: 沖縄県西表島

コガネムシタケ
Cordyceps scarabiicola Kobayasi:
埼玉県秩父

シロアリタケ
Cordyceps termitophila Kobayasi & Shimizu: 沖縄県西表島

タンポエゾセミタケ
Cordyceps toriharamontana Kobayasi:
山形県朝日岳

クロミノクチキムシタケ
Cordyceps uchiyamae Kobayasi & Shimizu: 東京都高尾山

エリアシタンポタケ
Cordyceps valvatostipitata Kobayasi:
宮城県蔵王町

ヤクシマセミタケ

Cordyceps yakusimensis Kobayasi：
鹿児島県屋久島
チャヒゲカワラタケ
Coriolopsis aspera (Jungh.) Teng：
沖縄県西表島、石垣島
ワニスタケ
Coriorus ochrotinctus (Berk. & Curt.)
Aoshima：本州以南
和名なし
Cornelia uberata Achar.：Fr.：高知県、
奈良県、鹿児島県屋久島
コウヤクマンネンハリタケ
Echinodontium japonicum Imazeki：
奈良県、宮崎県
マンネンハリタケ
Echinodontium tsugicola (Henn. &
Shirai) Imazeki：日光、赤城、秩父、八ヶ
岳
ラッコタケ
Inonotus flavidus (Berk.) Ryv.：本州
ヒジリタケ
Lignosus rhinocerus (Cke.) Ryv.：
沖縄県西表島、石垣島
コウヤムシタケモドキ
Neocordyceps kohyasanensis Kobayasi：
和歌山県高野山
ジャガイモタケ
Octaviania columellifera Kobayasi：関東
ホネタケ、オニゲナ菌
Onygena corvina Alb. & Schwein.；Fr.：
北海道、山形県
ツガマイタケ
Osteina obducta (Berk.) Donk：富士山
ヤエヤマキコブタケ
Phellinus pachyphloeus (Pat.) Pat.：
沖縄県西表島、石垣島
オオメシマコブ
Phellinus rimosus (Berk.) Pilat：四国、小
笠原
コカンバタケ
Piptoporus quercinus (Schrad.)
Karst.：静岡県、鳥取県
ヨコバエタケ
Podonectrioides cicadellidicola
(Kobayasi & Shimizu) Kobayasi：東北
タマチョレイタケ
Polyporus tuberaster Jacq.：Fr.：本州
ムカシオオミダレタケ
Protodaedalea hispida Imazeki：本州
和名なし
Protomyces pachydermus von
Thuemen：
ダイダイサルノコシカケ
Pyropolyporus albomarginatus (Zippoli

ex Lev.) Murr.：沖縄県西表島、石垣島
ツヤナシマンネンタケ
Pyrrhoderma sendaiense (Yasuda)
Imazeki：宮城県、新潟県、神奈川県、大
分県
サンチュウムシタケモドキ
Shimizuomyces paradoxus Kobayasi：
群馬県、長野県、宮城県、山形県
和名なし
Taphrina kusanoi Ikeno：千葉県清澄山
クモノオオトガリツブタケ
Torrubiella globosa Kobayasi & Shimizu：
山形県
エビタケ
Trachyderma tsunodae (Yasuda)
Imazeki：本州、九州

トゲホコリタケ
Bovistella yasudae Lloyd：
ハゲチャダイゴケ
Cyathus pallidus Berk. & Curt.：
エダウチホコリタケモドキ
Dendrosphaera eberhardtii Pat.：
鹿児島県屋久島、沖縄県西表島
ウスキキヌガサタケ
Dictyophora indusiata (Vent.；Pers.)
Fisch. f. lutea Kobayasi：宮崎県、広島
県、徳島県、京都府
スナタマゴタケ
Endoptychum agaricoides Czern.：
北海道小樽市、北陸
和名なし
Hypocrea cerebriformis Berk.：
北海道南部から東北
和名なし
Hypocrea splendens Phill. & Plowright：
東北
和名なし
Hypocrea subsplendens Doi：本州
ツキヨタケ
Lampteromyces japonicus (Kawamura)
Sing.：
ミヤベホコリタケ
Lycoperdon miyabei (Lloyd) Imai：
ツチグリカワタケ
Scleroderma polyrhizum Persoon

両生類

アベサンショウウオ Hynobius abei

ホクリクサンショウウオ
Hynobius takedai
ハクバサンショウウオ
Hynobius hidamontanus
イシカワガエル
Rana ishikawae
コガタハナサキガエル
Rana utsunomiyaorum

オオイタサンショウウオ
Hynobius dunni
オキサンショウウオ Hynobius okiensis
イボイモリ Tylototriton andersoni
ダルマガエル Rana porosa brevipoda
ハナサキガエル Rana narina
アマミハナサキガエル
Rana amamiensis
ナミエガエル Rana namiyei
オットンガエル Babina subaspera
ホルストガエル Babina holsti

ベッコウサンショウウオ
Hynobius stejnegeri
キタサンショウウオ
Salamandrella keyserlingii
オオサンショウウオ Andrias japonicus
シリケンイモリ Cynops ensicauda
オオハナサキガエル Rana supranarina

京都・大阪地域のカスミサンショウウオ
Hynobius nebulosus nebulosus
東京都のトウキョウサンショウウオ
Hynobius nebulosus tokyoensis
愛知県のトウキョウサンショウウオ
Hynobius nebulosus tokyoensis
本州・九州地域のオオダイガハラサン
ショウウオ Hynobius boulengeri

爬虫類

イヘヤトカゲモドキ
Goniurosaurus kuroiwae toyamai
キクザトサワヘビ
Opisthotropis kikuzatoi

爬虫類	絶滅危惧1B類
	EN

タイマイ *Eretmochelys imbricata*

マダラトカゲモドキ
Goniurosaurus kuroiwae orientalis

オビトカゲモドキ
Goniurosaurus kuroiwae splendens

ヤマシナトカゲモドキ
Goniurosaurus kuroiwae yamashinae

ヒメヘビ *Calamaria pfefferi*

爬虫類	絶滅危惧2類
	VU

アオウミガメ *Chelonia mydas*

アカウミガメ *Caretta caretta*

セマルハコガメ
Cuora flavomarginata evelynae

リュウキュウヤマガメ
Geoemyda japonica

クロイワトカゲモドキ
Goniurosaurus kuroiwae kuroiwae

キノボリトカゲ
Japalura polygonata polygonata

バーバートカゲ *Eumeces barbouri*

ミヤコトカゲ
Emoia atrocostata atrocostata

ミヤコヒバァ *Amphiesma concelarum*

ヨナグニシュウダ
Elaphe carinata yonaguniensis

ミヤラヒメヘビ
Calamaria pavimentata miyarai

爬虫類	準絶滅危惧
	NT

キシノウエトカゲ
Eumeces kishinouyei

イワサキセダカヘビ *Pareas iwasakii*

アマミタカチホヘビ *Achalinus werneri*

ヤエヤマタカチホヘビ
Achalinus formosanus chigirai

サキシマアオヘビ
Cyclophiops herminae

サキシマバイカダ
Lycodon ruhstrati multifasciatus

イワサキワモンベニヘビ
Hemibungarus macclellandi iwasakii

ヒャン *Hemibungarus japonicus japonicus*

ハイ *Hemibungarus japonicus boettgeri*

爬虫類	情報不足
	DD

スッポン *Trionyx sinensis*

爬虫類	絶滅のおそれのある地域個体群 LP

悪石島以北のトカラ諸島のニホントカゲ
Eumeces latiscutatus

三宅島、八丈島、青ヶ島のオカダトカゲ
Eumeces okadae

INDEX

HOW TO USE THE INDEX

Typography

Boldface type indicates entries for which there are articles in this book while standard type is used for words appearing within articles. If an article contains subheadings these are shown indented under the article title.

B

F

インデックス

インデックスの使い方

このインデックスは、本書に収録され
ている独立項目とその見出しおよび
本文から選んだ検索項目を五十音順
に配列したものである。

独立項目は太字で、検索項目は細字
で示した。ページ数は、独立項目は太
字(例**123**)、索引項目は細字(例123)で
示した。

音引(ー)、二重ハイフン(=)は
除いた。

を

かいていしんぱん　えいぶんにほんしょうじてん
改訂新版・英文日本小事典

Japan: Profile of a Nation revised edition

1999年3月26日　第1刷発行

編者	講談社インターナショナル株式会社
発行者	野間佐和子
発行所	講談社インターナショナル株式会社
	〒112-8652
	東京都文京区音羽1-17-14
	電話　03-3944-6493【編集部】
	03-3944-6492【営業部】

組版	Parastyle, Inc.
印刷所	大日本印刷株式会社
製本所	株式会社堅省堂
Output	Cytron (M) Sdn.Bhd (Malaysia)